Festschrift für

Thomas Rauscher

THOMAS E. RAUSCHER

EUROPÄISIERUNG DES ZIVILRECHTS

FESTSCHRIFT FÜR

THOMAS RAUSCHER

ZUM

70. GEBURTSTAG

Herausgegeben von

Guido Kosmehl

Steffen Pabst

István Varga

2025

C.H.BECK

Zitiervorschlag: Bearbeiter FS Rauscher, 2025, …

beck.de

ISBN 978 3 406 82703 7

Wilhelmstraße 9, 80801 München
info@beck.de
Druck und Bindung: Beltz Bad Langensalza GmbH
Am Fliegerhorst 8, 99947 Bad Langensalza

Satz: Jung Crossmedia Publishing GmbH, Lahnau
Umschlag: Druckerei C.H.Beck, Nördlingen

myclimate
shape our future

chbeck.de/nachhaltig
produktsicherheit.beck.de

Gedruckt auf säurefreiem, alterungsbeständigem Papier
(hergestellt aus chlorfrei gebleichtem Zellstoff)

GRUẞWORT

Der vorliegende Band ist unserem akademischen Lehrer, wissenschaftlichen Weggefährten und Kollegen, dem in der Welt der Rechtsvergleicher, Internationalprivatrechtler und Prozessrechtler hochgeschätzten *Thomas E. Rauscher* gewidmet, der am 7.2.2025 ein weiteres Jahrzehnt des ihm beschiedenen Erdenganges vollendete.

Diesem Geburtstag ist ein einmaliger wissenschaftlicher Werdegang vorausgegangen, der zunächst in München mit dem Studium der höheren Mathematik begann. Doch unmittelbar im Anschluss an das naturwissenschaftliche Studium beschloss der junge Diplom-Mathematiker, sich dem Studium der Rechtswissenschaften zuzuwenden, für dessen Abschluss er gerade einmal sechs Semester aufwenden musste. Innerhalb eines Bruchteils dieser Zeitspanne stellte er sodann auch seine Dissertationsschrift fertig – eine der ersten Abhandlungen zum Europäischen Zivilprozessrecht. Für die sich daran anschließende Habilitation fertigte er eine grundlegende Arbeit zum materiellen Erb- und Pflichtteilsrecht, dies jedoch nicht ohne in mehreren umfassenden rechtsvergleichenden Abschnitten den Blick in zahlreiche Rechtsordnungen des gesamten Globus zu werfen.

Sodann verabschiedete sich der junge *Thomas Rauscher* von seiner Münchener Lehrstube, um nach Vertretungssemestern in Frankfurt, Hamburg und Marburg 1993 einem Ruf nach Leipzig zu folgen. Dort gründete er im Jahr 1998 „sein" Institut für ausländisches und europäisches Privat- und Verfahrensrecht an der Juristenfakultät der Universität Leipzig. Dass Peter Schlosser zur Eröffnung den Festvortrag hielt, gab dem neuen rechtsvergleichenden Institut ersten Glanz, der mit der Arbeit über die kommenden Jahrzehnte immer heller strahlte.

Der akademische Weg brachte den *Jubilar* jedoch nicht in den Elfenbeinturm, vielmehr war er stets auf wissenschaftlich fundierte, praxisrelevante Hilfestellung bedacht. So startete er bereits in seinen Wanderjahren als Kommentator. Von Anfang an griff er dabei zum tiefer gehenden, die Praxisprobleme umfassend erläuternden Großkommentar. Seinen Einstieg fand er in Julius von Staudingers Kommentar zum Bürgerlichen Gesetzbuch, für den er Anfang der 1990er Jahre erstmals das neue, praktisch gerade hoch relevante Überleitungsrecht zur Wiedervereinigung Deutschlands übernahm. Drei Neubearbeitungen sollten über die kommenden 25 Jahre folgen, ebenso wie insgesamt fünf Bearbeitungen des Scheidungsrechts, drei des Umgangs- und Beistandschaftsrechts sowie vier des Abstammungsrechts.

Mit der Kompetenzrevolution von Amsterdam erkannte der *Jubilar* das Europäische Zivilprozessrecht als wichtigen, zunehmend Eigenständigkeit erlangenden und rapide wachsenden Teil des Zivilverfahrensrechts und begründete daher im Jahr 2000 den *Rauscher EuZPR* (die erste Auflage erschien 2003), der mit dem Fortschreiten der Aktivitäten des europäischen Verordnungsgebers in seiner 3. Auflage ab 2010 zum *Rauscher EuZPR/EuIPR* ausgebaut werden konnte. Hierfür suchte und fand er stets junge Mitstreiter, die dieses Rechtsgebiet perspektivisch prägen würden. Am Kommentar wirkten bisher 40 Kommentatoren mit. Von ihnen arbeiten aktuell 36, die in fünf mitteleuropäischen Staaten tätig sind, an der inzwischen in acht Bänden erscheinenden 5. Auflage des Werkes und schaffen so den einzigen umfassenden Großkommentar in diesem Spezialgebiet. Ein wahrhaft europäisches Projekt. Seine ganz eigene Handschrift verpasste er dabei dem europäischen Verfahrensrecht in Ehe- und Kindschaftssachen, indem er die Gesamtkommentierung der seinerzeit neuen Brüssel II-VO bzw. Brüssel IIa-VO übernahm.

Im Jahr 2006 gesellte sich ein zweites großes Kommentarprojekt dazu. Nach dem Ausscheiden von Gerhard Lüke als Gründungsherausgeber des Münchener Kommentars zur ZPO – liebevoll stets der „MüKoZPO" genannt – übernahm *Thomas Rauscher* ab der 3. Auflage die Mitherausgeberschaft. In diese Zeit fiel die Neukodifikation des Verfahrensrechts der Familiensachen und der Angelegenheiten der Freiwilligen Gerichtsbarkeit. Das seinerzeitige 6. und 9. Buch der ZPO und das FGG gingen im FamFG auf. *Thomas Rauscher* sah die weitreichende praktische Bedeutung dieser zweiten, umfassenden Verfahrensordnung für die ordentliche Gerichtsbarkeit und schuf gemeinsam mit dem sein Schaffen stets zuverlässig begleitenden Verlag C. H. Beck eine Gesamtkommentierung der neuen Verfahrensordnung zunächst als 4. Band des MüKoZPO. Dieser Teil konnte sich sodann in der folgenden Auflage zum eigenständigen MüKoFamFG emanzipieren und in der Folge zu einem nunmehr zweibändigen Werk wachsen. So betreut der *Jubilar* als Herausgeber heute fünf Bände Münchener Kommentar: gemeinsam mit Wolfgang Krüger drei Bände MüKoZPO und zwei weitere MüKoFamFG allein. Ein solches Großprojekt verlangt immer wieder nach neuen Autoren. Solche konnte *Thomas Rauscher* auch aus dem Kreis der Leipziger Kollegen und Schüler gewinnen. Selbstverständlich übernahm er auch selbst als Autor entscheidende Passagen.

Aber auch seine Lehrbücher prägten Generationen von Jurastudenten und Praktikern. Sein monumentales *Lehr- und Handbuch Familienrecht* suchte den Weg über die Ausbildung hinaus und setzte Maßstäbe. Es bleibt in Grundsatzfragen bis heute ein Referenzwerk ersten Ranges. Sein demnächst in der 6. Auflage erscheinendes, mit wissenschaftlichem Anspruch geschriebenes Lehrbuch *Internationales Privatrecht* darf gemeinsam mit dem didaktisch erstklassig vervollständigenden *Klausurenkurs* heute als das führende Werk des Rechtsgebiets gelten.

Beide Lehrwerke entstanden aus den und für die regelmäßigen Vorlesungen des *Jubilars,* der über ca. 20 Jahre sowohl das materielle Familienrecht als auch das internationale Privat- und Verfahrensrecht in all ihren Facetten an der Leipziger Fakultät vertrat. Dabei implementierte *Thomas Rauscher* immer neue Lehrmethoden und scheute sich nie vor dem Umgang mit neuen Medien. PowerPoint-Präsentationen nutze er bereits zu Zeiten von Windows 95. Der dafür notwendige Beamer, seinerzeit noch ein seltenes und teures, ca. 16 kg schweres Gerät von erheblichem Volumen, wurde aus Sondermitteln beschafft und nach einem genau ausgearbeiteten Plan von den Mitarbeitern des Instituts zu jeder Vorlesung in den Hörsaal transportiert und aufgebaut sowie im Anschluss wieder abgeholt. Um die Jahrtausendwende war dieser der einzige der Fakultät. Die erstellten PowerPoint-Folien nutzten die vollständige Farbpalette und vielfältige Animationsmöglichkeiten. Der *Jubilar* experimentierte, lernte selbst und suchte nach Möglichkeiten, den Lehrstoff modern zu vermitteln.

Die internationalen Aspekte der Lehre prägte *Thomas Rauscher* an der Leipziger Fakultät aber auch konzeptionell. Neben der grundständigen Ausbildung forcierte er die international-privatrechtliche Spezialisierung durch ein postgraduiertes LL.M.-Programm, indem er zuerst einen Magister-, nach der „Bologna-Reform" einen akkreditierten Masterstudiengang „Europäischer Privatrechtsverkehr" etablierte und als Erster regelmäßig auch englischsprachige Vorlesungen hielt. Er intensivierte den europäischen Studenten- wie Lehrkräfteaustausch. So sandte er auch die Leipziger Studenten, unter ihnen zwei der Herausgeber dieser Festschrift, nach Athen und Thessaloniki, um rechtsvergleichend die griechische Rechtsordnung kennenzulernen, und vermittelte in den Gesprächen nebenbei die Geographie der griechischen Inseln – Inselnamen wie Paros, Kos und Kalymnos wurden vertraute Begriffe, waren es doch die Orte, die er in jedem Frühjahr erwanderte und von denen er bis heute die Kraft für die nächsten wissenschaftlichen Projekte mitbringt. Er verantwortete nicht nur über Jahre das Erasmus-Programm an der Leipziger Fakultät, entsandte und empfing Austauschstudenten aus und in allen Studiengängen der Fakultät, sondern war als Gastdozent in Turku und Oslo selbst Teil des Programms und etablierte eine langjährige und tiefe Verbindung zur ELTE Budapest, an der er bis heute jährlich zum Europäischen Zivilprozessrecht lehrt und die dem *Jubilar* im Jahre 2016 den *doctor et professor honoris causa* verlieh. Von dort brachte er bereits vor der Jahrtausendwende den dritten Herausgeber dieser Festschrift als jungen Wissenschaftler nach Leipzig, um jährlich Lehrveranstaltungen zur Rechtsvergleichung und zur Internationalen Schiedsgerichtsbarkeit zu übernehmen. Dieser Austausch hält bis heute an.

Als Professor war *Thomas Rauscher* für seine Studenten stets ansprechbar. Die Zeit, die er in Leipzig weilte, gehörte uneingeschränkt der Universität. Das Seminar am Mittwochabend kollidierte nie mit anderen Veranstaltungen. Und eine unmittelbare Kommunikation per E-Mail war für *Thomas Rauscher* bereits im Jahr 2000 selbstverständlich. Kontakt, Austausch und Wissenstransfer benötigten bei ihm schon vor 25 Jahren keine permanente physische Präsenz. Wir sind uns sicher, gerade die konzentrierte Anwesenheit an der Universität, die strenge Organisation und Aufteilung der Woche in verschiedene Phasen des Arbeitens ermöglichten erst die unglaubliche Vielfalt seines Œuvres.

Und so ist sein Wirken von einem weiteren, dritten Bereich geprägt, der sich schon sehr früh dazu gesellte. Sein akademischer Lehrer, Werner Lorenz, hatte am Münchener Institut für Rechtsvergleichung eine Gutachtentätigkeit für deutsche Gerichte etabliert, wenn Rat im ausländischen materiellen Recht vonnöten war. Bereits in seiner Assistentenzeit begann *Thomas Rauscher* mit dieser Facette seines Schaffens. Die Recherche einer fremden – gleich wie weit entfernten – Rechtsordnung wird mit Akribie betrieben, Literatur im Zielland beschafft, Bekanntschaften für Recherche- und Übersetzungsleistungen vor Ort eingespannt. Der Zugang zu elektronischen Datenbanken wurde bereits in den Jahren gesucht, als diese noch in den Kinderschuhen steckten. Aufgebaut wurde so eine umfassende Bibliothek und herausragende Kompetenz. Irgendwann sprach es sich bei den Gerichten herum:

Wenn das Max-Planck-Institut am Hamburger Mittelweg, das Institut in der Münchener Veterinärstraße oder das Institut in der Heidelberger Augustinergasse abgesagt haben sollten, könnte man noch im Leipziger Institut anfragen, da saß jemand, der den Aufwand nicht scheute und ebenso die erforderliche Qualität liefern würde. Und kein spannender, interessanter Fall sollte durch widrige Umstände verloren gehen: Für die Gerichte wurde auch in Urlaubszeiten und zu Zeiten, in denen eine ständige weltweite Verfügbarkeit noch nicht selbstverständlich war, stets eine Kontaktmöglichkeit offengehalten. So entstanden Gutachten zum Recht Österreichs, der Schweiz und Lichtensteins oder Portugals, Spaniens und Griechenlands, aber auch Tschechiens, Rumäniens und Bulgariens oder Pakistans, Hong Kongs und Vietnams. Die Länderliste ließe sich vielfältig erweitern. Die praktische Bedeutung, das Lösen des relevanten Falles, die Anwendung wissenschaftlicher Methoden zur ganz konkreten Streitbewältigung, das begeistert *Thomas Rauscher*. Auch heute ist er als „Sachverständiger für ausländisches Privat- und Prozessrecht" tätig und pflegt den Kontakt zu freien Mitarbeitern im Ausland, die ihm die schnelle Beschaffung und Auswertung von Quellen ermöglichen, die in Deutschland nicht verfügbar sind.

Und die Gutachtenfälle finden dann wieder ihren Weg zurück in die Lehrtätigkeit – machen den Wissensstoff anschaulich, begeistern Studenten für das Rechtsgebiet, zeigen die Vielfalt des Rechts – aber auch in die Autorentätigkeit – bilden Grundlage von in Kommentaren behandelten Problemen –, so dass alle drei großen Tätigkeitsbereiche des *Thomas Rauscher* doch nie isoliert stehen, sondern eine große Schaffenseinheit bilden.

Den für all diese Tätigkeiten erforderlichen Ausgleich findet *Thomas Rauscher* bis heute in den Bergen Oberbayerns im Grenzgebiet zu Österreich, die sein ganz persönliches Zentrum wurden. Der Weg auf seinen Hausberg, den Brünnstein, – gleich ob zu Fuß oder mit dem Mountainbike – gibt ihm ebenso Kraft und Ideen, wie im Winter die Runden auf der Langlaufloipe um den Thiersee. Seine sportlichen Aktivitäten, die am Nachmittag die intensive Arbeit im Kiefersfeldener Panorama-Arbeitszimmer unterbrechen, spiegeln den Anspruch von *Thomas Rauscher* an Leistung und Leistungsbereitschaft: stets hart gegen sich selbst, bedingungslos das immer hoch angesetzte Ziel verfolgen. Davon wird auch auf Urlaubsreisen nicht abgerückt, die ihn zum Beispiel regelmäßig in die Berge des Himalaya in Nepal oder Bhutan führen. Die Bergwanderung räumt auch dort nicht nur den Kopf wieder frei, sondern stachelt unmittelbar zu sportlichen Höchstleistungen an. So geschieht es wohl von Zeit zu Zeit, dass der gut trainierte örtliche Guide den Gast dann doch ziehen lassen muss.

Dazu hebt *Thomas Rauscher* regelmäßig ab und lebt seine andere große Leidenschaft: das Fliegen. Hier ist er nicht nur Passagier – lange auf seinem persönlichen Arbeitsweg MUC-LEJ, „around the world" oder „long haul open jaw" wenn möglich in „executive or first" – als (heute nun Lifetime) Senator, sondern vor allem Privatpilot von Ein- und Zweimots VFR wie IFR fliegend. Und so lehrte der *Jubilar* nicht nur auf juristischem Gebiet: Eine Zusammenarbeit am Institut führte unweigerlich zu einem doch soliden Grundwissen der optimierten Gestaltungsmöglichkeiten von Flugreisen und zu gewissen Kenntnissen der privaten Flugorganisation und -durchführung, aber auch gelegentlich zu einer Praxiseinheit in der Luft.

Thomas Rauscher machen die Gegensätze aus: Im Alltag heimatverbunden in der oberbayerischen Natur verwurzelt und doch stets auf weiten Reisen unterwegs um die ganze Welt. Das Fremde entdeckend besinnt er sich auf die eigene Kultur und deren Bestand. Die nationalen Unterschiede schätzend liebt der *Jubilar* den Disput und die Provokation. In der Diskussion werden schon einmal polarisierende Meinungen vertreten, um Widerworte anzustacheln. Dies aber formt und bildet den kritischen, hinterfragenden Schüler. Dabei Irrwege zu beschreiten wird verziehen, das eigenständige Denken zu vergessen dagegen nicht.

Wir wünschen *Thomas Rauscher* Gesundheit und Schaffenskraft, stets den kritischen Geist, um Rechtswissenschaft wie Rechtspraxis voranzubringen, und die erforderliche Weitsicht und Milde auch gegenüber sich selbst, um auf Reisen Zeit zu finden zum Sammeln weiterer Eindrücke, die den Rechtsvergleicher, Internationalprivatrechtler und Prozessrechtler inspirieren. Ad multos annos!

Die Herausgeber im Februar 2025

INHALTSVERZEICHNIS

DAVID ABRAHAM

Minority Recognition, Universal Values and Constitutional Identity: The Conflict Over Circumcision and Its Lessons

How should a secular, formerly Christian or enlightened-Christian liberal democratic welfare state and society address its large and often tradition-oriented Muslim immigrant and Jewish citizen minority? Should the latter's requirement of male circumcision be tolerated as a matter of individual religious freedom? Should it be recognized as a valid group right in a multicultural society? Should it be tolerated as a matter of social peace or recognition of the "other"? Or should it, as an archaism, be opposed in the name of modern liberal values like autonomy, bodily integrity, science and public health? Or should it even be banned in the name of the state's duty to protect children, even as against their well-intentioned parents? The balance between the collective identity of Muslims and Jews, on the one hand, and that of the "entire" political community, on the other, was at issue in the Great German Circumcision Controversy analyzed here. The controversy ultimately addressed Germany's relations with its Muslim immigrants and fragile Jewish minority as well as the proper weightings of the relationship among parents, child, and state, and the deference owed medical thinking. Immigrant integration, religious freedom, group rights, and the meaning of "enlightenment" all remain sharply contested. Despite a brief reprieve, the issue of immigrant integration and adaptation to German norms, norms that are not static but, in fact evolve, sometimes imperceptibly, sometimes dramatically, remains a contentious and challenging issue as we saw again at the end of 2023.

One of the greatest pleasures of my 25-plus year career at the University of Miami School of Law was our Exchange Seminar with the Law Faculty of Leipzig University. Unusual in its format – five concentrated, non-stop days in Miami in the Winter and five concentrated, non-stop days in Leipzig in the Spring – a dozen or so students joined two or three faculty members from each institution for a round of intense and sometimes passionate discussion of salient legal issues. After the founding of the seminar by Dean *Prof. Rudolph Geiger* in 2001, for most of the years of the seminar, from roughly 2003 until Covid and retirements led to a winding down of the Seminar, the German team was led by *Prof. Dr. Thomas Rauscher. Thomas Rauscher* was joined at various times by several colleagues, including *Profs. Helmut Goerlich, Markus Kotzur, Christian Berger, Stephanie Schiedermair, Hendrik Schneider, Christoph Enders,* and a troop of dedicated assistants at various levels, *Steffen Pabst, Alexander Fehre, Sven Groschischka, Perrine Kobsik, Kristin Kißling, Valentin Pfisterer, Anna Mrozek, Nathalie Lörscher, Denise Wiedemann,* and others whose names time and age may be leading me to neglect. *Prof. Richard Williamson* was a constant partner of mine on the Miami team, along, at various times, with *Profs. Mario Barnes, Markus Wagner, Mary Coombs, Felix Mormann,* and *Donna Coker.* The number of students who benefitted from our efforts is certainly well over 300, and *Thomas Rauscher* is more than anyone to thank for that success.

With *Thomas Rauscher,* all of us witnessed the rebirth and transformation of Leipzig from the lost splendor and forlorn public spaces our exchange seminarians first encountered to the vibrant and dynamic city it had (again) become just a few years later. Our students were also introduced to the best of pre-war and GDR culture, high and low, and in our touring witnessed the problematic fate of declining parts of den Osten as well. In turn, German students were exposed to a very young Miami – both its attractive fast and indolent features – and its more serious offerings on land and sea. But not only the students enjoyed coming to Miami: *Thomas Rauscher* availed himself of the opportunity to indulge one of his favorite pastimes: flying, sometimes across the entire country before landing in Miami!

Never one to accept the Zeitgeist passively, a quality I also value and share, though from a different location on the political spectrum, *Thomas Rauscher* often accompanied his sedate commentary on civil procedure, family law, and commercial law with skeptical and critical reflections on political correctness and what has come to be called "wokeness." This sometimes left students and the uninitiated somewhat aghast – a response *Thomas Rauscher* at times up to a point enjoyed while also seeming at other times incredulous that anyone might take offense. Over the years, the range of "voices" contributing to discussion certainly expanded, but it is not clear that the tolerance for controversy expanded as well. Though *Thomas Rauscher* and I, coming from the Left, often disagreed deeply, we shared the spirit of intellectual inquiry and lively contention. And while our fields barely overlapped – my own specialties being immigration law and labor law along with German history – we regularly and readily exchanged views and interpretations of law and society. It is in that spirit that this contribution is offered.

I. Migrants Enter the Constitutional Order

On November 1, 2023, *Vice Chancellor Robert Habeck* sought to address both the terrible and destructive Israel-Hamas war in Gaza and the anti-Semitic and Islamophobic sentiments awakened by or aggravated by it in Germany. Although his main point was to underscore a special historical German obligation toward Israel and toward Jews, at one point *Habeck* put forward a more general admonition directed especially toward the (largely Muslim) immigrant population, old and new: "Whoever lives here does so according to the rules of this country. And whoever comes here must know that this is how it is and that this will be enforced."[1] As Saint Ambrose is said to have admonished Saint Augustine, in order neither to give offense

[1] Here according to the translation provided by the Bundesministerium für Wirtschaft und Klimaschutz, https://www.bmwk.de/Redaktion/DE/Downloads/M-O/manuskripte-habeck-ueber-israel-und-antisemitismus-en.pdf?__blob=publicationFile&v=4 (visited 11.5.2024).

nor be offended, "when in Rome, do as the Romans do." But not all issues are equally salient, and contemporary Germany is not a static society, and its Basic Law affords equal rights, dignity, and recognition under law to all citizens and residents of the country. In multiple respects, Germany has become a more pluralistic and diverse society, and the law has had to address, come to terms with, and help shape that transformation.

Arguably, no single factor has provided more impetus or generated greater challenges in the course of that transformation than immigration. The great waves of global migration into and out of Europe such as those that preceded World War I, followed World War II, and again drew our attention after 2015 and again in 2023 inevitably challenge the fixity or stability of a country's constitutional identity. Whether official ideologies are those of assimilation, integration, pluralism, or multiculturalism seems not to matter; challenges will arise no matter. Constitutional identities are not just ensembles of laws and an accumulated national jurisprudence. They are grounded in cultural configurations that evolve over long periods of time but are, for the most part, taken for granted. Thus, for example, a thoroughly secular constitution such as that of Germany (not to mention, France) nonetheless is built on a deep foundation, a vital layer of which is the Christian past.[2] Fundamental constitutional tenets of many a receiving country, such as the "separation of church and state," are barely thinkable outside the history of western Christianity. Indeed, they are even problematic in eastern Christianity, let alone Islam.

Migrants bring with them their own established social and cultural identities, sometimes more akin to that of the receiving country and sometimes less. In any event they become new passengers on a ship that has been sailing for quite some time. They become entitled, perhaps even before they become citizens but certainly once they do, to affect the whither, the *wohin* of that ship, but they are also called upon to acknowledge and defer to the whence, the *woher* of the vessel they have chosen or been forced to board. Consciously or otherwise, natives and immigrants both change, though which side bears how much burden is, obviously, a source of great political and social debate and stress.[3] Importantly, most liberal constitutional orders (and some illiberal ones) allow for a certain measure of legal pluralism, so that a fundamental secular constitutional identity or order is not necessarily threatened

---

[2] Laborde thus coined the term "Catho-laïque" to describe the Christian assumptions underlying the constitutionalism of utterly secular France; Laborde, Critical Republicanism: The Hijab Controversy and Political Philosophy, 2008.

[3] The turmoil within Germany engendered by side-taking in the Israel-Hamas war again inflamed the immigrant integration question, prompting the Integrationsbeauftragten in Berlin-Neukölln to write:

'Selbst die hoch idealistischen Verteidiger einer aktiven Migrationspolitik wollen sehr oft nicht wahrhaben, dass Migranten nicht immer per se gut und wichtig sind, sondern dass sie ein Land auch vor Herausforderungen stellen. Dieser Mangel an Aufrichtigkeit erzeugt bei vielen aus unseren Milieus einmal mehr das Gefühl, nicht wirklich ernst genommen zu werden. Eine Einwanderungsgesellschaft muss ständig dazulernen, kontinuierlich an Institutionen und Instrumenten der Integration arbeiten, sie muss Überzeugungsarbeit leisten. Sonst erzeugt Einwanderung nur Angst, gar Wut.', Balcı Süddeutsche Zeitung 8.2.2024, https://www.sueddeutsche.de/kultur/juden-hass-berlin-neukoelln-kann-ich-noch-auf-die-strasse-1.6345674?reduced=true (visited 11.5.2024).

by the existence of religious officials or tribunals in family disputes, the arbitration of commercial conflicts, or a range of other matters.[4]

In addition to recent migrants, minorities of long standing may hold to values different from or irritating to those of the majority – including values very much a part of group and individual identity. Here controversy may be a constant or recurring phenomenon with minorities enjoying certain rights guarantees but also being subjected to conformist pressures, legal and social.[5] With luck, a more capacious constitutional identity may be the outcome of such controversies; without it, existing social fissures may be exacerbated. And, of course, historical non-immigrant minorities, such as German speakers in Italy or French speakers in Canada or Catalans in Spain, may insist on federalism or regional or group rights.

The controversy over circumcision that I examine here combined a challenge to minority rights with "line drawing" intended to contain and transform practices of recent migrants, practices very much at the core of their identity but perceived by many in the majority as subversive of, if not directly contrary to, the constitutional identity of liberal Germany. In what follows, I examine the controversy and detail the legal and public conflict that it unleashed. I then turn to possible means of reconciling German constitutional identity with this important particular cultural practice of the Jewish and Muslim minorities, the former ancient but only recently reestablished and the latter a growing and "coming out" sector, for some representing a threat of a "great replacement."

II. Circumcision and Who "Belongs to Germany?"

The controversy began unspectacularly enough well back in November 2010. One Saturday morning, a four year-old Iraqi-German Muslim boy was brought to a local Cologne emergency room in an ambulance called by his mother, who was panicked over minor bleeding around the site of a circumcision performed two days earlier.[6] Due, it seems, to language shortcomings in explaining what had transpired and a possibly hostile on-call doctor, the conversation between mother

---

[4] It does, however, belong to the heated atmosphere of recent times that anxieties about being overwhelmed by sharia law or the like have gained real traction, not only in places like the Visegrad countries where demagogy is the coin of the political realm but also in firmly established constitutional democracies like Germany, Italy, Scandinavia, Canada, and the U.S. where Great Replacement ‚theories' and fantasies prosper: see, for example, Sarazin, Deutschland schafft sich ab, 2010; right wing German politicians like *Beatrix von Storch, Alexander Gauland, Petr Bystron* and others have played on this theme even more crudely.

[5] See, for example, Judd, Contested Rituals: Circumcision, Kosher Butchering, and Jewish Political Life in Germany 1843–1933, 2007.

[6] The circumcision was performed by an experienced, German-trained and licensed Syrian-German surgeon, *Dr. Omar Keeze,* to whom the family had been referred and who charged the going rate of €250. The procedure had been done two days earlier, and *Keeze* had made a routine house call that evening to treat the site. The family had a further check-in appointment with him scheduled for later that same Saturday. See Musharbash, Die Operation war einwandfrei, Die Zeit, 20.7.2012, p. 8. Other details are recounted in Fateh-Moghedan 13 German Law Journal 13 (2012), 1131.

and staff led to the police being called.[7] Two indictments followed: one of the parents for child abuse, soon dropped, and another, in January 2011, of the physician who had performed the circumcision for aggravated battery, "use of a dangerous instrument to physically abuse another and damage their well-being," through a violation of the infant's physical integrity.

The municipal trial court acquitted all parties and dismissed the indictments, finding circumcision "customarily socially acceptable." Any potential elements of the offense of bodily injury were justified or excused by the effective consent of the child's parents who, as properly responsible for the well-being of the child *(personensorgeberechtigt),* undertook the circumcision for the sake of the "well-being of the child."[8] In balancing the various interests involved – the right of parents to raise their children, their right to free exercise of their religion, and the right of a child to bodily integrity (all Constitutionally guaranteed) – the court asserted that it was important to start from the fact that circumcision served as a rite of passage to document cultural and religious membership in the Muslim community. Uncircumcised, the boy would face the threat of stigmatization in that community. As a final point, the court also noted that its own appointed expert as well as respected American practice saw in circumcision a positive medical benefit improving hygiene and perhaps helping to prevent certain diseases. In sum, the parents had given the doctor valid consent with the best social, religious, and health interests of the child in mind, thereby justifying what might otherwise arguably be construed as a criminal battery. As is often the case with lower court opinions, this court was very practically minded, with an ear to the ground and with an interest in disposing of problems brought to it.

Under German law, however, prosecutors have certain rights to appeal an acquittal, and here she persisted in pursuing the case against the physician. One must assume that the prosecutor fervently believed in her case, though there is some evidence that the prosecutor was encouraged by circumcision opponents in the legal academy – scholars, as we shall see, claiming to be standing up for and protecting the country's constitutional identity-to pursue a test case. In the event, on May 7, 2012, the District Court *(Landgericht)* in Cologne found that circumcision, notwithstanding parental consent, religious motivation, or community custom constituted a criminal bodily injury.[9] Tellingly, this court began its opinion with mention of anes-

[7] Whether calling the police was an obvious or reasonable response is difficult to reconstruct. The mother's German was weak: she apparently did not know the word for "scalpel" and said the procedure had been done with "scissors". She erroneously answered "no" when asked if there had been anesthesia. For his part, the on-call doctor's notes reported "normal range bleeding" but remarked that it had not been a good job and that the number of stitches had not been adequate. Later, at trial, he withdrew those accusations, though one can't know why.

[8] AG Köln 21.9.2011 – 528 Ds 30/11, BeckRS 2012, 13648, here citing § 1627 BGB (exercise of parental custody, best interests of the child). The concept of Sozialadäquanz is not easily rendered in English. The respective constitutional provisions on parenting (Art. 6 sec. 2 GG), religious exercise (Art. 4 sec. 1–2 GG), and bodily integrity (Art. 2 GG) are discussed below. It is characteristic of most "anti" literature that it begins graphically, sometimes luridly; this is also true in abortion debates.

[9] LG Köln 7.5.2012 – 151 Ns 169/11, NJW 2012, 2128, finding a violation of criminal code § 224 sec.2 StGB, "causing grievous bodily harm using a dangerous instrument." ("The child's

thetics, scalpels, stitches (4), and the fact that the procedure had been undertaken "without any indication of medical necessity." Although the surgeon committed no malpractice mistakes, this court quickly asserted that its expert appraisal found "at least in central Europe no medical need for or usefulness as a preventative healthcare measure."

The court then rejected the "customarily socially acceptable" *(Sozialadäquanz)* argument of the lower court and found that "the right of parents to a religious upbringing of their children does not outweigh the right of the child to bodily integrity and self-determination." The well-being of a child, who, as here is unable to give consent *(Einwilligung)*, may not be infringed or the law violated just because the infringement is "inconspicuous, generally approved of, or historically mandated." Further, "neither concern with avoiding ostracism within his own religious community nor parental authority over child rearing" renders circumcision compatible with the welfare of the child. Religious rites and freedom simply may not trump civil rights accorded by law.

As authority for these holdings, the court cited several scholars, long-time anti-circumcision activists who would come to play outsized roles in the controversy that followed.[10] Religiously-motivated circumcision, the court continued, was "disproportionate," a "permanent and irreparable" change to the body of the child that also undermined his ability later to decide himself what his religious preferences might be. It would not be too much of an imposition on the parents, the court finally concluded, to require them to "wait until their boy was of legal age and could decide for himself if he wished circumcision as a visible marker of Islamic belonging."

The court offered no explicit mention of the parties' migration status. But it did clearly disdain the alien, if not backward, practice of those whose religious or community motivations ignored or transgressed against the country's constitutional identity in which autonomy (even as against parents), consent, bodily integrity, and scientific enlightenment are core, premier values. A constitutional identity is more than an assemblage of the majority's preferences (let alone prejudices), the court suggested. Rather, for this court, if not entirely universalist, these values are Germany's and outweigh any valid claims of religious free exercise that are also part of Germany's constitutional identity, whether brought by minorities, migrants, or others.

What transpired in the months following was tumultuous. In the courts, in the Bundestag, in the press and other media, among legal scholars, NGOs and other pressure and anti-defamation groups, and within the medical disciplines, a whole

body is permanently and irreparably changed by the circumcision. This change conflicts with the child's [protected] interest of later being able to make his own decision ..."). Art. 2 sec. 2 GG, the Constitution, guarantees that "Every person shall have the right to life and physical integrity." Still, the doctor was himself cleared as under German law he could not have been expected to know of the subsequent finding of illegality (Verbotsirrtum), § 17 StGB. Such a finding is not available under U.S. law.

[10] In particular, Professors *Rolf Dieter Herzberg* (Bochum) and *Holm Putzke* (Passau). See Franz, Die Beschneidung von Jungen: Ein trauriges Vermächtnis, 2014; Putzke FS Herzberg, 2008, 669.

range of historical and contemporary fissures were laid bare – some for the first time, some a renewal of old conflicts. Circumcision and the debates over it offered a window onto a breadth of contemporary social issues, most notably how a secular, formerly Christian or enlightened-Christian liberal democratic welfare state and society should address its large and often observant or tradition-oriented Muslim immigrant and citizen minority: Should the latter's requirement of male circumcision be tolerated as a matter of individual religious freedom? Should it be recognized as a valid group right in a multicultural society? Should it be tolerated as a matter of social peace or recognition of the "other"? Or should it, as an archaism, be opposed in the name of modern liberal values like autonomy, bodily integrity, and public health? Or should it even be banned in the name of *ordre publique* and the state's duty to protect children, even as against their well-intentioned parents? The balance between the collective identity of Muslims and Jews, on the one hand, and of the "entire" political community, on the other, was at issue.

The tenuous position of Muslim immigrants and citizens in German society in recent years seemed to stand at the time in distinct contrast to the success of a reviving Jewish population. Indeed, Germany, decades later than the U.S. and particularly in conservative circles, had begun to adopt the language of a "Judeo-Christian tradition" *(christlich-jüdischen),* which at times was viewed as a simultaneous *instrumentalization* of Jews and *marginalization* of Muslims. As late as November 2010, the CDU could proclaim at its convention that "our cultural values, shaped by the philosophy of the ancient world, the Christian-Jewish tradition, the Enlightenment, and historical experiences form the basis of our social cohesion and constitute the dominant/mainstream *(Leitkultur)* of Germany." And, although in October 2011 *Bundespräsident Christian Wulff,* announced, controversially, that "in the meanwhile, Islam also has come to belong to Germany," he was criticized at the time and since. The rise and continued success of the AfD underscores the issue, with its *Chairman Gauland* announcing shortly before the September 2017 elections that Muslims and Islam were guided by sharia, "a political doctrine ... and as such incompatible with the free liberal-democratic ('*freiheitliche*')" constitutional identity of Germany and that consequently "Islam does not belong to [in] Germany" and is "not to be viewed" through the framework of "religious liberty."[11]

The rancorous circumcision debate took place in a variety of fora but never on a clean slate.[12] Beneath the surface lay an imperfectly scrubbed palimpsest; the Jewish narrative is omnipresent in Germany. To paraphrase *Marx,* on the brains of living German society lies a past nightmare – namely, the Holocaust. A key feature of (West) German *Vergangenheitsbewältigung* or *-aufarbeitung* (coming to terms with the

[11] CDU Program quoted in Bodenheimer, Haut Ab! Die Juden in der Beschneidungsdebatte, 2012, p. 15; Gauland, Süddeutsche Zeitung – SZ.de, 18.9.2017 19:28, http://www.sueddeutsche.de/politik/gauland-islam-gehoert-nicht-zu-deutschland-1.3672693 (no longer available).

[12] It should be noted that debates about circumcision are almost always rancorous and acrimonious. In the U.S., otherwise staid and even boring business law professors can turn lurid and violent on the subject. A good example is Miller Virginia Journal of Social Policy and Law 9 (2002), 497.

past), of its constitutional identity as well as its public culture, has been making Germany a place hospitable both to its tiny surviving Jewish population and to new waves of Jewish immigrants from eastern Europe, the former Soviet Union (FSU), and Israel. Since the circumcision of infant boys is arguably *the* core collective marker of Jewish ethnic identity, constitutive beyond any religious commitments,[13] to ban circumcision would be to break a core post-war and especially post-'68 taboo and to cross a pronounced red line.

A ban on circumcision would represent a dis-invitation to Jews, a hostile act akin to Holocaust denial, it would significantly reverse endless efforts at reconciliation. A century and longer ago, conflicts over Jewish rites like circumcision and kosher animal slaughter had been salient in the construction of a secular and enlightened (if imperfectly liberal) German nation state.[14] In the course of the recent controversies, virtually no one in Germany's political or cultural elite wished to revisit these matters – though some legal scholars and hundreds, perhaps thousands, of letters-to-the editor- writers seemed less inhibited and even eager for the opportunity to break free of the past and a perceived sense of coerced national self-denial.[15] Germany's political class seemed to sense that a Pandora's box was opening, and that a re-estrangement or new othering of Jews was threatening. And, indeed, in the immediate aftermath of the district court decision, several hospitals in Germany (and Austria and Switzerland) ceased performing circumcisions for fear of criminal liability, and in August 2012 the Chief Rabbi in Hof had criminal charges lodged against him by an irate citizen for performing a circumcision. Jews risked, once again, being included among the excluded.

On those occasions that German politicians did lift the lid on Pandora, it was not always pretty. Thus, one social democratic parliamentarian insisted that "respect for life is after all the lesson we draw from the Nazi period," and "the legalization of bodily injury to helpless children" on account of some biblical passage would violate that lesson – thus making the prohibition of a central Jewish practice into evidence of Germany's moral arrival after Nazi anti-Semitism. A Green Party deputy

[13] One might ask what the analogue is for Jewish females, but I shall not do so here. The question has been addressed: Cohen, Why Aren't Jewish Women Circumcised?: Gender and Covenant in Judaism, 2005, pp. 143–190. He argues both that Judaism was thoroughly patriarchal and less attentive to women and that circumcision was meant to bring men down a notch and also bind them to the Lord.

[14] Judd, Contested Rituals: Circumcision, Kosher Butchering, and Jewish Political Life in Germany 1843–1933, 2007.

[15] Some unknown portion of the German population is fed up with these taboos and would like to act out. But these taboos are very strong and carry other features of the post-war settlement with them, such as a pro-American orientation, anti-racism, etc. It is not impossible, it seems to me, that some of the itch to break the taboo is acted out on toward Muslim immigrants instead. One recalls the controversy begun in October 1998 when novelist *Martin Walser* unleashed a furor from the pulpit of the Paulskirche. *Walser* lamented that Germany continued to be constrained and extorted through its Holocaust guilt, a "moral cudgel" used – one wonders by whom? – to hold down the German people. Specifically, he condemned the "instrumentalization of Auschwitz" for contemporary purposes as "a permanent exhibit of our shame." On the other hand, is learning from history an "instrumentalization" of history? Is the past "unusable," an equally problematic and incapacitating proposition? See, Neiman, Learning from the Germans: Race and the Memory of Evil, 2019.

allowed as how "ultimately the burning of widows was also overcome" despite its cultural-religious validation, thereby equating the "harms" in question while also offering a probably unconscious nod in the direction of colonial and imperialist enlightenment.[16]

Along with the immigration, religion, and historical disputes unleashed by the circumcision debate, a more circumscribed legal debate was opened up as well, one suited for international and constitutional comparisons. Who may speak for an infant – or for any minor – when it comes to consent generally, as well as specifically for something like infant or boy-child[17] circumcision?

III. Protecting Children, Parents and the "Barbaric"

Here comparison with the U.S. is instructive. In the legal regimes of both countries, the state as well as parents bear responsibilities of many sorts for children, their safety, health, education, and general upbringing. Laws in both countries recognize this, with Germany even going so far as to constitutionalize the principles of primary and shared responsibility. Art. 6 sec. 2 GG, the Constitution, reads, "The care and upbringing of children is the natural right of parents and a duty primarily incumbent upon them. The state shall watch over them in the performance of this duty."[18] As a general proposition, it may be said that in the triangular relationship among parent, child, and state, the state-child leg is thicker in Germany than in the U.S., where the parent-child leg enjoys greater deference. Whereas parental rights in Germany are assessed for their "proportionality," those rights in the U.S. enjoy nearly "fundamental" status.

The greater power of a stronger, homogenizing German state as against a more private-power centered American constitutional regime is evident elsewhere in the parent/child/state triangle as well. To take another noisy example: "home schooling" is legal and widely well-regarded as an example of both parental engagement and prerogative in the U.S. but illegal in Germany. So substantial is the gap here that

[16] *Marlene Rupprecht* and *Irmingard Schewe-Gerigk,* respectively, quoted and characterized in Heins, Der Skandal der Vielfalt, 2013, pp. 152–153. Impressionistically, it seems that women are more outspoken on this question than men.

[17] Jewish practice is quite uniform in requiring circumcision 8 days after birth, barring extraordinary circumstances; Genesis 17:10–14, reaffirmed in Joshua 5:2–4; Silverman, From Abraham to America: A History of Jewish Circumcision, 2006. Circumcision was abandoned by the Christians as part of their focus on faith in Christ and their decision to appeal to heathens and Hellenists, Acts 15:19; Romans 1:25–29. Muslim practice varies, and the procedure is generally allowed anytime pre-puberty. Since the practice is not itself Koranic but comes from the hadît (sayings of the Prophet), there is considerable variation in the timing and details by country, class, and sect; Clotter, Die Beschneidung im Islam, Cibedo-Texte Nr. 23 (5/1983), 6, 11, Clotter goes so far as to say that, despite its cultural centrality, circumcision itself has "no religious significance or canonical mandate." Rather, "since all of social life is molded by Islam, a relatively important ritual like circumcision necessarily takes on a religious dimension." Still, it is a practice of Muslims rather than of Islam, a matter of community identity.

[18] See also Art. 5 sec. 1 GG. In addition, §§ 1601–1615, 1631 BGB (Civil Code) lay out the responsibilities of parents and children for one another. The District Court found circumcision a "disproportionate" exercise of the parental right to religious education of children.

German home-schoolers have (been organized and) moved to file for asylum in the U.S.[19] on the grounds of state persecution, much to the consternation and incredulity of Germans, who overwhelmingly endorse *Schulpflicht,* the obligation of parents to send their children to one of a large variety of available schools where they will meet and get to know others. In the U.S., this position has long been held to be an authoritarian, not to say tyrannical, appropriation of parental responsibility by an overweening state and reflects that different collective and constitutional identity.[20]

Parental child "abuse" is, of course, illegal in both countries, though Germans may be less willing than others to rely on moral opprobrium to do the primary preventive work. Thus, to cite perhaps similar instances, neither ear piercing nor tattooing is permitted in Germany below the age of 16, regardless of parental permission, and parental authorization is determinative for only the two years between 16 and 18.[21] U.S. laws on tattooing vary a great deal, though generally they take account of parental authorization while rarely if ever do state laws impede parents who wish to pierce even a baby's ears.[22] In the Cologne district court opinion, both the religious rights of the parents and their authority to educate and raise their child *(Sorgerecht)* were outweighed by the child's right to bodily integrity and self-determination in the future – rights the state was empowered, expected, and, here, compelled to enforce.

The circumcision debate, finally, also exposed rifts of subjectivity in the medical sciences or, at least, distinct national practice preferences in Germany and the U.S. Whereas pediatricians and public health professionals in Germany have long been resolute opponents of circumcision on evidence-based scientific grounds, their American peers have been staunch advocates on grounds presumptively equally scientific. Such sharp differences should not exist, or at least need to be accounted for. Insofar as medicine and public health are also social institutions, they have historically paid attention to or cast their gaze on "inferior" immigrant populations. These might be burdened with inherited customs needing enlightened upgrading, such as by being either dissuaded from primitive unhygienic customs like circumcision disdained by the majority culture in Germany or, alternatively, being intro-

[19] The case of the Romeikes, supported by Christian home schooling lobbies, drew worldwide attention; see, for example, BBC, 5.3.2014, http://www.bbc.com/news/world-us-canada-26454988 (visited 11.5.2024); University of St. Thomas Minnesota, Newsroom, 23.11.2012, http://www.stthomas.edu/news/hot-topics-cool-talk-german-home-schoolers (visited 11.5.2024); BBC, 6.11.2013, http://www.bbc.com/news/business-24804804 (visited 11.5.2024).

[20] See U.S. Supreme Court Pierce v Society of Sisters, 268 U.S. 510 (1925) (requiring public schooling of children violated parental liberty to direct education of their children); Meyer v Nebraska, 262 U.S. 390 (1923) (public interest in younger children being educated in English does not outweigh parental discretion); Milliken v Bradley, 418 U.S. 717 (1974) (state did not have authority to bus children out of their school district in order to desegregate); Yoder v. Wisconsin, 406 U.S. 205 (1972) (requirement that parents send their children to school to age 16 violated religious freedom of Mennonite parents).

[21] The Jugendschutzgesetz [Law for the Protection of Children and Youth] is "tougher" than any comparable U.S. law.

[22] In the U.S. this is particularly popular in communities of Hispanic background. On tattooing, Caplan, Written on the Body: The Tattoo in European and American History, 2000.

duced to its cleansing and disease-preventing benefits as construed when dealing with immigrants by the dominant American culture.[23]

At the fevered peak of the controversy, hundreds of German doctors, scientists, and lawyers published an open letter to the government and parliament in which they denounced the "exercise of sexual violence against non-consenting boys," drew a direct connection between male and female circumcision, and insisted that the real issue was "protecting Jewish and Islamic life within the framework of the German legal order"[24] against what one prominent ethicist, *Reinhard Merkel,* labeled the "barbaric," a shocking term usually reserved in German discourse for Nazism. Human Rights laws seem to underscore these enlightened scientific obligations as well, though circumcision's proponents were not lacking in medical-scientific arguments of their own.[25] German physicians made a distinct contribution to the "violent-archaic" argument, helping to propagate the sonorous but distinctly unpluralist notion that "whoever doesn't belong to our times, does not belong in our land."[26] Not only are immigrant and minority cultures barbaric but, apparently as bad from the perspective of German majority cultural identity, they are *archaic,* an unacceptable instance of Ungleichzeitigkeit der Gleichzeitigen.

IV. Repose without Resolution

For the time being, at least, the circumcision debate in Germany has been legislatively resolved in favor of those who might wish, even in the absence of any medical indication, to circumcise their male children for religious reasons. On July 19, 2012 the Bundestag passed a resolution intended to guarantee that "Jewish and Muslim religious life be viable in Germany" and on December 12th of that year a bill was passed that legislatively overrode the ruling of the Cologne District Court and established circumcision, not as *per se* legal, but as a non-punishable undertaking when undertaken for religious reasons by someone professionally trained to perform the procedure (and who need not be a doctor if the child is under six months

[23] It is necessary to establish numbers for various sub-populations, but overall, about 20% of males in Germany are circumcised compared to about 75% in the U.S. Numbers in the U.S. have declined some, partly because the practice is less common among the Latin American immigrants who dominate the current stream, because insurance companies are trying to pay for less and less, and possibly for other reasons to be explored. Numbers at the time in question in Germany seem to have risen to over 12% along with the Muslim population, Kamtsiuris/Bergmann/Rattay/Schlaud Bundesgesundheitsblatt 50 (2007), 836.

[24] Offener Brief zur Beschneidung "Religionsfreiheit kann kein Freibrief für Gewalt sein", FAZ, 21.7.2012, http:www.faz.net/aktuell/politik/inland/offener-brief-zur-beschneidung-11827590.html (visited 11.5.2024).

[25] Thus, in the Convention on the Rights of the Child, Art. 19.1 commits signatories to take all appropriate measures "to protect the child from all forms of physical ... violence, injury, or abuse" while Art. 24 requires them to "take all effective and appropriate measures with a view to abolishing traditional practices prejudicial to the health of children." Proponents regularly referred to well-documented hygienic and disease-prevention benefits.

[26] See Heins, Der Skandal der Vielfalt, 2013, p. 151.

of age).[27] Insofar as a legislature may be more immediately responsive to the public's sense of identity than either the courts or the academic professions, it would seem that German identity grew in capaciousness and toleration of diversity. A thoroughly konsequent commitment to Aufklärung can be oppressive.

Settled as the matter itself seems to be for now, the controversy has left us with extraordinary amounts of published and unpublished documentation from legal, elite, and popular sources. Sometimes the documentation reveals thoroughly incommensurable discourses with no translation keys; sometimes the confrontations seem very knowing and direct. Together with the professional social science, legal, and medical literature around the circumcision question, the debate addressed the four topics – and their ideological and professional expressions – adumbrated here, namely: 1) Germany's relations with its Muslim immigrants and citizens; 2) Germany's relations with its Jewish minority; 3) differences between German and American views of the relationship among parents, child, and state; and 4) differences between German and American medical thinking and practice in this area.

Although it might be thought that these issues, at least as viewed through the window of circumcision, are now "over" and closed, this is hardly the case. New and contradictory developments continue to take place in all four arenas. Thus, at the same moment that the AfD and other populist anti-Muslim and anti-immigrant groups grow on the basis of the claim that "the German way of life" is under siege, the German Constitutional Court has moved in the opposite direction, ruling that, absent a concrete danger, it was an infringement on personal and religious liberty for schools to ban teachers from wearing Muslim headscarves at work, particularly where a state had exempted similar display of "Christian and Western educational and cultural values or traditions" from any ban, thereby privileging a specific religion.[28]

At the same time that Jewish Germany has experienced a tremendous revival, anxieties as to community security have also been revived by an assortment of recent events, including sporadic right-wing violence and imbrication in the Israel-Palestine conflict, itself salient to many immigrants to Germany both before the migration crisis of 2015 and considerably exacerbated by the Israel-Hamas war of 2023-24. While that war produced a dramatic deterioration in relations between the two communities practicing circumcision, it led both to wonder about their "voice" and place in German society and the "lessons of German history."[29]

[27] The Resolution of Parliament appears at BT-Drs. 17/10331 while the law is codified at § 1631 d BGB (Civil Code) among the sections dealing with parental authority and near to § 1626 sec. 1 BGB, which states that "parental custody includes care of the person of the child." The if-under-six-months clause enables Jewish circumcisers (mohelim) to continue to pursue their vocation.

[28] BVerfG 27.1.2015 – 1 Bv R 471/10 und 1 BvR 1181/10, NJW 2015, 1359. The fallout from this decision has taken some time to settle, in both the courts and the schools.

[29] For a summary of that debate, see Deitelhoff/Forst/Günther/Habermas, Grundsätze der Solidarität,13.11.2023, https://www.normativeorders.net/2023/grundsatze-der-solidaritat/ (visited 11.5.2024); Tooze/Moyn/Srinivasan, The Guardian, 22.11.2023, https://www.theguardian.com/world/2023/nov/22/the-principle-of-human-dignity-must-apply-to-all-people (visited 11.5.2024) in response.

V. "Free Exercise" in a Post-Secular Culture

There has been considerable angst expressed in recent years as to how we live in a "post-secular" world,[30] one in which most are irreligious while others persistently attach their religion to national identity (truer in the U.S. and central and eastern Europe, for example, than in Germany). Yet secular liberals still find it hard to accept how seriously religious people take religious practice and attendant cultural practices like circumcision and what that means not only for culture-war issues but for social integration.[31] "Religious liberty," the right, especially of minorities, to exercise religious requirements, may not provide an adequate framework for today's conflicts. Migration and religious revival together have challenged the insulation of the state from religious demands, a prerequisite for existing liberal constitutional understandings of religious liberty as well as of public vs. private. From India to Israel to Turkey to Poland to the United States and beyond, existing "separation of church and state + free exercise of religion" regimes have suffered – -apparently, it might be noted, in some places at an accelerating pace.

Coming from a different direction, multiculturalism, especially in the strong sense of "group rights," is also averse to inherited liberal law and legal culture with their emphasis on the separation of public from private and unapologetic emphasis on individuals rather than groups. Even *Will Kymlicka's* seminal Multicultural Citizenship was initially intended to address historic national minorities, not voluntary immigrants.[32] Still, even those liberal theorists rejecting group rights accept that individual human rights also demand certain concessions to minorities *as groups.* Thus, it has been urged that nation states may "reproduce men and women of a certain sort: Norwegian, French, Dutch, or whatever," but on the condition that they allow "minorities an equal freedom to organize their members, express their cultural values, and reproduce their way of life."[33] Indeed, the International Covenant on Civil and Political Rights insists that "persons belonging to [ethnic, religious, or linguistic] minorities shall not be denied the right … to enjoy their own culture."[34] But no right can be unlimited, and the state certainly need not further that which it dare not deny. Where then might lines be drawn?

At times, High Courts have recognized that religious liberty cannot nullify laws of general applicability. Thus, 30-some years ago, in the U.S., it was still held that

[30] See, for example, Joppke, The Secular State under Siege: Religion and Politics in Europe and America, 2015.

[31] See Carol/Helbling/Michalowski, Gretchenfrage der Integration: Religiöse Praxis prägt das Zusammenleben starker als angenommen, WZB Mitteilungen Nr. 142 (December 2013), p. 18; Carol/Michalowski/HelblingSocial Forces 94 (2015), 647; Burchardt/Michalowski, Islam in Europe: Politics, Law and Religious Life, 2015.

[32] Kymlicka, Multicultural Citizenship: A Liberal Theory of Minority Rights, 2000, pp. 94–96, 114–115; Banting/Kymlicka, Multiculturalism and the Welfare State: Recognition and Redistribution in Contemporary Democracies, 2006.

[33] Gutman, Multiculturalism: Examining the Politics of Recognition/Walzer, 1994, pp. 99-101. Walzer is one of the more sovereigntist and communitarian of liberals.

[34] Art. 1, 27 International Covenant on Civil and Political Rights, adopted by the General Assembly of the United Nations in resolution 2200 (XXI) of 16.12.1966 and opened for signature on 19.12.1966; U.S. Senate Executive Report 102-23; 999 U.N.T.S. 171.

"if prohibiting the exercise of religion is not the object of the [law] but merely the incidental effect of a generally applicable and otherwise valid provision," religious freedom "has not been offended ... To make an individual's obligation to obey such a law contingent upon the law's coincidence with his religious beliefs, except where the State's interest is 'compelling,'" permits a person "by virtue of his beliefs," unacceptably "to become a law unto himself."[35]

More recently, however, responding to this post-secularism, legislatures in some places, including the U.S., have offered religious liberty or religious sentiments considerably greater protection or preference.[36] Indeed, the Congress of the United States in passing the "Religious Freedom Restoration Act" sought to overcome the *Smith* ruling and compel the courts to use a "strict scrutiny" and "compelling interest" test – the highest barriers – whenever a "free exercise of religion" claim was made against a law. The key provision of that Act states:

"Government shall not substantially burden a person's exercise of religion even if the burden results from a rule of general applicability, except ... [g]overnment may substantially burden a person's exercise of religion only if it demonstrates that application of the burden to the person (1) is in furtherance of a compelling governmental interest; (2) is the least restrictive means of furthering that compelling government interest."[37]

Ought this to be the framework through which any full or partial ban on male circumcision should be analyzed? Or does protection of religious exercise permit too much – as seems recently to have become the case in the U.S. – providing special rights and exemptions that undermine principles of equality? Certainly to its opponents, the Bundestag's endorsement of a right to religiously-motivated infant circumcision does just that.

Religion is one aspect of culture, and like culture generally, except in the ever-fewer societies of extreme homogeneity, religion is particularistic. Over the past generation, culture has largely replaced class as the idiom of political debate, largely

[35] U.S. Supreme Court Employment Division v Smith, 494 U.S. 872, 885 (1990) (per Scalia, J) (involving the religious use of peyote, a banned drug). At the time, J. Scalia was considered the right flank of the Court.

[36] The U.S. Congress in response in 1993 passed this so-called Religious Freedom Restoration Act (RFRA), precisely in order to require a compelling government purpose when religious interests are affected. 42 U.S.C. § 2000bb(1)-(4). Although highly valued in recent years by Christian Conservatives, RFRA was initially proposed by liberals seeking to protect Native American rituals involving ceremonial drugs as in the original Smith case. One might interpret the Bundestag's overwhelming endorsement in December 2012, (introducing § 1631d BGB through the "Gesetz über den Umfang der Personensorge bei einer Beschneidung des männlichen Kindes") in this vein as privileging religious freedom over normal government regulation with "incidental effects."

[37] 42 U.S.C. § 2000bb(1)(a)-(b). Subsequently, today's very religion-friendly U.S. Supreme Court has privileged religious belief over general and even over anti-discrimination legislation: U.S. Supreme Court Burwell v Hobby Lobby Stores, 573 U.S. 682 (2014) (allowing religious "free exercise" of fervently Christian employer to exclude birth control coverage from government-mandated employer-provided health insurance); and 303 Creative LLC v. Elenis, 600 U.S. 570 (2023) (which recently held that an anti-gay-marriage commercial web designer cannot be "compelled to speak" or sacrifice her religious views by designing a website for a gay marriage. She was, it seems, not discriminating against gay clientele, just refusing to publicize their gay marriage message.).

dissolving universalistic assumptions and undermining the core liberal distinction between private and public. With the decentering of identities, culture has taken much of the place of class, and various identity claims have displaced broad economic categories. Once, political economy was a virtuous way to organize conflict. In distributional matters, compromise was generally possible. Now however, many societies have arrived at a culturalization of social conflict, a situation where fixed group demographics and identity replace malleable class conflict as an explanation for electoral and political outcomes.[38]

VI. Homogeneity, Leitkultur, and Constitutional Identity

As the circumcision debate helped to make clear, the genie is out of the bottle and issues of culture and identity are not to be denied or returned to a private sphere separated successfully from a public one. Just as socially embedded capitalism, a hallmark of German society and economy for decades gave way to neo-liberalism, so social democracy has become social liberalism. From opposing perspectives, multiculturalists and nationalists alike have succeeded in this regard, and citizenship cannot be dissociated from culture. Outcomes as well as discourses change when state organs have to govern a society where religion, culture, and various other identities have been made objects of explicit demands for recognition. Unthinking majorities and the constitutional identities they have crafted over time are now confronted by both long-time minorities and even more alien new immigrants.

It was not all so long ago that Germany's liberal constitutional identity was still a work in progress – especially for West Germany's Catholics, themselves not fully comfortable with the country's advancing progressive secularism. To assure both majority constitutionalists and *Kulturkampf*-anxious Catholics, the distinguished Catholic legal thinker and jurist *Ernst Wolfgang Böckenförde* sought to show that West Germany was homogenous enough to accommodate all in a liberal constitutional state and society. He formulated this position, which came to be widely known as the "Böckenförde Paradox," to explain that conflict could and would be *real but self-limiting* because of the ultimate homogeneity and consensus of society. The paradox holds that liberal states sit atop value-laden societies:

"[t]he liberal, secularized state is nourished by presuppositions that it cannot itself guarantee. That is the great gamble that it has made for liberty's sake. On the one hand, it can only survive as a liberal state if the liberty it has allowed its citizens regulates itself from within, on the basis of the moral substance of the individual and the homogeneity of society. On the other hand, it cannot attempt to guarantee those internal regulatory forces by its own efforts – that is

[38] The fundamentals of this debate were captured already by Fraser/Honneth, Redistribution or Recognition?, 2003; see also Benhabib, The Claims of Culture: Equality and Diversity in the Global Era, 2002. *Pres. Obama's* 2012 election victory was explained, especially by media and academic supporters, as a triumph of identity demographics, not of class interests. Likewise, *Pres. Trump's* 2016 victory and his continued allure rest on replacing class identity with cultural. See Karp Jacobin 40 (2021), 99. The same might be said of the AfD in Germany, which abandoned its original economic critique in favor of a much more successful identitarian politics.

to say with the instruments of legal coercion and authoritative command – without thereby abandoning its liberalness and ... lapsing into that pretension to totality ... of the denominational civil wars."[39]

The liberality of the liberal state is, in other words, nourished by and dependent on a certain value consensus, one generally left undiscussed, except perhaps in times of revolution or constitution writing. In order to be able to dispute and fight democratically and stably over a certain range of matters, there needs to be a background consensus on numerous other matters, a consensus that goes sometimes to pre-political cultural as well as political values and not just rules, to justice and not just fairness. That agreement, in turn, cannot be limited to procedures or legality but must, *pace* both Rawls's overlapping or overarching consensus and Habermas's "constitutional patriotism," implicate historically and locally-produced sets of values, visions of justice, and a core of ethics. The homogeneity, however relative, that *Böckenförde* assumes, lies somewhere between constitutional patriotism and cultural uniformity.

Does this mean, or can this mean, that Germany is a country with a *Leitkultur,* one that is simultaneously modernist and Christian and which can therefore disfavor practices, such as circumcision, that are at odds with that *Leitkultur?* No one respectable explicitly makes such an argument.[40] At the same time, however, one must wonder why so many German ethicists and jurists cannot even imagine *infant baptism* as violating any of the legal-constitutional strictures they see transgressed by *circumcision*. Ultimately, secularism and liberal Protestantism are more closely tied than most advocates of either would care to acknowledge.

The reality of pluralism, the fact that consensus may be more an *overlapping* of different views than a single capacious *overarching* view, a fortiori commits the state itself to remain agnostic or neutral in its worldview and its conceptions of dignity or justice in matters large and small. For Habermasian liberals, the democratic constitutional state is self-sufficient, able by itself, without "pre-political" foundations, to supply normative justifications for loyalty and legitimacy. It is the democratic constitution and rational-discursive way of life itself that engenders legitimacy without metaphysics and while accommodating citizens with diverse beliefs. From such a perspective, that some people practice circumcision ought to be no problem. Were it were (still) so. Legitimacy maybe cannot spring from legality alone but comes also from places like culture and ethics.

In debating with the then-Pope, *Habermas* recognized that "pre-political" civil society energies are what motivate citizens to go beyond their selfish interests to

---

[39] Formulated in 1967, Böckenförde's Paradox was intended in part as a reminder of the salient role of religion in a democratic Germany. Bökenförde served on the Constitutional Court from 1983–1996. This English translation of Böckenförde is taken from the collection: Böckenförde, State, Society, and Liberty: Studies in Political Theory and Constitutional Law, 1991, p. 45. For a renewal of the Böckenförde discussion with reference to religious values, see Habermas/Ratzinger, The Dialectics of Secularization: On Reason and Religion, 2006, and Habermas et al., An Awareness of What Is Missing: Faith and Reason in a Post-Secular Age, 2010, pp. 18–19, 21.

[40] The rise of the AfD, of course, shows that more and more Germans actually think so, and though the explicit argument is not yet salonfähig, it is now in the Bundestag and several Länder governments. Indeed, the amorphous protest groups – like the Reichsbürger – that have emerged in the shadow of Covid take such an Urkultur for granted.

seek a common good and practice the solidarity and political virtue essential to a democracy: "liberal societal structures are dependent on the solidarity of their citizens." Further, "not only in their abstract substance, but very specifically out of the historical context" of each nation is anything like constitutional patriotism possible. In the end, concedes *Habermas,* "the cognitive process on its own does not suffice": "An abstract solidarity, mediated by the law, arises among citizens only when the principles of justice have penetrated more deeply into the complex of ethical orientations in a given culture."[41] At the same time, however, *Habermas* wants the diverse ethical and religious values that inform society to be expressed only in the shared language of a secular state. This attempt to square the circle – "ethical orientations in a given culture" and expression through the secular state – haunts efforts to govern the circumcision question through principles of religious freedom, which the secular state can only understand and support in a limited and culture majoritarian fashion.[42]

We come close, then, to saying that a certain measure of community *precedes* the legal and social contract. At the same time, as *Max Weber* noted, "It is primarily the political community, no matter how artificially organized, that inspires the belief in a common ethnicity."[43] German society then may, through its constitutional and give-and-take democratic political process, create the *Zusammengehörigkeitsgefühl* – the feeling of belonging together–necessary to accept and treat as German non-majoritarian practices like circumcision. Those feelings and practices of solidarity, of community feeling, *Gemeinsamkeitsgefühl,* in part on account of migration face great stress today in Germany as elsewhere while the law's respect for individual rights and religious freedoms tends in the opposite direction and may tolerate or even encourage a certain fractiousness.

It may be that religious liberty and toleration are no longer adequate principles or mechanisms. Were circumcision the practice of a fictitious group of Germans of about 200,000 or a random ¼ of 1% of the population, then, though objectionable to the majority, it could be tolerated as a matter of indifference, harmless to the society as a whole, like the horse and buggy primary-school-only beliefs of some Mennonite sects.[44] But the 200,000 in question are Jews, and freighted history does not allow "indifference" on either side of the relationship. "Mere toleration" on the majority's side would imply acceptance of a dependent, asymmetrical *inferior*

---

[41] Habermas/Ratzinger, The Dialectics of Secularization: On Reason and Religion, 2006, pp. 31, 32, 33, 34. Finally, it is "cultural resources that nourish citizens' consciousness of norms and their solidarity", p. 46.

[42] Habermas's vision of a secular state with religious people sounds quite idealized American and is, in any event, modeled on a very Protestant model of separation that does not work in most countries. Habermas, Wie viel Religion verträgt der liberale Staat, Neue Zürcher Zeitung, 6.8.2012, https://www.nzz.ch/wie-viel-religion-vertraegt-der-liberale-staat-ld.786772 (visited 11.5.2024).

[43] Roth/Wittich, Max Weber – Economy and Society, 1978, p. 389.

[44] The best known example of this approach is U.S. Supreme Court Wisconsin v. Yoder, 406 U.S. 205 (1972), a case in which the U.S. Supreme Court found that on account of their family's religious beliefs Amish children could not be forced to attend school to age 16 or past 8th grade. The Court (mis-)construed the Amish as a harmless, hermetically sealed sect of about 15,000 in Wisconsin.

position by the tolerated minority, which is given "permission" to be different.[45] And as *Rainer Forst* points out quoting *Goethe:* "Tolerance should be a temporary attitude only: it must lead to recognition. To tolerate means to insult."[46]

If toleration of Jewish circumcision via cool indifference does not work for historical reasons, it could not work for the Muslim population of 5 million or nearly 6% for numerical reasons alone. They are too many, and they are not charming. Further, since most of that population is still "becoming German," the issue is one of respect (or non-respect) as moral and political equals, of recognizing Muslims as belonging to a common framework of social life. If not, then circumcision may be banned as a violation of that common framework, just as the District Court had maintained. Can majority German society and its legal institutions accept the right to justify the practice of circumcision?

Can the "homogeneity" or bonding forces of society provide bridges to others? If that homogeneity is based on particularistic ethical foundations – like the modernist, secularized, liberal Christianity of the *Leitkultur* that animates so many German jurists and ethicists – then "no." *Too much toleration* would undermine the consensus that makes toleration and social solidarity possible to begin with. In the circumcision debates, the presumptive neutrality of science and the integrity of the individual and his will were the cultural and legal principles that served as the outer defense perimeter against particularistic or outsider challenges to that consensus. "Illiberal liberalism" at work, it seemed.[47] On the other hand, circumcision was, in the end, validated. If some shared sense of fairness, fairness toward different ethical views, can grow out of the experience of living together and be backed by political and social power to help make others listen to diverse justifications, then the constructed homogeneity of society will allow us to say, "yes, bonds and bridges are both possible." And *Vice Chancellor Habeck* may have fewer occasions to express disappointment and offer admonishment.

---

[45] This important point is made by Forst, The Limits of Toleration, Constellations 11:3 (2004), 312 (313, 315).

[46] Forst, The Limits of Toleration, Constellations 11:3 (2004), 312 (316), quoting Goethe, Maximen und Reflexionen, Werke 6, 1981, p. 507.

[47] Gray, Two Faces of Liberalism, 2002, he argues that liberalism contains two contradictory faces, one advocating progress and universal enlightenment, the other tolerance and peaceful coexistence.

MARIANNE ANDRAE

Vermögensrechtliche Ansprüche und Unterhaltspflichten zwischen Partnern faktischer Lebensgemeinschaften mit grenzüberschreitendem Bezug

I. *Problemstellung*

Die vermögensrechtlichen Wirkungen faktischer Lebensgemeinschaften im IZPR/IPR sind ein Dauerthema. Noch immer wird darum gestritten, ob diese von EU-Verordnungen und dem HUntStProt 2007[1], die einschlägig sein könnten, erfasst oder nicht erfasst sind. Auch in der vom *Jubiliar* herausgegebenen und allseitig geschätzten Kommentarreihe zum Europäischen Prozess- und Kollisionsrecht vertreten die Autoren hierzu unterschiedliche Auffassungen. Weitgehende Einigkeit besteht darin, dass die Verbindungen vom personellen Anwendungsbereich der beiden EU-Güterrechtsverordnungen ausgeschlossen sind.[2] Anders sieht es bezogen auf die anderen Rechtsinstrumente aus. Zu nennen ist hier zB ein Beitrag von *Winkler,*[3] in dem ausführlich das diesbezügliche materielle Recht Kroatiens, Sloweniens, Italiens, Spaniens und Litauens beschrieben wird. Bezogen auf die grenzüberschreitende Problematik wird dort konstatiert, dass die EU-LP-GüterVO nicht anwendbar sei und – ohne dies dann näher zu begründen – diese dem einzelstaatlichen Recht der Mitgliedstaaten überlassen ist. Dieser Beitrag wird durchaus die Rechtspraxis in den Mitgliedstaaten tangieren. Der Sammelband, in dem der Beitrag veröffentlicht ist, ist im Rahmen des von der EU kofinanzierten Projekts „E-Training zu EU-Familiengüterregimen" (EU-FamPro) verfasst worden. Die Monographie ist frei im Internet zugänglich.[4] Finanziert wurde dies durch das Förderprogramm „Justiz" der Europäischen Union (EU) für die Jahre 2014–2020.

Mit der Schlussfolgerung von *Winkler* gehen die Ausführungen von *Gruber* zur Reform des deutschen Kollisionsrechts hinsichtlich rein „faktischer" – auf Dauer angelegter – Lebensgemeinschaften konform.[5] Sein Vorschlag läuft darauf hinaus,

---

[1] Protokoll über das auf Unterhaltspflichten anzuwendende Recht v. 23.11.2007, Anhang zu Beschl. 2009/941/EG, ABl. 2009 L 331, 19.

[2] Ua Heiderhoff IPRax 2018, 1 (4); Coester, Besonderheiten der Verordnung für das Güterrecht eingetragener Paare, in: Dutta/Weber, Die europäischen Güterrechtsverordnungen, 2017, S. 111 Rn. 8; aA Dutta FamRZ 2016, 1973 (1976).

[3] Winkler, De Facto Couples: Between National Solutions and European Trends, in: Ruggeri/Limantė/Pogorelčnik Vogrinc, The EU Regulations on Matrimonial Property and Property of Registered Partnerships, 2022, S. 245

[4] https://www.intersentiaonline.com/library/the-eu-regulations-on-matrimonial-property-and-property-of-registered-partnerships (abgerufen 1.5.2024).

[5] Gruber IPRax 2021, 39 (50ff.).

dass ihre Wirkungen bei einer Neuregelung von Art. 14 EGBGB mit der Folge einer (primären) wandelbaren objektiven Anknüpfung an den jeweiligen gemeinsamen gewöhnlichen Aufenthalt erfasst werden sollten. Das läuft auf ein einheitliches Wirkungsstatut für faktische Lebensgemeinschaften in Anbindung an das für die Ehe hinaus.[6] Demgegenüber kommt *Cl. Mayer* in einem neueren Beitrag zu grenzüberschreitenden nicht formalisierten Paarbeziehungen zu dem Schluss, dass auf Ausgleichsansprüche bei Auflösung einer solchen Beziehung keine familienrechtlichen Kollisionsnormen – auch nicht im Wege der Analogie – anwendbar seien.[7] Die betreffenden Ausgleichsansprüche wären auf Grund ihrer schuldrechtlichen Natur von der Rom I-VO erfasst. Der Anwendungsvorrang der Verordnung hindere auch eine autonome kollisionsrechtliche Neuregelung.

II. Um was für Verhältnisse und Ansprüche geht es?

Gegenstand der Erörterung sind vermögensrechtliche Wirkungen, die ihren Grund in der faktischen Lebensgemeinschaft haben. Unter dem Begriff faktische Lebensgemeinschaft wird die stabile, auf Dauer (unbestimmte Zeit) angelegte Beziehung eines in einem gemeinsamen Haushalt lebenden Paares verstanden.[8] Die Partner sind nicht miteinander verheiratet und ihre Beziehung erfüllt auch nicht die Kriterien einer eingetragenen Lebenspartnerschaft iSd EU-LP-GüterVO. Für die Partnerschaft findet sich auch der Begriff nichteheliche Lebensgemeinschaft. Sie beruht auf dem freien Entschluss der Partner, ist nicht registriert und kann von ihnen jederzeit einverständlich oder einseitig ohne Rechtsgrund und ohne Einhaltung eines rechtlich vorgeschriebenen Verfahrens beendet werden. Charakteristisch ist die gewollte Nichtehelichkeit/Nichtinstitutionalisierung der Beziehung. Äußerlich muss die Lebensgemeinschaft durch einen gemeinsamen Haushalt in Erscheinung treten. Deshalb wird regelmäßig während des Bestehens der Gemeinschaft ein gemeinsamer Lebensmittelpunkt vorhanden sein. Die inneren, persönlichen Beziehungen müssen so gestaltet sein, dass sie über eine reine Haushalts- und Wirtschaftsgemeinschaft hinausgehen. Keine Bedeutung haben das Geschlecht und die sexuelle Orientierung der Partner.[9] Es geht also zusammengefasst um die vermögensrechtlichen Wirkungen einer gelebten, bereits längere Zeit bestehenden faktischen Lebensgemeinschaft zweier Personen mit grenzüberschreitendem Bezug,

[6] In der Tendenz auch Münchener Kommentar zum BGB/Coester, 9. Aufl. 2024, EGBGB Art. 17b Rn. 124; Sonnenberger FS Coester-Waltjen, 2015, 787 (807ff.); Beck'scher Online-Kommentar BGB/Mörsdorf, 69. Ed. 1.11.2023, EGBGB Art. 13 Rn. 19.

[7] Mayer, Die nichteheliche Paarbeziehung im Internationalen Privatrecht, in: Budzikiewicz/Heiderhoff/Klinkhammer/Niethammer-Jürgens, Europa als Taktgeber für das Internationale Familienrecht, Dialog internationales Familienrecht IV, 2022, S. 141 (insb. 159); hierzu Budzikiewicz/Heiderhoff IPRax 2022, 538 (539).

[8] Angelehnt an EGMR 22.7.2010 – 18984/02, BeckRS 2016, 12098 Rn. 30: „Die Beziehung der Bf. – ein im gemeinsamen Haushalt und in einer stabilen de facto-Beziehung lebendes, gleichgeschlechtliches Paar – fällt daher unter den Begriff «Familienleben», so wie dies auch im Falle eines heterosexuellen Paares zutreffen würde."

[9] So auch ua Münchener Kommentar zum BGB/Coester, 9. Aufl. 2024, EGBGB Art. 17b Rn. 122.

die als Geschlechts- und Wirtschaftsgemeinschaft geführt wird. Einbezogen sind auch solche Beziehungen, bei denen die Lebenspartnerschaft bereits begründet ist und sich aus den Umständen die feste Absicht der Partner ableiten lässt, eine beständige Lebensgemeinschaft führen zu wollen. Zu den vermögensrechtlichen Wirkungen zählen einerseits als unterhaltsrechtlich zu qualifizierende Verpflichtungen und zum anderen solche, die bezogen auf die Ehe/eingetragene Lebenspartnerschaft nach der EU-EheGüterVO/EU-LP-GüterVO unter den Begriff des Güterstandes fallen würden. Gemeint sind damit sämtliche vermögensrechtliche Regelungen, die zwischen den Partnern sowie in ihren Beziehungen zu Dritten direkt aufgrund der faktischen Lebensgemeinschaft oder deren Beendigung gelten. Das betrifft sowohl vermögensrechtliche Aspekte, die die Verwaltung des Hausstandes und des gemeinsamen Lebens im weiten Sinne im Alltag betreffen als auch die vermögensrechtliche Auseinandersetzung, insbesondere infolge der Trennung des Paares oder des Todes eines Partners. Das Merkmal der Unmittelbarkeit ist eher in einem weiten Sinne zu verstehen. Es reicht ein innerer Zusammenhang zur Lebensgemeinschaft oder ihrer Auflösung.[10] Vermögensrechtliche Beziehungen, die zwischen den Partnern bestehen, jedoch keinen solchen unmittelbaren Zusammenhang zur Lebensgemeinschaft oder ihrer Auflösung aufweisen, sind hinsichtlich der Zuordnung zu infrage kommenden europäischen Rechtsinstrumenten unproblematisch.[11] Auf sie finden die Normen des europäischen IZPR und IPR im Allgemeinen Anwendung. Das maßgebliche Recht für Ansprüche der Partner aus solchen einzelnen schuldrechtlichen Verträgen (Schenkung, Darlehen, Arbeitsvertrag, Übernahme einer Bürgschaft, einfache Gesellschaft) ist, wenn der direkte Bezug zur Gestaltung der nichtehelichen Lebensgemeinschaft fehlt, gesondert nach den einschlägigen Bestimmungen der Rom I-VO zu bestimmen.[12]

III. Verhältnisse, die mit der Ehe vergleichbare Wirkungen haben

Vermögensrechtliche Streitigkeiten zwischen den Partnern, die ihren Grund in der Lebensgemeinschaft haben, sind Zivilsachen iSd Brüssel Ia-VO.[13] Sie werden von ihrem sachlichen Anwendungsbereich erfasst, es sei denn, die Anwendung ist nach Art. 1 Abs. 2 Brüssel Ia-VO ausgeschlossen. Es geht dabei um den Ausschlusstatbestand der „ehelichen Güterstände oder Güterstände aufgrund von Verhältnissen, die nach dem auf diese Verhältnisse anzuwendenden Recht mit der Ehe ver-

---

[10] Vgl. Art. 3 lit. a EU-EheGüterVO; Zum Begriff des Güterstandes nach den EU-EheGüterVO ua: Köhler, Der sachliche Anwendungsbereich der Güterrechtsverordnungen und der Umfang des Güterstatuts, in: Dutta/Weber, Die europäischen Güterrechtsverordnungen, 2017, S. 147ff.; Mankowski NZFam 2021, 757; Andrae IPRax 2018, 221.

[11] Bezogen auf eheliche Beziehungen: EuGH 14.6.2017 – C-67/17, ECLI:EU:C:2017:459 Rn. 29 = BeckRS 2017, 122519, bereits EuGH 27.3.1979 – 143/78, ECLI:EU:C:1979:83 Rn. 7 (de Cavel).

[12] Staudinger, BGB/Mankowski, 2011, EGBGB Anh. zu Art. 13 Rn. 75; Schaal ZNotP 2009, 290 (297).

[13] EuGH 6.6.2019 – C-361/18, ECLI:EU:C:2019:473 = BeckRS 2019, 10517 (sachlich ging es um die Vermögensauseinandersetzung nach Beendigung der faktischen Lebensgemeinschaft).

gleichbare Wirkung entfalten". Einen solchen sehen auch Art. 1 Abs. 2 lit. c Rom I-VO und Art. 1 Abs. 2 lit b Rom II-VO vor.

Der EuGH[14] hat entschieden, dass die Vermögensauseinandersetzung der ehemaligen Partner einer faktischen Lebensgemeinschaft mangels ehelicher Verbindung nicht unter den Tatbestand der „ehelichen Güterstände" gemäß Art. 1 Abs. 2 lit. a Brüssel Ia-VO fällt. Dies begründet er einerseits mit der gebotenen engen Auslegung der Bereichsausnahmen. Andererseits argumentiert er dahingehend, dass die Erweiterung des Ausschlusstatbestandes auf Verhältnisse, die nach dem auf sie anzuwendenden Recht mit der Ehe vergleichbare Wirkungen entfalten, jede Bedeutung genommen wäre, wenn vermögensrechtliche Streitigkeiten faktischer Lebensgemeinschaften bereits unter den Tatbestand „eheliche Güterstände" subsumiert werden könnten. Daraus lässt sich folgern, dass der EuGH es jedenfalls nicht ausschließt, dass diese unter den erweiterten Tatbestand in Art. 1 Abs. 2 lit. a Brüssel Ia-VO fallen. Bereits ein Jahr davor war der EuGH mit Vorlagefragen seitens des österreichischen OGH in einem Fall befasst, in dem zunächst hätte geprüft werden müssen, ob die Bereichsausnahme bezogen auf die Brüssel Ia-VO zutrifft.[15] Es ging um die internationale Zuständigkeit für die Klage auf Gesamtschuldnerausgleich eines Partners gegen seine Partnerin nach Auflösung ihrer faktischen Lebensgemeinschaft. Die Partner hatten während des Bestehens der Lebensgemeinschaft gemeinsam mehrere Kredite zur Finanzierung gemeinsamen Wohneigentums aufgenommen. Nach Art. 27 lit. e EU-EheGüterVO gehören zur Reichweite des Güterstatuts die Teilung, Aufteilung oder Abwicklung des Vermögens. Vermögen umfasst nicht nur das aktive, sondern auch das passive Vermögen. Bei einer ordentlichen Prozessführung seitens einer verklagten Partei wird der Ausgleich nicht unabhängig von der nachpartnerschaftlichen Nutzung bzw. Verwertung des gemeinsamen Wohneigentums entschieden werden. Wären im Fall die Streitparteien ehemalige Ehegatten, würde es sich folglich um eine Streitigkeit aus „ehelichen Güterständen" handeln. Es kommt deshalb normativ darauf an, ob es sich bei faktischen Lebensgemeinschaften um Verhältnisse handelt, die nach dem auf diese Verhältnisse anzuwendenden Recht mit der Ehe vergleichbare Wirkungen entfalten. Zur Auslegung dieses Passus findet sich kein Hinweis in den Erwägungsgründen der Brüssel Ia-VO, jedoch in denen der Rom I-und Rom II-VO.[16] Danach sollte diese Frage nach dem Recht des Mitgliedstaates ausgelegt werden, in dem sich das angerufene Gericht befindet.[17] Das stimmt zwar nicht mit dem Wortlaut der Norm überein, ist jedoch die einzig sinnvolle Lösung, wenn die an sich zu bevorzugende einheitliche autonome Auslegung nach dem Wortlaut der Norm ausgeschlossen ist. Letztere wäre durchaus hinsichtlich der Zuordnung/Nichtzuordnung von vermögensrechtlichen Streitigkeiten, die ihren Grund in faktischen Lebensgemeinschaften haben, ohne komplizierten Vergleich zur Ehe bei funktio-

[14] EuGH 6.6.2019 – C-361/18, ECLI:EU:C:2019:473 = BeckRS 2019, 10517.

[15] EuGH 15.6.2017 – C-249/16, ECLI:EU:C:2017:472 = BeckRS 2017, 113096.

[16] ErwGr. 8 Rom I-VO; ErwGr. 10 Rom II-VO.

[17] Rauscher, EuZPR/EuIPR/Mankowski, 5. Aufl. 2021, Brüssel Ia-VO Art. 1 Rn. 93; beck-online.GROSSKOMMENTAR zum Zivilrecht/Paulus, Stand 1.12.2023, Rom I-VO Art. 1 Rn. 74; Rauscher, EuZPR/EuIPR/von Hein, 5. Aufl. 2023, Rom I-VO Art. 1 Rn. 26.

neller Betrachtung möglich. Für den Ausschluss vom Anwendungsbereich könnte angeführt werden, dass die Zuständigkeitsordnung der Brüssel Ia-VO keine sachnahen gesetzlichen Zuständigkeiten für lebenspartnerschaftliche Streitigkeiten vorsieht, die bezogen auf Ehegatten oder eingetragene Lebenspartner unter dem Begriff „Güterstand" zu subsumieren wären. Eine entsprechende Regelung wie in Art. 6 EU-EheGüterVO wäre funktionsadäquater, sie fehlt jedoch. Gegen einen Ausschluss lässt sich anführen, dass er mangels einer anderweitigen unionsrechtlichen einheitlichen Regelung dazu führen würde, dass sich die internationale Zuständigkeit nunmehr nach einzelstaatlichem Recht richten würde. Jedenfalls hält das deutsche IZVR für diese Art von Streitigkeiten keine funktionsadäquateren Bestimmungen zur internationalen Zuständigkeit im Vergleich zur Brüssel Ia-VO bereit. De lege lata zählen diese vermögensrechtlichen Streitigkeiten im deutschen Verfahrensrecht noch nicht einmal zu den sonstigen Familiensachen, vgl. § 266 FamFG. Für sie gilt die Zuständigkeitsordnung der ZPO unmittelbar, aus deren Vorschriften über die örtliche Zuständigkeit zugleich die internationale Zuständigkeit abgeleitet wird (Grundsatz der Doppellfunktionalität). Der Ausschluss hätte zudem zur Folge, dass die Bestimmungen der Verordnung zur Anerkennung und Vollstreckung von Entscheidungen, gerichtlichen Vergleichen und öffentlichen Urkunden aus einem Mitgliedstaat in den anderen Mitgliedstaaten keine Anwendung fänden und folglich nunmehr dem autonomen IZVR der Mitgliedstaaten unterliegen würden. Insgesamt wäre dies ein Rückschritt gegenüber der Rechtslage nach der Brüssel I-VO. Es ist deshalb funktionell betrachtet zu empfehlen, die vermögensrechtlichen Streitigkeiten zwischen Partnern oder ehemaligen Partnern einer faktischen Lebensgemeinschaft nicht aus dem Anwendungsbereich der Brüssel Ia-VO auszuklammern, auch wenn sie bezogen auf Ehegatten oder ehemalige Ehegatten zu den ehelichen Güterständen gehören und deshalb der EU-EheGüterVO unterliegen.[18] Aufgrund der gebotenen engen Auslegung der Bereichsausnahmen in Art. 1 Abs. 2 Brüssel Ia-VO steht dieses Ergebnis nicht im Widerspruch zum Wortlaut der normativen Regelung. Zu vergleichen sind nämlich nicht die vermögensrechtlichen Wirkungen einer faktischen Lebensgemeinschaft mit denen der Ehe, vielmehr geht es um die allgemeinen rechtlichen Wirkungen dieser Verbindungen. Der Vergleich ist nicht anhand des deutschen materiellen Rechts, sondern nach der im deutschen IPR anerkannten funktionellen Qualifikationsmethode vorzunehmen. In allen Mitgliedstaaten hat die Eheschließung, die im institutionellen Rahmen erfolgt und registrierungspflichtig ist, die Änderung des familienrechtlichen Status der Beteiligten zur Folge. Mit dem Tag der Eheschließung werden weitreichende gegenseitige gesetzliche Rechte und Pflichten der Ehegatten, zu denen Beistands- und Einstandspflichten gehören, begründet, wobei es nicht darauf ankommt, ob sie zusammenleben und einen gemeinsamen Hausstand haben. Auch nach faktischer Trennung besteht die Ehe mit gesetzlichen Rechten und Pflichten fort. Für ihre Auflösung sind gesetzlich institutionelle Verfahren und Auflösungs-

[18] Wie hier: Brosch FamRZ 2019, 1557 (1561); Mankowski NZFam 2019, 890; in der Tendenz für eine Zuordnung zu dem Ausschlusstatbestand: Rauscher, EuZPR/EuIPR/Mankowski, 5. Aufl. 2021, Brüssel Ia-VO Art. 1 Rn. 94.

gründe vorgeschrieben. Alles dies trifft auf die faktische Lebensgemeinschaft nicht zu, so dass ausreichend Argumente bestehen, eine Vergleichbarkeit der Wirkungen bezogen auf Art. 1 Abs. 2 lit. a Brüssel Ia-VO zu verneinen.[19] Daraus folgt, dass vermögensrechtliche Streitigkeiten von Partnern oder ehemaligen Partnern faktischer Lebensgemeinschaften, die unmittelbar ihren Grund in dieser Partnerschaft und ihrer Auflösung haben und die bezogen auf Ehegatten/ehemaligen Ehegatten als güterrechtlich zu qualifizieren wären, vom sachlichen Anwendungsbereich der Brüssel Ia-VO erfasst werden. Aus der gebotenen identischen Auslegung der Art. 1 Abs. 2 lit. c Rom I-VO/Art. 1 Abs. 2 lit. b Rom II-VO ergibt sich, dass dieser Ausschlusstatbestand dort nicht die faktische Lebensgemeinschaft einschließt. Für diese beiden Verordnungen kommt es deshalb darauf an, ob der Ausschusstatbestand der Art. 1 Abs. 2 lit. b Rom I -VO/Art. 1 Abs. 1 lit. a Rom II zutrifft.

IV. Familienverhältnis oder Verhältnis mit vergleichbaren Wirkungen

Art. 1 Abs. 2 lit. e Brüssel Ia-VO schließt Unterhaltspflichten aus, „die auf einem Familien-, Verwandtschafts- oder eherechtlichen Verhältnis oder Schwägerschaft beruhen". Für diese Bereichsausnahme in Art. 1 Abs. 2 Brüssel Ia-VO ist keine enge Auslegung erforderlich, denn es droht diesbezüglich keine Regelungslücke. Wortgleich ist der Anwendungsbereich der EG-UntVO in Art. 1 Abs. 1 EG-UntVO bestimmt. Eine übereinstimmende Auslegung ist angezeigt.[20] Diese liegt auch für das HUntStProt 2007 schon deshalb nahe, weil es über Art. 15 EG-UntVO in das unionsrechtliche Regelungssystem für grenzüberschreitende familienrechtliche Unterhaltspflichten einbezogen ist. Der europäische Verordnungsgeber hat im Laufe des Gesetzgebungsprozesses für die EG-UntVO eine Anpassung an die Umschreibung des personellen Geltungsbereichs des HUntStProt 2007 vorgenommen und damit auf einen Gleichlauf mit den Begriffen in den Ausschlusstatbeständen in Art. 1 Abs. 2 lit. b Rom I-VO und Art. 1 Abs. 2 lit. a Rom II-VO verzichtet.[21] Er hat mit der Verordnung das Ziel verfolgt, ein kohärentes unionsrechtliches Rechtsinstrument für Unterhaltssachen zu schaffen, das das Kollisionsrecht mit einschließt.[22] Der Begriff Familienbeziehung hat im Art. 1 HUntSt-

[19] EuGH 19.12.2019 – C-460/18P, ECLI:EU:C:2019:1119 = BeckRS 2019, 32149 hat in einem anderen Zusammenhang die Wirkungen der Ehe und der nichtehelichen Lebensgemeinschaft verglichen und verneint, dass sich nichteheliche Lebensgefährten hinsichtlich der Hinterbliebenenversorgung in vergleichbarer Situation wie Verheiratete oder wie Partner einer eingetragenen Partnerschaft bezogen auf das belgische Recht befinden. Hierzu prononciert der Vergleich der Wirkungen in den Schlussanträgen von Generalanwalt Pikamäe 29.7.2019 – C-460/18P, ECLI:EU:C:2019:646 Rn. 85ff.

[20] So auch Hilbig GPR 2011, 310 (313); aA Althammer NZFam 2016, 629 (631f.), wonach der Begriff Familienverhältnis für die EG-UntVO anders als für das HUntStProt 2007 ausschließlich unionsautonom auszulegen ist.

[21] Im Art. 1 Abs. 1 EG-UntVO-E (Europäische Kommission KOM (2005) 649 endgültig, 15) heißt es noch: „Diese Verordnung findet Anwendung auf Unterhaltspflichten, die sich aus einem Familienverhältnis ergeben oder aus Beziehungen, die nach einschlägigem Recht eine ähnliche Wirkung entfalten".

[22] ErwGr. 10 EG-UntVO.

Prot 2007 eine doppelte Bedeutung. Er steht zum einen für die zusammenfassende Charakterisierung der Beziehungen Ehe, Verwandtschaft und Schwägerschaft. Darüber hinaus werden auch andere Beziehungen erfasst,[23] dabei ist jedenfalls der vom Protokoll gewählte Begriff von Familie eher weit gemeint,[24] was in der differenzierten kollisionsrechtlichen Regelung, zugeschnitten auf die verschiedenen Familienbeziehungen, begründet ist.[25] Welche anderen Beziehungen gemeint sind, ist im Protokoll nicht bestimmt. Auch sind die Kollisionsnormen des Protokolls nicht auf die Frage anzuwenden, ob die betreffende Beziehung eine Familienbeziehung darstellt.[26] Insoweit ist hierfür eine *lex causae* Qualifikation ausgeschlossen. Folglich ist es den teilnehmenden Vertragsstaaten überlassen, welche anderen Beziehungen außer den normativ aufgezählten in die Kategorie Familienbeziehungen fallen. Das ist unter Berücksichtigung dessen zu verstehen, dass für das HUntStProt 2007 gegebenenfalls die EU und die Mitgliedstaaten gleichermaßen als Vertragsstaaten gelten, vgl. Art. 24 Abs. 5 HUntStProt 2007. In Betracht kommt bezogen auf die Mitgliedstaaten in erster Linie eine einheitliche autonome Auslegung, welche weiteren Beziehungen vom Begriff erfasst werden.[27] Möglich ist jedoch auch, dies den mitgliedstaatlichen Rechtsordnungen zu überlassen. Beide Methoden können kombiniert werden, indem bestimmte Beziehungen autonom einheitlich zu den Familienbeziehungen gezählt werden und im Übrigen die Zuordnung den mitgliedstaatlichen Rechtsordnungen zunächst überlassen wird, solange die autonome Begriffsbestimmung noch im Prozess ist. Dass dieser Weg langwierig und nicht abgeschlossen ist, zeigt sich in der unterschiedlichen Begriffsverwendung in den EU-Verordnungen. In der EG-UntVO wird der Begriff nicht näher bestimmt. In ErwGr. 11 EG-UntVO wird der Wortlaut von Art. 1 Abs. 1 EG-UntVO ohne nähere Erläuterung wiederholt. Außerdem ist bestimmt, dass der Begriff Unterhaltspflicht autonom auszulegen ist, ohne dies auch für den Begriff Familienbeziehungen zu reklamieren. Der entsprechende Ausschlusstatbestand in Art. 1 Abs. 2 lit. b

[23] U.a. für das HUntStProt 2007: Bonomi, Protokoll vom 23. November 2007 über das auf Unterhaltspflichten anwendbare Recht, Erläuternder Bericht, 2009, Rn. 29 (eher weiter Begriff, der nicht auf die aufgelisteten Beispiele begrenzt ist); Hilbig GPR 2011, 310 (312); Staudinger, BGB/Mankowski, 2021, HUP Art. 1 Rn. 79ff.; beck-online.GROSSKOMMENTAR zum Zivilrecht/Yassari, Stand 1.12.2022, HUP 2007 Art. 1 Rn. 41; Hausmann, Internationales und Europäisches Familienrecht, 2. Aufl. 2018, C Rn. 47; Rauscher, EuZPR/EuIPR/Andrae, 4. Aufl. 2016, HUntStProt 2007 Art. 1 Rn. 4ff.; Althammer NZFam 2016, 629 (630); für die EG-UntVO: beck-online.GROSSKOMMENTAR zum Zivilrecht/Wurmnest, Stand 1.11.2023, EU-UnterhaltsVO Art. 1 Rn. 91ff.; Münchener Kommentar zum FamFG/Lipp, 3. Aufl. 2019, EuUntVO Art. 1 Rn. 13.

[24] Bonomi, Protokoll vom 23. November 2007 über das auf Unterhaltspflichten anwendbare Recht, Erläuternder Bericht, 2009, Rn. 29

[25] Hilbig GPR 2011, 310 (312); Andrae, Internationales Familienrecht, 5. Aufl. 2024, § 10 Rn. 20, Staudinger, BGB/Mankowski, 2021, HUP Art. 1 Rn. 81.

[26] Bonomi, Protokoll vom 23. November 2007 über das auf Unterhaltspflichten anwendbare Recht, Erläuternder Bericht, 2009, Rn. 31, anders wohl Münchener Kommentar zum BGB/Staudinger, 9. Aufl. 2024, HUP Art. 1 Rn. 16.

[27] Ausschließlich für eine autonome einheitliche Auslegung ua Münchener Kommentar zum FamFG/Lipp, 3. Aufl. 2019, Art. 1 Rn. 14; Hausmann, Internationales und Europäisches Familienrecht, 2. Aufl. 2018, C Rn. 48; beck-online.GROSSKOMMENTAR zum Zivilrecht/Wurmnest, Stand 15.11.2023, EU-UnterhaltsVO Art. 1 Rn. 93.

Rom I-VO/Art. 1 Abs. 2 lit. a Rom II-VO umfasst neben Schuldverhältnissen aus Vermögensbeziehungen auch Unterhaltspflichten aus einem Familienverhältnis oder aus Verhältnissen, die nach dem auf diese Verhältnisse anzuwendenden Recht vergleichbare Wirkungen entfalten. Er ist angelehnt an den Wortlaut des Art. 1 Abs. 1 EG-UntVO-E, der in die Endfassung nicht übernommen wurde, wahrscheinlich um einen Gleichlauf zum HUntStProt 2007 herzustellen.[28] Art. 1 Abs. 2 lit. b RomÜbk[29], Vorläuferübereinkommen zur Rom I-VO, schloss von seinem Anwendungsbereich neben den ehelichen Güterständen auch Schuldverhältnisse aus, die Rechte und Pflichten betreffen, die auf einem Familien-, Verwandtschafts- oder eherechtlichen Verhältnis oder auf einer Schwägerschaft beruhen. Mit dieser Aufzählung sollte das gesamte Familienrecht aus dem Anwendungsbereich des Übereinkommens ausgeschlossen werden.[30] Der Begriff „Verhältnisse, die nach dem auf diese Verhältnisse anzuwendenden Recht vergleichbare Wirkungen entfalten“, ist auch in diesem Übereinkommen nicht anzutreffen. Um die Gleichbehandlung der betroffenen Verhältnisse in den europäischen Rechtsinstrumenten zu sichern, sollte eine Auslegung dahingehend erfolgen, dass es bei den durch Art. 1 Abs. 2 Rom I-VO/Rom II-VO vom Anwendungsbereich ausgeschlossenen Verhältnissen mit vergleichbaren Wirkungen um jene geht, die in den anderen Rechtsinstrumenten vom weiten Begriff Familienverhältnisse erfasst werden.[31] Es sind die sonstigen Familienverhältnisse, also die, die nicht auf Verwandtschaft, Ehe und Schwägerschaft beruhen. Ob es sich um ein solches handelt, soll gemäß ErwGr. 8 Rom I-VO und ErwGr. 10 Rom II-VO nach dem Recht des Mitgliedstaats ausgelegt werden, in dem sich das angerufene Gericht befindet. Das wird teilweise so verstanden, dass dies jeweils anhand des nach dem IPR der *lex fori* anwendbaren Sachrechts zu bestimmen ist.[32] Eher muss hier nach der funktionellen Qualifikationsmethode, die im IPR für ausländische Rechtsinstitute entwickelt wurde, vorgegangen werden.[33] Es sind zwei Schritte erforderlich. Zunächst ist das betreffende Rechtsverhältnis anhand des darauf anwendbaren Rechts hinsichtlich seiner charakteristischen Merkmale zu analysieren. Bezogen auf die faktische Lebensgemeinschaft besteht die Besonderheit, dass sie in vielen Staaten mit den oben dargestellten Merkmalen anzutreffen ist, so dass der erste Schritt übersprungen werden kann. Im zweiten Schritt ist dann zu fragen, ob eine Beziehung mit diesen Merkmalen als Familienverhältnis eingeordnet werden kann. Die Kriterien für den Vergleich sind grundsätzlich der *lex fori* zu entnehmen, um daraufhin die Frage zu entscheiden, welches der europäischen Rechtsinstrumente hinsichtlich der Hauptfrage anzuwen-

---

[28] Rauscher, EuZPR/EuIPR/Andrae, 4. Aufl. 2016, EG-UntVO Art. 1 Rn. 9ff.; Hilbig GPR 2011, 310; Althammer NZFam 2016, 629 (633).

[29] Übereinkommen über das auf vertragliche Schuldverhältnisse anzuwendende Recht idF des Beitrittsübereinkommens von 2005, ABl. 2005 C 334, 1.

[30] Giuliano/Lagarde, Bericht über das Übereinkommen über das auf vertragliche Schuldverhältnisse anzuwendende Recht, ABl. 1980 C 282, 1, Art. 1 Rn. 3.

[31] Wohl im Ergebnis ähnlich Hilbig GPR 2011, 310 (312).

[32] beck-online.GROSSKOMMENTAR zum Zivilrecht/Paulus, Stand 1.3.2023, Rom I-VO Art. 1 Rn. 74, 77; Münchener Kommentar zum BGB/Martiny, 8. Aufl. 2021, Rom I-VO Art. 1 Rn. 32; Staudinger, BGB/Magnus, 2021, Rom I-VO Art. 1 Rn. 56.

[33] Staudinger, BGB/Mankowski, 2021, HUP Art. 1 Rn. 66; Hilbig GPR 2011, 310 (311).

den ist. Da es um die Bestimmung des sachlichen Anwendungsbereiches von europäischen Rechtsinstrumenten und eines internationalen Vertrages geht, an dem die Europäische Union als Vertragspartner beteiligt ist, tritt an die Stelle der *lex fori* die einheitliche autonome unionsrechtliche Auslegung, wenn diese sich für das betreffende Verhältnis manifestieren lässt. Dabei ist das entscheidende mitgliedstaatliche Gericht hinsichtlich der Quellen nicht auf Entscheidungen und Lehrmeinungen zum EuZVR und EuIPR beschränkt. Was die faktische Lebensgemeinschaft betrifft, so ist nach der Rechtsprechung des EGMR das nach Art. 8 EMRK geschützte Familienleben nicht auf durch Eheschließung rechtlich formalisierte Bindungen („marriage-based relationships") beschränkt, sondern erfasst auch andere faktische Familienbindungen („de facto family ties"), bei denen die beiden Partner außerhalb des Ehestandes zusammenleben.[34] Dabei fällt sowohl ein im gemeinsamen Haushalt und in einer stabilen de facto-Beziehung lebendes, gleichgeschlechtliches Paar unter den Begriff «Familienleben», so wie dies auch im Falle eines heterosexuellen Paares zutrifft.[35] Der EGMR bezieht sich dabei darauf, dass eine signifikante Zahl der Vertragsstaaten inzwischen die gesetzliche Anerkennung dieser Paare ermöglicht und auch einige Bestimmungen des EU-Rechts die Tendenz zeigen, sie in den Begriff der Familie miteinzubeziehen. In einigen europäischen Staaten sind materiell- und/oder kollisionsrechtliche Regelungen bezogen auf die faktische Lebensgemeinschaft anzutreffen.[36] Hier kann von einem eigenständigen, familienrechtlichen Rechtsinstitut, teilweise in der Ausgestaltung der Ehe angenähert, gesprochen werden. Typisches Beispiel hierfür sind die Rechtsordnungen der Nachfolgestaaten des früheren Jugoslawiens, die die nichteheliche Lebensgemeinschaft in ihren Gesetzen über Ehe und Familienbeziehungen und selbst in den IPR-Gesetzen regeln.[37] In Schweden gibt es ein Gesetz über das gemeinsame Heim der in nichtehelicher Lebensgemeinschaft Zusammenlebenden.[38] In Italien wurde die nichteheliche Lebensgemeinschaft (convivenza) nunmehr gesetzlich geregelt,[39] in Spanien findet sich die rechtliche Ausgestaltung in Partikular- bzw. Foralrechten,[40] in Schottland wurden Regelungen zum Vermögensausgleich zwischen nichtehelichen Lebensgemeinschaften (cohabitation) gesetzlich eingeführt[41] und in dem

[34] EGMR 22.7.2010 – 18984/02, BeckRS 2016, 12098; hierzu Althammer NZFam 2016, 629 (632f.).

[35] EGMR 22.7.2010 –18984/02, BeckRS 2016, 12098.

[36] Siehe näher aus rechtsvergleichender: Sicht Staudinger, BGB/Mankowski, 2011, EGBGB Anh. zu Art. 13 Rn. 44–49; Hausmann/Hohloch, Das Recht der nichtehelichen Lebensgemeinschaft/Martiny, 2. Aufl. 2004, Kap. 12 Rn. 4–6.

[37] Hierzu Süß/Ring, Eherecht in Europa/Mikulić/Schön, 3. Aufl. 2017, Kroatien Rn. 104; Süß/Ring, Eherecht in Europa/Rudolf, 3. Aufl. 2017, Slowenien Rn. 81ff. Näheres, insbesondere zu Serbien, bei Abbas, Die Vermögensbeziehungen der Ehegatten und nichtehelichen Lebenspartner im serbischen Recht, 2011, S. 23ff.

[38] Hierzu Süß/Ring, Eherecht in Europa/Johansson, 3. Aufl. 2017, Schweden Rn. 142.

[39] Gesetz Nr. 76/2016, hierzu Süß/Ring, Eherecht in Europa/Cubeddu Wiedemann/Wiedemann, 3. Aufl. 2017, Italien Rn. 253ff.

[40] Spanien, Überblick bei Süß/Ring, Eherecht in Europa/Huzel, 3. Aufl. 2017, Spanien Rn. 102ff.

[41] Hierzu Süß/Ring, Eherecht in Europa/Odersky, 3. Aufl. 2017, Großbritannien: Schottland Rn. 21ff.

neuen ungarische IPRG finden sich spezielle Bestimmungen zu dieser Gemeinschaft.[42] Selbst im deutschen Sachrecht gewinnt der familienrechtliche Charakter der nichtehelichen Lebensgemeinschaft zunehmend an Gewicht. So sind in Bezug auf die vermögensrechtliche Abwicklung der Lebensgemeinschaft Veränderungen mit den Entscheidungen des BGH zur Innengesellschaft und zu gemeinschaftsbedingten Zuwendungen eingetreten, was zu einer Annäherung an das Nebengüterrecht im ehelichen Güterstand der Gütertrennung geführt hat.[43] Zusammengefasst kann davon gesprochen werden, dass die Tendenz besteht, diese Beziehung rechtlich als Familienbeziehung einzuordnen.[44] Dem persönlichen, in erster Linie nicht wirtschaftlichen Charakter solcher Beziehungen wird weder eine allgemein schuldrechtliche noch eine gesellschaftsrechtliche Qualifikation für das IZVR/IPR gerecht.[45]

Daraus folgt mE, dass die faktischen Lebensgemeinschaften im Grundsatz von dem weiten Begriff Familienverhältnis in den EU-Verordnungen zum IZVR[46] und IPR sowie im HUntStProt 2007[47] erfasst werden sollten. Dabei sollten die Merkmale gemeinsamer Haushalt und stabile de facto-Beziehung einheitlich autonom ausgelegt werden. Ob gleichgeschlechtliche faktische Lebensgemeinschaften vom Begriff Familienverhältnis erfasst werden, ist mE gegenwärtig jedenfalls dem Recht des Mitgliedstaates überlassen, dessen Gericht im konkreten Fall über die Anwendung des Rechtsinstruments entscheidet.[48] Das ist die notwendige Konsequenz daraus, dass die gleichgelagerte Frage bezogen auf die Auslegung des Begriffs der Ehe in den europäischen Rechtsinstrumenten des IZVR/IPR noch auf diese Weise gelöst wird. Ist ein deutsches Gericht angerufen, so hat es die Frage, ob gleichgeschlechtliche faktische Lebensgemeinschaften vom Begriff Familienverhältnis erfasst werden, positiv zu beantworten. Nicht selten kommt es vor, dass mindestens

---

[42] Hierzu Szeibert FamRZ 2017, 1487 (1488).

[43] U.a. BGH 10.3.2021 – XII ZR 54/20, BeckRS 2021, 6401; BGH 9.7.2008 – XII ZR 179/05, BGHZ 177, 193 = NJW 2008, 3277; BGH 25.11.2009 – XII ZR 92/06, BGHZ 183, 242 = NJW 2010, 998 zu diesem Zusammenhang auch Buschbaum RNotZ 2010, 149ff.

[44] Zu den unterschiedlichen Auffassungen zur Qualifikation der nichtehelichen Lebensgemeinschaft im Allgemeinen: v. Bar/Mankowski, Internationales Privatrecht II, 2. Aufl. 2019, § 4 Rn. 805ff. m.w.H.; Hausmann, Internationales und Europäisches Familienrecht, 2. Aufl. 2018, I Rn. 285f.; Schümann, Nichteheliche Lebensgemeinschaft und ihre Einordnung im Internationalen Privatrecht, 2001, S. 14ff.

[45] AA für die grundsätzliche Anwendung der Rom I-VO und Rom II-VO: Erman, BGB/Stürner, 17. Aufl. 2023, EGBGB Vorbem. Art 13 Rn. 25; Staudinger, BGB/Magnus, 2021, Rom I-VO Art. 1 Rn. 51.

[46] Für die EG-UntVO ua Hausmann, Internationales und Europäisches Familienrecht, 2. Aufl. 2018, C Rn. 49.

[47] Wie hier vom HUntStProt 2007 und von der EG-UntVO erfasst: Gruber IPRax 2010, 128 (130); Conti, Grenzüberschreitende Durchsetzung von Unterhaltsansprüchen in Europa, 2011, S. 46f.; Beck'scher Online-Kommentar BGB/Heiderhoff, 69. Ed. 1.5.2023, HUP 2007 Art. 1 Rn. 43, 44; nicht ganz eindeutig: beck-online.GROSSKOMMENTAR zum Zivilrecht/Yassari, Stand 1.12.2022, HUP 2007 Art. 1 Rn. 45–46; aA Staudinger, BGB/Magnus, 2021, Rom I-VO Art. 1 Rn. 51; Hilbig GPR 2011, 310 (316).

[48] AA Auffassung Rauscher, EuZPR/EuIPR/von Hein, 5. Aufl. 2023, Rom I-VO Art. 1 Rn. 26 (entscheidet sich nach dem Recht, das nach dem IPR der *lex fori* auf die Partnerschaft anwendbar ist).

ein Partner der faktischen Lebensgemeinschaft mit einer dritten Person verheiratet ist. In einem solchen Fall sollte die faktische Lebensgemeinschaft erst ab dem Zeitpunkt bezogen auf die europäischen Rechtsinstrumente in die Kategorie Familienbeziehung eingeordnet werden, ab dem die Ehe bestandskräftig aufgelöst ist.

V. Unterhaltspflichten

1. Vertraglich vereinbarte Unterhaltspflichten

Unterhaltspflichten zwischen den Partnern einer faktischen Lebensgemeinschaft können sich aus Gesetz oder aus Vertrag ergeben. Geklärt ist, dass die EG-UntVO und das HUntStProt 2007 die gesetzliche Unterhaltspflicht sowie Verträge erfassen, die Personen zur Erfüllung einer gesetzlichen Unterhaltspflicht schließen oder die sich aus der Familienbeziehung ergebende gesetzliche Unterhaltspflicht ändern, genauer bestimmen oder abdingen. Noch umstritten ist, ob diese Rechtsinstrumente auch in Bezug auf Unterhaltspflichten anzuwenden sind, die ausschließlich auf freiwillig übernommenen Verpflichtungen innerhalb der betreffenden Familienbeziehung beruhen. Im HUntStÜbk 1973[49] – mit entsprechenden Konsequenzen für das HUntAVÜbk 1973[50] – ist die Frage bewusst offengehalten worden, ob Unterhaltsverpflichtungen aus Verträgen in den Anwendungsbereich des Übereinkommens fallen. Den Gerichten der Teilnehmerstaaten ist es nach dem Bericht von *Verwilghen* überlassen, hierauf die Kollisionsnormen des Übereinkommens anzuwenden oder nicht anzuwenden.[51] Daran anschließend ist das RomÜbk[52] dahingehend ausgelegt worden, dass der Ausschluss von Unterhaltspflichten, die auf einem familienrechtlichen Verhältnis beruhen, nur für Verträge gelten soll, die Personen zur Erfüllung, Modifizierung oder Ausschluss einer gesetzlichen Unterhaltspflicht schließen. Alle übrigen vertraglichen Verpflichtungen, auch solche, die den Unterhalt eines Familienangehörigen betreffen, dem gegenüber keine gesetzliche Unterhaltspflicht besteht, sollten dagegen in den Anwendungsbereich des Übereinkommens fallen.[53] Für das EuGVÜ und die Brüssel I-VO gab es dieses Problem nicht, sie erstreckten sich auf alle Streitigkeiten aus Unterhaltspflichten unabhängig, ob sie auf Gesetz oder Vertrag beruhen.

Auch im HUntStProt 2007 ist nicht normativ bestimmt, ob es auf Unterhaltspflichten anzuwenden ist, die sich aus einer Vereinbarung über das Bestehen oder

[49] Übereinkommen über das auf Unterhaltspflichten anzuwendende Recht, BGBl. 1986 II 837.

[50] Übereinkommen über die Anerkennung und Vollstreckung von Unterhaltsentscheidungen, BGBl. 1986 II 826.

[51] Verwilghen, Übereinkommen über Unterhaltspflichten, Erläuternder Bericht, BT-Drs. 10/258, 56 Rn. 120.

[52] Übereinkommen über das auf vertragliche Schuldverhältnisse anzuwendende Recht idF des Beitrittsübereinkommens von 2005, ABl. 2005 C 334, 1.

[53] Giuliano/Lagarde, Bericht über das Übereinkommen über das auf vertragliche Schuldverhältnisse anzuwendende Recht, ABl. 1980 C 282, S. 1, Art. 1 Rn. 3; hierzu auch beck-online. GROSSKOMMENTAR zum Zivilrecht/Paulus, Stand 1.12.2023, Rom I-VO Art. 1 Rn. 67.

den Umfang einer Unterhaltsforderung ergibt.[54] Nach dem Bericht zum Protokoll ist es gerechtfertigt, die Kollisionsnormen auf Unterhaltsvereinbarungen anzuwenden, soweit diese darauf abzielen, eine sich aus Familienbeziehungen ergebende Unterhaltspflicht zu ändern oder genauer zu bestimmen. Das wird aus dem Zweck der Rechtswahl nach Art. 8 HUntStProt 2007 abgeleitet. Einer der wichtigsten Gründe für die Ermöglichung der Rechtswahl besteht gerade darin, den im Unterhaltsbereich zwischen Ehegatten oder anderen erwachsenen Personen getroffenen Vereinbarungen eine gewisse Stabilität zu verleihen. Wenn jedoch das von den Parteien nach dem Protokoll gewählte Recht auf Unterhaltsvereinbarungen anzuwenden ist, gilt die gleiche Schlussfolgerung zwangsläufig für das anhand einer objektiven Anknüpfung bestimmte Recht.[55] Diese Auslegung schließt jedoch Unterhaltsvereinbarungen nicht ein, die keine gesetzliche Unterhaltspflicht zum Gegenstand haben. Wie für das HUntStÜbk 1973 ist diese Frage offen.[56] Für die an das HUntStProt 2007 gebundenen Mitgliedstaaten ist sie einheitlich sowohl für das HUntStProt 2007 als auch für die EG-UntVO zu beantworten. Das folgt schon daraus, dass in der EG-UntVO die Bestimmungen über Kompetenzkonflikte, Kollisionsnormen und die grenzüberschreitende Vollstreckung der Entscheidungen zusammengeführt sind und – daraus folgend – der Begriff Unterhaltspflichten auch diesbezüglich einheitlich ausgelegt werden muss. Besonders deutlich wird das Erfordernis der Einheitlichkeit der Auslegung im Bereich der Vollstreckung. Die Anwendung des Kapitel IV Abschnitt 1 EG-UntVO setzt nicht nur voraus, dass der Ursprungsmitgliedstaat an das HUntStProt 2007 gebunden ist, sondern auch, dass die Unterhaltspflicht, auf den sich der vollstreckbare Titel bezieht, sowohl vom Anwendungsbereich der EG-UntVO als auch des HUntStProt 2007 erfasst wird. Für die Einbeziehung von Unterhaltsvereinbarungen insgesamt spricht zunächst der Wortlaut des ErwGr. 11 EG-UntVO, wonach sich der Anwendungsbereich der Verordnung auf sämtliche Unterhaltspflichten erstreckt, die auf einem Familienverhältnis beruhen. Mit dieser weiten Fassung werden auch solche Unterhaltspflichten eingeschlossen, die sich ausschließlich aus vertraglichen Vereinbarungen ergeben, vorausgesetzt, dass diese durch die familiäre Bindung der Vertragsschließenden ver-

---

[54] Bonomi, Protokoll vom 23. November 2007 über das auf Unterhaltspflichten anwendbare Recht, Erläuternder Bericht, 2009, Rn. 32; beck-online.GROSSKOMMENTAR zum Zivilrecht/Yassari, Stand 1.12.2022, HUP 2007 Art. 1 Rn. 39, 40.

[55] Bonomi, Protokoll vom 23. November 2007 über das auf Unterhaltspflichten anwendbare Recht, Erläuternder Bericht, 2009, Rn. 32.

[56] Für die Einbeziehung: Beck'scher Online-Kommentar BGB/Spickhoff, 68. Ed. 1.8.2023, Rom I-VO Art. 1 Rn. 37; beck-online.GROSSKOMMENTAR zum Zivilrecht/Yassari, Stand 1.12.2022, HUP 2007 Art. 1 Rn. 39, 40; Prütting/Helms, FamFG/Hau, 6. Aufl. 2022, § 110 Anh. 3 Rn. 7; Hausmann, Internationales und Europäisches Familienrecht, 2. Aufl. 2018, C Rn. 56; Grüneberg, BGB/Thorn, 82. Aufl. 2023, HUntStProt Art. 1 Rn. 8; Münchener Kommentar zum FamFG/Lipp, 3. Aufl. 2019, EG-UntVO Art. 1 Rn. 22 ff.; beck-online.GROSSKOMMENTAR zum Zivilrecht/Wurmnest, Stand 1.12.2020, EU-UnterhaltsVO Art. 1 Rn. 7; für die Nichteinbeziehung: Staudinger, BGB/Magnus, 2021, Rom I-VO Art. 1 Rn. 50; beck-online.GROSSKOMMENTAR zum Zivilrecht/Paulus, Stand 1.12.2023, Rom I-VO Art. 1 Rn. 67 (vom Geltungsbereich der Rom I-VO erfasst); Erman, BGB/Stürner, 17. Aufl. 2023, Rom I-VO Art. 1 Rn. 9; Beck'scher Online-Kommentar BGB/Heiderhoff, 69. Ed. 1.5.2023, HUP 2007 Art. 1 Rn. 46.

anlasst sind. Nur so wird Rechtssicherheit und Voraussicht für die Rechtsanwendung geschaffen. Wenn die Zulassung der Rechtswahl gerade dazu dient, die materiellrechtliche Vereinbarung abzusichern,[57] so spricht dies für die Einbeziehung von Unterhaltsvereinbarungen in den sachlichen Anwendungsbereich des HUntSt-Prot 2007 insgesamt.

Andernfalls müsste das mitgliedstaatliche Gericht, in dem das Ursprungsverfahren anhängig gemacht wird, bei Verfahrensbeginn prüfen, ob es um vertraglich vereinbarte Unterhaltspflichten geht, und – soweit dies zutrifft – ob eine gesetzliche Unterhaltspflicht nach dem Recht besteht, das gemäß kollisionsrechtlicher Verweisung berufen wird. Das könnte natürlich nur das nach dem HUntStProt 2007 anwendbare Recht sein.[58] In diesem Zusammenhang würde sich dann noch die Frage stellen, ob dies auf die betreffende Art von Familienbeziehungen oder auf den konkreten Sachverhalt bezogen sein soll. Vom Ergebnis wäre abhängig, ob der Streitfall der EG-UntVO und dem HUntStProt 2007 oder der Brüssel Ia-VO und der Rom Ia-VO aufgrund schuldvertraglicher Qualifikation unterliegen würde. Für eine solche Auslegung findet sich kein Hinweis in den Rechtsinstrumenten. Ohne Differenzierung werden vertragliche Unterhaltspflichten, die auf einem Familienverhältnis beruhen, vom Anwendungsbereich der Brüssel Ia-VO und der Rom I-VO ausgeschlossen, ohne dies zusätzlich davon abhängig zu machen, dass ein gesetzlicher Rechtsgrund für die Unterhaltspflicht besteht.

EG-UntVO und HUntStProt 2007 sind folglich in den an das HUntStProt 2007 gebundenen Mitgliedstaaten einheitlich autonom dahingehend so auszulegen, dass der sachliche Anwendungsbereich alle Unterhaltspflichten der Partner/ehemaligen Partner einer faktischen Lebensgemeinschaft, die ihren Grund in der Lebensgemeinschaft haben, unabhängig davon erfasst, ob sich diese aus Gesetz oder Vertrag ergeben.[59]

2. *Kollisionsrecht*

a) Rechtswahl

Möglich ist eine Rechtswahl der *lex fori* für die Durchführung eines konkreten Prozesses nach Art. 7 HUntStProt 2007. Für die Partner der faktischen Lebensgemeinschaften gibt es keine Besonderheiten. Art. 8 HUntStProt 2007 ermöglicht darüber hinaus eine Rechtswahl ohne diesen Zusammenhang, die durch folgende Merkmale gekennzeichnet ist: Die Rechtswahl ist für bestimmte Unterhaltsbeziehungen ausgeschlossen. Nur bestimmte Rechtsordnungen können gewählt werden, es besteht Formzwang und die Rechtswahl ist in verschiedener Hinsicht ein-

---

[57] Bonomi, Protokoll vom 23. November 2007 über das auf Unterhaltspflichten anwendbare Recht, Erläuternder Bericht, 2009, Rn. 32, 126.

[58] AA Rauscher, EuZPR/EuIPR/von Hein, 5. Aufl. 2023, Rom I-VO Art. 1 Rn. 27 (entscheidet sich nach dem Recht, das auf die nichteheliche Lebensgemeinschaft anwendbar ist).

[59] AA bezogen auf rein vertragliche Unterhaltspflichten Anwendung der Rom I-VO: Rauscher EuZPR/EuIPR/von Hein, 5. Aufl. 2023, Rom I-VO Art. 1 Rn. 27; Erman, BGB/Stürner, 17. Aufl. 2023, EGBGB Vorbem. Art 13 Rn. 22; beck-online.GROSSKOMMENTAR zum Zivilrecht/Paulus, Stand 1.12.2023, Rom I-VO Art. 1 Rn. 67, 76; Staudinger, BGB/Magnus, 2021, Rom I-VO Art. 1 Rn. 50.

geschränkt. Die Einschränkungen dienen in erster Linie dem Schutz der schwächeren Partei. Bezogen auf die wählbaren Rechtsordnungen sollen sie auch sichern, dass eine gewisse reale Verbindung zwischen dem gewählten Recht und der Unterhaltsbeziehung zur Zeit der Rechtswahl besteht. Während alle anderen Regelungen in Art. 8 HUntStProt 2007 für die faktische Lebensgemeinschaft passend sind, gilt dies nicht vollumfänglich für die Regelung zu den wählbaren Rechten. Klar ist, dass die Partner das Recht des Staates, dem beide oder einer von ihnen zum Zeitpunkt der Rechtswahl angehören, wählen können (Art. 8. Abs. 1 lit. a HUntStProt 2007). Gleichfalls steht das Recht des gewöhnlichen Aufenthalts beider oder eines der Partner zum Zeitpunkt der Rechtswahl zur Verfügung (Art. 8 Abs. 1 lit. b HUntStProt 2007). Ausgeschlossen ist die in Art. 8 Abs. 1 lit. d HUntStProt 2007 vorgesehene Verknüpfung des Unterhaltsstatuts durch Rechtswahl mit einem gewählten Scheidungsstatut oder mit dem auf die Scheidung tatsächlich angewandten Recht. Letztlich vorgesehen ist die Möglichkeit, das Recht zu wählen, das die Partner als „das auf ihren Güterstand anzuwendende Recht bestimmt haben, oder das tatsächlich darauf angewandte Recht“. Der Wortlaut von Art. 8 Abs. 1 lit. c HUntStProt 2007 nennt die erfassten Unterhaltsbeziehungen nicht ausdrücklich. Deshalb steht diese Rechtswahlmöglichkeit auch der faktischen Lebensgemeinschaft offen.[60] Erforderlich ist jedoch, dass es für diese ein vom allgemeinen Zivilrecht abgehobenes familienrechtlichen Charakter tragendes Vermögensregime *(property regime)* gibt, an dessen kollisionsrechtliches Statut der Unterhalt angebunden werden kann.[61] Das folgt daraus, dass der Begriff des Güterstandes hier eher im traditionellen engeren Sinne zu verstehen ist.

b) Objektive Anknüpfung

Mangels Rechtswahl bestimmen sich die partnerschaftlichen Unterhaltspflichten nach dem gewöhnlichen Aufenthalt des Partners, der den Unterhalt geltend macht, Art. 3 Abs. 1 HUntStProt 2007. Diese Grundanknüpfung wird durch die nachfolgenden Bestimmungen für einzelne Arten von Familienbeziehungen modifiziert. Für den Unterhalt, der seinen Grund in der Ehe hat, erfolgt dies gemäß Art. 5 HUntStProt 2007. Es steht im Ermessen jedes Vertragsstaates,[62] die Bestimmung auf Verbindungen anzuwenden, die der Ehe gleichgestellt oder ihr ähnlich sind.[63] Es kann offenbleiben, ob die Entscheidung bezogen auf die faktische Lebensgemeinschaft unionsrechtlich einheitlich zu sehen oder insoweit den gebundenen

---

[60] Einschränkend auf andere Formen verrechtlicher Partnerschaften Grüneberg, BGB/Thorn, 82. Aufl. 2023, HUntProt Rn. 30.

[61] Ähnlich Beck'scher Online-Kommentar BGB/Heiderhoff, 69. Ed.1.5.2023, HUP 2007 Art. 8 Rn. 8; beck-online.GROSSKOMMENTAR zum Zivilrecht/Yassari, Stand 1.12.2022, HUP 2007 Art. 8 Rn. 28.; Hausmann FS Martiny, 2014, 345 (353), Staudinger, BGB/Mankowski, 2021, HUP Art. 8 Rn. 42 (Formen persönlicher Verbindungen mit einem eigenen Güterrechtsregime).

[62] Vertragsstaat ist wiederum iSd Art. 24 Abs. 5 HUntStProt 2007 zu verstehen, bezieht sich also auf die EU und die durch sie gebundenen Mitgliedsstaaten.

[63] Hierzu Bonomi, Protokoll vom 23. November 2007 über das auf Unterhaltspflichten anwendbare Recht, Erläuternder Bericht, 2009, Rn. 93; Bonomi YB PIL 2008, 333 (350); Rauscher, EuZPR/EuIPR/Andrae, 4. Aufl. 2016, HUntStProt Art. 5 Rn. 7.

Mitgliedstaaten überlassen ist. Auf unionsrechtlicher Ebene muss die Auslegung konform mit der Formulierung „ mit der Ehe vergleichbare Wirkung" in Art. 1 Abs. 2 lit. a Brüssel Ia-VO, Art. 1 Abs. 2 lit. c Rom I-VO und Art. 1 Abs. 2 lit b Rom II-VO gehen (hierzu → III.). Auch vom Standpunkt des deutschen IPR ist aus denselben Gründen, aber auch schon wegen fehlender Institutionalisierung in Form der Registrierung der Lebensgemeinschaft eine Gleichstellung abzulehnen.[64] Die faktische Lebensgemeinschaft wird deshalb von Art. 6 HUntStProt 2007 erfasst. Das hat zur Folge, dass es bei der Verweisung nach Art. 3 HUntStProt 2007 bleibt, solange beide Partner im selben Staat ihren gewöhnlichen Aufenthalt haben. Nur wenn dieser in verschiedenen Staaten liegt, kann Art. 6 HUntStProt 2007 relevant sein. Typisch ist der Fall, dass im Zusammenhang mit der Trennung oder danach ein Partner in ein anderes Land verzieht. Dann kommt es darauf an, ob nach dem Recht des gewöhnlichen Aufenthalts des Partners, der einen Unterhaltsanspruch geltend macht, dieser besteht oder nicht besteht. Ergibt sich aus diesem Recht kein Anspruch, so ist dieses Ergebnis – vorbehaltlich des *ordre public* – endgültig. Gibt es danach einen Anspruch, so kann der Unterhaltspflichtige durch Erhebung einer Einrede diesen vernichten. Hierfür muss nach dem Recht seines gewöhnlichen Aufenthalts in dieser Konstellation überhaupt kein Anspruch bestehen und die Partner dürfen kein gemeinsames Heimatrecht haben, welches wiederum einen solchen Anspruch bejaht. Diese kollisionsrechtliche Lösung ist dadurch verursacht, dass teilnehmende Vertragsstaaten, wie auch Deutschland, gesetzliche Unterhaltspflichten ua zwischen Partnern faktischer Lebenspartnerschaften nicht vorsehen. Sie soll Unterhaltspflichtige mit engem Bezug zur eigenen Rechtsordnung durch ihren gewöhnlichen Aufenthalt und die inländische Staatsangehörigkeit vor der Inanspruchnahme schützen. Die Anwendung des Rechts des gewöhnlichen Aufenthalts des Unterhaltsberechtigten mit entgegengesetzter materiellrechtlicher Lösung wird jedoch dann akzeptiert, wenn der Unterhaltspflichtige die Möglichkeit der Einrede nicht nutzt oder der erforderliche enge Bezug zu Rechtsordnungen besteht, die in dieser Konstellation eine Unterhaltspflicht gesetzlich vorsehen.

c) *Unterhaltsvereinbarungen*

Das HUntStProt 2007 regelt das auf eine Unterhaltsvereinbarung anwendbare Recht nicht speziell. Vorrang hat eine von den Parteien getroffene und nach Art. 8 HUntStProt 2007 wirksame ausdrückliche oder konkludente Rechtswahl. Das gewählte Recht regelt das Zustandekommen und die Wirksamkeit der Unterhaltsvereinbarung, ihren Inhalt und die sich daraus ergebenden Pflichten, einschließlich der Änderungsmöglichkeiten bei veränderter Sachlage. Für die Formerfordernisse besteht eine Regelungslücke, die durch das einzelstaatliche Kollisionsrecht ausgefüllt werden muss. Ist ein deutsches Gericht angerufen, findet Art. 11 EGBGB Anwendung. Die im HUntStProt 2007 vorgesehenen objektiven Anknüpfungen sind

[64] Ablehnung der Einbeziehung: beck-online.GROSSKOMMENTAR zum Zivilrecht/Yassari, Stand 1.12.2022, HUP 2007 Art. 5 Rn. 8; Münchener Kommentar zum BGB/Staudinger, 9. Aufl. 2024, HUP Art. 5 Rn. 8; Hausmann, Internationales und Europäisches Familienrecht, 2. Aufl. 2018, C Rn. 609.

nicht auf Unterhaltsvereinbarungen zugeschnitten, das trifft vor allem auf die speziellen Regelungen in Art. 4–6 HUntStProt 2007 zu. Das anwendbare Recht auf eine Unterhaltsvereinbarung zwischen den Partnern einer faktischen Lebensgemeinschaft kann sich allein aus Art. 3 HUntStProt 2007 ergeben; Art. 6 HUntStProt 2007 bleibt außen vor. Um dem Zweck des Abschlusses von Unterhaltsvereinbarungen Rechnung zu tragen, ist der Grundsatz der wandelbaren Anknüpfung an den gewöhnlichen Aufenthalt des Unterhaltsberechtigten eingeschränkt. Zulässigkeit, Zustandekommen und materielle Wirksamkeit der Vereinbarung bestimmen sich nach dem Recht des gewöhnlichen Aufenthalts des Unterhaltsberechtigten zum Zeitpunkt des Vertragsabschlusses, die Formerfordernisse wiederum nach Art. 11 EGBGB. Ist danach eine wirksame Unterhaltsvereinbarung getroffen worden, so regeln sich die daraus folgenden Unterhaltspflichten nach dem Unterhaltsstatut zum Zeitpunkt des Vertragsabschlusses, auch wenn der Unterhaltsberechtigte seinen gewöhnlichen Aufenthalt in ein anderes Land verlegt hat.[65] Beiden Partnern steht es frei, bei Veränderung tatsächlicher Umstände, insbesondere bei grundlegenden Veränderungen hinsichtlich der Leistungsfähigkeit oder der Bedürftigkeit eines Partners, eine Anpassung des Vertrages für die Zukunft gegebenenfalls gerichtlich einzufordern. Ob die Voraussetzungen hierfür vorliegen, bestimmt sich nach dem zum Zeitpunkt der Änderungsentscheidung nach Art. 3 HUntStProt 2007 anwendbaren Recht.[66] Diese Lösung trägt einerseits der grundsätzlichen Wandelbarkeit des Unterhaltsstatuts und andererseits dem Rechnung, dass Verträge grundsätzlich unwandelbar angeknüpft werden. Außerdem kann hierfür auf die Lösung für die Abänderung von Unterhaltsentscheidungen verwiesen werden. Auch hier regeln sich die materiellrechtlich zu qualifizierenden Fragen der Abänderbarkeit nicht nach dem Unterhaltsstatut, das der ursprünglichen Entscheidung zugrunde lag, sondern nach dem Recht, das nach dem HUntStProt 2007 zum Zeitpunkt der Abänderungsentscheidung anzuwenden ist.[67]

Unterhaltsvereinbarungen regeln gegebenenfalls die Unterhaltspflichten nicht nur einseitig, sondern der Partner gegenseitig. Die Anknüpfung nach Art. 3 HUntStProt 2007 darf nicht dazu führen, dass für den Vertrag eine Statutenspaltung eintritt. Haben die Vertragsparteien zum Zeitpunkt des Vertragsabschlusses einen gemeinsamen gewöhnlichen Aufenthalt, löst sich die Frage des anwendbaren Rechts einfach, denn Art. 3 HUntStProt 2007 führt bezogen auf beide Partner zum selben Recht. Fehlt es daran, besteht eine Regelungslücke. In Art. 25 Abs. 2 EU-ErbVO ist das vergleichbare Problem für mehrseitige Erbverträge dahingehend geregelt, dass die Auswahl zwischen den beiden hypothetischen Erbstatuten nach

[65] OLG Hamm 27.08.1997 – 10 UF 410/96, FamRZ 1998, 1532; Grüneberg, BGB/Thorn, 82. Aufl. 2023, HUntStProt Art. 3 Rn. 13; Hausmann, Internationales und Europäisches Familienrecht, 2. Aufl. 2018, C Rn. 576; Münchener Kommentar zum BGB/Siehr, 5. Aufl. 2010, EGBGB Art. 18 Anh. I Rn. 233; Staudinger, BGB/Mankowski, 2021, HUP Art. 3 Rn. 79; beck-online.GROSSKOMMENTAR zum Zivilrecht/Yassari, Stand 1.12.2022, HUP 2007 Art. 3 Rn. 38.

[66] Andrae, Internationales Familienrecht, 5. Aufl. 2024, § 10 Rn 126; Staudinger, BGB/Mankowski, 2021, HUP Art. 3 Rn. 79.

[67] EuGH 20.9.2018 – C-214/17, ECLI:EU:C:2018:744 Rn. 43ff. = BeckRS 2018, 22240 (Mölk); hierzu mwH Andrae, Internationales Familienrecht, 5. Aufl. 2024, § 10 Rn. 337ff.

dem Prinzip der engsten Verbindung erfolgt. Ein solches Herangehen ist auch bezogen auf Unterhaltsverträge sinnvoll, die gegenseitige Unterhaltspflichten zum Gegenstand haben. Entsprechend ist auch das Änderungsstatut für die gerichtliche Anpassung des Vertrages an veränderte Umstände zu bestimmen.

VI. Anknüpfung vermögensrechtlicher Ansprüche

Vermögensrechtliche Beziehungen und die sich daraus ergebenden Ansprüche, die ihren Grund in der Lebensgemeinschaft oder ihrer Auflösung haben, sind vom Anwendungsbereich der Rom I-VO und Rom II-VO ausgeschlossen, weil die Lebensgemeinschaft ein Familienverhältnis bzw. ein vergleichbares Verhältnis iSd des Ausschlusstatbestandes in Art. 1 Abs. 2 beider Verordnungen ist.[68] Sie unterliegen dem autonomen Kollisionsrecht der Mitgliedstaaten. Im deutschen IPR gibt es leider für diese Beziehung keine normative Regelung.

Für die Anknüpfung sollte keine Aufspaltung in separate Rechtsbeziehungen vorgenommen werden. Vielmehr sollte von einem einheitlichen Vermögensstatut ausgegangen werden, das alle vermögensrechtlichen Beziehungen des Paares zueinander und im Verhältnis zu Dritten erfasst. Dabei müsste der Anwendungsbereich des Vermögensstatuts entsprechend dem des Güterstatuts für Ehen und eingetragene Lebenspartner in der EU-EheGüterVO/EU-LP-GüterVO gesehen werden. Rechtspraktisch geht es regelmäßig um die Vermögensauseinandersetzung sowie um Ausgleichsansprüche wegen Zuwendungen oder aufgenommener Kreditverbindlichkeiten während gelebter nichtehelicher Lebensgemeinschaft infolge der Trennung oder des Todes eines Partners. Unerheblich muss auf der Ebene des Kollisionsrechts sein, ob materiellrechtlich die Vermögensauseinandersetzung nach speziellen Regelungen erfolgt, wie im slowenischen Recht, oder allgemeine zivilrechtliche Institute, wie Gesamtschuldnerausgleich, Wegfall der Geschäftsgrundlage oder ungerechtfertigte Bereicherung zu Hilfe genommen werden. Erforderlich ist gegenüber den ehelichen Beziehungen eine eigenständige Anknüpfung, womit dem Rechnung getragen wird, dass die nichteheliche Lebensgemeinschaften als bewusste Form des Zusammenlebens zweier Menschen als Alternative zur Ehe etabliert ist. Art. 14 EGBGB ist m. E. schon deshalb nicht auf diese Beziehungen zu erstrecken, weil er die nichtvermögensrechtlichen Wirkungen der Ehe zum Gegenstand hat. Nur für Ehen, die intertemporal nicht den Kollisionsnormen der EU-EheGüterVO unterliegen, erfasst er auch einige vermögensrechtliche Wirkungen und zwar jene, die nicht Gegenstand des Art. 15 EGBGB aF direkt oder analog sind. Letzteres schließt Rechtsinstitute ein, die im deutschen materiellen Recht unter den Begriff des Nebengüterrecht zusammengefasst sind und auch bei der ver-

[68] Für eine familienrechtliche Qualifikation ua in Münchener Kommentar zum BGB/Coester, 9. Aufl. 2024, EGBGB Art. 17b Rn. 127; Staudinger, BGB/Mankowski, 2011, EGBGB Anh. zu Art. 13 Rn. 59ff.; Beck'scher Online-Kommentar BGB/Heiderhoff, 69. Ed. 1.5.2023, EGBGB Art. 17b Rn. 25; Hausmann, Internationales und Europäisches Familienrecht, 2. Aufl. 2018, I Rn. 286; Beck'scher Online-Kommentar BGB/Mörsdorf, 69. Ed. 1.11.2023, EGBGB Art. 14 Rn. 6; hierzu bereits → IV.

mögensrechtlichen Abwicklung faktischer Lebensgemeinschaften zur Anwendung kommen können.

Die Partner können für ihre Vermögensbeziehungen eine Rechtswahl zumindest im Rahmen des Art. 22 EU-EheGüterVO analog treffen.[69] Die Rechtswahl kann ausdrücklich, aber auch konkludent erfolgen. Die materielle Wirksamkeit bestimmt sich nach dem gewählten Recht. Für ihre Form gelten nicht die Anforderungen des Art. 23 EU-EheGüterVO analog, sondern die des Art. 11 EGBGB.[70] Das deutsche Recht schreibt keine Form vor.[71]

Mangels Rechtswahl ist die Anknüpfung an den gemeinsamen gewöhnlichen Aufenthalt der Partner auch dann zu favorisieren, wenn sie eine gemeinsame Staatsangehörigkeit besitzen.[72] Wesentliches Merkmal der nichtehelichen Lebensgemeinschaft ist die gemeinsame Haushaltsführung am gemeinsamen Lebensmittelpunkt. Die Gestaltung der Innenbeziehung und der Beziehungen der Gemeinschaft zu Dritten wird durch die Umgebung geprägt. Eine nichteheliche Lebensgemeinschaft unterscheidet sich durch ihren fehlenden statusrechtlichen Charakter und aufgrund der Freiheit der Gestaltung und der Beliebigkeit der Auflösung von der Ehe. Der Stetigkeit der Beziehung kommt deshalb für die Anknüpfung gegenüber der Ehe geringere Bedeutung zu. Für diese Anknüpfung spricht weiterhin, dass die objektive Anknüpfungsleiter in der EU-EheGüterVO mit dem gemeinsamen gewöhnlichen Aufenthalt beginnt. Heiratet das zunächst in nichtehelicher Lebensgemeinschaft lebende Paar, kommt es infolge der Eheschließung regelmäßig nicht zum Statutenwechsel.

Anders als das objektive Güterstatut für die Ehe unterliegt jedoch das Vermögensstatut für die nichteheliche Lebensgemeinschaft dem Statutenwechsel. Eine im Inland begründete und gelebte Lebensgemeinschaft richtet sich nach deutschem Recht. Bei Aufenthaltswechsel über die Grenze sind die allgemeinen Regeln für einen Statutenwechsel heranzuziehen. Eine am bisherigen ausländischen Aufenthaltsort wirksam begründete Gemeinschaft wird, wenn der Lebensmittelpunkt in das Inland verlegt wird, hier anerkannt. Die vermögensrechtlichen Wirkungen der Beziehungen bestimmen sich nunmehr nach inländischem Recht.[73] Einen gemein-

---

[69] Staudinger, BGB/Mankowski, 2011, EGBGB Anh. zu Art. 13 Rn. 85f.; Hausmann/Hohloch, Das Recht der nichtehelichen Lebensgemeinschaft/Martiny, 2. Aufl. 2004, Kap. 12 Rn. 19; iErg Münchener Kommentar zum BGB/Coester, 9. Aufl. 2024, EGBGB Art. 17b Rn. 116; Buschbaum RNotZ 2010, 149 (154); Schümann, Nichteheliche Lebensgemeinschaft und ihre Einordnung im Internationalen Privatrecht, 2001, S. 149.

[70] Hausmann/Hohloch, Das Recht der nichtehelichen Lebensgemeinschaft/Martiny, 2. Aufl. 2004, Kap. 12 Rn. 28; aA Staudinger, BGB/Mankowski, 2011, EGBGB Anh. zu Art. 13 Rn. 86.

[71] AA (für einfache Schriftform zu Beweiszwecken) Staudinger, BGB/Mankowski, 2011, EGBGB Anh. zu Art. 13 Rn. 86; Buschbaum RNotZ 2010, 149 (154) (notarielle Beurkundung).

[72] Hierfür ua: Münchener Kommentar zum BGB/Coester, 9. Aufl. 2024, EGBGB Art. 17b Rn. 128; Erman, BGB/Hohloch, 15. Aufl. 2017, EGBGB Vor Art. 13 Rn. 1ff.; NomosKommentar BGB/Andrae, 4. Aufl. 2021, EGBGB Art. 13 Anh. II Rn. 14; Hausmann, Internationales und Europäisches Familienrecht, 2. Aufl. 2018, I Rn. 288; Schümann, Nichteheliche Lebensgemeinschaft und ihre Einordnung im Internationalen Privatrecht, 2001, S. 150ff.; Beck'scher Online-Kommentar BGB/Mörsdorf, 69. Ed. 1. 11. 2023, EGBGB Art. 13 Rn. 19.

[73] Gruber IPRax 2021, 39 (51); Hausmann, Internationales und Europäisches Familienrecht, 2. Aufl. 2018, I Rn. 289; für eine unwandelbare Anknüpfung: Staudinger, BGB/Mankowski, 2011, EGBGB Anh. zu Art. 13 Rn. 84.

samen gewöhnlichen Aufenthalt wird es regelmäßig geben, hilfsweise ist auf den letzten gemeinsamen gewöhnlichen Aufenthalt bei Bestehen der Gemeinschaft abzustellen. Letzteres kommt in Betracht, wenn es nach der Auflösung der faktischen Lebensgemeinschaft um vermögensrechtliche Streitigkeiten im Zusammenhang mit ihrer Auflösung geht.[74] Die Verweisung ist eine Gesamtverweisung (Art. 4 Abs. 1 S. 1 EGBGB). Sinnvoll wäre es an sich, dies als Regelanknüpfung zu begreifen und sie durch eine Ausweichklausel in Gesamtanalogie zu Art. 5 HUntStProt 2007 und insbesondere zu Art. 26 Abs. 3 EU-EheGüterVO zu ergänzen. Jeder Partner sollte sich darauf berufen können, dass insbesondere das Recht eines früheren gemeinsamen gewöhnlichen Aufenthalts während bestehender Lebensgemeinschaft eine engere Beziehung aufweist und beide Partner bei der Regelung oder Planung ihrer vermögensrechtlichen Beziehungen auf dessen Geltung vertraut haben. Für Wohnung und Hausrat könnte die Lösung wie in Art. 17a EGBGB aF entsprechend erfolgen.[75]

Haben die Partner einen Partnerschaftsvertrag geschlossen, ohne eine Rechtswahl zu treffen, so unterliegt dieser hinsichtlich der vermögensrechtlichen Regelungen dem Vermögensstatut zum Zeitpunkt seines Abschlusses, um das Vertrauen auf die Wirksamkeit der Vereinbarung zu schützen.[76] Bezogen auf den Schutz Dritter im inländischen Rechtsverkehr mit einem Partner der Lebensgemeinschaft kann an eine Analogie zu Art. 12 EGBGB gedacht werden.

VII. Die faktische Lebensgemeinschaft als Vorfrage

Die faktische Lebensgemeinschaft kann kollisionsrechtliche oder materiellrechtliche Vorfrage sein. Als kollisionsrechtliche Vorfrage tritt sie auf, wenn es darum geht, ob überhaupt und dann welches europäische Rechtsinstrument, einschließlich des HUntStProt 2007, den Streitgegenstand aus der betreffenden Rechtsbeziehung erfasst. Wenn zB in einem Fall nachpartnerschaftlicher Unterhalt und Vermögensausgleich wegen Mitarbeit im Geschäft des anderen Partners ohne Arbeitsverhältnis geltend gemacht wird, geht es darum, ob es sich um Streitgegenstände handelt, die iSv HUntStProt 2007 und Rom I-VO/Rom II-VO aus einem Familienverhältnis resultieren. Die Kriterien, damit eine Beziehung als faktische Lebensgemeinschaft und als solches als Familienverhältnis einzuordnen ist, sind möglichst einheitlich autonom zu setzen, um dann die Subsumtion vorzunehmen. In Bezug auf das HUntStProt 2007 stellt sich bei positiver Beantwortung die Frage, ob neben Art. 3 noch Art. 5 oder 6 HUntStProt 2007 Anwendung finden. Für die faktische Lebensgemeinschaft sollte bezogen auf die vermögensrechtlichen Ansprüche, die wegen ihrer familienrechtlichen Qualifikation dem autonomen IPR zugewiesen sind, die Kriterien der autonomen Auslegung mit der Folge übernom-

[74] Ähnlich im Ergebnis Münch, Familienrecht in der Notar- und Gestaltungspraxis/Süß, 3. Aufl. 2020, § 20 Rn. 355 (rückwirkende Anwendung des gemeinsamen Aufenthaltsrechts bei Auflösung der Gemeinschaft).

[75] So wohl auch NomosKommentar BGB/Gruber, 3. Aufl. 2016, EGBGB Art. 17a Rn. 21.

[76] So auch im Prinzip Gruber IPRax 2021, 39 (51).

men werden, dass es zwar um ein Familienverhältnis geht, dieses aber keine mit der Ehe vergleichbare Wirkung zeitigt.

Das Bestehen oder die Beendigung einer faktischen Lebensgemeinschaft ist zugleich materiell-rechtliche Vorfrage, zT auch in Fällen, in denen sie sich als kollisionsrechtliche Vorfrage nicht stellt. Das ist dann der Fall, wenn durch das IPR in der Hauptfrage auf ein Recht verwiesen wird, das materiellrechtliche Regelungen speziell für die Lebensgemeinschaft vorsieht. In diesem Zusammenhang hat *der Jubiliar* zu Recht darauf hingewiesen, dass der Begriff der „nichtehelichen Lebensgemeinschaft" gegenwärtig im Gegensatz zur Ehe nicht wechselseitig zwischen den berührten Rechtsordnungen austauschbar ist.[77] Diese sehen andere tatsächliche Voraussetzungen vor, um eine die angeordneten materielle Rechtsfolgen rechtfertigende Paarbeziehung anzunehmen.[78] Daher ist die Frage nach den Anforderungen an die Lebensgemeinschaft dem Sachrecht des Staates zu unterstellen, das auf die Hauptfrage Anwendung findet, und nicht erneut (selbstständig oder unselbstständig) kollisionsrechtlich anzuknüpfen.[79] Insofern bedarf es praktisch keiner Kollisionsnorm im deutschen IPR für ein Begründungs- oder Auflösungsstatut der faktischen Lebensgemeinschaft.[80]

---

[77] Rauscher, Internationales Privatrecht, 5. Aufl. 2017, Rn. 888.

[78] Zu den unterschiedlichen Voraussetzungen nach den Familiengesetzen der jugoslawischen Nachfolgestaaten Abbas, Die Vermögensbeziehungen der Ehegatten und nichtehelichen Lebenspartner im serbischen Recht, 2011, S. 23 ff.

[79] Rauscher, Internationales Privatrecht, 5. Aufl. 2017, 4. Aufl. 2017, Rn. 888; Münchener Kommentar zum BGB/Coester, 9. Aufl. 2024, EGBGB Art. 17b Rn. 124; Hausmann, Internationales und Europäisches Familienrecht, 2. Aufl. 2018, I Rn. 290; Münch, Familienrecht in der Notar- und Gestaltungspraxis/Süß, 3. Aufl. 2020, § 20 Rn. 351; ähnlich, jedoch Art. 13 Abs. 1 EGBGB für die Frage nach Hindernissen heranziehend, Hausmann/Hohloch, Das Recht der nichtehelichen Lebensgemeinschaft/Martiny, 2. Aufl. 2004, Kap. 12 Rn. 18; aA (jeweiliger gewöhnlicher Aufenthalt der Partner) Sonnenberger FS Coester-Waltjen, 2015, 787 (807 ff.); Erman, BGB/Stürner, 17. Aufl. 2023, EGBGB Vorbem. Art 13 Rn. 22; Erman, BGB/Hohloch 15. Aufl., 2017, EGBGB Vor Art. 13 Rn. 19; Abbas, Die Vermögensbeziehungen der Ehegatten und nichtehelichen Lebenspartner im serbischen Recht, 2011, S. 201 f. (unselbstständige Anknüpfung); Gruber IPRax 2021, 39 (51).

[80] Mayer, Die nichteheliche Paarbeziehung im Internationalen Privatrecht, in: Budzikiewicz/Heiderhoff/Klinkhammer/Niethammer-Jürgens, Europa als Taktgeber für das Internationale Familienrecht, Dialog internationales Familienrecht IV, 2022, S. 141 (144); Münchener Kommentar zum BGB/Coester, 9. Aufl. 2024, EGBGB Art. 17b Rn. 124.

EKKEHARD BECKER-EBERHARD

Europäische Rechtsanwältinnen und Rechtsanwälte in Deutschland

I. *Einleitung*

Dass, wer in einem EU-Staat nach nationalem Recht als Rechtsanwalt zugelassen ist und damit die Voraussetzungen für die Ausübung des Anwaltsberufs in diesem Land erfüllt, unter gewissen Voraussetzungen auch in einem anderen EU-Staat anwaltliche Dienstleistungen erbringen und sich dort auch niederlassen darf, sollte unter der Geltung der Dienstleistungs- (Art. 56 AEUV) und der Niederlassungsfreiheit (Art. 49 AEUV) selbstverständlich sein. Es bestanden jedoch naheliegende Bedenken, beide Freiheiten für den Anwaltsberuf voraussetzungslos gelten zu lassen. Wie für andere Berufe wie etwa den Arztberuf[1] schuf man in Form von Richtlinien im europäischen Recht vielmehr auch für die grenzüberschreitende Ausübung des Anwaltsberufs Sonderregelungen. Zu nennen sind vor allem die Richtlinie 77/249/EWG vom 22.3.1977 zur Erleichterung der tatsächlichen Ausübung des freien Dienstleistungsverkehrs der Rechtsanwälte[2] und die Richtlinie 98/5/EG vom 6.2.1998 zur Erleichterung der ständigen Ausübung des Rechtsanwaltsberufs in einem anderen Mitgliedstaat als dem, in dem die Qualifikation erworben wurde.[3] Zu rechtfertigen sind diese Sonderregelungen[4] mit den erheblichen Unterschieden, die nach wie vor und bis auf Weiteres zwischen den Rechtsordnungen der Mitgliedstaaten bestehen.

Diese Richtlinien sind mittlerweile weitgehend umgesetzt, in Deutschland etwa durch das Gesetz über die Tätigkeit europäischer Rechtsanwälte (EuRAG) vom 9.3.2000[5], zuletzt geändert durch Gesetz vom 5.10.2021. Das EuRAG versteht in § 1 unter „europäischen Rechtsanwälten" „natürliche Personen, die berechtigt sind, als Rechtsanwalt unter einer der in der Anlage zu dieser Vorschrift genannten Berufsbezeichnungen selbständig tätig zu sein", wobei die Anlage die verschiedenen Bezeichnungen aufführt, unter denen Rechtsanwälte in Europa tätig sind. Der Un-

[1] Dazu die Richtlinie 93/16/EWG vom 5. April 1993 zur Erleichterung der Freizügigkeit für Ärzte und zur gegenseitigen Anerkennung ihrer Diplome, Prüfungszeugnisse und sonstigen Befähigungsnachweise (ABl. 1993 L 165, 1).

[2] ABl. Nr. 1977 L 78, 17.

[3] ABl. Nr. 1998 L 77, 36.

[4] Mit denen nach Henssler ZZP 115 (2002), 321, 344 im Bereich anwaltlicher Dienstleistungen ein Harmonisierungsgrad erreicht sei, der dem Tempo der Integration im Übrigen weit enteilt sei.

[5] BGBl. 2000 I 182.

terscheidung der beiden genannten Grundfreiheiten sowie der beiden genannten Richtlinien folgt auch die folgende Darstellung.

II. Dienstleistende europäische Rechtsanwälte

Grenzüberschreitende Dienstleistungen europäischer Rechtsanwälte betreffend soll hier danach unterschieden werden, welche Dienstleistungen grenzüberschreitend in einem anderen Staat als dem eigenen Herkunftsstaat zu erbringen erlaubt bzw. zu erlauben ist (→ II. 1.) und unter welchen Rahmenbedingungen dies erlaubt bzw. zu erlauben ist (→ II. 2.).

1. Befugnis zur Erbringung anwaltlicher Dienstleistungen und deren Reglementierungen

a) Die Richtlinie 77/249/EWG

Die Richtlinie 77/249/EWG geht der später erlassenen Richtlinie 2006/213/EG vom 12. Dezember 2006 über Dienstleistungen im Binnenmarkt[6] gemäß Art. 3 Abs. 1, Art. 17 Nr. 4 dieser Richtlinie zumindest vor; nach hM verdrängt sie die letztgenannte sogar vollständig.[7]

Zur Befugnis, grenzüberschreitende Dienstleistungen erbringen zu dürfen, ist die Richtlinie 77/249/EWG klar und unmissverständlich: In dieser Befugnis ist der ausländische Rechtsanwalt einem inländischen Berufsträger grundsätzlich gleichzustellen. Einschließlich der Vertretungen vor Gerichten und Behörden muss ihm wie inländischen Kollegen erlaubt werden, die gesamte Palette anwaltlicher Dienstleistungen ausschöpfen. Dafür kennt die Richtlinie 77/249/EWG nur eine Voraussetzung: Man muss in einem Staat der EU nach den dort gültigen Regeln zum Anwaltsberuf zugelassen sein.

Die Richtlinie 77/249/EWG erlaubt den Mitgliedsstaaten in Art. 5 insoweit nur eine Einschränkung: Sie können grenzüberschreitend tätigen Rechtsanwälten bei Tätigkeiten, die mit der Vertretung und der Verteidigung von Mandanten im Bereich der Rechtspflege verbunden sind, abverlangen, dass „sie im Einvernehmen entweder mit einem bei dem angerufenen Gericht zugelassenen Rechtsanwalt … oder mit einem bei diesem Gericht tätigen *„avoué“* oder *„procuratore“* handeln."

b) Umsetzung in Deutschland

Deutschland hat die Richtlinie 77/249/EWG zunächst durch das „Gesetz zur Durchführung der Richtlinie des Rates der Europäischen Gemeinschaften vom 22. März 1977 zur Erleichterung der tatsächlichen Ausübung des freien Dienstleistungsverkehrs der Rechtsanwälte" vom 6.3.1980[8] (RADG) umgesetzt. Dabei hat es von der Möglichkeit, dem ausländischen Rechtsanwalt vor Gericht und Behör-

---

[6] ABl. Nr. L 376, 36.
[7] Ausführlich Singer, Festschrift 60 Jahre Bundesrechtsanwaltskammer, 2019, 177 (195ff.).
[8] BGBl. 1980 I 1453.

den die Beiziehung eines Einvernehmensanwalts zu verlangen, so reichlichen Gebrauch gemacht, dass es bald vom EuGH gemaßregelt werden musste. Darauf wird unter → II. 3. a) zurückzukommen sein. Im Jahre 2000 wurde das RADG durch das EuRAG abgelöst.

c) Nur vorübergehende Tätigkeit im Aufnahmestaat

Die Richtlinie 77/249/EWG formuliert zwar selbst keine Beschränkung des Rechts zur grenzüberschreitenden Dienstleistung auf eine nur vorübergehende Tätigkeit. Das Europäische Primärrecht kennt sie aber seit jeher (jetzt Art. 57 Abs. 3 AEUV). Dementsprechend erlaubt § 25 EuRAG ebenfalls nur eine vorübergehende und gelegentliche Tätigkeit im Aufnahmestaat. Über diese Beschränkung vollzieht sich die Abgrenzung zur Niederlassung. Wer als europäischer Rechtsanwalt dauerhaft grenzüberschreitend dienstleisten will, soll sich dafür niederlassen und dabei die unter → III. dargestellten Voraussetzungen erfüllen müssen.

Die Kriterien für diese Abgrenzung wurden vom EuGH[9] maßgeblich in der Vorlagesache *Gebhard/Consiglio dell'Ordine degli Avvocati e Procuratori di Milano* entwickelt. Danach ist der vorübergehende Charakter einer Tätigkeit „nicht nur unter Berücksichtigung der Dauer der Leistung, sondern auch ihrer Häufigkeit, regelmäßigen Wiederkehr oder Kontinuität zu beurteilen."[10] „Der vorübergehende Charakter schließt nicht die Möglichkeit … aus, sich im Aufnahmemitgliedssaat mit einer bestimmten Infrastruktur (einschließlich eines Büros, einer Praxis oder einer Kanzlei) auszustatten, soweit diese Infrastruktur für die Erbringung der fraglichen Leistung erforderlich ist."[11]

2. Die übrigen Reglementierungen

a) Die Richtlinie

Die übrigen Reglementierungen, die die Richtlinie 77/249/EWG erlaubt, betreffen die Erbringung anwaltlicher Dienstleistungen nicht inhaltlich, sondern nur die Rahmenbedingungen, denen der ausländische Rechtsanwalt bei seiner grenzüberschreitenden Tätigkeit durch das nationale Recht unterworfen werden darf.

So soll der Rechtsanwalt (auch) in dem Staat, in dem er die Dienstleistung erbringt, unter der Berufsbezeichnung handeln, die er in seinem Herkunftsland führt (Art. 3 Richtlinie 77/249/EWG). Dadurch wird dem Dienstleistungsempfänger hinreichend vor Augen geführt, dass er es nicht mit einem Rechtsanwalt zu tun hat, der im Dienstleistungsland zugelassen ist. Zugleich wird damit kompensiert, dass der Rechtsanwalt auch außerhalb seines Herkunftslandes auf allen Rechtsgebieten tätig werden darf und nicht (nach dem Vorbild des § 206 BRAO) auf gewisse Rechte (etwa sein Heimatrecht und das Völkerrecht) beschränkt ist. Denn der Dienstleistungsempfänger kann anhand der ausländischen Berufsbezeichnung erkennen und sich darauf einstellen, dass bei seinem Rechtsanwalt gewisse Schwä-

---

[9] EuGH 30.11.1995 – C-55/94, NJW 1996, 579 = JZ 1996, 465.
[10] EuGH 30.11.1995 – C-55/94, NJW 1996, 579 Rn. 27 und 39.
[11] EuGH 30.11.1995 – C-55/94, NJW 1996, 579 Rn. 27.

chen in der Beherrschung der Rechtsordnung des Dienstleistungslandes und seiner Sprache vorhanden sein könnten.

Dass der Rechtsanwalt nach Art. 4 Abs. 1 Richtlinie 77/249/EWG bei mit der Vertretung oder der Verteidigung eines Mandanten im Bereich der Rechtspflege oder vor Behörden zusammenhängenden Tätigkeiten denselben Bedingungen unterliegt wie der im Dienstleistungsstaat niedergelassene Anwalt, versteht sich von selbst, ebenso, dass hiervon das Erfordernis eines Wohnsitzes sowie die Zugehörigkeit zu einer Berufsorganisation in diesem Staat ausgenommen sind. Zu letzterer hat der bloß dienstleistende Rechtsanwalt ja gerade keinen Zugang.

Weitere bei der Erbringung anwaltlicher Dienstleistung im Ausland zu beachtende Regeln betreffen die Standesregeln und sonstigen Verpflichtungen. Bei Tätigkeiten im Bereich der Rechtspflege und vor Behörden iSd Art. 4 Abs. 1 Richtlinie 77/249/EWG sollen gemäß Art. 4 Abs. 2 Richtlinie 77/249/EWG generell sowohl die Standesegeln des Aufnahmestaats als auch die Verpflichtungen im Herkunftsstaat einzuhalten sein. Bei sonstigen Tätigkeiten bleiben die im Herkunftssaat geltenden Bedingungen und Standesregeln einzuhalten, während von den Regeln im Aufnahmestaat nach Art. 4 Abs. 4 Richtlinie 77/249/EWG nur die über „die Ausübung des Berufs, gleich welchen Ursprungs, insbesondere in Bezug auf die Unvereinbarkeit zwischen den Tätigkeiten des Rechtsanwalts und anderen Tätigkeiten in diesem Staat, das Berufsgeheimnis, die Beziehungen zu Kollegen, das Verbot des Beistands für Parteien mit gegensätzlichen Interessen durch denselben Rechtsanwalt und die Werbung" einzuhalten sind. Allerdings sind diese Regeln nur anwendbar, „wenn sie von einem Rechtsanwalt beachtet werden können, der nicht in dem Aufnahmestaat niedergelassen ist, und nur insoweit, als ihre Einhaltung in diesem Staat objektiv gerechtfertigt ist, um eine ordnungsgemäße Ausübung der Tätigkeit des Rechtsanwalts sowie die Beachtung der Würde des Rechtsanwalts sowie die Beachtung der Würde des Berufs und der Unvereinbarkeiten zu gewährleisten."

Es soll also (anders als nach der Richtlinie 2006/213/EG über Dienstleistungen im Binnenmarkt, die zwar kein reines Herkunftslandsprinzip statuiert, aber dem Aufnahmestaat in Art. 16 Richtlinie 2006/213/EG nur eine dosierte Reglementierung des ausländischen Dienstleistenden durch sein eigenes Recht gestattet) weitgehend das „Prinzip der doppelten Standesregeln" *(„double deontologie")* herrschen. Auch auf die dabei entstehenden Probleme wird zurückzukommen sein.

b) Umsetzung in Deutschland

In Deutschland ist die Richtlinie 77/249/EWG mittlerweile in den §§ 25ff. EuRAG umgesetzt, wobei das deutsche Recht vom „dienstleistenden europäischen Rechtsanwalt" spricht. Der Richtlinie folgend verlangt § 26 Abs. 1 iVm § 5 Abs. 1 EuRAG vom Dienstleistenden, unter der Berufsbezeichnung des Herkunftslandes aufzutreten. Nach § 26 Abs. 2 EuRAG hat er seine Berechtigung, im Staat seiner Niederlassung den Anwaltsberuf auszuüben, dem Gericht oder der Behörde, vor der er auftritt, auf Verlangen nachzuweisen.

Das Recht, Mandanten im Bereich der Rechtspflege oder vor Behörden zu den gleichen Bedingungen zu vertreten oder zu verteidigen wie Inländer, setzt § 27 Abs. 1 EuRAG in der Weise um, dass dienstleistende europäische Rechtsanwälte im Zusammenhang mit der Vertretung oder Verteidigung eines Mandanten im Bereich der Rechtspflege oder vor Behörden die Stellung eines Rechtsanwalts, insbesondere dessen Rechte und Pflichten, haben, soweit diese nicht die Zugehörigkeit zu einer Rechtsanwaltskammer sowie die Kanzlei betreffen.

Auch bei der Einhaltung der Standesregeln und sonstigen Verpflichtungen befolgt Deutschland im § 27 EuRAG die Richtlinie 77/249/EWG und unterscheidet wie deren Art. 4 Abs. 2, 4 Richtlinie 77/249/EWG zwischen Tätigkeiten im Bereich der Rechtspflege und vor Behörden und sonstigen Tätigkeiten. Indem § 27 Abs. 1 EuRAG den dienstleistenden europäischen Rechtsanwalt denselben Pflichten unterwirft wie inländische Rechtsanwälte, sind sie wie in Art. 4 Abs. 2 Richtlinie 77/249/EWG vorgesehen pauschal dem deutschen Berufsrecht verpflichtet. Die differenzierende Regelung in Art. 4 Abs. 4 Richtlinie 77/249/EWG setzt Deutschland in § 27 Abs. 2 EuRAG um, indem es an die Stelle einiger der dortigen Formulierungen die in Deutschland eher gebräuchlichen, aber bedeutungsgleichen setzt und einige zu beachtende Normen der BRAO eigens aufführt. Anders als die Richtlinie 77/249/EWG verhält sich das EuRAG nicht zur Fortgeltung der Verpflichtungen im Herkunftsstaat, da eine Aussage dazu nicht in die Regelungskompetenz des deutschen Gesetzgebers fällt. Das deutsche Recht hat es allerdings grds. zu akzeptieren und akzeptiert es, wenn das Herkunftsland die Bindung seiner im Ausland dienstleistenden Rechtsanwälte an ihr heimatliches Berufsrecht aufrechterhält.

3. Probleme

a) Die Rolle des Einvernehmensanwalts

aa) Überschießende Umsetzung durch § 4 RADG in seiner ursprünglichen Fassung von 1980

Zur Beteiligung eines Einvernehmensanwalts sind mit der oben wiedergegebenen Formulierung im Art. 5 Richtlinie 77/249/EWG schon deren Vorgaben eher diffus. Auch das mag den deutschen Gesetzgeber mit dazu bewogen haben, die von der Richtlinie eröffnete Möglichkeit, die Beteiligung eines Einvernehmensanwalts zu verlangen, im deutschen Recht nicht nur aufzugreifen. Er hat die Notwendigkeit dieser Beteiligung in der ursprünglichen Fassung des § 4 RADG von 1980 auch zunächst einmal denkbar weitgehend festgelegt.

Der ausländische Anwalt sollte „in gerichtlichen Verfahren sowie in behördlichen Verfahren wegen Straftaten, Ordnungswidrigkeiten, Dienstvergehen oder Berufspflichtverletzungen als Vertreter und Verteidiger eines Mandanten nur im Einvernehmen mit einem Rechtsanwalt handeln, der selbst in dem Verfahren Vertreter oder Verteidiger ist." In einer mündlichen Verhandlung oder einer Hauptverhandlung sollte er nur in Begleitung des Rechtsanwalts auftreten dürfen. Diese Abwehrhaltung kam einer Verweigerung der Umsetzung der Richtlinie sehr nahe. Sie wurde vom EuGH in seinem Urteil vom 25.2.1988 in einem Vertragsverletzungsverfahren gegen Deutschland auch entsprechend quittiert und die Regelung in wesentlichen Punkten für nicht richtlinienkonform erklärt.[12]

Der EuGH akzeptierte die in § 4 RADG damaliger Fassung vorgesehene Notwendigkeit der Einschaltung von Einvernehmensanwälten zum einen nur dort, wo das deutsche Recht anwaltliche Vertretung verlangt. Wo dies nicht der Fall sei, müsse der ausländische Rechtsanwalt auch ohne Einvernehmensanwalt auftreten können. Zwar konstatierte der EuGH, dass Art. 5 Richtlinie 77/249/EWG nicht zwischen Verfahren mit und ohne Anwaltszwang unterscheide.[13] Er gab aber überzeugend zu bedenken, dass dort, wo nach deutschem Recht kein Anwaltszwang bestehe, die Partei die Sache selbst vertreten könne, aber auch ihre Vertretung einer Person überlassen könne, die nicht Anwalt ist, sofern diese (insoweit auf das damals noch geltende Rechtsberatungsgesetz blickend) nicht geschäftsmäßig tätig werde.[14] Dadurch werde der ausländische Rechtsanwalt diskriminiert, wenn er auch ohne Bestehen eines Anwaltszwangs nur mit einem Einvernehmensanwalt handeln könne.[15] Dass Nichtanwälten die Vertretung in diesen Fällen nur unter Beachtung des Rechtsdienstleistungsgesetzes erlaubt ist, muss, so ist der Argumentation des EuGH hinzuzufügen, unbeachtlich bleiben. Denn indem Art. 4 Abs. 1 Richtlinie 77/249/EWG und § 27 Abs. 1 EuRAG (und damals schon § 3 RADG) ausländischen Rechtsanwälten die Rechte eines Rechtsanwalts zubilligen, sind auch sie „berufene Berater und Vertreter in allen Rechtsangelegenheiten" iSd § 3 BRAO und als solche von den Beschränkungen des RDG gerade befreit. Die Entscheidung vom 25.2.1988 lag auf einer Linie mit einem schon 1974 auf eine Vorlage aus den Niederlanden ergangenen EuGH-Urteil.[16] Danach verstieß eine Beschränkung wie die Notwendigkeit eines ständigen Aufenthalts des Rechtsdienstleistenden im Inland gegen die damaligen Art. 59 Abs. 1 und Art. 60 Abs. 3 EWGV, wenn die nationalen Rechtsvorschriften die Erbringung dieser Dienstleistung von keiner besonderen Voraussetzung abhängig machen.

Aber auch da, wo Anwaltszwang herrsche, sei es von der Richtlinie 77/249/EWG nicht gedeckt zu verlangen, dass der Einvernehmensanwalt in den Verfahren selbst Bevollmächtigter oder Verteidiger ist und den ausländischen Anwalt bei Terminen begleitet. Ein solches Erfordernis gehe über das hinaus, was zur Erreichung der mit der Beiziehung eines Einvernehmensanwalts verfolgten Ziele notwendig sei.[17] Diese sieht der EuGH darin, den ausländischen Anwalt in die Lage zu versetzen „die Aufgaben, die ihm sein Mandant anvertraut hat, unter Wahrung der Erfordernisse einer geordneten Rechtspflege zu erfüllen." Das Einvernehmen mit einem inländischen Rechtsanwalt solle „die notwendige Unterstützung dafür geben, in einem anderen als dem ... vertrauten Rechtssystem tätig zu werden" Dem angerufenen Gericht solle „sie die Gewähr dafür bieten, daß der dienstleistende Rechts-

[12] EuGH 25.2.1988 – 427/85, NJW 1988, 887 = JZ 1988, 506.
[13] EuGH 25.2.1988 – 427/85, NJW 1988, 887 Rn. 10.
[14] EuGH 25.2.1988 – 427/85, NJW 1988, 887 Rn. 13.
[15] EuGH 25.2.1988 – 427/85, NJW 1988, 887 Rn. 13.
[16] EuGH 3.12.1974 – 33/74, NJW 1975, 1095.
[17] EuGH 25.2.1988 – 427/85, NJW 1988, 887 Rn. 26.

anwalt tatsächlich über diese Unterstützung verfügt und somit in der Lage ist, das geltende Verfahrensrecht und die geltenden Berufs- und Standesregeln voll und ganz einzuhalten.“[18]

Daraufhin besserte der deutsche Gesetzgeber im Jahre 1990 dem EuGH folgend nach und schuf in § 4 RADG eine Regelung, die nach dem Aufgehen des RADG im EuRAG weitestgehend dem heutigen § 28 EuRAG entspricht.[19]

Auch Frankreich versuchte, seine Anwaltschaft mit einer ähnlich weit gehenden Notwendigkeit der Einbeziehung eines inländischen Rechtsanwalts zu schützen und wurde dafür in einem Vertragsverletzungsverfahren durch den EuGH[20] ebenfalls gerügt. Zusätzlich hatte Frankreich den Versuch unternommen, eigene Staatsangehörige, die den Anwaltsberuf in einem anderen Mitgliedsstaat nach den dortigen Regeln ausüben, überhaupt von der grenzüberschreitenden Dienstleistung in Frankreich auszuschließen. Das nahm der EuGH ebenfalls nicht hin.[21]

bb) Anwendungsprobleme bei § 28 EuRAG

(1) Unterstützung durch den Einvernehmensanwalt. Die Lockerung der strengen Regeln über die Einschaltung von Einvernehmensanwälten zog in Deutschland aber in einigen Punkten Unklarheiten und Unschärfen nach sich.

Klar ist zunächst, dass der Einvernehmensanwalt jetzt nicht mehr selbst auch Bevollmächtigter des betreffenden Rechtssuchenden sein muss, weshalb zwischen ihm und diesem auch kein Mandantschaftsverhältnis bestehen muss. § 28 Abs. 3 EuRAG bringt dies unmissverständlich zum Ausdruck und bestimmt, dass zwischen dem Einvernehmensanwalt und dem Mandanten kein Vertragsverhältnis zustande kommt, wenn die Beteiligten nichts anderes bestimmt haben.

Die Rolle des Einvernehmensanwalts ist in § 28 Abs. 2 S. 2 EuRAG im Ausgangspunkt wie folgt beschrieben: „Ihm obliegt es, gegenüber dem dienstleistenden europäischen Rechtsanwalt darauf hinzuwirken, dass dieser bei der Vertretung oder Verteidigung die Erfordernisse einer geordneten Rechtspflege beachtet.“ Damit lehnt sich der deutsche Gesetzgeber eng an die an bereits oben wiedergegebenen Formulierungen des EuGH-Urteil vom 25.2.1988 an.[22]

Die Funktion des Einvernehmensanwalts besteht also darin, den dienstleistenden europäischen Anwalt in seiner Arbeit zu unterstützen. Worin unterstützt werden soll, wie die Unterstützung erfolgt und wie intensiv sie sein soll, äußert sich der deutsche Gesetzestext ebenso wie schon die Richtlinie jedoch nur sehr vage.

Deutlich wird immerhin so viel, dass die Unterstützung inhaltlich auf die Beachtung der Erfordernisse einer geordneten Rechtspflege gerichtet sein soll. Damit obliegt es dem Einvernehmensanwalt jedenfalls nicht, den dienstleistenden Rechtsanwalt bei der Anwendung des materiellen Rechts zu unterstützen. Dessen

---

[18] EuGH 25.2.1988 – 427/85, NJW 1988, 887 Rn. 23.

[19] Zur Historie der §§ 4 RADG und 28 EuRAG auch Henssler/Prütting, BRAO/Kilian, 6. Aufl. 2024, EuRAG § 28 Rn. 2.

[20] EuGH 10.7.1991 – C-294/89, NJW 1991, 3084.

[21] EuGH 10.7.1991 – C-294/89, NJW 1991, 3084.

[22] EuGH 25.2.1988 – 427/85, NJW 1988, 887 Rn. 23.

Anwendung fällt, so auch der EuGH,[23] allein in den Verantwortungsbereich des dienstleistenden Rechtsanwalts gegenüber seinem Mandanten. Denn dem stand es frei, seine Belange einem Rechtsanwalt seiner Wahl anzuvertrauen. Und er hat sich entschieden, sein Vertrauen einem Rechtsanwalt zu schenken, für den das im Verfahren anzuwendende materielle Recht (möglicherweise, denn das anwendbare Recht muss ja nicht zwingend die *lex fori* sein) nicht sein Heimatrecht ist. Und damit ihm das nicht entgeht, muss der dienstleistende Rechtsanwalt gemäß § 26 Abs. 1 iVm § 5 Abs. 1 EuRAG unter seiner heimatlichen Berufsbezeichnung auftreten.

Weder das EuGH-Urteil vom 22.2.1988[24] noch § 28 EuRAG beschreiben näher, was mit den Erfordernissen einer geordneten Rechtspflege gemeint ist. Gehören dazu nur die Grundlagen des im anstehenden Verfahren anzuwendenden Verfahrensrechts sowie der grobe Verfahrensablauf oder auch Details der möglichen Entwicklung des Verfahrens im Allgemeinen oder sogar des konkreten Verfahrens? Hier scheiden sich die Geister ebenso wie beim „Wie" und beim „Wie-intensiv" des Hinwirkens bzw. der Unterstützung durch den Einvernehmensanwalt. Die einen stellen insoweit keine hohen Anforderungen und halten schon die bloße Mitunterzeichnung des ersten Schriftsatzes an das Gericht für ausreichend.[25] Andere begnügen sich damit, den dienstleistenden Rechtsanwalt bei Aufnahme seiner Tätigkeit vorab über Formalien der Klageerhebung, einzuzahlende Kostenvorschüsse, den Lauf und die Bedeutung von Fristen sowie die Anforderungen an Antragstellung, Sachvortrag und Beweisantritt lediglich zu informieren,[26] und den Dingen danach ihren Lauf zu lassen. Andere verlangen vom Einvernehmensanwalt, darauf hinzuwirken, dass der Dienstleistende die Erfordernisse einer geordneten Rechtspflege beachtet, also sicher zu stellen, dass er die Formalien der Klageerhebung und etwaige Fristen beachtet.[27] Manche erwarten von ihm schließlich, die Rechtssache in all ihren denkbaren Verfahrensentwicklungen zu durchdenken und mit dem Dienstleistenden zu beraten. Darüber hinaus empfehlen sie abzusprechen, wie eine ausreichende Unterrichtung des Einvernehmensanwalts über den weiteren Verlauf der Angelegenheit sichergestellt werden kann, um erforderlichenfalls situationsentsprechende weitere unterstützende Ratschläge geben oder sein Einvernehmen widerrufen zu können.[28]

Ob angesichts der unterschiedlichen Entwicklungen, die ein Verfahren nehmen kann, und der unterschiedlichen jeweils gebotenen Maßnahmen eine detaillierte

---

[23] EuGH 25.2.1988 – 427/85, NJW 1988, 887 Rn. 27.

[24] EuGH 25.2.1988 – 427/85, NJW 1988, 887.

[25] BAG 13.12.2012 6 – AZR 303/12, NJW 2013, 1620 Rn. 22; Stein/Jonas, ZPO/Jacoby, 23. Aufl. 2016, § 78 Rn. 84; Zöller, ZPO/Althammer, 35. Aufl. 2024, § 78 Rn. 6.

[26] Henssler/Prütting, BRAO/Kilian, 6. Aufl. 2024, EuRAG § 28 Rn. 7; im Ansatz ähnlich Weyland, BRAO/Nöker, 11. Aufl. 2024, EuRAG § 28 Rn. 4; die Berufung der Genannten für diese Formulierung auf Raiser NJW 1991, 2049 (2055 f.) = AnwBl. 1991, 487 (494) geht insoweit fehlt, als dieser sich nicht mit einer bloßen Information begnügt, sondern von einer Überwachungspflicht spricht.

[27] Gaier/Wolf/Göcken, Anwaltliches Berufsrecht/Buchmann/Gerking, 3. Aufl. 2020, EuRAG § 28 Rn. 3

[28] Weyland, BRAO/Nöker, 11. Aufl. 2024, § EuRAG 28 Rn. 5; Gaier/Wolf/Göcken, Anwaltliches Berufsrecht/Buchmann/Gerking, 3. Aufl. 2020, EuRAG § 28 Rn. 4.

Vorabinformation überhaupt möglich ist, lässt sich bezweifeln. Immerhin mag man den dienstleistenden Anwalt mit einer schriftlichen Information darüber aufklären können, mit welchen Entwicklungen in Verfahren im Allgemeinen oder auch im Konkreten zu rechnen ist. Manche Reaktionen auf mögliche Entwicklungen sind jedoch so komplex, dass sie sich erst wirksam erklären lassen, wenn die entsprechende Prozesssituation tatsächlich eingetreten ist.

So etwa, wenn eine Situation eintritt, in der für die Klägerseite eine weitere Verfolgung des ursprünglichen Verfahrensziels aussichtslos ist. Ob man jetzt Klageverzicht nach § 306 ZPO, Klagerücknahme nach § 269 ZPO oder die Hauptsache für erledigt erklärt, setzt Kenntnisse im deutschen Prozessrecht voraus, die sich dem ausländischen Kollegen besser angesichts der eingetretenen Situation als vorab gewissermaßen „auf dem Trockenen" erläutern lassen. Ähnlich ist es bei den Regeln des Sachvortrages. Den nicht in allen Staaten gleichermaßen praktizierten Beibringungsgrundsatz mag man vorab abstrakt erklären können. Wie aber, wenn es von Präklusion bedroht Sachvortrag nachzutragen oder zu ändern gilt? Ist darauf hinzuweisen bzw. dabei zu unterstützen, wie man sich dabei verhält? Schließlich sind auch Säumnissituationen mitunter schwer zu handhaben.

Letztlich wird man darauf abstellen müssen, wie komplex das anstehende gerichtliche Verfahren ist. In einfachen Fällen mag es ausreichen, vorab auf die im Verfahren zu beachtenden wesentlichen Formalien hinzuweisen. Bei einer komplexen Wirtschaftssache kann es dagegen erforderlich werden, sich als Einvernehmensanwalt in regelmäßigen Abständen informieren zu lassen, um gegebenenfalls mit weiteren Hinweisen eingreifen zu können.

(2) Haftungsfragen. Für die Haftungsverhältnisse, die entstehen, wenn einem der beteiligten Rechtsanwälte bei der Wahrnehmung der im obliegenden Pflichten Fehler unterlaufen, gilt:

Zweifelsfrei ist zunächst, dass für seine eigenen Fehler ausschließlich der dienstleistende Rechtsanwalt dem Mandanten haftet, nicht aber der Einvernehmensanwalt.

Darüber hinaus hat der dienstleistende Rechtsanwalt dem Mandanten aber auch für Fehler des Einvernehmensanwalts einzustehen.[29] Denn der Dienstleistende schuldet dem Mandanten auch die Einhaltung der Erfordernisse einer geordneten Rechtspflege, also das, bei dessen Erfüllung der Einvernehmensanwalt ihn zu unterstützen hat. Damit ist der Einvernehmensanwalt Erfüllungsgehilfe des Dienstleistenden iSd § 278 BGB, womit die unter → II. 1. behandelte Frage nach der Reichweite seiner Pflichten keineswegs trivial ist.

Bei der Haftung des Einvernehmensanwalts ließe sich schon in Zweifel ziehen, ob er überhaupt (wem auch immer) haftet. Dagegen könnte die Formulierung in der Richtlinie 77/249/EWG sprechen, die den Einvernehmensanwalt in Art. 5 Richtlinie 77/249/EWG als jemanden bezeichnet, „der gegebenenfalls diesem Gericht gegenüber die Verantwortung übernimmt". Auch der EuGH greift diese For-

[29] Ebenso Raiser NJW 1991, 2049 (2055) = AnwBl. 1991, 487 (494); Henssler/Prütting BRAO/Kilian, 6. Aufl. 2024, EuRAG § 28 Rn. 9; Weyland, BRAO/Nöker, 11. Aufl. 2024, EuRAG § 28 Rn. 6.

mulierung im Urteil vom 25.2.1988 auf und spricht von einer Verantwortung gegenüber dem angerufenen Gericht und nicht gegenüber dem Mandanten.[30] Die damit auferlegte Verpflichtung solle dem Gericht die Gewähr dafür bieten, dass der dienstleistende Rechtsanwalt tatsächlich über die Unterstützung des Einvernehmensanwalts verfügt und somit in der Lage ist, das geltende Verfahrensrecht und die geltenden Berufs- und Standesregeln voll und ganz einzuhalten.[31] Damit, so ließe sich sagen, werde klargestellt, dass die Einschaltung des Einvernehmensanwalts nur Gerichts- und damit Allgemeininteressen diene, nicht aber denen der Beteiligten. Auf deutsches Schuldrecht übersetzt hieße das: Weder der Mandant noch der dienstleistende Rechtsanwalt fielen in den Schutzbereich der Tätigkeit des Einvernehmensanwalts, was notwendig dessen Haftung ihnen gegenüber ausschlösse.

Abgesehen davon, dass die Kategorie einer „Verantwortung gegenüber dem Gericht" dem mit Prozesslasten und nicht Prozesspflichten operierenden deutschen Prozessrecht fremd ist (ein Handeln gegenüber dem Gericht ist entweder unzulässig oder unbegründet und wird dementsprechend entweder zurück- oder abgewiesen), würden damit die genannten Formulierungen jedoch überbewertet. Es ist nicht anzunehmen, dass der Richtliniengeber sich mit ihnen in die nach den nationalen Rechtsordnungen begründbaren Haftungsverhältnisse einmischen wollte.

Deshalb wird sich jedenfalls der dienstleistende Rechtsanwalt, der wegen eines Fehlers dem Einvernehmensanwalt gegenüber dem Mandanten haftpflichtig wird, bei dem Einvernehmensanwalt erholen können.[32] Denn zwischen ihnen besteht als Grundlage für eine solche Haftung durch das hergestellte Einvernehmen ein Vertrag, zumindest aber ein Schuldverhältnis iSd § 311 Abs. 3 BGB. Und mit seinem Fehler hat der Einvernehmensanwalt seine Pflicht zur zutreffenden Unterstützung des dienstleistenden Rechtsanwalts verletzt.

Eine vertragliche Haftung des Einvernehmensanwalts für eigene Fehler gegenüber dem Mandanten scheitert allerdings schon daran, dass der Mandant nur mit dem dienstleistenden Rechtsanwalt in einem Vertragsverhältnis steht und § 28 Abs. 3 EuRAG ein solches zwischen dem Mandanten und dem Erstgenannten bei Fehlen anderslautender Vereinbarungen gerade ausschließt.

Das hindert jedoch nur eine Haftung aus zwischen ihnen bestehendem Vertrag. Eine Haftung aus dem Vertrag zwischen Einvernehmensanwalt und dienstleistendem Anwalt unter dem Gesichtspunkt eines Vertrags mit Schutzwirkung zugunsten Dritter ist dadurch aber zumindest nicht von vornherein ausgeschlossen.[33] Von deren Voraussetzungen[34] sind wesentliche erfüllt: Es besteht Leistungsnähe des Mandanten zu der vom Einvernehmensanwalt zu erbringenden Leistung, der dienstleis-

---

[30] EuGH 25.2.1988 – 427/85, NJW 1988, 887 Rn. 27.

[31] EuGH 25.2.1988 – 427/85, NJW 1988, 887 Rn. 23.

[32] Allg. Ansicht Raiser NJW 1991, 2049 (2055) = AnwBl. 1991, 487 (494); Henssler/Prütting, BRAO/Kilian, 6. Aufl. 2024, EuRAG § 28 Rn. 9; Weyland, BRAO/Nöker, 11. Aufl. 2024, EuRAG § 28 Rn. 6.

[33] Anders Henssler/Prütting, BRAO/Kilian, 6. Aufl. 2024, EuRAG § 28 Rn. 9 und die Stellungnahme der Bundesrechtsanwaltskammer BRAK-Mitt. 1988, 123 (124); wohl auch der Jahresbericht 1988/89 des Deutschen Anwaltsvereins AnwBl. 1989, 372 (375).

[34] Zu ihnen etwa BGH 17.11.2016 – III ZR 139/14, BGHZ 181, 12 = JZ 2010, 414 Rn. 16ff.; BGH 17.11.2016 – III ZR 139/14, NJW-RR 2017, 888 Rn. 17; Lorenz JuS 2021,

tende Rechtsanwalt hat ein Interesse an der Einbeziehung des Mandanten in den Schutzbereich des Vertrages und dem Einvernehmensanwalt ist beides bekannt. Zweifel bestehen lediglich bei der Schutzbedürftigkeit des Mandanten. Da der dienstleistende Anwalt nach § 278 BGB für das Fehlverhalten dem Einvernehmensanwalt einzustehen hat, hat der Mandant einen Anspruch gegen jenen. Das gilt gemeinhin als Ausschlusskriterium für einen Anspruch aus Vertrag mit Schutzwirkung zugunsten Dritter, vorausgesetzt, der Anspruch gegen den dienstleistenden Anwalt ist dem Anspruch gegen den Einvernehmensanwalt gleichwertig. Daran kann es durchaus einmal fehlen, etwa wenn der Mandant ein Inländer ist und seinen Anspruch gegen den dienstleistenden Rechtsanwalt im Ausland verfolgen müsste.

b) Beachtung der Berufsrechte

Anders, als ihr Wortlaut nahelegen könnte, und verbreitet formuliert[35], kann es kaum Sinn des Art. 4 Abs. 2, 4 Richtlinie 77/249/EWG sein, der Umsetzung vorzuschreiben, grenzüberschreitend dienstleistende Rechtsanwälte bei ihrer Tätigkeit im Ergebnis tatsächlich sowohl dem Berufsrecht ihres Herkunfts- als auch dem des Aufnahmestaats zu unterwerfen bzw. unterworfen zu halten. Vielmehr kann es nur darum gehen, es sowohl dem Herkunfts- als auch dem Aufnahmestaat zu erlauben, grenzüberschreitend dienstleistende Rechtsanwälte an der Befolgung ihres jeweiligen Berufs- und Standesrechts festzuhalten bzw. neu zu verpflichten.

Deutschland macht davon im Rahmen seiner Regelungsbefugnis in beide Richtungen Gebrauch. § 27 EuRAG verlangt von hier tätigen ausländischen Rechtsanwälten eine weitgehende Befolgung des deutschen Berufsrechts. Umgekehrt scheint es selbstverständlich zu sein, im Ausland dienstleistende deutschen Rechtsanwälte an der Pflicht zur Befolgung des deutschen Berufsrechts festzuhalten; denn sie sind ja nach wie vor deutsche Rechtsanwälte im Sinne von BRAO und BORA. Soweit ersichtlich halten es die anderen Mitgliedstaaten ebenso.

Materiell-rechtlich wirft diese parallele Bindung an die Berufsrechte des Herkunfts- und die des Aufnahmestaats keine Probleme auf, soweit sie im Einzelfall zu gleichen Ergebnissen kommen. Legt eines der beiden Rechte strengere Maßstäbe an, scheint auf den ersten Blick die Lösung nahe zu liegen, sich an das strengere halten zu müssen.[36] Das wäre aber nur unproblematisch, wenn das strengere das des Aufnahmestaates ist. Dann unterläge der dienstleistende Rechtsanwalt bei seiner Auslandstätigkeit denselben Beschränkungen wie die Kollegen des Aufnahmestaats. Wollte man im umgekehrten Fall den dienstleistenden Rechtsanwalt an seinem

817, 818ff.; Münchener Kommentar zum BGB/Gottwald, 9. Aufl. 2022, § 328 Rn. 167ff.; Staudinger, BGB/Klumpp, 2020, § 328 Rn. 112ff.

[35] Etwa Henssler NJW 2009, 1556, in Fn. 4 Art. 4 Richtlinie 77/249/EWG als Geltungsgrund für die Bindung auch an das Heimatberufsrecht zitierend; Henssler/Prütting, BRAO/Kilian, 6. Aufl. 2024, EuRAG § 27 Rn. 16 (Richtlinie „stellt klar“ dass beide Berufsrechte „zu beachten hat“); Weyland, BRAO/Nöker, 11. Aufl. 2024, EuRAG § 27 Rn. 2 („hat nach Art. 4 Abs. 2 RL 77/249/EWG“ beide Berufsrechte „einzuhalten“); Dauses/Ludwigs, Handbuch des EU-Wirtschaftsrechts/Stumpf, 59. EL Oktober 2023, Kap. E. II. Rn. 202; wohl auch Singer, Festschrift 60 Jahre Bundesrechtsanwaltskammer, 177 (200).

[36] Hellwig BRAK-Mitt. 2009, 50 (53).

strengeren Heimatrecht festhalten, so würde er schlechter behandelt als die Kollegen im Aufnahmestaat und damit diskriminiert. Das kann das europäische Recht aber nicht hinnehmen. Deshalb gibt es unter europarechtlichen Gerichtspunkten hier im Grunde nur eine Lösung: Der grenzüberschreitend dienstleistende Rechtsanwalt wird jedenfalls in diesem Falle von der Beachtung der strengeren Regeln seines Herkunftsstaates befreit und muss nur das Recht des Aufnahmestaats befolgen.[37]

Vollends problematisch wird es, wenn die Ergebnisse des Rechts im Herkunftsstaat und die des Rechts im Aufnahmestaat divergieren oder sich gar sich widersprechen.

Insoweit eine klare Antwort zu geben, fällt schwer. Denn bei dem dem Öffentlichen Recht zugehörigen Berufsrecht konnte sich ein Kollisionsrecht bislang noch nicht herausbilden. Ebenso wenig hilft die Richtlinie selbst weiter. Zum einen billigt sie die doppelte Bindung ja gerade. Außerdem will sie nicht die Berufsrechte harmonisieren, sondern nur die Anforderungen an die grenzüberschreitende anwaltliche Tätigkeit.[38] Da von zwei sich widersprechenden Regeln aber nicht beide gleichzeitig befolgt werden können, kann die Lösung nur sein, dass eines der beteiligten Berufsrechte entweder überhaupt zurücktritt oder sein internationaler Geltungsanspruch so weit modifiziert und auf seinen Kernbereich reduziert wird, dass dem Anwalt in der konkreten Situation eine sachgerechte Vertretung des Mandanten ermöglicht wird.[39]

Letztlich spricht vieles dafür und entspricht zunehmender Ansicht, wegen der größeren Sachnähe dem Recht des Aufnahmestaats den Vortritt zu lassen,[40] zumindest de lege ferenda. Ob sich die Herkunftsstaaten allerdings auf eine solche Vernachlässigung ihrer Berufsrechte einzulassen bereit sind, ist ungewiss. Bislang war eine entsprechende Kompromissbereitschaft eher nicht zu spüren. So fiel der vom Deutschen Anwaltsverein unterbreitete Vorschlag, in einem neu eingefügten § 59o Abs. 2 BRAO bei der Dienstleistung deutscher Rechtsanwälte im Ausland unter gewissen Umständen auf die Einhaltung deutschen Berufsrechts zu verzichten, beim deutschen Gesetzgeber bislang nicht auf fruchtbaren Boden.[41]

---

[37] Henssler/Prütting, BRAO/Kilian, 6. Aufl. 2024, EuRAG § 27 Rn. 17; siehe auch Singer, Festschrift 60. Jahre Bundesrechtsanwaltskammer, 177 (201, 206f.).

[38] Hellwig BRAK-Mitt. 2009. 50, 53.

[39] Im letzteren Sinne Knöfel AnwBl. 2003, 3 und Knöfel, Grundfragen der internationalen Berufsausübung von Rechtsanwälten, 2005, 442 (452ff.).

[40] Für die Rechtslage in Deutschland Henssler NJW 2009, 1556 (1558, 1559); Henssler/Prütting, BRAO/Kilian, 6. Aufl. 2024, EuRAG § 27 Rn. 16 mwN; Gaier/Wolf/Göcken, Anwaltliches Berufsrecht/Buchmann/Gerking, 3. Aufl. 2020, EuRAG § 27 Rn. 5; Weyland, BRAO/Nöker, 11. Aufl. 2024, EuRAG § 27 Rn. 2; Deckenbrock/Henssler, RDG/Deckenbrock, 5. Aufl. 2021, § 1 Rn. 49; wohl auch Henssler ZZP 115 (2002), 321 (349f.); für eine weitgehende teleologische Reduktion der Berufsregeln des Herkunftslandes auch Singer, Festschrift 60 Jahre Bundesrechtsanwaltskammer, 198ff. (271).

[41] AnwBl. 2007, 682 (687) und dazu Hellwig BRAK-Mitt. 2009, 50 (54) sowie Henssler NJW 2009, 1556 (1558).

III. Niedergelassene europäische Rechtsanwälte

1. Niederlassung nach der Richtlinie 98/5/EG vom 6.2.1988

Schon bei Erlass der Richtlinie 77/249/EWG war klar, dass einem bereits in einem EU-Staat zugelassenen Rechtsanwalt auf Dauer auch die Niederlassung in einem anderen Mitgliedsstaat nicht würde versagt bleiben können und eingehendere Maßnahmen erforderlich sein werden, um die tatsächliche Ausübung der Niederlassungsfreiheit zu erleichtern.[42] Besonders deutlich wurde dies im Jahre 1995 anhand der Vorlagesache *Gebhard/Consiglio dell'Ordine degli Avvocati e Procuratori di Milano.* Darin sprach der EuGH[43] unmissverständlich aus, dass die Mitgliedsstaaten einem im Ausland selbständig Tätigen unter gewissen Bedingungen eine Niederlassung im Inland zu ermöglichen haben. Diese Bedingungen seien vom Mitgliedsstaat festzulegen, und zwar diskriminierungsfrei und unter Wahrung der Verhältnismäßigkeit. So kam es letzten Endes zur Richtlinie 98/5/EG vom 6.2.1998 zur Erleichterung der ständigen Ausübung des Rechtsanwaltsberufs in einem anderen Mitgliedsstaat als dem, in dem die Qualifikation erworben wurde.

Die Richtlinie 98/5/EG kennt zwei verschiedene Arten der Niederlassung eines Rechtsanwalts in einem anderen Mitgliedsstaat als seinem Herkunftsland. Die Niederlassung kann gemäß Art. 2 und Art. 4 Richtlinie 98/5/EG entweder unter der heimischen Berufsbezeichnung stattfinden (Art. 2ff. Richtlinie 98/5/EG) oder in Gestalt einer vollständigen Gleichstellung mit den Rechtsanwälten des Aufnahmestaates (Art. 10 Richtlinie 98/5/EG).

a) Niederlassung unter der heimischen Berufsbezeichnung

In diesem Falle hat der Rechtsanwalt sich nach Art. 3 Abs. 1 Richtlinie 98/5/EG bei der zuständigen Stelle des Aufnahmestaats eintragen zu lassen. Einzige Voraussetzung für diese Eintragung ist nach Art. 3 Abs. 2 Richtlinie 98/5/EG die Vorlage einer Bescheinigung über seine Eintragung bei der zuständigen Stelle des Herkunftsstaates. Sodann darf er nach Art. 5 Abs. 1 Richtlinie 98/5/EG unter Verwendung seiner heimatlichen Berufsbezeichnung die gleichen beruflichen Tätigkeiten ausüben wie im Aufnahmestaat zugelassene Rechtsanwälte und kann „insbesondere Rechtsberatung im Recht seines Herkunftsstaates, im Gemeinschaftsrecht, im internationalen Recht und im Recht des Aufnahmestaats erteilen."

Nach Art. 5 Abs. 3 Richtlinie 98/5/EG kann allerdings vorgesehen werden, dass der ausländische Rechtsanwalt bei der Vertretung und Verteidigung von Mandaten vor Gerichten nur im Einvernehmen mit einem bei dem Gericht zugelassenen Rechtsanwalt handeln kann. Nach Art. 6 Abs. 1 Richtlinie 98/5/EG sind bei Tätigkeiten im Aufnahmestaat neben den im Herkunftsland geltenden Berufs- und Standesregeln auch die des Aufnahmestaats einzuhalten. Bei Verletzung der Regeln des Aufnahmestaates sind die dortigen Disziplinarmaßnahmen möglich (Art. 7 Abs. 1 Richtlinie 98/5/EG).

---

[42] Vgl. den zweiten Erwägungsgrund zu Richtlinie 77/249/EWG.
[43] EuGH 30.11.1995 – C-55/94, NJW 1996, 579.

b) Niederlassung unter Gleichstellung mit den Berufsträgern des Aufnahmestaats

Zur Erlangung einer völligen Gleichstellung mit den Kollegen des Aufnahmestaates sieht die Richtlinie 98/5/EG im Art. 10 zwei Wege vor:

Bei Nachweis einer mindestens dreijährigen effektiven und regelmäßigen Tätigkeit im Aufnahmestaat unter der ursprünglichen Berufsbezeichnung im Recht dieses Aufnahmestaats ist sie ohne weitere Voraussetzungen zu ermöglichen (Art. 10 Abs. 1 Richtlinie 98/5/EG). Bei ebenso langer Tätigkeit im Aufnahmestaat, aber kürzerer Tätigkeit in dessen Recht ist die Möglichkeit zu eröffnen, in einem Prüfverfahren und einem Gespräch ausreichende Kenntnisse und Erfahrungen im Recht des Ausnahmestaates darzulegen (Art. 10 Abs. 3 Richtlinie 98/5/EG).

Wer eines dieser Verfahren erfolgreich durchlaufen hat, wird im Aufnahmestaat wie ein inländischer Rechtsanwalt zur Rechtsanwaltschaft zugelassen und ist diesen vollständig gleichgestellt. Er darf neben der Berufsbezeichnung im Aufnahmestaat allerdings nach wie vor die Berufsbezeichnung aus seinem Heimatland führen, falls er die dortige Zulassung aufrechterhält (Art. 10 Abs. 6 Richtlinie 98/5/EG).

c) Unzulässigkeit weiter gehender Beschränkungen durch nationales Recht

Über die genannten hinausgehende Beschränkungen darf der nationale Gesetzgeber nicht vornehmen. Denn der Gemeinschaftsgesetzgeber hat durch Art. 3 Richtlinie 98/5/EG eine vollständige Harmonisierung der Voraussetzungen für die Niederlassung gemäß der Richtlinie vorgenommen.[44] Dementsprechend hat der EuGH im Urteil vom 19.9.2006[45] in einem Vertragsverletzungsverfahren eine Regelung in Luxemburg[46] beanstandet, die die Eintragung eines die Niederlassung in Luxemburg beabsichtigenden Rechtsanwalts davon abhängig machte, dass der Betreffende in einem Gespräch die ausreichende Beherrschung der in Luxemburg im rechtlichen Bereich relevanten Sprachen nachweist.

2. *Niederlassung nach der Richtlinie 2005/36/EG vom 7.9.2005*

Einen weiteren Weg zur voll integrierten Niederlassung als Rechtsanwalt in einem anderen Mitgliedsstaat als dem, in dem man die Qualifikation zum Anwaltsberuf erworben hat, bietet die Richtlinie 2005/36/EG vom 7.9.2005 über die Anerkennung von Berufsqualifikationen.[47] Er steht jedem offen, der in einem Mitgliedstaat die Voraussetzungen zur Zulassung zur dortigen Anwaltschaft erworben hat. Die Erfordernisse der Richtlinie 98/5/EG müssen nicht erfüllt sein. Dh es ist weder erforderlich, im Herkunftsstaat seiner Qualifikation folgend bereits zur Anwaltschaft zugelassen zu sein noch muss man den Anwaltsberuf im Aufnahmestaat bereits dienstleistend aufgenommen. Beides schadet aber auch nicht. Es kann also

[44] EuGH 19.9.2006 – C-193/05, BeckRS 2006, 70703 Rn. 36.
[45] EuGH 19.9.2006 – C-193/05, BeckRS 2006, 70703.
[46] Das zuvor bereits vergeblich versucht hatte, die Richtlinie 98/5/EG wegen Verstoßes vor allem gegen Art. 52 Abs. 2 EGV (jetzt Art. 49 Abs. 2 AEUV) vor dem EuGH insgesamt zu Fall zu bringen, vgl. EuGH 7.11.2000 – C-168/98, NJW 2001, 137.
[47] ABl. 2005 L 255, 22.

auch jemand diesen Weg jederzeit gehen, der in seinem Herkunftsland bereits zur Anwaltschaft zugelassen ist und im Aufnahmestaat unter der ursprünglichen Berufsbezeichnung vielleicht sogar dienstleistend tätig geworden ist, die in der Richtlinie 98/5/EG verlangte Tätigkeitsdauer aber noch nicht erreicht hat. Dieser Weg ist aber komplex und mühsam und kann hier nicht im Einzelnen dargestellt werden.

3. Umsetzung durch das EuRAG

a) Niederlassung unter der Berufsbezeichnung des Herkunftsstaates nach §§ 2–10 EuRAG

Die Richtlinie 98/5/EG bezüglich der Niederlassung unter der Berufsbezeichnung des Herkunftsstaates umzusetzen, geschehen durch die §§ 2–10 EuRAG, war vergleichsweise einfach. Auf Antrag, dem eine Eintragungsbescheinigung der zuständigen Behörde des Herkunftsstaates über die dortige Zulassung zur Anwaltschaft beizufügen ist (§ 3 EuRAG),[48] wird man bei der zuständigen deutschen Anwaltskammer als niedergelassener europäischer Anwalt eingetragen und dadurch Mitglied dieser Kammer. Sodann hat man die gleichen Rechte und Pflichten wie die deutschen Kollegen, ist also mit denselben Konsequenzen und Problemen wie unter → II. 3. b) dargestellt dem deutschen und dem heimischen Berufsrecht unterworfen. Außerdem hat man nach § 7 EuRAG eine Berufshaftpflichtversicherung zu unterhalten. Anders als manch anderer Mitgliedsstaat sieht Deutschland von der Möglichkeit ab, die Einschaltung eines Einvernehmensanwalts zu verlangen.

b) Eingliederung nach §§ 11–15 EuRAG

Kein großer Umsetzungsaufwand war in §§ 11–15 EuRAG auch hinsichtlich der vollstandigen Aufnahme in die deutsche Anwaltschaft nach dreijähriger effektiver und regelmäßiger Tätigkeit in Deutschland zu betreiben. Erfolgte die Tätigkeit auch im deutschen Recht, begnügt sich § 12 EuRAG mit der Darlegung und dem Nachweis von Dauer und Gegenstand dieser Tätigkeit. Bei nur kürzerer Tätigkeit im deutschen Recht ist nach § 13 EuRAG die Fähigkeit, diese Tätigkeit weiter auszuüben, nachzuweisen. Das geschieht gemäß § 14 EuRAG wiederum durch Darlegung und Nachweis der Voraussetzungen. Außerdem überprüft die zuständige Rechtsanwaltskammer nach § 15 EuRAG in einem Gespräch, „ob die antragstellende Person effektiv und regelmäßig als niedergelassener europäischer Rechtsanwalt in Deutschland auf dem Gebiet des deutschen Rechts tätig war und ob sie imstande ist, diese Tätigkeit weiter auszuüben.“

---

[48] Das EuRAG folgt nicht dem vor dem EuGH gescheiterten Versuch Luxemburgs, eine jährliche Erneuerung dieser Bescheinigung zu verlangen, vgl. EuGH 19.9.2006 – C-193/05, BeckRS 2006, 70703.

c) Aufnahme in die deutsche Anwaltschaft nach Feststellung einer gleichwertigen Berufsqualifikation §§ 16–24 EuRAG

Wie schon die zugrundeliegende Richtlinie 2005/36/EG selbst ist ihre Umsetzung durch die §§ 16ff. EuRAG bezüglich der Aufnahme in die deutsche Anwaltschaft nach Feststellung einer gleichwertigen Berufsqualifikation durchaus komplex und der Weg dahin mühsam. Das kann angesichts der sich nach wie vor erheblich unterscheidenden Berufswege in die Anwaltschaft in der EU kaum überraschen.

Im Mittelpunkt steht nach § 16 Abs. 1 S. 1 EuRAG die von einem Justizprüfungsamt zu treffende Feststellung, dass die von der antragstellenden Person erworbene Berufsqualifikation die Kenntnisse umfasst, die für die Ausübung des Anwaltsberufs in Deutschland erforderlich sind. In Zweifelsfällen erlegt das Prüfungsamt nach § 16a Abs. 3 EuRAG die Ablegung einer aus einem schriftlichen und einem mündlichen Teil besehenden deutschsprachigen (§ 21 Abs. 1 EuRAG) Eignungsprüfung auf, die nach § 17 EuRAG „ausschließlich die beruflichen Kenntnisse und Kompetenzen der antragstellenden Person betrifft und mit der ihre Fähigkeit, den Beruf eines Rechtsanwalts in Deutschland auszuüben, beurteilt werden soll.“

CHRISTIAN BERGER

Grenzüberschreitende Videobeweisaufnahmen

Aufgrund seiner Arbeiten zum nationalen, europäischen und internationalen Zivilprozessrecht zählt *Thomas Rauscher* zu den profiliertesten Vertretern der deutschen Zivilprozessrechtswissenschaft. In diesem Rahmen hat er sich auch mit der internationalen Beweisaufnahme befasst. Die folgenden Gedanken zur grenzüberschreitenden Videobeweisaufnahme, in deren Mittelpunkt die ganz neuen nationalen Bestimmungen (§ 284 Abs. 2 und Abs. 3 ZPO) und die noch recht jungen Regeln der Europäischen Beweisaufnahmeverordnung (Art. 20 EU-BewVO 2020) stehen, mögen daher auf sein Interesse stoßen.

I. Videobeweisaufnahme im Zivilprozess

1. Videovernehmung nach § 128a Abs. 2 ZPO

Das Bonmot, wonach im Zivilprozess „ein Lot Rechtsfragen auf einen Zentner Tatsachen" trifft, lässt den Stellenwert der Beweiserhebung im zivilgerichtlichen Verfahren erkennen. Im Grundsatz findet die Beweisaufnahme unmittelbar vor dem erkennenden Gericht statt (§ 355 Abs. 1 Satz 1 ZPO). Unmittelbarkeit bedeutete über viele Jahrhunderte hinweg die gleichzeitige physische Anwesenheit der Mitglieder des gerichtlichen Spruchkörpers, der Parteien und ihrer Vertreter sowie der Beweismittel am Ort der Verhandlung und Beweisaufnahme. Der mit dem Gesetz zur Reform des Zivilprozesses (Zivilprozessreformgesetz)[1] vom 27.7.2001 aufgrund einer Initiative des Rechtsausschusses neu geschaffene § 128a Abs. 1 ZPO relativierte mit Wirkung vom 1. Januar 2002 für die mündliche Verhandlung das Erfordernis gleichzeitiger körperlicher Präsenz von Richtern, Parteien, ihren Bevollmächtigten und Beiständen im Sitzungszimmer. Nach dem ebenfalls durch das Zivilprozessreformgesetz eingefügten § 128a Abs. 2 ZPO konnte das Gericht Zeugen, Sachverständigen und zu vernehmenden Parteien bei der Beweisaufnahme gestatten, sich an einem Ort außerhalb des Sitzungszimmers aufzuhalten. Die Verhandlung und die Vernehmung wurden durch zeitgleiche Bild- und Tonübertragung in das Sitzungszimmer und, falls Parteien, Bevollmächtigte oder Beweispersonen der Aufenthalt an einem anderen Ort gestattet war, auch dorthin übertragen. Voraussetzung der Teilnahme an der mündlichen Verhandlung und der Beweisaufnahme von einem anderen Ort aus war eine richterliche Gestattung, die zunächst das Einverständnis beider Parteien voraussetzte.

[1] BGBl. 2001 I 1887; dazu Stadler ZZP 115 (2002), 413 437.

Seit dem Jahre 2013 genügte der Antrag einer Partei.[2] Freilich schafft die Gestattung stets nur eine Option; Beweispersonen konnten gleichwohl an der Gerichtsstelle erscheinen.

Allerdings hatte die zeitgleiche Übertragung von Bild und Ton von dem anderen Ort in das Sitzungszimmer zunächst kaum praktische Bedeutung. Erst die mit der Corona-Pandemie einhergehenden Reise- und Kontaktverbote haben § 128a ZPO aus seinem Dornröschenschlaf erweckt.[3]

2. *Neuregelung der Videoverhandlung und Videobeweisaufnahme*

An diese Entwicklung anknüpfend stellt das Gesetz zur Förderung des Einsatzes von Videokonferenztechnik in der Zivilgerichtsbarkeit und den Fachgerichtsbarkeiten vom 15.7.2024[4] die Videoverhandlung und die Videobeweisaufnahme auf erweiterte normative Grundlagen. § 128a ZPO, dessen zweiter Absatz bislang die Videovernehmung umfasste, normiert künftig ausschließlich die mündliche Verhandlung in Form der Videoverhandlung. Normadressaten der Vorschrift zur Videoverhandlung sind die Verfahrensbeteiligten und das Gericht. Die neu in § 284 ZPO einzufügenden Absätze 2 und 3 behandeln nunmehr die Videobeweisaufnahme.

Nach dem neu gefassten § 128a Abs. 1 Satz 2 ZPO können nicht nur Verfahrensbeteiligte (dazu § 128a Abs. 1 Satz 3 ZPO), sondern auch Mitglieder des Gerichts von außerhalb des Sitzungszimmers an der Videoverhandlung teilnehmen, soweit erhebliche Gründe dafür vorliegen (§ 128a Abs. 5 Satz 2 ZPO). Zudem kann die Teilnahme an einer Videoverhandlung durch den Vorsitzenden nicht nur „gestattet", sondern „angeordnet" werden (§ 128a Abs. 2 Satz 1 ZPO); die Option, gleichwohl im Sitzungssaal zu erscheinen, ist entfallen, vorbehaltlich des Einspruchs nach § 128a Abs. 2 Satz 2 ZPO.

Rechtliche Grundlage der Beweisaufnahme per Bild- und Tonübertragung bildet zukünftig § 284 Abs. 2 ZPO. Die Norm verweist auf zentrale Bestimmungen des § 128a ZPO (§ 284 Abs. 2 Satz 3 und Satz 4 ZPO). Das Antragsrecht steht auch Zeugen und Sachverständigen zu (§ 284 Abs. 2 Satz 2 ZPO). Das beweiserhebende Gericht kann ferner amtswegig eine Videobeweisaufnahme anordnen und Beweispersonen anweisen, sich während der Vernehmung an einer bestimmten Gerichtsstelle einzufinden (§ 284 Abs. 3 ZPO). Nur für den Urkundsbeweis ist eine Videobeweiserhebung ausgeschlossen (§ 284 Abs. 2 Satz 5 ZPO).

---

[2] § 128a ZPO wurde dahingehend geändert durch das Gesetz zur Intensivierung des Einsatzes von Videokonferenztechnik in gerichtlichen und staatsanwaltschaftlichen Verfahren vom 25.4.2013 (BGBl. 2013 I 935); zur Gesetzesgeschichte Stein/Jonas, ZPO/Kern, 23. Aufl. 2016, § 128a vor Rn. 1.

[3] Zur Entwicklung Rauscher COVuR 2020, 2 (5f.).

[4] BGBl. 2024 I 237.

3. Unionsebene

Normativ befördert wird die Videobeweisaufnahme auch in der neu gefassten EU-BewVO 2020. Die ursprüngliche Fassung der EG-BewVO des Jahres 2001 sah in Art. 17 Abs. 4 Satz 3 EG-BewVO zunächst nur eine Unterstützungspflicht der Zentralstelle und der zuständigen Behörde für Kommunikationstechnologie bei Video- und Telekonferenzen vor. Die seit dem 1.7.2022 anzuwendende Neufassung[5] regelt in Art. 20 EU-BewVO 2020 nunmehr eingehend die Videovernehmung. Ziel ist die Förderung unmittelbarer Beweisaufnahmen per Videokonferenz im Interesse der Vereinfachung und Beschleunigung des Verfahrens.[6]

Eine geringere Bedeutung hat die nach Art. 9 Abs. 3 EG-BagatellVO[7] in Verbindung mit Art. 8 Abs. 1 Satz 2 EG-BagatellVO in Bagatellverfahren mögliche Beweisaufnahme per Videokonferenz (oder im Wege anderer Mittel der Fernkommunikation), zumal das Verfahren ohnehin vom Freibeweis geprägt ist.[8] Die EG-BagatellVO bleibt im Folgenden außerhalb der Betrachtungen.

4. Zwecke

Videoverhandlungen schonen Ressourcen.[9] Der Wegfall von Reisen zur Gerichtsstelle spart Parteien, ihren Bevollmächtigten und den Beweispersonen Zeit und Geld.[10] Zudem erwartet man prozessökonomische Verfahren und eine erleichterte Terminfindung.[11] Videokonferenzen sollen sogar zur nachhaltigen Entwicklung beitragen, indem sie die Leistungsfähigkeit der Justiz erhöhen.[12] Bei sich weit entfernt aufhaltenden und nicht reisewilligen oder -fähigen Beweispersonen erübrigen Videovernehmungen eine Beweiserhebung durch einen ersuchten Richter (§ 375 Abs. 1 ZPO). Videovernehmungen dienen damit der (mediatisierten) Unmittelbarkeit der Beweisaufnahme, indem das erkennende Gericht selbst die Beweisaufnahme durchführen kann (§ 355 Abs. 1 Satz 1 ZPO).[13] Für die Parteien erleichtert dies den Zugang zum Beweismittel (§ 357 Abs. 1 ZPO) als Ausprägung ihres Rechts auf Beweisführung. Insbesondere wenn sich Beweispersonen im Ausland aufhalten, mag die Videovernehmung eine Beweiserhebung erst ermöglichen.

---

[5] Verordnung (EU) 2020/1783 des europäischen Parlaments und des Rates vom 25.11.2020 über die Zusammenarbeit zwischen den Gerichten der Mitgliedstaaten auf dem Gebiet der Beweisaufnahme in Zivil- oder Handelssachen (Beweisaufnahme) (Neufassung) (ABl. 2020 L 405, 1)

[6] ErwGr. 21 EU-BewVO 2020.

[7] Verordnung (EG) Nr. 861/2007 des Europäischen Parlaments und des Rates vom 11.7.2007 zur Einführung eines europäischen Verfahrens für geringfügige Forderungen (ABl. 2007 L 199, 1).

[8] Rauscher, EuZPR/EuIPR/Varga, 4. Aufl. 2015, EG-BagatellVO Art. 9 Rn. 1ff.; Stein/Jonas, ZPO/Domej, 23. Aufl. 2021, § 1101 Rn. 1.

[9] Dazu Stein/Jonas, ZPO/Kern, 23. Aufl. 2016, § 128a Rn. 1f.

[10] BT-Drs. 14/6036, 116 und S. 119; BT-Drs. 20/8095, 1.

[11] BT-Drs. 20/8095, 59.

[12] BT-Drs. 20/8095, 1 und 32 nimmt Bezug auf „Ziel 16" der SGDs, das „friedliche und inklusive Gesellschaften" anstrebt.

[13] Stein/Jonas, ZPO/Kern, 23. Aufl. 2016, § 128a Rn. 5.

II. Der autonome Rechtsrahmen der (grenzüberschreitenden) Videobeweisaufnahme

Die Rechtsgrundlagen grenzüberschreitender Videobeweisaufnahmen sind – wie jede Beweisaufnahme mit Auslandsbezug – geprägt durch innerprozessuale beweisrechtliche Bestimmungen über die Zulässigkeit und das Verfahren der Beweiserhebung und des Beweismittels (§§ 128a, 284 Abs. 2 und Abs. 3 ZPO) sowie die gegenüber dem Belegenheitsstaat des Beweismittels zu beachtenden zwischenstaatlichen Regeln.

1. Stand und Entwicklung der Rechtsgrundlagen für Videobeweisaufnahmen

Innerstaatliche Grundlage für eine Videobeweisaufnahme war seit dem Jahre 2002 der § 128a Abs. 2 ZPO. Danach konnte das Prozessgericht Zeugen, Sachverständigen und Parteien auf Antrag gestatten, sich während ihrer Vernehmung an einem anderen Ort (als der Gerichtsstelle) aufzuhalten. Die Vernehmung wurde in Bild und Ton zeitgleich in das Sitzungszimmer und an den Aufenthaltsort der zu vernehmenden Person übertragen.

Das Gesetz zur Förderung des Einsatzes von Videokonferenztechnik in der Zivilgerichtsbarkeit und den Fachgerichtsbarkeiten[14] stellt die Videobeweisaufnahme in § 284 Abs. 2 und Abs. 3 ZPO auf eine neue gesetzliche Grundlage. Die aufgrund der technischen Bezüge zur Videoverhandlung zuvor in § 128a Abs. 2 ZPO aF verankerte Regelung wird ihrer beweisrechtlichen Bedeutung entsprechend rechtssystematisch zutreffend in § 284 ZPO eingefügt. Dafür spricht insbesondere, dass § 284 Abs. 2 ZPO nicht nur auf die Vernehmung von Beweispersonen, sondern auch auf den Augenscheins-, nicht aber den Urkundsbeweis (§ 284 Abs. 2 Satz 5 ZPO) erstreckt wird; auch im Wege des Freibeweises (§ 284 Abs. 1 Satz 2 ZPO) dürfte der Urkundsbeweis als Videobeweisaufnahme ausscheiden. Videoverhandlung und Videobeweisaufnahme fallen damit gesetzestechnisch und rechtssystematisch auseinander. Gleichwohl bleibt beides rechtlich insofern verknüpft, als § 284 Abs. 2 Satz 3 ZPO eine entsprechende Anwendung wesentlicher Bestimmungen der Videoverhandlung auch bei der Videobeweisaufnahme vorsieht.

Mit der Neufassung der Grundlagen der Videobeweisaufnahme in § 284 Abs. 2 und Abs. 3 ZPO sind eine Reihe von Lockerungen und Modifikationen verbunden, auf die im Folgenden kurz eingegangen werden soll.

2. Antragsrecht

Nach dem früheren § 128a Abs. 2 ZPO aF fand die Videobeweisaufnahme auf Antrag statt. Wer antragsbefugt war, ließ sich dem Wortlaut der Norm nicht entnehmen. Die herrschende Meinung ging von der Antragsbefugnis beider Parteien aus; jedoch musste nur eine Partei den Antrag stellen.[15] Einvernehmen herrschte,

---

[14] BGBl. 2024 I 237.

[15] Stein/Jonas, ZPO/Kern, 23. Aufl. 2016, § 128a Rn. 21; das Einverständnis beider Parteien, das ihnen ein Vetorecht einräumte, war seit dem 1.11.2013 nicht mehr erforderlich.

dass Zeugen und Sachverständige den Antrag auf Vernehmung im Wege einer Videokonferenz nach § 128a Abs. 2 ZPO aF nicht stellen konnten.[16] Der neue § 284 Abs. 2 Satz 2 ZPO erweitert das Antragsrecht auf Zeugen und Sachverständige und darüber hinaus (über den weiten Begriff der „Verfahrensbeteiligten") auch auf Nebenintervenienten, Bevollmächtigte, Vertreter und Beistände (§ 284 Abs. 2 Satz 2 i.V. mit § 128a Abs. 1 Satz 3 ZPO). Da es um die Art und Weise der Beweisaufnahme geht, wäre es indes folgerichtig gewesen, die Antragsbefugnis nur der beweisführenden Partei zuzusprechen. Werden Minderjährige, die das 16. Lebensjahr vollendet haben, als Partei vernommen (§ 455 Abs. 2 ZPO), sollte ihnen trotz ihrer fehlenden Prozessfähigkeit im Rahmen des § 284 Abs. 2 Satz 2 ZPO ein eigenes Antragsrecht zustehen.

3. *Amtswegige Anordnung und Einspruch*

Anders als unter dem bisherigen § 128a Abs. 2 ZPO aF kann das Gericht fortan eine Videobeweisaufnahme auch amtswegig anordnen (§ 284 Abs. 2 Satz 1 ZPO).[17] Beweispersonen, denen gegenüber die Anordnung ergangen ist, sind dann verpflichtet, sich über eine Videokonferenz vernehmen zu lassen. Sie haben aber ein Einspruchsrecht[18] (§ 284 Abs. 2 Satz 4 ZPO), können also nicht gegen ihren Willen zur Videovernehmung gezwungen werden. Wird Einspruch eingelegt, muss der Vorsitzende die Anordnung für alle Verfahrensbeteiligte aufheben (§§ 284 Abs. 2 Satz 3, 128a Abs. 4 Satz 1 ZPO) und zum Termin in den Sitzungssaal laden. Zugleich soll er Verfahrensbeteiligten, die keinen Einspruch eingelegt haben, die Teilnahme per Videokonferenz gestatten (§§ 284 Abs. 2 Satz 3, 128a Abs. 4 Satz 2 ZPO) mit der Folge, dass der Einspruchsführer zwar im Gerichtssaal erscheinen kann, aber gleichwohl von dort eine Bild- und Tonübertragung in Kauf nehmen muss.

Verfahrensbeteiligte können gegen die Anordnung der Videovernehmung auch dann Einspruch einlegen, wenn sie nicht ihr Adressat sind (§ 284 Abs. 2 Satz 4 ZPO). Noch im Regierungsentwurf des Gesetzes zur Förderung der Videokonferenztechnik war den Parteien und ihren Bevollmächtigten ein Einspruchsrecht versagt worden mit der Begründung, die Beweisaufnahme diene der Überzeugungsbildung des Gerichts und daher müsse das Gericht auch über

---

[16] Stein/Jonas, ZPO/Kern, 23. Aufl. 2016, § 128a Rn. 21.

[17] Dazu BT-Drs. 20/8095, 60. Eine amtswegige Anordnung war bislang in § 128a Abs. 2 ZPO aF nicht vorgesehen.

[18] Mit dem Einspruchsrecht für Parteien und Zeugen soll dem Umstand Rechnung getragen werden, dass die Befragung durch ein Gericht insbesondere für Privatpersonen häufig besonders belastend ist. Nach der Begründung im RegE des Gesetzes zur Förderung der Videokonferenztechnik treffe dies auf Sachverständige als „professionelle Beteiligte" nicht zu (BT-Drs. 20/8095, 60), denen daher zunächst kein Einspruchsrecht zugestanden worden war. Dies traf auf Kritik in der Stellungnahme des Bundesrates (BR-Drs. 228/23, 6f.). Die Beschlussempfehlung des Rechtsausschusses des Bundestages hat dies aufgenommen und ein Einspruchsrecht der Sachverständigen vorgesehen (vgl. BT-Drs. 20/9354, 39). Für den Fall der mündlichen Anhörung des Sachverständigen zur Erläuterung seines schriftlichen Gutachtens besteht allerdings weiterhin kein Einspruchsrecht gegen eine Videoverhandlung (vgl. BR-Drs. 604/23, 4).

die Art und Weise der Vernehmung entscheiden.[19] Diese Restriktion wurde im weiteren Gesetzgebungsverfahren zurecht fallen gelassen.[20] Das Beweisführungsinteresse der Parteien bestimmt auch die Art und Weise der Beweisaufnahme. Die Parteien haben daher ein Anrecht, auf die dem Unmittelbarkeitsgrundsatz (§ 355 Abs. 1 ZPO), der Parteiöffentlichkeit (§ 357 ZPO) und dem Fragerecht (§ 397 ZPO) regelmäßig förderliche persönliche Vernehmung zu bestehen.

4. *Ermessensausübung des Prozessgerichts*

Die Entscheidung über die Anordnung oder Gestattung einer Videobeweisaufnahme steht im Ermessen des Gerichts (§ 284 Abs. 2 Satz 1 ZPO), anders als bei der Entscheidung über die Videoverhandlung nicht nur des Vorsitzenden (§ 128a Abs. 2 Satz 1 ZPO). Das ist folgerichtig, da die sämtlichen Mitgliedern des Kollegialorgans obliegende Beweiswürdigung betroffen ist. Das Prozessgericht hat dazu die mit der Videovernehmung verbundene Terminerleichterung, Beschleunigung und Ressourcenschonung[21] abzuwägen gegen die Beurteilung von Glaubwürdigkeit der Beweisperson und Glaubhaftigkeit ihrer Aussage unter den technischen Bedingungen einer Videovernehmung.[22] Bei Sachverständigen dürfte eine Videovernehmung häufig in Betracht kommen.[23] Bei Zeugen kann die Beurteilung erschwert sein, wenn trotz technisch hochwertiger Übertragung der unmittelbare persönliche Eindruck fehlt.[24] Freilich können auf Bildschirmen auch Unterlagen „geteilt" werden. Möglich ist es daher, einem Zeugen Dokumente vorzuhalten und Fotos oder Videos vorzuspielen und dazu Nachfragen zu stellen, was die Grundlage für Glaubwürdigkeitserwägungen stärken kann. Hierdurch kommt der Ablauf einer Videovernehmung der Vernehmung in Präsenz durchaus nahe. Darüber hinaus mag die fehlende physische Konfrontation mit anderen Prozessbeteiligten eine wahrheitsgemäße Aussage im Einzelfall sogar fördern.[25] Wenn eine schriftliche Aussage (§ 377 Abs. 3 ZPO) in Betracht kommt, dürfte eine Videovernehmung häufig näher liegen. Ist die Beweisperson (beispielsweise infolge Erkrankung oder körperlicher Beeinträchtigung) nicht in der Lage, eine Reise zum Sitz des Prozessgerichts zu unternehmen, stärkt die Videovernehmung den beweisrechtlichen Unmittelbarkeitsgrundsatz (§ 355 Abs. 1 Satz 1 ZPO) im Vergleich zur Beweisaufnahme durch den ersuchten Richter (§ 375 Abs. 1 ZPO) oder einer schriftlichen Zeugenaussage (§ 377 Abs. 3 ZPO).[26] Befindet sich die Beweisperson im Ausland, kann ihre fehlende (und nicht mit Zwangsmitteln durchsetzbare) Reise-

---

[19] BT-Drs. 20/8095, 60.

[20] Die zu begrüßende Änderung geht auf den Rechtsausschuss zurück, vgl. Beschlussempfehlung und Bericht, BT-Drs. 20/9354, 39.

[21] BT-Drs. 20/8095, 59.

[22] Dazu Reuß JZ 2020, 1135 (1137); eher restriktiv Greger MDR 2020, 957 Rn. 18ff.; vgl. aber Prütting AnwBl 2013, 330 (332) („Es dürfte nämlich auch künftig leichter sein, wahrheitswidrige Behauptungen in eine Kamera als direkt in das Gesicht des Richters zu formulieren.").

[23] Lorenz MDR 2016, 956 (959).

[24] Dazu BT-Drs. 20/8095, 60; weitere Kriterien bei Stein/Jonas, ZPO/Kern, § 128a Rn. 24.

[25] Lorenz MDR 2016, 956 (959).

[26] Stein/Jonas, ZPO/Kern, 23. Aufl. 2016, § 128a Rn. 25.

willigkeit oder -fähigkeit durch die Anordnung der Videovernehmung kompensiert werden.

Auch wenn beide Prozessparteien eine Videobeweisaufnahme beantragen, bleibt es bei dem weiten „freien"[27] Ermessensspielraum des Gerichts; nach § 284 Abs. 2 Satz 3 ZPO, der nicht auf § 128a Abs. 3 ZPO verweist, kommt die für die Videoverhandlung vorgesehene Verengung des Entscheidungsspielraums auf eine „Soll"-Bestimmung bei der Videobeweisaufnahme nicht zum Zuge. Dem Gericht verbleibt der volle Ermessensspielraum, auch um die rechtlichen und tatsächlichen Voraussetzungen und Schwierigkeiten einer (grenzüberschreitenden) Videobeweisaufnahme mit in die Ermessensausübung einbeziehen zu können.

5. *Gerichtlich bestimmte Vernehmungsstelle*

Der frühere § 128 Abs. 2 ZPO aF normierte keine ausdrücklichen Vorgaben für den „anderen Ort", an dem sich die Beweisperson aufhalten kann.[28] Das Gericht konnte die Auswahl der Beweisperson überlassen. Insbesondere ließ sich der Norm eine Begrenzung auf einen von „Justizangehörigen administrierten Raum"[29] nicht entnehmen. Das Risiko der Einflussnahme Dritter bei einem nicht durch das Gericht vorgegebenen Vernehmungsort auf das Aussageverhalten war nur im Rahmen der Ermessensausübung zu berücksichtigen.[30]

Die Neuregelungen zur Beweisaufnahme in §§ 284 Abs. 2 Satz 3, § 128a Abs. 1 Satz 2 ZPO greifen das Merkmal „anderer Ort" nicht mehr auf, sondern stellen technisch auf die Teilnahme an einer Bild- und Tonübertragung ab, die eine örtliche Dislokation von Beweisperson und Gericht impliziert. Allerdings kann das Gericht nach § 284 Abs. 3 ZPO ergänzend anordnen, dass sich die Beweisperson zur Vernehmung an einer vom Gericht näher zu bestimmenden „Gerichtsstelle" einfindet und dort während der Einvernahme aufhält, insbesondere um sicherzustellen, dass ihre Aussage nicht beeinflusst wird.[31] Der Sitz des anderen Gerichts wird dann zur „Gerichtstelle", wie § 377 Abs. 2 Nr. 5 ZPO zu entnehmen ist.[32]

Liegt der Vernehmungsort im Ausland, muss eine Anordnung des Prozessgerichts gemäß § 284 Abs. 3 ZPO nach Art. 20 Abs. 2 Satz 2 EU-BewVO 2020 durch eine entsprechende Vereinbarung über die „praktischen Modalitäten" der Vernehmung flankiert werden. Für das HBÜ, das eine Videobeweisaufnahme durch das ersuchende Gericht nicht vorsieht, kommt auf der Grundlage des Art. 9 Abs. 2 HBÜ nur eine Vernehmung durch das ersuchte Gericht in Betracht, das der Beweisperson die Anwesenheit im Gerichtsgebäude vorgibt und den Mitgliedern

---

[27] BT-Drs. 20/8095, 60.
[28] Stein/Jonas, ZPO/Kern, 23. Aufl. 2016, § 128a Rn. 22.
[29] Zöller, ZPO/Greger, 34. Aufl. 2022, § 128a Rn. 8.
[30] Stein/Jonas, ZPO/Kern, 23. Aufl. 2016, § 128a Rn. 22.
[31] BT-Drs. 20/8095, 61.
[32] In diesem Sinne auch BT-Drs. 20/8095, 61 (oben).

des ersuchenden Gerichts die Möglichkeit einräumt, im Wege der Bild- und Tonübertragung Fragen zu stellen.[33]

6. *Aufenthaltsort der Mitglieder des Gerichts*

§ 128a Abs. 2 ZPO aF ermöglichte es allein Beweispersonen, nicht aber Mitgliedern des Prozessgerichts, sich während der Vernehmung an einem anderen Ort aufzuhalten. Die neue Regelung der Videobeweisaufnahme in §§ 284 Abs. 2 Satz 3, 128a Abs. 5 Satz 2 ZPO erlaubt es künftig, dass der Vorsitzende bei Vorliegen „erheblicher Gründe" auch Mitgliedern des Gerichts gestattet, nicht vom Sitzungssaal aus, sondern im Wege der Bild- und Tonübertragung an der Videobeweisaufnahme teilzunehmen. Schon bei der mündlichen Videoverhandlung liegt die Schwelle dafür hoch. Der spontane unmittelbare persönliche Austausch der Mitglieder des Spruchkörpers wird erschwert. Bei der richterlichen Interaktion im Rahmen einer Videobeweisaufnahme mag dies zusätzliches Gewicht bekommen.

Der Aufenthalt eines Mitglieds eines richterlichen Spruchkörpers während der Videobeweisaufnahme im Ausland scheidet schon aus völkerrechtlichen Gründen aus.[34] Die Teilnahme an der Beweisaufnahme vom Territorium eines anderen Staates aus verletzt dessen Souveränität. Die gerichtliche Beweisaufnahme ist Ausübung hoheitlicher Gewalt, auch wenn sie im Rahmen einer Videokonferenz erfolgt. Eine Gestattung der Mitwirkung eines im Ausland weilenden Richters nach der EU-BewVO 2020 kommt nicht in Betracht, wenn sich das Beweismittel im Forumstaat befindet.

III. *Unionsrechtlicher Rahmen der Videobeweisaufnahme*

1. *Ausgangspunkte*

Ausgangspunkt des autonomen Rechts der grenzüberschreitenden Beweisaufnahme ist § 363 ZPO, der parallel zur Anwendbarkeit der neu gefassten EU-BewVO 2020 mit Wirkung vom 1. Juli 2022[35] neu konzipiert worden ist.[36] Die Bestimmung sieht – in der Reihung abfallender Relevanz – drei Wege grenzüberschreitender Beweisaufnahme vor: Abs. 1 die Beweisaufnahme nach der EU-BewVO 2020 (mit Verweisung auf die Ausführungsbestimmungen in §§ 1072, 1073 ZPO), Abs. 2 die Beweiserhebung in Drittstaaten aufgrund völkerrechtlicher Rechtshilfeverträge (insbesondere des HBÜ) und schließlich in Abs. 3 die Beweisaufnahme im vertragslosen Zustand. Zentrale praktische Bedeutung dürfte § 363

---

[33] Musielak/Voit, ZPO/Stadler, 21. Aufl. 2024, § 128a Rn. 8; Stein/Jonas, ZPO/Berger, 23. Aufl. 2015, Anhang zu § 363, HBÜ Art. 9 Rn. 55; zurückhaltend Stein/Jonas, ZPO/Kern, 23. Aufl. 2016, § 128a Rn. 38.

[34] Dazu → III. 2. b) bb).

[35] Art. 35 Abs. 1 Satz 2 EU-BewVO 2020.

[36] Durch das Gesetz zur Durchführung ua der EU-BewVO 2020 und der EU-ZustVO 2020 (BGBl. 2022 I 959).

Abs. 1 ZPO zukommen, der die Beweisaufnahme nach der EU-BewVO 2020 eröffnet; diese steht daher im Mittelpunkt der folgenden Analyse.

2. *Videobeweisaufnahme als Beweismitteltransfer?*

Die EU-BewVO 2020 kommt allerdings nicht zur Anwendung, falls man das technische Format einer Videovernehmung nicht als förmliche Beweisaufnahme im Ausland, sondern als stets zulässigen Beweismitteltransfer ins Inland versteht.

a) EU-BewVO 2020 und Beweismittelbeschaffung

Im Ausgangspunkt entfaltet die EU-BewVO 2020 indes keine Sperrwirkung gegenüber einem Beweismitteltransfer ins Inland.[37] Der EuGH hat diese Auffassung für die Vorladung eines in einem anderen Mitgliedsstaat weilenden Zeugen,[38] für Untersuchungen eines Sachverständigen[39] und für schriftliche Zeugenaussagen[40] bestätigt. Ihr liegt der Gedanke zugrunde, die EU-BewVO 2020 ziele darauf ab, eine Beweisaufnahme in anderen Mitgliedsstaaten zu erleichtern. Mitgliedsstaatliche Gerichte seien aber nicht verpflichtet, von den in der EU-BewVO 2020 vorgesehenen Mitteln und Wegen Gebrauch zu machen, wenn sich eine Beweisaufnahme außerhalb der EU-BewVO 2020 als einfacher, schneller und wirksamer erweist.[41] Diese Einschränkung ist freilich nicht so zu verstehen, dass die Anwendung der EU-BewVO 2020 zur freien Disposition steht. Eine tragfähige Differenzierung ergibt sich mit Rücksicht auf die Doppelfunktion der EU-BewVO 2020. Sie regelt zum einen den eher rechtstechnischen Aspekt der grenzüberschreitenden justiziellen Zusammenarbeit bei der Beweisaufnahme. Ferner dient die EU-BewVO 2020 dazu, den sich aus der Territorialitätshoheit der Mitgliedsstaaten ergebenden Souveränitätsbedenken Rechnung zu tragen. Wenngleich Souveränitätsansprüchen der Mitgliedsstaaten in Brüssel wenig effektive Wirkung zukommt, sollte dieser zentrale Aspekt nicht ausgeblendet werden. Immerhin hat auch der EuGH die an sich außerhalb der EU-BewVO 2020 möglichen Ermittlungen eines Sachverständigen in einem anderen Mitgliedsstaat unter den Vorbehalt gestellt, dass der Weg der unmittelbaren Beweisaufnahme über die EU-BewVO 2020 einzuschlagen ist, falls die Untersuchungen an Orten vorgenommen werden, die mit der Ausübung hoheitlicher Gewalt des Beweisaufnahmestaats verbunden sind.[42]

---

[37] Münchener Kommentar zur ZPO/Rauscher, 6. Aufl. 2022, Vorbem. § 1072 Rn. 10; Rauscher, EuZP/EuIPR/v. Hein, 5. Aufl. 2022, EU-BewVO 2020 Art. 1 Rn. 13 (mit umfassenden Nachweisen in Fn. 81).

[38] EuGH 6.9.2012 – C-170/11, ECLI:EU:C:2012:540 Rn. 24ff. = BeckRS 2012, 81870 (Lippens/Kortekaas).

[39] EuGH 21.2.2013 – C-332/11, ECLI:EU:C:2013:87 Rn. 38ff. = BeckRS 2013, 80348 (ProRail BV/Xpedys NV ua).

[40] EuGH 8.9.2022 – C-188/22, ECLI:EU:C:2022:678 Rn. 26ff. (VP/KS).

[41] EuGH 8.9.2022 – C-188/22, ECLI:EU:C:2022:678 Rn. 26ff. (VP/KS).

[42] EuGH 21.2.2013 – C-332/11, ECLI:EU:C:2013:87 Rn. 47 = BeckRS 2013, 80348 (ProRail BV/Xpedys NV ua).

b) Videobeweisaufnahme und Staatensouveränität

Für die Videovernehmung einer sich in einem anderen Mitgliedsstaat aufhaltenden Person stellt sich daher die Frage, ob ihre Einvernahme per Videokonferenz die Territorialhoheit des Aufenthaltsstaats verletzen kann.

aa) Überblick

Vor dem Hintergrund völkerrechtlicher Regeln über die grenzüberschreitende Beweisaufnahme hatte sich schon während der Gesetzgebungsarbeiten eine Diskussion um die Reichweite der geplanten Bestimmungen in § 284 Abs. 2 ZPO zur Videobeweisaufnahme bei Verfahren mit Auslandsbezug entzündet.[43] Im Gesetzgebungsverfahren spielte das Thema nur am Rande eine Rolle.[44] Ausgangspunkt sind die aus dem völkerrechtlichen Souveränitätsanspruch abgeleiteten Grenzen der Beweisaufnahme auf fremdem staatlichem Territorium.[45] Die technischen Möglichkeiten der Videovernehmung werfen insofern neue Fragen auf, die bislang allerdings mangels praktischer Relevanz eher am Rande diskutiert wurden. Das ändert sich mit der zunehmenden praktischen Bedeutung und der eingehenderen Normierung der Videobeweisaufnahme.

Überwiegend erstreckt man die herkömmlichen völkerrechtlichen Regeln über die Beweisaufnahme mit Auslandsbezug auf die grenzüberschreitende Videobeweisaufnahme, die daher allein im Wege der Rechtshilfe möglich erscheint.[46] Die Gegenauffassung verneint einen Souveränitätseingriff.[47] Ihr prominenter Vertreter ist das Bundespatentgericht, das in einem patentrechtlichen Verfahren keine Bedenken hatte, einen im Ausland weilenden Zeugen mit dessen Einverständnis per Videokonferenz zu vernehmen.[48] Dies bietet Anlass, im hier vorgegebenen

[43] M. Stürner/J. Stürner JZ 2023, 340 (347f.) (mit Bezugnahme auf Heck ZIP 2022, 1529, der sich allerdings in erster Linie mit der mündlichen Videoverhandlung befasst).

[44] Der Regierungsentwurf des Gesetzes zur Förderung des Einsatzes von Videokonferenztechnik in der Zivilgerichtsbarkeit und den Fachgerichtsbarkeiten verhält sich zu dem Thema nichtssagend und widersprüchlich, wenn er betont, der Entwurf sei mit dem Recht der Europäischen Union und völkerrechtlichen Verträgen vereinbar (BT-Drs. 20/8095, 31). Allerdings liegt dem die Prämisse zugrunde, der Entwurf adressiere ohnehin nur Videoverhandlungen und Videobeweisaufnahmen, „bei denen sich die Verfahrensbeteiligten im Inland aufhalten“ (BT-Drs. 20/8095, 31). Dann aber stellen sich völkerrechtliche Fragen nicht.

[45] Dazu Stein/Jonas, ZPO/Berger, 23. Aufl. 2015, § 363 Rn. 6ff.; umfassend Leipold, Lex fori, Souveränität, Discovery: Grundfragen des Internationalen Zivilprozessrechts, 1989, S. 41 (48ff.).

[46] OLG Celle 20.2.2020 – 11 U 169/19, BeckRS 2020, 6544 Rn. 33; Rauscher, EuZPR/EuIPR/v. Hein, 5. Aufl. 2022, EU-BewVO 2020 Art. 20, Rn. 3 (mit weiteren Nachweisen in Fn. 13); Musielak/Voit, ZPO/Stadler, 20. Aufl. 2023, ZPO § 128a Rn. 8; Stein/Jonas, ZPO/Kern, 23. Aufl. 2016, § 128a Rn. 35 mit weiteren Nachweisen in Fn. 74. Eingehende Nachweise bei Knöfel RIW 2021, 247 (250) in Fn. 55 – Abweichend Münchener Kommentar zur ZPO/Rauscher, 6. Aufl. 2022, ZPO Vor § 1072 Rn. 10 (allerdings unter Hinweis darauf, dass die EU-BewVO 2020 die Videovernehmung „derzeit“ [gemeint: unter der früheren Fassung der EG-BewVO] nicht explizit regele; unter Art. 20 EU-BewVO 2020 müsse anders entschieden werden).

[47] Knöfel RIW 2021, 247 (250f.) (weil Beweismitteltransfer).

[48] BPatG 16.7.2002 – 23 W (pat) 32/98, GRUR 2003, 176 (Leiterplattennutzen – Trennvorrichtung/Videokonferenz).

Rahmen die völkerrechtlichen Leitlinien in Erinnerung zu rufen und ihre Bedeutung für grenzüberschreitende Videovernehmungen auszuloten.

bb) Territorialitätsprinzip und mögliche Beschränkungen

Das Thema berührt die Grundfrage, inwieweit ein Gericht außerhalb der Staatsgrenzen tätig sein darf, wenn sich Verfahrensbeteiligte oder Beweismittel im Ausland befinden. Die maßgebliche Grenze zieht hier der völkerrechtliche Souveränitätsgrundsatz und das daraus abgeleitete Territorialitätsprinzip.[49] Nach Art. 25 GG sind die allgemeinen Regeln des Völkerrechts Bestandteil des Bundesrechts.[50] Dazu zählt die aus dem Territorialitätsgrundsatz folgende staatliche Rechtsmacht, Rechte und Pflichten für Personen zu begründen und auch zwangsweise durchzusetzen, die sich auf dem Staatsgebiet aufhalten. Zugleich ergibt sich daraus der Achtungsanspruch der territorialen Souveränität anderer Staaten.[51] Gerichtshoheit, namentlich die Beweisaufnahme,[52] zählt nach kontinentaler Tradition zur Staatsgewalt und ist daher im Ausgangspunkt entsprechenden territorialen Schranken unterworfen. Extraterritoriale Handlungen sind nicht statthaft.[53] Gerichtliches Handeln *auf* fremdem Staatsgebiet ist mithin ausgeschlossen, selbst wenn keine Zwangsakte vorgenommen werden.[54] Auf das Einverständnis der Prozessbeteiligten kommt es nicht an. Daher ist auch die Vernehmung mit Zustimmung eines Zeugen im Ausland völkerrechtswidrig. Für die staatliche Gerichtsbarkeit folgt daraus, dass bei Ausübung der Gerichtshoheit außerhalb des Forumstaats stets Rechtshilfe in Anspruch zu nehmen ist.

Weniger klar ist die Rechtslage, wenn Gerichte vom Forumstaat aus mit Wirkung *in* fremdes Staatsgebiet hinein handeln. Insofern besteht weithin noch Einigkeit darüber, dass grenzüberschreitend keine Zwangsmaßnahmen angedroht, verhängt oder gar durchgesetzt werden können. Aber schon der der Möglichkeit späterer Vollziehung von Zwangsmaßnahmen im Forumstaat anhaftende Druck auf derzeit im Ausland weilende Beweispersonen ist schwierig einzuordnen.

Eine Leitlinie bietet der von *Leipold* herausgearbeitete Gedanke, wonach der territoriale Souveränitätsanspruch durch die *lex-fori*-Regel begrenzt werde. Staaten akzeptieren es grundsätzlich, dass im Ausland Zivilprozesse mit Inlandsbezug ablaufen, die sich aus dem Bündel von Pflichten und Obliegenheiten der Beteiligten eines

[49] Leipold, Lex fori, Souveränität, Discovery: Grundfragen des Internationalen Zivilprozessrechts, 1989, S. 13 (zu Beweisantrag und Beweismittelbeschaffung).

[50] Grundlage sind Rechtsquellen des Völkerrechts, Allgemeine Rechtsgrundsätze, Völkergewohnheits- und Völkervertragsrecht, Leipold, Lex fori, Souveränität, Discovery: Grundfragen des Internationalen Zivilprozessrechts, 1989, S. 35 f. Bedeutung Staatenpraxis Leipold, Lex fori, Souveränität, Discovery: Grundfragen des Internationalen Zivilprozessrechts, 1989, S. 37.

[51] Leipold, Lex fori, Souveränität, Discovery: Grundfragen des Internationalen Zivilprozessrechts, 1989, S. 34 f.

[52] Musielak/Voit, ZPO/Stadler, 20. Aufl. 2023, § 363 Rn. 2.

[53] Leipold, Lex fori, Souveränität, Discovery: Grundfragen des Internationalen Zivilprozessrechts, 1989, S. 9.

[54] Leipold, Lex fori, Souveränität, Discovery: Grundfragen des Internationalen Zivilprozessrechts, 1989, S. 40.

Zivilprozesses ergeben.[55] Dieser Grundsatz gelte aber nicht gegenüber den nicht am Prozessrechtsverhältnis beteiligten Zeugen, weil die Bestimmungen über die internationale Zuständigkeit nur die Tätigkeit des Gerichts gegenüber den Parteien rechtfertige.[56] Bereits die Beweismittelbeschaffung nehme dem Adressaten richterlicher Anordnungen den Schutz des Souveränitätsprinzips.[57] Eine unmittelbare Anordnung bedeute eine Umgehung des Rechtshilfeweges,[58] sogar schon dann, wenn Prozessparteien aufgefordert werden, Zeugen zu schriftlichen Auskünften zu veranlassen.[59]

Freilich darf man nicht übersehen, dass es auch bei im Ausland belegenen Beweismitteln um das Beweisführungsinteresse der im Forumstaat einen Zivilprozess führenden Parteien geht, so dass der *lex-fori*-Gedanke die Differenzierung zwischen Partei und Beweispersonen nicht ohne weiteres trägt. Nicht zuletzt hängt die Rechtsstellung des Zeugen – auch bezüglich Verweigerungsrechten – maßgeblich vom jeweils anwendbaren Prozessrecht ab, das durch die internationale Zuständigkeit bestimmt wird.

Auch wenn man danach *Leipolds* Überlegungen nicht in allen Konsequenzen folgen möchte, ist der Grundansatz doch tragfähig: Staatliche territoriale Souveränität ist in einen Ausgleich zu bringen mit dem Gedanken, dass Staaten wechselseitig die an den *lex-fori*-Grundsatz gebundene Ausübung von Gerichtsbarkeit anerkennen und insoweit Begrenzungen ihrer Territorialhoheit wechselseitig hinnehmen.

cc) Stellungnahme: Freiwillige Videovernehmung verletzt staatliche Souveränität nicht

Gegenüber seiner strengen Ausprägung im 19. Jahrhundert hat der völkerrechtliche Territorialitätsanspruch in Randbereichen Einschränkungen erfahren, die durch die Digitaltechnik weiter verschoben werden. Nicht jede Wirkung digitaler grenzüberschreitender Kommunikation staatlicher Einrichtungen erscheint völkerrechtswidrig. Das gilt zunächst für den Datentransfer; digitale gerichtliche Erklärungen über das Internet nehmen durchaus den Weg über das Ausland, sogar falls sich alle Beteiligten im Forumstaat befinden. Daher unterliegt auch die Recherche im Internet zum Zwecke richterlichen Augenscheins keinen völkerrechtlichen Bedenken;[60] ob die dabei abgerufenen Daten physisch im Inland oder im Ausland gespeichert sind, ist ohne Belang, zumal der Speicherort

[55] Leipold, Lex fori, Souveränität, Discovery: Grundfragen des Internationalen Zivilprozessrechts, 1989, S. 54f.

[56] Leipold, Lex fori, Souveränität, Discovery: Grundfragen des Internationalen Zivilprozessrechts, 1989, S. 56.

[57] Leipold, Lex fori, Souveränität, Discovery: Grundfragen des Internationalen Zivilprozessrechts, 1989, S. 58.

[58] Leipold, Lex fori, Souveränität, Discovery: Grundfragen des Internationalen Zivilprozessrechts, 1989, S. 59.

[59] Leipold, Lex fori, Souveränität, Discovery: Grundfragen des Internationalen Zivilprozessrechts, 1989, S. 66f. (Über die Partei ausgeübter Druck sei unzulässige Umgehung der Rechtshilfe).

[60] Stein/Jonas, ZPO/Berger, 23. Aufl. 2015, § 363 Rn. 14; Musielak/Voit, ZPO/Stadler, 20. Aufl. 2023, ZPO § 363 Rn. 10; allgemein zum „surfenden Richter" Greger, FS Stürner I, 2013, S. 289.

kaum zu bestimmen ist. Von daher ist es nur ein kleiner Schritt, die im analogen Zeitalter anerkannten extraterritorialen Wirkungen digital fortzuschreiben. Mit Blick auf die Auslandswirkungen unterscheidet sich die Videovernehmung als direkte Kommunikationsform zwischen Gericht und Beweisperson nicht wesentlich von einer schriftlichen Beantwortung der Beweisfrage. In beiden Fällen befragt das Gericht den im Ausland weilenden Zeugen, der dem Gericht direkt antwortet. Dass bei der Videovernehmung die Antwort im unmittelbaren Anschluss an die Frage digital übermittelt wird, bei der schriftlichen Aussage jedoch nur zeitlich verzögert, bedeutet für die berührten staatlichen Territorialitätsbelange und die Interessen der Beweisperson keinen Unterschied.[61] Anders als die schriftliche Aussage des § 377 Abs. 3 ZPO substituiert die Aufzeichnung der Vernehmung (§§ 284 Abs. 2, 128a Abs. 4 Satz 3, 160a Abs. 6 Satz 2 ZPO) das Beweismittel zwar nicht. Die Aufzeichnung ist indes eine Regelung autonomen deutschen Verfahrensrechts, die keinen völkerrechtlichen Bezug aufweist. Die Videovernehmung ist im Kern nichts anderes als die Wahrnehmung eines im Ausland stattfindenden Ereignisses.[62] Sie bewirkt keine Verletzung territorialer Hoheitsrechte, wenn und weil sich die Richter im Forumstaat aufhalten.[63] Anders als ein sich im Ausland in der Öffentlichkeit bewegender Richter eines fremden Staats beschränkt sich eine Videovernehmung auf die Kommunikation und Informationen über Bildschirme und Lautsprecher in geschlossenen Räumen; die Öffentlichkeit selbst wird nur im Forumstaat hergestellt. Der EuGH hat dementsprechend eine ohne Zwangsmaßnahmen auf freiwilliger Basis erfolgende schriftliche Zeugenvernehmung von der Genehmigung der Behörden des Aufenthaltsstaats freigestellt und die EG-BewVO insofern für nicht anwendbar erklärt.[64] Vergleichbares ist für die Videovernehmung zu erwarten.

Ein zentrales Argument für die Annahme, die Videobeweisaufnahme berühre die Gebietshoheit anderer Staaten, ist neuerdings ihre ausdrückliche Verankerung in Art. 20 EU-BewVO 2020 und die damit einhergehende Verweisung auf das Erfordernis einer Gestattung nach Art. 19 EU-BewVO 2020.[65] Allein die eingehende Normierung der Videobeweisaufnahme in Art. 20 EU-BewVO 2020 als Fall unmittelbarer Beweisaufnahme bedeutet aber nicht, dass das Prozessgericht diesen Weg auch beschreiten muss.[66] Die unionsrechtliche Regulierung der Videokonferenztechnik sagt noch nichts darüber aus, ob damit wirklich Souveränitätsvorbehalte mittelbar anerkannt (und abgebaut) werden oder ob es sich allein um eine Vereinfachung der justiziellen Zusammenarbeit handelt.[67] Letzteres dürfte anzunehmen sein: Die Videovernehmung ohne Androhung von Zwangsmitteln in

---

[61] BGH 10.5.1984 – III ZR 29/83, NJW 1984, 2039 hat die Videovernehmung eines in Ghana lebenden Zeugen abgelehnt, unter Hinweis auf die Auffassung von Leipold.

[62] Knöfel RIW 2021, 247 (250).

[63] Ähnlich, im Ergebnis freilich offen M. Stürner/J. Stürner JZ 2023, 340 (348).

[64] EuGH 8.9.2022 – C-188/22, ECLI:EU:C:2022:678 Rn. 23ff. (VP/KS), der allerdings die Frage der Videovernehmung trotz der darauf gerichteten Vorlagefrage ausklammert, Rn. 22f.

[65] Rauscher, EuZPR/EuIPR/v. Hein, 5. Aufl. 2022, EU-BewVO 2020 Art. 20 Rn. 3.

[66] AA dezidiert Knöfel RIW 2021, 247 (250), der Art. 20 EU-BewVO 2020 daher sehr kritisch sieht.

[67] Zur Doppelfunktion der Bestimmungen über internationale Beweisaufnahme → III.2.a).

privaten Räumen entspricht wie eben dargelegt der keinen Souveränitätsbedenken ausgesetzten schriftlichen Aussage eines Zeugen nach § 377 Abs. 3 ZPO. Art. 20 EU-BewVO 2020 steht einem Beweismitteltransfer durch Videovernehmung daher nicht entgegen.

In diese Richtung weisen auch die im Justizgewährungsanspruch und im Gebot effektiven Rechtsschutzes wurzelnden Beweisführungsinteressen der Parteien. Soweit die Verfahrensordnung des Prozessgerichts die Videovernehmung als Beweismittel vorsieht, gewinnt das „Recht auf Beweis“[68] der Prozessparteien gegenüber den Territorialitätsansprüchen anderer Staaten ein höheres Gewicht.[69] Der im Rahmen einer Videokonferenz aussagebereite Zeuge wäre als präsentes Beweismittel (§ 294 Abs. 2 ZPO) nicht zu vernehmen, wenn man auch präsente Beweise nur im Wege der zeitraubenden Rechtshilfe erheben könnte. Zudem eröffnet der Beweismitteltransfer durch Videovernehmung dem Prozessgericht die Möglichkeit, eine drohende Verzögerungslage durch vorbereitende Maßnahmen aufzulösen und eine Präklusion zu vermeiden,[70] wenn die Videovernehmung eines kooperationsbereiten im Ausland weilenden Zeugen ohne größeren zeitlichen Vorlauf in der mündlichen Verhandlung als „gestellter Zeuge“[71] möglich ist.

Nicht zuletzt ist hervorzuheben, dass mit einer Videovernehmung allenfalls geringfügige, im Regelfall für Dritte nicht erkennbare und daher kaum spürbare Wirkungen der Gerichtsbarkeit im Ausland verbunden sind.[72] Der überkommene völkerrechtliche Territorialitätsanspruch bedarf daher einer vernünftigen und realitätsnahen Modifikation mit Blick auf digitale Kommunikation. Selbstredend vermögen Staaten digitale Kommunikationsmittel zu missbrauchen, um ihren Wirkungsbereich auszudehnen, Meinungsbilder zu beeinflussen, Wahlen zu manipulieren oder auf sonstige Weise destabilisierend zu wirken. All dies ist völkerrechtlichen Schranken unterworfen. Bei digitaler Kommunikation im Rahmen der Ausübung der Zivilgerichtsbarkeit ist ein solcher Missbrauch nicht zu befürchten.

Es bleibt daher bei dem Grundsatz, dass der richterlichen Einvernahme eines im Ausland weilenden Zeugen keine völkerrechtlichen Bedenken entgegenstehen.[73] Selbstredend setzt die Anerkennung der Videovernehmung als bloßer Beweismitteltransfer voraus, dass das Prozessgericht keine Zwangsmaßnahmen androht, verhängt oder gar exekutiert. Einem nicht mitwirkungsbereiten Zeugen dürfen weder Kosten noch Ordnungsgelder und erst recht keine Ordnungs- und Zwangshaft auferlegt werden (§§ 380, 390 ZPO). Unberührt bleibt die Wahrheitspflicht (§ 5 Nr. 10 StGB). Auch bei einer Videovernehmung erfolgt die Aussage „vor Gericht“ (§ 153 StGB).

---

[68] Zu seiner gesetzlichen Verankerung im europäischen und nationalen Recht Scherpe ZZP 129 (2016), 153 (155f., 167ff.).

[69] In diese Richtung zutreffend Stein/Jonas, ZPO/Domej, 23. Aufl. 2021, § 1072 Rn. 4.

[70] Dazu BGH 12..7.1979 – VII ZR 284/78, NJW 1979, 1988 (unter 1.d).

[71] Dazu BGH 25.3.1980 – KZR 10/79, NJW 1980, 1848 (1849) (Zeuge im Ausland).

[72] Für eine Berücksichtigung der Eingriffsintensität bei der Verletzung der Territorialhoheit im Rahmen der Urkundenbeschaffung Stürner JZ 1987, 988 (989f.).

[73] So bereits Stein/Jonas, ZPO/Berger, 23. Aufl. 2015, § 363 Rn. 14.

Die Videovernehmung des Zeugen aufgrund einer Gestattung der Beweisaufnahme per Bild- und Tonübertragung nach § 284 Abs. 2 Satz 1 ZPO ist daher unbedenklich, wenn keine Zwangsmittel zum Einsatz kommen. Eine Anordnung nach § 284 Abs. 3 ZPO an den Zeugen, sich bei einer Gerichtstelle im Ausland einzufinden, ist hingegen nicht statthaft.

c) Exkurs: Augenschein

Der von der EU-BewVO 2020 nicht ausgeschlossene Beweismitteltransfer spielt auch beim Augenschein eine Rolle. Nach § 284 Abs. 2 ZPO kann das Gericht den Augenschein auch im Wege der Videobeweisaufnahme einnehmen. Dies eröffnet eine Diskrepanz zu Art. 20 EU-BewVO 2020, der jedenfalls seinem Wortlaut nach („Person“) nur persönliche Beweismittel umfasst.[74] Gleichwohl kann das deutsche Gericht eine Augenscheinseinnahme per Videokonferenz anordnen (§ 284 Abs. 2 Satz 1 ZPO) und einen entsprechenden Informationstransfer ins Inland bewirken.

3. Videovernehmung nach der EU-BewVO 2020

a) § 1072 ZPO verbietet keinen Beweismitteltransfer

Obgleich die EU-BewVO 2020 den Beweismitteltransfer in das Inland nicht sperrt, sieht § 1072 ZPO[75] diesen Weg nicht ausdrücklich vor. Die in der Norm enthaltene Aufzählung der drei nach der EU-BewVO 2020 möglichen Wege der Beweisaufnahme (Rechtshilfe, unmittelbare Beweisaufnahme, konsularische Vernehmung) schließt den Transfer eines Beweismittels vor das Prozessgericht freilich nicht aus. Nur bei einer Beweis*aufnahme* mit grenzüberschreitender Wirkung zwingen §§ 363 Abs. 1, 1072 ZPO zur Anwendung der dort genannten drei Möglichkeiten. Auch § 363 ZPO entfaltet daher keine Sperrwirkung gegenüber der extraterritorialen Beweisbeschaffung ins Inland.[76]

b) Gerichtliches Ermessen

Bestehen danach weder unionsrechtlich noch nach nationalem Prozessrecht Bedenken gegen den Beweismitteltransfer, ergeben sich für das deutsche Prozessgericht vier Wege der grenzüberschreitenden Beweisaufnahme:[77] Neben dem Beweismitteltransfer steht die Beweisaufnahme durch das ersuchte Rechtshilfegericht (Art. 12ff. EU-BewVO 2020), die unmittelbare Beweisaufnahme durch das Prozessgericht (Art. 20, 19 EU-BewVO 2020) und die – ohnehin nur im Ausnahmefall zulässige (§ 1072 Nr. 3 ZPO) und daher hier zu vernachlässigende – konsularische

---

[74] AA Rauscher, EuZPR/EuIPR/v. Hein, 5. Aufl. 2022, EU-BewVO 2020 Art. 20 Rn. 5.

[75] Die Funktion des zum 1.7.2022 ebenfalls neu gefassten § 1072 ZPO ist umstritten. Man spricht von einer „Freischaltung“ der EU-BewVO 2020 durch § 1072 ZPO (Rauscher, EuZPR/EuIPR/v. Hein, 5. Aufl. 2022, EU-BewVO 2020 Art. 1 Rn. 13). § 1072 ZPO dürfte demgegenüber nur eine klarstellende Brückenfunktion haben (Stein/Jonas, ZPO/Domej, 23. Aufl. 2021, § 1072 Rn. 1).

[76] Zu § 363 ZPO a. F. Stein/Jonas, ZPO/Berger, 23. Aufl. 2015, § 363 Rn. 5.

[77] Vgl. Rauscher, EuZPR/EuIPR/v. Hein, 5. Aufl. 2022, EU-BewVO 2020 Art. 1 Rn. 28, der allerdings die Videovernehmung nicht als bloßen Beweismitteltransfer versteht.

Beweisaufnahme zur Verfügung (Art. 21 EU-BewVO 2020). Die Auswahl zwischen diesen vier Wegen steht im pflichtgemäßen Ermessen des Prozessgerichts.[78] Hinzu treten Ermessensentscheidungen nach § 284 Abs. 2 ZPO[79] und ggf. nach Art. 20 Abs. 1 EU-BewVO 2020. Die Kriterien überschneiden sich zum Teil. Im Rahmen der Ermessensausübung sind die Parteien zu hören, nicht zuletzt mit Blick auf die Kostenlast.

Ist eine Beweisperson mitwirkungsbereit, sind also Zwangsmaßnahmen nicht erforderlich, dürfte im Regelfall die formlose Videovernehmung und damit der Beweismitteltransfer nahe liegen, zumal dieser Weg mit geringerem bürokratischen Aufwand verbunden ist als ein Vorgehen nach der EU-BewVO 2020 und die Mitwirkung der Parteien und ihrer Bevollmächtigten ohne weiteres ermöglicht. Mit Blick auf die Unmittelbarkeit der Beweisaufnahme (§ 355 Abs. 1 Satz 1 ZPO) ist der Beweismitteltransfer durch Videovernehmung der Beweisaufnahme durch ein ersuchtes Gericht (Art. 12ff. EU-BewVO 2020) deutlich überlegen und daher vorzugswürdig.[80]

c) Videobeweisaufnahme durch ersuchtes Gericht

Wirkt eine Beweisperson nicht freiwillig mit und sind Zwangsmaßnahmen geboten, bleibt nur die Videovernehmung durch ein ersuchtes Gericht im Wege der Rechtshilfe (Art. 12ff. EU-BewVO 2020), in deren Rahmen Zwangsmaßnahmen möglich sind (Art. 15 EU-BewVO 2020). Das ersuchte Gericht verfährt grundsätzlich nach seinem Recht (Art. 12 Abs. 2 EU-BewVO 2020), was ein Nachteil ist, der aber durch ein Ersuchen um eine besondere Form, die dem Recht des ersuchenden Gerichts entspricht, kompensiert werden kann (Art. 12 Abs. 3 EU-BewVO 2020). Der Aufwand ist insgesamt erheblich. Allerdings sieht Art. 12 Abs. 1 EU-BewVO 2020 eine Erledigung des Ersuchens innerhalb von 90 Tagen nach Eingang vor. Die Ablehnungsgründe sind schwächer ausgeprägt als bei der unmittelbaren Beweisaufnahme nach Art. 20 EU-BewVO 2020.

Eine Beweisaufnahme des ersuchten Gerichts durch Videokonferenz ist auch möglich, wenn sie im Recht des ersuchten Staats nicht vorgesehen ist; andernfalls wäre der Versagungsgrund in Art. 12 Abs. 4 Satz 2 Fall 1 EU-BewVO 2020 („unvereinbar") nicht recht erklärbar.[81] Die Parteien haben nach Maßgabe des Art. 13 Abs. 1 EU-BewVO 2020 das Recht zur Teilnahme an der Videokonferenz (Parteiöffentlichkeit); ihre aktive Beteiligung bestimmt sich nach Art. 13 Abs. 2–5 EU-BewVO 2020.[82] Die Parteien können danach zur Videokonferenz zugeschaltet werden, der Vernehmung folgen und Fragen stellen bzw. stellen lassen (§ 397

[78] Dazu Münchener Kommentar zur ZPO/Rauscher, 6. Aufl. 2022, vor § 1072 Rn. 9; Stein/Jonas, ZPO/Domej, 23. Aufl. 2021, § 1072 Rn. 3.

[79] Dazu → II. 4.

[80] Ahrens, Der Beweis im Zivilprozess, 2015, Kap. 58 Rn. 47ff.; Stein/Jonas, ZPO/Domej, 23. Aufl. 2021, § 1072 Rn. 6.

[81] Rauscher, EuZPR/EuIPR/v. Hein, 5. Aufl. 2022, EU-BewVO 2020 Art. 12 Rn. 30; wohl auch Münchener Kommentar zur ZPO/Rauscher, 6. Aufl. 2022, EG-BewVO Art. 10 Rn. 12.

[82] Eingehend Rauscher, EuZPR/EuIPR/v. Hein, 5. Aufl. 2022, EU-BewVO 2020 Art. 13 Rn. 2ff.

Abs. 2 ZPO). Innerstaatlich ist die nicht ganz geglückte Bestimmung des § 1073 Abs. 1 Satz 2 ZPO maßgeblich.[83]

Die Beteiligung der Richter des ersuchenden Prozessgerichts bestimmt sich nach Art. 14 EU-BewVO 2020. Innerstaatliche Rechtsgrundlage ist § 1073 Abs. 1 Satz 1 ZPO. Art. 14 Abs. 1 EU-BewVO 2020 ermöglicht das (passive) Zugegensein, also das Verfolgen der Videovernehmung durch das ersuchende Gericht. Obgleich dies im Regelfall vom Territorium des Forumstaats aus erfolgt, geht es um die Teilnahme an einer ausländischen Beweisaufnahme und bedarf daher der Mitteilung nach Art. 14 Abs. 3 EU-BewVO 2020. Damit wird das ersuchte Gericht in die Lage versetzt, nach Art. 14 Abs. 4 EU-BewVO 2020 im Rahmen der „Bedingungen für ihre Teilnahme" über die technischen Wege des Zuschaltens zur Videokonferenz zu informieren (Art. 14 Abs. 5 EU-BewVO 2020).

d) *Unmittelbare Videobeweisaufnahme durch das Prozessgericht*

Die Videobeweisaufnahme durch das ersuchende Gericht nach Art. 20 EU-BewVO 2020 steht hinter der Beweismittelbeschaffung zurück.[84] Sie kommt in Betracht, wenn Kooperationsvereinbarungen zu treffen sind (Art. 20 EU-BewVO 2020). Beispielsweise kann eine Anordnung an die Beweisperson, sich bei der Vernehmung an einer Gerichtsstelle des ersuchten Gerichts aufzuhalten (§ 284 Abs. 3 ZPO), im Rahmen des Art. 20 Abs. 2 EU-BewVO 2020 umgesetzt werden. Auch Unterstützung bei der Suche nach einem Dolmetscher ist hiernach möglich. Die Videobeweisaufnahme nach Art. 20 EU-BewVO 2020 erfolgt nach dem Recht des Forumstaats (Art. 19 Abs. 8 EU-BewVO 2020); die Parteien sind in die Videovernehmung einzubinden (§ 357 ZPO). Innerstaatlich ist § 1073 Abs. 2 ZPO die maßgebliche Rechtsgrundlage.

---

[83] Dazu Rauscher, EuZPR/EuIPR/v. Hein, 5. Aufl. 2022, EU-BewVO 2020 Art. 13 Rn. 14; Stein/Jonas, ZPO/Domej, 23. Aufl. 2021, § 1073 Rn. 2; günstiger die Bewertung bei Münchener Kommentar zur ZPO/Rauscher, 6. Aufl. 2022, § 1073 Rn. 14f.

[84] Dazu → III. 2.

BURKHARD BOEMKE

Illegale Arbeitnehmerüberlassung nach Deutschland – Sozialversicherungs- und Arbeitsvertragsstatut

I. Einleitung

Bei grenzüberschreitenden Sachverhalten stellt sich in rechtlicher Hinsicht häufig die Frage nach dem anwendbaren Recht. Dies ist maßgeblich dafür, welche Tatbestandsvoraussetzungen für das Eintreten von Rechtsfolgen maßgeblich sind oder für das Bestehen und Ausüben von Rechten gegeben sein müssen. Im Zivilrecht bestimmt sich das anwendbare Recht nach den Grundsätzen und Regelungen des internationalen Privatrechts, im Prozessrecht nach den Grundsätzen und Regelungen des Internationalen Zivilverfahrensrecht. Es handelt sich hierbei um Bereiche des Rechts, in denen der *Jubilar* besonders ausgewiesen ist und sich sowohl auf dem Gebiet der Wissenschaft[1] als auch der Lehre[2] besonders ausgezeichnet hat.

Einen Teilbereich des Internationalen Privatrechts bildet das Internationale Arbeitsrecht[3]. Nach dem anwendbaren Recht bestimmt sich schon, ob überhaupt ein Arbeitsverhältnis im konkreten Fall besteht und, wenn ja, welche Schutzbestimmungen zugunsten von Beschäftigten. Mit dem Arbeitsverhältnis einher geht oft der Schutz der Sozialversicherung, obwohl zumindest nach nationalem Recht Arbeits- und Sozialversicherungsverhältnis strikt zu unterscheiden, beide also nicht identisch sind[4]. Gerade bei grenzüberschreitenden Sachverhalten stellt sich für etwaige Beitragszahlungen die Frage nach dem zuständigen System der Sozialversicherung.

In jüngerer Zeit haben sich hier aus nationaler Sicht insbesondere Fragen im Zusammenhang mit der (illegalen) Arbeitnehmerüberlassung ohne Erlaubnis nach § 1

[1] Siehe nur Rauscher, Internationales Privatrecht, 5. Aufl. 2017; Rauscher, Europäisches Zivilprozess- und Kollisionsrecht – EuZPR/EuIPR I-V, 5. Aufl. 2021 ff.

[2] Siehe nur Rauscher, Klausurenkurs im Internationalen Privat- und Verfahrensrecht für Schwerpunktbereich und Masterprüfung, 4. Aufl. 2019.

[3] Siehe dazu nur Gamillscheg, Internationales Arbeitsrecht (1959); Junker, Internationales Arbeitsrecht im Konzern (1992).

[4] BAG 26.5.1999 – 5 AZR 664/98, BeckRS 1999, 30060750; BAG 30.8.2000 – 5 AZB 12/00, BeckRS 2000, 30129130 Rn. 11; BSG 14.11.2013 – B 2 U 15/12 R, BeckRS 2014, 67312 Rn. 14; BSG 23.1.2018 – B 12 KR 55/17 B, BeckRS 2018, 1249 Rn. 11; BSG 4.6.2019, B 12 R 2/18 R, NZS 2019, 785, 787 Rn. 15; BSG 4.6.2019 – B 12 R 11/18 R, BeckRS 2019, 12883 Rn. 19; beck-online.GROSSKOMMENTAR zum Kündigungsrecht/Boemke, Stand 1.3.2024, KSchG § 1 Rn. 56; Gercke/Kraft/Richter, Arbeitsstrafrecht, 3. Aufl. 2021, 1. Arbeitgeberbegriff Rn. 37; Erfurter Kommentar zum Arbeitsrecht/Rolfs, 23. Aufl. 2023, SGB IV § 7 Rn. 2; Schneider/Reich medstra 2019, 11 (15); beck-online.GROSSKOMMENTAR zum SGB/Zieglmeier, Stand 1.3.2022, SGB IV § 7 Rn. 14.

Abs. 1 S. 1 AÜG nach Deutschland hinein ergeben. In diesen Fällen sind in der Vergangenheit gegen den sog. „Entleiher" grds. Beitragsbescheide durch die DRV erlassen worden. Dieser sei gem. § 10 Abs. 1 S. 1 AÜG iVm § 9 Abs. 1 Nr. 1 AÜG Arbeitgeber der überlassenen Arbeitnehmenden geworden und müsse daher nach allgemeinen Grundsätzen Beiträge zur Sozialversicherung abführen.

Im Folgenden soll anhand eines Praxisbeispiels (→ II.) zunächst auf die Frage eingegangen werden, ob der sog. Entleiher bei illegaler Arbeitnehmerüberlassung ins Inland tatsächlich Arbeitgeber des überlassenen Arbeitnehmenden geworden ist (→ III.). Im Anschluss hieran wird die Frage geklärt, welches System der sozialen Sicherheit bei derartigen grenzüberschreitenden Sachverhalten einschlägig ist (→ IV.).

II. Der praktische Fall

Die Frage nach der illegalen Arbeitnehmerüberlassung stellt sich häufig beim sog. Drittpersonal- bzw. Fremdfirmenmitarbeitereinsatz. Hier bereitet die Abgrenzung selbstständiger Unternehmenstätigkeit unter Einsatz von Erfüllungsgehilfen (§ 278 BGB) zur Arbeitnehmerüberlassung Schwierigkeiten.

Hierzu ein Beispiel aus der Praxis[5]:

Der deutsche Frachtunternehmer F erteilt dem litauischen Frachtunternehmen U einen Unterfrachtvertrag. Wegen der Regelungen zum europäischen Kabotageverkehr (GüKGrKabotageV) werden U von F Fahrzeuge zur Verfügung gestellt, F übernimmt auch die Betriebskosten und erteilt U genaue Anweisungen bzgl. der Nutzung der Fahrzeuge, zB bei welchen Tankstellen die Fahrzeuge zu betanken und welche Routen zu nehmen sind. Die Vergütung bemisst sich auf Grundlage einer Stundenlohnvereinbarung nach den tatsächlichen Arbeitszeiten der von U eingesetzten Lkw-Fahrer.

U ist abseits dieses Auftrags ganz überwiegend in Litauen tätig und führt eigene Frachtaufträge innerhalb von Litauen durch. Hiermit erwirtschaftet U 85% seines Gesamtumsatzes. Nur gelegentlich stellt U innerhalb Litauens sowie grenzüberschreitend anderen Unternehmen Lkw-Fahrer zur Verfügung.

Nach einer Betriebsprüfung durch das zuständige HZA erlässt die DRV einen Beitragsbescheid in Höhe von 280.000 € inkl. Säumniszuschläge. Es läge illegale Arbeitnehmerüberlassung mit der Folge vor, dass zwischen F und den Lkw-Fahrern ein Arbeitsverhältnis kraft Gesetzes (§§ 10 Abs. 1 S. 1, 9 Abs. 1 Nr. 1 AÜG) zustande gekommen sei.

Auch das HZA ist nicht untätig geblieben und erlässt einen Einziehungsbescheid über ca. 450.000 € gemäß §§ 29a Abs. 2 S. 1 Nr. 1 und Abs. 5 iVm §§ 87, 19 OWiG wegen eines Verstoßes gegen § 21 Abs. 1 Nr. 7 MiLoG. Gemäß §§ 10 Abs. 1 S. 1, 9 Abs. 1 Nr. 1 AÜG habe zwischen F und den Lkw-Fahrern ein Arbeitsverhältnis bestanden. F habe nicht den Mindestlohn gezahlt und sich damit einen wirtschaftlichen Vorteil verschafft. Dieser müsse abgeschöpft werden und unterliege der Einziehung.

---

[5] In Anlehnung an SG Magdeburg 28.11.2023 – S 46 BA 45/21, juris.

III. Kein Arbeitsverhältnis mit dem Entleiher nach §§ 9 Abs. 1 Nr. 1, 10 Abs. 1 S. 1 AÜG

1. Unwirksamkeit des Leiharbeitsvertrags als Tatbestandsvoraussetzung

Bei Anwendbarkeit des deutschen Rechts richten sich Tatbestand und Rechtsfolge der unerlaubten Arbeitnehmerüberlassung nach dem AÜG. Einschlägig ist hier § 9 Abs. 1 Nr. 1 AÜG für die Unwirksamkeit des Arbeitsvertrags zwischen Leiharbeitnehmer. § 10 Abs. 1 S. 1 AÜG wiederum bestimmt für diesen Fall, dass zwischen Entleiher und Leiharbeitnehmer kraft Gesetzes ein Arbeitsverhältnis zustande kommt.[6]

Die drohende Unwirksamkeit soll den Verleiher dazu bewegen, sich gesetzeskonform die notwendige Erlaubnis zu verschaffen.[7] Die Unwirksamkeit tritt dann ein, wenn ein ansonsten wirksamer[8] Arbeitsvertrag geschlossen wurde, die erforderliche Erlaubnis zur Arbeitnehmerüberlassung aber nicht oder nicht mehr vorliegt[9] und der Arbeitnehmer tatsächlich zur Arbeit überlassen wurde.[10] Mit dem Fehlen oder dem Wegfall der Erlaubnis wird der Arbeitsvertrag *ex nunc* unwirksam.[11]

§ 10 Abs. 1 S. 1 AÜG wiederum setzt voraus, dass der Vertrag nach § 9 Abs. 1 Nr. 1 AÜG unwirksam ist.[12] Ist dies nicht der Fall, also bleibt der Leiharbeitsvertrag zwischen Leiharbeitnehmer und Verleiher wirksam, so besteht kein Bedürfnis für ein kraft Gesetzes begründetes Arbeitsverhältnis zum Entleiher.[13]

2. Arbeitnehmerüberlassung aus dem Ausland

a) Anwendbarkeit von §§ 9 Abs. 1 Nr. 1, 10 Abs. 1 S. 1 AÜG

Auch die Überlassung von Leiharbeitnehmern durch Verleiher mit Sitz im Ausland in ins Inland bedarf einer Erlaubnis nach § 1 Abs. 1 S. 1 AÜG.[14] Fehlt diese

---

[6] BAG 26.4.2022 – 9 AZR 228/21, BeckRS 2022, 22073 Rn. 19; Erfurter Kommentar zum Arbeitsrecht/Roloff, 24. Aufl. 2024, AÜG § 10 Rn. 1; Ungenau BAG 26.4.2022 – 9 AZR 139/21, BeckRS 2022, 22076 Rn. 33: gesetzliche Fiktion.

[7] BT-Drs. VI/2303, 13.

[8] Es sei denn der Unwirksamkeitsgrund steht auch dem Arbeitsverhältnis zum Entleiher entgegen: Erfurter Kommentar zum Arbeitsrecht/Roloff, 24. Aufl. 2024, AÜG § 10 Rn. 3.

[9] Boemke/Lembke, AÜG/Lembke, 3. Aufl. 2013, § 9 Rn. 46; Beck'scher Online Kommentar Arbeitsrecht/Kock, 71. Ed. 1.3.2024, AÜG § 9 Rn. 24.

[10] BAG 20.1.2016 – 7 AZR 535/13, AP AÜG § 1 Nr. 38; aA Ulber/Ulber, AÜG/Ulber, 6. Aufl. 2023, § 9 Rn. 25.

[11] Beck'scher Online Kommentar Arbeitsrecht/Kock, 71. Ed. 1.3.2024, AÜG § 9 Rn. 24; Schüren/Hamann, AÜG/Schüren, 6. Aufl. 2022, § 9 Rn. 41; Boemke/Lembke, AÜG/Lembke, 3. Aufl. 2013, § 9 Rn. 63; Ulber/Ulber, AÜG/Ulber, 6. Aufl. 2023, § 9 Rn. 31.; Ulrici, AÜG, 2017, § 9 Rn. 34.

[12] Schüren/Hamann, AÜG/Schüren, 6. Aufl. 2022, § 10 Rn. 34.

[13] BAG 26.4.2022 – 9 AZR 228/21, BeckRS 2022, 22073 Rn. 21 ff.; BAG 26.4.2022 – 9 AZR 139/21, BeckRS 2022, 22076 Rn. 40.

[14] BAG 26.4.2022 – 9 AZR 228/21, BeckRS 2022, 22073 Rn. 21; BT-Drs. VI/2303, 10; Boemke/Lembke, AÜG/Lembke, 3. Aufl. 2013, Einl. Rn. 14; Erfurter Kommentar zum Arbeitsrecht/Roloff, 24. Aufl. 2024, AÜG § 1 Rn. 8; Pingel RdA 2023, 180 (181).

Erlaubnis, so handelt es sich um illegale Arbeitnehmerüberlassung. Das BAG geht in seiner Rechtsprechung davon aus, dass § 10 Abs. 1 AÜG in Fällen unerlaubter Arbeitnehmerüberlassung aus dem Ausland nicht zur Anwendung kommt, wenn seine Anwendung zu einem „Nebeneinander von fortbestehendem Leiharbeitsvertrag und fingiertem Arbeitsverhältnis“ führt.[15] Es führt hierfür den Wortlaut von § 10 Abs. 1 S. 1 AÜG an, wonach der Vertrag zwischen Leiharbeitnehmer und Verleiher nach § 9 Abs. 1 AÜG unwirksam sein muss ohne Voraussetzungen und Rechtsfolge territorial zu begrenzen.[16]

Für seine Auslegung kann sich das BAG auch auf den Sinn und Zweck von § 10 Abs. 1 S. 1 AÜG berufen, der aus Sicht des Arbeitnehmers den Verlust des Vertragsverhältnisses zum Verleiher mit einem Vertragsverhältnis zum Entleiher kompensieren soll. Hierfür besteht keine Notwendigkeit, wenn der Arbeitsvertrag zum Verleiher nicht nach § 9 Abs. 1 Nr. 1 AÜG unwirksam wird.[17] Auch die Gesetzesmaterialien sprechen in diesem Sinne vom neuen Arbeitgeber nach § 10 Abs. 1 S. 1 AÜG als „alleinige[m] Arbeitgeber“.[18]

b) Bestimmung des Arbeitsvertragsstatuts gem. Art. 3, 8 Rom-I-VO

Entscheidend in Fällen der unerlaubten Arbeitnehmerüberlassung aus dem Ausland ist, ob § 9 Abs. 1 Nr. 1 AÜG überhaupt zur Anwendung kommt, was sich nach Art. 3, 8 der Rom I-VO bestimmt. Gemäß Art. 3, 8 Abs. 1 Rom I-VO ist für das Arbeitsvertragsstatut zunächst und vorrangig die Rechtswahl der Parteien entscheidend. Diese Wahlfreiheit und mit ihr die Privatautonomie steht allerdings unter der Einschränkung, dass die Rechtswahl nicht zu einem Unterschreiten von Schutzbedingungen des nach den objektiven Kriterien von Art. 8 Abs. 2–4 Rom I-VO anwendbaren Rechts führen darf (Art. 8 Abs. 1 S. 2 Rom I-VO).[19] Im Beispielsfall hatten die Parteien keine ausdrückliche Rechtswahl getroffen, eine solche kann sich aber auch aus den Umständen des Vertragsschlusses, zB aus den in Bezug genommenen Rechtsvorschriften, ergeben (Art. 3 Abs. 1 S. 2 Alt. 2 Rom I-VO).[20]

Haben die Parteien keine Rechtswahl – ausdrücklich oder konkludent – getroffen, so bestimmt sich das Arbeitsvertragsstatut nach dem sog. *lex loci labori,* also nach objektiven Kriterien, insbesondere dem Ort der gewöhnlichen Arbeitsleistung (Art. 8 Abs. 2 Rom I-VO).[21] Erst wenn hierüber keine Feststellung möglich ist,

[15] BAG 26.4.2022 – 9 AZR 228/21, BeckRS 2022, 22073 Rn. 21; BAG 26.4.2022 – 9 AZR 139/21, BeckRS 2022, 22076 Rn. 34 allerdings mit der Verwendung des Ausdrucks Leiharbeitsverhältnis.

[16] BAG 26.4.2022 – 9 AZR 228/21, BeckRS 2022, 22073 Rn. 23; BAG 26.4.2022 – 9 AZR 139/21, BeckRS 2022, 22076 Orientierungssatz. 3.

[17] BAG 26.4.2022 – 9 AZR 228/21, BeckRS 2022, 22073 Rn. 26.; aA: Brors/Schüren NZA 2022, 1310 (1312).

[18] BT-Drs. VI/2303, 13f.

[19] Münchener Kommentar zum BGB/Martiny, 8. Aufl. 2021, Rom I-VO Art. 8 Rn. 3.

[20] Vgl. BAG 26.4.2022 – 9 AZR 139/21, BeckRS 2022, 22076 Rn. 57; BAG 26.4.2022 – 9 AZR 228/21, BeckRS 2022, 22073 Rn. 32.

[21] Münchener Kommentar zum BGB/Martiny, 8. Aufl. 2021, Rom I-VO Art. 8 Rn. 5.

kann sich das Arbeitsvertragsstatut subsidiär nach der einstellenden Niederlassung richten (Art. 8 Abs. 3 Rom I-VO).[22]

Schließlich kann es ausnahmsweise zur Nichtberücksichtigung der objektiven Kriterien kommen, wenn sich aus der „Gesamtheit der Umstände [ergibt], dass der Vertrag eine engere Verbindung zu einem anderen … Staat aufweist" (Art. 8 Abs. 4 Rom I-VO).[23]

Im Beispielsfall ergibt sich litauisches und nicht deutsches Arbeitsvertragsstatut zumindest aus Art. 8 Abs. 2 Rom I-VO.

c) Keine Eingriffsnorm iSd § 2 Abs. 1 Nr. 4 AEntG

aa) Vorrang von § 2 Abs. 1 Nr. 4 AEntG

Ist das Arbeitsvertragsstaut nach Art. 3 und 8 Rom I-VO kein deutsches, so kann sich die Anwendbarkeit von § 9 AÜG daraus ergeben, dass es bei der Norm um eine Regelung handelt, die „Bedingungen für die Überlassung von Arbeitskräften, insbesondere durch Leiharbeitsunternehmen" (§ 2 Abs. 1 Nr. 4 AentG) enthält. § 2 Abs. 1 Nr. 4 AEntG dient der Umsetzung von Art. 3 RL 96/71/EG (Entsende-RL) und ist damit als spezielleres Gesetz vorrangig anzuwenden, soweit sein Anwendungsbereich eröffnet ist.[24] Diesem Grundsatz dient Art. 23 Rom I-VO, indem er „Bestimmungen […], die zum reibungslosen Funktionieren des Binnenmarkts beitragen sollen" (ErwGr. 40 Rom I-VO) entgegen den Regelungen von Art. 8 Rom I-VO zur Anwendung bringt.[25]

Das BAG schließt sich dem EuGH und der hL an und versteht § 2 Abs. 1 Nr. 4 AEntG als Kollisionsnorm iSv Art. 23 Rom I-VO.[26] § 2 Abs. 1 Nr. 4 AEntG erfasst aber mit „Bedingungen für die Überlassung von Arbeitskräften, insbesondere durch Leiharbeitsunternehmen" nicht die Unwirksamkeit des Leiharbeitsvertrags bei fehlender Erlaubnis nach § 9 Abs. 1 Nr. 1 AÜG.

bb) Nationale Betrachtung

§ 2 Abs. 1 Nr. 4 AEntG betrifft die Arbeits- und Beschäftigungsbedingungen von Leiharbeitnehmern sowie die die im Inland geltenden gewerbe-, vermittlungs- und erlaubnisrechtlichen Voraussetzungen der Arbeitnehmerüberlassung.[27] Der Wort-

---

[22] EuGH 15.12.2011 – C-384/10, NZA 2012, 227 (228) Rn. 26 (Jan Voogsgeerd/Navimer SA); EuGH 15.3.2011 – C-29/10, NZA 2011, 625 (628) Rn. 43ff. (Heiko Koelzsch/Großherzogtum Luxemburg); BAG 15.12.2016 – 6 AZR 430/15, NZA 2017, 502 (507) Rn. 57ff.

[23] BAG 26.4.2022 – 9 AZR 139/21, BeckRS 2022, 22076 Rn. 62; BAG 26.4.2022 – 9 AZR 228/21, BeckRS 2022, 22073 Rn. 39; vgl. zu Art. 6 Abs. 2 RomÜbk: EuGH 12.9.2013 – C-64/12, NZA 2013, 1163 (1164) Rn. 26.

[24] EuGH 8.12.2020 – C-626/18, BeckRS 2020, 33946 Rn. 130ff.; BAG 26.4.2022 – 9 AZR 139/21, BeckRS 2022, 22076 Rn. 41; BAG 26.4.2022 – 9 AZR 228/21, BeckRS 2022, 22073 Rn. 45; Münchener Kommentar zum BGB/Martiny, 8. Aufl. 2021, Rom I-VO Art. 23 Rn. 19; Rauscher, EuZPR/EuIPR/Thorn, 5. Aufl. 2023, Rom I-VO Art. 23 Rn. 6c.

[25] Rauscher, EuZPR/EuIPR/Thorn, 5. Aufl. 2023, Rom I-VO Art. 23 Rn. 2; Münchener Kommentar zum BGB/Martiny, 8. Aufl. 2021, Rom I-VO Art. 23 Rn. 1.

[26] BAG 26.4.2022 – 9 AZR 228/21, BeckRS 2022, 22073 Rn. 45; BAG 26.4.2022 – 9 AZR 139/21, BeckRS 2022, 22076 Rn. 43.

[27] BAG 26.4.2022 – 9 AZR 228/21, BeckRS 2022, 22073 Rn. 46.

laut von § 2 Abs. 1 Nr. 4 AEntG sei mit dem Begriff „Bedingungen" nicht weiter zielführend, jedoch zeige eine Gesamtschau aus der Überschrift von § 2 AEntG und den Gesetzgebungsmaterialien[28], dass es sich um „Arbeitsbedingungen" handeln soll.[29] Auch der Sinn und Zweck von § 2 AEntG würde dieses Ergebnis bestätigen, weil Ziel des AEntG nach § 1 AEntG die Schaffung und Durchsetzung angemessener Mindestarbeitsbedingungen sei. Mit diesen Zielen hat der Gesetzgeber die ErwGr. 5, 13, 14 Entsende-RL aufgegriffen, die ebenfalls auf die Sicherung von Mindestarbeitsbedingungen abzielen.[30]

Schließlich zeige die Zusammenschau mit § 2 Abs. 1 Nr. 1–3 und 5–7 AEntG, dass sich die Bestimmung nicht nur auf die Bedingungen „für" die Überlassung, sondern auch auf die gewerbe-, vermittlungs- und erlaubnisrechtlichen Voraussetzungen der Überlassung beziehe[31]. Sowohl Bedingungen als auch Voraussetzungen der Überlassung würden nicht die Vertragsbeziehungen der Beteiligten berühren oder mit den Sanktionen der Verletzung von § 1 Abs. 1 S. 1 AÜG in Zusammenhang stehen.[32]

cc) Unionsrechtskonforme Auslegung des § 2 Abs. 1 Nr. 4 AEntG

Da § 2 AEntG der Umsetzung der Entsende-RL dient, wird § 2 AEntG durch das BAG richtlinienkonform ausgelegt.[33] Sowohl Art. 3 Abs. 1 Hs. 1 Entsende-RL als auch Art. 3 Abs. 1 lit. d Entsende-RL beziehen sich auf die „Arbeits- und Beschäftigungsbedingungen" bzw. auf die „Bedingungen für die Überlassung von Arbeitskräften, insbesondere durch Leiharbeitsunternehmen".[34] Auch in der Rspr. des EuGH[35] werde Art. 3 Abs. 1 Entsende-RL als Instrument zur Garantie eines Mindestschutzes im Bereich der Arbeits- und Wirtschaftsbedingungen gesehen.[36]

Ausgehend von dieser Rechtsprechung zeige sich, dass Art. 3 Abs. 1 lit. a–g Entsende-RL die besondere Struktur der Vertragsbeziehungen im Bereich der Arbeitnehmerüberlassung unberührt lasse. Sie verpflichte die Nationalstaaten nicht, die bei der Verletzung erlaubnisrechtlicher Bestimmungen vorgesehenen Sanktionen unabhängig von der Geltung nationalen Rechts zur Anwendung zu bringen.[37]

Diese bestätige auch Art. 3 Abs. 1 a UAbs. 2 Entsende-RL, der die Sicherstellung von Mindestarbeitsbedingungen bei einer Entsendungsdauer von mehr als

[28] BT-Drs. 16/10486, 11.

[29] BAG 26.4.2022 – 9 AZR 228/21, BeckRS 2022, 22073 Rn. 49; BAG 26.4.2022 – 9 AZR 139/21, BeckRS 2022, 22076 Rn. 45.

[30] BT-Drs. 16/10486, 11.

[31] BAG 26.4.2022 – 9 AZR 139/21, BeckRS 2022, 22076 Rn. 43.

[32] BAG 26.4.2022 – 9 AZR 228/21, BeckRS 2022, 22073 Rn. 51.

[33] BAG 26.4.2022 – 9 AZR 228/21, BeckRS 2022, 22073 Rn. 53ff.; BAG 26.4.2022 – 9 AZR 139/21, BeckRS 2022, 22076 Rn. 47ff.

[34] BAG 26.4.2022 – 9 AZR 228/21, BeckRS 2022, 22073 Rn. 54.

[35] EuGH 12.2.2015 – C-396/13, NZA 2015, 345 (346) Rn. 29 mwN (Sähköalojen ammattiliitto ry/Elektrobudowa Spółka Akcyjna).

[36] BAG 26.4.2022 – 9 AZR 228/21, BeckRS 2022, 22073 Rn. 55; BAG 26.4.2022 – 9 AZR 139/21, BeckRS 2022, 22076 Rn. 46.

[37] BAG 26.4.2022 – 9 AZR 228/21, BeckRS 2022, 22073 Rn. 56; BAG 26.4.2022 – 9 AZR 139/21, BeckRS 2022, 22076 Rn. 49.

12 Monaten gerade nicht im Hinblick auf Abschluss und Beendigung des Arbeitsverhältnisses verlangt.[38]

Eine andere Betrachtungsweise würde auch nicht durch Art. 3 Abs. 10 Entsende-RL verlangt. Hiernach können die Mitgliedsstaaten über den Katalog von Art. 3 Abs. 1 Entsende-RL hinaus weitere Mindestarbeitsbedingungen festlegen, die aus dem Bereich der öffentlichen Ordnung stammen. § 9 Abs. 1 Nr. 1 AÜG und § 10 Abs. 1 S. 1 AÜG betreffen nach Ansicht des BAG aber nur das zugrunde liegende Vertragsgefüge und damit das Privatrecht, können also nicht als weitergehende Vorschrift iSv Art. 3 Abs. 10 Entsende-RL verstanden werden.[39]

dd) Stellungnahme

Die Auslegung des neunten Senats von § 2 Abs. 1 Nr. 4 AEntG als „Bedingung der Überlassung von Leiharbeitnehmern" ohne die Einbeziehung der vertraglichen Wirksamkeit der Überlassung überzeugt[40]. Der Senat kann sich auf gute Argumente aus Wortlaut und Systematik sowohl des AEntG als auch der Entsende-RL stützen. Zudem: Würde man Vorschriften über die Begründung des Leiharbeitsverhältnisses in den Anwendungsbereich von § 2 Abs. 1 Nr. 4 AEntG einziehen, so liefe dies auf eine Einbeziehung des gesamten AÜG hinaus.[41] Dies entspräche nicht dem gesetzgeberischen Willen des Richtliniengebers, der in ErwGr. 14 Entsende-RL ausdrücklich nur die Geltung eines „harten Kerns" von Schutzbestimmungen anordnet.

Gleichfalls überzeugend ist die Rechtsprechung des Senats im Hinblick auf die Bedingungen „für" die Überlassung, also die gewerbe-, vermittlungs- und erlaubnisrechtlichen Voraussetzungen. Hierzu zählt § 9 Abs. 1 AÜG gerade nicht, weil er nur die privatrechtliche Folge der fehlenden Erlaubnis regelt, nicht deren Voraussetzungen.[42]

Überzeugend ist insbesondere der Verweis auf den neu eingefügten Art. 3 Abs. 1 a UAbs. 2 Entsende-RL.[43] Dieser bezieht sich auf Abschluss und Beendigung des Arbeitsvertrags. Damit „wird das gesamte Recht der Anbahnung, des Abschlusses und der Beendigung des Arbeitsverhältnisses von dem Anwendungsbefehl des Art. 3 Abs. 1 a UAbs. 1 ausgenommen"[44]. § 9 Abs. 1 Nr. 1 AÜG lässt den Arbeitsvertrag mit Beginn der Überlassung[45] bzw. bei nachträglichem Wegfall der Erlaub-

[38] BAG 26.4.2022 – 9 AZR 228/21, BeckRS 2022, 22073 Rn. 56.

[39] BAG 26.4.2022 – 9 AZR 228/21, BeckRS 2022, 22073 Rn. 60.

[40] Zustimmend auch Erfurter Kommentar zum Arbeitsrecht/Franzen, 24. Aufl. 2024, AEntG § 2 Rn. 3; beck-online.GROSSKOMMENTAR zum Zivilrecht/Maultzsch, Stand 1.3.2024, Rom I-VO Art. 9 Rn. 232; Pingel RdA 2023, 180 (181 ff.); aA Brors/Schüren NZA 2022, 1310 (1311 f.).

[41] Pingel RdA 2023, 180 (181).

[42] Pingel RdA 2023, 180 (181).

[43] AA: BAG 26.4.2022 – 9 AZR 228/21, AP AÜG § 1 Nr. 42 mit Anmerkung Hamann/Rathmann zu II. 1.

[44] Franzen/Gallner/Oetker, Kommentar zum europäischen Arbeitsrecht/Krebber, 5. Aufl. 2024, RL 96/71/EG Art. 3 Rn. 29.

[45] Dazu Erfurter Kommentar zum Arbeitsrecht/Roloff, 24. Aufl. 2024, AÜG § 9 Rn. 6.

nis *ex nunc*[46] unwirksam werden. Die Unwirksamkeit des Arbeitsvertrags soll zur Beendigung des Arbeitsverhältnisses zwischen Verleiher und Leiharbeitnehmer[47] sowie nach § 10 Abs. 1 S. 1 AÜG zur Begründung eines Arbeitsverhältnisses kraft Gesetzes zwischen Leiharbeitnehmer und Entleiher führen. §§ 9 Abs. 1 Nr. 1 AÜG und § 10 Abs. 1 S. 1 AÜG sind somit „Bedingungen für den Abschluss und die Beendigung des Arbeitsvertrags" iSv Art. 3 Abs. 1a UAbs. 2 Entsende-RL.

d) Keine Eingriffsnorm iSd Art. 9 Rom-I-VO

In der Literatur werden die Entscheidungen des BAG auch deswegen kritisiert, weil BSG und der 7. Senat des BAG §§ 9, 10 AÜG bisher „auf ausländische Arbeitsverhältnisse erstreckt" hätten, „und zwar nicht in einem *obiter dictum,* sondern in den maßgeblichen Gründen"[48]. Diese Kritik geht bei genauerer Betrachtung fehl und könnte ihre Ursache in einer so genannten Leseschwäche haben.[49]

Die Entscheidung des BSG aus dem Jahr 1988 betraf einen Sachverhalt, der weit vor dem Inkrafttreten der Rom-I-VO spielte.[50] In der Entscheidung des BSG aus dem Jahr 2016 ging es um die Überlassung eines Arbeitnehmers von Luxemburg aus nach Deutschland für die Dauer von sieben Jahren in den Jahren 2001 bis 2007, also einem Zeitpunkt zu dem die Rom-I-VO ebenfalls noch nicht in Kraft getreten war.[51] Der 12. Senat hatte sich weder in der Entscheidung aus dem Jahr 1988 noch in der aus dem Jahr 2016 mit Fragen des Arbeitsvertragsstatuts beschäftigt, sondern seine Entscheidung auf allgemeine Erwägungen gestützt. Der 7. Senat des BAG hingegen befasste sich in seiner Entscheidung aus dem Jahr 2017[52] intensiv mit Art. 27ff. EGBGB und führte auch knapp zu § 2 AEntG aus. Letztlich war dies alles aber nicht entscheidungserheblich, weil der zu beurteilende Fall keine Arbeitnehmerüberlassung zum Gegenstand hatte.[53]

---

[46] Beck'scher Online-Kommentar Arbeitsrecht/Kock, 71. Ed. 1.3.2024, AÜG § 9 Rn. 24; Schüren/Hamann, AÜG/Schüren, 6. Aufl. 2022, § 9 Rn. 41; Boemke/Lembke, AÜG/Lembke, 3. Aufl. 2013, § 9 Rn. 63; Ulber/Ulber, AÜG/Ulber, 6. Aufl. 2023, § 9 Rn. 31.

[47] Beck'scher Online-Kommentar Arbeitsrecht/Kock, 71. Ed. 1.3.2024, AÜG § 9 Rn. 25; Schüren/Hamann, AÜG/Schüren, 6. Aufl. 2022, § 9 Rn. 41;.vgl. auch BAG 26.4.2022 – 9 AZR 228/21, BeckRS 2022, 22073 Rn. 22, sprachlich allerdings unsauber: ein Vertragsverhältnis kann Bestehen oder Nichtbestehen, aber nicht unwirksam sein. Letzteres ist das Privileg von Rechtsgeschäften, nicht von Rechtsbeziehungen.

[48] Brors/Schüren NZA 2022, 1310 (1313f.); Henssler/Willemsen/Kalb, Arbeitsrecht Kommentar/Höpfner, 11. Aufl. 2024, AÜG § 9 Rn. 3; Holler juris PR-ArbR 45/2022 Anm. 2 unter C. – Ähnlich Bissels/Singraven DB 2022, 2803; Tschöpe, Arbeitsrecht Handbuch/Bissels, 13. Aufl. 2023, 6. Teil D Rn. 216c.

[49] Grundlegend zur Leseschwäche im Rahmen juristischer Argumentationen Düwell jurisPR-ArbR 25/2011 Anm. 6; hieran anknüpfend Boemke DB 2012, 802 (803 Fn. 23). Siehe auch Boemke jurisPR-ArbR 30/2016 Anm. 2 unter C I 1; beck-online.GROSSKOMMENTAR zum Kündigungsrecht/Boemke, Stand 1.3.2024, KSchG § 1 Rn. 151 Fn. 434; zu einem Fall der Leseschwäche iVm Rechtsunkenntnis instruktiv Düwell jurisPR-ArbR 23/2015 Anm. 2 unter C.

[50] BSG 25.10.1988 – 12 RK 21/87, BeckRS 1988, 30728285.

[51] BSG 29.6.2016 – B 12 R 8/14 R, BeckRS 2016, 74709.

[52] BAG 21.3.2017 – 7 AZR 207/15, BeckRS 2017, 119476.

[53] BAG 21.3.2017 – 7 AZR 207/15, BeckRS 2017, 119476 Rn. 73ff.

Aber auch mit dem Verweis auf den gesetzgeberischen Willen hat die Entscheidung des BAG aus der Literatur Kritik erfahren.[54] So würden § 9 Abs. 1 Nr. 1 AÜG § 10 Abs. 1 S. 1 AÜG nicht allein und nicht vorrangig auf den Schutz oder die Kompensation des einzelnen Arbeitnehmers abzielen, sondern seien Teil eines Sanktionssystems, das vorrangig sozial- und ordnungspolitische Vorstellungen durchsetzen soll. Es handele sich somit um eine Eingriffsnorm iSv Art. 9 Rom I-VO sei.

Teilweise wurde die Auslegung des BAG aber auch als unionsrechtlich zwingend gesehen[55] und zustimmend aufgenommen.[56]

Eingriffsnormen iSv Art. 9 Rom I-VO sind nur solche Bestimmungen, die von einem Staat als entscheidend „für die Wahrung seines öffentlichen Interesses, insbesondere seiner politischen, sozialen oder wirtschaftlichen Organisation" angesehen werden, wobei nicht alle nationalen Bestimmungen, von denen nicht durch Vereinbarung abgewichen werden kann, hierunter zu fassen sind.[57]

Zwar ist festzustellen, dass auch § 9 AÜG eine national unabdingbare Vorschrift ist. Der Senat begründet die Nichtanwendung von § 9 AÜG über Art. 9 Rom I-VO aber zutreffend damit, dass das AÜG keinen über § 2 AEntG hinausgehenden Schutz bei Überlassung vom Ausland ins Inland fordert. Die Sicherung des öffentlichen Interesses erfolge demgegenüber durch § 16 Abs. 1 Nr. 1, 2 AÜG.[58] Ein überwiegender Teil der Literatur folgt dem mit Verweis auf die hauptsächlich privatrechtliche Sanktionierung.[59]

3. *Ergebnis*

Zu Recht geht das BAG davon aus, dass das Zustandekommen eines gesetzlich begründeten Arbeitsverhältnis nach § 10 Abs. 1 S. 1 AÜG die Unwirksamkeit des Arbeitsvertrages zwischen Leiharbeitnehmer und Verleiher nach § 9 Abs. 1 S. 1 AÜG voraussetzt und es demzufolge kein Nebeneinander von Arbeitsverträgen geben kann.

In grenzüberschreitenden Sachverhalten der illegalen Überlassung von Leiharbeitnehmern setzt dies also voraus, dass § 9 Abs. 1 S. 1 AÜG auf das Verhältnis Leiharbeitnehmer – Verleiher Anwendung findet. Ist dies nicht schon nach Art. 8 Rom I-VO der

---

[54] Brors/Schüren NZA 2022, 1310 (1312).

[55] BAG 26.4.2022 – 9 AZR 228/21, AP AÜG § 1 Nr. 42 mit Anmerkung Hamann/Rathmann zu II. 1.

[56] BAG 26.4.2022 – 9 AZR 228/21, AP AÜG § 1 Nr. 42 mit Anmerkung Hamann/Rathmann zu II. 1; NomosKommentar Gesamtes Arbeitsrecht/Ulrici, 2. Aufl. 2023, AÜG § 3 Rn. 4; Pingel RdA 2023, 180.

[57] Münchener Kommentar zum BGB/Martiny, 8. Aufl. 2021, Rom I-VO Art. 9 Rn. 12.

[58] BAG 26.4.2022 – 9 AZR 228/21, BeckRS 2022, 22073 Rn. 63f.; BAG 26.4.2022 – 9 AZR 139/21, BeckRS 2022, 22076 Rn. 52; aA noch BAG 21.3.2017 – 7 AZR 207/15, NJOZ 2018, 1744 (1754) Rn. 65ff.; Bähr DB 2022, 197; Brors/Schüren NZA 2022, 1310 (1312f.); Henssler/Willemsen/Kalb, Arbeitsrecht Kommentar/Höpfner, 11. Aufl. 2024, AÜG § 9 Rn. 3; Münchener Handbuch zum Arbeitsrecht I/Oetker, 5. Aufl. 2021, § 13 Rn. 134; Mankowski RdA 2018, 181 (186).

[59] Beck'scher Online-Kommentar Arbeitsrecht/Kock, 71. Ed. 1.3.2024, AÜG § 10 Rn. 10; Erfurter Kommentar zum Arbeitsrecht/Franzen, 24. Aufl. 2024, AEntG § 2 Rn. 3; Erfurter Kommentar zum Arbeitsrecht/Roloff, 24. Aufl. 2024, AÜG § 1 Rn. 8; NomosKommentar Gesamtes Arbeitsrecht/Ulrici, 2. Aufl. 2023, AÜG § 9 Rn. 4; Pingel RdA 2023, 180 (183f.); Riediger GWR 2017, 109ff. – Vgl. auch Bayreuther NZA 2019, 1256 (1257).

Fall, so kann sich die Anwendung der Normen des AÜG nur aus § 2 Abs. 1 Nr. 4 AEntG ergeben, welcher über Art. 23 Rom I-VO zur Anwendung kommt. Der neunte Senat des BAG legt allerdings entgegen der Rechtsprechung des siebten Senats und des BSG § 2 Abs. 1 Nr. 4 AEntG so aus, dass nur Arbeits- und Beschäftigungsbedingungen, sowie gewerbe-, vermittlungs- und erlaubnisrechtlichen Voraussetzungen der Überlassung von seinem Anwendungsbereich erfasst sind.

§ 9 Abs. 1 Nr. 1 AÜG ist nach Rechtsprechung des Senats auch keine Eingriffsnorm iSv Art. 9 Rom I-VO.

Daher kam im Ausgangsfall zwischen dem Frachtunternehmen F und den litauischen Kraftfahrern kein Arbeitsverhältnis zustande. Dementsprechend bestand keine Pflicht, den Mindestlohn nach deutschem Recht zu zahlen. Der Einziehungsbescheid war rechtswidrig.

IV. Sozialversicherungsstatut

1. Bestimmung der maßgeblichen Rechtsgrundlagen

a) Ausgangspunkt

Da das litauische Frachtunternehmen U aus dem Beispielfall mangels Anwendung des § 9 Abs. 1 Nr. 1 AÜG noch immer Arbeitgeber der überlassenen LKW-Fahrer ist und auch keine Arbeitsverhältnisse zwischen den Fahrern und dem deutschen Frachtunternehmer F gem. § 10 Abs. 1 AÜG begründet wurden, ist U für die Erbringung der Sozialversicherungsbeiträge in Anspruch zu nehmen. Fraglich ist aber, ob dies nach deutschem oder litauischem Sozialversicherungsrecht zu erfolgen hat. Insbesondere stellt dies eine von der Bestimmung des Arbeitsvertragsstatuts zu unterscheidende Frage dar.

b) Nationale Regelungen

Aus deutscher Sicht kommt zunächst die Anwendung der Vorschriften im Vierten Sozialgesetzbuch zum persönlichen und räumlichen Geltungsbereich in Betracht. Grundsätzlich gilt nach § 3 Nr. 1 SGB IV das sog. Territorialprinzip[60], wonach an den Beschäftigungsort iSd § 9 SGB IV – also den Ort der *tatsächlichen* Beschäftigung[61] – angeknüpft wird. Dies spräche zunächst für die Geltung des deutschen Sozialversicherungsrechts, weil die LKW-Fahrer tatsächlich in Deutschland eingesetzt werden.

Zu beachten ist allerdings die Ausnahmevorschrift § 5 Abs. 1 SGB IV: Demnach findet deutsches Sozialrecht bei einer Entsendung aus dem Ausland nach Deutschland dann keine Anwendung, „wenn die Entsendung infolge der Eigenart der Be-

---

[60] Dazu BSG 25.10.1988 – 12 RK 21/87, BeckRS 1988, 30728285; BSG 10.12.2019 – B 11 AL 1/19 R, BeckRS 2019, 35753 Rn. 23.

[61] BSG 23.2.2017 – B 11 AL 1/16 R, BeckRS 2017, 112711 Rn. 32; Knickrehm/Roßbach/Waltermann, Kommentar zum Sozialrecht/Hänlein, 8. Aufl. 2023, SGB IV §§ 1–6 Rn. 17; beck-online.GROSSKOMMENTAR zum SGB/Zieglmeier, Stand 15.11.2023, SGB IV § 3 Rn. 14.

schäftigung oder vertraglich im Voraus zeitlich begrenzt ist". So liegt der Fall hier; bei Anwendung des § 5 Abs. 1 SGB IV würde den nur vorläufig nach Deutschland entsendeten Beschäftigten, deren Arbeitsverhältnis mit dem entsendenden Unternehmen fortbesteht, das Sozialversicherungsrecht ihres Heimatstaats erhalten bleiben.[62]

c) Vorrangiges Unionsrecht

Die nationalen Regelungen gelten – wie § 6 SGB IV klarstellt – allerdings nur vorbehaltlich der Regelungen des über- und zwischenstaatlichen Rechts. Derartige vorrangige Regelungen sind für entsendete Personen innerhalb des Gebiets der Europäischen Union in der Sozialversicherungs-VO[63] sowie in der dazu ergangenen Durchführungs-VO[64] zu finden.[65]

Nach Art. 11 Abs. 1 Sozialversicherungs-VO unterliegen „Personen, für die diese Verordnung gilt, den Rechtsvorschriften nur eines Mitgliedsstaates". Grundsätzlich gelten – vergleichbar mit § 3 Nr. 1 SGB IV – gem. Art. 11 Abs. 3 lit. a Sozialversicherungs-VO die Rechtsvorschriften des Mitgliedstaats, in dem die Person ihre Beschäftigung ausübt. Ebenfalls vergleichbar zum deutschen Pendant ist aber gem. Art. 12 Abs. 1 Sozialversicherungs-VO im Falle einer zeitlich begrenzten Entsendung in einen anderen Mitgliedsstaat weiterhin das Sozialversicherungsrecht des Staats anwendbar, aus dem der Arbeitnehmer entsendet wurde, wenn die weiteren tatbestandlichen Voraussetzungen der Norm vorliegen. Hervorzuheben ist in diesem Zusammenhang allerdings, dass die Voraussetzungen, unter denen eine Entsendung iSd Art. 12 Abs. 1 Sozialversicherungs-VO vorliegt, sich nicht mit den Tatbestandsvoraussetzungen des § 5 Abs. 1 SGB IV decken (zu den Voraussetzungen → IV. 2. a)). Außerdem muss Art. 12 Abs. 1 Sozialversicherungs-VO von einer weiteren Ausnahmevorschrift, dem Art. 13 Abs. 1 lit. b) i) Sozialversicherungs-VO, abgegrenzt werden, der bei gleichzeitiger Beschäftigung von Arbeitnehmern in zwei Mitgliedsstaaten einschlägig ist (hierzu → IV. 3.).

2. Anwendung des Art. 12 Abs. 1 Sozialversicherungs-VO

a) Überblick

Die Anwendung von Art. 12 Abs. 1 Sozialversicherungs-VO ist an das Vorliegen dreier Positivmerkmale sowie das Nichtvorliegen zweier Negativmerkmale geknüpft:

---

[62] beck-online.GROSSKOMMENTAR zum SGB/Zieglmeier, Stand 15.11.2023, SGB IV § 5 Rn. 6, 11.

[63] Verordnung (EG) Nr. 883/2004 des Europäischen Parlaments und des Rates vom 29. April 2004 zur Koordinierung der Systeme der sozialen Sicherheit, ABl. 2004 L 166, 1.

[64] Verordnung VO (EG) 987/2009 des Europäischen Parlaments und des Rates vom 16. September 2009 zur Festlegung der Modalitäten für die Durchführung der Verordnung (EG) Nr. 883/2004 über die Koordinierung der Systeme der sozialen Sicherheit, ABl. 2009 L 284, 1.

[65] Beck'scher Online-Kommentar Sozialrecht/Wagner, 71. Ed 1.3.2024, SGB IV § 6 Rn. 4; Krauskopf, Soziale Krankenversicherung, Pflegeversicherung/Stäbler, 121. EL 2/2024, SGB IV § 6 Rn. 6; das verkennt SG Magdeburg 28.11.2023 – S 46 BA 45/21, juris Rn. 30.

1. die betroffene Person muss in einem Mitgliedsstaat eine Beschäftigung für Rechnung eines Arbeitgebers ausüben,
2. der Arbeitgeber muss gewöhnlich in diesem Mitgliedsstaat tätig sein und
3. diese Person muss vom Arbeitgeber in einen anderen Mitgliedsstaat entsandt werden, um dort eine Arbeit für dessen Rechnung auszuführen.

Weder darf

1. die voraussichtliche Dauer dieser Arbeit 24 Monate überschreiten,
2. noch darf diese Person eine andere entsandte Person ablösen.

Art. 12 Abs. 1 Sozialversicherungs-VO begünstigt die Arbeitnehmerfreizügigkeit sowie die Dienstleistungsfreiheit des entsendenden Unternehmens, indem die Entsendungen vereinfacht und von administrativem Aufwand befreit werden.[66] Um aber zu verhindern, dass Unternehmen nur deshalb ihren Sitz in einem Mitgliedsstaat wählen, damit sie in den Genuss der dort geltenden günstigen Sozialversicherungssystemen kommen, normiert die Norm einige Einschränkungen.[67] Um ununterbrochene bzw. Kettenentsendungen zu unterbinden, wurden die beiden entsprechenden Negativmerkmale eingefügt.[68] Von erheblicher Bedeutung zur Unterbindung von Rechtsmissbrauch ist zudem die Voraussetzung, dass der entsendende Arbeitgeber „gewöhnlich" im Herkunftsstaat tätig sein muss (näher dazu → IV. 2. c) bb) (3)).

b) Subsumtion der unproblematischen Tatbestandsmerkmale

Im Beispielsfall sind vier der fünf Tatbestandsvoraussetzungen offensichtlich erfüllt. Die LKW-Fahrer sind als Arbeitnehmer des litauischen Unternehmens U für dessen Rechnung in Litauen tätig und werden von U nach Deutschland – also ein anderes EU-Land – entsandt, um dort eine Arbeit für die Rechnung des U auszuführen. Insbesondere „ist davon auszugehen, dass eine Arbeit für Rechnung des Arbeitgebers des Entsendestaats ausgeführt wird, wenn feststeht, dass diese Arbeit für diesen Arbeitgeber ausgeführt wird und dass eine arbeitsrechtliche Bindung zwischen Arbeitnehmer und Arbeitgeber, der ihn entsandt hat, fortbesteht".[69] Wie bereits unter → III. 2. dargestellt, sind die Arbeitsverträge zwischen U und seinen Arbeitnehmern gerade nicht von der Unwirksamkeitsfolge des § 9 Abs. 1 Nr. 1 AÜG umfasst. Von einer Arbeitsausführung im EU-Ausland für Rechnung des U ist daher auszugehen. Auch die Ausnahmetatbestände greifen im Beispielsfall nicht ein. Weder werden die LKW-Fahrer länger als 24 Monate beim deutschen Unter-

---

[66] EuGH 17.12.1970 – 35/70, ECLI:EU:C:1970:120 = Celex 61970CJ0035 (Manpower); Eichenhofer, Sozialrecht der EU, 7. Aufl. 2018, Rn. 150; Tiedemann NZS 2011, 41.

[67] beck-online.GROSSKOMMENTAR zum SGB/Schreiber, Stand 15.2.2024, VO (EG) 883/2004 Art. 12 Rn. 11.

[68] Tiedemann NZS 2011, 41 (44f.); vgl. Beck'scher Online Kommentar Sozialrecht/Utz, 72. Ed 1.3.2024, VO (EG) 883/2004 Art. 12 Rn. 17.

[69] So die Verwaltungskommission für die Koordinierung der Systeme der sozialen Sicherheit in ihrem Beschluss Nr. A2 vom 12.6.2009 unter 1. Abs. 2; vgl. auch Tiedemann NZS 2011, 41 (44).

nehmer F tätig, noch lösen sie andere, von U entsandte LKW-Fahrer, ab. Fraglich bleibt letztlich nur, ob U als Unternehmen gewöhnlich in Litauen tätig ist.

c) Insbesondere: Arbeitgeber im Herkunftsland „gewöhnlich" tätig

aa) Konkretisierung in Art. 14 Abs. 2 Durchführungs-VO

In welchen Fällen ein Arbeitgeber im Herkunftsland „gewöhnlich" tätig wird, ist in Art. 14 Abs. 2 Durchführungs-VO konkretisiert.[70] Demnach muss der Arbeitgeber „gewöhnlich andere nennenswerte Tätigkeiten als reine interne Verwaltungstätigkeiten" in dem Mitgliedsstaat, in dem er seinen Sitz hat, ausüben. Dies ist im Rahmen einer Gesamtbetrachtung der Kriterien, welche die Tätigkeit des Unternehmens kennzeichnen, zu bewerten. Art. 14 Abs. 2 Hs. 2 Durchführungs-VO hebt hervor, dass dabei „die Besonderheiten eines jeden Arbeitgebers und die Eigenart der ausgeübten Tätigkeiten" berücksichtigt werden müssen. In einer nicht erschöpfenden Aufzählung hat die Verwaltungskommission in ihrem Beschluss Nr. A2 die für die Gesamtabwägung wesentlichen – quantitativ sowie qualitativ zu untersuchende[71] – Kriterien dargestellt:

- Ort des Sitzes und der Verwaltung des Unternehmens
- Zahl der Beschäftigten im Herkunftsland bzw. in dem oder den anderen Mitgliedsstaat(en) in der Verwaltung
- Ort der Einstellung der entsandten Arbeitnehmer
- Ort, wo der Großteil der Verträge mit den Kunden geschlossen wird
- Recht, dem die Verträge unterliegen, die das Unternehmen mit Arbeitnehmern bzw. Kunden abschließt
- Erzielter Umsatz in den jeweiligen Mitgliedsstaaten während eines „hinreichend charakteristischen Zeitraums"
- Zahl der im entsendenden Staat geschlossenen Verträge.[72]

In ihrem 2013 veröffentlichten praktischen Leitfaden konkretisierte die Verwaltungskommission das Kriterium des erzielten Umsatzes weiter und stufte einen im Herkunftsstaat erwirtschafteten Umsatzanteil von 25% als „nennenswerte Tätigkeit" iSd Art. 14 Abs. 2 Durchführungs-VO ein.[73] Dies ist insofern überzeugend, als der Wortlaut[74] zwar eine gewisse Erheblichkeit voraussetzt, aber keineswegs

---

[70] Insoweit stellt Art. 14 Abs. 2 Durchführungs-VO eine Normierung der Grundsätze dar, die der EuGH in vorherigen Entscheidungen aufgestellt hat: EuGH 10.2.2000 – C-202/97, NZS 2000, 291 (Fitzwilliam); EuGH 9.11.2000 – C-404/98, BeckRS 2004, 77068 (Plum); vgl. dazu Zeiske, Das Statut sozialer Sicherheit bei grenzüberschreitender Arbeitnehmerüberlassung, 2016, S. 143ff.

[71] Boemke/Brandt ZfA 2022, 249 (256).

[72] Verwaltungskommission für die Koordinierung der Systeme der sozialen Sicherheit in ihrem Beschluss Nr. A2 vom 12.6.2009 unter 1. Abs. 2; dem folgend beck-online.GROSSKOMMENTAR zum SGB/Schreiber, Stand 15.2.2024, VO (EG) 883/2004 Art. 12 Rn. 11.

[73] Verwaltungskommission, Praktischer Leitfaden, 2013, S. 9; freilich hat dieser Leitfaden keine Rechtsnormqualität und ist daher nicht bindend.

[74] „Nennenswert" im Deutschen, „substantiell" in anderen Sprachfassungen: „substantial activities" im Englischen, „activités substantielles" im Französischen, „attività sostanziali" im Italienischen.

eine „überwiegende" Tätigkeit fordert, die einen Grenzwert von 50% nach sich ziehen würde.[75] Allerdings dürfte der Grenzwert von 25% zu niedrig angesetzt sein. Dies folgt schon aus dem systematischen Vergleich mit Art. 14 Abs. 8 Durchführungs-VO, wo ein Anteil von 25% bereits als regelmäßig „wesentlich" eingeordnet wird. Für eine stets „nennenswerte" Tätigkeit muss angesichts dessen ein höherer Anteil verlangt werden, etwa – nach hiesigem Vorschlag – von mindestens einem Drittel. Letztlich obliegt es der Rechtsprechung, durch eine klar bezifferte Stellungnahme für Rechtssicherheit zu sorgen.[76]

bb) Leiharbeitsunternehmen

(1) Problematik. Besondere Schwierigkeiten bereitet die Anwendung der Definition des Art. 14 Abs. 2 Durchführungs-VO im Falle von Leiharbeitsunternehmen. Für die Frage, ob ein Leiharbeitsunternehmen im entsendenden Staat nennenswerte Tätigkeiten ausführt, muss zunächst geklärt werden, welche die ein solches Unternehmen kennzeichnenden Tätigkeiten sind. Fraglich ist insofern, ob schon allein durch die Auswahl und die Einstellung der Leiharbeitnehmer Tätigkeiten gegeben sind, die einen nennenswerten Anteil der Gesamttätigkeit des Leiharbeitsunternehmens begründen können. Denkbar ist aber auch, die Überlassung der Leiharbeitnehmer als eine der kennzeichnenden Tätigkeiten anzusehen. Dies hätte zur Folge, dass – zumindest zu einem „nennenswerten" Anteil – Arbeitnehmer innerhalb des Herkunftslands an Entleiher überlassen werden müssten, damit die Voraussetzungen des Art. 14 Abs. 2 Durchführungs-VO gegeben wären.

(2) Streitstand. Im Zuge der „Team Power Europe"-Entscheidung des EuGH, die am 3.6.2021 erging, wurden zu der aufgeworfenen Streitrage drei verschiedene Positionen vertreten.

Der Generalanwalt *Sánchez-Bordona* hat im Rahmen des Gerichtsverfahrens die Auffassung vertreten, dass Leiharbeitsunternehmen bereits allein durch die Auswahl und die Einstellung von Leiharbeitnehmern eine nennenswerte Tätigkeit im Mitgliedsstaat erbringen könnten.[77] Die Mitarbeiter des Unternehmens, die die Anwerbung, Auswahl und Einstellung der Leiharbeitnehmer im Herkunftsland übernähmen, erbrächten den „harten Kern der charakteristischen Tätigkeit" eines Leiharbeitsunternehmens.[78] Konträr hierzu vertrat eine Stimme aus der Literatur, dass Leiharbeitsunternehmen – im Gegensatz zu Unternehmen, die nur gelegentlich Arbeitnehmer überlassen – nie die Voraussetzungen des Art. 12 Sozialversicherungs-VO erfüllen könnten.[79] Das Geschäftsmodell eines gewerbsmäßig tätigen

---

[75] So aber Franzen/Gallner/Oetker, Kommentar zum europäischen Arbeitsrecht/*Steinmeyer*, 5. Auf. 2024, AEUV Art. 48 Rn. 40.

[76] So auch Hamann/Rathmann jurisPR-ArbR 31/2021 Anm. 3, unter D; einen festen Grenzbetrag hingegen ablehnend Zeiske, Das Statut sozialer Sicherheit bei grenzüberschreitender Arbeitnehmerüberlassung, 2016, S. 150.

[77] Generalanwalt Sánchez-Bordona 10.12.2020 – C-784/19, BeckRS 2020, 34418, Tenorvorschlag, Rn. 58ff.

[78] Generalanwalt Sánchez-Bordona 10.12.2020 – C-784/19, BeckRS 2020, 34418, Rn. 74, 76.

[79] Hlava/Höller/Klengel NZA 2021, 767 (771f.).

Leiharbeitsunternehmens bestehe gerade darin, Leiharbeitnehmer für andere tätig werden zu lassen, während es selbst insoweit „untätig“ bleibe.

In seiner Entscheidung vom 3.6.2021 schließt der EuGH Leiharbeitsunternehmen nicht vollständig vom Anwendungsbereich des Art. 12 Abs. 1 Sozialversicherungs-VO aus, fordert aber für das Vorliegen einer „gewöhnlichen Tätigkeit“ im entsendenden Staat, dass über die Auswahl und Einstellung hinaus auch die Überlassung von Leiharbeitnehmern im nennenswerten Umfang innerhalb des Mitgliedsstaats erfolgen muss.[80] Dieser Ansatz findet auch in der Literatur Anklang.[81]

(3) Argumentation des EuGH. Hierfür spreche zunächst der Wortlaut des Art. 14 Abs. 2 Durchführungs-VO, der „nennenswerte Tätigkeiten“ fordert und diese unter Einbeziehung der die Geschäftstätigkeit kennzeichnenden Kriterien bestimmt. Derartige, Leiharbeitsunternehmen kennzeichnende Tätigkeiten seien gerade nicht nur die Auswahl und die Einstellung, sondern auch die Überlassung von Leiharbeitnehmern. Schließlich seien die beiden erstgenannten Tätigkeiten lediglich vorbereitender Natur, während mit der eigentlichen Überlassung der tatsächliche Umsatz erwirtschaftet würde.[82]

Darüber hinaus folgert der EuGH aus dem Ausnahmecharakter des Art. 12 Abs. 1 Sozialversicherungs-VO gegenüber Art. 11 Abs. 3 lit. a Sozialversicherungs-VO, dass die Tatbestandsmerkmale der erstgenannten Norm eng auszulegen seien. Nur, wenn auch im Bereich der tatsächlichen Arbeitnehmerüberlassung nennenswerte Tätigkeiten stattfänden, könnte die Ausnahmevorschrift eingreifen.

Schließlich würde der Zweck des Art. 12 Abs. 1 Sozialversicherungs-VO – insbesondere der Schutz der Dienstleistungsfreiheit der entsendenden Unternehmen – verfehlt werden, wenn Leiharbeitsunternehmen trotz fehlender Arbeitnehmerüberlassungen im entsendenden Staat in den Genuss der dort geltenden Sozialversicherungsregelungen kommen würde. So könnten sich Leiharbeitsunternehmen Staaten mit den günstigsten Rechtsvorschriften suchen *(„forum shopping“)* und damit in anderen Mitgliedsstaaten bestehende Schutzniveaus unter einen Abwärtsdruck setzen sowie eine Wettbewerbsverzerrung zugunsten der Inanspruchnahme von Arbeitnehmerüberlassung herbeiführen.[83]

(4) Stellungnahme. Dem EuGH ist sowohl im Ergebnis als auch in der Argumentation zuzustimmen. Zur Vervollständigung des Auslegungskanons kann lediglich noch auf die historische Auslegung des Art. 12 Abs. 1 Sozialversicherungs-VO hingewiesen werden. Ihren Ursprung findet die Norm in der Entscheidung des EuGH in der Sache „Manpower“.[84] Schon hier hat der EuGH in einem Spagat zwischen Förderung der Dienstleistungsfreiheit und Arbeitnehmerfreizügigkeit einerseits und der Bekämpfung von Rechtsmissbrauch andererseits entschieden, dass die grenzüberschreitende Überlassung von Arbeitnehmern sehr wohl unter den Begriff

---

[80] EuGH 3.6.2021 – C-784/19, NZA 2021, 1461 (Team Power Europe).

[81] Becker ZESAR 2021, 467; Boemke/Brandt ZfA 2022, 249 (254ff.); Hamann/Rathmann jurisPR-ArbR 31/2021, Anm. 3; Niksova HSI-Report 2/2021, 4 (12); Plagemann EWiR 2021, 534.

[82] EuGH 3.6.2021 – C-784/19, NZA 2021, 1461 (1463) Rn. 44ff. (Team Power Europe).

[83] EuGH 3.6.2021 – C-784/19, NZA 2021, 1461 (1464) Rn. 57ff. (Team Power Europe).

[84] EuGH 17.12.1970 – 35/70, ECLI:EU:C:1970:120 = Celex 61970CJ0035 (Manpower).

der Entsendung fallen kann. Andererseits grenzte er die Anwendung auf die Fälle ein, in denen das Leiharbeitsunternehmen auch Herkunftsstaat „normalerweise" tätig ist.[85] Diese einschränkende Auslegung zur Bekämpfung von Rechtsmissbrauch setzte der EuGH auch in zwei Entscheidungen im Jahr 2000 fort und sprach nunmehr von der Ausübung „nennenswerter Tätigkeiten" im Herkunftsstaat.[86] Ebenjene Formulierung fand sodann Einzug in den Normwortlaut des Art. 14 Abs. 2 Durchführungs-VO, der der Konkretisierung des Art. 12 Abs. 1 Sozialversicherungs-VO dient.[87] Die aktuelle EuGH-Entscheidung fügt sich passend in die Entscheidungshistorie ein, weil durch die grundsätzliche Anwendungsmöglichkeit des Art. 12 Abs. 1 Sozialversicherungs-VO grenzüberschreitende Arbeitnehmerüberlassung recht unbürokratisch möglich ist, aber andererseits durch das einschränkende Verständnis der „nennenswerten Tätigkeit" dem Rechtsmissbrauch soweit wie möglich ein Riegel vorgeschoben wird.[88]

Im Übrigen muss den abweichenden Ansätzen bereits im Ansatz widersprochen werden. Beide Ansichten verkennen, dass Leiharbeitnehmer auch nach der Überlassung an den Entleiher weiterhin Arbeitnehmer des Verleihers bleiben bzw. betriebsverfassungsrechtlich dessen Betrieb zugeordnet sind.[89] Dies wird in § 14 Abs. 1 AÜG klargestellt, folgt aber auch aus allgemeinen Grundsätzen zur Bestimmung der Betriebszugehörigkeit: Trotz der Überlassung des Leiharbeitnehmers an den Entleiher verbleibt dem Verleiher ein übergeordnetes Weisungsrecht[90], welches eine fortbestehende Eingliederung und damit Betriebszugehörigkeit des Leiharbeitnehmers begründet.[91] Hieraus folgt zum einen, dass Leiharbeitnehmer entgegen der Ansicht des Generalanwalts nicht als „Gegenstände" der Dienstleistung des Verleihers angesehen werden können, sondern durch ihre Tätigkeit beim Entleiher weiterhin den arbeitstechnischen Zweck des Verleiherbetriebs erfüllen. Zum anderen wird deutlich, dass Leiharbeitsunternehmen – anders als von der vereinzelt gebliebenen Literaturansicht vertreten – mittelbar durch ihre überlassenen Leiharbeitnehmer im Einsatzstaat tätig werden, weil die Leiharbeitnehmer auf Weisung des Unternehmens dort tätig werden.

[85] EuGH 17.12.1970 – C-35/70, ECLI:EU:C:1970:120 = Celex 61970CJ0035 Rn. 14/16 (Manpower).

[86] EuGH 10.02.2000 – C-202/97, NZS 2000, 291 Rn. 40ff. (FTS); EuGH 9.11.2000 – C 404/98, AP EWG-Verordnung Nr. 1408/71 Nr. 9 Rn. 21 (Plum).

[87] Fuchs, Europäisches Sozialrecht/Steinmeyer, 8. Aufl. 2022, VO (EG) Nr. 883/2004 Art. 12 Rn. 5; Tiedemann NZS 2011, 41, 45; Zeiske, Das Statut sozialer Sicherheit bei grenzüberschreitender Arbeitnehmerüberlassung, 2016, S. 142.

[88] S. bereits Boemke/Brandt ZFA 2022, 249 (255).

[89] BAG 7.6.2016 – 1 ABR 25/14, NZA 2016, 1420 (1421) Rn. 13; Erfurter Kommentar zum Arbeitsrecht/Roloff, 24. Aufl. 2024, AÜG § 14 Rn. 2; Schüren/Hamann, AÜG/Hamann, 6. Aufl. 2022, § 14 Rn. 21.

[90] Der Verleiher bestimmt, ob der Arbeitnehmer an einen Entleiher überlassen wird und falls ja, an welchen; vgl. auch Urici AÜG, 2017, Schwerpunktbeitrag A: Leiharbeitsverhältnis Rn. 7.

[91] Boemke, Schuldvertrag und Arbeitsverhältnis, 1999, S. 282ff.; iE ebenso Scheider/Trümner FS Gnade, 1992, 175 (188ff.); Schüren/Hamann, AÜG/Hamann, 6. Aufl. 2022, § 14 Rn. 24; Ulrici, AÜG, 2017, § 14 Rn. 21; Ziemann AuR 1990, 58 (62, 64).

cc) Mischunternehmen

Im Beispielsfall ist zu berücksichtigen, dass neben der Arbeitnehmerüberlassung ins Ausland (15% der Tätigkeit) im Heimatstaat eigene Frachtaufträge (85%) durchgeführt werden. Es handelt sich somit um ein so genanntes Mischunternehmen (auch Mischbetrieb), das neben der Arbeitnehmerüberlassung im Rahmen seiner wirtschaftlichen und betrieblichen Tätigkeit weitere Zwecke verfolgt[92]. Hier stellt sich die Frage, ob für die Ermittlung, ob eine nennenswerte Tätigkeit im Heimatstaat ausgeübt wird, ausschließlich auf die Arbeitnehmerüberlassung abgestellt wird oder aber die sonstigen Tätigkeiten des Unternehmens zu berücksichtigen sind. In der Literatur wird mit dem Argument der Gesetzesumgehung die Auffassung vertreten, dass insoweit allein auf die Arbeitnehmerüberlassung abgestellt werden dürfe[93]. Hiergegen spricht aber, dass bei Mischbetrieben nach der Geprägetheorie maßgeblich ist, welche Tätigkeit den Unternehmen das Gepräge verleiht[94]. Überdies ist gemäß Art. 14 Abs. 2 Durchführungs-VO die Zuordnung „unter Berücksichtigung aller Kriterien, die die Tätigkeit des betreffenden Unternehmens kennzeichnen", zu treffen. Es ist die Tätigkeit des Unternehmens insgesamt und nicht nur die Arbeitnehmerüberlassung als bloßen Teilaspekt zu würdigen.

d) „Nennenswerte" Tätigkeit im Beispielsfall

Im Beispielsfall spricht zunächst für die Annahme einer nennenswerten Tätigkeit des Unternehmens U in Litauen, dass dort der Ort des Sitzes und der Verwaltung angesiedelt ist. Auch ist davon auszugehen, dass U seine Arbeitnehmer in Litauen am Unternehmenssitz eingestellt hat. Von entscheidender Bedeutung ist aber letztlich, in welchem Umfang U in Litauen tatsächlich tätig geworden ist: Welchen Anteil nehmen die im Herkunftsstaat geschlossenen Verträge mit Kunden ein und wie hoch ist der Anteil des dabei erzielten Umsatzes verglichen mit dem Gesamtumsatz des Unternehmens? (vgl. dazu → IV. 2. c) aa)). Nach hier vertretener Ansicht muss der Umsatz in Litauen mindestens ein Drittel des Gesamtumsatzes betragen, um sicher von einer nennenswerten Tätigkeit in Litauen ausgehen zu können. Diese Voraussetzung ist im vorliegenden Fall jedenfalls erfüllt, weil U 85% seines Umsatzes mit Frachtaufträgen innerhalb Litauens erwirtschaftet.

e) Zwischenergebnis

Im Beispielsfall sind die Anwendungsvoraussetzungen des Art. 12 Abs. 1 Sozialversicherungs-VO erfüllt. Insbesondere ist das litauische Unternehmen U gewöhnlich in Litauen tätig, weil es iSd Art. 14 Abs. 2 Durchführungs-VO nennenswerte Tätigkeiten, die keine rein interne Verwaltungstätigkeiten darstellen, ausübt. Mit-

---

[92] Zum Begriff BAG 5.9.1990 – 4 AZR 59/90, BeckRS 1990, 47080 Ls. 1; BSG 10.11.1994 – 12 RK 58/93, BeckRS 1994, 30751880; Boemke/Sachadae BB 2011, 1973.

[93] So Boemke/Brandt ZFA 2022, 249 (257).

[94] BAG 22.11.1988 – 1 ABR 6/87, NZA 1989, 561, 562; BAG 25.9.1996 – 1 ABR 4/96, BeckRS 1997, 40438; Boemke/Sachadae BB 2011, 1973; Henssler/Moll/Bepler, Der Tarifvertrag/Sittard, 2. Aufl. 2016, Teil 2 C Rn. 224.

hin hat U nach litauischen Recht Sozialversicherungsbeiträge zu erbringen. Deutsches Sozialversicherungsrecht ist also im konkreten Fall nicht anzuwenden, der Beitragsbescheid der DRV ist zu Unrecht ergangen und daher aufzuheben.

V. Zusammenfassung

1. Ein Arbeitsverhältnis wird nur dann gesetzlich gem. § 10 Abs. 1 S. 1 AÜG begründet, wenn der Leiharbeitsvertrag zwischen Verleiher und Leiharbeitnehmer gem. § 9 Abs. 1 AÜG unwirksam ist.

2. Gilt bei einer grenzüberschreitenden illegalen Arbeitnehmerüberlassung nach Deutschland hinein das Arbeitsvertragsstatut des Heimatstaats, findet § 9 Abs. 1 Nr. 1 AÜG keine Anwendung auf das Leiharbeitsverhältnis. § 9 Abs. 1 Nr. 1 AÜG stellt keine Eingriffsnorm iSd § 2 Nr. 4 AEntG oder Art. 9 Rom-I-VO.

3. Das Sozialversicherungsstatut bestimmt sich nicht nach nationalem Recht, sondern der Verordnung (EG) Nr. 883/2004 zur Koordinierung der Systeme der sozialen Sicherheit. Hierbei sind insbesondere Art. 12 Abs. 1 Sozialversicherungs-VO sowie Art. 13 Abs. 1 lit. b sublit. (i) Sozialversicherungs-VO zu beachten.

4. Für die Frage, ob der Arbeitgeber im Herkunftsland iSd Art. 12 Abs. 1 Sozialversicherungs-VO gewöhnlich tätig ist, muss konkretisierend Art. 14 Abs. 1 Durchführungs-VO herangezogen werden. Demnach muss der Arbeitgeber gewöhnlich andere nennenswerte Tätigkeiten als reine interne Verwaltungstätigkeiten in dem Mitgliedsstaat ausüben.

5. Ob eine solche gewöhnliche Tätigkeit vorliegt, muss im Wege einer Gesamtabwägung der Kriterien, die die Tätigkeit des Unternehmens kennzeichnen, ermittelt werden. Jedenfalls ausreichend für eine gewöhnliche Tätigkeit in einem Staat ist es, wenn das Unternehmen dort einen Umsatzanteil von mindestens einem Drittel erwirtschaftet.

6. Leiharbeitsunternehmen sind – über diese Voraussetzungen hinaus – nur dann im Herkunftsland gewöhnlich tätig, wenn sie einen nennenswerten Anteil – also zumindest ein Drittel – ihrer Arbeitnehmerüberlassungen innerhalb dieses Staats durchführen. Bei Mischunternehmen ist die Tätigkeit des Unternehmens insgesamt und nicht nur die Arbeitnehmerüberlassung als Teilaspekt zu würdigen

MARKUS FEHRENBACH

Das internationale Gesellschaftsrecht im Verhältnis zu Drittstaaten

I. Einleitung

Das internationale Gesellschaftsrecht Deutschlands ist nicht kodifiziert. Im Verhältnis zu den Mitgliedstaaten der Union soll das anwendbare Gesellschaftsrecht infolge der Entscheidungstrias des EuGH zur Niederlassungsfreiheit (Art. 49, 54 AEUV) in den Fällen *Centros,*[1] *Überseering*[2] und *Inspire Art*[3] jedoch nach der Gründungstheorie bestimmt werden,[4] die an den Staat der Inkorporation der Gesellschaft anknüpft.[5] Selbiges soll ebenso im Verhältnis zu den Mitgliedstaaten des EWR[6] sowie zu bestimmten Drittstaaten, insbesondere den USA,[7] aufgrund von Staatsverträgen gelten.[8] Im Verhältnis zu den übrigen Drittstaaten soll es nach der wohl noch überwiegend vertretenen,[9] wenn auch zuneh-

---

[1] EuGH 9.3.1999 – C-212–97, Slg. 1999, I-1459 = NJW 1999, 2027 (Centros).

[2] EuGH 5.11.2002 – C-208/00, Slg. 2002, I-9919 = NZG 2002, 1164 (Überseering).

[3] EuGH 30.9.2003 – C-167/01, Slg. 2003, I-10155 = NJW 2003, 3331 (Inspire Art).

[4] BGH 13.3.2003 – VII ZR 370/98, BGHZ 154, 185 (189f.) = NJW 2003, 1461 (Überseering); BGH 12.7.2011 – II ZR 28/10, BGHZ 190, 242 Rn. 15ff. = NJW 2011, 3372; BGH 21.7.2011 – IX ZR 185/10, BGHZ 190, 364 Rn. 22 = NJW 2011, 3784; BGH 14.3.2005 – II ZR 5/03, NJW 2005, 1648 (1649); BGH 11.1.2011 – II ZR 157/09, NJW 2011, 844 Rn. 16; BGH 8.9.2016 – III ZR 7/15, BeckRS 2016, 16911 = ZIP 2016, 2060 Rn. 12; OLG Düsseldorf 10.5.2010 – 24 U 160/09, NZG 2010, 1226 = ZIP 2010, 1852 (1853); OLG Köln 28.9.2010 – 18 U 3/10, BeckRS 2010, 24180 = ZIP 2010, 2016f.; zur vor dem Inkrafttreten des MoPeG umstrittenen Frage der Anwendbarkeit der Gründungstheorie auf Personengesellschaften siehe Schön ZHR 187 (2023), 123 (135ff.); Wertenbruch NZG 2023, 1343 (1345f.).

[5] Zu den verschiedenen Spielarten der Gründungstheorie hinsichtlich des Anknüpfungsmoments siehe NomosKommentar BGB/Hoffmann, 4. Aufl. 2021, EGBGB Anh. Art. 12 Rn. 37ff.; Kaulen IPRax 2008, 389 (390ff.).

[6] BGH 19.9.2005 – II ZR 372/03, BGHZ 164, 148 (151ff.) = NJW 2005, 3351 (im Verhältnis zu Liechtenstein).

[7] BGH 29.1.2003 – VIII ZR 155/02, BGHZ 153, 353 (355ff.) = NJW 2003, 1607; BGH 5.7.2004 – II ZR 389/02, NJW-RR 2004, 1618; BGH 13.10.2004 – I ZR 245/01, BeckRS 2004, 10662 = ZIP 2004, 2230 (2231) (GEDIOS Corporation); OLG Düsseldorf 15.12.1994 – 6 U 59/94, NJW-RR 1995, 1124 (1125); OLG Zweibrücken 13.10.1986 – 4 U 98/85, NJW 1987, 2168 (aufgrund des deutsch-amerikanischen Freundschafts-, Handels- und Schifffahrtsvertrages).

[8] Eidenmüller, Ausländische Kapitalgesellschaften im deutschen Recht/Rehm, 2004, § 2 Rn. 12ff.

[9] BGH 29.1.2003 – VIII ZR 155/02, BGHZ 153, 353 (355) = NJW 2003, 1607; BGH 27.10.2008 – II ZR 158/06, BGHZ 178, 192 Rn. 19 = NJW 2009, 289 (Trabrennbahn); BGH 22.11.2016 – II ZB 19/15, BGHZ 212, 381 Rn. 21 = NZG 2017, 347; BGH 8.9.2016 – III ZR 7/15, BeckRS 2016, 16911 = ZIP 2016, 2060 Rn. 12; OLG München 5.8.2021 – 29 U 2411/21, NZG 2021, 1518 = ZIP 2021, 2178, 2179; Koch, AktG, 17. Aufl. 2023, § 1 Rn. 36;

mend bestritten,[10] Auffassung aufgrund gewohnheitsrechtlicher Anerkennung[11] bei der Sitztheorie verbleiben, nach der das Gesellschaftsrecht an den tatsächlichen Verwaltungssitz angeknüpft wird.

Im Folgenden soll gezeigt werden, dass einerseits die Sitztheorie selbst im Verhältnis zu nicht privilegierten Drittstaaten nicht mehr zu überzeugen vermag, andererseits aber auch die Gründungstheorie im Verhältnis zu diesen Staaten Modifikationen bedarf. Bei einem Verwaltungssitz im Inland sind insoweit im Wege der Sonderanknüpfung die Vorschriften anzuwenden, die in Ermangelung einer ordnungsgemäßen Gründung eingreifen.

II. Die Sitztheorie

1. Der Stand der Sitztheorie

a) Grundlagen

Nach der Sitztheorie stellt der tatsächliche Verwaltungssitz der Gesellschaft das maßgebliche Anknüpfungsmoment dar. Das Gesellschaftsstatut richtet sich damit nach dem Recht des Staates, in dem der Verband seinen tatsächlichen Verwaltungssitz hat. Sinn und Zweck der Sitztheorie soll darin liegen, das Recht des Staates zur Anwendung kommen zu lassen, zu dem die Gesellschaft die engsten Beziehungen unterhält.[12] Die Sitztheorie verwirklicht mithin das Prinzip der engsten Verbindung.[13]

b) Folgen der Verlegung des Verwaltungssitzes

Zu Irritationen führt die Sitztheorie allerdings dann, wenn eine nach einem ausländischen Recht gegründete Gesellschaft ihren Verwaltungssitz aus dem Ausland ins Inland verlegt, denn damit tritt aus Sicht des Zuzugsstaates ein Statutenwechsel

---

Ebenroth/Boujong/Joost/Strohn, HGB/Wertenbruch, 4. Aufl. 2020, § 105 Rn. 380; Wertenbruch NZG 2023, 1343 (1347).

[10] Allgemein für die Hinwendung zur Gründungstheorie beispielsweise: Behrens IPRax 2003, 193 (205 f.); NomosKommentar BGB/Hoffmann, 4. Aufl. 2021, EGBGB Anh. Art. 12 Rn. 49, 148; Kieninger NJW 2009, 292 (293); Leible/Hoffmann RIW 2002, 925 (935 f.); Schmidt/Lutter, AktG/Ringe, 5. Aufl. 2023, IntGesR Rn. 80; Hopt/Roth, HGB, 42. Aufl. 2023, vor § 105 Rn. 29; Schmidt EuZW 2021, 613 (619). Im Detail ist vieles umstritten; so werden auch in den sachrechtlichen Regelungen des § 706 S. 2 BGB (siehe dazu Hoffmann/Horn RabelsZ 86 (2022), 65) sowie der § 5 AktG, § 4a GmbHG (Bayer/Schmidt ZHR 173 (2009), 735 (749 ff.); Hoffmann ZIP 2007, 1581 (1585 f.)) einseitige versteckte Kollisionsnormen gesehen.

[11] Münchener Kommentar zum BGB/Kindler, 8. Aufl. 2021, IntGesR Rn. 5, 155; Roth ZGR 2014, 168 (171).

[12] Vgl. OLG Nürnberg 7.6.1984 – 8 U 111/84, BeckRS 1984, 31137893 = IPRax 1985, 342; v. Bar, Internationales Privatrecht II, 1991, Rn. 621; Grüneberg, BGB/Thorn, 83. Aufl. 2024, EGBGB Anh. Art. 12 Rn. 1.

[13] BayObLG 7.5.1992 – 3Z BR 14/92, BayObLGZ 1992, 113 (115); Schmidt/Lutter, AktG/Ringe, 5. Aufl. 2023, IntGesR Rn. 6; Roth ZGR 2014, 168 (171, 191); Weller FS Goette, 2011, 583 (590).

ein.[14] Während vor der Verlegung auf den Verband ausländisches Gesellschaftsrecht zur Anwendung gelangte, ist es nach der Verlegung inländisches Gesellschaftsrecht.

Die Anwendung deutschen Gesellschaftsrechts auf einen nach einem fremden Recht gegründeten Rechtsträger meint zunächst, dass im Wege der Transposition auf das Recht derjenigen inländischen Rechtsform zurückgegriffen wird, die der ausländischen Gesellschaft am ehesten entspricht.[15] Handelt es sich bei der ausländischen Rechtsform um eine Personengesellschaft, für welche die Eintragung in das Register nicht konstitutiv ist, wird die Aufrechterhaltung der Rechtspersönlichkeit der Gesellschaft unter gewissen Änderungen der Verbandsverfassung und in Form der inländischen Rechtsform, die der ausländischen Rechtsform am ehesten entspricht, möglich sein.[16] Mit der Verlegung des Verwaltungssitzes findet also ein automatischer Formwechsel außerhalb des UmwG in eine inländische Personengesellschaft statt.[17] Handelt es sich jedoch um eine juristische Person, sieht das deutsche Recht vor, dass diese ihre Rechtsfähigkeit erst mit Eintragung in das jeweilige Register erlangt[18] und notwendigerweise mangelt es der ausländischen Rechtsform an der entsprechenden Eintragung. Ein automatischer Formwechsel kann bei registergebundenen Rechtsträgern folglich nicht stattfinden.

aa) Traditionelle Sitztheorie

Nach der Sitztheorie in ihrer traditionellen Ausprägung wurde hieraus geschlossen, dass die ausländische Gesellschaft als inexistent zu behandeln sei.[19]

Die Folge dieser Annahme liefe aber einerseits dem Gedanken der Schwerpunktanknüpfung zuwider, weil im Ergebnis gerade nicht das Gesellschaftsrecht des Staates des Verwaltungssitzes, sondern keines zur Anwendung käme und böte andererseits für niemanden einen gerechtfertigten Vorteil.[20] Die Negation des Zuordnungssubjekts müsste an sich das Verschwinden des gesamten Vermögens des Rechtsträgers mit sich bringen. Sachen würden spontan herrenlos und Gläubiger verlören ihren Schuldner. Allein die Schuldner der Gesellschaft könnten sich freuen, denn sie würden von ihren Verbindlichkeiten befreit.[21]

---

[14] OLG Hamburg 30.3.2007 – 11 U 231/04, NZG 2007, 597 = ZIP 2007, 1108 (1114); OLG München 6.5.1986 – 5 U 2562/85, NJW 1986, 2197 (2198); OLG Nürnberg 7.6.1984 – 8 U 111/84, BeckRS 1984, 31137893 = IPRax 1985, 342; Hellgardt/Illmer NZG 2009, 94; Jestädt, Niederlassungsfreiheit und Gesellschaftskollisionsrecht, 2005, S. 37; Kindler IPRax 2003, 41; Kindler NJW 2003, 1073 (1074); Leible FS Roth, 2011, 447 (452); Rauscher, Internationales Privatrecht, 5. Aufl. 2017, Rn. 630; Walden EWS 2001, 256 (258).

[15] OLG Hamburg 30.3.2007 – 11 U 231/04, NZG 2007, 597 = ZIP 2007, 1108 (1113); Eidenmüller/Rehm, ZGR 1997, 89 (90f.).

[16] Vgl. Oetker, HGB/Lieder, 8. Aufl. 2024, § 105 Rn. 187.

[17] Stiegler ZGR 2017, 312 (329f.).

[18] § 21 BGB (für den Verein), § 41 Abs. 1 S. 1 AktG (für die Aktiengesellschaft), § 11 Abs. 2 GmbHG (für die GmbH), § 13 GenG (für die Genossenschaft).

[19] OLG München 6.5.1986 – 5 U 2562/85, NJW 1986, 2197 (2198); OLG München 31.10.1994 – 26 U 2596/94, NJW-RR 1995, 703 (704); LG Aurich 11.7.1967 – Q 20/67, IPRspr. 1968, 31f. (Nr. 14); Staudinger, BGB/Großfeld, 1998, IntGesR Rn. 427.

[20] Vgl. Fischer IPRax 1991, 100 (104).

[21] Vgl. GmbHG Großkommentar/Behrens/Hoffmann, 3. Aufl. 2019, Einl. Rn. B 35.

Vor dem Hintergrund dieser desaströsen Konsequenzen wird der Sitztheorie primär ein generalpräventiv-repressiver Charakter zugeschrieben.[22] Gerade durch die als bekannt unterstellte Folge der Nichtanerkennung soll auf die Akteure Druck ausgeübt werden, sich dem inländischen Gesellschaftsrecht durch Neugründung anzupassen.[23]

Sollte der Verwaltungssitz der ausländischen Gesellschaft dessen ungeachtet aber dennoch ins Inland verlegt werden, laufen die Folgen der Anwendung der Sitztheorie ihrem erklärten Ziel, den inländischen Rechtsverkehr zu schützen, diametral entgegen. Daher werden gerade zur Verwirklichung des Schutzes des inländischen Rechtsverkehrs Korrekturen für erforderlich gehalten,[24] indem für den nicht existenten Rechtsträger ein Ersatzrecht geschaffen werden soll.[25] Insbesondere soll dieser nach „Rechtsscheingrundsätzen" im Prozess zumindest passiv parteifähig (§ 50 ZPO) sein[26] und die vom inexistenten Rechtsträger abgeschlossenen Verträge sollen „nach dem Zweck der Sitztheorie" wirksam sein.[27]

Überzeugen können diese Flickschustereien indes kaum. Geht man von der Prämisse aus, dass der Rechtsträger nicht existiert, kann kein noch so starker Rechtsschein diese Inexistenz überwinden. Hinzu kommt, dass dem Kläger mit einem obsiegenden Urteil nicht geholfen wäre, denn gegen einen bloßen Rechtsschein kann es nicht vollstreckt werden. Für den Fall der tatsächlichen Verlegung des Verwaltungssitzes, muss die Sitztheorie also ein amorphes Gebilde konstruieren, das zwar nicht ist, aber zugunsten des inländischen Rechtsverkehrs dennoch irgendwie als existierend betrachtet wird und setzt sich damit zwangsläufig in Widerspruch zur Grundprämisse der Inexistenz des Rechtsträgers.[28]

bb) Modifizierte Sitztheorie

Vor dem Hintergrund dieser Probleme verwundert es nicht, dass der Bundesgerichtshof sich veranlasst sah, die Sitztheorie zu modifizieren. Die Verlegung des tatsächlichen Verwaltungssitzes eines ausländischen Rechtsträgers ins Inland soll nun nicht mehr dazu führen, dass die ausländische Gesellschaft als inexistent betrachtet wird, sondern dazu, dass sie als rechtsfähige Personengesellschaft[29] zu behandeln ist.[30] Die ausländische Rechtsform wird also in eine inländische Gesell-

---

[22] Behrens IPRax 2003, 193 (194); Fischer IPRax 1991, 100 (104); Staudinger, BGB/Großfeld, 1998, IntGesR Rn. 48.

[23] Vgl. OLG München 6.5.1986 – 5 U 2562/85, NJW 1986, 2197 (2198); Staudinger, BGB/Großfeld, 1998, IntGesR Rn. 49; Süß/Wachter, Handbuch des internationalen GmbH-Rechts/Kienle/Dolzer, 4. Aufl. 2021, § 3 Rn. 9; Rehbinder IPRax 1985, 324.

[24] Kritisch zur Sitztheorie deshalb auch Knobbe-Keuk ZHR 154 (1990), 325 (328f., 335ff.).

[25] Staudinger, BGB/Großfeld, 1998, IntGesR Rn. 435f.

[26] OLG Nürnberg 7.6.1984 – 8 U 111/84, BeckRS 1984, 31137893 = IPRax 1985, 342, ähnlich BGH 21.3.1986 – V ZR 10/85, BGHZ 97, 269 (270f.) = NJW 1986, 2194 (passive Parteifähigkeit nach dem Rechtsgedanken des § 50 Abs. 2 ZPO a. F. bei Eintragung ins Grundbuch).

[27] Schuck BB 1994, 1538 (1539).

[28] Siehe insoweit auch die Kritik bei Leible/Hoffmann DB 2002, 2203 (2204).

[29] BGH 1.7.2002 – II ZR 380/00, BGHZ 151, 204 (206ff.) = NJW 2002, 3539 (Jersey Limited); BayObLG 20.2.2003 – 1Z AR 160/02, BeckRS 2003, 2439 = RIW 2003, 387, 388.

[30] Siehe zu früheren Ansätzen Lanzius, Anwendbares Recht und Sonderanknüpfungen unter der Gründungstheorie, 2005, S. 45ff.

schaftsform umqualifiziert; ihren Gesellschaftern wird gleichsam eine inländische Rechtsform untergeschoben, weshalb diese Variante der Sitztheorie auch als „Wechselbalgtheorie"[31] bekannt geworden ist.

Der Bundesgerichtshof hält mithin kollisionsrechtlich an der Sitztheorie fest, korrigiert aber deren Ergebnisse umfassend auf sachrechtlicher Ebene,[32] indem er den ausländischen Rechtsträger nach deutschem Sachrecht nicht mehr als inexistent betrachtet, sondern diesem nach dem deutschen *numerus clausus* der Gesellschaftsformen[33] die Rechtsform zuordnet, dessen Gründungserfordernisse er erfüllt. Hierbei soll eine ausländische Kapitalgesellschaft bei Betrieb eines Handelsgewerbes als oHG (§§ 105ff. HGB) oder andernfalls als Gesellschaft bürgerlichen Rechts (§§ 705ff. BGB) einzuordnen sein.[34] Hat die ausländische Kapitalgesellschaft nur einen Gesellschafter, so soll aus Perspektive des deutschen Rechts nur der Gesellschafter Zurechnungssubjekt sein.[35] Nach der modifizierten Sitztheorie ist es nun die drohende persönliche und unbeschränkte Haftung der Gesellschafter (§§ 721 BGB, 126 HGB), von der der Druck zur Anpassung an das inländische Recht ausgeht.

2. *Probleme der Sitztheorie*

a) *Das Problem des Anknüpfungsmerkmals*

aa) *Vagheit des Merkmals des effektiven Verwaltungssitzes*

Es versteht sich von selbst, dass die Anknüpfung des Gesellschaftsstatuts stets klar und bestimmt sein sollte. Allerdings vermag das Merkmal des effektiven Verwaltungssitzes diesem Anspruch oftmals nicht genügen.[36]

Als Verwaltungssitz wird nach der *Sandrock'schen* Formel der Ort angesehen, von welchem aus die grundlegenden Entscheidungen der Unternehmensleitung effektiv in laufende Geschäftsführungsakte umgesetzt werden.[37] Der mit dieser Definition verbundene Erkenntnisgewinn ist indes bescheiden.[38] Je nach Zuschnitt der

---

[31] Forsthoff DB 2002, 2471 (2476); Goette VGR 13 (2007), 1 (5); Paefgen DZWIR 2003, 441 (444).

[32] Vgl. Kindler IPRax 2003, 41 (42); Leible/Hoffmann DB 2002, 2203f.

[33] Siehe dazu Schmidt, Gesellschaftsrecht, 4. Aufl. 2002, S. 96ff. (§ 5 II 1).

[34] Eidenmüller/Rehm ZGR 1997, 89 (91); Großerichter DStR 2003, 159 (160); Lamsa BB 2009, 1416 (1417); Leible/Hoffmann DB 2002, 2203 (2204); Kindler IPRax 2003, 41 (42f.); Roth ZIP 2000, 1597 (1600); Walden EWS 2001, 256 (259); Weller FS Goette, 2011, 583 (592).

[35] OLG München 5.8.2021 – 29 U 2411/21, NZG 2021, 1518 = ZIP 2021, 2178, 2179; Binz/Mayer BB 2005, 2361 (2363); Bogler DB 1991, 848 (850); Lamsa BB 2009, 1416 (1417); Leible/Hoffmann DB 2002, 2203 (2204); Roth ZIP 2000, 1597 (1600).

[36] NomosKommentar BGB/Hoffmann, 4. Aufl. 2021, EGBGB Anh. Art. 12 Rn. 31.

[37] So zurückgehend auf Sandrock FS Beitzke, 1979, 669 (683); BGH 21.3.1986 – V ZR 10/85, BGHZ 97, 269 (272) = NJW 1986, 2194; BGH 15.3.2010 – II ZR 27/09, NJW-RR 2010, 1364 Rn. 16; BayObLG 18.7.1985 – BReg. 3 Z 62/85, BayObLGZ 1985, 272 (280) (Landshuter Druckhaus I); KG 13.6.1989 – 6 U 591/89, NJW 1989, 3100 (3101); OLG Düsseldorf 15.12.1994 – 6 U 59/94, NJW-RR 1995, 1124; OLG Frankfurt 23.6.1999 – 22 U 219/97, NJW-RR 2000, 1226; OLG Hamburg 21.1.1987 – 4 U 54/86, RIW 1988, 816; OLG Hamburg 30.3.2007 – 11 U 231/04, NZG 2007, 597 = ZIP 2007, 1108 (1110); OLG Hamm 4.10.1996 – 29 U 108/95, IPRax 1998, 358 (359); OLG Hamm 18.8.1994 – d 15 W 209/94, NJW-RR 1995, 469 (470); OLG Oldenburg 4.4.1989 – 12 U 13/89, NJW 1990, 1422.

[38] GmbHG Großkommentar/Behrens/Hoffmann, 3. Aufl. 2019, Einl. Rn. B 29.

Rechtsform können die „grundlegenden Entscheidungen" entweder vom Geschäftsführungsorgan oder von den Gesellschaftern getroffen werden. Maßgeblich soll dann schließlich doch nicht der Ort sein, an dem diese Entscheidungen getroffen werden, sondern der Ort, von dem aus sie in „laufende Geschäftsführungsakte" umgesetzt werden. Welche Geschäftsführungsakte damit konkret gemeint sind, bleibt unklar.[39] Das Schrifttum entgeht dieser Frage, indem es in der Regel den Tätigkeitsort der für das Tagesgeschäft zuständigen Mitglieder des Verwaltungsorgans für maßgeblich erachtet.[40] „Tagesgeschäft" betreibt die Gesellschaft allerdings auf allen Märkten, auf denen sie aktiv ist. Ebenso kann eine Person durchaus an mehreren Orten beschäftigt sein und nicht alle Mitglieder der Geschäftsführung brauchen am selben Ort tätig zu werden.[41] Schon jetzt dürfte der effektive Verwaltungssitz bisweilen nur schwer zu ermitteln sein[42] und es wurden bereits Fälle bekannt, in denen dieser überhaupt nicht feststellbar war.[43]

Hinzu kommt, dass inzwischen die Digitalisierung selbst völlig dezentrale Organisationsformen ermöglicht.[44] Relativ problemlos können sich Menschen heute in verschiedenen Ländern befinden und dennoch effektiv zusammenarbeiten. Treffen können in den virtuellen Raum verlegt und Daten über Cloudspeicher problemlos ausgetauscht werden. Wird eine Gesellschaft in dieser Weise organisiert, kann ein effektiver Verwaltungssitz schlicht nicht festgestellt werden.

bb) Teleologische Schwächen der Anknüpfung an den Verwaltungssitz

Verbände sind multipolare Interessengebilde. Dem Verbandsrecht fällt nach dem traditionellen Verständnis die Aufgabe zu, eine potentielle Vielzahl von Interessen zu ordnen und in Ausgleich zu bringen. Zu berücksichtigen sind insbesondere Interessengegensätze zwischen Mehrheit und Minderheit der Gesellschafter, zwischen Gründern und Kapitalanlegern, zwischen Gesellschaftern und Geschäftsführung, zwischen Kapitalgebern und Arbeitnehmern sowie zwischen Gesellschaftern und Gläubigern.[45] Wenn die Anknüpfung an den effektiven Verwaltungssitz eine Schwerpunktanknüpfung darstellen soll, so meint dies, dass das Verbandsrecht des Staates zur Anwendung berufen sein muss, in dessen Gebiet die Mehrzahl der Interessenträger ansässig ist.

---

[39] Vgl. Zimmer RabelsZ 67 (2003), 298 (300).

[40] OLG Hamm 18.8.1994 – d 15 W 209/94, NJW-RR 1995, 469 (470); OLG Köln 30.9.1999 – 2 Wx 22/98, MittBayNot 1999, 394 = IPRax 2000, 130, 131; Fedke ZIP 2019, 799 (802); Münchener Kommentar zum BGB/Kindler, 8. Aufl. 2021, IntGesR Rn. 459.

[41] Vgl. NomosKommentar BGB/Hoffmann, 4. Aufl. 2021, EGBGB Anh. Art. 12 Rn. 148; Breuninger/Krüger FS Rädler, 1999, 79 (80ff.) (mit Verweis auf polyzentrische Führungsstrukturen).

[42] OLG München 6.5.1986 – 5 U 2562/85, NJW 1986, 2197 (2198); Ebke FS Hellwig, 2010, 117 (139); Fedke ZIP 2019, 799 (804); Jestädt Niederlassungsfreiheit und Gesellschaftskollisionsrecht, 2005, S. 253.

[43] Siehe den Fall OLG Frankfurt 23.6.1999 – 22 U 219/97, NJW-RR 2000, 1226, in dem die Gesellschaft aus Piloten bestand, welche die Geschäfte der Gesellschaft von ständig wechselnden Orten aus betrieben. Beim heutigen Stand der Informationstechnologie sind ohne Weiteres Organisationsformen denkbar, die völlig ohne einen ständigen physischen Verwaltungssitz auskommen, siehe auch Wiepen, Digitalisierung und Lokalisierung im internationalen Gesellschaftsrecht, 2024, S. 43f.

[44] Siehe bereits Breuninger/Krüger FS Rädler, 1999, 79 (82f.).

[45] Vgl. Wiedemann, Gesellschaftsrecht I, 1980, S. 16ff. (§ 2 II 2).

Dieser Anforderung wird die Anknüpfung an den effektiven Verwaltungssitz aber nicht unbedingt gerecht. Die Verwaltungssitzanknüpfung führt dazu, dass das Gesellschaftsrecht des Staates zur Anwendung gelangt, in dem die Geschäftsführung domiziliert ist. An grenzüberschreitenden Geschäften ist diese jedoch nicht gehindert, sodass die übrigen Interessenträger auch unter Geltung der Sitztheorie ohne Weiteres der Anwendung fremden Gesellschaftsrechts ausgesetzt sein können. Für einen Vertragsschluss über das Internet spielt der Staat des Verwaltungssitzes einer Gesellschaft überhaupt keine Rolle und in Zeiten der Digitalisierung erscheint der physische Ort der Geschäftsführung zunehmend beliebig.

Letztendlich bedeutet die Entfaltung jeder grenzüberschreitenden Aktivität einer Gesellschaft, dass bezogen auf die Aktivität im jeweils betroffenen nationalen Markt das nationale Gesellschaftsrecht nicht beachtet wird. Die Sitztheorie entpuppt sich daher als Konstrukt für geschlossene Märkte.

b) Probleme der Umqualifizierung im Falle der Verlegung des Verwaltungssitzes

aa) Dogmatische Probleme

Die Umqualifizierung einer ausländischen Kapitalgesellschaft infolge der Verwaltungssitzverlegung ins Inland wird häufig als folgerichtige Anwendung des deutschen Gesellschaftsrechts begriffen. In der Behandlung als inländische Personengesellschaft soll nichts weiter liegen als die konsequente Einstufung in das Ordnungsgefüge des *numerus clausus* des deutschen Gesellschaftsrechts.[46] Die zugezogene Gesellschaftsform soll als das zu behandeln sein, „was sie nach deutschen Gesellschaftsrecht ist".[47]

Eine ausländische Gesellschaftsform ist aber zunächst eine Gesellschaftsform ausländischen Rechts. Ihre Existenz und ihre Struktur verdankt sie allein ihrer Heimatrechtsordnung. In den *numerus clausus* des deutschen Gesellschaftsrechts kann sie als solche nicht eingeordnet werden und erst recht lässt es sich kaum als schlichte Anwendung des deutschen Gesellschaftsrechts begreifen, wenn man einer ausländischen Kapitalgesellschaft eine völlig strukturverschiedene Rechtsform des deutschen Personengesellschaftsrechts unterschiebt.

Solchen Erwägungen liegt unausgesprochen die Prämisse zugrunde, dass sich hinter jeder juristischen Person ein Personenverband verbirgt, der ohne erfolgreiche Beschränkung der Haftung als Personengesellschaft einzuordnen ist. Eine einmal entstandene juristische Person ist aber von ihren Mitgliedern verselbstständigt und nicht mit der Summe ihrer Gesellschafter gleichzusetzen.[48] Die Anwendung des inländischen Personengesellschaftsrechts stellt daher keine konsequente Anwendung des deutschen Gesellschaftsrechts dar, sondern eine echte Umqualifizierung einer bestehenden juristischen Person in eine Personengesellschaft. Eine solche Umqualifizierung *ipso iure* ist dem deutschen Gesellschaftsrecht aber grundsätzlich fremd.

[46] Vgl. OLG Hamburg 30.3.2007 – 11 U 231/04, NZG 2007, 597 = ZIP 2007, 1108 (1111); Eidenmüller/Rehm ZGR 1997, 89 (90f.); Leible/Hoffmann DB 2002, 2203 (2204); Roth ZIP 2000, 1597 (1600); Zimmer RabelsZ 67 (2003), 298 (301).

[47] Leible/Hoffmann DB 2002, 2203 (2204).

[48] Flume, Allgemeiner Teil des Bürgerlichen Rechts I/2, 1983, S. 259 (§ 8 I).

Am ehesten lässt sich die Umqualifizierung als Spielart des Durchgriffs begreifen.[49] Im engeren Sinn versteht man hierunter die Außerachtlassung der Trennung von selbstständiger juristischer Person und Gesellschaftern. Die Normanwendung wird auf das personale Substrat der Gesellschaft bezogen; an die Stelle der juristischen Person treten ihre Mitglieder.[50] Unter der Prämisse eines umfassenden Durchgriffs ließe sich die juristische Person also unter Umständen als Personengesellschaft behandeln.

Eine Durchgriffslehre, welche die Normanwendung unmittelbar auf die Gesellschafter als personales Substrat bezieht, ist mit dem Konzept der juristischen Person, das sich gerade dadurch auszeichnet, dass der Rechtsträger von seinen Mitgliedern verselbstständigt ist, nicht zu vereinbaren.[51] Es existiert schlicht keine reale Personengesellschaft, die sich hinter dem „Schleier" des Konstrukts der juristischen Person verstecken könnte. Die diskutierten Fälle einer Durchgriffshaftung lassen sich regelmäßig systemkonform als Innenhaftung der Gesellschafter gegenüber der juristischen Person einordnen. Insoweit nimmt es nicht wunder, dass sich die Durchgriffslehren im engeren Sinne auf dem Rückzug befinden. Ganz in diesem Sinne hat der Bundesgerichtshof auch längst seine Rechtsprechung zum existenzvernichtenden Eingriff modifiziert und die ursprünglich auf die analoge Anwendung des § 126 HGB gestützte Außenhaftung[52] der Gesellschafter durch eine auf § 826 BGB gestützte Innenhaftung ersetzt.[53] In gleicher Weise hat unter dem Gesichtspunkt des Durchgriffs die Rechtsprechung die Haftung der Mitglieder eines eingetragenen Vereins nach dem Vorbild eines nicht eingetragenen Wirtschaftsvereins bei Überschreitung des Nebenzweckprivilegs verneint.[54]

bb) Sachrechtliche Folgeprobleme

Selbst wenn man von der dogmatischen Unbegründbarkeit einer Umqualifizierung absieht, führt diese auf sachrechtlicher Ebene dennoch zu unüberbrückbaren Schwierigkeiten.

(1) Folgen für das Haftungsregime

(a) Eintritt der persönlichen und unbeschränkten Haftung der Gesellschafter nach deutschem Recht. Verlegt eine ausländische Kapitalgesellschaft ihren Verwaltungssitz ins Inland, haften nach der Wechselbalgtheorie künftig deren Gesellschafter nach

[49] So GmbHG Großkommentar/Behrens/Hoffmann, 3. Aufl. 2019, Einl. Rn. B 34; vgl. auch im Rahmen der Sitztheorie in ihrer traditionellen Ausprägung von Falkenhausen RIW 1987, 818.

[50] Vgl. Flume, Allgemeiner Teil des Bürgerlichen I/2, 1983, S. 63ff. (§ 3 I)

[51] Vgl. Flume, Allgemeiner Teil des Bürgerlichen I/2 1983, S. 63ff. (§ 3 I); Wilhelm FS Flume II, 1978, 337 (394ff.); Wilhelm, Rechtsform und Haftung bei der juristischen Person, 1981, S. 291ff.

[52] BGH 24.6.2002 – II ZR 300/00, BGHZ 151, 181 (186ff.) = NJW 2002, 3024 (KBV); BGH 13.12.2004 – II ZR 206/02, NJW-RR 2005, 335 (Autovertragshändler); BGH 13.12.2004 – II ZR 256/02, NZG 2005, 214 = ZIP 2005, 250 (251) (Handelsvertreter).

[53] BGH 16.7.2007 – II ZR 3/04, BGHZ 173, 246 Rn. 17ff. = NJW 2007, 2689 (Trihotel); BGH 28.4.2008 – II ZR 264/06, BGHZ 176, 204 Rn. 10 = NJW 2008, 2437 (Gamma); BGH 9.2.2009 – II ZR 292/07, BGHZ 179, 344 Rn. 15 = NJW 2009, 2127 (Sanitary).

[54] BGH 10.12.2007 – II ZR 239/05, BGHZ 175, 12 Rn. 17ff. = NZG 2008, 670 (Kolpingwerk).

Maßgabe der §§ 721 BGB, 126 HGB persönlich und unbeschränkt für die Verbindlichkeiten der Gesellschaft. Dies wirkt durchaus gerechtfertigt, wenn alle Gesellschafter der Sitzverlegung zustimmen, denn dann nehmen sie es in Kauf, den Schutz ihrer Heimatrechtsordnung zu verlieren und einer anderen Rechtsordnung unterstellt zu werden.

Allerdings wird der Verwaltungssitz typischerweise durch das Handeln des Leitungsorgans und nicht durch die Gesellschafter geprägt. Damit kann die Verlegung des Verwaltungssitzes als tatsächlicher Vorgang unter Umständen ganz ohne Wissen und Zutun der Gesellschafter erfolgen. Zu rechtfertigen ist die Haftung der Gesellschafter unter diesen Umständen nicht.[55]

Diese Problematik wird auch in der Literatur gesehen. Zum Teil wird vorgeschlagen, die Haftung von Gesellschaftern, die keinerlei Leitungsfunktion ausüben, nach Art von Kommanditisten auf die Höhe der Einlage zu beschränken[56] oder bei Publikumsgesellschaften die nicht handelnden Minderheitsgesellschafter wie Mitglieder eines nicht rechtsfähigen Idealvereins zu behandeln.[57] Solche Ansätze mildern zwar die untragbaren Konsequenzen der Wechselbalgtheorie ab, doch setzen sie sich zur Grundannahme in Widerspruch, den ausländischen Verband nach dem *numerus clausus* des deutschen Gesellschaftsrechts zu erfassen. Stattdessen wird auch in dieser Spielart der Sitztheorie ein Ersatzrecht konstruiert, das weder dem Gründungsrecht noch dem deutschen Gesellschaftsrecht entspricht.

Höchst problematisch erscheint die Haftung der Gesellschafter für Altverbindlichkeiten, also für solche Verbindlichkeiten, die bereits vor dem Zeitpunkt der Verlegung des Verwaltungssitzes begründet wurden. Es ist wertungsmäßig kaum nachvollziehbar, warum die Gesellschafter einer ausländischen Kapitalgesellschaft auch für diese Verbindlichkeiten persönlich haften sollten. Die Altgläubiger haben mit einer ausländischen Kapitalgesellschaft, die ihren Verwaltungssitz im Ausland hatte, kontrahiert und durften nicht erwarten, dass ihnen mehr als nur das Gesellschaftsvermögen als Haftungsmasse zur Verfügung steht. Die persönliche Haftung der Gesellschafter ist für sie also ein *windfall profit*.[58] Auf der anderen Seite durften die Gesellschafter zum Zeitpunkt der Begründung der Verbindlichkeit darauf vertrauen, nicht persönlich zu haften.[59]

Vor diesem Hintergrund wird im Schrifttum vorgeschlagen, die Gesellschafter für Altverbindlichkeiten nicht haften zu lassen. Begründet wird dies mit zwei Erwägungen: Erstens entstehe die deutsche Personengesellschaft erst im Moment der Verwaltungssitzverlegung, wobei die ausländische Rechtsform aus Sicht der Gründungsrechtsordnung dennoch bestehen bleibe. Damit komme es zu einer Statutenverdopplung und die deutsche Personengesellschaft trete nur neben die ausländische Gesellschaft, sei aber nicht deren Rechtsnachfolgerin. Zweitens müsse die Maxime der *lex temporis actus* beachtet werden, nach welcher der spätere Wechsel des anwendbaren Rechts nicht nachträglich zu einem veränderten Beurteilungs-

[55] Zweifelnd auch Binz/Mayer BB 2005, 2361 (2364).
[56] Eidenmüller/Rehm ZGR 1997, 89 (103); Fischer IPRax 1991, 100 (101).
[57] Weller FS Goette, 2011, 583 (592).
[58] Freitag/Korch ZIP 2016, 1361 (1363).
[59] Weller FS Goette, 2011, 583 (598).

maßstab führen dürfe, sofern nicht ausnahmsweise das Bedürfnis nach einer späteren Rechtsangleichung überwiege.[60]

Beide Erwägungen können nicht überzeugen. Zu einer Statutenverdopplung kommt es lediglich bei einer globalen Betrachtungsweise. Aus Sicht des Herkunftsstaates besteht die Gesellschaft trotz Verlegung des Verwaltungssitzes in ihrer ursprünglichen Rechtsform fort. Aus Sicht des deutschen internationalen Gesellschaftsrechts führt hingegen die Verwaltungssitzverlegung ins Inland auf dem Boden der Sitztheorie zu einem Statutenwechsel. Folglich besteht unter der weiteren Annahme der Umqualifizierung aus inländischer Sicht die zugezogene Gesellschaft ab dem Zeitpunkt der Verwaltungssitzverlegung ausschließlich als deutsche Personengesellschaft fort. Verneint man die Identität zwischen dem ursprünglichen ausländischen Rechtsträger und der deutschen Personengesellschaft, so verneint man zugleich den Statutenwechsel und damit die Sitztheorie. Stattdessen fingiert man eine Neugründung, die mit dem ursprünglichen Rechtsträger nichts mehr zu tun hat. Auch das zweite Argument überzeugt nicht. Mit dem Statutenwechsel wird nicht nur die persönliche Haftung begründet, sondern zugleich entfallen die Kapitalschutzvorschriften des Herkunftsstaates. Dadurch erlangen die Gesellschafter einen unbeschränkten Zugriff auf das Gesellschaftsvermögen. Diese Zugriffsmöglichkeit muss gerade zum Schutze der Altgläubiger durch die persönliche und unbeschränkte Haftung der Gesellschafter kompensiert werden.[61]

(b) Entfall der nach ausländischem Recht bestehenden Vermögensbindung. Im Falle einer Kapitalgesellschaft haftet den Gesellschaftsgläubigern allein das Gesellschaftsvermögen. Ein Zugriff auf das Privatvermögen der Gesellschafter ist im Grundsatz ausgeschlossen. Privatgläubigern der Gesellschafter hingegen haftet unbeschränkt das Privatvermögen der Gesellschafter. Hierzu gehört auch deren Beteiligung an der Kapitalgesellschaft, wobei die Privatgläubiger bei der Verwertung der Beteiligung erst nach den Gesellschaftsgläubigern befriedigt werden. Im Ergebnis haftet das Vermögen der Gesellschaft vorrangig den Gesellschaftsgläubigern, während das Privatvermögen der Gesellschafter ausschließlich den Privatgläubigern haftet.[62]

Die Umqualifizierung in eine Personengesellschaft fegt dieses privatautonom begründete Haftungsregime beiseite. Aufgrund der jetzt eintretenden persönlichen und unbeschränkten Haftung der Gesellschafter können Gesellschaftsgläubiger auch auf das Privatvermögen der Gesellschafter zugreifen. Die Umqualifizierung verschafft daher den Gesellschaftsgläubigern einen Vorzug und verschlechtert die Stellung der Privatgläubiger, die nun mit dem wirtschaftlichen Risiko der Gesellschaft belastet werden. Diese Verschiebung des Haftungsgleichgewichts ist kaum zu rechtfertigen.[63]

Im Falle einer ausländischen Einmann-Kapitalgesellschaft treten sogar völlig zufällige Verschiebungen im Haftungsgefüge auf. Im Falle der Umqualifizierung der Gesellschaft in eine natürliche Person können nun Gesellschafts- und Privatgläu-

---

[60] Weller FS Goette, 2011, 583 (597).

[61] Vgl. BGH 7.4.2003 – II ZR 56/02, BGHZ 154, 370 (373f.) = NJW 2003, 1803 (zur akzessorischen Haftung für Altverbindlichkeiten beim Beitritt zu einer GbR).

[62] Vgl. König AcP 217 (2017), 611 (618).

[63] Behrens IPRax 2003, 193 (195f.) (zur traditionellen Sitztheorie).

biger gleichrangig sowohl in das ehemalige Gesellschafts- als auch in das Privatvermögen vollstrecken. Dies wirkt sich zugunsten der Gesellschaftsgläubiger aus, wenn es um die Vermögenslage der Gesellschaft schlecht und um die private Vermögenslage eher gut bestellt war, während im umgekehrten Fall die Privatgläubiger profitieren. Entsprechendes gilt bei Konzernsachverhalten, wo eine Vermögenskonsolidation stattfinden kann.

(2) Auswirkungen auf das Innenrecht. Mit der persönlichen und unbeschränkten Haftung des einzelnen Gesellschafters im Außenverhältnis korrespondiert im deutschen Personengesellschaftsrecht die starke Stellung des Gesellschafters im Innenverhältnis. So sieht das gesetzliche Normalstatut vor, dass im Recht der oHG grundsätzlich alle Gesellschafter zur Geschäftsführung befugt sind (§ 116 Abs. 1, Abs. 3 S. 1 HGB). Widerspricht ein geschäftsführungsbefugter Gesellschafter, hat die Geschäftsführungsmaßnahme zu unterbleiben (§ 116 Abs. 3 S. 3 HGB). Im Recht der GbR obliegt den Gesellschaftern im Grundsatz die Geschäftsführungsbefugnis sogar nur gemeinschaftlich (§ 715 Abs. 1, Abs. 3 S. 1 BGB). Jedem Gesellschafter stehen in oHG und GbR in den Angelegenheiten der Gesellschaft sehr weitreichende Informationsrechte zu (§ 717 BGB, § 105 Abs. 3 HGB). Beschlüsse der Gesellschafter müssen grundsätzlich einstimmig gefasst werden (§ 109 Abs. 3 HGB, § 714 BGB). Jeder Gesellschafter einer oHG unterliegt nach Maßgabe des § 117 HGB einem Wettbewerbsverbot. Die Mitgliedschaft ist jeweils nur mit Zustimmung aller Gesellschafter übertragbar (vgl. § 105 Abs. 3 HGB, § 711 Abs. 1 S. 1 BGB).

Unter Vernachlässigung der Unterschiede der jeweiligen nationalen Rechte ist das Innenrecht der Kapitalgesellschaften typischerweise dadurch gekennzeichnet, dass die Geschäftsführung in die Hände eines von den Gesellschaftern verschiedenen Geschäftsführungsorgans gelegt wird. Informationsrechte der Gesellschafter bestehen unter Umständen nur eingeschränkt, Beschlüsse werden mit Mehrheit gefasst, Wettbewerbsverbote gibt es meist nicht und die Mitgliedschaft ist frei übertragbar.

Stülpt man der ausländischen Kapitalgesellschaft die Rechtsform einer deutschen Personengesellschaft über, kommt das Prinzip der Selbstorganschaft zum Zuge, womit das Geschäftsführungsorgan entfällt. Stattdessen erhalten plötzlich Personen Geschäftsführungsbefugnisse, Widerspruchs- und Informationsrechte, welche die Mitglieder der ausländischen juristischen Person nie damit ausstatten wollten.[64] Gleichzeitig können sich Gesellschafter einem Wettbewerbsverbot ausgesetzt sehen, mit dem sie nie gerechnet haben. Ehemals frei übertragbare Mitgliedschaften können nur noch mit Zustimmung aller Gesellschafter übertragen werden.

Evident entspricht insoweit die Anwendung der Regelungen des deutschen Personengesellschaftsrechts nicht dem Parteiwillen der Gesellschafter der umqualifizierten ausländischen Kapitalgesellschaft und aus Perspektive des deutschen Rechts besteht im Prinzip auch kein Interesse daran, in das privatautonom begründete Innenverhältnis einzugreifen.

---

[64] Siehe auch die Kritik bei Heidenhain NZG 2002, 1141 (1142).

Diese Probleme erscheinen auf den ersten Blick allerdings überwindbar. Zwar haben die Gesellschafter der umqualifizierten Personengesellschaft für diese nie einen Gesellschaftsvertrag abgeschlossen, jedoch für die ausländische Rechtsform. Damit liegt es nahe, den in der Satzung der ausländischen Kapitalgesellschaft zum Ausdruck kommenden Willen der Gesellschafter im Rahmen des insoweit dispositiven deutschen Personengesellschaftsrechts aufrechtzuerhalten. Ist ein Gesellschafter für die ausländische Kapitalgesellschaft zugleich zum Geschäftsführer bestellt, böte es sich beispielsweise an, den Willen der Gesellschafter so auszulegen, dass dieser auch nach der Umqualifizierung zur Geschäftsführung berechtigt sein soll, während nicht geschäftsführende Gesellschafter der ausländischen Kapitalgesellschaft von der Geschäftsführung ausgeschlossen wären.

Auf einen zweiten Blick erscheint es indes höchst zweifelhaft, ob die möglichst weitgehende Aufrechterhaltung der inneren Verbandsverfassung der ausländischen Kapitalgesellschaft tatsächlich als von den Gesellschaftern gewollt angesehen werden kann. Schließlich stehen sich Innenrecht und Haftungsrecht nicht unverbunden gegenüber, sondern sind aufeinander bezogen. Mit der unbeschränkten Haftung des Gesellschafters im Außenverhältnis korrespondiert seine starke Stellung im Innenverhältnis. Wer unbeschränkt und persönlich für die Verbindlichkeiten der Gesellschaft einzustehen hat, wird eine solche Haftung typischerweise davon abhängig machen wollen, dass ihm im Innenverhältnis weitgehende Einwirkungs- und Informationsrechte eingeräumt werden. Sind diese aber erst einmal gewährt, liegt nicht nur das grundsätzliche Bedürfnis nach einem Wettbewerbsverbot auf der Hand, sondern gleichzeitig drängt die jetzt bestehende Interessenlage dazu, die Übertragung der Mitgliedschaft von der Zustimmung der anderen Gesellschafter abhängig zu machen. Folglich kann man einen Willen der Gesellschafter, die Satzung der ausländischen Kapitalgesellschaft so weit als möglich als Gesellschaftsvertrag einer deutschen Personengesellschaft aufrechtzuerhalten, nicht annehmen.

(3) Vertretungsrecht. Legt man die These von der Metamorphose der ausländischen Kapitalgesellschaft in eine inländische Personengesellschaft zugrunde, ändert sich mit der Verlegung des Verwaltungssitzes die organschaftliche Vertretung.

Ist das ursprüngliche Mitglied der Geschäftsführung zugleich Gesellschafter, folgt seine Vertretungsmacht nach der Umqualifizierung aus § 720 BGB oder aus § 124 HGB. Damit besteht nach dem dispositiven Recht in der GbR Gesamt- und in der oHG Einzelvertretungsmacht. Gerade die Vertretungsregel der GbR schützt insoweit die persönlich haftenden Gesellschafter. Daher kann eine Satzungsregelung der ursprünglichen Kapitalgesellschaft, nach der Alleinvertretungsmacht des Mitgliedes des Geschäftsführungsorgans besteht, nicht unbedingt in eine Regelung des Gesellschaftsvertrages der GbR umgedeutet werden, die Einzelvertretungsmacht gewährt.[65]

Ist das ursprüngliche Mitglied der Geschäftsführung Fremdgeschäftsführer, so wird in der Literatur angenommen, dass die Bestellung zum vertretungsbefugten Organmitglied in die Erteilung einer rechtsgeschäftlichen Vertretungsmacht um-

[65] AA wohl BGH 27.10.2008 – II ZR 158/06, BGHZ 178, 192 Rn. 25 = NJW 2009, 289 (Trabrennbahn); Gottschalk ZIP 2009, 948 (951); Weller FS Goette, 2011, 583 (593).

gedeutet werden könne.[66] Im Ausgangspunkt dürfte es in der Tat dem Willen der Gesellschafter entsprechen, die organschaftliche Vertretungsmacht jedenfalls als rechtsgeschäftliche aufrechtzuerhalten. Allerdings ermöglicht die ursprünglich bestehende organschaftliche Vertretungsmacht allein die Verpflichtung der juristischen Person mit ihrem eigenen Vermögen. Nach der Umqualifizierung haften für die Verbindlichkeiten der Gesellschaft nun auch die Gesellschafter nach § 721 BGB, § 126 HGB. Selbst wenn diese Haftung aus dem Gesetz folgt, würde die Umdeutung es also im wirtschaftlichen Ergebnis ermöglichen, nicht nur die Gesellschaft, sondern auch die Gesellschafter zu verpflichten. Ein solcher Wille kann den Gesellschaftern nicht ohne Weiteres unterstellt werden.[67] Eine Umdeutung ist deshalb in der Regel nicht möglich.[68]

cc) Kollisionsrechtliche und internationalzivilverfahrensrechtliche Folgeprobleme

Auch in kollisionsrechtlicher Hinsicht führt die modifizierte Sitztheorie zu höchst unbefriedigenden Ergebnissen. Jedenfalls dann, wenn der Wegzugsstaat das Gesellschaftsstatut gemäß der Gründungstheorie anknüpft, bleibt die ausländische Kapitalgesellschaft trotz Verlegung des Verwaltungssitzes aus Sicht des Wegzugsstaates als solche existent, während sie auf der Grundlage der Sitztheorie in Deutschland als Personengesellschaft besteht. Wann und wo immer also die Rechtsverhältnisse der Gesellschaft relevant werden, hängt die rechtliche Einordnung der Gesellschaft davon ab, ob das Gesellschaftsstatut gemäß der Gründungstheorie oder der Sitztheorie angeknüpft wird. Aus globaler Sicht kommt es nicht zu einem Statutenwechsel, sondern zu einer Statutenverdoppelung[69] mit der Folge eines hinkenden Rechtsverhältnisses.[70] Auf internationaler Ebene führt die Gesellschaft mithin ein Doppelleben:[71] Sie ist sowohl Kapital- als auch Personengesellschaft. Damit ist der äußere Entscheidungseinklang nicht gewährleistet und das Ordnungsinteresse des Internationalen Privatrechts verletzt.[72]

Dieses internationale Doppelleben der Gesellschaft vermag das deutsche Recht nicht völlig auszublenden. Wegen des Vorrangs des internationalen Zivilverfahrensrechts vor dem Kollisionsrecht setzt sich der Fortbestand der Gesellschaft als Kapitalgesellschaft auch im Inland durch, wenn das Internationale Privatrecht des Forumsstaates der Gründungstheorie folgt und die Entscheidung in Deutschland anzuerkennen ist.

---

66 Weller FS Goette, 2011, 583 (595f.).

67 Vgl. Eidenmüller/Rehm ZGR 1997, 89 (93f.); aA Weller FS Goette, 2011, 583 (595f.).

68 So im Ergebnis auch Lamsa BB 2009, 1416 (1418); zweifelnd Thölke DNotZ 2009, 389 (391).

69 Behrens IPRax 2003, 193 (200); Ebke JZ 2003, 927 (928); Gottschalk ZIP 2009, 948 (950); Jestädt, Niederlassungsfreiheit und Gesellschaftskollisionsrecht, 2005, S. 40 (94ff.); Münchener Kommentar zum GmbHG/Weller, 4. Aufl. 2022, Einl. Rn. 352; Weller FS Goette, 2011, 583 (593).

70 Münchener Kommentar zum GmbHG/Weller, 4. Aufl. 2022, Einl. Rn. 352; Weller FS Goette, 2011, 583 (593).

71 Gottschalk ZIP 2009, 948 (950); Walden EWS 2001, 256 (259ff.).

72 Siehe nur Kegel/Schurig, Internationales Privatrecht, 9. Aufl. 2004, S. 139f. (§ 2 III a).

c) Zwischenfazit

Einstweilen kann festgestellt werden: Die Sitztheorie kann weder in ihrer traditionellen noch in ihrer modifizierten Ausprägung überzeugen. Letztere vermeidet zwar das Problem der Inexistenz der zugezogenen Gesellschaft, führt aber selbst zu unüberbrückbaren Schwierigkeiten.

III. Die Gründungstheorie

1. Der Stand der Gründungstheorie

Die Gründungstheorie knüpft das Gesellschaftsstatut an das Recht des Staates an, nach dem die Gesellschaft gegründet wurde. Der große Vorteil dieser Anknüpfung liegt gewiss darin, dass das Merkmal stabil ist. Solange das Sachrecht dies zulässt, beeinträchtigt eine Verlegung des Verwaltungssitzes die Verfassung der Gesellschaft nicht. Vielmehr besteht die Gesellschaft, ohne ihre Existenz zu verlieren oder einer Umqualifizierung unterzogen zu werden, nach ihrem Gründungsrecht fort. Im Ausgangspunkt stellt die Gründungsanknüpfung damit zumindest für offene Märkte die überlegene Anknüpfung dar.

2. Probleme der Gründungstheorie

a) Problem des Anknüpfungsmerkmals

Anders als der tatsächliche Verwaltungssitz lässt sich der Staat der Inkorporation zumindest bei solchen Rechtsträgern, die im deutschen Rechtssystem als juristische Person angesehen werden, die also ihre Rechtspersönlichkeit von einem staatlichen Verleihungsakt, insbesondere durch Registereintragung, herleiten, leicht und sicher bestimmen.[73]

Bei Personengesellschaften kann dies jedoch anders aussehen. Ist diese deklaratorisch in ein Register einzutragen, so wird sich regelmäßig aus der Verknüpfung der Gesellschaft mit dem Register, die im deutschen Recht über den Satzungssitz (§ 707 Abs. 1 BGB, § 106 Abs. 1 HGB) hergestellt wird, das Gründungsrecht leicht ermitteln lassen.[74] Ist die Gesellschaft jedoch nicht eingetragen oder gar nicht eintragungsfähig, wird die Bestimmung des Gründungsrechts problematisch. Soweit allerdings vertreten wird, in diesem Fall sei die Sitztheorie anzuwenden,[75] kann dem schon deshalb nicht gefolgt werden, weil die Registereintragung Folge der Anwendung des Sachrechts ist, der das Kollisionsrecht vorgeschaltet ist. Daran ändert auch nichts, dass das Sachrecht in diesem Fall dennoch den Sitz der Gesellschaft an ihren Verwaltungssitz verorten kann (vgl. § 706 S. 1 BGB). Fehlt es an einer Registereintragung, sollte deshalb auf das Recht abgestellt werden, nach dem die Ge-

[73] Münchener Kommentar zum BGB/Kindler, 8. Aufl. 2021, IntGesR Rn. 371, Lieder/Kliebisch BB 2009, 338 (341); Schmidt EuZW 2021, 613 (619).

[74] Roth ZGR 2014, 168 (183, 195f.).

[75] Schön ZHR 187 (2023), 123 (137) (auch für die Zeit nach Inkrafttreten des MoPeG).

sellschaft organisiert ist.[76] Nach welchem Recht die Gesellschaft organisiert ist, kann mitunter schwierig zu beurteilen sein. Sieht der Gesellschaftsvertrag einen Sitz vor, ist das Recht des Sitzstaates maßgeblich. Ansonsten wird man auf den erkennbaren Willen der Gesellschafter und sonst auf die Rechtsordnung abstellen müssen, zu der die Gesellschaft zum Zeitpunkt ihrer Gründung[77] die engste Verbindung aufweist.

Letztendlich kann die Gründungstheorie zwar auch nicht in jedem Fall mit einem klaren Anknüpfungsmerkmal dienen, sollte aber der Sitztheorie insoweit dennoch deutlich überlegen sein.

b) Schutzdefizite

Bereits für die Sitztheorie wurde gezeigt, dass sie ihr Ziel, die in der Gesellschaft betroffenen Interessen zu wahren, nicht immer erreichen kann (→ II. 2. a) bb)). Dieses Problem stellt sich für die Gründungstheorie verschärft. Gerade unter ihrer Geltung können die Gründer eine Rechtsordnung wählen, in deren Rahmen der Schutz der betroffenen Interessen, insbesondere der Gläubiger, der Minderheitsgesellschafter oder der Arbeitnehmer deutlich schwächer ausgeprägt ist.[78]

aa) Relativierung der Schutzdefizite

Unbestreitbar ist, dass die Gründungstheorie insoweit zu Schutzlücken führt, doch lohnt sich durchaus die Frage, wie groß diese Lücke ist.

(1) Gläubigerschutz. Regelmäßig wird gegen die Gründungstheorie vorgebracht, sie laufe dem Gläubigerschutz zuwider[79] und sofern das Gründungsrecht ein niedrigeres Gläubigerschutzniveau als das deutsche Recht aufweist, kann dem kaum widersprochen werden.

Allerdings ist zu bemerken, dass viele Bereiche des Gläubigerschutzes längst nicht mehr gesellschaftsrechtlich, sondern insolvenzrechtlich qualifiziert werden. Gleichzeitig wurde der Standort dieser Regeln von den gesellschaftsrechtlichen Kodifikationen in die Insolvenzordnung verschoben. So wird die Insolvenzverschleppungshaftung (§ 823 Abs. 2 iVm § 15a InsO) insolvenzrechtlich qualifiziert[80] und die Insolvenzantragspflicht wurde mit dem MoMiG 2008 in die InsO verschoben. Selbiges gilt für die Ersatzpflicht für Zahlungen, die nach Eintritt der Insolvenzreife vorgenommen werden (§ 15b InsO),[81] die durch das SanInsFoG

[76] Roth ZGR 2014, 168 (183, 195).

[77] Roth ZGR 2014, 168 (196).

[78] Münchener Kommentar zum BGB/Kindler, 8. Aufl. 2021, IntGesR Rn. 371; Rauscher, Internationales Privatrecht, 5. Aufl. 2017, Rn. 628.

[79] BGH 27.10.2008 – II ZR 158/06, BGHZ 178, 192 Rn. 21 = NJW 2009, 289 (Trabrennbahn); Münchener Kommentar zum BGB/Kindler, 8. Aufl. 2021, IntGesR Rn. 362, 372.

[80] Schmidt, InsO/Brinkmann, 20. Aufl. 2023, EuInsVO Art. 7 Rn. 12; Münchener Kommentar zum BGB/Kindler, 8. Aufl. 2021, EuInsVO Art. 7 Rn. 58ff.; Uhlenbruck, InsO II/Knof, 16. Aufl. 2023, EuInsVO Art. 7 Rn. 118; Rauscher, EuZPR/EuIPR/Mäsch, 5. Aufl. 2022, EU-InsVO Art. 7 Rn. 20; Münchener Kommentar zur InsO/Reinhart, 4. Aufl. 2021, EuInsVO Art. 7 Rn. 9.

[81] EuGH 10.12.2015 – C-594/14, ECLI:EU:C:2015:806 = NJW 2016, 223 (Kornhaas); BGH 15.3.2016 – II ZR 119/14, NJW 2016, 2660 Rn. 14ff.; BGH 4.7.2017 – II ZR 319/15, NZG 2017, 1034 = ZIP 2017, 1619 Rn. 8; Schmidt, InsO/Brinkmann, 20. Aufl. 2023, EuInsVO Art. 7 Rn. 13; Münchener Kommentar zum BGB/Kindler, 8. Aufl. 2021, EuInsVO Art. 7 Rn. 87; Rau-

2020 in die Insolvenzordnung verschoben wurde. Ebenso hatte das MoMiG 2008 die auf der analogen Anwendung des Kapitalerhaltungsrechts beruhenden Rechtsprechungsregeln zum Kapitalersatzrecht beseitigt und in einen Insolvenzanfechtungsgrund (§ 135 InsO) umgeformt. Spätestens seither[82] ist eine insolvenzrechtliche Qualifikation vorzunehmen.[83] Die Existenzvernichtungshaftung wurde von der Rechtsprechung bereits 2007 von ihrer gesellschaftsrechtlichen Grundlage der Durchgriffshaftung gelöst und auf § 826 BGB gestützt.[84] Sie wird seither überwiegend als insolvenzrechtlich qualifiziert.[85] Im Falle einer insolvenzrechtlichen Qualifikation gelangt nach Art. 7 Abs. 1 EU-InsVO das Recht des Staates der Eröffnung des Insolvenzverfahrens zur Anwendung, wobei die internationale Zuständigkeit nach Art. 3 Abs. 1 EU-InsVO in dem Mitgliedstaat liegt, in dem der Schuldner den Mittelpunkt seiner hauptsächlichen Interessen hat, der wiederum dem Verwaltungssitz entsprechen sollte.[86] Das Ergebnis sollte also der Sitztheorie entsprechen.[87]

Gleichzeitig wurde das Gläubigerschutzrecht in Deutschland abgeschwächt. So kennt seit der Einführung der „Unternehmergesellschaft (haftungsbeschränkt)" (§ 5a GmbHG) durch das MoMiG 2008 das deutsche Kapitalgesellschaftsrecht kein zwingendes Mindestkapital mehr.

(2) Schutz der Minderheitsgesellschafter. Weiter wird gegen die Gründungstheorie vorgebracht, sie untergrabe den Schutz der Minderheitsgesellschafter.[88] Auch hier ist zwar zu konstatieren, dass der Minderheitenschutz ein zentrales Anliegen des Gesellschaftsrechts darstellt und nicht einfach zur Disposition der Gründer gestellt werden darf, doch muss man sich hier ebenso fragen, wie groß die Schutzlücke eigentlich ist.

Betrachtet man den Minderheitenschutz in einer deutschen GmbH oder einer deutschen Personengesellschaft, so fällt auf, dass das Innenrecht im weitesten Um-

---

scher, EuZPR/EuIPR/Mäsch, 5. Aufl. 2022, EU-InsVO Art. 7 Rn. 20; Münchener Kommentar zur InsO/Reinhart, 4. Aufl. 2021, EuInsVO Art. 7 Rn. 9.

[82] Bereits zu §§ 30a, 30b GmbHG aF: BGH 21.7.2011 – IX ZR 185/10, NJW 2011, 3784 Rn. 27ff.

[83] Schmidt, InsO/Brinkmann, 20. Aufl. 2023, EuInsVO Art. 7 Rn. 9; Hübner, Kollisionsrechtliche Behandlung von Gesellschaften aus „nicht-privilegierten" Drittstaaten, 2011, S. 211ff.; Münchener Kommentar zum BGB/Kindler, 8. Aufl. 2021, EuInsVO Art. 7 Rn. 96ff.; Uhlenbruck, InsO II/Knof, 16. Aufl. 2023, EuInsVO Art. 7 Rn. 121.

[84] BGH 16.7.2007 – II ZR 3/04, BGHZ 173, 246 Rn. 17ff. = NJW 2007, 2689 (Trihotel); BGH 28.4.2008 – II ZR 264/06, BGHZ 176, 204 Rn. 10 = NJW 2008, 2437 (Gamma); BGH 9.2.2009 – II ZR 292/07, BGHZ 179, 344 Rn. 15 = NJW 2009, 2127 (Sanitary).

[85] Kienle NotBZ 2008, 245 (256); Münchener Kommentar zum BGB/Kindler, 8. Aufl. 2021, EuInsVO Art. 7 Rn. 101; Uhlenbruck, InsO II Knof, 16. Aufl. 2023, EuInsVO Art. 7 Rn. 123; Lieder FS Pannen, 2017, 439 (460f.); Lieder DZWIR 2008, 145 (148); Rauscher, EuZPR/EuIPR/Mäsch, 5. Aufl. 2022, EU-InsVO Art. 7 Rn. 21; für eine deliktsrechtliche Qualifikation: Schmidt, InsO/Brinkmann, 20. Aufl. 2023, EuInsVO Art. 7 Rn. 10; für eine gesellschaftsrechtliche Qualifikation: GmbHG Großkommentar/Behrens/Hoffmann, 3. Aufl. 2019, Einl. Rn. B 117; Münchener Kommentar zur InsO/Reinhart, 4. Aufl. 2021, EuInsVO Art. 7 Rn. 7.

[86] Fehrenbach GPR 2016, 282 (288).

[87] Rauscher, EuZPR/EuIPR/Mäsch, 5. Aufl. 2022, EU-InsVO Art. 7 Rn. 18.

[88] BGH 27.10.2008 – II ZR 158/06, BGHZ 178, 192 Rn. 21 = NJW 2009, 289 (Trabrennbahn); Münchener Kommentar zum BGB/Kindler, 8. Aufl. 2021, IntGesR Rn. 372.

fang dispositiv ist[89] mit der Folge, dass sich ein Gesellschafter bei einem Beitritt ohnehin seiner Rechte vergewissern muss. Damit ist die Lage von der Beteiligung an einer ausländischen Gesellschaftsform nicht grundlegend verschieden.[90]

Anders verhält es sich bei börsennotierten Aktiengesellschaften, denn hier sind die Informationskosten in Relation zur Beteiligungshöhe häufig sehr hoch, weshalb der deutsche Gesetzgeber die Aktiengesellschaft durch das Prinzip der formalen Satzungsstrenge (§ 23 Abs. 5 AktG) gleichsam standardisiert hat.[91] Allerdings haben sich die Kapitalmärkte inzwischen internationalisiert und der Anlegerschutz hat sich vom Kapitalgesellschaftsrecht ins Kapitalmarktrecht verlagert.

(3) Umgehung des Mitbestimmungsrechts. Soweit die Umgehung des Mitbestimmungsrechts angeführt wird,[92] sollte es genügen festzustellen, dass dieses ohnehin einen löchrigen Flickenteppich von rechtsformspezifischen Einzelregelungen bildet und auch ohne die Verwendung einer ausländischen Rechtsform umgangen werden kann,[93] weshalb der Aspekt der unternehmerischen Mitbestimmung schwerlich entscheidend gegen die Gründungsanknüpfung sprechen kann.

bb) Abschwächung der Schutzdefizite im Binnenmarkt

Soweit der Binnenmarkt betroffen ist, sollte beachtet werden, dass das Gesellschaftsrecht zumindest in Teilen harmonisiert ist. Zwar mag die Harmonisierung in erster Linie das Aktienrecht betreffen,[94] doch kann erwartet werden, dass hiervon eine gewisse Modellwirkung für die Rechtsformen der geschlossenen Kapitalgesellschaft ausgeht. Im Ergebnis sollten daher die Gesellschaftsformen in der Union ein vergleichbares Schutzniveau aufweisen.

c) Zwischenfazit

Bezogen auf die Validierbarkeit des Anknüpfungsmerkmals führt die Gründungstheorie zu geringeren Schwierigkeiten als die Sitztheorie, doch gleichzeitig gewährt sie einen geringeren Schutz inländischer Interessenträger. Gegenwärtig erscheinen diese Schutzlücken indes nicht allzu groß und im Verhältnis zu den Mitgliedstaaten der Union letztlich zu vernachlässigen. Anders kann es sich aber im Verhältnis zu Drittstaaten verhalten, wo gegebenenfalls eher exotische Rechtsformen, die unter Umständen einen Interessenausgleich gar nicht anstreben,[95] zu deutlichen Schutzdefiziten führen können.

---

[89] Ebenroth/Boujong/Joost/Strohn, HGB/Born, 4. Aufl. 2020, § 109 Rn. 2; Münchener Kommentar zum GmbHG/Fleischer, 4. Aufl. 2022, Einl. Rn. 21 ff.; Münchener Kommentar zum BGB/Schäfer, 9. Aufl. 2023, § 705 Rn. 135; Staub, HGB III/Schäfer, 5. Aufl. 2009, vor § 105 Rn. 17; GmbHG Großkommentar/Ulmer/Habersack, 3. Aufl. 2019, Einl. Rn. A 21.

[90] Vgl. Hübner, Kollisionsrechtliche Behandlung von Gesellschaften aus „nicht-privilegierten" Drittstaaten, 2011, S. 234 f.

[91] Fehrenbach, Der fehlerhafte Gesellschafterbeschluss in der GmbH, 2011, S. 124.

[92] Münchener Kommentar zum BGB/Kindler, 8. Aufl. 2021, IntGesR Rn. 372.

[93] Siehe Fehrenbach ZHR 182 (2018), 191 (220).

[94] Münchener Kommentar GmbHG/Fleischer, 4. Aufl. 2022, Einl. Rn. 284; Jung/Krebs/Stiegler, Gesellschaftsrecht in Europa/Jung/Stiegler, 2019, § 18 Rn. 17 ff.

[95] Siehe Ebke ZVglRWiss 110 (2011), 2 (31).

IV. Gründungstheorie und Sonderanknüpfungen

Fragt man sich, wie das internationale Gesellschaftsrecht im Verhältnis zu Drittstaaten angeknüpft werden soll, liegt es angesichts der Schwächen der Sitztheorie nahe, zwar von der Gründungstheorie auszugehen, doch das Schutzdefizit abzumildern.

1. Modifizierte Verbandsverfassung mittels Sonderanknüpfungen

Insoweit wird häufig vertreten, die Wahrung berechtigter Interessen durch einseitige Sonderanknüpfungen sicherzustellen.[96] Allerdings gerät dieser Ansatz schnell an seine Grenzen und droht durch eine Kombination von Elementen verschiedener Gesellschaftsrechte Sinnzusammenhänge zu zerreißen. So ließe sich zwar das inländische Kapitalerhaltungsrecht mittels Sonderanknüpfung auf ausländische Gesellschaftsformen erstrecken,[97] doch führt dies zu Friktionen, wenn das ausländische Gründungsrecht Entnahmerechte gewährt, doch das inländische, im Wege einer Sonderanknüpfung zur Anwendung berufene Kapitalerhaltungsrecht diese verwehrt. Ähnlich ließen sich zum Schutz von Minderheitsgesellschaftern im Wege der Sonderanknüpfung Informationsrechte nach inländischem Recht begründen, doch könnte dies im Widerspruch zum Gründungsrecht stehen, das unter Umständen gerade wegen des Fehlens von Informationsrechten auf ein Wettbewerbsverbot verzichtet. Problematisch erscheint es auch, die unternehmerische Mitbestimmung im Wege der Sonderanknüpfung auf eine ausländische Gesellschaftsform zur Anwendung zu bringen,[98] denn die deutsche Mitbestimmung lässt sich nicht ohne Weiters implementieren, wenn das Gründungsrecht keinen Aufsichtsrat kennt.[99]

Hinzu tritt, dass sich die Gesellschaft dann in ähnlicher Weise wie nach der Wechselbalgtheorie in ein internationales Zwitterwesen verwandelt. Im Gründungsstaat und in Staaten, die der Gründungstheorie ohne die Beschränkung durch Sonderanknüpfungen folgen, bestünde die Gesellschaft in ihrer unmodifizierten, im Inland hingegen in ihrer modifizierten Gestalt. Auch bei diesem Ansatz wäre ein hinkendes Rechtsverhältnis die Folge.

2. Anwendung der Regeln zur Handelndenhaftung mittels Sonderanknüpfungen

Geeigneter, als die Schaffung einer hybriden Verbandsverfassung im Wege von Sonderanknüpfungen, erscheint es, im Falle einer nach dem Recht eines nicht privilegierten Drittstaates organisierten Gesellschaft, die Verbandsverfassung grundsätzlich unangetastet zu lassen und stattdessen im Falle der Feststellbarkeit eines in-

[96] NomosKommentar BGB/Hoffmann, 4. Aufl. 2021, EGBGB Anh. Art. 12 Rn. 148ff.; Lanzius, Anwendbares Recht und Sonderanknüpfungen unter der Gründungstheorie, 2005, S. 189ff.; Lieder/Hilser ZHR 185 (2021), 471 (500f.); Lieder/Kliebisch BB 2009, 338 (341ff.); Schmidt/Lutter, AktG/Ringe, 5. Aufl. 2023, IntGesR Rn. 80.

[97] Hierfür Altmeppen NJW 2004, 97 (103).

[98] Im Grundsatz dafür Altmeppen/Wilhelm DB 2004, 1083 (1089); Großfeld/Erlinghagen JZ 1993, 217; de lege ferenda für einführbar gehalten beispielsweise bei Eberspächer ZIP 2008, 1951; Thüsing ZIP 2004, 381 (382).

[99] Lieder/Kliebisch BB 2009, 338 (342).

ländischen Verwaltungssitzes allein die Vorschriften im Wege der Sonderanknüpfung zur Anwendung zu bringen, welche das Gesetz für eine nicht ordnungsgemäße Gründung vorsieht.

Anzuwenden wären im Falle einer juristischen Person die Vorschriften zur Handelndenhaftung (§ 54 Abs. 2 BGB, § 11 Abs. 2 GmbHG, § 41 Abs. 1 S. 2 AktG).[100] Damit würden die Handelnden einer nach dem Recht eines Drittstaates organisierten juristischen Person während der Zeit des Bestehens eines inländischen Verwaltungssitzes persönlich haften. Im Falle einer Personengesellschaft, bei der nicht alle Mitglieder persönlich und unbeschränkt für die Verbindlichkeiten der Gesellschaft haften, wäre § 176 Abs. 1 HGB anzuwenden, welcher die Gesellschafter persönlich und unbeschränkt haften lässt, wenn die Eintragung in das Handelsregister unterblieben ist.

Der Vorteil dieses Ansatzes im Vergleich zur klassischen oder modifizierten Sitztheorie besteht darin es, dass die Hereinverlegung des Verwaltungssitzes zu keinem Statutenwechsel führt. Gleichzeitig bewirkt die persönliche und unbeschränkte Haftung, dass Druck auf die Handelnden ausgeübt wird, sich einer Rechtsform des Staates des Verwaltungssitzes oder zumindest eines Mitgliedstaates zu bedienen und damit die missbräuchliche Rechtsformwahl unattraktiv zu machen. Der Ansatz stellt insoweit ein milderes Mittel dar, als die Verbandsverfassung des Gründungsrechts im Grundsatz unangetastet bleibt und nur um besondere Haftungsregeln ergänzt wird. In Anbetracht der kleiner werdenden Schutzlücke erscheint dies auch ausreichend. Der Vorteil im Vergleich zur reinen Gründungstheorie besteht indes darin, dass der verbleibenden Schutzlücke dennoch begegnet wird.

V. Ergebnisse

Betrachtet man die Problematik der Anknüpfung des Gesellschaftsrechts im Ver hältnis zu nicht privilegierten Drittstaaten, so ist zu beobachten, dass die Sitztheorie aufgrund des immer schlechter validierbaren Anknüpfungsmerkmals problematisch erscheint und der Situation, dass bei einer Gründung nach ausländischem Recht der Verwaltungssitz im Inland besteht, nicht gewachsen ist, überholt erscheint und aufgegeben werden sollte. Insoweit ist der Gründungstheorie der Vorzug einzuräumen. Deren Schutzdefizite, die heutzutage allerdings weniger schwer wiegen als zu früheren Zeiten, sind dadurch auszugleichen, dass im Falle der Nachweisbarkeit eines inländischen Verwaltungssitzes im Wege der Sonderanknüpfung die Regeln anzuwenden sind, die für die nicht ordnungsgemäße Gründung gelten, also bei der juristischen Person die Vorschriften zur Handelndenhaftung (§ 54 Abs. 2 BGB, § 11 Abs. 2 GmbHG, § 41 Abs. 1 S. 2 AktG) und bei Personengesellschaften zur Haftung beim Handeln vor Eintragung (§ 176 Abs. 1 HGB).

[100] Vgl. bereits Binz/Mayer BB 2005, 2361 (2366ff.).

ROBERT FREITAG

Internationale Rechtsfragen des Euro als gesetzliches Zahlungsmittel *de lege ferenda*

Thomas Rauscher hat sich insbesondere mit dem von ihm editierten Kommentar zum Europäischen Zivilprozess- und Kollisionsrecht nachhaltig um das unionale Kollisions- und Verfahrensrecht verdient gemacht: Der „Rauscher" erschließt diese komplexe Materie erstmals in ihrer Gesamtheit systematisch und macht sie so Praxis und Wissenschaft zugänglich. Darüber hinaus hat der *Jubilar* auch inhaltlich selbst Hand angelegt und im Internationalen Familienrecht, aber auch darüber hinaus namentlich mit seinem Lehrbuch, maßgeblich zur Durchdringung des einschlägigen Unionsrechts beigetragen. Freilich ist mit den zahlreichen Verordnungen, die im „Rauscher" so kenntnisreich kommentiert werden, das Ende der Geschichte nicht erreicht. Denn der europäische Gesetzgeber erlässt fast pausenlos neue Rechtsakte, die im Einzelfall im Konflikt mit dem bestehenden Korpus des EuIPR und EuZPR stehen, ohne dass man den Eindruck hätte, dass man sich Brüssel und Straßburg dieser Problematik bewusst wäre. Aus Sicht des Verfassers, der insoweit seinerseits vermutlich einen myopisch-verengten Blickwinkel hat, besteht dieses Defizit, das für die Wissenschaft unzweifelhaft ein Segen ist, insbesondere im internationalen Wirtschaftsrecht. Dies soll im Folgenden anhand einer sehr speziellen Problematik, die aus dem künftigen europäischen (Währungs-)Recht herrührt, näher belegt werden.

I. *Einführung*

Gem. Art. 128 Abs. 1 S. 3 AEUV, Art. 16 Abs. 1 S. 3 des Protokolls über die Satzung des Europäischen Systems der Zentralbanken und der Europäischen Zentralbank[1] bzw. Art. 10 S. 2 und Art. 11 S. 2 der Euro-EinführungsVO[2] kommt allein den von der EZB herausgegebenen Banknoten sowie den von den nationalen Zentralbanken der Mitgliedstaaten emittierten Euro-Geldmünzen der Status des „gesetzlichen Zahlungsmittels" *(legal tender, cours légal, moneta legale)* im Eurogebiet zu. Eine Definition dieses Zentralbegriffs wie auch eine Regelung seiner Implikationen im Recht der privaten und öffentlichen Geldschulden ist der Unionsgesetzgeber freilich bis zum heutigen Tage weitgehend schuldig geblieben: Abgesehen davon, dass Art. 11 S. 3 der Euro-EinführungsVO die Pflicht zur Annahme von Euro-Geldmünzen auf höchstens 50 Stück begrenzt und damit zugleich einen grundsätz-

[1] ABl. 2016 C 202, 230.

[2] Verordnung (EG) Nr. 974/98 des Rates vom 3. Mai 1998 über die Einführung des Euro, ABl. 1998 L 139, 1.

lichen Annahmezwang zumindest impliziert, existiert zu der Thematik bislang lediglich eine unverbindliche Empfehlung der Kommission aus dem Jahr 2010,[3] die auf Vorarbeiten einer Arbeitsgruppe von Vertretern der Kommission und der nationalen Zentralbanken sowie der EZB beruht.[4] Und auch der EuGH hatte sich überhaupt erst einmal in dem Urteil „Dieterich" mit der Thematik zu befassen und dies auch „nur" in einer öffentlich-rechtlichen Streitigkeit darüber, ob (und dass) die deutschen Länder den Bürgern die unbare Begleichung der Rundfunkgebühren vorschreiben können.[5] Am 28.6.2023, dh 24 Jahre nach der offiziellen Einführung des Euro als einheitlicher Währung und 21 Jahre nach Einführung des Euro-Bargeldes[6], hat die Kommission zwei Verordnungsvorschläge vorgelegt, die in dieser für die Währungsunion wichtigen Frage mehr Rechtsklarheit und damit -sicherheit schaffen sollen: Zum einen den Entwurf einer Verordnung über die Einführung des Digitalen Euro[7] (*Regulation on the establishment of the digital Euro,* kurz „Digital Euro-Regulation" oder „DER" genannt), zum anderen den Vorschlag für eine Verordnung über den Statuts des Euro-Bargeld als gesetzliches Zahlungsmittel[8] (Regulation on the legal tender of euro coins and banknotes, kurz „Euro Cash-Regulation" oder „ECR" genannt). Diese enthalten konkrete Regelungsvorschläge zu den Voraussetzungen und Rechtsfolgen der Qualifikation des bestehenden Euro-Bargeldes und des geplanten digitalen Euro als gesetzliche Zahlungsmittel, machen aber auch Aussagen zum sachlichen, persönlichen und räumlichen Anwendungsbereich der Vorschläge. An dieser Stelle ist zu Ehren des kollisionsrechtlich so ungemein versierten *Jubilars* selbstverständlich primär, wenn auch nicht ausschließlich, auf die internationalen und zum Teil auch international-privatrechtlichen Aspekte der Thematik einzugehen.

---

[3] Empfehlung der Kommission vom 22. März 2010 über den Geltungsbereich und die Auswirkungen des Status der Euro-Banknoten und -Münzen als gesetzliches Zahlungsmittel, ABl. 2010 C 83, 70.

[4] Bericht der „Euro Legal Tender Expert Group" (ELTEG) zu Definition, Anwendungsbereich und Auswirkungen des Konzepts des gesetzlichen Zahlungsmittels in Bezug auf Euro-Banknoten und -Münzen von 2010, http://ec.europa.eu/economy_finance/articles/euro/documents/elteg_en.pdf (abgerufen 28.2.2024).

[5] EuGH 26.1.2021 –C-422/19 und C-423/19, ECLI:EU:C:2021:63 = NJW 2021, 1081 (Dietrich u. Häring ./. Hessischer Rundfunk).

[6] Gem. Art. 2ff. Euro-EinführungsVO hatte der Euro mit Ende der dritten Stufe der Währungsunion bereits zum 1.1.1999 die nationalen Währungen ersetzt; bis zum 1.1.2002 war lediglich auf die Ausgabe eigenständiger Euro-Geldmittel verzichtet worden. Die während der vierjährigen Übergangszeit von 1999–2002 weiterhin zirkulierenden physischen Geldmittel in nationaler Währung galten daher rechtlich als Ausprägungen des Euro zum bereits zum 1.1.1999 endgültig fixierten Wechselkurs.

[7] Vorschlag der Kommission vom 28.6.2023 für eine Verordnung des Europäischen Parlaments und des Rates über die Einführung des digitalen Euro, COM(2023)369 endg.

[8] Vorschlag der Kommission vom 28.6.2023 für eine Verordnung des Europäischen Parlaments und des Rates über Euro-Banknoten und Euro-Münzen als gesetzliches Zahlungsmittel, COM (2023) 364 endg.

II. Grundlegendes Verhältnis zu bestehenden Regelungen

Wie bereits erwähnt sollen beide Verordnungsentwürfe das bislang nur sehr vage konturierte Konzept des „gesetzlichen Zahlungsmittels“ für die einheitlichen Währung näher präzisieren (ECR-Vorschlag) bzw. überhaupt erst auf den digitalen Euro erstrecken und diesen zugleich einführen (DER-Vorschlag). Weil Art. 128 Abs. 1 S. 3 AEUV für die Euro-Banknoten deren Status als gesetzliche Zahlungsmittel unmittelbar primärrechtlich festschreibt, war allerdings seit jeher unklar, ob der Sekundärgesetzgeber und/oder die Mitgliedstaaten in der Materie überhaupt regelungsbefugt sind.[9] Es wäre zumindest denkbar, bereits aus Art. 128 Abs. 1 S. 3 AEUV für die Euro-Banknoten sämtliche aus dem Konzept des „gesetzlichen Zahlungsmittels“ folgenden Rechtsfragen als unmittelbar und abschließend primärrechtlich geregelt anzusehen. Ein solches Verständnis strahlte auch auf die Euro-Münzen und gegebenenfalls den digitalen Euro aus. Denn zwar beruht bei diesen der Status des gesetzlichen Zahlungsmittels allein auf Sekundärrecht, allerdings wäre es zumindest für physische Euro-Münzen aus praktischer Sicht kaum erstrebenswert, diese kategorial anders zu behandeln als Euro-Banknoten.[10] Die Kommission folgt mit dem ECR-Vorschlag indes einer grundlegend anderen, bereits früher im Schrifttum[11] vertretenen und vom EuGH im Urteil „Dieterich“ bestätigten Auslegung des Art. 128 Abs. 1 S. 3 AEUV:[12] Danach enthält der Vertrag lediglich eine ausfüllungsfähige und -bedürftige Rahmenregelung, deren Konkretisierung dem Sekundärrechtsgeber (und nicht den Mitgliedstaaten) durchaus erlaubt ist. Unmittelbar aus dem Institut des gesetzlichen Zahlungsmittels folgen allerdings die in Nr. 1 der Kommissionsempfehlung von 2010 genannten zentralen Prinzipien des grundsätzlichen Annahmezwangs des Gläubigers sowie der Schuldbefreiung bei Leistung gesetzlicher Zahlungsmittel im Umfang ihres kumulierten Nominalbetrags.[13] Darüber hinaus freilich herrscht Unklarheit, die sich – unter anderem und insbesondere – auch auf die Einzelheiten des Annahmezwangs bezieht, namentlich auf die Ausnahmen von diesem.[14]

Aus dem Verhältnis zwischen Primär- und Sekundärrecht resultiert im Übrigen ein erstaunliches Defizit des ECR-Vorschlags: Zu Recht soll durch die künftige ECR dem Euro-Bargeld der Status des gesetzlichen Zahlungsmittels nicht selbst verliehen werden,[15] da dieser bereits aus den eingangs genannten, bereits existieren-

[9] Hierzu bereits Amtenbrink/Herrmann, The EU Law of Economic and Monetary Union/Freitag, 2020, Rn. 21.1, 21.53ff.

[10] Für den digitalen Euro als spezielles Buchgeld liegen die Dinge *ration materiae* anders, dazu unten III.3.a).

[11] Nachw. bei Amtenbrink/Herrmann, The EU Law of Economic and Monetary Union/Freitag, 2020, Rn. 21.59ff.

[12] EuGH 26.1.2021 – C-422/19 und C-423/19, ECLI:EU:C:2021:63 Rn. 51 = NJW 2021, 1081 (Dietrich u. Häring ./. Hessischer Rundfunk).

[13] EuGH 26.1.2021 –C-422/19 und C-423/19, ECLI:EU:C:2021:63 Rn. 46 = NJW 2021, 1081 (Dietrich u. Häring ./. Hessischer Rundfunk).

[14] Siehe erneut die Ergebnisse im Bericht der „Euro Legal Tender Expert Group“ (ELTEG) zu Definition, Anwendungsbereich und Auswirkungen des Konzepts des gesetzlichen Zahlungsmittels in Bezug auf Euro-Banknoten und -Münzen von 2010, http://ec.europa.eu/economy_finance/articles/euro/documents/elteg_en.pdf (abgerufen 28.2.2024), Ziffer 2.1.1.

[15] Vgl. in diesem Sinne explizit Art. 1 ECR-Vorschlag.

den Normen folgt. Vor diesem Hintergrund befremdet Art. 2 Abs. 2 des Vorschlags, wonach die künftige Verordnung auf Zahlungspflichten aus Fernabsatzverträgen nicht anwendbar sein soll. Offenbar meint die Kommission, bei Fernabsatzgeschäften komme eine Barzahlung aus praktischen Gründen nicht in Betracht oder werde durchgängig ex- oder wenigstens implizit abbedungen. Zwingend ist dies freilich nicht; so kommt eine Barzahlung auch im Fernabsatz durchaus in Betracht, etwa wenn die Abholung der Ware im Laden erfolgen soll oder Zahlung Zug-um-Zug bei Lieferung vereinbart ist. In diesen Fällen wäre das Euro-Bargeld zwar weiterhin nach den bestehenden Regelungen gesetzliches Zahlungsmittel, allerdings bliebe der Umfang des Annahmezwangs mangels sekundärrechtlicher Normierung auch weiterhin unklar. Art. 2 Abs. 2 ECR-Vorschlag ist daher zu streichen und sein Regelungsgehalt in die Ausnahmeregelungen der Artt. 5f. ECR-Vorschlag zu integrieren (zu diesen → III. 2.).

III. Überblick über das grundsätzliche Konzept des gesetzlichen Zahlungsmittels

1. Allgemeines

Seit jeher hat sich für die Bezeichnung der physischen Ausprägungen staatlicher Währungen im Sinne körperlicher Geldmünzen und Banknoten der Begriff des gesetzlichen Zahlungsmittels etabliert. Derartige, von staatlichen Hoheitsträgern emittierte Zahlungsmittel wurden und werden im jeweiligen Währungsgebiet rechtlich privilegiert, um die inländische Währung, deren physischer Ausdruck sie sind, gegenüber ausländischen Währungen zu stärken.[16] Zentrales Mittel hierfür ist die Anordnung eines gesetzlichen Annahmezwangs dergestalt, dass der Gläubiger einer (jedenfalls in der betreffenden Währung ausgedrückten[17]) Geldschuld grundsätzlich zur Entgegennahme ihm angebotener Zahlungsmittel im Umfang des Nominalbetrages der Schuld verpflichtet ist. Aus umgekehrter Perspektive impliziert der Annahmezwang ein Andienungsrecht für den Schuldner und bewirkt die Leistung von Geldmitteln im Umfang des nominalen Schuldbetrags die Befreiung des Schuldners von der Verbindlichkeit. Auch für das frühere autonome deutsche Währungsrecht war dieses Konzept des Annahmezwangs anerkannt. Zwar schrieb § 14 Abs. 1 S. 2 BundesbankG für die Deutsche Mark lediglich fest, dass die DM-Münzen und -Banknoten gesetzliches Zahlungsmittel waren, doch wollte der historische Gesetzgeber damit zugleich das Konzept des Annahmezwangs kodifizieren.[18] Ebenso hat der EuGH in der bereits erwähnten Entscheidung „Dietrich“ für die Euro-Banknoten zu Recht aus Art. 128 Abs. 1 S. 3 AEUV einen zumindest grundsätzlichen, wenn auch nicht unbeschränkten,

[16] Statt aller mit zahlr. Nachw. Freitag/Omlor, The Euro as Legal Tender/Siekmann, 2020, S. 1 (12f.).

[17] Zu Fremdwährungsschulden → IV. 4.

[18] Vgl. die Begründung des Entwurfs der Bundesregierung eines Gesetzes über die Deutsche Bundesbank, BT-Drs. 2/281, 34 (zu § 10 des Entwurfs). Siehe auch BVerwG 27.3.2019 – 6 C 5.18, BeckRS 2019, 10484 Rn. 22ff.

Annahmezwang abgeleitet.[19] Wohl von selbst versteht sich, dass die Barzahlung die Geldschuld in Höhe des kumulierten Nominalwertes der geleisteten Zahlungsmittel tilgt, auch wenn es bei unbaren Zahlungen ebenso liegt. Diese gesicherten Grundsätze hat die Kommission denn auch als Nr. 1 an den Anfang ihrer Empfehlung von 2010 gestellt.[20]

Demzufolge liegt der Schwerpunkt der rechtlichen Befassung mit dem Status traditioneller physischer Barmittel als gesetzliche Zahlungsmittel in der Bestimmung des exakten Umfangs des Annahmezwangs und des Kreises zulässiger Ausnahmen. Hierbei resultieren besondere Schwierigkeiten daraus, dass die Thematik am Schnittpunkt zwischen europäischem öffentlichem Währungsrecht und privatem und grundsätzlich nationalem Geld(schuld)recht angesiedelt ist – es ist gleichsam eine doppelte Matrix aus öffentlichem und privatem sowie aus unionalem und nationalem Recht zu bilden. Die bereits erwähnte Kommissionsempfehlung von 2010[21] und die vorbereitenden Erwägungen auf Arbeitsebene[22] haben die relevanten Fragestellungen[23] benannt: Sachrechtlich zu klären ist etwa, ob und bejahendenfalls unter welchen Voraussetzungen die Parteien die Erfüllung einer Geldschuld in den lokalen gesetzlichen Zahlungsmitteln abbedingen können, wobei bereits nach der Art und Weise der „Abbedingung" zwischen öffentlichem und privatem Recht zu unterscheiden ist.[24] Für das Privatrecht könnte weiter zwischen dem unternehmerischen und dem verbraucherischen Verkehr differenziert werden, ebenso zwischen individuell ausgehandelten und vorformulierten Vertragsbedin-

---

[19] EuGH 26.1.2021 – C-422/19 und C-423/19, ECLI:EU:C:2021:63 Rn. 29ff., insbes. Rn. 55f. = NJW 2021, 1081 (Dietrich u. Häring ./. Hessischer Rundfunk; ebenso zuvor BVerwG 27.3.2019 – 6 C 5.18, BeckRS 2019, 10484 Rn. 22ff.

[20] Vgl. Nr. 1 der Empfehlung der Kommission vom 22. März 2010 über den Geltungsbereich und die Auswirkungen des Status der Euro-Banknoten und -Münzen als gesetzliches Zahlungsmittel, ABl. 2010 C 83, 70; ebenso der Bericht der „Euro Legal Tender Expert Group" (ELTEG) zu Definition, Anwendungsbereich und Auswirkungen des Konzepts des gesetzlichen Zahlungsmittels in Bezug auf Euro-Banknoten und -Münzen von 2010, http://ec.europa.eu/economy_finance/articles/euro/documents/elteg_en.pdf (abgerufen 28.2.2024), S. 4.

[21] Empfehlung der Kommission vom 22. März 2010 über den Geltungsbereich und die Auswirkungen des Status der Euro-Banknoten und -Münzen als gesetzliches Zahlungsmittel, ABl. 2010 C 83, 70.

[22] Vgl. den Bericht der „Euro Legal Tender Expert Group" (ELTEG) zu Definition, Anwendungsbereich und Auswirkungen des Konzepts des gesetzlichen Zahlungsmittels in Bezug auf Euro-Banknoten und -Münzen von 2010, http://ec.europa.eu/economy_finance/articles/euro/documents/elteg_en.pdf (abgerufen am 28.2.2024).

[23] Hierzu auch instruktiv Principles, Definitions and Model Rules of European Private Law – Draft Common Frame of Reference (DCFR), https://www.law.kuleuven.be/personal/mstorme/european-private-law_en.pdf (abgerufen am 8.5.2024), S. 769ff. (Art. III.-2:108, Notes I. 1), deutsche Übersetzung des DCFR abrufbar unter https://www.elsi.uni-osnabrueck.de/fileadmin/documents/public/hsn/DCFR_%C3%9Cbersetzung_f%C3%BCr_Internet.pdf (abgerufen 8.5.2024).

[24] In dem der Entscheidung „Dietrich" zugrundeliegenden Sachverhalt hatte das für die betroffene Landesrundfunkanstalt maßgebliche Landesrecht die Barzahlung ausgeschlossen, was der EuGH aufgrund der Erfordernisse der Aufrechterhaltung des ordnungsgemäßen Funktionierens der öffentlichen Verwaltung trotz des grundsätzlich bestehenden Annahmezwangs für rechtmäßig erachtete, vgl. EuGH 26.1.2021 – C-422/19 und C-423/19, ECLI:EU:C:2021:63 Rn. 29ff. = NJW 2021, 1081 (Dietrich u. Häring ./. Hessischer Rundfunk").

gungen.[25] Weiter stellt sich die Frage nach einem Recht des Gläubigers zur Verweigerung der Annahme gesetzlicher Zahlungsmittel auch ohne Vorliegen einer diesbezüglichen Abrede, insbesondere weil die Barzahlung für ihn unzumutbar ist. Zumeist im internationalen Kontext zu erörtern ist ferner, ob die Parteien die Befugnis des Schuldners zur Begleichung seiner Schuld mit den am Erfüllungsort der Geldschuld kursierenden gesetzlichen Zahlungsmitteln dadurch wirksam ausschließen können, dass sie eine Fremdwährungsschuld vereinbaren oder ob nach dem Vorbild des § 244 BGB der Schuldner, der im Eurogebiet zu zahlen hat, allein deswegen (zumindest grundsätzlich) stets in Euro zahlen darf.

Für den digitalen Euro sind zusätzlich grundsätzliche Fragen dieses neuen Zahlungsmittels zu beantworten. Das betritt naturgemäß die technische Ausgestaltung und die Funktionalitäten des digitalen Euro, wobei auf beides hier nicht näher einzugehen ist.[26] Erwähnungsbedürftig ist freilich, dass der digitale Euro kontenbasiert ausgestaltet werden soll, wobei im Währungsgebiet ansässige Zahlungsdienstleister dazu berechtigt sind, entsprechende Konten für diejenigen Privatpersonen und Unternehmungen zu führen, denen Zugang zum digitalen Euro gewährt wird.[27] Aus diesem Ansatz folgt zugleich, dass der digitale Euro in Konkurrenz zum sonstigen bargeldlosen Zahlungsverkehr steht und die Zuerkennung seines Status als gesetzliches Zahlungsmittel dazu dient, ihn gegenüber klassischen kontenbasierten Bezahlmethoden in Euro zu privilegieren, insbesondere aber auch gegenüber den im letzten Jahrzehnt aufgekommenen „privaten Währungen“ im Sinne von *fungible tokens* wie etwa Bitcoin, Ethereum etc. Auch und insbesondere die (Möglichkeit der) Begrenzung des neuen gesetzlichen Zahlungsmittels auf das Territorium des Währungsgebietes wirft spezifische Probleme auf. Selbstverständlich ist, dass Staaten körperliche Geldmittel ihre Währung allein auf ihrem Staatsgebiet emittieren und ihnen den privilegierten Status des gesetzlichen Zahlungsmittels auch nur auf ihrem Territorium zuerkennen können. Digitale Währungseinheiten, gar solche, die mittels der Blockchain-Technologie begeben und übertragen werden, sind dagegen entmaterialisiert und damit potenziell ubiquitär. Hier muss daher festgelegt werden, welche anderweitigen Anknüpfungskriterien das klassische Territorialitätsprinzip ersetzen können.[28]

2. *Grundsätzlicher Annahmezwang nach den Verordnungsvorschlägen*

Gem. Art. 4 Abs. 1 ECR-Vorschlag und Art. 7 Abs. 2 DER-Vorschlag sollen beide Verordnungen eine Verpflichtung für den Gläubiger begründen, ihm angebotene physische bzw. digitale Euro-Zahlungsmittel mit schuldbefreiender Wirkung anzunehmen. Redundant formulieren die Art. 4 Abs. 2 ECR-Vorschlag und Art. 7 Abs. 3 DER-Vorschlag den Annahmezwang noch einmal dahingehend, dass

[25] Vgl. → III. 3.

[26] Hierzu etwa Strobel ZIP 2024, 377 (378 ff.); ausf. ECB, A stocktake on the digital euro – Summary report on the investigation phase and outlook on the next phase vom 18 Oktober 2023, https://www.ecb.europa.eu/paym/digital_euro/investigation/profuse/shared/files/dedocs/ecb.dedocs231018.de.pdf (abgerufen 28. 2. 2024).

[27] Vgl. Artt 2 Nr. 5, 13, 22, ErwGr. 9 DER-Vorschlag.

[28] Dazu näher → III. 3. b).

der Gläubiger ihm angebotene Euro-Zahlungsmittel nicht zurückweisen dürfe. Ebenfalls ohne weiteren Erkenntniswert schreiben Art. 4 Abs. 4 des ECR-Vorschlags und Art. 7 Abs. 5 DER-Vorschlag das Recht des Schuldners fest, sich durch Leistung gesetzlicher Euro-Zahlungsmittel von seiner Schuld zu befreien. Weiterhin wird für beide Erscheinungsformen des Euro in Einklang mit seit jeher geltenden Gepflogenheiten festgelegt, dass Euro-Geldschulden durch Leistung von Euro-Zahlungsmitteln im passenden Nennwert getilgt werden können (Art. 4 Abs. 3 S. 1 ECR-Vorschlag, Art. 7 Abs. 4 S. 1 DER-Vorschlag). Ergänzt wird dieses Nennwertprinzip durch ein Verbot der Erhebung von Gebühren oder zusätzlicher Entgelte auf Zahlungen in gesetzlichen Zahlungsmitteln, vgl. Art. 4 Abs. 3 S. 2 ECR-Vorschlag, Art. 7 Abs. 4 S. 2 DER-Vorschlag).

Das Verhältnis zwischen physischen und digitalen Euro-Geldmitteln regelt Art. 12 DER-Vorschlag dahingehend, dass dann, wenn nach beiden Rechtsakten eine Annahmepflicht besteht, der Schuldner entscheiden darf, ob er physische oder digitale Euro-Geldmittel leistet. Dass eine Annahmezwang nach beiden Regelungsregimes besteht, ist allerdings in der Tat keinesfalls zwingend, da die Verordnungen unterschiedlichen sachliche, persönliche und territoriale Anwendungsvoraussetzungen haben und auch die Ausnahmen vom Annahmezwang nicht inhaltsgleich geregelt sind.

3. Ausnahmen vom Annahmezwang

Die beiden Vorschläge regeln die Ausnahmen vom Annahmezwang zum Teil identisch, zum Teil unterschiedlich, wobei die Unterschiede den Besonderheiten des digitalen Euro als elektronischer Einheiten geschuldet sind.

a) ECR-Vorschlag

Nach Art. 5 ECR-Vorschlag ist der Gläubiger zur Ablehnung ihm angebotenen physischen Euro-Bargeldes in zwei Fällen befugt: Zum einen ist dies der Fall, wenn die Ablehnung in gutem Glauben, aus legitimen und vorübergehenden Gründen, im Einklang mit dem Grundsatz der Verhältnismäßigkeit und angesichts konkreter Umstände, auf die der Zahlungsempfänger keinen Einfluss hat, erfolgt (Art. 5 Abs. 1 lit. a ECR-Vorschlag). Art. 5 Abs. 2 ECR-Vorschlag konkretisiert dies beispielshaft dahingehend, dass entweder (i) der Wert der angebotenen Banknote in keinem angemessenen Verhältnis zum Wert des zu begleichenden Betrags steht, oder (ii) das Unternehmen zu dem Zeitpunkt, zu dem die Barzahlung angeboten wird, ausnahmsweise über kein Wechselgeld verfügt oder ihm infolge der betreffenden Zahlung kein ausreichendes Wechselgeld für seine normalen täglichen Geschäftsvorgänge zur Verfügung steht. Angeboten hätte es sich, auch den Fall der Zahlung sehr großer Beträge zu erwähnen, da hier die Verlust- und Diebstahlsrisiken im Einzelfall nicht mehr angemessen beherrscht werden können.

Zum anderen können die Parteien nach Art. 5 Abs. 1 lit. b ECR-Vorschlag auch vor der Zahlung einen abweichenden Zahlungsweg vereinbaren. Die letztgenannte Regelung wirft die Frage auf, ob bei derartigen Vereinbarungen zwischen dem Verkehr mit Verbrauchern im Sinne von B2C-Geschäften und sonstigen Verträgen

(B2B, C2C) zu unterscheiden ist[29] wie auch danach, ob die Abrede individualvertraglich erfolgt oder in einer vorformulierten Klausel enthalten ist. Hierzu liest man ärgerlicherweise nichts. Allerdings erwähnt Art. 2 Abs. 1 S. 2 ECR-Vorschlag, dass die Verordnung auch anwendbar sein solle, wenn ein einseitiger *ex ante* Ausschluss der Barzahlung vorliege *(ex ante unilateral exclusions of cash)*. Diese Formulierung, die sich jenseits aller privatrechtlichen Kategorien bewegt, ist grundsätzlich verfehlt: Nach der Legaldefinition des Art. 3 Nr. 4 ECR-Vorschlag soll eine *ex ante unilateral exclusion of cash* vorliegen, wenn ein Einzelhändler *(retailer)* oder Dienstleistungsanbieter *(serviceprovider)* die Barzahlung einseitig ausschließt, etwa durch ein „Kein Bargeld akzeptiert“-Schild. Hier liege, so Art. 2 Abs. 1 S. 2 ECR-Vorschlag, keine freie Vereinbarung über den Ausschluss der Barzahlung vor. Freilich handelt es sich in derartigen Fällen um den Ausschluss der Barzahlung mittels AGB und damit sehr wohl um eine vertragliche Abrede. Die Regelung sollte daher in Art. 5 ECR-Vorschlag verschoben und so formuliert werden, dass im Verkehr zwischen Unternehmern und Verbrauchern ein Ausschluss der Barzahlung in vom Unternehmer vorformulierten Geschäftsbedingungen entweder überhaupt nicht oder – was vorzugswürdig erscheint – nur gestattet ist, wenn der Unternehmer für eine solche Vereinbarung einen sachlichen Grund hat. In diesem Sinne ist zu Recht auch der Vorschlag für die DER formuliert: Dessen Art. 9 Abs. 1 lit. d, Art. 10 erklären AGB-Regelungen des Zahlungsempfängers für unwirksam, die den Gebrauch des digitalen Euro zur Begleichung von in Euro denominierten Geldschulden beschränken.

b) DER-Vorschlag

Der Vorschlag für die DER sieht in seinem Art. 9 zum Teil identische, zum Teil auch kategorial anders konzipierte Ausnahmen vom Annahmezwang vor. Mit Art. 5 Abs. 1 lit a ECR-Vorschlag wörtlich überein stimmt Art. 9 Abs. 1 lit. b DER-Vorschlag, der dem Gläubiger die Verweigerung der Annahme nach Treu und Glauben ermöglicht. Ebenfalls zugelassen ist die vertragliche Abbedingung der Annahme digitaler Euro (vgl. Art. 9 Abs. 1 lit. d DER-Vorschlag). Anders als der Vorschlag für die ECR sieht derjenige für die DER zusätzlich vor, dass Verbraucher, gemeinnützige Unternehmen und Kleinstunternehmen (jeweils wie in der Norm definiert) grundsätzlich nicht zur Entgegennahme von digitalen Euro verpflichtet sind (Art. 9 Abs. 1 lit. c DER-Vorschlag). Anderes gilt, falls diese Gläubiger digitale Euro oder sonstige vergleichbare digitale Zahlungsmittel auch sonst akzeptieren. Wann ein digitales Zahlungsmittel vergleichbar ist, ist freilich unklar und dürfte in Bezug gerade auf private Währungen (*bitcoin* und sonstige *stable coins*) erhebliche Auslegungsprobleme bereiten. Der Gesetzgeber will diesen als schützenswert erachteten „Kleingläubigern“ mit der Regelung die Obliegenheit zum Abschluss eines gegebenenfalls kostenpflichtigen, jedenfalls aber mit Verwaltungsaufwand behafte-

[29] Zu dieser Problematik vgl. Bericht der „Euro Legal Tender Expert Group“ (ELTEG) zu Definition, Anwendungsbereich und Auswirkungen des Konzepts des gesetzlichen Zahlungsmittels in Bezug auf Euro-Banknoten und -Münzen von 2010, http://ec.europa.eu/economy_finance/articles/euro/documents/elteg_en.pdf (abgerufen 28.2.2024), Ziffer 2.1.2.

ten Vertrages mit einem Zahlungsdienstleister über den Zugang zu digitalen Euro ersparen.

IV. Internationale Aspekte der Vorschläge

1. Allgemeines

Die vorgeschlagenen Neuregelungen werfen mehrere Fragestellungen im internationalen bzw. grenzüberschreitenden Kontext auf. Dabei muss zwischen den Regelungen zum räumlichen sowie zum persönlichen Anwendungsbereich der Verordnungen und klassisch kollisionsrechtlichen Aspekten differenziert werden, die freilich häufig miteinander verschränkt sind. Es versteht sich von selbst, dass beide Verordnungen aus sich heraus Geltung nur in den EU-Mitgliedstaaten beanspruchen können, da die EU nur auf ihrem eigenen Territorium Hoheitsgewalt ausüben und ihre Rechtsregeln durchsetzen kann. Während der Entwurf für eine Verordnung über den Status physischer Euro-Barmittel (ECR-Vorschlag) keine weitergehenden Vorgaben zu seinem räumlichen Anwendungsbereich enthält (zu der erforderlichen Beschränkung auf das Währungsgebiet sogleich unter → a)), enthält Art. 8 DER-Vorschlag in seinen beiden Absätzen explizite Regelungen dazu, unter welchen Voraussetzungen der digitale Euro im offline- und online-Einsatz gesetzliches Zahlungsmittel ist.

2. Der räumliche und persönliche Anwendungsbereich nach dem Vorschlag für eine ECR

Der Vorschlag für die ECR regelt ebenso wie etwa § 14 BundesbankG seinen räumlichen Anwendungsbereich nicht. Hieraus (und auch nicht aus dem Gegenschlusses zu dem sogleich zu erörternden Art. 8 DER-Vorschlags) folgt indes nicht, dass Euro-Bargeld gänzlich unabhängig von seinem Einsatz-, dh dem Zahlungsort, gesetzliches Zahlungsmittel werden soll. Infolge des oben erwähnten Territorialprinzips kann die Union den Euro-Barmitteln den Status des gesetzlichen Zahlungsmittels allein für das Unionsgebiet zuerkennen, will sie nicht in die Währungshoheit von Drittstaaten eingreifen. Hinzu kommt freilich eine weitergehende Begrenzung auf das Euro-Währungsgebiet, dh ausgeschlossen vom Anwendungsbereich sind diejenigen EU-Mitgliedstaaten, die die Voraussetzungen für die Einführung des Euro nicht erfüllen (vgl. Art. 139 AEUV), da auch in deren Hoheit nicht eingegriffen werden soll und darf.[30]

[30] Nach Art. 139 AEUV sind diese „Mitgliedstaaten, für die eine Ausnahmeregelung gilt", von den primärrechtlichen Bestimmungen des Rechts der Währungsunion ausgeschlossen.

3. *Der persönliche und räumliche Anwendungsbereich der DER nach dem Kommissionsvorschlag*

a) Allgemeines

Anders als der Verordnungsvorschlag für das Euro-Bargeld enthält derjenige für den digitalen Euro detaillierte Regelungen sowohl zu den persönlichen Voraussetzungen, die Personen und Unternehmen erfüllen müssen, um Zugang zum digitalen Euro zu erhalten, wie auch zum räumlichen Geltungsbereich des Annahmezwangs. Der diesbezügliche Regelungsbedarf beruht auf den technischen Besonderheiten dieses elektronischen Zahlungsmittels.[31] Bei Barmitteln einer Währung versteht es sich von selbst, dass diese nur im jeweiligen Währungsgebiet gesetzliche Zahlungsmittel sind und dass sie von wenn auch an beliebigen dort aufhältigen Personen und Unternehmen verwendet werden können. Auf die Konten, über die der digitale Euro verbucht wird, kann dagegen sowohl vom In- wie auch vom Ausland aus zugegriffen werden. Für ist ist zusätzlich zu klären, ob sie auch von Gebietsfremden eröffnet werden dürfen. Ohne Sonderregelung bestünde andernfalls das Risiko, dass selbst Drittstaater ohne jeden Bezug zum Euro-Währungsgebiet unmittelbar Zugang zum hiesigen Zentralbankgeld erhielten, was auch in die Währungshoheit ihrer Heimatstaaten einzugreifen drohte. Die Regelungen zum persönlichen Anwendungsbereich in Art. 13, 14 DER-Vorschlag sollen daher sicherstellen, dass nur Personen mit hinreichendem Bezug zum Währungsgebiet Zugang zur digitalen Währung erhalten (dazu sogleich → IV. 3. b)).

Hinsichtlich der Eigenschaft des digitalen Euro als gesetzliches Zahlungsmittel stellt sich die zudem die Frage nach der Lokalisierung einer Zahlungstransaktion: In der analogen Welt des Euro-Bargelds versteht sich von selbst, dass physische Einheiten der Währung nur auf dem Territorium des Währungsgebietes gesetzliches Zahlungsmittel sind (dazu → IV. 2.). Bei kontogebundenen und damit gleichsam ubiquitären Mitteln liegen die Dinge anders. Hier will Art. 8 DER-Vorschlag im Sinne einer „Bargeldanalogie" diejenigen territorialen Umstände definieren, die die Anwendung der aus dem Status des digitalen Euro als gesetzliches Zahlungsmittel folgenden Rechtsregeln gestatten.

b) Persönlicher Anwendungsbereich

Art. 13, 14 DER-Vorschlag befassen sich mit der grundsätzlichen Befähigung natürlicher Personen und von Unternehmen, Zugang zum digitalen Euro zu erhalten (Art. 13) bzw. gewähren gar einen diesbezüglichen Anspruch (Art. 14) gegen im Währungsgebiet ansässige Zahlungsdienstleister.[32]

Grundsätzlich bezugsberechtigt sind nach Art. 13 Abs. 1 UAbs. 1 lit. a DER-Vorschlag natürliche Personen mit „Aufenthalt" *(residence)* und Unternehmen mit „Niederlassung" *(establishment)* im Währungsgebiet. Für den Begriff des Aufenthalts

---

[31] Dazu bereits → III. 1.

[32] Art. 14 DER-Vorschlag begründet zu Gunsten natürlicher Personen im Sinne des Art. 13 Abs. 1 UAbs. 1 lit. a DER-Vorschlag einen Kontrahierungszwang ähnlich dem für Zahlungsverkehrskonten mit Basisfunktionen geltenden.

verweist die Legaldefinition des Art. 2 Nr. 16 DER-Vorschlag auf Art. 2 Nr. 2 der BasiskontenRiLi.[33] Letzterer stellt freilich in Bezug auf die danach anspruchsberechtigten Personen nicht auf die schlichte *residence* ab, sondern darauf, ob die betreffende Person sich *rechtmäßig* in der Union aufhält. Warum die Kommission das zusätzliche Erfordernis der Rechtmäßigkeit des Aufenthalts nicht in Art. 13 DER-Vorschlag aufgenommen hat, bleibt rätselhaft. Der Begriff der Niederlassung wird dagegen überhaupt nicht definiert. Er ist im üblichen wie auch im juristischen Sprachgebrauch vom (Satzungs-)Sitz *(seat)* abzugrenzen und dürfte damit alle rein tatsächlich im Währungsgebiet errichteten Geschäftseinheiten unabhängig davon erfassen, welchem Recht der Unternehmensträger unterliegt. Zugang haben ferner gem. lit. b natürliche und juristische Personen, die ein Konto für den digitalen Euro zu einer Zeit eröffnet haben, als sie ihren Aufenthalt oder ihre Niederlassung (beides im jeweils vorbezeichneten Sinne) in einem Mitgliedstaat hatten, dessen Währung der Euro ist und die ihren Aufenthalt bzw. ihre Niederlassung nicht länger im Währungsgebiet haben. Lit. c des Art. 13 Abs. 1 UAbs. 1 DER-Vorschlag gewährt zusätzlich der als Besucher *(visitors, visiteurs)* bezeichneten Gruppe Zugang zu digitalen Euro, wobei Art. 2 Nr. 22 DER-Vorschlag diesen Begriff in seiner Abgrenzung vom Aufenthalt näher erläutert. Diese Abgrenzung ist auch relevant, da gem. Art. 13 Abs. 1 UAbs. 2 in Verbindung mit Art. 16 Abs. 5[34] DER-Vorschlag nur Besuchern nach lit. c, nicht aber Nutzer nach lit. a, Beschränkungen bei der Verwendung des Euro als Medium zur Vermögensspeicherung auferlegt werden können. Schließlich kann der digitale Euro gem. Art. 13 Abs. 1 lit. d, e DER-Vorschlag auch an in anderen EU-Mitgliedstaaten sowie gar in Drittstaaten ansässigen Personen und Unternehmen ausgegeben werden, was freilich den Abschluss entsprechender Assoziierungsverträge zwischen der EU und den betreffenden Staaten nach Maßgabe des Art. 18 bzw. der Art. 19, 20 DER-Vorschlag erfordert.

c) Territorialer Anwendungsbereich

aa) Offline-Zahlungen

Gem. Art. 8 Abs. 1 DER-Vorschlag ist die Eigenschaft des digitalen Euro als gesetzliches Zahlungsmittel bei offline-Zahlungen explizit auf im Euro-Gebiet erfolgende Zahlungsvorgänge beschränkt. Das erfordert eine Lokalisierung der Transaktion, die indes voraussichtlich keine Probleme bereiten wird, da offline-Zahlungen nach der Legaldefinition in Art. 2 Nr. 15 DER-Vorschlag dergestalt erfolgen sollen, dass lokal in einer App (wallet) des Zahlers gespeicherte Währungseinheiten auf das in unmittelbarer Nähe befindliche Speichermedium des Zahlungsempfängers transferiert werden, was gem. ErwGr. 69 DER-Vorschlag durch Einsatz der NFC-Technologie geschehen soll. Grenzüberschreitende Sachverhalte dürften in Anbetracht dieser Übermittlungsmethode wohl allenfalls theoretisch denkbar sein.

---

[33] Richtlinie 2014/92/EU des Europäischen Parlaments und des Rates vom 23. Juli 2014 über die Vergleichbarkeit von Zahlungskontoentgelten, den Wechsel von Zahlungskonten und den Zugang zu Zahlungskonten mit grundlegenden Funktionen, ABl. 2014 L 257, 214.

[34] In Art. 13 Abs. 1 UAbs. 2 DER-Vorschlag wird stattdessen versehentlich auf Art. 16 Abs. 2 DER-Vorschlag verwiesen.

Zusätzlich verlangt Art. 8 Abs. 1 DER-Vorschlag, dass der Euro auch die sog. Schuldwährung ist, dh dass der Umfang der zu begleichenden Verbindlichkeit in Euro ausgedrückt ist.[35]

bb) Online-Zahlungen

Online-Zahlungen in digitalen Euro sollen kontogebunden zwischen Zahler und Zahlungsempfänger über die noch zu errichtende „digital euro settlement infrastructure" erfolgen, die einen Datenaustausch über das Internet erfordert (vgl. Art. 2 Nr. 14, Nr. 19 DER-Vorschlag). Bei derartigen Transaktionen schreibt Art. 8 Abs. 2 DER-Vorschlag dem digitalen Euro den Status des gesetzlichen Zahlungsmittels zu, wenn der Empfänger der Zahlung seinen Aufenthalt oder eine (beliebige) Niederlassung (wie unter → IV. 3. b) definiert) im Währungsgebiet hat. Keinerlei Rolle spielen demgegenüber der Ort des Aufenthalts bzw. der Hauptniederlassung oder der mit der Transaktionen befassten Niederlassung des Zahlers noch der – nach dem auf die Geldschuld anwendbaren Recht zu bestimmende – Zahlungsort im Sinne des Erfüllungsortes. Hinter der Anknüpfung an den Zahlungsempfänger dürfte der Wunsch nach einer Stärkung des digitalen Euro stehen, da Art. 8 Abs. 2 Vorschlag eine mittelbare Verpflichtung sämtlicher in der EU ansässiger (nicht Micro-)Unternehmen[36] begründet, sich Zugang zum digitalen Euro zu verschaffen. Erneut gilt auch diese Regelung nur für in Euro denominierte Schulden (dazu → IV. 4.).

Die räumliche Anknüpfung an den Aufenthalt bzw. die Niederlassung des Zahlungs*empfängers* wirft unterschiedliche Fragen auf: Unklar ist zunächst wie zu verfahren ist, wenn der konkrete Gläubiger die ihm angebotenen digitalen Euro aus technischen Gründen nicht entgegennehmen kann, weil er über kein entsprechendes Konto verfügt. Richtigerweise handelt es sich hier nicht um einen Fall der tatsächlichen Unmöglichkeit der Erfüllung, weil der Gläubiger sich in den von Art. 8 Abs. 2 DER-Vorschlag erfassten Konstellationen stets gem. Art. 13 Abs. 1 lit. a DER-Vorschlag einen entsprechenden Zugang zumindest verschaffen könnte. Es ist daher davon auszugehen, dass den Gläubiger nach Systematik und Telos des DER-Vorschlags eine diesbezügliche Obliegenheit trifft und er gegebenenfalls in den Annahmeverzug gerät. Umgekehrt gerät der Schuldner seinerseits nicht in den Schuldnerverzug, wenn er einem Unternehmer, der kein Micro-Unternehmer ist, die Begleichung der Schuld in digitalen Euro anbietet.

Nicht zu beanstanden ist auch, dass Art. 8 Abs. 2 DER-Vorschlag nicht voraussetzt, dass der Zahlungs*schuldner* seinerseits überhaupt über tatsächlichen oder zumindest potenziellen Zugang zu digitalen Euro verfügt. Denn der digitale Euro substituiert das physische Euro-Bargeld nicht, sondern tritt neben dieses. Zahlungspflichtige ohne Zugang zu digitalen Euro können damit ihre Verbindlichkeit stets in gesetzlichen Euro-Zahlungsmitteln erfüllen.

Gravierender ist ein weiterer gegen Art. 8 Abs. 2 DER-Vorschlag sprechender Einwand: Nach dieser Norm kann der Zahler die Leistung an den Gläubiger auf ein im Eurogebiet geführtes digitales Euro-Konto unabhängig davon leisten, ob

---

35 Zu Fremdwährungsschulden → IV. 4.

36 Zur Ausnahme der Verbraucher und Micro-Unternehmen vom Annahmezwang bereits → IV. 3. a).

die Gelder nach den einschlägigen Regelungen des Schuldstatuts (bzw. der vertraglichen Abrede) überhaupt in das Eurogebiet transferiert werden sollen. Letzteres aber ist selbst bei in Euro denominierten Geldschulden möglich, wenn Leistung auf ein einem Drittstaat geführtes Euro-Fremdwährungskonto des Gläubigers geschuldet ist. Richtigerweise sollte daher formuliert werden, dass der digitale Euro nur dann gesetzliches Zahlungsmittel ist, wenn der Zahlungserfolg im Sinne der Verbuchung des geschuldeten Betrages auf einem unmittelbar dem Zahler zugeordneten Konto im Währungsgebiet einzutreten hat. Freilich ist die defizitäre Formulierung des Vorschlags deswegen nicht von entscheidender Bedeutung, weil dann, wenn der Zahlungsbetrag nach dem Schuldstatut auf ein in Euro denominiertes Fremdwährungskonto des Empfängers in einem Staat außerhalb des Eurogebietes zu leisten ist, der Annahmezwang ohnedies wirksam gem. Art. 9 lit. d, Art. 10 DER-Vorschlag abbedungen wurde.

4. Insbesondere Fremdwährungsschulden

a) Allgemeines

Nur zum Teil geklärt ist das Verhältnis beider Verordnungsschläge zum Phänomen der Fremdwährungsschuld, dh zu solchen Zahlungspflichten, die aufgrund vertraglicher Abrede oder nach der einschlägigen gesetzlichen Bestimmung des in- oder ausländischen Schuldstatuts nicht in Euro, sondern in der Währung eines anderen Staates denominiert sind. Insoweit geht es um die Beantwortung der Frage, ob der Euro (in seiner physischen oder digitalen Ausprägung) „gesetzliches Zahlungsmittel" mit Annahmezwang für den Gläubiger auch dann ist, wenn zwar die territorialen und/oder persönlichen Voraussetzungen für die Anwendung der künftigen Verordnungen und damit für einen Annahmezwang vorliegen, die Schuld indes gar nicht in Euro zu begleichen ist. Diese Thematik liegt gleichsam quer zu den beiden Verordnungsvorschlägen. Diese befassen sich nach ihrem Wortlaut allein mit der Frage, ob der Schuldner in gesetzlichen Zahlungsmitteln leisten darf oder ob er gegebenenfalls einen anderen Zahlungsweg wählen muss, wobei insbesondere die Leistung von Buch- und E-Geld als Alternativen in Betracht kommen. Bei Fremdwährungsschulden geht es dagegen um die Frage, ob weitergehend jegliche Leistung in inländischer Währung ausgeschlossen sein soll und in der Folge in gesetzlichen Zahlungsmitteln oder sonstigen Emanationen einer ausländischen Währung zu leisten ist.

Auf der Ebene des Sachrechts wird üblicherweise differenziert zwischen „echten" und „unechten" Fremdwährungsschulden:[37] Bei der „unechten" Fremdwährungsschuld dient die (vertraglich vereinbarte oder vom Gesetz vorgegebene) Festlegung der Währung in Verbindung mit dem Betrag der Schuld primär oder allein der Bestimmung des Umfangs der den Schuldner treffenden Wertverschaffungspflicht. Dagegen spielt es aus Sicht der Parteien, insbesondere des Gläubigers, keine bzw. zumindest keine entscheidende Rolle, in welcher Währung die geschuldeten

[37] Zum Folgenden etwa beck-online.GROSSKOMMENTAR zum Zivilrecht/Freitag, Stand 15.3.2021, BGB § 244 Rn. 1.

Werte geleistet werden. Bei unechten Fremdwährungsschulden steht dem Schuldner daher etwa nach deutschem Sachrecht unter den Voraussetzungen des § 244 Abs. 1 Hs 1 BGB eine Ersetzungsbefugnis zu: Er kann eine Geldschuld, die im Inland zu erfüllen ist, in Euro als sog. Zahlungswährung selbst dann begleichen, wenn die (Wertverschaffungs-)Schuld in einer anderen Währung (sog. Schuldwährung) ausgedrückt ist.[38] Keine Ersetzungsbefugnis zu Gunsten der am Zahlungsort geltenden Währung ist dem Schuldner dagegen bei der „echten" bzw. effektiven Fremdwährungsschuld eingeräumt. Bei dieser kommt es den Parteien (dh in der Regel dem Gläubiger) entscheidend darauf an, dass effektiv Einheiten der Schuldwährung geleistet werden mit der Folge, dass Zahlungs- und Schuldwährung übereinstimmen müssen.

Umstritten und im Unionsrecht nicht geregelt ist bereits, welches Recht darüber entscheidet, in welcher Währung zu zahlen ist, dh ob eine echte oder eine unechte Fremdwährungsschuld vorliegt. Nach Art. 147 Abs. 3 des Schweizer IPRG ist dies das am Zahlungsort geltende Recht, während es im Inland zu Recht der herrschenden Ansicht entspricht, insoweit das Schuldstatut zu befragen.[39]

Anerkannt ist darüber hinaus, dass echte Fremdwährungsschulden ihrem Wesen nach dem Einsatz inländischer gesetzlicher Zahlungsmittel entgegen stehen.[40] In Bezug auf unechte Fremdwährungsschulden wurde dagegen bis zur Einführung des Euro aus der einseitigen Formulierung des § 244 BGB, wonach dem Schuldner eine Ersetzungsbefugnis bei Geldschulden zusteht, die im Inland (und damit nicht in anderen Währungsgebieten) zu erfüllen sind, die Ansicht vertreten, die Bestimmung sei zur Stärkung der hiesigen Währungen unabhängig vom Schuldstatut anzuwenden, wenn der Zahlungsort im Inland liege. Das wird freilich zumindest seit der Umstellung auf den Euro und spätestens seit Inkrafttreten der Rom I-VO vom ganz herrschenden Schrifttum abgelehnt.[41] Und auch der BGH geht davon aus, dass allein das Schuldstatut über das Vorliegen einer Ersetzungsbefugnis entscheidet.[42] Damit implizit auch der vereinzelt vertretenen These[43] eine Absage erteilt dass § 244 BGB als „Erfüllungsmodalität" im Sinne des Art. 12 Abs. 2 Rom I-VO anzusehen und daher bei Zahlungsort im Inland anzusehen sei.

[38] Näher beck-online.GROSSKOMMENTAR zum Zivilrecht/Freitag, Stand 15.3.2021, BGB § 244 Rn. 94ff.

[39] BGH 28.9.2022 – XII ZR 7/22, NJW 2022, 3644 Rn. 39; Münchener Kommentar zum BGB/Spellenberg, 8. Aufl. 2021, Rom I-VO Art. 12 Rn. 46; Staudinger, BGB/Hausmann, 2021, Rom I-VO Art. 12 Rn. 113.

[40] Vgl. BGH 28.9.2022 – XII ZR 7/22, NJW 2022, 3644 Rn. 38; Staudinger, BGB/Hausmann, 2021, Rom I-VO Art. 12 Rn. 117.

[41] Nachw. bei Rauscher, EuZPR/EuIPR/Freitag, 5. Aufl. 2023, Rom I-VO Art. 12 Rn. 26f.; Münchener Kommentar zum BGB/Martiny, 8. Aufl. 2021, Rom I-VO Anh. I zu Art. 9 Rn. 26; Münchener Kommentar zum BGB/Spellenberg, 8. Aufl. 2021, Rom I-VO Art. 12 Rn. 50 a. E.; Staudinger, BGB/Hausmann, 2021, Rom I-VO Art. 12 Rn. 117.

[42] Vgl. BGH 28.9.2022 – XII ZR 7/22, NJW 2022, 3644 Rn. 37ff., Rn. 41.

[43] Vertreten von Staudinger, BGB/Hausmann, 2021, Rom I-VO Art. 12 Rn. 117.

b) Beschränkung des DER-Vorschlags auf in Euro denominierte Geldschulden

Zumindest für den digitalen Euro ist die Bedeutung seiner Qualifikation als gesetzliches Zahlungsmittel bei Fremdwährungsschulden durch den Wortlaut des Art. 8 DER-Vorschlag geklärt: Denn zwar soll nicht der Status des digitalen Euro als gesetzliches Zahlungsmittel gem. Art. 1, wohl aber der Annahmezwang gem. Art. 8 DER-Vorschlag (und zwar unabhängig davon, ob online- oder offline gezahlt wird) davon abhängen, dass die betreffende Schuld in Euro denominiert ist. Auf Fremdwährungsschulden ist der DER-Vorschlag damit zumindest insoweit, als er den Annahmezwang normiert, von Vornherein unanwendbar. Warum dies allerdings so sein soll, dh warum der Gesetzgeber von Vornherein darauf verzichtet, den digitalen Euro zumindest als Zahlungswährung bei nicht effektiven Fremdwährungsschulden zu stärken, erfährt man bedauerlicherweise auch aus den Gesetzgebungsunterlagen nicht.

c) Fremdwährungsschulden und ECR-Vorschlag

Anders als der DER-Vorschlag enthält der Vorschlag für die ECR keine Begrenzung auf in Euro denominierte Geldschulden. Dies scheint im systematischen Gegenschluss zum DER-Vorschlag dafür zu sprechen, die physischen Euro-Geldmittel entgegen der bislang im Inland vertretenen Ansicht (dazu → IV. 4. a)) als gesetzliche Zahlungsmittel auch dann anzusehen, wenn die Schuld in fremder Währung ausgedrückt ist. Allerdings sind systematische Schlüsse im Unionsrecht in Anbetracht des teilweise zu beobachtenden Eklektizismus der europäischen Gesetzgebung häufig nur begrenzt tragfähig.[44] Vorliegend freilich stehen die beiden Verordnungsvorschläge ganz offensichtlich in ähnlich engem Zusammenhang wie die Rom-Verordnungen und sollen einander ergänzen: Das folgt nicht allein daraus, dass beide Vorschläge Bestandteil des einheitlichen „Digital Euro Package" der Kommission sind,[45] sondern auch aus Ziffer 1 der dem ECR-Vorschlag vorangestellten „Begründung"[46] wie auch aus der Konkurrenzregel des Art. 15 ECR-Vorschlag.[47] Dennoch beruhte die pauschale Annahme, dass die physischen Euro-Zahlungsmittel auch zur Tilgung von nicht in Euro denominierten Geldschulden eingesetzt werden dürfen und in diesem Fall anzunehmen sind, auf einem Trugschluss. Für die weitere Betrachtung ist dabei zwischen echten und unechten Fremdwährungsschulden zu differenzieren:

aa) Echte Fremdwährungsschulden

Jedenfalls der Wirksamkeit der Vereinbarung effektiver Fremdwährungsschulden steht der ECR-Vorschlag richtigerweise nicht entgegen. Dies folgt allerdings nicht zwingend aus der oben geschilderten grundsätzlichen Disponibilität des Annahmezwangs. Denn die Vereinbarung einer echten Fremdwährungsschuld geht in ihren

---

[44] Allg. zur interinstrumentellen Auslegung etwa Grundmann RabelsZ 75 (2011), 882ff.

[45] Vgl. https://finance.ec.europa.eu/publications/digital-euro-package_en (abgerufen 28.2. 2024).

[46] Europäische Kommission, COM(2023) 369 final, 1.

[47] Dazu → III. 2.

Wirkungen sehr viel weiter als die bloße Abbedingung der Zahlung in inländischen gesetzlichen Zahlungsmitteln; immerhin wird hier die Leistung in inländischer Währung vollständig ausgeschlossen. Allerdings gewährleisten die primärrechtliche Kapital- und Zahlungsverkehrsfreiheit gem. Art. 63 Abs. 1, Abs. 2 AEUV den grundsätzlich ungehinderten Kapitalfluss auch im Verkehr mit Drittstaaten. Ein freier Kapital- und Zahlungsverkehr (und im Übrigen ein funktionierender Außenhandel) aber setzt voraus, dass „Inländer" ihre Geldschulden unabhängig vom Zahlungsort und/oder dem Ort des Aufenthalts bzw. einer Niederlassung des Empfängers nicht nur in Euro (bzw. anderen mitgliedstaatlichen Währungen), sondern auch in sonstigen Währungen begleichen dürfen und dies bei Vorliegen entsprechender vertraglichen Abreden bzw. gesetzlicher Vorgaben selbst im Inland auch tun müssen.

bb) Unechte Fremdwährungsschulden

Im Hinblick auf nicht effektive Fremdwährungsschulden ist die Lage dagegen weniger evident und wäre eine entsprechende Klarstellung im endgültigen Verordnungstext (genauer: in den Erwägungsgründen) daher unbedingt wünschenswert. Sollte es hierzu nicht kommen, sprechen die erwähnten systematischen Überlegungen allerdings dafür, die ECR-Verordnung so zu verstehen, dass bei inländischem Zahlungsort auch in Euro gezahlt werden darf. Freilich ist dies mit dem Wortlaut des Art. 4 Abs. 1 ECR-Vorschlag nicht ohne weiteres vereinbar, weil dieser den Gläubiger zur Annahme in Höhe des Nennbetrages der ihm angebotenen Geldmittel zur Tilgung einer Gelschuld verpflichtet. Eine nicht in Euro denominierte Geldschuld lässt sich jedoch nicht ohne Währungsumrechnung überhaupt in Euro ausdrücken: Eine Schuld in Höhe 1.000 US-Dollar kann ersichtlich nicht durch Leistung von einhundert 10-Euro-Banknoten beglichen werden. Von dieser Umrechnung und dem hierfür erforderlichen Währungstausch aber ist im ECR-Vorschlag keine Rede. Es spricht daher viel dafür, dass die Frage des Vorliegens einer Ersetzungsbefugnis auf weiterhin gem. Art. 12 Abs. 1 lit. b Rom I-VO dem auf die Schuld anwendbaren Recht überantwortet wird.

V. Schlussbemerkungen

Die geplanten Regelungen zum Recht der bestehenden physischen und der noch zu schaffenden digitalen Euro-Zahlungsmittel werden für den Fall ihrer Verabschiedung eine empfindliche Lücke im Unionsrecht schließen und so für deutlich mehr Rechtssicherheit sorgen. Lässt man einmal die Frage dahinstehen, ob es eines digitalen Euro in Anbetracht des funktionierenden Euro-Buchgeldsystems überhaupt bedarf, sind die Vorhaben daher sehr begrüßenswert. Die besonderen Probleme der Fremdwährungsschulden hatte der Gesetzgeber allerdings nicht im Blick. Indem Art. 8 DER-Vorschlag die Geltung der künftigen Verordnung explizit auf in Euro denominierte Schulden begrenzt, schwächt er den Euro allerdings nicht nur gegenüber ausländischen Währungen, sondern auch gegenüber privaten Währungen im Sinne von *stable coins,* obwohl deren Emergenz den Bedarf an der Einführung des digitalen Euro in weiten Teilen überhaupt erst begründet haben dürfte. Dennoch ist an der selbstgewählten Beschränkung festzuhalten, da in einer Marktwirtschaft die Marktteilnehmer sollten bestimmen dürfen, in welchen Einheiten sie ihre Verbindlichkeiten denominieren.

THOMAS GARBER/MATTHIAS NEUMAYR

Zum Grundsatz der *perpetuatio fori internationalis* im Familienverfahrensrecht unter besonderer Berücksichtigung des KSÜ und der Brüssel IIb-VO

Auch wenn – wie der deutsche Mathematiker Georg *Cantor* (1845–1918) es formulierte – in der Mathematik die Kunst, eine Frage zu stellen, höher zu bewerten sei als die Kunst, diese zu lösen, müssen sowohl in der Mathematik als auch in den Rechtswissenschaften Fragen durch die Anwendung von Regeln und Formeln vollständig und ohne Widerspruch gelöst werden.[1] Anders als in der Mathematik ist in den Rechtswissenschaften das Ergebnis wertungsoffen. Fragen können unterschiedlich beantwortet, Gesetzestexte und Gerichtsentscheidungen ungleich interpretiert werden. In beiden Disziplinen sind allerdings Systematik und Logik von großer und entscheidender Bedeutung. Das analytische Denken und die präzise Herangehensweise des Mathematikers wendet der Jurist und Mathematiker *Thomas Rauscher* in seinem juristischen Werk an. Sein wissenschaftliches Schaffen ist bemerkenswert: Er ist nicht nur Verfasser zahlreicher Untersuchungen, sondern auch Herausgeber einer der größten und bedeutsamsten Kommentarreihe zum Europäischen Zivilprozess- und Kollisionsrecht, an der sowohl der Erst- und als auch der Zweitverfasser als Autoren mitwirken dürfen. Der vorliegende Beitrag ist dem Jubilar mit den herzlichsten Glückwünschen zu seinem Geburtstag gewidmet.

I. *Begriff und Bedeutung des Grundsatzes der perpetuatio fori*

Nach dem Grundsatz der *perpetuatio fori* genügt es, dass das Gericht zu Beginn des Verfahrens – in aller Regel im Zeitpunkt der Einreichung der Klage oder des verfahrenseinleitenden Antrags bei Gericht[2] oder, sofern das Verfahren von Amts wegen eingeleitet wird, im Zeitpunkt, in dem das Gericht eine erste Verfahrenshandlung vornimmt[3] – zuständig ist.[4] Der Umstand, dass die zuständigkeitsbegrün-

[1] Siehe auch Radbruch, Mathematik in den Geisteswissenschaften, 1989, passim; Risse, Mathematik, Statistik und die Juristerei, NJW 2020, 2383.

[2] Für Österreich siehe Fasching/Konecny, Kommentar zu den Zivilprozessgesetzen/Scheuer, 3. Aufl. 2013, JN § 29 Rn. 4; für Deutschland Musielak/Voit, ZPO/Foerste, 21. Aufl. 2024, § 261 Rn. 3 (Zustellung der Klage an den Gegner) sowie Münchner Kommentar zum FamFG/Pabst, 3. Aufl. 2018, § 2 Rn. 16. Im Anwendungsbereich der Europäischen Verordnungen wird der Zeitpunkt der Rechtshängigkeit unionsrechtlich autonom bestimmt (vgl. etwa Art. 17 lit. a und b Brüssel IIb-VO).

[3] Für Österreich § 12 AußStrG; in Deutschland ist in Verfahren in Familiensachen und in den Angelegenheiten der freiwilligen Gerichtsbarkeit der Zeitpunkt, in dem das Gericht Tatsachen er-

denden Umstände zu einem späteren Zeitpunkt entfallen, führt nicht zur Unzuständigkeit des angerufenen Gerichts; vielmehr wird die zu Beginn des Verfahrens bestehende örtliche, sachliche und internationale Zuständigkeit perpetuiert.

Die Aufrechterhaltung der Zuständigkeit des angerufenen Gerichts dient insbesondere der Verfahrensökonomie[5] und der Sicherstellung von Stabilität und Kontinuität der Zuständigkeit (dazu → III. 1. e)). Der Wechsel des Gerichts und die dadurch bedingte Neudurchführung des Verfahrens würden einen höheren Zeit- und Kostenaufwand verursachen.[6] Dies gilt umso mehr, wenn die Änderung der zuständigkeitsbegründenden Umstände die internationale Unzuständigkeit des Staats, dessen Gerichte angerufen wurden, bewirken würde. In diesem Fall gelten für das neu durchzuführende Verfahren möglicherweise ganz andere Bedingungen – wie etwa hinsichtlich der Einbringung der Klage, ihrer Form- und Inhaltsvoraussetzungen oder der Gerichtssprache.

Der Grundsatz der *perpetuatio fori* bewirkt allerdings nicht, dass ein bei Gerichtsanhängigkeit[7] unzuständiges Gericht unzuständig bleibt, wenn die fehlenden Zuständigkeitsmerkmale erst nach diesem Zeitpunkt eintreten. Änderungen, die dazu führen, dass das (zuvor unzuständige) Gericht zuständig wird, sind grundsätzlich zu beachten (dazu → VII.).

II. Geltung des Grundsatzes der perpetuatio fori

Während der Grundsatz der *perpetuatio fori* im innerstaatlichen Recht Österreichs (§ 29 JN)[8] und Deutschlands (§ 261 Abs. 3 dZPO, § 2 Abs. 2 FamFG)[9] für die ört-

---

fährt, die ein Einschreiten gebieten, entscheidend (Münchener Kommentar zum FamFG/Pabst, 3. Aufl. 2018, § 2 Rn. 17 mwN). Im Anwendungsbereich der Europäischen Verordnungen wird der Zeitpunkt der Rechtshängigkeit unionsrechtlich autonom bestimmt (vgl. etwa Art. 17 lit. a und c Brüssel IIb-VO).

[4] Zur Frage, ob der Grundsatz der *perpetuatio fori* auch bei der Zulässigkeit des Rechtswegs gilt, siehe Rechberger/Simotta, Grundriss des Zivilprozessrechts, 9. Aufl. 2017, Rn. 243 sowie Gitschthaler/Höllwerth, AußStrG/Kodek, 2. Aufl. 2019, § 1 Rn. 168; für Deutschland § 17 Abs. 1 GVG.

[5] Vgl. etwa Jacobs, Die perpetuatio fori im internationalen Recht des Zivilprozesses und der freiwilligen Gerichtsbarkeit, 1962 passim.

[6] BGH 1.2.1978 – IV ZR 142/77, BGHZ 70, 295 = NJW 1978, 949.

[7] Siehe Fn. 2 und 3.

[8] Der Grundsatz gilt in Österreich für die sachliche, örtliche und internationale Zuständigkeit (jedenfalls) im streitigen und außerstreitigen Verfahren (§ 29 JN), siehe Kodek/Oberhammer, ZPO-ON/Rassi, 2023, JN § 29 Rn. 9 ff.; Fasching/Konecny, Kommentar zu den Zivilprozessgesetzen/Scheuer, 3. Aufl. 2013, JN § 29 Rn. 4; zur ausnahmsweisen Durchbrechung siehe § 111 JN (für das Pflegschaftsverfahren) und § 120 JN (für das Firmenbuch und bestimmte gesellschaftsrechtliche Ansprüche).

[9] Der Grundsatz gilt in Deutschland nach § 261 Abs. 3 dZPO für die sachliche und örtliche und – zumindest nach hA – für die internationale Zuständigkeit (Löser, Zuständigkeitsbestimmender Zeitpunkt und perpetuatio fori im internationalen Zivilprozess, 2009, S. 36 ff.; Stein/Jonas, ZPO/Roth, 23. Aufl. 2016, § 261 Rn. 40; aA Damrau FS Bosch, 1976, 103 [112 ff.]) und nach § 2 Abs. 2 FamFG für die örtliche Zuständigkeit. Die Bestimmung ist analog auf die sachliche Zuständigkeit anzuwenden (vgl. Münchener Kommentar zum FamFG/Pabst, 3. Aufl. 2018, § 2 Rn. 36). Hinsichtlich der internationalen Zuständigkeit wird der Grundsatz im Anwendungsbereich des FamFG nur eingeschränkt anerkannt und dessen Geltung insbesondere bei Bestehen

liche und zumindest zum Teil für die sachliche und die internationale Zuständigkeit ausdrücklich normiert ist und auch – als ungeschriebenes Prinzip des Unionsrechts – uneingeschränkt im Anwendungsbereich der Brüssel Ia-VO[10] und anderer Verordnungen zum Europäischen Zivilverfahrensrecht[11] einschließlich der Verordnungen, die das Internationale Familienverfahrensrecht[12] betreffen, gilt, findet er in Verfahren hinsichtlich der elterlichen Verantwortung nicht in allen Fällen Anwendung.[13] Im Folgenden wird die Frage untersucht, ob und unter welchen Voraussetzungen der Grundsatz der *perpetuatio fori* in diesen Verfahren *de lege lata* gilt und *de lege ferenda* gelten soll.

III. Zum Grundsatz der perpetuatio fori in Verfahren betreffend die elterliche Verantwortung

1. Zum Grundsatz der perpetuatio fori bei Anknüpfung an den gewöhnlichen Aufenthalt des Kindes

a) Allgemeines

Nach Art. 1 MSA, Art. 5 KSÜ und Art. 7 Abs. 1 Brüssel IIb-VO sind für Verfahren betreffend die elterliche Verantwortung die Gerichte (bzw. Behörden) des Mitgliedstaats, in dem sich der gewöhnliche Aufenthalt des Kindes befindet, zuständig.[14] Die dadurch entstehende räumliche Nähe zwischen Forum und Kind dient

von Fürsorgeinteressen verneint (vgl. Münchener Kommentar zum FamFG/Pabst, 3. Aufl. 2019, § 2 Rn. 33 sowie Sternal, FamFG/Sternal, 21. Aufl. 2023, § 2 Rn. 32.

[10] Geimer/Schütze, EuZVR/Geimer, 4. Aufl. 2020, EuGVVO Art. 4 Rn. 173; Stadler JZ 1999, 1089 (1098); Stein/Jonas, ZPO/Roth, 23. Aufl. 2016 § 261 Rn. 40; Wilske/Kocher NJW 2000, 3550; in diese Richtung auch EuGH 5.2.2004 C-18/02,, ECLI:EU:C:2004:74 Rn. 37 (Danmarks Rederiforening); vgl. auch Schlosser/Hess, EU-ZPR/Schlosser, 5. Aufl. 2021, EuGVVO Vor Art. 4-35 Rn. 7, nach dessen Ansicht sich der Grundsatz der *perpetuatio fori* (wenn schon nicht nach der Verordnung selbst) aus dem autonomen Recht ergebe.

[11] Zur EuErbVO siehe Mayr, Handbuch des europäischen Zivilverfahrensrechts/Wittwer, 2. Aufl. 2023, Rn. 7.67.

[12] Zur Brüssel IIa-VO/Brüssel IIb-VO siehe für Ehesachen iSd Art. 1 Abs. 1 Brüssel IIa-VO/ Brüssel IIb-VO Gitschthaler, Internationales Familienrecht/Garber, 2019, Brüssel IIa-VO Art. 3 Rn. 6 und Rn. 78, Art. 4 Rn. 19, sowie Art. 6 Rn. 19; Mayr, Handbuch des europäischen Zivilverfahrensrechts/Neumayr/Weber, 2. Aufl. 2023, Rn. 4.106; zur EuUnterhaltsVO siehe Gitschthaler, Internationales Familienrecht/Fuchs, 2019, EuUVO Vorbem Kap II Rn. 16; zur EU-EheGüterVO und zur EU-LP-GüterVO siehe Gitschthaler, Internationales Familienrecht/Weber, 2019, EuEhegüterVO Vor Art. 4 Rn. 27 und EuPartnergüterVO Vor Art. 4 Rn. 27.

[13] Auch im Anwendungsbereich des ErwSÜ gilt der Grundsatz der *perpetuatio fori* nicht (siehe dazu Traar/Pesendorfer/Lagger-Zach/Fritz/Barth, Erwachsenenschutzrecht, 2. Aufl. 2023, HESÜ Vor Art 5 Rn. 7). Der OGH hat in seiner Entscheidung vom 26.5.2021, 2 Ob 45/21p (2 Ob 46/21k, 2 Ob 62/21p), NZ 2022, 97, hat – methodisch allerdings wenig überzeugend – den Grundsatz bei der internationalen Zuständigkeit nach dem Rechtshilfe-Vertrag zwischen der Republik Österreich und dem Fürstentum Liechtenstein über Rechtshilfe, Beglaubigung, Urkunden und Vormundschaft v. 13.3.1956 (BGBl. 1956/213 i.d.g.F.) für „Vormundschaft und Pflegschaft" angenommen (dazu krit. Garber NZ 2022, 74).

[14] Vgl. auch Kress, Internationale Zuständigkeit für elterliche Verantwortung in der Europäischen Union, 2006, S. 108.

dem Kindeswohl.[15] Das Kind kann nämlich unmittelbar vor dem Gericht gehört werden, ohne dass eine u. U. aufwändige und grenzüberschreitende Anreise zum Gericht erforderlich ist. Häufig, was freilich nicht zwingend der Fall ist, ist das Kind der Sprache des Staats, in dem es sich gewöhnlich aufhält, mächtig, sodass die Anhörung des Kindes durch das Gericht ohne Beiziehung eines Dolmetschers erfolgen kann. Die verfahrensbedingten Belastungen für das Kind werden durch die Zuständigkeit der Gerichte im Staat des gewöhnlichen Aufenthalts daher im Allgemeinen erheblich verringert.[16]

Durch die Zuständigkeit der Gerichte des Staats, in dem das Kind seinen gewöhnlichen Aufenthalt hat, soll zudem gewährleistet werden, dass das – zumindest in der Regel – sachnächste Gericht entscheidet.[17] Die Gerichte des Staats, in dem sich der gewöhnliche Aufenthalt des Kindes befindet, können in der Regel die familiären und sozialen Verhältnisse des Kindes am raschesten und am einfachsten klären.[18] Die Gerichte können grundsätzlich am schnellsten tätig werden[19] und die Rechtssache aufgrund der Sach- und Beweisnähe ohne Verzögerungen, die etwa durch eine grenzüberschreitende Beweisaufnahme entstehen würden, entscheiden.[20]

Da auch das Kollisionsrecht in vielen Fällen an den gewöhnlichen Aufenthalt des Kindes anknüpft, bewirkt die Zuständigkeit des Staats, in dem das Kind seinen gewöhnlichen Aufenthalt hat, einen Gleichlauf zwischen *forum* und *ius*.[21] Durch die Anknüpfung an den gewöhnlichen Aufenthalt des Kindes wird daher (zumindest grundsätzlich) auch eine Rechtsnähe gewährleistet.[22] Die Gerichte des Staats, in dem sich der gewöhnliche Aufenthalt des Kindes befindet, können die Rechtssache entscheiden, ohne ausländisches Recht anwenden zu müssen. Aus diesem Grund können sie in der Regel am schnellsten über die Rechtssache entscheiden. Der Gleichlauf zwischen Zuständigkeit und anwendbarem Recht führt auch zu einer höheren Richtigkeitsgewähr von Entscheidungen.[23]

---

[15] ErwGr. 20 Brüssel IIb-VO; vgl. auch Garber/Neumayr GS Mankowski (im Erscheinen).

[16] Coester-Waltjen FamRZ 2005, 241 (242); Münchener Kommentar zum FamFG/Gottwald, 3. Aufl. 2019, Brüssel IIa-VO Art. 8 Rn. 4; Hausmann, Internationales und Europäisches Familienrecht, 3. Aufl. 2024, F Rn. 95.

[17] Geimer/Schütze, Internationaler Rechtsverkehr/Dilger, 66. EL 1/2023, VO Nr 2201/2003 Art. 8 Rn. 1; Gitschthaler, Internationales Familienrecht/Garber, 2019, Brüssel IIa-VO Art. 8 Rn. 3; vgl. auch EuGH 23.12.2009 – C-403/09, ECLI:EU:C:2009:810 = BeckRS 2010, 90184 (Detiček/Sgueglia) sowie EuGH 27.10.2016 – C-428/15, ECLI:EU:C:2016:819 = BeckRS 2016, 82546 (Child and Family Agency/J. D.).

[18] Coester-Waltjen FamRZ 2005, 241 (242).

[19] Hausmann, Internationales und Europäisches Familienrecht, 3. Aufl. 2024, F Rn. 95 und 516; Rauscher, EuZPR/EuIPR/Rauscher, 4. Aufl. 2015, Brüssel IIa-VO Art. 8 Rn. 6.

[20] Vgl. auch Rauscher, EuZPR/EuIPR/Rauscher, 4. Aufl. 2015, Brüssel IIa-VO Art. 8 Rn. 6.

[21] Häufig wird das Gleichlaufprinzip allerdings ohnehin als Grundnorm statuiert (vgl. Art. 15 Abs. 1 KSÜ).

[22] Geimer/Schütze, Internationaler Rechtsverkehr/Dilger, 66. EL 2023, VO Nr 2201/2003 Art. 8 Rn. 1; Garber, Internationale Zuständigkeit für Verfahren betreffend die elterliche Verantwortung, in: Garber/Lugani, Die Brüssel IIb-Verordnung: Zuständigkeit, Anerkennung und Vollstreckung in Ehesachen und Kindschaftssachen einschließlich der internationalen Kindesentführung, 2022, Rn. 6/4.

[23] Dazu allgemein Hausmann, Internationales und Europäisches Familienrecht, 3. Aufl. 2024, F Rn. 394 und 460.

Zudem wird durch die Zuständigkeit der Gerichte des Staats, in dem das Kind seinen gewöhnlichen Aufenthalt hat, eine allfällig erforderliche Kommunikation zwischen den zuständigen Gerichten und dem Jugendamt, dem Kinder- und Jugendhilfeträger und anderen staatlichen Stellen erleichtert.[24]

b) KSÜ

aa) Grundregel und Ausnahmen

In Art. 5 Abs. 2 KSÜ wird ausdrücklich normiert, dass – mit Ausnahme des widerrechtlichen Verbringens eines Kindes – durch die Verlegung des gewöhnlichen Aufenthalts des Kindes von einem Vertragsstaat die Behörden des anderen Staats von diesem Zeitpunkt an international zuständig sind.[25] Dass der Grundsatz der *perpetuatio fori* nicht gilt, entspricht auch der herrschenden Ansicht[26] zum MSA, das – im Unterschied zum KSÜ – insofern keine ausdrückliche Regelung enthält.

Der Wechsel des gewöhnlichen Aufenthalts des Kindes entzieht daher den Behörden des Staats, in dem sich bislang der gewöhnliche Aufenthalt des Kindes befunden hat, unmittelbar die internationale Zuständigkeit;[27] dies gilt auch dann, wenn das Verfahren im früheren Aufenthaltsstaat des Kindes im Zeitpunkt des Aufenthaltswechsels bereits anhängig ist.[28] Der Vorschlag, die Zuständigkeit des Staats des bisherigen gewöhnlichen Aufenthalts des Kindes während einer bestimmten Zeitspanne aufrechtzuerhalten, fand keinen Eingang in die in Kraft getretene Fassung des Übereinkommens.[29]

---

[24] Garber, Internationale Zuständigkeit für Verfahren betreffend die elterliche Verantwortung, in Garber/Lugani, Die Brüssel IIb-Verordnung: Zuständigkeit, Anerkennung und Vollstreckung in Ehesachen und Kindschaftssachen einschließlich der internationalen Kindesentführung, 2022, Rn. 6/5 mwN.

[25] Im Rahmen der Vertragsverhandlungen zum KSÜ wurde vorgeschlagen, dass sich die Frage, ob der Grundsatz der *perpetuatio fori* gelte, nach innerstaatlichem Recht bestimmen solle (Lagarde, Übereinkommen vom 19. Oktober 1996 über die Zuständigkeit, das anzuwendende Recht, die Anerkennung, Vollstreckung und Zusammenarbeit auf dem Gebiet der elterlichen Verantwortung und der Maßnahmen zum Schutz von Kindern, Erläuternder Bericht, 1996, Rn. 42). Der dafür notwendige Rückgriff auf das innerstaatliche Recht hätte das Ziel des Übereinkommens, die internationale Zuständigkeit einheitlich zu regeln und dadurch Konflikte zwischen ihren Rechtssystemen in Bezug auf die Zuständigkeit zu verhindern, konterkariert.

[26] BGH 5.6.2002 – XII ZB 74/00, BGHZ 151, 63 = NJW 2002, 2955; siehe auch RIS-Justiz RS0046199 (T 1); NomosKommentar BGB/Benicke, 4. Aufl. 2021, MSA Art. 1 Rn. 3; Hausmann, Internationales und Europäisches Familienrecht, 3. Aufl. 2024, F Rn. 121 und 525.

[27] OLG Karlsruhe 12.11.2013 – 5 UF 139/11, BeckRS 2014, 4656 = FamRZ 2014, 1565; KG 2.3.2015 – 3 UF 156/14, BeckRS 2015, 5918 = IPRax 2016, 372 mzustAnm Heiderhoff IPRax 2016, 335 = NZFam 2015, 474 mAnm Rentsch; OLG Stuttgart 24.2.2020 – 18 WF 11/20, NJOZ 2020, 1356; siehe auch RIS-Justiz RS0128438; Benicke IPRax 2013, 44 (48); NomosKommentar BGB/Benicke, 4. Aufl. 2021, KSÜ Art. 5 Rn. 3; Gitschthaler, Internationales Familienrecht/Huter, 2019, KSÜ Art. 5 Rn. 68; Schulz FamRZ 2011, 156 (158); Münchener Kommentar zum FamFG/Wiedemann, 3. Aufl. 2021, KSÜ Art. 5 Rn. 18.

[28] KG 2.3.2015 – 3 UF 156/14, BeckRS 2015, 5918 = IPRax 2016, 372 mzustAnm Heiderhoff IPRax 2016, 335 = NZFam 2015, 474 mAnm Rentsch; Roth/Döring FuR 1999, 195 (199f.); Siehr RabelsZ 62 (1998), 464 (478).

[29] Näheres hierzu bei Lagarde, Übereinkommen vom 19. Oktober 1996 über die Zuständigkeit, das anzuwendende Recht, die Anerkennung, Vollstreckung und Zusammenarbeit auf dem Gebiet

Als Begründung für die Nichtgeltung des Grundsatzes der *perpetuatio fori* wird der Schutzzweck des Art. 5 KSÜ angeführt, dem der Gedanke zugrunde liegt, dass die Behörden im Staat des gewöhnlichen Aufenthalts die für Notwendigkeit, Art und Umfang von Schutzmaßnahmen maßgebenden sozialen und familiären Verhältnisse des Kindes am besten und schnellsten ermitteln können.[30] Durch die Verlegung des gewöhnlichen Aufenthalts entfällt die die Zuständigkeit legitimierende räumliche Nähe des Kindes zu der angerufenen Behörde.[31]

Die angerufene Behörde hat bei einem Wechsel des gewöhnlichen Aufenthalts des Kindes in einen anderen Vertragsstaat die Unzuständigkeit auszusprechen. Dies gilt auch im Rechtsmittelverfahren.[32] Zur Frage, ob bereits erlassene Entscheidungen Bestand haben, → III. 1. b) bb). Erlässt die Behörde trotz Wechsel des gewöhnlichen Aufenthalts im Verfahren erster Instanz eine Entscheidung, ist diese nichtig und daher aufzuheben.[33]

Das KSÜ sieht allerdings drei Fälle vor, in denen der Grundsatz der *perpetuatio fori* Anwendung findet:

– Die Verneinung der *perpetuatio fori* gilt zum einen nur für rechtmäßige Aufenthaltswechsel des Kindes innerhalb der Vertragsstaaten, während im Falle eines widerrechtlichen Aufenthaltswechsels des Kindes Art. 7 KSÜ eingreift und ein Zuständigkeitswechsel blockiert wird.[34] Art. 7 KSÜ stellt allerdings keine allgemeine Regelung der *perpetuatio fori* dar, weil die Zuständigkeit auch dann aufrecht bleibt, wenn noch kein Verfahren anhängig ist.[35]
– Der Grundsatz der *perpetuatio fori* wird von Art. 5 Abs. 2 KSÜ nur in einer Konstellation verneint, in welcher der Aufenthaltswechsel zwischen zwei Vertragsstaaten erfolgt, während bei einem Aufenthaltswechsel in einen Drittstaat unter Umständen *perpetuatio fori* eintreten kann (dazu → VI.).
– Bei Anwendung des Art. 10 KSÜ ist nach dessen ausdrücklichen Wortlaut ua maßgeblich, dass einer der Elternteile „zu Beginn des Verfahrens" seinen gewöhnlichen Aufenthalt in diesem Staat hat, sodass ein späterer Wechsel des gewöhnlichen Aufenthalts nicht schadet.[36]

---

der elterlichen Verantwortung und der Maßnahmen zum Schutz von Kindern, Erläuternder Bericht, 1996, Rn. 41.

[30] Hausmann, Internationales und Europäisches Familienrecht, 3. Aufl. 2024, F Rn. 524; Rauscher, EuZPR/EuIPR/Hilbig-Lugani, 4. Aufl. 2016, KSÜ Art. 5 Rn. 15.

[31] Gruber IPRax 2013, 409 (410); Hausmann, Internationales und Europäisches Familienrecht, 3. Aufl. 2024, F Rn. 24; Rauscher, EuZPR/EuIPR/Hilbig-Lugani, 4. Aufl. 2016, KSÜ Art. 5 Rn. 15.

[32] NomosKommentar BGB/Benicke, 4. Aufl. 2021, KSÜ Art. 5 Rn. 4; aA Geimer/Schütze, Internationaler Rechtsverkehr/Gruber, 66. EL 1/2023, KSÜ Art. 5 Rn. 5, wonach eine *perpetuatio fori* anzunehmen sei, wenn sich die Rechtsmittelinstanz allein auf eine rechtliche Nachprüfung beschränke.

[33] Rauscher, EuZPR/EuIPR/Hilbig-Lugani, 4. Aufl. 2016, KSÜ Art. 5 Rn. 13; OGH 20.12.2012 – 5 Ob 104/12y (5 Ob 201/12p), EF-Z 2013/156 mAnm Nademleinsky = EvBl 2013/71 = iFamZ 2013/77 mAnm Fucik = IPRax 2014, 183 mAnm Heindler IPRax 2014, 201.

[34] Dazu ausführlich Rauscher, EuZPR/EuIPR/Hilbig-Lugani, 4. Aufl. 2016, KSÜ Art. 7 Rn. 1 ff.

[35] Gitschthaler, Internationales Familienrecht/Huter, 2019, KSÜ Art. 7 Rn. 17 f.; Krah, Das Haager Kinderschutzübereinkommen, 2004, S. 158.

[36] Rauscher, EuZPR/EuIPR/Hilbig-Lugani, 4. Aufl. 2016, KSÜ Art. 10 Rn. 12.

bb) Zur Bestandskraft bereits erlassener Entscheidungen

Nach Art. 14 KSÜ bleiben, selbst wenn durch eine Änderung der Umstände – wie dem Wechsel des gewöhnlichen Aufenthalts – die Grundlage der Zuständigkeit wegfällt, die nach den Art. 5 bis 10 KSÜ getroffenen Maßnahmen innerhalb ihrer Reichweite so lange in Kraft, bis die nach diesem Übereinkommen zuständigen Behörden sie ändern, ersetzen oder aufheben (siehe auch die insofern vergleichbare Regelung des Art. 5 Abs. 1 MSA). Dadurch soll sichergestellt werden, dass nicht durch ein Entfallen einer bereits erlassenen Entscheidung eine Schutzlücke entsteht, bis die Behörde des Staats, in dem sich nunmehr der gewöhnliche Aufenthalt befindet, eine entsprechende Entscheidung erlassen hat.[37]

Die Beurteilung der Frage, ab welchem Zeitpunkt eine ihrem Bestand geschützte Entscheidung vorliegt, führt zu Friktionen.[38] Zum Teil wird vertreten, dass der Zeitpunkt der letzten mündlichen Verhandlung maßgeblich sei.[39] Die Auffassung ist nicht mit dem Wortlaut der Bestimmung, wonach eine Entscheidung bereits vorliegen muss (arg: „die […] getroffene Maßnahme"), vereinbar, weil zum Zeitpunkt der letzten mündlichen Verhandlung in aller Regel noch keine Entscheidung vorhanden ist.[40] Auch der Zeitpunkt, in dem die erste Instanz die Entscheidung erlässt, kann nicht maßgeblich sein;[41] andernfalls würde – gegen den Willen der Verfasser des KSÜ – eine versteckte *perpetuatio fori* eintreten: Ist das Gericht der zweiten (oder höheren) Instanz eine Tatsacheninstanz, könnte sie den Wechsel des gewöhnlichen Aufenthalts nicht unberücksichtigt lassen. Ist demgegenüber die Kompetenz des Rechtsmittelgerichts auf eine Prüfung von Rechtsfragen beschränkt, könnte sie die Tatsache des Wechsels des gewöhnlichen Aufenthalts nicht neu bewerten. Daraus ergibt sich, dass für Art. 14 KSÜ der Zeitpunkt der Erlassung der Entscheidung durch die letzte Tatsacheninstanz maßgeblich ist.[42] Nur unter der Voraussetzung, dass nach diesem Zeitpunkt ein Wechsel des gewöhnlichen Aufenthalts erfolgt, ist die Entschcidung in ihrem Bestand geschützt. Hat die Tatsacheninstanz – in erster oder höherer Instanz – in einem anhängigen Verfahren nach einem Aufenthaltswechsel noch keine Entscheidung erlassen, ist der Rechtsschutzantrag mangels internationaler Zuständigkeit zurückzuweisen.[43] Hat die letzte Tat-

---

[37] Rauscher, EuZPR/EuIPR/Hilbig-Lugani, 4. Aufl. 2016, KSÜ Art. 14 Rn. 1; Gitschthaler, Internationales Familienrecht/Huter, 2019, KSÜ Art. 14 Rn. 5; Roth/Döring JBl 1999, 758 (767).

[38] Ausführlich zum Meinungsstand Rauscher, EuZPR/EuIPR/Hilbig-Lugani, 4. Aufl. 2016, KSÜ Art. 5 Rn. 14.

[39] Zum MSA siehe OLG Rostock 25.5.2000 – 10 UF 126/00, BeckRS 2000, 9036 = IPRax 2001, 588 mAnm Baetge IPRax 2001, 573 (Zeitpunkt der letzten mündlichen Verhandlung in der Tatsacheninstanz). Vgl. hierzu auch die Nachweise bei Rauscher, EuZPR/EuIPR/Hilbig-Lugani, 4. Aufl. 2016, KSÜ Art. 5 Rn. 14 Fn 57.

[40] So treffend Rauscher, EuZPR/EuIPR/Hilbig-Lugani, 4. Aufl. 2016, KSÜ Art. 5 Rn. 14.

[41] So zum Anwendungsbereich des MSA OGH 30.11.1982 – 2 Ob 557/82, IPRax 1984, 164 mkritAnm Hoyer.

[42] BGH 29.10.1980 – IVb ZB 586/80, NJW 1981, 520; OLG Rostock 25.5.2000 – 10 UF 126/00, FamRZ 2001, 642 = NJWE-FER 2001, 93; BGH 22.6.2005 – XII ZB 186/03, NJW 2005, 3424 = FamRZ 2005, 1540; ausführlich zum Meinungsstand Rauscher, EuZPR/EuIPR/Hilbig-Lugani, 4. Aufl. 2016, KSÜ Art. 5 Rn. 14; siehe auch beck-online.GROSSKOMMENTAR zum Zivilrecht/Markwardt, Stand 1.3.2024, KSÜ Art. 5 Rn. 11.

[43] NomosKommentar BGB/Benicke, 4. Aufl. 2021, KSÜ Art. 5 Rn. 4.

sacheninstanz eine Entscheidung erlassen und erfolgt erst danach der Wechsel des gewöhnlichen Aufenthalts, bleibt die Entscheidung bestehen, bis die Behörden im neuen gewöhnlichen Aufenthalt eine abändernde Entscheidung treffen. Dies gilt auch dann, wenn das Verfahren in der Rechtsmittelinstanz noch anhängig ist.[44] Die Rechtsmittelinstanz hat in diesem Fall das Rechtsmittel wegen der nun fehlenden internationalen Zuständigkeit zurückzuweisen, weil die internationale Zuständigkeit auch in der Rechtsmittelinstanz von Amts wegen zu prüfen ist.[45] An die Stelle der Überprüfung einer solchen Entscheidung im Instanzenzug tritt die Möglichkeit der Beteiligten, durch geeignete Antragstellung im Staat des nunmehrig gewöhnlichen Aufenthalts eine diese ändernde, ersetzende oder aufhebende Maßnahme zu bewirken.[46]

c) Brüssel IIb-VO

Im Unterschied zum KSÜ und zum MSA wird in Art. 7 Abs. 1 Brüssel IIb-VO ausdrücklich normiert, dass sich der gewöhnliche Aufenthalt des Kindes „im Zeitpunkt der Antragstellung" in dem Mitgliedstaat, dessen Gerichte angerufen wurden, befinden muss. Da auf den Zeitpunkt der Antragstellung abgestellt wird, gilt im Anwendungsbereich des Art. 7 Abs. 1 Brüssel IIb-VO der Grundsatz der *perpetuatio fori*.[47] Liegt die internationale Zuständigkeit im Zeitpunkt des Art. 17 Brüssel IIb-VO vor, bleiben daher die Gerichte des Mitgliedstaats auch dann zuständig, wenn das Kind während des Verfahrens seinen gewöhnlichen Aufenthalt von einem Mitgliedstaat in einen anderen Mitgliedstaat verlegt; anderes gilt, wenn der gewöhnliche Aufenthalt in einen Nur-Vertragsstaat des KSÜ bzw. des MSA verlegt wird, in deren Anwendungsbereich der Grundsatz der *perpetuatio fori* nicht gilt (dazu → III. 1. b) aa) und → VI.).

Die Geltung des Grundsatzes der *perpetuatio fori* entspricht der Rechtslage nach Art. 8 Brüssel IIa-VO.[48] Nach dem Entwurf zur Neufassung der Brüssel

---

[44] Zur vergleichbaren Regelung nach dem ErwSÜ siehe OGH 23.11.2022 – 7 Ob 171/22f, BeckRS 2022, 41165 = EF-Z 2023/76 mAnm Huter.

[45] Vgl. NomosKommentar BGB/Benicke, 4. Aufl. 2021, KSÜ Art. 5 Rn. 4; Heindler IPRax 2014, 201 (202); aA Geimer/Schütze, Internationaler Rechtsverkehr/Gruber, 66. EL 1/2023, KSÜ Art. 5 Rn. 5, wonach eine *perpetuatio fori* anzunehmen sei, wenn sich die Rechtsmittelinstanz allein auf eine rechtliche Nachprüfung beschränke.

[46] Heindler IPRax 2014, 201 (202). Zur vergleichbaren Regelung nach dem ErwSÜ siehe OGH 23.11.2022 – 7 Ob 171/22f, BeckRS 2022, 41165 = EF-Z 2023/76 mAnm Huter.

[47] Garber, Internationale Zuständigkeit für Verfahren betreffend die elterliche Verantwortung, in Garber/Lugani, Die Brüssel IIb-Verordnung: Zuständigkeit, Anerkennung und Vollstreckung in Ehesachen und Kindschaftssachen einschließlich der internationalen Kindesentführung, 2022, Rn. 6/10; Köllensperger, Die Entstehung der Brüssel IIb-VO, in Garber/Lugani, Die Brüssel IIb-Verordnung: Zuständigkeit, Anerkennung und Vollstreckung in Ehesachen und Kindschaftssachen einschließlich der internationalen Kindesentführung, 2022, Rn. 2/12; Neumayr, Die Brüssel IIb-VO – Grundlagen und Ziele, in Garber/Lugani, Die Brüssel IIb-Verordnung: Zuständigkeit, Anerkennung und Vollstreckung in Ehesachen und Kindschaftssachen einschließlich der internationalen Kindesentführung, 2022, Rn. 3.18.

[48] OGH 23.10.2007 – 3 Ob 213/07, iFamZ 2008/52 mAnm Fucik = Zak 2008/30; BGH 17.2.2010 – XII ZB 68/09, BGHZ 184, 269 = FamRZ 2010, 720 mAnm Stößer = FR 2010, 182 mAnm van Els = JR 2011, 254 mAnm Probst = JuS 2010, 819 mAnm Wellenhofer = NJW 2010, 1351 mAnm Peschel-Gutzeit; OLG München 26.7.2011 – 33 UF 874/11, BeckRS 2011,

IIa-VO[49] (im Folgenden: Brüssel IIb-VO-E) sollte die Wendung gestrichen werden und die allgemeine Zuständigkeit um folgenden Satz ergänzt werden: „Zieht ein Kind rechtmäßig von einem Mitgliedstaat in einen anderen Mitgliedstaat um und erlangt dort einen neuen gewöhnlichen Aufenthalt, sind die Behörden des Mitgliedstaats des neuen Aufenthalts zuständig." Die Bestimmung sollte nach ErwGr. 15 zum Brüssel IIb-VO-E unabhängig davon Anwendung finden, ob ein Verfahren anhängig gewesen wäre oder nicht. Für den Fall, dass noch kein Verfahren anhängig ist, hätte die Regelung zu keiner Änderung der bisherigen Rechtslage geführt, denn maßgeblich sind die Umstände im Zeitpunkt der Antragstellung. Bei Anhängigkeit des Verfahrens hätte die Regelung im Vergleich zur Brüssel IIa-VO eine Änderung der Rechtslage bewirkt: Das Gericht, das im Zeitpunkt der Antragstellung zuständig gewesen wäre, hätte bei Verlegung des gewöhnlichen Aufenthalts des Kindes während des Verfahrens seine Unzuständigkeit aussprechen müssen.

Das Europäische Parlament hat – wenngleich ohne nähere Begründung – in seiner Stellungnahme zum Entwurf die gänzliche Streichung der vorgeschlagenen Ergänzung begehrt.[50] In der in Kraft getretenen Fassung der Brüssel IIb-VO wird in ErwGr. 21 Brüssel IIb-VO die Geltung des Grundsatzes der *perpetuatio fori* ausdrücklich betont: „Ist noch kein Verfahren betreffend die elterliche Verantwortung anhängig und ändert sich der gewöhnliche Aufenthalt des Kindes nach einem rechtmäßigen Umzug, so sollte die Zuständigkeit das Kind begleiten, damit die räumliche Nähe aufrechterhalten bleibt. Für bereits anhängige Verfahren rechtfertigen es die Rechtssicherheit und die Effizienz der Justiz, diese Zuständigkeit so lange aufrechtzuerhalten, bis in den betreffenden Verfahren eine rechtskräftige Entscheidung ergangen ist oder die Verfahren anderweitig abgeschlossen worden sind. Das Gericht, bei dem ein Verfahren anhängig ist, sollte jedoch unter bestimmten Umständen [nämlich bei Vorliegen der in Art. 12 Brüssel IIb VO genannten Kriterien[51]] berechtigt sein, die Zuständigkeit auf den Mitgliedstaat zu übertragen, in dem das Kind nach einem rechtmäßigen Umzug lebt."

d) *Ergebnis*

Im Ergebnis gilt im Anwendungsbereich des KSÜ der Grundsatz der *perpetuatio fori* nicht. Dies entspricht auch dem Inhalt des MSA und des ErwSÜ. Nach Art. 5

2743 = FamRZ 2011, 1887; OLG Stuttgart 12.4.2012 – 17 UF 22/12, BeckRS 2012, 10154 = FamRZ 2013, 49 = IPRax 2013, 441 mAnm Gruber IPRax 2013, 402; OGH 27.4.2016 – 3 Ob 56/16f, EF-Z 2016/136 mAnm Nademleinsky = JBl 2016, 543 = Zak 2016/315; dazu krit. Kress, Internationale Zuständigkeit für elterliche Verantwortung in der Europäischen Union, 2006, S. 111 ff.; Geimer/Schütze, EuZVR/Geimer, 4. Aufl. 2020, EuEheVO Art. 8 Rn. 22 f.; Münchener Kommentar zum FamFG/Gottwald, 3. Aufl. 2019, Brüssel IIa-VO Art. 8 Rn. 6; Köllensperger, Die Entstehung der Brüssel IIb-VO, in Garber/Lugani, Die Brüssel IIb-Verordnung: Zuständigkeit, Anerkennung und Vollstreckung in Ehesachen und Kindschaftssachen einschließlich der internationalen Kindesentführung, 2022, Rn. 2/12.

[49] Europäische Kommission, COM(2016) 411 final.

[50] Zwiefka, Rechtsausschuss, Europäisches Parlament, A8-0388/2017, 11 (zu ErwGr. 15).

[51] Ergänzung durch die Verfasser.

Abs. 2 ErwSÜ sind bei einem Wechsel des gewöhnlichen Aufenthalts des Erwachsenen in einen anderen Vertragsstaat die Behörden des Staats des neuen gewöhnlichen Aufenthalts zuständig. Auf völkerrechtlicher Ebene scheint der Grundsatz der *perpetuatio fori* nicht für die internationale Zuständigkeit für Materien zu gelten, die dem Schutz einer Person dienen.

Demgegenüber gilt der Grundsatz im Anwendungsbereich der Brüssel IIb-VO. Der OGH[52] hat die Geltung – methodisch allerdings wenig überzeugend – auf den Rechtshilfe-Vertrag zwischen der Republik Österreich und dem Fürstentum Liechtenstein über Rechtshilfe, Beglaubigung, Urkunden und Vormundschaft vom 13. März 1956[53] für „Vormundschaft und Pflegschaft" übertragen, sodass seiner Auffassung nach auch in dessen Anwendungsbereich der Grundsatz der *perpetuatio fori* gilt.

e) *Bewertung*

Hat sich das Gericht nach Verlegung des gewöhnlichen Aufenthalts für unzuständig zu erklären, weil die Zuständigkeit auf die Gerichte des neuen gewöhnlichen Aufenthaltsstaats übergeht, wird sichergestellt, dass die die Anknüpfung legitimierende räumliche Nähe zwischen Gericht und Kind aufrecht erhalten bleibt (vgl. auch ErwGr. 15 zum Brüssel IIb-VO-E). Für den Zuständigkeitswechsel können darüber hinaus alle Gründe für die Zuständigkeit des Staats, in dessen Hoheitsgebiet sich der gewöhnliche Aufenthalt des Kindes befindet, angeführt werden (dazu → III. 1. b) aa).

Allerdings führt die Durchbrechung des Grundsatzes der *perpetuatio fori* zu zahlreichen Nachteilen.[54] Ein Zuständigkeitswechsel bei bereits anhängigen Verfahren ist nämlich in den meisten Fällen kaum effizient.[55] Dies gilt insbesondere dann, wenn das Verfahren bereits weit fortgeschritten ist. Auch in diesem Fall muss das Verfahren ohne Sachentscheidung beendet werden und ein Rechtsschutzantrag im neuen Staat gestellt werden. Eine grenzüberschreitende Überweisung ist aufgrund der unterschiedlichen Verfahrensabläufe in den einzelnen Staaten nicht möglich.[56] Die erforderliche Neudurchführung des Verfahrens bewirkt, dass die Parteien (in aller Regel) erst zu einem späteren Zeitpunkt zu einer Sachentscheidung gelangen[57] und das Verfahren verteuert wird.[58] Durch die neuerliche Durchführung des Ver-

[52] OGH 26.5.2021 – 2 Ob 45/21p (2 Ob 46/21k, 2 Ob 62/21p), NZ 2022, 97; dazu kritAnm. Garber NZ 2022, 74.

[53] BGBl. 1956/213 i.d.g.F.

[54] Vgl. auch Gitschthaler, Internationales Familienrecht/Huter, 2019, KSÜ Art. 5 Rn. 75, wonach die „konsequente Verneinung der *perpetuatio fori* nach einem Aufenthaltswechsel sehr dramatische Konsequenzen haben kann".

[55] Antomo, Die Neufassung der Brüssel IIa-Verordnung – erfolgte Änderungen und verbleibender Reformbedarf, in Pfeiffer/Lobach/Rapp, Europäisches Familien- und Erbrecht, 2020, S. 13 (34).

[56] McGuire, ZfRV 2005, 83.

[57] Die Verzögerung wird auch durch den Umstand, dass die Parteien sich mit den im neuen Staat geltenden Rechtsnormen vertraut machen müssen und/oder erst einen geeigneten Rechtsvertreter beauftragen müssen.

[58] Vgl. BGH 1.2.1978 – IV ZR 142/77, BGHZ 70, 295 = NJW 1978, 949.

fahrens werden die verfahrensbedingten Belastungen für das Kind erhöht, wodurch das Kindeswohl konterkariert wird.

Wird die Zuständigkeit nicht aufrechterhalten, erhöht sich nicht nur der Zeit- und Kostenaufwand, sondern es besteht auch die Gefahr, dass der Anspruch – etwa aufgrund einer mittlerweile eingetretenen Verjährung – nicht mehr erfolgreich durchgesetzt werden kann,[59] wenngleich einzuräumen ist, dass in Verfahren betreffend die elterliche Verantwortung die Gefahr der Verjährung in aller Regel nicht von Bedeutung ist.

Dies gilt insbesondere dann, wenn der Wechsel des gewöhnlichen Aufenthalts erst nach einem langwierigen und möglicherweise auch kostspieligen Verfahren erst im Rechtsmittelstadium des Verfahrens erfolgt; der bisherige Aufwand war – sofern der Bestand der bisherigen Entscheidung nicht gewahrt wird (vgl. Art. 14 KSÜ, dazu → III. 1. b) bb) ohne Ergebnis.

Durch die Nichtgeltung des Grundsatzes der *perpetuatio fori* wird der Anreiz, einen Zuständigkeitswechsel durch Verlegung des gewöhnlichen Aufenthalts herbeizuführen, erhöht. Es besteht auch die Gefahr, dass der gewöhnliche Aufenthalt nur deshalb mehrfach verlegt wird, um eine Sachentscheidung zu verhindern. Eine Person, die über den gewöhnlichen Aufenthalt des Kindes bestimmen kann, hat die Möglichkeit, den gewöhnlichen Aufenthalt des Kindes zu verlegen, wenn sie mit einem ungünstigen Ausgang des Verfahrens rechnet.

Gegen ein Absehen vom Grundsatz der *perpetuatio fori* spricht auch, dass bei (möglichen) Wechseln des gewöhnlichen Aufenthalts die Frage der internationalen Zuständigkeit im Verfahren mehrfach aufgeworfen wird. Selbst wenn ein Gericht bereits das Vorliegen der Zuständigkeit geprüft und bejaht hat, kann im späteren Verfahren die Einrede der nunmehr vorliegenden internationalen Unzuständigkeit erhoben werden, indem behauptet wird, dass sich die zuständigkeitsbegründen Umstände geändert haben. Das Gericht hat eine neuerliche Prüfung der Frage vorzunehmen, die – aufgrund der Komplexität der Bestimmung des gewöhnlichen Aufenthalts[60] – u. U. zeitaufwändig ist. Eine Partei, die die Erlassung einer Sachentscheidung verzögern oder verhindern möchte, könnte die Einrede der Unzuständigkeit in bloßer Verschleppungsabsicht erheben. Demgegenüber bewirkt der Grundsatz der *perpetuatio fori,* dass ein möglicher Streit über die Zuständigkeit lediglich einmal und in aller Regel am Beginn des Verfahrens entschieden wird und die Parteien rascher zu einer Sachentscheidung gelangen können.

Die Anwendung des Grundsatzes der *perpetuatio fori* erscheint auch in Verfahren betreffend die elterliche Verantwortung sachgerecht.[61] Um die im konkreten Einzelfall bestehenden Härten, die durch den Grundsatz der *perpetuatio fori* eintreten

---

[59] Fasching/Konecny, Kommentar zu den Zivilprozessgesetzen/Simotta, 2. Aufl. 2010, EuEheKindVO Art. 3 Rn. 19.

[60] Ein Überblick zur reichhaltigen Rechtsprechung zum gewöhnlichen Aufenthalt findet sich etwa bei Gitschthaler, Internationales Familienrecht/Garber, 2019, Brüssel IIa-VO Art. 3 Rn. 17ff. Zahlreiche Fragen sind in diesem Zusammenhang noch offen, etwa, ob ein Kind im Fall einer grenzüberschreitenden Doppelresidenz in mehreren Staaten seinen gewöhnlichen Aufenthalt haben kann, siehe dazu Garber/Neumayr GS Mankowski (im Erscheinen).

[61] So bereits Neumayr, Die Brüssel IIb-VO – Grundlagen und Ziele, in Garber/Lugani, Die Brüssel IIb-Verordnung: Zuständigkeit, Anerkennung und Vollstreckung in Ehesachen und Kindschaftssachen einschließlich der internationalen Kindesentführung, 2022, Rn. 3.27.

können, zu verhindern, müssen allerdings Instrumente zur Verfügung gestellt werden, um die Nachteile für das Kind zu vermeiden.

2. *Wie können Nachteile der Nichtgeltung bzw Geltung der perpetuatio fori ausgeglichen werden?*

a) Bei Nichtanwendbarkeit des Grundsatzes der perpetuatio fori

Im Anwendungsbereich des KSÜ soll durch Art. 14 KSÜ, der den Bestand erlassener Entscheidungen schützt, Härten, die durch einen Wechsel der Zuständigkeit eintreten, verhindert werden. Es soll sichergestellt werden, dass nicht durch ein Entfallen einer bereits erlassenen Entscheidung eine Schutzlücke entsteht, bis die Behörde des Staats, in dem sich nunmehr der gewöhnliche Aufenthalt befindet, eine entsprechende Entscheidung erlassen hat (dazu → III. 1. b) bb). Die Regelung trägt dem Schutz des Kindes u. E. allerdings nicht ausreichend Rechnung. Bei Wechsel des gewöhnlichen Aufenthalts ist ein Verfahren auch dann zu beenden, wenn es bereits weit fortgeschritten, die Erlassung einer Sachentscheidung unmittelbar bevorsteht oder eine Sachentscheidung nicht nach Art. 14 KSÜ in ihrem Bestand gesichert ist. Auch in diesem Fall muss das Verfahren ohne Sachentscheidung beendet und im Zweitstaat neu durchgeführt werden.

Fraglich ist, ob die Nachteile durch einen Zuständigkeitstransfer nach Art. 8, 9 KSÜ verhindert werden können. Nach Art. 8 KSÜ können die Behörden des nunmehrigen gewöhnlichen Aufenthalts (ua) den Staat des bisherigen gewöhnlichen Aufenthalts[62] ersuchen, die Zuständigkeit zu übernehmen. Zudem können nach Art. 9 KSÜ die Behörden dieses Staats den nunmehr zuständigen Staat ersuchen, die Zuständigkeit auszuüben, um die von ihnen für erforderlich gehaltenen Schutzmaßnahmen zu treffen. Die von Teilen des Schrifttums vertretene Auffassung, die internationale Zuständigkeit könne über Art. 8, 9 KSÜ möglicherweise „fortgesetzt" werden,[63] überzeugt u. E. nicht.[64] Die Frage, ob das Rechtsschutzbegehren zurückzuweisen ist oder das anhängige Verfahren zu unterbrechen bzw. innezuhalten ist, bestimmt sich nach innerstaatlichem Recht. Nach österreichischem Recht hat ein unzuständiges Gericht nicht die Möglichkeit, das Verfahren zu unterbrechen (zu den Voraussetzungen siehe § 190 ZPO, § 25 AußStrG) bzw. innezuhalten (zu den Voraussetzungen siehe § 29 AußStrG), sodass die Klage zurückzuweisen ist.[65] Dies gilt auch für Verfahren, die weit fortgeschritten sind.

[62] Der Staat, in dem sich bislang der gewöhnliche Aufenthalt des Kindes befunden hat, wird in Art. 8 Abs. 2 KSÜ nicht ausdrücklich als ein Staat genannt, der um Übernahme der Zuständigkeit ersucht werden kann, allerdings ist er wohl von Art. 8 Abs. 2 lit. d KSÜ („Staat, zu dem das Kind eine enge Verbindung hat") erfasst (Rauscher, EuZPR/EuIPR/Hilbig-Lugani, 4. Aufl. 2016, KSÜ Art. 8, 9 Rn. 11).

[63] Krah, Das Haager Kinderschutzabkommen, 2004, S. 151.

[64] Siehe auch Gitschthaler, Internationales Familienrecht/Huter, 2019, KSÜ Art. 5 Rn. 75, wonach die Anwendung der Art. 8,9 KSÜ „gerade in solchen ‚Wegzugsfällen' […] eine lediglich theoretische Möglichkeit darstellen [dürfte]"

[65] Siehe zum vergleichbaren Fall, dass ein gerichtliches Aufteilungsverfahren vor Entstehen des Anspruchs eingeleitet wird, Fenyves/Kerschner/Vonkilch, Großkommentar zum ABGB – Klang-Kommentar/Garber, 3. Aufl. 2021, EheG § 95 Rn. 72.

Im Rahmen der Arbeiten zur Revision der Brüssel IIa-VO war man sich der Nachteile, die eine Nichtgeltung des Grundsatzes der *perpetuatio fori* bewirkt, bewusst. Um diese Nachteile zu verringern, sah ErwGr. 15 zum Brüssel IIb-VO-E vor, dass im Fall der Anhängigkeit des Verfahrens die Parteien im Interesse der Wirksamkeit der Justiz vereinbaren können, dass die Zuständigkeit bis zum Ergehen der endgültigen Entscheidung bei den Gerichten des Mitgliedstaats geblieben wäre, in dem das Verfahren anhängig gewesen war, sofern dies dem Wohl des Kindes entsprochen hätte. Die vorgeschlagene Regelung erschien nicht unproblematisch.[66] Zum einen fand die Möglichkeit einer abweichenden Vereinbarung im normativen Teil des Verordnungsentwurfs keinen Niederschlag – eine Vereinbarung wäre nur bei Vorliegen der in Art. 10 Brüssel IIb-VO-E normierten (zusätzlichen)[67] Voraussetzungen möglich gewesen[68] –, zum anderen wäre in der Praxis eine Vereinbarung wohl häufig gescheitert, weil die Partei, die mit einem ungünstigen Ausgang des Verfahrens rechnet, der Aufrechterhaltung der Zuständigkeit nicht zugestimmt hätte. Eine Vereinbarung ist u. E. nicht geeignet, um die Nachteile der Durchbrechung des Grundsatzes der *perpetuatio fori* der Zuständigkeit zu verhindern.

b) Bei Anwendung des Grundsatzes der perpetuatio fori

aa) Allgemeines

Die Brüssel IIb-VO sieht Instrumente vor, um sicherzustellen, dass im konkreten Einzelfall das Gericht des bisherigen gewöhnlichen Aufenthalts nicht entscheiden muss, sondern die Zuständigkeit auf das Gericht des neuen gewöhnlichen Aufenthalts übergeht.

bb) Zuständigkeitstransfer

Die Verordnung sieht in Art. 12 Brüssel IIb-VO die Möglichkeit eines Zuständigkeitstransfers vor. Ein nach der Verordnung zuständiges Gericht kann in Ausnahmefällen und im Interesse des Kindeswohls die Zuständigkeit für die Entscheidung ganz oder zum Teil an ein anderes Gericht transferieren. Durch die eingeräumte Flexibilität soll sichergestellt werden, dass das Kindeswohl im konkreten Einzelfall bestmöglich gewahrt ist.[69]

---

[66] Siehe auch Garber, Neuerungen im Ehe- und Familienrecht: Zur Revision der Brüssel IIa-VO und zu den Güterrechtsverordnungen, in: König/Mayr, Europäisches Zivilverfahrensrecht in Österreich V, 2018, S. 109 (S. 125f.); Weller IPRax 2017, 222 (223); aA Antomo in Pfeiffer/Lobach/Rapp, Familien- und Erbrecht S. 34f.

[67] So wäre nach Art. 10 Abs. 3 Brüssel IIb-VO-E erforderlich gewesen, dass nach dem Recht des betreffenden Mitgliedstaats eine Vereinbarung oder ausdrückliche Anerkennung der Zuständigkeit während des Verfahrens zulässig sein musste.

[68] Dazu ausführlich Garber, Neuerungen im Ehe- und Familienrecht: Zur Revision der Brüssel IIa-VO und zu den Güterrechtsverordnungen, in König/Mayr, Europäisches Zivilverfahrensrecht in Österreich V, 2018, S. 109 (127f.).

[69] Fasching/Konecny, Kommentar zu den Zivilprozessgesetzen/Neumayr, 2. Aufl. 2010, EuEheKindVO Art. 15 Rn. 2; Pirrung FS Schlosser, 2005, 695 (703).

Die Anwendung des Art. 12 Brüssel IIb-VO setzt voraus, dass das angerufene Gericht zuständig ist.[70] Sofern das angerufene Gericht unzuständig ist, hat es sich von Amts wegen für unzuständig zu erklären und die Klage zurückzuweisen. Ein unzuständiges Gericht kann daher keinen Zuständigkeitstransfer initiieren.[71]

Eine der Voraussetzung für den Zuständigkeitstransfer ist, dass das Kind eine besondere Bindung zu dem anderen Mitgliedstaat hat. In Art. 12 Abs. 4 Brüssel IIb-VO werden fünf Punkte genannt, die für eine Übertragung sprechen können. Nach Art. 12 Abs. 4 lit. a Brüssel IIb-VO besteht eine besondere Bindung zu einem anderen Mitgliedstaat etwa dann, wenn das Kind nach Anrufung der Gerichte des Erststaats seinen gewöhnlichen Aufenthalt im anderen Mitgliedstaat erworben hat.[72] Durch Art. 12 Abs. 4 lit. a Brüssel IIb-VO soll gewährleistet werden, dass ein Zuständigkeitstransfer erfolgen kann, wenn das zuerst angerufene Gericht aufgrund des gewöhnlichen Aufenthalts des Kindes in diesem Staat zuständig ist, das Kind aber während des Verfahrens seinen gewöhnlichen Aufenthalt in einem anderen Staat begründet. Die Bestimmung gewährleistet, dass Härten, die durch den Grundsatz der *perpetuatio fori* entstehen würden, verhindert werden.[73]

Ein Zuständigkeitstransfer bei Wechsel des gewöhnlichen Aufenthalts ist etwa dann in Betracht zu ziehen, wenn das Verfahren noch nicht weit fortgeschritten ist. Die Übertragung ist nicht von der Zustimmung der Verfahrensparteien abhängig und das Gericht kann die Umstände des Einzelfalls berücksichtigen.[74] Würde der Grundsatz der *perpetuatio fori* nicht gelten, hätte das Gericht – aufgrund der nunmehr bestehenden Unzuständigkeit – keine Möglichkeit, die Zuständigkeit zu übertragen. Die geordnete Verfahrensbeendigung und gleichzeitige Wiederaufnahme des Verfahrens in einem anderen Staat entspricht dem Kindeswohl mehr als die andernfalls zu erfolgende Zurückweisung wegen Unzuständigkeit.

cc) Anregung auf Zuständigkeitsübertragung

Art. 13 Brüssel IIb-VO ermöglicht es ua[75] dem Gericht des Staats, in dessen Hoheitsgebiet der gewöhnliche Aufenthalt verlegt wurde, und das nach der Verord-

---

[70] Dies gilt auch für Art. 8 KSÜ. Aus diesem Grund kann im Anwendungsbereich des KSÜ die Behörde des bisherigen gewöhnlichen Aufenthalts nicht die Zuständigkeit an das Gericht des Staats des neuen gewöhnlichen Aufenthalts transferieren, sie kann lediglich die Behörde des nunmehrigen gewöhnlichen Aufenthalts ersuchen, die Zuständigkeit auszuüben.

[71] OGH 13.7.2010 – 4 Ob 82/10b, EF-Z 2010/155 = iFamZ 2010/232; OGH 24.6.2015 – 9 Ob 14/15x, EF-Z 2016/25 mAnm Nademleinsky = EvBl 2016/8 mAnm Pesendorfer = iFamZ 2015/199 mAnm Fucik; Breuer, Ehe- und Familiensachen in Europa, 2008, Rn. 260; Geimer/Schütze, EuZVR/Geimer, 4. Aufl. 2020, EuEheVO Art. 15 Rn. 15; vgl. auch EuGH 2.4.2009 – C-523/07, ECLI:EU:C:2009:225 (A).

[72] Vgl. dazu OLG Karlsruhe BeckRS 2015, 19394.

[73] Gruber IPRax 2013, 409; Fasching/Konecny, Kommentar zu den Zivilprozessgesetzen/Neumayr V/2, 2. Aufl. 2010, EuEheKindVO Art. 15 Rn. 27; Althammer, Brüssel IIa – Rom III/Schäuble, 2014, Brüssel IIa-VO Art. 15 Rn. 1.

[74] Dazu ausführlich Garber, Internationale Zuständigkeit für Verfahren betreffend die elterliche Verantwortung, in Garber/Lugani, Die Brüssel IIb-Verordnung: Zuständigkeit, Anerkennung und Vollstreckung in Ehesachen und Kindschaftssachen einschließlich der internationalen Kindesentführung, 2022, Rn. 6/83 und Rn. 6/84ff.

[75] Das Kind muss zum Mitgliedstaat, dessen Gerichte um Übertragung der Zuständigkeit ersuchen, eine besondere Bindung gem Art. 12 Abs. 4 Brüssel IIb-VO besitzen, was bei einem

nung nicht zuständig ist, das Gericht des Mitgliedstaats des bisherigen gewöhnlichen Aufenthalts des Kindes um Übertragung der Zuständigkeit zu ersuchen.

Das ersuchte Gericht hat binnen sechs Wochen nach Eingang des Ersuchens zu entscheiden, ob es seine Zuständigkeit überträgt oder nicht. Nach Art. 13 Abs. 2 Brüssel IIb-VO hat das Gericht zu überprüfen, ob die Übertragung aufgrund der besonderen Umstände des Falls dem Kindeswohl entspricht. Es ist bei der Prüfung nicht an die Auffassung des ersuchenden Gerichts gebunden. Wenn das ersuchte Gericht der Übertragung seiner Zuständigkeit zustimmt, setzt es das ersuchende Gericht unverzüglich davon in Kenntnis. Gibt das ersuchte Gericht dem Ersuchen innerhalb der Frist nicht statt, dann wird das ersuchende Gericht nicht zuständig.[76]

Die Lösung, dass der Staat des nunmehrigen gewöhnlichen Aufenthalts des Kindes den Staat des bisherigen gewöhnlichen Aufenthalts um Übertragung der Zuständigkeit – und nicht wie im Anwendungsbereich des KSÜ in umgekehrter Weise – ersuchen muss, erscheint u. E. sinnvoll. Dadurch haben die Gerichte des bisherigen gewöhnlichen Aufenthalts die „stärkere" Position, was sachgerecht erscheint, weil sie mit den Umständen des Falls vertraut sind, während in dem Staat des nunmehrigen gewöhnlichen Aufenthalts in aller Regel noch keine (wesentlichen) Verfahrenshandlungen gesetzt worden sind. Dadurch wird aber vor allem sichergestellt, dass das Gericht des bisherigen gewöhnlichen Aufenthalts sich nicht sofort für unzuständig erklären muss, sondern es kann weitere Handlungen (einschließlich der Einleitung eines Zuständigkeitstransfers) setzen, ohne dass die bisherigen Ergebnisse des Verfahrens vernichtet werden.

dd) Ausschließliche Zuständigkeitsvereinbarung

Vereinzelt wird von Teilen der deutschen Lehre (zum innerstaatlichen Recht) vertreten, dass die Zuständigkeit wegfalle, wenn die Parteien nachträglich die ausschließliche Zuständigkeit eines anderen Gerichts vereinbaren.[77] Die deutsche Rechtsprechung[78] und die überwiegende Lehre[79] haben die Auffassung abgelehnt.[80] Fraglich ist, ob im Anwendungsbereich der Brüssel IIb-VO eine nachträgliche Prorogation zu

Mitgliedstaat, in dessen Hoheitsgebiet der gewöhnliche Aufenthalt verlegt wurde, vorliegt. Siehe dazu Garber, Internationale Zuständigkeit für Verfahren betreffend die elterliche Verantwortung, in Garber/Lugani, Die Brüssel IIb-Verordnung: Zuständigkeit, Anerkennung und Vollstreckung in Ehesachen und Kindschaftssachen einschließlich der internationalen Kindesentführung, 2022, Rn. 6/91.

[76] Zum Verfahren Garber, Internationale Zuständigkeit für Verfahren betreffend die elterliche Verantwortung, in Garber/Lugani, Die Brüssel IIb-Verordnung: Zuständigkeit, Anerkennung und Vollstreckung in Ehesachen und Kindschaftssachen einschließlich der internationalen Kindesentführung, 2022, Rn. 6/127f.

[77] LG Flensburg 13.12.1978 – 4 O 361/78, SchlHA 1979, 38; LG Waldshut-Tiengen. 31.8.1984 – 2 O 281/84, MDR 1985, 941; Münchener Kommentar zur ZPO/Becker-Eberhard, 6. Aufl. 2020, § 261 Rn. 92; Traub NJW 1963, 842.

[78] BGH 16.11.1962 – III ARZ 123/62, NJW 1963, 585 = JZ 1963, 754 mzustAnm Zeuner; BGH 6.10.1993 – XII ARZ 22/93, NJW-RR 1994, 126 = FamRZ 1994, 437; BGH 18.1.1995 – XII ARZ 36/94, NJW-RR 1995, 513 = FamRZ 1995, 729; BGH 18.2.2010 – Xa ARZ 14/10, NJW-RR 2010, 891.

[79] Stein/Jonas, ZPO/Bork, 23. Aufl. 2014, § 38 Rn. 62; Zöller, ZPO/Greger, 35. Aufl. 2024, § 261 Rn. 12.

[80] Zur nachträglichen Konsensprorogation nach österreichischem Recht siehe § 31a Abs 1 JN.

einem Wegfall der bereits begründeten Zuständigkeit führt. Gegen den Wegfall der Zuständigkeit kann angeführt werden, dass die Möglichkeit der Beendigung der *perpetuatio fori* durch eine ausschließliche Gerichtsstandsvereinbarung nicht ausdrücklich in ErwGr. 21 zur Brüssel IIb-VO genannt wird. Andererseits sieht Art. 20 Abs. 4 Brüssel IIb-VO vor, dass bei einer ausschließlichen Gerichtsstandsvereinbarung die Gerichte aller anderen Mitgliedstaaten (als desjenigen, auf den die Prorogation lautet) das Verfahren so lange auszusetzen haben, bis das auf der Grundlage der Gerichtsstandsvereinbarung angerufene Gericht erklärt hat, dass es gemäß der Vereinbarung nicht zuständig ist – auf den Zeitpunkt des Abschlusses der Gerichtsstandsvereinbarung wird aber nicht abgestellt. Da nach Ansicht des EuGH[81] zum EuGVÜ eine Gerichtsstandsvereinbarung lediglich eine Zuständigkeitsoption darstellt, die erst im Falle einer Klagseinbringung Wirkungen entfaltet, können auch durch eine nachträgliche Gerichtsstandsvereinbarung wohl die Wirkungen des Art. 20 Abs. 4 Brüssel IIb-VO ausgelöst werden, wenn bei dem nach der Vereinbarung zuständigen Gericht eine Klage erhoben bzw. ein Antrag gestellt. Eine Antwort auf diese Frage kann hier offen gelassen werden. Selbst wenn man der Auffassung folgt, dass eine nachträgliche Zuständigkeitsvereinbarung zur Durchbrechung des Grundsatzes der *perpetuatio fori* führt, darf im Anwendungsbereich der Brüssel IIb-VO dessen Art. 10 als *lex specialis* nicht außer Acht gelassen werden. Nach dieser Bestimmung haben die Parteien bei Vorliegen bestimmter, von der Verordnung vorgegebener Voraussetzungen[82] die Möglichkeit, eine ausschließliche Gerichtsstandsvereinbarung zu schließen und so die Unzuständigkeit des angerufenen Gerichts zu erreichen.

ee) Einstweilige Maßnahmen

Für die Zuständigkeit am aktuellen gewöhnlichen Aufenthalt wird vorgebracht, dass das Gericht (zumindest in der Regel[83]) am schnellsten über die Sache entscheiden kann. Überträgt das Gericht des ursprünglichen gewöhnlichen Aufenthalts nicht die Zuständigkeit an die Gerichte des aktuellen Aufenthalts, könnte das Verfahren zeitaufwändiger sein. Die dadurch allenfalls eintretenden Nachteile können – zumindest zum Teil – durch Art. 15 Brüssel IIb-VO verhindert werden. Die Bestimmung ermöglicht in dringenden Fällen die Erlassung einstweiliger Maßnahmen, die nach dem Recht dieses Mitgliedstaats vorgesehen sind, sofern sich das Kind in diesem Mitgliedstaat aufhält oder sich Vermögen des Kindes in diesem Mitgliedstaat befindet.[84] Die Gerichte des neuen gewöhnlichen Aufenthaltsstaats besitzen daher jedenfalls die Kompetenz, einstweilige Maßnahmen zu erlassen. Dies gilt – nach dem ausdrücklichen Wortlaut der Bestimmung[85] – auch dann, wenn das Verfahren in einem anderen Staat anhängig ist.

[81] EuGH 13.11.1979 – 25/79, ECLI:EU:C:1979:255, Rn. 6 (Sanicentral/Collin).

[82] Dazu ausführlich Garber, Internationale Zuständigkeit für Verfahren betreffend die elterliche Verantwortung, in Garber/Lugani, Die Brüssel IIb-Verordnung: Zuständigkeit, Anerkennung und Vollstreckung in Ehesachen und Kindschaftssachen einschließlich der internationalen Kindesentführung, 2022, Rn. 6/32ff.

[83] Dies gilt allerdings dann nicht, wenn das Verfahren vor dem Gericht des ursprünglichen gewöhnlichen Aufenthalts schon weit fortgeschritten ist.

[84] Zu der Bestimmung ausführlich Garber/Neumayr FS Thümmel, 2020, 173.

[85] Garber/Neumayr FS Thümmel, 2020, 173 (184f.).

ff) Möglichkeiten nach innerstaatlichem Recht

Sofern kein Zuständigkeitstransfer durchgeführt wird, obwohl die Parteien der Auffassung sind, dass die Gerichte am neuen gewöhnlichen Aufenthalt entscheiden sollen, können sie nach Maßgabe des innerstaatlichen Rechts die Klage bzw. den Antrag zurücknehmen und im neuen Staat eine entsprechende Klage einbringen. Zur Auffassung, dass eine ausschließliche Gerichtsstandsvereinbarung zur Durchbrechung des Grundsatzes der *perpetuatio fori* führt, → III. 2. b) dd).

IV. Zum Grundsatz der perpetuatio fori bei anderen Zuständigkeitsbestimmungen

Neben der Zuständigkeit am gewöhnlichen Aufenthalt des Kindes sehen sowohl das KSÜ als auch die Brüssel IIb-VO weitere Zuständigkeitsalternativen vor.[86]

Da im Anwendungsbereich des KSÜ bereits der Wechsel des gewöhnlichen Aufenthalts zur Unzuständigkeit führt, gilt dies erst recht für zuständigkeitsbegründende Umstände, die – wie der schlichte Aufenthalt des Kindes in einem Vertragsstaat (siehe Art. 6 Abs. 2 KSÜ) – eine geringere Verbindung des Kindes zu diesem Staat herstellen.

Im Anwendungsbereich der Brüssel IIb-VO ist fraglich, ob der Grundsatz der *perpetuatio fori* auch bei den anderen Zuständigkeitsalternativen Anwendung findet.[87] Die Geltung des Grundsatzes wird nämlich nur in Art. 7 Brüssel IIb-VO, dh bei der Anknüpfung an den gewöhnlichen Aufenthalt des Kindes, ausdrücklich normiert. Aus ErwGr. 21 Satz 2 zur Brüssel IIb-VO, wonach für bereits anhängige Verfahren die Rechtssicherheit und die Effizienz der Justiz es rechtfertigen, diese Zuständigkeit so lange aufrechtzuerhalten, bis in den betreffenden Verfahren eine rechtskräftige Entscheidung ergangen ist oder die Verfahren anderweitig abgeschlossen worden sind, kann u. E. geschlossen werden, dass der Grundsatz der *perpetuatio fori* immer gilt, sofern die Verordnung nicht ausdrücklich eine abweichende Regelung enthält. ErwGr. 21 zur Brüssel IIb-VO schränkt die Geltung des Grundsatzes der *perpetuatio fori* nämlich nicht auf besondere Zuständigkeitsbestimmungen ein.[88]

---

[86] Zum KSÜ siehe Siehr, DEuFamR 2000, 125; zur Brüssel IIb-VO siehe etwa Garber EF-Z 2023, 248.

[87] Zu Art. 8 Brüssel IIb-VO bzw. Art. 9 Brüssel IIa-VO bejahend Gitschthaler, Internationales Familienrecht/Garber, 2019, Brüssel IIa-VO Art. 9 Rn. 41f.; Mayr, Handbuch des europäischen Zivilverfahrensrechts/Neumayr/Weber, 2. Aufl. 2023, Rn. 4.139; verneinend Fasching/Konecny, Kommentar zu den Zivilprozessgesetzen/Pesendorfer, 2. Aufl. 2010, EuEheKindVO Art. 9 Rn. 23; zu Art. 11 Brüssel IIb-VO bzw. Art. 13 Brüssel IIb-VO bejahend Rauscher, EuZPR/EuIPR/Rauscher, 4. Aufl. 2015, Art. 13 Brüssel IIa-VO Rn. 10; verneinend Fleige, Die Zuständigkeit für Sorgerechtsentscheidungen und die Rückführung von Kindern nach Entführung nach europäischem IZVR, 2006, 262; Althammer, Brüssel IIa – Rom III/Schäuble, 2014, Brüssel IIa-VO Art. 13 Rn. 8. Zum Fall des widerrechtlichen Verbringens siehe Garber FS Fischer-Czermak, 2024, 207.

[88] Garber, Internationale Zuständigkeit für Verfahren betreffend die elterliche Verantwortung, in Garber/Lugani, Die Brüssel IIb-Verordnung: Zuständigkeit, Anerkennung und Vollstreckung

V. Ende der perpetuatio fori

Die Aufrechterhaltung der Zuständigkeit endet mit rechtskräftigem Abschluss des Verfahrens. Auch eine Beendigung des Verfahrens auf andere Weise – wie etwa durch Zurücknahme der Klage bzw. des verfahrenseinleitenden Antrags oder die Beendigung des Verfahrens durch Tod des Kindes – führt zu einem Ende der Zuständigkeitsperpetuierung. Zum Wechsel des gewöhnlichen Aufenthalts in einen anderen Staat → III. 1. b) aa) und c).

Zu beachten ist, dass nach Art. 9 Abs. 1 Brüssel IIb-VO bei Vorliegen bestimmter Voraussetzungen[89] die Gerichte des Mitgliedstaats, die eine Umgangsentscheidung erlassen haben, auch für die Änderung bzw. Anpassung dieser Entscheidung zuständig sind. Die Bestimmung führt zur Weiterentwicklung des Grundsatzes der *perpetuatio fori:*[90] Die Gerichte des Mitgliedstaats, die die Umgangsentscheidung erlassen haben, bleiben für die Änderung bzw. Anpassung zuständig, ohne dass im Zeitpunkt des Umzugs bereits ein Verfahren anhängig ist.

VI. Folgen der Divergenz zwischen KSÜ und Brüssel IIb-VO

Der Umstand, dass der Grundsatz der *perpetuatio fori* im Anwendungsbereich der Brüssel IIb-VO gilt, nicht aber im Anwendungsbereich des KSÜ, kann zu Friktionen führen.[91]

Hat das Kind seinen gewöhnlichen Aufenthalt in einem Mitgliedstaat der Brüssel IIb-VO, gilt der Grundsatz der *perpetuatio fori,* wenn das Kind während des Verfahrens seinen gewöhnlichen Aufenthalt in einen anderen Mitgliedstaat verlegt.[92] Anderes gilt, wenn der gewöhnliche Aufenthalt in einen Vertragsstaat des KSÜ verlegt wird, in deren Anwendungsbereich der Grundsatz der *perpetuatio fori* nicht gilt. Bei Wechsel des gewöhnlichen Aufenthalts in einen Drittstaat wird die Zuständigkeit aufrechterhalten, sofern kein vorrangig anzuwendender bi- oder multilateraler Vertrag Abweichendes vorsieht.[93]

---

in Ehesachen und Kindschaftssachen einschließlich der internationalen Kindesentführung, 2022, Rn. 6/23, 6/76.

[89] Dazu ausführlich Garber, Internationale Zuständigkeit für Verfahren betreffend die elterliche Verantwortung, in Garber/Lugani, Die Brüssel IIb-Verordnung: Zuständigkeit, Anerkennung und Vollstreckung in Ehesachen und Kindschaftssachen einschließlich der internationalen Kindesentführung, 2022, Rn. 6.14ff.

[90] Gitschthaler, Internationales Familienrecht/Garber, 2019, Brüssel IIa-VO Art. 9 Rn. 3.

[91] Siehe hierzu insbesondere die Kritik bei Neumayr, Die Brüssel IIb-VO – Grundlagen und Ziele, in Garber/Lugani, Die Brüssel IIb-Verordnung: Zuständigkeit, Anerkennung und Vollstreckung in Ehesachen und Kindschaftssachen einschließlich der internationalen Kindesentführung, 2022, Rn. 3.27 sowie Pirrung, Brüche zwischen internationaler und europäischer Rechtsvereinheitlichung, in: Freitag/Leible/Sippel/Wanitzek, Internationales Familienrecht im 21. Jahrhundert, 2005, 89 (94).

[92] OLG Stuttgart 12.4.2012 – 17 UF 22/12, BeckRS 2012, 10154 = FamRZ 2013, 49 = IPRax 2013, 111 mAnm Gruber IPRax 2013, 402; Andrae IPRax 2006, 82 (84f.); Nademleinsky EF-Z 2011, 85 (87).

[93] Geimer/Schütze, Internationaler Rechtsverkehr/Dilger, 66. EL 1/2023, VO Nr. 2201/2003 Art. 8 Rn. 13; Gruber IPRax 2013, 409 (411); Nademleinsky EF-Z 2011, 85 (87); Mayr, Hand-

Wechselt der gewöhnliche Aufenthalt des Kindes aus einem Vertragsstaat des KSÜ in einen Mitgliedstaat der Brüssel IIb-VO oder in einen Drittstaat, findet das KSÜ keine Anwendung mehr.[94] In diesem Fall bestimmt sich nach innerstaatlichem Recht einschließlich bi- und multilateraler Verträge, ob der Vertragsstaat die Zuständigkeit weiter ausüben darf. Vereinzelt wird angenommen, dass in diesem Fall aus der fehlenden *perpetuatio fori* im KSÜ im Unterschied zur Brüssel IIb-VO allenfalls ein Vorrang des KSÜ abgeleitet werden könnte.[95] Diese Auffassung überzeugt nicht, weil es sich hierbei nicht um eine Frage der *perpetuatio fori,* sondern um eine Frage der Abgrenzung vom Anwendungsbereich des KSÜ von dem der Brüssel IIb-VO handelt.[96]

VII. Fehlen des gewöhnlichen Aufenthalts bei Antragstellung

Fraglich ist, welche Folgen es bei Geltung des Grundsatzes der *perpetuatio fori* hat, wenn das Kind im Zeitpunkt der Antragstellung keinen gewöhnlichen Aufenthalt in dem Staat, dessen Gerichte angerufen worden sind, hat, dieser aber im Laufe des Verfahrens – vor Zurückweisung des Rechtsschutzbegehrens wegen Unzuständigkeit – begründet wird. Der Grundsatz der *perpetuatio fori* bewirkt – wie bereits unter → I. ausgeführt – nicht, dass ein bei Gerichtsanhängigkeit[97] unzuständiges Gericht unzuständig bleibt, wenn die fehlenden Zuständigkeitsmerkmale erst nach diesem Zeitpunkt eintreten. Änderungen, die dazu führen, dass das (zuvor unzuständige) Gericht zuständig wird, sind grundsätzlich zu beachten.[98] Entgegen dem Wortlaut des Art. 7 Abs. 1 Brüssel IIb-VO genügt es u. E., dass das Kind zum Zeitpunkt der Entscheidung des Gerichts seinen gewöhnlichen Aufenthalt im Mitgliedstaat hat, dessen Gerichte angerufen wurden. Dadurch wird verhindert, dass ein Antrag wegen Unzuständigkeit zurückgewiesen werden muss, obwohl die Voraussetzungen im Zeitpunkt der Entscheidung gegeben sind. Andernfalls müsste das Gericht die Klage zurückweisen; die Klage müsste daraufhin neuerlich in diesem Staat eingebracht werden, weil sich nunmehr der gewöhnliche Aufenthalt in diesem Staat befindet. Für die hier vertretene Auffassung sprechen insbesondere verfahrensökonomische Erwägungen. Anders verhält es sich nur dann, wenn zuvor ein Antrag bei den Gerichten eines international zuständigen Staats gestellt worden ist. In diesem Fall hat sich das zuerst angerufene Gericht für unzuständig zu erklären; andernfalls würde die Bestimmung des Art. 20 Abs. 2 Brüssel IIb-VO konterkariert werden.[99]

---

buch des europäischen Zivilverfahrensrechts/Neumayr/Weber, 2. Aufl. 2023, Rn. 4.133; aA Heinrich FamRZ 2002, 1185 (Entscheidungsanm.), nach dessen Auffassung das innerstaatliche Recht maßgeblich sein solle, ob es eine *perpetuatio fori* gebe oder nicht.

[94] Gitschthaler, Internationales Familienrecht/Huter, 2019, KSÜ Art. 5 Rn. 78.

[95] Nademleinsky EF-Z 2011, 85 (87); Traar iFamZ 2011, 44 (48).

[96] Heindler IPRax 2014, 201 (202); Gitschthaler, Internationales Familienrecht/Huter, 2019, KSÜ Art. 5 Rn. 77.

[97] Siehe Fn. 2 und 3.

[98] Vgl. Sternal, FamFG/Sternal, 21. Aufl. 2023, § 2 Rn. 33.

[99] Siehe dazu Gitschthaler, Internationales Familienrecht/Garber, 2019, Brüssel IIa-VO Art. 8 Rn. 48 mwN. Geimer/Schütze, EuZVR/Geimer, 4. Aufl. 2020, EuEheVO Art. 8 Rn. 22f.

Demgegenüber vertritt der OGH[100] die Auffassung, dass der Umstand, dass die Zuständigkeitstatbestände erst zu einem späteren Zeitpunkt eintreten, im Rechtsmittelverfahren, sofern Neuerungsverbot gilt, nicht mehr zu berücksichtigen sei und die Klage daher wegen des früheren Mangels der internationalen Zuständigkeit zurückgewiesen werden müsse. Eine Ausnahme vom Neuerungsverbot solle aufgrund des ausdrücklichen Wortlauts des § 42 Abs. 1 JN nämlich nur in Bezug auf solche Tatsachen bestehen, aus denen hervorgehe, dass die Rechtssache der internationalen Zuständigkeit entzogen sei. Für das positive Vorliegen der internationalen Zuständigkeit fehle eine entsprechende Vorschrift, weshalb Tatsachen, die im Rechtsmittelverfahren gegen eine Zurückweisung der Klage vorgebracht werden, dem Neuerungsverbot unterliegen würden. Demnach seien im Rechtsmittelverfahren nur der Wegfall der internationalen Zuständigkeit, nicht aber auch deren Eintritt zu berücksichtigen. Die Auffassung überzeugt nicht.[101] Die zu Unrecht erfolgte Bejahung der internationalen Zuständigkeit stellt nämlich keinen gravierenderen Mangel dar als ihre zu Unrecht erfolgte Verneinung. Zudem sind nach § 482 Abs. 2 ZPO neue Tatsachen und Beweismittel sowohl zur Dartuung als auch zur Widerlegung von Rechtsmittelgründen zulässig. Da die (nicht geheilte bzw. nicht heilbare) internationale Unzuständigkeit gem. § 42 Abs. 1 JN und § 477 Abs. 1 Ziff. 3 ZPO einen Nichtigkeitsgrund darstellt, sind auch Tatsachen, durch die der nachträgliche Wegfall der internationalen Unzuständigkeit dargetan werden soll, nicht vom Neuerungsverbot erfasst, weil dadurch das Vorliegen eines Nichtigkeitsgrundes widerlegt werden soll.[102] Wenn der nach Gerichtsanhängigkeit erfolgte Eintritt der internationalen Zuständigkeit von einer Partei in einem Rechtsmittel geltend gemacht werden kann, muss – bei Vorliegen eines zulässigen Rechtsmittels – der Wegfall der internationalen Unzuständigkeit auch von Amts wegen wahrgenommen werden können.[103]

Für die hier vertretene Auffassung können wiederum verfahrensökonomische Erwägungen angeführt werden: Könnte der im Rechtsmittelverfahren erfolgte Eintritt der internationalen Zuständigkeit nicht berücksichtigt werden, müsste die Klage mit Beschluss zurückgewiesen werden und der Kläger wäre gezwungen, eine neue Klage einzubringen. Dadurch erhöhen sich nicht nur der Zeit- und Kostenaufwand, sondern es besteht auch die Gefahr, dass der Kläger – etwa aufgrund der mittlerweile eingetretenen Verjährung – seinen Anspruch nicht mehr erfolgreich durchsetzen kann.[104]

---

[100] RIS-Justiz RS0053062; vgl auch Höllwerth/Ziehensack, ZPO/Stefula, 2019, JN § 76 Rn. 33.

[101] Fasching/Konecny, Kommentar zu den Zivilprozessgesetzen/Garber, 3. Aufl. 2013, JN § 42 Rn. 50; Garber EvBl 2022, 1152; Simotta FS Schütze, 1999, 831 (874f.); Simotta, Die internationale Zuständigkeit in Ehesachen nach der Brüssel IIb-VO, in Garber/Lugani, Die Brüssel IIb-Verordnung: Zuständigkeit, Anerkennung und Vollstreckung in Ehesachen und Kindschaftssachen einschließlich der internationalen Kindesentführung, 2022, Rn. 5/130.

[102] Fenyves/Kerschner/Vonkilch, Großkommentar zum ABGB – Klang-Kommentar/Garber, 3. Aufl. 2021, EheG § 46 Rn. 49 mwN.

[103] Garber EvBl 2022, 1152; Fasching/Konecny Kommentar zu den Zivilprozessgesetzen/Simotta, 2. Aufl. 2010, EuEheKindVO Art. 3 Rn. 14.

[104] Fasching/Konecny, Kommentar zu den Zivilprozessgesetzen/Simotta, 2. Aufl. 2010, EuEheKindVO Art. 3 Rn. 19.

VIII. Resümee

Die Anwendung des Grundsatzes der *perpetuatio fori* erscheint u. E. auch in Verfahren betreffend die elterliche Verantwortung sinnvoll. Es entspricht dem Kindeswohl, Verfahren – insbesondere solche, die bereits weit fortgeschritten sind – trotz Wegfall der die internationale Zuständigkeit begründeten Umstände zu Ende zu führen, andernfalls müsste in einem anderen Mitgliedstaat das Verfahren gänzlich neu durchgeführt werden, wodurch in aller Regel die verfahrensbedingten Belastungen für das Kind zunehmen.

Im Einzelfall bedarf es allerdings Instrumente, um im konkreten Einzelfall Härten, die durch die *perpetuatio fori* entstehen, zu vermeiden – dazu zählt insbesondere die Möglichkeit des Zuständigkeitstransfers vom Gericht des Staats, in dem sich bislang der gewöhnliche Aufenthalt des Kindes befunden hatte, zu dem Staat, in dem das Kind nunmehr über seinen gewöhnlichen Aufenthalt verfügt.

HERBERT GEISLER

Scheut der Bundesgerichtshof Vorlagen an den Europäischen Gerichtshof in Luxemburg am Beispiel der Dieselabgasfälle?

I. Sachverhalt

Unabhängig von den verschiedenen Sachverhaltsvarianten beruhen die Dieselabgasfälle auf folgendem Grundsachverhalt: Ein Kläger hat von einem Autohändler ein Fahrzeug erworben, welches mit einem Dieselmotor der mit der Schadstoffnorm Euro 5 ausgestattet ist. Für den Fahrzeugtyp wurde die Typgenehmigung nach der VO (EG) Nr. 715/2007 mit der Schadstoffklasse Euro 5 erteilt. Der Autohersteller hatte eine unzulässige Abschalteinrichtung eingebaut. Diese hatte den Zweck, beim Abgasprüfungstest die Messwerte dadurch zu manipulieren, dass der Abgasausstoß nur während der Prüfphase die vorgeschriebenen Abgaswerte erreicht. Im normalen Straßenverkehr werden diese Werte erheblich überschritten. Der Kläger verlangt im Wesentlichen die Rückzahlung des für das Fahrzeug gezahlten Kaufpreises nebst Zinsen Zug um Zug gegen Übergabe und Übereignung des Fahrzeugs.

II. Lösungsansätze des BGH zu den Haftungsgrundlagen

1. Gegen Verkäufer

Gegen den Verkäufer hat der Käufer eines mit einer Manipulationssoftware ausgestatteten Pkw grundsätzlich Gewährleistungsansprüche nach §§ 434ff. BGB. In den meisten Fällen war die kaufrechtliche Gewährleistungsfrist von 2 Jahren gem. § 438 Abs. 1 Nr. 3 BGB inzwischen abgelaufen bzw. 3 Jahren gem. § 438 Abs. 3 BGB mangels eigener Kenntnis des Händlers von der Manipulationssoftware und fehlender Zurechnung des arglistigen Verhaltens des Herstellers zum Vertragshändler.[1]

2. Gegen Hersteller

Mangels Vertragsbeziehung entfallen kaufrechtliche Gewährleistungsansprüche gegen den Fahrzeughersteller. Dem Käufer stellt sich sodann die Frage, ob er vom Fahrzeughersteller Rückzahlung des Kaufpreises aus deliktischen Schadensersatzansprüchen (§ 826 BGB; § 823 Abs. 2 iVm einem Schutzgesetz) verlangen kann.

---

[1] BGH 9.6.2020 – VIII ZR 315/19, NJW 2020, 3312 Rn. 18.

a) § 826 BGB

aa) Haftungsgrundsätze

Der BGH stellte im Urteil vom 25.5.2020[2] die Grundsätze auf zu den relevanten Fragen einer Haftung des Fahrzeugherstellers wegen Verwendung einer unzulässigen Abschalteinrichtung aus vorsätzlicher sittenwidriger Schädigung gemäß §§ 826, 31 BGB. Der Käufer sei veranlasst durch das einer arglistigen Täuschung gleichstehende sittenwidrige Verhalten des Herstellers eine ungewollte vertragliche Verpflichtung eingegangen. Darin liege sein Schaden, weil er ein Fahrzeug erhalten habe, das für seine Zwecke nicht voll brauchbar sei.[3] Er müsse sich aber die Nutzungsvorteile auf der Grundlage der gefahrenen Kilometer anrechnen lassen, weil er im Hinblick auf das schadensersatzrechtliche Bereicherungsverbot nicht bessergestellt werden dürfe als er ohne den ungewollten Vertragsschluss stünde.[4]

bb) Thermofenster

Nach der Rechtsprechung des BGH reicht der Umstand, dass die Abgasrückführung durch eine temperaturabhängige Steuerung des Emissionskontrollsystems reduziert und letztlich ganz abgeschaltet wird („Thermofenster"), für sich genommen nicht aus, um dem Verhalten der für die Hersteller handelnden Personen ein sittenwidriges Gepräge zu geben.[5] Bei einer Abschalteinrichtung, die im Grundsatz auf dem Prüfstand in gleicher Weise arbeitet wie im realen Fahrbetrieb und bei der die Frage der Zulässigkeit nicht eindeutig und unzweifelhaft beantwortet werden kann, müssen weitere Umstände hinzutreten, die das Verhalten der handelnden Personen als besonders verwerflich erscheinen lassen.[6]

cc) Wegfall der Verwerflichkeit ab September 2015

Mit der sittenwidrigen Haftung der Fahrzeughersteller hätten die Käufer zufrieden sein können. Doch die vom BGH angenommene Sittenwidrigkeit des Herstellers endete jedoch ab September 2015, nachdem VW und danach auch weitere Hersteller öffentlich in einer sog. Ad-hoc-Mitteilung die Verwendung einer entsprechenden Manipulationssoftware eingeräumt hatten. Darin sieht der BGH eine grundlegende Verhaltensänderung des Herstellers.[7] Eine Haftung des Herstellers aus § 826 BGB scheidet damit grundsätzlich aus, wenn der Käufer das Fahrzeug nach September 2015 erworben hat.[8]

dd) Verjährung

Keine Aussicht auf Schadensersatz haben diejenigen, die das Fahrzeug zwar vor September 2015 gekauft haben, im Jahr 2015 unzweifelhaft vom Dieselskandal wussten und erst nach dem Ablauf des Jahres 2018 geklagt haben. Die dreijährige

---

[2] BGH 25.5.2020 – VI ZR 252/19, BGHZ 225, 316 = NJW 2020, 1962.
[3] BGH 25.5.2020 – VI ZR 252/19, BGHZ 225, 316 = NJW 2020, 1962 Rn. 46.
[4] BGH 25.5.2020 – VI ZR 252/19, BGHZ 225, 316 = NJW 2020, 1962 Rn. 64ff.
[5] BGH 16.9.2021 – VII ZR 286/20, BeckRS 2021, 30338 Rn. 15
[6] BGH 24.3.2022 – III ZR 270/20, BeckRS 2022, 10055 Rn. 16.
[7] BGH 22.2.2022 – VI ZR 934/20, BeckRS 2022, 4978 Rn. 17 mwN.
[8] BGH 28.10.2021 – III ZR 261/20, NJW-RR 2022, 243 Rn. 17.

Verjährungsfrist des § 195 BGB beginnt mit Schluss des Jahres 2015 und kann durch eine nach 2018 erhobene Klage nicht mehr gehemmt werden. Ein Käufer hat die für den Verjährungsbeginn erforderliche allgemeine Kenntnis vom Dieselskandal durch die umfassende Medienberichterstattung aus dem Jahr 2015 spätestens bis Ende des Jahres 2015 erlangt, selbst wenn er nicht laufend die Pressemeldungen verfolgt hat. Ihn trifft der Vorwurf grob fahrlässiger Unkenntnis von der konkreten Betroffenheit seines Fahrzeugs gemäß § 199 Abs. 1 Nr. 2 Fall 2 BGB[9].

b) §§ 826, 831 BGB

Einen Anspruch aus §§ 826, 831 BGB gegen einen Verrichtungsgehilfen lehnt der BGH ab, weil auch die für den Hersteller tätigen Personen dem Kläger aus den vorstehenden Gründen nicht in einer gegen die guten Sitten verstoßenden Weise Schaden zugefügt haben[10].

c) § 852 BGB

Nach Verjährung des Anspruchs aus § 826 BGB steht dem Neuwagenkäufer[11] zu mindestens noch ein Restschadensersatzanspruch nach § 852 Satz 1 BGB gegen den Hersteller zu auf Herausgabe des von ihm Erlangten[12]. Das ist der Händlereinkaufspreis[13].

d) § 823 Abs. 2 BGB iVm § 263 StGB

Eine Haftung des Herstellers aus § 823 Abs. 2 BGB iVm § 263 StGB scheitere beim Kauf eines Gebrauchtwagens schon an der erforderlichen Stoffgleichheit des erstrebten rechtswidrigen Vermögensvorteils mit einem etwaigen Vermögensschaden[14].

e) § 823 Abs. 2 BGB iVm § 6 Abs. 1, § 27 Abs. 1 EG-FGV oder Normen der VO (EG) Nr. 715/2007

Kann ein Käufer die strengen Voraussetzungen einer Haftung wegen vorsätzlicher sittenwidriger Schädigung nach § 826 BGB nicht darlegen und beweisen oder wurde der Kaufvertrag erst nach der ad-hoc-Mitteilung vom 22.9.2015 abgeschlossen, versagte der BGH jeglichen Schadensersatz. Da die Rechtslage zur Legalität von Thermofenstern unsicher ist, sei allenfalls ein Fahrlässigkeitsvorwurf gerechtfertigt[15]. § 826 BGB setze jedoch Vorsatz voraus.

---

[9] BGH 10.2.2022 – VII ZR 692/21, BeckRS 2022, 4168 Rn. 23ff.; 10.2.2022 – VII ZR 679/21, BeckRS 2022,4167 Rn. 24ff.

[10] BGH 8.3.2021 – VI ZR 505/19, NJW 2021, 1669 Rn. 35.

[11] Nicht bei Kauf eines Gebrauchtwagens vgl. BGH 10.2.2022 – VII ZR 365/21, NJW 2022, 1311 Rn. 30f.; BGH 10.2.2022 – VII ZR 692/21, BeckRS 2022, 4168 Rn. 44f.; BGH 10.2.2022 – VII ZR 717/21, BeckRS 2022, 4153 Rn. 38f.

[12] BGH 3.4.2023 – VIa ZR 233/22, BeckRS 2023, 11374 Rn. 9 mwN.

[13] BGH 21.2.2022 – VIa ZR 57/21, NJW-RR 2022, 850 Rn. 14.

[14] BGH 30.7.2020 – VI ZR 5/20, NJW 2020, 2798 Rn. 24ff.

[15] BGH 16.9.2021 – VII ZR 190/20, NJW 2021, 3721 Rn. 31.

Deshalb stützten die Fahrzeugkäufer ihr Klagebegehren wegen einer fahrlässig verbauten illegalen Abschalteinrichtung auch auf Schutzgesetzverletzung aus § 823 Abs. 2 BGB iVm § 6 Abs. 1, § 27 Abs. 1 EG-FGV („Fahrzeuggenehmigungsverordnung“) oder Art. 5 Abs. 2 der VO (EG) Nr. 715/2007 („Fahrzeugemissionenverordnung“). Die VO (EG) Nr. 715/2007 verbietet ausdrücklich die Verwendung von Abschalteinrichtungen, die die Wirkung von Emissionskontrollsystemen unter normalen Nutzungsbedingungen verringern.

Dennoch lehnten die betroffenen Senate des BGH Schadensersatzansprüche wegen Schutzgesetzverletzung ab. Aus einem Verstoß gegen die vorgenannten Vorschriften könne kein auf Rückabwicklung eines Fahrzeugkaufvertrages gerichteter Schadensersatzanspruch hergeleitet werden, da das Interesse, nicht zur Eingehung einer ungewollten Verbindlichkeit veranlasst zu werden, nicht dem Schutz des Fahrzeugkäufers diene[16]. Die Käufer hätten mangels individualschützenden Charakters der Normen der VO (EG) Nr. 715/2007 keinen Anspruch darauf, sich von dem ungewollt geschlossenen Kaufvertrag zu lösen.

Damit hat der BGH den Käufern den „großen Schadensersatz“, also die Rückabwicklung der betroffenen Kaufverträge, versagt. Die unionsrechtlichen Regeln für Automobilhersteller, die Abschalteinrichtungen verbieten[17] und verlangen, dass Autos mit dem zugelassenen Typ übereinstimmen[18], seien nicht drittschützend im Sinne von § 823 Abs. 2 BGB[19]. Die betroffenen §§ 6, 27 Abs. 1 EG-FGV sowie Art. 5 Abs. 2 VO (EG) Nr. 715/2007 dienten dem Umweltschutz und der Luftqualität, bezweckten jedenfalls keinen Schutz der allgemeinen Handlungsfreiheit und speziell des wirtschaftlichen Selbstbestimmungsrechts der einzelnen Käufer[20]. Die Übereinstimmungserklärung nach Art. 18 iVm Anh. IX Richtlinie 2007/46/EG habe deshalb keine besondere Bedeutung. Anderes ergebe sich auch nicht aus dem Grundsatz der möglichst wirksamen Anwendung des Gemeinschaftsrechts (effet utile), da die Regelung weder individuelle Käuferinteressen im Blick habe noch dem Einzelnen Rechte verleihe. Ein Vorabentscheidungsersuchen lehnte der BGH ab, da die Rechtslage nach seiner Auffassung eindeutig (acte clair) sei. Es drängt sich die Frage auf, ob der BGH die Frage eines europarechtlichen Individualschutzes dem Europäischen Gerichtshof (EuGH) vorlegen musste.

III. Vorlagepflicht an den Europäischen Gerichtshof

1. Verhältnis EuGH/BGH

Der EuGH ist kein „Konkurrent“ zum BGH, da es sich um zwei verschiedene Gerichte handelt, die in unterschiedlichen Rechtsbereichen tätig sind.

---

[16] BGH 16.9.2021 – VII ZR 190/20, NJW 2021, 3721 Rn. 36 mwN.
[17] Art. 5 Abs. 2 VO (EG) Nr. 715/2007.
[18] Art. 18 EG-Richtlinie 2007/46.
[19] BGH 4.5.2022 VII ZR 733/21, BeckRS 2022, 14779 Rn. 14 mwN.
[20] BGH 10.2.2022 – III ZR 87/21, BeckRS 2022, 4565 Rn. 14 mwN.

Der BGH ist das höchste Gericht der ordentlichen Gerichtsbarkeit in Deutschland und ist zuständig für die Auslegung und Anwendung des deutschen Rechts.

Der EuGH ist hingegen das höchste Gericht in der Europäischen Union und ist zuständig für die Auslegung und Anwendung des EU-Rechts einschließlich der Verträge, der EU-Gesetze und EU-Verordnungen sowie der Entscheidungen und Handlungen der EU-Organe.

Der EuGH hat auch die Befugnis, über Vorabentscheidungsersuchen nationaler Gerichte zu entscheiden, die sich mit der Auslegung des EU-Rechts befassen. Die Einheit der Unionsrechtsordnung ist nämlich bedroht, wenn das Unionsrecht in den Mitgliedstaaten ungleich angewandt wird. Deshalb gliedert Art. 267 AEUV den EuGH funktional in die Gerichtsbarkeit der Mitgliedstaaten ein, soweit ihm im Interesse der Rechtssicherheit und der Rechtsanwendungsgleichheit die Auslegung und Anwendung des Unionsrechts aufgegeben ist[21].

Der EuGH ist zwar kein oberstes europäisches Berufungsgericht. Befasst sich der EuGH mit einer Vorlage, so beantwortet er idR eine abstrakte Rechtsfrage in Form eines Gutachtens, beschränkt sich hierbei jedoch auf die Auslegung europäischen Rechts. Er garantiert über das Vorabentscheidungsersuchen jedoch, dass das europäische Recht in der gesamten EU einheitlich ausgelegt wird. Faktisch kommt dies einer Normenkontrolle gleich, weil indirekt geprüft wird, ob nationales Recht mit europäischem Recht vereinbar ist.

Die Wirkung des Urteils des EuGH im Vorabentscheidungsverfahren auf jeweils nationale Gerichte ist nicht ausdrücklich geregelt. Ausgehend vom Zweck des Art. 267 AEUV binden Auslegungsentscheidungen das vorlegende Gericht und die beteiligten Instanzgerichte[22], nach hM gilt dies auch für andere Gerichtsverfahren[23]. Erklärt der EuGH einen Unionsrechtsakt im Vorabentscheidungsverfahren für ungültig, hat diese Entscheidung eine umfassende Bindungswirkung[24].

2. *Vorabentscheidungsverfahren nach Art. 267 AEUV*

Nach Art. 267 AEUV können nationale Gerichte dem EuGH in einem Vorabentscheidungsverfahren Rechtsfragen zur Auslegung und Gültigkeit europarechtlicher Bestimmungen vorlegen. Da der EuGH „gesetzlicher Richter" iSd Art. 101 GG ist, ist der BGH als letztinstanzliches nationales Gericht zur Aussetzung des Rechtsstreits und Herbeiführung einer Vorabentscheidung des EuGH wegen einer Frage zur Auslegung des Unionsrechts zur Vorlage verpflichtet[25], während Instanzgerichte die Wahl haben[26].

Die Nichtbeachtung der Vorlagepflicht verletzt das Recht des Rechtssuchenden auf den gesetzlichen Richter nach Art. 101 Abs. 1 Satz 2 GG. Nach der Rechtsprechung des BVerfG[27] wird aber nur die willkürliche Nichtvorlage verfassungsrecht-

---

[21] BVerfG 9.8.2023 – 2 BvR 558/22, BeckRS 2023, 22722 Rn. 25 mwN.
[22] Fink Heidelberger Beiträge zum Finanz- und Steuerrecht 13 (2019) , S. 141 f.
[23] Fink Heidelberger Beiträge zum Finanz- und Steuerrecht 13 (2019), S. 142 f.
[24] Fink Heidelberger Beiträge zum Finanz- und Steuerrecht 13 (2019), S. 144.
[25] Art. 267 Abs. 3 AEUV.
[26] Art. 267 Abs. 2 AEUV.
[27] BVerfG 30.9.2022 – 2 BvR 2222/21, NJW 2022, 3413 Rn. 52.

lich sanktioniert. Für die Frage nach einer Verletzung des Rechts auf den gesetzlichen Richter kommt es nicht in erster Linie auf die Vertretbarkeit der fachgerichtlichen Auslegung des für den Streitfall maßgeblichen materiellen Unionsrechts an, sondern auf die Beachtung oder Verkennung der Voraussetzungen der Vorlagepflicht nach der Vorschrift des Art. 267 Abs. 3 AEUV, die den gesetzlichen Richter im Streitfall bestimmt[28]. Die Nichteinleitung eines Vorlageverfahrens nach Art. 267 Abs. 3 AEUV kann demnach eine der einheitlichen Auslegung bedürftige Frage des Unionsrechts der Entscheidung des gesetzlichen Richters – des EuGH – vorenthalten und damit das Ergebnis der Entscheidung beeinflussen[29]. Von der Vorlagepflicht darf nur abgewichen werden, wenn die Frage nicht entscheidungserheblich ist, in der Rechtsprechung des EuGH eindeutig geklärt („acte éclairé") oder die richtige Auslegung von vornherein so ist, dass für vernünftige Zweifel kein Raum bleibt („acte clair")[30]. Bei der Beurteilung, ob ein solcher Fall vorliegt, sind die Eigenheiten und Schwierigkeiten des Unionsrechts zu berücksichtigen[31].

Art. 101 Abs. 1 Satz 2 GG ist jedoch verletzt, wenn der BGH als letztinstanzliches Hauptsachegericht den ihm in solchen Fällen notwendig zukommenden Beurteilungsrahmen in unvertretbarer Weise überschritten hat[32]. Dies ist insbesondere dann der Fall, wenn mögliche Gegenauffassungen zu der entscheidungserheblichen Frage des Unionsrechts gegenüber der vom BGH vertretenen Meinung eindeutig vorzuziehen sind[33]. Jedenfalls bei willkürlicher Annahme eines „acte clair" durch die Fachgerichte ist der Beurteilungsrahmen in unvertretbarer Weise überschritten[34].

In diesem Zusammenhang ist auch zu prüfen, ob sich das Gericht hinsichtlich des Unionsrechts ausreichend kundig gemacht hat. Etwaige einschlägige Rechtsprechung des EuGH muss es auswerten und seine Entscheidung hieran orientieren. Auf dieser Grundlage muss der BGH unter Anwendung und Auslegung des materiellen Unionsrechts die vertretbare Überzeugung bilden, dass die Rechtslage entweder von vornherein eindeutig („acte clair") oder durch Rechtsprechung in einer Weise geklärt ist, die keinen vernünftigen Zweifel („acte éclairé") offenlässt[35]. Hat er dies nicht getan, verkennt er regelmäßig die Bedingungen für die Vorlagepflicht. Zudem hat der BGH Gründe anzugeben, die dem Bundesverfassungsgericht eine Kontrolle am Maßstab des Art. 101 Abs. 1 Satz 2 GG ermöglichen[36].

---

[28] BVerfG 25.2.2010 – 1 BvR 230/09, BVerfGK 17, 108 Rn. 14ff. mwN.

[29] BVerfG 28.1.2014 – 2 BvR 1561/12, BeckRS 2014, 46295 Rn. 177 mwN.

[30] EuGH 6.10.2021 – C-561/19, Celex-Nr. 62019CJ0561 Rn. 33 = NJW 2021, 3303; BVerfG 28.8.2014 – 2 BvR 2639/09, NVwZ 2015, 52 Rn. 35.

[31] EuGH 6.10.2021 – C-561/19, NJW 2021, 3303 Rn. 41.

[32] BVerfG 28.1.2014 – 2 BvR 1561/12, BVerfGE 135, 155 Rn. 183.

[33] BVerfG 6.12.2006 – 1 BvR 2085/03, BVerfGK 10, 19 Rn. 30 mwN.

[34] BVerfG 19.12.2017 – 2 BvR 424/17, BVerfGE 147, 364 Rn. 43.

[35] BVerfG 20.4.2022 – 2 BvR 1713/21, BeckRS 2022, 9227 Rn. 47.

[36] BVerfG 19.12.2017 – 2 BvR 424/17, BVerfGE 147, 364 Rn. 41 mwN.

3. Vorabentscheidungsverfahren sind die häufigste Verfahrensart am EuGH

a) Vorabentscheidungsverfahren im Jahr 2022

Im Jahr 2022 waren von 806 neuen Rechtssachen am EuGH 546 Vorabentscheidungsersuchen (ca. 67%). Davon kamen 98 aus Deutschland. Damit lagen die deutschen Gerichte deutlich vor den Gerichten der anderen großen Mitgliedstaaten Italien (63), Bulgarien (43), Spanien (41), Polen (39) und Österreich (34).[37]

b) Vorabentscheidungsvorlagen der Zivilsenate des BGH von 2006 bis 2022

Obwohl sich die Neueingänge in Zivilsachen beim BGH zwischen 2006 (3319)[38] und 2022 (4933)[39] beträchtlich erhöht haben, nahmen dessen Vorlagen an den EuGH nicht im gleichen Verhältnis zu. Von „Ausreißern" abgesehen sind die Vorlagen nahezu gleichgeblieben.

In den 16 Jahren von 2006 bis 2022 gab es (einschließlich Strafsenate) 183 Vorlagen zwischen 4 Vorlagen im Jahr 2010 und 21 Vorlagen im Jahr 2013, also im Jahresdurchschnitt 11,44 Vorlagen. Diese verteilten sich nur auf die Zivilsenate wie folgt:

2022: 10 Vorlagen, davon 3 vom I. Zivilsenat, 1 vom VI. Zivilsenat, 1 vom IX. Zivilsenat, 2 vom X. Zivilsenat, 1 vom XI. Zivilsenat, 1 vom XII. Zivilsenat und 1 vom Kartellsenat

2021: 7 Vorlagen, davon 4 vom I. Zivilsenat, 2 vom X. Zivilsenat und 1 vom Kartellsenat

2020: 17 Vorlagen, davon 10 vom I. Zivilsenat, jeweils zwei vom VI. und IX. Zivilsenat und jeweils 1 vom VII., XI. und den XII. Zivilsenat

2019: 8 Vorlagen, davon 5 vom I. Zivilsenat und jeweils 1 vom II., XII. Zivilsenat sowie Kartellsenat

2018: 11 Vorlagen, davon 8 vom I. Zivilsenat und jeweils 1 vom III., V. und IX. Zivilsenat

2017: 17 Vorlagen, davon 14 vom I. Zivilsenat und jeweils 1 vom V., VIII. und X. Zivilsenat

2016: 11 Vorlagen, davon 7 vom I. Zivilsenat, 3 vom X. Zivilsenat und 1 vom Kartellsenat

2015: 7 Vorlagen, davon 3 vom I. Zivilsenat, 4 auf die übrigen Zivilsenate

2014: 7 Vorlagen, davon 3 vom I. Zivilsenat, 4 auf die übrigen Zivilsenate

2013: 18 Vorlagen, davon 6 vom I. Zivilsenat, 10 von anderen Zivilsenaten und 2 von Spezialsenaten

---

[37] Pressemitteilung des EuGH Nr. 42/23 vom 3.3.2023 S. 3, 4.

[38] BGH, Übersicht über den Geschäftsgang bei den Zivilsenaten des Bundesgerichtshofes im Jahre 2006 – Jahresstatistik, https://www.bundesgerichtshof.de/SharedDocs/Downloads/DE/Service/StatistikZivil/jahresstatistikZivilsenate2006.pdf?__blob=publicationFile&v=2 (abgerufen 13.5.2024).

[39] BGH, Übersicht über den Geschäftsgang bei den Zivilsenaten des Bundesgerichtshofes im Jahre 2022 – Jahresstatistik, https://www.bundesgerichtshof.de/SharedDocs/Downloads/DE/Service/StatistikZivil/jahresstatistikZivilsenate2022.pdf?__blob=publicationFile&v=3 (abgerufen (13.5.2024).

2012: 12 Vorlagen, davon 8 vom I. Zivilsenat, 2 vom IX. Zivilsenat und je eine vom IV. und vom XII. Zivilsenat.
2011: 16 Vorlagen, davon 9 vom I. Zivilsenat, 1 vom V. Zivilsenat, 3 vom VIII. Zivilsenat, 2 vom X. Zivilsenat und 1 vom Kartellsenat.
2010: 3 Vorlagen, davon 1 vom II. Zivilsenat und 2 vom Xa. Zivilsenat
2009: 8 Vorlagen, davon 2 vom I. Zivilsenat, 1 vom VI. Zivilsenat, 3 vom VIII. Zivilsenat, 1 vom Xa Zivilsenat und 1 vom XII. Zivilsenat
2008: 8 Vorlagen, davon 2 vom I. Zivilsenat, 1 vom II. Zivilsenat, 2 vom VIII. Zivilsenat und 3 vom X. Zivilsenat.
2007: 8 Vorlagen, davon 3 vom I. Zivilsenat und jeweils 2 vom X. Zivilsenat sowie vom Senat für Landwirtschaftssachen und 1 vom Zivilsenat.
2006: 6 Vorlagen, davon 2 vom I. Zivilsenat und jeweils 1 vom III., dem VI., vom VII. und vom VIII. Zivilsenat.

In Anbetracht der relativ großen Zahl der Vorlagen aller Gerichte aus Deutschland, auch durch die Zivilsenate des BGH, verwundert es, dass der BGH in den Dieselskandalfällen trotz der tangierten europarechtlichen Bestimmungen eine Vorlage nach Art. 267 AEUV und laufender Anregungen von den jeweiligen Klägern durchweg abgelehnt hat. Der BGH hatte doch nichts zu „befürchten", wenn seine Auffassung zutreffend gewesen wäre und er eine Bestätigung seiner Auffassung durch den EuGH erhalten hätte. Oder wollte der BGH einer seiner Rechtsauffassung entgegenstehenden Rechtsprechung des EuGH aus dem Weg gehen?

IV. Diskrepanz zwischen BGH und EuGH bei der Auslegung europarechtlicher Bestimmungen (als Drittschutz)

1. Stetige Ablehnung einer Vorlage durch den BGH

Eine Unsicherheit bei der Anwendung des EU-Rechts hat der BGH herbeigeführt mit seiner Verweigerung einer Vorlage an den EuGH zur Auslegung der einschlägigen Bestimmungen des Unionsrechts. Obwohl europarechtliche Bestimmungen die Grundlage dafür bilden, ob eine Abschalteinrichtung unzulässig ist oder die europarechtlichen Bestimmungen Drittschutz gewähren, haben alle betroffenen Senate des BGH sich auf eine Vorsatzhaftung nach § 826 BGB beschränkt und eine Vorlage an den EuGH zur Prüfung einer Haftung nach § 823 Abs. 2 BGB iVm einem Schutzgesetz stets abgelehnt. Eine Vorlage an den EuGH gemäß Art. 267 Abs. 1 und 3 AEUV sei entbehrlich, da die Unionsrechtslage so eindeutig sei (acte clair), dass keinerlei Raum für einen vernünftigen Zweifel an einer Entscheidung des EuGH bleibe[40].

Für einen vernünftigen Zweifel könnte aber nur dann kein Raum bestehen, wenn der BGH davon überzeugt wäre, dass auch für die Gerichte der übrigen Mitgliedstaaten und für den Gerichtshof der EuGH selbst die gleiche Gewissheit bestünde. Nur dann durfte der BGH von einer Vorlage absehen und die Frage in

[40] BGH 24.3.2022 – III ZR 270/20, BeckRS 2022, 10055 Rn. 29 mwN.

eigener Verantwortung lösen[41]. Hiervon konnte in den Dieselfällen nicht ausgegangen werden. Bereits vor den Entscheidungen des BGH zur deliktsrechtlichen Haftung drängte sich aufgrund eines Vorlagebeschlusses des LG Erfurt zur verbraucherschützenden Wirkung der europarechtlichen Bestimmungen eine Vorlage auf[42]. Mit der Auffassung anderer europäischer Gerichte und den Entscheidungen des EuGH zu unzulässigen Abschalteinrichtungen[43] hat sich der BGH nicht befasst. Der VI. Zivilsenat des BGH[44] hat das streiterhebliche Unionsrecht unvollständig und damit nicht vertretbar ausgelegt. Er führt ohne nähere Begründung aus:

„… Die Rechtslage ist sowohl im Hinblick auf § 6 Abs. 1, § 27 Abs. 1 EG-FGV (vgl. Senatsurteil vom 25. Mai 2020 – VI ZR 252/19, ZIP 2020, 1179 Rn. 77) als auch im Hinblick auf Art. 5 VO 715/2007/EG wie dargestellt von vornherein eindeutig („acte claire", vgl. EuGH, Urteil vom 6. Oktober 1982 – Rs 283/81, NJW 1983, 1257, 1258; BVerfG, NVwZ 2015, 52 Rn. 35). Anderes ergibt sich nicht aus dem Umstand, dass die Landgerichte Stuttgart (BeckRS 2020, 3558), Gera (7 O 1188/18, juris) und Erfurt (8 O 1045/18, juris) Vorabentscheidungsersuchen an den EuGH zur Auslegung der genannten Vorschriften gerichtet haben (vgl. EuGH, Urteil vom 9. September 2015 – C-72/14, C-197/14, juris Tz. 56–63".

Andere Senate haben sich der Rechtsauffassung des VI. Zivilsenats hinsichtlich eines „acte clair" angeschlossen[45].

2. *Vorlage trotz Ablehnung durch BGH*

Es kam dann, wie es kommen musste. Trotz wiederholter Ablehnung einer gebotenen Vorlage an den EuGH fassten Instanzgerichte den Mut, sich der Auffassung des BGH entgegenzustellen. Sie legten dem EuGH in Vorabentscheidungsverfahren Rechtsfragen zur Auslegung europarechtlicher Bestimmungen vor. Dies gab dem EuGH trotz der Ablehnung durch den BGH doch noch Gelegenheit zu entscheiden über die Vorlagefrage, ob § 6 Abs. 1, § 27 Abs. 1 EG-FGV, welche die Zulassung und Veräußerung von Fahrzeugen unter Beifügung der vom Hersteller

---

[41] BVerfG 25.2.2010 – 1 BvR 230/09, NJW 2010, 1268 Rn. 20.
[42] LG Erfurt 15.6.2020 – 8 O 1045/18, BeckRS 2020, 13203 Rn. 14.
[43] EuGH 17.12.2020 – C 693/18, ECLI:EU:C:2020:1040, Celex-Nr. 62018CJ0693, NJW 2021, 1216. Vorabentscheidungsersuchen der Juges d'instruction du tribunal de grande instance de Paris; EuGH 8.11.2022 – C-873/19, ECLI:EU:C:2022:857, Celex-Nr. 62019CA0873 Vorabentscheidungsersuchen des Schleswig-Holsteinischen Verwaltungsgerichts wegen Klagebefugnis der Deutschen Umwelthilfe für Klagen wegen unzulässiger Abschalteinrichtung; EuGH 14.7.2022 – C-128/20, ECLI:EU:C:2022:570, Celex-Nr. 62020CA0128 Vorabentscheidungsersuchen des LG Klagenfurt – Österreich; EuGH 14.7.2022 – C-134/20, ECLI:EU:C:2022:571, Celex-Nr. 62020CA0134 Vorabentscheidungsersuchen des LG Eisenstadt – Österreich und EuGH 14.7.2022 – C-145/20, ECLI:EU:C:2022:572, Vorabentscheidung auf Vorlage des Obersten Gerichtshof von Österreich wegen vertragswidriger Verwendung einer unzulässigen Abschalteinrichtung; EuGH 14.7.2022 – C-128/20, ECLI:EU:C:2022:570, Schadenersatz auch bei fehlender Sittenwidrigkeit.
[44] BGH 30.7.2020 – VI ZR 5/20, NJW 2020, 2798 Rn. 16.
[45] U. a. BGH 29.9.2021 – VII ZR 127/21, BeckRS 2021, 31184 Rn. 1; BGH 8.12.2021 – VIII ZR 190/19, JW 2022, 1238 Rn. 91; BGH 24.3.2022 – III ZR 270/20, BeckRS 2022, 10055 Rn. 29.

ausgestellten Übereinstimmungsbescheinigung regeln, den Schutz der allgemeinen Handlungsfreiheit und des wirtschaftlichen Selbstbestimmungsrechts des Käufers bezweckt und auch Art. 5 VO (EG) Nr. 715/2007, welcher die Verwendung von Abschalteinrichtungen untersagt, diesen Schutz gewährt. Mit den grundlegenden Erwägungen, die das LG Ravensburg[46] und das LG Erfurt[47] vorgebracht haben, hat sich der BGH nicht in hinreichender Weise auseinander gesetzt, obwohl er genügend Veranlassung hatte, seine europarechtswidrige Auffassung zu überprüfen. Umgekehrt hielt der BGH den vorlegenden Landgerichten vor, dass diese sich nicht mit den tragenden Erwägungen seiner eigenen Rechtsprechung auseinandersetzen würden. Er sehe keine Veranlassung, an der Annahme eines acte clair zu zweifeln.[48] Die europarechtlichen Bestimmungen schützten nicht den Käufer vor dem Abschluss eines ungewollten Vertrages.

Das Landgericht Ravensburg[49] setzte sich mit der Rechtsprechung des BGH sehr wohl auseinander. Es vertrat hinsichtlich des Individualrechtsschutzes der europarechtlichen Regelungen eine vom BGH mit Blick auf die europarechtlichen Aspekte abweichende Auffassung und zitierte auch andere Gerichte, die diese Auffassung teilten[50]. Das Landgericht Ravensburg hatte dem EuGH die Frage vorgelegt, ob sich der Hersteller Mercedes schon dann schadenersatzpflichtig gemacht habe, wenn die unzulässige Abschaltvorrichtung (Thermofenster) nur fahrlässig und nicht mit Vorsatz verwendet wurde, um die Einhaltung der Grenzwerte beim Emissionsausstoß zu umgehen. Dass die Auffassung des Landgerichts Ravensburg hinsichtlich der europarechtlichen Dimension nicht abwegig, sondern im Gegenteil durchaus gut vertretbar und aus der ex-post Perspektive sogar richtig war, bestätigt das auf Vorlage des LG Ravensburg[51] ergangene Urteil des EuGH[52]. In allen vom BGH abgelehnten Vorlagen an den EuGH lag bis dahin noch keine Entscheidung des EuGH über die Auslegung der für den Fall relevanten Regelungen des Unionsrechts vor. Dabei liegt die ausschließliche Zuständigkeit für die Auslegung des Unionsrechts beim EuGH.

Auch das Urteil des EuGH[53], in welchem er das Thermofenster als unzulässige Abschalteinrichtung qualifiziert hat, bewegte den BGH nicht zur Vorlage. Der EuGH erklärte die von VW im Motor EA 189 verbaute Abschaltvorrichtung sowie (obiter dictum) die meisten weiteren aktuell am Markt verwendeten Abschaltvorrichtungen für illegal. Auch die von VW nach Bekanntwerden des Abgasskandals neu entwickelte Motorsteuerung sei gesetzeswidrig, obwohl das Kraftfahrtbundes-

[46] EuGH-Vorlage vom LG Ravensburg 31.3.2021 – 2 O 339/19, BeckRS 2021, 7681 im Vorabentscheidungsverfahren C-240/21; EuGH-Vorlage vom LG Ravensburg 9.3.2021 – 2 O 366/20, BeckRS 2021, 4922 im Vorabentscheidungsverfahren C-178/21.

[47] EuGH-Vorlage vom LG Erfurt 9.8.2021 – 8 O 481/21, BeckRS 2021, 42707 im Vorabentscheidungsverfahren C-506/21; EuGH-Vorlage vom LG Erfurt 15.6.2020 – 8 O 1045/18, BeckRS 2020, 13203 im Vorabentscheidungsverfahren C-276/20.

[48] BGH 12.1.2022 – VII ZR 391/21, BeckRS 2022, 6626 Rn. 16–19.

[49] EuGH-Vorlage vom LG Ravensburg 31.3.2021 – 2 O 339/19, BeckRS 2021, 7681 Rn. 78 ff.

[50] EuGH-Vorlage vom LG Ravensburg 31.3.2021 – 2 O 339/19, BeckRS 2021, 7681 Rn. 83 ff.

[51] EuGH-Vorlage vom LG Ravensburg 12.2.2021 – 2 O 393/20, BeckRS 2021, 1938.

[52] EuGH 21.3.2023 – C-100/21, ECLI:EU:C:2023:229, EuZW 2023, 378.

[53] EuGH 17.12.2020 – C-693/18, ECLI:EU:C:2020:1040, NJW 2021, 1216.

amt diese Motorsteuerung zuvor gebilligt hatte. Nach EuGH[54] ist die von der Außentemperatur abhängige Steuerung der Abgasreinigung nicht gerechtfertigt. Nach EuGH[55] steht Käufern von Autos mit illegaler Motorsteuerung auch dann Schadenersatz zu, wenn dem Hersteller keine vorsätzliche und sittenwidrige Schädigung zur Last fällt. Schon der nur fahrlässige Verstoß gegen die EU-Zulassungsregeln führe dazu, dass Autohersteller die Käufer entschädigen müssen.

Die stetige Ablehnung einer Vorlage durch den BGH trotz dieser Rechtsprechung des EuGH kann daher nur als willkürliche Verletzung seiner Vorlagepflicht an den EuGH erachtet werden. Wollte der BGH nicht von der Unzulässigkeit einer Abschalteinrichtung sowie einem Individualschutzcharakter der Vorschriften zur Übereinstimmungsbescheinigung und einem durchsetzbaren Anspruch nach dem effet utile ausgehen, war er verpflichtet, die rechtsstreiterheblichen Fragen zur Auslegung, zum Inhalt und zum Erklärungsgehalt der Übereinstimmungsbescheinigung nach §§ 6 Abs. 1, 27 Abs. 1 der EG-FGV sowie der zu Grunde liegenden Richtlinie 2007/46/EG iVm Art. 5 Abs. 2 der VO (EG) Nr. 715/2007 dem EuGH nach Art. 267 AEUV vorzulegen. Der BGH hätte sich nicht der Blöße hingeben dürfen, dass Instanzgerichte „schlauer" sind als der BGH. Dass der BGH „daneben lag" und die Instanzgerichte die erheblichen Vorlagefragen richtig erkannt hatten, wurde bestätigt durch das Urteil des EuGH vom 21.3.2023.

V. Wie hat der EuGH entschieden?

1. Schutz des Käufers bei Einbau einer illegalen Abschalteinrichtung

Der EuGH hat mit Urteil vom 21.3.2023 – C-100/21 klargestellt, dass der Käufer eines mit einer unzulässigen Abschalteinrichtung versehenen Kraftfahrzeugs in den persönlichen Schutzbereich der §§ 6 Abs. 1 und 27 Abs. 1 EG-FGV in Verbindung mit Art. 5 der VO (EG) Nr. 715/2007 fällt. Unionsrecht schützt neben allgemeinen Rechtsgütern auch die Einzelinteressen des individuellen Käufers eines Kraftfahrzeugs gegenüber dessen Hersteller, wenn dieses Fahrzeug mit einer unzulässigen Abschalteinrichtung ausgestattet ist. Das Unionsrecht stellt eine unmittelbare Verbindung zwischen dem Automobilhersteller und dem individuellen Käufer eines Kraftfahrzeugs her mit der diesem gewährleistet werden soll, dass das Fahrzeug mit den maßgeblichen Rechtsvorschriften der Union übereinstimmt[56].

Art. 5 VO (EG) Nr. 715/2007 verbietet ausdrücklich die Verwendung von Abschalteinrichtungen, die die Wirkung von Emissionskontrollsystemen unter normalen Nutzungsbedingungen verringern. Dabei ist es egal, ob es um physische Bauteile oder Software geht, ob der Ausstoß von Schadstoffen durch Einfluss auf den Verbrennungsvorgang wie etwa bei der Rückführung von Abgasen oder nachträglich durch Einspritzung von AdBlue in die Abgase reguliert wird. Ein Emis-

[54] EuGH 8.11.2022 – C-873/19, ECLI:EU:C:2022:857, Celex-Nr. 62019CA0873, NJW 2022, 3769.
[55] EuGH 14.7.2022 – C-128/20, C-134/20 und C-145/20.
[56] EuGH 21.3.2023 – C-100/21, ECLI:EU:C:2023:229 Rn. 82.

sionskontrollsystem muss im normalen Fahrbetrieb genau so aktiv sein wie bei den Prüfstandsfahrten. Der vom Autohersteller vorgebrachte erhöhte Verschleiß oder zusätzliche Wartungsaufwand rechtfertigen es nicht, die Abgasreinigung zu verringern oder abzuschalten oder umgekehrt nur für Prüfstandbedingungen die Abgasreinigung zu verbessern.

Der Einbau einer unzulässigen Abschalteinrichtung kann eine Unsicherheit hinsichtlich der Möglichkeit hervorrufen, das Fahrzeug anzumelden, zu verkaufen oder in Betrieb zu nehmen, und letztlich beim Käufer eines mit einer unzulässigen Abschalteinrichtung ausgerüsteten Fahrzeugs zu einem Schaden führen[57]. Der Käufer hat einen Anspruch auf Schadensersatz, wenn ihm durch die Abschalteinrichtung ein Schaden entstanden ist[58]. Es ist jedoch Sache der Mitgliedstaaten, die Modalitäten des Schadensersatzes festzulegen[59]. Nationale Rechtsvorschriften dürfen es dem Käufer nicht praktisch unmöglich machen oder übermäßig erschweren, einen angemessenen Ersatz des Schadens zu erhalten (Grundsatz der Effektivität)[60]. Andererseits darf der Ersatz nicht zu einer ungerechtfertigten Bereicherung der Anspruchsberechtigten führen (Grundsatz der Verhältnismäßigkeit)[61]. Der EuGH hat auch die Frage einer Vorteilsanrechnung dem nationalen Gericht die Prüfung zugestanden, ob die Anrechnung noch eine angemessene Entschädigung gewährleistet[62].

Damit steht die deutsche Judikatur zur Schadenshöhe unter einem allgemeinen europäischen Angemessenheitsvorbehalt.

2. *Folgen für die Rechtsprechung des BGH*

Die bisherige Auffassung des BGH, aus der unionsrechtswidrigen Verwendung einer Abschalteinrichtung folge kein Anspruch aus § 823 Abs. 2 BGB, war mit den bisherigen Begründungsmustern nicht mehr haltbar. Die strengen Voraussetzungen der Sittenwidrigkeit und Vorsatz wie bei § 826 BGB müssen nicht nachgewiesen werden. Autohersteller können schon bei bloßer Fahrlässigkeit haften (§ 823 Abs. 2 BGB iVm dem drittschützenden Unionsrecht), wenn sie eine unzulässige Abschalteinrichtung verbauen. Das erleichtert die Durchsetzung von Schadenersatzansprüchen erheblich. Wie der BGH mit dieser aktuellen Rechtsprechung des EuGH vom 21.3.2023 umgeht, hat er in den drei Entscheidungen vom 26.6.2023[63] gezeigt. Diese stellen eine durch den EuGH erzwungene Wende und unionsrechtskonforme Anpassung seiner bisherigen Rechtsprechung dar.

---

[57] EuGH 21.3.2023 – C-100/21, ECLI:EU:C:2023:229 Rn. 84.
[58] EuGH 21.3.2023 – C-100/21, ECLI:EU:C:2023:229 Rn. 91.
[59] EuGH 21.3.2023 – C-100/21, ECLI:EU:C:2023:229 Rn. 92, 96.
[60] EuGH 21.3.2023 – C-100/21, ECLI:EU:C:2023:229 Rn. 93.
[61] EuGH 21.3.2023 – C-100/21, ECLI:EU:C:2023:229 Rn. 94.
[62] EuGH 21.3.2023 – C-100/21, ECLI:EU:C:2023:229 Rn. 95.
[63] BGH 26.6.2013 – VIa ZR 335/21, NJW 2023, 2259; 26.6.2023 – VIa ZR 533/21, NJW 2023, 2270; 26.6.2023 – VIa ZR 1031/22, NJOZ 2023, 1133.

a) § 826 BGB

Die Rechtsprechung zu den Voraussetzungen einer Haftung nach § 826 BGB bleibt bestehen. Ergänzend führt der Senat aus, dass die Tatbestandswirkung der EG-Typgenehmigung[64], durch Verwaltungsakt festgestellte Rechtmäßigkeit eines beschriebenen Fahrzeugtyps[65] oder eine zur EG-Typgenehmigung hinzutretende Übereinstimmungsbescheinigung einem Anspruch aus §§ 826, 31 BGB gegen den Fahrzeughersteller nicht entgegengehalten werden können[66].

b) § 823 Abs. 2 BGB

aa) Unzutreffende Übereinstimmungsbescheinigung

Der Käufer kann beim Erwerb eines Kraftfahrzeugs, das zur Serie eines genehmigten Typs gehört und mit einer Übereinstimmungsbescheinigung versehen ist, vernünftigerweise erwarten, dass die VO (EG) Nr. 715/2007 und insbesondere deren Art. 5 eingehalten ist. Wird er in diesem Vertrauen enttäuscht, kann er von dem Fahrzeughersteller, der die Übereinstimmungsbescheinigung ausgegeben hat, Schadensersatz verlangen.

Eine Übereinstimmungsbescheinigung ist unzutreffend, wenn das betreffende Fahrzeug mit einer gemäß Art. 5 Abs. 2 der VO (EG) Nr. 715/2007 unzulässigen Abschalteinrichtung ausgerüstet ist, weil die Bescheinigung dann eine tatsächlich nicht gegebene Übereinstimmung des konkreten Kraftfahrzeugs mit Art. 5 Abs. 2 der VO (EG) Nr. 715/2007 ausweist. Auf den Inhalt der zugrundeliegenden EG-Typgenehmigung kommt es dabei nicht an.

Die Darlegungs- und Beweislast für das Vorliegen einer unzulässigen Abschalteinrichtung als solcher im Sinne der Art. 3 Nr. 10, Art. 5 Abs. 2 Satz 1 der VO (EG) Nr. 715/2007 trifft nach allgemeinen Regeln den Käufer als Anspruchsteller. Dem Fahrzeughersteller obliegt dagegen die Darlegungs- und Beweislast dafür, dass eine festgestellte Abschalteinrichtung ausnahmsweise zulässig sei[67].

bb) Verschulden

Für die Haftung nach § 823 Abs. 2 BGB in Verbindung mit § 6 Abs. 1, § 27 Abs. 1 EG-FGV genügt ein fahrlässiger Verstoß[68]. Zwar trifft den Anspruchsteller die Darlegungs- und Beweislast hinsichtlich des Verschuldens als anspruchsbegründende Voraussetzung. Jedoch muss derjenige, der objektiv ein Schutzgesetz verletzt hat, Umstände darlegen und erforderlichenfalls beweisen, die geeignet sind, die daraus folgende Annahme seines Verschuldens in Form einer Fahrlässigkeit auszuräumen. Insofern besteht eine von der objektiven Schutzgesetzverletzung ausgehende Verschuldensvermutung[69].

---

[64] BGH 26.6.2023 – VIa ZR 335/21, NJW 2023, 2259 Rn. 10f.
[65] BGH 26.6.2023 – VIa ZR 335/21, NJW 2023, 2259 Rn. 14.
[66] BGH 26.6.2023 – VIa ZR 335/21, NJW 2023, 2259 Rn. 15.
[67] BGH 26.6.2023 – VIa ZR 335/21, NJW 2023, 2259 Rn. 53f.
[68] BGH 26.6.2023 – VIa ZR 335/21, NJW 2023, 2259 Rn. 37.
[69] BGH 26.6.2023 – VIa ZR 335/21, NJW 2023, 2259 Rn. 59.

Der Fahrzeughersteller, der sich unter Berufung auf einen unvermeidbaren Verbotsirrtum entlasten will, muss sowohl den Verbotsirrtum als solchen als auch die Unvermeidbarkeit des Verbotsirrtums konkret darlegen und beweisen[70]. Ein entlastend wirkender Verbotsirrtum kann vorliegen, wenn der Schädiger die Rechtslage unter Einbeziehung der höchstrichterlichen Rechtsprechung sorgfältig geprüft hat und er bei Anwendung der im Verkehr erforderlichen Sorgfalt mit einer anderen Beurteilung durch die Gerichte nicht zu rechnen brauchte[71]. Beruft sich der Fahrzeughersteller weder auf eine tatsächliche oder hypothetische Genehmigung der zuständigen Behörde noch auf einen externen qualifizierten Rechtsrat, sondern auf selbst angestellte Erwägungen, ist ihm eine Entlastung verwehrt, wenn eine nicht im Sinne des Fahrzeugherstellers geklärte Rechtslage hinreichend Anlass zur Einholung eines Rechtsrats bot oder sich der Hersteller mit Rücksicht auf eine nicht in seinem Sinn geklärte Rechtslage erkennbar in einem rechtlichen Grenzbereich bewegte und deshalb eine abweichende rechtliche Beurteilung seines Vorgehens in Betracht ziehen und von der eventuell rechtswidrigen Verwendung der Abschalteinrichtung absehen musste[72].

cc) Ersatz des Differenzschadens

Der Käufer kann keinen großen Schadensersatz, also Rückabwicklung des Kaufvertrages, beanspruchen[73]. Der Schutz erstreckt sich nicht auf das Interesse des Käufers, nicht an dem Vertrag festgehalten zu werden. Es bleibt bei dem allgemeinen Grundsatz, dass ein Schadensersatzanspruch eine Vermögensminderung durch die enttäuschte Vertrauensinvestition bei Abschluss des Kaufvertrags über das Kraftfahrzeug voraussetzt. Dass dem Käufer im Fall von Fahrlässigkeit nach § 823 Abs. 2 BGB nur ein sog. „mittlerer Schadensersatz" in Form des Differenzschadens zusteht, begründet der BGH mit den Besonderheiten des deutschen Rechts[74]. Bemerkenswert ist, dass er sich von der Entscheidung des Obersten Gerichtshofs Österreichs[75] abgrenzt, welcher ebenfalls in Reaktion auf das Urteil des EuGH vom 21.3.2023 nach dortigem nationalem Recht dem Käufer einen großen Schadensersatz zugesteht.

Zur Erwerbskausalität kann sich der Kläger auf den Erfahrungssatz stützen, dass er den Kaufvertrag zu diesem Kaufpreis nicht geschlossen hätte[76].

Der Vermögensschaden liegt nach der Differenzhypothese darin, dass der objektive Wert des erworbenen Fahrzeugs hinter dem Kaufpreis zurückbleibt. Die jederzeitige Verfügbarkeit eines Kraftfahrzeugs hat Geldwert. Deshalb erleidet der Käufer eines Fahrzeugs, das mit einer unzulässigen Abschalteinrichtung versehen ist, stets einen Schaden. Der Schaden liegt in dem Betrag, um den der Käufer das Fahrzeug mit Rücksicht auf die mit der unzulässigen Abschaltvorrichtung verbundenen

70 BGH v. 25.9.2023 – VIa ZR 1/23, NJW 2023, 3796 Rn. 13.
71 BGH 26.6.2023 – VIa ZR 335/21, NJW 2023, 2259 Rn. 63.
72 BGH 26.6.2023 – VIa ZR 335/21, NJW 2023, 2259 Rn. 69.
73 BGH 26.6.2023 – VIa ZR 335/21, NJW 2023, 2259 Rn. 19
74 BGH 26.6.2023 – VIa ZR 335/21, NJW 2023, 2259 Rn. 73.
75 OGH 25.04.2023 – 10 Ob 2/23a & 10 Ob 16/23k, ZVR 2023,315 (Kathrein).
76 BGH 26.6.2023 – VIa ZR 335/21, NJW 2023, 2259 Rn. 55ff.

Risiken der Möglichkeit einer Betriebsbeschränkung oder -stilllegung zu teuer erworben hat.

Der Tatrichter hat die Höhe des dem Käufer entstandenen Vermögensschadens nach § 287 ZPO unter Berücksichtigung aller Umstände des Einzelfalles innerhalb der unionsrechtlich vorgegebenen Bandbreite zu schätzen[77]. Bei der Schätzung des Schadens innerhalb eines vom BGH vorgegebenen Rahmens zwischen 5% und 15% sind für die Bestimmung des objektiven Werts des Fahrzeugs im Zeitpunkt des Vertragsschlusses[78] die mit der Verwendung einer unzulässigen Abschalteinrichtung verbundenen Nachteile zu berücksichtigen. Wie der BGH auf die Bandbreite von 5% bis 15% gekommen ist, lässt sich nicht ergründen. Zur Einholung eines Sachverständigengutachtens ist der Tatrichter bei seiner Schätzung innerhalb des genannten Rahmens nicht gehalten[79].

Nutzungsvorteile und der Restwert des Fahrzeugs sind nur insoweit schadensmindernd anzurechnen, als sie den Wert des Fahrzeugs bei Abschluss des Kaufvertrags (gezahlter Kaufpreis abzüglich Differenzschaden) übersteigen[80].

Damit hat der BGH den unteren Instanzen Leitlinien an die Hand gegeben und deutlich gemacht, dass geschädigte Käufer mit dem Ersatz eines Differenzschadens rechnen können. Gleichzeitig hat der BGH neuen Streit veranlasst, mit dem sich die Tatsacheninstanzen befassen müssen. Was sind die Grundlagen für einen Differenzschaden von 5 bis 15%? Kann der Geschädigte einen höheren nachweisbaren Schaden geltend machen? Ist eine unzulässige Technik verbaut? Ist ein Herstellerverschulden nachgewiesen? Demnach ist nach den Urteilen des EuGH vom 21.3.2023 und des BGH vom 26.6.2023 klar, dass nichts „clair" ist.

3. *Folgen der bisherigen Ablehnung der individuellen Interessen der Käufer*

Die bisherige Ablehnung des Individualschutzes in den einschlägigen europarechtlichen Bestimmungen hatte für die Autokaufer fatale Folgen. Diese haben nach rechtskräftiger Klageabweisung nach der bisherigen Rechtsprechung des BGH ihre Schadensersatzansprüche verloren. Da der BGH dem Fahrzeugkäufer nur einen Schadensersatzanspruch nach § 826 BGB bei vorsätzlicher sittenwidriger Schädigung zugestanden hatte, hat er sämtliche Rechtsmittel und damit auch die Klagen nach § 823 Abs. 2 BGB, die sich auch auf fahrlässige Schutzgesetzesverletzung stützten, abgewiesen. Der Schaden für den Rechtsbürger ist unübersehbar. Die rechtskräftig abgewiesenen Klagen können nach der Entscheidung des EuGH vom 21.3.2023 nicht mehr aufgegriffen werden. Der Rechtssuchende ist Opfer der gegenteiligen Rechtsauffassungen von EuGH und BGH, insbesondere wegen dessen verletzter Pflicht zur Vorlage an den EuGH. Der Schaden bleibt beim Rechtssuchenden. Lediglich in den noch nicht rechtskräftig abgeschlossenen Verfahren können die Autokäufer ihre Schadensersatzanprüche mit Hilfe des EuGH, wenn auch reduziert auf einen bloßen Differenzschaden, noch „retten".

---

[77] BGH 26.6.2023 – VIa ZR 335/21, NJW 2023, 2259 Rn. 71ff.
[78] BGH 26.6.2023 – VIa ZR 335/21, NJW 2023, 2259 Rn. 76.
[79] BGH 26.6.2023 – VIa ZR 335/21, NJW 2023, 2259 Rn. 78.
[80] BGH 24.1.2022 – VIa ZR 100/21, NJW-RR 2022, 1033.

Trotz ständiger Anregungen der Kläger auf Vorlage an den EuGH zur Auslegung der einschlägigen Bestimmungen beharrten die betroffenen Senate des BGH auf ihrer starren Verweigerungshaltung. Nur mit Hilfe eines Untergerichtes konnte eine Entscheidung des EuGH herbeigeführt werden. Vielleicht wurde der BGH endlich eines besseren belehrt und legt bei gegebenen künftigen Anlässen zur Auslegung der europarechtlichen Bestimmungen die erheblichen Rechtsfragen dem hierfür originär zuständigen EuGH vor.

Der BGH war in den Dieselfällen nicht bereit, die dem Schutz der Verbraucher dienenden europarechtlichen Bestimmungen als Schutzgesetz gemäß § 823 Abs. 2 BGB überhaupt zur Kenntnis zu nehmen. Er lehnte nicht nur den Anspruch als solchen ab, sondern unter Verweis auf einen acte clair auch eine Vorlage an den EuGH wie folgt ab[81]: „Weder Vorabentscheidungsersuchen einzelner Landgerichte noch die von der Nichtzulassungsbeschwerde vorgelegte Stellungnahme der Europäischen Kommission vom 19. Dezember 2019 (sj.h(2019)8760684) geben Anlass, an der Annahme eines acte clair zu zweifeln“.[82]

Statt den vorlegenden Landgerichten vorzuwerfen sich nicht mit den tragenden Erwägungen der höchstrichterlichen Rechtsprechung auseinanderzusetzen, hätte es der BGH vielleicht besser vorziehen sollen, sich den Argumenten des vorlegenden Gerichtes nicht zu entziehen und den EuGH zur Auslegung der europarechtlichen Bestimmungen zurate ziehen sollen.

Hätte sich der BGH entsprechend seiner Vorlagepflicht zur Auslegung der europarechtlichen Bestimmungen nicht gescheut, eine europarechtliche Klärung der vorstehenden Fragen durch den EuGH herbeizuführen, wäre der großen Zahl von betroffenen Fahrzeugkäufern zeit- und kostenaufwendige Rechtsstreitigkeiten erspart geblieben und die Gerichte hätten sich weniger über eine große Belastung von (unnötigen) Verfahren beklagen müssen[83]. Durch seine Ablehnungshaltung verweigerte der BGH den Klägern die Durchsetzung berechtigter Ansprüche mit dem lapidaren Hinweis auf einen acte clair, weil er meinte europarechtliche Bestimmungen besser auslegen zu können als der EuGH[84]. Dass die Rechtsauffassung des BGH nicht „clair“ war, hat das Urteil des EuGH vom 21.3.2023 bestätigt.

VI. Ergebnis

Die Anzahl der Vorlagen an den EuGH durch die von Dieselfällen nicht betroffenen übrigen Senate zeigt, dass beim BGH eine Bereitschaft besteht europarechtliche Auslegungsfragen dem EuGH vorzulegen. Lediglich in den Dieselfällen haben

[81] BGH 25.5.2020 – VI ZR 252/19, NJW 2020, 1962 Rn. 17; BGH 16.9.2021 – VII ZR 190/20, NJW 2021, 3721 Rn. 37.

[82] So BGH 23.3.2022 – VII ZR 444/21, BeckRS 2022, 8312 Rn. 1.

[83] 2018 rund 10.000 Verfahren; 2019 rund 40.000 Fälle; 2020 rund 30.000 neue Fälle; zitiert nach beck-aktuell vom 14.6.2021.

[84] Als „Umgehungsstrategie der Vorlagepflicht“ bezeichnet, vgl. Ehricke, Die Bindungswirkung von Urteilen des EuGH im Vorabentscheidungsverfahren nach deutschem Zivilprozessrecht und nach Gemeinschaftsrecht, 1997, https://europainstitut.de/fileadmin/schriften/364.pdf (abgerufen 11.5.2024), S. 11.

sich die betroffenen Senate mit der Beschränkung auf eine alleinige Haftung nach § 826 BGB in eine Sackgasse manövriert. Obwohl viele Fragen zur streitigen Problematik der Unzulässigkeit von Abschalteinrichtungen und des Drittschutzes europarechtlicher Bestimmungen bereits dem EuGH vorlagen, waren die Senate des BGH nicht bereit, die Fragen zur richtigen Auslegung des persönlichen Schutzbereichs der § 6 Abs. 1 und § 27 Abs. 1 EG-FGV im Lichte der Art. 3 Nr. 36, Art. 18 Abs. 1, Art. 26 Abs. 1 und Art. 46 der Richtlinie 2007/46/EG iVm Art. 5 Abs. 2 der VO (EG) Nr. 715/2007 angesichts ihres Wortlauts und ihrer Regelungssystematik sowie des Regelungszwecks durch den EuGH unionsrechtskonform beantworten zu lassen. Die Vorlage drängte sich nicht nur auf in Anbetracht der anhängigen tausenden Rechtsstreitigkeiten, sondern auch wegen der zahlreichen Erörterungen in der Literatur. Die stetige und ausdrückliche Ablehnung einer Vorlage an den EuGH in den Dieselfällen mag deshalb nur als einmaliger „Ausrutscher" bezeichnet werden. Es bleibt zu hoffen, dass der BGH sich einer notwendigen Vorlage weiter offen zeigt und dadurch die einheitliche Rechtsanwendung innerhalb der EU fördert.

ANDREAS GEROLDINGER

Zur Missbrauchskontrolle im Rahmen des Art. 8 Nr. 1 Brüssel Ia-VO – Überlegungen aus Anlass der Entscheidungen OGH 9 Ob 18/22w und 5 Ob 73/23f*

I. Einleitung

Mehrere Beklagte aufgrund eines sachlichen und/oder rechtlichen Zusammenhangs an einem Ort gemeinsam klagen zu können, hat in zahlreichen Zuständigkeitsordnungen lange Tradition (zB § 93 JN iVm § 11 öZPO,[1] § 36 Abs. 1 Nr. 3 dZPO[2]). Auf unionsrechtlicher Ebene eröffnet Art. 8 Nr. 1 Brüssel Ia-VO – als Nachfolgebestimmung von Art. 6 Nr. 1 EuGVÜ bzw Brüssel I-VO – einen solchen „Streitgenossengerichtsstand". Diesem wurde in jüngerer Zeit wieder verstärkte Aufmerksamkeit zuteil.[3] So dient gegenwärtig der österreichische Wohnsitz eines Aufsichtsratsmitglieds der Wirecard AG, die ihren Sitz in Deutschland hat und in einen Finanzskandal verwickelt ist, mehreren österreichischen Klägern dazu, die in dieser Causa als Rechnungsprüferin tätige Wirtschaftsprüfungskanzlei mit Sitz in Deutschland vor österreichischen Gerichten zu verklagen.[4] Dass dabei stets nur ein einziges Mitglied des Aufsichtsrats in Österreich geklagt wird, lässt – bei einer Causa, deren Epizentrum zweifellos in Deutschland liegt und die wohl weitgehend nach deutschem Recht zu beurteilen ist[5] – zumindest gewisse Zweifel daran aufkommen, dass die Hauptstoßrichtung der klägerischen Bemühungen dem österreichischen „Ankerbeklagten" gilt.[6]

Trotz mehrerer kritischer Stellungnahmen im Vorfeld bejahte der OGH in der Entscheidung 9 Ob 18/22w die Zuständigkeit österreichischer Gerichte für die Ansprüche gegen die Wirtschaftsprüferin; die Einleitung eines Vorabentschei-

* Dieser Beitrag geht auf eine Anfrage aus der Praxis zurück und baut auf einen daraus entstandenen Aufsatz auf, der im Vorfeld der hier zu besprechenden Entscheidungen des OGH erschienen ist (Geroldinger JBl 2022, 268).

[1] Siehe dazu (anstelle vieler) Kodek Zak 2022, 65 (65ff.).

[2] Siehe dazu (anstelle vieler) Musielak/Voit, ZPO/Heinrich, 21. Aufl. 2024, § 36 Rn. 16ff. mwN; OLG Köln 21.2.2012 – 8 AR 65/11, BeckRS 2012, 5038.

[3] Siehe dazu im Kontext der Causa Wirecard: Geroldinger JBl 2022, 268; Pimmer Zak 2022, 28; in anderen Zusammenhängen siehe etwa OLG Wien 28.02.2024 – 33 R 9/24x, ECLI:AT:OLG0009:2024:03300R00009.24X.0228.000.

[4] Siehe zB Der Standard, 21.2.2022, Geschädigte Wirecard-Aktionäre können in Österreich klagen.

[5] Pimmer Zak 2022, 31.

[6] Geroldinger JBl 2022, 186 (186); zum „wirtschaftlichen Zweck" der Klage gegen den Ankerbeklagten siehe Schlosser/Hess EU-Zivilprozessrecht/Schlosser, 5. Aufl. 2021, EuGVVO Art. 8 Rn. 2 mwN.

dungsverfahrens vor dem EuGH erachtete der 9. Senat für nicht angezeigt. Sowohl der Lösung der Zuständigkeitsfrage als auch der Einschätzung betreffend das Vorliegen eines acte claire haben sich inzwischen mehrere Senate des OGH angeschlossen.

Kaum eine deutschsprachige Entscheidung zu Rechtsakten der Europäischen Union auf dem Gebiet des Internationalen Privatrechts und des Internationalen Zivilverfahrensrechts kommt ohne Rückgriff auf den von *Thomas Rauscher* herausgegebenen Kommentar aus. Mit diesem Werk hat der Jubilar einen wichtigen Beitrag dazu geleistet, dass die darin behandelten Rechtsakte in Praxis und Wissenschaft ankommen und angewendet werden konnten. Mein Respekt vor diesem Verdienst, der die europäische Integration und Rechtsstaatlichkeit befördert, lässt mich dem Jubilar herzlich zum 70. Geburtstag gratulieren. In der Hoffnung, mit der bereits kurz skizzierten Themenwahl auf sein Interesse zu stoßen, soll der vorliegende Beitrag die erwähnte Judikaturlinie aufarbeiten.

II. Die Rechtsprechung des OGH zu Wirecard

1. OGH 9 Ob 18/22w und erste Folgeentscheidungen

Der Entscheidung des OGH zu 9 Ob 18/22w lag folgender Ausgangssachverhalt zugrunde:[7] Der Kläger begehrte von zwei Beklagten die Zahlung von rund 31.000 € zur ungeteilten Hand aus dem Titel des Schadenersatzes, Zug um Zug gegen die Rückgabe von 500 Stück Aktien der Wirecard AG. Der Erstbeklagte, der in Wien wohnte, war von 2009 bis 2020 Aufsichtsratsmitglied der Wirecard AG, die ihren Sitz in München hatte. In dieser Funktion habe er – dem Vorbringen des Klägers zufolge – die (ebenfalls in Deutschland ansässige) Zweitbeklagte mit der Prüfung des Jahresabschlusses und des Lageberichts der AG beauftragt. Zumindest ab 2015 seien wesentliche Teile des Umsatzes der Wirecard AG frei erfunden gewesen. Trotz zahlreicher Hinweise auf Malversationen („Luftbuchungen") ab 2008 hätte weder der Erstbeklagte seine Kontrollbefugnisse als Aufsichtsrat wahrgenommen noch die Zweitbeklagte konkrete Nachforschungen angestellt. Die Zweitbeklagte habe seit 2009 uneingeschränkte Bestätigungsvermerke erteilt, und zwar auch nach dem Bekanntwerden der Bilanzmanipulationen am 24.4.2019. Sowohl die Vorstände der Wirecard AG als auch die Beklagten als Aufsichtsratsmitglied bzw Abschlussprüferin hätten durch bewusstes und gewolltes Täuschen über kapitalmarktrelevante Tatsachen den Kläger dazu verleitet, Aktien zu erwerben, um dadurch sich oder die Wirecard AG zu bereichern. Hätten die Beklagten gesetzes- und pflichtgetreu gehandelt, wäre dem Kläger kein Schaden entstanden, weil die Bilanzmanipulationen vor seinem Investment bekannt geworden wären, und er dann nicht in die Aktien der Wirecard AG investiert hätte. Der Kläger habe auf die Vollständigkeit und Richtigkeit der Vermögens-, Finanz- und Ertragslage der Wirecard AG und auf das Funktionieren der Kontrollmechanismen (in Form von Aufsichtsrat

[7] OGH 19.5.2022 – 9 Ob 18/22w, ECLI:AT:OGH0002:2022:0090OB00018.22W.0519.000 Rn. 3.

und Abschlussprüfer) vertraut. Die Zuständigkeit österreichischer Gerichte begründete der Kläger einerseits mit Art. 7 Nr. 2 Brüssel Ia-VO (für beide Beklagten) und andererseits mit Art. 4 Brüssel Ia-VO (für den Erstbeklagten) sowie mit Art. 8 Nr. 1 Brüssel Ia-VO (für die Zweitbeklagte).

Während das Erstgericht seine Zuständigkeit hinsichtlich der Zweitbeklagten verneinte, hielt die zweite Instanz die Voraussetzungen des Streitgenossengerichtsstands nach Art. 8 Nr. 1 Brüssel Ia-VO für gegeben. Das Rechtsmittel an den OGH (einen außerordentlichen Revisionsrekurs) wies dessen 9. Senat mit der Begründung, dass keine „erhebliche Rechtsfrage“ iSd § 528 (iVm § 502) ZPO zu behandeln sei, als unzulässig zurück. Zwar anerkannte das Höchstgericht, dass in den beiden Klagen unterschiedliche materiell-rechtliche Anspruchsgrundlagen verfolgt wurden und sich die Prüfpflichten der beiden Beklagten unterscheiden. Unter Bezugnahme auf die Entscheidung 8 Ob 126/19s sowie die Judikate des EuGH in der Rs. *Freeport* und der Rs. *Painer* betonte der 9. Senat aber, dass ein Beruhen der erhobenen Klagen auf derselben Rechtsgrundlage nur einer von mehreren möglichen Faktoren des notwendigen Zusammenhangs iSd Art. 8 Nr. 1 Brüssel Ia-VO sei. In casu hätten beide Klagen „nicht nur ihren Ursprung im Fall ‚W.‘“, sondern behaupte der Kläger, dass ihm deshalb ein Schaden entstanden sei, weil unterbliebene Auskünfte über die für die Kaufentscheidung relevanten Tatsachen eine mangelfreie Entscheidung seinerseits verhindert haben; die Beklagten (und andere der Wirecard AG zuzurechnenden Personen) hätten ihn durch bewusstes Täuschen über kapitalmarktrelevante Tatsachen dazu verleitet, Wirecard-Aktien zu erwerben. Der Kläger stelle damit in den Raum, „dass beide Beklagten gemeinsam durch ihre jeweils – wenn auch aus rechtlichen Gründen heraus unterschiedlichen – Pflichtverletzungen (Unterlassungen von Kontroll- bzw Prüfpflichten) seinen Schaden herbeigeführt hätten (kumulative Kausalität) und ihm dafür solidarisch haften“.[8] Außerdem seien die beiden Klagen auf dasselbe Interesse gerichtet, nämlich Ersatz des Schadens Zug um Zug gegen Rückgabe der erworbenen Aktien. Es stelle sich ferner „gegenüber beiden Parteien die (Vor-)Frage, ob die Jahresabschlüsse des Zweitbeklagten tatsächlich unrichtig waren und nicht zuletzt, welches Investment der Kläger bei Kenntnis aller Umstände getätigt hätte“.[9] Das führt den 9. Senat zu folgender Schlussfolgerung: „In Bezug auf die diesbezüglichen Tat- und Rechtsfragen besteht daher sehr wohl die Gefahr von sich einander widersprechenden Entscheidungen. Der Umstand, dass dennoch das Ergebnis des Verfahrens für die beiden Beklagten unterschiedlich sein kann, schadet nicht“.[10]

Hinsichtlich der – in ErwGr. 15 Brüssel Ia-VO angesprochenen und vom EuGH beim Gerichtsstand der Streitgenossenschaft wiederholt betonten – Vorhersehbarkeit der Zuständigkeit hatte der Kläger vorgebracht, dass ein Abschlussprüfer nicht

---

[8] OGH 19.5.2022 – 9 Ob 18/22w, ECLI:AT:OGH0002:2022:0090OB00018.22W.0519.000 Rn. 19.

[9] OGH 19.5.2022 – 9 Ob 18/22w, ECLI:AT:OGH0002:2022:0090OB00018.22W.0519.000 Rn. 19.

[10] OGH 19.5.2022 – 9 Ob 18/22w, ECLI:AT:OGH0002:2022:0090OB00018.22W.0519.000 Rn. 19.

damit rechnen müsse, dass er von Aktionären in anderen EU-Mitgliedstaaten geklagt werde, weil ein Aufsichtsratsmitglied der von ihm geprüften AG seinen Wohnsitz im Wohnsitzstaat des Anlegers habe. Diesen Bedenken entgegnet der OGH, dass sie „die Besonderheit des Gerichtsstands der Streitgenossenschaft unberücksichtigt [ließen]. Immer wenn ein Geschädigter zwei oder mehrere Schädiger in einer Klage wegen kumulativer Herbeiführung des Schadens in Anspruch nimmt, ist es für den oder die Mitbeklagten nie gänzlich vorhersehbar, welche Schädiger der Kläger mit seiner Klage belangt und in welchem Staat der (Haupt-) Beklagte zum Zeitpunkt der Klagseinbringung seinen Wohnsitz hat. Es ist vielmehr objektiv [...] für einen Schädiger vorhersehbar, dass die Zuständigkeitsvorschrift des Art. 8 Nr. 1 [Brüssel Ia-VO] es einem Geschädigten ermöglicht, bei Vorliegen des erforderlichen Sachzusammenhanges zwischen den Klagen gegen mehrere Schädiger am jeweiligen Gerichtsstand jedes einzelnen Schädigers die Klage gegen alle Schädiger einbringen kann.“[11]

Und schließlich äußert sich der 9. Senat noch zum Einwand der Rechtsmissbräuchlichkeit: Unter Verweis auf die Entscheidung des EuGH in der Rs. *CDC* heißt es, dass bei einer auf Art. 8 Nr. 1 Brüssel Ia-VO gestützten Klage nicht gesondert festgestellt werden müsse, „dass die Klagen nicht nur erhoben worden sind, um einen der Beklagten den Gerichten seines Wohnsitzstaats zu entziehen.“ Eine Zweckentfremdung des Streitgenossengerichtsstands könne das Gericht nur dann feststellen, wenn das „Bestehen eines kollusiven Zusammenwirkens der betreffenden Parteien zu dem Zweck, die Voraussetzungen für die Anwendung dieser Bestimmung im Zeitpunkt der Klageerhebung künstlich herbeizuführen oder aufrechtzuerhalten,“ anhand beweiskräftiger Indizien dargelegt werde.[12]

Eine Vorabentscheidung erschien dem 9. Senat nicht angezeigt, „weil die unionsrechtlichen Grundlagen zum Gerichtsstand nach Art. 8 Nr. 1 EuGVVO hinreichend geklärt sind und deren Anwendung auf den konkreten Fall den nationalen Gerichten obliegt“.[13]

In verschiedenen Parallelverfahren haben mehrere Senate des OGH den jeweiligen Revisionsrekurs unter Verweis auf die Entscheidung zu 9 Ob 18/22w kurzerhand zurückgewiesen.[14] Nach Ansicht des 2. Senats seien die für die Missbrauchskontrolle maßgeblichen Kriterien vom 9. Senat hinreichend herausgearbeitet worden. „Ob ausreichend beweiskräftige Indizien dafür vorliegen, dass die Klage gegen den Erstbeklagten allein zu dem Zweck erhoben worden wäre, um der Zweitbeklagten ihre Sitzzuständigkeit zu entziehen (‚künstliche‘ Herbeiführung

[11] OGH 19.5.2022 – 9 Ob 18/22w, ECLI:AT:OGH0002:2022:0090OB00018.22W.0519.000 Rn. 22.

[12] OGH 19.5.2022 – 9 Ob 18/22w, ECLI:AT:OGH0002:2022:0090OB00018.22W.0519.000 Rn. 24.

[13] OGH 19.5.2022 – 9 Ob 18/22w, ECLI:AT:OGH0002:2022:0090OB00018.22W.0519.000 Rn. 26.

[14] OGH 14.09.2022 – 6 Ob 128/22z, ECLI:AT:OGH0002:2022:0060OB00128.22Z.0914.000; 25.10.2023 – 2 Ob 186/23a, ECLI:AT:OGH0002:2023:0020OB00186.23A.1025.000; 24.10.2022 – 8 Ob 113/22h, ECLI:AT:OGH0002:2022:0080OB00113.22H.1024.000.

des Gerichtsstands), kann […] regelmäßig nur anhand der Umstände des Einzelfalls beurteilt werden."[15]

2. *Erste Reaktionen im Schrifttum*

Während also die Senate 2, 6, 8 und 9 des OGH in trauter Einigkeit judizieren, fallen die Reaktionen des Schrifttums nahezu einhellig ablehnend aus. Einzig *Braza* hält das Ergebnis des 9. Senats für „vertretbar".[16] *Lehmann/Eichmüller* attestieren dem OGH hingegen, „mit dem Konnexitätskriterium [des Art. 8 Nr. 1 Brüssel Ia-VO] sehr locker umzugehen".[17] *Simotta* lehnt die Entscheidung dezidiert ab und vermutet, dass „der OGH österr[eichischen] Anlegern, die durch den Wirecard-Skandal geschädigt worden sind, unbedingt die Möglichkeit eröffnen [wollte], gestützt auf Art. 8 Nr. 1 [Brüssel Ia-VO] in Österreich ihre Schadenersatzklagen einzubringen".[18] Auch *Oberhammer* bilanziert, dass sich der OGH „von einem eigentlich missbräuchlichen anwaltlichen Kniff beeindrucken" habe lassen, und schließt seine Ausführungen mit folgender Beobachtung: „Dass hier nun im Ergebnis einzelne von insgesamt dem Vernehmen nach tausenden Fällen in Österreich entschieden werden, während der Großteil der Auseinandersetzungen naturgemäß in Deutschland stattfindet, mutet durchaus etwas paradox an, wenn man bedenkt, dass das zentrale Zweckkriterium der zuständigkeitsbegründenden Norm […] in der Verhinderung widersprechender Entscheidungen liegt."

3. *OGH 5 Ob 73/23f*

Neue Akzente setzt der OGH in seiner jüngsten einschlägigen Entscheidung. Zwar entspricht die Argumentation zur Zuständigkeit zu 5 Ob 73/23f jener des 9. Senats. Im Verfahren vor dem 5. Senat hatte aber die erste Instanz festgestellt, dass die Kläger die Klage gegen den Erstbeklagten „nur im Versuch erhoben haben, die Zuständigkeit des Gerichts für die Klage gegen die Zweitbeklagte zu begründen"[19]. Sowohl die erste als auch die zweite Instanz hatten die internationale Zuständigkeit der österreichischen Gerichte für die Ansprüche gegen die Wirtschaftsprüferin deshalb verneint. Damit war in dritter Instanz näher auf die Missbrauchskontrolle im Rahmen des Art. 8 Nr. 1 Brüssel Ia-VO einzugehen.

Der 5. Senat referiert zunächst die einschlägigen Ausführungen in 9 Ob 18/22w und erachtet es als „geklärt", dass „sich der EuGH einer Missbrauchskontrolle beim Gerichtsstand der Streitgenossenschaft nicht grundsätzlich ver-

---

[15] OGH 25.10.2023 – 2 Ob 186/23a, ECLI:AT:OGH0002:2023:0020OB00186.23A.1025.000 Rn. 3.

[16] Braza EvBl 2022/148; rein referierend Mayr, Handbuch des europäischen Zivilverfahrensrechts/Wittwer, 2. Aufl. 2023, Rn. 3.391. Braza und Simotta führen aus, dass auch Kolmasch die Entscheidung als vertretbar qualifiziere; tatsächlich handelt es sich bei dem zitierten Beitrag („Zak 2022/405") bloß um eine stark zusammenfassende Wiedergabe der Entscheidung.

[17] Lehmann/Eichmüller BKR 2023, 1 (6).

[18] Fasching/Konecny, Kommentar zu den Zivilprozessgesetzen/Simotta V/1, 3. Aufl. 2022, EuGVVO Art. 8 2012 Rn. 76/10 (Fn 178).

[19] OGH 22.2.2024 – 5 Ob 73/23f ECLI:AT:OGH0002:2024:0050OB00073.23F.0222.000 Rn. 15, 41.

schließt".[20] Wegen der Einzelfallabhängigkeit der Missbrauchskontrolle bestehe allerdings keine Notwendigkeit nach einem Vorabentscheidungsersuchen an den EuGH; „allgemein gültige Regeln dafür welche Verhaltensweisen eines Klägers als rechtsmissbräuchlich anzusehen sind und daher der Berufung auf den Gerichtsstand der Streitgenossenschaft entgegenstehen, lassen sich nicht aufstellen".[21]

Nach Ansicht des 5. Senats beschränkt sich der Tatsachengehalt der Feststellung des Erstgerichts auf die Motivation der Kläger:

„Die damit bewiesene Intention der Kläger, mit der gleichzeitigen Klageführung gegen den in Österreich wohnhaften Erstbeklagten auch eine internationale Zuständigkeit für eine Klage gegen die Zweitbeklagte zu bewirken, die in einem sachlichen Zusammenhang mit der Klage gegen den Erstbeklagten steht, bedeutet aber für sich allein keinen Rechtsmissbrauch. Die Kläger haben die Voraussetzungen für die Anwendung des Gerichtsstands der Streitgenossenschaft nach Art. 8 Nr. 1 EuGVVO damit nicht künstlich herbeigeführt oder aufrechterhalten, insbesondere haben sie nicht mit dem Ankerbeklagten kollusiv zusammengewirkt, um der Zweitbeklagten ihren allgemeinen Gerichtsstand zu entziehen. [...] Die Entscheidung der Kläger, ihre Rechte gleichzeitig auch gegenüber einem in Österreich wohnhaften Aufsichtsratsmitglied geltend zu machen und damit die internationale Zuständigkeit für die Zweitbeklagte ‚zu begründen', bedeutet im Sinn der dargestellten Rechtsprechung keine Zweckwidrigkeit und damit keinen Missbrauch des Gerichtsstands der Streitgenossenschaft. [...] Unter der Voraussetzung der schlüssigen Behauptung eines im objektiven Zusammenhang stehenden Anspruchs unternehmen die Kläger daher nicht den ‚Versuch', eine Zuständigkeit ‚zu begründen', sie nehmen vielmehr einen zulässigen Gerichtsstand in Anspruch."[22]

Dieses Ergebnis gilt es, in weiterer Folge zu hinterfragen; dazu sollen zunächst die allgemeinen Voraussetzungen des Art. 8 Nr. 1 Brüssel Ia-VO erörtert werden. Im Anschluss gilt es, auf die Möglichkeit einer Missbrauchskontrolle im Rahmen der Zuständigkeitsprüfung sowie auf die Anforderungen an das klägerische Vorbringen zum Zuständigkeitstatbestand einzugehen.

III. Konnexität iSd Art. 8 Nr. 1 Brüssel Ia-VO

1. Anhaltspunkte in Normtext und -genese

Die Anwendung von Art. 8 Nr. 1 Brüssel Ia-VO setzt zunächst voraus, dass zumindest einer der Beklagten – der sogenannte Ankerbeklagte – seinen Wohnsitz im Sprengel des angerufenen Gerichts hat und dieses nach Art. 4 Brüssel Ia-VO zuständig ist.[23]

[20] OGH 22.2.2024 – 5 Ob 73/23f ECLI:AT:OGH0002:2024:0050OB00073.23F.0222.000 Rn. 39.

[21] OGH 22.2.2024 – 5 Ob 73/23f ECLI:AT:OGH0002:2024:0050OB00073.23F.0222.000 Rn. 39.

[22] OGH 22.2.2024 – 5 Ob 73/23f ECLI:AT:OGH0002:2024:0050OB00073.23F.0222.000 Rn. 39.

[23] Czernich/Kodek/Mayr, Europäisches Gerichtsstands- und Vollstreckungsrecht/Heiss, 4. Aufl. 2015, EuGVVO Art. 8 Rn. 15; Wieczorek/Schütze, ZPO/Garber/Neumayr, 5. Aufl. 2022, Brüssel Ia-VO Art. 8 Rn. 18ff.

Zwischen den Klagen gegen die verschiedenen Beklagten muss gemäß Art. 8 Nr. 1 Brüssel Ia-VO eine so enge Beziehung bestehen, dass eine gemeinsame Verhandlung und Entscheidung geboten erscheint, um widersprechende Entscheidungen zu vermeiden.

Dieses Konnexitätserfordernis fehlte im Wortlaut des Art. 6 Nr. 1 EuGVÜ, wurde aber vom EuGH in Anlehnung an Art. 22 Abs. 3 EuGVÜ – mit knapper Begründung – als ungeschriebenes Element in diesen Zuständigkeitstatbestand hineininterpretiert.[24] In der Rs. *Kalfelis/Schröder* ua betonte der EuGH, dass Art. 6 Nr. 1 EuGVÜ eine Ausnahme vom Grundsatz der Maßgeblichkeit des Beklagtenwohnsitzes bilde und „*in einer Weise auszugestalten [sei], die das Bestehen des Grundsatzes selbst nicht in Frage stellen kann. Dies könnte dann der Fall sein, wenn es einem Kläger freistünde, eine Klage gegen mehrere Beklagte allein zu dem Zweck zu erheben, einen dieser Beklagten der Zuständigkeit der Gerichte seines Wohnsitzstaats zu entziehen. Wie [im Jenard-Bericht] hervorgehoben wird, muß eine solche Möglichkeit ausgeschlossen werden. Es ist deshalb erforderlich, daß zwischen den Klagen gegen die einzelnen Beklagten ein Zusammenhang besteht. Dazu ist darauf hinzuweisen, daß in dem genannten Bericht des Sachverständigenausschusses zur Begründung von Artikel 6 Nr. 1 ausdrücklich das Bestreben erwähnt wird, zu vermeiden, ‚daß in einzelnen Vertragsstaaten unter sich unvereinbare Entscheidungen ergehen‘. Es handelt sich im übrigen um ein Anliegen, dem das Übereinkommen in Artikel 22 selbst Ausdruck verliehen hat; dort ist der Fall geregelt, daß Klagen, die im Zusammenhang stehen, bei Gerichten verschiedener Vertragsstaaten erhoben werden. Die Vorschrift des Artikels 6 Nr. 1 greift somit ein, wenn die Klagen gegen die verschiedenen Beklagten bei ihrer Erhebung im Zusammenhang stehen, das heißt, wenn eine gemeinsame Verhandlung und Entscheidung geboten erscheint, um zu vermeiden, daß in getrennten Verfahren widersprechende Entscheidungen ergehen könnten. Es ist Sache des nationalen Gerichts, in jedem Einzelfall zu prüfen, ob diese Voraussetzung erfüllt ist.*“ Mit Art. 6 Nr. 1 Brüssel I-VO wurde die Passage aus Art. 22 Abs. 3 EuGVÜ ausdrücklich und in Übereinstimmung mit der „Auslegung des Gerichtshofes“ übernommen.[25]

An der Begründung des EuGH zeigt sich, dass schon das Konnexitätserfordernis selbst einen Teil jener Funktion übernimmt, die in Art. 8 Nr. 2 Brüssel Ia-VO festgeschrieben ist: Es soll verhindern, dass eine Klage nur deshalb abseits vom allgemeinen Gerichtsstand eingebracht wird, um dem Beklagten die Zuständigkeit der Gerichte seines Wohnsitzstaats zu entziehen.[26] Diese Formulierung entspricht im Kern jener des Missbrauchsvorbehalts im damaligen Art. 6 Nr. 2 EuGVÜ, der – wie aus dem *Jenard*-Bericht zum EuGVÜ erhellt – Vorbilder in „Artikel 181 der belgischen, französischen und luxemburgischen ZPO und Artikel 74 der niederländischen ZPO“ hatte.[27] Die aus Art. 22 Abs. 3 EuGVÜ übernommene Formulie-

[24] EuGH 27.9.2988 – C-189/87, NJW 1988, 3088 mAnm Geimer Rn 12 = RIW 1988, 901 mAnm Schlosser (Kalfelis/Schröder ua).

[25] Europäische Kommission, KOM(1999) 348 endg., 15.

[26] Jenard, Bericht zu dem Übereinkommen über die gerichtliche Zuständigkeit und die Vollstreckung gerichtlicher Entscheidungen in Zivil- und Handelssachen, ABl. 1997 C 59, 1 (26).

[27] Jenard, Bericht zu dem Übereinkommen über die gerichtliche Zuständigkeit und die Vollstreckung gerichtlicher Entscheidungen in Zivil- und Handelssachen, ABl. 1997 C 59, 1 (27).

rung liefert damit nur einen von mehreren Anhaltspunkten für die notwendige Intensität des Zusammenhangs. Der GA *Léger,* große Teile der Literatur und einzelne Entscheidungen des OGH bekunden daher zu Recht Sympathien dafür, die Anforderungen an den Zusammenhang in Art. 6 Nr. 1 EuGVÜ/Brüssel I-VO bzw Art. 8 Nr. 1 Brüssel Ia-VO „enger zu sehen" als in jener Bestimmung, aus der sie entlehnt wurden.[28] Für Art. 8 Nr. 1 Brüssel Ia-VO müsse *mindestens* ein solcher Zusammenhang bestehen, wie ihn Art. 30 Abs. 3 Brüssel Ia-VO fordert.[29] Der EuGH hat diese Frage allerdings bislang offengelassen.[30] Für eine engere Auslegung streiten neben der erwähnten Missbrauchsprävention noch ErwGr. 15 Brüssel Ia-VO, der die Vorhersehbarkeit der Gerichtsstände für den Beklagten fordert und die Bedeutung von dessen Wohnsitz als zentralen Anknüpfungspunkt unterstreicht, und ErwGr. 16 Brüssel Ia-VO, demzufolge ein Beklagter keinem Gerichtsstand unterworfen sein soll, mit dem er „vernünftigerweise nicht rechnen konnte". Außerdem wäre es vom europäischen Gesetzgeber alles andere als konsequent, einerseits die Gerichtspflicht des Beklagten zu begrenzen – und deshalb beispielsweise die sogenannten exorbitanten Gerichtsstände[31] mit der Begründung auszuschalten, sie seien für den Beklagten (mit Wohnsitz in der EU) unzumutbar (vgl. Art. 5 Brüssel Ia-VO) –, andererseits aber den Beklagten am Wohnsitz eines beliebigen anderen Beklagten ohne nennenswerte Schranke gerichtspflichtig zu machen. Der Grundsatz actor sequitur forum rei wäre in bedenklichem Maße ausgehöhlt.[32]

Vorhersehbarkeit der Gerichtspflicht für den Beklagten und Missbrauchsprävention sind damit dem *Tatbestand des Art. 8 Nr. 1 Brüssel Ia-VO immanente Wertungsmaßstäbe.* In der Rs. *CDC Hydrogen Peroxide* hat der EuGH auch eindeutig zu erkennen gegeben, dass er einem eigenständigen Korrektiv iS des Art. 8 Nr. 2 Brüssel Ia-VO – wie es schon vielfach in der Literatur gefordert und wiederholt von mitgliedstaatlichen Gerichten befürwortet wurde[33] – offen gegenübersteht. Dieser Standpunkt wurde in der Rs. *Beverage City Polska* weiter bekräftigt.[34]

---

[28] OGH 9.9.2008 – 10 Ob 79/08b, ECLI:AT:OGH0002:2008:0100OB00079.08B.0909.000; Generalanwalt Léger 08.12.2005 – C-539/03, ECLI:EU:C:2005:749 Rn. 80ff. (Roche Nederland); siehe die Nachweise zur Diskussion bei Oberhammer/Slonina IPRax 2008, 555 (557 Fn 14).

[29] Rauscher, EuIPR/EuZPR/Leible, 5. Aufl. 2021, Brüssel Ia-VO Art. 8 Rn. 10; so auch schon zur Brüssel I-VO Althammer IPRax 2008, 228 (230).

[30] EuGH 13.07.2006 – C-539/03, ECLI:EU:C:2006:458 Rn. 25 = EuZW 2006, 573 (Roche Nederland).

[31] Siehe dazu Jenard, Bericht zu dem Übereinkommen über die gerichtliche Zuständigkeit und die Vollstreckung gerichtlicher Entscheidungen in Zivil- und Handelssachen, ABl. 1997 C 59, 1 (7, 19ff.).

[32] Coester-Waltjen RabelsZ 79 (2015), 471 (496f.); Geimer/Schütze, EuZVR/Geimer, 4. Aufl. 2020, EuGVVO Art. 8 Rn. 33f. mwN.

[33] Siehe etwa LG Feldkirch 8.6.2004 – 1 R 175/04i, ECLI:AT:LG00929:2004:00300R00175.04I.0608.000; OGH 2.2.2005 – 9 Ob 95/04t, ECLI:AT:OGH0002:2005:0090OB00095.04T.0202.000 = RdW 2005, 430 = ZIK 2005/115; Coester-Waltjen FS Kropholler, 2008, 747 (752f.); Musielak/Voit, ZPO/Stadler, 21. Aufl. 2024, EuGVVO Art. 8 Rn. 4 mwN.

[34] EuGH 7.9.2023 – C-832/21, GRUR 2023, 1559 Rn 43ff. (Beverage City Polska).

2. *Anhaltspunkte in der Judikatur des EuGH*

Eine gefestigte Definition, wann die erforderliche Konnexität vorliegt, hat sich in der Rspr. des EuGH bislang nicht herausgebildet.[35] Zwar gibt es gar nicht so wenig einschlägige Judikate aus Luxemburg,[36] doch stecken sie den Rahmen des Art. 8 Nr. 1 Brüssel Ia-VO alles andere als trennscharf ab.[37] Der „Maßstab ist so flexibel wie unpräzise".[38] Nach mehreren „Entwicklungsschübe[n]"[39] finden sich in den neueren Entscheidungen immerhin einzelne Ansätze für eine Präzisierung.[40]

Für die Anwendung des Art. 8 Nr. 1 Brüssel Ia-VO können der jüngeren Judikatur des EuGH zufolge „Entscheidungen nicht schon deswegen als einander widersprechend betrachtet werden, weil es zu einer abweichenden Entscheidung der Rechtsstreitigkeiten kommt, sondern diese Abweichung muss außerdem bei derselben Sach- und Rechtslage auftreten".[41] Hinsichtlich des schon in älteren Entscheidungen aufgestellten Erfordernisses „derselben Sach- und Rechtslage" blieb allerdings unklar, ob es sich hier um kumulative oder doch alternative Elemente handelt.[42] Zuletzt arbeitete der EuGH freilich die beiden Kriterien wieder gesondert heraus.[43]

Speziell in den Entscheidungen in der Rs. *Freeport* und der Rs. *Painer* hat der EuGH keine vollständige Identität von Sach- und Rechtlage mehr verlangt; weder müsse dasselbe materielle Recht auf alle Ansprüche gegen die Streitgenossen zur Anwendung kommen,[44] noch müssen sie auf derselben Rechtsgrundlage (Delikt oder Vertrag) beruhen.[45] Dies gilt, so der EuGH in der Rs. *Painer,* jedenfalls dann,

---

[35] In diesem Sinne OLG Karlsruhe 31.5.2017 – 13 U 130/16 25, BeckRS 2017, 130011; Hess, Europäisches Zivilprozessrecht, 2. Aufl. 2021, Rn. 6.91; Rauscher, EuIPR/EuZPR/Leible, 5. Aufl. 2021, Brüssel Ia-VO Art. 8 Rn. 10; Burgstaller/Neumayr/Geroldinger/Schmaranzer, Internationales Zivilverfahrensrecht/Schmaranzer, EuGVO Art. 6 Rn. 6; Stadler/Klöpfer ZEuP 2017, 890 (917).

[36] Siehe insbesondere EuGH 27.9.1988 – C-189/87, BeckRS 2004, 72110 (Kalfelis/Schröder ua); 27.10.1998 – C-51/97, EuZW 1999, 59 (Réunion européenne); 13.7.2006 – C-103/05, EuZW 2006, 667 (Reisch Montage); 13.7.2006 – C-539/03, ECLI:EU:C:2006:458 Rn. 25 = EuZW 2006, 573 (Roche Nederland); 11.10.2007 – C-98/06, NJW 2007, 3702 (Freeport); 1.12.2011 – C-145/10, EuZW 2012, 182 (Painer); 12.7.2012 – C-616/10, EuZW 2012, 837 (Solvay); 11.4.2013 – C-645/11, NJW 2013, 1661 (Sapir ua); 21.5.2015 – C-352/13, BeckRS 2015, 80660 (CDC Hydrogen Peroxide); 20.4.2016 – C-366/13, BeckRS 2016, 80666 (Profit Investment SIM); 27.09.2017 –C-24/16 & C-25/16, BeckRS 2017, 126271 (Nintendo); 7.9.2023 – C-832/21, GRUR 2023, 1559 Rn. 29 (Beverage City Polska).

[37] Siehe auch aus dem Schrifttum Brandes, Der gemeinsame Gerichtsstand, 1998; Winter, Ineinandergreifen von EuGVVO und nationalem Zivilverfahrensrecht am Beispiel des Gerichtsstands des Sachzusammenhangs, Art. 6 EuGVVO, 2007.

[38] Schack, Internationales Zivilverfahrensrecht, 8. Aufl. 2021, Rn. 441.

[39] Hess, Europäisches Zivilprozessrecht, 2. Aufl. 2021, Rn. 6.91.

[40] Musielak/Voit, ZPO/Stadler, 21. Aufl. 2024, EuGVVO Art. 8 Rn. 3.

[41] EuGH 21.5.2015 – C-352/13, BeckRS 2015, 80660 Rn. 20 (CDC Hydrogen Peroxide); 20.4.2016 – C-366/13, BeckRS 2016, 80666 Rn. 65 (Profit Investment SIM); 27.9.2017 – C-24/16 & C-25/16, BeckRS 2017, 126271 Rn. 45 (Nintendo).

[42] Stadler/Klöpfer ZEuP 2017, 918.

[43] EuGH 7.9.2023 – C-832/21, GRUR 2023, 1559 Rn. 29, 32 (Beverage City Polska).

[44] EuGH 1.12.2011 – C-145/10, EuZW 2012, 182 Rn. 76ff. (Painer).

[45] EuGH 11.10.2007 – C-98/06, NJW 2007, 3702 Rn. 47 (Freeport); 1.12.2011 – C-145/10, EuZW 2012, 182 Rn. 81 (Painer); anders noch EuGH 27.10.1998 – C-51/9, EuZW 1999, 59

wenn „für die Beklagten vorhersehbar war, dass sie in dem Mitgliedstaat, in dem mindestens einer von ihnen seinen Wohnsitz hatte, verklagt werden könnten".[46] Die Vorhersehbarkeit wurde auch in der Rs. *CDC Hydrogen Peroxide* im Zusammenhang mit der Prüfung betont,[47] ob die Beklagten eine inhaltlich identische Handlung vorgenommen oder ob in Übereinkunft miteinander gehandelt haben. In der Rs. *Profit Investment SIM* stellte der EuGH noch klar,[48] dass es für den Sachzusammenhang der Klagen nicht ausreicht, wenn sich das Ergebnis eines Verfahrens auf ein anderes, etwa auf die Höhe des zu beanspruchenden Schadens, auswirken kann.[49] Rein prozessökonomischen Überlegungen hat der EuGH bereits in der Rs. *Roche Nederland* eine Absage erteilt: Auch wenn diese auf den ersten Blick für eine Konzentration mehrerer Klagen bei einem einzigen Gericht sprechen mögen, so würde gleichzeitig eine „Quelle neuer Risiken" geschaffen; schließlich würde es zu einer Häufung der potenziellen Gerichtsstände kommen, was die Vorhersehbarkeit der Zuständigkeitsregeln und den Grundsatz der Rechtssicherheit beeinträchtige.[50]

3. *Beispiele aus Literatur und Judikatur*

Bereits lange vor den letzten Ansätzen des EuGH zur (partiellen) Klarstellung der Tatbestandselemente hat sich in der österreichischen Judikatur folgender Rechtssatz herausgebildet und über gut zwei Jahrzehnte verfestigt: Der notwendige Zusammenhang iS des Art. 8 Nr. 1 Brüssel Ia-VO (bzw seiner Vorgängerbestimmungen) „wird zu bejahen sein, wenn die Klagen im Wesentlichen tatsächlich oder rechtlich gleichartig sind. Allgemein bejaht wird dieser Zusammenhang bei Gesamtschuldnerschaft und Bürgschaft. Der erforderliche Sachzusammenhang wird in der Regel immer dann vorliegen, wenn die Entscheidung über den einen Anspruch von dem anderen abhängt oder wenn beide Ansprüche von der Lösung einer gemeinsamen Vorfrage abhängen."[51]

Mehrere auf Basis dieses Rechtssatzes gelöste Fälle hat der OGH in jüngerer Vergangenheit in der Entscheidung zu 8 Ob 126/19s kompakt zusammengefasst.[52] Dieses Judikat selbst erging im Kontext von „Dieselgate", wobei ein deutscher Autohersteller über den „Gerichtsstand der Streitgenossen" am Sitz des österreichischen Autohändlers geklagt worden war; der OGH bejahte die erforderliche Kon-

---

(Réunion européenne) und unter Verweis darauf OGH 29.6.2004 – 5 Ob 188/03p, ECLI:AT:OGH0002:2004:0050OB00188.03P.0629.000 = RdW 2005, 31; vgl später aber OGH 9.9.2008 – 10 Ob 79/08b, ECLI:AT:OGH0002:2008:0100OB00079.08B.0909.000; 28.7.2010, 9 ObA 120/09a, ECLI:AT:OGH0002:2010:009OBA00120.09A.0728.000.

[46] EuGH 1.12.2011 – C-145/10, EuZW 2012, 182 Rn. 84 (Painer).

[47] EuGH 21.5.2015 – C-352/13, BeckRS 2015, 80660 Rn. 23 (CDC Hydrogen Peroxide).

[48] EuGH 20.4.2016 – C-366/13, BeckRS 2016, 80666 Rn. 66 (Profit Investment SIM).

[49] Stadler/Klöpfer ZEuP 2017, 917, 920.

[50] EuGH 13.7.2006 – C-539/03, ECLI:EU:C:2006:458 Rn. 36f. = EuZW 2006, 573 (Roche Nederland).

[51] RIS Justiz RS0115274; ähnlich Burgstaller/Neumayr/Geroldinger/Sschmaranzer, Internationales Zivilverfahrensrecht/Schmaranzer EuGVO, Art. 6 Rn. 6.

[52] OGH 6.12.2019 – 8 Ob 126/19s, ECLI:AT:OGH0002:2019:0080OB00126.19S.1216.000 = VbR 2020, 76.

nexität und damit die Zuständigkeit des österreichischen Gerichts auch gegenüber dem Autohersteller.

a) *Abhängigkeit von gemeinsamer Vorfrage*

Nach ständiger Rechtsprechung des OGH soll der Streitgenossengerichtsstand schon dann offenstehen, wenn „alle Ansprüche die Lösung einer gemeinsamen Vorfrage voraussetzen".[53] Auch in der Literatur wird als ausreichend erachtet, dass die Klagen „jeweils von der Entscheidung derselben Frage abhängen".[54]

Dieses Kriterium ist freilich seit jeher viel zu weit gefasst und benötigt zwingend einer Einschränkung. Denn nähme man es beim Wort, so könnte beispielsweise ein Unternehmer (Kaufmann) Geldzahlungsansprüche aus beiderseitig unternehmensbezogenen Geschäften am Gerichtsstand eines beliebigen, behauptetermaßen in Verzug befindlichen Geschäftspartners einklagen und alle ausländischen (der Brüssel Ia-VO unterfallenden) Schuldner dort mitverklagen. Denn in allen Prozessen ist die Frage zu lösen, ob der Kläger Unternehmer und damit zB der Anwendungsbereich des vierten Buchs des UGB (dHGB) eröffnet ist. Die Zuständigkeit wäre – bei wörtlicher Interpretation des Rechtssatzes – selbst dann zu bejahen, wenn die Unternehmereigenschaft des Klägers gar nicht strittig ist, weil sie sich zwanglos aus der Rechtsform ergibt (§ 2 UGB bzw HGB). Sogar der Unternehmensbezug des Rechtsgeschäfts ließe sich, wenn es sich um gleichartige Transaktionen handelt (zB jeweils Verkäufe von Motorenteilen an verschiedene Autohersteller), noch als gemeinsame Vorfrage verstehen.

Umgekehrt könnte ein Schuldner negative Feststellungsklagen über Zahlungsansprüche mit dem Argument, überall stelle sich die Frage nach seiner Unternehmereigenschaft, an einem für langwierige Prozesse bekannten Gerichtsstandort, an dem einer seiner (vielen) Gläubiger sitzt, bündeln; „Torpedoklagen"[55] wäre Tür und Tor geöffnet.

Es bedarf keiner näheren Begründung, dass ein solches Ergebnis überschießend wäre und klar gegen den Geist der Brüssel Ia-VO verstieße. In dieser Weite war der Rechtssatz zur gemeinsamen Vorfrage gewiss auch nie gemeint, der OGH will sie schließlich auch nur „in der Regel" genügen lassen.[56]

---

[53] OGH 14.2.2012 – 5 Ob 39/11p, ECLI:AT:OGH0002:2012:0050OB00039.11P.0214.000 = ecolex 2012, 392 mAnm Wilhelm = EvBl 2012/80; in diesem Sinn auch zu Art. 6 Nr. 1 EuGVÜ OGH 9.9.2008 – 10 Ob 79/08b, ECLI:AT:OGH0002:2008:0100OB00079.08B.0909.000; zu Art. 6 Nr. 1 Brüssel I-VO OGH 29.6.2004 – 5 Ob 188/03p, ECLI:AT:OGH0002:2004:0050OB00188.03P.0629.000; 15.1.2013 – 4 Ob 221/12x, ECLI:AT:OGH0002:2013:0040OB00221.12X.0115.000 = ecolex 2013, 358 mAnm Schumacher = MR 2013, 147 mAnm Thiele; zu Art. 8 Nr. 1 Brüssel Ia-VO OGH 6.12.2019 – 8 Ob 126/19s, ECLI:AT:OGH0002:2019:0080OB00126.19S.1216.000.

[54] Rauscher, EuIPR/EuZPR/Leible, 5. Aufl. 2021, Brüssel Ia-VO Art. 8 Rn. 10a; in diesem Sinne auch Czernich/Kodek/Mayr, Europäisches Gerichtsstands- und Vollstreckungsrecht/Heiss, 4. Aufl. 2015, EuGVVO Art. 8 Rn. 18; Hess, Europäisches Zivilprozessrecht, 2. Aufl. 2021, Rn. 6.90; Schack, Internationales Zivilverfahrensrecht, 8. Aufl. 2021, Rn. 441, je mwN.

[55] Siehe dazu Coester-Waltjen RabelsZ 79 (2015), 496; Schlosser/Hess, EU-Zivilprozessrecht/Schlosser, 5. Aufl. 2021, EuGVVO Art. 29 Rn. 4c f.

[56] OGH 6.12.2019 – 8 Ob 126/19s, ECLI:AT:OGH0002:2019:0080OB00126.19S.1216.000.

Weder von einem einheitlichen rechtserzeugenden Sachverhalt noch einer Verpflichtung aus demselben tatsächlichen Grund wurde zu 5 Ob 213/12b ausgegangen: Der Fall hatte die Montage von mangelhaftem Material zum Gegenstand, wobei der Werkunternehmer wegen Gewährleistung und der Hersteller aufgrund eines behaupteten konstitutiven Anerkenntnisses belangt wurde. Zur Durchsetzung des Anspruchs gegen den Hersteller kam es nach den Ausführungen des OGH weder auf das Vorhandensein von Mängeln noch auf die zwischen dem Kläger und dem Werkunternehmer getroffenen Vereinbarungen an. Weil hier die Begehren auf unterschiedliche Sachverhalte und verschiedene Rechtsgründe gestützt wurden, bestand die Gefahr von widersprechenden Entscheidungen iS von Art. 6 Nr. 1 Brüssel I-VO – auch wenn die Ansprüche zumindest partiell auf dasselbe Interesse (Rückzahlung des Kaufpreises) gerichtet waren – nicht.[57]

b) Solidarschuld

„Allgemein bejaht" wird nach der Darstellung des OGH, dass eine Gesamtschuldnerschaft als Basis für einen gemeinsamen Gerichtsstand nach Art. 8 Nr. 1 Brüssel Ia-VO hinreicht.[58] In der Tat findet sich dieses Beispiel schon im *Jenard*-Bericht zu Art. 6 Nr. 1 EuGVÜ und in zahlreichen Stellungnahmen.[59] Dem wird man in vielen Fällen auch zustimmen können, etwa bei wissentlich aufeinander abgestimmtem Fehlverhalten.[60] Gerade für das Schadenersatzrecht ist der Rechtssatz aber stark einschränkungsbedürftig: Wird ein Kind, das vor einem Hund fliehend auf die Straße läuft und dort von einem Auto erfasst wird, am Körper verletzt,[61] so haften der Hundehalter (§ 1320 ABGB; § 833 BGB) und der Halter des Fahrzeugs (§ 1 EKHG; § 7 StVG) solidarisch, sofern sich die haftungsbegründenden Vorwürfe im Prozess bestätigen (§§ 1301, 1302 ABGB; § 840 BGB, § 17 StVG). Haben die beiden (potenziellen) Schädiger ihren allgemeinen Gerichtsstand in unterschiedlichen Mitgliedstaaten, ist eine gemeinsame Klage jedenfalls am Ort des Schadenseintritts nach Art. 7 Nr. 2 Brüssel Ia-VO möglich. Warum aber beispielsweise der Hundehalter am Wohnsitz des Kfz-Halters gerichtspflichtig werden soll, ist nicht einzusehen – auch wenn sich einzelne Beweisergebnisse (zB zum Ausmaß der Verletzung) in beiden Verfahren verwerten lassen. Die Schädiger sind zwar Solidar-

---

[57] OGH 6.6.2013 – 5 Ob 213/12b, ECLI:AT:OGH0002:2013:0050OB00213.12B.0606.000 = JBl 2013, 732.

[58] RIS-Justiz RS0115274.

[59] Jenard, Bericht zu dem Übereinkommen über die gerichtliche Zuständigkeit und die Vollstreckung gerichtlicher Entscheidungen in Zivil- und Handelssachen, ABl. 1997 C 59, 1 (26); aus der Literatur etwa Auer in Geimer/Schütze, Internationaler Rechtsverkehr/Hau, 66. EL 1/2023, EuGVVO Art. 6 Rn. 23; Czernich/Kodek/Mayr, Europäisches Gerichtsstands- und Vollstreckungsrecht/Heiss, 4. Aufl. 2015, EuGVVO Art. 8 Rn. 22; Mayr, Europäisches Zivilprozessrecht, 2. Aufl. 2020, Rn. II/93; Burgstaller/Neumayr/Geroldinger/Schmaranzer, Internationales Zivilverfahrensrecht/Schmaranzer, EuGVO Art. 6 Rn. 6; Mayr, Handbuch des europäischen Zivilverfahrensrechts/Wittwer, 2. Aufl. 2023, Rn. 3.385.

[60] Zu Art. 6 Nr 1 EuGVÜ BayOLG 25.3.1997 – 1Z AR 2/97, BeckRS 1997, 3159 = RIW 1997, 596 (Schädigung durch bewusstes aufeinander abgestimmtes Unterdrücken von Tatsachen).

[61] Zum Sachverhalt siehe OLG Düsseldorf 25.5.1994 – 15 W 13/94, NJW-RR 1995, 281.

schuldner, mitnichten ist deshalb aber „immer" der nach Art. 8 Nr. 1 Brüssel Ia-VO erforderliche Sachzusammenhang gegeben.[62]

Eine Rolle für die Bejahung des Streitgenossengerichtsstands spielte das Vorbringen zum Vorliegen einer Solidarschuld nach § 89 UrhG etwa in der Entscheidung OGH 4 Ob 124/07z; entscheidend für die Konntexität war nach den Ausführungen des OGH aber das bewusste Zusammenwirken zwischen einem ausländischen Händler und dem inländischen Vertriebspartner, dessen er sich für die Abwicklung von Kaufgeschäften im Inland bediente; außerdem stand als weitere Anspruchsgrundlage die Haftung als Bürge und Zahler nach § 42b Abs. 3 Ziff. 1 UrhG im Raum.[63] Diese Argumentation zu § 89 UrhG liegt auf der Linie der jüngeren Rsp des EuGH, die im Falle eines Zusammenwirkens der Beklagten auch eine Vorhersehbarkeit der Gerichtspflicht am Wohnsitz eines Beteiligten annimmt. So verhält es sich auch mit der Anwendung von Art. 8 Nr. 1 Brüssel I-VO beim sittenwidrigen Abwerben von Vertriebspartnern in gemeinsamem Zusammenwirken zweier Beklagter[64] oder im Kontext einer sogenannten „Verletzerkette".[65] Für Liefer- bzw Verletzerketten verlangt der EuGH jedoch, dass dieselbe Sachlage „bei sämtlichen Tätigkeiten der verschiedenen Beklagten vorliegen" muss und sich nicht „auf bestimmte Gesichtspunkte oder bestimmte Teile dieser Tätigkeiten beschränken" darf.[66] In einer noch recht jungen Entscheidung hielt der EuGH allerdings fest, dass von „derselben Sachlage" ausgegangen werden könne, wenn „die Klageansprüche [...] gegen verschiedene Akteure gerichtet sind, die im Rahmen einer Kette von Verletzungshandlungen jeweils zur selben Verletzung einer Unionsmarke beigetragen haben".[67]

c) *Bürgschaft*

Ein Fall für den Streitgenossengerichtsstand nach Art. 8 Nr. 1 Brüssel Ia-VO wird regelmäßig die Klage gegen den Hauptschuldner und den Bürgen sein.[68] Dies kann bei einer akzessorischen Bürgschaft auch dann zutreffen, wenn Bürgschaft und

---

[62] So aber Czernich/Kodek/Mayr, Europäisches Gerichtsstands- und Vollstreckungsrecht/Heiss, 4. Aufl. 2015, EuGVVO Art. 8 Rn. 14.

[63] OGH 2.10.2007 – 4 Ob 124/07z, ECLI:AT:OGH0002:2007:0040OB00124.07Z.1002.000; 27.8.2013 – 4 Ob 142/13f, ECLI:AT:OGH0002:2013:0040OB00142.13F.0827.000 = ÖBl 2014, 33 mAnm Büchele.

[64] OGH 21.01.2003 – 4 Ob 298/02f, ECLI:AT:OGH0002:2003:0040OB00298.02F.0121.000.

[65] OGH 15.1.2013 – 4 Ob 221/12x, ECLI:AT:OGH0002:2013:0040OB00221.12X.0115.000 = ecolex 2013, 358 mAnm Schumacher = MR 2013, 147 mAnm Thiele; siehe dazu auch LG Nürnberg-Fürth 26.4.2018 – 19 O 3000/17, GRUR Int 2019, 57 Rn. 36.

[66] EuGH 27.9.2017 – C-24/16 & C-25/16, BeckRS 2017, 126271 Rn. 52 (Nintendo); Rauscher, EuIPR/EuZPR/Leible, 5. Aufl. 2021, Brüssel Ia-VO Art. 8 Rn. 14a.

[67] EuGH 7.9.2023 – C-832/21, GRUR 2023, 1559 Rn. 41 (Beverage City Polska); siehe auch OLG Wien 28.02.2024 – 33 R 9/24x, ECLI:AT:OLG0009:2024:03300R00009.24X.0228.000.

[68] Beispielsweise lag auch dem Ausgangsverfahren zur Rs. *Reisch Montage* eine Bürgschaft zugrunde; siehe EuGH 13.7.2006 – C-103/05, EuZW 2006, 667 Rn. 9 (Reisch Montage); vgl auch OGH 2.10.2007 – 4 Ob 124/07z, ECLI:AT:OGH0002:2007:0040OB00124.07Z.1002.000.

Hauptschuld unterschiedlichen Sachrechten unterfallen. Überzeugend hat in einem solchen Fall das OLG Karlsruhe zu Art. 6 Nr. 1 LugÜbk 2007 argumentiert: „Würde in getrennten Verfahren die Hauptschuld unterschiedlich beurteilt – sei es, dass sie in einem Verfahren als nicht bestehend oder als geringer bestehend angenommen würde als im anderen Verfahren – könnte sich ergeben, dass einerseits die Klage gegen die Hauptschuldner abgewiesen, der Klage gegen den Bürgen aber stattgegeben würde, weil die Entstehung der Hauptschuld von den Gerichten unterschiedlich beurteilt wird.“[69] Außerdem wurde die Vorhersehbarkeit der Gerichtspflicht für den Beklagten am Sitz der Hauptschuldnerin als eigenständiges Kriterium geprüft und bejaht; schließlich war der (in der Schweiz wohnhafte) Bürge der Geschäftsführer der Hauptschuldnerin, an deren Sitz die Klage eingebracht wurde.[70]

IV. Missbrauchskontrolle

Wie die vorstehenden Ausführungen gezeigt haben, herrscht – entgegen der Einschätzung des OGH – betreffend die Voraussetzungen der Konnexität iSd Art. 8 Nr. 1 Brüssel Ia-VO keineswegs hinreichende Klarheit im Sinne von *acte claire*. Dies gilt ganz besonders mit Blick auf die (dem Kriterium der Konnexität innewohnende) Missbrauchsschranke.[71] Wenn der EuGH zum wiederholten Male formuliert, dass ein Missbrauch von vornherein ausgeschlossen sei, wenn die Klagen gegen den Ankerbeklagten und gegen die Annexbeklagten miteinander in dem von Art. 8 Nr. 1 Brüssel Ia-VO geforderten Zusammenhang stünden,[72] ist damit wenig gewonnen.[73]

Zu Recht hatte die zweite Instanz im Verfahren zu 5 Ob 73/23f herausgearbeitet, dass ein Missbrauch im Rahmen des Art. 8 Nr. 1 Brüssel Ia-VO keineswegs zwingend ein kollusives Zusammenwirken des Klägers mit dem Ankerbeklagten erfordert.[74] Schließlich sind die Ausführungen des EuGH in der Rs. *CDC Hydrogen Peroxide* vor dem Hintergrund zu verstehen, dass im dortigen Ausgangsverfahren die Klage gegen den Ankerbeklagten aufgrund eines Vergleichs unmittelbar nach Klageeinbringung zurückgenommen wurde. Abgesehen von derartigen Fällen ist – speziell mit Blick auf die jüngste Entscheidung des EuGH in der Rs. *Beverage City Polska*[75] – weiterhin unklar, ob die Zuständigkeit gegenüber dem Annexbeklagten verneint werden kann, wenn die (schlüssige) Klage gegen den Ankerbeklagten

---

[69] OLG Karlsruhe 31.5.2017 – 13 U 130/16, BeckRS 2017, 130011 Rn. 37.

[70] OLG Karlsruhe 31.5.2017 – 13 U 130/16, BeckRS 2017, 130011.

[71] Stein/Jonas, ZPO/Thole, 23. Aufl. 2022, EuGVVO Art. 8 Rn. 44 („Eine Konkretisierung des Missbrauchsverbots steht bisher weitgehend noch aus“).

[72] EuGH 11.10.2007 – C-98/06, NJW 2007, 3702 Rn. 53 (Freeport); 7.9.2023 – C-832/21, GRUR 2023, 1559 Rn. 45 (Beverage City Polska).

[73] Stein/Jonas, ZPO/Thole, 23. Aufl. 2022, EuGVVO Art. 8 Rn. 44.

[74] OGH 22.2.2024 – 5 Ob 73/23f, ECLI:AT:OGH0002:2024:0050OB00073.23F.0222.000 Rn. 14f.

[75] EuGH 7.9.2023 – C-832/21, GRUR 2023, 1559 Rn. 45 (Beverage City Polska).

allein zu dem Zweck erhoben wurde, dem Annexbeklagten durch die gemeinsame Klage die Zuständigkeit der Gerichte seines Wohnsitzstaats zu entziehen.

Es sprechen gute Gründe dafür, für die Annahme einer missbräuchlichen Inanspruchnahme des Streitgenossengerichtsstands die Feststellung genügen zu lassen, dass die Klage gegen den Erstbeklagten nur erhoben worden sei, um einen Gerichtsstand gegen die Zweitbeklagte in Österreich zu konstruieren. Damit wäre der Fall in 5 Ob 73/23f geradezu prädestiniert gewesen, um zahlreiche Zweifelsfragen zu Art. 8 Nr. 1 Brüssel Ia-VO zu klären. Von acte claire konnte keine Rede sein, vielmehr wurde die Vorlagepflicht nach Art. 267 AEUV verletzt.

V. Behauptungs- und Beweislast, doppelrelevante Tatsachen

Für die Praktikabilität und das Missbrauchspotenzial des Art. 8 Nr. 1 Brüssel Ia-VO kommt es entscheidend darauf an, welche Anforderungen an das Vorbringen zum Zuständigkeitstatbestand gestellt werden. Nach hA kommt eine A-limine-Zurückweisung im Anwendungsbereich der Brüssel Ia-VO abseits von Art. 27 (iVm Art. 24) Brüssel Ia-VO nicht in Betracht. Die Klage ist dem Beklagten jedenfalls zuzustellen.[76] Bestreitet dieser die Zuständigkeit oder bleibt er passiv – kommt es also zu keiner rügelosen Einlassung iS des Art. 26 Brüssel Ia-VO –, muss das Gericht seine Zuständig näher prüfen.

Im Hinblick auf Art. 8 Nr. 1 Brüssel Ia-VO findet sich nun regelmäßig die Aussage, dass der Kläger die Darlegungs- und Beweislast für die Voraussetzungen der Konnexität trage,[77] für die Missbräuchlichkeit der Berufung auf Art. 8 Nr. 1 Brüssel Ia-VO hingegen der Beklagte.[78] Die Prüfung der Konnexität müsse anhand des gesamten Akteninhalts erfolgen.[79]

Weitgehend anerkannt ist ferner, dass man es im Hinblick auf den Annexbeklagten mit doppelrelevanten Tatsachen zu tun hat,[80] die man ansonsten vor allem mit Art. 7 Nr. 2 Brüssel Ia-VO assoziiert. Zu dieser Bestimmung hat der EuGH – wenngleich die Zuständigkeitsprüfung abseits der Vorgaben in Art. 27f. Brüssel Ia-VO im Wesentlichen vom nationalen Recht geregelt wird – im Interesse der praktischen Wirksamkeit des europäischen Zuständigkeitsrechts[81] bestimmte Leitlinien

[76] Zum LugÜbk 2007 OGH 26.6.2019 – 7 Ob 4/19t, ECLI:AT:OGH0002:2019:0070OB00004.19T.0626.000 = IPRax 2020, 468; siehe dazu Maultzsch IPRax 2020, 469 (473ff.).

[77] OGH 9.9.2008 – 10 Ob 79/08b, ECLI:AT:OGH0002:2008:0100OB00079.08B.0909.000; Geimer/Schütze, EuZVR/Geimer, 4. Aufl. 2020, EuGVVO Art. 8 Rn. 43a; Burgstaller/Neumayr/Geroldinger/Schmaranzer, Internationales Zivilverfahrensrecht/Schmaranzer, EuGVO Art. 6 Rn. 6.

[78] OGH 2.2.2005 – 9 Ob 95/04t, ECLI:AT:OGH0002:2005:0090OB00095.04T.0202.000 = RdW 2005, 430 = ZIK 2005/115.

[79] EuGH 12.7.2012 – C-616/10, EuZW 2012, 837 Rn. 83 (Solvay); Wieczorek/Schütze, ZPO/Garber/Neumayr, 5. Aufl. 2022, Brüssel Ia-VO Art. 8 Rn. 25.

[80] Münchener Kommentar zur ZPO/Gottwald, 6. Aufl. 2022, Brüssel Ia-VO Art. 8 Rn. 12; vgl. RIS-Justiz RS0116404 (T2).

[81] EuGH 28.1.2015 – C-375/13, EuZW 2015, 218 mAnm Müller = GWR 2015, 189 mAnm Müllejans = LMK 2015, 367447 mAnm Mankowski (Kolassa).

für die Prüfung doppelrelevanter Tatsachen herausgearbeitet.[82] Speziell für den Gerichtsstand der unerlaubten Handlung (Art. 7 Nr. 2 Brüssel Ia-VO) sind danach im Rahmen der Zuständigkeitsprüfung nicht die Zulässigkeit oder Begründetheit der Klage nach nationalem Recht zu prüfen, sondern „nur die Anknüpfungspunkte mit dem Staat des Gerichtsstands“ zu ermitteln.[83] Dabei dürfe das Gericht „die einschlägigen Behauptungen des Klägers zu den Voraussetzungen der Haftung aus unerlaubter Handlung“ grundsätzlich ohne Durchführung eines Beweisverfahrens „als erwiesen ansehen“, im Rahmen einer geordneten Rechtspflege aber „gegebenenfalls auch die Einwände des Beklagten“ berücksichtigen.[84] Jüngere Entscheidungen[85] werden von Teilen des Schrifttums als Pflicht zur Würdigung des Beklagtenvorbringens – und damit als Abkehr von der Lehre von den doppelrelevanten Tatsachen – gedeutet.[86]

Mäsch hat bereits vor geraumer Zeit darauf hingewiesen, dass man sich, um möglichem Missbrauch von Art. 8 Nr. 1 Brüssel Ia-VO einen Riegel vorzuschieben, „in diesem Kontext von der üblichen Behandlung doppelrelevanter Tatsachen verabschieden“ müsse: Zwar solle kein volles Beweisverfahren über den Zuständigkeitstatbestand abgeführt werden, praktikabel sei aber eine summarische Prüfung nach dem Vorbild des § 114 dZPO im Kontext der Prozesskostenhilfe. Demnach sei die Klage gegen den nicht im Gerichtsstaat ansässigen Beklagten nur dann zulässig, wenn das Gericht die Konnexität bejahe und nach einer überschlägigen Prüfung der Rechts- und Sachlage es zumindest für möglich hält, dass der Kläger mit seinem Begehren gegen den Beklagten durchdringt, dessen Wohnsitz im Gerichtsstaat den Weg zu Art. 6 Nr. 1 Brüssel I-VO öffne.[87] *Althammer* zufolge erfordert das Missbrauchspotential der Vorschrift „eine über die Prüfung der Schlüssigkeit des Tatsachenstoffes hinausgehende Glaubhaftmachung der tatsächlichen Grundlagen, ohne dass eine volle Begründetheitsprüfung durchzuführen wäre“.[88] Auch GA *Szpunar* hat in seinen Schlussanträgen zur Rs. *Kolassa* eine Prima-facie-Kontrolle der zuständigkeitsbegründenden Tatsachen gefordert.[89] *Geimer* verlangt offenbar

[82] Siehe dazu Maultzsch IPRax 2020, 470471; kritisch etwa Linke/Hau, Internationales Zivilverfahrensrecht, 8. Aufl. 2021, Rn. 4.72 mwN.

[83] EuGH 28.1.2015 – C-375/13, EuZW 2015, 218 Rn. 62 mAnm Müller = GWR 2015, 189 mAnm Müllejans = LMK 2015, 367447 mAnm Mankowski (Kolassa); 16.6.2016 – C-12/15, NJW 2016, 2167 mAnm Müller Rn. 44 = IWRZ 2016, 232 mAnm Pfitzner = LMK 2016, 381538m Anm Magnus (Universal Music International Holding).

[84] EuGH 28.1.2015 – C-375/13, EuZW 2015, 218 Rn. 64 mAnm Müller = GWR 2015, 189 mAnm Müllejans = LMK 2015, 367447 mAnm Mankowski (Kolassa); 16.6.2016 – C-12/15, NJW 2016, 2167 mAnm Müller Rn. 45 = IWRZ 2016, 232 mAnm Pfitzner = LMK 2016, 381538 m Anm Magnus (Universal Music International Holding).

[85] EuGH 10.03.2016 – C-94/14, BeckRS 2016, 80468 Rn. 63 (Flight Refund); 16.6.2016 – C-12/15, NJW 2016, 2167 mAnm Müller Rn. 46 = IWRZ 2016, 232 mAnm Pfitzner = LMK 2016, 381538m Anm Magnus (Universal Music International Holding).

[86] Klöpfer/Wendelstein JZ 2017, 99 (101f.).

[87] Mäsch IPRax 2005, 509 (514); zustimmend Coester-Waltjen FS Kropholler, 2008, 757.

[88] Althammer IPRax 2008, 232; in diesem Sinne auch Burgstaller/Neumayr/Geroldinger/Schmarantzer, Internationales Zivilverfahrensrecht/Schmaranzer, EuGVO Art. 6 Rn. 7; vgl. ferner LG Feldkirch 8.6.2004 – 1 R 175/04i, ECLI:AT:LG00929:2004:00300R00175.04I.0608.000.

[89] Generalanwalt Szpunar 3.9.2014 – C-375/13, ECLI:EU:C:2014:2135 Rn. 78 (Kolassa).

sogar den vollen Beweis der die Konnexität begründenden Faktoren, wenn der Beklagte diese bestreitet; allein die schlüssige Behauptung genüge nicht.[90]

Art. 7 Nr. 2 Brüssel Ia-VO und Art. 8 Nr. 1 Brüssel Ia-VO unterscheiden sich mit Blick auf die Doppelrelevanz-Problematik erheblich: Zur Rechtfertigung der Lehre von den doppelrelevanten Tatsachen wird üblicherweise darauf verwiesen, dass eine rechtskraftfähige klageabweisende Sachentscheidung für den Beklagten günstiger sei als ein Zurückweisung wegen Unzuständigkeit.[91] Im Kontext des Art. 8 Nr. 1 Brüssel Ia-VO zieht die Abweisung der Ankerklage aber keineswegs zwingend die negative Erledigung der Annexklage nach sich.[92] In diesem Sinne hat bereits der 1. Senat zu § 93 JN ausgeführt, dass die etablierten Begründungsmuster für die Behandlung doppelrelevanter Tatsachen „nicht ohne weiteres auf die Fälle der behaupteten Streitgenossenschaft wegen einer vermeintlichen Solidarverpflichtung [passen], wenn die Haftung der Streitgenossen auf unterschiedliche rechtliche Erwägungen gestützt wird. Dann liegt häufig keineswegs die Situation vor, dass auch schon gegenüber jener Partei, die die Zuständigkeit bestreitet, eine abschließende Sachentscheidung möglich wäre, die den Vorrang vor einer Zurückweisungsentscheidung haben soll."[93] Daher hat *Kodek* auch jüngst eine Prüfung der „tatsächliche[n] Plausibilität" des Vorbringens zum Streitgenossengerichtsstand gemäß § 93 JN vorgeschlagen.[94]

Die Zuständigkeit für den Ankerbeklagten ergibt sich außerdem ausschließlich aus dessen Wohnsitz. Nur im Hinblick auf den Annexbeklagten werden doppelrelevante Faktoren relevant, die keineswegs nur Tatsachenfragen betreffen müssen. Vielmehr muss der Prozessstoff, der sich aus den gegen den Ankerbeklagten in Betracht kommenden Anspruchsgrundlagen ergibt, jenem gegenübergestellt werden, der den Annexbeklagten betrifft, wozu die jeweilige lex causae konsultiert (und zunächst ermittelt) werden muss. Die Qualität und/oder Quantität der thematischen Überschneidungen entscheiden dann über die Konnexität iS des Art. 8 Nr. 1 Brüssel Ia-VO. Dieser Vorgang ist ungleich komplexer als die schlichte Prüfung doppelrelevanter Tatsachen im Kontext des Art. 7 Nr. 2 Brüssel Ia-VO.

Damit erscheint es aber unzulässig, die vom EuGH aufgestellten Leitlinien zur Prüfung doppelrelevanter Tatsachen auf Art. 8 Nr. 1 Brüssel Ia-VO zu übertragen.[95] Dementsprechend sollte die bloße Behauptung eines „Zusammenwirkens" der Beklagten nicht genügen, um „dieselbe Sachlage" anzunehmen und so einen Streitgenossengerichtsstand zu begründen.

---

[90] Geimer/Schütze, EuZVR/Geimer, 4. Aufl. 2020, EuGVVO Art. 8 Rn. 43a.

[91] Siehe dazu ausführlich Mankowski IPRax 2006, 454 (454ff.).

[92] Althammer IPRax 2008, 232 Fn 70.

[93] OGH 29.08.2013 – 1 Ob 132/13p, ECLI:AT:OGH0002:2013:0010OB00132.13P.0829.000; zustimmend Kodek Zak 2022, 68.

[94] Kodek Zak 2022, 68.

[95] Vgl. noch RIS-Justiz RS0116404 (T2).

VI. Fazit

Trotz einer Vielzahl einschlägiger EuGH-Judikate sind bis heute keine klaren Konturen des Erfordernisses der Konnexität iS der Art. 8 Nr. 1 Brüssel Ia-VO erkennbar. Vom Kriterium der „einheitlichen Rechtslage" bleibt in den neueren EuGH-Entscheidungen nur noch wenig übrig; zusehends mehr Gewicht erhält hingegen die Prüfung, ob ein konzertiertes Parallelverhalten im Raum steht.[96] In diese Richtung weist auch die jüngste Entscheidung des EuGH in der Rs. *Beverage City Polska,* in der es der EuGH für die Annahme „derselben Sachlage" nicht genügen ließ, dass mehrere Personen eine Unionsrechtsmarke in unterschiedlichen Mitgliedstaaten nur „parallel" verletzen.[97] Besonderes Gewicht kam „der Beziehung zwischen allen begangenen Verletzungshandlungen", insbesondere einer exklusiven Vertragsbeziehung zwischen zwei beklagten Gesellschaften und dem Betrieb zweier gemeinsamer Websites, zu.[98]

Wie *Stadler/Klöpfer* zutreffend festhalten, hat sich der EuGH vom Wortlaut des Art. 8 Nr. 1 Brüssel I-VO, der auf die Gefahr widersprechender Entscheidungen bei getrennter statt gemeinsamer Verhandlung abstellt, erheblich entfernt.[99] Damit erodiert auch das oft betonte Gebot der engen Auslegung von Gerichtständen,[100] die dem Beklagten seinen allgemeinen Gerichtstand entziehen, in bedenklichem Maße. Das Potenzial des Art. 8 Nr. 1 Brüssel Ia-VO dafür, Beklagten gänzlich unvorhersehbare und sachfremde Gerichtsstände aufzuzwingen, ist bereits seit langem bekannt.[101] Wie schon *Mock* in anderem Zusammenhang hervorgehoben hat, kann beispielsweise über die internationale Zuständigkeit für Klagen gegen Organmitglieder iVm Art. 8 Nr. 1 Brüssel Ia-VO zugleich eine Zuständigkeit für Klagen gegen die Gesellschaft begründet werden. Der Wohnsitz – und in gewissem Umfang auch der Arbeitsort – der Mitglieder der Gesellschaftsorgane würde so eine unzulässige Zuständigkeitsmanipulation ermöglichen.[102] Ein Wohnsitz eines Organmitglieds, der womöglich erst lange nach dem schadensstiftenden Ereignis im Ausland begründet wird, ist für die Gesellschaft oder mit ihr kooperierende Dienstleister schwerlich ein Ort, an dem mit der Gerichtspflicht gerechnet werden kann und muss; eine solche Zuständigkeit ist somit alles andere als „in hohem Maße vorhersehbar" (ErwGr. 15 Brüssel Ia-VO).[103] In der aktuellen Interpretation des OGH

---

[96] Stadler/Klöpfer ZEuP 2017, 919; vgl. EuGH 1.12.2011 – C-145/10, EuZW 2012, 182 Rn. 83 (Painer) („Dabei kann erheblich sein, ob die Beklagten, denen der Urheberrechtsinhaber inhaltlich identische Verletzungen seines Rechts vorwirft, unabhängig voneinander gehandelt haben oder nicht").

[97] So Hackbarth GRUR-Prax 2023, 631 (631).

[98] EuGH 7.9.2023 – C-832/21, GRUR 2023, 1559 Rn. 37 ff. (Beverage City Polska).

[99] Stadler/Klöpfer ZEuP 2017, 918.

[100] EuGH 20.4.2016 – C-366/13, BeckRS 2016, 80666 Rn. 62 f. (Profit Investment SIM); EuGH 7.9.2023 – C-832/21, GRUR 2023, 1559 Rn. 35 (Beverage City Polska).

[101] Siehe bereits zu Art. 6 Nr. 1 EuGVÜ Jenard, Bericht zu dem Übereinkommen über die gerichtliche Zuständigkeit und die Vollstreckung gerichtlicher Entscheidungen in Zivil- und Handelssachen, ABl. 1997 C 59, 1 (26).

[102] Mock IPRax 2010, 510 (512).

[103] Geroldinger JBl 2022, 186.

verliert das Kriterium der Vorhersehbarkeit (aufgrund eines Zirkelschlusses) viel an Bedeutung.

Ein präzise formuliertes Vorabentscheidungsersuchen im Verfahren zu 5 Ob 73/23f hätte das Potenzial gehabt, zahlreiche Zweifelsfragen im Zusammenhang mit Art. 8 Nr. 1 Brüssel Ia-VO zu klären. Zumal der OGH aber – wie *Simotta* treffend beobachtet – fest entschlossen erscheint, österreichischen Anlegern im Wirecard-Skandal (unter Verletzung der Vorlagepflicht) eine Zuständigkeit in Österreich zu eröffnen,[104] sei an dieser Stelle auf das Vorlagerecht unterer Instanzen nach Art. 267 AEUV hingewiesen. Selbst eine „ständige Rechtsprechung" des OGH und die (in casu ohnehin irrige) Annahme von *acte claire* durch das Höchstgericht stehen diesem Recht nicht entgegen.[105]

[104] Fasching/Konecny, Kommentar zu den Zivilprozessgesetzen/Simotta V/1, 3. Aufl. 2022, EuGVVO Art. 8 2012 Rn. 76/10 (Fn 178).

[105] Siehe dazu die Nachweise bei Geroldinger ZIK 2011, 208 (212).

ASTRID GRAUL

Das Schutzlandprinzip *(lex loci protectionis)* im Lichte ubiquitärer und multinationaler Verletzungen von unionsweiten Rechten des geistigen Eigentums*

Grenzenloses Internet und Globalisierung stellen das Kollisionsrecht vor neue Herausforderungen. Im Folgenden soll die traditionelle Anknüpfung von Verletzungen geistiger Eigentumsrechte an das Schutzlandprinzip *(lex loci protectionis)* unter dem Blickwinkel stetig zunehmender ubiquitärer und multinationaler Schutzrechtsverletzungen im Internet beleuchtet werden, das eine territoriale Begrenzung der Verletzungshandlung nicht kennt. Erscheint die Anknüpfung an das Schutzlandprinzip noch zeitgemäß oder sind Lockerungen hiervon angezeigt? Der Fokus soll hierbei auf Verletzungen der unionsweiten Schutzrechte der Unionsmarken und -designs und die Anknüpfung der Folgeansprüche einer Schutzrechtsverletzung gerichtet werden.

I. Lex loci protectionis als Anknüpfungspunkt für grenzüberschreitende Verletzungen von geistigen Eigentumsrechten

1. Territorialität geistiger Eigentumsrechte

Wesentlicher Pfeiler des Immaterialgüterrechts ist, national wie international, das Territorialitätsprinzip. Die Wirkung der Rechte des geistigen Eigentums ist auf das jeweilige nationale Territorium des Staates begrenzt, für das der Schutz der Rechte beansprucht wird. Das Territorialitätsprinzip geht mit einem Mosaik nationaler Rechte einher.[1]

Diese jahrhundertelange Tradition basiert auf dem Grundsatz der völkerrechtlichen Rücksichtnahme gegenüber den souveränen Regelungen anderer Staaten.[2] Gewerbliche Schutzrechte hängen grundsätzlich von einem staatlichen Akt der Erteilung oder Eintragung ab. Ein solcher Hoheitsakt kann nur in dem jeweiligen Territorium des Eintragungs- bzw. Erteilungsstaates Wirkung entfalten. Nur der Schutz gewährende Staat soll über die Entstehung und Wirkung der Schutzrechte entscheiden können.

---

* Die von der Autorin dargelegten Äußerungen und Meinungen sind persönliche Ansichten und binden unter keinen Umständen das EUIPO oder die Europäische Kommission.

[1] Münchener Kommentar zum BGB/Drexl, 8. Aufl. 2021, Rom II-VO Art. 8 Rn. 7.

[2] Münchener Kommentar zum BGB/Drexl, 8. Aufl. 2021, Rom II-VO Art. 8 Rn. 308.

Dies gilt für eingetragene Rechte des geistigen Eigentums, die im Hinblick auf Bestand, Umfang und Wirkung auf das Territorium beschränkt sind, für das der Schutz gewährt wurde, ebenso wie für geistige Eigentumsrechte, die nicht auf einem staatlichen Akt der Erteilung oder Eintragung beruhen, wie nicht eingetragene Marken.[3] Auch sie entfalten ihre Wirkung nur in dem Staat, der das Recht anerkennt.

Für die parallel zu den nationalen Marken- und Designrechten bestehenden Schutzrechte der Unionsmarken und -designs liegt der „Erteilungsakt" in der durch die jeweiligen Unionsrechtsakte der Unionsmarkenverordnung (UMV)[4] und der EU-Designverordnung (EUDV)[5] geregelten Eintragung beim Amt der Europäischen Union für geistiges Eigentum (EUIPO) in Alicante begründet bzw. für nicht eingetragene Unionsdesigns in der Offenbarung des Designs innerhalb der Union bei Vorliegen der materiellen Schutzvoraussetzungen.[6] Unionsschutzrechte stellen nach Art. 118 AEUV europäische Rechtstitel mit einheitlichem Schutz in den Unionsmitgliedstaaten dar. Der Schutz gilt länderübergreifend in dem gesamten Gebiet der Union, nicht jedoch darüber hinaus.

Weder eine Marke noch ein Design gewähren dem Inhaber damit einen universellen Schutz. Rechte an derselben Marke bzw. demselben Design können in verschiedenen Ländern von verschiedenen Inhabern erworben werden. Eine nationale Marke kann in Deutschland für A geschützt sein, während sie in Österreich für B rechtmäßig eingetragen ist und damit von B rechtmäßig in Österreich benutzt werden kann. Werden die von B mit der Marke versehenen Waren im geschäftlichen Verkehr jedoch in Deutschland benutzt, kann Markeninhaber A die Benutzung der Marke in Deutschland untersagen. Nach dem Territorialitätsprinzip endet das ausschließliche Recht einer Marke oder Designs in der Regel an der Grenze des jeweiligen Staatsgebiets, so dass auch eine Verletzung des Marken- oder Designrechts nur in dem das Recht gewährenden Land erfolgen kann. Außerhalb dessen Territoriums entfällt ein Schutz des von ihm verliehenen Rechts und damit auch eine Rechtsgutverletzung.[7]

2. *Schutzlandanknüpfung für grenzüberschreitende Verletzungen von Unionsmarken und -designs*

Der territorialen Begrenztheit der Immaterialgüterrechte entspricht auf der Ebene des Kollisionsrechts für grenzüberschreitende Sachverhalte die Anknüpfung an das Recht des Schutzlandes *(lex loci protectionis),* die das internationale Imma-

---

[3] Art. 3 Abs. 1 des Entwurfs einer Richtlinie des Europäischen Parlaments und des Rates betreffend den rechtlichen Schutz von Designs (Neufassung) sieht einen Schutz nicht eingetragener Designs in den Mitgliedstaaten der EU nicht mehr vor, Europäische Kommission, COM(2022) 667 final.

[4] Verordnung (EU) 2017/1001 des Europäischen Parlaments und des Rates vom 14. Juni 2017 über die Unionsmarke (ABl. 2017 L 154, 1).

[5] Entwurf einer Verordnung (EU) des Europäischen Parlaments und des Rates zur Änderung der Verordnung (EG) Nr. 6/2002 des Rates über das Gemeinschaftsgeschmacksmuster und zur Aufhebung der Verordnung (EG) Nr. 2246/2002 der Kommission, COM(2022)666 final

[6] Art. 11 Abs. 1 EUDV. Ein Schutz für nicht eingetragene Marken besteht auf Unionsebene nicht.

[7] Fezer/Hauck, MarkenR/Fezer, 5. Aufl. 2023, MarkenG, Einl. Rn. 391–394.

terialgüterrecht beherrscht.[8] Die *lex loci protectionis* beruft das Recht des Staates, für dessen Gebiet Immaterialgüterschutz beansprucht wird. Für die unionsweit geltenden Schutzrechte der Unionsmarken und -designs beruft die Anknüpfung an die *lex loci protectionis* damit das Recht der Union.[9]

Das Schutzlandprinzip gilt nicht nur für den Bestand, Umfang und die Wirkung der Rechte des geistigen Eigentums. Auch die Frage der Verletzung geistiger Eigentumsrechte, also ob und in welchem Umfang Schutz gegen eine grenzüberschreitende rechtsverletzende Benutzung gewährt wird, wird der *lex loci protectionis* unterstellt.[10] Insoweit ist die Anknüpfung an die *lex loci protectionis* von der Anknüpfung an die *lex fori* abzugrenzen, die das Recht am Sitz des angerufenen Gerichts beruft: A, mit Wohnsitz in Deutschland, ist Inhaber einer eingetragenen Marke in Österreich. Er verklagt B an B's Wohnsitz in Deutschland auf Schadensersatz wegen Verletzung seiner in Österreich eingetragenen Marke. B macht geltend, dass die Marke von A in Österreich nichtig sei. Deutsche Gerichte haben nach dem Schutzlandprinzip die Schutzrechtsverletzung nach österreichischem Recht zu beurteilen.

Nach Vereinheitlichung des Kollisionsrechts im Bereich der außervertraglichen Schuldverhältnisse auf Unionsebene findet das Schutzlandprinzip auch für Unionsschutzrechte seinen Ausdruck in Art. 8 Abs. 1 Rom II-VO[11]. Dieser regelt für Unionsschutzrechte deren Rechtsanwendung im Verhältnis zu Drittstaaten.[12] Art. 8 Abs. 1 Rom II-VO normiert bei grenzüberschreitenden Sachverhalten als Grundregel für das auf eine Schutzrechtsverletzung anzuwendende Recht die Geltung des Schutzlandprinzips, des Rechts des Staates, für den der Schutz beansprucht wird. Als Schutzland ist dabei das Territorium der gesamten Union zu verstehen.[13] Die Wahrung des allgemein anerkannten Grundsatzes der *lex loci protectionis* für die Verletzung von Rechten des geistigen Eigentums wird explizit von ErwGr. 26 Rom II-VO herausgestellt.

Für Verletzungen einer Unionsmarke sind nach Art. 17 Abs. 1 S. 1 UMV iVm Art. 129 Abs. 1 UMV primär die supranationalen Bestimmungen der UMV anwendbar. Dies gilt für die Feststellung, ob überhaupt eine Unionsmarkenverletzung vorliegt oder droht und den Anspruch auf Unterlassung, vollzogene Verletzungshandlungen fortzusetzen bzw. drohende Verletzungshandlungen aufzunehmen (Art. 130 Abs. 1 S. 1 UMV), was sich unmittelbar aus Art. 9 UMV ergibt. Aufgrund der Territorialität der unionsweiten Schutzrechte, die nur innerhalb des Unionsgebietes Wirkung entfalten und der Einheitlichkeit ihrer Wirkung im gesamten

[8] Münchener Kommentar zum BGB/Drexl, 8. Aufl. 2021, Rom II-VO Art. 8 Rn. 7.

[9] Münchener Kommentar zum BGB/Drexl, 8. Aufl. 2021, Rom II-VO Art. 8 Rn. 134.

[10] Münchener Kommentar zum BGB/Drexl, 8. Aufl. 2021, Rom II-VO Art. 8 Rn. 7.

[11] Verordnung (EG) Nr. 864/2007 des Europäischen Parlaments und des Rates vom 11. Juli 2007 über das auf außervertragliche Schuldverhältnisse anzuwendende Recht (ABl. 2007 L 199, 40). Die Verordnung gilt für alle Mitgliedstaaten mit Ausnahme Dänemarks (Art. 1 Abs. 4 Rom II-VO) seit dem 11. 1. 2009 (Art. 31, 32 Rom II-VO).

[12] Dauses/Ludwigs, Handbuch des EU-Wirtschaftsrechts/Kreuzer/Wagner/Reder, 59. EL Okt. 2023, R Rn. 378; Rauscher, EuZPR/EuIPR/Pabst, 5. Aufl. 2023, Rom II-VO Art. 8 Rn. 20.

[13] Münchener Kommentar zum BGB/Drexl, 8. Aufl. 2021, Rom II-VO Art. 8 Rn. 134; Dauses/Ludwigs, Handbuch des EU-Wirtschaftsrechts/Kreuzer/Wagner/Reder, 59. EL Okt. 2023, R Rn. 378; Rauscher, EuZPR/EuIPR/Pabst, 5. Aufl. 2023, Rom II-VO Art. 8 Rn. 20.

Unionsgebiet (Art. 1 Abs. 2 S. 1 UMV), sind Unterlassungsansprüche nur dann begründet, wenn die Verletzung innerhalb des räumlichen Schutzbereichs der betreffenden Unionsmarke erfolgt. Die territoriale Reichweite des Anspruchs ist dabei grundsätzlich europaweit[14], geht aber nicht über das Gebiet der Union hinaus. Darüber hinaus regelt die UMV lediglich spezifische Schadensersatzansprüche bei Verletzungshandlungen, nämlich vor Veröffentlichung der Marke (Art. 11 Abs. 2 UMV), Ansprüche gegen Verleger (Art. 12 UMV), Agenten oder Vertreter (Art. 13 UMV) und gegen Lizenznehmer (Art. 25 Abs. 2 UMV).

Für EU-Designs bestimmt Art. 88 Abs. 1 EUDV entsprechend primär die Anwendung der supranationalen Bestimmungen der EUDV. Ähnlich wie die UMV regelt die EUDV die dem Inhaber wegen Verletzung des EU-Designs zustehenden Ansprüche nicht abschließend. Art. 89 EUDV regelt in Abs. 1a–c autonom den Unterlassungsanspruch sowie Ansprüche auf Beschlagnahme verletzender Erzeugnisse sowie der zu ihrer Herstellung verwendeten Materialien und Werkzeuge.[15]

Soweit das das Schutzrecht begründende Unionsrecht keine eigenen Bestimmungen bzgl. der materiellen Rechtsfragen grenzüberschreitender Verletzungen unionsweiter Schutzrechte enthält, ist das anwendbare Recht auf der Grundlage von Art. 8 Abs. 2 Rom II-VO zu bestimmen. Art. 8 Abs. 2 Rom II-VO stellt eine Unteranknüpfung zur Lokalisierung der Schutzrechtsverletzung bereit, indem er auf das (Sach-)Recht[16] des Staates verweist, in dem die Verletzung begangen wurde.

Dieses gilt für die nicht explizit in der UMV und der EUDV geregelten Folgeansprüche einer Schutzrechtsverletzung auf Schadensersatz, auf Erteilung von Auskünften über die Verletzungshandlungen zum Zweck der Bestimmung des Schadens und Rechnungslegung.[17] Art. 17 Abs. 1 S. 2 UMV iVm Art. 129 Abs. 2 UMV bzw. Art. 88 Abs. 2 EUDV bestimmen, dass das Unionsmarken(-design)gericht in allen Marken- und Designfragen, die nicht durch die Verordnungen erfasst werden, das geltende nationale Recht anwendet.[18] Dieses ergibt sich aus der allgemein anwendbaren Rom II-VO (Art. 8 Abs. 2). Anwendbar ist damit grundsätz-

[14] EuGH 12.4.2011 – C-235/09, ECLI:EU:C:2011:238, Rn. 39ff. = GRUR 2011, 518 (DHL Express France/Chronopost); EuGH 19.10.2017 – C-231/16, ECLI:EU:C:2017:771, Rn. 50 = GRUR 2017, 1250 (Merck).

[15] Näher hierzu Jestaedt/Fink/Meiser, DesignG – GGV/Jestaedt, 7. Aufl. 2023, GGV Art. 89 Rn. 1, 3ff., 13ff.

[16] Art. 24 Rom II-VO.

[17] Nach der Rechtsprechung des EuGH gehören die Annexansprüche auf Auskunftserteilung, Rechnungslegung und Schadensersatz nicht zu den Sanktionen iSv Art. 130 UMV bzw. Art. 89 Abs. 1 EUDV, s. EuGH 3.3.2022 – C-421/20, ECLI:EU:C:2022:152 = GRUR 2022, 569, Rn. 31 (Acacia/BMW); EuGH 13.2.2014 – C-479/12, ECLI:EU:C:2014:75 = GRUR 2014, 368, Rn. 53, 54 (Gautzsch); Jestaedt/Fink/Meiser, DesignG – GGV/Jestaedt, 7. Aufl. 2023, GGV Art. 88 Rn. 5.

[18] Die in Art. 101 und 102 Abs. 1 GMV aF und Art. 88 Abs. 2 GGV (Verordnung (EG) Nr. 6/2002 des Rates vom 12. Dezember 2001 über das Gemeinschaftsgeschmacksmuster (ABl. 2002 L 003, 1)) enthaltenen Verweisungen auf das IPR der Mitgliedstaaten wurden gestrichen. Bei den Neufassungen des Art. 129 Abs. 2 UMV und Art. 88 Abs. 2 EUDV handelt es sich nicht mehr um Kollisionsnormen; s. Münchener Kommentar zum BGB/Drexl, 8. Aufl. 2021, Rom II-VO Art. 8 Rn. 142; Hildebrandt/Sosnitza, UMV/Hildebrandt, 2021, UMV Art. 129 Rn. 9.

lich das Recht des Verletzungsstaates.[19] Dieses berufen auch Art. 130 Abs. 2 UMV und Art. 89 Abs. 1 lit. d EUDV für das Recht der Sanktionen, nämlich Ansprüche auf Vernichtung und Beseitigung rechtsverletzender Waren, Rückruf und Urteilsveröffentlichung.[20] Demgegenüber enthalten Art. 130 Abs. 1 S. 2 UMV und Art. 89 Abs. 2 EUDV eine Kollisionsnorm, die für prozessuale Maßnahmen zur Einhaltung des Unterlassungsgebots das innerstaatliche Recht am Sitz des Unionsmarken(-design)gerichts beruft *(lex fori)*.[21]

Das Schutzlandprinzip erfährt für Verletzungen von Unionsmarken und -designs im Rahmen des Anwendungsbereichs der Rom II-VO eine weitere Intensivierung, als von der Anwendbarkeit des Schutzlandrechts nicht durch Parteivereinbarung abgewichen werden kann. Art. 8 Abs. 3 Rom II-VO schließt eine Rechtswahl für die Folgen von Schutzrechtsverletzungen ausdrücklich aus, um das Interesse des Schutzlandes nicht durch die Wahl einer anderen Rechtsordnung zu beeinträchtigen.[22]

3. Territorialität und „Mosaik-Ansatz" – Für und Wider einer Schutzlandanknüpfung bei Schutzrechtsverletzungen im Internet

Grundsätzlich wehrt das Schutzlandprinzip eine Anwendung ausländischen Rechts ab, indem es die Frage einer Schutzrechtsverletzung dem Recht des Staates unterstellt, für den der Schutz beansprucht wird. Für die Rechtsanwendung führt dies bei Verletzung inländischer Schutzrechte im Gebiet des Schutz gewährenden Staates zu einer Anwendung inländischen Rechts. Andererseits nimmt das Schutzlandprinzip Rücksicht auf die Regelungen anderer Staaten, indem es die Frage der Verletzung eines ausländischen Schutzrechts nach dem jeweiligen ausländischen Recht beurteilt.[23] Es folgt damit dem Interesse der einzelnen Staaten an einer abschließenden Regelung der Immaterialgüterrechte für ihr Staatsgebiet.

Werden Kennzeichen in rechtsverletzender Weise im Internet verwendet, droht eine Kollision verschiedener Rechtsordnungen. Während Markeninhaber A in Deutschland verhindern möchte, dass Inhaber B derselben oder einer verwechslungsfähigen Marke in Österreich die Verkehrskreise in Deutschland anspricht, muss er fürchten, seinen Internet-Auftritt durch Markeninhaber B in Österreich verboten zu bekommen. Hier kommt es darauf an, die Reichweite der Schutzrechte im Internet genau abzugrenzen. Werden eine Unionsmarke oder ein EU-Design verletzende Waren aus einem Drittstaat über eine an Verbraucher in der EU gerichtete Internetseite angeboten, bestimmt das Sachrecht des „Schutzlandes",

---

[19] Damit soll einem forum shopping entgegengewirkt werden, idS Hildebrandt/Sosnitza, UMV/Hildebrandt, 2021, UMV Art. 129 Rn. 10.

[20] Generalanwalt Bot 1.3.2017 – C-24/16, C-25/16, ECLI:EU:C:2017:146 = BeckRS 2017, 102566 Rn. 43–52 (Nintendo/BigBen).

[21] Münchener Kommentar zum BGB/Drexl, 8. Aufl. 2021, Rom II-VO Art. 8 Rn. 142; s. auch Jestaedt/Fink/Meiser, DesignG – GGV/Jestaedt, 7. Aufl. 2023, GGV Art. 89 Rn. 18.

[22] IdS Ingerl/Rohnke/Nordemann, MarkenG/Nordemann-Schiffel, 4. Aufl. 2023, MarkenG Einl. Rn. 44; Münchener Kommentar zum BGB/Drexl, 8. Aufl. 2021, Rom II-VO Art. 8 Rn. 272; kritisch Rauscher, EuZPR/EuIPR/Pabst, 5. Aufl. 2023, Rom II-VO Art. 8 Rn. 29; Maunsbach RabelsZ 78 (2014), 876, 877.

[23] Münchener Kommentar zum BGB/Drexl, 8. Aufl. 2021, Rom II-VO Art. 8 Rn. 308.

dh die den Schutz gewährenden Unionsrechtsakte der UMV oder der EUDV, ob eine Handlung zu einer Schutzrechtsverletzung im Unionsgebiet führt (Art. 8 Abs. 1 Rom II-VO). Generell besteht die Tendenz, dass Gerichte des Schutzlandes im Interesse eines effektiven Rechtsschutzes eigenes Recht selbst bei nur geringen Inlandsauswirkungen zur Anwendung bringen wollen, um die Regelungsinteressen des eigenen Gesetzgebers durchzusetzen und inländische Rechteinhaber zu schützen.[24] Daher kommt es darauf an, geeignete Kriterien für die Annahme einer „inländischen" Rechtsverletzung und Lokalisierung der Verletzungshandlung im Sachrecht des Schutzlandes zu entwickeln, um den Schutzbereich der eigenen Immaterialgüterrechte nicht über Gebühr auf ausländische Sachverhalte auszudehnen. Eine zu weite Ausdehnung der Annahme „inländischer" Schutzrechtsverletzungen birgt die Gefahr von Kompetenzstreitigkeiten und bringt für die Parteien Unsicherheiten hinsichtlich des anzuwendenden Rechts.

Auch auf kollisionsrechtlicher Ebene stößt die Anknüpfung an das Schutzlandprinzip für das anwendbare Recht bei Schutzrechtsverletzungen durch ubiquitäre Medien, wie das Internet, an ihre Grenzen. Werden eine Unionsmarke verletzende, in der EU produzierte Waren über eine Webseite in Frankreich, Deutschland und Spanien angeboten und macht der Markeninhaber Schadensersatz geltend, beurteilt sich die Anknüpfung des Folgeanspruchs auf Schadensersatz nach dem jeweiligen nationalen Recht, an dem die Verletzung begangen wurde, da es insoweit an einer einheitlichen Regelung in der UMV fehlt (Art. 8 Abs. 2 Rom II-VO). Nach dem Schutzlandprinzip wären damit alle nationalen Rechte, in denen eine Schutzrechtsverletzung stattgefunden hat, parallel anzuwenden (sog. Mosaik-Ansatz). Dies widerspricht zum einen der Konzeption der Unionsschutzrechte, die gerade von einer Einheitlichkeit auch der Rechtsverletzung in allen Mitgliedstaaten ausgehen[25] und erschwert zum anderen die Rechtsanwendung. In der Praxis kann dies für den Richter bedeuten, dass er bei Verletzung von unionsweiten Schutzrechten das Recht sämtlicher Rechtsordnungen, in denen Schutzrechtsverletzungen stattgefunden haben, zu ermitteln hat, möglicherweise mit Rechtfolgen, die dem nationalen Recht des entscheidenden Gerichts unbekannt sind. Dies hat bei unionsweiter internationaler Zuständigkeit der Unionsmarken(-design)gerichte oft erhebliche Probleme bereitet.[26] Auch für den Rechteinhaber ist die Durchsetzung seiner Rechte erheblich erschwert, als für sämtliche Rechte die Rechtslage in den verschiedenen Staaten dargelegt und bewiesen werden muss.

[24] Münchener Kommentar zum BGB/Drexl, 8. Aufl. 2021, Rom II-VO Art. 8 Rn. 319.
[25] Münchener Kommentar zum BGB/Drexl, 8. Aufl. 2021, Rom II-VO Art. 8 Rn. 138.
[26] Hildebrandt/Sosnitza, UMV/Hildebrandt, 2021, UMV Art. 129 Rn. 12 mwN.

II. Lokalisierung der Verletzungshandlung bei ubiquitären und multinationalen Schutzrechtsverletzungen

1. Ansätze zur Eingrenzung einer inländischen Verletzungshandlung im Sachrecht des Schutzlandes

Eine nicht abschließende Liste von Indizien zur Bestimmung der Annahme einer inländischen Verletzungshandlung nach den Regeln des anwendbaren Sachrechts des Schutzlandes findet sich bereits in der im Jahr 2001 von der WIPO und der Pariser Union zum Schutz des Geistigen Eigentums verabschiedeten „Joint Recommendation Concerning Provisions on the Protection of Marks, and Other Industrial Property Rights in Signs, on the Internet".[27] Im Einklang mit der Schutzlandanknüpfung versuchen diese, bei Markenverletzungen im Internet eine inländische Verletzungshandlung nach den Regeln des anwendbaren Sachrechts des Schutzlandes einzugrenzen, indem sie eine „wirtschaftliche Auswirkung" (commercial effect) der Benutzung des Zeichens im Internet in dem betreffenden Staat fordern (Art. 2).[28] Dabei stellen sie auf die Auswirkungen der Schutzrechtsverletzung auf die wirtschaftlichen Interessen des Markeninhabers, den Einfluss des Verletzers auf die Schutzrechtsverletzung, seinen Nutzen von der inländischen Erreichbarkeit sowie die Sichtbarkeit des Internetangebots für Inländer im Hinblick auf die verwendete Sprache, Währung, den Versand und eine Lieferung in das Schutzgebiet ab (Art. 3).

Auf europäischer Ebene urteilte der EuGH in „L'Oréal"[29] unter Betonung des Interesses an einer praktischen Wirksamkeit des Markenschutzes, dass Werbung auf einer an Verbraucher in der Union adressierten Ebay-Plattform und Verkauf aus Drittstaaten eingeführter rechtsverletzender Waren an Verbraucher in der Union eine Unionsmarkenverletzung nach der UMV darstellen, wenn sich das Angebot an Verbraucher im Schutzgebiet der Marke richtet. Die bloße Zugänglichkeit einer Website in dem durch die Marke erfassten Gebiet solle hierfür nicht ausreichend sein. Vielmehr habe das Gericht anhand „relevanter Indizien", wie der Angaben zu den geografischen Gebieten, in die der Verkäufer die Ware liefere, zu prüfen, ob sich das Angebot an Verbraucher im Schutzgebiet der geltend gemachten Marke richtet.[30] Weitere quantitative Anforderungen an den Bezug zum Schutzland stellt der EuGH nicht.

Restriktiver hingegen der BGH, der im Hinblick auf das Schutzlandprinzip das Vorliegen eines hinreichenden wirtschaftlich relevanten Inlandsbezugs der Angebote fordert, wobei er sich an den Empfehlungen der WIPO Joint Recommendation orientiert.[31] In seiner Begründung verweist der BGH ausdrücklich darauf, eine „uferlose Ausdehnung des Schutzes nationaler Kennzeichenrechte" und un-

---

[27] Assembly of the Paris Union for the Protection of Industrial Property and the General Assembly of WIPO, Thirty-Sixth Series of Meetings of the Assemblies of the Member States of WIPO, 2001, https://tind.wipo.int/record/28712?v=pdf (abgerufen 11.5.2024).

[28] Münchener Kommentar zum BGB/Drexl, 8. Aufl. 2021, Rom II-VO Art. 8 Rn. 353.

[29] EuGH 12.7.2011 – C-324/09, ECLI:EU:C:2011:474 = GRUR 2011, 1025 (L'Oréal SA and Others).

[30] EuGH 12.7.2011 – C-324/09, ECLI:EU:C:2011:474 Rn. 64, 65 = GRUR 2011, 1025 (L'Oréal SA and Others).

[31] BGH 13.10.2004 – I ZR 163/02 = GRUR 2005, 431 (433) (Hotel Maritime).

angemessene Beschränkung der wirtschaftlichen Aktivitäten ausländischer Unternehmen im Ausland zu vermeiden.[32]

Auch der US Supreme Court hat sich kürzlich in der Rechtssache Abitron Austria GmbH v. Hetronic International, Inc. für Verletzungshandlungen, die größtenteils in Europa stattfanden, gegen eine extraterritoriale Anwendung der markenrechtlichen Vorschriften des Lanham Act ausgesprochen und eine vorausgegangene Verurteilung der Beklagten durch den 10. Circuit Court zu Schadensersatz in Höhe von 96 Millionen US Dollar aufgehoben.[33] Die Normen des Lanham Act sollen sich nur auf Ansprüche erstrecken, bei denen die rechtsverletzende Nutzung im Handel im Inland erfolgt.

Die Annahme einer inländischen Verletzungshandlung auf der Ebene des Sachrechts des Schutzlandes in Fällen grenzüberschreitender Internetverletzungen einzugrenzen, erscheint nicht nur aus Gründen rechtspolitischer Rücksichtnahme geboten. Es gilt auch Kompetenzstreitigkeiten infolge der Anwendung mehrerer Rechte auf eine Rechtsverletzung und die damit verbundenen Risiken eines „forum shopping“ zu vermeiden. Zugleich stärkt dies die Voraussehbarkeit des anwendbaren Rechts. Die von der WIPO und der Pariser Union entwickelten Kriterien erscheinen auch nach über 20 Jahren noch durchaus als ein wertvoller Ansatz hierfür. Diese lassen sich weiter ergänzen -neben Kriterien der Sichtbarkeit des Internetangebots im Inland, wie die Verwendung der in dem betreffenden Mitgliedstaat gebräuchlichen Sprache, Währung, der Möglichkeit, Produkte oder Dienstleistungen zu bestellen, der Verwendung einer einschlägigen Top-Level-Domäne bzw. App im jeweiligen nationalen App-Store – durch Heranziehung von auf den betreffenden Mitgliedstaat ausgerichteten Dienstleistungsangeboten, wie der Schaltung lokaler Werbung, der Bereitstellung eines Kundendienstes in einer im betreffenden Mitgliedstaat verwendeten Sprache oder bestimmter nationaler Zustelldienstleister.[34]

2. Kollisionsrechtliche Ansätze zur Lokalisierung der Verletzungshandlungen in einer Rechtsordnung – Kyoto Guidelines

In den letzten Jahrzehnten sind auf internationaler Ebene verschiedene sog. Single-Law-Approachs diskutiert worden mit dem Ziel, bei ubiquitären Schutzrechtsverletzungen eine interessen- und praxisgerechte Lokalisierung der Verletzungshandlungen für die Bestimmung des anwendbaren Rechts zu erreichen und somit zur Anwendung einer einzigen Rechtsordnung zu gelangen. Damit soll die Rechtsanwendung der Gerichte und die Durchsetzung der geistigen Eigentumsrechte für den Rechteinhaber erleichtert werden.

---

[32] BGH 13.10.2004 – I ZR 163/02 = GRUR 2005, 431 (432) (Hotel Maritime); BGH 7.11.2019 – I ZR 222/17 = GRUR 2020, 647, Rn. 25–29, 37ff. (Club Hotel Robinson); grdl. EuGH 22.06.1994 – C-9/93 = GRUR Int. 1994, 614 (Ideal Standard II); Ingerl/Rohnke/Nordemann, MarkenG/Nordemann-Schiffel, 4. Aufl. 2023, MarkenG Einl. Rn. 44.

[33] U.S. Supreme Court 31.7.2023 – 21-1043, Abitron Austria GmbH et al. v. Hetronic International, Inc.; hierzu s. a. Witte GRUR 2023, 1235, 1238.

[34] Siehe auch ErwGr. 8 zur Verordnung (EU) 2022/2065 des Europäischen Parlaments und des Rates vom 19. Oktober 2022 über einen Binnenmarkt für digitale Dienste und zur Änderung der Richtlinie 2000/31/EG (Gesetz über digitale Dienste), ABl. 2022 L 277, 1.

Im Jahr 2020 wurde mit den Kyoto Guidelines für Geistiges Eigentum und Internationales Privatrecht auf internationaler Ebene von der International Law Association ein erfolgversprechender neuer Vorschlag globaler Prinzipien für das Kollisionsrecht des Immaterialgüterrechts verabschiedet.[35] Der Vorschlag baut auf den vom American Law Institute verabschiedeten ALI Principles für die kollisionsrechtliche Behandlung von geistigen Eigentumsrechten[36], den von der Europäischen Max-Planck-Gruppe für Internationales Privat- und Zivilprozessrecht des geistigen Eigentums aufgestellten CLIP Principles[37], dem Japanese Transparency Proposal[38] und den Japanese-Korean Principles[39] auf.

Im Einklang mit den früheren Empfehlungen halten auch die Kyoto Guidelines als Grundregel für Verletzungen von Rechten des geistigen Eigentums und deren Rechtsfolgen an dem Grundsatz einer Anknüpfung an die *lex loci protectionis* fest (Regel 25 Abs. 1).[40]

Zugunsten einer effizienten Gestaltung des Rechtsschutzes von Immaterialgüterrechten erfährt das Schutzlandprinzip jedoch diverse Einschränkungen. Die Kyoto Guidelines sehen zunächst in Durchbrechung des Schutzlandprinzips eine uneingeschränkte Rechtswahloption für die Parteien vor, das anwendbare Recht für die Rechtsfolgen einer Schutzrechtsverletzung zu wählen (Regel 25 Abs. 2).[41] Dies weicht von dem traditionellen Verständnis ab, welches auch Art. 8 Abs. 3 Rom II-VO zugrunde liegt, aufgrund des strikt territorialen Ansatzes für die Rechte des geistigen Eigentums eine Rechtswahl der Parteien auszuschließen. Den Parteien soll ein Ermessensspielraum eingeräumt werden, für Folgeansprüche einer Schutzrechtsverletzung ein Recht zu wählen, nicht aber für andere verletzungsbezogene oder eigentumsrechtliche Fragen. Durch die damit verbundene Reduzierung der anwendbaren Rechtsordnungen soll eine effizientere Rechtsanwendung in Fällen multinationaler Schutzrechtsverletzungen gewährleistet werden.[42]

Darüber hinaus ermöglicht Regel 26 der Kyoto Guidelines dem Gericht für ubiquitäre oder multinationale Schutzrechtsverletzungen ein Abweichen vom Schutzlandprinzip durch Anwendung des Rechts einer besonders engen Verbindung zu der weltweiten Verletzung. Als nicht abschließende Faktoren zur Bestimmung der

---

[35] Ancel/Binctin/Drexl ua JIPITEC 12 (2021), 44 (applicable law).

[36] American Law Institute, Intellectual Property: Principles Governing Jurisdiction, Choice of Law, and Judgments in Transnational Disputes, 2008, WIPO Lex No. US218.

[37] European Max Planck Group on Conflict of Laws in Intellectual Property (CLIP), Principles of Conflict of Laws in Intellectual Property, 2011.

[38] Japanese Transparency Proposal on Jurisdiction, Choice of Law, Recognition and Enforcement of Foreign Judgments in Intellectual Property, 2009, in: Basedow/Keno/Metzger, Intellectual Property in the Global Arena, 2010, Annex III.

[39] Japanese-Korean Principles of Private International Law on Intellectual Property Rights, Joined Proposal by Members of the Private International Association of Korea and Japan, The Quarterly Review of Corporation Law and Society, 2011, S. 112ff.

[40] Siehe §§ 301–302 ALI Principles; Art. 3:601, 3:602, 3:605, 3:606 CLIP Principles; Art. 301, 303, 304 Transparency Proposal; Art. 304–305 Joint Korean-Japanese Principles.

[41] Auch die Vorgängerprojekte schlugen in unterschiedlichem Umfang die Einführung einer Parteiautonomie vor, s. § 302 ALI Principles; Art. 3:606 CLIP Principles; Art. 304 Transparency Proposal; Art. 302 Joint Korean-Japanese Principles.

[42] Ancel/Binctin/Drexl ua JIPITEC 12 (2021), 44 Rn. 65.

besonders engen Verbindung führt Abs. 1 den Ort des substanziellen Schadens, den gewöhnlichen Aufenthalt oder Hauptgeschäftssitz der Parteien und den Ort, an dem wesentliche, die Rechtsverletzung unterstützende Tätigkeiten ausgeübt worden sind, an.

Damit folgen die Kyoto Guidelines der engen Lockerung des Schutzlandprinzips für ubiquitäre Rechtsverletzungen nach den CLIP Principles, die grundsätzlich das Schutzlandprinzip auch für Multistate-Verletzungen im Internet berufen. Der Richter kann hiervon jedoch abweichen und einheitlich an das Recht des Staates der engsten Verbindung anknüpfen (Artikel 3:603 CLIP Principles), wie das Recht am gewöhnlichen Aufenthalt des Verletzers, den Ort, von dem aus er seine Geschäfte tätigt oder wesentliche, die Rechtsverletzung unterstützende Tätigkeiten ausübt oder den Ort des substanziellen Schadenseintritts. Im Gegensatz hierzu sahen die ALI Principles für ubiquitäre Verletzungen von geistigen Eigentumsrechten im Internet eine weitreichendere Ausnahme vom Schutzlandprinzip vor mit einem weiten Ermessensspielraum für die Gerichte, das Recht der engsten Verbindung anzuwenden, welches sich ua an den Märkten, auf die die Parteien ihre Investitionen und ihre Tätigkeit gerichtet haben, orientierte (§ 321 ALI Principles). Hierdurch wurde eine extraterritoriale Anwendung von US-Recht begünstigt.[43]

Auch Regel 26 der Kyoto Guidelines verpflichtet die Gerichte nicht, die ubiquitäre Verletzungsregel anzuwenden. Der allgemeine Grundsatz der *lex loci protectionis* (Regel 25 Abs. 1) mit Anwendung der verschiedenen einzelnen Rechte kann auch für die Beurteilung ubiquitärer Verstöße herangezogen werden, was eine größere Flexibilität für die Rechtsanwender gewährleistet.

Zudem wird in Regel 26 Abs. 2 Kyoto Guidelines eine Ausnahme normiert, die es jeder Partei ermöglicht, sich auf das Recht eines anderen Staates, der von der Klage betroffen ist und eine anderweitige Regelung der Rechtsfolgen als das Recht der engsten Verbindung nach Abs. 1 enthält, für den Fall im Ganzen zu berufen. Diese ist von dem Gericht bei der Ausgestaltung der Rechtsfolgen zu berücksichtigen.[44]

Die Regelung der Kyoto Guidelines stellt einen ausgewogenen Kompromiss für die Schutzlandanknüpfung in ubiquitären Verletzungsfällen dar und ist sowohl im Hinblick auf das grundsätzliche Festhalten an der Anknüpfung an das Schutzlandprinzip als auch im Hinblick auf die gezielten Lockerungen der Anknüpfung durch Zulassung einer Rechtswahl und ein balanciertes Ausweichen auf das Recht einer besonders engen Verbindung bei ubiquitären oder multinationalen Schutzrechtsverletzungen zu begrüßen.[45] Hält man an einer Anknüpfung an die *lex loci protectionis* fest, kommt es darauf an, die Zahl der zur Anwendung berufenen Rechtsordnungen bei ubiquitären oder multinationalen Rechtsverletzungen zu begrenzen.[46] Zwar mag auch eine Berufung des Rechts einer besonders engen Verbindung in Einzelfällen verschiedene Rechte zur Anwendung bringen, etwa wenn eine enge

[43] Münchener Kommentar BGB/Drexl, 8. Aufl. 2021, Rom II-VO, Art. 8 Rn. 358; HWB-EuP 2009/Metzger, 2009, Geistiges Eigentum (Kollisionsrecht).

[44] Ancel/Binctin/Drexl ua JIPITEC 12 (2021), 44 Rn. 77, s. a. die vergleichbare Regelung in Art. 3:603 Abs. 3 CLIP Principles.

[45] IdS auch Drexl FS Schack, 2022, 123 (135).

[46] Münchener Kommentar zum BGB/Drexl, 8. Aufl. 2021, Rom II-VO Art. 8 Rn. 323.

Verbindung zu mehreren Rechtsordnungen besteht[47], und damit ein gewisses Risiko in sich bergen, dass das anwendbare Recht für den Kläger nicht ex ante bestimmbar ist. In der Mehrzahl der Fälle wird jedoch für ubiquitäre Rechtsverletzungen die Anwendung eines einzigen Rechts anstelle einer Mosaikbetrachtung möglich sein, was die Entscheidungsfindung in multinationalen Verletzungsfällen erheblich erleichtert.[48]

3. Kollisionsrechtliche Lokalisierung der Verletzungshandlungen durch den EuGH für Folgeansprüche bei Verletzung von Unionsmarken und -designs

Auf europäischer Ebene hat der EuGH in „Nintendo"[49] für Fälle, in denen die Handlungen einer Verletzung einer Unionsmarke bzw. -designs in mehreren Mitgliedstaaten begangen wurden, nunmehr Klarheit für die Lokalisierung der Verletzungshandlungen im Handlungsstaat nach Art. 8 Abs. 2 Rom II-VO gebracht. Das von Nintendo wegen Verletzung eines Gemeinschaftsgeschmacksmusters verklagte Unternehmen mit Sitz in Frankreich hatte rechtsverletzende Waren über die Webseite des Unternehmens unmittelbar an Verbraucher in Frankreich, Belgien und Luxemburg verkauft.

Bezüglich der nicht unionsweit geregelten Folgeansprüche etwa auf Auskunft und Schadensersatz verweist Art. 8 Abs. 2 Rom II-VO auf das nationale Recht des Staates, in dem die Verletzungshandlung begangen wurde. Bei Multi-State-Verletzungen kann bei unionsweiter Geltendmachung der Rechte die Anwendung des Rechts des Orts, an dem sich die Rechtsverletzung verwirklicht hat (Recht am tatbestandlichen Handlungsort) im unglücklichsten Fall zur parallelen Anwendung von 27 verschiedenen Rechten durch den Richter am zuständigen Unionsmarken (-design)gericht führen (sog. Mosaiklösung)[50], was auch die Einführung des Art. 8 Abs. 2 Rom II-VO nicht behoben hat.

Dem hat der EuGH in „Nintendo" eine Absage erteilt. Danach sind Sanktionen einer Schutzrechtsverletzung einheitlich nach dem Recht des Staates zu bestimmen, in dem das schadensbegründende Ereignis eingetreten ist, dh die rechtsverletzende Handlung begangen wurde (natürlicher Handlungsort). Der EuGH hat sich damit gegen eine Anwendung des Rechts am Ort, an dem sich die Rechtsverletzung verwirklicht hat, entschieden, die bei Multi-State-Verletzungen zu einer Mosaikbetrachtung führen würde. Im Wege einer Gesamtwürdigung des Verhaltens ist der Ort zu bestimmen, an dem die ursprüngliche Verletzungshandlung, auf die das vorgeworfene Verhalten zurückgeht, begangen worden ist oder droht.[51] Dies hat der EuGH ausdrücklich mit Gründen der Vorhersehbarkeit des Ausgangs der Rechts-

[47] Ancel/Binctin/Drexl ua JIPITEC 12 (2021), 44 Rn. 76.

[48] Ancel/Binctin/Drexl ua JIPITEC12 (2021), 44 Rn. 75.

[49] EuGH 27.9.2017 – C-24/16 und C-25/16, ECLI:EU:C:2017:146 = GRUR 2017, 1120 (Nintendo/BigBen).

[50] IdS noch EuGH 13.2.2014 – C-479/12, ECLI:EU:C:2014:75 = GRUR 2014, 368, Rn. 51ff., 55 – Gautzsch; Münchener Kommentar zum BGB/Drexl, 8. Aufl. 2021, Rom II-VO Art. 8 Rn. 138; Hildebrandt/Sosnitza, UMV/Hildebrandt, 2021, UMV Art. 129 Rn. 12.

[51] EuGH 27.9.2017 – C-24/16 und C-25/16, ECLI:EU:C:2017:146 = GRUR 2017, 1120, Rn. 102 (Nintendo/BigBen).

streitigkeiten, der Sicherheit in Bezug auf das anzuwendende Recht, der einheitlichen Anwendung der Verordnung in allen Mitgliedstaaten sowie einem angemessenen Interessenausgleich zwischen den Parteien des Rechtsstreits begründet.[52] Geht der Vertrieb rechtsverletzender Ware auf ein Online-Angebot zurück, soll auf den Ort, an dem der Prozess der Veröffentlichung des Angebots auf der Website in Gang gesetzt worden ist, abzustellen sein.[53] So soll aus Gründen der Effektivität des Rechtsschutzes ein einheitlicher Anknüpfungspunkt und damit die Anwendung eines einheitlichen Rechts erzielt werden.[54]

Zwar kann im Einzelfall nicht ausgeschlossen werden, dass selbst eine Gesamtwürdigung des Verhaltens keine eindeutige Bestimmung der ursprünglichen Verletzungshandlung ermöglicht, etwa wenn Verletzungshandlungen mehrere Rechtsordnungen erfassen oder der Ursprung der Verletzungshandlung nur schwierig einem bestimmten Ort zugeordnet werden kann, was insbesondere bei Internetverletzungen der Fall sein kann. Grundsätzlich wird die Anknüpfung jedoch, jedenfalls soweit die ursprüngliche Verletzungshandlung in einem EU-Mitgliedstaat vorgenommen wurde, zu praxisgerechten Ergebnissen führen und ein Großteil der Folgeansprüche aus Multi-State-Unionsmarken(-design)verletzungen sich einheitlich anhand einer Rechtsordnung bestimmen lassen.[55] Werden die rechtsverletzenden Erzeugnisse vom Verletzer in einem Mitgliedstaat hergestellt, wird der Ort deren Herstellung die ursprüngliche Verletzungshandlung reflektieren, da es ohne die Herstellung die Verletzungshandlung nicht gegeben hätte.[56] Bei mehreren Produktions- und Vertriebsorten innerhalb der EU wird auf den Ort der Entscheidung über die Vermarktung und den Vertrieb abzustellen sein.[57] Im Ergebnis wird die vom EuGH geforderte Gesamtwürdigung oftmals auf die Anwendung des Rechts des Staates hinauslaufen, in dem der vermeintliche Rechtsverletzer niedergelassen ist.[58]

Diese Grundsätze gelten jedoch nur bei Klagen mit unionsweiter Wirkung am allgemeinen Gerichtsstand des Beklagten (oder einem der weiteren unionsweiten Gerichtsstände nach Art. 125 Abs. 1–4 UMV bzw. Art. 82 Abs. 2–4 EUDV). Für den Tatortgerichtsstand stellt der EuGH in Abgrenzung zu „Nintendo“ in „Acacia/BMW“[59] klar, dass sich die Prüfung einer begangenen oder drohenden Schutzrechtsverletzung iRd Art. 8 Abs. 2 Rom II-VO auf das Hoheitsgebiet des Mitglied-

[52] EuGH 27.9.2017 – C-24/16 und C-25/16, ECLI:EU:C:2017:146 = GRUR 2017, 1120, Rn. 103 (Nintendo/BigBen).

[53] EuGH 27.9.2017 – C-24/16 und C-25/16, ECLI:EU:C:2017:146 = GRUR 2017, 1120, Rn. 108 (Nintendo/BigBen).

[54] EuGH 27.9.2017 – C-24/16 und C-25/16, ECLI:EU:C:2017:146 = GRUR 2017, 1120 Rn. 104 (Nintendo/BigBen); kritisch Hildebrandt/Sosnitza, UMV/Hildebrandt, 2021, UMV Art. 129 Rn. 15 wegen der Gefahr eines forum shoppings durch den Verletzer.

[55] Beck'scher Online-Kommentar MarkenR/Grüger, 36. Ed. 1.1.2024, UMV Art. 129 Rn. 27.

[56] Generalanwalt beim EuGH Schlussantrag v. 1.3.2017 – C 24/16, ECLI:EU:C:2017:146 Rn. 58 = GRUR 2017, 120 (Nintendo/BigBen).

[57] Jestaedt/Fink/Meiser, DesignG – GGV/Jestaedt, 7. Aufl. 2023, GGV Art. 88 Rn. 8a.

[58] Münchener Kommentar zum BGB/Drexl, 8. Aufl. 2021, Rom II-VO Art. 8 Rn. 140.

[59] EuGH 3.3.2022 – C-421/20, ECLI:EU:C:2022:152 = GRUR 2022, 569, Rn. 46 (Acacia/BMW).

staates beschränkt, in dem das Gericht am Tatortgerichtsstand nach Art. 82 Abs. 5 EUDV angerufen worden ist, bei dem die Kognitionsbefugnis des Gerichts auf Verletzungshandlungen im Gerichtsstaat beschränkt ist (Art. 126 Abs. 2 UMV bzw. Art. 83 Abs. 2 EUDV) und Verletzungen in anderen Mitgliedstaaten nicht Gegenstand des Rechtsstreits sind.[60] Der EuGH hält auch insoweit an dem im ErwGr. 26 Rom II-VO niedergelegten Grundsatz der *lex loci protectionis* fest und stärkt die Effektivität der Rechtsdurchsetzung aus Unionsmarken bzw. -designs für Folgeansprüche, indem er dem Inhaber die Möglichkeit eröffnet, durch Beschränkung seiner Ansprüche auf Verletzungshandlungen im deliktischen Wahlgerichtsstand, Rechtssicherheit in Bezug auf das auf Annexansprüche anwendbare Recht zu erhalten.

III. Schlüsse für die Behandlung von Folgeansprüchen bei ubiquitären und multinationalen Verletzungen von Unionsmarken und -designs

1. Kollisionsrechtliche Ebene

a) Hilfsanknüpfung an das Recht der engsten Verbindung

Weiterhin ungeklärt bleibt auch nach Lokalisierung der Verletzungshandlungen durch den EuGH die Bestimmung des anwendbaren Rechts für Folgeansprüche einer multinationalen Verletzung von Unionsschutzrechten, wenn der Ursprung der Verletzungshandlung außerhalb der Union liegt. In Fällen, in denen rechtsverletzende Waren im EU-Ausland hergestellt, von dort über eine Webseite in der EU angeboten und dorthin versandt werden, führt die vom EuGH vorgenommene Bestimmung des Orts der ursprünglichen Verletzungshandlung, auf die das vorgeworfene Verhalten zurückgeht, zum EU-Ausland.

Während die Regelungen der internationalen Zuständigkeit der Unionsmarkengerichte in Art. 125 Abs. 1–4 UMV einen Gerichtsstand für Rechtsstreitigkeiten im Zusammenhang mit Schutzrechtsverletzungen innerhalb der Union auch dann gewährleisten wollen, wenn weder Kläger noch Beklagter in der Union ansässig sind[61], verweist Art. 8 Abs. 2 Rom II-VO für das anwendbare Recht für die nicht in der UMV geregelten Folgeansprüche, wie Auskunft oder Schadensersatz, auf das Sachrecht eines Drittstaates als das Recht am Ort der ursprünglichen Verletzungshandlung. Nach Art. 3 Rom II-VO ist das nach dieser Verordnung bezeichnete Recht grundsätzlich auch dann anzuwenden, wenn es nicht das Recht eines Mitgliedstaats ist.

Dies erscheint als äußerst problematisch. Das Recht des EU-Auslands als anwendbares Recht zur Anwendung zu bringen, wäre mit dem Schutzlandprinzip nicht vereinbar. Der Schutz der Unionsrechte und deren Wirkung erstrecken sich

[60] EuGH 3.3.2022 – C-421/20, ECLI:EU:C:2022:152 = GRUR 2022, 569 Rn. 44, 49 (Acacia/BMW).

[61] Generalanwalt Szpunar 28.3.2019 – C-172/18, ECLI:EU:C:2019:276 Rn 53 = BeckRS 2019, 5185 (AMS Neve).

auf das Gebiet der Union, nicht jedoch darüber hinaus. Eine Verletzung eines Unionsrechts des geistigen Eigentums kann nur innerhalb des Schutz gewährenden Territoriums der Union erfolgen. Außerhalb des Territoriums der Union stellt deren Verletzung keinen sanktionsbegründenden Tatbestand dar.[62] Darüber hinaus ist auch das in den Mitgliedstaaten der EU durch Richtlinie 2004/48/EG zur Durchsetzung von Rechten des geistigen Eigentums (Enforcement-Richtlinie)[63] gewährleistete Bestehen der Mindeststandards für Auskunftsansprüche, Schadensersatz sowie Rückruf, Entfernung aus den Vertriebswegen und Vernichtung rechtsverletzender Waren in Drittstaaten nicht garantiert.[64]

Gerade bei Schutzrechtsverletzungen im Internet mag es auch zweifelhaft erscheinen, ob die vom EuGH befürwortete Veranlassung der Internetseite tatsächlich den Schwerpunkt der ursprünglichen Verletzungshandlung bildet, zumal der Verletzer, der Werbung und Verkaufsangebote außerhalb der Union ins Internet stellt, leicht der Anwendung von Art. 9 UMV entgehen und dessen praktische Wirksamkeit beeinträchtigen kann.[65] Bei Verletzungshandlungen aus Drittstaaten wäre es im Hinblick auf die Vorhersehbarkeit des anwendbaren Rechts für den Kläger in vielen Fällen übermäßig erschwert, wenn nicht gar unmöglich, von dem Ort Kenntnis zu erlangen, an dem der Verletzer die Entscheidungen und technischen Maßnahmen zur Schaltung der Anzeige im Internet getroffen hat.[66]

Art. 8 Abs. 2 Rom II-VO muss daher im Hinblick auf das Schutzlandprinzip dahingehend eingeschränkt werden, dass er nur die Rechtsvorschriften der EU-Mitgliedstaaten als anwendbares Recht beruft. Liegt der Schwerpunkt der ursprünglichen Verletzungshandlung im EU-Ausland, was gerade bei ubiquitären Schutzrechtsverletzungen nicht selten vorkommen wird, muss aufgrund der Einschränkung des Art. 8 Abs. 2 Rom II-VO im Einklang mit dem Schutzlandprinzip versucht werden, einen einheitlichen Anknüpfungspunkt innerhalb des Schutzgebietes der Union festzustellen.[67] Insoweit ist als Reserveanknüpfung das sachnächste Recht eines Mitgliedstaates zur Anwendung zu bringen.[68]

Die Vorschläge der Kyoto-Guidelines, nach deren Regel 26 Abs. 1 für Schutzrechtsverletzungen durch ubiquitäre oder multinationale Medien, das Recht des

[62] Generalanwalt Szpunar 28.10.2021 – C-421/20, ECLI:EU:C:2021:886, Rn. 82f. = GRUR-RS 2021, 32333 (Acacia/BMW); Jestaedt/Fink/Meiser, DesignG – GGV/Jestaedt, 7. Aufl. 2023, GGV Art. 88 Rn. 1, 8c; Ruhl/Tolkmitt, GGV/Tolkmitt, 3. Aufl. 2018, Art. 88 Rn. 9; Kur GRUR 2018, 358, 363f.

[63] Richtlinie 2004/48/EG des Europäischen Parlaments und des Rates vom 29.4.2004 zur Durchsetzung der Rechte des geistigen Eigentums.

[64] Kur GRUR 2018, 358 (363f.).; idS auch Münchener Kommentar zum BGB/Drexl, 8. Aufl. 2021, Rom II-VO Art. 8 Rn. 139

[65] EuGH 5.9.2019 – C-172/18, ECLI:EU:C:2019:674 Rn. 48 = GRUR 2019, 1047 (AMS Neve).

[66] So auch EuGH 5.9.2019 – C-172/18, ECLI:EU:C:2019:674 Rn. 51 = GRUR 2019, 1047 (AMS Neve) (für internationale Zuständigkeit); s. a. Ruhl/Tolkmitt, GGV/Tolkmitt, 3. Aufl. 2018, Art. 88 Rn. 9.

[67] Für eine teleologische Reduktion des Anwendungsbereichs des Art. 8 Abs. 2 Rom II-VO auch Münchener Kommentar zum BGB/Drexl, 8. Aufl. 2021, Rom II-VO Art. 8 Rn. 139, denn die Funktion der Vorschrift beschränkt sich auf eine Unteranknüpfung für das Territorium der EU.

[68] Münchener Kommentar zum BGB/Drexl, 8. Aufl. 2021, Rom II-VO Art. 8 Rn. 139.

Staates einer besonders engen Verbindung zu der Rechtsverletzung im Ganzen zur Anwendung gebracht werden kann, bieten hierfür eine gute Orientierung.[69] Der Ort, an dem wesentliche, die Verletzung unterstützende Tätigkeiten in einem Mitgliedstaat ausgeführt wurden, kann etwa in der Einfuhr oder dem Vertrieb der rechtsverletzenden Waren in die Union liegen.[70] Dies entspricht dem Ort der ursprünglichen Verletzungshandlung in der Union.[71]

Wurden Verletzungshandlungen in mehreren Mitgliedstaaten begangen, ohne dass sich eine besonders enge Verbindung zu einem der Mitgliedstaaten feststellen lässt, wurden die Waren bspw. aus dem EU-Ausland in verschiedene Mitgliedstaaten eingeführt und dort vertrieben, versagt das Abstellen auf den Einfuhrstaat als einheitlicher Anknüpfungspunkt im Schutzland der EU. Insoweit lässt sich ein Zurückgreifen auf die „Mosaik-Lösung" vertreten, dh das Recht der jeweiligen Mitgliedstaaten zur Anwendung zu bringen.[72] Als angebrachter erscheint es jedoch, im Interesse einer effektiven Rechtsanwendung für Richter, einer erleichterten Rechtsdurchsetzung für den Verletzten und eines gerechten Interessenausgleichs, das Recht am gewöhnlichen Aufenthalt bzw. der Hauptniederlassung des Klägers als Verletzten zur Anwendung zu berufen.[73]

De lege ferenda wäre es daher zu begrüßen, Art. 8 Abs. 2 Rom II-VO für den Fall, dass der Verletzer außerhalb der Union gehandelt hat, entsprechend der Vorschläge der Kyoto-Guidelines zu ergänzen und neben der Berufung des Rechts des Mitgliedstaates, in dem die Verletzung begangen wurde, das Recht einer besonders engen Verbindung zu einem Mitgliedstaat zur Anwendung zu bringen.

b) Lockerung der Anknüpfung an das Schutzlandprinzip für Folgeansprüche durch Einräumung einer Rechtswahlmöglichkeit

Darüber hinaus macht gerade für die Bestimmung des anwendbaren Rechts für Folgeansprüche einer multinationalen Schutzrechtsverletzung unionsweiter Rechte des geistigen Eigentums (wie Unterlassung, Schadensersatz oder Beschlagnahme

---

[69] Generalanwalt Szpunar 28.10.2021 – C-421/20, ECLI:EU:C:2021:886, Rn. 85, 86 = GRUR-RS 2021, 32333 (Acacia/BMW): Es müsse versucht werden, eine ursprüngliche oder zentrale Verletzungshandlung im Gebiet der Union festzustellen … Recht eines Mitgliedstaats, in dem die Verletzungshandlung ihre Wirkungen entfaltet habe, oder aber das Recht eines Mitgliedstaats, der in engem Zusammenhang mit dem Verstoß gegen die Rechte des geistigen Eigentums stehe; s. a. Ruhl/Tolkmitt, GGV/Tolkmitt, 3. Aufl. 2018, Art. 88 Rn. 9; Münchener Kommentar zum BGB/Drexl, 8. Aufl. 2021, Rom II-VO, Art. 8 Rn. 139: für eine Anknüpfung an den Marktort in Bezug auf die Verletzungshandlung aufgrund des dadurch erzielten Gleichlaufs mit dem Marktortprinzip nach Art. 6 Abs. 1 Rom II-VO im Bereich des Lauterkeitsrechts.

[70] Kur GRUR 2018, 358 (363f.).

[71] Beck'scher Online-Kommentar MarkenR/Grüger, 36. Ed. 1.1.2024, UMV Art. 129 Rn. 32; so auch Hildebrandt/Sosnitza, UMV/Hildebrandt, 2021, UMV Art. 129 Rn. 17.

[72] Münchener Kommentar zum BGB/Drexl, 8. Aufl. 2021, Rom II-VO Art. 8 Rn. 139; Beck'scher Online-Kommentar MarkenR/Grüger, 36. Ed. 1.1.2024, UMV Art. 129 Rn. 32; vgl. Kur GRUR Int 2014, 746 (758); kritisch Jestaedt/Fink/Meiser, DesignG – GGV/Jestaedt, 7. Aufl. 2023, GGV Art. 88 Rn. 8c.

[73] So auch Hildebrandt/Sosnitza, UMV/Hildebrandt, 2021, UMV Art. 129 Rn. 18.

und Vernichtung rechtsverletzender Waren) eine Konkretisierung der Schutzlandanknüpfung durch Zulassung einer Rechtswahl Sinn.[74]

Für diese Ansprüche fehlt es an einer einheitlichen sachrechtlichen Regelung in den Unionsrechtsakten der UMV und EUDV, die nach Art. 8 Abs. 2 Rom II-VO dem jeweiligen nationalen Recht am Handlungsort der Verletzungshandlungen unterliegen und somit zu einer Mosaikbetrachtung aufgrund der parallelen Anwendung verschiedener Rechtsordnungen führen können. Eine Rechtswahl für Folgeansprüche würde vor allem bei Multistate-Delikten eine Mosaikbetrachtung vermeiden und eine Entscheidung nach einer Rechtsordnung ermöglichen, während das Schutzlandprinzip zur Bestimmung des anwendbaren Rechts der Rechtsverletzung unberührt bliebe. So ließe sich die Durchsetzung unionsweiter Rechte des geistigen Eigentums für die Rechteinhaber und die Rechtsanwendung für die Gerichte erleichtern.

Der in Art. 8 Abs. 3 Rom II-VO normierte Ausschluss einer Rechtswahl spiegelt den traditionellen Ansatz der Territorialität für Schutzrechtsverletzungen wider. Soweit jedoch das Recht eines EU-Mitgliedstaates gewählt wird, kann für unionsweite Rechte des geistigen Eigentums das Schutzlandprinzip durch eine Rechtswahl nicht konterkariert werden.[75] Unabhängig davon ist auch insoweit kein Grund ersichtlich, eine zumindest eingeschränkte Rechtswahl nach Eintritt des schadensbegründenden Ereignisses nicht zuzulassen, da die Parteien den Rechtsstreit jederzeit auch im Wege eines Vergleichs beilegen können. Auch einige nationale Rechtsordnungen, wie Art. 110 Abs. 2 des Schweizerischen Bundesgesetzes über das Internationale Privatrecht, lassen im Falle von Ansprüchen aus einer Verletzung von Rechten des geistigen Eigentums eine Rechtswahl der Parteien nach Eintritt der schadensverursachenden Handlung zugunsten des Rechts des Staates des angerufenen Gerichts zu.

2. *Sachrechtliche Ebene*

Denkbar wäre es auch, die durch die europäische Rechtsprechung nur bedingt ausgeräumten nachteiligen Auswirkungen der Fragmentierung des anwendbaren Rechts für Folgeansprüche einer Unionsmarken- bzw. -designverletzung auf sachrechtlicher Ebene anzugehen, nämlich durch Schaffung eines einheitlichen Sanktionenkatalogs auf Unionsebene.[76] Bereits im Vorfeld der Unionsmarkenreform hatte das Max-Planck-Institut in seiner Studie zum Funktionieren des europäischen Markensystems im Jahr 2011 vorgeschlagen, in die UMV alle materiell- und verfahrensrechtlichen Rechtsfolgen aufzunehmen, die Bestandteil der Enforcement-Richtlinie 2004/84/EC sind, und somit einen einheitlichen Sanktionenkatalog für Unionsmarken im Hinblick auf einen selbständigen Auskunftsanspruch, Schadensersatz sowie Rückruf, Entfernung aus den Vertriebswegen und Vernichtung rechts-

---

[74] IdS auch Münchener Kommentar zum BGB/Drexl, 8. Aufl. 2021, Rom II-VO Art. 8 Rn. 272.

[75] Siehe Rauscher, EuZPR/EuIPR/Pabst, 5. Aufl. 2023, Rom II-VO Art. 8 Rn. 29.

[76] Kur ILC 2021, 52(5), 579; idS auch Münchener Kommentar zum BGB/Drexl, 8. Aufl. 2021, Rom II-VO Art. 8 Rn. 156; Beck'scher Online-Kommentar UMV/Müller, 31. Ed. 15.2.2022, UMV Art. 129 Rn. 8.

verletzender Waren bereitzustellen.[77] Entsprechendes sollte aufgrund der horizontalen Natur für die Gemeinschaftsgeschmacksmusterverordnung gelten.[78] Dies ließ sich bislang jedoch nicht verwirklichen.

Erstrebenswert wäre es daher zumindest, durch eine Harmonisierung der Rechtsfolgen nationaler Schutzrechtsverletzungen so weit wie möglich gleiche Bedingungen für die Ausübung und Durchsetzung von Rechten des geistigen Eigentums auf Unionsebene zu schaffen, da der Grad der Harmonisierung der Rechtsfolgen bei Verletzungen nationaler Rechte des geistigen Eigentums in der Enforcement-Richtlinie 2004/84/EC nur auf einem de-minimis-Ansatz beruht.[79] Somit ließe sich selbst bei einem „Mosaik-Ansatz" in Bezug auf Folgeansprüche einer Unionsmarken- oder -designverletzung die Rechtsanwendung und Ermittlung des ausländischen nationalen Rechts der Mitgliedstaaten in der Praxis erleichtern.[80]

IV. Fazit

Insgesamt herrscht auch im Internet-Zeitalter die Schutzlandanknüpfung global weiter vor. Trotz stetiger Zunahme grenzüberschreitender Schutzrechtsverletzungen im Internet hat die Forderung, das Schutzlandprinzip für Fälle der weltweiten Verletzung geistiger Eigentumsrechte im Internet aufzugeben, bislang keinen Widerhall in Gesetzgebung und Rechtsprechung gefunden.[81] Die Rechtsprechung konkretisiert das Schutzlandprinzip nur näher, ohne es jedoch grundlegend in Frage zu stellen. Dies ist Ausdruck des berechtigten Interesses der Staaten, der Preisgabe des eigenen Regelungsanspruchs für Rechte des geistigen Eigentums auch und gerade im Internet-Zeitalter zu entgegnen.

Um die Rechtsanwendung bei Schutzrechtsverletzungen im Internet jedoch zu erleichtern, erscheint es angebracht, in diesen Fällen gewisse Einschränkungen vom Schutzlandprinzip zuzulassen und eine einzelne Rechtsordnung über die u. U. zahlreichen parallelen Schutzrechtsverletzungen entscheiden zu lassen. Die Kyoto Guidelines der International Law Association bieten hierfür eine gute Orientierungshilfe. Aus legislativer Perspektive sollten diese auf kollisionsrechtlicher Ebene für die Anknüpfung von Folgeansprüchen bei Verletzungen unionsweit geltender Schutzrechte im Rahmen des Art. 8 Abs. 2 Rom II-VO jedenfalls für Fälle herangezogen werden, in denen der Ursprung der Verletzungshandlung im EU-Ausland liegt. Auch erscheint eine Lockerung des Rechtswahlausschlusses in Art. 8 Abs. 3 Rom II-VO als angebracht, um die Rechtsfolgen der gesamten globalen Schutz-

---

[77] MPI, Study on the Overall Functioning of the European Trade Mark System, 2011, Rn. 3.149, 3.150 sowie Teil VII Conclusions, Rn. 64.

[78] MPI, Study on the Overall Functioning of the European Trade Mark System, 2011, Rn. 3.151.

[79] Rosati, The Localization of IP Infringements in the Online Environment: From Web 2.0 to Web 3.0 and the Metaverse, WIPO, 2023, 7. Conclusion, S. 35.

[80] Beck'scher Online-Kommentar UMV/Müller, 31. Ed. 15.2.2022, UMV Art. 129 Rn. 8; vgl. a. OLG Frankfurt 31.5.2012 – 6 U 10/11, GRUR-RR 2012, 473 (475) – Joop!

[81] HWB-EuP 2009/Metzger, 2009, Geistiges Eigentum (Kollisionsrecht).

rechtsverletzung nach Maßgabe eines einzigen anwendbaren Rechts beurteilen zu können und so eine gewisse Flexibilität für die Bestimmung des anwendbaren Rechts für Folgeansprüche zu erzielen und die Durchsetzung von Rechten geistigen Eigentums bei globalen Verletzungen zu erleichtern.[82]

Auf sachrechtlicher Unionsebene wäre in Ermangelung eines unionsweit einheitlichen Sanktionenkatalogs für Folgeansprüche einer Unionsmarken- oder -designverletzung jedenfalls eine umfassendere Harmonisierung der Mindeststandards für Rechtsfolgen von Verletzungen nationaler Schutzrechte in der Enforcement-Richtlinie begrüßenswert. Durch diese ließe sich die Rechtsanwendung und Ermittlung des ausländischen nationalen Rechts der Mitgliedstaaten auch in Bezug auf Folgeansprüche einer Unionsmarken- oder -designverletzung in der Praxis erleichtern.

[82] Ancel/Binctin/Drexl ua JIPITEC 12 (2021), 44 Rn. 72.

SVEN GROSCHISCHKA

Der Gerichtsstand des gewöhnlichen Arbeitsortes in der Brüssel Ia-VO und dessen Bestimmung beim fliegenden Personal

Eines der schwierigsten und gleichzeitig spannendsten Felder des Arbeitsrechts ist das (internationale) Arbeitsprozessrecht. Insbesondere im Zusammenhang mit der internationalen Zuständigkeit am gewöhnlichen Arbeitsort bestehen vielfältige Fragestellungen, die den Rechtsanwender in der Praxis vor große Herausforderungen stellen. In dem nachfolgenden Beitrag soll sich einigen dieser wichtigen, jedoch in der alltäglichen Beratungspraxis oftmals unterschätzten Probleme gewidmet werden. Hierdurch bietet sich gleichzeitig die Möglichkeit, zwei der wesentlichen Wirkungs- und Interessengebiete des beruflichen und privaten Schaffens des Jubilars miteinander zu verbinden – das Europäische Zivilprozessrecht und die (internationale) Luftfahrt.

I. Einführung

In Art. 21 Brüssel Ia-VO ist die Zuständigkeit in Arbeitssachen mit internationalem Bezug geregelt. Die Regelung betrifft Aktivklagen eines Arbeitnehmers[1] gegen seinen Arbeitgeber und beinhaltet drei zum Teil alternativ anwendbare, ansonsten jedoch grundsätzlich ausschließliche Gerichtsstände.[2] Eine Anwendung der Regelungen zum allgemeinen internationalen Gerichtsstand (Art. 4 Brüssel Ia-VO) und den besonderen Gerichtsständen nach Art. 7f. Brüssel Ia-VO ist – mit Ausnahme der ausdrücklich in der Verweisung in Art. 20 Abs. 1 Brüssel Ia-VO für anwendbar erklärten Vorschriften – ausgeschlossen.

1. Einzelne Gerichtsstände für Klagen gegen den Arbeitgeber

Hierbei steht die Zuständigkeit nach Art. 21 Abs. 1 lit. a Brüssel Ia-VO („Wohnsitz" des Arbeitgebers als eine Art allgemeiner Gerichtsstand) alternativ zu den Zuständigkeiten nach Art. 21 Abs. 1 lit. b Brüssel Ia-VO. Die hierin geregelten Gerichtsstände nach Art. 21 Abs. 1 lit. b sublit. (i) Brüssel Ia-VO (am gewöhnlichen Arbeitsort) und Art. 21 Abs. 1 lit. b sublit. (ii) Brüssel Ia-VO (Ort der einstellenden

---

[1] Gemeint sind Personen jeder Geschlechtsidentität. Um der leichteren Lesbarkeit willen wird im Beitrag die grammatikalisch männliche Form verwendet.

[2] Saenger, ZPO/Dörner, 10. Aufl. 2023, EuGVVO Art. 21 Rn. 1; Geimer/Schütze, Internationaler Rechtsverkehr/Paulus, 66. EL Januar 2023, VO (EG) 1215/2012 Art. 21 Rn. 1; Rauscher, EuZPR/EuIPR/Mankowski, 5. Aufl. 2021, Brüssel Ia-VO Art. 21 Rn. 1.

Niederlassung) schließen sich dagegen strikt gegenseitig aus.[3] Insoweit ist vorrangig ein etwaiger gewöhnlicher Arbeitsort zu prüfen. Erst wenn ein solcher nicht festgestellt werden kann, ist der Anknüpfungspunkt der einstellenden Niederlassung heranzuziehen.[4]

a) *„Vorrang" des gewöhnlichen Arbeitsortes gegenüber dem Gerichtsstand der einstellenden Niederlassung*

Der Gerichtsstand der Niederlassung knüpft – anders als der Gerichtsstand des gewöhnlichen Arbeitsortes – an ein Merkmal des Arbeitgebers an und kann daher von diesem auch entsprechend beeinflusst werden. Dies steht in gewissem Widerspruch zu der Zielstellung der Regelungen in Art. 20ff. Brüssel Ia-VO, die den Schutz des Arbeitnehmers bezwecken.[5]

Daher ist die Rechtsprechung des EuGH deutlich von dem Versuch geprägt, den Anwendungsbereich des Gerichtsstands der den Arbeitnehmer einstellenden Niederlassung so gering wie möglich zu halten und stattdessen auf den Gerichtsstand des gewöhnlichen Arbeitsortes zurückzugreifen.[6] Im Zuge dessen legt der EuGH ein sehr extensives Verständnis des gewöhnlichen Arbeitsortes zugrunde.[7] Dies führt zu einer gezielten Marginalisierung des Gerichtsstands der Niederlassung.[8]

b) *Kein Gerichtsstand der Ausweichklausel*

Anders als bei den Regelungen zur Bestimmung des anwendbaren Rechts (vgl. Art. 8 Abs. 4 Rom I-VO, Art. 6 Abs. 2 Hs. 2 RomÜbk, Art. 30 Abs. 2 Hs. 2 EGBGB a.F.) besteht kein Gerichtsstand einer etwaigen engeren Verbindung des Arbeitsvertrages oder des Arbeitsverhältnisses zu einem anderen Mitgliedstaat. Zwar orientiert sich der Wortlaut der Regelung in Art. 21 Abs. 1 lit. b Brüssel Ia-VO an der Regelung in Art. 8 Abs. 2, Abs. 3 Rom I-VO, so dass überlegt werden könnte, auch einen Gerichtsstand zur Regelung atypischer Sachverhalte vorzusehen, sofern einzelne Fallkonstellationen nicht adäquat über die Gerichtsstände in Art. 21 Abs. 1 lit. b Brüssel Ia-VO gelöst werden könnten.

Hiervon wurde jedoch abgesehen, um nicht zu Lasten der Arbeitnehmer Unsicherheiten zu schaffen, so dass der Gerichtsstand auch bei atypischen Sachverhal-

---

[3] EuGH 15.12.2011 – C-384/10, NZA 2012, 227 Rn. 26 (noch zu Art. 6 RomÜbk); Rauscher, EuZPR/EuIPR/Mankowski, 5. Aufl. 2021, Brüssel Ia-VO Art. 21 Rn. 3; Geimer/Schütze, Internationaler Rechtsverkehr/Paulus, 66. EL Januar 2023, VO (EG) 1215/2012 Art. 21 Rn. 3.

[4] EuGH 15.12.2011 – C-384/10, EuZW 2012, 61 Rn. 32, 39; Junker EuZW 2021, 41 (42); Knöfel IPRax 2014, 130 (131).

[5] EuGH 15.3.2011 – C-29/10, EuZW 2011, 302 Rn. 46 unter Verweis auf ErwGr. 23 Rom I-VO (vgl. zum Auslegungszusammenhang zwischen der Rom I-VO und der Brüssel Ia-VO ErwGr. 7 Rom I-VO); Junker FS Gottwald, 2014, 293 (298); Knöfel IPRax 2014, 130 (131).

[6] EuGH 15.12.2011 – C-384/10, EuZW 2012, 61 Rn. 39f.; Junker FS Gottwald, 2014, 293 (296); Mankowski EuZA 2017, 267 (271).

[7] EuGH 15.3.2011 – C-29/10, EuZW 2011, 302 Rn. 43, 45, 47; vgl. auch BAG 15.12.2016 – 6 AZR 430/15, NZA 2017, 502 Rn. 56.

[8] Rauscher, EuZPR/EuIPR/Mankowski, 5. Aufl. 2021, Brüssel Ia-VO Art. 21 Rn. 4.

ten vorhersehbar bleiben soll.[9] Im Übrigen bestünde hierfür angesichts der Wahlmöglichkeiten bei Klagen des Arbeitnehmers ohnehin kein Bedürfnis, da die bestehenden Gerichtsstände in Art. 21 Brüssel Ia-VO die Anküpfungspunkte für eine enge Verbindung bereits abdecken. Im Rahmen der internationalen Zuständigkeit genügt insoweit eine enge Verbindung, die ggf. auch zu mehreren Gerichtsständen bestehen kann. Eine engste Verbindung wie im IPR bedarf es hierbei nicht.[10]

c) *Spezieller Gerichtsstand bei Arbeitnehmerentsendung*

Neben den Zuständigkeiten in Art. 21 Brüssel Ia-VO sind ferner nach Art. 67 Brüssel Ia-VO die Spezialgerichtsstände aus der RL 96/71/EG (EntsendeRL) anwendbar.

In Art. 3 EntsendeRL werden entsandten Arbeitnehmern – unabhängig von dem auf das jeweilige Arbeitsverhältnis anwendbaren Recht – bestimmte Arbeits- und Beschäftigungsbedingungen garantiert. Zur Durchsetzung dieser Arbeits- und Beschäftigungsbedingungen kann nach Art. 6 EntsendeRL eine Klage in dem Mitgliedstaat erhoben werden, in dessen Hoheitsgebiet der Arbeitnehmer entsandt ist oder war. Dies wurde im nationalen Recht in § 15 AEntG umgesetzt.

Dabei soll jedoch nicht nur Arbeitnehmern der Gerichtsstand nach Art. 6 EntsendeRL eröffnet sein. Vielmehr sollen auch Sozialkassen hiernach Klage erheben können, da diese die Mindestarbeitsbedingungen absichern und zu diesem Zweck Beiträge (bei den Arbeitgebern) einfordern können.[11]

2. *Sachliche Reichweite des Gerichtsstands des gewöhnlichen Arbeitsortes*

Die Gerichtsstände in Art. 21 Brüssel Ia-VO sind nach Art. 20 Abs. 1 Brüssel Ia-VO sachlich nur in Arbeitssachen anwendbar. Dh, Gegenstand des Rechtsstreits müssen Streitigkeiten aus einem Arbeitsverhältnis zwischen einem Arbeitnehmer und einem Arbeitgeber sein.[12]

a) *Arbeitnehmer*

Der Begriff des Arbeitnehmers wird in der Brüssel Ia-VO jedoch nicht näher definiert.

---

[9] Franzen/Gallner/Oetker, Kommentar zum europäischen Arbeitsrecht/Krebber, 5. Aufl. 2024, VO (EU) 1215/2012 Art. 21 Rn. 12f.; Rauscher, EuZPR/EuIPR/Mankowski, 5. Aufl. 2021, Brüssel Ia-VO Art. 21 Rn. 3; Ulrici jurisPR-ArbR 30/2011 Anm. 3.

[10] Mankowski FS Heldrich, 2005, 867 (868ff.).

[11] Geimer/Schütze, EuZVR/Geimer, 4. Aufl. 2020, EuGVVO Art. 20 Rn. 25; Wiesehügel/Saal, Die Sozialkassen der Bauwirtschaft und die Entsendung innerhalb der Europäischen Union/Birk, 1998, 111 (117f.); Preis/Temming, Die Urlaubs- und Lohnausgleichskassen im Kontext des Gemeinschaftsrechts, 2006, 195; Zöller, ZPO/Geimer, 35. Aufl. 2024, VO (EU) 1215/2012 Art. 21 Rn. 7; aA: Eichenhofer IPRax 2008, 109 (111).

[12] Geimer/Schütze, Internationaler Rechtsverkehr/Paulus, 66. EL Januar 2023, VO (EG) 1215/2012 Art. 21 Rn. 11.

aa) Begrifflichkeit

Nach der Rechtsprechung des EuGH ist ein Arbeitnehmer eine Person, die während einer bestimmten Zeit für eine andere Person nach deren Weisungen Leistungen erbringt, für die sie als Gegenleistung eine Vergütung erhält.[13]

Die Weisungsgebundenheit muss sich insbesondere auf die fehlende Freiheit bei der Wahl von Zeit, Ort und Inhalt der Arbeitsleistung beziehen.[14] Ferner wird eine gewisse Abhängigkeit zum Arbeitgeber vorausgesetzt.[15] Die Person des Arbeitnehmers muss in das Unternehmen des Arbeitgebers eingegliedert sein und es gerade an einem eigenen unternehmerischen Risiko fehlen.[16]

Die für die Erbringung der Arbeitsleistung durch den Arbeitnehmer anfallende Gegenleistung muss dabei nicht zwingend in der Zahlung eines Geldbetrages liegen. Vielmehr reicht die Verschaffung irgendeines geldwerten Vorteils aus.[17] Auch kann eine bloß erfolgsabhängige Vergütung genügen.[18]

bb) Beispiele

Danach unterfallen neben „normalen" Arbeitnehmern (Arbeiter und Angestellte) auch leitende Angestellte dem Arbeitnehmerbegriff.[19] Selbstverständlich stellen auch Leiharbeitnehmer – im Verhältnis zu ihrem Vertragsarbeitgeber und nicht zum Entleiher – Arbeitnehmer iSd. Brüssel Ia-VO dar. Auch Auszubildene, Praktikanten und Referendare sind Arbeitnehmer nach Art. 20 Abs. 1 Brüssel Ia-VO.[20]

Auch neuere Arbeitsformen wie Work on Demand[21] oder Crowdworking[22] können danach eine Arbeitnehmerstellung im europarechtlichen Verständnis begründen, sofern die vorstehenden Anforderungen der Rechtsprechung an ein Arbeitsverhältnis erfüllt sind.

cc) Organe einer Gesellschaft

Nach der Rechtsprechung des EuGH sollen auch Organe von juristischen Personen und Gesellschaften, insbesondere Geschäftsführer einer GmbH oder ver-

---

[13] EuGH 10.9.2015 – C-47/14, EuZW 2015, 922 Rn. 41; 11.11.2010 – C-232/09, EuZW 2011, 74 Rn. 39; 3.7.1986 – 66/85, NVwZ 1987, 41.

[14] EuGH 4.12.2014 – C-413/13, NZA 2015, 55 Rn. 36; 13.1.2004 – C-256/01, NZA 2004, 201 Rn. 72; BAG 20.10.2015 – 9 AZR 525/14, NZA 2016, 254 Rn. 18.

[15] EuGH 10.9.2015 – C-47/14, EuZW 2015, 922 Rn. 40.

[16] EuGH 4.12.2014 – C-413/13, NZA 2015, 55 Rn. 36; BAG 20.10.2015 – 9 AZR 525/14, NZA 2016, 254 Rn. 18; LAG Rheinland-Pfalz 8.10.2019 – 6 Sa 97/19, BeckRS 2019, 39431 Rn. 31.

[17] Vgl. EuGH 5.10.1988 – 196/87, NVwZ 1990, 53 Rn. 12.

[18] Geimer/Schütze, Internationaler Rechtsverkehr/Paulus, 66. EL Januar 2023, VO (EG) 1215/2012 Art. 20 Rn. 37; Rauscher, EuZPR/EuIPR/Mankowski, 5. Aufl. 2021, Brüssel Ia-VO Art. 20 Rn. 21.

[19] BAG 8.12.2010 – 10 AZR 562/08, NZA-RR 2012, 320 Rn. 27.

[20] EuGH 17.3.2005 – C-109/04, NJW 2005, 1481 Rn. 13; 26.2.1992 – C-3/90, NZA 1992, 736 Rn. 15ff.; 3.7.1986 – 66/85, NVwZ 1987, 41.

[21] Hierbei handelt es sich um Verträge, bei denen die Arbeits-/Dienstleistung nicht kontinuierlich, sondern nur auf Abruf bzw. Anforderung erbracht wird.

[22] Bei dieser Arbeitsform (auch Plattformarbeit genannt) werden inhaltlich und zeitlich begrenzte Tätigkeiten über Onlineplattformen vergeben.

gleichbarer ausländischer Rechtsformen, Arbeitnehmer im europarechtlichen Sinne sein. Dies setze voraus, dass die betreffende Person in ihrer Eigenschaft als Geschäftsführer/Organ während einer bestimmten Zeit für die Gesellschaft und nach deren Weisung Leistungen erbringt, für die sie als Gegenleistung eine Vergütung erhält und sie zu dieser Gesellschaft in einer dauerhaften Beziehung steht, durch die sie in einer bestimmten Weise in deren Betrieb eingegliedert wurde.[23]

Dabei ist insbesondere die Weisungsgebundenheit in jedem Einzelfall anhand aller Gesichtspunkte und aller Umstände, die die Beziehungen zwischen den Parteien kennzeichnen, zu prüfen. Insoweit kommt es darauf an, ob der Geschäftsführer in der Lage ist, auf die Willensbildung des Verwaltungsorgans der Gesellschaft Einfluss zu nehmen. Hierbei ist festzustellen, wer befugt ist, dem Geschäftsführer Weisungen zu erteilen und deren Umsetzung zu kontrollieren. Sofern die Einflussmöglichkeit des Geschäftsführers auf dieses Organ „nicht unerheblich" ist, sei nicht von einem Unterordnungsverhältnis auszugehen.[24]

Danach sind nach deutschem Recht jedenfalls Fremdgeschäftsführer (vgl. § 6 Abs. 3 S. 1 Alt. 2 GmbHG) aufgrund der Weisungsgebundenheit gegenüber der Gesellschafterversammlung Arbeitnehmer im europarechtlichen Sinne, während ein Vorstandsmitglied einer deutschen Aktiengesellschaft aufgrund der fehlenden Weisungsgebundenheit (vgl. § 76 Abs. 1 AktG) keine Arbeitnehmer-Stellung inne hat.[25] Inwiefern das jeweilige Organ tatsächlich den Weisungen der Gesellschaft bzw. des hierfür zuständigen Verwaltungsorgans unterworfen ist, beurteilt sich nach dem Gesellschaftsstatut und ist damit eine Vorfrage im Rahmen der Bestimmung der internationalen Zuständigkeit.[26] Demgegenüber sind Organe mit Unternehmensbeteiligung, also insbesondere Gesellschafter-Geschäftsführer, dann keine Arbeitnehmer, wenn diese aufgrund ihres Anteils an der Gesellschaft einen beherrschenden Einfluss ausüben können und damit selbst über Inhalt und Erteilung von Weisungen entscheiden.[27]

Festzuhalten bleibt mithin, dass der Begriff des Arbeitnehmers im europarechtlichen Sinne deutlich weiter reicht als die Einordnung als Arbeitnehmer nach nationalem Recht (vgl. § 611 a BGB). Inwiefern dies angesichts des vom EuGH immer wieder bemühten umfassenden Schutzes der Arbeitnehmer beispielsweise mit Blick auf Geschäftsführer in der Praxis tatsächlich gerechtfertigt erscheint, darf zumindest bezweifelt werden und widerspricht auch in erheblicher Weise dem Selbstverständnis vieler Geschäftsführer/CEO und der gelebten Praxis innerhalb der Unternehmen.

---

[23] EuGH 10.9.2015 – C-47/14, EuZW 2015, 922 Rn. 45.

[24] EuGH 10.9.2015 – C-47/14, EuZW 2015, 922 Rn. 47.

[25] Kindler IPRax 2016, 115 (116); Geimer/Schütze, Internationaler Rechtsverkehr/Paulus, 66. EL Januar 2023, VO (EG) 1215/2012 Art. 20 Rn. 42; Rauscher, EuZPR/EuIPR/Mankowski, 5. Aufl. 2021, Brüssel Ia-VO Art. 20 Rn. 71.

[26] Rauscher, EuZPR/EuIPR/Mankowski, 5. Aufl. 2021, Brüssel Ia-VO Art. 20 Rn. 63; Geimer/Schütze, Internationaler Rechtsverkehr/Paulus, 66. EL Januar 2023, VO (EG) 1215/2012 Art. 20 Rn. 42; Kindler IPRax 2016, 115 (117).

[27] Geimer/Schütze, Internationaler Rechtsverkehr/Paulus, 66. EL Januar 2023, VO (EG) 1215/2012 Art. 20 Rn. 43; Kindler IPRax 2016, 115 (119); Rauscher, EuZPR/EuIPR/Mankowski, 5. Aufl. 2021, Brüssel Ia-VO Art. 20 Rn. 67.

b) Arbeitgeber

Auch der Begriff des Arbeitgebers wird in der Brüssel Ia-VO nicht definiert. Arbeitgeber ist im Umkehrschluss zum Arbeitnehmer-Begriff, wer gegenüber dem Arbeitnehmer die Weisungsbefugnis innehat.[28] Entscheidend ist, wem die Arbeitsleistung normativ-rechtlich zusteht, nicht wem sie faktisch erbracht wird.[29]

c) Keine Beschränkung auf vertragliche Ansprüche

Fraglich ist, ob sich der Gerichtsstand des Arbeitsorts allein auf vertraglich zu qualifizierende Streitigkeiten aus dem Arbeitsverhältnis beschränkt oder auch deliktische Ansprüche umfasst sind.

Nach einer Auffassung soll der Gerichtsstand auf vertraglich zu qualifizierende Ansprüche und Streitigkeiten zu beschränken sein.[30] Die Regelung in Art. 21 Brüssel Ia-VO gewähre keine Annexkompetenz für etwaige deliktische Ansprüche, beispielsweise aufgrund eines Arbeitsunfalls. Dies folge aus der allgemeinen Systematik der Brüssel Ia-VO.

Demgegenüber erstreckt sich der Gerichtsstand nach zutreffender Auffassung auch auf konkurrierende deliktische Ansprüche.[31] Insoweit ist es in konsequenter Berücksichtigung des Schutzzwecks des Gerichtsstands in Art. 21 Brüssel Ia-VO geboten, einen einheitlichen Gerichtsstand zu gewähren. Hierfür spricht auch, dass etwaige deliktische Ansprüche des Arbeitnehmers gegen den Arbeitgeber bei vernünftiger Betrachtungsweise ihren Grund im jeweiligen Arbeitsvertrag haben.[32]

3. Arbeitnehmer als Partei des Verfahrens

Anders als beim Verbrauchergerichtsstand nach Art. 18 Brüssel Ia-VO wird in Art. 21 Brüssel Ia-VO nicht ausdrücklich vorausgesetzt, dass ein Arbeitnehmer auch Partei des konkreten Verfahrens sein muss. Wenn beispielsweise im Wege der Legalzession Ansprüche eines Arbeitnehmers gegen den (früheren) Arbeitgeber wegen des zwischenzeitlich bezogenen Arbeitslosengelds teilweise auf die Bundesagentur für Arbeit übergegangen sind (vgl. § 115 SGB X), so stellt sich die Frage, ob dann auch der Bundesagentur für Arbeit als Dritter der Gerichtsstand nach

---

[28] Münchener Kommentar zum BGB/Martiny, 8. Aufl. 2021, Rom I-VO Art. 8 Rn. 24; Geimer/Schütze, Internationaler Rechtsverkehr/Paulus, 66. EL Januar 2023, VO (EG) 1215/2012 Art. 20 Rn. 47.

[29] Rauscher, EuZPR/EuIPR/Mankowski, 5. Aufl. 2021, Brüssel Ia-VO Art. 20 Rn. 25.

[30] Geimer/Schütze, Internationaler Rechtsverkehr/Paulus, 66. EL Januar 2023, VO (EG) 1215/2012 Art. 21 Rn. 15; Kropholler/von Hein, Europäisches Zivilprozessrecht, 9. Aufl. 2011, EuGVVO Art. 18 Rn. 3; Junker FS Schlosser, 2005, 299 (303).

[31] Rauscher FS Schütze, 1999, 695 (706); Saenger, ZPO/Dörner, 10. Aufl. 2023, EuGVVO Art. 20 Rn. 5; Franzen/Gallner/Oetker, Kommentar zum europäischen Arbeitsrecht/Krebber, 5. Aufl. 2024, VO (EU) 1215/2012 Art. 21 Rn. 11; Münchener Kommentar zur ZPO/Gottwald, 6. Aufl. 2022, Brüssel Ia-VO Art. 20 Rn. 7; Däubler NZA 2003, 1297 (1299); wohl auch Schlosser/Hess, Europäisches Zivilprozessrecht/Schlosser, 5. Aufl. 2021, Brüssel Ia-VO Art. 20 Rn. 6.

[32] OGH 11.8.2015 – 4 Ob 78/15x, BeckRS 2015, 111280 = IPRax 2017, 105 Rn. 10f.; vgl. auch LAG Niedersachen 29.6.2016 – 13 Sa 1152/15, NZA-RR 2016, 611 Rn. 40.

Art. 21 Brüssel Ia-VO offen steht. Dasselbe gilt für Fälle, in denen der Arbeitnehmer sonstigen Dritten etwaige Forderungen gegenüber dem Arbeitgeber abtritt.

Insoweit wird die Auffassung vertreten, dass die Zuständigkeit nach Art. 21 Brüssel Ia-VO voraussetze, dass an dem konkreten Verfahren ein Arbeitnehmer als Kläger teilnehme.[33] Dies folge aus dem Normzweck der Regelungen in Art. 20ff. Brüssel Ia-VO, die gerade eine verfahrensrechtliche Privilegierung des Arbeitnehmers zum Ziel hätten. Klagen von Rechtsnachfolgern von Arbeitnehmern könnten danach nicht an dem Gerichtsstand nach Art. 21 Brüssel Ia-VO erhoben werden.

Hiergegen wird angeführt, dass der Anknüpfungspunkt des Gerichtsstands des Arbeitsorts sachbezogen sei und gerade nicht an die Person des Arbeitnehmers selbst anknüpfe. Dies spreche dafür, dem Zessionar den Gerichtsstand nach Art. 21 Abs. 1 lit. b Brüssel Ia-VO zu eröffnen.[34] Insoweit sei kein Unterschied zu dem Zessionar einer Vertragsforderung zu machen, dem ebenfalls der Erfüllungsortgerichtsstand nach Art. 7 Nr. 1 Brüssel Ia-VO offen stehe.

Dies überzeugt jedoch nicht. Insoweit ist kein Grund ersichtlich, weshalb auch ein Dritter, dem die Forderung des Arbeitnehmers abgetreten wurde, hinsichtlich der internationalen Zuständigkeit privilegiert werden sollte. Der Gerichtsstand des Arbeitsortes wurde gerade zum individuellen Schutz des Arbeitnehmers geschaffen. Dieser Schutzzweck ist bei Klagen Dritter nicht gegeben, so dass keine Rechtfertigung dafür bestünde, diese gegenüber Arbeitgebern als Beklagten über Gebühr zu privilegieren.

Unabhängig davon besteht aber jedenfalls Einigkeit darüber, dass Klagen einer Gewerkschaft, auch wenn es sich hierbei ursprünglich um Rechtsstreitigkeiten aus einer Arbeitnehmersache handeln sollte, nicht an den Arbeitnehmergerichtsständen geltend gemacht werden können.[35]

II. Grundsätze des Gerichtsstands des gewöhnlichen Arbeitsorts

Die Regelung in Art. 21 Abs. 1 lit. b sublit. (i) Brüssel Ia-VO umfasst hinsichtlich des gewöhnlichen Arbeitsortes vier verschiedene Tatbestandsalternativen, zwischen denen in der Praxis nicht immer trennscharf unterschieden wird. Danach kommen folgende Anknüpfungen in Betracht:

- Ort, an dem der Arbeitnehmer gewöhnlich seine Arbeit verrichtet;
- Ort, von dem aus der Arbeitnehmer gewöhnlich seine Arbeit verrichtet;
- Ort, an dem der Arbeitnehmer seine Arbeit zuletzt gewöhnlich verrichtet hat;

---

[33] Geimer/Schütze, Internationaler Rechtsverkehr/Paulus, 66. EL Januar 2023, VO (EG) 1215/2012 Art. 21 Rn. 13; Schlosser/Hess, Europäisches Zivilprozessrecht/Hess, 4. Aufl. 2015, EuGVVO Art. 20 Rn. 1; Münchener Kommentar zur ZPO/Gottwald, 4. Aufl. 2013, EuGVVO Art. 18 Rn. 4; Geimer/Schütze, EuZVR/Geimer, 3. Aufl. 2010, EuGVVO Art. 19 Rn. 40; Wagner RIW 2023, 245 (253); Abele FA 2013, 357 (360).

[34] Rauscher, EuZPR/EuIPR/Mankowski, 5. Aufl. 2021, Brüssel Ia-VO Art. 21 Rn. 112.

[35] Münchener Kommentar zur ZPO/Gottwald, 6. Aufl. 2022, Brüssel Ia-VO Art. 20 Rn. 9; Geimer/Schütze, Internationaler Rechtsverkehr/Paulus, 66. EL Januar 2023, VO (EG) 1215/2012 Art. 20 Rn. 46; Zöller, ZPO/Geimer, 35. Aufl. 2024, VO (EU) 1215/2012 Art. 21 Rn. 16.

– Ort, von dem aus der Arbeitnehmer seine Arbeit zuletzt gewöhnlich verrichtet hat.

Der Gerichtsstand nach Art. 21 Abs. 1 lit. b sublit. (i) Brüssel Ia-VO wird mithin am derzeitigen oder am letzten gewöhnlichen Arbeitsort des Arbeitnehmers festgelegt. Hierbei wird neben der internationalen auch die örtliche Zuständigkeit geregelt.[36]

1. *Zweck des Gerichtsstands*

Durch den Arbeitsortgerichtsstand nach Art. 21 Abs. 1 lit. b sublit. (i) Brüssel Ia-VO soll einem Arbeitnehmer eine kostengünstige Durchsetzung seiner Ansprüche gegenüber seinem Arbeitgeber ermöglicht werden. Denn in vielen Fällen wird der Gerichtsstand des Arbeitsortes der für den Arbeitnehmer nächstgelegene Gerichtsstand sein.[37]

Zweck der Norm sind ferner die Beweisnähe, vor allem aber auch die Leichtigkeit des Zugangs zu Gericht. Denn hierdurch muss sich ein Arbeitnehmer nicht an die unter Umständen weit entfernten Gerichte am Sitz des Arbeitgebers wenden.[38] Vielmehr kann ein Arbeitnehmer in der gewohnten Umgebung klagen, deren Umfeld ihm bekannt und vertraut ist.

Schließlich fördert der Gerichtsstand des Arbeitsortes potenziell den Gleichlauf von Zuständigkeit und anwendbarem Recht und dient damit letztlich auch der Rechtsnähe.[39] Das Gericht des Ortes, an dem der Arbeitnehmer die vereinbarte Tätigkeit auszuüben hat, soll dabei am besten zur Entscheidung eines Rechtsstreits in der Lage sein, der sich aus dem Arbeitsvertrag ergeben kann.[40] Jedoch ist es für den gewöhnlichen Arbeitsort nicht maßgeblich, welches Recht in der Sache anwendbar ist.[41]

Demzufolge schlägt sich in dem Gerichtsstand des Arbeitsortes der Schutz des Arbeitnehmers als das tragende Prinzip der Regelung in Art. 21 Brüssel Ia-VO umfassend nieder.

---

[36] Saenger, ZPO/Dörner, 10. Aufl. 2023, EuGVVO Art. 21 Rn. 4; Geimer/Schütze, Internationaler Rechtsverkehr/Paulus, 66. EL Januar 2023, VO (EG) 1215/2012 Art. 21 Rn. 21; Zöller, ZPO/Geimer, 35. Aufl. 2024, VO (EU) 1215/2012 Art. 21 Rn. 8.

[37] Musielak/Voit, ZPO/Stadler/Krüger, 21. Aufl. 2024, EuGVVO Art. 21 Rn. 2; Geimer/Schütze, Internationaler Rechtsverkehr/Paulus, 66. EL Januar 2023, VO (EG) 1215/2012 Art. 21 Rn. 21.

[38] Geimer/Schütze, EuZVR/Geimer, 4. Aufl. 2020, EuGVVO Art. 21 Rn. 5; Beck'scher Online-Kommentar ZPO/Spohnheimer, 52. Ed. 1.3.2024, Brüssel Ia-VO Art. 21 Rn. 8; Garber FS Kaissis, 2012, 221 (222).

[39] Musielak/Voit, ZPO/Stadler/Krüger, 21. Aufl. 2024, EuGVVO Art. 21 Rn. 2; Franzen/Gallner/Oetker, Kommentar zum europäischen Arbeitsrecht/Krebber, 5. Aufl. 2024, VO (EU) 1215/2012 Art. 21 Rn. 8; Geimer/Schütze, Internationaler Rechtsverkehr/Paulus, 66. EL Januar 2023, VO (EG) 1215/2012 Art. 21 Rn. 21.

[40] EuGH 10.4.2003 – C-437/00, EuZW 2003, 412 Rn. 17; 9.1.1997 – C-383/95, NZA 1997, 225 Rn. 16.

[41] Rauscher, EuZPR/EuIPR/Mankowski, 5. Aufl. 2021, Brüssel Ia-VO Art. 21 Rn. 13; Geimer/Schütze, Internationaler Rechtsverkehr/Paulus, 66. EL Januar 2023, VO (EG) 1215/2012 Art. 21 Rn. 22.

2. *Begriffsbestimmung*

a) *Auslegungsgrundsätze*

Der Arbeitsort ist in autonomer und weiter Auslegung zu bestimmen.[42] Hierbei sind die zu Art. 8 Rom I-VO entwickelten Grundsätze heranzuziehen, da der Wortlaut der Regelung in Art. 21 Abs. 1 lit. b Brüssel Ia-VO an die Formulierungen in Art. 8 Abs. 2 Rom I-VO angelehnt ist.[43] Der gewöhnliche Arbeitsort ist damit „der Ort, an dem oder von dem aus der Arbeitnehmer gewöhnlich seine Arbeit verrichtet".

Dem Begriff kann ein marktorientiertes Auslegungsmodell mit der Testfrage unterlegt werden, auf welchem national begrenzt gedachten Arbeitsmarkt der Arbeitgeber hypothetisch Ersatz für den konkreten Arbeitnehmer rekrutieren würde. Durch dieses stark faktisch geprägte Kriterium erscheint der Arbeitsort als sehr resistent gegenüber etwaigen Manipulationen.[44]

aa) *Fokus auf die Person des Arbeitnehmers*

Bei der Auslegung des Begriffs steht grundsätzlich ausschließlich der Arbeitnehmer im Fokus. Alle Aktivitäten auf Seiten des Arbeitgebers haben bei der Bestimmung des gewöhnlichen Arbeitsortes keine Relevanz, so dass es auch nicht darauf ankommt, ob der Arbeitgeber an dem Arbeitsort einen Betrieb oder sonstige Infrastruktur unterhält.[45]

Ferner kommt Verträgen des Arbeitgebers mit dessen Kunden im Außenverhältnis keine unmittelbare Rolle zu, da der Arbeitnehmer selbst an diesen nicht als Partei beteiligt ist. Auch wenn der Arbeitnehmer nach außen gegenüber Kunden des Arbeitgebers als Erfüllungsgehilfe bei dessen unternehmerischer Tätigkeit auftritt, ist der Erfüllungsort dieser Verträge ohne Bedeutung im Innenverhältnis zwischen Arbeitnehmer und Arbeitgeber und schlägt damit nicht auf das Arbeitsverhältnis bzw. den gewöhnlichen Arbeitsort durch.[46]

---

[42] EuGH 15.12.2011 – C-384/10, NZA 2012, 227 Rn. 35; 9.1.1997 – C-383/95, NZA 1997, 225 Rn. 12; Beck'scher Online-Kommentar ZPO/Spohnheimer, 52. Ed. 1.3.2024, Brüssel Ia-VO Art. 21 Rn. 8.

[43] Münchener Kommentar zur ZPO/Gottwald, 6. Aufl. 2022, Brüssel Ia-VO Art. 21 Rn. 6; Franzen/Gallner/Oetker, Kommentar zum europäischen Arbeitsrecht/Krebber, 5. Aufl. 2024, VO (EU) 1215/2012 Art. 21 Rn. 8; Beck'scher Online-Kommentar ZPO/Spohnheimer, 52. Ed. 1.3.2024, Brüssel Ia-VO Art. 21 Rn. 8.

[44] Rauscher, EuZPR/EuIPR/Mankowski, 5. Aufl. 2021, Brüssel Ia-VO Art. 21 Rn. 14; Mankowski IPRax 1999, 332 (336ff.); Gebauer/Wiedmann, Europäisches Zivilrecht/Gebauer, 3. Aufl. 2021, Kap. 26 Rn. 96.

[45] Rauscher, EuZPR/EuIPR/Mankowski, 5. Aufl. 2021, Brüssel Ia-VO Art. 21 Rn. 20; Geimer/Schütze, Internationaler Rechtsverkehr/Paulus, 66. EL Januar 2023, VO (EG) 1215/2012 Art. 21 Rn 31; Münchener Kommentar zur ZPO/Gottwald, 6. Aufl. 2022, Brüssel Ia-VO Art. 21 Rn. 6.

[46] BAG 27.1.2011 – 2 AZR 646/09, NZA 2011, 1309 Rn. 32f.; Geimer/Schütze, Internationaler Rechtsverkehr/Paulus, 66. EL Januar 2023, VO (EG) 1215/2012 Art. 21 Rn. 22; Rauscher, EuZPR/EuIPR/Mankowski, 5. Aufl. 2021, Brüssel Ia-VO Art. 21 Rn. 22.

bb) Örtlicher Anknüpfungspunkt bei Weisungen

Der EuGH hat demgegenüber teilweise die Auffassung vertreten, dass – neben anderen Kriterien – auch auf den Ort abzustellen sei, von dem aus der Arbeitnehmer Weisungen erhalte.[47] Richtigerweise sollte jedoch vielmehr auf den Ort des Empfangs der Weisungen abgestellt werden.[48]

Dies ist wiederum Ausprägung des Grundsatzes, dass es für die Auslegung des Begriffs des gewöhnlichen Arbeitsortes allein auf die Person des Arbeitnehmers ankommen kann und nicht auf den Arbeitgeber. Ferner ist dies insoweit konsequent, als dass es sich bei dem Empfang von Weisungen ebenfalls um eine Arbeitsleistung handelt. Demgegenüber ist der Ausspruch von Weisungen der Sphäre des Arbeitgebers zuzurechnen und ist daher als Kriterium eher dem – gegenüber dem Gerichtsstand des gewöhnlichen Arbeitsortes nachrangigen – Gerichtsstand der einstellenden Niederlassung zuzuordnen.

b) Mittelpunkt der Arbeitstätigkeit

Arbeitsort ist danach der Ort, welchen der Arbeitnehmer zum tatsächlichen Mittelpunkt seiner Arbeitstätigkeit gemacht hat[49] bzw. an dem oder von dem aus – unter Berücksichtigung sämtlicher Umstände des Einzelfalles – er den wesentlichen Teil seiner Verpflichtungen gegenüber dem Arbeitgeber tatsächlich erfüllt.[50] Hierbei handelt es sich in der Regel um den Ort, an dem der Arbeitnehmer tatsächlich die meiste Arbeitszeit verbringt.[51]

aa) Unerheblichkeit der vertraglichen Vereinbarungen

Dies ist unabhängig von den arbeitsvertraglichen Vereinbarungen.[52] Zwar kann eine Festlegung im Arbeitsvertrag den Ausgangspunkt für die weitere Beurteilung bilden und insoweit ein wichtiges Indiz darstellen. Eine weitreichendere Bindung an die vertraglichen Regelungen würde jedoch einer Gerichtsstandsvereinbarung gleichkommen und wäre daher an den Vorgaben in Art. 23 Brüssel Ia-VO zu messen. Entscheidend ist folglich nicht die vertragliche Vereinbarung, sondern vielmehr

---

[47] EuGH 15.12.2011 – C-384/10, NZA 2012, 227 Rn. 38; 15.3.2011 – C-29/10, EuZW 2011, 302 Rn. 49; dem zustimmend: Franzen/Gallner/Oetker, Kommentar zum europäischen Arbeitsrecht/Krebber, 5. Aufl. 2024, Rom I-VO Art. 8 Rn. 37.

[48] EuGH 14.9.2017 – C-168/16 & C-169/16, NZA 2017, 1477 Rn. 63; Generalanwältin beim EuGH (Trstenjak), Schlussantrag v. 16.12.2010 – C-29/10, BeckRS 2010, 91454 Rn. 96; Geimer/Schütze, Internationaler Rechtsverkehr/Paulus, 66. EL Januar 2023, VO (EG) 1215/2012 Art. 21 Rn 31; Mankowski/Knöfel EuZA 2011, 521 (529); Rauscher, EuZPR/EuIPR/Mankowski, 5. Aufl. 2021, Brüssel Ia-VO Art. 21 Rn. 21.

[49] Dies wird vereinzelt als zu subjektives Kriterium zurückgewiesen, vgl. Junker ZZP Int 3 (1998), 179 (195); s. hierzu auch die untenstehenden Ausführungen zur vertragswidrigen Verlegung des Arbeitsortes durch den Arbeitnehmer.

[50] EuGH 15.12.2011 – C-384/10, EuZW 2012, 61 Rn. 37; 15.3.2011 – C-29/10, EuZW 2011, 302 Rn. 39; 9.1.1997 – C-383/95, NZA 1997, 225 Rn. 23.

[51] EuGH 27.2.2002 – C -37/00, NZA 2002, 459 Rn. 50, 58.

[52] Beck'scher Online-Kommentar ZPO/Spohnheimer, 52. Ed. 1.3.2024, Brüssel Ia-VO Art. 21 Rn. 9; Rauscher, EuZPR/EuIPR/Mankowski, 5. Aufl. 2021, Brüssel Ia-VO Art. 21 Rn. 15; Garber FS Kaissis, 2012, 221 (223).

die tatsächliche Durchführung des Arbeitsverhältnisses. Es kommt also darauf an, wie das Arbeitsverhältnis tatsächlich gelebt wird.

Dem vertraglich vereinbarten Arbeitsort kommt nur in Ausnahmefällen bei der Bestimmung des gewöhnlichen Arbeitsortes eine weitreichendere Bedeutung zu, wenn der Arbeitnehmer (beispielsweise bei einer ausschließlichen Tätigkeit im Homeoffice) vertragswidrig einen anderen Arbeitsort gewählt hat und – oftmals unbemerkt vom Arbeitgeber – von dort aus tätig geworden ist. Denn andernfalls könnte der Arbeitnehmer durch sein vertragswidriges Verhalten einen Gerichtsstand einseitig festlegen.[53]

Hierbei kann es auch nicht darauf ankommen, ob der Arbeitgeber konkrete Kenntnis von der absprachewidrigen Verlegung des Arbeitsortes hatte.[54] Zum einen kann einer bloßen Duldung eines Verhaltens kein rechtserheblicher Erklärungswert entnommen werden. Zum anderen müsste dann konsequenterweise weiter danach gefragt werden, auf wessen Kenntnis es hierbei ankommen soll. Dabei könnte es auf die Kenntnis des Vorgesetzten des Arbeitnehmers ankommen. In entsprechender Anwendung der Grundsätze im Rahmen des nationalen Kündigungsrechts könnte demgegenüber auch mit guten Argumenten ausschließlich auf eine etwaige Kenntnis der vertretungsberechtigten Person(en) abzustellen sein. Allein schon zur Vermeidung derartiger Unsicherheiten sollte daher vorzugswürdig in diesen Konstellationen auf den vertraglich vereinbarten Arbeitsort abgestellt werden.[55]

bb) Anteil der Arbeitszeit

Entscheidendes Kriterium ist danach die Zeit, welche der Arbeitnehmer in Ausübung seiner vertraglichen Tätigkeit an bestimmten Orten oder in bestimmten Staaten verbringt. Der gewöhnliche Arbeitsort setzt danach das Überschreiten einer Mindestschwelle voraus. Nach der in Rechtsprechung und Literatur hierzu entwickelten Faustformel soll es für das Vorliegen eines gewöhnlichen Arbeitsortes grundsätzlich ausreichen, wenn ein Arbeitnehmer mindestens etwa 60% seiner Arbeitszeit an einem bestimmten Ort verbringt bzw. hierzu jedenfalls nach dem Vertrag angehalten wäre.[56]

Hierbei soll eine Betrachtung der gesamten Tätigkeit des Arbeitnehmers im Rahmen des bestehenden Arbeitsverhältnisses vorzunehmen sein.[57] Dies würde jedoch dazu führen, dass der gewöhnliche Arbeitsort erst *ex post* festgelegt und so aktuellen Planungserwartungen der Parteien während des laufenden Arbeitsverhältnisses nicht gerecht werden würde. Dies erscheint nicht interessengerecht und ist

---

[53] Domröse DB 2008, 1626 (1628f.); Rauscher, EuZPR/EuIPR/Mankowski, 5. Aufl. 2021, Brüssel Ia-VO Art. 21 Rn. 16; Reinhard/Böggemann NJW 2008, 1263 (1265); Beck'scher Online-Kommentar ZPO/Spohnheimer, 52. Ed. 1.3.2024, Brüssel Ia-VO Art. 21 Rn. 9a.

[54] AA: Staudinger, BGB/Magnus, 2002, EGBGB Art. 30 Rn. 101.

[55] So im Ergebnis auch Domröse DB 2008, 1626 (1628f.).

[56] EuGH 9.1.1997 – C-383/95, NZA 1997, 225 Rn. 25 (2/3 des Zeitraums der ausgeübten Tätigkeit); OGH 10.07.2008 – 8 ObA 33/08y, BeckRS 2010, 1640 (63% des Zeitraums der ausgeübten Tätigkeit); Saenger, ZPO/Dörner, 10. Aufl. 2023, EuGVVO Art. 21 Rn. 5; Münchener Kommentar zur ZPO/Gottwald, 6. Aufl. 2022, Brüssel Ia-VO Art. 21 Rn. 6; Geimer/Schütze, EuZVR/Geimer, 4. Aufl. 2020, EuGVVO Art. 21 Rn. 9.

[57] EuGH 27.2.2002 – C-37/00, NZA 2002, 459 Rn. 52.

daher richtigerweise abzulehnen.[58] Denn der Gerichtsstand des gewöhnlichen Arbeitsorts soll eine Klageerhebung nur an dem Ort ermöglichen, an dem zum Zeitpunkt der Klageerhebung der Schwerpunkt des Arbeitsverhältnisses des Arbeitnehmers liegt. Dieser kann sich aber entsprechend im Laufe des Arbeitsverhältnisses ändern, ohne dass der Zeitraum der Tätigkeit am „neuen" gewöhnlichen Arbeitsort gegenüber dem Zeitraum der Tätigkeit an dem bisherigen gewöhnlichen Arbeitsort – gemessen an der Gesamtdauer des Arbeitsverhältnisses – überwiegen würde.

Unabhängig davon ist die vorstehend genannte Faustformel freilich nicht schematisch anzuwenden. Vielmehr sind – wie bereits eingangs ausgeführt – stets auch qualitative und organisatorische Aspekte des Einzelfalles zu beachten.[59]

3. Base rule – Ort des gewöhnlichen Arbeitsantritts

Durch ein ausschließliches Abstellen auf den Ort, an dem der Arbeitnehmer überwiegend tätig geworden ist, konnten Arbeitnehmer, bei denen eine internationale Mobilität wesentlicher Teil der Arbeitsleistung ist, von dem Gerichtsstand des Arbeitsorts nach dem ausdrücklichen Wortlaut der bisherigen Regelung nicht erfasst werden, wodurch der durch den Gerichtsstand des Arbeitsorts beabsichtigte umfassende Arbeitnehmerschutz nicht (mehr) gewahrt wurde. Daher wurde mit der Reform durch die Brüssel Ia-VO – wiederum parallel zu der Regelung in Art. 8 Abs. 2 Satz 1 Rom I-VO – in Umsetzung der von der Rechtsprechung des EuGH[60] entwickelten Ausprägungen des Begriffs des Arbeitsorts zusätzlich ein Gerichtsstand am Ort des gewöhnlichen Arbeitsantritts eingeführt (sog. base rule).[61] Hierdurch wird zum Ausdruck gebracht, dass ein Staat für einen Arbeitnehmer auch eine Art Stützpunkt oder Basis sein kann.[62]

Jedoch stehen die Anknüpfungen an den Arbeitsort, „an dem" der Arbeitnehmer seine Arbeit verrichtet oder zuletzt verrichtet hat und „von dem aus" der Arbeitnehmer seine Arbeit verrichtet oder zuletzt verrichtet hat, in einem Subsidiaritätsverhältnis zueinander. Primäre Anknüpfung ist der Arbeitsort, „an dem" die Tätigkeit verrichtet wird. Erst wenn ein solcher Ort, an dem gewöhnlich die Arbeit verrichtet wird, nicht festgestellt werden kann, gelangt die base rule zur Anwendung.[63]

---

[58] Domröse DB 2008, 1626 (1629); Mankowski IPRax 2003, 21 (23); aA: Kropholler/von Hein, Europäisches Zivilprozessrecht, 9. Aufl. 2011, EuGVVO Art. 19 Rn. 5.

[59] Rauscher, EuZPR/EuIPR/Mankowski, 5. Aufl. 2021, Brüssel Ia-VO Art. 21 Rn. 17; Musielak/Voit, ZPO/Stadler/Krüger, 21. Aufl. 2024, EuGVVO Art. 21 Rn. 2.

[60] Vgl. EuGH 14.9.2017 – C-168/16 & C-169/16, NZA 2017, 1477 Rn. 62.

[61] Münchener Kommentar zur ZPO/Gottwald, 6. Aufl. 2022, Brüssel Ia-VO Art. 21 Rn. 12; Beck'scher Online-Kommentar ZPO/Spohnheimer, 52. Ed. 1.3.2024, Brüssel Ia-VO Art. 21 Rn. 12; Temming NZA 2017, 1437 (1438); dies wurde vom EuGH bis dahin noch offengelassen, vgl. EuGH 14.9.2017 – C-168/16 & C-169/16, NZA 2017, 1477 Rn. 60.

[62] Münchener Kommentar zum BGB/Martiny, 8. Aufl. 2021, Rom I-VO Art. 8 Rn. 56; Rauscher, EuZPR/EuIPR/Mankowski, 5. Aufl. 2021, Brüssel Ia-VO Art. 21 Rn. 29; Knöfel RdA 2006, 269 (274).

[63] Ulrici jurisPR-ArbR 41/2013 Anm. 2; Wieczorek/Schütze, ZPO/Temming, 5. Aufl. 2022, VO (EU) 1215/2012 Art. 21 Rn. 3; Knöfel GPR 2019, 43 (45).

Für die Begründung eines Gerichtsstands am Ort, von dem aus gewöhnlich die Arbeit verrichtet wird, darf es sich hierbei nicht nur um den bloßen Rückkehrort handeln. Vielmehr muss dieser eine gewisse Bedeutung für das Arbeitsverhältnis in zeitlicher und fachlicher Hinsicht haben.[64] So können beispielsweise dort regelmäßig getätigte Vorbereitungshandlungen oder die Verwahrung von Arbeitskleidung oder anderer Arbeitsmittel Indizien sein, damit der Rückkehrort eine den Anforderungen nach Art. 21 Abs. 1 lit. b sublit. (i) Brüssel Ia-VO genügende „Einsatz- bzw. Operationsbasis" darstellen kann.[65]

4. *Letzter gewöhnlicher Arbeitsort*

Demgegenüber überdauert der Anknüpfungspunkt des letzten gewöhnlichen Arbeitsortes das Arbeitsverhältnis und greift folglich auch dann ein, wenn das Arbeitsverhältnis im Zeitpunkt der Klageerhebung nicht mehr besteht.[66]

a) Reichweite der Anknüpfung

Noch nicht abschließend geklärt ist jedoch die konkrete Reichweite des Gerichtsstands des letzten gewöhnlichen Arbeitsorts. Nach überwiegender Auffassung umfasst dieser zutreffender Weise (allein) Streitigkeiten zwischen Arbeitgeber und Arbeitnehmer, die nach Beendigung des Arbeitsverhältnisses entstanden sind.[67]

Wenn das Arbeitsverhältnis im Zeitpunkt der Klageerhebung noch besteht, ist demgegenüber allein der aktuelle gewöhnliche Arbeitsort maßgeblich.[68] Auf frühere gewöhnliche Arbeitsorte kann es nicht ankommen. Insoweit kommt dem Arbeitnehmer auch kein Wahlrecht zu.[69]

---

[64] Beck'scher Online-Kommentar ZPO/Spohnheimer, 52. Ed. 1.3.2024, Brüssel Ia-VO Art. 21 Rn. 13; Generalanwältin beim EuGH (Trstenjak), Schlussantrag v. 16.12.2010 – C-29/10, BeckRS 2010, 91454 Rn. 94; Rauscher, EuZPR/EuIPR/Mankowski, 5. Aufl. 2021, Brüssel Ia-VO Art. 21 Rn. 33.

[65] Geimer/Schütze, Internationaler Rechtsverkehr/Paulus, 66. EL Januar 2023, VO (EG) 1215/2012 Art. 21 Rn. 27.

[66] Münchener Kommentare zur ZPO/Gottwald, 6. Aufl. 2022, Brüssel Ia-VO Art. 21 Rn. 10; Geimer/Schütze, EuZVR/Geimer, 4. Aufl. 2020, EuGVVO Art. 21 Rn. 22; Wieczorek/Schütze, ZPO/Temming, 5. Aufl. 2022, VO (EU) 1215/2012 Art. 21 Rn. 115.

[67] Geimer/Schütze, EuZVR/Geimer, 4. Aufl. 2020, EuGVVO Art. 21 Rn. 23; Rauscher, EuZPR/EuIPR/Mankowski, 5. Aufl. 2021, Brüssel Ia-VO Art. 21 Rn. 83; Wieczorek/Schütze, ZPO/Temming, 5. Aufl. 2022, VO (EU) 1215/2012 Art. 21 Rn. 112; Geimer/Schütze, Internationaler Rechtsverkehr/Paulus, 66. EL Januar 2023, VO (EG) 1215/2012 Art. 21 Rn. 18.

[68] Rauscher, EuZPR/EuIPR/Mankowski, 5. Aufl. 2021, Brüssel Ia-VO Art. 21 Rn. 83; Wieczorek/Schütze, ZPO/Temming, 5. Aufl. 2022, VO (EU) 1215/2012 Art. 21 Rn. 112; Geimer/Schütze, EuZVR/Geimer, 4. Aufl. 2020, EuGVVO Art. 21 Rn. 23; Hausmann EuLF 2000/2001, 40, 47; Burgstaller/Neumayr, Internationales Zivilverfahrensrecht/Garber, 2015, EuGVVO Art. 21 Rn. 10.

[69] Kropholler/von Hein, Europäisches Zivilprozessrecht, 9. Aufl. 2011, EuGVVO Art. 19 Rn. 6; Rauscher, EuZPR/EuIPR/Mankowski, 5. Aufl. 2021, Brüssel Ia-VO Art. 21 Rn. 81; Thüsing NZA 2003, 1303 (1310).

b) *Entsendung von Arbeitnehmern*

Durch eine bloß vorübergehende Entsendung wird der bisher bestehende gewöhnliche Arbeitsort jedoch nicht bereits aufgehoben.[70] Dies folgt jedenfalls aus der Regelung in Art. 8 Abs. 2 S. 2 Rom I-VO, wonach der Staat, in dem die Arbeit gewöhnlich verrichtet wird, nicht wechselt, wenn der Arbeitnehmer seine Arbeit vorübergehend in einem anderen Staat verrichtet.[71] Andernfalls hätte es der Arbeitgeber in der Hand, durch eine kurzfristige und vorübergehende Entsendung auf Grundlage seines Direktionsrechts den wesentlichen Gerichtsstand des Arbeitnehmers zu verlegen.[72]

Offen ist jedoch, ab welcher Zeitdauer keine nur vorübergehende Entsendung mehr vorliegen soll. Gemäß ErwGr. 36 S. 1 Rom I-VO soll die Erbringung der Arbeitsleistung in einem anderen Staat als vorübergehend gelten, wenn von dem Arbeitnehmer erwartet wird, dass er nach seinem Arbeitseinsatz im Ausland seine Arbeit im Herkunftsstaat wieder aufnimmt. Daher wird überwiegend angenommen, dass erst eine endgültige Verlagerung zu einem Wechsel des gewöhnlichen Arbeitsortes führen könne.[73] Demgegenüber wird teilweise auf bestimmte Zeitgrenzen abgestellt.[74]

Richtigerweise ist hierbei jedoch wiederum auf die Umstände des Einzelfalles abzustellen.[75] Indizien, die für eine nur vorübergehende Natur der Entsendung sprechen, können beispielsweise die vertragliche Vereinbarung einer von beiden Parteien beabsichtigten Rückkehr des Arbeitnehmers sein[76] oder die tatsächlich bestehende Möglichkeit des Arbeitnehmers zur Rückkehr an den bisherigen gewöhnlichen Arbeitsort aufgrund des Vorhaltens eines Arbeitsplatzes durch den Arbeitgeber.[77] Sofern der Arbeitnehmer lediglich zur Verrichtung von Tätigkeiten im

---

[70] ArbG Bielefeld 2.12.2008 – 3 Ca 2703/08, BeckRS 2008, 58340; Saenger, ZPO/Dörner, 10. Aufl. 2023, EUGVVO Art. 21 Rn. 5; Burgstaller/Neumayr, Internationales Zivilverfahrensrecht/Garber, 2015, EuGVVO Art. 21 Rn. 25.

[71] Geimer/Schütze, Internationaler Rechtsverkehr/Paulus, 66. EL Januar 2023, VO (EG) 1215/2012 Art. 21 Rn. 29; Wieczorek/Schütze, ZPO/Temming, 5. Aufl. 2022, VO (EU) 1215/2012 Art. 21 Rn. 71; Kropholler/von Hein, Europäisches Zivilprozessrecht, 9. Aufl. 2011, EuGVVO Art. 19 Rn. 7.

[72] Burgstaller/Neumayr, Internationales Zivilverfahrensrecht/Garber, 2015, EuGVVO Art. 21 Rn. 25; Rauscher, EuZPR/EuIPR/Mankowski, 5. Aufl. 2021, Brüssel Ia-VO Art. 21 Rn. 23; Wieczorek/Schütze, ZPO/Temming, 5. Aufl. 2022, VO (EU) 1215/2012 Art. 21 Rn. 71.

[73] Geimer/Schütze, EuZVR/Geimer, 4. Aufl. 2020, EuGVVO Art. 21 Rn. 11; Franzen/Gallner/Oetker, Kommentar zum europäischen Arbeitsrecht/Krebber, 5. Aufl. 2024, VO (EG) 593/2008 Art. 8 Rn. 38.

[74] Vgl. Geimer/Schütze, Internationaler Rechtsverkehr/Paulus, 66. EL Januar 2023, VO (EG) 1215/2012 Art. 21 Rn. 29, wonach jedenfalls eine Entsendung von bis zu einem Jahr noch unschädlich sein soll; vgl. auch Art. 12 Abs. 1 VO (EG) Nr. 883/2004, wonach die Entsendung von bis zu 24 Monaten das Sozialversicherungsstatut unberührt lässt.

[75] Münchener Kommentar zum BGB/Martiny, 8. Aufl. 2021, Rom I-VO Art. 8 Rn. 66; Wieczorek/Schütze, ZPO/Temming, 5. Aufl. 2022, VO (EU) 1215/2012 Art. 21 Rn. 73.

[76] Hierbei sind jedoch die Grenzen des Rechtsmissbrauchs zu beachten, beispielsweise wenn der Arbeitgeber trotz langjähriger Auslandsentsendung weiter auf einem zeitlich unbefristet vereinbarten Rückrufrecht bestehen sollte, um einen Wechsel des gewöhnlichen Arbeitsortes zu verhindern; vgl. LAG Hessen 28.5.2008 – 8 Sa 2179/06, BeckRS 2008, 55973 Rn. 27.

[77] Däubler RIW 1987, 249 (251); Schmidt-Hermesdorf RIW 1988, 938 (940); Rauscher, EuZPR/EuIPR/Mankowski, 5. Aufl. 2021, Brüssel Ia-VO Art. 21 Rn. 24.

Rahmen eines konkreten Projektes entsendet wird, spricht dies ebenfalls für eine nur vorübergehende Entsendung.[78]

c) *Wechsel des gewöhnlichen Arbeitsortes aufgrund von Homeoffice*

In der Praxis kommt es – spätestens seit der vorübergehenden Einführung einer entsprechenden Pflicht für bestimmte Arbeitnehmergruppen während der Corona-Pandemie – vermehrt zu Konstellationen, bei denen Arbeitnehmer überwiegend vom Homeoffice aus tätig sind. Dabei kann dies insbesondere bei Grenzgängern dazu führen, dass die Tätigkeiten in diesen Fällen von einem ausländischen Wohnsitz aus erbracht werden. Gleiches gilt für Fälle des sog. Workation, bei denen Arbeitnehmer vor, nach oder zwischen Urlaubstagen vor Ort im Ausland Arbeitstätigkeiten im Rahmen von mobiler Arbeit verrichten.

Die Tätigkeit im ausländischen Homeoffice kann – in Fällen von Workation nur bei zeitlich sehr ausgedehnten Auslandsaufenthalten – dazu führen, dass der gewöhnliche Arbeitsort sodann am Standort der Homeoffice-Tätigkeit besteht.[79] Denn insoweit kommt es auf den Ort der Erbringung der Arbeitsleistung und nicht auf den Ort, an den die Arbeitsergebnisse versendet werden, an.[80]

Arbeitgebern sollte daher bewusst sein, dass in Fällen einer all zu großzügigen Handhabung der Homeoffice-Tätigkeit ihrer Arbeitnehmer hierdurch auch – neben den ebenfalls besonders zu beachtenden steuer- und sozialversicherungsrechtlichen Implikationen einer Tätigkeit aus dem Ausland – der gewöhnliche Arbeitsort wechseln und folglich ein nicht vorgesehener Gerichtsstand im Ausland (sowie im Falle einer fehlenden Rechtswahl u. U. auch ein Wechsel des anwendbaren Rechts) entstehen kann. In diesen Konstellationen wird freilich der von dem Gerichtsstand des Arbeitsortes eigentlich bezweckte Schutz der Arbeitnehmer stark überstrapaziert.

5. *Fehlende Feststellbarkeit eines gewöhnlichen Arbeitsortes*

Jedoch führt nicht jeder tatsächliche Arbeitsort auch zum Vorliegen eines gewöhnlichen Arbeitsortes. Denn einen tatsächlichen oder relativ überwiegenden Arbeitsort wird es immer geben, so dass die – nachrangig anzuwendende – Anknüpfung an den Ort der einstellenden Niederlassung (Art. 21 Abs. 1 lit. b sublit. (ii) Brüssel Ia-VO) andernfalls obsolet werden würde.[81] Daher bedarf es zur Feststellung eines gewöhnlichen Arbeitsortes einer besonderen und spezifischen Qualität und Ortsbezogenheit.

So fehlt es beispielsweise an einem gewöhnlichen Arbeitsort, wenn der Arbeitnehmer seine Tätigkeit an zwei oder mehr gleich bedeutsamen Arbeitsorten aus-

---

[78] Junker ZIAS 1995, 564 (568); Hänlein ZIAS 1996, 21 (38); Rauscher, EuZPR/EuIPR/Mankowski, 5. Aufl. 2021, Brüssel Ia-VO Art. 21 Rn. 26.

[79] Vgl. LAG Niedersachsen 12.7.2021 – 12 Sa 1341/20, BeckRS 2021, 26119 Rn. 54ff.; Kuhn/Marceau/Rosemann NZA 2023, 393 (396).

[80] Beck'scher Online-Kommentar ZPO/Spohnheimer, 52. Ed. 1.3.2024, Brüssel Ia-VO Art. 21 Rn. 9a; Geimer/Schütze, EuZVR/Geimer, 4. Aufl. 2020, EuGVVO Art. 21 Rn. 9, 20; Wieczorek/Schütze, ZPO/Temming, 5. Aufl. 2022, VO (EU) 1215/2012 Art. 21 Rn. 82, 84.

[81] Rauscher, EuZPR/EuIPR/Mankowski, 5. Aufl. 2021, Brüssel Ia-VO Art. 21 Rn. 16.

führt und folglich kein Ort festgestellt werden kann, an dem hauptsächlich die Arbeitsleistungen erbracht werden.[82] Gleiches gilt, wenn an keinem der tatsächlichen Arbeitsorte ein hinreichend fester und intensiver Bezug zu der geleisteten Arbeit festgestellt werden kann, so dass keiner dieser Arbeitsorte als Hauptbezugsort angesehen werden kann.[83]

Wenn sich der gewöhnliche Arbeitsort jedoch nur deshalb nicht bestimmen lässt, weil mehrere Orte innerhalb desselben Mitgliedstaates in Betracht kommen, gilt dies freilich nicht. In derartigen Fallkonstellationen ist die internationale Zuständigkeit der (Arbeits-)Gerichte dieses Mitgliedstaates dessen ungeachtet nach Art. 21 Abs. 1 lit. b sublit. (i) Brüssel Ia-VO zu bejahen.[84] Andernfalls würde dem Arbeitnehmer die internationale Zuständigkeit des Mitgliedstaates, in dem er gewöhnlich gearbeitet hat, verwehrt. Die Auswahl eines konkreten gewöhnlichen Arbeitsortes wird insoweit erst bei der örtlichen Zuständigkeit relevant. Diesbezüglich ist dann eine wertende Schwerpunktbetrachtung vorzunehmen.

III. Bestimmung des gewöhnlichen Arbeitsortes bei fliegendem Personal

Bei der Bestimmung des gewöhnlichen Arbeitsortes bei fliegendem Personal findet – mangels einer ortsfesten Ausübung der Tätigkeiten des Flugpersonals im Ansatz zutreffend – die sog. base rule Anwendung.[85] Insoweit legen Historie und Genese der Regelung deren Anwendung auf das fliegende Personal nahe.[86]

1. Anknüpfung an Heimatbasis

In Anwendung der base rule soll es bei Arbeitnehmern des internationalen Luftverkehrs grundsätzlich auf denjenigen Ort ankommen, „von dem aus" regelmäßig die Pilotentätigkeit, Flugbegleitung oder Transporttätigkeit etc. stattfindet. Daher sollen Angehörige des fliegenden Personals ihren gewöhnlichen Arbeitsort regelmäßig am Ort ihrer Einsatz- bzw. Heimatbasis haben.[87]

Die Heimatbasis ist nach OPS 1.1095 Ziff. 1.7. Anh. III VO (EWG) 3922/91 (Verordnung zur Harmonisierung der technischen Vorschriften und der Verwaltungsverfahren in der Zivilluftfahrt) der vom Luftfahrtunternehmer gegenüber dem Besatzungsmitglied benannte Ort, wo das Besatzungsmitglied normalerweise eine Dienstzeit oder eine Abfolge von Dienstzeiten beginnt und beendet und wo der Luft-

[82] Zöller, ZPO/Geimer, 35. Aufl. 2024, VO (EU) 1215/2012 Art. 21 Rn. 6; Geimer/Schütze, Internationaler Rechtsverkehr/Paulus, 66. EL Januar 2023, VO (EG) 1215/2012 Art. 21 Rn. 35.

[83] Geimer/Schütze, EuZVR/Geimer, 4. Aufl. 2020, EuGVVO Art. 21 Rn. 10; Zöller, ZPO/Geimer, 35. Aufl. 2024, VO (EU) 1215/2012 Art. 21 Rn. 6.

[84] Beck'scher Online-Kommentar ZPO/Spohnheimer, 52. Ed. 1.3.2024, Brüssel Ia-VO Art. 21 Rn. 11; Rauscher, EuZPR/EuIPR/Mankowski, 5. Aufl. 2021, Brüssel Ia-VO Art. 21 Rn. 28.

[85] Pfeiffer EuZW 2008, 622 (627).

[86] Rauscher, EuZPR/EuIPR/Mankowski, 5. Aufl. 2021, Brüssel Ia-VO Art. 21 Rn. 54.

[87] Geimer/Schütze, Internationaler Rechtsverkehr/Paulus, 66. EL Januar 2023, VO (EG) 1215/2012 Art. 21 Rn. 34; Saenger, ZPO/Dörner, 10. Aufl. 2023, EuGVVO Art. 21 Rn. 5; Schlosser/Hess, EU-Zivilprozessrecht/Schlosser, 5. Aufl. 2021, Brüssel Ia-VO Art. 21 Rn. 1; Bayreuther NZA 2010, 262 (265); Magnus IPRax 2010, 27 (41).

fahrtunternehmer normalerweise nicht für die Unterbringung des betreffenden Arbeitnehmers verantwortlich ist.[88] D. h., die Heimatbasis ist nach dieser Legaldefinition derjenige Ort, an dem Angehörige des fliegenden Personals systematisch ihren Arbeitstag beginnen und beenden und dem Arbeitgeber zur Verfügung stehen, so dass diese für gewöhnlich auch ihren Wohnsitz in der Nähe der Heimatbasis haben werden. Die Heimatbasis ist nach OPS 1.1090 Ziff. 3.1. Anh. III VO (EWG) 3922/91 durch den Luftfahrtunternehmer für jedes Besatzungsmitglied anzugeben.[89] Dies könnte daher mit der Verpflichtung des Arbeitgebers nach nationalem Recht gemäß § 2 Abs. 1 S. 2 Nr. 4 NachwG zur Angabe des Arbeitsortes in der Niederschrift der wesentlichen Vertragsbedingungen des Arbeitsverhältnisses gleichzusetzen sein.

Aus den vorstehend genannten Regelungen der VO (EWG) 3922/91 (bzw. VO (EU) Nr. 83/2014) wird gefolgert, dass von der Heimatbasis aus der wesentliche Teil der Verpflichtungen erfüllt werde, da die Flüge von dort aus beginnen und auch beendet werden. Auch würden die Weisungen des Arbeitgebers dort entgegengenommen werden. Deshalb sei auf die Heimatbasis als gewöhnlichen Arbeitsort abzustellen.[90] Insoweit sei von einem übergreifenden Prinzip der Anknüpfung an die Heimatbasis auszugehen.[91]

Hierfür ließe sich ferner anführen, dass die Heimatbasis zentraler Bezugspunkt der arbeitszeitrechtlichen Regelungen für Besatzungsmitglieder ist. So knüpfen die bei Besatzungsmitgliedern einzuhaltenden Ruhezeiten an die Heimatbasis an (vgl. ORO.FTL.235 Anh. II VO (EU) Nr. 83/2014 bzw. OPS 1.1110 Ziff. 1 Anh. III VO (EWG) 3922/91). Jedoch gehören Ruhezeiten gerade nicht zur Arbeitszeit und sind daher für die – allein auf die Arbeitsverpflichtung – abstellende Bestimmung des gewöhnlichen Arbeitsortes irrelevant.

Darüber hinaus ist die Heimatbasis gemäß Art. 11 Abs. 5 VO (EG) 883/2004 idF der VO (EU) 465/2012 auch Anknüpfungspunkt zur Bestimmung der für Besatzungsmitglieder geltenden sozialrechtlichen Vorschriften. Hierdurch soll nach ErwGr. 18b VO (EG) 883/2004 idF der VO (EU) 465/2012 bei Besatzungsmitgliedern die Kontinuität bei der Anwendung der sozialrechtlichen Vorschriften gesichert werden. Dieser Zweck könnte ebenso auf den auf einen möglichst umfassenden Schutz der Arbeitnehmer ausgerichteten Gerichtsstand des Arbeitsortes übertragen werden.[92]

2. *Heimatbasis nur mit Indizwirkung*

Nach der Rechtsprechung des EuGH kann die Heimatbasis jedoch nicht ohne Weiteres mit dem gewöhnlichen Arbeitsort bei fliegendem Personal gleichgesetzt werden.[93] Für den gewöhnlichen Arbeitsort sei vielmehr zu ermitteln, in welchem Mitgliedstaat der Ort liegt, von dem aus der Arbeitnehmer seine Verkehrsdienste erbringt, an den er danach zurückkehrt, an dem er Anweisungen dazu erhält und

[88] S. hierzu auch ORO.FTL.105 Ziff. 14 Anh. II VO (EU) Nr. 83/2014.
[89] S. hierzu auch ORO.FTL.200 Anh. II VO (EU) Nr. 83/2014.
[90] BAG 20.12.2012 – 2 AZR 481/11, NZA 2013, 925 Rn. 24, 26.
[91] Knöfel GPR 2019, 43 (47).
[92] Demgegenüber stellt der EuGH allein auf ErwGr. 1 VO (EG) 883/2004 und das darin formulierte Ziel der Verbesserung des Lebensstandards und der Arbeitsbedingungen ab.
[93] EuGH 14.9.2017 – C-168/16 & C-169/16, NZA 2017, 1477 Rn. 65f.

seine Arbeit organisiert und an dem sich die Arbeitsmittel befinden. Ferner sei der Ort zu berücksichtigen, an dem die Flugzeuge stationiert sind, in denen die Arbeit gewöhnlich verrichtet wird.[94]

Gleichwohl stellt die Heimatbasis auch nach der jüngeren Rechtsprechung ein gewichtiges Indiz für die Bestimmung des Ortes, an dem der Arbeitnehmer gewöhnlich seine Arbeit verrichtet, dar.[95] Danach soll die Heimatbasis im Ergebnis immer dann gewöhnlicher Arbeitsort sein, sofern kein außergewöhnlicher Fall vorliegt, bei dem eine engere Verbindung zu einem anderen Ort besteht, der dann als gewöhnlicher Arbeitsort anzusehen sei.[96] Gemeint ist hiermit aber wohl eher, dass der gewöhnliche Arbeitsort ein anderer Ort als die Heimatbasis sein kann, wenn die den gewöhnlichen Arbeitsort ausfüllenden tatsächlichen Umstände im Einzelfall anderswo verwirklicht sind.[97] Denn anders als im IPR kommt es im Rahmen des Gerichtsstands des Arbeitsorts gerade nicht auf eine engere Verbindung an. Eine solche Ausweichklausel kann den Zuständigkeiten in Art. 21 Brüssel Ia-VO – wie bereits oben dargestellt – nicht entnommen werden.

Die nur indizielle Bedeutung der Heimatbasis ist dabei mit Blick auf den Arbeitnehmerschutz konsequent. Denn bei einer automatischen Gleichsetzung des gewöhnlichen Arbeitsortes mit der Heimatbasis könne dies zu rechtsmissbräuchlichen Gestaltungen durch den Arbeitgeber führen, da dieser den Ort der Heimatbasis einseitig bestimmen kann.[98] Ob diese Bedenken angesichts der etwaige Gestaltungsmöglichkeiten der Arbeitgeber erheblich einschränkenden praktischen Erfordernisse tatsächlich durchgreifen, erscheint zumindest zweifelhaft.

3. *Anknüpfung an Registerstaat*

Demgegenüber wird teilweise die Auffassung vertreten, es sei auf den Registerstaat des jeweiligen Flugzeugs abzustellen. Nach Art. 17 Chicago Convention[99] haben Luftfahrzeuge die Staatszugehörigkeit des Staates, in dem sie eingetragen sind. Das fliegende Personal habe seinen gewöhnlichen Arbeitsort an Bord des jeweiligen Flugzeugs und damit im Registerstaat.[100] Hier werden von dem Bordpersonal gerade die spezifischen Tätigkeiten des Arbeitsverhältnisses verrichtet. Im Übrigen sei die Anknüpfung

---

[94] EuGH 14.9.2017 – C-168/16 & C-169/16, NZA 2017, 1477 Rn. 63f.; BAG 7.5.2020 – 2 AZR 692/19, NZA 2021, 225 Rn. 27.

[95] EuGH 14.9.2017 – C-168/16 & C-169/16, NZA 2017, 1477 Rn. 69; BAG 7.5.2020 – 2 AZR 692/19, NZA 2021, 225 Rn. 28; aA: Winkler v. Mohrenfels EuZA 2018, 236 (245).

[96] Franzen/Gallner/Oetker, Kommentar zum europäischen Arbeitsrecht/Krebber, 5. Aufl. 2024, VO (EU) 1215/2012 Art. 21 Rn. 8; EuGH 14.9.2017 – C-168/16 & C-169/16, NZA 2017, 1477 Rn. 70; BAG 7.5.2020 – 2 AZR 692/19, NZA 2021, 225 Rn. 29; in diese Richtung auch bereits Lüttringhaus IPRax 2011, 554 (557).

[97] Knöfel GPR 2019, 43 (47).

[98] Ulrici EuZW 2017, 947 (948).

[99] Chicago Convention on International Civil Aviation of 7 December 1944, BGBl. 1956 II 411 (442); Art. 17 Chicago Convention lautet: „Luftfahrzeuge haben die Staatszugehörigkeit des Staates, in dem sie eingetragen sind".

[100] Zöller, ZPO/Geimer, 35. Aufl. 2024, VO (EU) 1215/2012 Art. 21 Rn. 9; Münchener Kommentar zur ZPO/Gottwald, 6. Aufl. 2022, Brüssel Ia-VO Art. 21 Rn. 9; Geimer/Schütze, EuZVR, 4. Aufl. 2020, EuGVVO Art. 21 Rn. 19; Burgstaller/Neumayr, Internationales Zivilverfahrensrecht/Garber, 2015, EuGVVO Art. 21 Rn. 31; Kropholler/v. Hein, Europäisches Zivilpro-

an die base rule subsidiär und könne nur dann greifen, wenn es keinen Ort gebe, an dem die Tätigkeiten für gewöhnlich verrichtet werden. Die Tätigkeiten im Flugzeug würden danach den Tätigkeiten am Boden faktisch und normativ gegenüberstehen.[101]

Dieser Ansatz wird jedoch von der Rechtsprechung und weiten Teilen der Literatur abgelehnt. Danach soll bei Flugpersonal eine Anknüpfung an den Registerstaat für die Bestimmung des gewöhnlichen Arbeitsorts iSv. Art. 21 Abs. 1 lit. b sublit. (i) Brüssel Ia-VO nicht in Betracht kommen, da der Begriff des Ortes, an dem oder von dem aus der Arbeitnehmer gewöhnlich seine Arbeit verrichtet, mit keinem anderen Begriff gleichgesetzt werden könne, auch in Bezug auf die „Staatszugehörigkeit" von Flugzeugen.[102] Für die internationale Zuständigkeit gelte gerade kein Flaggen- bzw. Registerprinzip.[103] Im Übrigen sei den Bestimmungen der Chicago Convention kein Regelungsgehalt hinsichtlich des gewöhnlichen Arbeitsortes oder ein Zusammenhang zwischen Registerstaat und gewöhnlichem Aufenthalt zu entnehmen.[104] Vielmehr regele das darin enthaltene Registerprinzip die Zugehörigkeit dieses Transportmittels zu einem bestimmten Staat, um insbesondere die Ausübung staatlicher Hoheitsmacht über dieses Objekt und auf diesem in staatsfreien Räumen völkerrechtlich zu legitimieren und sicherzustellen.[105]

4. *Grenzen der Anknüpfung an Heimatbasis*

Hierbei wird jedoch übersehen, dass die Einsatzbasis nur dann in konsequenter Anwendung der base rule den gewöhnlichen Arbeitsort bilden kann, wenn hier auch ein wesentlicher Teil der Arbeitsleistung verrichtet wird. Denn der Einsatzbasis muss insoweit eine gewisse Bedeutung für das Arbeitsverhältnis in zeitlicher und fachlicher Hinsicht zukommen. Dies kann bei Piloten der Fall sein, wenn diese an der Heimatbasis die Vor- und Nachbereitung der Flüge, insbesondere sicherheitsrelevante Vorbereitungen oder Briefings und Nachbesprechungen des jeweiligen Flugeinsatzes, durchführen.[106] Ferner können Schulungen, Fortbildungen oder andere verpflichtende Termine, die am Ort der Einsatzbasis vorgenommen werden, hierbei eine Rolle spielen.[107] Hierbei ist jedoch zu berücksichtigen, dass die wesent-

zessrecht, 9. Aufl. 2011, EuGVVO Art. 19 Rn. 9b; offen gelassen bei Winkler von Mohrenfels EuZA 2018, 236 (246).

[101] Wurmnest EuZA 2009, 481 (496f.); Garber FS Schütze II, 2014, 81 (89).

[102] EuGH 14.9.2017 – C-168/16 & C-169/16, NZA 2017, 1477 Rn. 75f.; BAG 7.5.2020 – 2 AZR 692/19, NZA 2021, 225 Rn. 34; noch offen gelassen von BAG 20.12.2012 – 2 AZR 481/11, NZA 2013, 925 Rn. 28.

[103] Beck'scher Online-Kommentar ZPO/Spohnheimer, 52. Ed. 1.3.2024, Brüssel Ia-VO Art. 21 Rn. 13.2; Wieczorek/Schütze, ZPO/Temming, 5. Aufl. 2022, VO (EU) 1215/2012 Art. 21 Rn. 108.

[104] Generalanwalt beim EuGH (Saugmandsgaard Øe), Schlussantrag v. 27.4.2017 – C-168/16 & C-169/16, BeckRS 2017, 118644 Rn. 123ff.; Temming NZA 2017, 1437 (1440).

[105] Wieczorek/Schütze, ZPO/Temming, 5. Aufl. 2022, VO (EU) 1215/2012 Art. 21 Rn. 89: Generalanwalt beim EuGH (Saugmandsgaard Øe), Schlussantrag v. 27.4.2017 – C-168/16 & C-169/16, BeckRS 2017, 118644 Rn. 126.

[106] BAG 7.5.2020 – 2 AZR 692/19, NZA 2021, 225 Rn. 34; 20.12.2012 – 2 AZR 481/11, NZA 2013, 925 Rn. 27; LAG Berlin-Brandenburg 27.2.2018 – 6 SHa 140/18, NZA-RR 2018, 442 Rn. 25; LAG Rheinland-Pfalz 8.10.2019 – 6 Sa 97/19, BeckRS 2019, 39431 Rn. 33.

[107] Mankowski EWiR 2017, 739 (740).

lichen Tätigkeiten des fliegenden Personals oftmals nicht bereits an der Heimatbasis aufgenommen werden. Vielmehr ist durchaus üblich und wird in den Flugplänen entsprechend festgelegt, dass der Flug an einem anderen Flughafen als der Heimatbasis des fliegenden Personals startet. Dann beginnt zwar an der Heimatbasis die Dienstzeit, die schwerpunktmäßigen Tätigkeiten werden jedoch erst von einem anderen Ort aus aufgenommen, wenn dort das Einsatzflugzeug bestiegen wird (vgl. insoweit auch die Unterscheidung zwischen Dienstzeit und Flugdienstzeit gemäß OPS 1.1095 Ziff. 1.5. und Ziff. 1.6. Anh. III VO (EWG) 3922/91).

Bei denjenigen Arbeitnehmern des fliegenden Personals, die jedoch keine Arbeitstätigkeiten in entsprechendem Umfang an der Einsatzbasis verrichten, kann insoweit folgerichtig kein gewöhnlicher Arbeitsort an der Einsatzbasis begründet werden.[108] Wenn sich die von den Angehörigen des fliegenden Personals zu verrichtenden Tätigkeiten bei wertender Betrachtung keinem bestimmten Ort am Boden zuordnen lassen, ist das Transportmittel selbst der Arbeitsort und damit dem Land zuzurechnen, dessen „Staatsangehörigkeit" (vgl. Art. 17 Chicago Convention) in Bezug auf das Luftfahrzeug eingetragen ist.

Für diese Arbeitnehmer ist folglich auf den Registerstaat des Flugzeugs zurückzugreifen. Dem kann auch nicht pauschal ein potentieller Missbrauch durch etwaige Umgehungsstrategien seitens des Arbeitgebers entgegengehalten werden. Mag die Ablehnung der Anknüpfung an den Registerstaat auch aus sozialpolitischen Erwägungen und den Aspekten eines umfassenden Schutzes des strukturell schwächeren Arbeitnehmers wünschenswert sein,[109] so wäre in diesen Fällen aus dogmatischen Gründen eine Anknüpfung an einen vermeintlichen gewöhnlichen Arbeitsort am Boden verfehlt.

Im Übrigen wird auch in anderen Regelungsbereichen – wie beispielsweise bei Versetzungen des Kabinenpersonals im Sinne des nationalen Arbeitsrechts – an das Flugzeug als gewöhnlichen Arbeitsort des fliegenden Personals angeknüpft,[110] wenngleich diese Grundsätze aufgrund der vorzugswürdigen autonomen Auslegung selbstverständlich nicht ohne Weiteres auf die Bestimmung des gewöhnlichen Arbeitsortes im Rahmen der internationalen Zuständigkeit übertragen werden können.

5. *Wechseldienst*

Bei (ständigem) Wechseldienst bei verschiedenen Fluglinien fehlt es dagegen – unabhängig davon, ob an die Heimatbasis, verschiedene Indizien oder an den Registerstaat angeknüpft wird – an einem gewöhnlichen Arbeitsort.[111]

---

108 Garber FS Schütze II, 2014, 81 (89); wohl auch: Geimer/Schütze, Internationaler Rechtsverkehr/Paulus, 66. EL Januar 2023, VO (EG) 1215/2012 Art. 21 Rn. 34, 27; in diese Richtung wohl auch tendierend: Ulrici, jurisPR-ArbR 43/2017 Anm. 5 (C. II. 2. b)); aA wohl Rauscher, EuZPR/EuIPR/Mankowski, 5. Aufl. 2021, Brüssel Ia-VO Art. 21 Rn. 55f.

109 Ulrici jurisPR-ArbR 43/2017 Anm. 5 (D.); Wieczorek/Schütze, ZPO/Temming, 5. Aufl. 2022, VO (EU) 1215/2012 Art. 21 Rn. 108; Rauscher, EuZPR/EuIPR/Mankowski, 5. Aufl. 2021, Brüssel Ia-VO Art. 21 Rn. 62.

110 BAG 30.11.2016 – 10 AZR 11/16, NZA 2017, 1394 Rn. 23; 21.7.2009 – 9 AZR 404/08, NZA 2009, 1369 Rn. 20.

111 Zöller, ZPO/Geimer, 35. Aufl. 2024, VO (EU) 1215/2012 Art. 21 Rn. 9; Burgstaller/Neumayr, Internationales Zivilverfahrensrecht/Garber, 2015, EuGVVO Art. 21 Rn. 31; Geimer/

In diesen Fällen greift folglich – neben dem Wohnsitz des Arbeitgebers – allein der Gerichtsstand der einstellenden Niederlassung.

IV. Fazit

In Zeiten wachsender wirtschaftlicher Verflechtungen auf internationaler Ebene nimmt die Zahl der Arbeitsverhältnisse mit grenzüberschreitendem Bezug stetig zu. Insoweit ist davon auszugehen, dass sich die Rechtsprechung künftig noch umfassender mit dem Gerichtsstand des (internationalen) gewöhnlichen Arbeitsortes auseinandersetzen wird. Hierbei bleibt zu hoffen, dass die von dem EuGH bisher eher schlagwortartig angeführte indiziengeprägte Abwägung der Umstände des Einzelfalles gerade im Hinblick auf einzelne besondere Fallgruppen noch stärker akzentuiert wird.

Insbesondere mit Blick auf das fliegende Personal erscheint die nach der sich nunmehr als herrschend herausgebildeten Auffassung vorzunehmende Orientierung an der Heimatbasis in Fällen, in denen – anders als bei den Fluglinien, die bisher Gegenstand der höchstrichterlichen Rechtsprechung gewesen sind – prägende Tätigkeiten gerade nicht an der Einsatzbasis ausgeübt werden, als dogmatisch nicht überzeugend. Insoweit bleibt abzuwarten, ob der EuGH künftig entweder – ergebnisorientiert mit Blick auf den gebotenen umfassenden Schutz der Arbeitnehmer vor (vermeintlichen) Umgehungstrategien der Luftfahrtunternehmen – diesbezüglich von seiner ursprünglichen Definition des Arbeitsortes als tatsächlichen Mittelpunkt der Tätigkeit, an dem die wesentlichen Verpflichtungen erfüllt werden, weiter abrücken oder in diesen Fällen doch das Flugzeug als Arbeitsort und damit den Registerstaat stärker in den Fokus rücken wird. Andernfalls bliebe nur die Annahme, dass es bei fliegendem Personal ohne hinreichenden Tätigkeitsbezug zur Heimatbasis an einem gewöhnlichen Arbeitsort fehlt und die betroffenen Arbeitnehmer folglich entweder am Ort der einstellenden Niederlassung oder am Sitz des Arbeitgebers klagen müssten. Ein Ergebnis, dass die Rechtsprechung bisher unter Zugrundlegung eines extensiven Verständnisses des Begriffs des gewöhnlichen Arbeitsorts strikt versucht hat, zu vermeiden.

Schütze, EuZVR, 4. Aufl. 2020, EuGVVO Art. 21 Rn. 19; Rauscher, EuZPR/EuIPR/Mankowski, 5. Aufl. 2021, Brüssel Ia-VO Art. 21 Rn. 61.

ANNA GÜRTLER

Anerkennungsfähigkeit polnischer Gerichtsurteile nach der Brüssel Ia-VO nach Inkrafttreten der Justizreformen

I. Einführung

„Die Europäisierung des Rechts" ist nicht nur das Leitthema dieser Festschrift, sondern auch eine Entwicklung, die nicht alle Mitgliedsstaaten der Europäischen Union ohne Weiters hinzunehmen bereit sind – wohl aus Sorge um den Verlust der eigenen Souveränität. Die Schaffung und Aufrechterhaltung eines „europäisierten" Raums ohne Binnengrenzen sind allerdings nur möglich, wenn sich die Mitgliedstaaten gegenseitig vertrauen. Konkret verlangt der Grundsatz des gegenseitigen Vertrauens, namentlich in Bezug auf den Raum der Freiheit, der Sicherheit und des Rechts, von jedem Mitgliedstaat, abgesehen von außergewöhnlichen Umständen, davon auszugehen, dass alle anderen Mitgliedstaaten das Unionsrecht und insbesondere die im Unionsrecht anerkannten Grundrechte beachten.[1] Laut EuGH sei es das gegenseitige Vertrauen der EU-Mitgliedstaaten in die allseitige Absicht und Fähigkeit, das Unionsrecht zu wahren, das die Voraussetzung für das Entstehen und Funktionieren der Europäischen Union darstelle.[2] Der Grundsatz des gegenseitigen Vertrauens – so der EuGH – hat *„im Unionsrecht fundamentale Bedeutung [...], da er die Schaffung und Aufrechterhaltung eines Raums ohne Binnengrenzen ermöglicht. Dieser Grundsatz verlangt aber, namentlich in Bezug auf den Raum der Freiheit, der Sicherheit und des Rechts, von jedem Mitgliedstaat, dass er, abgesehen von außergewöhnlichen Umständen, davon ausgeht, dass alle anderen Mitgliedstaaten das Unionsrecht und insbesondere die dort anerkannten Grundrechte beachten"*.[3] In einer Situation zunehmend erodierenden gegenseitigen Vertrauens für die Unionsrechtstreue ist die Frage nicht nur des politischen sondern auch des rechtlichen Umgangs mit Mitgliedstaaten zu stellen, die dem Grundsatz zuwiderhandeln. Die hier interessierende Frage lautet, wie sich die im Jahr 2015 begonnen polnischen Justizreformen unter Berücksichtigung des Grundsatzes des gegenseitigen Vertrauens auf die gegenseitige Anerkennung von Entscheidungen im Geltungsbereich der Brüssel Ia-VO auswirken. Die mit dem Inkrafttreten der Brüssel Ia-VO erfolgte Abschaffung des Exequaturverfahrens hin zur unmittelbaren Anerkennung und Zwangsvollstreckung wird als Herzstück der

---

[1] EuGH 25.7.2018 – C-216/18 PPU, ECLI:EU:C:2018:586 Rn. 36 = BeckEuRS 2018, 572779.

[2] Müller, Der Grundsatz des gegenseitigen Vertrauens im Mehrebenensystem der Europäischen Union, S. 35.

[3] EuGH 18.12.2014, Gutachten 2/13 (EMRK-Beitritt II) – C-2/13, ECLI:EU:C:2014:2454 Rn. 191 = BeckRS 2015, 80256.

damaligen Reform bezeichnet.[4] Zwar gilt der Grundsatz nicht uneingeschränkt, wie sich an der Kodifizierung des sog. *ordre public* des Anerkennungsstaates in Art. 45 Abs. 1 lit. a Brüssel Ia-VO zeigt. Die Reformen des polnischen Justizsystems und die dazu ergangene Rechtsprechung des EuGH geben Anlass, sich erneut mit der Thematik des anerkennungsrechtlichen *ordre public*-Vorbehalts und des Vertrauensgrundsatzes zu befassen. Mit Urteil vom 5.6.2023 attestiert der EuGH der Republik Polen, dass ihre Justizreform von 2019 gegen das Unionsrecht verstößt, da das maßgebliche Änderungsgesetz die Unabhängigkeit der Richter beeinträchtige und die Republik Polen gegen ihre Verpflichtungen aus Art. 19 Abs. 1 UAbs. 2 EUV in Verbindung mit Art. 47 GRCh und Art. 267 EUV und dem Grundsatz des Vorrangs des Unionrechts verstoße.[5] Insoweit ist die Frage berechtigt, ob Entscheidungen polnischer Gerichte, die in den Anwendungsbereich der Brüssel Ia-VO fallen, angesichts dieser Rechtsprechung des EuGH noch anerkennungsfähig sind, oder ob sie gegen den *ordre public*-Vorbehalt nach Art. 45 Abs. 1 lit. a Brüssel Ia-VO verstoßen. Dass solche konkreten praktischen Auswirkungen sehr viel mehr in den Fokus gerückt werden müssen als bisher, zeigt sich schon daran, dass keine der bisher ergriffenen Maßnahmen der Europäischen Union und keines der Urteile des EuGH in der Lage war, etwas an der Situation in Polen zu ändern. Die autokratische Regierung unter der Führung der PIS-Partei in Polen hat sehr schnell verstanden, dass, wenn sie genug Tempo bei der Implementierung ihrer Ideologie macht, vor Ort Fakten schaffen kann, an denen die EU nicht mehr rütteln kann.[6] Es bleibt also fast nur noch zu fragen, was das polnische Justizdrama für die übrigen Akteure der Europäischen Wertegemeinschaft bedeutet. Dieser pragmatische Blick auf die Realität war auch für die wissenschaftliche Arbeit von *Thomas Rauscher* prägend. Der von ihm stets praktizierte Blick über den Tellerrand der eigenen Rechtsordnung hinaus, wie er dem Internationalen und Europäischen Privatrecht immanent ist, lehrt, dass es Wege braucht, mit Rechtsordnungen umzugehen, die der deutschen Rechtsordnung wesensfremd sind. Einen solchen Weg des Umgangs mit Urteilen der polnischen Gerichte zu finden, ist auch das erklärte Ziel dieser Untersuchung.

II. Die Justizreformen in Polen

Um die Frage untersuchen zu können, ob die polnischen Justizreformen Ausfluss auf den *ordre public*-Vorbehalt haben können, werden diese zunächst allgemein skizziert. Eine eingehende Analyse würde den Rahmen dieser Untersuchung sprengen, sodass hier der Augenmerkt auf die wesentlichen Regelungsfelder und die Entscheidung des EuGH vom 5.6.2023 gelegt wird.

---

[4] Rauscher, EuZPR/EuIPR/Mankowski, 5. Aufl. 2022, Brüssel Ia-VO Vor Art. 39–41, Rn. 1.

[5] EuGH 5.6.2023 – C-204/21, ECLI:EU:C:2023:442 = NJW 2023, 2837 Rn. 102 = BeckEuRS 2023, 761766.

[6] Kovács/Scheppele, Rechtsstaat unter Druck. Ungarn, Polen und die Rolle der EU, APuZ https://www.bpb.de/apuz/herrschaft-des-rechts-2021/340009/rechtsstaat-unter-druck-ungarn-polen-und-die-rolle-der-eu (abgerufen 3.3.2024).

1. *Allgemeiner Abriss*

Die umfangreichen Reformen des polnischen Justizwesens nahmen ihren Lauf mit der erstmaligen Erringung der Parlamentsmehrheit der PiS-Partei im Jahr 2015. Die wichtigsten Reformschritte des polnischen Justizwesens lassen sich chronologisch in drei Stufen einteilen, nämlich 2015, 2017 und 2019.[7] Den Beginn machten die Reformen der Staatsanwaltschaften. Mit dem entsprechenden Gesetz wurde die Zusammenlegung des Amtes des Justizministers mit dem des Generalstaatsanwalts vollzogen, was Bedenken hinsichtlich der Weisungsabhängigkeit und der Versetzung von Staatsanwälten gab.[8] Im gleichen Schritt wurden mit dem Gesetz über das Verfassungstribunal („Trybunał Konstytucyjny"), das die Reform der Ernennung von Richtern zum Ziel hatte, die zuvor ordnungsgemäß durch *Sejm* (1. Kammer des polnischen Parlaments) gewählt wurde, ihres Amtes enthoben und an ihrer Stelle neue Richter ernannt. Obwohl das Verfassungstribunal, das zu diesem Zeitpunkt noch mit den „alten" Richtern besetzt war, die Verfassungswidrigkeit dieses Gesetzes erklärte, verweigerte die Regierung die Veröffentlichung dieses Urteils und schenkte ihm auch in der Folge keine Beachtung.[9] Weitere Gesetzesänderungen betrafen die Art und Weise der Berufung von Richtern, vor allen von Gerichtsdirektoren und -präsidenten sowie die Organisation und die Arbeitsweise des Obersten Gerichtshofes, des Nationalen Richterrates, der ordentlichen Gerichtsbarkeit und der Nationalen Hochschule für das Justizwesen. 2017 wurde ein Gesetz erlassen, mit dem das Renteneintrittsalter der Richter von 70 auf 65 abgesenkt wurde, wodurch ca. 40% aller aktiven Richter vorzeitig in den Ruhestand versetzt wurden. Das eröffnete dem polnischen Präsidenten die Möglichkeit, neue Richter zu benennen, und zwar durch den neu berufenen Landesrichterrat, der aus Mitgliedern bestand, die durch *Sejm* berufen wurden.[10] Im gleichen Schritt

[7] Blanke/Sander EuR 2023 54 (66).

[8] Venedig-Kommission, Opinion on the Draft Act amending the Act on the National Council of the Judiciary; on the Draft Act amending the Act of the Supreme Court, proposed by the President of Poland, and on the Act on the Organisation of Ordinary Courts, CDL-AD (2017) 031, Rn. 14.

[9] Gemäß Art. 190 plVerfassung sind Entscheidungen des Verfassungsgerichtshofes allgemein bindend und endgültig. Sie werden „unverzüglich" in der amtlichen Veröffentlichung bekannt gemacht. Die Entscheidung des Verfassungsgerichtshofes tritt am Tag der Verkündung in Kraft. Insoweit ist es rechtsdogmatisch in der polnischen Verfassungslehre ungeklärt, welche Wirkungen die fehlende Veröffentlichung tatsächlich entfaltet. Die Richterinnen und Richter des Obersten Gerichtshofes sahen sich allerdings angesichts der unterlassenen Veröffentlichung veranlasst einen Beschluss zu erlassen, in dem sie feststellen, dass die Entscheidungen des Verfassungsgerichtshofes unverzüglich zu veröffentlichen seien sowie dass auch eine nicht veröffentlichte Entscheidung, die die Verfassungswidrigkeit eines Normativaktes feststellt, die Vermutung der Verfassungsmäßigkeit bereits zum Zeitpunkt der Verkündung widerlegt, s. Beschluss vom 26.4.2016. Welche Folgen die verweigerte Veröffentlichung konkret mit sich bringt, ist in der polnischen Literatur gleichwohl umstritten.

[10] Wegen der Zwangspensionierungen wurde durch die Europäische Kommission ein Vertragsverletzungsverletzungsverfahren eingeleitet. Der EuGH bestätigte daraufhin, dass die neuen Vorschriften in Verbindung mit den neuen Vorschriften über die Verlängerung der Dienstzeit nur mit Zustimmung des Präsidenten mit den Erfordernissen der richterlichen Unabhängigkeit nicht vereinbar sind und erließ zwei einstweilige Anordnungen, die die Regelungen mit sofortiger Wirkung außer Kraft setzten, vgl. EuGH 24.6.2019 – C-619/18, ECLI:EU:C:2019:531

wurden am Obersten Gerichtshof zwei weitere Kammern eingerichtet: die Disziplinarkammer sowie die Kammer für außerordentliche Überprüfung und öffentliche Angelegenheiten. Beide Kammern wurden mit Richtern besetzt, die durch den neuen Richterrat ausgewählt wurden. Schließlich wurde im Jahr 2019 die Disziplinarordnung für Richter verändert.[11] Zudem wurden Richter verpflichtet, Informationen über ihre Mitgliedschaften und Vereinen, Stiftungen etc. offen zu legen. Dieses Gesetzespaket wird auch als „Maulkorbgesetz" *(„ustawa kagańcowa")* bezeichnet.

2. *Die Reformen in der Rechtsprechung des EuGH*

Der EuGH hat sich in einer Reihe von Entscheidungen mit den polnischen Justizreformen beschäftigt, wobei für diese Untersuchung insbesondere die Entscheidung vom 05.06.2023 von Bedeutung ist, da diese die Reformen vollumfassend untersucht. Die übrigen Entscheidungen, soweit sie für die hier untersuchte Fragestellung von Relevanz sind, können angesichts der Komplexität der Reformvorhaben und der durchaus unterschiedlichen Reformstadien, die ihnen zu Grunde lagen, nicht ausführlich dargestellt werden. Soweit sich das Urteil des EuGH vom 3.6.2023 auf die vorgehergehenden Entscheidungen bezieht, werden sie des Verständnisses wegen grob skizziert.

a) Zuständigkeit des EuGH

Die Frage der Zuständigkeit des Gerichtes erhielt im gegenständlichen Verfahren eine ganz besondere Brisanz, da Polen unter Bezugnahme auf die *ultra vires* Rechtsprechung des EuGH die Überschreitung der Kompetenzen des Gerichtes rügte. Dabei berief sich Polen auf ein in der polnischen Literatur höchst umstrittenes und kritisiertes Urteil des polnischen Verfassungstribunals vom 14.7.2021[12], wonach dieses bei Grundsatzsachen, die die polnische Verfassungsordnung beträfen, das „letzte Wort" haben müsse. Polen sah hier eine Missachtung des unionsrechtlichen Grundsatzes der begrenzten Einzelermächtigung, da die ausschließliche Zuständigkeit im Bereich der Organisation der ordentlichen Gerichte bei polnischen Gerichten läge. Dieser Auslegung setzte der EuGH eine klar abweichende Meinung entgegen und bestätigte einleitend seine uneingeschränkte Zuständigkeit für die Prüfung, ob ein Mitgliedstaat Werte und Grundsätze wie Rechtsstaatlichkeit, wirksamen Rechtsschutz und Unabhängigkeit der Justiz beachtet. Demnach sind die in Art. 2 EUV niederlegten Werte wie Achtung der Menschenwürde, Freiheit, Demokratie, Gleichheit, Rechtsstaatlichkeit und die Wahrung der Menschenrechte, diejenigen, auf die sich die Union gründe. Art. 47 GRCh schreibe eine weitere Verpflichtung vor, wonach jede Person, deren durch das Recht der Union garantierte Rechte oder Freiheiten verletzt worden sind, das Recht hat, einen wirksamen

---

= BeckEuRS 2019, 606707; EuGH 5.11.2019 – C-192/18, ECLI:EU:C:2019:924 = BeckRS 2019, 26608.

[11] Ustawa z dnia 20 grudnia 2019 r. o zmianie ustawy – Prawo o ustroju sądów powszechnych, ustawy o Sądzie Najwyższym oraz niektórych innych ustaw, Polnisches Amtsblatt 2020, S. 190.

[12] PlVerfG 14.7.2021 –RS P 7/20, https://trybunal.gov.pl/s/p-7–20 (abgerufen 3.3.2024).

Rechtsbehelf einzulegen, der von einem unabhängigen, unparteiischen und zuvor durch Gesetz errichteten Gericht in einem fairen Verfahren öffentlich und innerhalb angemessener Frist verhandelt wird. Art. 19 UAbs. 2 EUV bestimmt indes, dass die Mitgliedstaaten die erforderlichen Rechtsbehelfe schaffen, damit ein wirksamer Rechtsschutz in den vom Unionsrecht erfassten Bereichen gewährleistet ist.

b) Fehlende Unabhängigkeit und Unparteilichkeit der Disziplinarkammer

Im Hinblick auf die vom EuGH zuerst geprüfte Rüge (die durch die Kommission als vierte Rüge vorgelegt wurde) der fehlenden Unabhängigkeit und Unparteilichkeit der Disziplinarkammer beantragte die Kommission die Feststellung eines Verstoßes gegen Art. 19 Abs. 1 UAbs. 1 und UAbs. 2 des EUV. Mit der Rüge macht die Kommission im Wesentlichen geltend, dass die Disziplinarkammer in Anbetracht des besonderen Kontexts, in dem sie entstanden ist, nicht den in Art. 19 Abs. 1 UAbs. 2 EUV aufgestellten Anforderungen an die Unabhängigkeit und Unparteilichkeit eines Gerichtes genüge. In Anbetracht der Gesamtheit der durchgeführten Reformen sei eine systemische Diskontinuität eingetreten, die geeignet ist, bei den Rechtssubjekten berechtigte Zweifel im Hinblick auf die Unabhängigkeit und Unparteilichkeit hervorzurufen. Hier seien aus Sicht der Kommission mehrere Umstände zu beachten, wie zum Beispiel die Zusammensetzung der Disziplinarkammer die Berufung aller Richter durch den neuen Richterrat sowie der Umstand einer überdurchschnittlich guten finanziellen Absicherung, der der Kammer einige Freiheiten verschaffe. Die polnische Seite hingegen berief sich darauf, dass die Richter nach wie vor in einem geordneten, gesetzlich festgelegten Verfahren berufen werden würden. Die Stellen würden öffentlich ausgeschrieben, es erfolge ein Auswahlverfahren mit einer Empfehlung des Richterrates und schließlich die Ernennung durch den Präsidenten, der an die Empfehlung nicht gebunden sei. Die Zusammensetzung des Richterrates sei zudem durch das Polnische Verfassungstribunal bereits für rechtmäßig befunden worden und unterschiede sich kaum von den Landesrichterräten in den anderen Mitgliedstaaten der Europäischen Union. Überraschungen waren bei dieser Rüge insoweit nicht zu erwarten gewesen, als der EuGH bereits mit Urteil vom 15.7.2022[13] bestätigte, dass die neu geschaffene Disziplinarkammer unter besonderer Berücksichtigung ihrer Entstehungsgeschichte und ihrer Besonderheiten im Vergleich zu den bereits existierenden beiden anderen Kammern des Obersten Gerichtshofes, nicht den Eindruck vermittle, unabhängig und unparteiisch zu sein. Dadurch sei das Vertrauen beeinträchtigt, das die Justiz in einer demokratischen Gesellschaft bei den Rechtsunterworfenen schaffen müsse. Der Dreh- und Angelpunkt war hier also herauszuarbeiten, weswegen ein Normativakt, der so ähnlich auch in anderen Mitgliedstaaten der Europäischen Union zu finden ist, in Bezug auf die Republik Polen gegen Art. 19 Abs. 1 UAbs. 2 EUV verstößt. Erwähnt sei in dem Zusammenhang das Urteil des EuGH vom 9.7.2020 gegen das Land Hessen,[14] wonach der

[13] EuGH 15.7.2021 – C-791/19, ECLI:EU:C:2021:596 = BeckRS 2001, 18354.

[14] EuGH 9.7.2020 – C-272/19, ECLI:EU:C:2020:535 Rn. 55, 56 = BeckEuRS 2020, 641412.

Umstand, dass sich ein Landesrichterrat, der am Auswahlverfahren von Richtern beteiligt ist, vorwiegend aus Mitgliedern der Legislative zusammensetzt, noch nicht entscheidungserheblich sei bei der Beantwortung der Frage nach Unparteilichkeit und Unabhängig der so gewählten Personen. Entscheidend sei aus Sicht des EuGH im Fall Polens die Gesamtschau aller Umstände, unter denen die Kammer entstand, sowie die Art und Weise, wie ihre Mitglieder ernannt werden.[15] Die ausschlaggebenden Umstände seien aus Sicht des EuGH, dass der neu geschaffenen Disziplinarkammer gemäß Art. 27, Art. 73 § 1, Art. 97 § 3 des neuen Gesetzes über den Obersten Gerichtshof und Art. 110 § 1 des Gesetzes über die ordentliche Gerichtsbarkeit eigens eine ausschließliche Zuständigkeit eingeräumt wurde sowohl für die Entscheidung über Disziplinarsachen als auch für die Entscheidung über arbeits- und sozialversicherungsrechtliche Streitigkeiten sowie Ruhestandsangelegenheiten, die Richter des Obersten Gerichtshofes betreffen, sowie die Zuständigkeit für die Entscheidung über Disziplinarsachen, die Richter der ordentlichen Gerichtsbarkeit betreffen – je nach Fall – entweder im zweiten Rechtszug oder im ersten und im zweiten Rechtszug. Die Übertragung dieser Zuständigkeit an die Disziplinarkammer erfolgte ua parallel zum Erlass von Bestimmungen des neuen Gesetzes über den Obersten Gerichtshof, mit denen das Ruhestandsalter für Richter des Obersten Gerichtshofes herabgesetzt und diese Maßnahme auf die amtierenden Richter dieses Gerichts für entsprechend anwendbar erklärt wurde. Zugleich wurde dem Präsidenten der Republik Polen die Befugnis verliehen, den aktiven Dienst dieser Richter über das neu festgelegte Ruhestandsalter hinaus nach freiem Ermessen zu verlängern.[16] Darüber hinaus stellte der EuGH fest, dass die Disziplinarkammer zwar organisatorisch als eine weitere Kammer des Obersten Gerichtshofes eingerichtet wurde, sie allerdings im Vergleich zu den beiden anderen Kammern über eine besonders weitgehende organisatorische, funktionelle und finanzielle Autonomie verfügt. Von Bedeutung war zudem der Umstand, dass die Richter der Disziplinarkammer einen Anspruch auf eine etwa 40% höhere Vergütung haben, als die Richter der anderen Kammern des Oberstes Gerichtshofes. Darüber hinaus rügte der EuGH, dass die Disziplinarkammer des Obersten Gerichtshofes bei ihrer erstmaligen Einrichtung nur aus neuen Richtern bestehen durfte, die vom Präsidenten der Republik auf Vorschlag des neuen Richterrates ernannt wurden. Es bestand also keine Möglichkeit der Versetzung bereits beim Obersten Gerichtshof tätiger Richter in diese Kammer, obwohl solche Versetzungen von Richtern von einer Kammer in eine andere Kammer des Obersten Gerichtshofes nach diesem Gesetz grundsätzlich zulässig sind. Der Richterrat, der die neuen Richter der Disziplinarkammer berief, wurde vor den Ernennungen vollständig neu gebildet.[17]

[15] EuGH 5.6.2023 – C-204/21, ECLI:EU:C:2023:442 = NJW 2023, 2837 Rn. 102 = BeckEuRS 2023, 761766.

[16] In seinem Urteil vom 24.6.2019 hat der EuGH insoweit entschieden, dass die Republik Polen durch den Erlass dieser nationalen Bestimmungen die Unabsetzbarkeit und Unabhängigkeit der Richter des Sąd Najwyższy (Oberster Gerichtshof) beeinträchtigt und gegen ihre Verpflichtungen aus Art. 19 Abs. 1 UAbs. 2 EUV verstoßen hat, vgl. EUGH 24.6.2019 – C-619/18, ECLI:EU:C:2019:531 = BeckEuRS 2019, 606707.

[17] EuGH 15.7.2021 – C-791/19, ECLI:EU:C:2021:596 Rn. 89–94 = BeckEuRS 2021, 743836.

Nach der entsprechenden Reform wurden 15 der dem Gremium angehörenden Richter nicht mehr durch die Richterschaft selbst gewählt, sondern durch das Parlament. Unter Berücksichtigung dessen befand der EuGH, dass die Gesamtschau des „besonderen Kontextes" und der objektiven Bedingungen, unter denen die Disziplinarkammer geschaffen wurde, ihrer Merkmale sowie der Art und Weise der Ernennung ihrer Mitglieder geeignet ist, bei den Rechtsunterworfenen berechtigte Zweifel an ihrer Unempfänglichkeit für äußere Faktoren aufkommen zu lassen, insbesondere für unmittelbare oder mittelbare Einflussnahme durch die Legislative und Exekutive. Hierdurch könne das Vertrauen beeinträchtigt werden, das die Justiz in einer demokratischen Gesellschaft bei den Rechtsunterworfenen schaffen muss.[18] Insoweit sei ein Verstoß gegen Art. 19 Abs. 1 UAbs. 2 EUV, das heißt gegen die Verpflichtung Polens, die Unabhängigkeit und Unparteilichkeit der Disziplinarkammer zu gewährleisten, festzustellen.

c) *Inhalt des Gerichtsurteils als Disziplinarverstoß*

Die erste Rüge der Kommission (die durch den EuGH an dritter Stelle geprüft wurde) betraf die Vereinbarkeit des Art. 107 § 1 des Änderungsgesetzes und des Art. 72 § 1 Nr. 2 und 3 des Gesetzes über den Obersten Gerichtshof mit Art. 19 Abs. 1 UAbs. 1 und UAbs. 2 des EUV. Nach Auffassung der Kommission verstoßen die zitierten Vorschriften gegen Art. 19 Abs. UAbs. 2 EUV iVm Art. 47 GRCh, da sie darauf gerichtet seien, alle betroffenen Richter unter Androhung von Disziplinarstrafen, die bis hin zu ihrer Abberufung gehen, daran zu hindern, Entscheidungen zu treffen, die sie nach dem europäischen Recht zu treffen verpflichtet sind. Die Kommission befürchtete eine politische Kontrolle von gerichtlichen Entscheidungen durch die Neufassung der Gesetze. Art. 107 § 1 des geänderten Gesetzes über die ordentliche Gerichtsbarkeit bestimmt indes, dass ein Richter für Fehlverhalten im Amt (Disziplinarvergehen) disziplinarisch belangt werden kann, unter anderem für: 1) die offensichtliche und grobe Missachtung von Rechtsvorschriften, 2) Handlungen oder Unterlassungen, die das Funktionieren eines Organs der Rechtsprechung unmöglich machen oder wesentlich erschweren können, 3) Handlungen, mit denen das Bestehen des Dienstverhältnisses eines Richters oder die Legitimität eines Verfassungsorgans der Republik Polen in Frage gestellt wird. Gleiches sieht Art. 72 § 1 des geänderten Gesetzes über den Obersten Gerichtshof für Richter des Obersten Gerichtshofes vor. Zudem genügten die Vorschriften nicht dem Bestimmtheitsgebot, soweit die Begriffe des „unmöglich machen" und „wesentlich erschweren können" verwendet werden würden. Erfasst wären demnach nicht nur Handlungen, die das Infragestellen der Gültigkeit der Ernennung eines Richters betreffen, sondern ganz allgemein jede negative Beurteilung des ordnungsgemäßen Ablaufs des Verfahrens zur Ernennung eines Richters im Rahmen der Überprüfung, ob die Anforderungen der Union in Bezug auf die zuvor durch Gesetz errichtetes Gericht gewahrt seien. So könne zum Beispiel vom Vorliegen eines disziplinarischen Vergehens ausgegangen werden, wenn ein im zweiten Rechtszug entscheidendes

[18] EuGH 5.6.2023 – C-204/21, ECLI:EU:C:2023:442 = NJW 2023, 2837 Rn. 102 = BeckEuRS 2023, 761766.

Gericht feststelle, dass das erstinstanzliche Gericht aufgrund der Modalitäten der Ernennung der in diesem Gericht entscheidenden Richter kein zuvor durch Gesetz errichtetes Gericht darstellt und deshalb die Entscheidung des erstinstanzlichen Gerichts aufhebt.[19] Der Verstoß gegen Art. 267 AEUV hingegen ergebe sich aus Sicht der Kommission bereits aus der Formulierung der gerügten Vorschriften. Danach genüge für die Einstufung als Disziplinarverstoß allein der Umstand, dass ein nationales Gericht ein anhängiges Verfahren aussetze und den Gerichtshof Fragen zur Auslegung der sich aus dem Unionsrecht ergebenden Anforderungen an einen wirksamen Rechtsschutz vorlege, zum Beispiel weil es Zweifel habe, ob die einem nationalen Gericht oder dem neuen Richterrat als Verfassungsorgan übertragenen Kompetenzen oder Zuständigkeiten mit diesen Anforderungen vereinbar seien. Dieser Argumentation folgte der EuGH und lehnte die von Polen vorgetragene Sichtweise ab, wonach sich die Bestimmungen ausschließlich auf Rechtsprechungshandlungen bezögen, die eine Entscheidung über die Gültigkeit der Ernennung eines Richters zum Gegenstand haben. Das Gericht sah hier hingegen eine ganze Bandbreite von Handlungen als dem Tatbestand unterfallend an. Aus Sicht des EuGH seien die Formulierungen derart weit gefasst und ungenau, dass sie insbesondere in Fällen, in denen die betroffenen Richter prüfen und entscheiden, ob sie selbst oder das Gericht, dem sie angehören, den Anforderungen des Art. 19 Abs. 1 UAbs. 2 AEUV und Art. 47 GRCh genügen, zur Anwendung der beanstandeten nationalen Bestimmungen und zur Einleitung von Disziplinarverfahren gegen sie führen können. In Bezug auf die Verhaltensweisen, die als Disziplinarvergehen von Richtern eingestuft werden können, hat der Gerichtshof festgestellt, dass die Wahrung dieser Unabhängigkeit zwar nicht dazu führen dürfe, dass eine disziplinarische Verantwortlichkeit völlig ausgeschlossen sei. Sie müsse aber, um die richterliche Unabhängigkeit zu wahren und den Missbrauch durch eine etwaige politische Kontrolle auszuschließen, auf ganz außergewöhnliche Fälle beschränkt bleiben.[20] Bemerkenswerterweise verzichtete der EuGH an dieser Stelle auf eine Auseinandersetzung mit der Argumentation Polens, wonach sich die eigeführten Definitionen kaum von der Regelungen der anderen Mitgliedstaaten unterscheiden. In seinem Schlussantrag bestätigte der EuGH-Generalanwalt Tanchev, dass es zwar keine einheitliche Linie der Mitgliedstaaten gäbe und die Einführung der Kategorie der „offensichtlichen" und „groben Missachtung von Rechtsvorschriften" per se noch nicht geeignet sei, die Unabhängigkeit und Unparteilichkeit der Richter zu begründen. Allerdings waren auch hier aus Sicht des EuGH die Gesamtschau und der Kontext entscheidend. Es seien nämlich „die besonderen Umstände und der spezielle Kontext des Erlasses der genannten nationalen Bestimmungen zu berücksichtigen, um die Tragweite dieser Bestimmungen zu verdeutlichen.[21] Zu sehen ist insoweit laut EuGH zum einen die Eile, in der das Gesetzespaket verabschiedet wurde: dieses

[19] EuGH 5.6.2023 – C-204/21, ECLI:EU:C:2023:442 = NJW 2023, 2837 Rn. 110–111 = BeckEuRS 2023, 761766.

[20] EuGH 5.6.2023 – C-204/21, ECLI:EU:C:2023:442 = NJW 2023, 2837 Rn. 127 = BeckEuRS 2023, 761766.

[21] EuGH 5.6.2023 – C-204/21, ECLI:EU:C:2023:442 = NJW 2023, 2837 Rn. 139 = BeckEuRS 2023, 761766.

ist der Ersten Kammer des Parlaments – „Sejm" – am 12.12.2019 vorgelegt und bereits am 20.12.2019 beschlossen worden. Zudem sei hier die zeitliche Nähe zum Urteil vom 19.11.2019[22] zu sehen, in dem es im Wesentlichen darum ging, ob die polnischen Gerichte berechtigt sind, dem EuGH Fragen vorzulegen, wenn sie Zweifel haben, ob in Anbetracht der nationalen Vorschriften über die Schaffung einer speziellen Einrichtung wie der Disziplinarkammer, eine solche Einrichtung und ihre Mitglieder den Anforderungen an die Unabhängigkeit und Unparteilichkeit genügen, die ein Gericht nach Art. 47 GRCh erfüllen muss. Zum gleichen Zeitpunkt hat der Oberste Gerichtshof selbst[23] als unmittelbare Folge des Urteils des EuGH festgestellt, dass der neu berufene Richterrat in der neuen Zusammensetzung kein von der polnischen Legislative und Exekutive unabhängiges Organ sei und die Disziplinarkammer kein Gericht im Sinne des Art. 47 GRCh, Art. 7 EMRK und Art. 45 der polnischen Verfassung. Eine solche Entscheidung war zu dem Zeitpunkt ihres Erlasses in der polnischen Verfassung einmalig.[24] Zudem lagen dem Gerichtshof zum Zeitpunkt des Erlasses des beanstandeten Gesetzes mehrere Vorlagefragen polnischer Gerichte vor zur Auslegung des Art. 19 Abs. 1 UAbs. 2 AEUV.[25] All diese Umstände seien aus Sicht des Gerichtshofes geeignet, ein Dis-

---

[22] EUGH 19.11.2019 – C-585/18, C-624/18 und C-625/18, ECLI: EU:C:2019:982 = BeckEuRS 2019, 621848; Art. 47 GRCh und Art. 9 Abs. 1 der Richtlinie 2000/78/EG des Rates vom 27. November 2000 zur Festlegung eines allgemeinen Rahmens für die Verwirklichung der Gleichbehandlung in Beschäftigung und Beruf sind dahin auszulegen, dass sie dem entgegenstehen, dass Rechtsstreitigkeiten über die Anwendung des Unionsrechts in die ausschließliche Zuständigkeit einer Einrichtung fallen können, die kein unabhängiges und unparteiisches Gericht im Sinne von Art. 47 GRCh ist. Es ist Sache des vorlegenden Gerichts, unter Berücksichtigung aller ihm zur Verfügung stehenden erheblichen Erkenntnisse zu ermitteln, ob dies bei einer Einrichtung wie der Disziplinarkammer des Obersten Gerichtshofes der Fall ist. In einem solchen Fall ist der Grundsatz des Vorrangs des Unionsrechts dahin auszulegen, dass er das vorlegende Gericht dazu verpflichtet, die Bestimmung des nationalen Rechts, die die Zuständigkeit für die Entscheidung über die Ausgangsrechtsstreitigkeiten dieser Einrichtung vorbehält, unangewendet zu lassen, damit die Rechtsstreitigkeiten von einem Gericht verhandelt werden können, das den oben genannten Anforderungen an die Unabhängigkeit und Unparteilichkeit genügt und in dem betreffenden Bereich zuständig wäre, stünde diese Bestimmung dem nicht entgegen.

[23] Polnischer Oberster Gerichtshof 5.12.2019 – III PO 7/18.

[24] Michał Ziółkowski European Papers 5/1 (2020), 347.

[25] Natürlich war auch insoweit zu einem späteren Zeitpunkt durch die Kammer für außerordentliche Überprüfung und öffentliche Angelegenheiten des polnischen Obersten Gerichtshofes eine völlig andere Interpretation des Urteils des EuGH festgestellt worden. In der Entscheidung plOG 8.1.2020 – I NOZP 3/19 (englische Übersetzung: https://ruleoflaw.pl/wp-content/uploads/2020/02/I-NOZP-3-19-2_English.pdf, abgerufen 13.5.2024) schränkte der Oberste Gerichtshof die Durchsetzung des EuGH-Urteils ein durch eine ganz eigene (regierungsfreundliche) Interpretation der Verfassung. Dem Beschluss zufolge könne sich die mangelnde Unabhängigkeit und Unparteilichkeit des Richterrates sowie eine etwaige mangelnde Unabhängigkeit oder Unparteilichkeit der Kandidaten gegenüber der Exekutive während des Ernennungsverfahrens nicht auf die Unabhängigkeit der gewählten Richter auswirken. Die Meinungsverschiedenheiten zwischen den beiden Kammern des Obersten Gerichtshofes führten zu einer beispiellos kuriosen Situation in einer Entscheidung vom 23.1.2020 (Polnischer Oberster Gerichtshof 23.1.2020 – BSA I-4110-1/20, englische (...): plOG 23.1.2020 – BSA I-4110-1/20 (englische Übersetzung: https://forumfws.eu/bsa-i-4110–1_20_english.pdf, abgerufen 13.5.2024), verabschiedeten sechzig Richter des Obersten Gerichtshofes nach einer außerordentlichen gemeinsamen Sitzung der drei „alten" Kammers einen neuen Beschluss, der im Wesentlichen den Ausführungen aus Polnischer Oberster Gerichtshof 5.12.2019 – III PO 7/18 folgte. Dies kümmerte aber

ziplinarvergehen zu begründen, da sie sich im Wesentlichen auf die Frage konzentrierten, ob es sich bei den durch den neuen Richterrat ausgewählten Richtern um unabhängige und unparteiliche Richter handelt.

d) *Alleinentscheidungskompetenz der Kammer für außerordentliche Überprüfung und öffentliche Angelegenheiten des Obersten Gerichtshofes*

Schließlich ging es in der zweiten Rüge der Kommission, die vom Gericht als vierte geprüft wurde, um die ausschließliche Zuständigkeit der Kammer für außerordentliche Überprüfung und öffentliche Angelegenheiten für die Prüfung der Frage der Unabhängigkeit anderer Gerichte. Die Kommission machte die Verletzung des Art. 19 Abs. 1 UAbs. 2 EUV iVm Art. 47 GRCh durch die Einführung der Art. 42a §§ 1 und 2 und Art. 55 § 4 des geänderten Gesetzes über die ordentliche Gerichtsbarkeit, Art. 26 § 3 und Art. 29 §§ 2 und 3 des geänderten Gesetzes über das Oberste Gericht geltend. Art. 42a § 1 des geänderten Gesetzes über die ordentliche Gerichtsbarkeit bestimmt, dass die Gerichte im Rahmen ihrer Tätigkeit die Legitimität der Gerichte, der Verfassungsorgane des Staates und der Organe zur Kontrolle und zum Schutz des Rechts nicht in Frage stellen dürfen. Art. 42a § 2 ergänzt, dass ein ordentliches Gericht oder ein anderes Organ der Staatsgewalt die Rechtsmäßigkeit der Ernennung eines Richters oder der sich daraus ergebenden Befugnis zur Wahrnehmung von Aufgaben im Bereich der Rechtsprechung weder feststellen noch beurteilen darf. Art. 55 § 4 bestimmt hinsichtlich der Zuständigkeit des Richters, dass dieser zwar über alle Sachen an seinem Dienstort und in den gesetzlich vorgesehenen Fällen in anderen Gerichten entscheiden kann. Es wird ihm aber untersagt darüber zu entscheiden, ob ein Spruchkörper ordnungsgemäß besetzt ist oder ob eine Person an der Entscheidung beteiligt war, die dazu nicht befugt oder nicht zuständig ist. Vielmehr sieht Art. 26 §§ 2–6 des geänderten Gesetzes über den obersten Gerichtshof die Bildung der Kammer für außerordentliche Überprüfung und öffentliche Angelegenheiten vor, dass diese ausschließlich zuständig ist für Anträge oder Erklärungen betreffend die Ablehnung eines Richters oder die Bestimmung des Gerichts, bei dem ein Verfahren geführt werden soll, wenn die Unabhängigkeit des Gerichts oder des Richters gerügt wird. Nach Art. 26 § 3 wird der Antrag nach Art. 26 § 2 allerdings nicht geprüft, wenn er die Feststellung und die Beurteilung der Rechtmäßigkeit der Ernennung eines Richters oder seiner Ermächtigung zur Wahrnehmung von Aufgaben im Bereich der Rechtsprechung betrifft. Art. 29 §§ 2 und 3 runden die Regelungsmaterie dadurch ab, dass sie festlegen, dass im Rahmen der Tätigkeiten des Obersten Gerichtshofes oder seiner Organe die Legitimität der Gerichte, der Verfassungsorgane des Staates und der Organe zur Kontrolle und zum Schutz des Rechts nicht infrage gestellt werden können (Art. 29 § 2). Zudem darf der Oberste Gerichtshof oder ein anderes Organ der Staatsgewalt die Rechtmäßigkeit der Ernennung eines Richters oder die sich daraus ergebenden Befugnis zur Wahrnehmung von Aufgaben im Bereich der Rechtsprechung weder feststellen, noch beurteilen (Art. 29 § 3). Ergänzend hinzuweisen ist auf eine weitere Vorschrift

---

weder die Kammer für außerordentliche Überprüfung und öffentliche Angelegenheiten noch den Richterrat. In Folge trat das hier besprochene Gesetz über die Dienstvergehen in Kraft.

dieses Regelungskomplexes, nämlich Art. 88 §§ 2–5 des geänderten Gesetzes über den Obersten Gerichtshof. Diese bestimmen neben der bereits genannten ausschließlichen Zuständigkeit, dass diese Kammer zudem beim Erlass eines entsprechenden Beschlusses an keine andere Entscheidung des Obersten Gerichtshofes gebunden ist und dass die Beschlüsse dieser Kammer für alle anderen Spruchkörper des Obersten Gerichtshofes verbindlich sind. Problematisch war hier aus Sicht des EuGH nicht die Vielzahl der möglichen Verhaltensweisen, die unter die Vorschrift subsumierbar wären. Sie könnte nämlich grundsätzlich auch dann greifen, wenn die Gerichte unter Umständen prüfen müssten, ob sie selbst oder andere Richter oder Gerichte, die über Sachverhalte mit Bezug zum Unionsrecht zu entscheiden haben oder entschieden haben, die Erfordernisse gemäß Art. 19 Abs. 1 UAbs. 2 AEUV und Art. 47 GRCh in Bezug auf Unabhängigkeit, Unparteilichkeit und vorherige Errichtung durch Gesetz erfüllen.[26] Entscheidungserheblich war vielmehr auch hier der Kontext. Die Bündelung von Zuständigkeit bei einem überörtlichen höherrangigen Gericht begegnet zwar an sich keinen Bedenken, da sie grundsätzlich geeignet ist, Verfahren zu beschleunigen und die nötige Fachkompetenz zu steigern. Der Gerichtshof hat aber festgestellt, dass jedwede Norm mit dem Unionsrecht unvereinbar ist, die die Gerichte dazu veranlasst, Vorschriften anzuwenden, die mit dem Unionsrecht unvereinbar sind. Das wäre bereits nach der früheren Rechtsprechung des Gerichts dann der Fall, wenn bei einem Widerspruch zwischen einer unionsrechtlichen Bestimmung und einem nationalen Gesetz die Lösung dieses Normenkonflikts einem über ein eigenes Ermessen verfügenden Organ als dem Gericht, das für die Anwendung des Unionsrechts zu sorgen hat, vorbehalten wäre.[27] Aus Sicht des EuGH ist insoweit unionsrechtlich zwingend geboten, jedem Gericht selbst die Prüfung zu überlassen, ob es in Anbetracht seiner Zusammensetzung ein solches Gericht ist, und wenn hieran ernsthafte Zweifel bestehen, prüfen zu können, ob eine Vorschriftswidrigkeit des Verfahrens zur Ernennung eines Richters zu einer Verletzung dieses Grundrechts führen kann.[28] Es bestand auch hier aus Sicht des EuGH angesichts der Eile in der die Reform beschlossen wurde und des Zeitpunktes des Erlasses, zu dem mehrere Vorabscheidungsverfahren am EuGH zu den gegenständlichen Fragen vorlagen, die Gefahr, dass sich die Versuche der polnischen Behörden, die nationalen Gerichte davon abzuhalten oder daran zu hindern, den Gerichtshof um Vorabentscheidung und Auslegung von Art. 19 Abs. 1, UAbs. 2 und Art. 47 GRCh im Zusammenhang mit den jüngsten Gesetzesreformen zu ersuchen, die Unabhängigkeit der polnischen Justiz und den Grundsatz des Vorrangs des Europarechts gefährden.[29]

---

[26] EuGH 5.6.2023 – C-204/21, ECLI:EU:C:2023:442 = NJW 2023, 2837 Rn. 201 = BeckEuRS 2023, 761766.

[27] EuGH 5.6.2023 – C-204/21, ECLI:EU:C:2023:442 = NJW 2023, 2837 Rn. 273 = BeckEuRS 2023, 761766; EuGH 4.12.2018 – C-378/17, ECLI:EU:C:2018:979 = BeckEuRS 2018, 602424; EuGH 8.9.2010 – C-409/06, ECLI:EU:C:2010:503 = BeckRS 2010, 91036.

[28] EuGH 5.6.2023 – C-204/21, ECLI:EU:C:2023:442 = NJW 2023, 2837 Rn. 276 = BeckEuRS 2023, 761766.

[29] Schließlich ging es im Urteil des EuGH um die Frage, ob die nationalen Bestimmungen, die die Richter verpflichten, eine schriftliche Erklärung mit Angaben zu ihrer etwaigen Mitgliedschaft in einem Verein, einer Stiftung ohne Gewinnzweck oder einer politischen Partei vorzulegen, und

III. Fehlendende Unabhängigkeit der Richter und der ordre public-Vorbehalt

Es stellt sich vor dem Hintergrund die Frage, ob die festgestellten Verstöße, die die Unparteilichkeit und Unabhängigkeit der polnischen Gerichte in Frage stellen, zwingend dazu führen müssten, dass die Urteile solcher Gerichte nicht mehr anerkennungsfähig sind, weil sie gegen den ordre public-Vorbehalt verstoßen.

1. Grundsatz der gegenseitigen Anerkennung

Dabei ist im Grundsatz gemäß Art. 36 Abs. 1 Brüssel Ia-VO davon auszugehen, dass die in einem Mitgliedstaat ergangenen Entscheidungen in den anderen Mitgliedstaaten anerkannt werden, ohne dass es hierfür eines besonderen Verfahrens bedarf. Darüber hinaus sind gemäß Art. 39 Brüssel Ia-VO in einem Mitgliedstaat ergangene Entscheidungen, die in diesem Mitgliedstaat vollstreckbar sind, in den anderen Mitgliedstaaten vollstreckbar, ohne dass es einer Vollstreckbarerklärung bedarf. Eines besonderen vorherigen Exequaturverfahrens bedarf es nicht.[30] Im Geltungsbereich der Brüssel Ia-VO fungiert der Antrag auf Versagung der Anerkennung nach Art. 36 Abs. 2 Brüssel I-VO (bzw. Art. 46 Brüssel Ia-VO) als funktionales Äquivalent zu den Beschwerdemöglichkeiten des Schuldners nach altem Recht. Auf einen solchen Antrag hin kann im Hinblick auf die Anerkennung einer ausländischen Entscheidung ein Versagungsgrund aus Art. 45 Brüssel Ia-VO festgestellt werden, der nach Art. 45 Abs. 1, 46 Brüssel Ia-VO die Anerkennung und Vollstreckung hindert. Ansonsten werden im Anerkennungs- und Vollstreckungsstaat weder Versagungsgründe der Brüssel Ia-VO geprüft, noch beurteilt das ersuchte Vollstreckungsorgan in irgendeiner Weise die Anerkennungsfähigkeit und Vollstreckbarkeit nach dem nationalen Recht.[31] Dies entspricht auch dem Telos der Brüssel Ia-VO, die ausweislich des Erwägungsgrundes 26 Satz 3 eine Gleichbehandlung der von den Gerichten eines Mitgliedstaats erlassenen Entscheidung mit einer im ersuchten Mitgliedstaat ergangen Entscheidung bezweckt, womit die ausländische Gerichtsentscheidung ohne weitere Prüfung einer inländischen gleichgesetzt werden soll.[32]

---

die Veröffentlichung dieser Angaben im Internet vorsehen, die Grundrechte der betreffenden Richter auf Schutz personenbezogener Daten und auf Achtung des Privatlebens verletzen. Da diese Ausführungen für die hier untersuchte Frage nicht von Relevanz sind, wir auf ihre Erläuterung verzichtet.

[30] Musielak/Voit, ZPO/Stadler/Krüger, 20. Aufl. 2023, EuGVVO Art. 39 Rn. 1; Vor Durchführung konkreter Vollstreckungsmaßnahmen wird im ersuchten Staat (Art. 2 lit. e Brüssel Ia-VO) lediglich geprüft, ob der zeitliche und räumliche Anwendungsbereich der Brüssel Ia-VO eröffnet ist, eine Mitgliedstaatenentscheidung iSv Art. 36 Brüssel Ia-VO iVm Art. 2 lit. a Brüssel Ia-VO vorliegt, diese Entscheidung im Ursprungsstaat (Art. 2 lit. d Brüssel Ia-VO) vollstreckbar ist und alle notwendigen Bescheinigungen und die Entscheidung selbst gemäß Art. 43 Brüssel Ia-VO an den Schuldner zugestellt wurden.

[31] Saenger, ZPO/Dörner, 10. Aufl. 2023, EuGVVO Art. 39 Rn. 3.

[32] Beck'scher Online-Kommentar ZPO/Neumayr, 52. Ed. 1.3.2024, Brüssel Ia-VO Art. 39 Rn. 30 a.

2. *Ordré public-Vorbehalt*

Doch auch im Geltungsbereich der Brüssel Ia-VO ist das Vertrauen nicht grenzenlos. Die Verordnung hält eine Regelung parat, die dem Umstand Rechnung trägt, dass die mitgliedstaatlichen Verfahrens- und Sachrechte bisher noch nicht vereinheitlicht sind und gewährt Schutz vor Entscheidung anderer Mitgliedstaaten, die mit der „öffentlichen Ordnung" des Anerkennungsstaates schlechterdings unvereinbar sind.[33] Art. 45 Abs. 1 lit. a Brüssel Ia-VO regelt für diesen Fall, dass die Anerkennung eines Urteils eines Mitgliedstaates versagt wird, wenn die Anerkennung der öffentlichen Ordnung *(ordre public)* des ersuchten Mitgliedstaats offensichtlich widersprechen würde. Was der öffentlichen Ordnung unterliegt, legt das nationale Recht fest.[34] Eine solche Unvereinbarkeit kann dabei in zweierlei Hinsicht entstehen: Zum einen kann am Inhalt der Entscheidung Anstoß genommen werden *(materiellrechtlicher ordre public)*. Zum anderen aber kann die Art und Weise des Zustandekommens der ausländischen Entscheidung gegen wesentliche Grundsätze des deutschen Rechts verstoßen *(verfahrensrechtlicher ordre public)*.[35] Wenngleich die Hauptfunktion beider Klauseln ähnlich sein mag, nämlich die inländische Rechts- und Sittenordnung, die unverzichtbaren Grundgedanken der jeweiligen deutschen Gesetzgebung und die dahinterstehenden fundamentalen Interessen- und Gerechtigkeitswertungen zu schützen[36], ist ihre Struktur durchaus unterschiedlich. Prüfungsfrage bei der Anwendung des kollisionsrechtlichen *ordre public* ist nicht der abstrakte ausländische Rechtssatz oder die hinter dem jeweiligen Rechtssatz stehenden Prinzipien, sondern das Ergebnis der ausländischen Rechtsanwendung im Einzelfall.[37] Tertium comparationis bei dem anerkennungsrechtlichen *ordre public* hingegen ist weder die fremde Entscheidung selbst, noch der Rechtssatz, auf dem sie beruht oder die dahinter stehenden Prinzipien, sondern die potentielle Situation nach der Anerkennung.[38] Trotz der Orientierung an der nationalen Rechtsordnung ist der Begriff der öffentlichen Ordnung aufgrund des Ausnahmecharakters der Norm international im Kontext des unionsrechtlichen Rahmens auszulegen. Außerdem erfasst er als Auffang- und Ausnahmetatbestand nicht sämtliche Abweichungen vom verfahrens- oder materiellen Recht des Anerkennungsstaates, sondern verhindert eine Anwendung der Brüssel Ia-VO nur in solchen Fällen, in denen die Anerkennung offensichtlich untragbar wäre. Angesichts der weiterreichenden Feststellungen des EuGH zu der Lage des Rechtsstaates in Polen stellt sich die Frage, ob die festgestellten Verstöße, die dazu geführt haben, dass die Unabhängigkeit und Unparteilichkeit der Gerichte nicht mehr gewährleistet ist und dazu führen, dass der Grundsatz des Geltungs- und Anwendungsvorrangs des Unionsrechts untergraben wird, dazu führen, dass aus Sicht Deutschlands als Anerkennungsstaates die Anerkennungsfähigkeit solcher Entscheidungen versagt werden

---

[33] Rauscher, EuZPR/EuIPR/Leible, 5. Aufl. 2022, Brüssel Ia-VO Art. 45 Rn. 5.
[34] Münchener Kommentar zur ZPO/Gottwald, 6. Aufl. 2022, Brüssel Ia-VO Art. 45 Rn. 12.
[35] Stürner DGVZ 2016, 215.
[36] So im Ergebnis Völker, Zur Dogmatik des ordre public, 1998, S. 67.
[37] Völker, Zur Dogmatik des ordre public, 1998, S. 67.
[38] Völker, Zur Dogmatik des ordre public, 1998, S. 67.

müsste. Zur Klärung dieser Frage ist zunächst ein Blick auf die Definition des Begriffs des *ordre public*-Vorbehalts durch den EuGH und den BGH zu lenken, um sodann der Frage nachzugehen, ob die Auswirkungen der Reformen unter diese Definition subsumierbar sind.

a) Definition des EuGH und Vorgaben des BGH

Die Anwendung der Vorbehaltsklausel des Art. 45 Abs. 1 lit. a Brüssel Ia-VO kommt nur in Betracht, wenn die Anerkennung oder Vollstreckung (dann über die Verweisung in Art. 46 Brüssel Ia-VO) der in einem anderen Mitgliedstaat erlassenen Entscheidung gegen einen wesentlichen Rechtsgrundsatz verstieße und deshalb in einem nicht hinnehmbaren Gegensatz zur Rechtsordnung des Vollstreckungsstaates stünde. Damit das Verbot der Nachprüfung der ausländischen Entscheidung auf ihre Gesetzmäßigkeit gewahrt bleibt, muss es sich bei diesem Verstoß um eine offensichtliche Verletzung einer in der Rechtsordnung des Anerkennungsstaates als wesentlich geltenden Rechtsnorm oder eines dort als grundlegend anerkannten Rechts handeln.[39] Die Ausfüllung des Begriffs des *ordre public* obliegt den Mitgliedstaaten, es ist auf ihre Sicht als die Sicht des Anerkennungsstaates bei der Auslegung des Begriffs „öffentliche Ordnung" abzustellen. Auch wenn die Gerichte des Anerkennungsstaates demnach selbst bestimmen können, welchen Anforderungen ausländische Entscheidungen entsprechen müssen, gehört die Auslegung selbst gleichwohl noch zur Auslegung der Verordnung.[40] Folglich kann der EuGH die Grenzen des Begriffs nicht definieren, wacht aber über die Grenzen der Auslegung. Die gerügten Verfahrensverstöße und ihre mögliche Kausalität für das gefundene Ergebnis müssen offen zu Tage treten. Im Hinblick auf die hier einzig in Frage kommenden verfahrensrechtlichen Verstöße käme es im Ergebnis demnach darauf an, ob die Entscheidungen polnischer Gerichte auf einem Verfahren beruhen, das von den Grundprinzipien des deutschen Verfahrensrechts in einem Maße abweicht, dass sie nach der deutschen Rechtsordnung nicht als in einer geordneten rechtsstaatlichen Weise ergangenen angesehen werden können.[41] Es kommt ausdrücklich nicht darauf an, ob bei gleicher Verfahrensweise auch die deutschen Gerichte gegen tragende Grundsätze des Verfahrensrechts verstoßen hätten. Eine wesentliche, unerträgliche Abweichung kann sich demnach nicht bereits aus der Andersartigkeit der Verfahrensvorschriften ergeben. Zu betrachten sind zudem nicht etwa einzelne Verfahrensabschnitte oder -handlungen, sondern das Verfahren als Ganzes und an-

[39] EuGH 2.4.2009 – C-167/08, ECLI:EU:C:2009:263 Rn. 27 = BeckEuRS 2009, 496934; EuGH 28.4.2009 – C-420/07, ECLI:EU:C:2009:271 Rn. 59 = BeckRS 2009, 70441.

[40] Rauscher, EuZPR/EuIPR/Leible, 5. Aufl. 2022, Brüssel Ia-VO Art. 45 Rn. 6.

[41] Rauscher, EuZPR/EuIPR/Leible, 5. Aufl. 2022, Brüssel Ia-VO Art. 45 Rn. 15; BGH 18.10.1967 – VIII ZR 145/66, BGHZ 48, 331; BGH 25.3.1970 – VIII ZR 202/69, BGHZ 53, 359; BGH 7.3.1979 – IV ZR 30/78, BGHZ 73, 378 (386); BGH 15.5.1986 – III ZR 192/84, BGHZ 98, 70 (73); BGH 4.6.1992 – IX ZR 149/91, BGHZ 118, 312; BGH 26.8.2009 – XII ZB 169/07, BGHZ 182, 188 (204) Rn. 25; BGH 19.9.1977 – VIII ZR 120/75, NJW 1978, 1114 = WM 1977, 1232; BGH 27.3.1984 – IX ZR 24/83, NJW 1984, 2765 = WM 1984, 749; BGH 21.3.1990 – XII ZB 71/89, NJW 1990, 2001 = IPRax 1992, 33; BGH 26.8.2009 – XII ZB 169/07, NJW 2009, 3308; OLG Hamm 27.6.1996 – 1 W 102/95, IPRax 1998, 203; OLG Frankfurt 31.1.2002 – 12 W 229/01, IPRax 2002, 523.

hand sämtlicher Umstände. Diese weitgehenden Anforderungen sind durchaus auf den Vertrauensgrundsatz zurückzuführen, wonach – so jedenfalls die abstrakte Annahme – in allen Mitgliedstaaten gerichtliche Entscheidungen regelmäßig in einem rechtsstaatlichen Verfahren ergehen. Im Hinblick auf den hier letztlich interessierenden verfahrensrechtlichen *ordre public*-Vorbehalt ist somit zu fragen, ob die ausländische Entscheidung in einem Verfahren zustande gekommen ist, das dermaßen von zwingenden Bestimmungen des deutschen Gerichtsverfassungs- und Verfahrensrechts abweicht, dass sie nicht mehr als Ergebnis eines geordneten, rechtsstaatlichen Verfahrens angesehen werden kann.[42] Dabei ist anerkannt, dass sich der Begriff nicht nur aus nationalen Vorschriften speist. Der Kernbestand der öffentlichen Ordnung wird vielmehr auch durch völkerrechtliche und supranationale Rechtssätze determiniert. Unstreitig sind vor allem die verfahrensrechtlichen Garantien maßgebend, aus dem der EuGH den allgemeinen gemeinschaftsrechtlichen Grundsatz herleitet, dass jedermann Anspruch auf einen fairen Prozess hat.[43] Zu einer weiteren elementaren verfahrensrechtlichen Garantie zählt der Grundsatz der Unabhängigkeit und Unparteilichkeit der Gerichte.[44] Dies hat der EuGH klargestellt und das Erfordernis der richterlichen Unabhängigkeit zum Wesensgehalt des in Art. 47 Abs. 2 GRCh verbürgten Grundrechts auf ein faires Verfahren erklärt.[45] Jede die richterliche Unabhängigkeit berührende Einschränkung dieses Grundrechts ist nach Art. 52 Abs. 1 S. 1 GRCh wegen Missachtung seines Wesensgehalts ausgeschlossen. Auch bei einer Berufung auf die EMRK und die Grundrechtecharta gilt gleichwohl, dass ein Grundrechtsverstoß allein nicht genügt, sondern dieser zu einer offensichtlichen Unvereinbarkeit mit dem *ordre public* des Anerkennungsstaates führen muss. Es lohnt zunächst ein Blick auf die Grundsätze selbst, um dann in einem zweiten Schritt zu untersuchen, welche Prüfungsmaßstäbe aus den bisherigen Entscheidungen herangezogen werden können.

aa) Art. 47 Grundrechtecharta

Art. 47 GRCh ist Ausweis der Union als Rechtsgemeinschaft, indem er den Anspruch auf einen wirksamen Rechtsschutz bei einem Gericht rechtsstaatlich verbürgt.[46] Die Vorschrift garantiert erstens, dass es einen Rechtsweg gibt, schreibt zweitens vor, dass dieser Rechtsweg zu einem unabhängigen, unparteiischen und auf gesetzlicher Grundlage errichteten Gericht führen muss, und verlangt drittens ein Verfahren, das fair, öffentlich und innerhalb angemessener Frist erfolgt sowie unter Gewährleistung der Möglichkeit der Beratung, Verteidigung und Vertre-

[42] BGH 6.4.2017 – IX ZB 19/16, EuZW 2017, 623; Linke/Hau, Internationales Zivilverfahrensrecht, 7. Aufl. 2018, Rn. 13, 38.

[43] EuGH 17.12.1998 – C-185/95 P, ECLI:EU:C:1998:608 Rn. 20f. = BeckRS 2004, 74773; EuGH 11.1.2000 – verb. Rs. C-174/98 P und C-189/98 P, ECLI:EU:C:2000:1 Rn. 17 = BeckRS 2004, 74687; EuGH 28.3.2000 – C-7/98, ECLI:EU:C:2000:164 Rn. 26 = BeckRS 2000, 70116; EuGH 2.4.2009 – C-394/07, ECLI:EU:C:2009:219 Rn. 28 = BeckRS 2009, 70383; Rauscher, EuZPR/EuIPR/Leible, 5. Aufl. 2022, Brüssel Ia-VO Art. 45 Rn. 12.

[44] Rauscher, EuZPR/EuIPR/Leible, 5. Aufl. 2022, Brüssel Ia-VO Art. 45 Rn. 16.

[45] EuGH 25.07.2018 – C-216/18 PPU, ECLI:EU:C:2018:586 Rn. 59, 63 = BeckRS 2018, 16206.

[46] Calliess/Ruffert, EUV – AEUV/Blanke, 6. Aufl. 2022, AEUV Art. 47 Rn. 1.

tung.[47] Damit schlägt die Vorschrift den Bogen zu weiteren justizgrundrechtlich abgesicherten Verfahrensgarantien. Gleichzeitig betont der EuGH in seiner neueren Rechtsprechung, dass die Unabhängigkeit der Gerichte zum Wesensgehalt des Art. 47 Abs. 2 GRCh gehört. Der EuGH versteht Art. 47 Abs. 2 GRCh als Konkretisierung des Rechtsstaatsprinzips aus Art. 2 EUV.[48] Zudem reichert Art. 47 Abs. 2 GRCh die objektiv-rechtlich im Rechtsstaatsprinzip verankerte Garantie der Unabhängigkeit der Gerichte um ein subjektives Recht an, auf das sich Betroffene vor mitgliedstaatlichen Gerichten und im Rahmen der eingeschränkten Möglichkeiten von Direktklagen auch vor dem EuGH berufen können.[49]

bb) Unionsgerichtsbarkeit

Art. 19 EUV beschreibt als Grundsatzbestimmung die wesentlichen Aufgaben sowie die Struktur der Unionsgerichtsbarkeit und trifft die zentralen Aussagen über den Rechtsschutz in der Europäischen Union.[50] Der hier im Fokus stehenden Art. 19 Abs. 1 UAbs. 2 EUV auferlegt dem EuGH die Aufgabe der „Wahrung des Rechts bei der Auslegung und Anwendung der Verträge, womit ihm die Funktion einer der Einhaltung des Rechts kontrollierenden dritten Gewalt zukommt.[51] Die Vorschrift steht damit im engen Zusammenhang zur unionsrechtlichen Rechtsschutzgarantie. Der EuGH hebt diesen Zusammenhang deutlich hervor, wenn er einerseits ausführt, dass Art. 19 Abs. 1 UAbs. 2 EUV eine Konkretisierung von Art. 2 EUV darstellt, andererseits Art. 47 Abs. 2 GRCh als Bestätigung der Vorgaben aus Art. 19 Abs. 1 UAbs. 2 EUV begreift. Die mit dem Vertrag von Lissabon geschaffene Vorschrift bekräftigt die Dezentralität des unionsrechtlichen Rechtsschutzsystems, in dem die Unionsgerichte und die mitgliedstaatlichen Gerichte gemeinsam die rechtsprechende Gewalt ausüben und Rechtsschutz gewähren. Die Einbindung der mitgliedstaatlichen Gerichte in einen Rechtsprechungsverbund mit der Unionsgerichtsbarkeit kommt insbesondere in Art. 267 AEUV zum Ausdruck, der das Recht und in bestimmten Konstellationen die Pflicht mitgliedstaatlicher Gerichte begründet, dem EuGH im Wege des Vorabentscheidungsverfahrens Fragen nach der Auslegung und Gültigkeit des Unionsrechts vorzulegen. Damit wird die Ausgestaltung der mitgliedstaatlichen Gerichtsbarkeit zum Regelungsgegenstand des Unionsrechts.[52] Art. 19 Abs. 1 UAbs. 2 EUV sieht in der Folge vor, dass die Mitgliedstaaten die erforderlichen Rechtsbehelfe schaffen müssen, um wirksamen Rechtsschutz in den vom Unionsrecht erfassten Bereichen zu gewährleisten. Auch wenn die konkrete Ausgestaltung von Gerichtsorganisation und Ge-

---

[47] von der Groeben/Schwarze/Hatje, Europäisches Unionsrecht/Lemke, 7. Aufl. 2015, GRC Art. 47 Rn. 5ff.

[48] EuGH 25.07.2019 – C-216/18 PPU, ECLI:EU:C:2018:586 Rn. 48 = BeckRS 2018, 16206; EuGH 5.6.2023 – C-204/21, ECLI:EU:C:2023:442 = NJW 2023, 2837 Rn. 354 = BeckEuRS 2023, 761766.

[49] Payandeh JuS 2021, 481.

[50] von der Groeben/Schwarze/Hatje, Europäisches Unionsrecht/Gaitanides, 7. Aufl. 2015, EUV Art. 19 Rn. 1.

[51] von der Groeben/Schwarze/Hatje, Europäisches Unionsrecht/Gaitanides, 7. Aufl. 2015, EUV Art. 19 Rn. 3.

[52] Payandeh JuS 2021, 481.

richtsverfahren im Kompetenzbereich der Mitgliedstaaten verbleibt, führt die Einbindung der mitgliedstaatlichen Gerichte in den europäischen Gerichtsverbund zu unionsrechtlichen Vorgaben für die judikative Gewalt in den Mitgliedstaaten.[53] Dementsprechend leitet der EuGH aus Art. 19 Abs. 1 UAbs. 2 EUV – wie auch aus Art. 267 AEUV – ab, dass die mit dem unionsrechtlich determinierten Rechtsschutz beauftragten Gerichte unabhängig sein müssen, damit wirksamer gerichtlicher Rechtsschutz gewährleistet ist. Damit schlägt der EuGH die Brücke von den unionsrechtlichen Anforderungen an die innerstaatliche Gerichtsbarkeit, die sich aus der Einbindung der mitgliedstaatlichen Gerichte in das europäische Rechtsschutzsystem ergeben, zu der unionsgrundrechtlichen Rechtsschutzgarantie des Art. 47 Abs. 1 GRCh.

cc) Völkerrechtliche Verpflichtungen

Das unionsverfassungsrechtliche Rechtsstaatsprinzip wird schließlich durch völkerrechtliche Vorgaben beeinflusst. Auch wenn die Europäische Union selbst, anders als ihre Mitgliedstaaten, weder Mitglied des Europarats noch Vertragspartei der EMRK ist, beeinflussen die rechtsstaatlichen Gehalte der EMRK in ihrer Ausgestaltung durch die Rechtsprechung des EGMR das unionsrechtliche Verständnis von Rechtsstaatlichkeit seit jeher ebenso wie andere im institutionellen Gefüge des Europarats, insbesondere von der Venedig-Kommission, entwickelte Standards. Im Hinblick auf die Unionsgrundrechte ist dieser Einfluss in Art. 6 Abs. 3 EUV und Art. 52 Abs. 3 GRCh explizit angeordnet, so dass insbesondere Art. 47 Abs. 2 GRCh im Lichte von Art. 6 EMRK auszulegen ist.[54] Er wird aber auch darüber hinaus für das Verständnis des unionsverfassungsrechtlichen Rechtsstaatsprinzips vom EuGH ebenso wie von der Europäischen Kommission angenommen.[55]

dd) Rechtsstaatlichkeit

Art. 2 EUV normiert die Rechtsstaatlichkeit (im Englischen *rule of law,* in der französischen Fassung *l'État de droit,* in Polen geht es um den Begriff *praworządność*) nun als Wert, auf den sich die Union gründet, und erkennt damit die Rechtsstaatlichkeit als eigenständiges unionsverfassungsrechtliches Prinzip. Das Rechtsstaatsprinzip ist auf Konkretisierung angelegt und angewiesen, so dass in der Rechtsanwendung die einzelnen Ausprägungen des Rechtsstaatsprinzips – seien sie explizit in den Verträgen normiert oder als ungeschriebene Grundsätze anerkannt – im Vordergrund stehen. Zu diesen konkreteren unionsrechtlichen Vorgaben bildet das Rechtsstaatsprinzip die unionsverfassungsrechtliche Grundlage, beeinflusst ihre Auslegung und ihr Verständnis. Diese Grundrechte und verfassungsrechtlichen Garantien des Art. 6 EMRK sind im Hinblick auf die Prüfung eines Verstoßes gegen den anerkennungsrechtlichen *ordre public*-Vorbehalt von grundlegender Relevanz.

---

53 Payandeh JuS 2021, 481.

54 Calliess/Ruffert, EUV – AEUV/Kingreen, 6. Aufl. 2022, GRC Art. 52 Rn. 21.

55 Payandeh JuS 2021, 481.

b) Rechtsprechung des EuGH und des BGH

Wann die geforderte offensichtliche Unvereinbarkeit anzunehmen ist, ist Auslegungsfrage. Eine weitere Frage ist, ob es einer konkreten Betroffenheit bedarf oder ein allgemeines Berufen auf die durch den EuGH zuletzt im Urteil vom 5.6.2023 festgestellten Missstände ausreichend ist. Zu klären wäre zudem, ob alle Entscheidungen der polnischen Gerichte, die in den Anwendungsbereich der Brüssel Ia-VO fallen, umfasst wären, oder vielmehr nur solche mit Bezügen zum Europarecht, da die Unionsgrundrechte die die Mitgliedstaaten nur bei Durchführung von Unionsrecht, das heißt in erster Linie bei allen unionsrechtlichen Fallgestaltungen binden. Entsprechende Entscheidungen des EuGH oder des BGH, die sich zu diesen konkreten Fragen verhalten, sind noch nicht ergangen. Es gibt aber eine Reihe von Entscheidungen, die einen Hinweis darauf geben, in welche Richtung der Weg eingeschlagen werden könnte.

aa) Krombach gegen Bamberski

Wichtige Anhaltspunkte liefert das Urteil des EuGH vom 28.3.2022 in der Sache Dieter Krombach gegen André Bamberski[56], ergangen im Rahmen eines Vorabentscheidungsersuchens des BGH.[57] Darin definierte der EuGH erstmals in seiner Rechtsprechung für das Brüsseler Übereinkommen EuGVÜ den Begriff „Verstoß gegen den *ordre public*". Mit der hier relevanten zweiten Vorlagefrage wollte der BGH wissen, ob im Rahmen des *ordre public*-Vorbehalts berücksichtigt werden dürfe, dass das Ausgangsgericht im zivilrechtlichen Adhäsionsverfahren die Verteidigung des Beklagten durch einen Rechtsanwalt zurückgewiesen habe. Dabei verwies der BGH auf Art. II des Protokolls zum EuGVÜ vom 27.9.1968, wonach Personen, die in einem anderen Vertragsstaat als dem ihres Wohnsitzes und ihrer Staatsangehörigkeit wegen einer fahrlässig begangenen Straftat verfolgt werden, das Recht haben, sich von dazu befugten Personen verteidigen zu lassen, auch wenn sie vor dem ausländischen Gericht nicht persönlich erscheinen. Der EuGH beantwortete die im Ergebnis die Frage dahingehend, dass in dem Ausschluss der Verteidigung durch einen Rechtsanwalt eine offensichtliche Grundrechtsverletzung liegt. Dabei verwies er auf das durch die Europäische Menschenrechtskonvention garantierte Recht auf einen fairen Prozess und den dazu gehörenden Anspruch auf rechtliches Gehör. Den Begriff eines Verstoßes gegen den *ordre public*-Vorbehalt definierte der EuGH dahingehend, dass dieser nur in Betracht komme, wenn eine in der Rechtsordnung des Vollstreckungsstaats als wesentlich geltende Rechtsnorm oder ein dort als grundlegend anerkanntes Recht offensichtlich verletzt wird. Die Rechtsverletzung muss offensichtlich sein, da ansonsten das Verbot der *révision au fond* gem. Art. 29 und Art 34 Abs. 3 EuGVÜ missachtet würde. Diese sehr enge Auslegung, die der EuGH auch in späteren Urteilen bestätigte[58], sei schon deswegen erforderlich, weil es sich hierbei um Hindernisse für eines der grundlegenden Ziele des Übereinkommens – die Freizügigkeit der Urteile, handle. Diese zum

[56] EuGH 28.3.2000 – C-7/98, ECLI:EU:C:2000:164 = BeckRS 2000, 70116.
[57] BGH 8.3.2012 – IX ZB 144/10, NJW 2012 1472 = IPRspr 2012, Nr. 263, 590–594.
[58] EuGH 11.5.2000 – C 38/98, ECLI:EU:C:2000:225 = BeckRS 2004, 76889.

Zeitpunkt der Entscheidung geforderte „offensichtliche" Verletzung von Rechtsprinzipien, die der Wortlaut des Art. 27 Nr. 1 EuGVÜ noch nicht enthielt, ist nun in Art. 45 Brüssel Ia-VO kodifiziert.

bb) Vollstreckung eines europäischen Haftbefehls in Polen

Als jedenfalls eine mögliche Richtung weisend könnten die Vorabentscheidungsersuchen des irischen High Court zu Europäischen Haftbefehlen aus Polen herangezogen werden. Die betroffene Person machte dort unter Berufung auf den begründeten Vorschlag der Kommission nach Art. 7 Abs. 1 EUV[59] geltend, ihr drohe bei Übergabe an die polnischen Gerichte angesichts der dortigen Justizreformen die echte Gefahr eines gegen Art. 6 Abs. 1 EMRK verstoßenden unfairen Strafverfahrens, was zu entsprechenden Vorlagefragen des High Court führte.[60] Im Ergebnis stellte der EuGH fest, dass es nicht genügt, wenn die zuständige Behörde feststellt, dass das Grundrecht auf ein faires Verfahren in seinem Wesensgehalt verletzt wird, weil die Justiz dieses Mitgliedstaates systemische oder allgemeine Mängel aufweist, die die Unabhängigkeit seiner Gerichte gefährden könnten. Vielmehr müsse die zur Vollstreckung berufene Justizbehörde in einem zweiten Schritt konkret und genau prüfen, ob es unter den gegebenen Umständen ernsthafte, durch Tatsachen bestätigte Gründe für die Annahme gebe, dass gerade die konkret betroffene Person einer solchen Gefahr ausgesetzt sein werde.[61] Deshalb müsste die vollstreckende Justizbehörde nur dann, wenn der Europäische Rat unter den Voraussetzungen des Art. 7 Abs. 2 EUV eine schwerwiegende und anhaltende Verletzung der in Art. 2 EUV genannten Grundsätze wie derjenigen, die der Rechtsstaatlichkeit inhärent sind, im Ausstellungsmitgliedstaat festgestellt hat und die Anwendung entsprechender Vorschriften gegenüber dem betroffenen Staat ausgesetzt hat (im vom EuGH zu entscheidenden Fall die des Rahmenbeschlusses 2002/584/JI[62]), ohne Weiteres ablehnen, ohne in irgendeiner Weise konkret prüfen zu müssen, ob die betroffene Person der echten Gefahr ausgesetzt ist, dass ihr Grundrecht auf ein faires Verfahren in seinem Wesensgehalt angetastet wird.[63] In allen übrigen Fällen, in denen es einen solchen Beschluss des Rates noch nicht gibt, verlangt der EuGH in der genannten Entscheidung eine konkrete und genaue Prüfung des Einzelfalls, ob es ernsthafte und durch Tatsachen bestätigte Gründe für die Annahme gibt, dass die betroffene Person einer echten Gefahr ausgesetzt sein wird, dass ihr Grundrecht auf ein unabhängiges Gericht verletzt und damit der Wesensgehalt ihres Grundrechts auf ein faires Verfahren angetastet wird. Im Fall der Anerkennung der Entscheidung eines polnischen Gerichtes hieße dies wohl, dass im Rahmen der Prüfung eines

[59] Europäische Kommission, COM(2017) 835 final.

[60] EuGH 25.7.2018 – C-216/18 PPU, ECLI:EU:C:2018:586 Rn. 34 = BeckRS 2018, 16206; Hummer EuR 2018 653ff.

[61] EuGH 25.7.2018 – C-216/18 PPU, ECLI:EU:C:2018:586 Rn. 66 = BeckRS 2018, 16206.

[62] Rahmenbeschluss des Rates vom 13.6.2002 über den Europäischen Haftbefehl und die Übergabeverfahren zwischen den Mitgliedstaaten – Stellungnahmen bestimmter Mitgliedstaaten zur Annahme des Rahmenbeschlusses, ABl. 2002 L 1901.

[63] EuGH 25.7.2018 – C-216/18 PPU, ECLI:EU:C:2018:586 Rn. 72 = BeckRS 2018, 16206.

etwaigen Antrages nach Art. 45 Abs. 1 lit. a Brüssel Ia-VO zu prüfen wäre, ob in dem konkreten Verfahren, in dem die Entscheidung, um deren Anerkennung es geht, ergangen ist, konkrete Gefahren bestanden. Es geht also um die Frage, ob die festgestellten Mängel dieses konkrete Gericht berühren können.

cc) Vorlagefragen des LG Aachen vom 06. 12. 2021 und Entscheidung des EuGH vom 09. 11. 2023

Im Rahmen eines Vorabentscheidungsersuchens des LG Aachen vom 6. 12. 2021[64] wurde die Frage der Ablehnung der Anerkennung des Urteils aus Polen diskutiert, wobei im Vordergrund die Frage des Verstoßes der Justizreformen gegen das Rechtsstaatsprinzip stand. Mit seinen Fragen möchte das vorlegende Gericht im Wesentlichen wissen, ob Art. 3 Abs. 4 und Art. 8 des Rahmenbeschlusses 2008/909 dahin auszulegen sind, dass das Gericht des Vollstreckungsmitgliedstaats es von sich aus ablehnen kann, die von einem Gericht eines anderen Mitgliedstaats ausgesprochene Verurteilung zu einer strafrechtlichen Sanktion anzuerkennen und zu vollstrecken, wenn es über Anhaltspunkte dafür verfügt, dass in diesem Mitgliedstaat systemische oder allgemeine Mängel in Bezug auf das Recht auf ein faires Verfahren und in einem weiteren Sinne das Funktionieren des Justizsystems und die Einhaltung der Rechtsstaatlichkeit bestehen. Insbesondere war für das LG Aachen die Frage von Bedeutung, ob es einer konkreten Betroffenheit bedarf, wie sie der EuGH in Fall des irischen High Court gefordert hatte. Da es um die Anerkennung einer strafrechtlichen Entscheidung ging, war der rechtliche Rahmen durch Art. 8 des Rahmenbeschlusses 2008/909/JI des Rates vom 27. 11. 2008 über die Anwendung des Grundsatzes der gegenseitigen Anerkennung auf Urteile in Strafsachen, durch die eine freiheitsentziehende Strafe oder Maßnahme verhängt wird, für die Zwecke ihrer Vollstreckung in der Europäischen Union abgesteckt. Der Rahmenbeschluss kennt zwar bestimmte Versagungsgründe, die eine Anerkennung verhindern, einen *ordre public*-Vorbehalt enthalten die Regelungen allerdings nicht. Zur Begründung berief sich das LG Aachen im Wesentlichen auf die Urteile des EuGH vom 5. 11. 2019, vom 19. 11. 2019 und vom 2. 3. 2021, in denen dieser bereits entsprechende Verstöße Polens gegen den Grundsatz der Rechtsstaatlichkeit feststellte. Erwähnung fand zudem der begründete Vorschlag der Europäischen Kommission vom 20.12.217 nach Art. 7 Abs. 1 EUV zur Rechtsstaatlichkeit in Polen.[65] Es stellte dann, hier vor allem interessierende Frage, ob die vom EuGH im oben erwähnten Fall verlangte zweistufige Prüfung auch für die Frage der Anerkennung der Entscheidung gelte. LG Aachen war der Meinung, dass eine solche konkrete Prüfung der Gefährdung – der zweite Schritt also – nicht angezeigt sei. Es sei nämlich „schlechterdings kein Verfahren denkbar", in dem angesichts der durch den EuGH festgestellten strukturellen Eingriffe in das Justizsystem die Verletzung des Grund-

[64] LG Aachen 6. 12. 2021 – 33 O StVK 1055/21, ECLI:DE:LGAC:2021:1206.33OSTVK 1055.21.00 = BeckRS 2021, 45066.

[65] Europäische Kommission, COM(2017) 835 final. In seiner Entschließung vom März 2018 unterstützte das Europäische Parlament das Vorhaben, Entschließung des Europäischen Parlaments, 1.3.2018, P8_TA(2018)0055. Weitere wesentliche Entwicklungen gab es seitdem allerdings nicht.

rechts auf ein faires Verfahren ausgeschlossen werden könnte. Im Unterschied zu der Auslieferung sei bei der Frage der Anerkennung außerdem zu bedenken, dass dort die Frage der Prognose des zu erwartenden Verfahrensverlaufs nach Vollstreckung des europäischen Haftbefehls zu klären war. Eine solche Prognoseentscheidung sei aber bei der Frage der Anerkennung nicht relevant, da das Verfahren mit der Entscheidung über die Vollstreckbarerklärung im bilateralen Verhältnis zwischen der Bundesrepublik und Polen abgeschlossen sei. Einer solcher Sichtweise erteilte der EuGH in der rauf folgenden Entscheidung schließlich eine Absage und blieb bei der Forderung einer zweistufigen Prüfung.[66] Bei festgestellten Mängeln müsse der Vollstreckungsmitgliedsstaat in einem zweiten Schritt konkret und genau untersuchen, inwieweit sich die im ersten Prüfungsschritt festgestellten Mängel auf das Funktionieren der für die Verfahren gegen die betroffene Person zuständigen Gerichte des Ausstellungsmitgliedsstaats auswirken konnten und ob es in Anbetracht der persönlichen Situation dieser Person sowie des zugrunde liegenden Sachverhalts ernsthafte und durch Tatsachen bestätigte Gründe für die Annahme gibt, dass im konkreten Fall eine solche Gefahr tatsächlich eingetreten sei.[67] Es sei nämlich darauf hinzuweisen, dass sich die Existenz systemischer oder allgemeiner Mängel nicht zwangsläufig auf alle Entscheidungen auswirkt, die von den Gerichten dieses Mitgliedstaates in jedem Einzelfall erlassen werden. Der EuGH fürchtete eine Aushöhlung des Grundsatzes des gegenseitigen Vertrauens, würde die Möglichkeit zugelassen werden, sämtliche Anträge auf Anerkennung von Urteilen und auf Vollstreckung strafrechtlicher Sanktionen aus dem von diesen Mängeln betroffenen Mitgliedstaat aus Prinzip ablehnen.

dd) Zweistufige Prüfung auch bei systemischen Mängeln

Es kann festgehalten werden, dass ein Verstoß gegen den *ordre public*-Vorbehalt nach der bisherigen Rechtsprechung nur in Betracht kommt, wenn eine in der Rechtsordnung des Vollstreckungsstaats als wesentlich geltende Rechtsnorm oder ein dort als grundlegend anerkanntes Recht offensichtlich verletzt wird – dies dürfte mittlerweile als gesicherte und ständige Rechtsprechung des EuGH und des BGH gelten. Ob eine allgemeine Berufung auf systemische Mängel – vom EuGH als solche bereits in zahlreichenden Urteilen als gegeben anerkennte – ausreicht, um einen *ordre public*-Verstoß zu begründen oder ob konkret geprüft werden müsse, ob sich diese Mängel in der konkret anzuerkennenden Entscheidung niedergeschlagen haben, ist jedenfalls für den Anwendungsbereich der Brüssel Ia-VO im Hinblick auf die Justizreformen in Polen bisher nicht entschieden worden. Für die strafrechtlichen Sanktionen fordert der EuGH zum Schutz des Grundsatzes des gegenseitigen Vertrauens eine solche konkrete Betroffenheit.

---

[66] EuGH 9.11.2023 – C-819/21, ECLI:EU:C:2023:841 Rn. 29 = BeckRS 2023, 31012.
[67] EuGH 9.11.2023 – C-819/21, ECLI:EU:C:2023:841 Rn. 30 = BeckRS 2023, 31012.

3. *Folgen für die Anerkennung*

Gerichte müssen unabhängig sein, damit sie im Gefüge der Gewaltenteilung die Kontrolle über Akte der Exekutive und auch der Legislative am Maßstab der Verfassung ausüben können. Der Grundsatz der Unabhängigkeit der Gerichte geht auf eine Forderung der Aufklärung seit Mitte des 18. Jahrhunderts zurück.[68] Sowohl historisch als auch systematisch ist die richterliche Unabhängigkeit unlösbar mit der Gewaltenteilung und mit dem Rechtsstaatsprinzip verbunden. Die Mitgliedstaaten erfüllen nur bei vollständiger Gewährleistung der Unabhängigkeit ihrer Gerichte die Rechtstaatlichkeitsanforderungen des Art. 2 EUV, die als unteilbar zu betrachten sind. Ein Mitgliedstaat kann nicht in den vom Unionsrecht erfassten Bereichen rechtsstaatlich und ansonsten unrechtsstaatlich strukturiert sein und umgekehrt.[69] Der Vertrauensgrundsatz ist nicht uferlos, das zeigt sich schon daran, dass der *ordre public*-Vorbehalt in der Brüssel Ia-VO überhaupt kodifiziert wurde. Das Vertrauen kann auch nur dann dem anderen Mitgliedstaat entgegengebracht werden, wenn sich dieses wiederum an die grundlegenden Übereinkünfte der Europäischen Union als Wertegemeinschaft hält. Seit dem Lissaboner Vertrag ist in Art. 2 EUV ein Kodex jener Werte enthalten, dazu zählt auch die Rechtsstaatlichkeit. Der Wert der Rechtsstaatlichkeit ergibt sich aus dem Charakter einer Rechtsgemeinschaft.

Die Europäische Union hat das Recht, in ihren von den Mitgliedstaaten übertragenen Zuständigkeiten eine eigene Rechtsordnung zu schaffen. Dieses Unionsrecht ist eine eigenständige Kategorie, sie entwickelt sich gegenüber den Rechtsordnungen der Mitgliedstaaten autonom. Der EuGH hat schon in seiner frühzeitigen Rechtsprechung den Grundsatz des Vorranges des EU-Rechts gegenüber dem nationalen Recht der Mitgliedstaaten judiziert.[70] Ein bedeutendes Instrument europäischer Rechtsstaatlichkeit ist die Kompetenz des EuGH zur Vorabentscheidung. Dadurch soll die Homogenität der Auslegung und Anwendung des Gemeinschaftsrechts gewährleistet werden. Einen besonderen Tiefpunkt erreichte der Rechtsstaatskonflikt mit Polen durch ein Urteil des polnischen Verfassungsgerichtes vom 2.10.2021. In diesem Urteil, das durch einen Antrag des polnischen Ministerpräsidenten ausgelöst wurde, stellte das Gericht fest, dass der EU-Vertrag in wesentlichen Punkten im Widerspruch zur polnischen Verfassung stehe. Es ist eine Verpflichtung der Europäischen Union klarzustellen, was der europäische Rechtsstaat ist. Er gibt den Rechtssuchenden das Recht, gegen das Unrecht der Politik vorzugehen. Dazu braucht es die Unabhängigkeit von Gerichten. Eine zweistufige Prüfung scheint angesichts der eklatanten Mängel nicht nur nicht angezeigt, sondern kaum praktikabel. Damit hinge eine Prüfung zusammen, ob das Gericht, das die anzuerkennende Entscheidung erlassen hat, unparteilich und unabhängig ist und von den dargestellten Reformen nicht betroffen ist. Eine solche Prüfung ist kaum möglich. Die Reformen betreffen alle Richterinnen und Richter der Zivilgerichtsbarkeit. Theoretisch denkbar wäre eine zweistufige Vorgehensweise dahin-

---

[68] Kadelbach JA 2023, 1250.
[69] Giegerich ZEuS 2019, 61 (72).
[70] EuGH 15.7.1964 – C-6/64, ECLI:EU:C:1964:66 = BeckRS 1964, 105086.

gehend, ob es um die Entscheidung eines Gerichtes geht, das von einer der durch EuGH in seiner Entscheidung vom 5.6.2023 geprüften Fallkonstellationen betroffen war. Ging es zB um ein Gericht, in dem Richter zu entscheiden hatten, die durch den neuen Richterrat berufen wurden. Auch könnte die Frage von Relevanz sein, ob es ggf. um eine Frage des Unionsrechts geht und das Gericht angesichts der drohenden disziplinarischen Folgen die Vorlage an den EuGH im Rahmen eines Vorabentscheidungsersuchens unterlies, wie auch immer eine solche Frage in der Praxis zu klären wäre. Solch weitgehenden Prüfungen würden nicht mehr zumutbar sein.

JAN VON HEIN

Neues zum Kollisionsrecht der Patientenverfügung

I. Einführung

Das deutsche materielle Recht kennt schon seit geraumer Zeit das Institut der Patientenverfügung, deren Kodifikation bereits 2009 durch das dritte Betreuungsrechtsänderungsgesetz[1] in § 1901a BGB aF erfolgte und die seit dem 1.1.2023 in § 1827 BGB zu finden ist.[2] Inhaltlich blieb die Vorschrift bei der jüngsten umfassenden Reform des Betreuungsrechts unverändert.[3] Als Patientenverfügung i.S. der sachrechtlichen Legaldefinition gilt folglich eine Erklärung, in der „ein einwilligungsfähiger Volljähriger für den Fall seiner Einwilligungsunfähigkeit schriftlich festgelegt [hat], ob er in bestimmte, zum Zeitpunkt der Festlegung noch nicht unmittelbar bevorstehende Untersuchungen seines Gesundheitszustands, Heilbehandlungen oder ärztliche Eingriffe einwilligt oder sie untersagt" (§ 1827 Abs. 1 S. 1 BGB). Hat ein Erwachsener eine Patientenverfügung errichtet, muss der Betreuer prüfen, ob die darin enthaltenen Festlegungen auf die aktuelle Lebens- und Behandlungssituation des Betreuten zutreffen (§ 1827 Abs. 1 S. 1 BGB). Ist dies zu bejahen, hat der Betreuer den Willen des Betreuten zu befolgen und zu verwirklichen (§ 1827 Abs. 1 S. 2 BGB). Obwohl im Zuge der jüngsten Reform des Betreuungsrechts auch das autonome IPR für dieses Gebiet neu geregelt wurde,[4] fehlt es bislang an einer auf die Patientenverfügung zugeschnittenen Kollisionsnorm. Dies könnte dem Vorrang internationaler Rechtsakte i.S. des Art. 3 EGBGB geschuldet sein. Zwar existiert auf dem Gebiet des Internationalen Betreuungsrechts bislang keine einschlägige EU-Verordnung (Art. 3 Nr. 1 EGBGB). Deutschland ist aber wie einige andere EU-Mitgliedstaaten Vertragsstaat des Haager Erwachsenenschutzübereinkommens.[5] Dieses Übereinkommen wurde am 13.1.2000 geschlossen und trat am 1.1.2009 zwischen Frankreich, Deutschland und dem Vereinigten Königreich (allerdings beschränkt auf Schottland) in Kraft. Heute ist das Überein-

---

[1] BGBl. 2009 I 2286.

[2] Gesetz zur Reform des Vormundschafts- und Betreuungsrechts vom 4.5.2021 (BGBl. 2021 I 882); zur Entstehungsgeschichte näher Münchener Kommentar zum BGB/Schneider, 9. Aufl. 2024, BGB § 1827 Rn. 1; zur Rechtslage in anderen europäischen Ländern Bergamini/Bercea/Verteş-Olteanu Yb PIL 24 (2022/2023), 1 (3ff.).

[3] Münchener Kommentar zum BGB/Schneider, 9. Aufl. 2024, BGB § 1827 Rn. 1.

[4] Hierzu monographisch Meyer, Die Anknüpfung internationaler Fürsorgeverhältnisse nach der Reform des Art. 24 EGBGB, 2023; zur Einführung Thorn/Varón Romero IPRax 2021, 15; Wagner FamRZ 2022, 405; speziell zu Art. 15 EGBGB Croon-Gestefeld FamRZ 2021, 1939.

[5] Haager Übereinkommen über den internationalen Schutz von Erwachsenen vom 13.1.2000 (BGBl. 2007 II 323).

kommen auch in der Schweiz, Finnland, Estland, der Tschechischen Republik, Österreich, Monaco, Lettland, Portugal, Zypern, Belgien, Griechenland, Malta und Irland in Kraft. Die Niederlande, Italien, Luxemburg und Polen haben das Übereinkommen unterzeichnet, es jedoch noch nicht ratifiziert. In den Niederlanden wird das Übereinkommen allerdings bereits von den Gerichten als Teil des niederländischen autonomen Rechts angewendet.[6] Insgesamt ist der Status der Ratifizierungen des ErwSÜ ein knappes Vierteljahrhundert nach seinem Abschluss eher unbefriedigend, da bisher nur 13 der heutigen EU-Mitgliedstaaten dem Übereinkommen beigetreten sind. Zudem ist zweifelhaft, ob und ggf. hinsichtlich welcher Aspekte das ErwSÜ auf Patientenverfügungen überhaupt anwendbar ist (→ II.). Probleme bereitet insbesondere die Abgrenzung von der Vorsorgevollmacht, für die in Art. 15 ErwSÜ eine spezielle Kollisionsnorm besteht (→ II. 2.), sowie das Verhältnis zur Rom I- und II-VO, deren Kollisionsnormen insbesondere für das auf die Arzthaftung anwendbare Recht maßgebend sind (→ III.). Am 31.5.2023 hat die Europäische Kommission einen Vorschlag für eine Verordnung über die Zuständigkeit, das anwendbare Recht, die Anerkennung und Durchsetzung von Maßnahmen und die Zusammenarbeit in Angelegenheiten des Erwachsenenschutzes (im Folgenden: EU-Erwachsenenschutzverordnungsentwurf – EU-ErwSVO-E) vorgelegt, der das ErwSÜ innerhalb der EU überlagern und ergänzen soll, um den internationalen Erwachsenenschutz im Kreise der Mitgliedstaaten zu verbessern.[7] Die EU selbst kann dem ErwSÜ im Gegensatz zu neueren Haager Konventionen nicht selbst beitreten.[8] Um die Ratifikation des ErwSÜ zu beschleunigen, wird der Verordnung deshalb ein Ratsbeschluss beigefügt, mit dem die Mitgliedstaaten (außer Dänemark) ermächtigt werden, im Interesse der EU Vertragsparteien des ErwSÜ zu werden oder zu bleiben.[9]

Im vorliegenden Beitrag soll der Frage nachgegangen werden, wie die Patientenverfügung im Rahmen dieser dynamischen Gemengelage aus verschiedenen Rechtsquellen kollisionsrechtlich einzuordnen ist. Diese Ausführungen sind *Thomas Rauscher* anlässlich seines 70. Geburtstags gewidmet. Ich habe bereits als Student im Sommersemester 1992 an der Universität Hamburg meinen späteren Kollegen kennengelernt, wo er seinerzeit ein Seminar zu den Auswirkungen der Wiedervereinigung auf das deutsche Privatrecht veranstaltete. Seitdem ist der wissenschaftliche Kontakt nicht abgerissen, und heute bin ich *Thomas Rauscher* vor allem als Kommentator der EU-BewVO und Teilen der Rom I-VO in dem von ihm herausgege-

---

[6] Hoge Raad 2.2.2018 – 17/00757, ECLI:NL:HR:2018:147.

[7] Vorschlag für eine Verordnung des Europäischen Parlaments und des Rates über die Zuständigkeit, das anwendbare Recht, die Anerkennung und Vollstreckung von Maßnahmen und die Zusammenarbeit in Fragen betreffend den Schutz Erwachsener vom 31.5.2023, COM(2023) 280 final; hierzu Bergamini/Bercea/Verteş-Olteanu Yb PIL 24 (2022/2023), 1 (15ff.); Kohler/Pintens FamRZ 2023, 1409 (1412ff.).

[8] John/Gulati/Köhler, The Elgar Companion to the Hague Conference on Private International Law/Frimston, 2020, 226 (235).

[9] Vorschlag für einen Beschluss des Rates zur Ermächtigung der Mitgliedstaaten, im Interesse der Europäischen Union Vertragsparteien des Übereinkommens vom 13. Januar 2000 über den internationalen Schutz von Erwachsenen zu werden oder zu bleiben vom 31.5.2023, COM (2023) 281 final.

benen Werk zum Europäischen IPR/IZVR verbunden.[10] Mit dem Internationalen Betreuungsrecht hat sich Rauscher ebenfalls befasst, ua als Kommentator,[11] Lehrbuchautor[12] und als Doktorvater der einschlägigen Dissertation von *Kobsik.*[13] Es ist daher zu hoffen, dass die folgenden Zeilen auf ein wohlwollendes Interesse des verehrten *Jubilars* stoßen mögen.

II. Das Haager Erwachsenenschutzübereinkommen

1. Die vom ErwSÜ erfassten Schutzmaßnahmen

Gem. Art. 1 Abs. 1 ErwSÜ ist das Übereinkommen „bei internationalen Sachverhalten auf den Schutz von Erwachsenen anzuwenden, die aufgrund einer Beeinträchtigung oder der Unzulänglichkeit ihrer persönlichen Fähigkeiten nicht in der Lage sind, ihre Interessen zu schützen".[14] Dieser Schutz kann erstens durch die in Art. 1 Abs. 2 lit. a ErwSÜ angesprochenen gerichtlichen oder behördlichen Maßnahmen verwirklicht werden; zweitens kommt eine Vertretung des Erwachsenen aufgrund einer privatautonom erteilten Vorsorgevollmacht in Betracht (Art. 1 Abs. 2 lit. c iVm Art. 15 ErwSÜ). Fraglich ist, wie die Patientenverfügung in diesen Dualismus einzuordnen ist. Die Maßnahmen, auf die in Art. 1 ErwSÜ Bezug genommen wird, werden in Art. 3 ErwSÜ näher definiert und aufgezählt. Als Einfallstor für die Patientenverfügung scheint prima facie Art. 3 lit. g Alt. 1 ErwSÜ in Betracht zu kommen, der als Schutzmaßnahme die Erlaubnis eines bestimmten Einschreitens zum Schutz der Person nennt. Als Beispiele für einen punktuellen Eingriff iSd Art. 3 lit. g ErwSÜ wird etwa eine chirurgische Behandlung des Betroffenen genannt.[15] In Bezug auf individuelle Heilbehandlungen ist aber zwischen der medizinischen Anordnung als solcher (der Verschreibung eines Medikaments, der Ansetzung einer Operation) einerseits, der rechtlichen Schutzmaßnahme, die diesen Eingriff erst ermöglicht, andererseits, zu unterscheiden.[16] Der medizinische Eingriff als solcher wird nicht erfasst.[17] Dies ergibt sich aus dem Rückbezug des

[10] Rauscher, EuZPR/EuIPR/v. Hein, 5. Aufl. 2022, EU-BewVO; Rauscher, EuZPR/EuIPR/v. Hein, 5. Aufl. 2023, Einl., Art. 1–3, 8, 11, 17, 24–26 Rom I-VO.

[11] Münchener Kommentar zum FamFG/Rauscher, 3. Aufl. 2018, FamFG §§ 104ff.

[12] Rauscher, Internationales Privatrecht, 5. Aufl. 2017, Rn. 1055ff.

[13] Kobsik, Antizipierte Erklärungen in Gesundheitsangelegenheiten im grenzüberschreitenden Verkehr, 2020.

[14] Näher Staudinger, BGB/v. Hein, 2022, ErwSÜ Art. 1 Rn. 1ff.

[15] Lagarde, Protection of Adults Convention – Explanatory Report, New and Revised Edition, 2017, Rn. 26.

[16] Practical Handbook, Prel. Doc. Nr. 6, Juli 2022, Rn. 3.49, https://assets.hcch.net/docs/339879fd-13de-4f74-aba7–697ee92213c1.pdf (abgerufen 13.5.2024); Bucher SZIER 2000, 37 (42); Kobsik, Antizipierte Erklärungen in Gesundheitsangelegenheiten im grenzüberschreitenden Verkehr, 2020, S. 321; Staudinger, BGB/v. Hein, 2022, ErwSÜ Art. 4 Rn. 11; skeptisch Frimston/Ruck Keene/van Overdijk, The International Protection of Adults/Ruck Keene, 2015, Rn. 8.45.

[17] Bucher SZIER 2000, 37 (42ff.); Clive Yb PIL 2 (2000), 1 (20); Budzikiewicz/Heiderhoff/Klinkhammer/Niethammer-Jürgens, Vorsorge und Verantwortung im Internationalen Familienrecht/Lipp, 2023, 103 (108); Siehr RabelsZ 64 (2000) 715 (720).

Art. 3 ErwSÜ auf den Art. 1 ErwSÜ, der in lit. a allein von behördlichen Maßnahmen spricht. Art. 3 lit. g ErwSÜ hat lediglich die Funktion klarzustellen, dass als Schutzmaßnahme iSd Art. 1 Abs. 2 lit. a ErwSÜ nicht nur die umfassende Einrichtung zB einer Betreuung (zB nach § 1814 Abs. 1 BGB) in Betracht kommt, sondern dass hierzu auch die behördliche oder gerichtliche Autorisierung einer ärztlichen Behandlung im Einzelfall (zB gem. § 1829 BGB) gehört.[18] Ebenso wenig findet das ErwSÜ Anwendung auf Entscheidungen medizinischer Fachgremien, die etwa an einer Klinik zur Beurteilung ethisch komplexer Fragen – zB der Triage im Falle einer Pandemie[19] – eingesetzt werden.[20] Besondere Bedeutung für die internationale Zuständigkeit in Bezug auf ärztliche Eingriffe haben die Art. 10 und 11 ErwSÜ, die es ermöglichen, im Bedarfsfall die zur Autorisierung nötigen Schutzmaßnahmen am Ort des schlichten Aufenthalts des Betroffenen anzuordnen.[21]

2. *Vorsorgevollmacht und Patientenverfügung*

Art. 15 ErwSÜ enthält eine Kollisionsnorm für das auf die Vorsorgevollmacht anwendbare Recht. Maßgebend ist insoweit grundsätzlich der gewöhnliche Aufenthalt des Betroffenen (Art. 15 Abs. 1 ErwSÜ), doch kann das anwendbare Recht auch nach Maßgabe des Art. 15 Abs. 2 ErwSÜ gewählt werden. Abgrenzungsfragen wirft das Verhältnis der Vorsorgevollmacht zur Patientenverfügung auf. Unproblematisch werden von Art. 15 ErwSÜ diejenigen Fälle erfasst, in denen der Betroffene lediglich bestimmt, wer ihn in Angelegenheiten der Gesundheitssorge vertreten darf, dem Bevollmächtigten i. Ü. aber freie Hand lässt. Verbindet der Betroffene die Erteilung einer Vorsorgevollmacht mit besonderen Weisungen an den Bevollmächtigten, zB der Einleitung lebensverlängernder Maßnahmen nicht zuzustimmen, fällt auch dieses Mandat unter Art. 15 ErwSÜ.[22] Die erteilten Restriktionen der Einwilligungsbefugnis des Bevollmächtigten auf die von einer Vollmacht ausdrücklich umfassten ärztlichen Maßnahmen (§ 1829 Abs. 5 BGB) können als Einschränkungen des „Umfangs" der Vollmacht iSd Art. 15 Abs. 1 ErwSÜ eingestuft werden.[23] Nach anderer Ansicht soll es sich hier-

[18] Münchener Kommentar zum BGB/Lipp, 9. Aufl. 2024, ErwSÜ Art. 1–4 Rn. 25; vgl. auch Lagarde, Protection of Adults Convention – Explanatory Report, New and Revised Edition, 2017, Rn. 42; Practical Handbook, Prel. Doc. Nr. 6, Juli 2022, Rn. 3.49; Bucher SZIER 2000, 37 (42).

[19] Hierzu BVerfG 16.12.2021 – 1 BvR 1541/20, NJW 2022, 380.

[20] Bucher SZIER 2000, 37 (42ff.).

[21] Staudinger, BGB/v. Hein, 2022, ErwSÜ Art. 10 Rn. 2, Art. 11 Rn. 4f.

[22] Lagarde, Protection of Adults Convention – Explanatory Report, New and Revised Edition, 2017, Rn. 96; Erman BGB/Stürner, 17. Aufl. 2023, ErwSÜ Art. 15 Rn. 1; Deixler-Hübner/Schauer, Handbuch Erwachsenenschutzrecht/Heindler, 2018, Rn. 14.52; Helms FamRZ 2008, 1995 (1999 in Fn. 55); Lemmerz, Die Patientenverfügung, 2014, 132; Jayme FS Spellenberg, 2010, 203 (208); Schaub IPRax 2016, 207 (209); Schwander AJP/PJA 2014, 1351 (1368f.); Spickhoff FS Coester-Waltjen, 2015, 825 (827); Wedemann FamRZ 2010, 785 (786); aA v. Bar/Mankowski, Internationales Privatrecht II, 2. Aufl. 2019, § 6 Rn. 89; Barth/Ganner, Handbuch des Erwachsenenschutzrechts/Traar, 3. Aufl. 2019, 948 (1005).

[23] Vgl. Lagarde, Protection of Adults Convention – Explanatory Report, New and Revised Edition, 2017, Rn. 96; Bucher SZIER 2000, 37 (53f.); Fagan Elder Law Journal 10 (2002) 329 (347ff.); Guttenberger, Das Haager Übereinkommen über den internationalen Schutz von

bei um Fragen der Ausübung der Vertretungsmacht handeln, die sich nach Art. 15 Abs. 3 ErwSÜ richten.[24]

Für die Art und Weise der Ausübung der Vollmacht sieht Art. 15 Abs. 3 ErwSÜ eine Sonderanknüpfung an das Recht des Staates vor, in dem die Vollmacht ausgeübt wird. Die Abgrenzung des Anwendungsbereichs der Art. 15 Abs. 1, 2 ErwSÜ von Art. 15 Abs. 3 ErwSÜ bereitet jedoch Probleme.[25] Art. 15 Abs. 3 ErwSÜ dient grundsätzlich ebenso wie Art. 14 ErwSÜ, der eine vordergründig ähnliche Regelung in Bezug auf die Durchführung von Schutzmaßnahmen trifft,[26] praktischen Zwecken:[27] Bloße Modalitäten der Ausübung einer Vertretungsmacht sollen dem Recht des Ortes unterworfen werden, an dem von dieser Vollmacht Gebrauch gemacht wird, um für eher technische Fragen die Notwendigkeit der zeit- und kostenaufwendigen Ermittlung ausländischen Rechts zu vermeiden. Es ist aber bei der Auslegung des Art. 15 Abs. 3 ErwSÜ zu beachten, dass die letztgenannte Vorschrift bewusst enger gefasst worden ist als Art. 14 ErwSÜ.[28] Während Art. 14 ErwSÜ allgemein die „Bedingungen", unter denen eine Schutzmaßnahme durchgeführt wird, dem Recht des Durchführungsstaates unterwirft, beschränkt sich Art. 15 Abs. 3 ErwSÜ auf die „Art und Weise der Ausübung" der Vollmacht. Diese absichtlich restriktiver gehaltene Formulierung resultiert daraus, dass auf der Haager Konferenz einige Delegationen für eine weitere Fassung des Art. 15 Abs. 3 ErwSÜ mit der Begründung eintraten, es müsse verhindert werden, dass ausländische Bevollmächtigte ihre Vertretungsmacht ausübten, um entgegen den Voraussetzungen des lokalen Rechts zB Organtransplantationen oder Bluttransfusionen zu erlauben.[29] Dieser Antrag wurde jedoch mit der Begründung abgelehnt, dass hierfür angesichts des ordre-public-Vorbehalts (Art. 21 ErwSÜ) kein Bedürfnis bestehe.[30] Hinzu kommt der Schutz, der bei einem Missbrauch der Vertretungsmacht durch die in Art. 16 ErwSÜ vorgesehene Aufhebungs- bzw. Änderungsbefugnis gewährt wird. Schließlich sind Eingriffsnormen des Staates, in dem sich der Erwachsene befindet, im Rahmen des Art. 20 ErwSÜ zu beachten.

Rechtspolitisch mag man durchaus bezweifeln, ob es sachgerecht ist, das auf Fragen der Ausübung einer Vertretungsmacht anwendbare Recht unterschiedlich an-

Erwachsenen, 2004, S. 152; Lemmerz, Die Patientenverfügung, 2014, 138; Kobsik, Antizipierte Erklärungen in Gesundheitsangelegenheiten im grenzüberschreitenden Verkehr, 2020, S. 423; Münchener Kommentar zum BGB/Lipp, 9. Aufl. 2024, ErwSÜ Art. 15 Rn. 24.

[24] So Schwander AJP/PJA 2014, 1351 (1369); Wedemann FamRZ 2010, 785 (789); ebenso, aber kritisch, Hill IntCompLQ 58 (2009) 469 (474f.).

[25] Vgl. auch v. Bar/Mankowski, Internationales Privatrecht II, 2. Aufl. 2019, § 6 Rn. 74; Salm, Protection of Vulnerable Adults, European Added Value Assessment Accompanying the European Parliament's Legislative Initiative Report/Curry-Sumner, 2016, Annex I, 18 (65).

[26] Näher Staudinger, BGB/v. Hein, 2022, ErwSÜ Art. 14 Rn. 1ff.

[27] Ebenso Münchener Kommentar zum BGB/Lipp, 9. Aufl. 2024, ErwSÜ Art. 15 Rn. 45.

[28] Dutoit FichesJurSuisses 2011, 1 (16); Helms FamRZ 2008, 1995 (2000); Kobsik, Antizipierte Erklärungen in Gesundheitsangelegenheiten im grenzüberschreitenden Verkehr, 2020, S. 392; aA speziell zu Patientenverfügungen Wedemann FamRZ 2010, 785 (789).

[29] Lagarde, Protection of Adults Convention – Explanatory Report, New and Revised Edition, 2017, Rn. 106.

[30] Lagarde, Protection of Adults Convention – Explanatory Report, New and Revised Edition, 2017, Rn. 106.

zuknüpfen, je nachdem, ob es sich um einen behördlich bestellten Betreuer (dann gilt für die Ausübung insgesamt Art. 14 ErwSÜ) oder um einen rechtsgeschäftlich Bevollmächtigten handelt, für den nur der enger gefasste Art. 15 Abs. 3 ErwSÜ maßgeblich ist.[31] Wertungsmäßig ist diese Divergenz zwar plausibel, wenn man sie mit dem größtmöglichen Schutz der Privatautonomie des Betroffenen rechtfertigt.[32] Im materiellen Recht werden privatautonom Bevollmächtigte und gerichtlich bestellte Betreuer allerdings überwiegend gleichbehandelt, soweit es um die Autorisierung ärztlicher Maßnahmen geht (vgl. §§ 1827 Abs. 6, 1829 Abs. 5 BGB). Angesichts des mehrfach gestaffelten kollisionsrechtlichen Schutzwalls gegen anstößige Vorsorgevollmachten (Art. 16, 20, 21 ErwSÜ) ist es jedoch angezeigt, den Wortlaut und die Entstehungsgeschichte des Art. 15 Abs. 3 ErwSÜ ernst zu nehmen, dh den Anwendungsbereich der Vorschrift strikt auf bloße Modalitäten der Vollmachtsausübung zu begrenzen.[33] Der „Umfang" der Vollmacht, der sich nach dem durch Art. 15 Abs. 1 und 2 ErwSÜ bestimmten Recht richtet, darf hierdurch nicht eingeschränkt werden. Dies ist auch nicht unbillig gegenüber dem Vorsorgebevollmächtigten, der bereits vor dem Eintritt des Vorsorgefalls weiß, nach welchem Recht sich seine Vollmacht richtet und der infolgedessen nicht unvorbereitet bei einem akuten Behandlungsbedarf des Vollmachtgebers mit einem ihm unbekannten Recht konfrontiert wird. Auch die im Rahmen der Spezialkommission der Haager Konferenz zum ErwSÜ eingesetzte Arbeitsgruppe hat sich insoweit für die Anwendung von Art. 15 Abs. 1 ErwSÜ ausgesprochen.[34]

3. *Die isolierte Patientenverfügung*

Eine sog. „isolierte" Patientenverfügung, in welcher der Betroffene lediglich seinen allgemeinen Willen in Bezug auf eine ärztliche Behandlung festhält (§ 1827 Abs. 1 BGB), ohne zugleich eine Bevollmächtigung einer anderen Person vorzunehmen, wird nach bisher h. M. mangels Erteilung einer Vertretungsmacht nicht von Art. 15 ErwSÜ erfasst.[35] Die Vorschrift ist insoweit auch nicht analog anwendbar, weil es mangels Vertretungsmacht an einer Vergleichbarkeit der Sachverhalte

---

[31] Wedemann FamRZ 2010, 785 (789).

[32] Vgl. Guttenberger, Das Haager Übereinkommen über den internationalen Schutz von Erwachsenen, 2004, S. 160f.

[33] V. Bar/Mankowski, Internationales Privatrecht II, 2. Aufl. 2019, § 6 Rn. 75; Gebauer/Isomura/Kansaku/Nettesheim, Alternde Gesellschaften im Recht/Gebauer, 2015, S. 59 (68); Lemmerz, Die Patientenverfügung, 2014, S. 137.

[34] Spezialkommission zum ErwSÜ, Prel. Doc. Nr. 6, April 2022, https://assets.hcch.net/docs/a7ffa46d-a1bd-4a75-a1a6-fd939da97e60.pdf (abgerufen 11.5.2023), Rn. 36.

[35] NomosKommentar BGB/Benicke, 4. Aufl. 2021, ErwSÜ Art. 15 Rn. 9; Budzikiewicz/Heiderhoff/Klinkhammer/Niethammer-Jürgens, Vorsorge und Verantwortung im Internationalen Familienrecht/Croon-Gestefeld, 2023, 75 (80f.); Grüneberg, BGB/Thorn, 83. Aufl. 2024, EGBGB Art. 24 Anh. Rn. 8; Helms FamRZ 2008, 1995 (1999); Lemmerz, Die Patientenverfügung, 2014, 140; Münchener Kommentar zum BGB/Lipp, 9. Aufl. 2024, ErwSÜ Art. 15 Rn. 20; Lipp, Handbuch der Vorsorgeverfügungen/Röthel, 2009, § 20 Rn. 26; Rolland/Ruck Keene, Interpreting the 2000 Hague Convention on the International Protection of Adults Consistently with the 2007 UN Convention on the Rights of Persons with Disabilities, 2021, 7; Schaub IPRax 2016, 207 (209); Schwander AJP/PJA 2014, 1351 (1369); anders offenbar, aber ohne Begründung, Rocha Ribeiro Revista do Ministério Público 125 (2011), S. 13 (56 in Fn. 97).

fehlt.[36] Fraglich ist deshalb, nach welchem Recht sich bestimmt, ob und in welchem Umfang ein Betreuer an eine Patientenverfügung des Erwachsenen gebunden ist (vgl. § 1827 BGB Abs. 1–3 BGB). Zum Teil wird dafür plädiert, diese Frage nach dem Gleichlaufprinzip an die Zuständigkeit des die Betreuung anordnenden Staates gem. Art. 13 Abs. 1 ErwSÜ anzuknüpfen.[37] Dies kann jedoch zu praktischen Schwierigkeiten führen, wenn der Staat, in dem die Betreuung angeordnet wurde, und der Staat, in dem die medizinische Behandlung erfolgen soll, auseinanderfallen, und infolgedessen die Ermittlung ausländischen Rechts erforderlich wird. Zwar mag man, ebenso wie bei Vermögensangelegenheiten,[38] insoweit bisweilen mit der Ausweichklausel des Art. 13 Abs. 2 ErwSÜ die Anwendung oder Berücksichtigung des Rechts am Behandlungsort ermöglichen und so im Einzelfall ein angemessenes Ergebnis erzielen können. Die besseren Argumente dürften aber dafür sprechen, die Bindung des Betreuers an eine Patientenverfügung generell als eine Bedingung der Ausübung der aufgrund einer behördlich angeordneten Schutzmaßnahme entstandenen Vertretungsmacht zu qualifizieren, die folglich nach Art. 14 ErwSÜ an den Durchführungsort anzuknüpfen ist.[39] Eine solche Anknüpfung gewährleistet in der Regel einen wünschenswerten Gleichlauf mit der Beurteilung der Patientenverfügung nach Internationalem Strafrecht und trägt so auch dazu bei, das ärztliche Personal vor Pflichtenkollisionen zu bewahren.[40]

4. Ein Haager Vorstoß zur Einbeziehung der isolierten Patientenverfügung in Art. 15 ErwSÜ

Wie die voranstehende Analyse gezeigt hat, ist die Behandlung von Patientenverfügungen im Rahmen des ErwSÜ von einer gewissen Rechtsunsicherheit und Uneinheitlichkeit gekennzeichnet.[41] Es verwundert daher nicht, dass in jüngerer Zeit Bemühungen zu verzeichnen sind, den Anwendungsbereich des Art. 15 ErwSÜ mithilfe einer großzügigen Auslegung auszudehnen. Die Spezialkommission der Haager Konferenz zum ErwSÜ hat im April 2022 ein von einer Arbeitsgruppe in Zusammenarbeit mit dem Permanent Bureau vorbereitetes Arbeitspapier vorgelegt, in dem dafür plädiert wird, Art. 15 ErwSÜ auch auf isolierte Patientenverfügungen anzuwenden.[42] Die Arbeitsgruppe begründet dies damit, dass Art. 15

---

[36] Anders aber Lurger/Melcher, Handbuch Internationales Privatrecht, 2021, § 2 Rn. 46.

[37] Dafür aber Jayme FS Spellenberg, 2010, 203 (208); Lemmerz, Die Patientenverfügung, 2014, 143.

[38] Vgl. BGH 18.8.2021 – XII ZB 145/21, FamRZ 2021, 1918 mAnm v. Hein/Gialeli FamRZ 2021, 1919.

[39] V. Bar/Mankowski, Internationales Privatrecht II, 2. Aufl. 2019, § 6 Rn. 97; Helms FamRZ 2008, 1995 (1999); Staudinger, BGB/v. Hein, 2022, ErwSÜ Art. 15 Rn. 16; Wedemann FamRZ 2010, 785 (786); einschränkend Münchener Kommentar zum BGB/Lipp, 9. Aufl. 2024, ErwSÜ Art. 15 Rn. 23: nur bei Notwendigkeit einer Genehmigung; zweifelnd Lipp, Handbuch der Vorsorgeverfügungen/Röthel, 2009, § 20 Rn. 26; aA Lemmerz, Die Patientenverfügung, 2014, S. 142f.

[40] Zur international-strafrechtlichen Einordnung der Patientenverfügung Heggen ZNotP 2008, 184 (195).

[41] So auch Bergamini/Bercea/Verteş-Olteanu Yb PIL 24 (2022/2023), 1 (18).

[42] Spezialkommission zum ErwSÜ, Prel. Doc. Nr. 6, April 2022, https://assets.hcch.net/docs/a7ffa46d-a1bd-4a75-a1a6-fd939da97e60.pdf (abgerufen 11.5.2023), Rn. 38ff.

ErwSÜ weit und autonom zu verstehen sei;[43] der Vorschrift lasse sich kein Erfordernis entnehmen, dass eine bestimmte Person als Vertreter bezeichnet werde.[44] Weiter wird darauf verwiesen, dass der Kreis der in Art. 3 ErwSÜ aufgezählten Schutzmaßnahmen nicht abschließend sei, was sich aus dem Wort „insbesondere" ergebe.[45] Die Arbeitsgruppe nimmt insoweit vor allem Bezug auf Art. 3 lit. d ErwSÜ.[46] Dieser Teil der Vorschrift entspricht dem gleichen Buchstaben des Art. 3 KSÜ; demnach regelt das nach dem ErwSÜ anwendbare Recht auch die Bestimmung und den Aufgabenbereich jeder Person oder Stelle, die für die Person oder das Vermögen des Erwachsenen verantwortlich ist, den Erwachsenen vertritt oder ihm beisteht.[47] Da Art. 3 lit. d ErwSÜ dahingehend offen formuliert sei, wer als Vertreter des Erwachsenen oder als für ihn verantwortliche Person bestimmt werde, lasse sich auch die isolierte Patientenverfügung einbeziehen, bei der niemand namentlich bezeichnet werde.[48] Zwar stellt die Arbeitsgruppe klar, dass die isolierte Patientenverfügung selbst keine Schutzmaßnahme i. S. des Art. 3 lit. d ErwSÜ bilde, sondern lediglich bei der Konkretisierung des Aufgabenbereichs im Rahmen einer behördlichen Maßnahme zu beachten sei.[49] Zugleich will die Arbeitsgruppe die isolierte Patientenverfügung aber als eine besondere Form der Vorsorgevollmacht gem. Art. 15 ErwSÜ einstufen.[50] Daraus leitet die Arbeitsgruppe zudem ab, dass eine Bescheinigung nach Art. 38 ErwSÜ auch über eine isolierte Patientenverfügung ausgestellt werden könne.[51]

Die Stellungnahmen der Vertragsstaaten der Haager Konferenz zu diesem Vorschlag sind allerdings ganz überwiegend ablehnend. Deutschland,[52] Frankreich,[53] und die Schweiz[54] betonen übereinstimmend, dass es bei einer isolierten Patientenverfügung schlicht an einer „Vertretungsmacht" i. S. des Art. 15 Abs. 1 ErwSÜ fehle und die Vorschrift daher sowohl nach ihrem Wortlaut als auch nach ihrem Sinn und

---

[43] Spezialkommission zum ErwSÜ, Prel. Doc. Nr. 6, April 2022, https://assets.hcch.net/docs/a7ffa46d-a1bd-4a75-a1a6-fd939da97e60.pdf (abgerufen 11.5.2023), Rn. 4.

[44] Spezialkommission zum ErwSÜ, Prel. Doc. Nr. 6, April 2022, https://assets.hcch.net/docs/a7ffa46d-a1bd-4a75-a1a6-fd939da97e60.pdf (abgerufen 11.5.2023), Rn. 4, 30 und 39.

[45] Spezialkommission zum ErwSÜ, Prel. Doc. Nr. 6, April 2022, https://assets.hcch.net/docs/a7ffa46d-a1bd-4a75-a1a6-fd939da97e60.pdf (abgerufen 11.5.2023), Rn. 17.

[46] Spezialkommission zum ErwSÜ, Prel. Doc. Nr. 6, April 2022, https://assets.hcch.net/docs/a7ffa46d-a1bd-4a75-a1a6-fd939da97e60.pdf (abgerufen 11.5.2023), Rn. 20; ebenso Bergamini/Bercea/Verteş-Olteanu Yb PIL 24 (2022/2023), 1 (12).

[47] Näher Dutoit FichesJurSuisses 2011, 1 (3).

[48] Spezialkommission zum ErwSÜ, Prel. Doc. Nr. 6, April 2022, https://assets.hcch.net/docs/a7ffa46d-a1bd-4a75-a1a6-fd939da97e60.pdf (abgerufen 11.5.2023), Rn. 20.

[49] Spezialkommission zum ErwSÜ Prel. Doc. Nr. 6, April 2022, https://assets.hcch.net/docs/a7ffa46d-a1bd-4a75-a1a6-fd939da97e60.pdf (abgerufen 11.5.2023), Rn. 38.

[50] Spezialkommission zum ErwSÜ, Prel. Doc. Nr. 6, April 2022, https://assets.hcch.net/docs/a7ffa46d-a1bd-4a75-a1a6-fd939da97e60.pdf (abgerufen 11.5.2023), Rn. 38 und 41.

[51] Spezialkommission zum ErwSÜ, Prel. Doc. Nr. 6, April 2022, https://assets.hcch.net/docs/a7ffa46d-a1bd-4a75-a1a6-fd939da97e60.pdf (abgerufen 11.5.2023), Rn. 49.

[52] Comments of Germany on Prel. Doc. No 6, https://assets.hcch.net/docs/9a47762e-b8b5–49ce-a411–128041e1cf4b.pdf (abgerufen 11.5.2023).

[53] Comments of France on Prel. Doc. No 6, https://assets.hcch.net/docs/dcd6b9a0–815a-4255-9672-40f0cfe68dc1.pdf (abgerufen 11.5.2023).

[54] Comments of Switzerland on Prel. Doc. No 6, https://assets.hcch.net/docs/68d3a652-dc57–4e07-b314–1dabcb32313d.pdf (abgerufen 11.5.2023).

Zweck nicht zur Anwendung kommen könne. Dem hat sich Kanada angeschlossen, welches das ErwSÜ bislang nicht gezeichnet hat.[55] Die Argumentation der Arbeitsgruppe wird letztlich – angesichts des bei der Haager Konferenz üblichen diplomatischen Sprachgebrauchs recht deutlich – als rechtspolitisches Wunschdenken ohne dogmatische Basis verworfen.[56] Einzig Italien hat die Subsumtion isolierter Patientenverfügungen unter Art. 15 ErwSÜ gebilligt.[57] Die von der Arbeitsgruppe befürwortete Einbeziehung isolierter Patientenverfügungen in Art. 38 ErwSÜ ist, soweit auf diese Frage ausdrücklich eingegangen wird, ebenfalls mehrheitlich auf Ablehnung gestoßen.[58]

III. Die Rom I- und Rom II-Verordnungen

1. Arzthaftung

Patientenverfügungen können nicht nur für den Umfang der Vertretungsmacht eines Betreuers oder Vorsorgebevollmächtigten von Bedeutung sein, sondern im Falle von isolierten Patientenverfügungen unmittelbar die Haftung eines Arztes beeinflussen, der einen Erwachsenen behandelt, der weder unter Betreuung steht noch eine Vorsorgevollmacht errichtet hat. Überwiegend werden solche Verfügungen dem auf das ärztliche Behandlungsverhältnis anwendbaren Recht unterworfen, das sich nach der Rom I- bzw. Rom II-VO richtet.[59] Hierfür müsste der sachliche Anwendungsbereich der Rom I- und II-Verordnungen eröffnet sein. Insoweit könnte fraglich erscheinen, ob der Ausschluss von Fragen des Personenstandes sowie der Rechts-, Geschäfts- und Handlungsfähigkeit nach Art. 1 Abs. 2 lit. a Rom I-VO der Anwendung der Verordnung auf eine isolierte Patientenverfügung entgegensteht.[60] Denn der EuGH hat entschieden, dass Fragen der Vormundschaft, Pflegschaft und Betreuung vom Anwendungsbereich der Brüssel Ia-VO gem. Art. 1

[55] Comments of Canada on Prel. Doc. No 6, https://assets.hcch.net/docs/46b1fe25-0921-42b2-b095-90a45102d5d7.pdf (abgerufen 11.5.2023).

[56] Vgl. die Schweiz (→ Fn. 54), S. 1: „[A] very extensive teleological interpretation of the Convention has been made without any really sharp and convincing arguments"; Kanada (→ Fn. 55), S. 1: „[A] teleological interpretation of the Convention that seems to be focused on a desired outcome and […] not supported, in our view, by the text of the Convention, the Explanatory Report or the proceedings of the diplomatic session."

[57] https://assets.hcch.net/docs/918a61f4-4fce-4806-9116-79003dd5f876.pdf; ebenso Bergamini/Bercea/Verteş-Olteanu Yb PIL 24 (2022/2023), 1 (13f.).

[58] Deutschland (→ Fn. 52) S. 1f.; Kanada (→ Fn. 55) S. 3.

[59] V. Bar/Mankowski, Internationales Privatrecht II, 2. Aufl. 2019, § 6 Rn. 92ff.; Kobsik, Antizipierte Erklärungen in Gesundheitsangelegenheiten im grenzüberschreitenden Verkehr, 2020, S. 428ff.; Mäsch FS Coester-Waltjen, 2015, 149 (158f.); Meyer, Die Anknüpfung internationaler Fürsorgeverhältnisse nach der Reform des Art. 24 EGBGB, 2023, S. 174; Münchener Kommentar zum BGB/Lipp, 9. Aufl. 2024, ErwSÜ Art. 15 Rn. 21; Spickhoff FS Coester-Waltjen, 2015, 825 (828); ebenso aus schweizerischer Sicht Basler Kommentar IPRG/Schwander, 4. Aufl. 2021, Art. 85 IPRG Rn. 166; Schwander AJP/PJA 2014, 1351 (1369).

[60] Hierzu Kobsik, Antizipierte Erklärungen in Gesundheitsangelegenheiten im grenzüberschreitenden Verkehr, 2020, S. 430f.; Lemmerz, Die Patientenverfügung, 2014, S. 245f.

Abs. 2 lit. a Brüssel Ia-VO ausgenommen sind.[61] Dieser Ausschluss von Betreuungssachen ist wegen des Gebots der harmonischen Auslegung (ErwGr. 7 Rom I-VO) grundsätzlich auch auf Art. 1 Abs. 2 lit. a Rom I-VO zu übertragen.[62] Jedoch führt dies nicht notwendigerweise zur Nicht-Anwendbarkeit der Rom I-VO auf die isolierte Patientenverfügung.[63] Zwar ist die Patientenverfügung materiellrechtlich (§ 1827 BGB) im deutschen Betreuungsrecht angesiedelt;[64] allein daraus lässt sich aber nicht zwingend ihre entsprechende kollisionsrechtliche Einordnung ableiten, weil im Rahmen der Rom I-VO eine autonome Qualifikation maßgebend ist.[65] Insoweit ist entscheidend, dass die isolierte Patientenverfügung kein betreuungsähnliches Fürsorgeverhältnis in Bezug auf den Patienten begründet, sondern lediglich eine antizipierte Einwilligung in bzw. die Untersagung bestimmter ärztlicher Heileingriffe enthält. Die Rom I-VO ist folglich sachlich anwendbar.[66]

Diese Überlegungen gelten erst recht für die Rom II-VO, die keine explizite Bereichsausnahme für Fragen der Rechts-, Geschäfts- und Handlungsfähigkeit wie in Art. 1 Abs. 2 lit. a Rom I-VO enthält.[67] Im Rahmen der Rom II-VO könnte indes der Ausschluss von Persönlichkeitsrechtsverletzungen (Art. 1 Abs. 2 lit. g Rom II-VO) tangiert sein, sofern man die Missachtung des in einer Patientenverfügung ausgedrückten Willens als eine Verletzung des Allgemeinen Persönlichkeitsrechts des Patienten betrachtet.[68] Diese Frage sollte aus Gründen systematischer Kohärenz nicht anders entschieden werden als für das Recht, das auf die Haftung für ärztliche Aufklärungspflichtverletzungen anwendbar ist. Für die letztgenannte Frage ist die Ansicht ganz herrschend, dass die primär durch Uneinigkeiten bei der Behandlung von Mediendelikten motivierte Bereichsausnahme des Art. 1 Abs. 2 lit. g Rom II-VO eng auszulegen und auf nichtkörperliche Schädigungen zu begrenzen ist.[69] Die Vorschrift steht daher einer Anwendung der Rom II-VO auf isolierte Patientenverfügungen nicht entgegen.[70]

---

[61] EuGH 3.10.2013 – C-386/12, ECLI:EU:C:2013:633 = FamRZ 2013, 1873 mAnm Wendenburg FamRZ 2013, 1874 = IPRax 2015, 235, mAnm v. Hein IPRax 2015, 198 = Rev crit dr i p 103 (2014) 182 mAnm Corneloup Rev crit dr i p 103 (2014) 182 – Siegfried János Schneider; hierzu auch Kümmerle GPR 2014, 170.

[62] Rauscher, EuZPR/EuIPR/v. Hein, 5. Aufl. 2023, Rom I-VO Art. 1 Rn. 22f.

[63] Vgl. auch Lemmerz, Die Patientenverfügung, 2014, S. 246.

[64] Hierauf stellten noch Jayme/Seeger IPRax 2015, 479 (480) ab.

[65] Zur autonomen Qualifikation im Rahmen der Rom I-VO Rauscher, EuZPR/EuIPR/v. Hein, 5. Aufl 2023, Rom I-VO Einl. Rn. 54, mwN; im Erg. auch Lemmerz, Die Patientenverfügung, 2014, S. 251.

[66] So im Erg. auch Kobsik, Antizipierte Erklärungen in Gesundheitsangelegenheiten im grenzüberschreitenden Verkehr, 2020, S. 430f.

[67] Im Erg. auch Kobsik, Antizipierte Erklärungen in Gesundheitsangelegenheiten im grenzüberschreitenden Verkehr, 2020, S. 456f.; Lemmerz, Die Patientenverfügung, 2014, S. 159.

[68] Erwogen, aber letztlich verneint von Lemmerz, Die Patientenverfügung, 2014, S. 161f.; ablehnend auch Kobsik, Antizipierte Erklärungen in Gesundheitsangelegenheiten im grenzüberschreitenden Verkehr, 2020, S. 456f.

[69] Näher Spickhoff FS v. Hoffmann, 2011, 437 (442f.); ebenso Münchener Kommentar zum BGB/Junker, 8. Aufl. 2021, Rom II-VO Art. 1 Rn. 43; NomosKommentar BGB/Knöfel, 3. Aufl. 2019, Rom II-VO Art. 1 Rn. 55; Rauscher, EuZPR/EuIPR/Scheller, 5. Aufl 2023, Rom II-VO Art. 1 Rn. 68.

[70] Kobsik, Antizipierte Erklärungen in Gesundheitsangelegenheiten im grenzüberschreitenden Verkehr, 2020, S. 456f.; im Erg. auch v. Bar/Mankowski, Internationales Privatrecht II, 2. Aufl.

Die Rom II-VO unterwirft in Art. 15 lit. b Rom II-VO auch die Gründe für einen Haftungsausschluss explizit dem Deliktsstatut, unter das daher sowohl tatbestandsausschließende Faktoren als auch Rechtfertigungsgründe fallen.[71] Da hierzu im Arzthaftungsrecht die Einwilligung des Patienten zählt, erscheint es sachgerecht, auch den actus contrarius, dh die Verweigerung oder Modifikation einer Einwilligung in die Heilbehandlung durch eine Patientenverfügung, diesem Recht zu unterwerfen.[72]

Ebenso ist für vertragliche Ansprüche anerkannt, dass Haftungsausschlussgründe nach dem Vertragsstatut zu beurteilen sind, wobei die Frage müßig ist, ob dies im Einzelnen aus Art. 12 Abs. 1 lit. b Rom I-VO (Erfüllung der durch den Vertrag begründeten Verpflichtungen) oder aus Art. 12 Abs. 1 lit. c Rom I-VO (Folgen der Nichterfüllung dieser Verpflichtungen) folgt.[73]

Die Heranziehung der Rom I- und II-VO führt in der Regel zur Anwendung des Rechts am Behandlungsort, die sich für vertragliche Ansprüche grundsätzlich aus Art. 4 Abs. 1 lit. b Rom I-VO – gewöhnlicher Aufenthalt des Erbringers der geschuldeten Dienstleistung – ergibt.[74] Zwar können auch ärztliche Behandlungsverträge Verbraucherverträge i. S. des Art. 6 Abs. 1 Rom I-VO darstellen, was im Ausgangspunkt zur Anwendbarkeit des Rechts am gewöhnlichen Aufenthalt des Verbrauchers führen würde.[75] Liegt der Behandlungsort aber außerhalb des Verbraucherstaates, wird in der Regel die Bereichsausnahme für ausschließlich im Ausland erbrachte Dienstleistungen (Art. 6 Abs. 4 lit. a Rom I-VO) eingreifen, sodass es im Ergebnis zumeist doch bei der Anwendung des Rechts am Behandlungsort verbleibt.[76]

Für deliktische Ansprüche ist nach der Grundregel des Art. 4 Abs. 1 Rom II-VO das Recht am Erfolgsort – dh, der Ort an dem der schädigende Erfolg eintritt – maßgeblich.[77] Fallen der Behandlungsort und der Erfolgsort ausnahmsweise nicht

2019, § 6 Rn. 92ff.; Mäsch FS Coester-Waltjen, 2015, 149 (158f.); Münchener Kommentar zum BGB/Lipp, 9. Aufl. 2024, ErwSÜ Art. 15 Rn. 21; Spickhoff FS Coester-Waltjen, 2015, 825 (828).

[71] Münchener Kommentar zum BGB/Junker, 8. Aufl. 2021, Rom II-VO Art. 15 Rn. 12; Soergel, Bürgerliches Gesetzbuch XXVII/2/Pfeiffer, 13. Aufl. 2019, Rom II-VO Art. 15 Rn. 28.

[72] Kobsik, Antizipierte Erklärungen in Gesundheitsangelegenheiten im grenzüberschreitenden Verkehr, 2020, S. 432ff.; Mäsch FS Coester-Waltjen, 2015, 149 (158f.); Spickhoff FS Coester-Waltjen, 2015, 825 (828).

[73] Für Art. 12 Abs. 1 lit. b Rom I-VO zB Magnus/Mankowski, Rome I Regulation/Ferrari, 2016, Rom I-VO Art. 12 Rn. 18; Münchener Kommentar zum BGB/Spellenberg, 8. Aufl. 2021, Rom I-VO Art. 12 Rn. 83; für Art. 12 Abs. 1 lit. c Rom I-VO zB NomosKommentar BGB/Leible, 3. Aufl. 2019, Rom I-VO Art. 12 Rn. 20; Reithmann/Martiny, Internationales Vertragsrecht/Martiny, 9. Aufl. 2022, Rn. 3.139.

[74] Lemmerz, Die Patientenverfügung, 2014, S. 157; Rauscher, EuZPR/EuIPR/Thorn, 5. Aufl. 2023, Rom I-VO Art. 4 Rn. 34; Spickhoff, Medizinrecht/Spickhoff, 4. Aufl. 2022, Rom II-VO Art. 26 Rn. 14.

[75] Lemmerz, Die Patientenverfügung, 2014, S. 157f.; Spickhoff, Medizinrecht/Spickhoff, 4. Aufl. 2022, Rom II-VO Art. 26 Rn. 13.

[76] Lemmerz, Die Patientenverfügung, 2014, S. 158; Spickhoff, Medizinrecht/Spickhoff, 4. Aufl. 2022, Rom II-VO Art. 26 Rn. 13; zu denkbaren Ausnahmen bei ärztlicher Onlineberatung („Telemedizin") Rauscher, EuZPR/EuIPR/Heiderhoff, 5. Aufl 2023. Rom I-VO Art. 6 Rn. 76.

[77] Mäsch FS Coester-Waltjen, 2015, 149 (158).

zusammen – zB bei einer Selbstmedikation des Patienten in Deutschland nach dessen vorheriger ärztlicher Anleitung in der Schweiz –, kommt eine vertragsakzessorische Anknüpfung nach Art. 4 Abs. 3 Rom I-VO in Betracht.[78]

Zum Teil ist allerdings vorgeschlagen worden, die wirksame Errichtung einer Patientenverfügung als Vorfrage selbstständig an das Personalstatut des Patienten anzuknüpfen.[79] Hierfür wird geltend gemacht, dass es bei einer Unterwerfung der Patientenverfügung unter das Vertrags- oder Deliktsstatut für den Betroffenen nicht vorhersehbar sei, nach welchem Recht seine Verfügung im später eintretenden Fall einer Behandlung im Ausland (etwa auf einer Reise oder nach einem Umzug) beurteilt werde.[80] Dagegen ist in dogmatischer Sicht wiederum eingewendet worden, dass die Suche nach einem „Errichtungsstatut" in die Irre führe, weil es sich bei der Patientenverfügung nicht um eine auf den Abschluss eines Rechtsgeschäfts gerichtete Willenserklärung handele.[81] Dieser Einwand erscheint allerdings im Lichte des geschilderten Vorhersehbarkeitsinteresses des Betroffenen als allzu begrifflich. Selbst wenn man einräumt, dass es sich bei der Patientenverfügung nicht um ein Rechtsgeschäft handelt,[82] wäre eine selbstständige Anknüpfung an ein Errichtungsstatut durchaus konstruktiv denkbar.[83] Nach der Reform des Art. 7 EGBGB, die ebenfalls zum 1.1.2023 in Kraft getreten ist, müsste man allerdings klären, ob es insoweit – wie bei der Rechtsfähigkeit – auf die Staatsangehörigkeit des Patienten (vgl. Art. 7 Abs. 1 S. 1 EGBGB) oder – wie bei der Geschäftsfähigkeit – auf seinen gewöhnlichen Aufenthalt (vgl. Art. 7 Abs. 2 S. 1 EGBGB) ankommen soll.[84] Die Staatsangehörigkeit wird zwar in Art. 15 Abs. 2 lit. a ErwSÜ als ein wählbares Recht für die Vorsorgevollmacht genannt, spielt aber im IPR der Schuldverhältnisse nur eine ganz untergeordnete Rolle.[85] Die Ermittlung des Heimatrechts würde zudem für den behandelnden Arzt eine kaum zumutbare Belas-

[78] Näher (noch zu Art. 41 Abs. 2 Nr. 1 EGBGB) BGH 9.7.2011 – VI ZR 217/10, BGHZ 190, 301 = NJW 2011, 3584; zur entsprechenden Lösung nach Art. 4 Abs. 3 Rom II-VO v. Hein Yb PIL 13 (2011), 523ff.; Mäsch FS Coester-Waltjen, 2015, 149 (159).

[79] Dafür Jayme FS Spellenberg, 2010, 203 (204ff.); Jayme/Seeger IPRax 2015, 479 (480); Körtner/Kopetzki/Kletečka-Pulker, Das österreichische Patientenverfügungsgesetz: ethische und rechtliche Aspekte/Ofner, 2007, 185 (191f.); im Ausgangspunkt auch Deixler-Hübner/Schauer, Handbuch Erwachsenenschutzrecht/Heindler, 2018, Rn. 14.52.

[80] Jayme FS Spellenberg, 2010, 203 (204); Körtner/Kopetzki/Kletečka-Pulker, Das österreichische Patientenverfügungsgesetz: ethische und rechtliche Aspekte/Ofner, 2007, 185 (191).

[81] Mäsch FS Coester-Waltjen, 2015, 149, 157.

[82] Zur Rechtsnatur näher Münchener Kommentar zum BGB/Schneider, 9. Aufl 2024, BGB § 1827 Rn. 2.

[83] Vgl. zum österreichischen IPR vor 2018 Deixler-Hübner/Schauer, Handbuch Erwachsenenschutzrecht/Heindler, 2018, Rn. 14.52.

[84] Jayme/Seeger IPRax 2015, 479 (480) verwiesen noch recht pauschal auf „Art. 7 –11 EGBGB [a. F.]"; deutlicher für die Staatsangehörigkeit Jayme FS Spellenberg, 2010, 203 (204); dafür in Anlehnung an § 15 IPRG a. F. (für Österreich) auch Körtner/Kopetzki/Kletečka-Pulker, Das österreichische Patientenverfügungsgesetz: ethische und rechtliche Aspekte/Ofner, 2007, 185 (191f.).

[85] Vgl. zur Staatsangehörigkeit als Indiz für eine konkludente Rechtswahl Rauscher, EuZPR/EuIPR/v. Hein, 5. Aufl. 2023, Rom I-VO Art. 3 Rn. 38; zur Begründung eines Auslandsbezuges Rauscher, EuZPR/EuIPR/v. Hein, 5. Aufl. 2023, Rom I-VO Art. 3 Rn. 109; zur Ersetzung der Staatsangehörigkeit durch den gewöhnlichen Aufenthalt bei der Auflockerung des Deliktsstatuts Calliess/Renner, Rome Regulations/v. Hein, 3. Aufl. 2020, Rom II-VO Art. 4 Rn. 36.

tung bedeuten.[86] Denn der Arzt sähe sich – anders als der Vorsorgebevollmächtigte nach Art. 15 Abs. 2 lit. a ErwSÜ – regelmäßig erst im akuten Behandlungsfall einem für ihn fremden Recht gegenüber. Die Anknüpfung der isolierten Patientenverfügung an den gewöhnlichen Aufenthalt des Patienten dürfte häufiger, muss aber nicht notwendigerweise zu dem am Behandlungsort geltenden Recht führen.[87] Dies gilt erst recht, wenn man die Anknüpfung an den gewöhnlichen Aufenthalt unwandelbar auf den Zeitpunkt der Errichtung der Patientenverfügung fixieren will.[88] Auch diese Lösung überzeugt daher allenfalls bedingt, denn auch hier wäre das ärztliche Personal in komplizierten Fällen mit Auslandsbezug damit überfordert, das auf eine isolierte Patientenverfügung anwendbare ausländische Recht zeitnah zu ermitteln und korrekt anzuwenden.[89] Letztlich gewichtet die h. M. die Verkehrsinteressen im Gesundheitswesen zum Zeitpunkt der ärztlichen Behandlung höher als das Interesse des Patienten, bereits zum Zeitpunkt der Errichtung der Patientenverfügung das im Behandlungsfall anwendbare Recht vorhersehen zu können.[90]

Einen vermittelnden, de lege ferenda zu verstehenden Vorschlag hat schließlich *Lemmerz* entwickelt.[91] Sie möchte – vorbehaltlich einer Rechtswahl – das Bestehen und die Änderung einer Patientenverfügung nach dem Recht am gewöhnlichen Aufenthalt des Patienten im Zeitpunkt der Errichtung der Verfügung beurteilen.[92] Der Inhalt und die Bindungswirkung der Verfügung sollen sich hingegen nach dem Recht am Behandlungsort richten.[93] Die Form der Patientenverfügung soll wiederum grundsätzlich entsprechend Art. 11 EGBGB behandelt werden.[94] *Lemmerz* erkennt allerdings selbst, dass ein so komplexes Anknüpfungssystem zahlreiche Abgrenzungsfragen aufwirft, welche die behandelnden Ärzte vor intrikate Probleme stellen würden.[95] Diese Bedenken versucht sie dadurch zu entkräften, dass bei medizinischen Notfällen stets das Recht des Behandlungsortes berufen werden soll und überdies die Eingriffsnormen des Behandlungsortes gesondert angeknüpft werden sollen.[96] Die differenzierende Systematik ihres Vorschlags erinnert stark an Art. 24 EGBGB a. F., der für die Betreuung zwischen der Anknüpfung des Werdegangs der Betreuung einerseits (Art. 24 Abs. 1 S. 1 EGBGB aF) und ihres Inhalts andererseits (Art. 24 Abs. 3 EGBGB aF) unterschied sowie überdies eine Sonderregel

[86] Lemmerz, Die Patientenverfügung, 2014, 218ff.; Lipp, Handbuch der Vorsorgeverfügungen/Röthel, 2009, § 20 Rn. 28; Spickhoff FS Coester-Waltjen, 2015, 825 (827).

[87] Lipp, Handbuch der Vorsorgeverfügungen/Röthel, 2009, § 20 Rn. 28; zum österreichischen IPR vor Inkrafttreten des § 1 Abs. 3 PatVG (dazu sogleich → IV. 1.) noch Deixler-Hübner/Schauer, Handbuch Erwachsenenschutzrecht/Heindler, 2018, Rn. 14.52.

[88] So noch zum österreichischen IPR Deixler-Hübner/Schauer, Handbuch Erwachsenenschutzrecht/Heindler, 2018, Rn. 14.52; vgl. auch Lemmerz, Die Patientenverfügung, 2014, S. 259f.

[89] So bereits Lipp, Handbuch der Vorsorgeverfügungen/Röthel, 2009, § 20 Rn. 28.

[90] Lipp, Handbuch der Vorsorgeverfügungen/Röthel, 2009, § 20 Rn. 28; Spickhoff FS Coester-Waltjen, 2015, 825 (827); vgl. auch Lemmerz, Die Patientenverfügung, 2014, S. 225ff.

[91] Lemmerz, Die Patientenverfügung, 2014, S. 300f.

[92] Lemmerz, Die Patientenverfügung, 2014, S. 300.

[93] Lemmerz, Die Patientenverfügung, 2014, S. 300.

[94] Lemmerz, Die Patientenverfügung, 2014, S. 300f.

[95] Lemmerz, Die Patientenverfügung, 2014, S. 301.

[96] Lemmerz, Die Patientenverfügung, 2014, S. 301.

für vorläufige Maßregeln enthielt (Art. 24 Abs. 3 EGBGB aF). Die Reform des autonomen IPR der Fürsorgeverhältnisse im Jahre 2021 hat diesen komplexen Ansatz aber nicht zuletzt wegen der damit verbundenen Abgrenzungsschwierigkeiten aufgegeben.[97] Auch für die Patientenverfügung überzeugt eine übermäßige Differenzierung der Anknüpfung nicht. Die besondere Anknüpfung für Notfallmaßnahmen trägt den Verkehrsinteressen nicht genügend Rechnung. Wie sich an Art. 11 ErwSÜ ablesen lässt, sind insbesondere bei Alterserkrankungen Situationen denkbar, in denen die Durchführung eines medizinischen Eingriffs im Ausland zwar durchaus ratsam erscheinen mag, aber nicht unbedingt ein Notfall vorliegt.[98] Die Öffnungsklausel für Eingriffsnormen wirft schließlich die schwierige Frage auf, welche Teile der §§ 1827 ff. BGB in diesem Sinne zu qualifizieren sind (dazu → IV.1.).

2. *Haftung von Betreuern*

Von der kollisionsrechtlichen Behandlung der Patientenverfügung im Rahmen der Arzthaftung ist die Frage zu unterscheiden, nach welchem Recht ein Betreuer haftet, der entgegen einer wirksamen Patientenverfügung in eine medizinische Behandlung einwilligt. Bei einem vom Betreuungsgericht nach Art. 13 Abs. 1 ErwSÜ oder Art. 24 Abs. 2 S. 1 EGBGB iVm § 1814 Abs. 1 BGB bestellten Betreuer dürfte es bereits an einem Vertragsverhältnis mit dem Betreuten i. S. des Art. 1 Abs. 1 Rom I-VO fehlen. Hierfür wäre nach der Rechtsprechung des EuGH eine freiwillig eingegangene Verpflichtung erforderlich.[99] Zwar darf gemäß § 1814 BGB ein Betreuer nicht gegen den freien Willen des Betreuten bestellt werden. Die vom Betreuungsgericht ausgewählte Person ist aber grundsätzlich dazu verpflichtet, die Betreuung zu übernehmen (§ 1819 Abs. 1 BGB). Die Grundlage der Haftung aus § 1826 BGB sind zudem „die sich aus dem öffentlich-rechtlich installierten, aber privatrechtlich gestalteten Betreuungsverhältnis ergebenden gesetzlichen Pflichten des Betreuers gegenüber dem Betreuten".[100] Selbst wenn man diese Qualifikationsfrage anders sehen wollte, würde der bereits (→ III. 1.) genannte Ausschluss nach Art. 1 Abs. 2 lit. a Rom I-VO eingreifen, der auch die Haftung des Betreuers erfasst. Für die Haftung des Betreuers ist deshalb allein das Betreuungsstatut maßgebend.[101] Soweit der Betreute gegen den Betreuer wegen der Missachtung der Patientenverfügung konkurrierende deliktische Ansprüche geltend macht, bleibt zu klären, ob das anwendbare Recht insoweit nach Art. 40 Abs. 1 EGBGB oder nach der Rom II-VO zu bestimmen ist. Obwohl die Rom II-VO keine Art. 1 Abs. 2 lit. a Rom I-VO ent-

---

[97] Staudinger, BGB/v. Hein, 2022, EGBGB Art. 24 Rn. 40.

[98] Näher Staudinger, BGB/v. Hein, 2022, ErwSÜ Art. 11 Rn. 1; vgl. auch zur Operation eines Grauen Stars in der Türkei LSG Niedersachsen-Bremen 19.12.2023 – L 16 KR 196/23, BeckRS 2023, 37804 Rn. 26: „Der typische Verlauf einer Alterserkrankung kann nicht als Notfall gesehen werden."

[99] EuGH 21.1.2016 – C-359/14, ECLI:EU:C:2016:40 Rn. 44 = NJW 2016, 1005.

[100] Münchener Kommentar zum BGB/Schneider, 9. Aufl 2024, BGB § 1826 Rn. 1.

[101] Münchener Kommentar zum BGB/Lipp, 9. Aufl. 2024, ErwSÜ Art. 14 Rn. 11 (für Art. 13 Abs. 1 ErwSÜ); Staudinger, BGB/v. Hein, 2022, EGBGB Art. 24 Rn. 81; differenzierend zur Abgrenzung zw. Art. 13 und 14 ErwSÜ NomosKommentar BGB/Benicke, 3. Aufl. 2019, ErwSÜ Art. 14 Rn. 5; BGB/v. Hein, 2022, ErwSÜ Art. 14 Rn. 9.

sprechende Bereichsausnahme enthält, spricht der enge sachliche Zusammenhang mit dem Betreuungsrecht für einen Ausschluss nach Art. 1 Abs. 2 lit. a Rom II-VO (vergleichbare Wirkungen wie ein Familienverhältnis),[102] zumindest aber für eine akzessorische Anknüpfung (Art. 4 Abs. 3 Rom II-VO) an das Betreuungsstatut.

3. *Haftung von Vorsorgebevollmächtigten*

Auch für die Haftung des Vorsorgebevollmächtigten, der eine Patientenverfügung des Vollmachtgebers ignoriert, stellt sich die Frage nach dem anwendbaren Recht. Art. 15 ErwSÜ erfasst allein das Außenverhältnis aufgrund der Bevollmächtigung, nicht aber das Innenverhältnis (Auftrag, Geschäftsbesorgungsvertrag) zwischen dem Vollmachtgeber und dem Bevollmächtigten.[103] In Bezug auf das Innenverhältnis kommt grundsätzlich die Heranziehung der Rom I-VO in Betracht.[104] Der Ausschluss der Stellvertretung durch Art. 1 Abs. 2 lit. g Rom I-VO steht dem nicht entgegen, weil diese Bereichsausnahme sich ebenfalls nicht auf das Innenverhältnis zwischen Vollmachtgeber und Bevollmächtigten erstreckt.[105] Fraglich ist aber wiederum, ob der Ausschluss von Betreuungsangelegenheiten (Art. 1 Abs. 2 lit. a Rom I-VO) auch insoweit eingreift. Denn die Pflichtenstellung des Vorsorgebevollmächtigten wird entscheidend dadurch modifiziert, dass § 1827 Abs. 6 BGB die entsprechende Anwendung der für den Betreuer geltenden Absätze 1–3 des § 1827 BGB auch auf den Vorsorgebevollmächtigten anordnet. Missachtet der Vorsorgebevollmächtigte die Patientenverfügung, verstößt er damit folglich nicht (allein) gegen eine Pflicht aufgrund des allgemeinen Auftrags- oder Geschäftsbesorgungsrechts, sondern gegen eine spezifische, in Anlehnung an das Betreuungsrecht ausgestaltete Verpflichtung. Dies lässt es naheliegend erscheinen, auch diese Frage nicht nach der Rom I-VO anzuknüpfen, sondern dem nach Art. 15 ErwSÜ bestimmten Recht zu unterwerfen. In einem geeigneten Fall müsste dem EuGH die Frage nach der autonomen Auslegung dieser Vorschriften vorgelegt werden.[106]

IV. *Eingriffsnormen und autonomes IPR*

1. *Eingriffsnormen*

Sofern die Anwendung des Rechts am inländischen Behandlungsort nicht ohnehin aus den Regelanknüpfungen der Rom I- und II-VO folgt (→ III. 1), bleibt zu prüfen, ob das nationale IPR Eingriffsnormen enthält, die einem ausländischen

---

[102] Staudinger, BGB/v. Hein, 2022, EGBGB Art. 24 Rn. 81.

[103] Mäsch Liber Amicorum Schurig, 2012, 147 (157); Münchener Kommentar zum BGB/Lipp, 9. Aufl. 2024, ErwSÜ Art. 15 Rn. 14; Schaub IPRax 2016, 207, 209; Staudinger, BGB/v. Hein, 2022, ErwSÜ Art. 15 Rn. 11.

[104] Vgl. zur Brüssel Ia-VO in Bezug auf den Aufwendungsersatz des Vorsorgebevollmächtigten OLG München 23.6.2021 – 20 U 6587/20, ZEV 2022, 232 = FamRZ 2022, 40 mAnm Mankowski FamRZ 2022, 12.

[105] Münchener Kommentar zum BGB/Martiny, 8. Aufl. 2021, Rom I-VO Art. 1 Rn. 76; Rauscher, EuZPR/EuIPR/v. Hein, 5. Aufl. 2023, Rom I-VO Art. 1 Rn. 49.

[106] Zur Auslegungskompetenz des EuGH auch für das ErwSÜ → V. 2.

Vertrags- oder Deliktsstatut nach Art. 9 Abs. 2 Rom I-VO bzw. Art. 16 Rom II-VO vorgehen.[107] Hier kommt zB in Österreich § 1 Abs. 3 PatVG zum Zug.[108] Gemäß dieser Vorschrift richten sich die Voraussetzungen, das Bestehen, der Umfang, die Wirkungen, die Änderung und die Beendigung einer Patientenverfügung für Behandlungen in Österreich nach österreichischem Recht. Dem ärztlichen Personal soll die Ermittlung ausländischen Rechts erspart bleiben, um schnell die erforderlichen medizinischen Entscheidungen treffen zu können.[109] Ob § 1 Abs. 3 PatVG im Falle einer Heilbehandlung im Ausland verallseitigt werden kann, ist noch nicht abschließend geklärt.[110] Die UbG-IPRG-Novelle von 2022 hat diese Spezialvorschrift unberührt gelassen.[111] Auch das ErwSÜ steht nationalen Eingriffsnormen in Bezug auf die Beachtlichkeit von Patientenverfügungen nicht entgegen, wie sich Art. 20 ErwSÜ entnehmen lässt.[112]

Allerdings fehlt es im deutschen IPR bislang an einer besonderen Kollisionsnorm für die Patientenverfügung, sodass die Einstufung der §§ 1827 f. BGB umstritten ist. Zugunsten einer Einordnung des § 1827 BGB als Eingriffsnorm wird angeführt, die Regeln über die Patientenverfügung hätten starke öffentlich-rechtliche und strafrechtliche Implikationen und einen besonderen ordre-public-Gehalt.[113] In der Tat konkretisieren die zivilrechtlichen Regelungen zum Schutz der Selbstbestimmung des Patienten durch eine Patientenverfügung letztlich die verfassungsrechtliche Garantie der Menschenwürde (Art. 1 Abs. 1 GG).[114] Dies lässt einen eingriffsrechtlichen Charakter naheliegend erscheinen,[115] denn die Menschenwürde ist nicht nur ein individuelles Grundrecht, sondern zugleich ein für die verfassungsrechtliche Ordnung des GG konstituierendes Grundprinzip.[116] Das vermeintliche argumentum ad absurdum, im Falle einer Qualifikation des § 1827 BGB als Eingriffsnorm müsste man alle zivilrechtlichen Institute, die eine Ausprägung grundrechtlich geschützter Positionen darstellten, wie etwa die Vertragsfreiheit (§§ 145 ff. BGB), eingriffsrechtlich einordnen, überzeugt daher nicht.[117] Zudem zeigt das bereits genannte Beispiel des österreichischen § 1 Abs. 3 PatVG, dass ein Gesetzgeber durchaus die zwingende Geltung des eigenen Patientenverfügungsrechts für Inlands-

---

[107] Vgl. Kobsik, Antizipierte Erklärungen in Gesundheitsangelegenheiten im grenzüberschreitenden Verkehr, 2020, 448 ff. (Art. 9 Rom I-VO), 463 f. (Art. 16 Rom II-VO).

[108] Patientenverfügungs-Gesetz, öBGBl. I Nr 55/2006, zuletzt geändert durch die PatVG-Novelle 2018, öBGBl. I Nr 12/2019; hierzu Lurger FS 40 Jahre IPRG, 2020, 79 (118 f.); Traar iFamZ 2019, 55.

[109] Lurger FS 40 Jahre IPRG, 2020, 79 (118).

[110] Näher Lurger FS 40 Jahre IPRG, 2020, 79 (118 f.).

[111] Unterbringungsgesetz- und IPR-Gesetz-Novelle 2022, öBGBl. 2022 I Nr. 147; hierzu Uitz iFamZ 2021, 94; v. Hein FS Neumayr, 2023, 793 (801).

[112] Münchener Kommentar zum BGB/Lipp, 9. Aufl. 2024, ErwSÜ Art. 20 Rn. 5; Staudinger, BGB/v. Hein, 2020, ErwSÜ Art. 20 Rn. 4.

[113] Lipp, Handbuch der Vorsorgeverfügungen/Röthel, 2009, § 20 Rn. 27.

[114] Näher Hufen JuS 2010, 1 (4).

[115] Staudinger, BGB/v. Hein, 2022, ErwSÜ Art. 20 Rn. 4; im Erg. auch Münchener Kommentar zum BGB/Lipp, 9. Aufl. 2024, ErwSÜ Art. 20 Rn. 5.

[116] Zur verfassungsrechtlichen Diskussion näher Böckenförde JZ 2003, 809 ff.; Hufen JuS 2010, 1 f.; beide mwN.

[117] Anders Lemmerz, Die Patientenverfügung, 2014, S. 199.

behandlungen anordnen kann, ohne dass dieser Ansatz auf das gesamte Zivilrecht ausstrahlt.

Dagegen wird vielfach vorgebracht, dass die §§ 1827 f. BGB keine Allgemeininteressen i. S. der Legaldefinition des Art. 9 Abs. 1 Rom I-VO, sondern lediglich Individualinteressen schützten.[118] Diese Sichtweise erscheint allerdings bei rechtsvergleichender und systematischer Betrachtung zu eng. Soweit deutsche Autoren sich zur Verneinung des Eingriffsnormcharakters der Vorschriften über die Patientenverfügung auf einen österreichischen Aufsatz aus dem Jahr 2007 stützen,[119] ist darauf hinzuweisen, dass die heutige österreichische Rechtslage durch § 1 Abs. 3 PatVG für Behandlungen in der Alpenrepublik gegenteilig ausgestaltet ist (→ IV. 1.). Soweit auch im heutigen österreichischen Schrifttum der Eingriffsnormencharakter des § 1 Abs. 3 PatVG bestritten und lediglich von einer „einseitige[n] Kollisionsnorm“ gesprochen wird,[120] wird verkannt, dass in diesem Fall österreichisches Recht entgegen einer anderslautenden Rechtswahl im Behandlungsvertrag (Art. 3 Abs. 1 Rom I-VO) wegen des Vorrangs der Rom I-VO gar nicht angewendet werden dürfte. Der Normzweck, Ärzten die Ermittlung ausländischen Rechts zu ersparen, um rasche Entscheidungen zu ermöglichen und eine übermäßige Belastung des Gesundheitswesens zu vermeiden, kann durchaus als ein hinreichendes öffentliches Interesse angesehen werden.

Auch die jüngere Entwicklung des deutschen IPR zeigt ähnliche Tendenzen. Für die gesetzliche Vertretungsbefugnis von Ehegatten in medizinischen Angelegenheiten gilt in Deutschland seit dem 1. 1. 2023 ein neuer Art. 15 EGBGB, der bestimmt: „In Angelegenheiten der Gesundheitssorge, die im Inland wahrgenommen werden, ist § 1358 des Bürgerlichen Gesetzbuchs auch dann anzuwenden, wenn nach anderen Vorschriften insoweit ausländisches Recht anwendbar wäre.“ Art. 15 EGBGB erhebt die deutsche Vorschrift über die Ex-lege-Befugnisse von Ehegatten (§ 1358 BGB) zur Eingriffsnorm.[121] Die Bundesregierung begründete dieses Vorgehen damit, dass „[i]m Interesse der Gesundheit einzelner, der Ehegatten und des Gesundheitswesens […] die vorgeschlagene Regelung sicherstellen [soll], dass in schwierigen und unvorhersehbaren Situationen mit Auslandsbezug zeitnah insbesondere wichtige medizinische Entscheidungen getroffen und sofort umgesetzt werden können. Vor diesem Hintergrund ordnet der neue Artikel 15 EGBGB-E an, dass § 1358 BGB-E in inländischen Angelegenheiten der Gesundheitssorge selbst dann anzuwenden ist, wenn diesbezüglich aufgrund anderer Kollisionsnor-

[118] v. Bar/Mankowski, Internationales Privatrecht II, 2. Aufl. 2019, § 6 Rn. 91; Lemmerz, Die Patientenverfügung, 2014, 201; Mäsch FS Coester-Waltjen, 2015, 149 (158); Spickhoff FS Coester-Waltjen, 2015, 825 (828).

[119] Körtner/Kopetzki/Kletečka-Pulker, Das österreichische Patientenverfügungsgesetz: ethische und rechtliche Aspekte/Ofner, 2007, 185 (192); zitiert zB von Mäsch FS Coester-Waltjen, 2015, 149 (158); Spickhoff FS Coester-Waltjen, 2015, 825 (828).

[120] So Traar iFamZ 2019, 55 f.

[121] Zur letztlich müßigen Streitfrage, ob Art. 15 EGBGB selbst (Begr RegE BT-Drs. 19/24445, 319; Thorn/Varón Romero IPRax 2021, 15 (28), Wagner FamRZ 2022, 405 (411)) oder § 1358 BGB (Croon-Gestefeld FamRZ 2021, 1939 (1943 ff.); Erman, BGB/Stürner, 17. Aufl. 2023, EGBGB Art. 15 Rn. 5; Münchener Kommentar zum BGB/Lipp, 9. Aufl. 2024, EGBGB Art. 15 Rn. 3) eine Eingriffsnorm ist, s. Staudinger, BGB/v. Hein, 2022, EGBGB Art. 24 Rn. 19.

men an und für sich ausländisches Recht anwendbar wäre."[122] Zu beachten ist, dass Art. 15 EGBGB für die gesetzliche Vertretungsmacht von Ehegatten auf den gesamten § 1358 BGB verweist, dh auch auf § 1358 Abs. 6 BGB, der wiederum den für die Patientenverfügung geltenden § 1827 Abs. 1–3 BGB in Bezug nimmt. Zwar ließe sich konstruktiv auch insoweit die selbstständige Anknüpfung der Vorfrage nach einer wirksamen Patientenverfügung erwägen (→ III. 1.); nach Sinn und Zweck des Art. 15 EGBGB, ein rasches ärztliches Handeln zu ermöglichen, erscheint es aber geboten, auf diesen Aspekt bei einer Behandlung im Inland ebenfalls allein deutsches Recht anzuwenden.

Fraglich bleibt daher nur, ob auch für Patientenverfügungen außerhalb des § 1358 Abs. 6 BGB eine zwingende Anknüpfung an den inländischen Behandlungsort gerechtfertigt ist. Der Grundgedanke, dass es Ärzten ermöglicht werden soll, „in schwierigen und unvorhersehbaren Situationen mit Auslandsbezug" schnell Entscheidungen zu treffen, ließe sich *mutatis mutandis* auch in Bezug auf Patientenverfügungen in anderen Konstellationen anführen. Dagegen könnte wiederum e contrario sprechen, dass der deutsche Gesetzgeber mit der Reform des Jahres 2021 das deutsche IPR der Fürsorgeverhältnisse umfassend reformiert hat, dabei aber nur für die gesetzliche Vertretungsbefugnis von Ehegatten eine spezielle Eingriffsnorm geschaffen hat. Ein solcher Umkehrschluss überzeugt jedoch nur bedingt, denn grundsätzlich ist für die Qualifikation einer Sachnorm als Eingriffsnorm kein expliziter, kodifizierter kollisionsrechtlicher Anwendungsbefehl erforderlich: „In den meisten Fällen sagt ein Gesetzgeber nicht, ob eine Norm unabhängig von einem an sich berufenen Sachstatut angewendet werden muss."[123] Dieses Ergebnis kann vielmehr auch durch die Auslegung der Sachnorm selbst gewonnen werden.[124]

Als Fazit ist daher festzuhalten: Sowohl die Rom I- und II-Verordnungen als auch das ErwSÜ lassen es zu, Vorschriften zur Beachtlichkeit von Patientenverfügungen bei einem hinreichenden Inlandsbezug als Eingriffsnormen auszugestalten. Ob dies der Fall ist, muss das jeweilige nationale Recht entscheiden.

2. *Sonstiges autonomes IPR*

Die isolierte Patientenverfügung stellt mangels Erteilung einer Vertretungsmacht kein rechtsgeschäftlich begründetes Fürsorgeverhältnis iSd Art. 24 Abs. 1 EGBGB dar.[125] Die isolierte Patientenverfügung ist lediglich bei der „Ausübung" eines anderweitig begründeten Fürsorgeverhältnisses, zB im Rahmen einer angeordneten Betreuung nach deutschem Recht (Art. 24 Abs. 2 S. 1 EGBGB), zu berücksich-

---

[122] BT-Drs. 19/24445, 318f.

[123] Leible/Unberath, Brauchen wir eine Rom 0-Verordnung?/Sonnenberger, 2013, 429 (433).

[124] Näher Köhler, Eingriffsnormen – Der „unfertige Teil" des europäischen IPR, 2013, S. 106ff.; Rauscher, Internationales Privatrecht, 5. Aufl. 2017, Rn. 1323; Leible/Unberath, Brauchen wir eine Rom 0-Verordnung?/Sonnenberger, 2013, S. 429 (433).

[125] Erman, BGB/Stürner, 17. Aufl. 2023, EGBGB Art. 24 Rn. 15; Meyer, Die Anknüpfung internationaler Fürsorgeverhältnisse nach der Reform des Art. 24 EGBGB, 2023, 174; Münchener Kommentar zum BGB/Lipp, 9. Aufl. 2024, EGBGB Art. 24 Rn. 113; Staudinger, BGB/v. Hein, 2022, EGBGB Art. 24 Rn. 24.

tigen.[126] Ob die Patientenverfügung wirksam ist oder nicht, unterliegt folglich dem auf die Ausübung des jeweiligen Fürsorgeverhältnisses anzuwendenden Recht.[127]

V. Der Vorschlag einer EU-Erwachsenenschutzverordnung

1. Überlagerung und Ergänzung des Haager Erwachsenenschutzübereinkommens

Wie bereits oben (→ I.) erwähnt, soll die EU-ErwSVO-E den grenzüberschreitenden Erwachsenenschutz in der EU verbessern. Die Verordnung soll das ErwSÜ zum Teil ersetzen und im Übrigen ergänzen, eine Vorrangregelung, die nach Art. 49 Abs. 2 und 3 ErwSÜ zulässig ist. In Bezug auf die internationale Zuständigkeit (Art. 5–7 EU-ErwSVO-E) und das anwendbare Recht (Art. 8 EU-ErwSVO-E) folgt der Verordnungsentwurf weitgehend dem ErwSÜ. Erleichtert wird aber die internationale Urteilsvollstreckung, für die entsprechend dem Vorbild der neueren EU-Verordnungen die Notwendigkeit eines Exequaturs abgeschafft wird (Art. 11 EU-ErwSVO-E).[128] Eigenständige Regelungen sind insbesondere für die Beweiskraft öffentlicher Urkunden (Art. 16f. EU-ErwSVO-E) und die grenzüberschreitende Unterbringung (Art. 21 EU-ErwSVO-E) vorgesehen. Ferner soll ein Europäisches Vertretungszertifikat eingeführt werden, um die grenzüberschreitende Ausübung von Vertretungsbefugnissen in der EU zu erleichtern (Art. 34ff. EU-ErwSVO-E).

2. Sachlicher Anwendungsbereich

Der sachliche Anwendungsbereich der EU-ErwSVO-E ähnelt im Wesentlichen dem des ErwSÜ. Art. 1 EU-ErwSVO-E umreißt den „Gegenstand" der Verordnung. Demnach dienen die Vorschriften der Verordnung ua dazu, den Mitgliedstaat zu bestimmen, dessen Behörden zuständig sind, Maßnahmen zum Schutz der Person oder des Vermögens des Erwachsenen zu treffen (lit. a), das von diesen Behörden bei der Ausübung ihrer Zuständigkeit anzuwendende Recht zu definieren (lit. b), das auf die Vertretung des Erwachsenen anzuwendende Recht festzulegen (lit. c), die Annahme öffentlicher Urkunden in allen Mitgliedstaaten sicherzustellen (lit. e) sowie ein europäisches Vertretungszertifikat einzuführen (lit. h). Eine ausdrückliche Bezugnahme auf Patientenverfügungen findet sich insoweit nicht, doch

---

[126] Erman BGB/Stürner, 17. Aufl. 2023, EGBGB Art. 24 Rn. 15; Meyer, Die Anknüpfung internationaler Fürsorgeverhältnisse nach der Reform des Art. 24 EGBGB, 2023, 174; Münchener Kommentar zum BGB/Lipp, 9. Aufl. 2024, EGBGB Art. 24 Rn. 114; Staudinger, BGB/v. Hein, 2022, 24 EGBGB Art. Rn. 24; im Erg ebenso schon zu Art. 24 EGBGB aF v. Bar/Mankowski, Internationales Privatrecht II, 2. Aufl. 2019, § 6 Rn. 97; Kobsik, Antizipierte Erklärungen in Gesundheitsangelegenheiten im grenzüberschreitenden Verkehr, 2020, 465f.; Lemmerz, Die Patientenverfügung, 2014, 250ff.; Mäsch FS Coester-Waltjen, 2015, 149 (157ff.); Spickhoff FS Coester-Waltjen, 2015, 825 (826ff.); aA Jayme/Seeger IPRax 2015, 479 (480).

[127] Münchener Kommentar zum BGB/Lipp, 9. Aufl. 2024, EGBGB Art. 24 Rn. 113; Staudinger, BGB/v. Hein, 2022, EGBGB Art. 24 Rn. 24.

[128] Zur Abschaffung des Exequaturs im Europäischen Zivilverfahrensrecht s. die Beiträge in v. Hein/Kruger, Informed Choices in Cross-Border Enforcement, 2021, 3ff.

stellt ErwGr. 29 Satz EU-ErwSVO-E klar, dass auch Patientenverfügungen öffentliche Urkunden i. S. des Art. 3 Nr. 5 EU-ErwSVO-E bilden können, sodass sich ihre formelle Beweiskraft ggf. nach Art. 16 EU-ErwSVO-E richtet (→ V. 4.). Art. 2 Abs. 3 EU-ErwSVO-E, der sich eng an Art. 3 ErwSÜ anlehnt, beschreibt die im Rahmen der Verordnung in Betracht kommenden Schutzmaßnahmen. Art. 2 Abs. 3 lit. d EU-ErwSVO-E entspricht dem Art. 3 lit. d ErwSÜ (→ II. 4.); Art. 2 Abs. 3 lit. g EU-ErwSVO-E spiegelt Art. 3 lit. g ErwSÜ wider (→ II. 1.). Es ist daher davon auszugehen, dass diese Bestimmungen gleichlautend ausgelegt werden. Insoweit ist zu bedenken, dass der EuGH nicht nur für die Auslegung der EU-ErwSVO-E zuständig sein wird, sondern dass das ErwSÜ aufgrund des Ermächtigungsbeschlusses der EU und der darauf folgenden Ratifikation durch die Mitgliedstaaten sekundäres Unionsrecht bilden wird, für das dem EuGH die Auslegungskompetenz zusteht.[129]

3. *Kollisionsnormen*

Zur Bestimmung des anwendbaren Rechts verweist Art. 8 EU-ErwSVO-E auf Kapitel III ErwSÜ. Insoweit ändert sich daher nichts an der oben (→ II.) zum ErwSÜ beschriebenen Rechtslage.[130]

4. *Öffentliche Urkunden*

Art. 16 EU-ErwSVO-E regelt die Annahme öffentlicher Urkunden. Wie bereits (→ V. 2.) erwähnt, können auch Patientenverfügungen öffentliche Urkunden i. S. der Verordnung darstellen. Art. 16 EU-ErwSVO-E beruht auf dem Regelungsvorbild des Art. 59 EU-ErbVO.[131] Nach Art. 16 Abs. 1 EU-ErwSVO-E hat „eine in einem Mitgliedstaat errichtete öffentliche Urkunde [...] in einem anderen Mitgliedstaat die gleiche formelle Beweiskraft wie im Ursprungsmitgliedstaat oder die damit am ehesten vergleichbare Wirkung, sofern dies der öffentlichen Ordnung (ordre public) des betreffenden Mitgliedstaats nicht offensichtlich widerspricht". Art. 17 EU-ErwSVO-E sieht die Möglichkeit vor, bei der zuständigen Behörde des Ursprungsmitgliedstaats die Ausfüllung des Formblatts II im Anhang der EU-ErwSVO-E zu beantragen, in dem die förmliche Beweiskraft der öffentlichen Urkunde näher beschrieben wird.

Ebenso wie Art. 59 Abs. 1 EU-ErbVO stellt Art. 16 Abs. 1 EU-ErwSVO-E lediglich eine verfahrensrechtliche Kollisionsnorm dar, welche die formelle Beweiskraft einer öffentlichen Urkunde betrifft.[132] Die Vorschrift bewirkt daher keine ma-

---

[129] COM(2023) 281 final 6.

[130] So auch Bergamini/Bercea/Verteş-Olteanu Yb PIL 24 (2022/2023), 1 (16), die allerdings dem Bericht der Haager Arbeitsgruppe (Spezialkommission zum ErwSÜ, Prel. Doc. Nr. 6, April 2022, https://assets.hcch.net/docs/a7ffa46d-a1bd-4a75-a1a6-fd939da97e60.pdf [abgerufen 11.5.2023]) folgen wollen.

[131] Zur „Prägewirkung" des Art. 59 EU-ErbVO für weitere Legislativakte bereits Buschbaum FS Martiny, 2014, 259 (270ff.).

[132] S. zu Art. 59 Abs. 1 EU-ErbVO Dutta/Weber, Internationales Erbrecht/Bauer/Weber, 2. Aufl. 2021, Art. 59 EuErbVO Rn. 2ff.; Mansel Liber Amicorum Kohler, 2018, 301 (303ff.);

terielle Rechtslagenanerkennung.[133] Eine Pflicht zur materiellen Anerkennung einer Patientenverfügung aus anderen EU-Mitgliedstaaten (ob mit oder ohne Vorsorgevollmacht) lässt sich auch nicht unmittelbar aus den EU-Grundfreiheiten ableiten.[134] Ob und in welchem Umfang ein Arzt, Betreuer oder Vorsorgebevollmächtigter inhaltlich an die Vorgaben einer Patientenverfügung gebunden ist, unterliegt deshalb weiterhin den oben (→ III.) geschilderten Kollisionsnormen. Aufgrund der engen Anlehnung an das aus Art. 59 EU-ErbVO sowie Art. 58 EU-EheGüterVO/EU-LP-GüterVO bekannte Konzept der „Annahme“ öffentlicher Urkunden wird man sich bei der Auslegung des Art. 16 EU-ErwSVO-E an diesen Regelungsvorbildern orientieren können. Allerdings werden damit auch die aus diesen Verordnungen bekannten, zahlreichen Streit- und Abgrenzungsfragen in die EU-ErwSVO-E hineingetragen.[135] Schließlich dürfte die praktische Reichweite der Vorschrift dadurch begrenzt werden, dass Patientenverfügungen vielfach lediglich privatschriftlich errichtet werden (zB nach § 1827 Abs. 1 BGB), sodass eine Einstufung als öffentliche Urkunde in diesen Fällen von vornherein ausscheidet.

5. Europäisches Vertretungszertifikat

Eine weitere Neuerung findet sich in Kapitel VII. Mit der Verordnung wird eine Europäische Vertretungsbescheinigung (Art. 34 EU-ErwSVO-E) eingeführt, welche die Bescheinigung gemäß Art. 38 ErwSÜ ersetzen wird. Die Bescheinigung wird zur Verwendung durch Vertreter ausgestellt, die in einem anderen Mitgliedstaat ihre Befugnisse zur Vertretung eines schutzbedürftigen Erwachsenen geltend machen müssen (Art. 35 Abs. 1 EU-ErwSVO-E). Mit der Bescheinigung kann nachgewiesen werden, dass der Vertreter aufgrund einer Maßnahme oder einer bestätigten Vertretungsmacht befugt ist, den Erwachsenen in verschiedenen, in Art. 1 EU-ErwSVO-E genannten Angelegenheiten zu vertreten (Art. 35 Abs. 2 EU-ErwSVO-E). Für den Begriff der „Vertretungsmacht“ ist deren Legaldefinition in Art. 3 Nr. 3 EU-ErwSVO-E maßgebend, die sich auf Befugnisse beschränkt, die von einem Erwachsenen entweder durch eine Vereinbarung oder ein einseitiges Rechtsgeschäft für den Fall eingeräumt werden, dass er selbst nicht in der Lage ist, seine Interessen zu schützen. Das Europäische Vertretungszertifikat wird also über Vorsorgevollmachten ausgestellt werden können, die mit einer Patientenverfügung kombiniert sind (→ II. 2.). Isolierte Patientenverfügungen werden davon hingegen

---

Münchener Kommentar zum BGB/Dutta, 9. Aufl. 2024, EU-ErbVO Art. 59 Rn. 1 ff.; Rauscher, EuZPR/EuIPR/Hertel, 4. Aufl. 2016, EU-ErbVO Art. 59 Rn. 1 ff., jeweils mwN.

[133] Vgl. zu Art. 59 Abs. 1 EU-ErbVO Dutta/Weber, Internationales Erbrecht/Bauer/Weber, 2. Aufl. 2021, EuErbVO Art. 59 Rn. 7; Mansel Liber Amicorum Kohler, 2018, 301 (303 ff.); Münchener Kommentar zum BGB/Dutta, 9. Aufl. 2024, Art. 59 EU-ErbVO Rn. 3; Rauscher, EuZPR/EuIPR/Hertel, 4. Aufl. 2016, EU-ErbVO Art. 59 Rn. 5, jeweils mwN.

[134] Jayme FS Spellenberg, 2010, 203 (209 f.); Lemmerz, Die Patientenverfügung, 2014, S. 312 ff.; Ramser, Grenzüberschreitende Vorsorgevollmachten in Europa im Lichte des Haager Übereinkommens über den internationalen Schutz von Erwachsenen vom 13. Januar 2000, 2010, S. 133 ff.; Röthel FPR 2007, 79, 82.

[135] Sehr kritisch zu Art. 59 EU-ErbVO Dutta/Weber, Internationales Erbrecht/Bauer/Weber, 2. Aufl. 2021, EuErbVO Art. 59 Rn. 1: „Art. 59 gehört zu den problematischsten Vorschriften der Verordnung.“

nicht erfasst, weil es insoweit wiederum am Element der Bevollmächtigung fehlt (→ II. 3. zu Art. 15 ErwSÜ).

VI. Ergebnisse und Ausblick

In Bezug auf Patientenverfügungen fallen die mit der EU-ErwSVO-E zu erwartenden Fortschritte bescheiden aus. Die einzig relevante Neuerung auf diesem Gebiet stellen die Vorschriften zur Annahme öffentlicher Urkunden (Art. 16f. EU-ErwSVO-E) dar, deren Wirkung aber auf die formelle Beweiskraft begrenzt bleibt. Die kollisionsrechtlichen Unsicherheiten bei der Behandlung der Patientenverfügung zwischen ErwSÜ, Rom I- und II-Verordnungen sowie nationalen Eingriffsnormen bleiben insoweit bestehen. Das ist insbesondere für die betroffenen Patienten misslich, die nicht sicher vorhersehen können, nach welchem Recht sich die Wirkungen einer von ihnen errichteten Patientenverfügung bei einer späteren Behandlung im Ausland richten werden. Allerdings ist zweifelhaft, ob sich dieser Erwartung mit den Methoden des Kollisionsrechts überhaupt adäquat Rechnung tragen lässt, ohne die berechtigten Verkehrsschutzinteressen des Gesundheitswesens zu missachten. De lege ferenda sollte daher verstärkt über eine sachrechtliche Lösung nachgedacht werden. Ein standardisiertes EU-Formular mit Kästchen zum Ankreuzen, das sich automatisch übersetzen ließe und innerhalb der EU eine einheitliche Wirkung hätte, könnte zumindest als Option für grenzüberschreitende Patientenverfügungen entwickelt werden.

CHRISTIAN HERTEL

Formerfordernisse und Auslandsbeurkundung

I. *Fragestellung*

Grundfrage des IPR ist immer: Welches Recht ist auf eine bestimmte Rechtsfrage anwendbar? Sinnvollerweise kann nach dem jeweiligen IPR jeweils nur eine Rechtsordnung auf die jeweilige Rechtsfrage anzuwenden sein. So ist auf die Erbfolge – je nach anwendbarem IPR – meist entweder das Heimatrecht (Staatsangehörigkeitsrecht) des Erblassers oder das Recht an dessen letztem gewöhnlichen Aufenthalt/Wohnsitz anwendbar. Das jeweilige IPR muss sich entscheiden, welche Anknüpfung es vorsieht.

Bei der Frage nach der Formwirksamkeit ist dies anders: Hier kann das IPR vorsehen, dass ein Rechtsgeschäft formwirksam ist, wenn es entweder den Formerfordernissen der Rechtsordnung des Staates A oder denen der Rechtsordnung des Staates B genügt – klassischerweise entweder der Ortsform (am Ort der Vornahme des Rechtsgeschäftes) oder der Geschäftsform (dh des materiell auf das betreffende Rechtsgeschäft anwendbaren Rechts), wie dies im autonomen deutschen IPR Art. 11 Abs. 1 EGBGB als Grundnorm regelt.

Erfordert eine der (möglicherweise) anwendbaren Rechtsordnungen (notarielle) Beurkundung für das betreffende Rechtsgeschäft, so stellt sich die weitere Frage, ob dieses Beurkundungserfordernis auch durch eine ausländische Urkundsperson und auch durch Einhaltung (nur) des ausländischen Beurkundungsverfahrens erfüllt werden kann. Denn das Beurkundungserfordernis stellt nicht nur Anforderungen an die Urkunde selbst, sondern auch an die Urkundsperson und an das Verfahren zur Erstellung der Urkunde.

Nachfolgend will ich die verschiedenen denkbaren IPR-Regelungen für die Formwirksamkeit im Allgemeinen und bei beurkundungsbedürftigen Rechtsgeschäften im Besonderen systematisch vergleichen und die Vor- und Nachteile der verschiedenen Regelungen darstellen – nicht als Kommentierung der Einzelvorschriften, sondern in einem kurzen systematischen Vergleich.

II. *Mögliche IPR-Regelungen*

1. *Mögliche IPR-Regelungen zur allgemeinen Formwirksamkeit*

Meist regeln IPR-Normen auch die Formwirksamkeit durch Anknüpfung an ein Kriterium wie den Ort der Vornahme des Rechtsgeschäfts oder (indirekt) das auf das Rechtsgeschäft anwendbare Geschäftsrecht etc. Denkbar ist aber auch, die Formerfordernisse unmittelbar inhaltlich in der IPR-Norm zu regeln – oder eine

Kombination von Anknüpfungsregel und materiellen Mindest- oder Maximalerfordernissen. Als Beispiel für unmittelbar inhaltlich die Formerfordernisse regelnde IPR-Normen wollen wir das Schriftformerfordernis nach Art. 23 Abs. 1, 25 Abs. 1 EU-EheGüterVO betrachten, das Mindesterfordernisse für eine Rechtswahl des Güterrechts bzw. für ehegüterrechtliche Vereinbarungen aufstellt.

Regelt der IPR-Gesetzgeber hingegen (wie meist) die Formwirksamkeit durch Verweis auf eine nach Anknüpfungskriterien bestimmte Rechtsordnungen, so kann er entweder nur ein einziges Anknüpfungskriterium vorsehen, so dass das Rechtsgeschäft den Formerfordernissen dieser Rechtsordnung genügen muss, oder er kann alternativ zwei oder mehrere Anknüpfungskriterien zulassen, so dass die Erfüllung der Formerfordernisse einer der so bestimmten Rechtsordnungen alternativ für die Formwirksamkeit genügt – oder er kann regeln, dass umgekehrt kumulativ die Anforderungen mehrerer Rechtsordnungen erfüllt sein müssen.

Als Anknüpfungskriterien bieten sich insbes. Ortsform und/oder Geschäftsform an, daneben aber etwa auch das Heimatrecht oder Wohnsitzrecht/Recht des gewöhnlichen Aufenthalts (insbes. bei personen-, familien- und erbrechtlichen Rechtsgeschäften).

Denkbar ist auch eine Kombination beider Regelungstypen, etwa dass zwar grundsätzlich mehrere Anknüpfungen zugelassen werden, zugleich aber inhaltlich bestimmte Mindestanforderungen vorgeschrieben werden – oder dass grundsätzlich nur ein Mindeststandard vorgeschrieben ist, aber wenn bestimmte Anknüpfungspunkte vorliegen, höhere Formerfordernisse dieses Rechts einzuhalten sind (wie etwa in Art. 23 und 25 EU-EheGüterVO geregelt ist).

2. *Zusätzliche Sonderfragen bei Beurkundungserfordernissen*

Verlangt das für die Formerfordernisse maßgebliche Recht eine (notarielle) Beurkundung, so ist weiter zu fragen, ob nur eine Beurkundung durch eine nach diesem Recht zuständige Urkundsperson (etwa nur durch einen inländischen Notar) und nur nach dem für diese Urkundsperson anzuwendenden Beurkundungsrecht genügt – oder ob und unter welchen Voraussetzungen auch eine Beurkundung durch eine ausländische Urkundsperson (Auslandsbeurkundung) genügt.

III. *Vergleich möglicher IPR-Regelungen zur Formwirksamkeit*

Betrachten wir Beispiele für die einzelnen Fallgruppen.

1. *Formerfordernisse in der IPR-Norm selbst inhaltlich geregelt*

Denkbar, aber selten sind IPR-Normen, die die Anforderungen an die Form nicht durch Verweisung auf eine Rechtsordnung, sondern inhaltlich in der IPR-Norm selbst regeln.[1] Ein Beispiel hierfür sind Art. 23 Abs. 1 und 25 Abs. 1 EU-

---

[1] Vor Kodifizierung des IPR fehlte in vielen Rechtsordnungen jegliche IPR-Regelung der anwendbaren Form. Dann war ggf. die für inländische Rechtsgeschäfte vorgeschriebene Form ein-

EheGüterVO, die für die ehegüterrechtlich Rechtswahl bzw. für Regelungen zum Ehegüterrecht mindestens Einhaltung der Schriftform verlangen.

Allerdings sind die Formerfordernisse damit nicht abschließend geregelt. Vielmehr sind nach Art. 23 Abs. 2–4 bzw. Art. 25 Abs. 2–3 EU-EheGüterVO zusätzlich weitergehende Formerfordernisse des Aufenthalts- bzw. (bei einer güterrechtlichen Vereinbarung) des Geschäftsrechts ebenfalls einzuhalten. Art. 23 Abs. 1 und 25 Abs. 1 EU-EheGüterVO regeln nur die Mindestanforderungen. Diese Mindestanforderungen sind allerdings so gering – und schließen im Wesentlichen nur einen mündlichen Vertragsschluss aus, dass sie neben den einzuhaltenden Formvorschriften des Aufenthalts- bzw. Geschäftsrechts nur selten eine Rolle spielen dürften.

Dass Beispiele für eine unmittelbare inhaltliche Regelung der Formerfordernisse in einer IPR-Norm selten sind, dürfte daran liegen, dass eine solche Regelung wenig praktikabel ist. Fordert der Gesetzgeber nur geringe Formanforderungen, kann er es gleich bleiben lassen. Fordert er höhere Anforderungen, könnte die kumulative Einhaltung der Geschäftsform (damit das Rechtsgeschäft auch in dem Staat, dessen Recht anwendbar ist, als formwirksam angesehen wird) schwierig werden.

2. *Anknüpfung*

a) Alternative Anknüpfung, insbes. an Orts- oder Geschäftsform

Als deutscher Jurist denkt man bei der Anknüpfung des Formstatuts natürlich sofort an die Grundregel des Art. 11 Abs. 1 EGBGB, wonach für die Formwirksamkeit alternativ entweder die Einhaltung der Ortsform oder der Geschäftsform genügt. Inhaltsgleich, wenngleich mit Hervorhebung des Geschäftsstatuts galt dies bereits bei Inkrafttreten des BGB.

In Europa ist die alternative Anknüpfung an Orts- oder Geschäftsform, jedenfalls für schuldrechtliche Rechtsgeschäfte, die übliche Regelung. Sie findet sich in Art. 9 Rom I-Übk[2] (an dessen Formulierung sich die jetzige mit der IPR-Kodifikation 1986 eingeführte Fassung des Art. 11 Abs. 1 EGBGB anlehnt) bzw. jetzt in Art. 11 Abs. 1 Rom I-VO. Ebenso findet sie sich – und fand sie sich vielfach auch schon vor dem RomÜbk und der Rom I-VO – etwa in Art. 11 BGB Griechenland, Art. 26 IPRG Italien 1942 (vgl. jetzt Art. 56 Abs. 3 IPRG Italien 1995), Art. 12 IPRG Polen 1965, Art. 36 IPRG Portugal, Art. 124 IPRG Schweiz, Art. 11 CC Spanien (zusätzlich genügt auch Heimatrecht), Art. 6 IPRG Türkei 1982, § 30 IPRG Ungarn 1979.[3] Dieselbe alternative Anknüpfung findet sich auch in diversen außereuropäischen Rechtsordnungen, zB Art. 36 CC Angola, Art. 8 Horei Japan,

zuhalten. Dies war aber idR nicht als international-privatrechtliche Anwendung der jeweiligen nationalen Formvorschrift anzusehen, sondern als (gewohnheitsrechtliche) Anwendung der lex fori.

[2] Übereinkommen über das auf vertragliche Schuldverhältnisse anzuwendende Recht vom 19. 6. 1980 (BGBl. 1986 II 810).

[3] Text bzw. deutsche Übersetzung in: Riering, IPR-Gesetze in Europa, 1997; Staudinger, BGB/Schäuble, 2024, EGBGB Anh. zu Art. 11.

Art. 3109 CC Quebec (auch Wohnsitzrecht), Art. 2094 CC Peru, § 5 IPRG Taiwan, Art. 68 IPRG Tunesien.[4]

Historisch älter als diese alternative Anknüpfung ist aber die Grundregel „locus regit actum", die nur die Ortsform zulässt.[5] Sie findet sich als Grundregel des Formstatuts etwa noch im IPR verschiedener lateinamerikanischer Staaten (so zB Art. 12 CC Argentinien, Art. 13 CC Kuba, Art. 23 CC Paraguay, ebenso Art. 17 CC Philippinen). Teilweise enthalten diese Rechte aber zumindest den Zusatz, dass für die Form auch eine „Unterwerfung" (Rechtswahl) unter das inländische Recht möglich ist (zB Art. 13 Abs. 4 CC Distrito Federal Mexiko, Art. 7 CC Panama) – und damit zumindest eine beschränkte Zulassung der Geschäftsform.

Umgekehrt sehen die (nahöstlichen) Rechtsordnungen, die auf dem Vorbild des maßgeblich von Al-Sanhuri entworfenen ägyptischen Zivilgesetzbuchs von 1948 aufbauen, neben der alternativen Anknüpfung an Orts- oder Geschäftsform zusätzlich die Möglichkeit einer „Unterwerfung" unter Wohnsitzrecht oder Heimatrecht vor (Art. 20 ZGB Ägypten, ebenso zB Art. 31 ZGB Jemen, Art. 21 ZGB Jordanien, Art. 21 ZGB Syrien, ähnlich aber auch Art. 71 IPRG Rumänien 1992). Hier hatte der Gesetzgeber bei Schaffung der Grundnorm wohl neben dem Schuldvertragsrecht auch die Formerfordernisse im Familien- und Erbrecht im Auge.

Schon die weltweite Verbreitung der alternativen Anknüpfung jedenfalls an Orts- und Geschäftsform zeigt, dass sich diese Grundregel bewährt hat.

b) Ausschließliche Geltung der Geschäftsform

aa) Sachenrechtliche Verfügungen

Eine klassische Ausnahme von der alternativen Anknüpfung ist die ausschließliche Geltung der Geschäftsform für dingliche Rechtsgeschäfte jedenfalls bei Grundstücken. Soweit hier die lex rei sitae besondere Formerfordernisse vorsieht, dürften diese nach dem jeweiligen IPR nahezu immer zwingend unabhängig vom Vornahmeort gelten.

Im deutschen IPR schreibt Art. 11 Abs. 4 EGBGB die ausschließliche Geltung der Geschäftsform nicht nur für unbewegliche, sondern auch für bewegliche Sachen vor.

bb) Gesellschaftsrecht

Ob im deutschen IPR die Ortsform nach Art. 11 Abs. 1 EGBGB auch für gesellschaftsrechtliche Rechtsgeschäfte genügt, ist umstritten. Der BGH ließ die Frage bisher offen (und prüfte jeweils die Gleichwertigkeit der Auslandsbeurkundung).[6] In der übrigen Rechtsprechung und in der Literatur wird teils Art. 11 Abs. 1 EGBGB uneingeschränkt angewendet und die Einhaltung der Ortsform immer für

---

[4] Text bzw. deutsche Übersetzung in: Kropholler/Krüger/Riering/Samtleben/Siehr, Außereuropäische IPR-Gesetze, 1999; Staudinger, BGB/Schäuble, 2024, EGBGB Anh. zu Art. 11.

[5] Staudinger, BGB/Schäuble, 2024, EGBGB Art. 11 Rn. 3ff.

[6] BGH 16.2.1981 – II ZB 8/80, BGHZ 80, 76 = DNotZ 1981, 451 = NJW 1981, 1160; indirekt auch BGH 17.12.2013 – II ZB 6/13, BGHZ 199, 270 = DNotZ 2014, 457 = NJW 2014, 2026; BGH 21.10.2014 – II ZR 330/13, BGHZ 203, 68, BGH DNotZ 2015, 207 = NJW 2015, 336; ebenso OLG München 19.11.1997 – 7 U 2511/97, NJW-RR 1998, 758.

ausreichend gehalten[7], teils wird nur für Verfassungsakte (Gründung, Satzungsänderung, Umwandlung) die Ortsform ausgeschlossen[8], teils für alle gesellschaftsrechtlichen Vorgänge, auch für GmbH-Geschäftsanteilsabtretungen[9].

Wortlaut und Systematik scheinen zunächst für die Geltung von Art. 11 EGBGB zu sprechen, weil sich keine ausdrückliche Ausnahme findet (während dingliche Verfügungen über Sachen nach Art. 11 Abs. 4 EGBGB ausdrücklich ausgenommen sind). Die Entstehungsgeschichte spricht aber dagegen. In der Begründung des Regierungsentwurfs für die IPR-Kodifikation heißt es: „Aus dem Standort – der Abschnitt betrifft sonst nur das Recht natürlicher Personen – und der Entstehungsgeschichte der Bestimmung – das EG-Schuldvertragsübereinkommen erfasst das Gesellschafts- und Vereinsrecht nicht, ebenso wenig der vorliegende Entwurf insgesamt, … – ergibt sich dagegen, dass Art 11 EGBGB nicht die Form von Vorgängen regelt, die sich auf die Verfassung von Gesellschaften und juristischen Personen beziehen.“[10] Richtig erscheint mir daher, dass im Gesellschaftsrecht die Ortsform nicht genügt (außer für schuldrechtliche Verpflichtungen, etwa zur Abtretung von GmbH-Anteilen).[11]

c) Alternative Zulassung diverser Anknüpfungspunkte

Umgekehrt gibt es Regelungen, die noch diverse weitere Anknüpfungspunkte für die Formwirksamkeit vorsehen. Am weitesten dürfte Art. 1 Abs. 1 des Haager Testamentsformübereinkommens (HTestFormÜbk)[12] gehen, der fünf verschiedene Anknüpfungspunkte für die Testamentsform zulässt (Errichtungsort, Staatsangehörigkeit, Wohnsitz, gewöhnlicher Aufenthalt sowie Belegenheit für Immobilien), davon die drei persönlichen Anknüpfungen jeweils noch wahlweise zur Zeit der Errichtung der Verfügung von Todes wegen bzw. zur Zeit des Todes, so dass insgesamt acht Anknüpfungen zu prüfen sind (auch wenn diese praktisch nie zu acht unterschiedlichen Rechtsordnungen führen dürften). Ziel dieser sehr weitgehenden Regelung ist der favor testamenti: Möglichst alle Verfügungen von Todes wegen, die nur an irgendein halbwegs einschlägiges Kriterium anknüpfen, sollen formwirksam sein. Weil die Haager Konferenz aber erkannte, dass die Weite der zulässigen Formen einige Staaten von der Ratifikation abhalten könnte, lässt sie in

---

[7] OLG Düsseldorf 25.1.1989 – 3 Wx 21/89, NJW 1989, 2200; Dutta RIW 2005, 98 (100); Loritz DNotZ 2000 (90); Odendahl RIW 2014, 189 (193f.); beck-online.GROSSKOMMENTAR zum Zivilrecht/Gebauer, Stand 1.3.2023, EGBGB Art. 11 Rn. 77; Grüneberg/Thorn, 83. Aufl. 2024, EGBGB Art. 11 Rn. 10; Münchener Kommentar zum BGB/Spellenberg, 9. Aufl. 2024, EGBGB Art. 11 Rn. 194ff.

[8] KG 24.1.2018 – 22 W 25/16, NJW 2018, 1828; Cramer DStR 2018, 746 (748); Goette DStR 1996, 709 (714); Ludwig NotBZ 2003, 90 (97); Stenzel GmbHR 2014, 1024 (1031).

[9] Herrler NJW 2018, 1787; Kindler BB 2010, 74 (75); Lieder ZIP ZIP 2018, 805 (808); Süss DNotZ 2011, 414 (416); Weber MittBayNot 2018, 215; juris PraxisKommentar BGB/Süß, 10. Aufl. 2023, EGBGB Art. 11 Rn. 59ff.; Staudinger, BGB/Schäuble, 2024, Art. 11 EGBGB Rn. 249ff.

[10] BT-Drs. 10/504, 49.

[11] Staudinger, BGB/Hertel, 2023, BeurkG Rn. 856 (860ff.).

[12] Haager Übereinkommen über das auf die Form letztwilliger Verfügungen anzuwendende Recht vom 5.10.1961 (BGBl. 1965 II 1145).

Art. 10 und 11 HTestFormÜbk Vorbehalte gegenüber mündlichen Testamenten zu sowie gegenüber der Ortsform, sofern die Beziehung zum Vorbehaltsstaat deutlich enger war (durch Staatsangehörigkeit und Heimatrecht) als zum Errichtungsstaat. Diese Weite der Anknüpfung war wohl auch der Hauptgrund, warum selbst etliche europäische Staaten das Haager Testamentsformübereinkommen bis heute nicht ratifiziert haben.[13]

Art. 27 EU-ErbVO, der im Wesentlichen auf Art. 1 Abs. 1 HTestFormÜbk aufbaut, erfasst daher bewusst nur „schriftliche" Verfügungen von Todes wegen, nicht mündliche.

d) *Kumulativ Erfüllung der Formerfordernisse mehrerer Rechtsordnungen erforderlich*

Selten sind Regelungen, die kumulativ die Erfüllung mehrerer Formerfordernisse verlangen. So erfordert Art. 25 Abs. 2 EU-EheGüterVO für Vereinbarungen über den ehelichen Güterstand die Einhaltung der Formerfordernisse des Aufenthaltsrechts, wenn zumindest einer der Ehegatten seinen gewöhnlichen Aufenthalt in einem EU-EheGüterVO-Mitgliedstaat hat. Art. 25 Abs. 3 EU-EheGüterVO erfordert auch die Einhaltung zusätzlicher Formvorschriften des anwendbaren Rechts (= Geschäftsrechts). Nach dem Wortlaut der Norm und nach dem Verständnis der Literatur sind die Anforderungen der Absätze 2 und 3 kumulativ einzuhalten.[14] Der europäische Gesetzgeber hat den möglichen Konflikt zwischen zwei unterschiedlichen Aufenthaltsrechten gesehen (und in Art. 25 Abs. 2 S. 2 EU-EheGüterVO bestimmt, dass die Einhaltung der Formerfordernisse eines der beiden EU-EheGüterVO-Aufenthaltsstaaten genügt). Zum Konflikt zwischen Absätzen 2 und 3 hat er hingegen nichts geregelt.

Das hieße etwa, dass zwei Briten, die ab dem 29.1.2019 geheiratet haben und beide ihren gewöhnlichen Aufenthalt in Deutschland haben, und in einem Ehevertrag güterrechtliche Vereinbarungen nach englischem Recht treffen wollen, die Rechtswahl nach deutschem Recht beurkunden müssen (Art. 23 Abs. 2 EU-EheGüterVO imV § 1410 BGB – hierfür ist das anwendbare Recht irrelevant) und für die materiellen güterrechtlichen Vereinbarungen neben dem deutschen Beurkundungserfordernis (Art. 25 Abs. 2 S. 1 EU-EheGüterVO imV § 1410 BGB) auch die Formanforderungen des gewählten englischen Rechts einhalten müssen (Art. 25 Abs. 3 EU-EheGüterVO). Insbes. ist etwa noch eine vorherige Beratung beider Ehegatten durch je einen nur dem betreffenden Ehegatten verpflichteten Anwalt erforderlich (obwohl auch der zur Unparteilichkeit verpflichtete Notar belehrt), sofern man das Erfordernis des *independent legal advice* als Form iSd Art. 23, 25 EU-EheGüterVO qualifiziert.[15] (Persönlich würde ich dies aber nicht als Formerfordernis, sondern als materiell-rechtliches Formerfordernis einstufen. Denn zum einen

---

[13] Von den EU-Mitgliedstaaten haben Bulgarien, Italien, Lettland, Litauen, Malta, Portugal, Rumänien, die Slowakei, Tschechien, Ungarn und Zypern das Haager Testamentsformübereinkommen nicht ratifiziert – Italien und Portugal, obwohl sie es schon unterzeichnet hatten.

[14] Dutta FamRZ 2016, 1973 (1984); Heiderhoff IPrax 2018, 1 (8); Münchener Kommentar zum BGB/Looschelders, 9. Aufl. 2024, EuGüVO Art. 25 Rn. 12; Hausmann, Internationales und Europäisches Familienrecht, 3. Aufl. 2024, B Rn. 427.

[15] Vgl. Dutta/Weber, Die Europäischen Güterrechtsverordnungen/Süß, 2017, S. 85 (98 Rn. 49ff.).

ist es in andere materiell-rechtliche Anforderungen eingebettet, wie etwa die Offenlegung der Vermögensverhältnisse. Zum anderen würde man bei einem Formerfordernis erwarten, dass man die Einhaltung der Form unmittelbar aus der Urkunde prüfen kann.)[16]

Die ratio hinter Art. 25 Abs. 3 EU-EheGüterVO ist verständlich und sinnvoll: Die Norm will sicherstellen, dass die Vereinbarung auch vor den Gerichten des Staates als formwirksam angesehen wird, dessen Ehegüterrecht anzuwenden ist. Art. 25 Abs. 2 EU-EheGüterVO will hingegen sicherstellen, dass die Schutzgesetze des Aufenthalts- und voraussichtlichen Gerichtsstaates eingehalten werden.

Folgt man der Rechtsauffassung von Süß, so wäre die rechtssichere Gestaltung für unser britisches Ehepaar, dass sie sich jeweils durch einen englischen Anwalt beraten lassen (das geht ja ggf. auch telefonisch oder online) und von diesen einen Vertragsentwurf erstellen lassen, den der deutsche Notar dann beurkundet. Denn der deutsche Notar wird sich kaum trauen, einen Vertragsentwurf zu dem ihm unbekannten englischen Recht zu erstellen. Das ist rechtssicher, aber umständlich. (Eine Beurkundung des Ehevertrags in England würde hingegen daran scheitern, dass die dortigen Notare den deutschen nicht gleichwertig sind.)

Wie man sieht, wird der Gesetzgeber kumulative Formerfordernisse nur verlangen, wenn er besondere Schutzzwecke erfüllt. Denn die Erfüllung kann schwierig werden. (Sehr häufig wird die Kumulation aber keine Probleme aufwerfen, weil das Aufenthaltsrecht auch Geschäftsrecht ist und nicht abgewählt wird.)

3. *Kombination von Anknüpfung und inhaltlichen Erfordernissen*

Art. 23 und 25 EU-EheGüterVO sind auch ein Beispiel für eine Kombination von inhaltlichen Erfordernissen (mindestens Schriftform nach dem jeweiligen Absatz 1) und einer IPR-Anknüpfung (zusätzliche Einhaltung der Formerfordernisse des Aufenthaltsrechts nach Art. 23 Abs. 2–4 bzw. Art. 25 Abs. 2 EU-EheGüterVO sowie – nur bei einer materiellen Vereinbarung zum Güterrecht – auch des Geschäftsrechts nach Art. 25 Abs. 3 EU-EheGüterVO). Die Mindestanforderungen der Schriftform nach Art. 23 Abs. 1 bzw. Art. 25 Abs. 1 EU-EheGüterVO sind aber sehr gering. Selbst ein Austausch von E-Mails würde hierfür genügen.[17] Fallstricke können sich allerdings daraus ergeben, dass die Schriftform nach Art. 23 Abs. 1 und 25 Abs. 1 EU-EheGüterVO auch die Datierung verlangt und daher eine Rechtswahl oder güterrechtliche Vereinbarung ohne Datumsangabe formunwirksam ist - und jedenfalls nach einer Meinung auch bei falscher Datumsangabe formunwirksam ist.[18] Praktisch relevant sind daher meist nur die Formerfordernisse des Aufenthaltsrechts (und ggf. des Geschäftsrechts).

---

[16] Beck'scher Online-Großkommentar zum BGB/Hertel, Stand 10/2024, EuGüVO Art. 24 Rn. 6.

[17] Grüneberg, BGB/Thorn, 83. Aufl. 2024, EuGüVO Art. 23 Rn. 2; Hausmann, Internationales und Europäisches Familienrecht, 3. Aufl. 2024, B Rn. 399.

[18] Dutta/Weber, Die Europäischen Güterrechtsverordnungen/Döbereiner, 2017, S. 63 (69 Rn. 21); Münchener Kommentar zum BGB/Loooschelders, 9. Auf. 2024, EuGüVO Art. 23 Rn. 4.

IV. Vergleich möglicher IPR-Regelungen zur Auslandsbeurkundung

Kommen wir zu den Fällen, in denen die Einhaltung der Ortsform nicht genügt und das als Geschäftsrecht anwendbare deutsche Recht eine Beurkundung vorschreibt. Heißt dies automatisch, dass dann ein deutscher Notar beurkunden muss oder ist auch eine Beurkundung durch einen ausländischen Notar erforderlich – und wenn unter welchen Voraussetzungen?

1. Ausschließliche Zuständigkeit

In bestimmten Fällen sind ausschließlich deutsche Notare (oder deutsche Konsularbeamte) für die Beurkundung zuständig.

a) Auflassung

So entschied der BGH, dass die Auflassung für ein in Deutschland belegenes Grundstück nur vor einem deutschen Notar erklärt werden kann (oder vor einem deutschen Konsularbeamten) (§ 925 Abs. 1 S. 2 BGB). Eine vor einem ausländischen Notar erklärte Auflassung ist unwirksam[19]. Dies entsprach auch zuvor der mehrheitlichen Literaturmeinung[20].

Argument des BGH ist zum einen die Entstehungsgeschichte: Nachdem die Auflassung nach der ursprünglichen Fassung des BGB gegenüber dem Grundbuchamt erklärt werden musste und Notare nur nach Maßgabe fortbestehender landesrechtlicher Vorschriften zuständig waren – und nur für im betreffenden Land bzw. Rechtsgebiet belegene Grundstücke, wurde die Zuständigkeit später auf „jeden" (deutschen) Notar erweitert. Dass eine Zuständigkeitsregelung nur für deutsche Amtsträger gelten sollte, nicht für ausländische Amtsträger, war zu selbstverständlich, um es ausdrücklich zu regeln.

Weiteres Argument des BGH ist aber auch die Kontrolle und Richtigkeitsgewähr durch die inländischen Notare, die ausländische Notare nicht bieten können. Diese Kontrollfunktion wurde nach Ergehen der BGH-Entscheidung noch verstärkt, da jetzt zur Kontrolle des Barzahlungsverbots nach § 16a Geldwäschegesetz beim Grundstückserwerb das Grundbuchamt eine Auflassung nur mehr vollziehen darf,

---

[19] BGH 13.2.2020 – V ZB 3/16, DNotZ 2020, 742 = NJW 2020, 1670; in diese Richtung bereits BGH 10.6.1968 – III ZR 15/66, BB 1969, 197 = WM 1968, 1170; dazu auch Lieder NZG 2020, 1081; OLG Hamm 1.2.1974 – 15 Wx 6/74, NJW 1974, 1057; ebenso KG 27.5.1986 – 1 W 2627/85, OLGZ 1986, 319 = DNotZ 1987, 44 = Rpfleger 1986, 428; OLG Köln 29.11.1971 – 2 Wx 78/71, OLGZ 1972, 321 = DNotZ 1972, 489 = Rpfleger 1972, 134; LG Ellwangen 26.11.1999 – 1 T 205/99, BWNotZ 2000, 45 = MittRhNotK 2000, 252.

[20] Armbrüster/Preuss/Renner, BeurkG/Armbrüster, 8. Aufl. 2020, BeurkG § 1 Rn. 57; Bausback DNotZ 1996, 254; Blumenwitz DNotZ 1968, 712 (736); Döbereiner ZNotP 2001, 465; Jakobs MittRhNotK 1985, 57 (58); Kanzleiter DNotZ 2007, 222 (227f.); Kropholler ZHR 140 (1976) 394 (410); Reithmann DNotZ 1995, 360 (362f.); Riedel DNotZ 1955, 521; Schütze DNotZ 1992, 66 (67); Weber NJW 1955, 1784 (1786); Demharter GBO § 20 Rn. 15; Grüneberg/Herrler BGB § 925 Rn 2; Grüneberg/Thorn, 83. Aufl. 2024, EGBGB Art. 11 Rn. 10; Staudinger/Hertel, 2023, BeurkG Rn. 855; aA – Gleichwertigkeit der ausländischen Beurkundung genügt: Heinz ZNotP 2001, 460; Mann NJW 1955, 1177; Mann ZHR 138 (1974) 448 (456); Münchener Kommentar zum BGB/Spellenberg, 9. Aufl. 2020, EGBGB Art. 11 Rn. 183.

wenn der Vollzug von einem (deutschen) Notar beantragt wird (§ 13 Abs. 1 S. 3 GBO[21]).

Auch die Verpflichtung zur Veräußerung oder zum Erwerb eines Grundstücks bedarf nach § 311c Abs. 1 BGB der notariellen Beurkundung. Für diese schuldrechtliche Verpflichtung genügt aber nach Art. 11 Abs. 1 EGBGB alternativ auch die Einhaltung der Ortsform am Abschlussort.

b) Vollstreckungsunterwerfung (§ 794 Abs. 1 Nr. 5 ZPO)

Ebenso gilt § 794 Abs. 1 Nr. 5 ZPO, wonach sich der Schuldner zu notarieller Urkunde rechtsgeschäftlich der sofortigen Zwangsvollstreckung unterwerfen und so einen Vollstreckungstitel schaffen kann (etwa eine vollstreckbare Grundschuld), nur für eine Vollstreckungsunterwerfung vor einem deutschen Notar[22]. Denn die Zivilprozessordnung regelt das Verfahren vor deutschen Gerichten. Ob und unter welchen Voraussetzungen auch ausländische Vollstreckungstitel in Deutschland vollstreckbar sind, ist anderweitig geregelt (insbes. in §§ 1079 ff. ZPO und der Verordnung (EG) Nr. 85/2004 zur Einführung eines europäischen Vollstreckungstitels für unbestrittene Forderungen).

Bei Erlass des BGB sah der Gesetzgeber die Erklärung der Auflassung ebenso als einen Akt gegenüber einer Behörde an – ähnlich wie die Vollstreckungsunterwerfung.

2. Gleichwertigkeit der Auslandsbeurkundung

a) Konzept des BGH

Verlangt hingegen das allein maßgebliche deutsche Geschäftsrecht zwar eine Beurkundung, sind hierfür aber nicht ausschließlich deutsche Notare zuständig, so lässt der BGH in ständiger Rechtsprechung eine Auslandsbeurkundung zur Erfüllung des deutschen Beurkundungserfordernisses genügen – und zwar als Substitution der deutschen Beurkundung, wenn die ausländische Beurkundung der deutschen gleichwertig ist.[23]

Gleichwertig muss sowohl die Urkundsperson wie das Beurkundungsverfahren sein. Oder, wie der BGH formuliert: „Gleichwertigkeit ist gegeben, wenn die ausländische Urkundsperson nach Vorbildung und Stellung im Rechtsleben eine der Tätigkeit des deutschen Notars entsprechende Funktion ausübt und für die Errichtung der Urkunde ein Verfahrensrecht zu beachten hat, das den tragenden Grundsätzen des deutschen Beurkundungsrechts entspricht.“[24]

---

[21] Eingefügt durch Art. 16 Nr. 2 Gesetz vom 19.12.2022 (BGBl. 2022 I 2606) mWv 28.12.2022.

[22] Anders/Gehle, ZPO/Schmid, 82. Aufl. 2024, ZPO § 794 Rn. 32; Musielak, ZPO/Voit/Lackmann, 21. Aufl. 2024, ZPO § 794 Rn. 29.

[23] BGH 16.2.1981 – II ZB 8/80, BGHZ 80, 76 = DNotZ 1981, 451 = NJW 1981, 1160; BGH 17.12.2013 – II ZB 6/13, BGHZ 199, 270 = DNotZ 2014, 457 = NJW 2014, 2026; BGH 21.10.2014 – II ZR 330/13, BGHZ 203, 68 = DNotZ 2015, 207 = NJW 2015, 336; ebenso OLG München 19.11.1997 – 7 U 2511/97, NJW-RR 1998, 758.

[24] BGH 16.2.1981 – II ZB 8/80, BGHZ 80, 76 = DNotZ 1981, 451 = NJW 1981, 1160.

Erforderlich ist nur, dass Urkundsperson und Beurkundungsverfahren in abstracto diese Kriterien erfüllen. Prüfungsmaßstab ist das ausländische Gesetz, nicht die konkrete Beurkundung. Denn wenn dem Gericht oder dem Rechtsverkehr die ausländische Urkunde vorliegt, kann man zwar prüfen, was das ausländische Gesetz erfordert, nicht aber, was in der konkreten Beurkundung passiert ist. Für die Gleichwertigkeit genügt daher nicht, wenn die ausländische Urkundsperson im Einzelfall höhere Anforderungen erfüllt als eigentlich für die Urkundsperson oder das betreffende ausländische Beurkundungsverfahren vorgeschrieben sind. Umgekehrt schaden einzelne Verstöße gegen das anwendbare ausländische Beurkundungsverfahren nicht, solange sie nicht die Beurkundung nach dem anwendbaren Recht unwirksam machen.

Gleichwertigkeit der Urkundsperson erfordert insbes. eine vergleichbare juristische Ausbildung, den Charakter als öffentliches Amt, sachliche Unabhängigkeit und Neutralitätspflicht bei der Amtsführung, das Bestehen entsprechender Berufspflichten und deren Kontrolle durch Standesorgane und Justizverwaltung. Für die Ausbildung wird man entweder ein juristisches Hochschulstudium oder eine fachspezifische Ausbildung verlangen (vgl. wie bei den früheren württembergischen Amtsnotaren), wohl auch eine zusätzliche praktische Ausbildung vor der Ernennung. Damit ist etwa ein US notary public nicht gleichwertig, wenn dies nach dem Recht des betreffenden US-Staates auch ein Nicht-Jurist sein kann, der nur eine Zusatzausbildung auf dem Niveau einer Sekretariatskraft oder eines Rechtsanwaltsgehilfen erfolgreich absolvieren muss (egal, ob die konkrete Urkundsperson Jura studiert hat).

Hinsichtlich des Beurkundungsverfahrens prüfte der BGH als wesentliche Punkte „die Prüfungs- und Belehrungspflicht des Notars, die Identitätsfeststellung der Beteiligten, die Verhandlungsniederschrift, das Vorlesen, Genehmigen und Unterzeichnen der Urkunde durch die Beteiligten sowie Siegeln und Unterzeichnen durch den Notar“.[25]

Zu Recht nennt der BGH an erster Stelle die notarielle „Prüfungs- und Belehrungspflicht“. Denn die notarielle Rechtsbelehrung ist die raison d'être der Beurkundung, das Grundgesetz des Notars. Ein Notar, der nicht belehrt, ist kein Notar. Die notarielle Belehrungspflicht ist daher für die Gleichwertigkeit unverzichtbar. Sie findet sich in allen Staaten des lateinischen Notariats.[26] Der Begriff der Belehrung ist noch zu eng, weil der Notar in aller Regel nicht nur über einen von Dritten vorgegebenen Urkundeninhalt informiert, sondern den Inhalt der Urkunde selbst nach den Angaben der Beteiligten formuliert. Auch eine solche vertrags-

---

[25] BGH 16.2.1981 – II ZB 8/80, BGHZ 80, 76 = DNotZ 1981, 451 = NJW 1981, 1160.

[26] Belgien Art. 9 Abs. 1 Notargesetz; Bulgarien Art. 25 Notargesetz; Estland § 30 Abs. 1 Notargesetz; in Frankreich nicht ausdrücklich gesetzlich geregelt, aber durch die Rechtsprechung gefordert, vgl zB Cour de cassation 15.5.2007 – Nr. 06–15.318, ECLI:FR:CCASS:2007:C100622; Italien Art. 47 Notargesetz aF; Lettland Art. 87 Notargesetz; Litauen Art. 30 Notargesetz; Malta Art. 25 Notargesetz; Niederlande jedenfalls aus Rechtsprechung; Österreich § 52–53 Notariatsordnung; Polen Art. 80 Notargesetz; Rumänien Art. 6 Abs. 1 und Art. 7 Notargesetz Nr. 36/1995; Slowakei; Slowenien Art. 42 Notargesetz; Spanien Art. 147 Notarordnung – *Reglamento Notarial* vom 2.6.1944; in Tschechien nicht ausdrücklich im Gesetz geregelt, aber in der Rechtsprechung insbes aus der Pflicht zur Unparteilichkeit abgeleitet.

gestaltende Funktion des Notars (bzw. Verantwortlichkeit für den rechtlichen Inhalt der Urkunde) dürfte nach dem Maßstab des BGH für die Gleichwertigkeit erforderlich sein.

Bei der Belehrungspflicht lässt der BGH genügen, wenn das anwendbare Beurkundungsrecht eine Belehrung zum inländischen Recht des Urkundsstaates erfordert; eine Belehrung über das ausländische Recht ist nicht erforderlich. Denn sonst wäre eine Auslandsbeurkundung fast nie gleichwertig, da viele Beurkundungsrechte keine Belehrung zum Inhalt des ausländischen Rechts verlangen (so wie auch der deutsche Notar zwar hinweisen muss, wenn – möglicherweise – ausländisches Recht anwendbar ist, er aber nicht über dessen Inhalt belehren muss, § 17 Abs. 3 BeurkG). Diesem Kriterium des BGH genügen die Rechtsordnungen des lateinischen Notariats daher meist unproblematisch.

Problematisch für die Vergleichbarkeit des Beurkundungsverfahrens kann v. a. das Verlesen sein. Manche Stimmen fordern für die Gleichwertigkeit eine vollständige Verlesung wie nach deutschem Recht.[27] Die vollständige Verlesung der Niederschrift ist aber keineswegs in allen Rechtsordnungen des lateinischen Notariats vorgeschrieben.[28] In manchen Staaten können die Beteiligten auf die Verlesung verzichten[29] oder genügt auch das das leise Selbstlesen durch die Beteiligten[30]. In anderen Staaten genügt eine kommentierte teilweise Verlesung.[31] Ich würde daher die Verlesung zwar als wichtiges Indiz werten, dass tatsächlich eine Beurkundung vorliegt und nicht nur eine Beglaubigung. Aber ein geringerer Umfang der Verlesung kann m. E. für die Gleichwertigkeit durch anderweitige Hinweise auf die Verfahrensleitung durch den Notar ausgeglichen werden, etwa dass der Urkundenentwurf typischerweise vom Notar kommt und dass er den Urkundeninhalt nach dem Beurkundungsrecht mit den Beteiligten ausführlich besprechen und sie über den Inhalt belehren muss.[32]

Als weiteren Punkt neben Urkundsperson und Beurkundungsverfahren wird man wohl auch die Rechtsqualität und Rechtswirkungen der notariellen Urkunde in der betreffenden Rechtsordnung heranziehen, also ob sie eine öffentliche Urkunde mit voller Beweiskraft und (jedenfalls potentiell) vollstreckbar ist. Ein Staat, der den eigenen notariellen Urkunden im innerstaatlichen Rechtsverkehr diese Rechtsqualität verweigert, dessen Urkunden können im zwischenstaatlichen Rechtsverkehr kaum als gleichwertig angesehen werden.

---

[27] OLG Bamberg 21.11.2001 – 2 UF 200/01, FamRZ 2002, 1120 = NJW-RR 2002, 1153; Brambring NJW 1975, 1255 (1260); Knoche, FS Rhein. Notariat, 1998, 297 (314).

[28] Eine vollständige Verlesung notarieller Niederschriften wie in Deutschland verlangen etwa Bulgarien, Estland (§ 13 BeurkG), Lettland (Art. 88 Notargesetz), Österreich (§§ 52–53 Notarordnung) und Polen (Art. 92 Abs. 1 Nr. 7 Notargesetz).

[29] ZB Italien, Schweiz.

[30] Eine vollständige Verlesung notarieller Niederschriften wie in Deutschland verlangen etwa Bulgarien, Estland (§ 13 BeurkG), Lettland (Art. 88 Notargesetz), Österreich (§§ 52–53 Notarordnung) und Polen (Art. 92 Abs. 1 Nr. 7 Notargesetz).

[31] Belgien Art. 12 Notargesetz seit 1.1.2000; In den Niederlanden ist die Verlesung nur vorgeschrieben, wenn zwei Zeugen zugezogen werden müssen, wie zB bei einem Testament (Art. 43 Notargesetz).

[32] Staudinger, BGB/Hertel, 2023, BeurkG Rn. 872.

b) Kritik: Echte Gleichwertigkeit gibt es mangels Rechtskenntnis nicht

Achillesferse des Konzepts der Gleichwertigkeit ist die notarielle Rechtsbelehrung. Das Problem daran ist, dass der ausländische Notar, jedenfalls der lateinische Notar, diese Belehrungsfunktion und Vertragsgestaltung zwar bei Anwendung inländischen Rechts wahrnimmt, aber bei Auslandsbeurkundung meist gerade nicht. Wenn ich beurkunde und (möglicherweise) ausländisches Recht anwendbar ist, belehre ich über die (mögliche) Anwendbarkeit ausländischen Rechts, weise aber zugleich darauf hin, dass ich keine näheren Kenntnisse des ausländischen Rechts habe und dazu nicht belehren muss und nicht belehre (§ 17 Abs. 3 BeurkG). Ähnliches gilt, wenn ein Schweizer Notar in einem ausländischen Recht beurkundet.[33] Und selbst wenn ein ausländisches Beurkundungsrecht auch eine Belehrung zum ausländischen Recht verlangt, wird der Notar dies in aller Regel mangels hinreichender Rechtskenntnis nicht wirklich leisten können.

Es hilft den Beteiligten und dient der entstehenden Urkunde nur begrenzt, wenn die Urkundsperson eine honorige Person ist und Fachkenntnisse in ihrer eigenen Rechtsordnung hat, wenn sie aber vom anwendbaren Recht nichts versteht. Wenn mir etwa ab und an eine Urkunde zur Veräußerung eines österreichischen Grundstücks zur Unterschriftsbeglaubigung (sic!) vorgelegt wird, so schaue ich mir die Urkunde mit Interesse an und verstehe auch so ungefähr, was die einzelnen Klauseln bezwecken sollen – aber die Beteiligten näher belehren oder gar über alternative Gestaltungsmöglichkeiten beraten könnte ich nicht. Aber das muss ich ja auch nicht, sondern ich muss nur die Personalien der Beteiligten feststellen und bescheinigen. Viel mehr würde ich auch nicht machen, wenn ich das als Auslandsbeurkundung vorlesen und beurkunden müsste.

Noch ein Beispiel: Ich beurkunde immer wieder spanischsprachige Vollmachten. Denn Spanien und viele lateinamerikanische Länder erfordern für bestimmte Rechtsgeschäfte eine notariell beurkundete Vollmacht und lassen eine bloße Unterschriftsbeglaubigung nicht genügen. Dann bitte ich, mir den von dem Notarkollegen im Empfangsstaat erstellten Urkundsentwurf zuzusenden. Ich ergänze Urkundseingang und -schluss mit den nach deutschem Beurkundungsgesetz erforderlichen Angaben, also insbes. Beurkundungszeitpunkt und -ort, Bezeichnung des Notars und der Beteiligten (§ 9 BeurkG), den Hinweis zur Sprachkunde der Beteiligten (§§ 5, 16 BeurkG), die erforderlichen Abschriften und Ausfertigungen sowie den Schlussvermerk (§ 13 BeurkG). Natürlich bringt die Beurkundung den Beteiligten einen Mehrwert gegenüber einer bloßen Unterschriftsbeglaubigung, nicht nur durch meine mündliche Übersetzung, falls die Beteiligten nicht hinreichend Spanisch verstehen, sondern ich kann den Beteiligten auch etwas zur Vollmacht sagen und zu den konkret geregelten Punkten. Aber das stößt schnell an Grenzen. Haben die Beteiligten Rückfragen über den Urkundstext hinaus, muss ich passen.

Die Auslandsbeurkundung kann etliche Funktionen der Beurkundung erfüllen, etwa die Personenfeststellung und die Feststellung des Willens der Beteiligten, sie

---

[33] Vgl. die Nachweise zur Schweizer Literatur und zur Rechtslage in den einzelnen Kantonen bei Weber MittBayNot 2018, 215 (219f.).

schafft eine beweiskräftige Urkunde – aber die Belehrungsfunktion kann sie nur rudimentär erfüllen.

Gleichwertig kann also nur der ausländische Notar, das ausländische Beurkundungsverfahren und die ausländische notarielle Urkunde sein. Die Auslandsbeurkundung kann nie gleichwertig sein – oder allenfalls, falls der betreffende Notar zufällig fundierte Kenntnisse des anwendbaren ausländischen Rechts hat.[34] Es kann aber nicht auf den Einzelfall ankommen, weil man der Urkunde die spezielle Rechtskenntnis des ausländischen Notars nicht ansieht, sondern die Gleichwertigkeit muss für ein bestimmtes Land entweder generell oder gar nicht bestehen.

Der BGH[35] weist zwar richtig darauf hin, dass dann eine Auslandsbeurkundung nie gleichwertig wäre und damit eine ausschließliche Zuständigkeit deutscher Notare bestünde. Das Argument fehlender Belehrung zum deutschen Recht wird man daher nicht als Kriterium zur Prüfung der Gleichwertigkeit verwenden, sondern es ist ein grundsätzliches Argument gegen das Konzept der Gleichwertigkeit.

Zumindest schief ist das Argument des BGH, die Beteiligten verzichteten durch die Auslandsbeurkundung indirekt auf die Belehrung.[36] Denn die Belehrung ist nicht parteidispositiv – ebenso wenig wie die Form als solche. Gemeint ist, dass die Beteiligten mit der Auslandsbeurkundung bewusst auf den Schutz durch die inländische Beurkundung und die mit ihr verbundene Belehrung verzichten. Die Auslandsbeurkundung ist eine Beurkundung ohne Belehrung oder nur mit rudimentärer Belehrung und ohne rechtliche Kontrolle durch den Notar.

3. Formzweck als Zusatzkriterium

a) Erfüllt die Auslandsbeurkundung Formzweck und Formwirkung?

Wenn aber die Auslandsbeurkundung – trotz Gleichwertigkeit von Urkundsperson, Beurkundungsverfahren und Rechtsqualität der Urkunde – eine Beurkundung ohne rechtliche Kontrolle und ohne Rechtsbelehrung durch den Notar ist, so fragt sich, ob die Gleichwertigkeit allein für die Substitution einer inländischen Beurkundung genügt. Ich halte die Gleichwertigkeit der Auslandsbeurkundung für eine zwar notwendige, aber nicht hinreichende Voraussetzung für die Substitution. Eine Auslandsbeurkundung kann m. E. nur dann ein deutsches Beurkundungserfordernis erfüllen, wenn sie nicht nur gleichwertig ist, sondern auch der Formzweck bzw. die Formwirkungen[37] des betreffenden deutschen Beurkundungserfordernisses trotz fehlender Belehrung und Rechtskontrolle durch eine (gleichwertige) Aus-

---

[34] Und auch dann bräuchte er eine hinreichende Praxis im betreffenden Recht. Ich habe etwa in den USA studiert und das Anwaltsexamen *(bar exam)* in New York mit gutem Erfolg abgelegt – würde mir aber mangels Praxis nie zutrauen, selbst einen Vertrag nach dem Recht von New York zu entwerfen.

[35] BGH 16.2.1981 – II ZB 8/80, BGHZ 80, 76 = DNotZ 1981, 451 = NJW 1981, 1160.

[36] BGH 16.2.1981 – II ZB 8/80, BGHZ 80, 76 = DNotZ 1981, 451 = NJW 1981, 1160.

[37] Zur Terminologie vgl. Staudinger/Hertel, 2023, BGB § 125 Rn. 34. Der Begriff Formzweck ist mir etwas zu eng, weil er v. a. auf die historischen Gründe für die Einführung des jeweiligen Formerfordernisses abstellt. Terminologisch besser erscheint mir, von Formwirkungen zu sprechen und damit auch die Bedeutung des Formerfordernisses im Gesamtsystem auch später erlassener Rechtsnormen zu betrachten.

landsbeurkundung bei wertender Betrachtung erfüllt werden können. Auch das kann man nicht im Einzelfall entscheiden, sondern nur allgemein für das jeweilige Beurkundungserfordernis.

Ich würde v.a. danach unterscheiden, inwieweit die Rechtskontrolle durch den Notar bei der Beurkundung auch einer öffentlichen Kontrolle dient – etwa als Vorstufe für eine Eintragung in Grundbuch oder Handels- und andere Register, oder durch Kontroll- und Meldepflichten des Notars, etwa nach Geldwäschegesetz. Das sind Punkte, die gegen die Möglichkeit einer Substitution sprechen, weil der ausländische Notar diesen Pflichten nicht unterliegt und damit diese Schutzfunktion oder Schutzwirkung der Beurkundung nicht erreicht werden kann.

Umgekehrt wird man eine Substitution (Gleichwertigkeit abgesehen von der Rechtsbelehrung vorausgesetzt) eher bei Beurkundungserfordernissen bejahen, bei denen die Rechtsbelehrung primär dem Schutz der Beteiligten selbst dient – evtl. mit Ausnahmen, wo es v.a. um den Schutz einer der beiden Vertragsparteien geht, der sonst durch Wahl der Auslandsbeurkundung ausgehebelt werden könnte.

In die Abwägung würde ich auch einbeziehen, inwieweit – abstrakt gesehen – ein schutzwürdiges Interesse an der Zulassung einer Auslandsbeurkundung für die betreffende Beurkundung besteht. So muss etwa für Vollmachten immer eine Auslandsbeurkundung möglich sein, weil sonst ein im Ausland ansässiger Beteiligter möglicherweise generell von bestimmten Beurkundungen ausgeschlossen wäre (wobei im deutschen Recht für die Vollmacht nur selten eine Beurkundung erforderlich ist – und für die Nachgenehmigung nie).

b) *Auslandsbeurkundung erfüllt Beurkundungszweck bei Ehevertrag und Verfügung von Todes wegen*

Betrachten wir ein paar wichtige Beurkundungserfordernisse, zunächst Ehevertrag (§ 1410 BGB) sowie Testament und Erbvertrag (§§ 2232, 2276 BGB).

Für Verfügungen von Todes wegen genügt nach Art. 27 Abs. 1 lit. a EU-ErbVO auch die Einhaltung der Ortsform. Daher kann man im Ergebnis dahinstehen lassen, ob die Auslandsbeurkundung auch die deutsche Beurkundung substituieren würde. ME ist die Möglichkeit einer Substitution aber ohne weiteres zu bejahen. Dafür spricht der *favor testamenti* und das praktische Bedürfnis, dass der Erblasser an seinem Wohn- oder Aufenthaltsort eine Verfügung von Todes wegen errichten kann. Formzweck, warum das deutsche Recht entweder eigenhändige Errichtung oder notarielle Beurkundung verlangt, ist v.a. die Rechtssicherheit, dass die Verfügung tatsächlich vom Erblasser stammt und seinen Willen zuverlässig und unbeeinflusst wiedergeben.[38] Dies ist auch bei einer Auslandsbeurkundung gewährleistet.

Auch bei einem Ehevertrag stellte sich das Problem bisher nicht, da bisher Art. 11 Abs. 1 EGBGB für den Ehevertrag die Ortsform genügen ließ. Jetzt erfor-

[38] BGH 21.5.1951 – IV ZR 11/50, BGHZ 2, 172; BGH 4.4.1962 – V ZR 110/60, BGHZ 37, 79 = NJW 1962, 1149; BGH 9.4.1981 – IVa ZB 4/80, BGHZ 80, 242 (246) = DNotZ 1982, 321 = NJW 1981, 1737; BayObLG FamRZ 2001, 771; Münchener Kommentar zum BGB/Sticherling, 9. Aufl. 2022, BGB § 2231 Rn. 1; Staudinger, BGB/Baumann, 2022, BGB § 2231 Rn. 25f.

dern aber Art. 25 Abs. 2 und Abs. 3 EU-EheGüterVO (für ab 29.1.2019 abgeschlossene Neuehen, Art. 69 Abs. 3 EU-EheGüterVO) die Einhaltung des Aufenthaltsrechts (wenn zumindest einer der Ehegatten seinen gewöhnlichen Aufenthalt in einem EU-EheGüterVO-Staat hat) und zusätzlich die Einhaltung der Geschäftsform.[39] Ein Bedürfnis für eine Auslandsbeurkundung sehe ich v. a., wenn in Deutschland ansässige Eheleute ihr ausländisches Heimatrecht wählen wollen. Dann sollten sie den Ehevertrag besser in ihrem Heimatland beurkunden lassen (oder sich zumindest den Entwurf von einem Juristen ihres Heimatlandes erstellen lassen). Schutzzweck des Beurkundungserfordernisses nach § 1410 BGB ist v. a., die rechtliche Beratung der Ehegatten sicherzustellen, auch durch Übereilungsschutz, daneben auch die Beweis- und Klarstellungsfunktion.[40] Die Beratung ist zwar nicht sichergestellt, wenn die Eheleute in einem anderen Staat als dem des anwendbaren Rechts beurkunden lassen (etwa um Kosten zu sparen[41]). Aber da das Beurkundungserfordernis primär dem Schutz der beiden Eheleute selbst dient, können sie auf diesen Schutz verzichten. Von den Vereinbarungen in einem (vermögensrechtlichen) Ehevertrag oder einer Scheidungsfolgenvereinbarung sind nur die beiden den Vertrag schließenden Ehegatten selbst betroffen. Wenn ein Ehegatte nachher merkt, dass er mangels Belehrung etwas für ihn Ungünstiges unterschrieben hat, ohne es zu merken, so ist dies zunächst einmal nur sein Problem. Öffentliche Schutzgüter sind nur indirekt berührt, etwa wenn unklare Vereinbarungen streitanfällig sind und damit mehr Kapazitäten der Justiz binden – oder auch bei der Frage, inwieweit der staatliche Durchsetzungsapparat auch für möglicherweise unfaire Vereinbarungen genutzt werden kann. Aber der Schwerpunkt liegt ganz eindeutig auf dem Individualschutz. Daher ist eine Substitution durch eine Auslandsbeurkundung m. E. zulässig.

c) Auslandsbeurkundung erfüllt Beurkundungszwecke vieler gesellschaftsrechtlicher Normen nicht

Im Gesellschaftsrecht dienen Beurkundungserfordernisse dagegen häufig auch dem Schutz des Rechtsverkehrs, insbes. bei Verfassungsakten der Gesellschaft (Gründung, Satzungsänderung, Umwandlung). So wird bei der Gründung einer GmbH oder Aktiengesellschaft durch die notarielle Beurkundung der Satzungstext rechtssicher festgestellt und der Satzungsinhalt rechtlich geprüft (auch wenn das Registergericht dies z. T. nochmals zusätzlich prüft). Priester hatte dies als „Rechtspflegefunktion" bezeichnet.[42] Diese Kontrolle kann der ausländische Notar mangels Kenntnis des deutschen Gesellschaftsrechts nicht wahrnehmen. Daher ist hier m. E. keine Substitution durch eine Auslandsbeurkundung möglich.

---

39 → III. 2. d).

40 Einsele NJW 1998, 1206; Münchener Kommentar zum BGB/Münch, 9. Aufl. 2022, BGB § 1410 Rn. 1 f.; Staudinger, BGB/Löhnig, 2023, § 1410 BGB Rn. 2.

41 Opris NZFam 2020, 501.

42 Scholz, GmbHG/Priester, 9. Aufl. 2002, GmbHG § 53 Rn. 72; ähnlich jetzt Scholz, GmbHG/Tebben, 12. Aufl. 2020, GmbHG § 53 Rn. 75.

Bei der Satzungsänderung einer GmbH sehe ich keinen Wertungsunterschied zwischen der Beurkundung der Satzung bei Gründung und der Satzungsänderung; in beiden Fällen genügt m. E. eine Auslandsbeurkundung nicht.

Dasselbe gilt mE bei Umwandlungsvorgängen jedenfalls für den Verschmelzungsvertrag und den Spaltungs- bzw. Übernahmevertrag. Denn Formzweck des Beurkundungsbedürfnisses nach § 6 UmwG ist – wie bei der Gründung der Kapitalgesellschaften – v. a. Rechtssicherheit und Richtigkeitsgewähr der Umwandlung, also ein öffentliches Interesse. Auch dies kann der ausländische Notar mangels Rechtskenntnis nicht leisten.

Für die Beurkundung der Zustimmungserklärungen (§ 13 UmwG) gilt derselbe Formzweck. Eine korrekte Beurkundung des Versammlungsbeschlusses setzt aber noch keine Rechtskenntnis voraus. Die korrekte Beurkundung der Versammlung kann man auch von einem des anwendbaren Gesellschaftsrechts unkundigen ausländischen lateinischen Notar erwarten.[43] Daneben ist aber Formzweck auch die „Kontrolle des Notars, der die Verantwortung dafür übernimmt, dass die Versammlung der Anteilsinhaber ordnungsgemäß abgewickelt wird“[44]. Diese Kontrolle kann nur ein des anwendbaren Gesellschaftsrechts kundiger Notar übernehmen. Je nachdem wie hoch man die inhaltliche Richtigkeitskontrolle durch den Notar wertet, wird man eine Substitution durch Auslandsbeurkundung für möglich halten oder nicht.

An die dingliche Abtretung eines GmbH-Geschäftsanteils (§ 15 Abs. 3 GmbHG) knüpft das Gesetz jetzt die Verpflichtung des Notars zur Einreichung einer neuen Gesellschafterliste an (§ 40 Abs. 2 GmbHG). Diese Liste begründet einen (wenngleich begrenzten) Gutglaubensschutz (§ 16 Abs. 3 GmbHG). Der ausländische Notar ist zur Einreichung einer Gesellschafterliste jedenfalls nicht verpflichtet. Dies spricht m. E. gegen eine Substituierbarkeit. Allerdings ist das Argument schwächer als bei der Beurkundung von Verfassungsakten der Gesellschaft. Denn nach dem Gesetz ist bei Veränderungen bei den Gesellschaftern zunächst der Geschäftsführer zur Einreichung einer neuen Gesellschafterliste verpflichtet. Der BGH lässt daher bekanntlich eine gleichwertige ausländische Beurkundung der GmbH-Geschäftsanteilsabtretung genügen; der ausländische Notar könne dann auch eine neue Gesellschafterliste einreichen.[45]

Für die schuldrechtliche Verpflichtung zur Abtretung von GmbH-Geschäftsanteilen genügt die Einhaltung der Ortsform nach Art. 11 Abs. 1 Rom I-VO. (Zwar gilt die Rom I-VO nach ihrem Art. 1 Abs. 2 lit. f) nicht für gesellschaftsrechtliche Fragen und daher auch nicht für die dingliche Geschäftsanteilsabtretung. Die schuldrechtliche Verpflichtung zur Übertragung ist aber nicht aus dem Anwendungsbereich ausgenommen und unterfällt der Rom I-VO.[46])

---

[43] Vgl. auch die Argumentation BGH 21.10.2014 – II ZR 330/13, BGHZ 203, 68 = DNotZ 2015, 207 = NJW 2015, 336 (Beurkundung der Hauptversammlung einer deutschen Aktiengesellschaft im Ausland).

[44] BT-Drs. 12/6699, 86.

[45] BGH 17.12.2013 – II ZB 6/13, BGHZ 199, 270 = DNotZ 2014, 457 = NJW 2014, 2026.

[46] Mankowski NZG 2010, 201 (206); Hausmann/Odersky, Internationales Privatrecht in der Notar- und Gestaltungspraxis/Schäuble, 4. Aufl. 2021, § 16 Rn. 152.

d) Auflassung

Wir hatten schon besprochen, dass eine Auflassung nach § 925 BGB nur vor einem deutschen Notar erklärt werden kann.[47] Der BGH begründet dies v. a. mit der Entstehungsgeschichte der Vorschrift, die die Erklärung der Auflassung als Verfahrenshandlung gegenüber einer Amtsperson behandelt. Als zweites Argument führt der BGH aber auch die Kontrolle und Richtigkeitsgewähr bei der Beurkundung durch deutsche Notare an. Diese Kontrolle dient dem öffentlichen Interesse an einem rechtssicheren Grundbuch. Außerdem sieht das Gesetz vor, dass die Eigentumsumschreibung beim Grundbuchamt nur durch einen Notar beantragt werden kann (§ 13 Abs. 1 S. 3 GBO). Damit will es sicherstellen, dass die Notare das Barzahlungsverbot (§ 16a GwG[48]) prüfen können. Auch dies spricht dagegen, bei der Auflassung eine Auslandsbeurkundung zuzulassen.

V. Fazit

Ich habe zu zeigen versucht, dass das Konzept der Rechtsprechung, wonach eine Auslandsbeurkundung bei Gleichwertigkeit (also bei Beurkundung durch lateinische Notare) immer eine deutsche Beurkundung substituieren kann, daran krankt, dass zwar der ausländische lateinische Notar, sein Beurkundungsverfahren und seine Urkunde als solche (theoretisch) gleichwertig sind, dass die Auslandsbeurkundung aber mangels Rechtskontrolle und Rechtsbelehrung nie wirklich gleichwertig ist.

ME muss man daher zunächst fragen, ob die Formzwecke bzw. Formwirkungen des jeweiligen Beurkundungserfordernisses sich überhaupt durch eine Auslandsbeurkundung erreichen lassen. ME ist dies für Beurkundungserfordernisse über die Verfassung einer Gesellschaft (Gründung, Satzungsänderung, Umwandlung) und die dingliche GmbH-Geschäftsanteilsabtretung zu verneinen, bei Beurkundung von Eheverträgen und Verfügungen von Todes wegen hingegen zu bejahen.

---

[47] → III. 2. b) aa).

[48] IdF durch das Gesetz vom 19.12.2022 (BGBl. 2022 I 2606) mWv 28.12.2022.

ABBO JUNKER

Gesetzlicher und vertraglicher Unterhalt in grenzüberschreitenden Sachverhalten

I. Einleitung

Thomas Rauscher ist einer der profiliertesten Vertreter des deutschen Internationalen Privat- und Prozessrechts. Sein Interessengebiet umfasst das gesamte Spektrum der kollisions- und verfahrensrechtlichen Gegenstände, die in privatrechtlichen Sachverhalten mit Auslandsberührung eine Rolle spielen. Einer der Schwerpunkte des wissenschaftlichen Werks von *Thomas Rauscher* liegt, wie schon die Gliederung seines Lehrbuchs zeigt,[1] im Internationalen Personen-, Familien- und Erbrecht. Es besteht daher die begründete Hoffnung, den Jubilar mit einer unterhaltsrechtlichen Abhandlung erfreuen zu können.

In dem Lehrbuch heißt es: „Vertragliche Unterhaltsansprüche (Alimentationsverträge) sowie Unterhaltsansprüche aufgrund Delikt (Tötung Unterhaltsverpflichteter) erfasst das [Unterhaltsstatut] nicht; sie unterliegen dem Vertrags- bzw. Deliktsstatut."[2] Dieser Satz ist unbestreitbar richtig, gilt aber nicht – wie auch *Thomas Rauscher* unausgesprochen voraussetzt – für vertragliche Abreden, die einen gesetzlichen Unterhaltsanspruch beschränken, ausgestalten oder erweitern; sie unterliegen dem Unterhaltsstatut.[3] Der folgende Beitrag handelt von der Abgrenzung solcher Abreden und ihren verfahrens- und kollisionsrechtlichen Besonderheiten in grenzüberschreitenden Sachverhalten.

II. Gesetzlicher und vertraglicher Unterhalt

Im Zentrum dieses Beitrags steht die vertragliche Vereinbarung, die sich auf einen gesetzlichen Unterhaltsanspruch bezieht. In grenzüberschreitenden Sachverhalten ist die Rechtsquelle für die internationale Zuständigkeit der Gerichte die Europäische Unterhaltsverordnung,[4] hier abgekürzt als EG-UntVO. Die kollisionsrechtliche Frage, welcher Rechtsordnung eine Unterhaltsvereinbarung mit Aus-

---

[1] Rauscher, Internationales Privatrecht, 5. Aufl. 2017, Rn. 604–1036.

[2] Rauscher, Internationales Privatrecht, 5. Aufl. 2017, Rn. 925.

[3] Bonomi, Explanatory Report on the Hague Protocol of 23 November 2007 on the Law Applicable to Maintenance Obligations, 2009, Rn. 32.

[4] Verordnung (EG) Nr. 4/2009 des Rates vom 18.12.2008 über die Zuständigkeit, das anwendbare Recht, die Anerkennung und Vollstreckung von Entscheidungen und die Zusammenarbeit in Unterhaltssachen (ABl. 2009 L 7, 1).

landsbezug unterliegt, beantworten kraft Verweisung durch Art. 15 EG-UntVO die Kollisionsnormen des Haager Unterhaltsprotokolls,[5] hier abgekürzt als HUntStProt 2007.

1. *Räumlicher Anwendungsbereich der relevanten Vorschriften*

Die *Unterhaltsverordnung* gilt in sämtlichen Mitgliedstaaten der EU, da sich am Zuständigkeitskapitel auch die Republik Irland und das Königreich Dänemark beteiligt haben. Der Anwendungsbereich ist unabhängig davon eröffnet, ob der Antragsgegner seinen gewöhnlichen Aufenthalt in einem Mitgliedstaat oder einem Drittstaat hat (ErwGr. 15 EG-UntVO). Eine Restzuständigkeit nach dem autonomen Recht der Mitgliedstaaten existiert in Unterhaltssachen nicht mehr („Totalvereinheitlichung").

Das *Unterhaltsprotokoll* gilt in den Mitgliedstaaten der Europäischen Union außer Dänemark sowie in zahlreichen Drittstaaten. Für den deutschen Rechtsanwender spielt der räumliche Geltungsbereich des Unterhaltsprotokolls wegen des Prinzips der universellen Verweisung keine Rolle: Das Protokoll ist als *loi uniforme* unabhängig davon anzuwenden, ob die Unterhaltsvereinbarung Bezüge zu einem Vertragsstaat des Unterhaltsprotokolls oder einem Nichtvertragsstaat aufweist (Art. 2 HUntStProt 2007).

Ein *autonomes deutsches Kollisionsrecht* gibt es für den Anknüpfungsgegenstand „Unterhaltspflichten" nicht mehr, jedoch haben bestehende völkerrechtliche Verträge den Vorrang vor dem Unterhaltsprotokoll (Art. 19 HUntStProt 2007). Dieser Vorrang betrifft das *Deutsch-iranische Niederlassungsabkommen,* das Unterhaltsansprüche zwischen iranischen Staatsangehörigen dem iranischen Recht unterstellt (Art. 8 Abs. 3 S. 1 des Abkommens).

Ob die Vereinbarung über den Unterhalt Bezüge zu einem Vertragsstaat des Unterhaltsprotokolls aufweist oder zu einem Nichtvertragsstaat, kann relevant werden, wenn die Parteien eine Rechtswahl getroffen haben (→ IV.): Die Anerkennung einer Rechtswahl ist in einem Nichtvertragsstaat des HUntStProt 2007 keineswegs gesichert.[6] Das betrifft in der Praxis nicht Art. 7 UntStProt 2007, denn gegen die Wahl seiner *lex fori* wird der Gerichtsstaat kaum etwas einzuwenden haben, wohl aber die Rechtswahl nach Art. 8 HUntStProt 2007.

2. *Sachlicher Anwendungsbereich der relevanten Vorschriften*

Die *Unterhaltsverordnung* findet Anwendung auf Unterhaltspflichten, die auf einem Familien-, Verwandtschafts- oder eherechtlichen Verhältnis oder auf Schwägerschaft beruhen (Art. 1 Abs. 1 EG-UntVO). Das *Unterhaltsprotokoll* nennt Unterhaltspflichten, die sich aus Beziehungen der Familie, Verwandtschaft, Ehe oder Schwägerschaft ergeben (Art. 1 Abs. 1 HUntStProt 2007). Der sachliche Anwendungsbereich der beiden Rechtsakte hat nicht nur einen ähnlichen Wortlaut, sondern ist auch inhaltlich identisch: Das Protokoll bildet einen Bestandteil des Uni-

---

[5] Protokoll über das auf Unterhaltspflichten anzuwendende Recht (ABl. 2009 L 331, 19).

[6] von Bar/Mankowski, Internationales Privatrecht II, 2. Aufl. 2019, § 4 Rn. 844.

onsrechts[7] und kann – ebenso wie die Verordnung – Gegenstand von Vorabentscheidungen des EuGH sein (Art. 267 AEUV). Sie sind allerdings nur für die EU-Mitgliedstaaten verbindlich, nicht aber für die anderen Vertragsstaaten des Haager Protokolls.[8] Die Auslegung zielt auf einen Gleichklang zwischen der Unterhaltsverordnung und dem Unterhaltsprotokoll.[9]

a) Begriff der Unterhaltspflicht

Der Schlüssel zum sachlichen Anwendungsbereich der Unterhaltsverordnung und des Unterhaltsprotokolls ist das Rechtsverhältnis „Unterhaltspflicht". Dieses Rechtsverhältnis verschafft einer Person den Anspruch, die Mittel zur Bestreitung ihres Lebensbedarfs ganz oder teilweise von einer anderen Person zu verlangen.[10] In verordnungs- bzw. staatsvertragsautonomer Auslegung sind zwei Kriterien entscheidend für die Qualifikation einer Verbindlichkeit als Unterhaltspflicht: Zum einen muss es um die Pflicht zur Befriedigung der natürlichen Bedürfnisse eines Menschen gehen. Zum anderen muss diese Pflicht – wie sich aus Art. 14 HUntSt-Prot 2007 schließen lässt – auf die Bedürftigkeit des Berechtigten und die Leistungsfähigkeit des Verpflichteten zugeschnitten sein.[11]

b) Kategoriale Begrenzung

Die Unterhaltsverordnung und das Unterhaltsprotokoll besagen in unterschiedlicher Formulierung, aber inhaltlich übereinstimmend, dass die Unterhaltspflicht auf einem familien-, verwandtschafts- oder eherechtlichen Verhältnis oder auf Schwägerschaft beruhen muss (Art. 1 Abs. 1 EG-UntVO, Art. 1 Abs. 1 HUntStProt 2007). Der Anwendungsbereich der beiden Rechtsakte wird daher in dreifacher Hinsicht weiter gezogen als der Kreis der gesetzlichen Unterhaltspflichten des deutschen materiellen Rechts. Eingeschlossen sind erstens Unterhaltspflichten gegenüber Verwandten in der Seitenlinie (anders § 1601 BGB), zweitens Unterhaltspflichten, die sich aus der Schwägerschaft ergeben (anders § 1590 BGB), und drittens – als familienrechtliche Verhältnisse – Unterhaltspflichten gegenüber Stief- oder Pflegekindern sowie solche aus nichtehelichen Lebensgemeinschaften.

Auf den ersten Blick überrascht die Einbeziehung von *nichtehelichen Lebensgemeinschaften* in den Anwendungsbereich der relevanten Vorschriften, denn die herrschende Meinung zum Haager Unterhaltsübereinkommen von 1973 qualifizierte Unterhaltsansprüche aufgrund nichtehelicher Lebensgemeinschaft nicht als famili-

---

[7] NomosKommentar BGB/Gruber, 3. Aufl. 2019, HUP Vor Art. 1 Rn. 14.

[8] EuGH 12.5.2022 – C-644/20, NJW-RR 2022, 937 = FamRZ 2022, 1029; EuGH 1.8.2022 – C-501/20, BeckRS 2022, 18673 = FamRZ 2022, 1466.

[9] Münchener Kommentar zum BGB/Staudinger, 8. Aufl. 2020, HUP Art. 5 Rn. 8; Hilbig GPR 2011, 310 (313).

[10] Staudinger, BGB/Klinkhammer, 2022, BGB Vorb. zu §§ 1601 ff. Rn. 1; Schwab, Familienrecht, 30. Aufl. 2022, Rn. 1050.

[11] Staudinger, BGB/Mankowski, 2021, HUP Art. 1 Rn. 2; NomosKommentar BGB/Gruber, 3. Aufl. 2019, HUP Vor Art. 1 Rn. 13.

enrechtlich.[12] Der Widerspruch löst sich aber, wie sogleich zu zeigen ist (→ II. 2. c), über das Kriterium der „Gesetzlichkeit" der Unterhaltspflicht bzw. des korrespondierenden Unterhaltsanspruchs.

Nach dem materiellen deutschen Recht können Unterhaltsansprüche von Partnerinnen oder Partnern nichtehelicher Lebensgemeinschaften nur durch eine Unterhaltsvereinbarung begründet werden,[13] so dass die Anwendung des Unterhaltsübereinkommens und des Unterhaltsprotokolls ausscheidet. Besteht jedoch in einem Staat eine gesetzliche Unterhaltspflicht, so scheitert die Anwendung der europäischen Rechtsakte nach heutigem Verständnis nicht an der erforderlichen „Familienrechtlichkeit" der Beziehung.[14]

c) Gesetzliche Unterhaltspflicht

Den Materialien zum Haager Unterhaltsprotokoll lässt sich entnehmen, dass Unterhaltsvereinbarungen in den Anwendungsbereich des Protokolls (und damit auch in denjenigen der Unterhaltsverordnung) fallen, wenn sie sich in den Kategorien Familie, Verwandtschaft, Ehe und Schwägerschaft auf eine gesetzliche Unterhaltspflicht beziehen.[15] Dem entspricht auch die Systematik des Unterhaltsprotokolls: Es wäre merkwürdig, wenn das Protokoll zwar den Unterhaltsverzicht einer besonderen Anknüpfung unterstellen (Art. 8 Abs. 4 HUntStProt 2007), aber Vereinbarungen, die den gesetzlichen Unterhalt anderweitig modifizieren, nicht erfassen würde.[16] Auf der anderen Seite unterliegen Unterhaltsvereinbarungen, die keinen Bezug zu einer gesetzlichen Unterhaltspflicht haben, nach ganz herrschender Ansicht nicht den Unterhaltsgerichtsständen und dem Unterhaltsstatut.[17]

Die Gegenansicht will das Unterhaltsprotokoll auf alle Unterhaltsansprüche aus Verträgen erstrecken, die ihren Grund in einer familienrechtlichen Bindung haben, ohne Rücksicht darauf, ob der Unterhaltsanspruch rein rechtsgeschäftlich begründet wird oder auf gesetzlicher Grundlage beruht.[18] Wenn der Onkel seinem Neffen aufgrund eines Vertrages Unterhalt für ein Studium gewährt, unterläge dieser Vertrag nicht den allgemeinen Vertragskollisionsnormen, sondern den unterhaltsrechtlichen Regeln einschließlich der Sachnorm des Art. 14 HUntStProt 2007. Als Begründung wird „in erster Linie die Zulassung der Parteiautonomie" durch das Unterhaltsprotokoll (→ IV. 3.) genannt.[19] Die Parteiautonomie wird jedoch nicht

---

[12] Nachweise bei Staudinger, BGB/Mankowski, 2021, HUP Art. 1 Rn. 84; Hilbig GPR 2011, 310 (316).

[13] Staudinger, BGB/Klinkhammer, 2022, BGB Vorb. zu §§ 1601 ff. Rn. 137, § 1602 Rn. 26–28.

[14] Staudinger, BGB/Mankowski, 2021, HUP Art. 1 Rn. 64 ff.; Hilbig GPR 2011, 310 (316).

[15] Bonomi, Explanatory Report on the Hague Protocol of 23 November 2007 on the Law Applicable to Maintenance Obligations, 2009, Rn. 32.

[16] Staudinger, BGB/Mankowski, 2021, HUP Art. 1 Rn. 92.

[17] Prütting/Wegen/Weinreich, BGB/Martiny, 16. Aufl. 2021, HUP Art. 1 Rn. 3; Erman, BGB/Stürner, 16. Aufl. 2020, HUP Art. 1 Rn. 2; NomosKommentar BGB/Gruber, 3. Aufl. 2019, HUP Art. 1 Rn. 12; Münchener Kommentar zum BGB/Staudinger, 8. Aufl. 2020, HUP Art. 1 Rn. 33.

[18] Rauscher, EuZPR/EuIPR/Andrae, 4. Aufl. 2016, HUntStProt 2007 Art. 1 Rn. 8.

[19] Rauscher, EuZPR/EuIPR/Andrae, 4. Aufl. 2016, HUntStProt 2007 Art. 1 Rn. 9.

nur zugelassen, sondern ist viel größer, wenn die Kollisionsnormen der Rom I-Verordnung[20] (Rom I-VO) zur Anwendung kommen (Art. 3 Rom I-VO). Die Gegenansicht verdient daher schon mangels tragfähiger Begründung keine Zustimmung.

Die Abgrenzung zwischen gesetzlich und rechtsgeschäftlich begründeten Unterhaltspflichten fällt allerdings nicht so leicht, wie es auf den ersten Blick scheint, denn es existiert ein Graubereich. So bejaht die deutsche Rechtsprechung zum Beispiel einen stillschweigend abgeschlossenen Unterhaltsvertrag zugunsten des Kindes, wenn ein mit der Mutter nicht verheirateter zeugungsunfähiger Mann in eine heterologe Insemination einwilligt.[21] Bei einer Mitmutterschaft gilt das Gleiche in Bezug auf die Ehefrau oder Partnerin der Mutter eines Kindes.[22] Solche richterrechtlich entwickelten Regeln lassen sich den gesetzlichen Unterhaltspflichten gleichstellen.

Man kann somit den Begriff der „(gesetzlichen) Unterhaltspflicht" in der Weise autonom europäisch auslegen, dass auch in einem Mitgliedstaat richterrechtlich entwickelte Unterhaltspflichten unter diesen Systembegriff fallen. Ob die Unterhaltspflicht, um die es in der konkreten Vereinbarung geht, gesetzlich oder rein rechtsgeschäftlich begründet wird, kann sich jedoch nur aus dem staatlichen Recht ergeben. Damit stellt sich die Frage, welche Rechtsordnung die vertragsgegenständliche Unterhaltspflicht – zum Beispiel eine solche gegen den nichtehelichen Lebenspartner – gesetzlich vorsehen muss: das Recht des angerufenen Gerichts oder das hypothetisch zur Anwendung berufene Unterhaltsstatut? Ob Unterhaltspflichten eine gesetzliche Grundlage haben, ist entweder der *lex fori* oder der hypothetischen *lex causae* zu entnehmen.[23]

Der Verordnungsgeber ist bei der Auswahl keine große Hilfe: So soll zum Beispiel die Bezugnahme des Art. 1 Abs. 2 lit. b Rom I-VO auf „Verhältnisse, die einem Familienverhältnis vergleichbare Wirkungen entfalten," gemäß dem ErwGr. 8 S. 2 Rom I-VO nach der *lex fori* ausgelegt werden. Die Vorschrift selbst verweist jedoch auf das „auf diese Verhältnisse anzuwendende Recht", also auf die hypothetische *lex causae* des fraglichen Verhältnisses.[24] Bis zu einer abschließenden Entscheidung auf europäischer Ebene lassen sich somit beide Wege beschreiten: die Bestimmung der „Gesetzlichkeit" *lege causae,* das heißt nach dem hypothetischen Statut der Unterhaltspflicht, oder die Bestimmung *lege fori,* das heißt nach dem Recht des angerufenen Gerichts.[25] Im letztgenannten Fall kann die klagende Partei, wenn Ge-

[20] Verordnung (EG) Nr. 593/2008 des Rates vom 17.6.2008 über das auf vertragliche Schuldverhältnisse anzuwendende Recht (ABl. 2008 L 177, 6).

[21] BGH 23.9.2015 – XII ZR 99/14, BGHZ 207, 135 = NJW 2015, 3434 = FamRZ 2015, 2134 Rn. 9ff. mAnm Wellenhofer.

[22] OLG Brandenburg 26.10.2020 – 9 UF 178/20, NJW 2021, 1889 = FamRZ 2021, 1196 Rn. 20ff.; s. auch Reinken NZFam 2021, 424.

[23] Allgemein Münchener Kommentar zum BGB/von Hein, 8. Aufl. 2020, Einl. IPR Rn. 143; Junker, Internationales Privatrecht, 5. Aufl. 2022, § 7 Rn. 17ff.

[24] Vorschläge zur Auflösung dieses Widerspruchs bei Münchener Kommentar zum BGB/von Hein, 8. Aufl. 2020, EGBGB Art. 4 Rn. 125.

[25] Junker, Internationales Privatrecht, 5. Aufl. 2022, § 7 Rn. 45; Mansel FS Canaris, 2017, 739 (751).

richtsstände konkurrieren, durch Auswahl des Forumstaats unter Umständen Einfluss darauf nehmen, ob die dem Unterhaltsberechtigten freundlich gesonnenen Kollisionsnormen des Unterhaltsprotokolls zur Anwendung kommen oder die Vertragskollisionsnormen der Rom I-VO.

3. *Behandlung rechtsgeschäftlich begründeter Unterhaltspflichten*

Eine Unterhaltsvereinbarung, die das nicht gesetzlich entstandene Rechtsverhältnis „Unterhaltspflicht" erst begründet, unterliegt weder der Unterhaltsverordnung noch dem Unterhaltsprotokoll (→ II. 2.). Praktische Anwendungsfälle beschäftigen die deutsche Judikatur selten. Der Grund mag sein, dass ein Anlass zum Abschluss einer Unterhaltsvereinbarung in der Regel nur in Sachverhalten besteht, in denen auch der Gesetzgeber ein Schutzbedürfnis erkennt. Im deutschen materiellen Recht streitet eine Vermutung gegen eine vom Gesetz losgelöste Unterhaltsregelung mit eigenem Schuldgrund: Ein Wille der Parteien, den Unterhaltsanspruch völlig auf eine vertragliche Grundlage zu stellen und ihn damit des Wesens eines gesetzlichen Unterhaltsanspruchs zu entkleiden, könne – so der BGH – nur bei Vorliegen besonderer Anhaltspunkte angenommen werden.[26]

Die *internationale Zuständigkeit* der Gerichte für die Entscheidung über rein rechtsgeschäftlich begründete Unterhaltsansprüche folgt aus der Europäischen Gerichtsstands- und Vollstreckungsverordnung[27] (Brüssel Ia-VO). In Betracht kommen insbesondere der allgemeine Gerichtsstand im Wohnsitzstaat des Beklagten (Art. 4 Brüssel Ia-VO) und der besondere Gerichtsstand des Erfüllungsorts (Art. 7 Nr. 1 lit. a, c Brüssel Ia-VO).[28] Der Verbrauchergerichtsstand des Art. 18 Abs. 1 Brüssel Ia-VO wird in der Regel daran scheitern, dass keine der Parteien den Unterhaltsvertrag zu einem Zweck geschlossen hat, der ihrer beruflichen oder gewerblichen Tätigkeit zugerechnet werden kann (Art. 17 Abs. 1 Brüssel Ia-VO).[29]

Das *anwendbare Recht* bestimmt bei rechtsgeschäftlich begründeten Unterhaltsansprüchen grundsätzlich die Rom I-Verordnung. Das führt zu der objektiven Anknüpfung an das Recht des Staates, in dem der Unterhaltsgläubiger seinen gewöhnlichen Aufenthalt hat (Art. 4 Abs. 2 Rom I-VO), denn ebenso wie der Schenker (§ 518 BGB)[30] oder derjenige, der eine Leibrente verspricht (§ 561 BGB), erbringt auch der Unterhaltsverpflichtete die charakteristische Leistung. Die Ausweichklausel kann auf einen anderen Staat verweisen (Art. 4 Abs. 3 Rom I-VO). Bei einer Rechtswahl sind die Parteien nach Art. 3 Rom I-VO wesentlich freier als nach dem Unterhaltsprotokoll.

---

[26] BGH 26.9.1990 – XII ZR 87/89, NJW-RR 1991, 388 = FamRZ 1991, 673 (674); BGH 21.9.2011 – XII ZR 173/09, NJW 2012, 1356 = FamRZ 2012, 699 Rn. 19 mAnm Bergschneider.

[27] Verordnung (EU) Nr. 1215/2012 des Europäischen Parlaments und des Rates vom 12.12.2012 über die gerichtliche Zuständigkeit und die Anerkennung und Vollstreckung von Entscheidungen in Zivil- und Handelssachen, ABl. 2012 L 351, 1.

[28] Siehe zur Bestimmung des Erfüllungsorts nach dieser Vorschrift Junker, Internationales Zivilprozessrecht, 6. Aufl. 2023, § 6 Rn. 34ff.

[29] EuGH 5.12.2013 – C-508/12, NJW 2014, 841 Rn. 33 (Vapenik); krit. Stadler IPRax 2015, 202 (207); zust. Mankowski EWiR 2014, 371 (372).

[30] Münchener Kommentar zum BGB/Martiny, 8. Aufl. 2021, Rom I-VO Art. 4 Rn. 214.

III. Internationale Zuständigkeit der Gerichte

Im Folgenden geht es nur noch um Abreden, die Unterhaltspflichten ausgestalten, welche kraft Gesetzes entstanden sind oder entstehen können. Solche Abreden werden als Unterhaltsvereinbarung – und nicht als Unterhaltsvertrag – bezeichnet, weil sie in der Regel nicht isoliert erfolgen, sondern in ein anderes Rechtsgeschäft wie einen Ehevertrag oder einen Scheidungsfolgenvergleich eingebettet sind. Die internationale Zuständigkeit für solche Vereinbarungen regelt die Unterhaltsverordnung.

1. Vereinbarungen über gesetzliche Unterhaltspflichten

Die vertragliche Ausgestaltung eines gesetzlichen Unterhaltsanspruchs ist der in der gerichtlichen Praxis weitaus häufigste Typus einer Unterhaltsvereinbarung. In der deutschen Rechtsprechung stehen zwei Konstellationen im Vordergrund: Vereinbarungen über die Begrenzung des *Trennungsunterhalts,* in der Regel integriert in einen Ehevertrag,[31] und Vereinbarungen über den Ausschluss oder die Begrenzung des *nachehelichen Unterhalts,* häufig integriert in einen Scheidungsfolgenvergleich.[32] Ein weiterer Anwendungsfall ist eine *Freistellungsvereinbarung,* durch die zum Beispiel ein Ehegatte den anderen für den Fall der Scheidung von der Unterhaltspflicht gegenüber gemeinsamen Kindern befreit.[33]

2. Verordnungszuständigkeiten in Unterhaltssachen

Hat die Unterhaltsvereinbarung eine gesetzliche Unterhaltspflicht zum Gegenstand, so wird der Unterhaltsgläubiger, ähnlich wie ein Verbraucher oder ein Arbeitnehmer (Art. 17ff., 20ff. Brüssel Ia-VO), zuständigkeitsrechtlich als die schwächere Partei angesehen, der ein Klägergerichtsstand *(forum actoris)* zur Verfügung steht (Art. 3 lit. b EG-UntVO). Im Einzelnen sind nach Art. 3 EG-UntVO für Entscheidungen über Unterhaltsvereinbarungen in den Mitgliedstaaten der Europäischen Union alternativ zuständig

a) das Gericht des Ortes, an dem der *Beklagte* seinen gewöhnlichen Aufenthalt hat,
b) das Gericht des Ortes, an dem der *Unterhaltsberechtigte* seinen gewöhnlichen Aufenthalt hat,
c) das Gericht, das seinem Recht über eine Personenstandssache – vor allem eine *Ehescheidung* – zu befinden und eine Verbundzuständigkeit für den Unterhalt hat, und

---

[31] BGH 29.1.2014 – XII ZB 303/13, NJW 2014, 1101 = FamRZ 2014, 727; BGH 30.9.2015 – XII ZB 1/15, NJW 2015, 3715 = FamRZ 2015, 2131 mAnm Bergschneider/Wolf.

[32] BGH 11.2.2015 – XII ZB 66/14, NJW 2015, 1242 = FamRZ 2015, 734 mAnm Bergschneider; BGH 15.3.2017 – XII ZB 109/16, NZFam 2017, 408 = FamRZ 2017, 884 = JuS 2017, 1209 mAnm Wellenhofer.

[33] Münchener Kommentar zum BGB/Langeheine, 8. Aufl. 2020, BGB § 1614 Rn. 13; Staudinger, BGB/Klinkhammer, 2022, BGB § 1614 Rn. 135.

d) das Gericht, das nach seinem Recht für ein Verfahren über die *elterliche Verantwortung* für Kinder zuständig ist und eine Verbundzuständigkeit für den Unterhalt besitzt.[34]

Diese Zuständigkeiten betreffen nicht nur Klagen des Unterhaltsberechtigten, sondern auch solche des Unterhaltsverpflichteten, wie zum Beispiel eine Abänderungsklage (Art. 8 Abs. 1 EG-UntVO) oder eine Klage auf Feststellung, dass keine Unterhaltspflicht besteht.[35] Bei Vereinbarungen über den Trennungs- oder Scheidungsunterhalt eröffnet die akzessorische Zuständigkeit des Scheidungsgerichts (Art. 3 lit. c EG-UntVO) dem Unterhaltsverpflichteten die Möglichkeit, auf die internationale Zuständigkeit Einfluss zu nehmen.[36]

Wenn zum Beispiel in dem sogenannten Zahnarztfall des BGH der Ehemann Zweifel hegt, ob der im Ehevertrag vorgesehene Unterhaltsverzicht der Ehefrau vor deutschen Gerichten Bestand hat,[37] kann er davon profitieren, dass beide Ehegatten Angehörige eines anderen Mitgliedstaats sind, indem er dort nach der Brüssel IIb-Verordnung[38] (Brüssel IIb-VO) den Scheidungsantrag anhängig macht (Art. 3 lit. b Brüssel IIb-VO) und, wenn der Trennungsunterhalt Streitgegenstand ist, die internationale Verbundzuständigkeit des ausländischen Gerichts für den Trennungsunterhalt begründen (Art. 3 lit. c EG-UntVO).

3. *Vereinbarungen über die Gerichtszuständigkeit*

Derartige Überraschungen lassen sich durch eine Wahl des Gerichtsstands für die Unterhaltsvereinbarung vermeiden, denn es besteht – wenn die Parteien nichts Gegenteiliges vereinbaren – die Vermutung für eine ausschließliche Zuständigkeit des prorogierten Gerichts (Art. 4 Abs. 1 UAbs. 3 EG-UntVO). Die Prorogation ist allerdings zum Schutz des Unterhaltsberechtigten (ErwGr. 19 EG-UntVO) nach Art. 4 Abs. 1 UAbs. 1 EG-UntVO beschränkt auf

a) ein Gericht oder die Gerichte eines Mitgliedstaats, in dem (mindestens) eine Partei der Unterhaltsvereinbarung ihren *gewöhnlichen Aufenthalt* hat,
b) ein Gericht oder die Gerichte eines Mitgliedstaats, dessen *Staatsangehörigkeit* (mindestens) eine der Parteien der Unterhaltsvereinbarung besitzt, oder
c) bei Unterhaltspflichten zwischen Ehegatten das für die Ehesache zuständige Gericht sowie das oder die Gerichte des letzten gemeinsamen gewöhnlichen Aufenthalts.[39]

Der für die Prüfung, ob eine dieser Voraussetzungen erfüllt ist, maßgebende Zeitpunkt bezieht sich alternativ auf das Datum des Abschlusses der Gerichtsstands-

---

[34] Erläuterungen bei Junker, Internationales Zivilprozessrecht, 6. Aufl. 2023, § 17 Rn. 21, 25.
[35] Rauscher, EuZPR/EuIPR/Andrae, 4. Aufl. 2015, EG-UntVO Art. 3 Rn. 1.
[36] Allgemein Rauscher, EuZPR/EuIPR/Andrae, 4. Aufl. 2015, EG-UntVO Art. 3 Rn. 46 ff.
[37] BGH 30.9.2015 – XII ZB 1/15, NJW 2015, 3715 = FamRZ 2015, 2131 mAnm Bergschneider/Wolf.
[38] Verordnung (EU) 2009/1111 des Rates vom 25.6.2019 über die Zuständigkeit, die Anerkennung und Vollstreckung von Entscheidungen in Ehesachen und in Verfahren betreffend die elterliche Verantwortung und über internationale Kindesentführungen (ABl. 2019 L 178, 1).
[39] Erläuterungen bei Junker, Internationales Zivilprozessrecht, 6. Aufl. 2023, § 17 Rn. 26, 27.

vereinbarung oder den Termin der Anrufung des Gerichts (Art. 4 Abs. 1 UAbs. 2 EG-UntVO). Die Gerichtsstandsabrede bedarf der Schriftform oder der elektronischen Form (Art. 4 Abs. 2 EG-UntVO). Sie ist ausgeschlossen bei Streitigkeiten über eine Unterhaltspflicht gegenüber einem Kind, das noch nicht das 18. Lebensjahr vollendet hat (Art. 4 Abs. 3 EG-UntVO).

Diese Vorschrift spielt eine Rolle für eine *Freistellungsvereinbarung,* durch die eine Person eine andere von der Unterhaltspflicht gegenüber einem minderjährigen Kind befreit. Die herrschende Meinung zur Parallelvorschrift des Art. 8 Abs. 3 HUntStProt 2007 (Ausschluss der Rechtswahl für Unterhaltspflichten betreffend Minderjährige) hält es für hinreichend, dass sich die Vereinbarung auf Unterhaltsansprüche von Minderjährigen bezieht; der Minderjährige müsse, damit Art. 4 Abs. 3 EG-UntVO und Art. 8 Abs. 3 HUntStProt 2007 einschlägig sei, nicht Partei der Gerichtsstands- oder Rechtswahlvereinbarung sein.[40] Dem ist zuzustimmen, denn die Schutzbedürftigkeit des Minderjährigen und die Gefahr eines Interessenkonflikts bestehen auch, wenn der Minderjährige nicht Partei der Vereinbarung ist.

IV. Objektive Anknüpfung und Rechtswahl

Vereinbarungen, die Unterhaltspflichten ausgestalten, welche kraft Gesetzes entstanden sind oder entstehen können, werden nach dem Unterhaltsprotokoll angeknüpft. Es unterscheidet zwischen objektiven Anknüpfungen (Art. 3ff. HUntStProt 2007) und der Wahl des anzuwendenden Rechts (Art. 7f. HUntStProt 2007). Bei den Verweisungen des Haager Protokolls handelt es sich um Sachnormverweisungen mit der Folge, dass Rück- und Weiterverweisungen (Renvoi) ausgeschlossen sind (Art. 12 HUntStProt 2007).

1. Regelanknüpfung der Unterhaltspflichten und Ausnahmen

Unterhaltspflichten richten sich grundsätzlich nach dem Recht des Staates, in dem der Unterhaltsberechtigte seinen gewöhnlichen Aufenthalt hat (Art. 3 Abs. 1 HUntStProt 2007). Diese Grundregel ermöglicht einen Gleichlauf mit der internationalen Zuständigkeit nach Art. 3 lit. b EG-UntVO (→ III. 1.). Wechselt der Unterhaltsberechtigte den gewöhnlichen Aufenthalt, so ist ab dem Zeitpunkt des Wechsels das Recht des neuen gewöhnlichen Aufenthalts anzuwenden (Art. 3 Abs. 2 HUntStProt 2007). Das Statut der Regelanknüpfung ist somit wandelbar; der Aufenthaltswechsel führt zu einem Statutenwechsel.[41] Die Regelanknüpfung an den gewöhnlichen Aufenthalt des Unterhaltsberechtigten dient dem Ziel, das Recht des Staates heranzuziehen, in welchem der

[40] NomosKommentar BGB/Bach, 3. Aufl. 2019, HUP Art. 8 Rn. 5; Staudinger, BGB/Mankowski, Neubearbeitung 2021, HUP Art. 8 Rn. 69; Münchener Kommentar zum BGB/Staudinger, 8. Aufl. 2020, HUP Art. 8 Rn. 21.

[41] Erman, BGB/Stürner, 16. Aufl. 2020, HUP Art. 3 Rn. 4; Prütting/Wegen/Weinreich, BGB/Martiny, 16. Aufl. 2021, HUP Art. 3 Rn. 3; Junker, Internationales Privatrecht, 5. Aufl. 2022, § 19 Rn. 11.

Unterhaltsbedarf entsteht.[42] Bei einem Aufenthaltswechsel bleibt eine gerichtlich festgestellte Unterhaltspflicht wirksam, bis sie durch eine neue Entscheidung abgeändert wird.[43]

Die Grundanknüpfung des Art. 3 HUntStProt 2007 wird durch die besonderen Anknüpfungen des Art. 4 HUntStProt 2007 überlagert. Sie verwirklichen zum Vorteil bestimmter als typischerweise besonders schutzwürdig angesehener Unterhaltsberechtigter *(favor alimenti)* das Günstigkeitsprinzip als Instrument zum Schutz des Schwächeren. Das betrifft Unterhaltsansprüche von Kindern gegen ihre Eltern, von Eltern gegen ihre Kinder und von Berechtigten unter 21 Jahren gegen andere Personen als ihre Eltern, wenn es sich nicht um Ehegattenunterhalt im Sinne des Art. 5 HUntStProt 2007 handelt (Art. 4 Abs. 1 HUntStProt 2007). Das Grundprinzip besteht darin, subsidiäre Anknüpfungen zu berufen, wenn das primär anzuwendende Recht für die betreffende familienrechtliche Beziehung entweder überhaupt keinen Anspruch vorsieht oder die Voraussetzungen des Anspruchs nicht erfüllt sind.[44] Für Unterhaltsvereinbarungen spielt diese Vorschrift in der Praxis kaum eine Rolle.

2. *Ausweichklausel bei Trennungs- und Scheidungsunterhalt*

Unterhaltsvereinbarungen beziehen sich häufig auf den Trennungs- oder Scheidungsunterhalt zwischen Ehegatten oder früheren Ehegatten. Für diese Unterhaltspflichten hat die Ausweichklausel des Art. 5 HUntStProt 2007 Bedeutung. Sie ist als kollisionsrechtliche Einrede ausgestaltet.[45] Wenn eine der Parteien der Unterhaltsvereinbarung sich gegen die Anknüpfung nach Art. 3 HUntStProt 2007 wendet und das Recht eines anderen Staates, „insbesondere des Staates ihres letzten gemeinsamen gewöhnlichen Aufenthalts“, eine engere Verbindung zu der Ehe aufweist, ist das Recht dieses anderen Staates anzuwenden (Art. 5 HUntStProt 2007).

Diese Vorschrift wirft die Frage auf, ob die Verbindung zu dem „anderen Staat“ bloß – wie der Wortlaut nahelegt – eine *engere Verbindung* sein muss, oder ob – wie bei den Ausweichklauseln des Art. 4 Abs. 3 Rom I-VO und des Art. 4 Abs. 3 Rom II-VO – eine *offensichtlich engere Verbindung* zu verlangen ist, die „ein ganz besonderes Gewicht haben“ muss.[46] Ferner stellt sich die Frage nach der Bedeutung des letzten gemeinsamen gewöhnlichen Aufenthalts der Eheleute, den die Vorschrift hervorhebt.

Der BGH hatte einen Fall zu entscheiden, in welchem die deutschen Ehegatten, bedingt durch den Beruf des Ehemannes in der Ölbranche, nach der Eheschlie-

---

[42] EuGH 7.6.2018 – C-83/17, BeckRS 2018, 1469 = IPRax 2019, 530 Rn. 41f. (KE/LO); von Bar/Mankowski, Internationales Privatrecht II, 2. Aufl. 2019, § 4 Rn. 893.

[43] Staudinger, BGB/Mankowski, 2021, HUP Vorb. Rn. 43ff.; NomosKommentar BGB/Gruber, 3. Aufl. 2019, HUP Art. 1 Rn. 20ff.; Junker, Internationales Privatrecht, 5. Aufl. 2022, § 19 Rn. 7.

[44] Münchener Kommentar zum BGB/Staudinger, 8. Aufl. 2020, HUP Art. 4 Rn. 8; NomosKommentar BGB/Bach, 3. Aufl. 2019, HUP Art. 4 Rn. 9, 10.

[45] von Bar/Mankowski, Internationales Privatrecht II, 2. Aufl. 2019, § 4 Rn. 919; Bonomi, Yb PIL 10 (2008), 333 (346ff.).

[46] Münchener Kommentar zum BGB Martiny, 8. Aufl. 2021, Rom I-VO Art. 4 Rn. 298; Pfeiffer EuZW 2008, 622 (626).

ßung, die in den Niederlanden stattfand, nacheinander jeweils vier Jahre in den Niederlanden, im Sultanat Brunei und im US-Bundesstaat Texas lebten. Dort wurde die Ehe geschieden. Die Ehefrau übersiedelte von Texas nach Deutschland und verlangte Unterhalt nach deutschem Recht (Art. 3 Abs. 1 HUntStProt 2007). Der Ehemann berief sich nach Art. 5 HUntStProt 2007 auf das Recht des letzten gemeinsamen gewöhnlichen Aufenthalts (Texas).[47]

Der BGH räumt dem letzten gemeinsamen gewöhnlichen Aufenthalt in Texas keinen hohen Stellenwert ein, weil dieser Aufenthalt – wie die früheren Aufenthalte in den Niederlanden und im Sultanat Brunei – von vornherein als vorübergehend angelegt waren. Art. 5 HUntStProt 2007 verlange eine wertende Gesamtbetrachtung. Darin sei das „insbesondere"-Kriterium lediglich ein Faktor.[48] Der Sache nach vertritt der BGH damit eine enge Auslegung des Art. 5 HUntStProt 2007, vergleichbar den Ausweichklauseln der Rom I- und Rom II-Verordnungen.

Der restriktive Ansatz des BGH verdient Zustimmung. Ausweislich der Materialien soll es Art. 5 HUntStProt 2007 einem Ehegatten erschweren, das Bestehen und den Inhalt der Unterhaltspflicht durch einen einseitigen Wechsel des gewöhnlichen Aufenthalts auf unfaire Weise zu beeinflussen.[49] Davon kann nicht die Rede sein, wenn eine Ehefrau, die ihren Mann in regelmäßig wechselnde Einsatzländer begleitet hat, nach dem Scheitern der Ehe in ihren Heimatstaat zurückkehrt und nach dem Recht dieses Staates Unterhalt verlangt.

Bei Unterhaltsvereinbarungen hat die Ausweichklausel Bedeutung, wenn eine Vereinbarung zu einer Zeit geschlossen wurde, zu der mit einem Statutenwechsel nicht gerechnet werden konnte. In diesem Fall kann bei objektiver Anknüpfung nur die Ausweichklausel unangemessene Ergebnisse verhindern. Dies ist aber nur die zweitbeste Lösung, denn Art. 5 HUntStProt 2007 ist dispositiv. Eine nach Art. 7, 8 HUntStProt 2007 wirksame Rechtswahl der Parteien der Unterhaltsvereinbarung verdrängt Art. 5 HUntStProt 2007. Die Unsicherheiten einer Anwendung der Ausweichklausel werden dadurch vermieden.[50]

3. Vereinbarungen über die anwendbare Rechtsordnung

Während die Wahl des Gerichtsstands für eine Unterhaltsvereinbarung der Risikovorsorge dient (→ III. 3.), kann die Wahl des Vereinbarungsstatuts die Rechtssicherheit fördern. Das Unterhaltsprotokoll eröffnet zwei Möglichkeiten der Rechtswahl:

Art. 7 HUntStProt 2007 bezweckt einen Gleichlauf von *forum* und *ius* „für die Zwecke eines einzelnen Verfahrens" und erlaubt, auch als Konzession an die Staaten, die rechtspolitisch generell die Anwendung des Forumrechts befürworten,[51]

[47] BGH 11.5.2022 – XII ZB 543/20, NJW 2022, 2403 = FamRZ 2022,1278 mAnm Lugani.

[48] BGH 11.5.2022 – XII ZB 543/20, NJW 2022, 2403 Rn. 18ff.; zust. Yassari NJW 2022, 2372 (2374).

[49] Bonomi, Explanatory Report on the Hague Protocol of 23 November 2007 on the Law Applicable to Maintenance Obligations, 2009, Rn. 78.

[50] Staudinger, BGB/Mankowski, Neubearbeitung 2021, HUP Art. 5 Rn. 55.

[51] NomosKommentar BGB/Bach, 3. Aufl. 2019, HUP Art. 7 Rn. 2; Erman, BGB/Stürner, 16. Aufl. 2020, HUP Art. 7 Rn. 1.

nur die Wahl der *lex fori;* der Verordnungsgeber glaubte, auf Vorschriften zum Schutz der schwächeren Partei verzichten zu können.

Art. 8 HUntStProt 2007 ermöglicht den Parteien weitergehend, für den Fall des Aufenthaltswechsels Vorsorge zu treffen und den Gleichklang des Unterhaltsstatuts mit dem Ehegüter- oder Ehescheidungsstatut herzustellen, enthält aber zum Ausgleich Schutzvorschriften,[52] insbesondere für den bei Unterhaltsvereinbarungen sehr häufigen Fall des Unterhaltsverzichts.

a) Wahl der lex fori für ein einzelnes Verfahren

Die Parteien können *für ein einzelnes Verfahren* in einem bestimmten Staat das Recht dieses Staates zum Unterhaltsstatut berufen. Notwendig ist eine *ausdrückliche Erklärung;* die stillschweigende Rechtswahl im Prozess ist somit ausgeschlossen (Art. 7 Abs. 1 HUntStProt 2007). Eine Rechtswahl *vor der Verfahrenseinleitung* erfordert darüber hinaus eine von beiden Parteien unterschriebene Vereinbarung in Schriftform oder auf einem Datenträger (Art. 7 Abs. 2 HUntStProt 2007).

Die Rechtswahl nach Art. 7 HUntStProt 2007 ist dadurch gekennzeichnet, dass keine Regelungen zum Schutz des Schwächeren bestehen. Die Einschränkungen des Art. 8 HUntStProt 2007 finden keine Anwendung: Die Wahl der *lex fori* ist anders als nach Art. 8 Abs. 3 HUntStProt 2007 selbst für Kindesunterhalt möglich, der Unterhaltsverzicht unterliegt entgegen Art. 8 Abs. 4 HUntStProt 2007 keiner besonderen Anknüpfung, und eine kollisionsrechtliche Inhaltskontrolle nach Art. 8 Abs. 5 HUntStProt 2007 entfällt.[53]

Da die Sicherungen zum Schutz des Schwächeren wegfallen, erlaubt Art. 7 HUntStProt 2007 keine Wahl einer eventuell zukünftigen *lex fori* im Sinne einer pauschalen Koppelung des anwendbaren Rechts an das dem Kläger gegebenenfalls offenstehende Forum.[54] Die Reichweite der Vorschrift beschränkt sich auf ein konkretes, bereits anhängiges (Abs. 1) oder ein nach der Rechtswahl eingeleitetes Verfahren (Abs. 2). Daraus schließen manche, der Gläubiger oder der Schuldner müsse „im Begriff sein", bei einem bestimmten Gericht zu klagen.[55]

Nach der Gegenansicht soll es auf den Zeitabstand zwischen der Rechtswahl und der Verfahrenseinleitung nicht ankommen; auch die Eintrittswahrscheinlichkeit eines Verfahrens soll für die Wirksamkeit der Rechtswahl keine Rolle spielen.[56] Die Parteien können nach dieser Ansicht eine Gerichtsstandsvereinbarung „für ein

[52] NomosKommentar BGB/Bach, 3. Aufl. 2019, HUP Art. 8 Rn. 1; Rauscher, EuZPR/EuIPR/Andrae, 4. Aufl. 2016, HUntStProt 2007, HUP Art. 8 Rn. 1.

[53] EuGH 20.9.2018 – C-214/17, NJW 2018, 3433 Rn. 39 = FamRZ 2018, 1753 mAnm Brosch (Mölk/Mölk).

[54] Bonomi, Explanatory Report on the Hague Protocol of 23 November 2007 on the Law Applicable to Maintenance Obligations, 2009, Rn. 120; NomosKommentar BGB/Bach, 3. Aufl. 2019, HUP Art. 7 Rn. 9.

[55] Bonomi, Explanatory Report on the Hague Protocol of 23 November 2007 on the Law Applicable to Maintenance Obligations, 2009, Rn. 115; NomosKommentar BGB/Bach, 3. Aufl. 2019, HUP Art. 7 Rn. 10.

[56] Bonomi, Explanatory Report on the Hague Protocol of 23 November 2007 on the Law Applicable to Maintenance Obligations, 2009, Rn. 121; Staudinger, BGB/Mankowski, 2021, HUP Art. 7 Rn. 18; Gruber FS Spellenberg, 2010, 177 (189).

künftig zwischen uns eintretendes Verfahren" treffen (Art. 4 EG-UntVO) und sie mit der Wahl des Rechts am vereinbarten Forum kombinieren (Art. 7 HUntStProt 2007). Diese Ansicht ist jedoch kaum mit den anderen Sprachfassungen des Art. 7 Abs. 1 HUntStProt 2007 in Einklang zu bringen, die sich nicht auf ein „einzelnes", sondern auf ein „bestimmtes" *(particular, particulière)* Verfahren beziehen.

Eine zurückhaltende Anwendung des Art. 7 HUntStProt 2007 ist umso mehr geboten, als die Rechtswahl nach dieser Vorschrift nicht nur die objektiven Anknüpfungen des Vereinbarungsstatuts verdrängt (das sind sowohl die Regelanknüpfung als auch das Privileg des Art. 4 HUntStProt 2007 und die Einrede des Art. 5 HUntStProt 2007), sondern auch die Sicherungen des Art. 8 Abs. 3 bis 5 HUntStProt 2007 unterläuft.[57] Dass die schwächere Partei die Möglichkeit habe, sich über den Inhalt der *lex fori* zu informieren, ist als Begründung für eine weite Auslegung des Art. 7 HUntStProt 2007 weniger überzeugend als das für den enge Auslegung vorgebrachte Argument, dass sich die Gefahrenpotenziale im Vergleich zur Rechtswahl nach Art. 8 HUntStProt 2007 nicht grundsätzlich unterscheiden.[58]

b) Beschränkte Rechtswahl in anderen Fällen

Die Parteien können *unabhängig von einem Verfahren* nach Art. 8 HUntStProt 2007 jederzeit eine der folgenden Rechtsordnungen zum Unterhaltsstatut berufen

a) das Recht des Staates, dessen Staatsangehörigkeit zumindest eine Partei zur Zeit der Rechtswahl besitzt,
b) das Recht des gewöhnlichen Aufenthalts (mindestens) einer der Parteien im Zeitpunkt der Rechtswahl,
c) im Fall von Ehegatten der früheren Ehegatten das gewählte oder tatsächlich angewandte *Ehegüterstatut* oder
d) das für den Fall der Ehescheidung von den Parteien gewählte oder tatsächlich angewandte *Ehescheidungsstatut.*[59]

Die Rechtswahl bedarf, ebenso wie im Fall des Art. 7 HUntStProt 2007 (→ IV. 3. a)), einer von beiden Parteien unterschriebenen Vereinbarung in Schriftform oder auf einem Datenträger (Art. 8 Abs. 2 HUntStProt 2007). Die Vereinbarung muss, anders als bei Art. 7 HUntStProt 2007, nicht ausdrücklich erfolgen. Erfüllt ein Dokument zwischen den Parteien das Formerfordernis des Art. 8 Abs. 2 HUntStProt 2007, so kann in ihm eine *stillschweigende Rechtswahl* enthalten sein.[60] Trifft zum Beispiel ein Ehepaar in einem notariell beurkundeten Ehevertrag, der auf Vorschriften des BGB Bezug nimmt, Regelungen über den Trennungsunter-

---

[57] von Bar/Mankowski, Internationales Privatrecht II, 2. Aufl. 2019, § 4 Rn. 848; siehe zum Verhältnis von Art. 7 und 8 HUntStProt 2007, wenn unklar ist, auf welche Vorschrift die Parteien die Rechtswahl stützen wollten, NomosKommentar BGB/Bach, 3. Aufl. 2019, HUP Art. 8 Rn. 29.

[58] Überblick über den Meinungsstand bei Staudinger, BGB/Mankowski, 2021, HUP Art. 7 Rn. 17 ff.

[59] Erläuterungen bei Junker, Internationales Privatrecht, 5. Aufl. 2022, § 19 Rn. 22; von Bar/Mankowski, Internationales Privatrecht II, 2. Aufl. 2019, § 4 Rn. 863.

[60] Prütting/Wegen/Weinreich, BGB/Martiny, 16. Aufl. 2021, HUP Art. 8 Rn. 3; NomosKommentar BGB/Bach, 3. Aufl. 2019, HUP Art. 8 Rn. 22.

halt, kann die Bezugnahme auf das deutsche Recht eine stillschweigende Rechtswahl bedeuten (Art. 8 Abs. 1 HUntStProt 2007). Sie gilt dann aber nur für den Trennungsunterhalt, nicht aber für den nachehelichen Unterhalt.[61]

Die Rechtswahl nach Art. 8 Abs. 1 HUntStProt 2007 hat für die Parteien einer Unterhaltsvereinbarung vor allem in drei Konstellationen Bedeutung. Die erste liegt in der Möglichkeit, das Aufenthaltsrecht des *Unterhaltsschuldners* zu wählen (Art. 8 Abs. 1 lit. b HUntStProt 2007). Da der leistungsfähige Unterhaltsverpflichtete gegenüber dem bedürftigen Unterhaltsberechtigten häufig die stärkere Partei ist, betreffen die Rechtswahlschranken besonders diesen Fall.[62] Zweitens können die Parteien, indem sie das Aufenthaltsrecht des *Unterhaltsgläubigers* berufen (ebenfalls Art. 8 Abs. 1 lit. b HUntStProt 2007), das Unterhaltsrecht auf den Zeitpunkt der Rechtswahl fixieren und dadurch einen Statutenwechsel nach Art. 3 Abs. 1 HUntStProt 2007 vermeiden.[63]

Schließlich ermöglicht die Rechtswahl nach Art. 8 Abs. 1 HUntStProt 2007 die gemeinsame Behandlung zusammenhängender Sachverhalte, nämlich des Unterhalts und des Güterrechts (Art. 8 Abs. 1 lit. c HUntStProt 2007) sowie des Unterhalts und der Scheidung (Art. 8 Abs. 1 lit. d HUntStProt 2007).[64] Die Kollisionsregel des Art. 8 Abs. 1 lit. d HUntStProt 2007 trägt damit dem Umstand Rechnung, dass einige Rechtsordnungen, zum Beispiel das englische Recht (sections 21–26 Matrimonial Causes Act 1973), die vermögensrechtlichen Fragen der Scheidung nicht unterscheiden, sondern in eine Gesamtentscheidung einfließen lassen.[65]

c) Abweichende Anknüpfung des Unterhaltsverzichts

Vereinbarungen über den Trennungs- oder den nachehelichen Unterhalt laufen häufig auf einen Unterhaltsverzicht hinaus. Ein solcher Verzicht ist *ungeachtet des gewählten Rechts* nur zulässig, wenn das des Staates, in dem die berechtigte Person im Zeitpunkt der Rechtswahl ihren gewöhnlichen Aufenthalt hat, diesen Verzicht billigt (Art. 8 Abs. 4 HUntStProt 2007).[66] Die besondere Anknüpfung des Unterhaltsverzichts betrifft nach herrschender Meinung – über den Wortlaut der Vorschrift hinaus – nicht nur das „Ob“, sondern auch den zulässigen Umfang und die materiellen Voraussetzungen des Verzichts, zum Beispiel die Zahlung einer Abfindung. Auf diese Weise soll der Unterhaltsberechtigte umfassend vor der Wahl einer „verzichtsfreundlichen“ Rechtsordnung geschützt werden.[67]

---

[61] Beispiel nach Hausmann FS Martiny, 2014, 345 (348).

[62] Staudinger, BGB/Mankowski, 2021, HUP Art. 8 Rn. 35.

[63] Bonomi, Explanatory Report on the Hague Protocol of 23 November 2007 on the Law Applicable to Maintenance Obligations, 2009, Rn. 133; Hausmann FS Martiny, 2014, 345 (353).

[64] von Bar/Mankowski, Internationales Privatrecht II, 2. Aufl. 2019, § 4 Rn. 857f.

[65] Rauscher, EuZPR/EuIPR/Andrae, 4. Aufl. 2016, HUntStProt 2007 Art. 8 Rn. 11.

[66] Münchener Kommentar zum BGB/Staudinger, 8. Aufl. 2020, HUP Art. 8 Rn. 23; Staudinger, BGB/Mankowski, 2021, HUP Art. 8 Rn. 72.

[67] Bonomi YbPIL 10 (2008), 333 (356f.); s. zum wechselseitigen Verzicht Rauscher, EuZPR/EuIPR/Andrae, 4. Aufl. 2016, HUntStProt 2007 Art. 8 Rn. 22.

Eine sachrechtliche Inhaltskontrolle ergänzt die besondere Anknüpfung des Unterhaltsverzichts. Das gewählte Unterhaltsstatut ist nicht anzuwenden, wenn seine Anwendung für eine der Parteien offensichtlich unbillige oder unangemessene Folgen hätte (Art. 8 Abs. 5 Hs. 1 HUntStProt 2007). Diese Vorschrift wirkt beidseitig, das heißt sowohl zugunsten eines *Unterhaltsberechtigten,* der schlechter gestellt wird als nach dem objektiven anzuwendenden Recht, als auch zugunsten des *Unterhaltsverpflichteten,* wenn der Umfang seiner Verpflichtung nach dem gewählten Recht bedeutend größer ist oder die Unterhaltspflicht nach diesem Recht überhaupt erst begründet wird.[68]

Eine Inhaltskontrolle des Rechts, dem die Unterhaltsvereinbarung durch Rechtswahl unterstellt wurde, findet nicht statt, wenn die Parteien im Zeitpunkt der Rechtswahl umfassend unterrichtet und sich der Folgen ihrer Wahl vollständig bewusst waren (Art. 8 Abs. 5 Hs. 2 HUntStProt 2007). Diese Voraussetzung ist bei einer rechtsunkundigen Person in der Regel nur nach Rechtsberatung erfüllt. Der Vergleichsmaßstab für die Unbilligkeit oder Unangemessenheit der Folgen ist die Rechtslage unter Geltung des objektiven Unterhaltsstatuts.[69] Art. 8 Abs. 5 HUntStProt 2007 ist eine Sachnorm im IPR und keine Ordre public-Klausel, denn es kommt ersatzweise die *lex fori* und nicht das objektive Unterhaltsstatut zur Anwendung.[70]

V. Zusammenfassung

Der Beitrag behandelt vertragliche Vereinbarungen über gesetzliche Unterhaltsansprüche. Derartige Vereinbarungen sind sachlich von der Europäischen Unterhaltsverordnung und dem Haager Unterhaltsprotokoll erfasst, wobei die Qualifikation von Unterhaltspflichten als „gesetzlich" eine Herausforderung darstellt. Dies betrifft zum Beispiel nichteheliche Paarbeziehungen (→ II.). Bei der internationalen Zuständigkeit der Gerichte wirft die akzessorische Zuständigkeit des Scheidungsgerichts für Vereinbarungen über den Trennungs- oder Scheidungsunterhalt Fragen auf. Die Prorogation für eine Freistellungsvereinbarung ist kritisch, wenn es um den Unterhalt von Minderjährigen geht (→ III.).

Für die objektive Anknüpfung einer Unterhaltsvereinbarung hat die Ausweichklausel des Art. 5 HUntStProt 2007 zentrale Bedeutung. Die Rechtswahl kann Rechtssicherheit schaffen, stößt aber bei dem in Unterhaltsvereinbarungen häufig enthaltenen Unterhaltsverzicht an Grenzen. Lässt sich die besondere Anknüpfung des Unterhaltsverzichts an den gewöhnlichen Aufenthalt des Berechtigten *im Zeitpunkt der Rechtswahl* gemäß Art. 8 Abs. 4 HUntStProt 2007 noch einigermaßen kalkulieren, so tut die kollisionsrechtliche Inhaltskontrolle in einem Günstigkeitsvergleich mit dem objektiven Unterhaltsstatut *im Zeitpunkt des Unterhaltsbedarfs* nach Maßgabe des Art. 8 Abs. 5 HUntStProt 2007 der Rechtssicherheit einen ganz erheblichen Abbruch (→ IV.).

---

[68] von Bar/Mankowski, Internationales Privatrecht II, 2. Aufl. 2019, § 4 Rn. 870; Rauscher, EuZPR/EuIPR/Andrae, 4. Aufl. 2016, HUntStProt 2007 Art. 8 Rn. 25; Hausmann FS Martiny, 2014, 345 (361).

[69] NomosKommentar BGB/Bach, 3. Aufl. 2019, HUP Art. 8 Rn. 39.

[70] von Bar/Mankowski, Internationales Privatrecht II, 2. Aufl. 2019, § 4 Rn. 869.

PERRINE KOBSIK

Die Europäisierung des Erwachsenenschutzrechts

Am 31.5.2023 schlug die Europäische Kommission zwei Maßnahmen vor, mittels derer der Schutz von Erwachsenen in grenzüberschreitenden Situationen innerhalb der Europäischen Union gestärkt werden sollte. Zum einen liegt ein Vorschlag für eine Verordnung des Europäischen Parlaments und des Rates über die Zuständigkeit, das anwendbare Recht, die Anerkennung und Vollstreckung von Maßnahmen und die Zusammenarbeit in Fragen betreffend den Schutz Erwachsener (im Folgenden EU-ErwSVO-E)[1] vor, zum anderen ein Vorschlag für einen Beschluss des Rates zur Ermächtigung der Mitgliedstaaten, im Interesse der Europäischen Union (EU) Vertragsparteien des Übereinkommens vom 13.1.2000 über den internationalen Schutz von Erwachsenen zu werden oder zu bleiben[2]. Die dieser Festschrift ihren Titel gebende Europäisierung im Zivilrecht sollte damit nunmehr auch auf dem Gebiet des grenzüberschreitenden Erwachsenenschutzes voranschreiten.

I. Notwendigkeit der (einheitlichen) Regelung des Erwachsenenschutzes in grenzüberschreitenden Fällen

Die grenzüberschreitende Mobilität der Menschen in der Europäischen Union nimmt stetig zu und betrifft nicht nur gesunde und junge Menschen, sondern auch ältere Menschen und/oder solche mit Beeinträchtigungen. So kehren beispielsweise (innereuropäische) Migranten, die in frühen Jahren auf der Suche nach Arbeit ihr Heimatland verließen, nach Eintritt in den Ruhestand nicht in dieses zurück. Andere zieht es erst im fortgeschrittenen Alter in ein anderes Land, in welchem sie ihren Lebensabend verbringen wollen. Wieder andere besitzen Immobilien oder Vermögen im Ausland. Geraten diese Personen in einen Zustand, in dem sie nicht mehr in der Lage sind, ihre Interessen selbst zu schützen, sind Maßnahmen des Erwachsenenschutzes erforderlich – in Form von hoheitlicher Fürsorge oder privatautonomer Vorsorge. Im Vergleich zu anderen Politikfeldern betrifft der Erwachsenenschutz, insbesondere in grenzüberschreitenden Fällen, noch verhältnismäßig wenige und steht daher auf den politischen Agenden nicht weit oben. Die Zahl der Betroffenen wächst jedoch. In dem gemeinsam mit dem Verordnungsvorschlag vorgelegten Folgenabschätzungsbericht wurde die Zahl der Erwachsenen, die im

---

[1] COM(2023) 280 final.
[2] COM(2023) 281 final/2.

Jahr 2020 eines grenzüberschreitenden Erwachsenenschutzes bedurften auf 145.000 bis 780.000 geschätzt, für das Jahr 2030 bereits auf 190 000 bis 1.100 000.[3] Schutzbedürftige Erwachsene, oder solche, die für diesen Fall vorsorgen möchten und deren Angehörige sehen sich aufgrund der unterschiedlichen Regelungen im autonomen internationalen Privat- und Verfahrensrecht der EU-Mitgliedstaaten zum Teil komplexen internationalprivatrechtlichen Problemen gegenüber: Die Gerichte oder Behörden welches Mitgliedstaates sind zuständig, um über Maßnahmen zum Schutz der Person des Erwachsenen oder seines Besitzes zu entscheiden? Welches Recht findet auf solche hoheitlichen Schutzmaßnahmen oder auf eine diese ersetzende privatautonome Vorsorge Anwendung? Und wie verhält es sich mit der Anerkennung und gegebenenfalls Vollstreckung von im Ausland getroffenen Entscheidungen oder erteilten Vollmachten?

Das Haager Übereinkommen vom 13.1.2000 über den internationalen Schutz von Erwachsenen (ErwSÜ) hat zum Ziel, eben diese Fragen zu beantworten, indem es die internationale Zuständigkeit, das anwendbare Recht sowie Anerkennung und Vollstreckung sowohl für hoheitliche Schutzmaßnahmen als auch für die gewillkürte Stellvertretung regelt. Es ist anzuwenden bei internationalen Sachverhalten betreffend den Schutz Erwachsener, die aufgrund einer Beeinträchtigung oder der Unzulänglichkeit ihrer persönlichen Fähigkeiten nicht in der Lage sind, ihre Interessen zu schützen (sog. Schutzbedürftigkeit). Der Begriff der Unzulänglichkeit soll hierbei körperliche und geistige Behinderungen erfassen, derjenige der Beeinträchtigung einer Behinderung ähnliche Einschränkungen der persönlichen Fähigkeiten, die eher auf einer Alterserkrankung, etwa der Alzheimer-Krankheit, beruhen.[4]

Das ErwSÜ ist mittlerweile 25 Jahre alt und seit dem 1.1.2009 in Kraft. Noch immer hat es bedauernswert wenige Staaten vorzuweisen, die es ratifiziert haben. Im Januar 2024 war es erst in 15 Staaten in Kraft getreten, darunter 12 Mitgliedstaaten der Europäischen Union – Belgien, Deutschland, Estland, Frankreich, Finnland, Griechenland, Lettland, Malta, Österreich, Portugal, Tschechien und Zypern.[5] Mehr als die Hälfte der EU-Mitgliedstaaten waren damit bislang nicht Teil eines einheitlichen Rechtsrahmens für den internationalen Schutz von Erwachsenen.

Eine Verpflichtung zur Regelung grenzüberschreitender Fälle des Erwachsenenschutzes ergibt sich aus Art. 12 Abs. 4 der Behindertenrechtskonvention der Vereinten Nationen[6] (UN-BRK), der sowohl die EU-Mitgliedstaaten als auch die EU selbst als Vertragsstaaten verpflichtet sind. Demnach haben die Vertragsstaaten bezüglich aller die Ausübung der Rechts- und Handlungsfähigkeit betreffenden Maß-

[3] SWD(2023) 155 final, 72 (80).

[4] Lagarde, Protection of Adults Convention, Explanatory Report, https://assets.hcch.net/docs/1509ab33-c2fe-4532–981c-7aa4dad9ba45.pdf (abgerufen 13.3.2024), Rn. 9.

[5] Unterzeichnet, jedoch zu diesem Zeitpunkt noch nicht in Kraft getreten zudem von den EU-Mitgliedstaaten Niederlande, Irland, Italien und Polen. Vgl. zum aktuellen Ratifikationsstand https://www.hcch.net/en/instruments/conventions/status-table/?cid=71 (abgerufen 13.3.2024).

[6] Übereinkommen der Vereinten Nationen über die Rechte von Menschen mit Behinderungen vom 13.12.2006.

nahmen im Einklang mit den internationalen Menschenrechtsnormen geeignete und wirksame Vorkehrungen zu treffen, die gewährleisten, dass bei den Maßnahmen betreffend die Ausübung der Rechts- und Handlungsfähigkeit die Rechte, der Wille und die Präferenzen der betreffenden Person geachtet werden, dass es nicht zu Interessenkonflikten und missbräuchlicher Einflussnahme kommt, dass die Maßnahmen verhältnismäßig und auf die Umstände der Person zugeschnitten sind, dass sie von möglichst kurzer Dauer sind, einer regelmäßigen Überprüfung durch eine zuständige, unabhängige und unparteiische Behörde oder gerichtliche Stelle unterliegen und im Hinblick auf das Ausmaß, in dem diese Maßnahmen die Rechte und Interessen der Person berühren, verhältnismäßig sind.

Dieser Auftrag an die Vertragsstaaten der UN-BRK betrifft nicht nur das materielle Recht der Vertragsstaaten, sondern vor allem auch deren internationales Privatrecht und internationales Zivilverfahrensrecht sowie, mit Blick auf die Europäische Union, deren Vereinheitlichung, um Kompetenzkonflikte zu vermeiden und die wirksame Umsetzung privat oder behördlich getroffener Erwachsenenschutzmaßnahmen zu gewährleisten, sowie die Schaffung effektiver Mechanismen der Kooperation und Kommunikation.

Warum eine diesbezügliche Vereinheitlichung für einen effektiven internationalen Erwachsenenschutz nicht nur, aber insbesondere, innerhalb der Europäischen Union so wichtig ist, sollen einige kurze Beispiele verdeutlichen.

Ein wesentliches Hindernis für einen grenzüberschreitend gewährleisteten Schutz Erwachsener, die nicht mehr in der Lage sind, ihre Interessen selbst zu schützen, ist die unterschiedliche Anknüpfung des Erwachsenenschutzes im internationalen Privat- und Zivilverfahrensrecht der EU-Mitgliedstaaten an die Staatsangehörigkeit des schutzbedürftigen Erwachsenen einerseits oder dessen gewöhnlichen Aufenthalt andererseits.

In Fragen der internationalen Zuständigkeit kann dies insbesondere zu positiven Kompetenzkonflikten führen. Wenn es etwa um einen italienischen Staatsangehörigen mit gewöhnlichem Aufenthalt in Deutschland geht, würden sowohl deutsche als auch italienische Behörden bzw. Gerichte ihre Zuständigkeit bejahen, erstere aufgrund von Art. 5 ErwSÜ und letztere gestützt auf Art. 3 legge 31 maggio 1995, n. 218 (im Folgenden: italIPRG)[7].

In Bezug auf Vorsorgevollmachten – nach Art. 15 Abs. 1 ErwSÜ[8] von einem Erwachsenen durch eine Vereinbarung oder einseitiges Rechtsgeschäft eingeräumte Vertretungsmachten, die ausgeübt werden sollen, wenn dieser Erwachsene nicht mehr in der Lage ist, seine Interessen zu schützen – kann dies dazu führen, dass die Verwirklichung des Selbstbestimmungsrechts des schutzbedürftigen Erwachsenen gefährdet wird. Errichtet der Italiener des obigen Beispiels noch in Deutschland wirksam eine Vorsorgevollmacht nach deutschem Recht und verlegt später, noch

[7] Für dringliche und vorübergehende Maßnahmen statuiert Art. 44 italIPRG ebenfalls eine Zuständigkeit italienischer Behörden bzw. Gerichte. Für die internationale Zuständigkeit ebenfalls an die Staatsangehörigkeit anknüpfend beispielsweise auch Luxemburg, Schweden, Slowenien, vgl. Adriaenssens/Borrett/Fialon et al., Study on the cross-border legal protection of vulnerable adults in the EU, 2022, S. 89ff. (Abschnitt 2.3.2.).

[8] Sowie Art. 3 Nr. 1 EU-ErwSVO-E.

vor Eintritt des Vorsorgefalls[9], seinen gewöhnlichen Aufenthalt nach Frankreich, so würde diese Vorsorgevollmacht dort als wirksam anerkannt werden, da Frankreich als Vertragsstaat des ErwSÜ deren Wirksamkeit entsprechend Art. 15 Abs. 1 ErwSÜ nach dem Recht am gewöhnlichen Aufenthalt im Errichtungszeitpunkt beurteilt. Kehrt er jedoch in sein Heimatland Italien zurück, würde seine Vorsorgevollmacht nicht die gewünschte Wirkung entfalten können, da dort deren Wirksamkeit in Anwendung von Art. 43 italIPRG und damit nach dem italienischen Heimatrecht beurteilt wird, welches eine hoheitliche Schutzmaßnahmen entbehrlich machende gewillkürte Stellvertretung noch immer nicht kennt.[10] Gleichsam können die Staatsangehörigen all jener Staaten, deren Recht eine den Vorsorgefall überdauernde Bevollmächtigung nicht kennt[11], in Staaten, deren autonomes Kollisionsrecht an das Heimatrecht anknüpft, von einer zuvor wirksam nach dem Recht am gewöhnlichen Aufenthalt errichteten Vorsorgevollmacht nicht profitieren – sofern nicht aufgrund eines vorrangigen Übereinkommens oder Verordnungsrechts an das Recht des gewöhnlichen Aufenthalts angeknüpft wird. Dabei besteht insbesondere bei einem langfristigen gewöhnlichen Aufenthalt eine wesentliche Verbindung zum Recht dieses Staates.

Vergleichbare Probleme ergeben sich im Bereich der hoheitlichen Schutzmaßnahmen. Art. 24 Abs. 1 EGBGB wurde mit Wirkung zum 1.1.2023 in Anpassung an das ErwSÜ[12] geändert und knüpft nunmehr für kraft Gesetzes oder durch Rechtsgeschäft entstehende Fürsorgeverhältnisse an den gewöhnlichen Aufenthalt des Fürsorgebedürftigen[13] an[14]. Wie zuvor Art. 24 Abs. 1 EGBGB aF, wird jedoch etwa im italienischen Kollisionsrecht noch immer an die Staatsangehörigkeit angeknüpft, vgl. Art. 43 italIPRG[15].

---

[9] Dh des Zeitpunkts, in dem oder ab dem der Vollmachtgeber nicht mehr selbst in der Lage ist, für seine Interessen zu sorgen und die Vertretungsmacht des Vorsorgebevollmächtigten greifen soll.

[10] Vgl. Franzina, L'evoluzione del diritto internazionale privato della protezione degli adulti tra iniziative dell'Unione, modelli universali e norme interne, JUS-ONLINE 4/2022, 212 (217f.); zum Meinungsstand bezüglich der Anwendbarkeit von Art. 43 italIPRG in Abwesenheit einer spezifischen Kollisionsnorm vgl. Kobsik, Antizipierte Erklärungen in Gesundheitsangelegenheiten im grenzüberschreitenden Verkehr, 2020, S. 410f.

[11] Dies betrifft die folgenden EU-Mitgliedstaaten: Bulgarien, Estland, Griechenland, Italien, Zypern, Lettland, Litauen, Niederlande, Polen, Slowenien und Slowakei. Vgl. zur Verbreitung eines der Vorsorgevollmacht vergleichbaren Rechtsinstituts auch Staudinger, BGB/von Hein, 2022, ESÜ Art. 15 Rn. 2–5.

[12] Vgl. BT-Drs. 19/24445, 320.

[13] Die Regelanknüpfung nach Art. 24 EGBGB nF ist Gesamtverweisung in das Recht des Staates des gewöhnlichen Aufenthalts des Fürsorgebedürftigen, Art. 24 Abs. 2 und 3 EGBGB nF enthalten dagegen jeweils Sachnormverweisungen, Staudinger, BGB/von Hein, 2022, EGBGB Art. 24 Rn. 100ff.; Maßgeblicher Zeitpunkt ist hier die Entstehung des Fürsorgeverhältnisses, Staudinger, BGB/von Hein, 2022, EGBGB Art. 24 Rn. 49.

[14] Für den Erwachsenenschutz an den gewöhnlichen Aufenthalt anknüpfend zB Rumänien, Art. 2578 Codul civil.

[15] Insoweit an die Staatsangehörigkeit anknüpfend ebenfalls etwa Albanien, Art. 11 des Gesetzes Nr. 10.1428 vom 2.6.2011. Ausschließlich an die Staatsangehörigkeit anknüpfend auch Griechenland, Luxemburg und Slowenien, vgl. Adriaenssens/Borrett/Fialon et al., Study on the cross-border legal protection of vulnerable adults in the EU, 2022, S. 89ff. (Abschnitt 2.3.2.).

Will der nunmehr in Italien lebende, nicht schutzbedürftige Italiener des obigen Beispiels mit seiner rumänischen Ehefrau, die seit einiger Zeit unter einer Schutzbetreuung (amministrazione di sostegno) steht, in deren Heimat umziehen, so fehlt es dem italienischen Richter schlicht an Gesprächskanälen[16] um sicherzustellen, dass die notwendigen Schutzmaßnahmen zugunsten der Ehefrau auch in Rumänien ergriffen werden, etwa indem ihr dort ein Betreuer nach rumänischem Recht bestellt wird, der nahtlos die Aufgaben seines italienischen Vorgängers übernehmen kann.

Diese Beispiele zeigen auch, dass fehlende Rechtssicherheit in Bezug auf die Vorhersehbarkeit der internationalen Zuständigkeit, des anzuwendenden Rechts und der mit den notwendigen Verfahren zur Anerkennung und Vollstreckung verbundenen Kosten und die damit einhergehende fehlende Planbarkeit einer privatautonomen Vorsorge letztlich das Recht auf Freizügigkeit von Menschen mit Behinderung, wozu auch im oben genannten Sinne schutzbedürftige Erwachsene zählen, beeinträchtigen. Diese massive Beeinträchtigung des Rechts der Personenfreizügigkeit[17] aufgrund der bislang zu verzeichnenden Ineffektivität des Erwachsenenschutzes in grenzüberschreitenden Fällen und der Schwierigkeiten, denen Betroffene sich auf diesem Gebiet gegenübersehen, stellt neben der aus der UN-BRK folgenden Verpflichtung der EU einen weiteren Grund für eine europäische Regelung dar.

II. Kombinierte Vorschläge der Kommission im Mai 2023

Das ErwSÜ wird allgemein als gelungenes Instrument angesehen, um den Schutz Erwachsener, die aufgrund einer Beeinträchtigung oder Unzulänglichkeit ihrer persönlichen Fähigkeiten nicht in der Lage sind, ihre eigenen Interessen zu schützen, in grenzüberschreitenden Angelegenheiten zu gewährleisten und ist, wie oben dargelegt, zumindest für zwölf EU-Mitgliedstaaten bereits geltendes Recht. In Verbindung mit den bereits in der Praxis gesammelten Erfahrungen und dem demnächst erscheinenden Praxishandbuch[18] bildet das Übereinkommen somit eine gute Grundlage für die der Verpflichtung aus der UN-BRK gerecht werdende Regelung des europäischen internationalen Privat- und -verfahrensrechts des Erwachsenenschutzes.

Das ErwSÜ ist jedoch nicht offen für einen Beitritt von supranationalen Organisationen, es fehlt an einer entsprechenden Klausel, wie sie neuere Haager Übereinkommen beinhalten. Möglich und richtig ist es daher, dass die EU ihre Mitgliedstaaten auffordert, dem Übereinkommen im Interesse der Union beizutreten (dies betrifft etwa Italien) oder Vertragsstaat zu bleiben[19] (dies gilt für Deutschland) – so

---

[16] Franzina, L'evoluzione del diritto internazionale privato della protezione degli adulti tra iniziative dell'Unione, modelli universali e norme interne, JUS-ONLINE 4/2022, 212 (218).

[17] Vgl. hierzu schon die Entschließung des Europäischen Parlaments vom 1.6.2017 mit Empfehlungen an die Kommission zum Schutz schutzbedürftiger Erwachsener (2015/2085(INL)), ABl. 2018 C 307, 154 (Erwägung D).

[18] Vgl. die bereits jetzt auf der Website der Haager Konferenz abrufbare Entwurfsfassung https://assets.hcch.net/docs/af8b7c86-6130-490d-b1fd-e3760da670d0.pdf (abgerufen 13.3.2024).

[19] COM(2023) 281 final/2.

wie sie es bereits für das in weiten Teilen vergleichbare Haager Kinderschutzübereinkommen[20] (KSÜ) getan hat. Die hierzu vorgeschlagene Ratsentscheidung soll zu einem einheitlichen Rechtsrahmen zwischen den EU-Mitgliedstaaten und Drittstaaten[21] führen, die Vertragsstaaten des ErwSÜ sind, und trägt damit letztlich auch der noch immer schleppenden Ratifikation des ErwSÜ auch durch die EU-Mitgliedstaaten Rechnung. Zahlreiche Initiativen der Kommission sowie des Rats der Europäischen Union seit dem Jahr 2008 hatten hier kaum einen Fortschritt bewirkt.[22]

2019 durfte ich meine unter dem Jubilar als Doktorvater entstandene Dissertation zum Thema antizipierter Erklärungen in Gesundheitsangelegenheiten im grenzüberschreitenden Verkehr verteidigen. Eine europäische Regelung zum Erwachsenenschutzrecht in Form einer Verordnung war schon damals in Wissenschaft und Praxis, sowie im Jahr 2017 ausdrücklich auch vom Europäischen Parlament[23], gefordert und auch von mir im Ergebnis der rechtsvergleichenden Betrachtung insbesondere mit Blick auf die unterschiedlichen internationalprivatrechtlichen Regelungen in den EU-Mitgliedstaaten befürwortet worden.

Allein durch eine in der Folge der vorgeschlagenen Ratsentscheidung künftig unionsweite Anwendung des ErwSÜ würden die Möglichkeiten des europäischen Rechtsraumes auch nach Ansicht der Kommission nicht ausgeschöpft. Vielmehr kann und soll die Zusammenarbeit innerhalb der Mitgliedstaaten auf der Grundlage des Grundsatzes des gegenseitigen Vertrauens zwischen den Mitgliedstaaten und der Erfahrungen mit der Harmonisierung anderer Bereiche der justitiellen Zusammenarbeit in Zivilsachen vertieft werden.[24] Die von der Kommission vorgeschlagene Verordnung über die Zuständigkeit, das anwendbare Recht, die Anerkennung und Vollstreckung von Maßnahmen und die Zusammenarbeit in Fragen betreffend den Schutz Erwachsener[25] soll ein EU-einheitliches Regelwerk schaffen und enthält auch Maßnahmen zur Erleichterung der digitalen Kommunikation, der Einführung eines europäischen Vertretungszertifikats, zur Einrichtung vernetzter Register mit Angaben zum Schutzstatus des Erwachsenen und zur Förderung einer engen Zusammenarbeit zwischen den zuständigen Behörden. Erklärte Ziele der EU-ErwSVO-E sind die Verbesserung des Schutzes der Rechte Erwachsener in grenzüberschreitenden Situationen in der EU und der Wirksamkeit und Schnelligkeit grenzüberschreitender Verfahren zum Schutz von Erwachsenen sowie die Erhöhung der diesbezüglichen Rechtssicherheit und Vorhersehbarkeit.[26]

---

[20] Haager Übereinkommen über die Zuständigkeit, das anzuwendende Recht, die Anerkennung, Vollstreckung und Zusammenarbeit auf dem Gebiet der elterlichen Verantwortung und der Maßnahmen zum Schutz von Kindern vom 19.10.1996.

[21] Dies sind bis dato lediglich Schottland, die Schweiz und Monaco.

[22] Vgl. hierzu COM(2023) final/2, 2f.

[23] Entschließung des Europäischen Parlaments vom 1.6.2017 mit Empfehlungen an die Kommission zum Schutz schutzbedürftiger Erwachsener (2015/2085(INL)) (ABl. 2018 C 307, 154).

[24] Vgl. die Pressemitteilung der Europäischen Kommission vom 31.5.2023, https://ec.europa.eu/commission/presscorner/detail/de/IP_23_2955 (abgerufen 13.3.2024).

[25] COM(2023) 280 final.

[26] Vgl. COM(2023) 280 final, ErwGr. 69.

Die Idee hinter den im Mai 2023 gemeinsam vorgelegten Vorschlägen der Kommission war es daher, dass die internationalprivatrechtlichen Normen des ErwSÜ für Drittstaaten unmittelbare Anwendung finden, während zwischen den Mitgliedstaaten der Europäischen Union die Regelungen des Übereinkommens mit den Abwandlungen und Ergänzungen der zu schaffenden EU-Verordnung gelten. Das ErwSÜ selbst gestattet gemäß seinem Art. 49 Abs. 2, dass Vertragsstaaten Vereinbarungen treffen, die in Bezug auf Erwachsene mit gewöhnlichem Aufenthalt in einem dieser Vertragsstaaten Bestimmungen über im ErwSÜ geregelte Angelegenheiten enthalten. Ebenso setzt das ErwSÜ bezüglich der Wirksamkeit der Schutzmaßnahmen und der Kooperation zwischen den Behörden nur einen Minimalstandard, der im Sinne der Verwirklichung der Ziele des Übereinkommens durch regionale Vereinbarungen durchaus heraufgesetzt werden darf.[27]

Ratsbeschluss und Verordnung sollen sich auf die Rechtsgrundlage des Art. 218 Abs. 6 AEUV iVm Art. 81 Abs. 2 AEUV betreffend die justizielle Zusammenarbeit in Zivil- und Handelssachen stützen.[28] Beide Vorschläge der Kommission haben es jedoch vor den Europawahlen im Juni 2024 nicht mehr in die Plenarebene geschafft und fallen damit nach Art. 240 GOEP dem Grundsatz der Diskontinuität anheim. Es ist nun an der Konferenz der Präsidenten zu Beginn der neuen Wahlperiode darüber zu entscheiden, ob diese „unerledigten Angelegenheiten" von vorn zu beginnen oder fortzusetzen sind. Die Verordnung würde nach Ablauf von 18 Monaten nach ihrer Veröffentlichung im Amtsblatt der Europäischen Union anwendbar und damit in den Mitgliedstaaten der EU unmittelbar anwendbares Recht. Nach Annahme des Ratsbeschlusses hätten diejenigen Mitgliedstaaten, die noch nicht Vertragsparteien des ErwSÜ sind, zwei Jahre Zeit, um dem Übereinkommen beizutreten. Zudem würde mit Annahme des Beschlusses das ErwSÜ zu einem Teil des Unionsrechts, was die Befugnis des Gerichtshofs der Europäischen Union mit sich bringen würde, dieses im Lichte der allgemeinen Grundsätze der Europäischen Union sowie der UN-BRK auszulegen[29].

III. Der Vorschlag einer Erwachsenenschutzverordnung (EU-ErwSVO-E)

Wie bereits dargelegt, ist es Ziel des vorgelegten Verordnungsvorschlages, dass zwischen den Mitgliedstaaten der EU die Regelungen des ErwSÜ mit Abwandlungen und Ergänzungen gelten. Die Abweichung von den Regelungen dieses Übereinkommens ist zum Teil völlig unproblematisch, zieht in anderen Bereichen jedoch Abgrenzungsschwierigkeiten nach sich. Neben einer summarischen Dar-

---

[27] So auch Franzina, Verso una più efficace protezione degli adulti fragili nell'unione europea, SIDIBlog, http://www.sidiblog.org/2023/07/06/verso-una-piu-efficace-protezione-degli-adulti-fragili-nellunione-europea (abgerufen 13.3.2024).

[28] Dies wird zum Teil kritisiert und stattdessen die Rechtsgrundlage betreffend das Familienrecht befürwortet, beispielsweise in Italien, vgl. Franzina, L'evoluzione del diritto internazionale privato della protezione degli adulti tra iniziative dell'Unione, modelli universali e norme interne JUS-ONLINE 4/2022, 212 (249 Fn. 63).

[29] Vgl. hierzu auch COM(2023) 280 final, ErwGr. 10 und 15.

stellung des Inhalts der EU-ErwSVO-E soll im Folgenden daher in der für den hiesigen Beitrag gebotenen Kürze insbesondere auf diese Friktionen eingegangen werden.

1. *Anwendungsbereich*

Der sachliche und persönliche Anwendungsbereich der Verordnung sind identisch mit dem des ErwSÜ, vgl. Art. 1 bis 3 EU-ErwSVO-E. Erwachsen im Sinne der Verordnung ist, wie auch im Rahmen des Übereinkommens, wer das 18. Lebensjahr vollendet hat, auch wenn nach dem Heimatrecht vor diesem Alter die Geschäftsfähigkeit erlangt worden sein sollte. Damit soll insbesondere eine Überschneidung mit dem Anwendungsbereich der Brüssel IIa-VO vermieden werden.[30] Wie im Anwendungsbereich des ErwSÜ ist jedoch auch hier die Anwendbarkeit für solche Maßnahmen gegeben, die für einen nunmehr Erwachsenen zu einem Zeitpunkt getroffen worden sind, in welchem er das 18. Lebensjahr noch nicht vollendet hatte. Der oben beschriebene Begriff der Schutzbedürftigkeit ist für ErwSÜ und EU-ErwSVO-E ebenfalls übereinstimmend auszulegen.

Maßgeblicher Anknüpfungspunkt für den räumlichen Anwendungsbereich der Verordnung ist gemäß Art. 59 Abs. 1 lit. a EU-ErwSVO-E in Anlehnung an das ErwSÜ der gewöhnliche Aufenthalt des schutzbedürftigen Erwachsenen in einem EU-Mitgliedstaat. Damit greift auch die EU-ErwSVO-E auf das nunmehr im europäischen Kollisionsrecht dominierende Anknüpfungsmoment des gewöhnlichen Aufenthalts[31] zurück.

Intertemporal sieht Art. 65 EU-ErwSVO-E die Geltung für nach dem Geltungsbeginn der Verordnung getroffene Maßnahmen, förmlich errichtete oder eingetragene Urkunden und bestätigte Vertretungsmachten vor. Vergleichbar dem ErwSÜ soll die Verordnung jedoch ab ihrem Inkrafttreten auch für zuvor erteilte Vertretungsmachten gelten, sofern diese zuvor unter Bedingungen erteilt wurden, die denen des Art. 15 ErwSÜ entsprechen.

2. *Zuständigkeit und anwendbares Recht*

a) Ergänzung des Zuständigkeitssystems des ErwSÜ um die Möglichkeit der Prorogation

Hinsichtlich der Zuständigkeitsregelungen verweist Art. 5 EU-ErwSVO-E zunächst vollständig auf die Zuständigkeitsregelungen des ErwSÜ, ergänzt diese sodann jedoch in den Art. 6 und 7 um eine nicht ausschließliche Zuständigkeit aufgrund einer Wahl des Erwachsenen. Diese soll gemäß Art. 6 Abs. 1, 4 EU-ErwSVO-E gleichrangig neben der Aufenthaltszuständigkeit nach Art. 5, 6 ErwSÜ stehen.

Die Möglichkeit der Prorogation ist insbesondere mit Blick auf die Kollisionsnorm des ErwSÜ zur Vorsorgevollmacht, die eine begrenzte Rechtswahl zulässt, eine begrüßenswerte Erweiterung für diejenigen, deren gewöhnlicher Aufenthalt

---

[30] Vgl. COM(2023) 280 final, ErwGr. 65.

[31] Vgl. Staudinger, BGB/von Hein, 2022, EGBGB Art. 24 Rn. 6.

sich zum Zeitpunkt der Errichtung der Vorsorgevollmacht bzw. der Wahl der zuständigen Behörden in einem Mitgliedstaat der Europäischen Union befindet. Sie bringt jedoch im Zusammenhang mit der Verweisung der Verordnung auf die Regelungen des ErwSÜ zum anwendbaren Recht Schwierigkeiten mit sich, auf die noch näher einzugehen sein wird.

b) Unveränderte Übernahme der Kollisionsregeln des Übereinkommens durch Verweisung auf Kapitel III des ErwSÜ

In Bezug auf das anwendbare Recht verweist Art. 8 EU-ErwSVO-E vollumfänglich auf die diesbezüglichen Regelungen in Kapitel III, mithin Art. 13 bis 21, des ErwSÜ. Damit wird es nach dem Vorschlag der Kommission auch der Verordnung an einer Kollisionsnorm zur Bestimmung des anwendbaren Rechts in Bezug auf gesetzliche Vertretungsbefugnisse, wie etwa die gegenseitige Vertretung von Ehegatten in Angelegenheiten der Gesundheitssorge nach § 1358 BGB, Art. 378 des Schweizerischen Zivilgesetzbuches, § 268 des österreichischen Allgemeinen Bürgerlichen Gesetzbuches oder Art. 7 Abs. 1 des Lettischen Patientenrechtegesetzes, fehlen.[32] Auch für isolierte Patientenverfügungen, also solche, die nicht mit einer Vorsorgevollmacht oder einer Betreuungsverfügung verbunden sind, fehlt es dann nach wie vor an einer einheitlichen europäischen Regelung, da weder des ErwSÜ[33] noch die EU-ErwSVO-E diese – in Gänze[34] – erfassen.

aa) Geltung des Gleichlaufprinzips

Sowohl im ErwSÜ als auch in der EU-ErwSVO-E gilt aufgrund der umfänglichen Verweisung der Verordnung auf die Regelungen des Übereinkommens das Prinzip des Gleichlaufs von forum und ius. Dies folgt letztlich aus dem Bestreben, den Erwachsenenschutz wirksam und unter denkbar geringem Aufwand, umfassend und schnell zu gewährleisten. Dazu trägt die Anwendung des eigenen Rechts durch die zuständigen Gerichte oder Behörden[35] ganz erheblich bei. Zusammen mit der Regelanknüpfung an den gewöhnlichen Aufenthalt des Erwachsenen wird damit zumeist auch diejenige Rechtsordnung berufen, zu der in aller Regel die

[32] Für das ErwSÜ vgl. Lagarde, Protection of Adults Convention, Explanatory Report, https://assets.hcch.net/docs/1509ab33-c2fe-4532–981c-7aa4dad9ba45.pdf (abgerufen 13.3.2024), Rn. 90; Staudinger, BGB/von Hein, 2022, ESÜ Art. 4 Rn. 5 mwN; Kobsik, Antizipierte Erklärungen in Gesundheitsangelegenheiten im grenzüberschreitenden Verkehr, 2020, S. 322f.; in Bezug auf den Verordnungsentwurf daher von einer verpassten Chance sprechend Franzina, Verso una più efficace protezione degli adulti fragili nell'unione europea, SIDIBlog, http://www.sidiblog.org/2023/07/06/verso-una-piu-efficace-protezione-degli-adulti-fragili-nellunione-europea (abgerufen 13.3.2024).

[33] Vgl. Staudinger, BGB/von Hein, 2022, ESÜ Art. 15 Rn. 16 mwN.

[34] ErwSÜ und dem folgend EU-ErwSVO-E erfassen lediglich die Bindung von hoheitlichen Fürsorgepersonen insgesamt und von gewillkürten Stellvertretern in Gesundheitsangelegenheiten im Außenverhältnis an die in einer Patientenverfügung enthaltenen Erklärungen, vgl. näher Kobsik, Antizipierte Erklärungen in Gesundheitsangelegenheiten, S. 423f.

[35] Das ErwSÜ spricht im Allgemeinen von Behörden, seien es Gerichte oder Verwaltungsbehörden, vgl. Art. 5 Abs. 1 ErwSÜ. Im Folgenden wird daher der Begriff Behörden gleichsam als Oberbegriff verwendet. Gemäß COM(2023) 280 final, ErwGr. 18, soll der Begriff „Behörde" in der Verordnung ebenso zu verstehen sein.

aktuell engste Beziehung besteht, da hier der Lebensmittelpunkt liegt und das Schutzbedürfnis ent- bzw. besteht.

bb) Problem der Anwendbarkeit der Kollisionsnormen des ErwSÜ bei Zuständigkeit (nur) aufgrund der EU-ErwSVO-E

Die Geltung des Gleichlaufprinzips im ErwSÜ wirft im Zusammenhang mit der EU-ErwSVO-E die gleiche Frage auf, die sich bereits im Verhältnis des KSÜ zur Brüssel IIb-VO[36] stellt, namentlich ob die Kollisionsnormen des Übereinkommens auch dann anwendbar sind, wenn sich eine Zuständigkeit nach dem ErwSÜ nicht ergibt.

Im Gegensatz zur Brüssel IIb-VO fehlt es der EU-ErwSVO-E gänzlich an einer Regelung zu der Frage, inwiefern in einem solchen Fall die Kollisionsnormen des ErwSÜ Anwendung finden sollen. Weder Art. 59 EU-ErwSVO-E noch die Erwägungsgründe verhalten sich zu dieser Problematik.[37]

Da Art. 5 EU-ErwSVO-E auf die Zuständigkeitsregelungen des ErwSÜ verweist, sind insoweit auch Art. 13, 14 ErwSÜ ohne Weiteres als Kollisionsnormen anwendbar. Jedoch enthält Art. 6 EU-ErwSVO-E mit der Möglichkeit der Prorogation eine zusätzliche, im ErwSÜ jedenfalls nicht primär vorgesehene Zuständigkeitsnorm.

Im Einklang mit der im Praxis-Handbuch für die Anwendung des KSÜ niedergelegten Auffassung[38], sollten die Art. 13, 14 ErwSÜ, welchem das KSÜ als Vorbild diente, als Kollisionsnormen nur dann angewendet werden, soweit sich eine fiktive Zuständigkeit nach dem ErwSÜ ergäbe.[39] Die nach der EU-ErwSVO-E bestehende Zuständigkeit müsste demnach auf der Basis eines Zuständigkeitsgrundes bestehen, der sich auch im ErwSÜ findet. Nur so würde die in Art. 13 Abs. 1 ErwSÜ ausgedrückte Zuständigkeitswertung – Anwendung der *lex fori* des/der vom Übereinkommen für zuständig gehaltenen Gerichts/Behörde – hinreichend beachtet[40]. Findet sich kein entsprechender Zuständigkeitsgrund im ErwSÜ, müsste das anwendbare Recht im Fall der Prorogation *lege fori* bestimmt werden.[41]

---

[36] Vgl. hierzu Kobsik, Antizipierte Erklärungen in Gesundheitsangelegenheiten im grenzüberschreitenden Verkehr, 2020, S. 327–333.

[37] In ErwGr. 92 Brüssel IIb-VO findet sich die Maßgabe, dass der Verweis in Art. 15 Abs. 1 KSÜ auf die „Bestimmungen des Kapitels II" dieses Übereinkommens vor den Gerichten eines Mitgliedstaates als Verweis auf die Bestimmungen der Brüssel IIb-VO verstanden werden sollte.

[38] Praxis-Handbuch für die Anwendung des Haager Übereinkommens vom 19.10.1996 über die Zuständigkeit, das anzuwendende Recht, die Anerkennung, Vollstreckung und Zusammenarbeit auf dem Gebiet der elterlichen Verantwortung und der Maßnahmen zum Schutz von Kindern, https://assets.hcch.net/docs/b48321ba-0d95-44b8-8fbe-2a105e02dd78.pdf (abgerufen 29.12.2023), Rn. 9.1 Fn. 251 mit Verweis noch auf die Brüssel IIa-VO. In dem noch im Entwurfsstadium befindlichen Praxis-Handbuch für das ErwSÜ, finden sich bislang keine Ausführungen zu dieser Problematik, vgl. Revised Draft Practical Handbook on the Operation of the 2000 Protection of Adults Convention, Prel. Doc. No 4 of July 2023 (second revised edition), https://assets.hcch.net/docs/af8b7c86-6130-490d-b1fd-e3760da670d0.pdf (abgerufen 13.3.2024).

[39] AM Rauscher, EuZPR/EuIPR/Hilbnig-Lugani, 4. Aufl. 2016, KSÜ Art. 15 Rn. 2ff.

[40] So zum KSÜ Rauscher, EuZPR/EuIPR/Rauscher, 4. Aufl. 2015, Brüssel-IIa VO Art. 8 Rn. 24, jurisPK-BGB/Duden, 2023 EGBGB Art. 21 Rn. 39; OLG Karlsruhe 26.08.2015 – 18 UF 92/15, juris Rn. 18.

[41] Vgl. für das Verhältnis von KSÜ zur Brüssel IIa-VO Rauscher, EuZPR/EuIPR/Rauscher, 4. Aufl. 2015, Brüssel IIa-VO Art. 8 Rn. 25.

Es stellt sich somit die Frage, ob die Zuständigkeitswahl nach der EU-ErwSVO-E einen Zuständigkeitsgrund darstellt, der sich auch im ErwSÜ findet. Dafür müssen zunächst deren Voraussetzungen nach dem Verordnungsentwurf näher betrachtet werden.

Nach dem Konzept der Art. 6, 7 EU-ErwSVO-E handelt es sich um eine konkurrierende Zuständigkeit, wonach die gewählten Behörden eines Mitgliedstaates der Europäischen Union zuständig sein sollen, wenn die nach den Art. 5–8 ErwSÜ zuständigen Behörden ihre Zuständigkeit nicht ausgeübt haben. Weitere, kumulativ zu erfüllende, Voraussetzungen der Prorogation sind, dass der Erwachsene im Zeitpunkt der Wahl noch in der Lage war, seine Interessen zu schützen und dass die Wahrnehmung dieser Zuständigkeit im Interesse des Erwachsenen liegt. In formeller Hinsicht verlangt Art. 6 Abs. 3 EU-ErwSVO-E eine datierte und vom Erwachsenen unterzeichnete schriftliche Erklärung. Elektronische Übermittlungen, die die dauerhafte Aufzeichnung der Wahl der Zuständigkeit ermöglichen, sind der Schriftform gleichgestellt.

Dem ErwSÜ ist eine Zuständigkeit von Behörden, die der Erwachsene gewählt hat, jedenfalls nicht gänzlich fremd. Auch das Übereinkommen kennt eine die Selbstbestimmung des Erwachsenen anerkennende und fördernde[42] Wahl des Gerichtsstandes durch den Erwachsenen, wie Art. 8 Abs. 2 lit. d ErwSÜ zeigt. Eine solche Wahl der zuständigen Behörden hat nach den Regelungen des Übereinkommens jedoch lediglich zur Folge, dass die derart von dem Erwachsenen benannten Behörden von den nach Art. 5, 6 des Übereinkommens zuständigen Behörden ersucht werden können, Maßnahmen zum Schutz des Erwachsenen zu treffen, wenn erstere der Meinung sind, dass dies dem Wohl des Erwachsenen dient.[43] Die Zuständigkeit vom Erwachsenen gewählter Behörden ist damit nach dem ErwSÜ eine subsidiäre, die erst auf ein Ersuchen der sonst zuständigen Behörden bzw. mit deren Einverständnis auf ein Ersuchen der gewählten Behörden hin, ausgeübt werden kann. Zu beachten ist dabei allerdings, dass das ErwSÜ in Art. 8 Abs. 1 und der Präambel einen Vorrang des Selbstbestimmungsrechts des Erwachsenen gebietet. Dies sollte dazu führen, dass die Zuständigkeitswahl des Erwachsenen regelmäßig zu befolgen ist und diese sich damit gegen die Primärzuständigkeit der Behörden nach Art. 5 und 6 ErwSÜ durchsetzt.[44] Dadurch kann auch in Bezug auf eine Vorsorgevollmacht, für die nach Art. 15 Abs. 1, 2 ErwSÜ eine beschränkte Rechtswahl möglich ist, der das Übereinkommen prägende Gleichlauf von Zuständigkeit und anzuwendendem Recht hergestellt werden. Auch wenn das ErwSÜ damit keine echte Zuständigkeit kraft Prorogation kennt[45], so weisen die direkte Prorogation

---

[42] Vgl. Revised Draft Practical Handbook on the Operation of the 2000 Protection of Adults Convention, Prel. Doc. No 4 of July 2023 (second revised edition), https://assets.hcch.net/docs/af8b7c86-6130-490d-b1fd-e3760da670d0.pdf (abgerufen 13.3.2024), Ziffer 5.8; Lagarde, Protection of Adults Convention, Explanatory Report, https://assets.hcch.net/docs/1509ab33-c2fe-4532–981c-7aa4dad9ba45.pdf (abgerufen 13.3.2024), Rn. 71.

[43] Umgekehrt könnten die von dem Erwachsenen gewählten Behörden die nach Art. 5, 6 ErwSÜ zuständigen Behörden ersuchen, tätig zu werden, Art. 8 Abs. 1 ErwSÜ.

[44] So Münchener Kommentar zum BGB/Lipp, 9. Aufl. 2024, ESÜ Art. 8 Rn. 16.

[45] So auch Staudinger, BGB/von Hein, 2022, ESÜ Art. 8 Rn. 11 „limitierte Prorogationsfreiheit“; Helms FamRZ 2008, 1995 (1997) „keine echte Prorogation“.

nach Art. 6 EU-ErwSVO-E und die nur mittelbare Prorogationsmöglichkeit nach Art. 8 Abs. 2 lit. d ErwSÜ doch etliche Gemeinsamkeiten auf.

Voraussetzung der Ausübung dieser Zuständigkeit ist in beiden Fällen, dass dies dem Wohl bzw. Interesse des Erwachsenen dient. Ferner sind die Wirksamkeitsvoraussetzungen der Rechtswahl im Wesentlichen gleich. Sowohl nach Art. 8 Abs. 2 lit. d ErwSÜ als auch nach Art. 6 Abs. 1 EU-ErwSVO-E, ist eine ausdrückliche Erklärung in Schriftform erforderlich.[46] In beiden Fällen ist zudem erforderlich, dass der Erwachsene eine solche Erklärung überhaupt wirksam abgeben konnte. Diese Voraussetzung findet sich ausdrücklich in Art. 6 Abs. 1 lit. a EU-ErwSVO-E, wonach verlangt wird, dass die Wahl in einem Zeitpunkt getroffen wurde, in welchem der Erwachsene noch selbst in der Lage war, seine Interessen zu schützen. Art. 15 ErwSÜ stellt zwar ausdrücklich keine solche Bedingung auf, jedoch ist nach allgemeinen Regeln für Zustandekommen und Wirksamkeit einer Rechtswahl, ebenso wie für die Wahl der zuständigen Behörden, eine gewisse Einsichtsfähigkeit erforderlich. Deren Vorliegen ist im Rahmen der Rechtswahl nach Art. 15 Abs. 1, 2 ErwSÜ nach überwiegender Meinung nach dem gewählten Recht zu beurteilen.[47] Gleiches erscheint auch im Rahmen von Art. 6 Abs. 1 EU-ErwSVO-E sachgerecht. Schließlich findet sich in Art. 6 Abs. 1 lit. c EU-ErwSVO-E mit der Maßgabe, dass die Zuständigkeit kraft Prorogation nur ausgeübt werden darf, wenn die nach den Art. 5–8 ErwSÜ zuständigen Behörden ihre Zuständigkeit nicht ausgeübt haben, eine Wertung, die sich auch in Art. 8 ErwSÜ findet: Die Behörden des Staates, in dem der Erwachsene seinen gewöhnlichen Aufenthalt hat, sind in der Regel am besten geeignet, über Schutzmaßnahmen zu entscheiden.

Insgesamt berufen sich Behörden von EU-Mitgliedstaaten, wenn sie ihre Zuständigkeit auf Art. 6 EU-ErwSVO-E stützen damit auf einen Zuständigkeitsgrund, der so – wenn auch in anderer Ausprägung – im ErwSÜ zu finden ist. Daher sind auch im Fall der Prorogation nach Art. 6 EU-ErwSVO-E die Art. 13, 14 ErwSÜ als Kollisionsnormen heranzuziehen.[48] Somit gilt auch insoweit der Gleichlauf von forum und ius und führt eine nach Art. 6 EU-ErwSVO-E wirksame Prorogation zugleich zur Anwendung der lex fori durch die hiernach zuständigen Behörden.

3. *Anerkennung und Vollstreckung*

Die Maßnahmen des Erwachsenenschutzes, die von den Behörden eines Mitgliedstaates getroffen wurden, werden nach Art. 9 Abs. 1 EU-ErwSVO-E, wie im Rahmen des Art. 22 Abs. 1 ErwSÜ, in den anderen Mitgliedstaaten anerkannt,

---

[46] Für das ErwSÜ vgl. Revised Draft Practical Handbook on the Operation of the 2000 Protection of Adults Convention, Prel. Doc. No 4 of July 2023 (second revised edition), https://assets.hcch.net/docs/af8b7c86-6130-490d-b1fd-e3760da670d0.pdf (abgerufen 13.3.2024), Ziffer 2.15; Staudinger, BGB/von Hein, 2022, ESÜ Art. 8 Rn. 11.

[47] Staudinger, BGB/von Hein, 2022, ESÜ Art. 15 Rn. 24 mwN.

[48] So auch von Hein, Towards an EU Regulation on the International Protection of Adults, veröffentlicht am 5.6.2023 auf Conflict of Laws.net https://conflictoflaws.net/2023/towards-an-eu-regulation-on-the-international-protection-of-adults/ (abgerufen 13.3.2024), allerdings ohne nähere Begründung.

ohne dass es hierfür eines besonderen Verfahrens bedarf[49]. Gleichwohl kann jede betroffene Person, einschließlich des betroffenen Erwachsenen eine Entscheidung über die Anerkennung oder Nichtanerkennung beantragen. Artikel 10 EU-ErwSVO-E enthält einen abschließenden[50] Katalog von Gründen, bei deren Vorliegen die Anerkennung – zum Schutz insbesondere der Grundrechte des Erwachsenen[51] – versagt werden darf. Dies ist der Fall, wenn außer in dringenden Fällen, der Erwachsene im Rahmen eines Gerichtsverfahrens oder Verwaltungsverfahrens vor Erlass der Maßnahme nicht gehört worden ist, die Anerkennung dem ordre public des Mitgliedstaats, indem sie beantragt wurde, offensichtlich widerspricht, wenn die Maßnahme – bei Vorliegen der übrigen Anerkennungsvoraussetzungen im ersuchten Mitgliedstaat – mit einer später in einem nach Artikel 5 oder 6 der EU-ErwSVO-E zuständigen Drittstaat getroffenen Maßnahme unvereinbar ist oder das Verfahren nach Art. 14 EU-ErwSVO-E nicht eingehalten wurde. Nach der Verordnung soll somit – im Gegensatz zum ErwSÜ – insbesondere die Zuständigkeit der Behörden des Ursprungsmitgliedstaates nicht überprüft werden.[52] Auch dies soll auf der Grundlage des Gegenseitigen Vertrauens zwischen den EU-Mitgliedstaaten der Erleichterung und Beschleunigung dienen und damit zu einem wirksamen grenzüberschreitenden Erwachsenenschutz führen.

Was die Vollstreckung angeht, so wird durch Art. 11 EU-ErwSVO-E das in Art. 25 ErwSÜ erforderliche Verfahren der Vollstreckbarerklärung einer in einem Vertragsstaat getroffenen und dort vollstreckbaren Maßnahme (Exequatur) im Verhältnis zwischen den Mitgliedstaaten der EU abgeschafft.[53] Somit wird innerhalb des europäischen Rechtsraumes die Vollstreckung vereinfacht, was einen weiteren Schritt zur von der Kommission angestrebten vorbehaltlosen Anerkennung und Vollstreckung von Entscheidungen anderer EU-Staaten markiert[54]. Das Verfahren der Vollstreckung von in einem anderen Mitgliedstaat getroffenen Maßnahmen richtet sich nach der lex fori des Vollstreckungsmitgliedstaates, Art. 12 EU-ErwSVO-E.

Sowohl für die Anerkennung als auch für die Vollstreckung schließt Art. 13 EU-ErwSVO-E eine Nachprüfung in der Sache aus, beschreibt Art. 14 EU-ErwSVO-E weitere Einzelheiten zum Verfahren und schafft Art. 15 EU-ErwSVO-E die Rechtsgrundlage für eine Bescheinigung, aus der der Inhalt der jeweiligen Maß-

[49] Von den EU-Mitgliedstaaten, die nicht Vertragsstaaten des ErwSÜ sind, sehen lediglich Dänemark, Italien, Polen und Slowenien eine solche Anerkennung kraft Gesetzes vor, vgl. Adriaenssens/Borrett/Fialon et al., Study on the cross-border legal protection of vulnerable adults in the EU, 2022, S. 94ff. (Abschnitt 2.3.2.2.).

[50] Vgl. COM(2023) 280 final, ErwGr. 26.

[51] COM(2023) 280 final, 11.

[52] Vgl. COM(2023) 280 final, ErwGr. 25, sowie Art. 22 Abs. 2 lit. a, 25 Abs. 3 ErwSÜ.

[53] In Angelegenheiten des Erwachsenenschutzes sehen Dänemark, Griechenland, Ungarn und Schweden bereits jetzt grundsätzlich kein Verfahren der Vollstreckbarerklärung vor, vgl. Adriaenssens/Borrett/Fialon et al., Study on the cross-border legal protection of vulnerable adults in the EU, 2022, S. 96ff. (Abschnitt 2.3.2.3).

[54] Die Verwirklichung der Abschaffung des Exequaturverfahrens zeigt sich unter anderem in der Brüssel Ia- und Brüssel IIb-VO sowie in der „zweiten Generation" der EuZPR-Verordnungen – den Vollstreckungstitel-/Mahn-/Bagatell- und Unterhaltsverordnungen [Begriff nach Frattini ZEuP 2006, 225 (230)].

nahme hervorgeht, wofür ein Formblatt nach Anhang I der Verordnung zu verwenden sein soll.

Die Nichtüberprüfung der Zuständigkeit des Ursprungsmitgliedstaates sowie die Abschaffung des Exaquaturverfahrens sind Ausprägung des gegenseitigen Vertrauens zwischen den Mitgliedstaaten und dürften zu einer wesentlichen Vereinfachung und Beschleunigung der Anerkennung und Vollstreckung, insbesondere zur Vermeidung unnötiger Verfahren innerhalb des europäischen Rechtsraumes beitragen.

4. *Beweiskraft öffentlicher Urkunden*

Nach Art. 16 EU-ErwSVO-E haben in einem Mitgliedstaat errichtete öffentliche Urkunden in einem anderen Mitgliedstaat die gleiche formelle Beweiskraft wie im Ursprungsmitgliedstaat oder die damit am ehesten vergleichbare Wirkung, es sei denn, dies widerspricht offensichtlich dem ordre public des betreffenden Mitgliedstaates. Um dies zu erleichtern sieht Art. 17 EU-ErwSVO-E die Ausstellung einer Bescheinigung unter Verwendung eines Formblatts nach Anhang II der Verordnung vor. Ziel ist es, dass öffentliche Urkunden, die auf den Schutz von Erwachsenen und ihren Interessen ausgerichtet sind, in allen Mitgliedstaaten anerkannt werden. Dies soll etwa Vorsorgevollmachten und Patientenverfügungen erfassen.[55] Vorausgesetzt, derartige Erklärungen sind im Wege einer öffentlichen Urkunde errichtet worden, würde dies deren Umlauffähigkeit signifikant erhöhen. Für Vorsorgevollmachten soll diese Regelung auch eine Alternative zur Verwendung des durch die EU-ErwSVO-E geschaffenen Europäischen Vertretungszertifikats darstellen[56] und Bestehen, Art und Umfang der Vertretungsmacht beweisen können. Eine in einer öffentlichen Urkunde verkörperte Patientenverfügung könnte Beweis darüber erbringen, dass der Verfasser zum Zeitpunkt der Erklärung einwilligungsfähig war und welche Wünsche er in Bezug auf bestimmte medizinische Behandlungen zu diesem Zeitpunkt wirksam geäußert hat.

5. *Europäisches Vertretungszertifikat*

Ein Novum findet sich in den Art. 34 bis 44 EU-ErwSVO-E mit dem Europäischen Vertretungszertifikat („European Certificate of Representation“, im Folgenden EuVZ), welches die Bescheinigung nach Art. 38 ErwSÜ ersetzen soll, die bislang in der Praxis eine eher unbedeutende Rolle spielt.[57] Ähnlich der Bescheinigung nach dem ErwSÜ soll das EuVZ nach Art. 35 Abs. 1 EU-ErwSVO-E der Verwendung durch Vertreter dienen, die in einem anderen Mitgliedstaat ihre Befugnisse zur Vertretung von Erwachsenen geltend machen müssen, die aufgrund einer Beeinträchtigung oder Unzulänglichkeit nicht in der Lage sind, ihre Interessen zu schützen. Die Verwendung des EuVZ durch den Vertreter ist nicht verpflichtend, der Vertreter kann seine Vertretungsmacht auch in anderer Art und

---

[55] Vgl. COM(2023) 280 final, ErwGr. 19.

[56] Vgl. COM(2023) 280 final, ErwGr. 37.

[57] Franzina, Verso una più efficace protezione degli adulti fragili nell'unione europea, SIDIBlog, http://www.sidiblog.org/2023/07/06/verso-una-piu-efficace-protezione-degli-adulti-fragili-nellunione-europea (abgerufen 13.3.2024).

Weise nachweisen. Auch ersetzt das EuVZ nicht innerstaatliche vergleichbare Schriftstücke (Subsidiaritätsprinzip). Das EuVZ entfaltet jedoch nach seiner Ausstellung im Inland die gleichen Wirkungen, wie in dem Mitgliedstaat, für den es ausgestellt worden ist. Es kann eine Vertretungsmacht nachweisen, die auf einer Maßnahme oder einer bestätigten Vollmacht beruht. Art. 35 Abs. 2 EU-ErwSVO-E listet nicht abschließend mögliche nachzuweisende Vertretungsbefugnisse auf, darunter auch medizinische Entscheidungen, einschließlich der Erteilung und Verweigerung der Einwilligung zu einer medizinischen Behandlung. In dem in Anhang III der EU-ErwSVO-E vorgegebenen Formblatt finden sich noch weit mehr Beispiele für Vertretungsbefugnisse in Gesundheitsangelegenheiten, aber auch betreffend etwa die Vermögenssorge oder die Unterbringung des Erwachsenen, die durch Ankreuzen ausgewählt werden können. Inhaltlich enthält das EuVZ zudem Angaben darüber, welche Befugnisse der Vertreter hat und gegebenenfalls welche nicht sowie zu Einschränkungen dieser Befugnisse oder Bedingungen, die an die Befugnisse geknüpft sind, Art. 39 EU-ErwSVO-E.

Für die Ausstellung des EuVZ zuständig ist der Mitgliedstaat, in dem die Maßnahme ergriffen oder die Vertretungsmacht bestätigt wurde. Sie erfolgt auf einen Antrag eines Vertreters, der aufgrund einer in diesem Mitgliedstaat getroffenen Maßnahme oder einer dort bestätigten Vertretungsmacht berechtigt ist, den Erwachsenen zu vertreten, Art. 36, 37 EU-ErwSVO-E. In der Zusammenschau mit ErwGr. 36 EU-ErwSVO-E ergibt sich, dass eine solche Antragstellung damit erst ab dem Zeitpunkt möglich sein soll, in dem der Erwachsene insoweit schutzbedürftig ist, seine Interessen also nicht mehr selbst schützen kann. Antragstellung und Ausstellung „für den Fall, dass …" sind somit ausgeschlossen. Dies mag einerseits einer Missbrauchsgefahr vorbeugen, andererseits bedeutet dies jedoch auch einen Verlust an Geschwindigkeit für den schutzbedürftigen Erwachsenen. Angesichts der Aufnahme von etwaigen Beschränkungen der Vertretungsbefugnisse oder Bedingungen, die an diese geknüpft sind, erscheint diese im Ergebnis Zeit kostende Einschränkung wenig sachgerecht. Eine zeitsparende Alternative dürfte hier die Errichtung einer Vorsorgevollmacht in öffentlicher Urkunde darstellen, die aufgrund der Regelungen in Art. 16, 17 EU-ErwSVO-E im Vorsorgefall unmittelbar die dort genannten Wirkungen entfalten kann.

Vor Ausstellung des EuVZ nimmt die ausstellende Behörde eine umfangreiche Prüfung nach Art. 38 Abs. 1 EU-ErwSVO-E vor. Für das EuVZ ist das Formblatt nach Anhang III der Verordnung zu verwenden.[58] Das mit sechzehn Seiten sehr umfangreiche Formblatt wird in sämtlichen Amtssprachen der EU zur Verfügung stehen. Allein hierdurch wird der Gebrauch von Vorsorgevollmachten im europäischen Rechtsraum erheblich vereinfacht und beschleunigt, da Zeit und Kosten einer sonst erforderlichen Übersetzung eingespart werden können. Die Gültigkeitsdauer des EuVZ ist grundsätzlich auf ein Jahr zu befristen, im Einzelfall kann hier-

[58] Es wird grundsätzlich in der Sprache des Mitgliedstaats der ausstellenden Behörde ausgefüllt, auf Ersuchen des Antragstellers kann es jedoch auch in einer anderen Amtssprache der EU ausgestellt werden.

von nach oben oder unten abgewichen werden, Art. 38 Abs. 9 EU-ErwSVO-E. Hier kann unter anderem eine Rolle spielen, ob eine Änderung der Umstände in Bezug auf die Schutzbedürftigkeit des Erwachsenen wahrscheinlich ist. Mit der begrenzten Gültigkeit soll gewährleistet werden, dass die ausstellende Behörde regelmäßig überprüft, ob sich die Rechtslage in Bezug auf den Erwachsenen geändert hat, etwa durch eine nachfolgende behördliche Maßnahme oder einen Widerruf der Vertretungsbefugnis.

Nach Art. 40 EU-ErwSVO-E entfaltet das EuVZ in allen Mitgliedstaaten seine Wirkung, ohne dass es eines besonderen Verfahrens bedürfte. Es bildet zwar keinen vollstreckbaren Titel, begründet jedoch die Vermutung, dass es festgestellte Sachverhalte[59] zutreffend aufweist und der benannte Vertreter über die darin beschriebenen Befugnisse verfügt sowie keine nicht genannten Beschränkungen oder Bedingung gelten. Insoweit wird auch ein Gutglaubensschutz gewährt. Aufgrund der Wirkung des EuVZ können unterschiedliche Wirksamkeitsvoraussetzungen nach den nationalen Rechtsordnungen überwunden werden, aber auch das Nichtvorhandensein eines vergleichbaren Rechtsinstituts autonomer Vorsorge. Die Wirkung des Art. 40 EU-ErwSVO-E tritt unabhängig davon ein, ob der Staat, in dem das EuVZ verwendet werden soll, in seinem nationalen Recht ein vergleichbares Rechtsinstitut vorsieht. Grenzen setzt dieser Wirkung allenfalls der nationale ordre public.

Berichtigung, Änderung und Widerruf des EuVZ sind in Art. 42 EU-ErwSVO-E geregelt, Art. 43 EU-ErwSVO-E sieht zudem die Schaffung von Rechtsbehelfen in den Mitgliedstaaten im Zusammenhang mit der Ausstellung des EuVZ vor. Im Zusammenspiel mit Art. 42, 43 EU-ErwSVO-E regelt Art. 44 EU-ErwSVO-E die Möglichkeit der Aussetzung der Wirkungen des EuVZ.

6. *Zentrale Behörden, Errichtung und Vernetzung von Schutzregistern*

Art. 18–32 EU-ErwSVO-E regeln die Schaffung und die Aufgaben von Zentralen Behörden in den Mitgliedstaaten. Hierdurch soll insbesondere die Zusammenarbeit der Behörden untereinander gefördert werden. Es ist davon auszugehen, dass Mitgliedstaaten, die bereits Vertragsstaaten des ErwSÜ sind, die bereits hierfür zuständigen Zentralen Behörden auch mit dieser Aufgabe betrauen werden. Die Einrichtung und Vernetzung von öffentlichen Registern zu Vertretungsbefugnissen und deren gegenseitige Vernetzung ist eine weitere Modifikation der Regelungen des ErwSÜ im Verordnungsvorschlag, die keine Abstimmungsprobleme mit sich bringen dürfte. Nach Art. 45 bis 48 EU-ErwSVO-E sind sogenannte Schutzregister zu schaffen in denen die Mitgliedstaaten Informationen über die auf ihrem Hoheitsgebiet getroffenen Schutzmaßnahmen und, wenn die lex fori die Bestätigung von Vertretungsmachten vorsieht, über solche Vertretungsmachten gespeichert werden. Bereits bestehende elektronische Register über andere, von einer zuständigen Behörde registrierte Vertretungsmachten, für die das nationale Recht keine Bestätigung vorsieht, müssen angepasst werden, um mit den Schutzregistern nach

---

[59] Soweit sie in den Anwendungsbereich der EU-ErwSVO-E fallen, Art. 40 Abs. 2 EU-ErwSVO-E am Ende.

Art. 45 EU-ErwSVO-E interoperabel zu sein.[60] Die Kommission soll im Wege von Durchführungsakten für eine Vernetzung der Register sorgen, auch eine Suchfunktion in allen Amtssprachen der Union soll zur Verfügung gestellt werden, Art. 47, 48 EU-ErwSVO-E. Die Errichtung, Führung und Vernetzung der Schutzregister sollen den kontinuierlichen Schutz des Erwachsenen in grenzüberschreitenden Situationen in der Union und damit Rechtssicherheit gewährleisten. Interoperabilität und Verfügbarkeit der dort hinterlegten Informationen sollen auch verhindern, dass parallele Verfahren eingeleitet werden oder bestehende Vertretungsbefugnisse nicht berücksichtigt werden.[61]

Art. 49–54 EU-ErwSVO-E schließlich enthalten Regelungen zur digitalen Kommunikation und zum Datenschutz, auf die hier nicht näher eingegangen werden soll.

IV. Fazit

25 Jahre nach Abschluss des Haager Übereinkommens über den Internationalen Schutz von Erwachsenen bestehen auf diesem Gebiet leider noch immer den Maßgaben des Art. 12 UN-BRK und auch der unionsrechtlichen Personenfreizügigkeit nicht gerecht werdende Schutzlücken bei Sachverhalten mit internationalem Bezug. Die von der Kommission vorgeschlagene Ratsentscheidung, die die Mitgliedstaaten unter Fristsetzung ermächtigt, dem ErwSÜ beizutreten oder im Interesse der Union Vertragsstaat dieses Übereinkommens zu bleiben, ist längst überfällig. Zahlreiche Kampagnen der Vergangenheit haben schließlich nicht zu einer signifikanten Steigerung der Zahl der Vertragsstaaten des ErwSÜ geführt, obwohl es generell als gelungenes Instrument zum Schutz von Erwachsenen in grenzüberschreitenden Situationen gilt, die nicht mehr selbst für ihre Interessen sorgen können.

Die vorgeschlagene Verordnung wurde in Wissenschaft und Praxis ebenfalls seit geraumer Zeit gefordert und gibt die Möglichkeit, im Verhältnis der EU-Mitgliedstaaten endlich den für einen effektiven internationalen Erwachsenenschutz benötigten einheitlichen Rechtsrahmen zu schaffen. Die in weiten Teilen geplante Übernahme der Regelungen des ErwSÜ ist aus den oben genannten Gründen folgerichtig, die Abwandlung zum Zwecke der Intensivierung der justiziellen Zusammenarbeit innerhalb der EU sinnvoll, jedoch nicht einhundertprozentig ausgereift, was sich insbesondere an der fehlenden Abstimmung von internationaler Zuständigkeit und anwendbarem Recht in Bezug auf die in der EU-ErwSVO-E vorgesehene Prorogationsmöglichkeit zeigt. Zu bedauern ist, dass nach dem vorliegenden Entwurf die Chance vergeben wurde, Einheitlichkeit auch in Bezug auf die kollisionsrechtliche Behandlung von Patientenverfügungen und ex lege-Vertretungen im Bereich des Erwachsenenschutzes zu schaffen. Damit müsste das auf

---

[60] Dies dürfte in Deutschland das von der Bundesnotarkammer geführte Zentrale Vorsorgeregister betreffen, in welchem Vorsorgevollmachten, Patientenverfügungen und Widersprüche gegen das Ehegattennotvertretungsrecht ihrem wesentlichen Inhalt nach typisiert registriert werden.

[61] Vgl. COM(2023) 280 final, ErwGr. 44, 47.

Patientenverfügungen anwendbare Recht, sofern sie nicht in Verbindung mit einer hoheitlichen Fürsorgemaßnahme oder einer Vorsorgevollmacht stehen, weiterhin nach der Rom I-VO bzw. Rom II-VO bestimmt werden.[62] In Bezug auf gesetzliche Vertretungsbefugnisse müsste nach der Beziehung des Vertreters zum schutzbedürftigen Erwachsenen und dem Inhalt der Vertretungsbefugnisse qualifiziert und an das jeweilige Wirkungsstatut angeknüpft werden. Es verbliebe damit im Hinblick auf diese Rechtsinstrumente bei einer Rechtsunsicherheit, die sich negativ auf die Verwirklichung des Selbstbestimmungsrechts des schutzbedürftigen Erwachsenen auswirkt. Die Zäsur der Diskontinuität ist daher zwar bedauerlich, bietet jedoch auch eine Chance, diese Defizite zu beheben.

Das Selbstbestimmungsrecht schutzbedürftiger Erwachsener wird nicht nur durch die Uneinheitlichkeit des europäischen Kollisionsrechts auf diesem Gebiet eingeschränkt, sondern in Teilen auch durch die materiellrechtlichen Regelungen des Erwachsenenschutzes in den EU-Mitgliedstaaten. Weder das ErwSÜ noch eine Erwachsenenschutzverordnung der EU wollen ihre Vertragsstaaten zwingen, sich vollkommen und ohne jegliche Einschränkungen fremder Rechtsakte betreffend den Erwachsenenschutz zu öffnen. Im Geiste der UN-BRK sollen jedoch die Schwierigkeiten, die die Internationalität eines Sachverhalts mit sich bringt weitestgehend minimiert werden, insbesondere das Problem der Diskontinuität des Erwachsenenschutzes und eines unkoordinierten Nebeneinanders verschiedener Schutzmaßnahmen in Bezug auf denselben Erwachsenen – sei es aufgrund einer von verschiedenen Staaten gleichzeitig angenommenen Zuständigkeit, der Unverträglichkeit der materiellen Rechtswirkungen von Schutzmaßnahmen in verschieden Staaten oder der fehlenden Kommunikation zwischen den Behörden dieser Staaten. Die beiden Vorschläge der Kommission sollen sich als Ausprägung des Subsidiaritätsprinzips ausdrücklich nicht auf die materiellrechtlichen Vorschriften der Mitgliedstaaten auswirken. Gleichwohl bleibt zu hoffen, dass durch die Annahme sowohl des Ratsbeschlusses als auch des Verordnungsentwurfes diejenigen Mitgliedstaaten, die bislang ihr nationales Recht (einschließlich des autonomen Kollisionsrechts) noch nicht im Sinne der UN-BRK reformiert haben, dies zum Anlass nehmen, um sich dieser wichtigen Materie anzunehmen und den eigenen Staatsangehörigen auch nach ihrem Heimatrecht insbesondere ermöglichen, privatautonome Vorsorge für den Fall der eigenen Schutzbedürftigkeit zu treffen. Die Umsetzung der beiden Vorschläge der Kommission in der neuen Wahlperiode könnte somit neben einer weiteren Europäisierung des internationalen Privat- und Verfahrensrechts der Mitgliedstaaten auch zu einer Modernisierung des Sachrechts der Mitgliedstaaten im Sinne der Ziele der UN-BRK führen.

[62] Vgl. hierzu Kobsik, Antizipierte Erklärungen in Gesundheitsangelegenheiten im grenzüberschreitenden Verkehr, 2020, S. 464.

GUIDO KOSMEHL

Post BREXIT – das Internationale Zivilverfahrensrecht im Verhältnis zum Vereinigten Königreich

Der Autor erlebte *Thomas Rauscher* erstmals im Wintersemester 1996/97 in der Vorlesung zum Internationalen Privatrecht an der Juristenfakultät Leipzig. Damals weckte der *Jubilar* das Interesse für das „Fremde Recht" und die „Internationalisierung". Es folgten viele weitere Vorlesungen, Seminare im Internationalen und Europäischen Privat- und Verfahrensrecht und schließlich die Anstellung als wissenschaftlicher Mitarbeiter an „seinem" Lehrstuhl für Internationales Privatrecht, Europäisches Privatrecht sowie Bürgerliches Recht.

Thomas Rauscher hat gleich zu Beginn seines wissenschaftlichen Wirkens[1] das Europäische Zivilprozessrecht in den Blick genommen und im Laufe der Jahre ist das Europäische Privat- und Verfahrensrecht zu einem seiner Schwerpunkte geworden.[2] Dabei hat er zugleich stets auch die Entwicklungen im Internationalen Zivilverfahrensrecht begleitet[3] und etwa das völkervertragliche Zustellungsrecht kommentiert.[4]

Mit dem zum 31.1.2020 vollzogenen BREXIT – oder juristisch ausgedrückt – dem Ausstritt des Vereinigten Königreichs Großbritannien und Nordirland aus der Europäischen Union,[5] hat das Vereinigte Königreich Großbritannien und Nordirland[6] nicht nur den europäischen Binnenmarkt und die (politische) EU verlassen, sondern auch die über viele Jahrzehnte geschaffenen Regelungen des Europäischen Zivilprozessrechts hinter sich gelassen.[7]

Nach Ablauf des Übergangszeitraums sind seit dem 1.1.2021 die verschiedenen Verordnungen des EuZPR im Verhältnis zum Vereinigten Königreich nicht mehr anwendbar. Folglich müssen Sachverhalte zwischen einem Mitgliedsstaat der Europäischen Union und dem Vereinigten Königreich – aus Sicht des internationalen

---

[1] Rauscher, Verpflichtung und Erfüllungsort in Art. 5 Nr. 1 EUGVÜ, unter besonderer Berücksichtigung des Vertragshändlervertrages, 1984 (Dissertation).

[2] Als Herausgeber und Autor des mittlerweile in 5. Aufl. erscheinenden Kommentar zum Europäischen Zivilprozess- und Kollisionsrecht.

[3] Siehe auch Rauscher, Internationales Privatrecht mit internationalem Verfahrensrecht, 5. Aufl. 2017, sowie Rauscher, Klausurenkurs im Internationalen Privat- und Verfahrensrecht, 4. Aufl. 2019.

[4] Münchener Kommentar zur ZPO/Rauscher, 6. Aufl. 2022, Völkervertragliches Zustellungsrecht.

[5] Abkommen über den Austritt des Vereinigten Königreichs Großbritannien und Nordirland aus der Europäischen Union und der Europäischen Atomgemeinschaft, ABl. 2019 C 66 I/01.

[6] Im Folgenden Vereinigtes Königreich genannt.

[7] Bemerkenswert auch, dass der Beitritt des Vereinigten Königreich in die damalige Europäische Wirtschaftsgemeinschaft zum 1.1.1973 einen Monat vor Inkrafttreten des EuGVÜ geschah.

Zivilverfahrensrecht – auf eine „andere“ oder „neue“ Grundlage gestellt bzw. mit anderen Instrumenten gelöst werden.

In Betracht kommen die völkervertragliche Erstreckung des Lugano-Übereinkommens und/oder die Anwendung der Übereinkommen der Haager Konferenz für Internationales Privatrecht. Nachfolgende Überlegungen sind dem *Jubilar* in weiterhin[8] dankbarer Verbundenheit gewidmet.

I. Beitritt zum Lugano-Übereinkommen

1. Das Lugano-Übereinkommen

Nachdem mit dem am 27.9.1968 in Brüssel unterschriebenen und am 1.2.1973 in Kraft getretenen Übereinkommen über die gerichtliche Zuständigkeit und Vollstreckung gerichtlicher Entscheidungen in Zivil- und Handelssachen (EuGVÜ)[9] ein einheitliches und bindendes Regelwerk für die Mitgliedsstaaten der Europäischen Gemeinschaft (EG) geschaffen wurde, wurde erstmals bereits 1973 und sodann mit Erfolg ab 1981 auf Initiative Schwedens und der Schweiz ein Parallelübereinkommen zum EuGVÜ erarbeitet.[10]

Ziel war es die Staaten der Europäischen Freihandelsassoziation (EFTA)[11] in das erfolgreiche europäische Zivilprozessrecht einzubeziehen.[12] Weil das EuGVÜ als „geschlossenes“ Übereinkommen konzipiert war, dh keine Drittstaaten Vertragsstaat werden konnten, bestand auch aus Sicht der EFTA-Staaten Handlungsbedarf, um wirtschaftliche Nachteile zu vermeiden.[13]

Der eingesetzte Sachverständigenausschuss, dem Experten aus den Mitgliedsstaaten der EG und der EFTA angehörten, legte der diplomatischen Konferenz in Lugano den Vorschlag für ein Übereinkommen sowie 3 Protokolle und Erklärungen vor.[14] Das

---

[8] Schon vor 20 Jahren Kosmehl, Welchen Wert hat der Gerichtsstand der unerlaubten Handlung im europäischen Zivilprozeßrecht?, LA Rauscher, 2005, 79.

[9] ABl. 1972 L 299, 32. Geändert durch mehrere Beitrittsübereinkommen, zuletzt durch das 4. Beitrittsübereinkommen vom 29.11.1996 (BGBl 1998 II 1412). Mit Wirkung vom 1.3.2002 wurde das EuGVÜ weitestgehend durch die VO (EG) Nr. 44/2001 vom 22.12.2000 über die gerichtliche Zuständigkeit und die Anerkennung und Vollstreckung von Entscheidungen in Zivil- und Handelssachen (Brüssel I-VO; ABl. 2001 L 12, 1) ersetzt, die ihrerseits durch die Verordnung (EU) Nr. 1215/2012 des Europäischen Parlaments und des Rates vom 12.12.2012 über die gerichtliche Zuständigkeit und die Anerkennung und Vollstreckung von Entscheidungen in Zivil- und Handelssachen (Brüssel Ia-VO; ABl. 2012 L 351, 1) ersetzt wurde.

[10] Rauscher, EuZPR/EuIPR/Staudinger, 5. Aufl. 2021, Brüssel Ia-VO Einl. Rn 25; Kropholler/von Hein, Europäisches Zivilprozessrecht, 9. Aufl. 2011, EuGVO Einl. Rn. 85; Dassner/Oberhammer, LugÜ/Markus, 3. Aufl. 2021, Vor Art. 1 Rn. 4; Schnyder, LugÜ/Grolimund, 2011, Allgemeine Einleitung Rn. 4; Basler Kommentar LugÜ/Oetiker/Weibel/Fountonlakis, 3. Aufl. 2024, Einleitung Rn. 5.

[11] Also Finnland, Island, Norwegen, Österreich Schweden und die Schweiz. EFTA Mitglied Lichtenstein hat sich nicht beteiligt.

[12] Dassner/Oberhammer, LugÜ/Markus, 3. Aufl. 2021, Vor Art. 1 Rn. 1; Kropholler/von Hein, Europäisches Zivilprozessrecht, 9. Aufl. 2011, EuGVO Einl. Rn. 82; Basler Kommentar LugÜ/Oetiker/Weibel, 2. Aufl. 2016, Einleitung Rn. 10.

[13] Schnyder, LugÜ/Grolimund, 2011, Allgemeine Einleitung Rn. 4.

[14] Jenard/Möller-Bericht [zum LugÜbk 1988] (ABl. 1990 C 189, 57 (65)).

Übereinkommen wurde am 16.9.1988[15] verabschiedet und zur Unterzeichnung ausgelegt. Unmittelbar unterzeichnet haben das LugÜbk 1988 zehn Staaten: die EG-Mitgliedstaaten Belgien, Dänemark, Griechenland, Italien, Luxemburg und Portugal sowie die EFTA-Mitgliedstaaten Island, Norwegen, Schweden und die Schweiz.[16] Das LugÜbk 1988 trat am 1.1.1992 in Kraft. Das Vereinigte Königreich hat das LugÜbk 1988 am 18.9.1989 gezeichnet und am 5.2.1992 ratifiziert.[17] Die Bundesrepublik Deutschland hat das LugÜbk 1988 am 23.10.1989 gezeichnet und am 14.12.1994 ratifiziert.[18] Das LugÜbk 1988 ist ein „beschränkt offenes“ Übereinkommen.[19] Dh auch Drittstaaten (also weder EG noch EFTA Mitglied) können Vertragsstaat des LugÜbk 1988 werden, so einzig vollzogen mit Polen.[20]

Inhaltlich zeichnet das LugÜbk 1988 das EuGVÜ in der Fassung des 2. Beitrittsübereinkommen[21] nach. Es wird daher häufig auch als Parallelübereinkommen bezeichnet.[22] Es geht aber an einigen Stellen über das geltende EuGVÜ idF des 2. Beitrittsübereinkommen hinaus, was nach Abschluss des LugÜbk 1988 durch die Änderung des EuGVÜ im Rahmen des 3. Beitrittsübereinkommen[23] wieder in einen gewissen Gleichlauf gebracht wurde. Wie das EuGVÜ umfasst das LugÜbk 1988 Regelungen zu gerichtlichen Zuständigkeiten, wie auch zur Anerkennung und Vollstreckung gerichtlicher Entscheidungen in Zivil- und Handelssachen.

2. *Revision und LugÜbk 2007*

Mit dem Beitritt der bisherigen EFTA Mitglieder Finnland, Schweden und Österreich zur Europäischen Gemeinschaft wurde, wie immer auch ein neues Beitrittsübereinkommen zum EuGVÜ geschlossen. Zugleich wurde deutlich, dass der Anpassungsbedarf aber auch die Änderungswünsche über den üblichen Rahmen eines Beitrittsübereinkommen hinausgehen. Daher wurde eine Gesamtrevision des EuGVÜ in Betracht gezogen. Um den Gleichlauf zwischen EuGVÜ und LugÜ zu

---

[15] Übereinkommen über die gerichtliche Zuständigkeit und die Vollstreckung gerichtlicher Entscheidungen in Zivil- und Handelssachen, zur Unterzeichnung aufgelegt am 16.9.1988 (ABl. 1988 L 319, 9; ber. ABl. 1989 L 20, 38, ABl. 2001 L 148, 86). Dieses wird nach dem Tagungsort der Konferenz als Lugano-Übereinkommen (LugÜbk 1988) bezeichnet.

[16] Jenard/Möller-Bericht [zum LugÜbk 1988] (ABl. 1990 C 189, 57 (65)).

[17] Inkrafttreten des LugÜbk 1988 im Vereinigten Königreich am 1.5.1992. Siehe https://www.bj.admin.ch/bj/de/home/wirtschaft/privatrecht/lugue-2007/lugue-1988.html (abgerufen 27.6.2024).

[18] BGBl 1994 II 2658. Für Deutschland am 1.3.1995 in Kraft getreten.

[19] Dassner/Oberhammer, LugÜ/Domej, 3. Aufl. 2021, Art. 70–73 Rn. 1; Orell Füssli Kommentar IPRG/LugÜ/Kren Kostkiewicz, 2. Aufl. 2019, LugÜ Art. 70 Rn. 2; Basler Kommentar LugÜ/Weibel/Mata, 3. Aufl. 2024, Art. 70–72 Rn. 2.

[20] Ratifiziert am 1.11.1999 und in Kraft getreten am 1.2.2000.

[21] Übereinkommen über den Beitritt der Republik Griechenland zum Übereinkommen über die gerichtliche Zuständigkeit und die Vollstreckung gerichtlicher Entscheidungen in Zivil- und Handelssachen sowie zum Protokoll betreffend die Auslegung dieses Übereinkommens durch den Gerichtshof [...], unterzeichnet am 25.10.1982 (ABl. 1982 L 388, 1).

[22] Geimer, IZPR, 9. Aufl. 2024, Rn. 247s; Schack, Internationales Zivilverfahrensrecht, 8. Aufl. 2021, § 3 Rn. 138, hält diesen Begriff für „trügerisch“.

[23] Übereinkommen über den Beitritt des Königreichs Spanien und der Portugiesischen Republik zum Übereinkommen über die gerichtliche Zuständigkeit und die Vollstreckung gerichtlicher Entscheidungen in Zivil- und Handelssachen sowie zum Protokoll betreffend die Auslegung dieses Übereinkommens durch den Gerichtshof [...], unterzeichnet am 26.5.1989 (ABl. 1989 L 285, 1).

erhalten, wurde auch eine Revision des LugÜbk. 1988 angestrebt.[24] Der Ständige Ausschuss nach Protokoll Nr. 2 gab im September 1996 die formelle Empfehlung zur Revision ab.[25] Eine aus den 15 EG-Mitgliedsstaaten und den verbliebenen EFTA-Staaten[26] gebildete EG-EFTA-Arbeitsgruppe legte bereits 1999 einen revidierten Vorschlag für beide Übereinkommen vor.

Der Abschluss der beiden revidierten Übereinkommen verzögerte sich in der Folge. Zum einen wurde durch den Vertrag von Amsterdam der Bereich der justiziellen Zusammenarbeit in Zivil- und Handelssachen „vergemeinschaftet", was zur Folge hatte, dass nunmehr die Europäische Gemeinschaft die Rechtssetzungskompetenz hat und Regelungen, als Gemeinschaftsmaßnahme im Wege einer Verordnung erlassen werden konnten. Die Kommission machte davon Gebrauch und legte den Vorschlag für eine Brüssel I-VO[27] vor. Diese trat nach Durchlaufen des europäischen Verordnungsgebungsverfahrens am 1.3.2002 in Kraft.

Vor Abschluss eines revidierten Lugano Übereinkommens musste noch die Frage geklärt werden, ob die die Europäische Gemeinschaft die alleinige Außenvertretungskompetenz zum Abschluss eines neuen Lugano-Übereinkommen besitzt. Hierzu wurde ein Gutachten des EuGH[28] eingeholt. Im Ergebnis sieht der EuGH eine alleinige (Außenvertretungs)Kompetenz bei der Europäischen Gemeinschaft.[29] Des Weiteren musste noch die Rolle Dänemarks in Bezug auf ein revidiertes Lugano-Übereinkommen geklärt werden. Da Dänemark nicht an der justiziellen Zusammenarbeit in Zivil- und Handelssachen teilnimmt, besitzt die Europäische Gemeinschaft keine Kompetenz auch im Namen Dänemarks das Lugano-Übereinkommen abzuschließen. Für die Brüssel I-VO wurde hierfür das EU-DK Abk, als völkerrechtlicher Vertrag geschlossen.[30] Da Dänemark Vertragsstaat des LugÜbk 1988 war, konnte (und wollte) Dänemark auch Vertragsstaat im revidierten Lugano-Übereinkommen bleiben. Somit sind vier Staaten und die EU Vertragsparteien.[31]

Das revidierte Lugano Übereinkommen (LugÜbk 2007)[32] wurde auf der Diplomatischen Tagung in Lugano am 30.10.2007 unterzeichnet[33] und trat ab dem

[24] Dassner/Oberhammer, LugÜ/Markus, 3. Aufl. 2021, LugÜ Vor Art. 1 Rn. 11ff.

[25] Basler Kommentar LugÜ/Oetiker/Weibel, 2. Aufl. 2016, Einleitung Rn. 11.

[26] Lichtenstein beteiligte sich erneut nicht. Polen, dass dem LugÜbk 1988 beitreten wollte, nahm als Beobachter an den Verhandlungen teil.

[27] Europäische Kommission, Vorschlag vom 14.7.1999, KOM(1999) 348; VO (EG) Nr. 44/2001 vom 22.12.2000 über die gerichtliche Zuständigkeit und die Anerkennung und Vollstreckung von Entscheidungen in Zivil- und Handelssachen (ABl. 2001 L 12, 1).

[28] EuGH 7.2.2006 – Gutachten 1/03, ECLI:EU:C:2006:81 = BeckEuRS 2006, 421995.

[29] EuGH 7.2.2006 – Gutachten 1/03, Rn. 173, ECLI:EU:C:2006:81 = BeckEuRS 2006, 421995.

[30] ABl. 2005 L 299, 62; Rauscher, EuZPR/EuIPR/Pabst, 5. Aufl. 2024, EU-DK Abk Art. 2 Rn. 1.

[31] Die Europäische Union, Island, Norwegen, Schweiz und – als eigenständige Vertragspartei – Dänemark. Das LugÜbk 2007 verwendet nunmehr den Begriff „Vertragspartei" statt Vertragsstaat, um die Europäische Union einzubeziehen.

[32] Übereinkommen über die gerichtliche Zuständigkeit und die Anerkennung und Vollstreckung von Entscheidungen in Zivil- und Handelssachen, unterzeichnet am 30.10.2007 (ABl. 2009 L 147, 5, ber. ABl. 2009 L 147, 44, ABl. 2011 L 115, 31, ABl. 2014 L 18, 70).

[33] Pocar-Bericht [zum LugÜbk. 2007] (ABl. 2009 C 319, 1 (3)). Zunächst nur von Island, Norwegen, der Schweiz und der Europäischen Union. Dänemark unterzeichnete am 5.12.2007.

1.1.2010 in Kraft.[34] Zu gleich wird das LugÜbk. 1988 vollständig ersetzt und ist damit erloschen. Daher ist mit Blick auf das Vereinigte Königreich nach dem BREXIT auch die Frage, ob ein Wiederaufleben der ursprünglichen (eigenen) Mitgliedschaft des Vereinigten Königreichs im LugÜbk 1988 in Betracht käme, mit Nein zu beantworten.[35]

Der inhaltliche Regelungsgehalt des LugÜbk 2007 entspricht der Brüssel I-VO, die am 1.3.2002 in Kraft getreten war.[36]

Der Bedarf einer erneuten Revision des Lugano-Übereinkommens wächst, zumal seit Inkrafttreten der aktuellen Brüssel Ia-VO zum 1.10.2015, der ursprünglich mit der Ersetzung des LugÜbk 1988 durch das LugÜbk 2007 erreichte Gleichlauf beider Instrumente entfallen ist.[37] Dies führt unvermeidlich auch zu Auslegungsschwierigkeiten.[38] Eine erneute Revision wäre dringend notwendig.[39]

3. Wiederbeitritt des Vereinigten Königreichs zum LugÜbk 2007

Mit Antrag vom 8.4.2020 begehrte das Vereinigte Königreich den Beitritt zum LugÜbk. 2007.[40] Der angestrebte Beitritt zum LugÜbk 2007 wurde bereits frühzeitig in einem *„A future Partnership Paper"*[41] veröffentlicht. Zugleich betonte das Vereinigte Königreich immer wieder die Wichtigkeit des Lugano-Übereinkommen.[42]

Grundsätzlich stehen gem. Art. 70 LugÜbk 2007 nach Inkrafttreten des Übereinkommens verschiedene Wege für einen Beitritt zum Übereinkommen zur Verfügung. Entweder als neues Mitglied der Europäischen Freihandelsassoziation (Art. 70 Abs. 1 lit. a LugÜbk 2007) oder „jeder andere Staat" (Art. 70 Abs. 1 lit. c iVm Art. 72 LugÜbk 2007). Das Vereinigte Königreich hat sich für den zweiten Weg entschieden.[43] Somit war gemäß Art 72 LugÜbk 2007 die Zustimmung aller Vertragsstaaten des Übereinkommens erforderlich. Nicht mehr erforderlich war eine formelle Einladung eines Vertragsstaates zum Beitritt, wie sie noch Art. 60

---

[34] Zuerst zwischen der EU, Dänemark und Norwegen. Zum 1.1.2011 dann auch im Verhältnis zur Schweiz und am 1.5.2011 im Verhältnis zu Island.

[35] Dasser/Oberhammer, Lugano-Übereinkommen/Domej, 3. Aufl. 2021, LugÜ Art. 63 Rn. 27.

[36] Nach den Erweiterungen der EG 2004 und 2007, galt die Brüssel I-VO ab dem 1.1.2007 für alle Mitgliedsstaaten der EG mit Ausnahme Dänemarks.

[37] Basler Kommentar LugÜ/Oetiker/Weibel, 2. Aufl. 2016, Einleitung Rn. 26.

[38] Basler Kommentar LugÜ/Oetiker/Weibel, 2. Aufl. 2016, Einleitung Rn. 31 b.

[39] So auch Schack, Internationales Zivilverfahrensrecht, 8. Aufl. 2021, § 3 Rn. 138.

[40] Nach dem BREXIT, aber vor Ablauf des Übergangszeitraums. Siehe Lein N.Y.U. J. Int'l L. & Pol. 56 (2023), 263 (271).

[41] HM Government, 22.8.2017, Policy paper, Providing a cross-border civil judicial cooperation framework – a future partnership paper, S. 6, https://assets.publishing.service.gov.uk/government/uploads/system/uploads/attachment_data/file/868874/The_Future_Relationship_with_the_EU.pdf (abgerufen 28.6.2024).

[42] „This is an important convention for UK businesses, the legal services sector, individuals and families (due to the inclusion of family maintenance arrangements within its scope).", https://www.gov.uk/government/news/support-for-the-uks-intent-to-accede-to-the-lugano-convention-2007 (abgerufen 28.6.2024).

[43] Lein N.Y.U. J. Int'l L. & Pol. 56 (2023), 263 (271).

lit. c LugÜbk 1988 vorsah.[44] Diese Voraussetzung wurde mit der Revision im neuen Art. 70 LugÜbk 2007 gestrichen.

Die Schweiz als Depositar der Luganer Übereinkommen[45] informierte die Vertragsparteien der des Übereinkommens am 14.4.2020 über das Beitrittsgesuch und bat um Zustimmung binnen eines Jahres.[46]

Eine Zustimmung zum Beitrittsgesuch des Vereinigten Königreichs erfolgte durch die Schweiz[47], Island[48] und Norwegen[49].

Eine erste Mitteilung der Europäischen Union ging am 25.3.2021 ein.[50] Darin teilte die Europäische Kommission mit, dass sie die Jahresfrist des Art. 72 Abs. 3 LugÜbk 2007 nicht einhalten könne. Allerdings heißt es in Art. 72 Abs. 3 S. 1 LugÜbk 2007 nur: „Die Vertragsparteien sind bestrebt, ihre Zustimmung spätestens innerhalb eines Jahres nach der Aufforderung durch den Verwahrer zu erteilen." Insofern hat eine spätere Antwort der Europäischen Union keine Auswirkung. Die finale Notifikation der Europäischen Union erreichte den Depositar mit Schreiben vom 28.6.2021.[51]

Die Europäische Kommission teilte mit, dass sie ihre Zustimmung zum Beitritt des Vereinigten Königreiches nicht erteilen könne.[52] Eine Begründung enthält die

---

[44] Basler Kommentar LugÜ/Weibel/Hosang, 2. Aufl. 2016, Art. 70–72 Rn. 3; Schnyder, LugÜ/Siehr, 2011, Art 70 Rn. 4.

[45] Übersichtsseite zum LugÜbk. unter: https://www.fdfa.admin.ch/eda/fr/dfae/politique-exterieure/droit-international-public/traites-internationaux/depositaire/autres-conventions/convention-concernant-la-competence-judiciaire-la-reconnaissance-et-l-execution-des-decisions-en-mati%C3%A8re-civile-et-commerciale.html (abgerufen am 28.6.2024).

[46] „to give their consent at the latest within one year after this notification." Dokument Nr. 612-04-04-01 – LUG 2/20 – https://www.fdfa.admin.ch/eda/fr/dfae/politique-exterieure/droit-international-public/traites-internationaux/depositaire/autres-conventions/convention-concernant-la-competence-judiciaire-la-reconnaissance-et-l-execution-des-decisions-en-mati%C3%A8re-civile-et-commerciale.html (abgerufen am 28.6.2024).

[47] 11.9.2020 siehe Dokument Nr. 612-04-04-01 – LUG 1/21 – https://www.fdfa.admin.ch/eda/fr/dfae/politique-exterieure/droit-international-public/traites-internationaux/depositaire/autres-conventions/convention-concernant-la-competence-judiciaire-la-reconnaissance-et-l-execution-des-decisions-en-mati%C3%A8re-civile-et-commerciale.html (abgerufen 28.6.2024).

[48] 26.2.2021 Dokument Nr. 612-04-04-01 – LUG 2/21 – https://www.fdfa.admin.ch/eda/fr/dfae/politique-exterieure/droit-international-public/traites-internationaux/depositaire/autres-conventions/convention-concernant-la-competence-judiciaire-la-reconnaissance-et-l-execution-des-decisions-en-mati%C3%A8re-civile-et-commerciale.html (abgerufen 28.6.2024).

[49] 30.3.2021 Dokument Nr. 612-04-04-01 – LUG 3/21 – https://www.fdfa.admin.ch/eda/fr/dfae/politique-exterieure/droit-international-public/traites-internationaux/depositaire/autres-conventions/convention-concernant-la-competence-judiciaire-la-reconnaissance-et-l-execution-des-decisions-en-mati%C3%A8re-civile-et-commerciale.html (abgerufen 28.6.2024).

[50] Dokument Nr. 612-04-04-01 – LUG 3/21 – https://www.fdfa.admin.ch/eda/fr/dfae/politique-exterieure/droit-international-public/traites-internationaux/depositaire/autres-conventions/convention-concernant-la-competence-judiciaire-la-reconnaissance-et-l-execution-des-decisions-en-mati%C3%A8re-civile-et-commerciale.html (abgerufen 28.6.2024).

[51] Dokument Nr. 612-04-04-01 – LUG 4/21 vom 1.7.2021 – https://www.fdfa.admin.ch/eda/fr/dfae/politique-exterieure/droit-international-public/traites-internationaux/depositaire/autres-conventions/convention-concernant-la-competence-judiciaire-la-reconnaissance-et-l-execution-des-decisions-en-mati%C3%A8re-civile-et-commerciale.html (abgerufen 28.6.2024).

[52] „not to be in a position to give its consent" siehe Dokument Nr. 612-04-04-01 – LUG 4/21 vom 1.7.2021 – https://www.fdfa.admin.ch/eda/fr/dfae/politique-exterieure/droit-international-public/traites-internationaux/depositaire/autres-conventions/convention-concernant-la-

Mitteilung nicht. Dagegen hat die Europäische Kommission in einer Mitteilung gegenüber dem Rat und dem Europäischen Parlament eine „Bewertung zum Ersuchen des Vereinigten Königreichs Großbritannien und Nordirland um Beitritt zum Lugano-Übereinkommen von 2007“ abgegeben.[53] Die Mitteilung der Europäischen Kommission ist schon in ihrem Umfang aber auch hinsichtlich der Argumentationstiefe nicht geeignet, dem Rat und dem Europäischen Parlament als Adressaten, eine fundierte Entscheidungsgrundlage zu bieten. Nicht nachvollziehbar ist es, dass die Europäische Kommission als Alternative zum Beitritt/Nichtbeitritt zum Lugano-Übereinkommen nur auf die Haager Übereinkommen verweist und so beispielsweise den Abschluss eines bilateralen Vertrages EU-VK nicht in Erwägung zieht.

Weder der Rat noch das Europäische Parlament, als Adressaten der Mitteilung, haben zur Mitteilung offiziell Stellung genommen. Mit Blick auf den Zeitablauf, am 4.5.2021 Mitteilung der Europäischen Kommission an Rat und EP und finale Notifizierung der Ablehnung durch die Europäische Kommission gegenüber dem Depositar am 28.6.2021, konnte, in der für Beratungsabläufe auf europäischer Ebene üblicherweise notwendige Zeit, davon auch kaum ausgegangen werden. Es bleibt dennoch bedauerlich, dass der „Europäische Gesetzgeber“ in einer solch wichtigen Angelegenheit schweigt.

Das Ergebnis der Einschätzung der Europäischen Kommission beruht auf (nur) zwei Erwägungen: Zum einen der Verweis auf das Wesen des Lugano-Übereinkommens: „[es] spiegelt die Vorschriften der EU über die internationale Zuständigkeit und ihr quasiautomatisches System der Anerkennung und Vollstreckung von Entscheidungen in Zivil- und Handelssachen gegenüber EFTA-Staaten wider“.[54] Zudem sei das Lugano-Übereinkommen „eine flankierende Maßnahme für die Wirtschaftsbeziehungen der EU zu den EFTA-/EWR-Staaten.“[55]

Zum anderen verweist die Europäische Kommission auf den Ansatz der EU, dass „der geeignete Rahmen für die justizielle Zusammenarbeit mit Drittstaaten in Zivilsachen die multilateralen Haager Übereinkommen sind“.[56] Dabei benennt sie konkret das HProrogÜbk 2005 und das HAVÜ 2019.

Die von der Europäischen Kommission im Namen der Europäischen Union mitgeteilte Nichtzustimmung hat deutliche Kritik hervorgerufen.[57] Besonders der Hinweis der Europäischen Kommission „das Lugano-Übereinkommen unterstützt die Beziehungen der EU zu Drittstaaten, die im Regelungsbereich besonders eng mit der EU verbunden sind“[58] impliziert, dass das Vereinigte Königreich keine „enge Verbindung“ zur Europäischen Union hätte. Dabei verkennt die Kommis-

---

competence-judiciaire-la-reconnaissance-et-l-execution-des-decisions-en-mati%C3%A8re-civile-et-commerciale.html (abgerufen 28.6.2024).

[53] Europäische Kommission, Mitteilung vom 4.5.2021, COM(2021) 222 final.

[54] Europäische Kommission, Mitteilung vom 4.5.2021, COM(2021) 222 final, S. 2.

[55] Europäische Kommission, Mitteilung vom 4.5.2021, COM(2021) 222 final, S. 2.

[56] Europäische Kommission, Mitteilung vom 4.5.2021, COM(2021) 222 final, S. 3.

[57] Kohler ZEuP 2021, 781; Lein N.Y.U. J. Int'l L. & Pol. 56 (2023), 263 (278 ff.); Basedow EuZW 2021, 777.

[58] Europäische Kommission, Mitteilung vom 4.5.2021, COM(2021) 222 final, S. 3 (abgerufen 28.6.2024).

sion die lange Zeitspanne in denen Regelungen des EuZPR wie auch das Lugano-Übereinkommen zwischen dem Vereinigten Königreich und der Europäischen Union bzw. ihren Mitgliedsstaaten galt.[59]

In der Politischen Erklärung zur Festlegung des Rahmens für die künftigen Beziehungen zwischen der Europäischen Union und dem Vereinigten Königreich finden die engen wirtschaftlichen Beziehungen dagegen mehrfach Erwähnung.[60] Die Europäische Kommission betont, dass die Mitglieder des Lugano Übereinkommen enge wirtschaftliche Beziehungen zur EU aufweisen.[61] Es ist aber anzunehmen, dass solche wirtschaftlichen Beziehungen – abseits einer formalen Mitgliedschaft in EFTA oder EWR – etwa als Ergebnis des über viele Jahre wirkenden Binnenmarkt, im Verhältnis zum Vereinigten Königreich bestehen.

Basedow bemängelt, dass die Kommission keine vergleichende Untersuchung der Rechtslage (hier HAVÜ 2019, LugÜbk 2007 und Brüssels Ia-VO) angestellt habe und weist darauf hin, dass „dieses Haager Übereinkommen eine massive Verkürzung des individuellen Rechtsschutzes im Verhältnis zum Vereinigten Königreich darstelle".[62] Denn der sachliche Anwendungsbereich des HAVÜ 2019 ist wesentlich kleiner (auch wegen Art 2 HAVÜ 2019) als beim LugÜbk 2007 und das HAVÜ 2019 regelt als *convention simple* nur Anerkennung und Vollstreckung.

Das Vereinigte Königreich ist sicher kein „normaler" Drittstaat,[63] dennoch stellt sich die (auch politische) Frage, ob ein Beitritt zum Lugano-Übereinkommen der richtige Weg wäre. Folgt man dem Mantra der Regierung des Vereinigten Königreich „Brexit means Brexit"[64] ist es inkonsequent, beim Austritt der EU, dem gemeinsamen Binnenmarkt und letztlich auch aus den Instrumenten des EuZPR, einen Wiedereintritt – zumindest in den Reglungskreis des Lugano-Übereinkommens 2007 – anzustreben. Anderseits ist es aus Sicht der Europäischen Union zwar nachvollziehbar, dass mit dem gewollten Austritt in der Konsequenz auch der Verzicht auf verbindliche Regelungen zur gerichtlichen Zuständigkeit, Anerkennung und Vollstreckung gerichtlicher Entscheidungen verbunden ist. Diese im unmittelbaren Nachgang wieder zu „vereinbaren" ist – wohl aus Sicht der Europäischen Kommission – eine kaum zumutbare Rosinenpickerei oder treffender „Cherry-picking".

Aber ist die Nichtzustimmung auch im Sinne der ca. drei Millionen Bürger und unzähligen Unternehmen der Europäischen Union, die im Vereinigten Königreich leben und ansässig sind bzw. die ca. eine Million britische Staatsangehörige und

[59] Lein N.Y.U. J. Int'l L. & Pol. 56 (2023), 263 (278).

[60] Politische Erklärung zur Festlegung des Rahmens für die künftigen Beziehungen zwischen der Europäischen Union und dem Vereinigten Königreich (ABl. 2020 C 134, 178) siehe insb. in den Ziffer 3, 5 und 16.

[61] Europäische Kommission, Mitteilung vom 4.5.2021, COM(2021) 222 final, S. 3f. (abgerufen 28.6.2024).

[62] Basedow EuZW 2021, 777 (778).

[63] Deutlicher: Lein N.Y.U. J. Int'l L. & Pol. 56 (2023), 263 (278): „The United Kingdom is not, and never will be ‚just another third country'."; Basedow EuZW 2021, 777 (778): „in Zukunft der bedeutendste Nachbar der Union".

[64] Siehe https://www.bbc.com/news/uk-politics-36782922 (abgerufen 20.6.2024).

viele Unternehmen, die in der Europäischen Union leben und ansässig sind. Sie brauchen klare und verlässliche Regelungen. Das LugÜbk 2007 hätte das leisten können. Gerade die Europäische Kommission als „Hüterin der Verträge" muss bei Entscheidungen auch die Interessen der Bürger und Unternehmen an einem (funktionierenden) individuellen Rechtsschutz beachten. Die Entscheidung der Europäischen Kommission, dem Gesuch des Vereinigten Königreichs zum Beitritt zum LugÜbk 2007 keine Zustimmung zu geben, war ein Fehler.

Den Beitritt zum Lugano-Übereinkommen zu unterstützen, wäre im Übrigen auch die konsequente Anwendung des Beschlusses des Rates vom 4.5.2010 des Stockholmer Programm[65]. Darin heißt es wörtlich:

„Der Europäische Rat ist der Auffassung, dass es im Hinblick auf den Rechtsverkehr mit Drittländern in einem sicheren rechtlichen Umfeld sehr wichtig ist, die externen Interessen und Prioritäten der Union im Bereich der justiziellen Zusammenarbeit in Zivilsachen eindeutig zu definieren.

Das Lugano-Übereinkommen von 1988 über die gerichtliche Zuständigkeit und die Vollstreckung gerichtlicher Entscheidungen in Zivil- und Handelssachen steht anderen Staaten zum Beitritt offen; die Union sollte in Zusammenarbeit mit den anderen Vertragsparteien prüfen, welche Drittländer zum Beitritt ermutigt werden könnten."[66]

Daraus ist abzuleiten, dass eine (formale) Mitgliedschaft in EFTA oder EWR aus Sicht des Rates gerade nicht Bedingung für einen Beitritt zum Lugano-Übereinkommen sein soll. Das Beitrittsgesuch des Vereinigten Königreich wäre die Gelegenheit gewesen, diesen Worten auch Taten folgen zu lassen.

Für den Beitritt zum LugÜbk 2007 hätte das Vereinigte Königreich selbstverständlich ein klares Bekenntnis zu den Regelungen des LugÜbk 2007 und auch der Zusatzprotokolle, wie das Protokoll Nr. 2 über die einheitliche Auslegung des Übereinkommens und den Ständigen Ausschuss, abgeben müssen. Dazu war das Vereinigte Königreich auch bereit.

4. *Zwischenergebnis*

Der Weg über einen Beitritt nach Art. 70 Abs. 1 lit. c, Art. 72 LugÜbk 2007 Vertragspartei des Lugano-Übereinkommens zu werden, ist somit derzeit versperrt. Es bleibt fraglich, ob sich die Auffassung der Europäischen Kommission in absehbarer Zeit ändern wird. Ein erneuter Anlauf oder ggfs. auch über den Weg des Beitritts zur Europäischen Freihandelsassoziation stünde dem Vereinigten Königreich aber weiterhin – dann über Art. 70 Abs. 1 lit. a, Art 71 LugÜbk 2007 offen. Hierbei ist keine Zustimmung der anderen Vertragsparteien notwendig.[67]

---

[65] Europäischer Rat [Stockholmer Programm] (ABl. 2010 C 115, 1).
[66] Europäischer Rat [Stockholmer Programm] (ABl. 2010 C 115, 1 (17)).
[67] Basler Kommentar LugÜ/Weibel/Hosang, 2. Aufl. 2016, LugÜ Art. 70–72 Rn. 5.

II. Die Haager Konferenz für internationales Privatrecht

1. Beginn und Entwicklung

Die Haager Konferenz für internationales Privatrecht[68] ist erstmals auf Einladung der niederländischen Regierung 1893 zusammengetreten.[69] In den nunmehr mehr als 130 Jahren des Bestehens wurden insgesamt 22 Diplomatische Tagungen abgehalten.[70] An der ersten Konferenz 1893 beteiligten sich 13 Staaten.[71] Die zunächst schwungvoll begonnenen Arbeiten, mit immerhin vier Diplomatischen Tagungen binnen 10 Jahren,[72] gerieten Anfang des 20. Jahrhunderts trotz erster Ergebnisse ins Stocken. Wohl auch durch die Erkenntnis, dass das ursprüngliche Ziel einer Gesamtkodifikation des Internationalen Privatrechts sich so zügig nicht verwirklich lässt. In der Folge wurden eher kleinere Teilbereiche verhandelt und zu einem Abschluss gebracht. Letztlich machte auch der Erste Weltkrieg und dessen Folgen ein „kontinuierliches" Tagen unmöglich. Erst 1925 wurde mit der fünften Diplomatischen Tagung die Arbeit der Haager Konferenz fortgesetzt. Zugleich wurde dabei auch das Ziel einer (Be)Ständigkeit[73] der Haager Konferenz selbst ausgerufen, ohne dass es eine förmliche Satzung gab. Es folgte noch die sechste Diplomatische Tagung 1928, ehe zumindest mit Blick auf die Diplomatischen Tagungen die Haager Konferenz erneut für längere Zeit zum Erliegen kam.

Mit Blick auf das Zivilverfahrensrecht, dass in diesem Beitrag im Focus stehen soll, sind aus der „ersten" Phase des Bestehens der Haager Konferenz das Übereinkommen vom 17.7.1905 über den Zivilprozess[74] sowie ein Vorschlag über die Anerkennung und Vollstreckung gerichtlicher Entscheidungen[75] als Ergebnisse zu erwähnen.

2. Neustart nach dem Zweiten Weltkrieg

Nach dem Ende des Zweiten Weltkriegs fand vom 9. bis 31.10.1951 die siebte Diplomatische Tagung statt. Auf dieser wurde erstmals auch eine Satzung für die

---

[68] Im Folgenden als Haager Konferenz bezeichnet.

[69] Kahn, Die einheitliche Kodifikation des Internationalen Privatrechts durch Staatsverträge, 1904, S. 14, Kahn verweist zudem auch auf die vorhergehenden Bemühungen von Mancini und Asser; ähnlich auch Asser, Grundrisse des Internationalen Privatrecht/Gödan, Nachdruck 2008, Vorbemerkung.

[70] Einen allgemeinen Überblick bis zur 18. Tagung gibt Schack RabelsZ 57 (1993), 224; zu den Ergebnissen der fünften Tagung siehe Volkmar JZ 1926, 307; Anmerkungen bis zur zehnten Tagung Arnold JZ 1965, 708; kurze historische Einordnung Basedow RabelsZ 82 (2018), 922 (923ff.); im Übrigen siehe: Proceedings of the HCCH, https://www.hcch.net/de/publications-and-studies/publications2/proceedings-of-the-diplomatic-sessions (abgerufen 28.6.2024).

[71] Das Deutsche Reich, Belgien, Dänemark, Frankreich, Italien, Luxemburg, die Niederlande, Österreich-Ungarn, Portugal, Rumänien, Russland, die Schweiz und Spanien.

[72] Diplomatische Tagungen 1893, 1894, 1900 und 1904. Nachweise bei Schack RabelsZ 57 (1993), 224 sowie Kahn, Die einheitliche Kodifikation des Internationalen Privatrechts durch Staatsverträge, 1904, S. 14.

[73] Arnold JZ 1965, 708.

[74] Ersetzt das Übereinkommen von 1896 nebst Protokoll. Das Übereinkommen 1905 wurde seinerseits später durch das Übereinkommen vom 1.3.1954 über den Zivilprozess ersetzt.

[75] Abgedruckt bei Volkmar JW 1926, 309 (313).

Haager Konferenz beschlossen.[76] Darin heißt es in Art. 1: „Die Haager Konferenz hat die Aufgabe, an der fortschreitenden Vereinheitlichung der Regeln des Internationalen Privatrechts zu arbeiten." Rechtsvereinheitlichung ist aber nur ein Teilaspekt. Der andere – aus meiner Sicht – noch wichtigere Teil ist Rechtssicherheit. Auch diesen Aspekt hat die Haager Konferenz im Blick, wenn sie als „Vision" ausführt: „Für eine Welt zu arbeiten, in der Individuen, Familien aber auch Gesellschaften und andere juristische Personen, deren Leben und Wirken die Grenzen zwischen verschiedenen Rechtsordnungen überschreiten, sich eines hohen Grades an Rechtssicherheit erfreuen können; Die ordnungsgemäße und effiziente Lösung von Konflikten, ordnungsgemäße Verfahrensführung und rechtliches Gehör unter Anerkennung der Unterschiede der Rechtstraditionen zu fördern."[77]

Die Haager Konferenz wirkte fortan als zwischenstaatliche Organisation.[78] Die auf der siebten Diplomatischen Tagung beschlossene Satzung ist 1955 – also dem Geburtsjahr des *Jubilars* – in Kraft getreten.[79] Waren zu Beginn der Arbeiten der Haager Konferenz nur kontinentaleuropäische Staaten beteiligt (mit Ausnahme Japans,[80] welches ab 1904 Teilnehmer war), beteiligten sich ab 1951 auch vermehrt außereuropäische Staaten an der Haager Konferenz.[81] Seit dem Jahr 2000 ist eine deutliche Zunahme an Mitgliedern zu verzeichnen, die auch mit einer breiteren regionalen Verteilung einhergeht.[82] Trotz der bemerkenswerten Gesamtzahl an bisher geschlossenen Übereinkommen, darf nicht unerwähnt bleiben, dass der Geltungsbereich einzelner Übereinkommen sehr unterschiedlich ist.[83]

III. Die Haager Konferenz als Brücke von und nach Europa?

Mit Blick auf die Tatsache, dass zu Beginn, wie auch zum formalen „Neustart" 1955, fast alle Teilnehmer bzw. Mitgliedsstaaten der Haager Konferenz vom europäischen Kontinent stammten, kann man die Haager Konferenz per se als Brücke von und nach Europa bezeichnen. Die Haager Übereinkommen können für das

---

[76] Aktuelle Fassung abrufbar unter: https://www.hcch.net/de/instruments/conventions/full-text (abgerufen 28.6.2024).

[77] https://www.hcch.net/de/about/vision-and-mission (abgerufen 28.6.2024).

[78] Kreuzer, FS 600 Jahre Würzburger Juristenfakultät, 2002, S. 247 (261): bezeichnet sie als „... die einzige internationale Organisation, die sich satzungsgemäß um die globale Integration des IZVR bemüht".

[79] Inkrafttreten der Satzung am 15.7.1955. Die Satzung ist für die Bundesrepublik Deutschland am 14.12.1955 in Kraft getreten (BGBl. 1959 II 981).

[80] Mitglied ist Japan aber erst seit 27.6.1957.

[81] Mitgliedschaft zB USA 15.10.1964, Australien 1.11.1973, Mexiko 18.3.1986, China 3.7.1987, Russland 6.12.2001, Singapur 9.4.2014.

[82] Aktuell hat die Haager Konferenz 91 Mitglieder: 90 Staaten und die Europäische Union, siehe https://www.hcch.net/de/states/hcch-members (abgerufen 25.5.2024), weitere 66 Nichtmitgliedsstaaten sind Vertragspartei mindestens eines Übereinkommens, https://www.hcch.net/de/states/other-connected-parties (abgerufen 25.5.2024).

[83] Die Spanne reicht von noch nicht in Kraft getreten bis hin zu 126 Vertragsstaaten (Haager Übereinkommen vom 5.10.1961 zur Befreiung ausländischer öffentlicher Urkunden von der Legalisation). Skeptisch Kreuzer, FS 600 Jahre Würzburger Juristenfakultät, 2002, S. 247 (261): „... nicht von einer globalen Rechtsintegration sprechen".

Verhältnis des Vereinigten Königreich zu den Mitgliedsstaaten der Europäischen Union eine tragfähige Grundlage zur Lösung von Rechtsfragen dienen und die Haager Konferenz wieder stärker an Bedeutung gewinnen.

Nach dem 1955 nicht alle Mitgliedsstaaten der Europäischen Wirtschaftsgemeinschaft (EWG) Mitglied der Haager Konferenz waren,[84] sind knapp 70 Jahre später die aktuellen 27 Mitgliedsstaaten der Europäischen Union alle zugleich auch Mitglieder der Haager Konferenz. Am Mitgliedsstatus in der Haager Konferenz hat auch der Beitritt der Europäischen Union zur Haager Konferenz nichts geändert.[85] Die Haager Konferenz hat seit 1955 für verschiedenen Aspekte des Zivilverfahrensrechts – so auch zur Zuständigkeit, Anerkennung und Vollstreckung gerichtlicher Entscheidungen – Übereinkommen[86] verhandelt oder sogar abgeschlossen. Darüber hinaus auch weitere Übereinkommen, von denen die familienrechtlichen Übereinkommen[87] durchaus einen gewissen Bekanntheitsgrad und eine große Bedeutung erlangt haben. Zuletzt wurde 2019 das Übereinkommen über die Anerkennung und Vollstreckung ausländischer Entscheidungen in Zivil- und Handelssachen[88] (HAVÜ 2019) verabschiedet und zur Zeichnung aufgelegt.

1. *Das Vereinigte Königreich und die Haager Konferenz*

Das Vereinigte Königreich ist seit dem 15.7.1955 Mitglied der Haager Konferenz und ist Vertragspartei von 14 Haager Übereinkommen.[89] Es hat ein weiteres Übereinkommen[90] gezeichnet. Mit Blick auf das internationale Zivilverfahrensrecht und die Regelungsinhalte europäischer Verordnungen im Rahmen der justi-

---

[84] Gründungsstaaten der am 25.3.1957 in Rom gegründeten EWG waren Frankreich, Italien, die Niederlande, Belgien, Luxemburg und die Bundesrepublik Deutschland. Mitglieder der Haager Konferenz waren die Bundesrepublik Deutschland seit 14.12.1955, die Niederlande und Belgien seit 15.7.1955 sowie Luxemburg seit 12.3.1956. Italien trat am 26.6.1957 und Frankreich erst am 20.4.1964 der Haager Konferenz bei.

[85] → III. 2.

[86] Beispielhaft seien hier erwähnt: Haager Übereinkommen vom 1.3.1954 über den Zivilprozess (HZPÜ) BGBl 1956 II 576, Haager Übereinkommen vom 15.11.1965 über die Zustellung gerichtlicher und außergerichtlicher Schriftstücke im Ausland in Zivil- oder Handelssachen (HZÜ), Haager Übereinkommen vom 18.3.1970 über die Beweisaufnahme im Ausland in Zivil- oder Handelssachen (HBÜ), Haager Anerkennungs- und Vollstreckungsübereinkommen (HAVÜ 1971).

[87] Haager Übereinkommen vom 25.10.1980 über die zivilrechtlichen Aspekte internationaler Kindesentführung; Haager Übereinkommen vom 29.5.1993 über den Schutz von Kindern und die Zusammenarbeit auf dem Gebiet der internationalen Adoption (KSÜ); Haager Übereinkommen vom 19.10.1996 über die Zuständigkeit, das anzuwendende Recht, die Anerkennung, Vollstreckung und Zusammenarbeit auf dem Gebiet der elterlichen Verantwortung und der Maßnahmen zum Schutz von Kindern; Haager Übereinkommen vom 13.1.2000 über den internationalen Schutz von Erwachsenen (ESÜ).

[88] Angenommen auf der 22. Diplomatischen Tagung am 2.7.2019.

[89] Siehe Statustabelle unter https://www.hcch.net/de/states/hcch-members/details1/?sid=75 (abgerufen 28.6.2024).

[90] Haager Übereinkommen vom 2.10.1973 über die internationale Nachlassverwaltung, dieses dürfte auch angesichts von aktuell nur 3 Vertragsstaaten auch nicht mehr ratifiziert werden.

ziellen Zusammenarbeit, welche bis zum BREXIT galten, sind folgende Übereinkommen[91] von Interesse:

- Übereinkommen vom 5.10.1961 zur Befreiung ausländischer öffentlicher Urkunden von der Legalisation,
- Übereinkommen vom 15.11.1965 über die Zustellung gerichtlicher und außergerichtlicher Schriftstücke im Ausland in Zivil- oder Handelssachen (HZÜ),
- Übereinkommen vom 1.6.1970 über die Anerkennung von Ehescheidungen und Ehetrennungen,
- Übereinkommen vom 18.3.1970 über die Beweisaufnahme im Ausland in Zivil- oder Handelssachen (HBÜ),
- Übereinkommen vom 2.10.1973 über die Anerkennung und Vollstreckung von Unterhaltsentscheidungen (HUntAVÜbk 1973),
- Übereinkommen vom 25.10.1980 über die zivilrechtlichen Aspekte internationaler Kindesentführung (HKindEntfÜbk),
- Übereinkommen vom 29.5.1993 über den Schutz von Kindern und die Zusammenarbeit auf dem Gebiet der internationalen Adoption (HAdoptÜbk 1993),
- Übereinkommen vom 19.10.1996 über die Zuständigkeit, das anzuwendende Recht, die Anerkennung, Vollstreckung und Zusammenarbeit auf dem Gebiet der elterlichen Verantwortung und der Maßnahmen zum Schutz von Kindern (KSÜ),
- Übereinkommen vom 13.1.2000 über den internationalen Schutz von Erwachsenen (ESÜ),
- Übereinkommen vom 30.6.2005 über Gerichtsstandsvereinbarungen (HProrogÜbk 2005),
- Übereinkommen vom 23.11.2007 über die internationale Geltendmachung der Unterhaltsansprüche von Kindern und anderen Familienangehörigen (HUntVerfÜbk 2007),
- Übereinkommen vom 2.7.2019 über die Anerkennung und Vollstreckung ausländischer Entscheidungen in Zivil- und Handelssachen (HAVÜ 2019).

Nach dem BREXIT[92] aber noch vor Ablauf des BREXIT Übergangszeitraums[93] zum 31.12.2020 hat das Vereinigte Königreich dabei von der Möglichkeit Gebrauch gemacht, in eigenem Namen Haager Übereinkommen zu unterzeichnen bzw. zu ratifizieren.[94] So wurden zwei von der Europäischen Union ratifizierten

---

[91] Das Vereinigte Königreich ist auch Vertragsstaat des Haager Übereinkommens vom 5.10.1961 über das auf die Form letztwilliger Verfügungen anzuwendende Recht und des Haager Übereinkommens vom 1.7.1985 über das auf Trusts anzuwendende Recht und über ihre Anerkennung.

[92] Abkommen über den Austritt des Vereinigten Königreichs Großbritannien und Nordirland aus der Europäischen Union und der Europäischen Atomgemeinschaft (ABl. 2020 L 29, 7).

[93] Art. 126, 127 Abs. 1 des Abkommen über den Austritt des Vereinigten Königreichs Großbritannien und Nordirland aus der Europäischen Union und der Europäischen Atomgemeinschaft (ABl. 2020 L 29, 7).

[94] Gemäß Art. 129 Abs. 4 Austrittsabkommen: „während des Übergangszeitraums internationale Übereinkünfte aushandeln, unterzeichnen und ratifizieren, die es in Bereichen der ausschließlichen Zuständigkeit der Union eigenständig schließt".

Übereinkommen, das HProrogÜbk 2005 und das HUntVerfÜbk 2007, erneut und im eigenen Namen ratifiziert.[95] In diesem Zusammenhang hatte das Vereinigte Königreich bereits angekündigt, auch das HAVÜ 2019 unterschrieben und ratifizieren zu wollen.[96]

2. *Die Europäische Union und die Haager Konferenz*

Die Europäische Kommission legte dem Rat ein Vorschlag zum Beitritt der Europäischen Gemeinschaft zur Haager Konferenz vor,[97] der vom Rat am 5.10.2006 beschlossen wurde.[98] Die Kompetenz der Europäischen Gemeinschaft hierzu ergab sich aus der Kompetenzzuweisung des Art 61 AEUV, dies wird auch durch die Ausführungen des EuGH in seinem Gutachten[99] zu einem Beitritt der EG zum Lugano-Übereinkommen gestützt. Damit entscheidet das EuZPR über die Kompetenz der EU zum Abschluss der Haager Übereinkommen.

Für die Mitgliedschaft der Europäischen Union war zunächst aber eine Änderung der Satzung der Haager Konferenz notwendig. In Art. 3 Abs. 1 der Satzung wurde die Möglichkeit eröffnet, dass Organisationen der regionalen Wirtschaftsintegration Mitglied der der Haager Konferenz werden können. Gemäß Art. 3 Abs. 2 müssen bestimmte Voraussetzungen für die Anerkennung als eine Organisation der regionalen Wirtschaftsintegration erfüllt sein, wie ein Zusammenschluss souveräner Staaten, die Zuständigkeiten übertragen haben und die an die Beschlüsse der Organisation der regionalen Wirtschaftsintegration auch gebunden sind.[100] Diese Voraussetzungen treffen für Europäische Union zu. Die Änderung der Satzung wurde am 30.6.2005 beschlossen.[101]

Mit Wirkung vom 3.4.2007 ist die Europäische Gemeinschaft Mitglied der Haager Konferenz geworden.[102]

Die Europäische Union ist seit ihrem Beitritt zur Haager Konferenz Vertragsstaat von vier Haager Übereinkommen[103] geworden. Mit Blick auf das In-

---

[95] In Kraft getreten war das HProrogÜbk 2005 bereits am 1.10.2015. Die Ratifikation des Vereinigten Königreichs erfolgte am 28.11.2020 im Rahmen einer Änderung des Private International Law (Implementation of Agreements) Act 2020. In diesem Gesetz wurde mit dem HUntVerfÜbk 2007 ein weiteres Haager Übereinkommen ratifiziert.

[96] Siehe Ministry of Justice, The Hague Convention of 2 July 2019 on the Recognition and Enforcement of Foreign Judgments in Civil or Commercial Matters (Hague 2019) Response to consultation, S. 27 https://assets.publishing.service.gov.uk/media/6554c926046ed400148b992a/The_Hague_Convention_Response_to_Consultation__web_.pdf (abgerufen am 28.6.2024).

[97] Europäische Kommission, Vorschlag vom 9.12.2005, KOM(2005) 639 endgültig.

[98] Beschluss des Rates (2006/719/EG; ABl. 2006 L 297, 1).

[99] EuGH 7.2.2006 – Gutachten 1/03, ECLI:EU:C:2006:81 = BeckEuRS 2006, 421995.

[100] Siehe Text der Satzung unter https://www.hcch.net/de/instruments/conventions/full-text (abgerufen 28.6.2024).

[101] In Kraft getreten zum 1.1.2007, https://www.hcch.net/en/news-archive/details/?var event=125 (abgerufen 28.6.2024).

[102] Möglich wurde dies durch eine Satzungsänderung die am 30.6.2005 in Kraft getreten war. Nach der Art 3 Abs. 1 nF Satzung der Haager Konferenz können auch „Organisationen der regionalen Wirtschaftsintegration" Mitglieder werden.

[103] Siehe Statustabelle unter: https://www.hcch.net/de/states/hcch-members/details1/?sid=220 (abgerufen 28.6.2024).

ternationale Zivilverfahrensrecht sind folgende Übereinkommen[104] von Interesse:
- Übereinkommen vom 30.6.2005 über Gerichtsstandsvereinbarungen,[105]
- Übereinkommen vom 23.11.2007 über die internationale Geltendmachung der Unterhaltsansprüche von Kindern und anderen Familienangehörigen,[106]
- Übereinkommen vom 2.7.2019 über die Anerkennung und Vollstreckung ausländischer Entscheidungen in Zivil- und Handelssachen.[107]

Es ist davon auszugehen, dass die Europäische Union auch in der Zukunft an der Erarbeitung weiterer Haager Übereinkommen beteiligt.

3. „Gemeinsame" Haager Übereinkommen

Vor dem Beitritt der Europäischen Union 2007 haben die Mitgliedsstaaten selbst darüber entschieden, welche Haager Übereinkommen sie zeichnen und ggfs. auch ratifizieren. Diese sind ebenfalls im Verhältnis des jeweiligen Mitgliedsstaates (als Vertragsstaat) zum Vertragsstaat Vereinigtes Königreich zu beachten.

Wie ist also der Stand, hinsichtlich einer „gemeinsamen" Mitgliedschaft des Vereinigten Königreiches und der Mitgliedsstaaten der Europäischen Union (als eigener Vertragsstaat oder abgeleitet über die Europäische Union als Vertragsstaat) in den verschiedenen Haager Übereinkommen?

Ausgehend vom aktuellen Vertragsstatus des Vereinigten Königreich bestehen Gemeinsamkeiten hinsichtlich folgender Haager Übereinkommen:
- Übereinkommen vom 5.10.1961 zur Befreiung ausländischer öffentlicher Urkunden von der Legalisation – alle 27 EU-Mitgliedsstaaten,
- Übereinkommen vom 15.11.1965 über die Zustellung gerichtlicher und außergerichtlicher Schriftstücke im Ausland in Zivil- oder Handelssachen (HZÜ) – alle 27 EU Mitgliedsstaaten,
- Übereinkommen vom 1.6.1970 über die Anerkennung von Ehescheidungen und Ehetrennungen – 12 EU-Mitgliedsstaaten,[108]
- Übereinkommen vom 18.3.1970 über die Beweisaufnahme im Ausland in Zivil- oder Handelssachen (HBÜ) – 23 EU-Mitgliedsstaaten,[109]
- Übereinkommen vom 2.10.1973 über die Anerkennung und Vollstreckung von Unterhaltsentscheidungen (HUntAVÜbk 1973) – 16 EU-Mitgliedsstaaten,[110]

---

[104] Protokoll vom 23.11.2007 über das auf Unterhaltspflichten anzuwendende Recht; Beschluss des Rates (2009/941/EG; ABl. 2009 L 331, 17); in Kraft seit 1.8.2013.

[105] Beschluss des Rates 2014/887/EU vom 4.12.2014 über die Genehmigung — im Namen der Europäischen Union — des Haager Übereinkommens über Gerichtsstandsvereinbarungen vom 30.6.2005 (ABl. 2014 L 353, 5).

[106] Beschluss des Rates (2011/220/EU; ABl. 2011 L 93, 9).

[107] Beschluss des Rates (2022/1206/EU; ABl. 2022 L 187, 1).

[108] Vertragsstaaten sind die EU-Mitgliedsstaaten: Dänemark, Estland, Finnland Italien, Luxemburg, Niederlande, Polen, Portugal, Schweden, Slowakei, Tschechische Republik, Zypern.

[109] Nicht Vertragsstaaten sind die EU-Mitgliedsstaaten: Belgien, Finnland, Irland und Österreich.

[110] Nicht Vertragsstaaten sind die EU-Mitgliedsstaaten: Belgien, Bulgarien, Irland, Kroatien, Lettland, Malta, Österreich, Rumänien, Slowenien, Ungarn, Zypern.

- Übereinkommen vom 25.10.1980 über die zivilrechtlichen Aspekte internationaler Kindesentführung (HKindEntfÜbk) – alle 27 EU-Mitgliedsstaaten,
- Übereinkommen vom 29.5.1993 über den Schutz von Kindern und die Zusammenarbeit auf dem Gebiet der internationalen Adoption (HAdoptÜbk 1993) – alle 27 EU-Mitgliedsstaaten,
- Übereinkommen vom 19.10.1996 über die Zuständigkeit, das anzuwendende Recht, die Anerkennung, Vollstreckung und Zusammenarbeit auf dem Gebiet der elterlichen Verantwortung und der Maßnahmen zum Schutz von Kindern (KSÜ) – alle 27 EU-Mitgliedsstaaten,
- Übereinkommen vom 13.1.2000 über den internationalen Schutz von Erwachsenen (ESÜ) – 13 EU-Mitgliedsstaaten,[111]
- Übereinkommen vom 30.6.2005 über Gerichtsstandsvereinbarungen (HProrogÜbk 2005) – alle 27 EU-Mitgliedsstaaten,
- Übereinkommen vom 23.11.2007 über die internationale Geltendmachung der Unterhaltsansprüche von Kindern und anderen Familienangehörigen (HUntVerfÜbk 2007) – 26 EU-Mitgliedsstaaten,[112]
- Übereinkommen vom 2.7.2019 über die Anerkennung und Vollstreckung ausländischer Entscheidungen in Zivil- und Handelssachen (HAVÜ 2019) – 26 EU-Mitgliedsstaaten.[113]

Die Übersicht zeigt, dass einige Haager Übereinkommen, in denen das Vereinigte Königreich Vertragsstaat ist, auch alle EU-Mitgliedsstaaten Vertragsstaaten sind. Damit kann eine Anwendung der verschiedenen Haager Übereinkommen gegenüber einer Vielzahl von EU-Mitgliedsstaaten erfolgen. Die Anwendbarkeit Haager Übereinkommen durch das Vereinigte Königreich und die Mitgliedsstaaten der Europäische Union schafft Rechtsklarheit, Vorhersehbarkeit und vor allem Rechtsicherheit.[114]

Besonders wichtig ist dies beispielweise bei den Haager Übereinkommen aus dem Bereich der Rechtshilfe. HZÜ und HBÜ wurden schon vor Schaffung der jeweiligen europäischen Verordnungen (EG-ZustVO und EG-BewVO), als zu beachtende Regelungen des Internationalen Zivilverfahrensrecht,[115] angewendet. Damit kommt ein bekannter, einheitlicher Rahmen, wenn auch abgeschwächt im Vergleich zu den auf der vertieften Integration beruhenden europäischen Verordnungen nunmehr wieder zur Anwendung.

Mit dem HZÜ steht eine gute und praxistaugliche Rechtsgrundlage zur Verfügung. Natürlich ist bei der Anwendung des HZÜ an Stelle der (bisher genutzten EG-ZustVO 2007) zu beachten, dass die EG-ZustVO 2007 (wie auch ihre Nach-

[111] Vertragsstaaten sind die EU-Mitgliedsstaaten: Belgien, Deutschland, Estland, Finnland, Frankreich, Griechenland, Irland, Lettland, Malta, Österreich, Portugal, Spanien, Tschechische Republik, Zypern. Immerhin gezeichnet haben weitere 4 EU-Mitgliedsstaaten: Italien, Luxemburg, Niederlande und Polen.

[112] Nicht Vertragsstaat ist EU-Mitgliedsstaat Dänemark.

[113] Nicht Vertragsstaat ist EU-Mitgliedsstaat Dänemark.

[114] So mit Hinweis auf das HZÜ: Schlosser/Hess, EuZPR/Schlosser/Hess, 5. Aufl. 2021, EuZVO 2022 Art. 29 Rn. 2; Rauscher, EuZPR/EuIPR/Urici, 5. Aufl. 2024, EU-ZustVO 2020 Einl. Rn. 46.

[115] Rauscher, Internationales und Europäisches Zivilverfahrensrecht, 1. Aufl. 1999, S. 12.

folgerin EU-ZustVO 2020) für bestimmte Zustellungen andere (höhere) Voraussetzungen vorsieht.[116] Neben dem HZÜ können aber auch bilaterale Abkommen wieder zur Anwendung gelangen, so lebt im Verhältnis Vereinigtes Königreich zu Deutschland das deutsch-britische Rechtshilfeabkommen wieder auf.[117]

Aber auch die Anwendungen der familienrechtlichen Haager Übereinkommen (KSÜ, ESÜ, HUntVerfÜbk 2007) im Verhältnis des Vereinigten Königreichs zu den EU-Mitgliedsstaaten und umgekehrt, ist positiv zu bewerten. Wobei es sicher nicht schadet, weitere EU-Mitgliedstaaten zu animieren, auch Vertragsstaat des ESÜ zu werden.

Auch die beiden aus dem sogenannten „jurisdiction project"[118] entstandenen Haager Übereinkommen: das HProrogÜbk 2005 und das HAVÜ 2019[119] dürften schnell an Bedeutung gewinnen. Das für die EU bereits am 1.9.2023 in Kraft getretene HAVÜ 2019[120] hat das Vereinigte Königreich gezeichnet und am 27.6.2024 auch die Ratifizierungsurkunde hinterlegt.[121] Das HAVÜ 2019 wird im Verhältnis zum Vereinigten Königreich am 1.7.2025 in Kraft treten. Dann könnten gerichtliche Entscheidungen in Zivil- und Handelssachen zukünftig vereinfachter anerkannt und vollstreckt werden können.[122]

IV. Der Blick nach vorn

Als Status Quo ist somit festzuhalten, dass durch den Austritt des Vereinigten Königreiches aus der Europäischen Union und dem (verweigerten) Beitritt zum Lugano-Übereinkommen 2007 sich gemeinsame Rechtsgrundlagen zwischen dem Vereinigten Königreich und einem Mitgliedsstaat der Europäischen Union auf internationale Abkommen, wie die Haager Übereinkommen, beschränken.

Zumindest für einen Teil der mittlerweile kaum zu überschauenden Vielzahl an europäischen Verordnungen, können die Haager Übereinkommen, wenn auch nicht gleichwertigen Ersatz bieten.

Es bleibt zu hoffen, dass das Vereinigten Königreich – aber auch die Europäischen Union – sich auch zukünftig an der Erarbeitung weiterer Haager Übereinkommen beteiligen und den Abschluss dieser Abkommen zugleich auch als verlässliche Verbindung zwischen ihnen verstanden wird.

---

[116] Zu Einzelheiten siehe Rauscher, EuZPR/EuIPR/Urici, 5. Aufl. 2024, EU-ZustVO 2020 Einl. Rn. 10.

[117] Münchener Kommentar zur ZPO/Rauscher, 6. Aufl. 2022, ZPO Vor § 1067 Rn. 7.

[118] Zu den Entwicklungen und dem aktuellen Stand siehe https://www.hcch.net/de/projects/legislative-projects/jurisdiction-project (abgerufen 28.6.2024).

[119] Eine erste Kommentierung des HAVÜ 2019 bei: Rauscher, EuZPR/EuIPR/Weller, 5. Aufl. 2022, HAVÜ 2019; siehe auch Jacobs, Das Haager Anerkennungs- und Vollstreckungsübereinkommen vom 2. Juli 2019, 2021.

[120] Kritisch zum Abschluss des HAVÜ 2019: Schack IPRax 2020, 1; Huber FS Schack, 2022, 451; Schack ZEuP 2023, 285; dagegen positiv zum HAVÜ 2019 Jacobs/Lützi ZEuP 2024, 15 (16).

[121] Pressemitteilung, https://www.hcch.net/de/news-archive/details/?varevent=985 (abgerufen 28.6.2024).

[122] Allerdings bleibt festzuhalten, dass das HAVÜ 2019 kein Ersatz für das LugÜbk 2007 ist.

Soll es dauerhaft bei dieser Beschränkung bleiben? Ist die enge Verbundenheit und Tatsache, dass zwischen dem Vereinigten Königreich und der Europäischen Union über mehr als 40 Jahre ein gemeinsames Europäisches Zivilprozessrecht galt, nicht Grund genug auch über einen Sonderweg neben Lugano-Übereinkommen und Haager Übereinkommen nachzudenken?

Gerade weil aber die „wirtschaftlichen" wie auch die „persönlichen" Verbindungen zwischen dem Vereinigten Königreich und der Europäischen Union bzw. deren Mitgliedsstaaten gewachsen und sehr eng sind, sollte in der Zukunft – auf beiden Seiten – darüber nachgedacht werden, wie das Vereinigte Königreich wieder enger an das Europäische Zivilprozessrecht binden könnte.

Hierzu werden im Schrifttum bereits einige Ideen diskutiert. *Sonnentag* etwa untersuchte schon 2017 verschiedene Szenarien für bilaterale Abkommen nach Norwegischen oder Schweizer Vorbild.[123] Für *Lein* käme auch ein bilaterales Übereinkommen EU-UK nach Vorbild des EU-DK Abkommen in Betracht.[124]

Grundsätzlich wäre ein völkerrechtliches Abkommen zwischen der Europäischen Union und dem Vereinigten Königreich möglich. Allerdings dürfte das EU-DK Abkommen als Blaupause nicht taugen, denn trotz der Tatsache, dass Dänemark sich nicht an der justiziellen Zusammenarbeit in der EU beteiligt, so ist es dennoch Teil des gemeinsamen europäischen Binnenmarktes. Gerade diesen gemeinsamen Binnenmarkt wollte das Vereinigte Königreich verlassen.

Aussichtsreicher dürfte es sein, doch nochmal einen neuen Anlauf für einen Beitritt zum Lugano-Übereinkommen zu unternehmen. Dies könnte etwa im Zuge einer hoffentlich bald auf den Weg zu bringenden Revision des LugÜbk 2007 geschehen. Vielleicht sind dann – auf beiden Seiten – die Gedanken mehr einer gemeinsamen Zusammenarbeit gewidmet als dem Begleichen alter Rechnungen.

Bis dahin können die verschiedenen Haager Übereinkommen, die mit dem Austritt aus der Europäischen Union entstandene Lücke teilweise schließen. Ein gleicher wertiger Ersatz zum EuZPR sind die Haager Übereinkommen jedoch nicht.

---

[123] Sonnentag, Die Konsequenzen des BREXIT für das Internationale Privat- und Zivilverfahrensrecht, 2017.

[124] Lein ZVglRWiss (120) 2021, 1 (10ff.); so auch Basler Kommentar LugÜ/Weibel/Mata, 3. Aufl. 2024, Art. 70–72 Rn. 7.

MARKUS KOTZUR

Toleranzdenken, Toleranzerwartungen, Toleranzgrenzen – Diskursimpulse aus völkerrechtlicher Sicht

I. Vorbemerkung

Der folgenden, vom großen Toleranzgedanken eines *Thomas von Aquin, Gotthold Ephraim Lessing* oder *Voltaire* inspirierten völkerrechtlichen Miniatur aus Anlass des 70. Geburtstags von *Thomas Rauscher* sei eine persönliche Vorbemerkung vorangestellt. Der Verfasser durfte während seiner Leipziger Zeit (von 2004 bis 2012) gemeinsam mit dem Jubilar sowie den Kollegen *Richard L. Williamson, David Abraham* und *Markus Wagner* (alle University of Miami) ein Kooperationsseminar betreuen, für dessen didaktische Konzeption schon *Rudolf Geiger*[1] mitverantwortlich zeichnete: das „Miami-Leipzig-Seminar"[2]. Jährlich identifizierten die beiden beteiligten Fakultäten aktuelle, immer auch grundlegende Themen aus dem Internationalen Privatrecht und dem Völkerrecht. Sie wurden jeweils von einem Tandem einer Leipziger Studentin/eines Leipziger Studenten und einer Studentin/eines Studenten aus Miami bearbeitet. Gute Englischkenntnisse waren für das englischsprachige Seminar auch auf deutscher Seite Voraussetzung. Im Januar/Februar (am Ende des deutschen Wintersemesters) reiste die deutsche Gruppe nach Florida, im Mai/Juni erfolgte der Gegenbesuch in Sachsen. Angeleitet von den Betreuerinnen/Betreuern erarbeiteten die Studierenden zu dem ihnen vorgegeben Oberthema eine eigene Forschungsfrage, die es dann aus vergleichender Perspektive und auch mit Gespür für die außerrechtlichen Zusammenhänge zu behandeln galt.

Der Ertrag dieses komparatistisch und diskursiv angelegten, nicht zuletzt vom „law in context"-Ansatz getragenen Seminars war für die Studierenden wie Lehrenden gleichermaßen groß. Jeder Lehrende wurde zum Lernenden (der Völkerrechtler mit Blick auf das Internationale Privatrecht, die deutschen mit Blick auf die US-amerikanischen Kolleginnen/Kollegen und vice versa), jede(r) Lernende zum/zur Lehrenden auf Grundlage ihrer/seiner jeweiligen Fach- und Rechtskultur: eine interkulturell wie interdisziplinär gelebte „universitas litterarum" aus spezifisch rechtswissenschaftlicher und damit notwendig normativer Perspektive. Dass es dabei auch zu pointierten Positionierungen und fruchtbaren „contestations"[3] kam, versteht sich für die freie Wissenschaft innerhalb einer offenen Wissensgesell-

---

[1] Lehrstuhlvorgänger des Verfassers an der Universität Leipzig.

[2] Siehe auch Kotzur, Werkstatt Seminar – Überlegungen zur Konzeptionalisierung einer forschungsbasierten, kompetenz- und diskursorientierten Lehrform, in: Krüper, Rechtswissenschaft lehren. Handbuch der juristischen Fachdidaktik, 2022, § 27, S. 682ff.

[3] Wiener, A Theory of Contestation, 2014.

schaft von selbst. Es waren vor allem die großen, im Verlauf der Jahre immer wiederkehrenden Themen, die zum Nach-, Fort- und Weiterdenken anregten. Das gilt insbesondere für das hier angerissene Toleranzpostulat. In zahlreichen Seminargesprächen wurde immer wieder deutlich, dass sich sowohl das Internationale Privatrecht, zu dessen kollisionsrechtlicher Natur *Thomas Rauscher* Grundsätzliches beiträgt[4], als auch das Völkerrecht im Sinne einer Toleranzordnung deuten lassen, damit aber die Fragen nach dem Verhältnis von verbindlichem Recht und (außer-)rechtlicher Toleranz nur benannt, aber gewiss nicht gelöst sind. Lösungen kann auch vorliegende Skizze nicht anbieten, sie will nur, verbunden mit den besten Geburtstagswünschen, vorläufige Überlegungen zur kritischen Diskussion stellen.[5]

II. Toleranz, Duldsamkeit und Kompromiss – vom „Sich-Ertragen" und dessen Grenzen

Begonnen sei mit einer wertebezogenen Toleranzbehauptung aus Art. 2 EUV, deren indikativische Formulierung nicht über ihre normative Stoßrichtung und ihren Appellcharakter hinwegtäuschen darf: „Die Werte, auf die sich die Union gründet, sind die Achtung der Menschenwürde, Freiheit, Demokratie, Gleichheit, Rechtsstaatlichkeit und die Wahrung der Menschenrechte einschließlich der Rechte der Personen, die Minderheiten angehören. Diese Werte sind allen Mitgliedstaaten in einer Gesellschaft gemeinsam, die sich durch Pluralismus, Nichtdiskriminierung, Toleranz, Gerechtigkeit, Solidarität und die Gleichheit von Frauen und Männern auszeichnet." Der so gebrauchte Toleranzbegriff rekurriert auf das vorrechtliche Ideal einer toleranten Gesellschaft, will dieses Gesellschaft aber zugleich durch die Mittel des Rechts ermöglichen und garantieren.[6] Eine solche Steuerungsdialektik findet sich nicht nur im Unionsrecht, sondern auch auf vielen Teilgebieten des Völkerrechts. Es nimmt in den unterschiedlichsten Zusammenhängen Bezug auf vielfältige vorrechtliche Toleranzideen respektive Toleranzideale[7], ohne die Toleranz explizit zu einer eigenen (normativen) Kategorie oder gar einem übergeordneten Rechtsprinzip (vgl. Art. 38 Abs. 1 lit. c IGH-Statut) auszuformen. Nichtsdestoweniger will es mit dem Ziel praktizierter Toleranz normativ steuern. Besonders aussagekräftig ist die Präambel der Charta der Vereinten Nationen in ihrer authentischen englischen Sprachfassung[8]: „to practice tolerance and live to-

---

[4] Etwa als Herausgeber des mittlerweile in 5. Aufl. erscheinenden achtbändigen Kommentars zum Europäischen Zivilprozess- und Kollisionsrecht (EuZPR/EuIPR); weiterhin Rauscher, Internationales Privatrecht. Mit internationalem Verfahrensrecht, 5. Aufl. 2017.

[5] Sie gehen zurück auf Kotzur, Toleranzdenken im Völkerrecht, in: Toleranz! Interdisziplinäre Zugänge zu einem Kernthema der Menschheitsgeschichte, Kieler Schriften zur Regionalgeschichte, Band 10, 2023, S. 79ff.; Kotzur AVR 48 (2010), 163ff.; Kotzur, Toleranz statt Ordnung im Völkerrecht?, in: Enders/Kahlo, Diversität und Toleranz. Toleranz als Ordnungsprinzip?, 2010, S. 229ff.

[6] Vgl. Reimer ZG 2003, 208; Calliess JZ 2003, 1033; Kotzur DÖV 2005, 313.

[7] Siehe auch Bobbio, Gründe für die Toleranz, in: Bobbio, Das Zeitalter der Menschenrechte, 1998, S. 87ff.

[8] Authentische Sprachfassungen der Charta sind nach ihrem Art. 111 Chinesisch, Französisch, Russisch, Englisch und Spanisch. Zur normativen Bindungswirkung der Präambel Kotzur, Theo-

gether in peace with one another as good neighbours." Die deutsche Übersetzung verzichtet überraschenderweise auf den Toleranzbegriff, unterstreicht vielmehr in etwas altertümlich anmutender Formulierung den der Toleranz immanenten Aspekt geduldigen Ertragens: „Duldsamkeit zu üben und als gute Nachbarn in Frieden miteinander zu leben."

Dieser Duldsamkeitsaspekt ist schon im Modell des Gesellschaftsvertrages angelegt. Ganz gleich, ob fiktiv gedacht oder real praktiziert, bleibt sein Ziel ein „immer neues Sich-Vertragen und Sich-Ertragen aller" in einer wie auch immer definierten, national, regional oder international angelegten politischen Gemeinschaft.[9] Dieses „Sich-Vertragen" und „Sich-Ertragen" fordert vor allem die Gewaltfreiheit aller relevanten Akteure, wie sie Art. 2 Nr. 4 mit dem Gewaltverbot als völkerrechtliches ius cogens[10] festschreibt und friedliche Streitbeilegung (Art. 2 Nr. 3). Ein solch normativ ausbuchstabierter Wunsch nach friedlichem Zusammenleben ignoriert aber nicht die Konflikte, die allen (pluralistischen) Gesellschaften und Gemeinschaften notwendig immanent sind.[11] Weil, individuell wie kollektiv gedacht, die Freiheit des/der Einen immer mit der Freiheit des/der Anderen kollidieren wird, bedarf es eines durch Recht bestimmten Koordinatensystems, das „pluralistische Initiativen und Alternativen"[12] erlaubt und, wie eben gesagt, Raum für das streitige, aber gewaltlose Austragen von Konflikten gibt[13]. Toleranz und kluge Politik teilen einen gemeinsamen Nenner: ihr Modus ist der Kompromiss[14]. Die Kompromissbereitschaft kann, um noch einmal an die Formel vom „Sich-Vertragen" und „Sich-Ertragen" aller anzuknüpfen, bis an die Grenzen des Erträglichen heranreichen. Das „Unerträgliche zu ertragen" würde Toleranzpraxen, wie sie die vorstehend genannten Normen anmahnen, indes in ihr Gegenteil verkehren. Das Erträgliche zu ertragen ist ein stabilisierender, ordnungsbildender Faktor, das Unerträgliche zu Ertragen – sei es aus Ohnmacht, Hilflosigkeit oder Gleichgültigkeit – wirkt destabilisierend und ordnungszersetzend. Die Grenzen zwischen dem Noch- und dem Nicht Mehr Erträglichen verschwimmen oft in Grauzonen. So gibt es kein Patentrezept, wie freiheitliche Demokratien mit autoritären Staaten umgehen sollen, heute geläufige Begriffe wie „De-Coupling" und „De-Risking"[15] stehen für schmale Gradwanderungen und befeuern ihrerseits politische Kontroversen. Bei al-

---

rieelemente des internationalen Menschenrechtsschutzes. Das Beispiel der Präambel des Internationalen Paktes über bürgerliche und politische Rechte, 2001.

[9] Häberle, Verfassungslehre als Kulturwissenschaft, 2. Aufl. 1998, S. 621.

[10] Statt aller Kadelbach, Zwingendes Völkerrecht, 1992.

[11] Häberle, Die „Kultur des Friedens" – Thema der universalen Verfassungslehre. Oder: das Prinzip Frieden, 2017, S. 178, bezeichnet die Toleranz als „friedensnahen Begriff" und ordnet sie als „funktionales Äquivalent" für das Prinzip Frieden ein.

[12] Hesse, Grundzüge des Verfassungsrechts der Bundesrepublik Deutschland, 20. Aufl. 1999 (Neudruck 2020), Rn. 130.

[13] Grundlegend aus politikwissenschaftlicher Sicht Wiener, A Theory of Contestation, 2014.

[14] Nicht zuletzt deshalb gilt Toleranz als ein tragender Grundsatz der freiheitlichen Demokratie, BVerfG 11.4.1972 – 2 BvR 75/71, BVerfGE 33, 23 (32) = NJW 1972, 1183 (Eidesverweigerung aus Glaubensgründen).

[15] Müller, De-Risking. Das neue Konzept zur Abkoppelung von China. Es klingt weniger dramatisch, wird jedoch weiter Streit verursachen, www.sueddeutsche.de/meinung/china-derisking-decoupling-1.5946671 (zuletzt besucht am 28.4.2024).

len von Toleranz geleiteten Abwägungsnotwendigkeiten darf „Duldsamkeit" indes niemals die Antwort auf einen eindeutigen Völkerrechtsbruch sein (wie etwa den seit Februar 2022 von Russlands Machthaber *W. Putin* verantworteten völkerrechtswidrigen Angriffskrieg der Russischen Föderation gegen die Ukraine[16]). Auch dort, wo wie beim Terrorschlag der Hamas gegen Israel vom Oktober 2023, Terror beim Namen genannt werden muss, verbietet sich jedes relativierende „Ja, aber (...)" – womit, auch das sei klargestellt, noch keine Aussage über die Verhältnismäßigkeit der Gegenschläge getroffen ist.[17]

III. Toleranz als Konfliktbegriff

Aus dem Gezeigten sei eine erste generelle Schlussfolgerung gezogen: Toleranz ist ein Konfliktbegriff, sie setzt Konflikte voraus und muss im Konflikt immer auch seine eigenen Grenzen ausloten.[18] Daraus leitet sich eine weitere Konsequenz ab: Der facettenreiche Konfliktbegriff der Toleranz bleibt definitorisch schwer erfassbar; es geht eher um unterschiedlich konnotierte Toleranzbegriffe im Plural als den einen Toleranzbegriff im Singular. Hier nur einige Variationen zum Thema: Positiv besetzt ist die Toleranz als Identitätszuschreibung offener Gesellschaften, als (unerreichbares) Ideal, als politische Praxis, als ein normatives Sollen, mitunter sogar im positiven Recht verbürgt, negativ besetzt ist die Toleranz als Indifferenz, Beliebigkeit, Unentschiedenheit, laissez faire. Besonders schwer wiegt, individualrechtlich wie in Rechtsbeziehungen zwischen Kollektiven, bloße „Toleranz" statt echter Anerkennung bei asymmetrischen Machtkonstellationen.[19] So verschieden die Toleranzbegriffe, so unterschiedlich sind die Toleranzsubjekte- bzw. Toleranzakteure (Individuen, Kollektive, „die Gesellschaft", „der Staat", „die internationale Gemeinschaft") und Toleranzobjekte (Überzeugungen, Überzeugungssysteme/Ideologien, Religionen, Weltanschauungen, Personen oder persönliche Eigenschaften, Handlungsweisen, Gewohnheiten etc.). Auch Toleranzpraktiken können differenzierte Gestalt annehmen (negative Duldung, positive Anerkennung, aktive Förderung).[20]

Wie kann angesichts von Diversität und Konflikt[21] dennoch einen begriffskonkretisierende Annäherung gelingen? *R. Frost* spricht von „eine(r) Haltung bzw. eine(r) Praxis, die nur in einem Konflikt erforderlich wird".[22] Diesen Konflikt-

[16] Zur Einordnung siehe Schmahl NJW 2022, 969 und Walter JZ 2022, 473.

[17] Asseburg/Wiese, Die Gräueltaten der Hamas, Israels Reaktion und das völkerrechtliche Primat zum Schutz der Zivilbevölkerung, verfassungsblog.de/die-graueltaten-der-hamas-israels-reaktion-und-das-volkerrechtliche-primat-zum-schutz-der-zivilbevolkerung/ (zuletzt besucht am 28.4.2024).

[18] Grundlegend zum Folgenden Frost, Toleranz im Konflikt. Geschichte, Gehalt und Gegenwart eines umstrittenen Begriffs, 6. Aufl. 2020.

[19] Yovel, Tolerance as Grace and as Rightful Recognition, Social Research 65 (1998) 897.

[20] Frost, Toleranz im Konflikt. Geschichte, Gehalt und Gegenwart eines umstrittenen Begriffs, 6. Aufl. 2020, S. 31.

[21] Siehe auch McKinnon/Castiglione, The Culture of Toleration in Diverse Societies, 2003.

[22] Frost, Toleranz im Konflikt. Geschichte, Gehalt und Gegenwart eines umstrittenen Begriffs, 6. Aufl. 2020, S. 12.

begriff der Toleranz erschließt *Frost* in vier Bedeutungsschichten: Toleranz als von wechselseitiger Akzeptanz geprägtes „Miteinander im Dissens"; Toleranz als eine Forderung, die aus Konflikten entsteht; Toleranz als eine Forderung, die selbst Gegenstand von Konflikten ist und bestritten wird; Toleranz als „ein Konzept", das aber aus einer „Fülle von Konzeptionen" und Toleranzbegründungen lebt.[23] In eine für die rechtswissenschaftliche Auseinandersetzung zentrale Steuerungsperspektive übersetzt geht es um Mechanismen des Vielfaltsmanagement bzw. der „diversity governance". Das Recht arbeitet dabei dialektisch. Es sucht manche Konflikte normativ verbindlich zu entscheiden, andere bewusst in der Schwebe zu halten. Bei diesem „In-der-Schwebe-Halten" wirken außerrechtliche und durch das Recht eröffnete Toleranz diametral gegensätzlich. Toleranz will die Freiheit der Einen mit der Freiheit der Anderen dadurch in Ausgleich bringen, dass sie „Miteinander im Dissens" ermöglicht. Die Einen sollen die Anderen „ertragen" – tolerare – ohne dazu verpflichtet zu sein. In diesem Sinne gibt das Leitmotiv der Europäischen Union „in Vielfalt geeint" ein Toleranzversprechen. Recht hingegen will die Freiheit der Einen ebenso wie die Freiheit der Anderen durch subjektive Rechte garantieren und den Widerstreit der jeweiligen Freiheitsrechte durch ihrerseits wiederum verbindliche Regeln der Abwägung und des Ausgleichs lösen. Es weiß, dass es dazu auf Toleranzspielräume als Steuerungsmittel nicht verzichten kann. Liegt umfassende Verrechtlichung vor, besteht für außerrechtliche Toleranz kein Bedürfnis mehr, bleibt für Toleranz nurmehr der Raum eröffnet, den das Recht bewusst in der Schwebe hält. Anders formuliert: Wo Duldung oder Anerkennung rechtlich geboten, zur Rechtspflicht geworden sind, ist die Toleranz *Voraussetzung* des Rechts, werden Toleranzerwartungen verrechtlich. Aber auch wo eine solche Verrechtlichung (noch) nicht stattgefunden hat und Recht nur an Toleranz appelliert, bleibt sie eine Sollenskategorie, mag das Sollen seinen Grund in der Moral, in politischer Klugheit, in Nützlichkeitserwägungen, Gegenseitigkeitserwartungen oder anderem haben.

IV. Pragmatische Toleranz und Vielseitigkeitsmanagement im Völkerrecht

„Toleranzdenken" ist dem Recht von seiner Steuerungslogik her also stärker immanent, als es die außerrechtliche bzw. vorrechtliche Konzeption der Toleranz vermuten lässt. Das Völkerrecht macht diesbezüglich keine Ausnahme, im Gegenteil: Die Diversität der Rechtskulturen, mit denen es umgehen, die Diversität der Rechtsordnungen, die es im Sinne einer regelbasierten internationalen Ordnung einhegen, und Diversität der Machtinteressen, denen es sich wirklichkeitsbewusst stellen muss, verlangt nach einem „accomodating diversity" – aber auch danach, das Unerträgliche außerhalb des Rechts zu stellen.

Die religiöse Toleranz liefert dafür ein gutes Beispiel. Toleranz, seinerzeit verstanden als von der Hoheitsmacht einseitig gewährte, daher auch jederzeit wieder rück-

[23] Frost, Toleranz im Konflikt. Geschichte, Gehalt und Gegenwart eines umstrittenen Begriffs, 6. Aufl. 2020, S. 12–14.

nehmbare Freiheit, findet etwa im *Mailänder Toleranzedikt* (313) oder im *Edikt von Nantes* (1598) Niederschlag.[24] Dabei geht es zunächst nur um einen pragmatischen „Modus der Konfliktvermeidung"[25] – solange die Religion der Minderheit deren Privatsache bleibt und keine öffentliche Anerkennung fordert, besteht keine Gefahr für die öffentliche Ordnung nach Vorstellungen der Mehrheit. Toleranz als „Sich-Ertragen" ist hier noch lange nicht ausgeformt. Vom heutigen Individualrecht der Religionsfreiheit bleibt dieses Verständnis denkbar weit entfernt. Erst wo die Religionsfreiheit als unveräußerliches Recht anerkannt wird, folgt daraus ein Anerkennungsanspruch[26], der dem Staat vorausliegt und über den der Staat nicht mehr verfügen kann.[27] Im Staat-Bürger-Verhältnis geht es nicht mehr um Toleranz, sondern um Grundrechtsberechtigung und Grundrechtsverpflichtung. Über die Drittwirkungslehre[28] und die Schutzpflichtendimension[29] wirkt die Verpflichtungswirkung in den innergesellschaftlichen Bereich hinein. Soweit aber im Bürger-Bürger-Verhältnis Fragen religiöser Freiheit noch nicht verrechtlich sind, erwartet der religiös neutrale freiheitliche Verfassungsstaat von der ihn konstituierenden Bürgergesellschaft religiöse Toleranz.[30] Der einleitend zitierte Art. 2 EUV macht das für den europäischen Verfassungsverbund[31] mehr als deutlich.

Pragmatische Toleranz macht sich das Völkerrecht auch jenseits der Religion zu eigen. In der Idee friedlicher Koexistenz ist sie schon der Sache nach mitangelegt. Das Koexistenzvölkerrecht fragt weder nach den materiellen Legitimationsvoraussetzungen noch den tatsächlichen Machtgrundlagen der Souveränität, sondern verlangt, die jeweils andere Machtbegründungskonzeption, gleich ob freiheitlicher Verfassungs- oder autoritärer Gottesstaat, gleich ob absolute Monarchie oder freiheitliche Demokratie, zu *tolerieren* – selbst wenn die tatsächlichen Machtverhältnisse, die *tatsächliche Dominanz* politischer, wirtschaftlicher oder militärischer Natur *Intoleranz* zuließen. Genau das besagt Art. 2 Nr. 1 UN-Charta: „Die Organisation beruht auf dem Grundsatz der souveränen Gleichheit aller ihrer Mitglieder." Die (völkerrechtlich weiterhin umstrittene) *Toleranzgrenze* ist allenfalls dort erreicht, wo nach schwersten Menschenrechtsverletzungen („gross violations of human rights") die humanitäre Intervention der internationalen Gemeinschaft als ultima ratio mi-

---

[24] Rottmann FS der Juristenfakultät zum 600jährigen Bestehen der Universität Leipzig, 2009, S. 551 (562f.).

[25] Rottmann FS der Juristenfakultät zum 600jährigen Bestehen der Universität Leipzig, 2009, S. 551 (562f.) unter Verweis auf den Text des Ediktes von Nantes: „Um keinen Anlass zu Unruhen und Streitigkeiten zwischen unseren Untertanen bestehen zu lassen", zit. nach Heerdtle/Leeb, Toleranz – Texte zu Theorie und politischer Praxis, 1987, S. 59.

[26] Grundlegend Honneth, Anerkennung. Eine europäische Ideengeschichte, 2018.

[27] Locus classicus ist Jellinek, Die Erklärung der Menschen- u. Bürgerrechte. Ein Beitrag zur Verfassungsgeschichte, 1895.

[28] Kroemer, Drittwirkung der Grundrechte. Die Unterscheidung zwischen Staat und Gesellschaft als staatstheoretische Bedingung der Drittwirkungsproblematik, 2024.

[29] Siehe zB Jaeckel, Schutzpflichten im deutschen und europäischen Recht, 2001.

[30] Siehe zB Püttner, Toleranz als Verfassungsprinzip, 1977; Debus, Das Verfassungsprinzip der Toleranz unter besonderer Berücksichtigung der Rechtsprechung des Bundesverfassungsgerichts, 1999; weiterhin Goerlich, Säkularität – Religiosität – Egalität – in einer nicht nur auf die Grenzen verfasster Rechte fixierten Perspektive (2011), in: Goerlich, Zur zugewandten Säkularität – Beiträge auf dem Weg dahin. Ausgewählte Schriften, 2014, S. 235.

[31] Prägend Pernice VVDStRL 60 (2001) 148 (163).

litärisches Einschreiten erlaubt[32] und formale Souveränität materieller Gerechtigkeit zu weichen hat.

Warum das Völkerrecht so reich an Toleranztexten ist, vermag sich vor diesem Hintergrund besser zu erschließen. Schon in der bereits zitierten Präambel zur UN-Charta bekennen die Mitglieder den „Glauben an die Grundrechte des Menschen, an Würde und Wert des Einzelnen, Rechtsgleichheit von Mann und Frau sowie von großen und kleinen Nationen" und bekunden sodann, das sei hier nochmals unterstrichen, ihren Entschluss, „Duldsamkeit zu üben und als gute Nachbarn zusammenzuleben": „to practice tolerance". Das Toleranzpostulat der „guten Nachbarschaft" wird in der „Friendly Relations Declaration", einer Resolution der UN-Generalversammlung und daher bloßes „soft law", aufgegriffen.[33] Den häufigsten Niederschlag findet Toleranz in menschenrechtlichen Verbürgungen. Ein erstes Beispiel auf universeller Ebene ist Art. 26 Nr. 2 AEMR (1948).[34] Ihm zufolge soll Erziehung ausgerichtet sein auf „Verständnis, Toleranz und Freundschaft zwischen den Nationen und Religionen". Ein menschheitsumspannendes Erziehungsziel[35] zur Toleranz wird formuliert und findet später sein normativ verbindliches Pendant in Art. 13 Abs. 1 IPWSKR (UN-Sozialpakt) (explizit bezogen auf nationale, ethnische und religiöse Gruppierungen). Nach Art. 10 der Erklärung über die Rechte des Kindes (1959)[36] sollen Kinder „im Geist des Verständnisses, der Toleranz und Völkerfreundschaft, des Friedens und der Brüderlichkeit sowie im vollen Bewusstsein erzogen werden, dass [sie ihre] Kräfte und Fähigkeiten im Dienst der Menschen einsetzen [sollen]." Das universelle Völkerrecht kennt auch den Gegenbegriff zur Toleranz, den der *Intoleranz,* etwa in der „Erklärung zur Beseitigung aller auf Religionen oder Überzeugungen beruhenden Formen von Intoleranz und Diskriminierung" (1981).[37]

Für den regionalen Menschenrechtsschutz sei, um nicht in der europäisch-atlantischen Welt stehen zu bleiben, exemplarisch auf die Arabische Menschenrechtscharta aus (2004) verwiesen. Bei aller Bezogenheit auf den Islam als rechtliche Maxime konstitutioneller Einheit[38] heißt es dort im zweiten Passus der Präambel: „in furtherance of the eternal principles of fraternity, equality and tolerance among hu-

[32] v. Schorlemer Internationale Politik 2/2000; Schmalenbach JZ 2005, 637; Schaber ARSP 92 (2006), 295; Lange-Bertalot, Weltbürgerliches Völkerrecht: Kantianische Brücke zwischen konstitutioneller Souveränität und humanitärer Intervention, 2007; zum menschenrechtlich bedingten Wandel des Souveränitätsbegriffs Müller, Wandel des Souveränitätsbegriffs im Lichte der Grundrechte, in: Symposion L. Wildhaber, 1997, S. 45 (61); daran anknüpfend Kotzur, Theorieelemente des internationalen Menschenrechtsschutzes, 2001, S. 322.

[33] UN-Generalversammlung Res. 2625 (XXV) vom 24. 10. 1970.

[34] Zur AEMR jüngst Fassbender, Die Menschenrechtserklärung der Vereinten Nationen von 1948 – eine Einführung in ihre Entstehung, Bedeutung und Wirkung, in: Fassbender, Menschenrechtserklärung. Neuübersetzung, Synopse, Erläuterung, Materialien, 2009, S. 1 ff.; Kotzur, 60 Jahre Allgemeine Erklärung der Menschenrechte – Reflexionen zur Entstehungsgeschichte, Ideengeschichte und Wirkungsgeschichte, MenschenRechtsMagazin, 2008, S. 184 ff.

[35] UN-Generalversammlung Res. 2625 (XXV) vom 24. 10. 1970.

[36] Von der UN-Generalversammlung in Res. 1386 (XIV) am 20. 11. 1959 verkündet.

[37] Ausführliche Nachweise zu deren Genese bei Roca FS Starck, 2007, 905 (908 f.).

[38] Allgemein Ebert, Die Interdependenz von Staat, Verfassung und Islam im Nahen und Mittleren Osten in der Gegenwart, 1991.

man beings consecrated by the noble Islamic religion and the other divinely-revealed religions". Der operative Vertragstext greift in Art. 1 Abs. 2 das Toleranzpostulat als Erziehungsziel auf: „teaching people in the Arab States pride in identity, loyalty to their home country, and tolerance towards others".

Auch in der Art und Weise, wie Völkerrecht entsteht, ist Toleranzdenken präsent. Der Vertrag ist die praktisch wichtigste formelle Quelle (Art. 38 Abs. 1 lit. a IGH-Statut) des Völkerrechts und zugleich Hauptrechtssetzungsinstrument zur Fortentwicklung der internationalen Ordnung.[39] Diesem Rechtsinstrument wohnt selbst ein Moment des „tolerare", des „Sich-Vertragens" und „Sich-Ertragens" inne[40], jedenfalls wenn es sich nicht um bloße Austauschbeziehung („contract treaties"), sondern um die Setzung grundlegender Normen für die Völkerrechtsgemeinschaft handelt („law-making treaties").[41] Damit ist freilich zunächst nur ein sehr unspezifisches „Tolerieren" in einem weiteren Sinne bezeichnet. Konkreter greifbar werden Toleranzmechanismen vor allem im Sinne einer *tolerierten* Abweichung vom vertraglichen Konsens. Dass alle Staaten der Welt einem Vertrag mit universellem Geltungsanspruch zustimmen, muss Illusion bleiben. Dennoch gilt es Gestaltungsinstrumente zu schaffen, die Zustimmung zu universellen Vertragswerken erleichtern, indem sie einzelnen Parteien partielle Abweichungen erlauben, also deren „Nicht-Gebundensein-Wollen" *tolerieren,* ohne den *Gesamtkonsens* schlechthin in Frage zu stellen. Zu nennen sind hier Vorbehalte und sog. „opt-out-Mechanismen", aber auch Toleranzspielräume bei der Vertragsauslegung. Neben den bislang vorgestellten rechtsimmanenten Toleranzmomenten mag Toleranz schließlich auch dort zum Tragen kommen, wo bewusst auf (jede Form von) Verrechtlichung verzichtet oder partielle Nichtbefolgung von bindendem Recht in Kauf genommen wird. Für ersteres gibt das „soft law"[42], für letzteres die Entscheidung „ex aequo et bono"[43] ein Beispiel.

V. Eine Kultur der Toleranz

Damit seien die folgende Thesen als Diskussionsimpulse formuliert: Das Völkerrecht kennt Toleranz erstens als Voraussetzung und Modus normativer Ordnungsbildung: der Territorialstaat als Produkt religiöser Toleranz. Das Völkerecht kennt Toleranz zweitens als Inhalt von Recht: souveräne Gleichheit, Selbstbestimmung, menschenrechtliche Garantien verdeutlichen das. Und das Völkerrecht kennt drit-

[39] Ipsen, Völkerrecht/Heintschel v. Heinegg, 5. Aufl. 2004, 3. Kap., Rn. 4; Graf Vitzthum, Völkerrecht/Graf Vitzthum, 4. Aufl. 2007, 1. Abschn., Rn. 113ff.

[40] So, bezogen auf eine kontraktualistische Verfassungskonzeption, die Formulierung bei Häberle, Verfassungslehre als Kulturwissenschaft, 2. Aufl. 1998, S. 621.

[41] Zu dieser nicht unumstrittenen Differenzierung Ipsen, Völkerrecht/Heintschel v. Heinegg, 5. Aufl. 2004, § 9 Rn. 7.

[42] Max Planck Encyclopedia of Public International Law/Thürer, www.mpepil.com, 2009, Soft Law.

[43] Garner, Black's Law Dictionary, 8. Aufl. 2004, S. 600; Brownlie, Principles of Public International Law, 7. Aufl. 2008, S. 26; Max Planck Encyclopedia of Public International Law/Kotzur, www.mpepil.com, 2009, Ex aequo et bono.

tens Toleranz im Umgang mit Recht: durch Auslegung, durch Vorbehalte und opt-out Möglichkeiten, durch „margins of appreciation" und Verhältnismäßigkeitserwägungen bei der Menschenrechtsrealisierung. Das Völkerrecht toleriert viertens Nicht-Recht (soft law) und Entscheiden jenseits des Rechts („ex aequo et bono"). Je fragmentierter globale Ordnungsmuster, je diverser Gesellschaften werden, je stärker neue Nationalismen den Multilateralismus herausfordern und neue Populismen, ohne vor Verschwörungsmythen zurückschrecken[44], das demokratische zu einem identitären Prinzip und den Citoyen zum Wutbürger[45] pervertieren, umso nachdrücklicher müssen wir uns vor Augen halten, dass sich nicht in der Exklusion, sondern im Aushalten von Differenz die Stärke einer politischen Gemeinschaft zeigt. Eine Kultur der Toleranz ist allemal besser als eine Kultur der Empörung.[46]

[44] Kotzur, Wenn Argumente Scheitern. Aufklärung in Zeiten des Populismus, 2018.
[45] Massing, Wutbürger, 2017.
[46] Mayer, Empörung als Bildungsproblem oder -impuls?, in: Mayer/Schäfer, Populismus – Aufklärung – Demokratie, 2019, S. 245 ff.

WOLFGANG KRÜGER

Zuständigkeitsfragen aus revisionsrechtlicher Sicht

I. *Warum gerade ich*

Es ist eine weit verbreitete, je nach Sichtweise: Sitte oder Unsitte, dass die Älteren den Jüngeren gute oder wenigstens gut gemeinte Ratschläge erteilen. Zu Beginn eines richterlichen Berufslebens erhält man viele solcher Empfehlungen von erfahrenen Kollegen, darunter mit ziemlicher Sicherheit den folgenden Tipp: Bevor Sie eine Akte in die Hand nehmen, um sich über den darin unterbreiteten Rechtsfall den Kopf zu zerbrechen, sollten Sie sich zunächst immer die wichtigste aller Fragen stellen: Warum gerade ich? Und damit der mit dem Ratschlag Bedachte den Witz dieser maßvoll originellen Formulierung auch ja nicht verpasse, versieht der Ratgeber seine Mission mit einem Schmunzeln, Lächeln oder Grinsen und nicht selten mit dem Ausdruck wohlwollender Väterlichkeit.[1]

Dem Anfänger erschließt sich schnell der praktische Sinn dieser Mahnung. Man hat genug zu tun und sollte sich nur mit dem befassen, für das man zuständig ist, und nicht noch die Arbeit anderer verrichten. Was aber eigentlich hinter der Frage „Warum gerade ich" steckt und viel bedeutsamer ist, das erfasst man zumeist erst nach und nach. Es geht um den gesetzlichen Richter, es geht um ein Gebot mit Verfassungsrang, Art. 101 Abs. 1 S. 2 GG, § 16 S. 2 GVG. Nur der nach Gesetz und richterlicher Geschäftsverteilung zuständige Richter ist befugt, eine Rechtssache zu behandeln und zu entscheiden. Verstöße gegen diesen Grundsatz unterliegen in der Regel im Rechtsmittelzug der Aufhebung. War das Berufungsgericht nicht vorschriftsmäßig besetzt, liegt ein absoluter Revisionsgrund vor, § 547 Nr. 1 ZPO, ist der Fehler in der ersten Instanz entstanden, kann dies nach § 538 Abs. 2 Nr. 1 ZPO zur Aufhebung durch das Berufungsgericht und Zurückverweisung führen.[2] War das angerufene Gericht örtlich oder sachlich nicht zuständig, kann die Abweisung der Klage als unzulässig nur durch einen Antrag auf Verweisung an das zuständige Gericht abgewendet werden, § 281 Abs. 1 ZPO.[3]

Der Grundsatz, dass nur der nach Gesetz und Geschäftsverteilung zuständige Richter zur Befassung und Entscheidung berufen ist, kollidiert mit einem Gedanken, der für die Prozessparteien nicht weniger bedeutsam ist, nämlich mit dem Ge-

---

[1] Mütter gab es zu meinen Anfangszeiten kaum.

[2] Nämlich dann, wenn aufgrund des Verfahrensmangels eine umfangreiche oder aufwendige Beweisaufnahme notwendig ist; dazu BGH 17.3.2008 – II ZR 313/06, NJW 2008, 1672.

[3] Ob die Vorschrift auch bei fehlender funktioneller Zuständigkeit (analog) angewendet werden kann, ist umstritten, s. nur Münchener Kommentar zur ZPO/Prütting, 6. Aufl. 2020, ZPO § 281 Rn. 25 mwN. Auch wenn die Norm nicht gilt, muss eine formlose Abgabe möglich sein, der freilich keine Bindungswirkung zukommt.

danken der Prozesswirtschaftlichkeit und dem Interesse an einer kurzen Verfahrensdauer. Nur schnelles Recht ist gutes Recht. Diesem Gedanken trägt das Gesetz ebenfalls Rechnung, indem es die Überprüfbarkeit der Zuständigkeit im Instanzenzug Einschränkungen unterwirft. So kann nach den Vorschriften der §§ 348 Abs. 4, 348a Abs. 3, 526 Abs. 3 ZPO ein Rechtsmittel nicht darauf gestützt werden, dass der Rechtsstreit unter Verletzung der dafür maßgeblichen Verfahrensregelungen vom Einzelrichter entschieden wurde.[4] Und ganz allgemein kann weder die Berufung noch die Revision darauf gestützt werden, dass das Gericht des ersten Rechtszuges nicht zuständig war, §§ 513 Abs. 2, 545 Abs. 2 ZPO. Geht es um die Zulässigkeit des Rechtswegs, sehen die Vorschriften des § 17a Abs. 1–4 GVG ein besonderes Vorabverfahren mit Beschwerdemöglichkeit vor; im Hauptsacheverfahren ist in den Rechtsmittelinstanzen demgegenüber nicht mehr zu prüfen, ob der beschrittene Rechtsweg zulässig ist, § 17a Abs. 5 GVG.

Welche Bedeutung diesen Regelungen in der Revisionsinstanz zukommt, wollen wir im Folgenden näher untersuchen.

II. Die Grundsätze des § 545 Abs. 2 ZPO

Nach § 545 Abs. 2 ZPO kann die Revision nicht darauf gestützt werden, dass das Gericht des ersten Rechtszuges seine Zuständigkeit zu Unrecht angenommen oder verneint hat.

1. Der Begriff der Zuständigkeit

a) Allgemeine Grundsätze

Zuständigkeit im Sinne der Norm meint – im Einklang mit der früheren Rechtslage (§ 549 Abs. 2 ZPO aF) – die örtliche und die sachliche Zuständigkeit,[5] seit der ZPO-Reform[6] aber entgegen früherem Recht auch die funktionelle Zuständigkeit.[7] Entscheidungen, die die Frage der funktionellen Zuständigkeit revisionsrechtlicher Überprüfung für zugänglich hielten,[8] sind daher nicht mehr einschlägig. Nicht erfasst ist die internationale Zuständigkeit.[9] Nicht immer eindeutig wird die Frage beantwortet, was man unter funktioneller Zuständigkeit zu verstehen hat. Im Gesetz selbst nicht geregelt, wird dieser Zuständigkeitskategorie im Wesentlichen die Aufgabenverteilung innerhalb eines Gerichts zugerechnet, also

[4] Ausgenommen hiervon sind willkürliche Verstöße gegen gerichtliche Zuständigkeitsvorschriften, die einen beachtlichen Verstoß gegen Art. 101 Abs. 1 S. 2 GG begründen, s. nur BGH 12.12.2006 – VI ZR 4/06, BGHZ 170, 180 Rn. 5 = NJW 2007, 1466; BGH 17.3.2023 – V ZR 109/22, NJW-RR 2023, 715 Rn. 9ff., 15 mwN. Näheres später im Text.

[5] S. nur Münchener Kommentar zur ZPO/Krüger, 6. Aufl. 2020, ZPO § 545 Rn. 16.

[6] Durch Gesetz vom 27.7.2001 (BGBl. 2001 I 1887).

[7] BGH 26.6.2003 – III ZR 91/03, NJW 2003, 2917.

[8] ZB BGH 13.12.1991 – LwZR 2/91, NJW-RR 1992, 1152 (Landwirtschaftsgericht im Verhältnis zum allgemeinen Zivilgericht).

[9] BGH 16.12.2003 – XI ZR 474/02, NJW 2004, 1456; BGH 28.11.2002 – III ZR 102/02, NJW 2003, 426.

beispielsweise die Unterscheidung, ob das Amtsgericht als Prozessgericht, Vollstreckungsgericht, Insolvenzgericht oder Arrestgericht tätig wird.[10] Auch wenn das Amtsgericht in Wohnungseigentumssachen entscheidet, geht es um die funktionelle Zuständigkeit.[11] Ferner gehört zur funktionellen Zuständigkeit die Frage, ob der Einzelrichter oder das Kollegialgericht, der Rechtspfleger oder der Urkundsbeamte der Geschäftsstelle zuständig ist.[12]

b) Landwirtschaftsgericht und FamFG

Wie es sich mit dem Amtsgericht als Landwirtschaftsgericht, als Familiengericht und als Gericht in den Angelegenheiten der freiwilligen Gerichtsbarkeit verhält wird nicht ganz einheitlich beurteilt oder findet in der Kommentarliteratur keine oder nur teilweise Erwähnung.[13] Im Ergebnis ist allerdings davon auszugehen, dass alle diese Fälle von § 545 Abs. 2 ZPO erfasst werden, sei es nun unter dem Gesichtspunkt der funktionellen oder der sachlichen Zuständigkeit.[14] Beim Familiengericht ist allerdings zu beachten, dass nach § 17a Abs. 6 GVG die vorstehenden Absätze der Norm auch für die Abgrenzung von ZPO- zu FamFG-Verfahren gelten.[15] Die Regelungen über die Bindungswirkung der Rechtswegentscheidung werden für entsprechend anwendbar erklärt und passen auch nur entsprechend, weil sich der Konflikt innerhalb eines Gerichts, also nicht rechtswegübergreifend, entfaltet.[16] Dasselbe gilt für die Abgrenzung zwischen dem Prozessgericht und dem Amtsgericht als Gericht der freiwilligen Gerichtsbarkeit. Die Regelungen treten damit aber in ein Konkurrenzverhältnis zu der Vorschrift des § 545 Abs. 2 ZPO (dazu → II. 2. b)).

---

[10] S. nur Münchener Kommentar zur ZPO/Wöstmann, 6. Aufl. 2020, ZPO § 1 Rn. 9; Zöller, ZPO/Schutzky, 35. Aufl. 2023, ZPO § 1 Rn. 6.

[11] Anders/Gehle, ZPO/Gehle, 82. Aufl. 2024, ZPO Vor § 1 Rn. 12; hiervon geht auch BGH 20.2.2014 – V ZB 116/13, NJW 2014, 1879 Rn. 15, aus; nicht mehr einschlägig ist die Entscheidung BGH 30.6.1995 – V ZR 118/94, BGHZ 130, 159 (162f.) = NJW 1995, 2851, in der der BGH auf der Grundlage des damaligen Rechts, das die Wohnungseigentumssachen der freiwilligen Gerichtsbarkeit zuordnete, den Zuständigkeitsstreit zwischen Prozessgericht und Wohnungseigentumsgericht wie eine Rechtswegstreitigkeit behandelte und § 17a GVG, nicht aber § 549 Abs. 2 ZPO aF, anwandte.

[12] Thomas/Putzo, ZPO/Hüßtege, 45. Aufl. 2024, ZPO § 1 Rn. 2; Münchener Kommentar zur ZPO/Wöstmann, 6. Aufl. 2020, ZPO § 1 Rn. 9; Stein/Jonas, ZPO/Roth, 24. Aufl. 2024, ZPO § 1 Rn. 60; Wieczorek/Schütze, ZPO/Prütting/Winter, 5. Aufl. 2021, ZPO § 545 Rn. 65.

[13] Vgl. Thomas/Putzo, ZPO/Hüßtege, 45. Aufl. 2024, ZPO Vorb § 1 Rn. 2; nur das Familiengericht, nicht aber das Landwirtschaftsgericht, erwähnen: Musielak/Voit, ZPO/Heinrich, 21. Aufl. 2024, ZPO § 1 Rn. 7; Anders/Gehle, ZPO/Gehle, 82. Aufl. 2024, ZPO § 1 Rn. 12.

[14] Für das Landwirtschaftsgericht ist der BGH zum früheren Recht von einer funktionellen Zuständigkeit ausgegangen, die damals allerdings noch revisionsrechtlicher Prüfung unterlag, BGH 13.12.1991 – LwZR 2/91, NJW-RR 1992, 1152. Für das Familiengericht ohne Klassifizierung der Art der Zuständigkeit: BGH 5.11.2008 – XII ZR 103/07, NJW-RR 2009, 434. Von einer sachlichen Zuständigkeit in den im FamFG geregelten Fällen geht aus Münchener Kommentar zur ZPO/Wöstmann, 6. Aufl. 2020, ZPO § 1 Rn. 8.

[15] Münchener Kommentar zur ZPO/Pabst, 6. Aufl. 2022, GVG § 17a Rn. 40.

[16] Siehe Münchener Kommentar zur ZPO/Pabst, 6. Aufl. 2022, GVG § 17a Rn. 40.

c) Arbeitsgerichtsbarkeit

Es müsste sich eigentlich von selbst verstehen, dass es bei der Abgrenzung von Amtsgericht zu Arbeitsgericht allein um § 17a GVG, hingegen nicht um § 545 Abs. 2 ZPO geht. Denn wir haben es mit einem klassischen Fall der Rechtswegzuständigkeit zu tun, und nicht mit funktioneller Zuständigkeit. Soweit in Entscheidungen des BGH die Frage der arbeitsgerichtlichen Zuständigkeit für nicht überprüfbar gehalten wird,[17] beruhen diese Entscheidungen auf dem früheren Rechtszustand, also auf § 549 Abs. 2 ZPO aF. Die Norm lautete: „Das Revisionsgericht prüft nicht, ob das Gericht des ersten Rechtszuges sachlich oder örtlich zuständig war, ob die Zuständigkeit des Arbeitsgerichts begründet war oder ob eine Familiensache vorliegt." Das geltende Recht, § 545 Abs. 2 ZPO, hat den die Zuständigkeit des Arbeitsgerichts betreffenden Teil nicht übernommen. Ball hält § 545 Abs. 2 ZPO gleichwohl für grundsätzlich anwendbar, meint aber, die Regelung werde „weitgehend durch § 17a Abs. 5 GVG verdrängt."[18] Dem ist nicht zu folgen. Was sollte man sich unter einer weitgehenden Verdrängung vorstellen? Wie weitgehend? Und was soll eine Norm, die weitgehend verdrängt wird? Ich denke, hier wird nichts verdrängt; vielmehr ist die Abgrenzung klar: § 545 Abs. 2 ZPO handelt von der sachlichen, der örtlichen und der funktionellen Zuständigkeit, § 17a GVG von der Rechtswegzuständigkeit (mit den Besonderheiten in Abs. 6). Alles andere führt ins Unklare und Verschwommene.

2. Die Regelung des § 17a GVG

a) Anwendungsbereich der Norm

Die Vorschrift des § 17a GVG ist wie § 545 Abs. 2 ZPO dem Gedanken der Prozesswirtschaftlichkeit verpflichtet.[19] Sie funktioniert aber anders. Sie verknüpft Elemente des § 281 ZPO und des § 545 Abs. 2 ZPO und ergänzt sie um eigenständige Regelungen. Im Mittelpunkt der Norm steht die Möglichkeit und uU die Notwendigkeit, vorab über die Frage der Rechtswegzuständigkeit zu entscheiden. Die Grundsätze, nach denen sich dies beurteilt, sind die folgenden. Hält das angerufene Gericht den Rechtsweg für zulässig, *kann* es dies vorab aussprechen, § 17a Abs. 3 S. 1 GVG; rügt eine Partei die Zulässigkeit des Rechtswegs, *muss* das Gericht darüber vorab entscheiden, § 17a Abs. 3 S. 2 GVG. Hält das angerufene Gericht den Rechtsweg für unzulässig, trifft es die Entscheidung darüber von Amts wegen und verweist den Rechtsstreit mit bindender Wirkung an das zuständige Gericht, § 17a Abs. 2 GVG. In allen diesen Fällen gibt es eine Beschwerdemöglichkeit nach den allgemeinen Vorschriften, im Zivilprozess also gegen eine erstinstanzliche Entscheidung die sofortige Beschwerde, § 17a Abs. 4 S. 3 GVG, und gegen eine zweit-

[17] BGH 23.6.1988 – IX ZR 172/87, BGHZ 105, 34 (39) = NJW 1989, 170; BGH 30.6.1995 – V ZR 118/94, BGHZ 130, 159 (164) = NJW 1995, 2851.

[18] Musielak/Voit, ZPO/Ball, 21. Aufl. 2024, ZPO § 545 Rn. 14.

[19] Vgl. Münchener Kommentar zur ZPO/Pabst, 6. Aufl. 2022, GVG § 17a Rn. 1; Musielak/Voit, ZPO/Wittschier, 21. Aufl. 2024, GVG § 17a Rn. 1.

instanzliche Entscheidung die – zulassungsbedürftige – Rechtsbeschwerde, § 17a Abs. 4 S. 4–6 GVG.[20]

Für das Revisionsgericht bedeutet das Folgendes. Mit Rechtskraft der Vorabentscheidung tritt Bindungswirkung ein. Wird die Zulässigkeit des Rechtswegs bejaht, ergibt sich die Bindungswirkung aus § 17a Abs. 1 GVG; erklärt das Gericht den eingeschlagenen Rechtsweg für unzulässig und verweist die Sache an das Gericht des zulässigen Rechtswegs, so folgt die Bindung aus § 17a Abs. 2 S. 3 GVG. Diese Bindungswirkung hindert im Hauptsacheverfahren eine erneute Überprüfung der Rechtswegfrage, § 17a Abs. 5 GVG. Die Entscheidung darüber kann daher auch nicht mit den Mitteln der Revision angefochten werden.

Ist eine Vorabentscheidung in der unteren Instanz unterblieben, so ist zu unterscheiden. Hat das Gericht erster Instanz in der Sache entschieden, so liegt darin konkludent eine Entscheidung auch über den eingeschlagenen Rechtsweg. Das hat grundsätzlich die Bindungswirkung nach § 17a Abs. 5 GVG zur Folge, es sei denn, die Zuständigkeit des Rechtswegs ist von einer Partei gerügt worden. Denn in jenem Fall muss das Gericht vorab entscheiden. Verstößt es hiergegen, nimmt es der Partei die Beschwerdemöglichkeit, was nicht von § 17a Abs. 5 GVG überspielt werden kann.[21] Vielmehr ist unter diesen Umständen eine Vorabentscheidung in zweiter Instanz nachzuholen.[22] Die Rechtskraft erst dieser Entscheidung hat die Bindungswirkung zur Folge. Hat auch das Berufungsgericht die infolge der Rechtswegrüge gebotene Vorabentscheidung unterlassen, so tritt ebenfalls keine Bindung ein; der BGH kann aber nicht selbst entscheiden, sondern muss die Sache zur Nachholung der Vorabentscheidung an das Berufungsgericht zurückverweisen.[23] Hiervon kann nur dann ausnahmsweise abgesehen werden, wenn das Berufungsgericht im Falle einer nach Zurückverweisung und erneuter Bejahung des Rechtswegs, nun im Rahmen einer Vorabentscheidung, nicht gehalten wäre, die Rechtsbeschwerde zuzulassen.[24] Darüber hinausgehend, hat sich der BGH auch dann für befugt gehalten, über die Rechtswegfrage selbst zu entscheiden, wenn sich das Berufungsgericht – unrichtigerweise – an einer nachgeholten Vorabentscheidung durch die im Urteil konkludent bejahte Zuständigkeit durch das erstinstanzliche Gericht gehindert gesehen hat, weil es von einer Bindungswirkung ausgegangen ist.[25] Ob diese Ausdehnung der Befugnisse des Revisionsgerichts vom Gesetz gedeckt ist, kann man mit mE guten Gründen in Zweifel ziehen. Denn ob das Berufungsgericht die Vorabentscheidung deswegen unterlässt, weil es sich für gebunden erachtet oder weil es einfach durchentschieden hat, ist für den Umstand, dass der Partei, die den Rechtsweg gerügt hat, der Beschwerderechtsweg genommen

---

[20] Näheres etwa bei Thomas/Putzo, ZPO/Hüßtege, 45. Aufl. 2024, GVG § 17a Rn. 18ff.; Münchener Kommentar zur ZPO/Pabst, 6. Aufl. 2022, GVG § 17a Rn. 23ff.

[21] BGH 19.11.1993 – V ZR 269/92, NJW 1994, 387.

[22] BGH 3.7.1997 – IX ZB 116/96, NJW 1998, 231.

[23] BGH 18.11.1998 – VIII ZR 269/97, NJW 1999, 651; BGH 29.3.1996 – V ZR 326/94, BGHZ 132, 245 (248) = NJW 1996, 1890.

[24] BGH 29.3.1996 – V ZR 326/94, BGHZ 132, 245 (248) = NJW 1996, 1890.

[25] BGH 25.2.1993 – III ZR 9/92, BGHZ 121, 367 (372) = NJW 1993, 1799; BGH 30.6.1995 – V ZR 118/94, BGHZ 130, 159 (163f.) = NJW 1995, 2851; s. auch BGH 18.11.1998 – VIII ZR 269/97, NJW 1999, 651.

wird, ohne Belang. Freilich entsprach das Vorgehen des BGH in den genannten Fällen[26] dem Gedanken der Prozesswirtschaftlichkeit, da der BGH die Zuständigkeitsfrage wie die Vorinstanzen entschied und dadurch ein zeitaufwendiges Beschwerdeverfahren, das zum selben Ergebnis geführt haben würde, vermied. Insoweit besteht Ähnlichkeit zu den Fällen, in denen die Vorinstanzen eine Vorabentscheidung unterlassen haben, ohne dass sich das Berufungsgericht an die Entscheidung des Gerichts erster Instanz gebunden erachtet hat.

b) Verhältnis zu § 545 Abs. 2 ZPO

Infolge der Regelung in § 17a Abs. 6 GVG ergibt sich ein Konkurrenzverhältnis zwischen dieser Vorschrift und § 545 Abs. 2 ZPO. Denn Familiensachen und Angelegenheiten der freiwilligen Gerichtsbarkeit unterfallen unter dem Gesichtspunkt der funktionellen oder sachlichen Zuständigkeit der Vorschrift des § 545 Abs. 2 ZPO (→ II. 1. b)). Es ist davon auszugehen, dass die spezielleren Vorschriften des § 17a GVG vorgehen. Während § 545 Abs. 2 BGB schlicht eine Bindung des Revisionsgerichts an die in erster Instanz angenommene Zuständigkeit vorgibt, hält § 17a GVG ein differenziertes Prüfungskonzept in einem Vorabverfahren mit Beschwerdemöglichkeit vor. Dies wäre hinfällig, könnte allein auf § 545 Abs. 2 ZPO abgestellt werden.

3. Die Befugnisse des Revisionsgerichts

a) Bedeutung der Norm

Der Wortlaut der Norm ist in zweierlei Hinsicht missverständlich. Zum einen erweckt sie den Anschein, als gehe es darum, auf welche Gründe eine Revision gestützt werden kann, und zum anderen, als schlösse sie nur die revisionsrechtliche Überprüfung der Entscheidung des Gerichts erster Instanz über die Zuständigkeit aus. Es besteht indes Einigkeit, dass der Wortlaut missglückt ist und die Bindung des Revisionsgerichts an die in den Vorinstanzen bejahte oder verneinte örtliche, sachliche und funktionelle Zuständigkeit umfassend ist. Das heißt, es geht nicht um die Frage, worauf die Revision gestützt werden kann, sondern generell um die Prüfungsbefugnis der gerichtlichen Zuständigkeit selbst. Und es geht auch nicht nur um die Entscheidung des Gerichts erster Instanz; die Norm hindert auch die revisionsrechtliche Überprüfung der Entscheidung des Berufungsgerichts, sei es, dass dies die Zuständigkeitsfrage wie das Erstgericht beurteilt hat, sei es, dass es sie für falsch gehalten und deswegen die Erstentscheidung aufgehoben hat.[27] Unter dem Regime der Vorgängerbestimmung, § 549 Abs. 2 ZPO aF, bestand darüber Einigkeit.[28] Die Reform hatte erklärtermaßen nicht zum Ziel, die revisionsrechtliche

---

[26] BGH 25.2.1993 – III ZR 9/92, BGHZ 121, 367 (372) = NJW 1993, 1799; BGH 30.6.1995 – V ZR 118/94, BGHZ 130, 159 (163f.) = NJW 1995, 2851.

[27] Zum Vorstehenden insbesondere BGH 26.6.2003 – III ZR 91/03, NJW 2003, 2917; BGH 5.11.2008 – XII ZR 103/07, NJW-RR 2009, 434 Rn. 8; aus der Lit. Münchener Kommentar zur ZPO/Krüger, 6. Aufl. 2020, ZPO § 545 Rn. 13; Thomas/Putzo, ZPO/Hüßtege, 45. Aufl. 2024, ZPO § 545 Rn. 13; Musielak/Voit, ZPO/Ball, 21. Aufl. 2024, ZPO § 545 Rn. 12; Stein/Jonas, ZPO/Jacobs, 23. Aufl. 2018, ZPO § 545 Rn. 29.

[28] S. die Nachw. bei BGH 26.6.2003 – III ZR 91/03, NJW 2003, 2917.

Überprüfungsmöglichkeit in irgendeiner Hinsicht zu eröffnen bzw. hinter der Vorgängerregelung zurückzubleiben.[29] Im Gegenteil, das Verbot wurde ausgedehnt, indem jetzt auch die funktionelle Zuständigkeit erfasst ist. Ob man dieses Ergebnis auf eine die Gesetzesmaterialien berücksichtigende erweiternde Auslegung des § 545 Abs. 2 ZPO stützt,[30] oder auf eine entsprechende Anwendung des § 513 Abs. 2 ZPO (iVm § 565 S. 1 ZPO),[31] ist ohne Belang.[32]

Es versteht sich von selbst, dass das Verbot der Überprüfbarkeit nicht dadurch ausgehebelt werden kann, dass das Berufungsgericht die Revision zum Zwecke der Klärung der Zuständigkeit zulässt.[33] Die Revision ist dann aus diesem Grund zwar nicht unzulässig, aber unbegründet.[34]

b) Ausnahme: Willkür

Der Umstand, dass dem Revisionsgericht verwehrt ist, die örtliche, sachliche und funktionelle Zuständigkeit der Vorinstanzen zu überprüfen, bedeutet keine Einschränkung des von der Verfassung geschützten Rechts auf den gesetzlichen Richter. Denn dieser Schutz ist nur im Rahmen der (Verfahrens)Gesetze gewährleistet. Untersagt das Zivilprozessrecht die Überprüfung der Zuständigkeit des Richters der Vorinstanz, dann war dieser Richter der gesetzliche Richter auch dann, wenn sein Tätigwerden von den Vorschriften über die Zuständigkeit nicht gedeckt war. Die Frage ist, ob dies ausnahmslos gilt oder ob eine Bindung des Revisionsgerichts, zu verneinen ist, wenn in den Vorinstanzen bewusst die Regeln über die Zuständigkeit außer Acht gelassen wurden.

Der BGH hat dies in Fällen, in denen es um eine gebotene, aber unterlassene Vorlage des Einzelrichters an den gesamten Spruchkörper geht, § 526 Abs. 2 S. 1 Nr. 1 ZPO, dann bejaht, wenn der Verstoß objektiv willkürlich war.[35] Beispielhaft sei ein jüngst entschiedene Fall geschildert.[36] Der Einzelrichterin war der Rechtsstreit von der Kammer des Berufungsgerichts zur Entscheidung übertragen worden, § 526 Abs. 1 ZPO. Aufgrund einer nach der Übertragung eingetretenen Gesetzesänderung war die Einzelrichterin zu der Überzeugung gelangt, dass der Sache nunmehr grundsätzliche Bedeutung zukomme. Sie entschied in der Sache und ließ die

---

[29] BGH 26.6.2003 – III ZR 91/03, NJW 2003, 2917; BGH 22.2.2005 – KZR 28/03, NJW 2005, 1660.

[30] So die die amtliche Begründung der Vorschrift zitierende (BT-Drs.14/4722, 106) Entscheidung BGH 26.6.2003 – III ZR 91/03, NJW 2003, 2917.

[31] BGH 22.2.2005 – KZR 28/03, NJW 2005, 1660.

[32] Auch der Wortlaut des § 513 Abs. 2 ZPO, entsprechend angewendet auf das Revisionsgericht, verfehlt in gleicher Weise wie § 545 Abs. 2 ZPO das vom Gesetzgeber angestrebte Ziel, vgl. BGH 22.2.2005 – KZR 28/03, NJW 2005, 1660.

[33] BGH 7.3.2006 – VI ZR 42/05, NJW-RR 2006, 930; BGH 16.3.2010 – VIII ZR 341/09, NJW-RR 2011, 72.

[34] BGH 7.3.2006 – VI ZR 42/05, NJW-RR 2006, 930 mwN.

[35] BGH 12.12.2006 – VI ZR 4/06, BGHZ 170, 180 Rn. 5 = NJW 2007, 1466; BGH 25.11.2015 – XII ZB 105/13, MDR 2016, 413 Rn. 9 (sachlich vergleichbarer Verstoß gegen § 68 Abs. 4 FamFG); BGH 18.11.2016 – V ZR 221/15, NJW-RR 2017, 260 Rn. 7; BGH 10.11.2022 – III ZR 13/22, BGHZ 235, 93 Rn. 16 = NJW 2023, 922; BGH 17.3.2023 – V ZR 109/22, NJW-RR 2023, 715 Rn. 8ff., 14f.

[36] BGH 17.3.2023 – V ZR 109/22, NJW-RR 2023, 715.

Revision gegen ihr Urteil nach § 543 Abs. 2 Nr. 1 ZPO zu. Dies war verfahrensfehlerhaft. Der Einzelrichter hat den Rechtsstreit dem Berufungsgericht zur Entscheidung über eine Übernahme vorzulegen, wenn infolge einer wesentlichen Änderung der Prozesslage die Rechtssache grundsätzliche Bedeutung erlangt, § 526 Abs. 2 Nr. 1 ZPO.[37] Ein – hier vorliegender – bewusster Rechtsverstoß reicht allerdings nicht aus, um Willkür anzunehmen. Hinzukommen muss vielmehr, dass die Entscheidung unter keinem denkbaren rechtlichen Gesichtspunkt mehr vertretbar ist, so dass sich der Schluss aufdrängt, dass sachfremde Erwägungen eine Rolle gespielt haben (Verstoß gegen Art. 3 Abs. 1 GG).[38] Soweit die Senate von Willkür ausgegangen sind, fehlen regelmäßig nähere Darlegungen zu den Voraussetzungen der Willkür.[39] Im soeben geschilderten Fall hat der Senat diese Voraussetzungen, ohne sie ausdrücklich zu benennen, mit der Begründung bejaht, dass das Vorgehen der Einzelrichterin unter einem nicht auflösbaren Widerspruch leide. Einerseits habe sie bei ihrer Zulassungsentscheidung die Grundsatzbedeutung bejaht, sie andererseits aber auch implizit verneint, indem sie eine Vorlage an den Spruchkörper unterließ.[40] Das ist an sich nicht mehr als die Feststellung eines bewussten Verstoßes gegen die Vorlagepflicht. Es wäre indes falsch anzunehmen, dass jeder bewusste Verstoß zugleich Willkür bedeutet, auch wenn die Zurückhaltung in den Begründungen der BGH-Entscheidung diesen Eindruck erwecken kann. Zu Recht findet sich darin nämlich zumeist auch der Hinweis, dass bei der Annahme von Willkür Zurückhaltung geboten sei; nicht jede unterlassene Vorlage rechtfertige diesen (objektiven) Vorwurf.[41] Es muss sich – und davon geht der BGH offensichtlich aus – um eine unter keinem rechtlichen Gesichtspunkt vertretbare Entscheidung handeln. Nur dann verstößt sie gegen die Verfassung, weil sie den Parteien den gesetzlichen Richter entzieht. Wegen der Schwere des Verstoßes hat das Revisionsgericht den Mangel von Amts wegen zu berücksichtigen; es bedarf also keiner Verfahrensrüge.[42]

Diese für einen willkürlichen Verstoß gegen § 526 Abs. 2 S. 1 Nr. 1 ZPO angenommene Ausnahme von der Vorschrift des § 545 Abs. 2 ZPO ist auf andere willkürliche Verfahrensverstöße, die die Zuständigkeit betreffen, übertragbar. Die Frage ist allerdings umstritten[43] und vom BGH bislang offengelassen wor-

---

[37] Änderung der Rechtslage wird als Unterfall der Änderung der Prozesslage begriffen, BGH 17.3.2023 – V ZR 109/22, NJW-RR 2023, 715 Rn. 12.

[38] S. nur BGH 27.3.2003 – V ZR 291/02, BGHZ 154, 288 (299 f.) = NJW 2003, 1943 mwN, insbesondere aus der Rspr. des BVerfG.

[39] S. zB BGH 10.11.2022 – III ZR 13/22, BGHZ 235, 93 Rn. 20 f. = NJW 2023, 922.

[40] BGH 17.3.2023 – V ZR 109/22, NJW-RR 2023, 715 Rn. 14.

[41] S. zB BGH 17.3.2023 – V ZR 109/22, NJW-RR 2023, 715 Rn. 14.

[42] BGH 10.11.2022 – III ZR 13/22, BGHZ 235, 93 Rn. 11 = NJW 2023, 922; BGH 17.3.2023 – V ZR 109/22, NJW-RR 2023, 715 Rn. 8.

[43] Wie hier Kessal-Wulf in Beck'scher Online-Kommentar ZPO/Kessal-Wulf, 53. Ed. 1.7.2024, ZPO § 545 Rn. 18; Stein/Jonas, ZPO/Jacobs, 23. Aufl. 2018, ZPO § 545 Rn. 31; Wieczorek/Schütze, ZPO/Prütting/Winter, 5. Aufl. 2021, ZPO § 545 Rn. 67; zu der Parallelnorm § 513 Abs. 2 ZPO ebenso: OLG Oldenburg 26.3.1998 – 8 U 215/97, NJW-RR 1999, 865; Münchener Kommentar zur ZPO/Rimmelspacher, 6. Aufl. 2020, ZPO § 513 Rn. 22; Stein/Jonas, ZPO/Althammer, 23. Aufl. 2018, ZPO § 513 Rn. 11; aA Beck'scher Online-Kommentar ZPO/Wulf, 53. Ed. 1.7.2024, ZPO § 513 Rn. 11.

den.[44] Es gibt indes keinen Grund für eine Unterscheidung. Ein Verstoß gegen das Willkürverbot, Art. 3 Abs. 1 GG, verlangt unabhängig davon eine Sanktion, um welchen Verfahrensverstoß es sich handelt. Wenn ein Gericht willkürlich und rechtswidrig seine Zuständigkeit bejaht oder verneint, entzieht es den Parteien den gesetzlichen Richter in gleich gravierender Weise wie in den zu § 526 Abs. 2 S. 1 Nr. 1 ZPO vom BGH entschiedenen Fällen. Würde dies nicht auf der Ebene der Fachgerichte korrigiert, bliebe nur die Verfassungsbeschwerde.[45] Das aber ist nach der Rechtsprechung des BVerfG nicht der in unserem Rechtssystem verfassungsrechtlich hinnehmbare Weg.[46]

c) § 547 Nr. 1 ZPO

Erforderlich ist auch eine Abgrenzung zu § 547 Nr. 1 ZPO. Nach dieser Vorschrift stellt es einen absoluten Revisionsgrund dar, wenn das erkennende Gericht nicht vorschriftsmäßig besetzt war. Als im weitesten Sinn falsch besetzt könnte man auch einen örtlich, sachlich oder funktionell unzuständigen Spruchkörper oder Einzelrichter ansehen. So ist die Norm aber nicht zu verstehen und ließe sich auch nicht in Einklang bringen mit § 545 Abs. 2 ZPO. Denn was nach dieser Norm nicht der Überprüfung unterliegt, kann nach jener nicht zur Aufhebung wegen eines absoluten Revisionsgrundes führen.

aa) In einem Fall gibt es indes eine Überschneidung. Er betrifft den Zuständigkeitskonflikt zwischen Einzelrichter und Kollegium, den wir soeben behandelt haben. Entscheidet der nicht dazu befugte Einzelrichter[47] oder das entgegen § 568 S. 1 ZPO nicht dazu berufene Kollegialgericht,[48] so ist das Gericht nicht vorschriftsmäßig besetzt iSv § 547 Nr. 1 ZPO.[49] Zugleich ist in diesen Fällen der funktionell nicht zuständige Richter tätig geworden.[50] Die Folge ist ein gesetzlicher Konflikt: unter dem Gesichtspunkt des § 547 Nr. 1 ZPO liegt ein auf Rüge hin[51] zu beachtender absoluter Revisionsgrund vor, unter dem Gesichtspunkt des § 545 Abs. 2 ZPO findet, wie schon in den Vorinstanzen[52] auch eine revisionsrechtliche Überprüfung der Zuständigkeit des erkennenden Richters nicht statt. Wie ist dieser Konflikt aufzulösen? Auszugehen ist davon, dass § 547 Nr. 1 ZPO nur verfassungs-

---

44 BGH 17.3.2015 – VI ZR 11/14, NJW-RR 2015, 941 Rn. 19; BGH 23.11.2016 – IV ZR 50/16, NJW 2017, 393 Rn. 10.

45 Münchener Kommentar zur ZPO/Rimmelspacher, 6. Aufl. 2020, ZPO § 513 Rn. 22; Wieczorek/Schütze, ZPO/Prütting/Winter, 5. Aufl. 2021, ZPO § 545 Rn. 67.

46 BVerfG 30.4.2003 – 1 PBvU 1/02, BVerfGE 107, 395 = NJW 2003, 1924 (ergangen zu einem Verstoß gegen Art. 103 Abs. 1 GG).

47 BGH 19.10.1988 – IVb ZR 10/88, BGHZ 105, 270 (276) = NJW 1989, 229; BGH 25.1,2001 – VII ZR 32/99, NJW 2001, 1357.

48 BGH 11.2.2003 – VIII ZB 56/02, NJW 2003, 1875; BGH 21.9.2017 – IX ZB 84/16, WM 2017, 2035 Rn. 13.

49 BGH 25.11.2015 – XII ZB 105/13, NJW-RR 2016, 388 Rn. 10; BGH 17.11.2022 – VII ZR 297/21, NJW 2023, 925 Rn. 16; BGH 17.3.2023 – V ZR 109/22, NJW-RR 2023, 715 Rn. 16; Musielak/Voit, ZPO/Ball, 21. Aufl. 2024, ZPO § 547 Rn. 3; Münchener Kommentar zur ZPO/Krüger, 6. Aufl. 2020, ZPO § 547 Rn. 8.

50 Vgl. BGH 23.4.2015 – I ZB 73/14, NJW 2015, 2194 Rn. 4.

51 S. nur Münchener Kommentar zur ZPO/Krüger, 6. Aufl. 2020, ZPO § 547 Rn. 10 mwN.

52 §§ 348 Abs. 4, 348a Abs. 3, 526 Abs. 3, 568 Satz 3 ZPO.

rechtlich bedeutsame Verstöße erfasst; es geht um den Grundsatz, dass niemand seinem gesetzlichen Richter entzogen werden darf (Art. 101 Abs. 1 S. 2 GG).[53] Nicht jeder Fehler bei der Bestimmung des zuständigen Richters, etwa durch den Geschäftsverteilungsplan, durch einen aus besonderem Anlass erfolgten Präsidiumsbeschluss oder durch die spruchkörperinternen Mitwirkungsgrundsätze (§ 21g Abs. 1 S. 1 GVG) führt zu einer gesetzwidrigen Besetzung des Gerichts und damit zu einem Verstoß gegen Art. 101 Abs. 1 S. 2 GG.[54] Erforderlich ist vielmehr, dass der Verstoß so schwer wiegt, dass die Grenze zur (objektiven) Willkür überschritten ist.[55] Damit im Einklang steht die Rechtsprechung zum Einzelrichter/Kollegium-Konflikt. Denn die Verstöße in diesem Bereich führen nur bei Willkür zur Aufhebung durch das Revisionsgericht (→ II. 3. b)). Bei einem Verfassungsverstoß müssen die Regelungen, die eine Überprüfung der Zuständigkeit im Instanzenzug ausschließen, zurücktreten. Das Verhältnis der Normen zueinander lässt sich folglich widerspruchsfrei auflösen.

bb) Es bleibt eine letzte Abgrenzungsfrage. Unterhalb der Willkürgrenze sind Verstöße gegen das Gebot der vorschriftsmäßigen Besetzung nicht sanktionslos. Sie müssen lediglich gerügt werden[56] und führen dann als absolute Revisionsgründe zur Aufhebung im Revisionsverfahren, § 547 Nr. 1 ZPO. Das kann indes, will man nicht in einen unauflösbaren Widerspruch geraten, nur für die Fälle der nicht vorschriftsmäßigen Besetzung gelten, die nicht von den Vorschriften der §§ 348 Abs. 4, 348a Abs. 3, 526 Abs. 3 ZPO erfasst werden. Denn in diesen Fällen führt – wie dargelegt – nur ein willkürlicher Verstoß gegen Vorschriften, die die Zuständigkeiten zwischen Einzelrichter und Kollegialgericht regeln, zu einem Verfassungsverstoß und fällt nur dann unter § 547 Nr. 1 ZPO. Dass auch Verstöße dieser Art, die unterhalb der Willkürgrenze bleiben, zur Aufhebung führen sollten, freilich nur bei entsprechender Verfahrensrüge, wäre nicht vermittelbar. Zum einen bliebe dann kein Anwendungsbereich für die die Überprüfbarkeit der Zuständigkeit des Einzelrichters bzw. des Kollegialgerichts ausschließenden Normen, und zum anderen unterfielen Fälle der Aufhebung, die von Verfassungs wegen gerade nicht zu beanstanden sind; § 547 Nr. 1 ZPO erfasst aber nur verfassungswidrige Fehlbesetzungen.[57]

Welche Fälle bleiben demnach für § 547 Nr. 1 ZPO übrig? Das sind zunächst die Fälle, bei denen die nicht vorschriftsmäßige Besetzung per se verfassungswidrig ist, ohne dass die Frage, ob ein willkürlicher Verstoß vorliegt, sinnvollerweise gestellt werden könnte. Dazu gehören die Fälle eines nicht befähigten oder nicht wirksam ernannten Richters.[58] Der Richter etwa, dem die Befähigung zum Richteramt fehlt oder der nicht nach den Vorschriften der §§ 8ff. DRiG bestellt worden ist, ist unter

[53] Siehe nur Beck'scher Online-Kommentar ZPO/Kessal-Wulf, 53. Ed. 1.7.2024, ZPO § 547 Rn. 7.

[54] BGH 22.11.1994 – X ZR 51/92, NJW 1995, 332; Beck'scher Online-Kommentar ZPO/Kessal-Wulf, 53. Ed. 1.7.2024, ZPO § 547 Rn. 11.

[55] BGH 5.5.1994 – VGS 1–4/93, BGHZ 126, 63 (71) = NJW 1994, 1735 mwN.

[56] S. nur BGH 3.2.2016 – XII ZB 221/15, NJW-RR 2016, 510 Rn. 6; Münchener Kommentar zur ZPO/Krüger, 6. Aufl. 2020, ZPO § 547 Rn. 10 mwN.

[57] Beck'scher Online-Kommentar ZPO/Kessal-Wulf, 53. Ed. 1.7.2024, ZPO § 547 Rn. 7, 11.

[58] Dazu Münchener Kommentar zur ZPO/Krüger, 6. Aufl. 2020, ZPO § 547 Rn. 6.

keinen Umständen der gesetzliche Richter, wie auch immer es zu seinem Tätigwerden gekommen ist. Dasselbe gilt für die Konstellationen, bei denen das Gericht entgegen § 21f GVG nicht ordnungsgemäß besetzt war[59] oder die Besetzung nicht den Anforderungen des § 29 DRiG genügte.[60] In diesen Fällen führt die Rüge im Revisionsverfahren ohne weiteres zur Aufhebung. Die Regelung des § 545 Abs. 2 ZPO ist von vornherein nicht betroffen. Es geht nicht um Zuständigkeitsfragen im Sinne dieser Norm, sondern um Besetzungsfragen.

Nicht vorschriftsmäßig besetzt ist das Gericht schließlich auch, wenn die Besetzung auf einem fehlerhaft aufgestellten oder angewandten Geschäftsverteilungsplan[61] oder auf den Anforderungen des § 21g GVG nicht genügenden Mitwirkungsgrundsätzen[62] beruht. Bei Verstößen in dem Bereich der Geschäftsverteilung (Plan oder Mitwirkungsgrundsätze) ist wiederum eine Besonderheit zu beachten. Hier führt nicht jeder Verstoß automatisch zu einem absoluten Revisionsgrund iSv § 547 Nr. 1 ZPO. Das Verfassungsgebot des Art. 101 Abs. 1 S. 2 GG ist erst dann verletzt, die Voraussetzung des § 547 Nr. 1 ZPO erst dann zu bejahen, wenn der Verstoß schwer wiegt, also auf einer nicht mehr hinnehmbaren Rechtsansicht beruht und damit objektiv willkürlich ist.[63] Auch insoweit geht es nicht um Zuständigkeit im Sinne von § 545 Abs. 2 ZPO. Im Interesse einer widerspruchsfreien Anwendung der Normen, sollte bei diesen Verstößen, die Willkür voraussetzen, auf eine Verfahrensrüge verzichtet werden, so wie ja auch in anderen auf Willkür beschränkten Normverstößen eine Berücksichtigung von Amts wegen erfolgt (→ II. 3. b)).

III. Zusammenfassung

Die Vorschrift des § 545 Abs. 2 ZPO schließt eine Überprüfung der örtlichen, sachlichen und funktionellen Zuständigkeit der Gerichte der Vorinstanz aus. Ausgenommen sind nur willkürliche Verstöße gegen Zuständigkeitsbestimmungen, die von Verfassungs wegen nicht hingenommen werden können, Art. 3 Abs. 1 GG. Willkür setzt mehr als eine vorsätzliche Verletzung der jeweiligen die Zuständigkeit regelnden Vorschrift voraus. Hinzukommen muss, dass die Entscheidung schlechthin unvertretbar ist und den Schluss zulässt, dass sie von sachfremden Erwägungen getragen wird. Die Ausnahme wegen Willkür gilt nicht nur für die Fälle, in denen es um die Verletzung von Normen geht, die die Zuständigkeit des Einzelrichters und des Kollegialgerichts regeln und die in der Rechtsprechung des BGH ein-

---

[59] S. etwa die Fälle BGH 11.7.1985 – VII ZB 6/85, BGHZ 95, 246 = NJW 1985, 2337 (Besetzungsfehler wegen Haushaltssperre); BGH 12.3.2015 – VII ZR 173/13, NJW 2015, 1685 (unzulässige Vertretungsregelung bei dauerhafter Verhinderung des Vorsitzenden).

[60] BGH 13.7.1995 – V ZB 6/94, BGHZ 130, 304 (307) = NJW 1995, 2791.

[61] Vgl. BGH 10.7.1963 – VIII ZR 204/61, BGHZ 40, 91 = NJW 1963, 2071; BVerwG 2.7.1987 – 9 CB 7/87, NJW 1988, 1339.

[62] Vgl. BGH 5.5.1994 – VGS 1–4/93, BGHZ 126, 63 = NJW 1994, 1735; BGH 22.11.1994 – X ZR 51/92, NJW 1995, 332.

[63] BGH 5.5.1994 – VGS 1–4/93, BGHZ 126, 63 (71) = NJW 1994, 1735; BGH 22.11.1994 – X ZR 51/92, NJW 1995, 332 (335).

gehend Beachtung gefunden haben, sondern auch in allen anderen Fällen, in denen es um Verletzung von Zuständigkeitsnormen geht. Verfassungsrechtlich bedeutsame Verstöße können von § 545 Abs. 2 ZPO nicht legitimiert werden.

Geht es um die Frage des zulässigen Rechtswegs, ist nicht § 545 Abs. 2 ZPO einschlägig, sondern § 17a GVG. Diese Norm hat auch Vorrang, wenn das Verhältnis vom Prozessgericht zum Familiengericht oder dem in Angelegenheiten der freiwilligen Gerichtsbarkeit zuständigen Spruchkörper im Streit ist. An sich handelt es sich um unterschiedliche funktionelle Zuständigkeit. Wegen des Verweises in § 17a Abs. 6 GVG sind indes auch hier die spezielleren Vorschriften der den Rechtsweg abgrenzenden Norm anzuwenden.

Zu § 547 Nr. 1 ZPO gibt es Überschneidungen. Die Norm geht stehts vor, wenn die nicht vorschriftsmäßige Besetzung auf Willkür beruht. Dann bedarf es auch keiner Verfahrensrüge. Ist die Willkürgrenze nicht überschritten, kommt die Norm nicht in Betracht in den Fällen der speziellen Regelungen über die Zuständigkeit des Einzelrichters im Verhältnis zum Kollegialgericht. Bei anderen Besetzungsfehlern greift § 547 Nr. 1 ZPO auf Rüge ein.

Die gesetzlichen Regelungen lassen insgesamt einen überzeugenden Ausgleich zwischen dem Postulat der Prozesswirtschaftlichkeit und dem Verfassungsgrundsatz, dass niemand seinem gesetzlichen Richter entzogen werden darf, erkennen. Zuständigkeitsfragen sind grundsätzlich in den unteren Instanzen zu klären und vom Revisionsgericht nicht zu überprüfen. So wird vermieden, dass der Rechtsstreit nach Aufhebung und Zurückverweisung noch einmal, nun vor dem eigentlich zuständigen Gericht geführt werden muss. Dieser Grundsatz hat seine Grenze, wenn der Verstoß gegen Zuständigkeitsregeln willkürlich und damit von Verfassungs wegen zu beachten ist.

ALEXANDER METZING

Die Forderungsabtretung als Element der Unternehmensfinanzierung im internationalen Rechtsverkehr

I. Einleitung

Um international wettbewerbsfähig bleiben zu können, müssen Wirtschaftsunternehmen ihre laufenden Ausgaben decken und Investitionen in die Zukunft ihres Betriebs tätigen können. Neben der Verwendung vorhandenen Eigenkapitals und der Aufnahme von Krediten können, insbesondere für Großunternehmen, aber auch für klein- und mittelständige Unternehmen, auch strukturierte Finanzierungen und Verbriefungen sowie Factoring alternative Mittel der Unternehmensfinanzierung sein. Wesentliches Element dieser Finanzierungsformen ist die Forderungsabtretung. Der Beitrag beleuchtet im Folgenden die Elemente der Forderungsabtretung im deutschen Recht, die eine solche forderungsbasierte Unternehmensfinanzierung ermöglichen, und gibt einen Überblick über die Bestimmung des auf die Forderungsabtretung anwendbaren Rechts bei grenzüberschreitenden Sachverhalten. An geeigneter Stelle wird aufgezeigt, welche Rolle diese Prinzipien im Rahmen der forderungsbasierten Unternehmensfinanzierung spielen und wie die Forderungsabtretung für Finanzierungszwecke nutzbar gemacht werden kann.

II. Forderungsabtretung nach deutschem Recht

1. Allgemeines

Die Abtretung von Forderungen unterliegt im deutschen Recht den §§ 398 ff. BGB. Danach kann eine (bereits bestehende) Forderung durch Vertrag vom Zedenten (bisheriger Forderungsgläubiger) auf den Zessionar (neuer Forderungsgläubiger) übertragen werden, sofern diese existiert, bestimmt (oder im Falle von zukünftigen Forderungen bestimmbar) ist und ihre Abtretung nicht kraft Gesetzes oder aufgrund vertraglicher Vereinbarung ausgeschlossen ist. Der Abtretungsvertrag kann zwischen dem jeweiligen Zedenten und Zessionar ohne Mitwirkung oder Information des Forderungsschuldners geschlossen werden.

2. Bestehen der Forderung, Bestimmtheitserfordernis, gutgläubiger Erwerb

Die Forderungsabtretung ist nur wirksam, wenn die abzutretende Forderung auch besteht und hinreichend bestimmt ist. Im Zusammenhang mit einer forderungsbasierten Unternehmensfinanzierung spielt das Bestehen in mehrfacher Hinsicht eine besondere Rolle. Grundsätzlich gilt, dass, solange die Forderung nicht entstanden ist, die Abtretung ins Leere geht und der Zessionar keine Rechte gegenüber dem Forderungsschuldner erworben hat.

a) Gegenwärtige und zukünftige Forderungen

Die §§ 398ff. BGB sind nicht nur auf die Abtretung gegenwärtiger, sondern auch auf die Abtretung künftiger Forderungen anwendbar, unabhängig, ob diese aus einem im Zeitpunkt der Abtretungserklärung bereits existierenden Rechtsverhältnis entstammen oder die Rechtsgrundlage für das Entstehen der Forderung erst später gelegt wird.[1] Zur wirksamen Abtretung künftiger Forderungen ist es erforderlich, dass die Forderung ausreichend bestimmt oder jedenfalls bestimmbar ist.[2] Eine Forderung ist grundsätzlich bestimmt, wenn aus dem Abtretungsvertrag hinreichend hervorgeht, um welche Ansprüche es sich handelt, in welcher Höhe bzw. welchem Umfang diese bestehen und gegen wen diese gerichtet sind. Mit Blick auf künftige Forderungen können diese Anforderungen nicht in jedem Fall erfüllt werden. Es ist daher insbesondere nicht erforderlich, dass der künftige Schuldner im Abtretungszeitpunkt bestimmt werden kann; es muss allerdings gefordert werden, dass die zum tatsächlichen Entstehen der Forderung führenden Umstände im Zeitpunkt der Abtretung bereits beschrieben werden können und die Forderung jedenfalls im Entstehungszeitpunkt nach Gegenstand und Umfang bestimmbar ist.[3] Ist die abzutretende Forderung entsprechend wenigstens bestimmbar (und sind alle anderen Voraussetzungen des Abtretungstatbestands bereits erfüllt), ist die Abtretung im Sinne eines Verfügungsgeschäfts bereits vollendet.[4] Da die Forderung in diesem Zeitpunkt aber nicht besteht, ist der Rechtserwerb durch den Zessionar noch nicht erfolgt. Dies ist erst dann der Fall, wenn die Forderung zur Entstehung gelangt ist.[5]

Ungeachtet des Vorgenannten spielt auch die Abtretung künftiger Forderungen eine bedeutende Rolle im Wirtschaftsverkehr. Insbesondere zum Zweck der laufenden Finanzierung kann es von Vorteil sein, bereits mit Abschluss der Finanzierungsvereinbarung alle bestehenden und zukünftigen Forderungen (aus dem gesamten Geschäftsbetrieb des Zedenten oder aus bestimmten Geschäftszweigen (unter der Voraussetzung der ausreichenden Bestimmbarkeit)) an den Forderungserwerber zu übertragen. Hierdurch kann insbesondere der mögliche Finanzierungsumfang erweitert und der administrative Aufwand einer auf Dauer angelegten Finanzierung reduziert werden. Insbesondere mit Blick auf Letzteres ist nämlich zu bedenken, dass sich Zedent und Zessionar nicht jedes Mal von Neuem auf den Forderungsübergang einigen müssen.

---

[1] Münchener Kommentar zum BGB/Kieninger, 9. Aufl. 2022, BGB § 398 Rn. 78.

[2] BGH 22.6.1989 – III ZR 72/88, NJW 1989, 2383 (2385).

[3] BGH 6.5.2020 – VIII ZR 120/19, BeckRS 2020, 11460 Rn. 82; BGH 20.9.2012 – IX ZR 208/11, NJW-RR 2013, 248.

[4] BGH 17.12.2020 – IX ZR 205/19, NJW-RR 2021, 173 (174).

[5] BGH 17.12.2020 – IX ZR 205/19, NJW-RR 2021, 173 (174).

b) Inhaberschaft der Forderung, kein Gutglaubenserwerb von Forderungen

Eine Forderung kann nur von deren Inhaber abgetreten werden; ein gutgläubiger Forderungserwerb ist in Ermangelung eines entsprechenden Rechtsscheins nicht möglich.[6] Etwas anderes gilt nur im Fall der Vorlegung einer Abtretungsurkunde (§ 405 BGB).[7] In diesem Fall besteht zwar ebenfalls keine Forderung, jedoch kann sich der Forderungsschuldner gegenüber dem neuen Forderungsgläubiger nicht darauf berufen, dass die Eingehung oder das Anerkenntnis eines Schuldverhältnisses, über welches er eine Urkunde erstellt hat, nur zum Schein erfolgt sei oder die Abtretung durch Vereinbarung mit dem Zedenten ausgeschlossen ist, es sei denn, der Zessionar kannte diese Umstände. Mithin wird durch die Abtretungsurkunde der Anschein einer bestehenden Schuld gesetzt, gegenüber der sich der Forderungsschuldner nicht auf die Einwendungen gem. §§ 399 Alt. 2 BGB bzw. 117 BGB berufen kann.[8] Der Schutz des § 405 BGB wirkt auch nach der Eröffnung des Insolvenzverfahrens über das Vermögen des Ausstellers der Abtretungsurkunde fort, sofern diese nur vor der Verfahrenseröffnung ausgestellt und weitergegeben wurde; die Forderung wird als bereits mit der unter Urkundenvorlegung erfolgten Abtretung vor Insolvenzeröffnung als entstanden betrachtet.[9]

Als Urkunde über die Abtretung einer Forderung sind beispielsweise Schuldscheine oder andere über eine Forderung ausgestellte Wertpapiere anzusehen, die mit dem Willen des Ausstellers in den Rechtsverkehr gebracht worden sind.[10] Im Fall des national und international als Alternative zu einfachen Bankkrediten und Anleihen etablierten Schuldscheins vermag § 405 BGB dennoch nicht darüber hinwegzuhelfen, dass über den Darlehensrückzahlungsanspruch eines Kreditgebers bzw. Finanzierers bereits vor dessen Auszahlung ein Schuldschein zwar ausgestellt wurde, das Darlehen aber nie zur Auszahlung gelangte.[11] Der Schuldner stellt in einem solchen Fall den Schuldschein regelmäßig in Erwartung der Valutierung des Darlehens und damit nicht nur zum Schein im Sinne von 117 BGB aus.[12]

Zur Bedeutung von Schuldscheinen im Zusammenhang mit forderungsbasierten Finanzierungen → IV. 2. a).

3. *Offenlegung der Abtretung*

Die Forderungsabtretung ist dem Forderungsschuldner im deutschen Recht – anderes als beispielsweise in anderen Rechtsordnungen (zB Portugal) – nicht an-

---

[6] Staudinger, BGB/Busche, 2022, Einl. zu § 398 ff. Rn. 26.

[7] Staudinger, BGB/Busche, 2022, Einl. zu § 398 ff. Rn. 27.

[8] Schulze, BGB/Fries/Schulze, 11. Aufl. 2021, BGB § 405 Rn. 1; Erman, BGB/Martens, 17. Aufl. 2023, BGB § 405 Rn. 7.

[9] RG 21.12.1915 – III 244/15, RGZ 87, 420 (422); Staudinger, BGB/Busche, 2022, BGB § 405 Rn. 18.

[10] Staudinger, BGB/Busche, 2022, BGB § 405 Rn. 5; Langenbucher/Bliesener/Spindler, Bankrechts-Kommentar/Haertlein, 3. Aufl. 2020, BGB § 405 Rn. 25.

[11] Münchener Kommentar zum BGB/Kieninger, 9. Aufl. 2022, BGB § 405 Rn. 9; Reichsgerichtsrätekommentar/Weber, 12. Aufl. 1976, BGB § 405 Rn. 11.

[12] RG 12.1.1904 – VI 109/04, RGZ 60, 21 (22); Staudinger, BGB/Busche, 2022, BGB § 405 Rn. 18.

zuzeigen. Von dieser Möglichkeit der so genannten „stillen Zession" wird im Wirtschaftsverkehr regelmäßig Gebrauch gemacht. Die stille Zession ist deshalb von Bedeutung, weil der Zedent dadurch einen möglichen einen Reputationsverlust durch Offenlegung der Abtretung vermeiden kann, insbesondere, soweit ein Bekanntwerden der Abtretung die Vermutung nahelegen könnte, der Zedent befinde sich in wirtschaftlichen Schwierigkeiten.[13]

Ist von den Parteien des Abtretungsvertrags eine solche stille Zession gewollt, sind die Bestimmungen des – auch formlos abschließbaren – Abtretungsvertrags dahingehend auszulegen, dass der Zedent weiterhin zur Einziehung der betreffenden Forderungen ermächtigt sein soll.[14] Dies hindert den Zessionar grundsätzlich nicht, die Forderung auch selbst beim Forderungsschuldner einzuziehen. Hierzu ist er kraft eigenen Rechts (infolge der Abtretung) berechtigt. Um dem Geheimhaltungsinteresse des Zedenten Rechnung zu tragen, wird in der Regel jedoch vereinbart sein, dass der Zessionar die Benachrichtigung des Forderungsschuldners von der Abtretung bis zum Eintritt vordefinierter Ereignisse unterlässt. Zu derartigen Ereignissen zählt unter anderem die Eröffnung des Insolvenzverfahrens über das Vermögen des Zedenten. In diesem Fall erlischt auch dessen – gegebenenfalls konkludent erteilte – Einziehungsermächtigung.[15]

Um in einem solchen Fall jedoch nicht dem Problem gegenübergestellt zu sein, dass der Forderungsschuldner die Zahlung mit der Begründung verweigert, er kenne den neuen Forderungsgläubiger nicht und um einer darauf gestützten Hinterlegung durch den Forderungsschuldner wegen Ungewissheit über die Person des Gläubigers (vgl. Voraussetzungen gem. §§ 372 BGB) entgegenzuwirken, wird in Finanzierungstransaktionen der Zedent regelmäßig verpflichtet, dem Zessionar eine Blanko-Benachrichtigung sowie eine Vollmacht zum Ausfüllen und gegebenenfalls zur Vervielfältigung der Blanko-Benachrichtigung zur Verfügung zu stellen. Nach einer entsprechenden Benachrichtigung des Forderungsschuldners kann dieser nicht mehr unter dem Schutz des § 407 Abs. 1 BGB (siehe im Einzelnen unten) an den Zedenten leisten.[16]

Die stille Zession resultiert in einem vollwertigen Übergang der Forderung vom Zedenten auf den Zessionar, sodass eine nach der Abtretung erfolgende Pfändung oder Insolvenz den Erwerb der Forderung beim Zessionar grundsätzlich unberührt lassen.[17] Je nach Hintergrund der Forderungsabtretung kann jedoch der Insolvenzverwalter berechtigt sein, die Forderung weiterhin einzuziehen (zB im Fall der Sicherungsabtretung gem. § 166 Abs. 2 InsO).[18]

Haben bisheriger und neuer Forderungsgläubiger kein Interesse an einer Geheimhaltung, kann die Abtretung von diesen formfrei offengelegt werden. In

---

[13] Hamann/Sigle/Grub, Gesellschaftsrecht, Finanzierung und Unternehmensnachfolge/Dippmann, 3. Aufl. 2022, § 10 Rn. 136.

[14] BGH 9.12.1992 – XIII ZR 218/91, NJW 1993, 1396 (1398).

[15] BGH 6.4.2000 – IX ZR 422/98, NJW 2000, 1950 (1952).

[16] Langenbucher/Bliesener/Spindler, Bankrechts-Kommentar/Haertlein, 3. Aufl. 2020, Kap. 27 Einl. Rn. 23.

[17] Soergel, BGB/Schreiber, 13. Aufl. 2010, BGB § 398 Rn. 13; beck-online.GROSSKOMMENTAR zum Zivilrecht/Lieder, BGB § 398 Rn. 62.

[18] Ellenberger/Bunte, Bankrechts-Handbuch/Ganter, 6. Aufl. 2022, § 75 Rn. 88.

einem solchen Fall verhindert die Anzeige im Ergebnis, dass der Schuldner weiterhin mit schuldbefreiender Wirkung leisten kann (vgl. § 407 Abs. 1 BGB).

4. Kein Abtretungsausschluss

Der Rechtserwerb durch den Zessionar ist nur dann erfolgreich, wenn die Abtretung nicht ausgeschlossen ist.

a) § 399 BGB: Inhaltsänderung oder vertragliches Abtretungsverbot

Gem. § 399 BGB schlägt die Abtretung fehl, wenn hierdurch der Inhalt des Schuldverhältnisses geändert wird (§ 399 Alt. 1 BGB) oder die Abtretung aufgrund einer Vereinbarung mit dem Forderungsschuldner ausgeschlossen ist (§ 399 Alt. 2 BGB).

aa) Abtretungsverbot wegen Inhaltsänderung (§ 399 Alt. 1 BGB)

Abtretungsverbote wegen Inhaltsänderung werden – insoweit für Finanzierungszwecke regelmäßig irrelevant – virulent mit Blick auf Ansprüche, bei denen die Person des Gläubigers eine wesentliche Rolle spielt (sog. höchstpersönliche Ansprüche), bzw. Ansprüche aus Schuldverhältnissen, bei denen aus Vertrauensgesichtspunkten dem Schuldner ein Wechsel in der Person des Gläubigers nicht zugemutet werden kann.[19] Bedeutung kann der Abtretungsausschluss nach § 399 Alt. 1 BGB allerdings dann erlangen, wenn die in Frage stehende Forderung zweckgebunden ist. Vorstellbar ist ein Abtretungsausschluss nach Alternative 1 nämlich auch in Fällen, in denen die Zweckbindung der Forderung durch deren Abtretung verloren geht. Dies kann beispielsweise der Fall bei staatlichen Zuwendungen je nach deren konkreter Ausgestaltung sein.[20] Eine Abtretung von Fördermitteln kann jedoch dann möglich sein, wenn der mit der Subvention angestrebte Zweck erreicht wird. Finanzierungsmodelle, denen die Abtretung staatlicher Subventionen zugrunde liegen, bedürfen daher einer genauen Betrachtung des mit der Subvention verfolgten Zwecks im Einzelfall.

bb) Vertragliches Abtretungsverbot (§ 399 Alt. 2 BGB)

Für die Möglichkeit der Inanspruchnahme forderungsbasierter Finanzierungsformen von größerer Bedeutung ist die Frage, ob die Parteien des Vertrags, aus dem die zur Abtretung vorgesehene Forderung entspringt, ein Abtretungsverbot iSv § 399 Alt. 2 BGB vereinbart haben. Ist dies der Fall, ist die Forderung grundsätzlich nicht wirksam übertragbar. Dass ein solches Abtretungsverbot, welches häufig in allgemeinen Geschäftsbedingungen zu finden ist, geeignet ist, Unternehmen ein wichtiges Finanzierungsinstrument zu entziehen, erkannte bereits der Gesetz-

---

[19] Münchener Kommentar zum BGB/Kieninger, 9. Aufl. 2022, BGB § 399 Rn. 2; Erman, BGB/Martens, 17. Aufl. 2023, BGB § 399 Rn. 3f.; Beck'scher Online-Kommentar BGB/Rohe, Stand 1.11.2023, BGB § 399 Rn. 4f.

[20] BGH 29.10.1969 – I ZR 72/67, BeckRS 1969, 31368020; OVG Weimar 3.2.2004 – 2 KO 434/03, BeckRS 2004, 19173 Rn. 31ff.; VG Bayreuth 4.4.2007 – B 4 K 05.699, BeckRS 2007, 35521 Rn. 31.

geber.[21] Um es Unternehmen, insbesondere solchen mit ausgezeichneter Bonität, dennoch zu ermöglichen, Forderungen als Kreditsicherungsmittel oder im Übrigen zu Finanzierungszwecken einzusetzen, schuf der Gesetzgeber mit § 354a HGB eine Vorschrift, die derart gebundene Forderungen dennoch der Kreditfinanzierung zugänglich macht, ohne schutzwürdige Belange Dritter nachteilig zu berühren.[22]

§ 354a HGB ist anwendbar, wenn es sich bei den Parteien des zugrunde liegenden Vertrags um Kaufleute und bei dem Geschäft folglich um ein beiderseitiges Handelsgeschäft im Sinne von § 354a Abs. 1 HGB handelt. Diese Vorschrift spielt insbesondere dann eine Rolle, wenn die Abtretung durch Vereinbarung mit dem Forderungsschuldner ausgeschlossen ist, der Forderungsgläubiger jedoch kein Interesse hat, dem Schuldner die Abtretung anzuzeigen, mithin von den Finanzierungsparteien eine stille Zession (siehe oben) beabsichtigt ist. Soweit gem. § 354 Abs. 1 S. 3 HGB abweichende Vereinbarungen unwirksam sind, vermag § 354a HGB auch solche vertragliche Vereinbarungen zu überwinden, die nicht ausdrücklich als Abtretungsausschluss ausgestaltet sind, jedoch in ihren Wirkungen einem Abtretungsausschluss gleichkommen. Dazu zählen beispielsweise schuldrechtlich vereinbarte Zustimmungs- oder Anzeigeerfordernisse.[23] In analoger Anwendung von § 354a Abs. 1 S. 3 HGB sind sodann auch vertragliche Bestimmungen, die den Zedenten im Falle der Abtretung zum Schadensersatz verpflichten oder diesem eine Vertragsstrafe auferlegen, unwirksam, soweit diese es dem Zedenten ebenfalls unmöglich machen, die betreffenden Forderungen wirtschaftlich sinnvoll zu verwerten.[24] Folgerichtig kann der bisherige Forderungsgläubiger daher auch nicht aufgrund gesetzlicher Bestimmungen (insbesondere gem. 280ff. BGB) zum Schadensersatz verpflichtet sein, wenn er die Forderung entgegen des vereinbarten Abtretungsverbots abtritt.

Nicht in jedem Fall hilft jedoch § 354a HGB über ein vertraglich vereinbartes Abtretungsverbot hinweg. Dies ist einerseits der Fall, soweit es sich bei der abzutretenden Forderung nicht um eine Geldforderung handelt. Aus diesem Grund können beispielsweise Forderungen aus einem Versicherungsvertrag vor Eintritt des Versicherungsfalls nicht ohne Mitwirkung der Versicherung abgetreten werden. Andererseits sind aber auch Forderungen aus Darlehensverträgen nicht abtretbar, wenn es sich bei dem Zedenten um ein Kreditinstitut im Sinne von § 1 Abs. 1 KWG handelt, § 354a Abs. 2 HGB. Letztgenannter Absatz wurde 2008 durch das Risikobegrenzungsgesetz[25] vor dem Hintergrund des Verhaltens von Kreditinstituten und Finanzinvestoren im Zusammenhang mit der Veräußerung notleidender Kredite eingeführt.[26] Soweit Kreditinstitute dennoch ein berechtigtes Interesse an

[21] BT-Drs. 12/7912, 24.

[22] BT-Drs. 12/7912, 25.

[23] BGH 26.1.2005 – VIII ZR 275/03, NJW-RR 2005, 624 (626); OLG Celle 1.12.1998 – 16 U 13/98, NJW-RR 1999, 618 (619); Röhricht/Graf von Westphalen/Haas/Mock/Wöstmann, HGB/Steimle/Dornieden, 6. Aufl. 2023, HGB § 354a Rn. 12.

[24] Röhricht/Graf von Westphalen/Haas/Mock/Wöstmann, HGB/Steimle/Dornieden, 6. Aufl. 2023, HGB § 354a Rn. 14.

[25] BGBl. 2008 I 1666.

[26] Münchener Kommentar zum HGB/K. Schmidt/Langenbucher, 5. Aufl. 2021, HGB § 354a Rn. 44.

der Refinanzierung ausgereichter bzw. auszureichender Darlehen haben, vertraute der Gesetzgeber darauf, dass diese bereits im Zusammenhang mit der Aushandlung der Darlehen aufgrund ihrer Stellung und Verhandlungsposition in der Lage sein würden, die Vereinbarung eines Abtretungsverbots zu verhindern.[27] Im Zusammenhang mit der Abtretung von Darlehensforderung findet diese Bereichsausnahme jedoch keine Anwendung, sofern das Kreditinstitut lediglich als Zwischenerwerber agiert und die Darlehensforderung in der Folge selbst weiterveräußert.[28] Zudem ist § 354a Abs. 2 HGB gem. § 20 Abs. 1 S. 5 Wirtschaftsstabilisierungsbeschleunigungsgesetz (WStBG) nicht anzuwenden auf Übertragungen unter anderem von Darlehensforderungen an den Finanzmarkstabilisierungsfonds; diese Bestimmung hat jedoch mit der Auflösung des Finanzmarktstabilisierungsfonds (auch bekannt unter der Bezeichnung „SoFFin" oder „Bankenrettungsfonds") an Bedeutung verloren.[29] Soweit diese Bestimmung schon aufgrund ihres Ausnahmecharakters nicht analogiefähig ist, können sich Kreditinstitute auf diese auch nicht im Zusammenhang mit der Abtretung notenbankfähiger Ansprüche an die Bundesbank berufen.[30]

Der Schuldner ist im Fall der Anwendung des § 354a HGB jedoch nicht schutzlos gestellt. Laut § 354a Abs. 1 S. 2 HGB ist er weiterhin berechtigt, mit befreiender Wirkung an den bisherigen Gläubiger zu leisten. Dies ist insbesondere insoweit von Bedeutung, als es dafür anders als nach § 407 Abs. 1 BGB nicht auf die Kenntnis des Forderungsschuldners von der Abtretung ankommt. Die Vorschrift bedingt ein Wahlrecht des Schuldners: Er kann entweder unter Berufung auf § 354a Abs. 1 S. 2 HGB seine Forderung weiterhin gegenüber dem Zedenten begleichen oder unmittelbar mit befreiender Wirkung an den Zessionar leisten.[31] Grenzen setzen diesem Wahlrecht jedoch die aus §§ 138, 242, 826 BGB abgeleiteten Rechtsprinzipien, sodass eine Leistung an den Zedenten in Schädigungsabsicht oder Kenntnis von der bevorstehenden Insolvenz bzw. eine Leistung in der Erwartung der Nichtweiterleitung von Zahlungen durch den Zedenten an den Zessionar als rechtsmissbräuchlich anzusehen ist.[32]

b) Abtretungsverbot aufgrund allgemeiner gesetzlicher Verbote

Für die Abtretung gelten die allgemeinen gesetzlichen Beschränkungen, insbesondere § 134 BGB. Besonders praxisrelevant ist dabei die Frage, ob die Abtretung von Forderungen aus Rechtsgeschäften von zur Verschwiegenheit verpflichteten Personen eine Nichtigkeit wegen Gesetzesverstoßes nach § 203 StGB nach sich

---

[27] Lieder Ticaret ve Fikri Mülkiyet Hukuku Dergisi (TFM) 3 (2017), 83 (88).

[28] Oetker, HGB/Maultzsch, 8. Aufl. 2024, HGB § 354a Rn. 10; beck-online.GROSSKOMMENTAR zum Handelsrecht/Feldhusen, Stand 15.1.2024, HGB § 354a Rn. 129.

[29] Oetker, HGB/Maultzsch, 8. Aufl. 2024, HGB § 354a Rn. 9.

[30] Heer, Die Abtretung von Darlehensforderungen durch Banken zu Refinanzierungszwecken, 2011, 151f.

[31] BGH 21.3.2018 – VIII ZR 17/17, NJW 2018, 2254 (2258); BGH 26.1.2005 – VIII ZR 275/03, NJW-RR 2005, 624 (626).

[32] Heymann, HGB, 2. Aufl. 2005, HGB § 354a Rn. 11; Ebenroth/Boujong/Joost/Strohn, HGB/Wagner, 4. Aufl. 2020, HGB § 354a Rn. 15.

zieht.[33] Darüber hinaus und gerade auch im Kontext der Abtretung von (Verbraucher-)Darlehensforderungen zum Zwecke der Refinanzierung spielen das Bankengeheimnis und datenschutzrechtliche Beschränkungen nach Bundesdatenschutzgesetz und Datenschutzgrundverordnung eine besondere Rolle.[34] Mittlerweile ist höchstrichterlich anerkannt, dass eine Abtretung von Darlehensforderungen nicht zwangsläufig eine Nichtigkeit nach § 134 BGB bedingt.[35] Um verbliebenen Rechtsunsicherheiten zu begegnen, kann außerdem ein Datentreuhänder dazwischengeschaltet werden, der nur den „Schlüssel“ zu einer die für die Einziehung erforderlichen Kundendaten enthaltenden Datei nur dann freigibt, wenn die Einzugsermächtigung des Zedenten erlischt und die Forderungen durch den Zessionar eingezogen werden (sollen). Die Einschaltung eines Datentreuhänders spielt bei Verbriefungstransaktionen insbesondere insoweit eine Rolle, als die Abtretung der zugrundeliegenden Forderungen dem Forderungsschuldner in der Regel nicht offengelegt wird (zu Verbriefungen → IV. 3.).

5. *Wirkungen der Abtretung*

Gem. § 398 S. 2 BGB geht die Forderung mit der Abtretung vom bisherigen auf den neuen Forderungsinhaber über. Die Abtretung als Verfügungsgeschäft über die Forderung bewirkt dabei gleichzeitig auch einen Übergang aller mit der Forderung in Verbindung stehenden Neben- und Vorzugsrechte gem. § 401 BGB, während selbstständige Gestaltungsrechte (zB Anfechtungs-, Kündigungs- und Rücktrittsrechte) grundsätzlich nicht automatisch auf den Zessionar übergehen.[36] In Finanzierungstransaktionen wird deren Übergang daher im Forderungskaufvertrag regelmäßig ausdrücklich geregelt; andernfalls müsste der Zessionar ausdrücklich zur Ausübung der betreffenden Gestaltungsrechte ermächtigt werden.

6. *Schutzbedürfnis des Forderungsschuldners*

Obwohl die Zession absolute Wirkung hat, dh auch Dritten gegenüber wirksam ist, ist der an der Abtretung nicht unmittelbar beteiligte Forderungsschuldner nicht schutzlos gestellt. Die §§ 404 ff. BGB sorgen für einen angemessenen Ausgleich zwischen dem Geheimhaltungsinteresse der am Abtretungsvertrag Beteiligten einerseits und dem Informations- und Schutzbedürfnis des Forderungsschuldners andererseits.

Gemäß § 404 BGB kann der Forderungsschuldner dem Zessionar die Einwendungen entgegenhalten, die im Zeitpunkt der Abtretung gegen den Zedenten begründet waren. Im Fall der Vorausabtretung zukünftiger Forderungen ist dabei nicht der Zeitpunkt des Abschlusses des Abtretungsvertrags sondern der Zeitpunkt der Entstehung der Forderung und damit des Wirksamwerdens der Abtretung maßgebend. § 404 BGB erfasst nicht nur rechtshindernde und rechtsvernichtende Einwendungen sondern auch jegliche Einreden, die gegen den Anspruch beschränken

[33] Staudinger, BGB/Busche, 2022, Einl. zu §§ 398 ff. Rn. 44 ff.
[34] Ellenberger/Bunte, Bankrechts-Handbuch/Rinne, 6. Aufl. 2022, § 95 Rn. 52.
[35] BGH 27.2.2007 – XI ZR 195/05, NJW 2007, 2106.
[36] Staudinger, BGB/Busche, 2022, BGB § 398 Rn. 81.

oder dessen Durchsetzung hindern.[37] Daneben kann sich der Forderungsschuldner über § 404 BGB auch auf prozessuale Einreden wie beispielsweise die Vereinbarung eines ausschließlichen Gerichtsstands,[38] eine Schiedsabrede[39] oder das Bestehen eines Vollstreckungsvertrags[40] berufen. In Abtretungsketten, wie sie im Zusammenhang mit Finanzierungstransaktionen insbesondere dann vorkommen, wenn der Forderungserwerber die Forderungen auf einen Sicherheitentreuhänder weiterüberträgt, stehen dem Schuldner gegenüber dem Letzterwerber der Forderung alle Einwendungen und sonstigen Einreden zu, die im Verlauf der Abtretung gegen Zwischenerwerber der Forderungen begründet waren, es sei denn, es handelte sich um höchstpersönliche Einwendungen.[41]

Dem Schutz des Forderungsschuldners dient des Weiteren § 406 BGB, der es diesem erlaubt, mit einer ihm gegen den bisherigen Gläubiger zustehenden Forderung auch gegenüber dem neuen Gläubiger aufzurechnen. § 406 BGB bewirkt damit eine Durchbrechung des Prinzips der Gegenseitigkeit aus § 387 BGB.[42] Dies ist nur dann nicht der Fall, wenn der Forderungsschuldner bei dem Erwerb der Forderung Kenntnis von der Abtretung hatte oder die Forderung erst nach Erlangung der Kenntnis und später als die abgetretene Forderung fällig geworden ist. Entgegen von § 406 Hs. 2 BGB lässt die hM allerdings auch dann noch eine Aufrechnung gegenüber dem Zessionar zu, wenn es sich bei Haupt- und Gegenforderung um Forderungen aus demselben einheitlichen Rechtsverhältnis handelt, selbst wenn die Gegenforderung erst nach Erlangung der Kenntnis von der Abtretung entstanden ist und/oder zeitlich danach fällig wird.[43]

Forderungsbezogene Rechtshandlungen, welche der Schuldner dem Zedenten gegenüber vornimmt, insbesondere solche, die der Erfüllung der abgetretenen Forderung dienen, behalten auch nach der Abtretung ihre Bedeutung, es sei denn, dieser kannte die Abtretung, § 407 Abs. 1 BGB. Eine bloß fahrlässige Unkenntnis der Abtretung bzw. der den Forderungsübergang bewirkenden Tatsachen im Zeitpunkt der betreffenden Rechtshandlung genügt nicht. Kenntnis erhält der Schuldner insbesondere durch Anzeige der Abtretung. Im Fall der Anzeige durch den ursprünglichen Gläubiger (§ 409 Abs. 1 S. 1 BGB) oder aufgrund einer durch diesen errichteten Urkunde, unabhängig davon, wer diese vorlegt (§ 409 Abs. 1 S. 2 BGB), muss sich der ursprüngliche Gläubiger die Abtretung entgegenhalten lassen, auch wenn diese tatsächlich nicht erfolgt oder unwirksam gewesen ist.[44] Im Übrigen ist die Frage, ob der Schuldner eine den Schutz des § 407 Abs. 1 BGB vernichtende Kenntnis erlangte, anhand der Umstände des Einzelfalles zu beurteilen. Insbeson-

---

[37] juris PraxisKommentar BGB/Rosch, 10. Aufl. 2023, BGB § 404 Rn. 5f.

[38] Schulze, BGB/Fries/Schulze, 11. Aufl. 2022, BGB § 398 Rn. 12,

[39] BGH 2.3.1978 – III ZR 99/76, NJW 1978, 1585; Stein/Jonas, ZPO/Schlosser, 23. Aufl. 2014, BGB § 1040 Rn. 5.

[40] Staudinger, BGB/Löwisch, 2022, BGB § 398 Rn. 32.

[41] Vgl. OLG Rostock 20.11.2008 – 3 U 158/08, BeckRS 2009, 2345.

[42] Münchener Kommentar zum BGB/Kieninger, 9. Aufl. 2022, BGB § 406 Rn. 1.

[43] BGH 19.12.1974 – II ZR 27/73, NJW 1975, 1022 (1023f.); Münchener Kommentar zum BGB/Kieninger, 9. Aufl. 2022, BGB § 406 Rn. 11; Schulze, BGB/Fries, 12. Aufl. 2024, BGB § 406 Rn. 3.

[44] Beck'scher Online-Kommentar BGB/Rohe, 68. Ed. 1.11.2023, BGB § 409 Rn. 3ff.

dere einer Anzeige des Zessionars braucht der Forderungsschuldner nicht ohne Weiteres Glauben zu schenken und selbst bei Zweifeln keine weiteren Ermittlungen anzustellen, solange der Zedent ihm die Abtretung nicht bestätigt oder eine Abtretungsurkunde vorgelegt wird.[45] Etwas anderes gilt nur dann, wenn dem Zessionar bzw. der Information ein besonderer Vertrauensgehalt zuzumessen ist und beispielsweise die wirtschaftliche Lage oder die sonstigen Umstände die Befürchtung einer Täuschung bezüglich der Abtretung nicht aufkommen lassen.[46] Um derartige Unsicherheiten auszuschließen, lassen sich Forderungserwerber im forderungsbasierten Finanzierungsgeschäft regelmäßig nicht nur Blankonotifikationen durch den Forderungsverkäufer ausstellen, sondern auch eine zugehörige Vollmacht, um diese Benachrichtigung im Namen des Zedenten ausfüllen und dem Forderungsschuldner zukommen zu lassen, da nur in diesem Fall vor dem oben beschriebenen Hintergrund die für den Zessionar vorteilhafte Wirkung des § 409 Abs. 1 BGB herbeigeführt werden kann.

III. Das Internationale Privatrecht der Forderungsabtretung

Die vorgenannten Grundsätze und Prinzipien sind nur anzuwenden, wenn auf die der Finanzierungstransaktion zugrundeliegende Forderungsabtretung bzw. mit Blick auf deren Drittwirkungen deutsches Recht anzuwenden ist. Die Bestimmung des anwendbaren Rechts erfolgt durch Rückgriff auf internationale Konventionen, EU-Verordnungen oder nationale Kollisionsnormen. Innerhalb der EU ist die Verordnung (EG) Nr. 593/2008 des Europäischen Parlaments und des Rates vom 17. Juni 2008 über das auf vertragliche Schuldverhältnisse anzuwendende Recht („Rom I-VO") maßgeblich, die in Art. 14 Rom I-VO spezifische Regelungen für die Forderungsabtretung vorsieht.

1. Abtretungsstatut (Art. 14 Abs. 1 Rom I-VO)

Art. 14 Abs. 1 Rom I-VO regelt, welches Recht das Verhältnis zwischen dem Zedenten und dem Zessionar anwendbar ist (so genanntes Abtretungsstatut). Die Vorschrift betrifft dabei anders als die Vorgängerregelung in Art. 33 Abs. 1 EGBGB und Art. 12 EVÜ nicht nur den der Abtretung zugrundeliegenden schuldrechtlichen Vertrag und die sich daraus ergebenden Verpflichtungen der Parteien, mithin die Verpflichtung des Zedenten, die Forderung an den Zessionar abzutreten, sondern vielmehr das gesamte „Verhältnis" zwischen dem Zedenten und dem Zessionar.[47]

a) Verpflichtungsgeschäft

Unstrittig ist das auf die Verpflichtungen aus dem Grundgeschäft (wie beispielsweise einem Forderungskaufvertrag oder dem Vertrag zur Sicherungsabtretung

---

[45] Münchener Kommentar zum BGB/Kieninger, 9. Aufl. 2022, BGB § 407 Rn. 16.
[46] BGH 19.10.1987 – II ZR 9/87, NJW 1988, 700 (702); OLG Düsseldorf 25.3.1975 – 21 U 156/74, WM 1975, 397 (399).
[47] Münchener Kommentar zum BGB/Martiny, 8. Aufl. 2021, Rom I-VO Art. 14 Rn. 12.

einer Forderung) anzuwendende Recht nach Art. 14 Abs. 1 Rom I-VO zu ermitteln. Auf das Grundgeschäft ist mithin das nach Art. 4 Rom I-VO ermittelte Recht anzuwenden, wenn die Parteien nicht die Anwendung eines anderen Rechts vereinbart haben; insoweit hat die Vorschrift des Art. 14 Abs. 1 Rom I-VO gegenüber Art. 3ff. Rom I-VO nur klarstellenden Charakter.[48] Vorbehaltlich einer anderweitigen Rechtswahl gem. Art. 3 Rom I-VO unterliegen die hier näher betrachteten Forderungskaufverträge dem Recht am Sitz des Verkäufers gem. Art. 4 Abs. 1 lit. a Rom I-VO.[49] Etwas anderes kann jedoch mit Blick auf Forderungskäufe im Rahmen von Factoring angenommen werden, soweit man Factoring als Dienstleistung im Sinne von Art. 4 Abs. 2 lit. b Rom I-VO ansehen möchte; in diesem Fall ist auf den gewöhnlichen Aufenthalt des Factors (dh des Forderungskäufers) abzustellen.[50]

b) Verfügungsgeschäft

Auch nach der Neuregelung in Art. 14 Abs. 1 Rom I-VO bleibt hingegen unklar, welches Recht auf die dinglichen Wirkungen der Abtretung anzuwenden ist. Betrachtet man allein die Änderung des Wortlauts von „Verpflichtungen" zwischen Zedenten und Zessionar hin zu „Verhältnis" zwischen Zedenten und Zessionar, liegt es nahe, das Abtretungsstatut auch insoweit anzuwenden, als es die dinglichen Wirkungen der Abtretung zwischen dem Zedenten und dem Zessionar, also insbesondere die Frage, ob die Abtretung auch tatsächlich erfolgt ist, betrifft. Aber auch die sonstigen Voraussetzungen der Abtretung der Forderung, das Zustandekommen des Übertragungsgeschäfts und die unmittelbare Wirkung der Abtretung zwischen den Parteien des Abtretungsvertrags soll sich nach Art. 14 Abs. 1 Rom I-VO bestimmen.[51] Konsequenterweise könnten Zedent und Zessionar in diesem Fall auch das auf die dingliche Übertragung anzuwendende Recht gem. Art. 3 Rom I-VO wählen.[52] Diese Auslegung stünde auch im Einklang mit ErwGr. 38, der vorsieht, dass auch „die dinglichen Aspekte des Vertrags zwischen Zedent und Zessionar" dem Abtretungsstatut unterstellt werden sollen, „wenn eine Rechtsordnung dingliche und schuldrechtliche Aspekte trennt". Was genau mit „dinglichen Aspekten" gemeint sein sollte, bleibt jedoch umstritten.[53] Einig ist man sich indes, dass von Art. 14 Abs. 1 Rom I-VO in keinem Fall der Abtretung vorgelagerte Fragestellungen erfasst sein sollen (so ausdrücklich ErwGr. 38). Der EuGH hat hierzu ausgeführt, dass dazu beispielweise die Frage gehört, ob eine abgetretene Forderung bereits zuvor einmal abgetreten wurde oder nicht.[54] Dient eine Vorschrift indes

[48] beck-online.GROSSKOMMENTAR zum Zivilrecht/Hübner, Stand 1.8.2022, Rom I-VO Art. 14 Rn. 15.

[49] Ferrari/Kieninger/Mankowski, Internationales Vertragsrecht/Kieninger, 3. Aufl. 2018, Rom I-VO Art. 14 Rn. 6, 14.

[50] Ferrari/Kieninger/Mankowski, Internationales Vertragsrecht/Kieninger, 3. Aufl. 2018, Rom I-VO Art. 14 Rn. 6, 14; vgl. auch Basedow ZEuP 1997, 615 (619f.).

[51] Erman, BGB/Stürner, 17. Aufl. 2023, Rom I-VO Art. 14 Rn. 7f.

[52] Flessner IPRax 2009, 35 (38).

[53] Zum Meinungsstand juris PraxisKommentar BGB/Rosch, Rom I-VO, 10. Aufl. 2023, Art. 14 Rn. 25ff.

[54] EuGH 9.10.2019 – C 548/18, ECLI:EU:C:2019:848, NJW 2019, 3368 (3369).

dem Schutz des Zedenten, des Zessionars oder einer Drittpartei, unterfällt diese nicht unmittelbar dem Anwendungsbereich des Art. 14 Abs. 2 Rom I-VO.

2. *Forderungsstatut (Art. 14 Abs. 2 Rom I-VO)*

Abweichend von Art. 14 Abs. 1 Rom I-VO bestimmt nicht das Recht, dem der Abtretungsvertrag unterliegt, sondern gem. Art. 14 Abs. 2 Rom I-VO das Recht, dem die übertragene Forderung unterliegt, ihre Übertragbarkeit, das Verhältnis von Zessionar und Schuldner, die Voraussetzungen, unter denen die Übertragung dem Schuldner entgegengehalten werden kann und die befreiende Leistung durch den Schuldner an den Zedenten gegenüber dem Zessionar. Hierdurch wird dem Schutz des Schuldners – der insbesondere im deutschen Recht oft zunächst keine Kenntnis von der Abtretung hat (Stichwort stille Zession) – Rechnung getragen.

Vor dem Hintergrund der Intention des europäischen Gesetzgebers, mittels Art. 14 Abs. 2 Rom I-VO den Schutz des Schuldners zu bewirken, sind nur solche Regelungen dem Forderungsstatut zu unterstellen, die diesen Schutz auch tatsächlich bewirken sollen. Dazu zählen insbesondere (i) die doppelfunktionale Frage der Übertragbarkeit der Forderung, (ii) die Wirksamkeit von Abtretungsverboten, (iii) der Erhalt von Einreden und Einwendungen, (iv) unter welchen Voraussetzungen eine Leistung des Drittschuldners auch dem Zessionar gegenüber schuldbefreiende Wirkung hat, (v) ob und wie der Schuldner von der Abtretung zu benachrichtigen ist und (vi) wann die Abtretung dem Schuldner entgegengehalten werden kann (insbesondere bestimmt sich nach Art. 14 Abs. 2 Rom I-VO also die Anwendbarkeit der §§ 404ff. BGB).[55] Sinn und Zweck der Vorschrift bedingen es daher auch, dass das Forderungsstatut selbst nicht durch Wahl des anzuwendenden Rechts durch Zedent und Zessionar verändert werden kann; Stimmt der Drittschuldner zu, soll dies aber möglich sein.[56]

3. *Drittwirkung der Forderungsabtretung*

Ein besonders umstrittenes Thema im Zusammenhang mit dem auf die Forderungsabtretung anzuwendenden Recht und vielleicht „das am intensivsten diskutierte des gesamten IPR, national und international,“[57] ist die Frage, nach welchem Recht sich die Drittwirkung der Forderungsabtretung bestimmt. Diese spielt insbesondere im Zusammenhang mit der forderungsbasierten Unternehmensfinanzierung eine besondere Rolle, weil sie insbesondere dann relevant wird, wenn Dritte die abgetretene Forderung vollstrecken wollen oder den (vorrangigen) Erwerb einer Forderung, die Gegenstand einer Mehrfachabtretung wurde, geltend machen.[58]

Aus diesem Grund ist die Drittwirkung der Forderungsabtretung insbesondere auch im Rahmen des Factoring von besonderer Bedeutung. Sie wird nicht nur re-

[55] juris PraxisKommentar BGB/Rosch, 10. Aufl. 2023, Rom I-VO Art. 14 Rn. 35ff.; Erman, BGB/Stürner, 17. Aufl. 2023, Rom I-VO Art. 14 Rn. 16.
[56] Erman, BGB/Stürner, 17. Aufl. 2023, Rom I-VO Art. 14 Rn. 13.
[57] Kieninger NJW 2019, 3353 (3354).
[58] juris PraxisKommentar BGB/Rosch, 10. Aufl. 2023, Rom I-VO Art. 14 Rn. 42ff.

levant, wenn Gläubiger des Factoring-Kunden versuchen, auf die dem Factor abgetretene Forderung im Wege der Zwangsvollstreckung zuzugreifen, sondern die Forderungsabtretung kann auch ein Mittel zur Entlastung der Bilanz des Forderungsverkäufers sein. Wird die Forderung im Wege des echten Factorings, also unter Übertragung des Delkredererisikos vom Forderungsverkäufer auf den Factor übertragen, verringert sich zudem seitens des Forderungsverkäufers das Forderungsausfallrisiko.

Eine ausdrückliche Regelung der Drittwirkung der Forderungsabtretung im grenzüberschreitenden Rechtsverkehr findet sich in Art. 14 Rom I-VO trotz ihrer besonderen Bedeutung nicht. Zwar wurde teilweise bisher vertreten, der europäische Gesetzgeber habe diese Frage implizit mitgeregelt und dass sich die Drittwirkungen der Forderungsabtretung nach dem Abtretungsstatut, dh nach Art. 14 Abs. 1 Rom I-VO bestimmen. Dieser Ansicht hat der EuGH in seiner Entscheidung vom 9.10.2019 zuletzt jedoch eine Absage erteilt; er geht insoweit davon aus, dass „das Fehlen von Kollisionsnormen zur Frage der Drittwirkung von Forderungsübertragungen auf einer bewussten Entscheidung des Unionsgesetzgebers beruhte".[59]

Zwar hatte der europäische Gesetzgeber die Notwendigkeit der Regelung des auf die Drittwirkungen der Forderungsabtretung anwendbaren Rechts schon im Vorfeld des Inkrafttretens der Rom I-VO erkannt; der Vorschlag einer Regelung scheiterte jedoch am Widerstand des Vereinigten Königreichs, weshalb man sich lediglich auf eine Überprüfung und erneuten Auseinandersetzung nach Inkrafttreten der Rom I-VO verständigte (vgl. Art. 27 Abs. 2 Rom I-VO).[60] Erst mit der Vorlage eines Entwurfs einer Verordnung über das auf die Drittwirkung von Forderungsübertragungen anzuwendende Recht im März 2018[61] wurde eine Schließung der vom EuGH wenige Zeit später explizit festgestellten Lücke seitens des Unionsgesetzgebers wieder in Angriff genommen. Von den zur Diskussion stehenden Lösungsmöglichkeiten im Rahmen des Verordnungsvorschlags blieben zuletzt nur noch die (seitens der Kommission offenbar favorisierte und als Regelanknüpfung ausgestaltete) Anknüpfung an das am Sitz des Zedenten geltende Recht und die Anknüpfung an das Forderungsstatut Gegenstand der Diskussion.[62] Solange diese Lücke allerdings durch den Unionsgesetzgeber nicht gefüllt wurde, sollte die Frage nach dem anwendbaren Recht unter Rückgriff auf das nationale Kollisionsrecht und mit der bisher geltenden Meinung dahingehend entschieden werden, dass sich die Drittwirkungen der Forderungsabtretung nach dem Forderungsstatut bestimmen.[63] Aus Finanzierungssicht, aber auch Gründen der Rechtssicherheit, spricht

---

[59] EuGH 9.10.2019 – C 548/18, ECLI:EU:C:2019:848 = NJW 2019, 3368 (3369); Stefer IPRax 21, 155.

[60] beck-online.GROSSKOMMENTAR zum Zivilrecht/Hübner, Stand 1.8.2022, Rom I-VO Art. 14 Rn. 25.

[61] EU COM(2018) 96 endg.

[62] Erman, BGB/Stürner, 17. Aufl. 2023, Rom I-VO Art. 14 Rn. 21.

[63] OLG Saarbrücken 20.02.2020 – 4 U 109/17, BeckRS 2020, 2943. Zur bisherigen Rechtsprechung s. BGH 20.6.1990 – VIII ZR 158/89, NJW 1991, 637 (638); OLG Hamburg 28.4.1992 – 7 U 59/91, NJW-RR 1993, 40 (41) = VersR 1992, 685 (686); OLG München 5.11.1997 – 7 U 2989/97, NJW-RR 1998, 549 (550).

hierfür insbesondere die mit dieser Anknüpfung verbundene Rechtssicherheit im Zeitpunkt der Abtretung. Anders als bei einer Anknüpfung an den Zedentensitz, ist das Recht, nach welchem sich die Drittwirkungen bestimmen, im Fall der Anwendung des Forderungsstatuts nicht wandelbar, sondern steht aufgrund der Rechtswahl oder objektiver Anknüpfung im Zeitpunkt des Abschlusses des der Forderung zugrundeliegenden Vertrags endgültig und unveränderlich fest; mithin wird somit eine einheitliche kollisionsrechtliche Behandlung der Drittwirkungen der Forderungsabtretung gewährleistet.[64] Teilweise wird auch vorgeschlagen, im Zusammenhang mit Verbriefungstransaktionen dem Zedenten und Zessionar ein Wahlrecht zugunsten des Forderungsstatuts hinsichtlich des auf die Drittwirkungen anwendbaren Rechts einzuräumen; dies spiegelt sich auch in Art. 4 Abs. 3 des Verordnungsentwurfs.[65]

IV. Die Forderungsabtretung als Finanzierungsmittel

1. Factoring

Factoring ermöglicht es Unternehmen, Zugang zu sofortiger Liquidität zu erhalten, ohne auf die Zahlung durch ihre Debitoren warten zu müssen. Dies ist besonders dann attraktiv, wenn das jeweilige Unternehmen üblicherweise lange Zahlungsziele vereinbart oder mit Kunden kontrahiert, die üblicherweise spät zahlen. Durch den Verkauf ihrer Forderungen an den Factor kommt das Unternehmen sofort zu Barmitteln, welche es für laufende Betriebskosten, Investitionen oder zur Schuldentilgung verwenden kann.[66]

Ein wesentlicher Aspekt, der im Rahmen des Factorings zu berücksichtigen ist, ist die Bonität der Drittschuldner, da der Factor jedenfalls im Zuge des echten Factorings das Risiko des Forderungsausfalls übernimmt. Die Übernahme dieses so genannten Delkredererisikos ist eine wesentliche Voraussetzung dafür, dass die Forderungsübertragung auch in einer späteren Insolvenz des Forderungsverkäufers, dh des Factoringkunden, Bestand hat und der Factor gegenüber dem Insolvenzverwalter des Factoringkunden ein Aussonderungsrecht an der Forderung gem. § 47 InsO[67] oder ein Ersatzaussonderungsrecht an einer ggf. bereits erfolgten Einziehung gem. § 48 InsO geltend machen kann.

In der Regel wird der Factor die Forderungen nicht zum vollen Nennwert kaufen, sondern einen Abschlag (Discount) vom Forderungskaufpreis vornehmen, der das Risiko des Forderungsausfalls des Factors widerspiegelt. Dieser Abschlag ist so zu bemessen, dass er eine Übertragung des Delkredererisikos vom Forderungsverkäufer auf den Forderungskäufer nicht verhindert. Andernfalls handelt es sich bei dem Forderungsverkauf nicht um echtes, sondern lediglich um unechtes Factoring.

---

64 Schmitt EuZW 2019, 940 (941); OLG Saarbrücken 20.02.2020 – 4 U 109/17, BeckRS 2020, 2943.

65 S. dazu Hübner ZEuP 2019, 41 (56).

66 Vgl. auch Ellenberger/Bunte, Bankrechts-Handbuch/Rinne, 6. Aufl. 2022, § 81 Rn. 2.

67 Schmidt, InsO/Thole, 20. Aufl. 2023, InsO § 47 Rn. 77.

Als Anhaltspunkt, ob die ein Abschlag in einer bestimmten Höhe einer Übertragung des Delkredererisikos entgegensteht, kann die historische Ausfallrate des zu übertragenden Forderungsportfolios herangezogen werden. Übersteigt der Abschlag die historische Ausfallrate wesentlich, ist das Risiko groß, dass das Factoring als unechtes Factoring eingestuft und der Forderungsverkauf in ein gesichertes Darlehen umqualifiziert wird mit der Folge, dass dem Forderungskäufer kein (Ersatz-) Aussonderungsrecht zusteht, sondern die Forderungen vielmehr als zur Sicherheit dieses Darlehens übertragen angesehen werden. Diese darf der Insolvenzverwalter gem. § 166 Abs. 2 InsO verwerten und vom Verwertungserlös seine Kosten in Höhe von 9% für die Feststellung und Verwertung der Forderung vorweg aus der Insolvenzmasse entnehmen, § 170 Abs. 1, § 171 InsO. Unechtes Factoring ist daher insbesondere dann attraktiv, wenn das Risiko eines Zahlungsausfalls unter der Forderung relativ gering ist.

2. *Verbriefungen*

a) *Rechtliche Grundlagen*

Die Forderungsabtretung ist ebenfalls Kernelement von Verbriefungstransaktionen. Diese zeichnen sich dadurch aus, dass Forderungen verschiedenster Assetklassen (Handelsforderungen, Darlehensforderungen, Leasingforderungen, etc.) vom Forderungsverkäufer, dem so genannten Originator, an eine eigens zu diesem Zweck gegründete Zweckgesellschaft (sog. *Special Purpose Vehicle, SPV*) auf Grundlage eines Forderungskaufvertrags (sog. *Receivables Purchase Agreement*) übertragen werden. Die Zweckgesellschaft finanziert den Kauf dieser Forderungen beispielsweise durch die Ausgabe von Inhaber- oder Namensschuldverschreibungen oder den Abschluss von (Schuldschein-) Darlehen, die von Investoren gezeichnet bzw. gewährt werden. Die Zahlungen auf die zugrundeliegenden Forderungen dienen als Cashflow für die Bedienung von Zins und Tilgung unter den Wertpapieren bzw. Darlehen.

Die Wirksamkeit der Abtretung ist in diesem Zusammenhang von wesentlicher Bedeutung. Nur wenn die Abtretung rechtlich wirksam und durchsetzbar ist, können die Forderungen tatsächlich vom Vermögen des Originators getrennt und auf das SPV übertragen werden. Dies ist insbesondere im Falle einer Insolvenz des Originators von Bedeutung, da die abgetretenen Forderungen dann nicht zur Insolvenzmasse gehören und somit vor dem Zugriff der Gläubiger des Originators geschützt sind. Dies ist das Ziel jeder Verbriefungstransaktion, da nur auf diese Weise der Fortbestand der Cashflows aus den Forderungen trotz einer möglichen Insolvenz des Originators den Investoren zugute kommt. Ein wichtiger Aspekt bei der Beurteilung, ob die Forderungen vom Vermögen des Originators getrennt wurden, ist die Frage, ob es sich um einen sogenannten „true sale" handelt. Dieses Prinzip hat zwar keine exakte Entsprechung im deutschen Recht, jedoch greift man zur Beurteilung der „true sale"-Eigenschaft einer Transaktion auf zivil- und insolvenzrechtliche Grundsätze des deutschen Rechts zurück. Von einem „true sale" spricht man insoweit, wenn es sich bei der Forderungsveräußerung um echtes Factoring handelt und die Übertragung der Forderung gerade nicht als besichertes Darlehen *(secured loan)* bzw. unechtes Factoring mit Rückgriff auf den Forderungsverkäufer interpretiert werden kann.

b) *Verbriefungen als Finanzierungsmittel*

In dieser Trennung der Forderungen vom Originator liegt das große Potential von Verbriefungen zur Finanzierung. Die vom SPV emittierten Wertpapiere werden daher auch als forderungsbesicherte Wertpapiere bezeichnet *(asset backed securities)*, da die Wertpapiere eben in keiner rechtlichen und wirtschaftlichen Verbindung mit dem Originator mehr stehen, sondern lediglich durch die Forderungen besichert und wirtschaftlich mit Leben erfüllt werden. Ratingagenturen bzw. in letzter Konsequenz die Investoren müssen bei der Risikobewertung so lediglich das Ausfallrisiko der Forderungen bewerten. Eine Investition in beispielsweise Unternehmensanleihen erfordert eine ungleich aufwendigere Risikobewertung, da hier das gesamte Unternehmen und dessen gesamtes Marktumfeld mitbetrachtet werden muss.

Außerdem wird kleinen und mittelständischen Unternehmen, die mangels Ratings oder schlechter Finanzkennzahlen keinen Zugang zum Kapitalmarkt erhalten würden, die Möglichkeit eröffnet, sich mittelbar am Kapitalmarkt refinanzieren.[68] In dieser Erweiterung des möglichen Investorenkreises liegt im Übrigen auch der Unterschied zum Factoring, bei dem für den Forderungskauf nur Factors mit entsprechender Erlaubnis durch die BaFin nach § 32 Abs. 1 Satz 1 KWG in Frage kommen.[69]

Dennoch lohnt sich eine Verbriefungstransaktion für kleine und mittelständische Unternehmen nicht in jedem Fall. Durch ihr Komplexität und die Vielzahl der beteiligten Akteure ist eine Verbriefung kostenintensiv und lohnt sich erst ab einem Forderungsvolumen von 250–300 Mio. Euro. Für geringere zu verbriefende Forderungsvolumina kann sich allerdings die Nutzung bereits aufgesetzter Verbriefungsstrukturen lohnen (sog. Conduit-Programme, aufgesetzt beispielsweise von bestimmten investierenden Banken).[70]

3. *Forderungsabtretung als Mittel der Unternehmensrestrukturierung*

Die Abtretung von Forderungen kann ein effektives Mittel zur Restrukturierung eines Unternehmens sein, insbesondere wenn es darum geht, die Liquidität zu verbessern und die Bilanz zu stärken. Unter Restrukturierung soll hier der Prozess der Neugestaltung der finanziellen, operativen oder rechtlichen Strukturen eines Unternehmens zum Zweck der Erreichung finanzieller Stabilität und zur Sicherung langfristiger Rentabilität verstanden werden.

Im Kontext der Restrukturierung bietet die Abtretung von Forderungen diverse Vorteile. Durch den Forderungsverkauf erhält das Unternehmen sofortige Liquidi-

---

[68] Ellenberger/Bunte, Bankrechts-Handbuch/Rinne, 6. Aufl. 2022, § 95 Rn. 1, 25.

[69] BaFin Merkblatt Factoring, Stand 5.1.2009, VI; der Forderungsankauf durch Zweckgesellschaften ist dabei von der Erlaubnispflicht ausgenommen, s. BaFin Merkblatt Factoring, Stand 5.1.2009, IV.

[70] Ellenberger/Bunte, Bankrechts-Handbuch/Rinne, 6. Aufl. 2022, § 95 Rn. 16.

tät, die zur Erfüllung dringender Verbindlichkeiten, zur Erhöhung des Betriebskapitals oder zur Investition in das Kerngeschäft nuten kann. Außerdem kann die Übertragung von Forderungen dazu beitragen, Bilanzkennzahlen zu verbessern und damit die Attraktivität des Unternehmens für Investoren und Kreditgeber zu erhöhen. Die Forderungsabtretung ermöglicht es dem Forderungsverkäufer außerdem, sich auf das Kerngeschäft zu fokussieren, anstatt Ressourcen für das Forderungsmanagement und Inkasso zu binden. Das Outsourcing des Forderungsmanagements vermag es außerdem, die Verwaltungskosten zu reduzieren, soweit die Einziehung der Forderungen durch den die Forderung erwerbenden Forderungskäufer erfolgt. Dieser Schritt muss jedoch wohl überlegt sein, da eine Benachrichtigung des Forderungsschuldners die Gefahr eines Reputationsverlustes birgt, insbesondere dann, wenn die Forderungsabtretung im ohnehin schon finanziell schwierigen Umfeld des Forderungsverkäufers erfolgt.

V. Schlussfolgerung/Ausblick

Die Forderungsabtretung ist Grundbaustein für vielseitige und effektive Finanzierungsinstrumente. Fast immer geht es dabei um die Minimierung bzw. Auslagerung des Debitoren-Ausfallrisikos. Dieses Risiko, zusammen mit der Wartezeit auf vollständige Begleichung der Forderung, wird mit entsprechendem Abschlag gegen sofortige Liquidität eingetauscht.

Die Transformationsprozesse, die Unternehmen im Zuge sich verändernder sozialer, wirtschaftlicher und klimatischer Umstände abverlangt wird, müssen finanziell gestemmt werden. Die Verfügbarkeit von Liquidität ist dafür unerlässlich. Die Forderungsabtretung kann dabei in ihren verschiedenen Erscheinungsformen eine wichtige Rolle spielen.

RALF MÜLLER-FELDHAMMER

Das Unternehmen als Adressat von Geldbußen im deutschen und europäischen Kartellrecht

I. Einleitung

Mit jeder Novelle des GWB schreitet die Angleichung des nationalen Kartellrechts an das europäische Kartellrecht unaufhörlich voran. Mit der 9. GWB Novelle 2017 hat der deutsche Gesetzgeber zwei aus dem europäischen Kartellrecht stammende Grundsätze übernommen, die von grundlegenden Vorstellungen des deutschen Unternehmensrechts abweichen. Es sind dies die Grundsätze der Haftung der wirtschaftlichen Einheit und der wirtschaftlichen Unternehmenskontinuität.

Der Grundsatz der Haftung der wirtschaftlichen Einheit besagt, dass eine Geldbuße nicht dem Rechtsträger, dh der das Unternehmen tragenden natürlichen oder juristischen Person, sondern dem Unternehmen, welches von zwei oder mehreren Personen getragen werden kann, zugerechnet wird. Die wirtschaftliche Unternehmenskontinuität bedeutet, dass bei Übertragungsvorgängen die Haftung für eine Geldbuße mit dem Unternehmen verbunden ist, so dass der übernehmende Rechtsträger für die Geldbuße – neben dem übertragenden Rechtsträger – haftet.

Beide Grundsätze kommen naturgemäß dem *effet utile,* dh der effektiven Durchsetzung des Kartellrechts, zugute, weil jeweils zwei oder mehrere Rechtsträger als Haftungssubjekte zur Verfügung stehen. Beide Grundsätze sind jedoch mit dem Rechtsträgerprinzip nicht in Übereinstimmung zu bringen, dh der grundlegenden Vorstellung, dass Rechte und Verbindlichkeiten dem Rechtsträger des Unternehmens zugerechnet werden.[1] Dieser Grundsatz ist notwendige Folge der herrschenden Vorstellung, dass das Unternehmen selbst nicht rechtsfähig ist. Die Entscheidung des deutschen Gesetzgebers die genannten Prinzipien in das GWB zu übernehmen, hat damit weittragende Folgen auch für andere Rechtsbereiche als das Kartellrecht.

II. Das Unternehmen als wirtschaftliche Einheit

1. Das Unternehmen als Täter einer Kartellordnungswidrigkeit

Art. 23 Abs. 1, 2 VO 1/2003 als Grundnorm des europäischen Kartellbußgeldrechts ordnet die Bußgeldverhängung dem Wortlaut nach gegen Unternehmen oder Unternehmensvereinigungen an. Der Unternehmensbegriff des europäischen

[1] Teilweise auch als Trennungsprinzip bezeichnet.

Kartellrechts ist, wie derjenige des deutschen Kartellrechts, bewusst weit gefasst. Nach der Rechtsprechung des EuGH gilt als Unternehmen jede eine wirtschaftliche Tätigkeit ausübende Einrichtung, unabhängig von ihrer Rechtsform und der Art ihrer Finanzierung. Eine wirtschaftliche Tätigkeit wird dabei als jede Tätigkeit definiert, die darin besteht, Güter oder Dienstleistungen entgeltlich anzubieten.[2]

Verstößt eine solche Einrichtung gegen die Wettbewerbsregeln, hat sie nach dem Grundsatz der persönlichen Verantwortung für diese Zuwiderhandlung einzustehen. Der Begriff des Unternehmens im Sinne der Wettbewerbsbestimmungen des Vertrages setzt dabei nicht voraus, dass die betreffende wirtschaftliche Einheit eine eigene Rechtspersönlichkeit hat.[3] Der Begriff der wirtschaftlichen Einheit unterscheidet sich von dem Begriff des Unternehmens im Sinne des EU-Kartellrechts dadurch, dass auch zwei oder mehrere Einrichtungen, soweit sie unter einheitlicher Leitung stehen, eine wirtschaftliche Einheit begründen können. Mit diesem funktionalen Unternehmensbegriff soll ein Handeln von Wirtschaftssubjekten tatbestandlich möglichst umfassend erfasst werden.

Auch das Kartellverbot des § 1 GWB knüpft auf der Tatbestandsseite an Unternehmen und Unternehmensvereinigungen an. Tatbestandlich können durch das deutsche Kartellrecht daher ebenfalls Unternehmensgruppen erfasst werden.[4] § 81 Abs. 1 GWB lässt jedoch die Frage der bußgeldrechtlichen Verantwortlichkeit für einen Verstoß offen. § 30 OWiG ordnet, anders als Art. 23 VO 1/2003, nicht die bußgeldrechtliche Verantwortung des Unternehmens, sondern der juristischen Person oder der Personenvereinigung an, deren vertretungsberechtigtes Organ, Mitglied eines Organs oder Gesellschafter gehandelt hat. Eine Anwendung dieser Norm über ihren Wortlaut hinaus wird von der Rechtsprechung abgelehnt. Daher wurde seitens des BGH einer bußgeldrechtlichen Konzernhaftung mangels einer ausdrücklichen gesetzlichen Bestimmung eine Absage erteilt.[5]

Damit sind die Ausgangspunkte des deutschen und des europäischen Rechts diametral verschieden. Das deutsche Recht knüpfte vor der 9. GWB Novelle auf der Tatbestandsseite des Kartellverbots an das Unternehmen an, auf der Rechtsfolgenseite rechnete es die Handlungen entweder gem. § 130 OWiG dem Betriebs- oder Unternehmensinhaber oder gem. § 30 OWiG dem Rechtsträger zu. Die Rechtsprechung lehnt eine Anwendung des § 130 OWiG auf eine Haftung der Obergesellschaft für das Verhalten der Tochtergesellschaft ab, weil letztere mit eigener Rechtspersönlichkeit ausgestattet und als solche Inhaberin des Gesellschaftsvermögens ist.[6] Das europäische Kartellrecht knüpft demgegenüber auf der Tatbestands- und der Rechtsfolgenseite an den Unternehmens-

[2] EuGH 1.7.2008 – C 49/07, ECLI: EU:C:2008:376, Slg. 2008, I-4683, Rn. 21f. (MOTOE); EuGH 26.3 2009 – C-113/07 P, ECLI:EU:C:2009:191, Slg. I-2207 Rn. 69 (SELEX).

[3] EuGH 10.4.2014 – C-434/13 P, ECLI:EU:C:2014:2456, Rn. 39ff. (Parker Hannifin); EuGH 28.6.2005 – C-189/02 P, ECLI:EU:C:2005:408 = Slg. 2005, I-5425 Rn. 113f. (Dansk Roerindustri); Kling WRP 2010, 506 (507).

[4] Kling WRP 2010, 506 (507) Fn. 21.

[5] BGH 10.8.2011 – KRB 55/10, BGHSt 57, 193–202 Tz. 16, 24 (Versicherungsfusion).

[6] BGH 1.12.1981 – KRB 3/79, WuW/E BGH 1871 (1876) Rn. 29 (Transportbeton-Vertrieb).

begriff an.[7] Dies ist für den EuGH, wie dieser auch in neuerer Zeit nochmals betont hat, Ausgangspunkt für die Entwicklung der Rechtsfigur der wirtschaftlichen Einheit.[8] Dabei gehen die Unionsorgane zweistufig vor.[9] Sie stellen zunächst fest, welche wirtschaftliche Einheit für die Zuwiderhandlung verantwortlich ist und bestimmen in einem zweiten Schritt den Adressaten des Bußgeldbescheides, welcher zur Vollstreckung zivilrechtliche Rechtsfähigkeit aufweisen muss.[10] Der Vorgang der Haftungszuweisung findet damit im europäischen Kartellrecht auf einer zweiten Ebene statt.[11]

Die Rechtsprechung des EuGH hat aus dieser Vorgabe Zurechnungsgesichtspunkte abgeleitet, die sich zum Teil an Gesichtspunkte anlehnen, welche aus der Diskussion um die Rechtssubjektivität des Unternehmens bekannt sind, so zB das Kriterium der wirtschaftlichen Kontinuität, welches auch in das deutsche Kartellrecht Eingang gefunden hat.[12]

2. *Die wirtschaftliche Einheit als Adressat der Geldbuße*

Sowohl das deutsche als auch das europäische Kartellrecht gehen auf der Tatbestandsseite von dem funktionalen, weiten Unternehmensbegriff aus, mit dem umfassend für das Kartellrecht relevante Formen wirtschaftlichen Handelns erfasst werden sollen. Art. 23 Abs. 2 VO 1/2003 regelt jedoch auch die Rechtsfolgenseite insofern, als die Verhängung von Geldbußen gegen Unternehmen und Unternehmensvereinigungen angeordnet werden kann. Da Art. 299 AEUV lediglich die Vollstreckung, nicht auch die Zurechnung von Kartellrechtsverstößen dem nationalen Recht zuweist, erfolgt der Vorgang der Zurechnung des Kartellrechtsverstoßes an ein Rechtssubjekt durch die Kommission im Rahmen ihrer Entscheidung. Der Vorgang der Zurechnung erfolgt dabei häufig implizit, dh ohne Erörterung in der Kommissionsentscheidung bzw. dem Urteil.[13]

Nach dem oben dargestellten zweistufigen Vorgehen wird das kartellrechtswidrige Verhalten zunächst einer wirtschaftlichen Einheit zugeordnet, dies ohne Rücksicht auf die Rechtssubjektivität dieser Einheit. Mehrere natürliche oder juristische Personen können eine wirtschaftliche Einheit bilden. Aufgrund des weiten Unter-

---

[7] So bereits Art. 15 Abs. 1 VO 17/62; VO 17/62, ABl.1962 P 13, 204, sollte ursprünglich nur Sanktionen für Verfahrensverstöße vorsehen, vgl. dazu Immenga/Mestmäcker, Wettbewerbsrecht/Biermann, 6. Aufl. 2019, VO 1/2003 Vor Art. 23 Rn. 4.

[8] EuGH 6.10.2019 – C-882/19, ECLI:EU:C:2019:800 Rn. 19 (Sumal).

[9] Zum einstufigen Verfahren, bei dem als Adressat nur ein Rechtssubjekt in Frage kommt vgl. Grabitz/Hilf/Nettesheim, EUV/AEUV/Stockenhuber, 64. ErgLfg 2018, AEUV Art. 101 Rn. 52.

[10] EuG 20.4.1999 – T-305/94, ECLI:EU:T:1999:80, Slg. 1999 II-931 Rn. 979–981 (Limburgse Vinyl Maatschappij); Europäische Kommission 13.7.1994 – IV/C/33.833, ABl. 1994 L 243, 1 Rn. 141–146 (Karton); EuGH 11.12.2007 – C-280/06, ECLI:EU:C:2007:775, Slg. 2007, I-10893 Rn. 46–52 (ETI); Frankfurter Kommentar zum Kartellrecht/Roth/Ackermann, 101. Aktualisierung 2022, AEUV Art. 101 Rn. 105.

[11] Kritisch Immenga/Mestmäcker, Wettbewerbsrecht/Biermann, 6. Aufl. 2019, VO 1/2003 Vor Art. 23 Rn. 78; van Vormizeele WuW 2010, 1008 (1012 f.).

[12] § 81 Abs. 3a-3d GWB aF, heute § 81a Abs. 1–4 GWB.

[13] Vgl. dazu EuGH 23.4.1991, – C-41/90, ECLI:EU:C:1991:161 = Slg. 1999, I-1979 Rn. 21 (Höfner und Elser); Steinle FS Bechtold, 2006, 541 (543).

nehmensbegriffs werden Unternehmen und wirtschaftliche Einheit gleichgesetzt.[14] Eine wirtschaftliche Einheit liegt vor, wenn die Beteiligten nicht die Möglichkeit haben, wirtschaftlich selbständig zu handeln. Dabei kommt es darauf an, dass die Muttergesellschaft im Kartellzeitraum die Vertriebs- und Preispolitik der Tochtergesellschaft entscheidend beeinflussen konnte, diesen Einfluss auch tatsächlich ausgeübt hat und die Tochtergesellschaft unternehmerisch tätig ist. Dass die Muttergesellschaft als Holding fungiert, schadet dabei nicht. Nicht entscheidend ist, dass die Muttergesellschaft auf das kartellrechtswidrige Verhalten der Tochtergesellschaft tatsächlich Einfluss genommen hat oder von diesem Kenntnis hatte.[15]

Das Verhalten der Tochtergesellschaft kann der Muttergesellschaft dann zugerechnet werden kann, wenn diese trotz eigener Rechtspersönlichkeit ihr Marktverhalten nicht autonom bestimmt, sondern im Wesentlichen Weisungen der Muttergesellschaft befolgt, dies vor allem wegen der wirtschaftlichen, organisatorischen und rechtlichen Bindungen. Zwar soll erforderlich sein, dass die einheitliche Leitung tatsächlich ausgeübt wird, diese ergibt sich jedoch aus einer Gesamtbetrachtung aller wirtschaftlichen, organisatorischen und rechtlichen Bindungen zwischen Mutter- und Tochtergesellschaft.[16] Unerheblich ist, ob die Muttergesellschaft ein strategischer oder ein Finanzinvestor ist.[17] Die Kommission ist jedoch nicht verpflichtet, gegen sämtliche Personen, die für die Beteiligung persönlich haftbar gemacht werden können, eine Geldbuße zu verhängen.

Auf diese Weise wird das Unternehmen von einem Zuschreibungsobjekt zu einem Handlungssubjekt gemacht. Das Haftungssubjekt wird wirtschaftlich-funktional danach bestimmt, wer am Wirtschaftsleben teilnimmt und als Entität die Fähigkeit besitzt, den Wettbewerb zu beschränken.[18] In diesem Fall soll eine widerlegbare Vermutung dafür bestehen, dass die Muttergesellschaft auf die Tochtergesellschaft einen bestimmenden Einfluss ausübt.[19]

Diese Rechtsprechung hat der EuGH dahingehend erweitert, dass auch Konstellationen unterhalb einer 100% Beteiligung zu einer wirtschaftlichen Einheit führen können und das Bestehen einer wirtschaftlichen Einheit aus einem Bündel übereinstimmender Umstände hergeleitet werden kann, auch wenn keiner dieser Um-

[14] EuGH 28.6.2005, – C-189/02 P ua, ECLI:EU:C:1991:161 = Slg. 2005, I-5425 Rn. 113 (Dansk Roerindustrie); EuGH 10.4.2014 – C-231/11 P bis C-233/11, ECLI:EU:C:2014:256 Rn. 43 (Siemens Österreich); zur Entwicklung dieses Konzepts aus des Kommissionspraxis vgl. Immenga/Mestmäcker, Wettbewerbsrecht/Biermann, 6. Aufl. 2019, VO 1/2003 Vor Art. 23 Rn. 84.

[15] EuGH 16.11.2000 – C-286/98 P, ECLI:EU:C:2000:630 = Slg. 2000, I-9925 Rn. 26–29 (Stora Kopparbergs Bergslags); EuGH 10.9.2009 – C-97/08 P, ECLI:EU:C:2009:536 = Slg. 2010, I-8237 Rn. 74 (Akzo Nobel); Kellerbauer WuW 2014, 1173 (1176).

[16] Vgl. Langen/Bunte, Kartellrecht/Hengst, 13 Aufl. 2018, AEUV Art. 101 Rn. 43.

[17] Bosch/Brinker, EU-Kartellrecht, 4. Aufl. 2023, AEUV Art. 101 Rn. 33.

[18] Vgl. zu den zugrunde liegenden theoretischen Modellen Frankfurter Kommentar zum Kartellrecht/Meyer, 105. Aktualisierung 2023, AEUV Art. 101 Bußgeldrechtliche Folgen, Rn. 25–27, der dies als unternehmensbezogenes Solidarverantwortungsmodell bezeichnet; zustimmend Frankfurter Kommentar zum Kartellrecht/Roth/Ackermann, 101. Aktualisierung 2022, AEUV Art. 101 Rn 106a.

[19] EuGH 10.9.2009 – C-97/08 P, ECLI:EU:C:2009:536 = Slg. 2010, I-8237 Rn. 58 (Akzo Nobel); zur Haftung einer Holding für die Tochtergesellschaft einer Zwischenholding EuGH 20.1.2011 – C 90/09 P, ECLI:EU:C:2010:389 = Slg. 2011, I-1, Rn. 86, 88 (General Quimica).

stände für sich allein genügt, das Bestehen einer solchen Einheit zu belegen.[20] Nicht nur im Verhältnis zwischen Mutter- und Tochtergesellschaften soll eine Haftung in Betracht kommen, vielmehr können alle Teile einer wirtschaftlichen Einheit gesamtschuldnerisch zur Haftung herangezogen werden. Dies leitet der EuGH direkt aus dem Unternehmensbegriff ab.[21] Von diesem scheinbar klaren Ausgangspunkt weicht der Gerichtshof jedoch wieder ab und bezeichnet die wirtschaftliche Einheit als „Schuldverband" und verlangt, dass bei der Bestimmung des Außenverhältnisses dieses Verbandes der Grundsatz der individuellen Straf- und Sanktionsfestsetzung zu beachten sei, wonach der Betrag der verhängten Geldbuße anhand der Schwere der dem betroffenen Unternehmen individuell zur Last gelegten Zuwiderhandlung und ihrer Dauer bestimmt wird.[22]

Als Begründung für diese Rechtsprechung führt der EuGH lediglich an, dass einer Einheit die Verantwortung für das Verhalten einer anderen rechtlichen Einheit auferlegt werden kann, sofern diese ihr Marktverhalten nicht autonom bestimmt.[23] Der EuGH und ihm folgend das EuG sowie die Kommission leiten eine Verantwortlichkeit der Muttergesellschaft für das Handeln der Tochtergesellschaft somit direkt aus dem funktionalen Unternehmensbegriff des Kartellrechts ab.[24] Der EuGH begründet dieses Ergebnis nicht mit Erwägungen aus Haftungsgesichtspunkten, sondern mit dem Umstand, dass die betroffenen Gesellschaften ein einziges Unternehmen darstellen. Eine Zurechnung findet aus Sicht des EuGH nicht statt, vielmehr stellt sich aus seiner Sicht das rein praktische Erfordernis, dass die Kommission ihre Bußgeldentscheidung an die juristischen Personen richtet, aus denen das Unternehmen besteht.[25]

Soweit im Schrifttum diese Rechtsprechung als eine willkürliche Einzelbetrachtung kritisiert wird bzw. eine dogmatische Differenzierung zwischen der Verhaltenszurechnung bei unterschiedlichen Rechtssubjekten gefordert wird, ist Ausgangspunkt dieser Kritik das Rechtsträgerprinzip.[26] Tatsächlich bedürfte auf der

---

[20] EuGH 1.7.2010, – C-407/08 P, ECLI:EU:C:2010:389 = Slg. 2010, I-6375 Rn. 65, 82 (Knauf-Gips); vgl. hierzu ausführlich Langen/Bunte, Kartellrecht/Hengst, 13. Aufl. 2018, AEUV Art. 101 Rn. 43–46.

[21] EuGH 10.4.2014 – C-247/11 P u. C-253/11 P, ECLI:EU:C:2014:257 Rn. 122 (Areva); EuGH 11.7.2013, – C-440/11 P, ECLI:EU:C:2013:514 = NZKart 2013, 367 Rn 44 (Kommission/Stichting Administratiekantoor Portielje).

[22] EuGH 10.4.2014 – C-231/11 P bis C-233/11, ECLI:EU:C:2014:256 Rn. 53 (Siemens Österreich); EuGH 28.6.2005 – C-189/02 P, C-202/02 P, C-205/02 P bis C-208/02 P und C-213/02 P, ECLI:EU:C:2005:408 = Slg. 2005, I-5425 Rn. 242 (Dansk Roerindustri ua/Kommission).

[23] EuGH 11.7.2013, – C-440/11 P, ECLI:EU:C:2013:514 = NZKart 2013, 367 Rn 42 (Kommission/Stichting Administratiekantoor Portielje); vgl. zur Sicherstellung einer einheitlichen Leitung durch Budgetkontrolle EuGH 8.5.2013 – C-508/11 P, ECLI:EU:C:2013:289 Rn. 64 (Eni).

[24] Vgl. dazu aus Sicht des Rechtsträgerprinzips van Vormizeele WuW 2010, 1008 (1012).

[25] EuGH 29.9.2011 – C-521/09 P, ECLI:EU:C:2013:644 = Slg. 2011, I-8947 Rn. 88 (Elf Aquitaine/Kommission); EuGH 10.4.2014 – C-247/11 P u. C-253/11 P, ECLI:EU:C:2014:247 Rn. 55 (Areva).

[26] So Kling, WRP 2010, 506 (512); Immenga/Mestmäcker, Wettbewerbsrecht/Zimmer, 6. Aufl. 2019, AEUV Art. 101 Abs. 1 Rn. 32; ferner in Langen/Bunte, Kartellrecht/Hengst, 13. Aufl. 2018, AEUV Art. 101 Rn. 36f.; Kersting WuW 2014, 1156 (1159); Monopolkommission, Strafrechtliche Sanktionen bei Kartellverstößen (Sondergutachten 72), 2015, Rn. 66.

Basis des Rechtsträgerprinzips die Begründung einer Haftung der Muttergesellschaft für Handlungen der Tochtergesellschaft einer Rechtfertigung, welche über den Aspekt einer gesellschaftsrechtlichen Beteiligung und über die rein kartellrechtliche Erwägung eines nicht selbständigen Auftretens der Tochtergesellschaft am Markt hinausgeht. Die Erwägung des EuGH, dass die Tochtergesellschaft trotz eigener Rechtspersönlichkeit ihr Marktverhalten nicht autonom bestimmen kann, lässt sich anerkannten Zurechnungsprinzipien, dem Veranlassungsprinzip, der Verschuldenshaftung, oder dem Risikoprinzip nicht zuordnen, zumal auch ein Haftungsgrund über den Effektivitätsgrundsatz hinaus nicht erkennbar ist.[27]

3. *Teilrechtsfähigkeit der wirtschaftlichen Einheit*

Die Methode des EuGH, aus dem kartellrechtlichen Unternehmensbegriff eine Haftung der wirtschaftlichen Einheit für Handlungen seiner Mitglieder zu entwickeln, wirft ua die Frage auf, ob damit dieser Einheit Teilrechtsfähigkeit zukommt.[28] Diese Konsequenz liegt nahe, weil dann, wenn gegenüber der wirtschaftlichen Einheit als Unternehmen das Bußgeld verhängt wird, sie Trägerin kartellrechtlicher Pflichten und einer verfahrensrechtlichen Rechtsstellung sein muss.

Diese Konsequenz wird im Schrifttum überwiegend nicht gezogen. So wird von einer Verbandsverantwortlichkeit sui generis gesprochen, bei der die Bestimmung des Ahndungssubjekts mit der objektiven Zurechnung zusammenfällt, bzw. von einem täterschaftlichen Unternehmensbegriff gesprochen.[29] Eine Verantwortlichkeit unterhalb der Haftung ist jedoch logisch nicht vorstellbar. Zudem schließt die Ableitung der Haftung der wirtschaftlichen Einheit aus dem Unternehmensbegriff eine Zurechnung aus, weil der funktionale Unternehmensbegriff formal ist, denn er knüpft maßgeblich an die unternehmerische Tätigkeit an.

Teilweise wird im Schrifttum schlicht darauf verwiesen, dass die wirtschaftliche Einheit kein Rechtssubjekt sei.[30] Andere gehen von einer Rechtsfähigkeit der wirtschaftlichen Einheit nur dann aus, wenn sich Unternehmen zu einem Konzern in der Form einer Außengesellschaft zusammengeschlossen haben.[31] In diesem Fall wäre jedoch der Konzern als solcher Adressat des Kartellverbots und damit, vertreten durch die Konzernobergesellschaft, auch des Bußgeldbescheids. Unter dieser Voraussetzung könnte – im Gegensatz zur Rechtsprechung des EuGH – auf den

---

[27] Vgl. zu den Zurechnungsprinzipien: Canaris, Die Vertrauenshaftung im deutschen Privatrecht, 1971, S. 467ff.; zum Fehlen eines theoretisch belastbaren Haftungskonzepts Frankfurter Kommentar zum Kartellrecht/Kindhäuser/Meyer, 105. Aktualisierung 2023, AEUV Art. 101 Bußgeldrechtliche Folgen, Rn 31.

[28] Weitere Fragen, zB die Vereinbarkeit mit den Grundrechten, sollen in diesem Beitrag nicht erörtert werden.

[29] Frankfurter Kommentar zum Kartellrecht/Kindhäuser/Meyer, 105. Aktualisierung 2023, AEUV Art. 101 Bußgeldrechtliche Folgen, Rn. 29; Frankfurter Kommentar zum Kartellrecht/Roth/Ackermann, 101. Aktualisierung 2022, AEUV Grundfragen des Art. 101 Rn. 116.

[30] Kersting WuW 2014, 1156 (1158); anders in Immenga/Mestmäcker, Wettbewerbsrecht/Biermann, 6. Aufl. 2019, VO 1/2003 Vor Art. 23 Rn. 87, der von einer bußgeldrechtlichen Rechtspersönlichkeit ausgeht.

[31] Vgl. Immenga/Mestmäcker, Wettbewerbsrecht/Zimmer, 6. Aufl. 2019, AEUV Art. 101 Abs. 1 Rn. 31.

Nachweis verzichtet werden, dass die Konzernobergesellschaft einen bestimmenden Einfluss auf die Geschäftspolitik der handelnden Gesellschaft genommen hat.[32]

Den Weg einer konzernrechtlichen Außenhaftung – in der Form einer Handlungshaftung der Konzernobergesellschaft – geht der EuGH jedoch ausdrücklich nicht. Selbst dann, wenn etwa eine Weisung der Muttergesellschaft an die Tochtergesellschaft vorliegt, das kartellrechtliche Verhalten vorzunehmen, rechtfertigt der EuGH die Haftung der Muttergesellschaft mit der wirtschaftlichen Einheit des gebildeten Konzerns. Zur Begründung führt der Gerichtshof an, die sich aus der Verschiedenheit der Rechtspersönlichkeit ergebende formelle Trennung zwischen Muttergesellschaft und Tochtergesellschaft hindere nicht, dass ihr Verhalten auf dem Markt für die Anwendung der Wettbewerbsregeln als Einheit angesehen wird.[33] Daraus ist zu schließen, dass der Gerichtshof das Rechtsträgerprinzip nicht beachtet, dies aus Gründen einer effektiven Rechtsdurchsetzung.[34] Dies geht, nimmt man den EuGH wörtlich, so weit, dass nicht nur strukturelle Verflechtungen zwischen den Unternehmen zu einer wirtschaftlichen Einheit führen, sondern auch ein Verhalten.[35] Zusätzlich arbeitet die EuGH Rechtsprechung mit der widerlegbaren Vermutung, dass dann, wenn die Muttergesellschaft das gesamte oder nahezu das gesamte Kapital ihrer Tochtergesellschaft unmittelbar oder mittelbar hält, sie tatsächlich einen bestimmenden Einfluss auf die Tochtergesellschaft ausübt. Die Muttergesellschaft kann diese Vermutung widerlegen, indem sie alle Angaben in Bezug auf die organisatorischen, wirtschaftlichen und rechtlichen Verbindungen zwischen ihr und ihrer Tochtergesellschaft vorlegt, die dem Nachweis dienen können, dass Mutter- und Tochtergesellschaft keine wirtschaftliche Einheit bilden.[36]

Diese Äußerungen des EuGH sind in sich inkonsistent, weil sie strukturelle Verflechtungen zwischen Mutter- und Tochtergesellschaft mit Verhaltenselementen – tatsächliche Ausübung der Leitungsmacht und Verhalten auf dem Markt – verknüpfen, ohne, dass eine zugrundeliegende Wertung zu Tage tritt. Hinzu tritt, dass Leitungsmacht bzw. ein wettbewerblich erheblicher Einfluss auch bei Kapitalanteilen unter 100% bzw. annähernd 100% ausgeübt werden kann. Soweit der EuGH es als eine Prämisse bezeichnet, dass einer rechtlichen Einheit die Verantwortung für das

---

[32] Vgl. hierzu EuGH 10.9.2009, – C-97/08 P, ECLI:EU:C:2009:536 = Slg. 2010, I-8237 Rn. 26 (Akzo Nobel).

[33] Vgl. EuGH 14.7.1972 – C-48/69, ECLI:EU:C:1972:70 Rn. 140 (ICI/Kommission); EuG 20.3.2002 – T-9/99, ECLI:EU:T:2002:70 = Slg. 2002, II-1497, Rn. 66 (HFB Holding/Kommission).

[34] Vgl. zum *effet utile* EuGH 12.2.1992 – C-48/90, ECLI:EU:C:1992:63 = Slg. 1992, I 565, 635 Rn. 28 (Eilkurierdienstleistungen).

[35] Vgl. EuGH 26.9.2013 – C-179/12 P, ECLI:EU:C:2013:605 Rn. 23, 54 (Dow Chemical Company/Kommission); EuGH 15.6.2012 – C-494/11 P, ECLI:EU:C:2012:356 Rn. 42 (Otis Luxemburg).

[36] EuGH 16.6.2016 – C-155/14 P, ECLI:EU:C:2016:446 NZKart 2016, 325 Rn. 32–40 (Evonik Degussa ua/Kommission); EuGH 5.3.2015 – C-93/13 P und C-123/13 P, ECLI:EU:C:2015:150 Rn. 40 (Kommission/Versalis ua); EuGH 20.1.2011 – C-90/09 P, ECLI:EU:C:2011:21 Rn. 51 (General Química ua/Kommission); vgl. auch Kling WRP 2010, 506 (510), der von einer „Konzernzustandshaftung" ausgeht; zu den Einzelheiten vgl. Frankfurter Kommentar zum Kartellrecht/Roth/Ackermann, 101. Aktualisierung 2022, AEUV Grundfragen des Art. 101 Rn. 120b-120h.

Verhalten einer anderen rechtlichen Einheit auferlegt werden kann, sofern diese ihr Marktverhalten nicht autonom bestimmt, argumentiert der Gerichtshof zudem auf der Grundlage des Rechtsträgerprinzips und widerspricht damit dem eigenen Ausgangspunkt.[37]

Nach EuGH ist es nicht die handelnde rechtliche Einheit, welcher die Verantwortlichkeit für das wettbewerbswidrige Handeln auferlegt wird, sondern die wirtschaftliche. Jedoch kann nur dann, wenn die wirtschaftliche Einheit teilrechtsfähig ist, darauf verzichtet werden, innerhalb dieser Einheit die Zurechnung des Handelns eines Rechtssubjekts an ein anderes Rechtssubjekt zu rechtfertigen. Zudem betrifft die Haftung der wirtschaftlichen Einheit nur das Außenverhältnis zur Kommission, die Bestimmung der Anteile der Gesamtschuldner im Innenverhältnis überantwortet der EuGH dem nationalen Recht und den nationalen Gerichten.[38] Auch spricht für die Teilrechtsfähigkeit die Rechtsprechung, nach welcher das Bußgeld gegenüber Teilen der Einheit verhängt werden kann, jedoch nicht muss. Unerheblich ist dabei, ob alle rechtlichen Einheiten, welche das Unternehmen bilden, selbst wirtschaftlich aktiv sind und für sich genommen den Unternehmensbegriff erfüllen.[39] Eine Verhängung des Bußgeldes gegen Teile der wirtschaftlichen Einheit kann nur gerechtfertigt werden kann, wenn die Einheit als teilrechtsfähig angesehen wird und grundsätzlich aus dieser Teilrechtsfähigkeit eine Haftung aller Teile für das Bußgeld folgt.

Dieser Annahme scheint zu widersprechen, dass nach Auffassung des EuGH die wirtschaftliche Einheit im Hinblick auf den Gegenstand der fraglichen Vereinbarung besteht. Weitere Voraussetzung soll allerdings sein, dass zwischen den juristischen oder natürlichen Personen Interessengleichheit besteht und sie von derselben – ebenfalls an der Vereinbarung beteiligten – Person kontrolliert werden, so dass ein Wettbewerb unter diesen Personen unmöglich ist.[40] Bezieht sich die wirtschaftliche Einheit auf den Gegenstand der Absprachen, könnte gerade nicht jede einem Konzern angehörige Gesellschaft als Teil der wirtschaftlichen Einheit in Anspruch genommen werden, sondern nur solche Gesellschaften, die von dem Gegenstand der Kartellabsprachen profitieren oder an ihm partizipieren. In seiner jüngeren Rechtsprechung hält es der EuGH – wohl zur Begrenzung privatrechtlicher Ansprüche gegenüber „konglomeraten" Unternehmensgruppen – für möglich, dass eine Muttergesellschaft Teil mehrerer wirtschaftlicher Einheiten sein kann.[41] Diese Aufteilung der wirtschaftlichen Einheit in wirtschaftliche Teileinheiten widerspricht naturgemäß dem Ausganspunkt, nach welchem die wirtschaftliche Einheit nach ihrem Auftreten im Markt zu bestimmen ist. Dass „konglomerate"

---

[37] So EuGH 11.7.2013 – C-440/11 P, ECLI:EU:C:2013:540 Rn. 42 (Kommission/Stichting Adminstratiekantoor Portielje).

[38] EuGH 10.4.2014 – Rs. C-231/11-C 233/11 P, ECLI:EU:C:2014/256 Rn. 39–62 (Kommission/Siemens AG Österreich ua).

[39] EuGH 11.7.2013 – C-440/11 P, ECLI:EU:C:2013/514 Rn. 36–43 (Kommission/Stichting Administratiekantoor Portielje).

[40] EuGH 12.7.1985 – Rs. 170/83, ECLI:EU:C:1984:271 = Slg. 1984, 2000 (Hydrotherm Gerätebau); EuGH 14.7.1972 – Rs. 48/69, ECLI:EU:C:1972:70 Rn. 136 (ICI/Kommission).

[41] So bei konglomeraten Unternehmensgruppen EuGH 6.10.2021 – C-882/19, ECLI:EU:C:1021:800 (Sumal).

Konzerne wirtschaftlich nach außen hin nicht als Einheit auftreten, dürfte generell nicht zutreffen. Die Aufspaltung der wirtschaftlichen Einheit entlang von Produktmärkten führt zudem zu schwierigen Abgrenzungsfragen. Dies widerspricht erneut dem Ausgangspunkt der Rechtsprechung, dem *effet utile*.

Insgesamt wird damit die wirtschaftliche Einheit als Adressat kartellrechtlicher Verpflichtungen aus dem Kartellverbot, dh als primär haftendes Rechtssubjekt, von der europäischen Rechtsprechung angesehen. Bei fehlender Autonomie im Marktverhalten bilden rechtliche Einheiten im Hinblick auf den Gegenstand der Vereinbarung eine wirtschaftliche Einheit.[42] Eine Zurechnung individueller Tatanteile findet nur im Innenverhältnis der rechtlichen Einheit statt. Die Außenhaftung der wirtschaftlichen Einheit resultiert unmittelbar aus dem kartellrechtlichen Unternehmensbegriff des europäischen Rechts. Die wirtschaftliche Einheit wird damit von den europäischen Gerichten als teilrechtsfähig behandelt.[43]

III. Rechtsträgerprinzip und wirtschaftliche Unternehmenskontinuität

1. Das Rechtsträgerprinzip im deutschen Recht

Eine Schwachstelle des Rechtsträgerprinzips hat sich im deutschen Recht unter der umgangssprachlichen Bezeichnung „Wurstlücke“ aufgetan.[44] Gemäß §§ 9, 30 OWiG kommt eine Verhängung von Bußgeldern gegen juristische Personen in Betracht, wenn ein für diese handelnder Leitungsverantwortlicher oder sonstiger Mitarbeiter zurechenbar eine Ordnungswidrigkeit begangen hat. Aufgrund des Rechtsträgerprinzips, welches §§ 9, 30 OWiG zugrunde liegt, konnten Unternehmen, die sich in einem Bußgeldverfahren befanden, der Geldbuße durch Umstrukturierungen entgehen, indem sie Produktionsmittel auf andere Rechtsträger übertrugen und den betroffenen Rechtsträger liquidierten. Nach einer ständigen Rechtsprechung des BGH konnten Geldbußen im Fall von Umstrukturierungen, zB dem Verkauf des Vermögens der betroffenen Gesellschaft und deren anschließender Löschung, nur dann gegen ein Unternehmen in Rechtsnachfolge verhängt werden, wenn das haftende Vermögen weiterhin von dem Vermögen der verantwortlichen natürlichen Person getrennt war, in gleicher oder ähnlicher Weise wie bisher eingesetzt wurde und in der neuen juristischen Person einen wesentlichen

---

42 Zustimmend Langen/Bunte, Kartellrecht/Hengst, 13. Aufl. 2018, AEUV Art. 101 Rn. 43 mwN; Kling WRP 2010, 506 (514, 518).

43 Vgl. dazu EuGH 10.4.2014 – C -231/11 P bis C-233/11, ECLI:EU:C:2014:256 Rn. 55 (Siemens Österreich), wonach es einem rein praktischen Erfordernis entspringt, dass die Kommission ihre Bußgeldentscheidung zwingend an juristische Personen richtet; Brettel/Thomas WuW 2016, 336 (337).

44 Vgl. dazu BKartA, Pressemitteilung v. 19.10.2016, https://www.bundeskartellamt.de/SharedDocs/Meldung/DE/Pressemitteilungen/2016/19_10_2016_ClemensToennies_Gruppe_Wurst.html (abgerufen am 9.8.2024); die Bezeichnung bezieht sich auf die Anwendung der aus dem Rechtsträgerprinzip folgenden Grundsätze in einem Bußgeldverfahren gegen einen Fleischbetrieb; vgl. auch Monopolkommission, Strafrechtliche Sanktionen bei Kartellverstößen (Sondergutachten 72), 2015, S. 3.

Teil des gesamten Vermögens ausmachte. Eine extensive Auslegung der Bestimmung wurde von der Rechtsprechung abgelehnt.[45]

Bis zur 8. GWB Novelle enthielt das Gesetz keine ausdrücklichen Regelungen über eine Rechtsnachfolge in die Bußgeldhaftung. Durch die 8.GWB-Novelle wurde § 30 Abs. 2a OWiG eingeführt, wonach im Fall einer Gesamtrechtsnachfolge oder partiellen Gesamtrechtsnachfolge das Bußgeld gegen den oder die Rechtsnachfolger festgesetzt werden konnte. Erfasst wurde von dieser Regelung jedoch weder die Übertragung des Vermögens der Gesellschaft, noch eine Abspaltung oder Ausgliederung nach UmwG.[46] Auch kam eine Ersatzhaftung weiterer Konzerngesellschaften nicht in Betracht.[47] Es wurde daher als Regelungsdefizit angesehen, dass Kartellverstöße nicht allen Teilen eines Unternehmens zugerechnet werden konnten.[48]

2. *Der Grundsatz der wirtschaftlichen Kontinuität*

Mit entsprechenden dogmatischen Problemen haben die europäischen Gerichte nicht zu kämpfen. Der europäische Gerichtshof leitet aus dem Prinzip des *effet utile* den Grundsatz der wirtschaftlichen Kontinuität ab. Rechtliche oder organisatorische Änderungen einer Einrichtung, die gegen Wettbewerbsregeln verstoßen hat, sollen nicht zwingend dazu führen, dass eine von der Haftung für die Handlungen des Vorgängers befreite Einheit entsteht. Werden wirtschaftliche Tätigkeiten auf eine andere Einheit übertragen, kann der Einheit, auf welche die Tätigkeit übertragen wurde, eine Sanktion auferlegt werden, wenn zwischen dem handelnden und dem zur Haftung herangezogenen Rechtsträger eine wirtschaftliche Identität nachweisbar ist.[49]

Die Rechtsprechung zur wirtschaftlichen Kontinuität hatte ihre Grundlage in einem Sachverhalt, dem eine formwechselnde Umwandlung nach dem deutschen UmwG zugrunde lag, so dass eine Rechtsnachfolge unstreitig war. Dennoch hat der Gerichtshof bereits in dieser Entscheidung ein eigenes Rechtsprinzip entwickelt, indem er auf die Fortführung der wirtschaftlichen Tätigkeit des Unternehmens abstellt und von einer Haftung des neuen Unternehmens für die rechtswidrigen Handlungen des alten Unternehmens bei wirtschaftlicher Identität der beiden Unternehmen spricht.[50] Damit löst sich der Gerichtshof von der Vorstellung des

---

[45] BGH 11.3.1986 – KRB 8/85, WuW/E BGH 2265, 2266. – Rechtsnachfolge; BGH 23.11.2004 – KRB 23/04, NJW 2005, 1381 (1382) (Handelsregisterauszug); BGH 10.8.2011 – KRB 55/10, WuW/E DE-R 3455, 3457. – Versicherungsfusion; ablehnend gegenüber der Rechtsprechung Heinichen WRP 2012, 159 (163f.); Krohs/Timmerbeil BB 2012, 2447.

[46] Vgl. Beschlussempfehlung des Ausschusses für Wirtschaft und Technologie, BT-Drs. 17/11053, S. 22f.; Bischke/Brack NZG 2012, 1140 (1141f.).

[47] BGH 10.8.2011 – KBR 2/10 Rn. 16, 18–20 (Transportbeton Elskes).

[48] Vgl Monopolkommission, Strafrechtliche Sanktionen bei Kartellverstößen (Sondergutachten 72), 2015, S. 3f. mwN.

[49] Vgl. EuGH 11.12.2007 – C-280/06, ECLI:EU:C:2007:775 = Slg.2007, I-10893 Rn. 83 (Autoritá Garante della Concurrenza e del Mercato/ETI ua); EuGH 24.9.2009 – C-125/07 P, ECLI:EU:C:2009:576 = Slg. 2009, I-1843 Rn. 81–84 (Erste Group Bank).

[50] EuGH 28.03.1984 – 29/83 und 30/83, ECLI:EU:C:1984:130 = Slg. 1984, 1679 Rn. 9 (Compagnie royale asturienne des mines und Rheinzink/Kommission); EuGH 7.1.2004 – C-204/00 P, ECLI:EU:C:2004:6 Rn. 59 (Aalborg Portland ua/Kommission).

deutschen Umwandlungsrecht, wonach bei einer formwechselnden Umwandlung der Rechtsträger erhalten bleibt und lediglich ein neues „Kleid" erhält, so dass es auf eine Fortführung der wirtschaftlichen Tätigkeit nicht angekommen wäre. Die Kommissionspraxis und Teile der Literatur befürworten denn auch, dass Lösungen für organisatorische Änderungen im Rahmen des Unionsrechts nicht durch Anwendung nationalen Gesellschaftsrechts zu entwickeln seien.[51]

Besteht die handelnde Tochtergesellschaft rechtlich fort, firmiert sie um oder wechselt ihre Form, bedarf es keines Rückgriffs auf die wirtschaftliche Kontinuität, da keine Auswirkungen auf die eigentliche Geschäftstätigkeit vorliegen.[52] Überträgt sie ihre Aktivitäten auf eine andere Gesellschaft und besteht sie fort, bleibt sie Bußgeldadressat.[53] Besteht die Tochtergesellschaft nicht fort, kommt der Grundsatz der wirtschaftlichen Kontinuität zur Anwendung. Eine Mithaftung derjenigen Einheit kommt in Betracht, welche als Nachfolger die wirtschaftliche Tätigkeit der bisherigen Einheit fortführt. Die rechtliche oder organisatorische Änderung der Einrichtung, die gegen Wettbewerbsregeln verstoßen hat, hat nicht zwingend zur Folge, dass ein von der Haftung für Handlungen des Vorgängers befreites Unternehmen entsteht, sofern die beiden Einheiten wirtschaftlich gesehen identisch sind.[54] Auf einen Einsatz des Vermögens der ursprünglich haftenden juristischen Person in gleicher oder ähnlicher Weise wie bisher, wie es der BGH zu § 30 OWiG verlangt, kommt es nicht an.[55]

Eine Haftung des erwerbenden Rechtsträgers soll jedoch auch dann in Betracht kommen, wenn die juristische Person, deren Leitungsorgan die Ordnungswidrigkeit begangen hat, fortbesteht und zwischen dem übertragenden und dem übernehmenden Unternehmen strukturelle Beziehungen bestehen, dh vor allem in Konzernsachverhalten. Dann sei von einer wirtschaftlichen Identität beider Rechtsträger auszugehen.[56] Die wirtschaftliche Nachfolge erfasst auch eine wiederholte oder mittelbare Nachfolge. Ist der Vorgänger noch existent, tritt der Nachfolger als weiterer Beteiligter hinzu.[57] Auch der Begriff der wirtschaftlichen Kontinuität ist durch eine kartellrechtliche Betrachtungsweise geprägt und wird direkt dem kartellrechtlichen Unternehmensbegriff entnommen.[58] Teilweise vermischen sich die

[51] Vgl. EuGH 14.3.2019 – C-724/17, ECLI:EU:C:2019:204 Rn. 47–51 (Skanska); Frankfurter Kommentar zum Kartellrecht/Roth/Ackermann, 101. Aktualisierung 2022, AEUV Art 101 Rn. 111a mwN.

[52] EuGH 16.11.2000 – C- 297/98 P, ECLI:EU:C:2000:633 = Slg. 2000,I-10101 Rn 29 (SCA Holding).

[53] EuGH 16.11.2000 – C- 279/98, ECLI:EU:C:2000:626 = Slg. 1999, I-9693 Rn. 79 (Cascades).

[54] EuGH 16.12.1975, – 40/73, ECLI:EU:C:1975:174 = Slg. 1975, 1663 Rn. 84, 87 (Suiker Unie); EuGH 28.3.1984, – 29/83, ECLI:EU:C:1984:130 = Slg. 1984, 1679 Rn. 9 (CERAM und Rheinzink); EuGH 11.12.2007 – C-280/06, ECLI:EU:C:2007:775 Rn. 42–44 (Autoritá Garante della Concorrenza e del Mercato/ETI ua).

[55] Langen/Bunte, Kartellrecht/Hengst, 13. Aufl. 2018, AEUV Art. 101 Rn. 72.

[56] EuGH 7.1.2004 – C-204/00 P, ECLI:EU:C:2004:6 = Slg. 2004, I-123 Rn. 356–359 (Aalborg Portland); EuGH 18.12.2014 – C-434/13 P, ECLI:EU:C:2014:2456 Rn. 48–53 (Parker Hannifin); Langen/Bunte, Kartellrecht/Hengst, 13. Aufl. 2018, AEUV Art. 101 Rn. 71, 74.

[57] EuGH 18.12.2014, – C-434/13 P, ECLI:EU:C:2014:2456 Rn. 54 (Parker Hannifin).

[58] Vgl zusammenfassend EuGH 18.12.2014, – C-434/13 P, ECLI:EU:C:2014:2456 Rn. 40f. (Parker Hannifin); Immenga/Mestmäcker, Wettbewerbsrecht/Zimmer, 6. Aufl. 2019, AEUV

Aspekte der wirtschaftlichen Kontinuität und der wirtschaftlichen Einheit bei Konzernsachverhalten in der Argumentation des EuGH.[59]

Die Voraussetzung einer wirtschaftlichen Identität liegt vor, wenn zwischen den beiden Einheiten strukturelle Beziehungen bestehen, dh sie der Kontrolle derselben Person unterstehen und sie aufgrund der bestehenden engen Bindungen im Wesentlichen dieselben geschäftlichen Leitlinien angewendet haben. Von wirtschaftlicher Kontinuität ist auszugehen, wenn die Übertragung von Tätigkeiten während des Zeitraums der Zuwiderhandlungen oder nach der Abstellung der Zuwiderhandlungen erfolgt, soweit die strukturellen Verbindungen zwischen den Einrichtungen zum Zeitpunkt der Zuwiderhandlung bestanden.

Überträgt die zuwiderhandelnde Einheit ihre Aktivitäten und hört danach auf zu existieren, kann der aufnehmenden Einheit die Haftung für die Zuwiderhandlung auferlegt werden.[60] Die Muttergesellschaft haftet ebenfalls weiter für den Verstoß, soweit sie zur Zeit der Zuwiderhandlung mit der Tochtergesellschaft eine wirtschaftliche Einheit bildete.[61] Dies, dh die Haftung der aufnehmenden Einheit, soll aus Gründen der Abschreckung auch dann gelten wenn diese Einheit die maßgebenden wirtschaftlichen Aktivitäten nicht mehr entfaltet, weil eine Sanktion gegen ein Unternehmen ohne wirtschaftliche Aktivitäten unter dem Gesichtspunkt der Abschreckung kaum wirksam wäre.[62]

Rechtsfolge dieser Grundsätze ist nach dem vom EuGH betonten Prinzip der persönlichen Verantwortung, dass das übertragende Unternehmen für diejenigen Zuwiderhandlungen zeitanteilig haftet, welche vor der Übertragung vorgenommen wurden.[63] Gleichzeitig entsteht mit der Übertragung des relevanten Tätigkeitsbereichs ein neues, von der Haftung für wettbewerbswidrige Handlungen seines Vorgängers nicht befreites Unternehmen, soweit die beiden Einheiten wirtschaftlich gesehen identisch sind. Soweit das Verhalten, für welches die ursprüngliche Muttergesellschaft und die aufnehmende Gesellschaft haften, dieselben Zuwiderhandlungen betrifft, wird von einer gesamtschuldnerischen Haftung auszugehen sein.[64] Den Kreis der in diesen Vorgang einzubeziehenden Unternehmen leitet der EuGH direkt aus dem funktionalen Unternehmensbegriff unter Rückgriff auf den *effet utile* ab.

Damit lockert der EuGH auch in Übertragungsfällen das Rechtsträgerprinzip insofern, als er davon ausgeht, dass durch eine Übertragung „kartellbefangener" Ak-

---

Art. 101 Abs. 1 Rn. 43; Langen/Bunte, Kartellrecht/Hengst, 13. Aufl. 2018, AEUV Art. 101 Rn. 71.

[59] Vgl. dazu EuGH 11.12.2007 – C-280/06, ECLI:EU:C:2007:775 = Slg. 2007 I-10893 Rn 48 (ETI).

[60] So EuGH 8.7.1999 – C-49/92 P, ECLI:EU:C:1999:356 Rn. 146 (Komm/Anic ua).

[61] EuGH 16.11.2000 – C-286/98 P, ECLI:EU:C:2000:630 = Slg 2000 I-9925 Rn. 37–39 (Stora Kopparbergs Bergslags).

[62] EuGH 11.12.2007 – C-280/06, ECLI:EU:C:2007:775 Rn. 41 (Autoritá Garante/Eti Spa ua)

[63] EuGH 8.7.1999 – C-49/92 P, ECLI:EU:C:1999:356 Rn. 145 (Komm/Anic ua); Immenga/Mestmäcker, Wettbewerbsrecht/Zimmer, 6. Aufl. 2019, AEUV Art. 101 Abs. 1 Rn. 44; zur persönlichen Verantwortlichkeit Brömmelmeyer WuW 2017, 174.

[64] Immenga/Mestmäcker Wettbewerbsrecht/Zimmer, 6. Aufl. 2019, AEUV Art 101 Abs. 1 Rn. 44.

tivitäten eine Haftung des neuen Rechtsträgers entstehen kann. Eine konstruktive Grundlage des Prinzips der wirtschaftlichen Kontinuität lässt sich nur in dem weit ausgelegten funktionalen Unternehmensbegriff finden, indem die europäischen Gerichte den übertragenen wirtschaftlichen Aktivitäten eine Teilrechtsfähigkeit zubilligen, so dass die übertragenen Aktivitäten im Wege eines Verschmelzungsaktes zu einer Haftungsbegründung des aufnehmenden Rechtsträgers führen. Das sich aus den übertragenen Aktivitäten und dem verbleibenden Mutterunternehmen zusammensetzende, nicht mehr bestehende Unternehmen wird nach wirtschaftlicher Betrachtungsweise als fortbestehend angesehen, ohne dass das übernommene Vermögen innerhalb des übernehmenden Rechtsträgers das Gesamtvermögen prägen müsste.[65]

Ist das Prinzip der wirtschaftlichen Kontinuität auf den funktionalen Unternehmensbegriff zurückzuführen, kann dieser jedoch die fortbestehende Haftung des übertragenden Rechtsträgers nicht rechtfertigen, weil auch unter Zugrundelegung der Auffassung des EuGH durch die Trennung der Aktivitäten von der ursprünglichen Einheit ein teilrechtsfähiges neues Unternehmen oder ein neuer Unternehmensteil entstehen würde.

3. Übernahme der wirtschaftlichen Einheit in das deutsche Kartellrecht

Die durch die 8. GWB Novelle eingeführte Regelung des § 30 Abs. 2a OWiG wurde aus dem Gesichtspunkt der Kartellrechtsdurchsetzung als lückenhaft angesehen.[66] Die Neuregelung des Komplexes durch die 9. GWB-Novelle von 2017 hat die europarechtlichen Grundsätze der Haftung des Unternehmens als wirtschaftliche Einheit und die Rechtsfigur der wirtschaftlichen Unternehmenskontinuität in § 81 Abs. 3a–3e, 4a GWB aF (heute § 81a, § 81d Abs. 2 GWB) übernommen. § 81 Abs. 3a GWB aF (heute § 81a Abs. 1 GWB) übernimmt den Begriff der wirtschaftlichen Einheit, indem er die bußgeldrechtliche Verantwortlichkeit auf weitere juristische Personen oder Personenvereinigungen ausdehnt, die das Unternehmen zum Zeitpunkt der Begehung gebildet haben und auf die diejenige Person oder Personenvereinigung unmittelbar oder mittelbar einen bestimmenden Einfluss ausgeübt haben, deren Leitungsperson die Ordnungswidrigkeit begangen hat. § 81 Abs. 3c GWB aF (heute § 81a Abs. 3 GWB) übernimmt die Rechtsfigur der wirtschaftlichen Kontinuität im Wortlaut. Danach kann die Geldbuße auch gegen juristische Personen oder Personenvereinigungen festgesetzt werden, die das Unternehmen in wirtschaftlicher Kontinuität fortführen.

Der deutsche Gesetzgeber hielt die Übernahme der wirtschaftlichen Kontinuität zur Vermeidung von Umgehungsmöglichkeiten für erforderlich.[67] Liegt Gesamtrechtsnachfolge vor, trifft das Bußgeld den Rechtsnachfolger nur dann, wenn die

---

[65] Vgl. dazu BT-Drs. 18/10207, 92.

[66] Vgl. Stellungnahme des Bundeskartellamtes zum Regierungsentwurf zur 8 GWB-Novelle, Bonn 22.6.2012, S. 13–15; Monopolkommission, Strafrechtliche Sanktionen bei Kartellverstößen (Sondergutachten 72), 2015, Tz. 16.

[67] BT-Drs. 18/10207, 88.

Voraussetzungen der wirtschaftlichen Identität vorliegen.[68] Der Gesetzgeber rechtfertigt die Übernahme der wirtschaftlichen Unternehmenskontinuität damit, dass die Wirtschaftsgüter der juristischen Person oder Personenvereinigung, deren Leitungspersonal die Ordnungswidrigkeit begangen hat, übernommen werden und das verantwortliche Unternehmen – in anderer Zusammensetzung – weiterbetrieben wird. Getroffen werden soll das zu bestimmten wirtschaftlichen Zwecken eingesetzte Vermögen der Wirtschaftsteilnehmer, die von der Ordnungswidrigkeit profitieren.[69]

Die Übernahme der Rechtsfigur der wirtschaftlichen Einheit des EuGH und die über den einzelnen Rechtsträger hinausgehende Betrachtungsweise begründet der Gesetzgeber damit, dass die effektive Rechtsdurchsetzung gegenüber Unternehmen bei der Rechtsnachfolge und bei Konzernstrukturen durch Defizite des nationalen Regelungsrahmens erheblich beeinträchtigt werde. Die Abkehr vom Rechtsträgerprinzip wird damit begründet, dass im Kartellrecht das Unternehmen in seiner Gesamtheit Normadressat sei. Das Wirtschaftssubjekt, das auf den Wettbewerbsprozess Einfluss nimmt, sei bei Konzernen die unternehmerische Einheit.[70] Zudem werde bei der Bußgeldzumessung auch auf die Umsätze des Gesamtunternehmens abgestellt.[71] Es werde so ein notwendiger Gleichlauf von Verantwortung für rechtswidriges Verhalten und der Kontrolle und Lenkungskapazität hergestellt.[72].

Der Gesetzgeber war sich wohl bewusst, dass die materielle Verantwortlichkeit vom einzelnen Rechtsträger gelöst und auf das Unternehmen im Sinne einer wirtschaftlichen Einheit bezogen wird. Ziel der Verbandsgeldbuße sei es, das Vermögen desjenigen zu treffen, dem die finanziellen Vorteile einer in seinem Interesse vorgenommenen Betätigung zufließen. Eine hinsichtlich ihres Wettbewerbsverhaltens steuerungsfähige Einheit stelle ein der Schuldzurechnung fähiges Subjekt dar.[73]

4. *Konsequenzen der Übernahme*

Soweit die materielle Verantwortlichkeit vom einzelnen Rechtsträger gelöst wird, ist sie notwendigerweise einem anderen Rechtsträger zuzuordnen, entweder der wirtschaftlichen Einheit oder dem übernehmenden Rechtsträger. Die wirtschaftliche Einheit wird damit teilrechtsfähig als Trägerin kartellrechtlich begründeter Pflichten und Verfahrensrechten. Jedoch wird nicht die wirtschaftliche Einheit in ihrer Gesamtheit, dh alle Mitglieder der wirtschaftlichen Einheit, sondern lediglich die Mutter- und die handelnde Tochtergesellschaft mit einem Bußgeld belegt.

---

[68] OLG Düsseldorf 28.11.2012 – V-4 Kart 3/12 (OWi), NZKart 2013, 254; BGH 11.3.1986 – KRB 8/85, WuW/E BGH 2265, 2266.

[69] BT-Drs. 18/10207, 88; vgl. zu den angeblichen Lücken des deutschen Rechts Stellungnahme des Bundeskartellamts zum Diskussionsentwurf des Bundesministeriums der Justiz zur Regelung der Rechtsnachfolge in die Bußgeldhaftung (25.5.2012), S. 2f., abzurufen unter: www.bundeskartellamt.de/DE/UberUns/Publikationen/Stellungnahmen/stellungnahmen_mode.html.

[70] Zustimmend Langen/Bunte, Kartellrecht/Hengst, 13. Aufl. 2018, AEUV Art. 101 Rn. 40.

[71] BT-Drs. 18/10207, 4f.; vgl. auch Monopolkommission, Strafrechtliche Sanktionen bei Kartellverstößen (Sondergutachten 72), 2015, Tz. 27ff.

[72] Vgl. auch Timmerbeil/Blome BB 2017, 1544 (1549).

[73] BT-Drs. 18/10207, 87.

Zudem handelt es sich um eine scheinbare Rechtssubjektivität, da vollstreckungsrechtlich endgültig die Einstandspflicht einem rechtlich anerkannten Rechtsträger im Sinne des jeweiligen nationalen Gesellschaftsrechts zugeordnet werden muss. Die Rechtssubjektivität der wirtschaftlichen Einheit bildet so eine Art Durchgangsstadium. Die Regelung bleibt damit auf halbem Wege zwischen Rechtsträgerprinzip und Unternehmenshaftung stehen.[74]

Die tieferliegende Problematik des zweistufigen Vorgehens der europäischen Gerichte liegt darin, dass dann, wenn der wirtschaftlichen Einheit Rechtsubjektivität in Bezug auf einen Kartellrechtsverstoß zuerkannt wird, eine juristisch plausible Rechtfertigung dafür erfolgen muss, dass die Rechtsfolgen des Handelns dieser Einheit ein anderes Rechtssubjekt tragen muss. Darüber hinaus stellen sich Probleme bei der Bußgeldzumessung. Diesbezüglich geht der EuGH von dem Grundsatz der individuellen Zumessung aus. Ist die wirtschaftliche Einheit primärer Adressat der Geldbuße, müsste sich die konkrete Zumessung der Geldbuße nach den Verhältnissen der wirtschaftlichen Einheit richten. Dies ist jedoch nicht der Fall, vielmehr greift der EuGH insoweit auf die zu der wirtschaftlichen Einheit gehörenden Gesellschaften zurück, so dass die Höhe der Geldbuße für diese jeweils individuell festgelegt werden soll, dies unter Berücksichtigung der individuellen Schwere und Dauer der Zuwiderhandlung.[75]

Tatsächlich geht der EuGH davon aus, dass die wirtschaftliche Einheit – als solche – gegen Wettbewerbsregeln verstoßen kann und sie dann für diesen Verstoß nach dem Grundsatz der der persönlichen Verantwortlichkeit einzustehen hat.[76] Geht man vom Rechtsträgerprinzip aus, spricht dies für eine Teilrechtsfähigkeit, negiert man dieses, kann auch von einer nicht näher qualifizierten Adressatenstellung auszugehen sein.[77] Der Begriff der Sanktionsadressaten, der sich bei den Befürwortern der Linie des EuGH eingebürgert hat, verschleiert jedoch die Zurechnungsproblematik. Der Sanktionsadressat – als notwendig rechtsfähige natürliche oder juristische Person – ist Haftungsschuldner des Bußgeldes und nach neuerer Rechtsprechung auch Haftungsschuldner für privatrechtliche Schadensersatzansprüche. Angesichts der Höhe der von der Kommission verhängten Bußgelder und der potentiellen Höhe privater Schadensersatzforderungen, unterliegt der Sanktionsadressat damit einem erheblichen realen Insolvenzrisiko.[78] Warum eine von dem Normadressaten verschiedene Entität diesem Risiko unterworfen ist, bleibt unerklärlich.

---

[74] BT-Drs. 18/10207, 91, 93; dazu Brettel/Thomas WuW 2016, 336 (338).

[75] EuGH 10.4.2014 – C-247/11 P und C-253/11 P, ECLI:C:EU:2014:257 Rn. 127, 133 (Arreva).

[76] EuGH 10.4.2014, – C-231/11 P bis C-233/11 P, WuW/E EU-R 2970–2983 Rn. 44 (Kommission/Siemens); EuGH 11.7.2013, – C-440/11 P, ECLI:EU:C:2013:514 Rn. 37 (Kommission/Stichting Aministratiekantoor Portielje).

[77] Zur Adressatenstellung Frankfurter Kommentar zum Kartellrecht/Roth/Ackermann, 101. Aktualisierung 2022, AEUV Grundfragen des Art. 101 Abs. 1 Rn. 106.

[78] Vgl. zur Terminologie Frankfurter Kommentar zum Kartellrecht/Roth/Ackermann, 101. Aktualisierung 2022, AEUV Grundfragen des Art. 101 Abs. 1 Rn. 123; EuGH 6.10.2021 – C-882/19, ECLI:EU:C:1021:800 Rn. 44 (Sumal); diese Entscheidung enthält wiederum Anklänge an das Rechtsträgerprinzip, als der EuGH von einer „Haftungszuweisung an einen Teil der wirtschaftlichen Einheit“ spricht.

Dadurch, dass der EuGH jedoch – wohl – davon ausgeht, dass die wirtschaftliche Einheit keine Rechtspersönlichkeit haben muss, wird das Konzept vollends widersprüchlich.[79] Ist die wirtschaftliche Einheit nicht wenigstens teilrechtsfähig, ist sie rechtlich eine Fiktion und kann nicht Adressat rechtlicher Normen sein. Wird sie vom europäischen Normengeber oder der Rechtsprechung zum Adressaten von Normen gemacht, ist sie insoweit teilrechtsfähig, weil sie Pflichtiger der kartellrechtlichen Verhaltensnormen ist. Ist die wirtschaftliche Einheit Normadressat und die zu ermittelnde verantwortliche Person Sanktionsadressat, wird die Rechtssubjektivität in einen Normadressaten und einen Sanktionsadressaten gespalten und die Verantwortlichkeit verschoben.[80] Dass der europäische Gesetzgeber mit der Verwendung des Begriffs „Unternehmen" so weitreichende Konsequenzen in Kauf nehmen wollte, erscheint fernliegend. Unbestritten ist, dass es dem EuGH freisteht, ein autonomes Konzept im Hinblick auf die Rechtsfähigkeit zu verfolgen.[81] Ein solches Konzept ist jedoch nur tragfähig, wenn es in sich widerspruchsfrei ist.

Rechtssubjektivität ist nicht teilbar, in dem Sinne, dass die wirtschaftliche Einheit Trägerin der kartellrechtlichen Pflichten ist, Vollstreckungssubjekt jedoch ein Rechtsträger der nationalen Rechte ist. Eine solche Auffassung verschleiert die Problematik der Zurechnung, die sich zwangsläufig stellt, wenn zwei verschiedene Rechtssubjekte betroffen sind. Fallen kartellrechtliche Verantwortlichkeit und Bußgeldhaftung auseinander, wird der Zweck der Verhängung der Sanktion verfehlt, es sei denn, es bestehen klare Zurechnungsregeln. Entsprechendes gilt für die Teilung der Rechtssubjektivität in eine kartellrechtliche Teilrechtsfähigkeit und eine Rechtsfähigkeit für Zwecke des Verfahrens bzw. eine Adressatenstellung. Dies hätte eine Art Prozessstandschaft zur Folge, für welche jedoch die materielle Berechtigung Vorfrage wäre.[82] Ebenso wenig tragbar erscheint die Auffassung, ein Unternehmen könne mehrere Rechtsträger haben.[83] Damit wäre eine einheitliche Willensbildung innerhalb des Unternehmens nicht möglich, spiegelbildlich wären auch Verantwortlichkeit und Haftung unklar.

Eine vollständige Abkehr von dem Rechtsträgerprinzip würde voraussetzen, dass der wirtschaftlichen Einheit Vollrechtsfähigkeit, dh auch die Fähigkeit Vollstreckungssubjekt zu sein, zuerkannt würde. Ein solcher Schritt erscheint theoretisch denkbar, würde jedoch voraussetzen, dass der Umfang der wirtschaftlichen Einheit klar definiert wird und das der Vollstreckung unterliegende Vermögen sowie die der Vollstreckung unterliegenden Einheiten klar umrissen sind. Dies ist nach der

---

[79] EuGH 28.6.2005 – C-189/02 P ua, ECLI:EU:C:2005:08 Rn. 112–118 (Dansk Roerindustrie).

[80] Vgl. zu dieser Differenzierung Frankfurter Kommentar zum Kartellrecht/Roth/Ackermann, 101. Aktualisierung 2022, AEUV Grundfragen des Art. 101 Rn. 106: BT-Drs. 18/10207, 87: Lösung der materiellen Verantwortlichkeit vom einzelnen Rechtsträger und Bezug auf das Unternehmen im Sinne einer wirtschaftlichen Einheit.

[81] So wohl Frankfurter Kommentar zum Kartellrecht/Roth/Ackermann, 101. Aktualisierung 2022, AEUV Grundfragen des Art. 101 Rn. 106a.

[82] So Frankfurter Kommentar zum Kartellrecht/Roth/Ackermann, 101. Aktualisierung 2022, AEUV Grundfragen des Art. 101 Abs. 1 Rn. 116, Fn. 1; Kersting WuW 2014, 1156.

[83] So Generalanwältin Kokott 29.11.2012 – C-440/11 P, ECLI:EU:C: 2012:763 Rn. 32 (Kommission/Stichting Aministratiekantoor Portielje).

Rechtsprechung des EuGH nicht der Fall. Außerdem müssten die nationalen europäischen Gesetzgeber Regelungen für eine Vollstreckung gegen wirtschaftliche Einheiten schaffen, da eine bloße gesamtschuldnerische Haftung, dh eine Haftung mehrerer juristischer oder natürlicher Personen, einen Rückfall in das Rechtsträgerprinzip bedeutet.

5. *Das Unternehmen als Rechtsträger*

Eine vom Rechtsträger ganz oder teilweise gelöste Unternehmenshaftung wird seit geraumer Zeit im deutschen und österreichischen Handelsrecht ausgehend von der Problematik eines Verständnisses des Gesetzeszwecks des § 25 HGB unter dem Stichwort der Haftungskontinuität diskutiert. Die These bleibt zwar auf dem Boden des Rechtsträgerprinzips, relativiert dieses Prinzip allerdings in der Weise, dass sie die das Unternehmen betreffenden Rechtsverhältnisse zwar dessen Träger zuordnet, mit einem Wechsel der Rechtsträgerschaft aber auch einen Übergang der unternehmensbezogenen Rechtsverhältnisse postuliert. Ähnlich der Betrachtungsweise des EuGH bei der wirtschaftlichen Einheit, geht diese Auffassung beim Unternehmensübergang von einem Funktionsübergang aus, bei welchem das Unternehmen als Funktionseinheit übertragen wird.

Diese These geht – unausgesprochen – von einer Verselbständigung des Unternehmens gegenüber seinem Rechtsträger aus und führt über die Zuordnung der unternehmensbezogenen Verbindlichkeiten zum Unternehmen zu einer Aufhebung der Subjektbindung dieser Verbindlichkeiten und damit zu ähnlichen Rechtsfolgen wie eine Rechtssubjektivität des Unternehmens. Sie weist damit deutliche Parallelen zu der Rechtsprechung des EuGH im Bereich der Übertragung wirtschaftlicher Einheiten auf, bei denen die kartellrechtliche Bußgeldhaftung mit der wirtschaftlichen Aktivität auf einen neuen Rechtsträger übergeht. Durch eine vollständige Rechtsfähigkeit des Unternehmens würde jedoch eine in sich ruhenden Vermögensmasse gebildet, die keinem unternehmerischen Zweck dient und damit keinen eigenen Willen zu bilden in der Lage wäre oder wenigstens ein eigenes Interesse vorzuweisen hätte, außer dem Zweck des eigenen Erhalts. Erst durch die Bildung eines unternehmerischen Zwecks und die Bindung des Unternehmens an diesen Zweck kann für das Unternehmen ein unternehmerischer Wille gebildet werden. Nach dieser Auffassung wird das Unternehmen aus der dauernden Betätigung der Unternehmerpersönlichkeit, aus dem Niederschlag dieser Leistung in Gestalt eines Tätigkeitsbereiches sowie aus materiellen, immateriellen und personellen dem Unternehmen gewidmeten Mitteln gebildet.[84]

Dagegen definiert der EuGH das Unternehmen als einheitliche Organisation persönlicher, materieller und immaterieller Mittel, die dauerhaft einen bestimmten wirtschaftlichen Zweck verfolgt und die an einer Zuwiderhandlung im Sinne von Art. 101 AEUV beteiligt sein kann. Dabei geht der EuGH davon aus, dass Konzerne nicht immer wirtschaftliche Einheiten bilden, sondern zB solche des Typs „Konglomerat“, die in mehreren wirtschaftlichen Bereichen tätig sind, mehrere wirtschaft-

[84] Vgl. Müller-Feldhammer, Die Erwerberhaftung bei rechtsgeschäftlicher Unternehmensübertragung, 2001, S. 247, 901 ff., 910.

liche Einheiten bilden.[85] Damit folgt der EuGH eher dem organisationssoziologischen Ansatz, welcher versucht, das Unternehmen als soziales und wirtschaftliches Phänomen juristisch zu erfassen, wobei die juristische Form sich der Realität des Unternehmens unterzuordnen hat. Die Betonung des Unternehmens als Organisation begünstigt tendenziell die Vorstellung einer „Unabhängigkeit" des Unternehmens von seinem Träger und damit einer Rechtssubjektivität des Unternehmens.[86]

Damit offenbart die Rechtsprechung Widersprüche, die kaum aufzulösen sind. Ist die Tätigkeit in ein und demselben wirtschaftlichen Bereich Voraussetzung für das Bestehen einer wirtschaftlichen Einheit, muss das auch für das Verhältnis zwischen Mutter- und Tochtergesellschaft, nicht nur für das Verhältnis der verschiedenen Tochtergesellschaften untereinander gelten. Lässt man in diesem Verhältnis die Unterordnung der Tochtergesellschaft genügen, entfernt man sich von dem Ausgangspunkt, dem einheitlichen Auftreten am Markt, der aus dem funktionalen Unternehmensbegriff folgt.[87]

Stellt man im Verhältnis der Tochtergesellschaften untereinander auf die Unterordnung der Tochtergesellschaft und die Weisungsabhängigkeit ab, spielt die Frage des wirtschaftlichen Tätigkeitsbereiches der Tochtergesellschaften keine Rolle. Stellt man umgekehrt auf den Tätigkeitsbereich der Tochterunternehmen und ihr Auftreten am Markt ab, kommt es auf die wirtschaftlichen, organisatorischen und rechtlichen Beziehungen zwischen Mutter- und Tochtergesellschaft ebenso wenig an, wie auf eine Unterwerfung unter Weisungen. Fordert man eine Kumulation dieser Merkmale, ist zunächst der sachliche Markt, auf welchem die Tochtergesellschaften tätig sind, festzustellen. Dieser wird häufig unterschiedlich sein, weil eine rechtliche Trennung wirtschaftlicher Einheiten, die auf demselben sachlichen Markt tätig sind, i. d. R. wirtschaftlich nicht sinnvoll ist. Damit ist die wirtschaftliche Einheit als Rechtsfigur nicht in der Lage Konzernsachverhalte zu erfassen. Die Bedeutung dieser Rechtsfigur reduziert sich damit auf eine quasi Konzernhaftung der Muttergesellschaft für die Tochtergesellschaft, die sich einzig aus dem Anteilsverhältnis von 100% oder nahezu 100% speist.

Auch die Lockerung des Rechtsträgerprinzips durch Annahme einer – scheinbaren – Teilrechtsfähigkeit oder in Gestalt der Annahme unternehmensbezogener Rechte und Verbindlichkeiten im Sinne der wirtschaftlichen Kontinuität unterliegt Bedenken. Das Rechtsträgerprinzip ist nicht nur ein formales Ordnungsprinzip, sondern ist die natürliche Folge der Zweckbindung des Unternehmens. Es handelt sich damit um ein grundlegendes Zurechnungsprinzip im Bereich des Unternehmensrechts, in welchem das Prinzip der Selbstverantwortung der – natürlichen oder juristischen – Person für ihr Verhalten und für ihren Geschäftskreis zum Ausdruck kommt.[88] Wird das Rechtsträgerprinzip relativiert, indem das Unternehmen für

---

[85] EuGH 6.10.2021 – C-882/19, ECLI:EU:C:2021:800 Rn. 41, 44 = NZKart 2019, 626 (627 ff.) (Sumal).

[86] Vgl. dazu grundlegend Raiser, Das Unternehmen als Organisation, 1969; Müller-Feldhammer, Die Erwerberhaftung bei rechtsgeschäftlicher Unternehmensübertragung, 2001, S. 165 ff., 213.

[87] Vgl. hierzu Zandler NZKart 2016, 98 (101).

[88] Vgl. van Vormizeele WuW 2010, 1008 (1013) unter dem Gesichtspunkt des Schuldprinzips.

nicht rechtsträgerbezogene Verbindlichkeiten haftet, greift man in das Prinzip der Selbstverantwortung ein.

Das Rechtsträgerprinzip ist wirtschaftlich und rechtlich von erheblicher Bedeutung, indem es die Möglichkeit gibt, Risiken einem Rechtsträger zuzuordnen und diese im Zusammenwirken mit den gesellschaftsrechtlichen Haftungsbeschränkungen zu begrenzen. Lockert man diese Zuordnung oder spaltet man die Rechtssubjektivität in nicht näher umrissene Adressatenstellungen auf, durchbricht man das von den nationalen Gesetzgebern geschaffene System privatautonom begründeter Rechtspersönlichkeiten und deren voller oder beschränkter Verantwortlichkeit.[89] Teil dieses Systems sind auch Konzernstrukturen, dh rechtlich eigenständige Gesellschaften, welche durch tatsächliche Umstände, zB eine einheitliche Leitung, oder rechtliche Beziehungen, zB Anteilsverhältnisse oder Unternehmensverträge, miteinander verflochten sind. Damit ist auch die Haftungsbegrenzung innerhalb von Konzernen Teil dieses Systems, zB die „Auslagerung" wirtschaftlicher, rechtlicher oder tatsächlicher Risiken auf speziell hierfür geschaffene Gesellschaften, etwa auf Projektgesellschaften, welche speziell zur Haftungsbegrenzung gegründet werden. Die aus dem *effet utile* abgeleitete Begründung der Rechtsprechung des EuGH, Konzerne sollten sich nicht hinter kleinen Tochtergesellschaften „verstecken" können, erscheint daher nicht überzeugend.[90]

Hat zB die Tochtergesellschaft eines Konzerns eine kartellbußgeldrechtliche Sanktion veranlasst und wird die Muttergesellschaft im Rahmen einer wirtschaftlichen Einheit hierfür in Anspruch genommen, können die Anteilsverhältnisse der Mutter- und der Tochtergesellschaft differieren. Dies wäre etwa der Fall, wenn an der Muttergesellschaft konzernfremde Minderheitsgesellschafter beteiligt sind. Es liegt dann ein Eingriff in die Rechtsstellung der Minderheitsgesellschafter vor, der einer Rechtfertigung bedarf. Entsprechendes gilt für Übertragungsfälle, soweit sich zB ein latentes kartellrechtliches Bußgeldrisiko – etwa bei einem Asset Deal – in der Person des Übernehmers verwirklicht und der Übernehmer für dieses infolge der wirtschaftlichen Kontinuität haftet.

Die Statuierung der wirtschaftlichen Einheit aus dem funktionalen Unternehmensbegriff und des Prinzips der wirtschaftlichen Kontinuität führt damit zu einer zurechnungsfreien Haftung von Unternehmensträgern, ohne dass – mit Ausnahme des *effet utile* – die zugrundeliegenden Wertungen erkennbar wären.[91] Auf diese Weise wird der Zugriff in Vermögensmassen gestattet, die einer anderen, privatautonom eingegangenen Zweckbindung unterliegen.[92] Soweit demgegenüber argumentiert wird, dass sich die Verhaltensnormen des Wettbewerbsrechts an die Akteure richten sollten, die wettbewerblich am Markt tätig sind, wird dies dadurch

[89] Ähnlich van Vormizeele WuW 2010, 1008, (1015).

[90] Kokott/Dittert WuW 2012, 670 (674); zustimmend Langen/Bunte, Kartellrecht/Hengst, 13. Aufl. 2018, Rn. 47.

[91] Ähnlich Frankfurter Kommentar zum Kartellrecht/Meyer, 105. Aktualisierung 2023, AEUV Art. 101 Bußgeldrechtliche Folgen Rn. 31.

[92] Vgl. Timmerbeil/Blome BB 2017, 1544 (1549); aA Immenga/Mestmäcker, Wettbewerbsrecht/Biermann, 6. Aufl. 2020) GWB § 81 Rn. 342–344; Ost/Kallfaß/Rosen NZKart 2016, 456; Podszun/Kreifels/Schmieder WuW 2017, 114 (115); zur Verfassungswidrigkeit aus dem Gesichtpunkt des Schuldprinzips Brettel/Thomas WuW 2016, 336 (337).

sichergestellt, dass die wettbewerblichen Normen am Unternehmen anknüpfen.[93] Dies erfordert jedoch nicht die Schaffung einer künstlichen Einheit, die Adressat dieser Normen ist.

Folgt man der oben skizzierten These vom Unternehmen als Immaterialgut, wird zudem deutlich, dass das Unternehmen nicht als Vollstreckungssubjekt im Sinne einer Vollrechtsfähigkeit geeignet ist, weil die Widmung der materiellen und immateriellen Mittel durch die Unternehmerpersönlichkeit die Bildung eines unternehmerischen Zwecks voraussetzt. Die Begründung des deutschen Gesetzgebers für die Übernahme dieser Grundsätze des EuGH, durch die Verbandsgeldbuße solle das Vermögen desjenigen getroffen werden, dem die Vorteile einer in seinem Interesse vorgenommenen Betätigung zufließen, weist demgegenüber deutliche Parallelen zu Vorstellungen auf, die das Unternehmen als Haftungsfonds oder Zweck- bzw. Sondervermögen charakterisieren.[94] Diese Thesen sind als überholt anzusehen, da sie jeweils nur Teilaspekte des Unternehmens abbilden.[95]

IV. Ausblick

Die Haftung eines Rechtsträgers für eine Kartellbuße eines anderen Rechtsträgers aufgrund einer Konzernverbundenheit oder in Übertragungsfällen übersteigt in seiner Schwere den gesellschaftrechtlichen Haftungsdurchgriff, welcher in den nationalen Gesellschaftsrechten der europäischen Staaten entweder nicht vorgesehen oder auf eng umrissene Fallgruppen beschränkt ist.[96] Während der Haftungsdurchgriff innerhalb der haftungsbeschränkten Rechtspersönlichkeit auf dessen Rechtsträger zugreift, greift die Haftung infolge Konzernverbundenheit oder in Übertragungsfällen auf eine rechtlich selbständige Rechtspersönlichkeit zu.

Dieser Zugriff bedarf einer Rechtfertigung, weil er in die nationalen Gesellschafts- und Unternehmensrechte eingreift. Die wirtschaftliche Verflechtung von Mutter- und Tochtergesellschaft in Konzernfällen wird kartellrechtlich bereits im Rahmen der Bußgeldbemessung gemäß Art. 23 Abs. 2 S. 2 VO 1/2003 berücksichtigt. Die Obergrenze des Bußgeldes von 10% des jeweiligen im vorangegangenen Geschäftsjahr erzielten Gesamtumsatzes des Unternehmens bezieht sich auf den weltweiten Umsatz der Unternehmensgruppe, dh in Konzernfällen auf den Umsatz aller zurechenbaren Gesellschaften, einschließlich Tochter- und Schwestergesellschaften, und ist damit Teil der Bußgeldbemessung.[97]

Das Argument der effektiven Kartellrechtsdurchsetzung ist daher nicht durchschlagend. Konzernsachverhalte werden generell im Rahmen der Bußgeldhöhe be-

---

[93] Vgl. Frankfurter Kommentar zum Kartellrecht/Roth/Ackermann, 101. Aktualisierung 2022, AEUV Grundfragen des Art. 101 Rn. 106a.

[94] BT-Drs. 18/10207, 87.

[95] Vgl. dazu zusammenfassend Müller-Feldhammer, Die Erwerberhaftung bei rechtsgeschäftlicher Unternehmensübertragung, 2001, S. 26ff., 52ff., 334ff.

[96] Vgl. dazu rechtsvergleichend van Vormizeele WuW 2010, 1008 (1016f.)

[97] Vgl. dazu in Immenga/Mestmäcker, Wettbewerbsrecht/Biermann, 6. Aufl. 2019, VO 1/2003 Art. 23 Rn. 116; zum deutschen Kartellrecht vgl. § 81 Abs. 4 S. 2, 3 GWB aF (heute § 81c Abs. 2, 5 S.1 GWB).

rücksichtigt. Die Rechtsprechung des EuGH ist in sich nicht plausibel, weil mit der wirtschaftlichen Einheit nicht eine vollstreckungsfähige Einheit gebildet und insgesamt in Anspruch genommen wird, sondern ein scheinbar teilrechtsfähiges Gebilde entsteht, welches die Haftung auf vollstreckungsfähige natürliche oder juristische Personen durch leitet. Es wäre Sache der nationalen Gesetzgeber, Lücken im Rahmen der nationalen Gesellschafts- und Umwandlungsrechte zu schließen, soweit sich im Rahmen der Vollstreckung kartellrechtlicher Bußgelder Schutzlücken ergeben sollten.

Der Unternehmensbegriff wird seit dem 19. Jahrhundert diskutiert, ohne dass sich eine einheitliche Linie abzeichnet. Der funktionale Unternehmensbegriff des Kartellrechts ist damit nicht der richtige Ausgangspunkt für die Beurteilung von Konzernsachverhalten.[98] Dieser Unternehmensbegriff ist formal und kann nicht die sich auf der Rechtsfolgenseite zwangsläufig stellende Problematik der Zurechnung des kartellrechtswidrigen Verhaltens an ein vollstreckungsfähiges Rechtssubjekt angemessen lösen. Da die Bildung der wirtschaftlichen Einheit als unmittelbares Haftungssubjekt direkt aus dem funktionalen Unternehmensbegriff abgeleitet wird, enthält sie keine wertenden Kriterien in der Form von Zurechnungsgesichtspunkten. Entsprechende Gesichtspunkte sind von dem EuGH auch nicht entwickelt worden. Das Konstrukt der wirtschaftlichen Einheit ist folgerichtig in sich höchst widersprüchlich.

Der EuGH selbst versteht das Kriterium des maßgebenden wirtschaftlichen Einflusses, das Voraussetzung einer Konzernbildung ist, denn auch nicht als Zurechnungskriterium, nachdem er dem Vorgang der Zurechnung rein praktische Bedeutung zuweist. Eine Haftung konzernangehöriger Gesellschaften bedarf jedoch der Rechtfertigung und damit einer Zurechnung anhand der bekannten Zurechnungskriterien, weil ein Eingriff in die Selbstverantwortung privatautonom begründeter Rechtspersönlichkeiten vorliegt. Damit böte gerade das vom EuGH betonte Prinzip der persönlichen Verantwortung einen Ansatz für die Herausarbeitung tragfähiger Zurechnungskriterien.[99]

Anstelle der Bildung scheinbar teilrechtsfähiger Haftungseinheiten bedarf es daher der Zurechnung des kartellrechtswidrigen Verhaltens an ein vollstreckungsfähiges Rechtssubjekt anhand anerkannter Zurechnungsprinzipien. Zu diesen gehört vor allem die Verhaltenszurechnung, dh der Grundsatz, dass Verbänden die Taten ihrer Organe und leitenden Repräsentanten wie eigene Handlungen zugerechnet werden, sowie die Haftung für Aufsichts- und Organisationsversagen.[100] Eine – auch der Höhe nach – differenzierte Zurechnung wird jedoch dadurch erschwert, dass das europäische Recht über die Täterschaft hinaus keine Regelung einer bußgeldrechtlichen Verantwortung für Beihilfehandlungen vor-

[98] Ebenso Bosch/Brinker, EU-Kartellrecht, 4. Aufl. 2021, AEUV Art. 101 Rn. 39.

[99] Vgl. dazu Kling WRP 2010, 506 (514); Zimmer/Paul WuW 2007, 970 (971 f.); Canaris, Die Vertrauenshaftung im deutschen Privatrecht, 1971, S. 468, wonach das rechtsethische Prinzip der Selbstverantwortung sich im Gedanken der Zurechnung verwirklicht.

[100] Vgl. Frankfurter Kommentar zum Kartellrecht/Meyer, 105. Aktualisierung 2023, AEUV Art. 101 Bußgeldrechtliche Folgen, Rn. 25–29; für das Verschuldensprinzip vgl. hierzu Zandler NZKart 2016, 98 (103 f.).

sieht.[101] Eine Korrektur der europäischen Rechtsprechung ist daher nicht zu erwarten. Die Übernahme der vom EuGH entwickelten Rechtsfiguren in die nationalen Rechtsordnungen lässt daher die Herausbildung eines kartellrechtlichen Sonderbußgeldrechts erwarten, welches, dem Grundsatz der Einheit der Rechtsordnung folgend, auf andere Rechtsbereiche, etwa das Gesellschaftsrecht, ausstrahlen könnte und möglicherweise der Diskussion um die Rechtsfähigkeit des Unternehmens neuen Auftrieb geben wird.[102]

---

[101] Vgl. dazu Immenga/Mestmäcker, Wettbewerbsrecht/Zimmer, AEUV Vor Art. 23 Rn. 132ff.

[102] Vgl. dazu Immenga/Mestmäcker, Wettbewerbsrecht/Zimmer, AEUV Art. 101 Abs. 1 Rn. 32, der für eine Verhaltenszurechnung bei unterschiedlichen Rechtssubjekten und die Anerkennung der einheitlichen Unternehmenseigenschaft eines Konzerns plädiert.

CSONGOR ISTVÁN NAGY

Der „kleinste gemeinsame Nenner“ der europäischen Verbandsklagen: die Richtlinie über Verbandsklagen zum Schutz der Kollektivinteressen der Verbraucher

I. *Einführung*

Obwohl die Rechtsgeschichte der Gruppenklagen[1] in der EU ungefähr vor drei Jahrzehnten angefangen hat,[2] ist der erste und einzige verbindliche EU-Rechtsakt auf diesem Gebiet die Richtlinie 2020/1828 über Verbandsklagen zum Schutz der Kollektivinteressen der Verbraucher (VerbandsklageRL).[3]

Die VerbandsklageRL wurde mit der Hoffnung erwartet, dass sie eine neue Qualität im Bereich des kollektiven Rechtsschutzes bringen wird. Diese Hoffnung erwies sich aber als unbegründet. Die VerbandsklageRL hat einen begrenzten Anwendungsbereich, ist voll von unverbindlichen Vorschriften, geht nicht über den bereits bestehenden europäischen „kleinsten gemeinsamen Nenner“ hinaus. Der einzige Mehrwert der VerbandsklageRL besteht in dem Erfordernis, dass in jedem Mitgliedstaat ein kollektiver Mechanismus zur Verfügung stehen soll. Das stellt aber keinen wesentlichen Rechtsentwicklungsmehrwert dar, da solche Mechanismen in der Mehrheit der Mitgliedstaaten schon zur Verfügung stehen und die Vorschriften der VerbandsklageRL sich auf die bloße Anerkennung des gemeinsamen Kerns der mitgliedstaatlichen Rechte beschränken. Die VerbandsklageRL verwandelt den

---

[1] In diesem Beitrag bezeichnet „Gruppenklage” die kollektiven Rechtschutzmechanismen, die die Durchsetzung von Geldforderungen ermöglichen.

[2] Die erste offizielle Anerkennung erfolgte im Jahr 2005, mit der Veröffentlichung des Grünbuchs über Schadensersatzklagen wegen Verletzung des EU-Wettbewerbsrechts (Europäische Kommission, KOM(2005) 672 endgültig), dem drei Jahre später das Weißbuch gleichen Titels gefolgt ist (Europäische Kommission, KOM(2008) 165 endgültig). 2013 hat die Europäische Kommission „Gemeinsame Grundsätze für kollektive Unterlassungs- und Schadensersatzverfahren in den Mitgliedstaaten bei Verletzung von durch Unionsrecht garantierten Rechten“ veröffentlicht (Empfehlung der Kommission 2013/396/EU, ABl. 2013 L 201, 60); für einen Überblick über die Empfehlung siehe Carballo Piñeiro REDI (Revista española de derecho internacional) 65/2 (2013), 395; Stadler ZfPW 2015, 61; Nagy MJ (Maastricht Journal of European and Comparative Law) 22 (2015), 530. Die Empfehlung ist einem konservativen Ansatz gefolgt und hatte sehr geringen Einfluss auf das Recht der Mitgliedstaaten, s. Europäische Kommission, COM(2018) 40 final, 2.

[3] Richtlinie (EU) 2020/1828 des Europäischen Parlaments und des Rates vom 25. November 2020 über Verbandsklagen zum Schutz der Kollektivinteressen der Verbraucher und zur Aufhebung der Richtlinie 2009/22/EG (ABl. 2020 L 409, 1); siehe Visscher/Faure Journal of Consumer Policy 44 (2021), 455; Gsell CMLR 58 (2021), 1365; Hornkohl EuCML 10 (2021), 189; Gascón Inchausti GPR 2021, 61; Vollkommer MDR 2021, 129; Nagy EuZW 2022, 637; Schuschnigg EuZW 2022, 1043.

schon bestehenden regulatorischen gemeinsamen Kern in ein normatives „regulatorisches Minimum."

Dieser Beitrag stellt diesen „kleinsten gemeinsamen Nenner" der europäischen Verbandsklagen dar. Er gibt einen Überblick über die VerbandsklageRL im Lichte der regulatorischen Kernfragen und der einschlägigen europäischen Debatte. Im ersten Schritt stellt er den Anwendungsbereich und die Grundzüge der VerbandsklageRL und die aus deren Anwendungsbereich ausgelassenen Fragen dar. Im zweiten Schritt untersucht er die Vorschriften über Klagebefugnis und qualifizierte Einrichtungen. Im dritten Schritt beschäftigt er sich mit der „Vertretung ohne Ermächtigung" (der legislativen Wahl zwischen dem Opt-in und Opt-out-Prinzip). Im vierten Schritt untersucht und bewertet der Beitrag die „regulatorischen Sicherheitsvorkehrungen", die die VerbandsklageRL gegen die missbräuchliche Verwendung der Verbandsklagen errichtet. Schließlich identifiziert der Beitrag den Mehrwert der VerbandsklageRL, dh die Elemente, die im Vergleich zur Rechtslage vor der VerbandsklageRL eine Fortentwicklung darstellen, und stellt seine Schlussfolgerungen vor.

II. Anwendungsbereich und Grundzüge

Die VerbandsklageRL ist nicht in allen Verbraucherangelegenheiten anwendbar, ihr Anwendungsbereich beschränkt sich auf 66 Verbraucherschutzrichtlinien.[4] Es ist bedauerlich, dass der EU-Gesetzgeber nicht die Gelegenheit ergriffen hat, im Gegensatz zur Empfehlung der Kommission 2013/396/EU einen kollektiven Mechanismus für die Gesamtheit des Unionsrechts zu errichten. Es ist das Grundinteresse der EU, die Wirksamkeit des Unionsrechts in den Mitgliedstaaten zu erhöhen, und die Gruppenklagen wären ein hervorragendes Mittel dafür. Mit der teilweisen Privatisierung der Durchsetzung des Unionsrechts könnte die Rechtsdurchsetzung mehr Kraftressourcen in Anspruch nehmen.

Die VerbandsklageRL gilt nicht für Wettbewerbsrechtsklagen. Das heißt, dass sie unter keinen kollektiven Mechanismus fallen, da die Kartellschadensersatzrichtlinie diese Frage von seinem Anwendungsbereich ausschloss. Das kann als eine schiefe Lage angesehen werden. Der Gedanke des kollektiven Rechtsschutzes entstand ja im Wettbewerbsrecht als Teil der Bewegung für private Rechtsdurchsetzung: es war die private Rechtsdurchsetzung des Wettbewerbsrechts, die die Notwendigkeit von Gruppenklagen in den öffentlichen Diskurs einbrachte. Am Ende hat der EU-Gesetzgeber jedoch diese Frage in der Kartellschadensersatzrichtlinie wissentlich ausgelassen. Grund dafür war sehr wahrscheinlich, dass Gruppenklagen ein horizontales Thema sind und daher in einem Rechtsinstrument allgemeinerer Anwendung behandelt werden sollten. Die VerbandsklageRL erfüllt diese Erwartung nicht. Darüber hinaus ist diese Unterlassung auch aus sehr wichtigen rechtspolitischen Gründen bedauerlich. Das System der privaten Rechtsdurchsetzung im Wettbewerbsrecht besteht aus verschiedenen geschädigtenfreundlichen Regeln, die

[4] Anh. I VerbandsklageRL.

die Geltendmachung von Schadensersatzklagen bedeutend erleichtern und die Funktionsfähigkeit der kollektiven Rechtsdurchsetzung gewähren würden.

Die VerbandsklageRL ergibt keinen wesentlichen regulatorischen Mehrwert.

Erstens verlangt sie nicht mehr von den Mitgliedstaaten als das, was in Europa im Wesentlichen schon zur Verfügung steht. Sie ist ein Rechtsinstrument, das die Sitten an die Gewohnheiten und nicht die Gewohnheiten an die Sitten anpasst. Sie schreibt das vor, was die mitgliedstaatlichen Rechte großenteils schon enthalten. Die Erwartungen, die die VerbandsklageRL an die Mitgliedstaaten stellt, sind ganz minimalistisch. Gruppenklagen sind in etwa 60% der Mitgliedstaaten verfügbar,[5] und die meisten dieser Rechtssysteme gehen weit über die Anforderungen der VerbandsklageRL hinaus.[6]

Zweitens sind viele der Vorschriften der VerbandsklageRL unverbindlich und stellen bloße Empfehlungen dar, was sie zu einer „Empfehlung 2.0"[7] machen. In dem Kerntext der VerbandsklageRL, der aus 16 Artikeln (Art. 4-20 VerbandsklageRL) besteht, wird das Wort „können" bezüglich der zu verabschiedenden mitgliedstaatlichen Maßnahmen 15-mal verwendet. Während die VerbandsklageRL bezüglich der verbindlichen Vorschriften nicht wesentlich über die Empfehlung der Kommission 2013/396/EU hinausgeht, hat sie einen engeren Anwendungsbereich. Obwohl die Empfehlung keine verbindlichen Vorschriften enthält, ist sie zumindest allgemein anwendbar und gilt für alle Verstöße gegen das EU-Recht.

Drittens behindert die VerbandsklageRL sogar die Mitgliedstaaten, den kollektiven Rechtsschutz fördernde Maßnahmen zu verabschieden und damit Gruppenklagen funktionsfähig zu machen. Während die Mehrheit der positiven Vorschriften nicht verbindlich, sondern lediglich „empfohlen" ist, sind die negativen Vorschriften, die die regulatorische Förderung der Gruppenklagen ausschließen, verbindlich. Das deutet darauf hin, dass der EU-Gesetzgeber die Gruppenklagen viel mehr fürchtete, als dass er sie ermöglichen wollte. Ein ähnlicher Widerspruch kann zwischen den in der VerbandsklageRL genannten Zielen und den detaillierten Vorschriften wahrgenommen werden. Obwohl die VerbandsklageRL die Einführung der Verbandsklagen bezweckt um „das Vertrauen der Verbraucher [zu] stärken, sie in der Wahrnehmung ihrer Rechte [zu] bestärken, einen Beitrag zu einem faireren Wettbewerb [zu] leisten und gleiche Ausgangsbedingungen für die auf dem Binnenmarkt tätigen Unternehmer [zu] schaffen.",[8] spiegeln die detaillierten Vorschriften eine Denkweise wider, die ihr eigenes Geschöpf fürchtet.

---

[5] Nagy, Collective Actions in Europe – A Comparative, Economic and Transsystemic Analysis, 2014, S. 73–74.

[6] Nagy, Collective Actions in Europe – A Comparative, Economic and Transsystemic Analysis, 2014, S. 73–74.

[7] Azar-Baud/Sousa Ferro, Op-Ed: „Directive on consumer representative actions: a sheep in wolf's clothing?", EU Law Live (4. 12. 2020), https://eulawlive.com/op-ed-directive-on-consumer-representative-actions-a-sheep-in-wolfs-clothing-by-maria-jose-azar-baud-and-miguel-sousa-ferro/ (abgerufen 11. 5. 2024).

[8] ErwGr. 7 VerbandsklageRL.

III. Klagebefugnis

Die VerbandsklageRL sieht vor, dass zumindest qualifizierte Einrichtungen (Non-Profit-Nichtregierungsorganisationen und, wenn der Mitgliedstaat so wünscht, öffentliche Stellen[9]) befugt sein sollen, Verbandsklagen zu erheben.[10] Art. 4 Abs. 1 VerbandsklageRL besagt: „Die Mitgliedstaaten stellen sicher, dass die in dieser Richtlinie vorgesehenen Verbandsklagen von hierzu von den Mitgliedstaaten benannten qualifizierten Einrichtungen erhoben werden können."

Die VerbandsklageRL schließt nicht aus, dass die Mitgliedstaaten die Klagebefugnis weiter bestimmen und auch „nicht-qualifizierten" natürlichen und juristischen Personen eine Klagebefugnis gewähren, sie kann aber diese legislative Wahl mittelbar beschränken. Die Botschaft der VerbandsklageRL ist eindeutig, und es ist zu erwarten, dass die Auswirkungen auf das Recht der Mitgliedstaaten haben wird. Wichtiger noch, behindern die konservativen Vorschriften der VerbandsklageRL über die Klagebefugnis und die verschiedenen Schutzmaßnahmen, die die VerbandsklageRL gegen den Missbrauch des kollektiven Mechanismus errichtet, darüber hinaus mittelbar die Möglichkeiten der Mitgliedstaaten, die Klagebefugnis auszuweiten.

Die VerbandsklageRL unterscheidet zwischen inländischen und grenzüberschreitenden Verbandsklagen. Diese Unterscheidung beruht nicht auf den Merkmalen des Rechtsstreits oder des Beklagten, sondern auf den Merkmalen des Gruppenvertreters. Klagen, die von ausländischen Entitäten erhoben werden, gelten als „grenzüberschreitend", während inländische Entitäten inländische Verbandsklagen erheben können.[11] In Bezug auf inländische Verbandsklagen überlässt die VerbandsklageRL die Bestimmung der Klagebefugnis den Mitgliedstaaten. Grenzüberschreitende Verbandsklagen werden aber den detaillierten Anforderungen von Art. 4 Abs. 3 VerbandsklageRL unterworfen, die keinen Zweifel daran lassen, dass nur non-profit juristische Personen als qualifizierte Einrichtungen benannt werden können, und deuten darauf hin, dass bei grenzüberschreitenden Verbandsklagen Gruppenmitglieder und gewinnorientierte Entitäten nicht als Gruppenvertreter auftreten können.

Das steht im Widerspruch zum in Art. 1 Abs. 2 VerbandsklageRL festgelegten Nichtregression-Grundsatz. Die Mitgliedstaaten sollen sicherstellen, dass sie mindestens einen kollektiven Mechanismus haben, der „den Anforderungen dieser Richtlinie entspricht." Die VerbandsklageRL hindert sie jedoch nicht daran, über die Anforderungen der VerbandsklageRL hinauszugehen und „auf nationaler Ebene verfahrensrechtliche Mittel zum Schutz der Kollektivinteressen der Verbraucher zu erlassen oder beizubehalten." Die Umsetzung der VerbandsklageRL darf

[9] Art. 4 Abs. 7 VerbandsklageRL.

[10] Art. 4 Abs. 1 VerbandsklageRL. Gemäß Art. 3 Abs. 4 VerbandsklageRL umfasst der Begriff von „qualifizierter Einrichtung" jede Organisation oder öffentliche Stelle, die die Interessen der Verbraucher vertritt und von einem Mitgliedstaat als qualifiziert für die Erhebung von Verbandsklagen gemäß der VerbandsklageRL benannt wird.

[11] Art. 3 Abs. 6–7 VerbandsklageRL.

nicht als Rechtfertigung dafür dienen, das Verbraucherschutzniveau in den [betroffenen] Bereichen zu senken."

Obwohl die Mitgliedstaaten nicht verpflichtet sind, die oben genannten Regeln auch auf inländische Verbandsklagen anzuwenden,[12] ist es ziemlich schwer vorstellbar, dass sie unterschiedliche Maßnahmen für inländische und grenzüberschreitende Verfahren einführen werden. Art. 4 Abs. 4 VerbandsklageRL deutet darauf hin, dass die Klagebefugnis bei inländischen Verbandsklagen nicht radikal von den für grenzüberschreitende Klagen geltenden Regeln abweichen darf („Die Mitgliedstaaten stellen sicher, dass die Kriterien, die sie für die Benennung einer Organisation als qualifizierte Einrichtung für die Zwecke der Erhebung innerstaatlicher Verbandsklagen heranziehen, mit den Zielen dieser Richtlinie im Einklang stehen, um ein wirksames und effizientes Funktionieren dieser Verbandsklagen zu gewährleisten.").

Darüber hinaus können die Mitgliedstaaten „eine Organisation als qualifizierte Einrichtung auf deren Antrag hin ad hoc für die Erhebung einer bestimmten innerstaatlichen Verbandsklage benennen," aber nur dann, „wenn diese Organisation die im nationalen Recht vorgesehenen Kriterien für die Benennung als qualifizierte Einrichtung einhält."[13] Die Benennung von Gruppenmitgliedern ist per Definition ad hoc. Wenn die Mitgliedstaaten Anforderungen gegen die ständigen Benennungen als qualifizierte Einrichtungen errichten, müssen sie diese auch auf Ad-Hoc-Benennungen anwenden, einschließlich der Benennung von Gruppenmitgliedern als Gruppenvertreter.

Der obige Ansatz steht im Widerspruch zu den Ergebnissen, die die Mitgliedstaaten auf dem Gebiet der Gruppenklagen bereits erreicht haben. Obwohl die Helden der europäischen Gruppenklagen zweifellos Non-Profit-Organisationen sind, ist die Klagebefugnis nicht nur ihnen vorbehalten. In mehreren Mitgliedstaaten sind neben den Non-Profit-Organisationen und öffentlichen Stellen, auch Gruppenmitglieder klagebefugt, und nur wenige Rechtsysteme schließen ihre Klagebefugnis aus. Das gilt selbst dann, wenn es eine klare Tendenz ist, „schwierige Fälle", die bedeutende Rechtsanwendungsherausforderungen und ein erhöhtes Risiko des Missbrauchs darstellen, öffentlichen Stellen und qualifizierten Zivilorganisationen vorzubehalten.[14]

IV. Die Wahl zwischen Opt-in und Opt-out

Der Unterschied zwischen dem Opt-in und dem Opt-out liegt darin, ob die Gruppenmitglieder ohne ihre ausdrückliche Ermächtigung vertreten werden können. In dem Opt-in-System müssen die Gruppenmitglieder ausdrücklich, durch eine explizite Erklärung (Opt-in) in die Gruppe eintreten, um von dem Gruppenvertreter vertreten zu werden. Im Gegenteil basiert das Opt-out-System auf „Ver-

[12] Art. 4 Abs. 5 VerbandsklageRL.
[13] Art. 4 Abs. 6 VerbandsklageRL.
[14] Nagy, Collective Actions in Europe – A Comparative, Economic and Transsystemic Analysis, 2014, S. 95.

tretung ohne Ermächtigung" und die Mitglieder nur dann eine Erklärung abgeben, wenn sie die Gruppe verlassen und aus dem kollektiven Verfahren aussteigen wollen (Opt-out).

Die Annehmbarkeit der „Vertretung ohne Ermächtigung" (Opt-out-Prinzip) ist wahrscheinlich die umstrittenste Frage der Gruppenklagen in Europa. Die VerbandsklageRL behielt die konservative Auffassung des Unionsrechts bei und macht das Opt-out-Prinzip nur in jenen Fällen obligatorisch, wo der kollektive Mechanismus offensichtlich nicht wirksam ist. Betreffend die Fälle, wo dieser Mechanismus wirklich erfolgreich sein könnte, sollen die Mitgliedstaaten die Wahl treffen.

Die VerbandsklageRL verpflichtet die Mitgliedstaaten, den Opt-out-Mechanismus in Zivilsachen zu ermöglichen, aber nur für Unterlassungsklagen. Art. 8 Abs. 3 VerbandsklageRL stellt das klar: „Damit eine qualifizierte Einrichtung eine Unterlassungsentscheidung erwirken kann, müssen einzelne Verbraucher nicht ihren Willen äußern, sich durch diese qualifizierte Einrichtung repräsentieren zu lassen." Wenn es jedoch um Geldforderungen geht („Abhilfe in Form von Schadenersatz, Reparatur, Ersatzleistung, Preisminderung, Vertragsauflösung oder Erstattung des gezahlten Preises"),[15] wird die Wahl zwischen dem Opt-out und Opt-in den Mitgliedstaaten überlassen.[16] Damit behält die VerbandsklageRL einen auffälligen Regelungswiderspruch bei, der seit der Einführung der kollektiven Unterlassungsklage durch Richtlinie 98/27/EG besteht.[17]

Die Aufrechterhaltung dieser Rechtslage ist umso bedauerlicher, als die Opt-out-Gruppenklage in vielen Mitgliedstaaten verfügbar ist: etwa 60% der Mitgliedstaaten haben kollektiven Mechanismen eingeführt, die auch für Geldforderungen gelten, und mehr als die Hälfte dieser hat ein Opt-out-System angenommen.[18] Im Lichte dieser Lage kann das Opt-in-Prinzip nicht mehr als Europas ausschließliches oder sogar vorherrschendes Model angesehen werden. Der Ansatz der VerbandsklageRL in Bezug auf das Opt-out-Prinzip ist besonders enttäuschend, wenn man sich vor Augen führt, dass die Europäische Kommission vor mehr als einem Jahrzehnt einen Vorschlag für ein Opt-out-System vorlegte,[19] den sie schließlich zurücknahm.

Wenn es um Unterlassungs- und Feststellungsklagen geht, können qualifizierte Einrichtungen im Namen einer Gruppe von nicht identifizierten Verbrauchern auftreten, ohne dass eine individuelle Genehmigung oder Zustimmung erforderlich sei. Bezüglich Klagen, die keine Geldforderung umfassen, wirft die „Vertretung ohne Ermächtigung" keine Sorge auf. Was die VerbandsklageRL in dieser Hinsicht ermöglicht ist obendrein noch schlimmer als das Opt-out-Prinzip: der bezüglich Unterlassungs- und Feststellungsklagen vorgeschriebene Mechanismus folgt im buchstäblichen Sinne des Wortes nicht dem Opt-out, da es den Gruppenmitglie-

[15] Art. 3 Abs. 10 VerbandsklageRL.

[16] Art. 9 Abs. 1–2 VerbandsklageRL.

[17] Richtlinie 98/27/EG wurde von Richtlinie 2009/22/EG kodifiziert, die diese Rechtslage aufrechterhalten hat.

[18] Nagy, Collective Actions in Europe – A Comparative, Economic and Transsystemic Analysis, 2014, S. 73–85.

[19] Siehe Ioannidou CompLRev 8 (2011), 59 (78–80).

dern keine Möglichkeit gewährt, die Gruppe zu verlassen. Sie können aus der Gruppe (dem Verfahren) nicht aussteigen, selbst wenn sie es wollen. Dennoch, sobald es um Geldforderungen geht, hegt die VerbandsklageRL Argwohn gegen die „Vertretung ohne Ermächtigung." Begrifflich und auch aus der Sicht der Rechtsüberlieferung sollte es keinen Unterschied zwischen Geldforderungen und anderen zivilrechtlichen Ansprüchen geben. Schließlich handelt es sich bei beiden um zivilrechtliche Ansprüche, die im Allgemeinen in demselben verfahrensrechtlichen Rahmen, anhand derselben zivilprozessrechtlichen Regeln durchgesetzt werden.

Der Grund dieser Ungleichbehandlung ist vermutlich die Angst vor der eventuellen Privatisierung der Durchsetzung des öffentlichen Interesses, was der europäischen Zivilrechtstradition eindeutig fremd ist, und man kann die Gruppenklagen, wenn sie Geldforderungen betreffen, ja als ein solches Mittel ansehen. Obwohl die Gruppenklagen in Europa, ohne das besondere US-Amerikanische Rechtsumfeld (Strafschadensersatz, Erfolgshonorare usw.), einfach nicht in der Lage sind, eine ähnliche oder gar vergleichbare Rolle wie in den Vereinigten Staaten zu spielen, scheint es so aus, dass diese Angst die europäische Rezeption bedeutend beeinflusst.[20]

Obwohl die VerbandsklageRL grundsätzlich die Festlegung den kleinsten gemeinsamen europäischen Nenner bezweckt, ohne die Freiheit der Mitgliedstaaten einzuschränken, enthält sie eine sehr wichtige Einschränkung für Opt-out-Verbandsklagen. Art. 9 Abs. 3 VerbandsklageRL sieht vor, dass die Verbraucher, die ihren gewöhnlichen Aufenthalt außerhalb des betroffenen Mitgliedstaates haben, an dem Verbandsklageverfahren nur in dem Opt-in-System teilnehmen können.

„Ungeachtet des Absatzes 2 stellen die Mitgliedstaaten sicher, dass einzelne Verbraucher, die ihren gewöhnlichen Aufenthaltsort nicht in dem Mitgliedstaat des Gerichts oder der Verwaltungsbehörde haben, vor dem beziehungsweise vor der eine Verbandsklage erhoben worden ist, ihren Willen, bei der Klage repräsentiert zu sein, ausdrücklich äußern müssen, damit diese Verbraucher an das Ergebnis des Verbandsklageverfahrens gebunden sind."

Mit anderen Worten: im Allgemeinen können die Mitgliedstaaten zwischen dem Opt-in- und dem Opt-out-System wählen, aber wenn es um Gruppenmitglieder außerhalb des Mitgliedstaates geht, müssen sie dem Opt-in-Prinzip folgen. Diese Vorschrift ist ein großer Rücktritt für den kollektiven Rechtsschutz in Europa. Obwohl diese Einschränkung in Europa nicht völlig unbekannt ist,[21] sind die Opt-out-Gruppenklagen in vielen Mitgliedstaaten sowohl für inländische, als auch für ausländische Gruppenmitglieder verfügbar. Infolge von Art. 9 Abs. 3 VerbandsklageRL müssen diese nationalen Gesetze, zumindest in den Angelegenheiten, die unter den Anwendungsbereich der VerbandsklageRL fallen, die Verfügbarkeit der Opt-out-Gruppenklage einschränken und ausländische Kläger daraus ausschließen. Gemäß ErwGr. 11 VerbandsklageRL „sollte [die Richtlinie] bestehende nationale Verbandsklageverfahren zum Schutz der Kollektivinteressen oder der individuellen In-

[20] Nagy, Collective Actions in Europe – A Comparative, Economic and Transsystemic Analysis, 2014, S. 39.

[21] Nagy, Collective Actions in Europe – A Comparative, Economic and Transsystemic Analysis, 2014, S. 81–82.

teressen der Verbraucher nicht ersetzen“ und können die Mitgliedstaaten frei entscheiden, ob sie einen separaten, auf der VerbandsklageRL basierenden Mechanismus schaffen oder den auf der VerbandsklageRL basierenden Mechanismus zum Teil eines bestehenden Mechanismus machen. Unabhängig davon, welchen Ansatz sie wählen, müssen sie sicherstellen, dass der auf der VerbandsklageRL basierende Mechanismus den verbindlichen Vorschriften der VerbandsklageRL entspricht, einschließlich der Vorschrift, dass die Vorteile des Opt-out-Systems den ausländischen Gruppenmitgliedern entzogen werden sollen.

Es ist sehr schwierig, diese Diskriminierung zu rechtfertigen. Sicherlich gibt es technische und rechtliche Fragen, die in Bezug auf inländische Gruppenmitglieder leichter gelöst werden können. Es ist jedoch äußerst fraglich, ob diese wirklich so zwingend sind, die Ungleichbehandlung von Gruppenmitgliedern aufgrund ihres gewöhnlichen Aufenthalts zu rechtfertigen. Darüber hinaus hat diese Regel zur Folge, dass unabhängig davon, für welches Modell (Opt-in oder Opt-out) sich die Mitgliedstaaten aufgrund von Art. 9 Abs. 1 und 2 VerbandsklageRL entscheiden, das auf der VerbandsklageRL beruhende Verfahren in grenzüberschreitenden Angelegenheiten, die auch ausländische Verbraucher betreffen, nicht in vollem Umfang nach dem Opt-out-Prinzip stattfinden kann.

V. Schutzmaßnahmen gegen den Missbrauch der Verbandsklage

Wie bereits erwähnt, ist ein großer Teil der Regeln der VerbandsklageRL, die positive Vorschriften für die Gestaltung des bezweckten Mechanismus bestimmen, unverbindlich und sie können (aber müssen nicht) von den Mitgliedstaaten umgesetzt werden. Zu gleicher Zeit sind die negativen Vorschriften verbindlich.

Erstens sind, wie schon erwähnt, ausländische Verbraucher von dem Opt-out-Prinzip ausgeschlossen.

Zweitens ermächtigt die VerbandsklageRL die Gerichte oder Verwaltungsbehörden, „offensichtlich unbegründete Klagen in einem möglichst frühen Verfahrensstadium nach dem nationalen Recht ab[zu]weisen.“[22] Die Botschaft und der Nutzen dieser Vorschrift sind zweifelhaft. Sie macht deutlich, dass Gruppenkläger, im Vergleich zu Einzelklägern, Bürger zweiter Klasse sind, obwohl Einzelklagen über einen hohen Wert ebenso geneigt (oder nicht geneigt) sind missbraucht zu werden, wie hochwertige Gruppenklagen. Noch wichtiger ist jedoch, dass, angesichts des ausgesprochen minimalistischen Ansatzes der VerbandsklageRL und der übertriebenen (oder unnötigen) Garantien, die obige Aussiebungspflicht überflüssig scheint.

Drittens enthält Art. 10 VerbandsklageRL Regeln über die Drittfinanzierung. Diese Vorschriften bestimmen nicht, wie, sondern wie Gruppenklagen nicht finanziert werden können. Der Zweck dieser Regeln ist nicht, einen praktikablen Finanzierungsmechanismus zu schaffen. Ganz im Gegenteil, sie legen Verbote und Einschränkungen fest. Das ist umso bedauerlicher, als die Finanzierung eine

[22] Art. 7 Abs. 7 VerbandsklageRL.

entscheidende oder sogar die entscheidende Frage der Gruppenklagen ist.[23] Die VerbandsklageRL versucht nicht, die finanzielle Lebensfähigkeit der Verbandsklagen sicherzustellen, sondern legt es fest, wie diese nicht finanziert werden können. Sie schließt marktbasierte private Finanzierungssysteme tatsächlich aus, ohne einen Ersatz anzubieten. Die VerbandsklageRL legt nahe, dass die beste Finanzierungmethode das öffentliche Geld und philanthropische Spenden sind. Diese sind zwar ideale Quellen, aber können die nachhaltige Finanzierung von kollektiven Mechanismen nicht sicherstellen. Wenn die Finanzierung aus dem öffentlichen Haushalt erfolgt, stellt sich zudem die Frage, ob der Staat nicht einfach private Verträge nutzt, um seine eigenen Pflichten zu erfüllen.

Viertens, als Teil der Anstrengung, die Missbräuche auszuschließen, warnt die VerbandsklageRL nachdrücklich vor Strafschadensersatz und verbietet die Befreiung des Gruppenvertreters von der Haftung für Prozesskosten.

Der Ausschluss des Strafschadensersatzes wird im Haupttext der VerbandsklageRL nicht erwähnt, aber in der Präambel eindeutig gemacht. Laut ErwGr. 10 VerbandsklageRL: „Um den Missbrauch von Verbandsklagen zu verhindern, sollte die Gewährung von Strafschadenersatz vermieden werden und Vorschriften zu bestimmten Verfahrensaspekten, wie der Benennung und der Finanzierung qualifizierter Einrichtungen, festgelegt werden." ErwGr. 42 VerbandsklageRLfügt hinzu, dass die VerbandsklageRL „es nicht ermöglichen [sollte], dem zuwiderhandelnden Unternehmer nach nationalem Recht Strafschadenersatz aufzuerlegen."

Art. 12 Abs. 1 VerbandsklageRL lautet: „Die Mitgliedstaaten stellen sicher, dass die in einer Verbandsklage auf Abhilfeentscheidungen unterliegende Partei die von der obsiegenden Partei getragenen Verfahrenskosten nach Maßgabe der im geltenden nationalen Recht für Gerichtsverfahren im Allgemeinen vorgesehenen Bedingungen und Ausnahmen zahlt." Es ist zu betonen, dass diese Vorschrift für den Gruppenvertreter gilt, während Art. 12 Abs. 2 VerbandsklageRL die einzelnen Gruppenmitglieder von der Tragung der Verfahrenskosten ausdrücklich befreit. Ausnahmen von dieser Regel sind „die durch Vorsatz oder Fahrlässigkeit des einzelnen Verbrauchers verursacht[en]" Kosten.[24] Darüber hinaus können die Mitgliedstaaten vorschreiben, dass beitretende Gruppenmitglieder „eine moderate Beitrittsgebühr oder eine vergleichbare Gebühr" zahlen sollen.[25]

Der Strafschadensersatz, inklusive der „Punitive damages" und „Treble damages (dreifacher Schadensersatz), und die asymmetrische Haftung für Prozesskosten sind eine Besonderheit des US-Amerikanischen Rechts und werden zum Teil für die angeblichen Funktionsstörungen der „Class actions" verantwortlich gemacht.[26] Der Strafschadensersatz durchbricht den Grundsatz der ungerechtfertigten Bereicherung und gewährt dem Geschädigten einen höheren Schadensersatz als er für den erlittenen Schaden bekommen könnte. In den Vereinigten Staaten, gilt die asymmetrische Haftung für Prozesskosten auf bestimmten Gebieten, wie zB im

[23] Nagy CJEL (Columbia Journal of European Law) 19/3 (2013), 469 (482–483).
[24] Art. 12 Abs. 3 VerbandsklageRL.
[25] Art. 20 Abs. 3 VerbandsklageRL.
[26] Siehe Nagy CJEL 19/3 (2013), 469 (483–485); Udvary, Pro Actione Collectiva, 2015, S. 177–198.

Kartellrecht, und impliziert, dass für die Prozesskosten nur der Beklage haftet, die er im Falle seiner Sachfälligkeit zu erstatten hat, während der Kläger die Anwaltskosten des Beklagten nicht zu erstatten hat, auch wenn er sachfällig wird. Der Ausschluss dieses Rechtsinstituts erschien schon in der Empfehlung,[27] Dessen Rechtfertigung ist aber höchst fraglich und zweifelhaft: sie stellt ein gutes Beispiel für „regulatorisches Schattenboxen" dar. Die VerbandsklageRL bringt keinen wirksamen kollektiven Mechanismus zustande und schreibt nichts vor, was über das europäische Minimum hinausgehen würde. Das von der VerbandsklageRL ins Leben gerufene System braucht keine Schutzmaßnahmen gegen Missbrauch, da es unter wesentlichen Funktionsfähigkeitsproblemen leidet. Darüber hinaus sind der Strafschadensersatz und die asymmetrische Haftung für Prozesskosten in Europa im Grunde genommen ohnehin unbekannt.

VI. Schlussfolgerungen: Was ist eigentlich der Mehrwert der VerbandsklageRL?

Alles in allem stehen die Vorschriften der VerbandsklageRL im Widerspruch zu ihrem Ziel, ein praktikables System zu schaffen. Das von ihr eingeführte System bleibt hinter den bereits bestehenden Regulierungsergebnissen der Europäischen Mitgliedsstaaten zurück. Fast zwei Drittel der Mitgliedstaaten haben eine Gruppenklageordnung und die Mehrheit dieser übersteigt das konservative und minimalistische Model der VerbandsklageRL.[28] Darüber hinaus ist ein großer Teil der positiven Regeln der VerbandsklageRL eher unverbindlich und legt nur Regulierungsmöglichkeit fest, die die Mitgliedstaaten umsetzen „können." Das steht im Gegensatz zu dem verbindlichen Charakter der negativen Regeln, die Schutzmaßnahmen gegen die eventuellen Missbräuche bestimmen. Glücklicherweise schränkt die VerbandsklageRL die Mitgliedstaaten nicht ein, kollektive Verfahrenssysteme ihrer Wahl und Präferenz zu haben, unter der Voraussetzung, dass sie über mindestens einen, der VerbandsklageRL entsprechenden kollektiven Mechanismus verfügen. Gemäß Art. 1 Abs. 2 VerbandsklageRL sollen die Mitgliedstaaten sicherstellen, „dass *mindestens ein Verfahrensmechanismus,* der es qualifizierten Einrichtungen ermöglicht, sowohl Unterlassungs- als auch Rechtsbehelfsklagen zu erheben, mit dieser Richtlinie in Einklang steht."[29] Darüber hinaus enthält die VerbandsklageRL einen Nichtregression-Grundsatz („Rückschrittverbot"), im Sinne dessen zielt die VerbandsklageRL nicht darauf ab, die bereits bestehenden Errungenschaften der Bewegung für kollektiven Rechtsschutz zu beeinträchtigen.[30]

Im Einklang mit diesem Minimalismus in der VerbandsklageRL ist die Festlegung „angemessener Schutzmaßnahmen zur Verhinderung von Klagemiss-

---

[27] Empfehlung der Kommission 2013/396/EU, Abs. 13 und 29–31, ABl. 2013 L 201, 60; laut der Empfehlung können Erfolgshonorare nur ausnahmsweise zugelassen werden.

[28] Nagy, Collective Actions in Europe – A Comparative, Economic and Transsystemic Analysis, 2014, S. 71-112.

[29] Hervorhebung hinzugefügt.

[30] Art. 1 Abs. 2 VerbandsklageRL.

brauch"[31] ebenso wichtig, wie die Verfügbarkeit des kollektiven Rechtsschutzes. In diesem Zusammenhang spielt der „Zugang der Verbraucher zur Justiz"[32] lediglich eine zweitrangige Rolle.

Ungeachtet dessen kann die VerbandsklageRL den kollektiven Rechtsschutz in Europe fördern, auch wenn sie hinter den Erwartungen offensichtlich zurückbleibt.

Der Großteil des Mehrwerts der VerbandsklageRL ist darauf zurückzuführen, dass dank der VerbandsklageRL, mindestens ein kollektiver Mechanismus in Verbraucherangelegenheiten zur Verfügung stehen muss (zumindest bezüglich der in Anh. I VerbandsklageRL aufgeführten Unionsrechtsakten). In einem Drittel der Mitgliedstaaten gibt es keinen kollektiven Rechtsschutzmechanismus.[33] In diesen Mitgliedstaaten wird die VerbandsklageRL einen wesentlichen Fortschritt bringen. Darüber hinaus kann die VerbandsklageRL als „regulatorischer Katalysator" betrachtet werden, da sie zur Überarbeitung der nationalen Rechte und zu einem erneuten grenzüberschreitenden Meinungs- und Erfahrungsaustausch führen kann.

Darüber hinaus enthält die VerbandsklageRL eine Reihe von Vorschriften von geringerer Bedeutung, die die Durchsetzung von Gruppenklagen erleichtern können.

Erstens sieht Art. 13 Abs. 5 VerbandsklageRL vor, dass die Kommunikationskosten des Gruppenvertreters zu den rechtlich anerkannten Prozesskosten gehören und somit erstattungsfähig sind. Die Kosten für die Gruppenvertreter mögen erheblich sein, insbesondere bei Opt-in-Verfahren und fraglich ist, ob diese Ausgaben, ohne spezifische Regeln, als Prozesskosten angesehen werden können. Gemäß Art. 13 Abs. 5 VerbandsklageRL sollen die Mitgliedstaaten sicherstellen, „dass die obsiegende Partei sich die Kosten für die Bereitstellung von Informationen für die Verbraucher im Rahmen der Verbandsklage (…) erstatten lassen kann."

Zweitens bestimmt Art. 16 VerbandsklageRL klare gläubigerfreundliche Regeln bezüglich der Verjährung. Verbandsklagen sollen die Verjährung hemmen oder unterbrechen. Obwohl diese Regel nicht völlig neu ist und aus den allgemeinen zivilrechtlichen Regeln über Verjährung abgeleitet werden können, macht Art. 16 VerbandsklageRL die Rechtslage deutlich.

Drittens errichtet Art. 18 VerbandsklageRL eine schwache Variante der US-amerikanischen „Discovery" (dh der gerichtlich angeordneten Vorlage von Beweismitteln), die ansonsten in den europäischen Zivilprozessrechten nicht allgemein verfügbar ist. Die Wirksamkeit dieser Regeln wird durch Sanktionen untermauert.[34]

Viertens stärkt Art. 19 VerbandsklageRL das Gewicht von Unterlassungsmaßnahmen, die in zivilrechtlichen Ländern ansonsten lediglich den allgemeinen Regeln der gerichtlichen Vollstreckung unterliegen, durch die Einführung von „wirksam[en], verhältnismäßig[en] und abschreckend[en]" Sanktionen.

---

[31] Art. 1 Abs. 1 VerbandsklageRL.

[32] Art. 1 Abs. 1 VerbandsklageRL.

[33] Nagy, Collective Actions in Europe – A Comparative, Economic and Transsystemic Analysis, 2014, S. 76.

[34] Art. 19 Abs. 1 lit. b VerbandsklageRL.

LINE OLSEN-RING

Elternschaftsvermutung und Implikationen im internationalen Privat- und Prozessrecht am Beispiel des schwedischen Rechts

I. *Einleitung*

Im Zuge veränderter Familienmuster, einer wachsenden Anerkennung der Geschlechtervielfalt, Innovationen der Fortpflanzungsmedizin sowie aufgrund einer gesteigerten Zahl geschlechtsverändernder Eingriffe und Therapien gerät das Abstammungsrecht vielerorts zum Gegenstand von Diskussionen und Reformüberlegungen. Die rechtliche Definition der Begriffe „Mutter“, „Vater“ und „Elternteil“ folgt in vielen Rechtsordnungen nicht mehr dem traditionellen Sprachgebrauch.

Während das Abstammungsrecht in Deutschland gegenwärtig keine gemeinsame Elternschaft gleichgeschlechtlicher Paare vorsieht, und gleichgeschlechtliche Eheleute bzw. eingetragene Lebenspartnerinnen und Lebenspartner nur über das Behelfskonstrukt einer (Stiefkind-)Adoption eine gemeinsame rechtliche Elternschaft erlangen können, hat der schwedische Gesetzgeber zum 1.1.2022 im Elterngesetz *(föräldrabalken)*[1] ein System der Elternschaftsvermutung für alle Verheiratete eingeführt. Weniger als ein Jahr später sind in Schweden auch die damit einhergehenden international-privat- und -prozessrechtlichen Bestimmungen zur Elternschaft verabschiedet worden.

Vor dem Hintergrund, dass in Deutschland die weitreichenden abstammungsrechtlichen Reformvorhaben im Koalitionsvertrag der Ampel-Regierung[2] noch nicht konkretisiert und aktuell rechtspolitische Diskussionen im Gange sind[3], mag ein Blick auf die schwedische Rechtslage von Interesse sein. Auch auf Gemeinschaftsebene ist die international-privat- und -prozessrechtliche Problemstellung der Thematik „Elternschaft“ durch den im Dezember 2022 von der EU-Kommission angenommenen Vorschlag für eine Verordnung des Rates über die Zuständigkeit, das anzuwendende

[1] Gesetz 1949:381.

[2] Womit auch „ein Kind, das in die Ehe zweier Frauen geboren wird, … automatisch zwei rechtliche Mütter haben [soll], sofern nichts anderes vereinbart ist“; nähere Informationen zu dem Reformvorhaben finden sich auf der Homepage des Bundesjustizministeriums, https://www.bmj.de/SharedDocs/Gesetzgebungsverfahren/DE/2024_Reform_Abstammungsrecht.html?nn=110518 (abgerufen am 19.8.2024), vgl. dort auch das entsprechende Eckpunktepapier des BMJ vom 16.1.2024.

[3] So haben bspw. im Mai 2023 der Deutsche Juristinnenbund (djb), die Initiative Nodoption (ein Zusammenschluss queerer Familien mit unterschiedlichen Elternkonstellationen), die Bundesarbeitsgemeinschaft Schwule Juristen (BASJ) und der Lesben- und Schwulenverband (LSVD), unterstützt ua vom Deutschen Kinderhilfswerk, den Bundestag zu einer Reform des geltenden Abstammungs- und Sorgerechts aufgefordert, näher Eydlin, Juristinnenverbände fordern Reform von Gesetzen zur Elternschaft, ZEIT ONLINE, 5.5.2023.

Recht, die Anerkennung von Entscheidungen und die Annahme öffentlicher Urkunden in Elternschaftssachen sowie zur Einführung eines europäischen Elternschaftszertifikats[4] in den Blickpunkt von Regelungsbestrebungen geraten.

II. Vaterschaft, Mutterschaft und „Elternschaft" nach dem schwedischen Elterngesetz

1. Vorbemerkungen

Das schwedische Elterngesetz (fortan: FB) regelt in seinem ersten Kapitel die „Vaterschaft und Mutterschaft eines Kindes". Die einschlägigen Vorschriften sind in den letzten Jahrzehnten mehrfach geändert worden, um die Konsequenzen für zulässig erklärte geschlechtsverändernde und reproduktionsmedizinische Methoden in abstammungsrechtlicher Hinsicht nachzuvollziehen. Die Fortschritte der (Reproduktions-)Medizin und die innerhalb kürzester Zeit geänderten gesellschaftlichen Vorstellungen darüber, was als ethisch vertretbar und rechtlich erlaubt anzusehen ist, sind im Gesetz selbst förmlich ablesbar. Der Regelungsgehalt des ersten Kapitels FB ist kontinuierlich angewachsen und mittlerweile nicht mehr ganz leicht überschaubar.

In zweierlei Hinsicht mag die ansonsten sehr modern ausgestaltete schwedische Gesetzgebung dem Leser allerdings eher konservativ erscheinen: Das schwedische Recht erkennt zum einen auch heute noch nur zwei Geschlechter – männlich und weiblich – an. Angesichts der grundsätzlichen Bereitschaft des schwedischen Gesetzgebers, auch umwälzende Änderungen im Familien- und Abstammungsrecht vorzunehmen, dürfte dies weniger politisch-ethischen Vorstellungen, denn vor allem praktischen Überlegungen geschuldet sein[5].

Zum anderen kann ein Kind nach wie vor höchstens zwei rechtliche Elternteile *(föräldra)* haben. Mit der rechtlichen Elternschaft sind vor allem die elterliche Sorge und die Vormundschaft für das Kind (und damit bspw. auch akzessorische sozialsicherungsrechtliche Rechte), das Erbrecht des Kindes und jenes der Eltern sowie Unterhaltspflichten gegenüber dem Kind[6] verbunden.

---

[4] COM(2022) 695 final.

[5] Größere Schwierigkeiten dürfte bspw. das schwedische Personenidentifikationssystem bereiten. In Schweden wird (wie in den übrigen nordischen Staaten auch), allen im Land registrierten Personen eine Personenidentifikationsnummer zugewiesen, die in vielfältigsten Zusammenhängen zur Anwendung gelangt. An der Identifikationsnummer ist bereits an einer Chiffre erkennbar, ob die in Rede stehende Person männlich oder weiblich ist. Im Bericht einer von der Regierung eingesetzten Expertenkommission, die Vorschläge für eine Stärkung und verbesserte Lebensbedingungen von Transpersonen in Schweden erarbeiten sollte (SOU 2017:92, *Transpersoner i Sverige, Förslag för stärkt ställning och bättre levnadsvillkor*), wurde ua eine Neuausrichtung des Systems angeregt, wonach das Geschlecht einer Person nicht länger an deren Identifikationsnummer ablesbar sein soll. Eine solche Umstellung dürfte, so die Stellungnahme der für die Melderegister zuständigen schwedischen Steuerverwaltung *(Skatteverket),* allerdings eine längere Vorlaufzeit erfordern. Dabei seien auch Aufwand und Kosten – nötige Neuentwicklung einschlägiger IT-Systeme usw. – mit zu berücksichtigen. Vgl. näher SOU 1917:92, abrufbar auf der Homepage der schwedischen Regierung (Stichwort: Remiss SOU 2017:92).

[6] In Schweden, wie in den übrigen nordischen Staaten auch, bestehen hingegen keine Unterhaltspflichten des Kindes gegenüber seinen Eltern.

2. *Vaterschaftsvermutung bei ungeänderter Geschlechtszugehörigkeit*

In Bezug auf die Vaterschaft gilt nach römischrechtlichem Vorbild eine *pater est*-Regel. So bestimmt 1:1 S. 1 Hs. 1 FB Folgendes: „Ist die Mutter im Zeitpunkt der Geburt des Kindes mit einem Mann verheiratet, wird dieser als der Vater angesehen". Dies gilt gemäß 1:1 S. 2 FB gleichermaßen, „falls die Mutter Witwe ist, und das Kind innerhalb eines solchen Zeitraums nach dem Tod des Mannes geboren wird, dass es von ihm gezeugt sein kann".

Die Vaterschaftsvermutung nach 1:1 FB kann zunächst in besonderen Konstellationen gerichtlich entkräftet werden. Gemäß 1:2 I FB ist die Vermutung dann widerlegt,

- wenn feststeht, dass die Mutter während der Empfängniszeit einem anderen Mann beigewohnt hat und es unter Berücksichtigung aller Umstände wahrscheinlich ist, dass das Kind durch diese Beiwohnung gezeugt wurde;
- es aufgrund der genetischen Eigenschaften des Kindes bzw. eines anderen besonderen Umstandes als sicher angesehen werden kann, dass der Ehemann nicht der Vater des Kindes ist; bzw.
- wenn das Kind vor der Ehe oder während des Getrenntlebens der Eheleute gezeugt wurde und es unwahrscheinlich ist, dass diese während des Zeitraums, in dem das Kind gezeugt worden sein kann, einander beigewohnt haben.

Die Vaterschaftsvermutung kann außerdem dadurch widerlegt werden, dass der Ehemann die Anerkennung der Vaterschaft oder der Elternschaft nach 1:9 FB bzw. der Mutterschaft nach 1:14 FB, die von einer anderen Person erklärt worden ist, formgerecht bestätigt. Die betreffende Anerkennung muss jedoch immer von der Mutter schriftlich genehmigt werden (1:2 II FB).

Die Vaterschaftsvermutung für den Ehemann gilt auch im Falle einer Insemination oder künstlichen Befruchtung außerhalb des Körpers.

Bezüglich einer assistierten Reproduktion sei noch darauf hingewiesen, dass im Zusammenhang mit der Anerkennung[7] oder Feststellung einer Vaterschaft (nach Maßgabe von 1:2–1:5 FB) der Ehemann bzw. der mit der Mutter in eheähnlicher Lebensgemeinschaft lebende Partner (fortan: *sambo*)[8] gemäß 1:8 I FB als Vater des

---

[7] Ist das Kind minderjährig (dh hat es noch nicht das 18. Lebensjahr vollendet), muss die Vaterschaftsanerkennung – die auch bereits vor der Geburt des Kindes ausgesprochen werden kann – zwar gemäß 1:4 FB grundsätzlich schriftlich und persönlich vor der Sozialbehörde, *Socialnämnd,* erfolgen. Die anschließende Bestätigung der Behörde darf aber nur erteilt werden, wenn anzunehmen ist, dass der Mann tatsächlich der Vater des Kindes ist. Ist das Kind volljährig, muss die Anerkennung schriftlich erfolgen, von zwei Personen bezeugt und anschließend schriftlich vom Kind selbst genehmigt werden. Seit dem 1.1.2022 ermöglicht 1:4a FB aber auch eine einfache digitale Vaterschaftsanerkennung, wenn Mutter und Vater beide im Zeitpunkt der Geburt in Schweden wohnhaft gemeldet sind, und dies im Zeitpunkt der Abgabe der Vaterschaftsanerkennung ebenfalls für das Kind gilt. Diese Vaterschaftsanerkennung muss – ebenfalls digital – von der Mutter genehmigt werden; Anerkennung und Genehmigung haben spätestens vierzehn Tage nach der Geburt des Kindes zu erfolgen.

[8] Im schwedischen Recht werden unter dem Begriff *sambor* nach § 1 des Gesetzes über Zusammenlebende (Gesetz 2003:376 – *sambolag*) zwei Personen verstanden, die als Paar (unabhängig von ihrer sexuellen Orientierung) dauerhaft (unter eheähnlichen Verhältnissen) zusammenwohnen und einen gemeinsamen Haushalt führen. Nach den Gesetzesvorarbeiten soll das Kriterium der

Kindes anzusehen ist, wenn sich die Mutter einer entsprechenden Behandlung mit Zustimmung ihres Ehemanns bzw. *sambo* unterzogen hatte, und es unter Berücksichtigung sämtlicher Umstände wahrscheinlich ist, dass das Kind durch diese Behandlung gezeugt wurde. Erfolgte die Behandlung mit Samen eines anderen Mannes, gelten weitere Voraussetzungen: Der Ehemann bzw. *sambo* wird dann nur als Vater des Kindes angesehen, wenn die Behandlung in Übereinstimmung mit den Vorgaben des Gesetzes über die genetische Integrität[9] oder aber an einer zuständigen Einrichtung im Ausland erfolgt ist, und das Kind berechtigt ist, Zugang zu Informationen über den Samenspender zu erhalten (1:8 II FB).

3. *Mutterschaftsvermutung bei ungeänderter Geschlechtszugehörigkeit*

In Schweden gilt als ungeschriebene Mutterschaftsvermutung, dass die Frau, die ein Kind gebärt, als dessen Mutter anzusehen ist *(mater est quam gestatio demonstrat).*

Im Jahre 2002 wurde erstmalig eine Bestimmung über die Mutterschaft in das FB aufgenommen[10]. Dies geschah im Zusammenhang mit Änderungen der rechtlichen Rahmenbedingungen für eine künstliche Befruchtung, womit eine Eizellenspende erlaubt wurde[11]. Die damit geschaffene legale Möglichkeit einer Frau, ein Kind zu gebären, ohne dessen genetische Mutter zu sein, hat den Gesetzgeber zur Aufnahme einer Mutterschaftsregel in FB veranlasst. Statt die allgemeine ungeschriebene Mutterschaftsvermutung zu kodifizieren[12] wurde in 1:7 FB bestimmt, dass „eine Frau [die] ein Kind gebärt, das durch eine außerhalb des Körpers erfolgte Befruchtung einer von einer anderen Frau stammenden Eizelle gezeugt worden ist, wonach das Ei in ihren Körper eingeführt worden ist, als Mutter des Kindes“ gilt.

1:7 FB beinhaltet in der Praxis nach schwedischem materiellem Recht die Unzulässigkeit einer Leihmutterschaft. Ein ausdrückliches gesetzliches Verbot einer solchen Mutterschaft existiert hingegen nicht[13].

Dauerhaftigkeit bereits dann erfüllt sein, wenn die Partner beabsichtigen, dauerhaft zusammen zu leben.

[9] *Lag 2006:351 om genetisk integritet m.m.*

[10] *Lag 2002:251 om ändring i föräldrabalken.*

[11] *Lag 2002:252 om ändring i lagen (1988:711) om befruktning utanför kroppen.*

[12] Nach Ansicht des schwedischen Gesetzgebungsrats *(lagrådet)* sei eine solche allgemeine Kodifizierung „nicht notwendig“, Prop. 2001/02:89, 4.6.1.

[13] Obwohl die Anerkennung einer ausländischen Feststellung einer Vater- oder Elternschaft in Schweden nach der Rechtsprechung prinzipiell eine ausdrückliche Gesetzesgrundlage verlangt (NJA 1974, 324), hat das schwedische Oberste Gericht *(Högsta Domstolen)* in zwei Fällen ein ausländisches Urteil, das jeweils der sog. „Wunschmutter“ nach einer im Ausland erfolgten Leihmutterschaft die Mutterschaft zusprach, anerkannt (NJA 2019, 504 und NJA 2019, 969). In einem späteren, von der schwedischen Regierung in Auftrag gegebenen, Kommissionsbericht, SOU 2021:56, Neue Regeln über ausländische Elternschaft und Adoptionen in gewissen Fällen, *Nya regler om utländska föräldraskap och adoption i vissa fall,* ist vorgeschlagen worden, im internationalen Abstammungsrecht zu bestimmen, dass eine Frau, die nach dem Gesetz des Staates, in dem das Kind geboren wurde, als dessen Mutter anzusehen ist, obwohl sie das Kind nicht geboren hat und auch nicht mit der gebärenden Frau verheiratet oder deren *sambo* gewesen ist, auch in Schweden als die Kindesmutter gilt, wenn sie im Zusammenhang mit der Geburt mindestens ein Jahr lang ihren Wohnsitz und ununterbrochenen Aufenthalt in dem ausländischen Staat hatte (§ 2c LFI-

4. „Elternschaftsvermutung“ bei ungeänderter Geschlechtszugehörigkeit

Durch eine Gesetzesreform zum 1.1.2022[14] ist nunmehr auch für verheiratete weibliche Paare eine Elternschaftsvermutung eingeführt worden. Ist die Mutter mit einer Frau verheiratet bzw. lebt sie mit einer Frau in registrierter Partnerschaft zusammen, wird ihre Ehefrau/registrierte Partnerin nach 1:9 I FB nunmehr automatisch als (zweiter) Elternteil des Kindes angesehen. Dies gilt gleichermaßen, „falls die Mutter Witwe ist, und das Kind innerhalb eines solchen Zeitraums nach dem Tod der Frau der Mutter geboren wird, dass es vor dem Todeszeitpunkt gezeugt sein kann“. Es gilt damit ein parallel zur *pater est*-Regel ausgestaltetes Modell.

Der schwedische Gesetzgeber hat dabei die Verwendung der Bezeichnung „Elternteil“ *(förälder)* statt „Mutter“ *(mor)* für die Ehefrau/registrierte Partnerin der gebärenden Person gewählt, um Missverständnisse bei der Anwendung anderer gesetzlicher Vorschriften, welche auf die gebärende Person Bezug nehmen, zu vermeiden.

Zuvor waren im Jahre 2005 Bestimmungen über eine gemeinsame „Elternschaft“ *(föräldraskap)* für registrierte Partnerinnen und *sambor* im Falle einer künstlichen Befruchtung eingeführt worden. Deren Inhalt wurde parallel zur damaligen Regelung der Vaterschaft bei assistierter Reproduktion abgefasst. Diese Vorschriften sind gleichzeitig mit der Einführung des Rechtsinstituts der geschlechtsneutralen Ehe im Jahre 2009[15] auf Ehepartnerinnen erweitert worden. Sie finden sich in 1:9 FB.

Gemäß 1:9a FB muss iÜ gerichtlich erklärt werden, dass eine Frau, die nach der Vermutungsregel in 1:9 FB als zweiter Elternteil anzusehen wäre, dennoch nicht Elternteil des Kindes ist, wenn eine Insemination oder eine Befruchtung außerhalb des Körpers der Mutter stattgefunden hat, die Behandlung aber die gesetzlichen Anforderungen hierfür nicht erfüllt hat, oder die Mutter eine solche Behandlung nicht erhalten hat (1:9a I FB). Die vermutete Elternschaft kann außerdem – parallel zur Regelung bei der Vaterschaft – dadurch widerlegt werden, dass die zweite Frau die Anerkennung der Vaterschaft oder der Elternschaft nach 1:9 FB bzw. der Mutterschaft gemäß 1:14 FB, die von einer anderen Person formgerecht erklärt worden ist, bestätigt. Die betreffende Anerkennung muss jedoch immer von der Mutter schriftlich genehmigt werden (1:9a II 2 FB).

Entwurf); vgl. näher SOU 2021:56, 145ff. Damit sollte einerseits dem Kinder- und Familienschutz Rechnung getragen werden und andererseits eine allzu leichte Umgehung des nationalen materiellen Rechts, das keine Leihmutterschaft vorsieht, verhindert werden. Diesen Vorschlag hat die Regierung aber *nicht* aufgegriffen.

[14] *Lag 2021:783 om ändring av föräldrabalken.*

[15] *Lag 2009:253 om ändring i äktenskapsbalken.*

5. *Vaterschaft und Mutterschaft bei geänderter Geschlechtszugehörigkeit*

a) Vorgeschichte

Als weltweit erstes Land verabschiedete Schweden im Jahre 1972 ein Gesetz, das die Änderung des rechtlichen Geschlechts einer Person[16] (fortan: Gesetz über die Geschlechtszugehörigkeit) ermöglichte. Eine Geschlechtsänderung wurde allerdings an die Erfüllung tiefgreifender Voraussetzungen geknüpft. Bis zum Jahr 2013[17] (!) musste eine Person, um die Feststellung einer geänderten Geschlechtszugehörigkeit beantragen zu können, (§ 1 des Gesetzes über die Geschlechtszugehörigkeit aF), zeugungsunfähig sein. Die Aufhebung dieser Verpflichtung erfolgte erst, nachdem der Menschenrechtskommissar des Europarats im Jahre 2009 hieran Kritik geäußert und Ende 2012 das Oberverwaltungsgericht Stockholm[18] festgestellt hatte, dass die Zeugungsunfähigkeitsvoraussetzung sowohl gegen das schwedische verfassungsrechtliche Verbot eines aufgezwungenen körperlichen Eingriffs (2:6 RF) als auch gegen Art. 8 und Art. 14 der EMRK verstößt. Entsprechende Reformüberlegungen hatte die schwedische Regierung zwar auch schon selbst im Frühjahr 2012 angestellt[19]. Man hielt jedoch zunächst an der Voraussetzung fest, um im Vorfeld einer Änderung des Gesetzes über die Geschlechtszugehörigkeit kompatible abstammungsrechtliche Regeln im FB zu erarbeiten. Nachdem das Urteil des Oberverwaltungsgerichts ergangen war, schaffte der Gesetzgeber dann aber doch zeitnah und ohne gleichzeitige Änderung des Abstammungsrechts die Verpflichtung ab mit dem Hinweis, dass die bisherigen Bestimmungen und Prinzipien „analog Anwendung finden" könnten. In der Praxis löste die Neuregelung allerdings anfänglich Probleme bei der Personenregistrierung aus. So hatte die Steuerverwaltung *(Skatteverket)* – die in Schweden für die Führung der Personenstandsbücher zuständig ist – eine Person, die nach der Änderung ihres Geschlechts von weiblich auf männlich ein Kind geboren hatte, zunächst in Übereinstimmung mit dem Prinzip *mater semper est quam gestatio demonstrat* als Mutter des Kindes registriert. Im Jahre 2016 änderte die Verwaltung allerdings ihre Praxis und registrierte fortan die gebärende Person als „Vater" oder „Mutter" in Übereinstimmung mit der von ihr gewählten und registrierten juristischen Geschlechtszugehörigkeit[20].

b) Abstammungsrechtliche Neuregelungen

Eine gesetzliche Klarstellung erfolgte erst zum 1.1.2019, als in 1:10–1:14 FB Vorschriften zur „Vaterschaft und Mutterschaft bei geänderter Geschlechtszugehörigkeit" eingeführt wurden[21]. Relevant sind diese dann, wenn eine oder

---

[16] Gesetz 1972:119 über die Feststellung der Geschlechtszugehörigkeit in bestimmten Fällen *(Lag om fastställande av könstillhörighet i vissa fall)*.

[17] *Lag 2013:405 om ändring af lag om fastställande av könstillhörighet i vissa fall.*

[18] *Kammerrätten Stockholm,* mål nr. 1968-12.

[19] Gesetzentwurf zur Änderung des Gesetzes über die Geschlechtszugehörigkeit, prop. 2011/12:142.

[20] Prop. 2017/18:155, 57 mit Verweis auf die Stellungnahme der Steuerverwaltung.

[21] *Lag 2018:1279 om ändring av föräldrabalken.*

beide Personen ihr juristisches Geschlecht geändert hat/haben aber in biologischer Hinsicht noch ihrem alten Geschlecht zugehört/zugehören.

Für Personen, die nach Änderung ihrer juristischen Geschlechtszugehörigkeit als Mann zu qualifizieren sind (in den gesetzlichen Vorarbeiten als „Frau auf Mann" bezeichnet; fortan: FaM), bestimmt 1:11 FB seitdem Folgendes: „Wenn ein Mann ein Kind gebärt, ist er als Vater des Kindes anzusehen. Für den Mann gilt jedoch das, was in anderen Kapiteln des FB sowie in anderen Gesetzen über die Mutter und die Mutterschaft bestimmt ist". Ein Mann, der die Voraussetzungen in 1:5 FB (Vaterschaftsfeststellung im Urteilswege) oder 1:8 FB (Vaterschaftsfeststellung im Falle einer künstlichen Befruchtung) erfüllt, ist als Vater des Kindes anzusehen.

Für eine Person, die nach einer Änderung der Geschlechtszugehörigkeit als Frau zu qualifizieren ist (fortan: MaF) – aber durch eigene Spermien zur Zeugung des Kindes beigetragen hat, bzw. die Einwilligung in eine künstliche Befruchtung ihrer Ehepartnerin/ihres Ehepartners bzw. *sambo* erteilt hat – gilt nach 1:14 FB eine parallele Regelung. 1:14 I FB lautet wie folgt: „Eine Frau, die die Voraussetzungen nach 1:5 bzw. 1:8 FB erfüllt [dh Vaterschaftsfeststellung durch Urteil oder im Falle einer künstlichen Befruchtung] ist als Mutter des Kindes anzusehen. Für die Frau gilt jedoch das, was in anderen Kapiteln des FB sowie in anderen Gesetzen über den Vater und die Vaterschaft bestimmt ist".

Nach 1:14 II FB wird die Mutterschaft der MaF bei nicht-verheirateten Paaren durch Anerkennung bzw. im Urteilswege festgestellt. Geht es um eine Mutterschaftsanerkennung, finden die Vorschriften in 1:4–4b FB über die Vaterschaftsanerkennung entsprechend Anwendung.

In einer Paarbeziehung – gebärende Person und MaF – kann es nach der schwedischen Rechtsterminologie also zwei Mütter geben. Von der Begrifflichkeit „Mutter und [zweiter] Elternteil", die auf lesbische Paare Anwendung findet, in denen keine der beiden Personen eine geänderte Geschlechtszugehörigkeit hat, wird in diesem Fall also abgewichen. Im Abstimmungsrecht ist es somit nicht nur in gesetzessystematischer, sondern auch in sprachlicher Hinsicht zu einem „Flickenteppich" gekommen.

Bereits im Zusammenhang mit der Ausarbeitung der Vorschriften über Vaterschaft und Mutterschaft bei geänderter Geschlechtszugehörigkeit war überlegt worden, eine geschlechtsneutrale, für alle verheiratete Paare geltende Elternschaftsvermutung einzuführen. Der Gesetzgeber nahm aber zum damaligen Zeitpunkt letzten Endes hiervon Abstand und verwies dabei vor allem darauf, dass die Vaterschaftsvermutung auf dem Gedanken aufbaut, dass durch die *pater est*-Regel in den meisten Fällen der genetische Vater auch der rechtliche Vater des Kindes sein wird[22].

Wenige Jahre später wurde die Bedeutung der genetischen Verbindung zwischen Eltern und Kind neu bewertet. Der Gesetzgeber betonte jetzt, dass bereits nach geltender Rechtslage im Falle einer künstlichen Befruchtung sowohl die Begründung einer Vaterschaft als auch die Begründung einer anderen Elternschaft im Umstand der Einwilligung des Partners/der Partnerin lag, und dass die *pater est*-Regel auch

[22] Prop. 2017/18:155, 60.

dann griff, wenn die Befruchtung durch die Samenspende eines Dritten erfolgt war. Konsequenterweise sollte das Fehlen einer genetischen Verbindung zwischen Kind und angedachtem Elternteil daher kein Hindernis mehr für eine Elternschaftsvermutung sein[23].

Zum 1.1.2022 wurde dann der große Schritt vollzogen: Es gilt seitdem im Hinblick auf alle Ehepaare eine Vater- bzw. Mutter- oder Elternschaftsvermutung für die nicht-gebärende Person. Durch die Gesetzesreform[24] wurde nach der vorab beschriebenen Elternschaftsvermutung bei gleichgeschlechtlichen weiblichen Ehepaaren (1:9 I FB) nach 1:11a FB auch eine Elternschaftsvermutung für Ehepaare eingeführt, bei denen eine oder beide Personen die Geschlechtszugehörigkeit geändert hat/haben.

Bezweckt wird damit eine grundsätzliche abstammungsrechtliche Gleichstellung, bei der „nicht ohne Vorliegen schwerwiegender Gründe Unterscheidungen aufgrund der sexuellen Veranlagung oder des Geschlechts" vorgenommen werden sollen[25]. Im Fokus hatte der Gesetzgeber dabei auch das Recht auf Schutz des Privat- und Familienlebens nach der EMRK und die Vorgaben der UN-Kinderrechtskonvention über Antidiskriminierung[26]. Sowohl die EMRK als auch die UN-Kinderrechtskonvention gelten in Schweden mit Gesetzesrang.

Für den Fall, dass die mit der gebärenden Person verheiratete Person ein Mann ist, bestimmt 1:11a I FB Folgendes: „Wenn die Person, die das Kind geboren hat, im Zeitpunkt der Geburt mit einem Mann verheiratet ist, ist der Mann als Vater des Kindes anzusehen. Dasselbe gilt dann, wenn die Person, die das Kind geboren hat, Witwe oder Witwer ist, und das Kind innerhalb eines solchen Zeitraums nach dem Tod des Mannes geboren wird, dass es vor diesem Zeitpunkt gezeugt sein kann". Für den Fall, dass die mit der gebärenden Person verheiratete Person eine Frau ist, gilt nach der Parallelregelung des 1:11a II FB Folgendes: „Wenn die Person, die das Kind geboren hat, im Zeitpunkt der Geburt mit einer Frau verheiratet ist, ist die Frau als Mutter des Kindes anzusehen. Dasselbe gilt dann, wenn die Person, die das Kind geboren hat, Witwe oder Witwer ist, und das Kind innerhalb eines solchen Zeitraums nach dem Tod der Frau geboren wird, dass es vor dieser Zeit gezeugt sein kann. Für die Frau gilt jedoch das, was in anderen Kapiteln des FB sowie in anderen Gesetzen über den Vater und die Vaterschaft geregelt wird".

Die nach 1:11a FB vermutete Vater- oder Mutterschaft kann nach Maßgabe von 1:11b–d FB parallel zur Regelung in Konstellationen, in denen keine geänderte Geschlechtszugehörigkeit vorliegt, widerlegt werden.

---

[23] Prop. 2020/21:176, 26. Es sei noch angemerkt, dass es nach dem Gesetz über die genetische Integrität seit dem Jahre 2019 auch erlaubt ist, innerhalb des schwedischen Gesundheitswesens eine Befruchtung außerhalb des Körpers mit nur gespendetem Erbgut – Samen *und* Ei – durchführen zu lassen. Somit muss zwischen keinem Elternteil und dem Kind mehr eine genetische Verbindung bestehen.

[24] *Lag 2021:783 om ändring av föräldrabalken.*

[25] Prop. 2020/21:176, S. 25.

[26] Prop. 2020/21:176, S. 25. Daneben wollte der Gesetzgeber das Recht des Kindes, so weit wie möglich darüber Kenntnis erlangen zu können, wer dessen Eltern sind und unter deren Fürsorge stehen zu können, schützen.

Bei nicht-verheirateten Paarbeziehungen, in denen eine oder beide Personen ihre Geschlechtszugehörigkeit geändert haben, wird die Vater- oder Mutterschaft wie bei anderen Paaren ohne Trauschein durch Anerkennung bzw. im Urteilswege festgestellt[27].

III. Implikationen einer Elternschaftsvermutung im internationalen Privat- und Prozessrecht

Einleitungsweise sei angemerkt, dass das schwedische internationale Privat- und Prozessrecht keine Gesamtkodifikation erfahren hat. Es bestehen hingegen viele Einzelgesetze zu kleineren oder größeren Teilgebieten des IPR/IZPR. In einigen Bereichen ist Hauptrechtsquelle auch nicht die Gesetzgebung, sondern die Rechtsprechung – wobei die Anzahl von Entscheidungen allerdings überschaubar ist, und der oft rezitierende Stil der Urteilsbegründungen „Anlass zu vorsichtigen Spekulationen im Schrifttum gibt"[28].

Das internationalprivat- und -prozessrechtliche Familienrecht gehört aber zu den umfassend kodifizierten Bereichen. Im Abstammungsrecht finden sich drei einschlägige Gesetze, die alle – gut ein halbes Jahr nach Einführung der geschlechtsneutralen Elternschaftsvermutung im FB – zum 1.8.2022 geändert worden sind und in ihrem Titel nunmehr jeweils statt „Vaterschaft" die Begrifflichkeit „Elternschaft" tragen. Davon werden alle Eltern im Rechtssinne erfasst. In den Einzelvorschriften wird allerdings – wie im FB – jeweils von „Vaterschaft" und „Elternschaft" gesprochen.

Es handelt sich dabei um folgende Einzelgesetze:

- Gesetz 1985:367 über die Elternschaft in internationalen Verhältnissen (*lag om föräldraskap i internationella situationer,* fortan: LFI),
- Gesetz 1979:1001 über die Anerkennung nordischer Elternschaftsentscheidungen *(lag om erkännande av nordiska föräldraskapsavgöranden),* das innerhalb seines Anwendungsbereichs bei innernordischen Sachverhalten eine Anwendung der Vorschriften des Gesetzes 1985:367 verdrängt, sowie
- Gesetz 1977:595 über die Anerkennung und Vollstreckung nordischer Urteile auf dem Gebiet des Privatrechts *(lag om erkännande och verkställighet av nordiska domar på privaträttens område).*

---

[27] Geht es dabei um eine Vaterschaftsanerkennung einer FaM, bestimmt 1:13 II FB, dass die Vorschriften in 1:4–4b FB über die Vaterschaftsanerkennung in Fällen, in denen keine Änderung der Geschlechtszugehörigkeit vorliegt, entsprechende Anwendung finden. Geht es um die Mutterschaft einer MaF, werden die Vorschriften in 1:4–4b FB über die Vaterschaftsanerkennung gleichermaßen entsprechend herangezogen (1:14 II FB). Bei der Anwendung von 1:4 FB und 1:4a FB (Vaterschaftsanerkennung vor der Sozialbehörde bzw. auf digitalem Wege), 1:5 FB (Vaterschaftsfeststellung im Urteilswege) und 1:8 FB (Vaterschaftsfestellung im Falle einer künstlichen Befruchtung) gilt das, was in diesem Rahmen für eine Mutter bestimmt ist, (auch) für eine nach 1:11 FB als Mann zu qualifizierende Person (1:14 Abs 3 FB).

[28] So treffend Bogdan/Wong, Swedish Legal System, 2. Aufl. 2022, S. 448.

Die beiden letztgenannten Gesetze stellen niedrigere Anforderungen an die Anerkennung einer Elternschaftsentscheidung aus einem anderen nordischen Staat[29] als das LFI an entsprechende Entscheidungen anderer Staaten. Diese Unterscheidung erleichtert Familienumzüge innerhalb des Nordens und beruht auf der Annahme, dass die grundlegenden familien- und prozessrechtlichen Prinzipien in Verfahren der nordischen Staaten beachtet worden sind.[30]

Um Probleme und Unsicherheiten beim Zuzug von Familien nach Schweden entgegenzuwirken und Diskriminierungen aufgrund von Geschlecht oder sexueller Veranlagung zu verhindern, wurde im Lichte der Neuregelung von Sachverhalten mit reinem Inlandsbezug eine möglichst gleichförmige Regulierung für internationale Fallgestaltungen bezweckt. Für grenzüberschreitende Sachverhalte wurde aber neben der EMRK und der UN-Kinderrechtskonvention auch das Recht auf Freizügigkeit innerhalb der EU in den Blick genommen.

Die gesetzgeberische Intention rankt sich um die Schlagworte Gleichstellung, Inklusion und Zweckmäßigkeit[31]. Hingegen sollte aber ausdrücklich *nicht* „die Etablierung aller denkbaren Formern einer ausländischen Elternschaft" in Schweden ermöglicht werden[32]. Die Vorschriften über die Elternschaft in internationalen Verhältnissen nehmen auch keinen Bezug auf registrierte Partnerschaften und andere hiermit vergleichbare Institute. Bereits im Zusammenhang mit der Einführung der geschlechtsneutralen Ehe in Schweden im Jahre 2009 war der Gesetzgeber zum Ergebnis gekommen, dass die Frage, unter welchen Umständen ein im Ausland erlangter rechtlicher Status in Schweden anerkannt werden und welche Rechtswirkungen ein solcher Status nach sich ziehen soll, am sinnvollsten von den Gerichten beantwortet werden kann – so wie dies iÜ auch im Hinblick auf viele andere international-privatrechtliche Fragestellungen in Schweden gehandhabt wird[33]. Dabei sollten Vorschriften, die auf Ehepaare Anwendung finden, aber grundsätzlich gleichermaßen für eheähnliche Partnerschaften gelten[34].

Die Frage, wie zu verfahren ist, wenn es in einer Familie mit Auslandsbezug mehr als zwei rechtliche Elternteile des Kindes geben sollte, hat der Gesetzgeber noch offengelassen – ua mit Verweis darauf, dass gegenwärtig kein EU-Land eine solche Konstellation erlaubt. Sollten die neuen IPR- und IZPR-Vorschriften ausnahmsweise die Folge auslösen, dass mehr als zwei Personen rechtliche Eltern eines Kindes sind, müsse durch eine Rechtsanwendung (konkret: durch die Gerichten) entschieden werden, inwieweit ausländisches Recht nicht zur Anwendung gelangt

[29] Finnland, Norwegen, Dänemark und Island.

[30] Vgl. iÜ zum innernordischen IPR und IZPR Ring/Olsen-Ring, Einführung in das skandinavische Recht, 2. Aufl. 2014, Rn. 924ff.

[31] Kommentierter Gesetzentwurf „Gleichartige Bestimmungen über Elternschaft in internationalen Verhältnissen", *Lagrådsremiss Jämlika regler om föräldraskap i internationella situationer* (fortan: Gesetzentwurf zur Elternschaft in internationalen Verhältnissen), 21.

[32] Gesetzentwurf zur Elternschaft in internationalen Verhältnissen, 22.

[33] Gesetzentwurf zur Elternschaft in internationalen Verhältnissen, 22f. mit Verweis auf 202008/09:CU19, S. 22, und prop. 2018/19:50, 36.

[34] Gesetzentwurf zur Elternschaft in internationalen Verhältnissen, 22 mit Verweis auf 202008/09:CU19 S. 22. und prop. 2018/19:50, 36.

oder aber die Anerkennung einer ausländischen Entscheidung oder (Elternschafts-) Feststellung unter *ordre public*-Gesichtspunkten verweigert werden muss[35].

Durch die Neufassung des LFI ist erstmalig eine Elternschaftsvermutung für die nicht-gebärende Frau in einer gleichgeschlechtlichen Ehe mit Auslandsbezug anerkannt worden. Der Regelungsbedarf ging allerdings noch weiter: Vor dem 1.8.2022 konnte nämlich bei gleichgeschlechtlichen Paaren eine ausländische Elternschaftsfeststellung/-anerkennung der nicht-gebärenden Frau in Schweden nicht anerkannt werden. Sonstige Regelungen über eine Elternschaft dieser Frau fehlten ebenfalls[36]. Die nicht-gebärende Frau war daher selbst für den Fall, dass sie im Ausland rechtliche Elternschaft besaß, auf den Versuch angewiesen, in Schweden entweder ihre Elternschaft nach den Verfahrensvorschriften des FB feststellen zu lassen, oder aber das (eigene) Kind zu adoptieren.

Die Elternschaftsvermutung der Frau erfolgt nunmehr unter denselben Voraussetzungen wie bei einer Vaterschaftsvermutung. So bestimmt § 2a LFI parallel zur bereits früher geltenden Vaterschaftsvermutung in § 2 I LFI Folgendes: „Eine Frau, die mit der Mutter eines Kindes verheiratet ist oder gewesen ist, ist als Elternteil des Kindes anzusehen, wenn dies aus dem Gesetz des Staates folgt, in dem das Kind bei der Geburt seinen Wohnsitz erlangt hat, oder, falls nach diesem Gesetz neben der Mutter keine Frau als Elternteil des Kindes anzusehen ist, wenn dies aus dem Gesetz eines Staates folgt, dessen Staatsangehörigkeit das Kind bei der Geburt erlangte. Falls das Kind bei der Geburt seinen Wohnsitz in Schweden erlangt hat, ist die Frage jedoch stets nach schwedischem Recht zu beurteilen". Im letztgenannten Fall greifen somit die Vater- und Elternschaftsvermutungen des FB[37]. Dadurch soll vermieden werden, dass neben der Mutter des Kindes mehr als eine Person die rechtliche Elternschaft erhält[38].

In einem Punkt wird im LFI allerdings vom Prinzip der Geschlechtsneutralität abgewichen, nämlich in Bezug auf die Vorfrage, ob eine Ehe besteht oder bestanden hat. Dies wird allein im Zusammenhang mit der Vaterschaftsvermutung beantwortet. Nach § 2 II LFI ist die Frage, ob ein Mann mit der Mutter des Kindes verheiratet ist oder gewesen ist, nach dem Gesetz zu entscheiden, das nach § 2 I LFI für die Vaterschaftsvermutung gilt – womit eine auf ausländischem Recht direkt beruhende Vaterschaftsvermutung in Schweden selbst bei fehlender Anerkennung der Ehe in Schweden Bestand hat, wenn die Ehe in dem Land, in dem das Kind im Zeitpunkt der Geburt seinen Wohnsitz oder seine Staatsangehörigkeit erlangt hat, gültig ist. § 2 II LFI wurde zum 1. Juli 2021 eingeführt, um unbeabsichtigten Folgen von zwei jüngst erfolgten Reformen des schwedischen internationalen Eherechts[39], mit denen ein allgemeines Verbot der Anerkennung einer Mehrehe[40]

---

[35] Gesetzentwurf zur Elternschaft in internationalen Verhältnissen, 22.

[36] Vgl. näher Gesetzentwurf zur Elternschaft in internationalen Verhältnissen, 20.

[37] Vgl. näher Gesetzentwurf zur Elternschaft in internationalen Verhältnissen, 28.

[38] Gesetzentwurf zur Elternschaft in internationalen Verhältnissen, 26f., mit Verweis auf prop. 1984/85:124, 22.

[39] Geregelt in Gesetz 1904:26 über bestimmte zwischenstaatliche Rechtsverhältnisse betreffend Ehe und Vormundschaft (*lag om vissa internationella rättsförhållanden rörande äktenskap och förmynderskap,* fortan: LIÄ).

[40] Änderungsgesetz 2021:465 zum LIÄ (1:8a LIÄ).

sowie einer Minderjährigenehe[41] nach ausländischem Recht statuiert worden war, entgegenzuwirken. Durch § 2 II LFI sollte vor allem aus kinderschutzrechtlichen Gesichtspunkten verhindert werden, dass infolge dieser Verbote die Begründung einer Vaterschaft nach der *pater est*-Regel in gewissen Fällen völlig ausgeschlossen wird[42]. Der schwedische Gesetzgeber fand es hingegen nicht angebracht, eine entsprechende Regelung für gleichgeschlechtliche Mehrehen und Minderjährigenehen aufzustellen, da solche Konstellationen in der Praxis nicht vorkommen dürften, und es iÜ auch „keinen Grund zur Annahme gibt, dass ausländische gleichgeschlechtliche Ehen in nennenswertem Umfang nicht in Schweden anerkannt werden sollten“[43].

Wird ein Verfahren über die Aufhebung der vermuteten Vater- oder Elternschaft angestrengt, ergibt sich die Zuständigkeit eines schwedischen Gerichts aus § 4 LFI. Danach ist in Verfahren über die Vaterschaft bzw. über die Elternschaft einer Person, die mit der Mutter des Kindes verheiratet bzw. deren *sambo* sie ist oder gewesen ist, ein schwedisches Gericht dann zuständig, wenn

- das Kind seinen Wohnsitz *(hemvist)* in Schweden hat,
- das Verfahren gegen einen Mann bzw. gegen eine Frau oder gegen mehrere Männer bzw. gegen mehrere Frauen, die seinen/ihren Wohnsitz in Schweden hat/haben, geführt wird, oder
- angesichts der [engen] Beziehungen seitens des Kindes, der Mutter, des Mannes oder der Frau zu Schweden besondere Gründe dafür sprechen, den Fall in Schweden prüfen zu lassen.

Nach § 5 III LFI ist die Frage der Aufhebung einer vermuteten Vater- oder Elternschaft aufgrund der Feststellung, dass eine andere Person der Vater bzw. der Elternteil des Kindes ist, nach dem Gesetz zu beurteilen, das bei der (ursprünglichen) Vater- bzw. Elternschaftsfeststellung zur Anwendung gelangte. Gemäß § 5 I S. 1 LFI findet auf ein entsprechendes Verfahren in Schweden das Gesetz des Staates Anwendung, in dem das Kind im Zeitpunkt der erstinstanzlichen Entscheidung seinen Wohnsitz hatte. Es wird also auch in dieser Beziehung auf das Recht, zu dem das Kind die engste Verbindung hat[44], abgestellt.

Nach § 7 I LFI wird eine rechtskräftige ausländische Entscheidung, wonach eine Vaterschaft oder Elternschaft festgestellt oder aufgehoben wird, in Schweden (nur) anerkannt, wenn aufgrund des Wohnsitzes, der Staatsangehörigkeit oder einer anderen [engen] Verbindung einer Verfahrenspartei erhebliche Gründe dafür sprechen, dass das Verfahren im ausländischen Staat stattfand. § 7 II LFI statuiert eine Reihe von Fällen, in denen die Anerkennung einer ausländischen Entscheidung

---

[41] Änderungsgesetz 2018:1973 zum LIÄ (1:8a LIÄ).

[42] Näher prop. 2020/21:149, 36f.

[43] Gesetzentwurf zur Elternschaft in internationalen Verhältnissen, 28f. Auch hier wird die Herangehensweise der nordischen Gesetzgeber erkennbar, bei der oft, statt „allumfassende“ Regelungen anzustreben, bewusst Spielräume für eine richterliche Interpretation, die auch aktuellen gesellschaftlichen Vorstellungen und Gegebenheiten Rechnung tragen soll, geschaffen werden; näher Ring/Olsen-Ring, Einführung in das skandinavische Recht, 2. Aufl. 2014, Rn. 19ff.

[44] Vgl. näher Gesetzentwurf zur Elternschaft in internationalen Verhältnissen, 29.

gänzlich ausgeschlossen ist, so bspw. wenn die beklagte Partei keine angemessene Gelegenheit bekommen hat, ihre Sache vor Gericht zu vertreten (§ 7 II Nr. 1 LFI), die ausländische Entscheidung einem schwedischen Urteil widerspricht (§ 7 II Nr. 2 LFI), oder in Schweden bereits ein Gerichtsverfahren bezüglich der Vater- bzw. der Elternschaft anhängig ist (§ 7 II Nr. 5 LFI). Daneben statuiert § 12 LFI einen generellen *ordre public*-Vorbehalt, wonach eine ausländische Gesetzgebung bzw. gerichtliche wie außergerichtliche Entscheidungen in Schweden nicht angewandt werden können/nicht gelten, wenn dies der öffentlichen Ordnung Schwedens widersprechen würde.

IV. Ausblick

Mit der Einführung der geschlechtsneutralen Elternschaftsvermutung ist in Schweden eine grundlegende Weiterentwicklung des Abstammungsrechts erfolgt. Da mittlerweile mehr als die Hälfte aller in Schweden geborenen Kinder nicht-verheiratete Eltern haben[45], könnte allerdings überspitzt von einem „großen Wurf für eine kleine Gruppe" gesprochen werden. Macht es dann überhaupt noch Sinn, in Fragen der Elternschaft zwischen Verheirateten und Nicht-Verheirateten zu unterscheiden? Der Gesetzgeber hat – obwohl dies im Rahmen der Anhörung zur Gesetzgebung teilweise angeregt worden war[46] – weder überlegt, gesetzliche Elternschaftsvermutungen ganz aufzugeben noch diese alternativ auf *sambor* zu erweitern. Stattdessen hat man sich vorläufig darauf beschränkt, weitestmöglich eine geschlechtliche Gleichstellung zu schaffen. Gleichzeitig ist für *sambor* die Anerkennung einer Elternschaft auf äußerst einfachem digitalem Wege ermöglicht worden. Damit dürfte allen Parteien grundsätzlich gedient sein. Für Eltern, Kind und Gesellschaft wird in effizienter Weise anfängliche Klarheit geschaffen – bei verheirateten Eltern durch die Verbindung Trauschein und Elternschaftsvermutung per Automatik, bei *sambor* in aller Regel durch Elternschaftsanerkennung per Mausklick.

Mit der Elternschaftsvermutung wird allerdings, vor allem aus kinderrechtlicher Perspektive gesehen, ein nicht unerhebliches Risiko für eine Fehleranfälligkeit in Kauf genommen. So sollen bereits heute ungefähr 82 Prozent aller Gerichtsverfahren über die Aufhebung einer Elternschaft eine vermutete Vaterschaft zum Gegenstand haben. Es kommt auch wesentlich häufiger vor, dass eine durch die *pater est*-Regel vermittelte Vaterschaft „falsch" ist, als dies bei einer nach einer Vaterschaftsanerkennung vermittelten Vaterschaft der Fall ist[47]. Die absoluten Zahlen der Vaterschaftsprozesse haben sich allerdings auch in den letzten zehn Jahre stabil[48] gehalten.

---

[45] Vgl. prop. 2020/21:176, S. 33.

[46] So hatte etwa die Juristische Fakultät der Universität Göteborg den Nutzen der Vermutungsregeln in Frage gestellt; ähnlich der Verein Vater und Kind *PappaBarn;* der Reichsverband für sexuelle Information, *Riksförbundet för sexuell upplysning,* sprach sich hingegen für eine Erweiterung der Elternschaftsvermutungen auf *sambor* aus, vgl. näher prop. 2020/21:176, S. 24.

[47] Näher SOU 2022:38; Gute Elternschaft – ein starker Schutz des Familienlebens von Kindern, *Alle tiders föräldraskap – ett stärkt skydd för barns familjeliv,* 430 ff.

[48] Bei jählich ungefähr 1.200 Verfahren.

Die Einführung einer Elternschaftsvermutung für die nicht-gebärende Frau in einer gleichgeschlechtlichen Beziehung dürfte angesichts der gesetzlichen Vorgaben zur assistierten Befruchtung kaum zu verschärften Problemen führen.

Der durch die Reform des LFI geschaffene Gleichklang zum nationalen materiellen Recht Schwedens erscheint folgerichtig und auch verwaltungsökonomisch sinnvoll.

In gesetzestechnischer Hinsicht wird gegenwärtig eine Neustrukturierung und Vereinfachung der abstammungsrechtlichen Vorschriften des FB überlegt, bei der ua die Bezeichnung „Vaterschaft“ und „Mutterschaft“ durch „Elternschaft“ ersetzt werden soll. Das internationale Abstammungsrecht soll möglicherweise in einem Gesetz konzentriert werden[49].

Während das schwedische Recht die Voraussetzung einer genetischen Verbindung zwischen Kind und Eltern ganz aufgegeben hat, wird im nationalen wie im internationalen Abstammungsrecht an der Forderung einer persönlichen Beziehung zwischen den Elternteilen festgehalten. Auch das Klarheit, Stabilität und Abgrenzbarkeit dienende Prinzip, dass ein Kind höchstens zwei rechtliche Elternteile haben kann, wird offensichtlich noch als ganz zentral erachtet[50]. Diskutiert wird allerdings, ob „sozialen Elternteilen“ in Familien, in denen mehr als zwei Erwachsene eine elterliche Verantwortung ausüben, etwa sorgerechtliche Befugnisse und Informationsrechte in Bezug auf das Kind eingeräumt werden sollen[51].

Sollte die vorgeschlagene EU-Verordnung zum internationalen Abstammungsrecht Wirklichkeit werden und eine in einem Mitgliedstaat begründete Elternschaft grundsätzlich ohne besonderes Verfahren in allen anderen Mitgliedstaaten anerkannt werden, dürfte auch das schwedische Prinzip der Gleichstellung von nationalen und internationalen Fällen herausgefordert sein.

---

[49] Vgl. näher SOU 2022:38.

[50] SOU 2022:38, 26.

[51] Vgl. SOU 2022:38, S. 559 ff., wo diesbezüglich sehr detaillierte Überlegungen angestellt werden.

STEFFEN PABST

EuZPR – Die Entstehung eines Rechtsgebietes

Donostia – San Sebastián. Was für ein Klang. Mit diesen Worten begeisterte der *Jubilar* in seinen Vorlesungen der 1990er Jahre zum Internationalen Zivilprozessrecht und vermittelte den jungen Studenten zugleich Weltläufigkeit, Internationalität und Aufbruch zu neuen Zielen.

Donostia – San Sebastián, das meinte in diesem Zusammenhang natürlich das Dritte Beitrittsübereinkommen zum Europäischen Gerichtsstands- und Vollstreckungsübereinkommen, kurz zum EuGVÜ, mit dem gerade Spanien und Portugal beigetreten waren und welches am 26.5.1989 in gerade jener baskischen Stadt während der spanischen Ratspräsidentschaft von allen Mitgliedstaaten der damaligen EWG unterzeichnet wurde.

Die Idee zu diesem Artikel entstand dann viele Jahre später bei einer Reise des Autors in gerade jenes Donostia – San Sebastián. Die Vorlesung zum IZPR, die harte spanische Aussprache des *Jubilars* und die Träume des jungen Studenten, die Welt zu entdecken, waren wieder präsent. Und die Gedanken wanderten weiter: Woher kam das EuZPR, bis es Station in Donostia – San Sebastián machte und wohin entwickelte es sich immer rasanter danach? Und was hat der *Jubilar* zu dieser Reise beigetragen?

Die Lebenszeit des *Jubilars* erfasst nicht nur die gesamte Entwicklung des EuZPR. Er hat es auch selbst entscheidend mitgeprägt und dabei – beginnend mit seiner Dissertationsschrift im Jahr 1983[1] – wichtige Ecksteine gesetzt, welche die heutige Bedeutung und Begrenzung dieses Rechtsgebietes schufen. Und so will dieser Beitrag chronistisch zurückblicken und erinnern, mit etwas Abstand die Entwicklungen zusammenfassen, um am Ende durch Rückbesinnen auf Bewährtes dieses für die Zukunft nutzbar zu machen.

I. Völkervertragliche Rechtsetzung zwischen Nationalstaaten

1. Gründung der Europäischen Gemeinschaften und Schaffung des EuGVÜ

Als der *Jubilar* im Jahr 1955 diese Welt betrat, war der Grundstein unserer heutigen Europäischen Union gerade gelegt worden – die erste Gemeinschaft, die EGKS,[2] war etwa 3 Jahre zuvor gegründet worden. Etwa 3 Jahre später begann mit der Grün-

[1] Rauscher, Verpflichtung und Erfüllungsort in Art. 5 Nr. 1 EuGVÜ (1984), soweit ersichtlich eine der ersten Monografien, die sich mit einem Problem des EuGVÜ und damit des EuZPR beschäftigte.

[2] Vertrag über die Gründung der Europäischen Gemeinschaft für Kohle und Stahl, unterzeichnet am 18.4.1951 (BGBl. 1952 II 447), in Kraft getreten am 23.7.1952 (BGBl. 1952 II 978).

dung der zwei weiteren Gemeinschaften, der EWG[3] und der EAG[4], der Aufbau der multithematischen europäischen Institutionen. Aus den Präambeln aller drei Gründungsverträge folgt die Überzeugung, dass die europäischen Staaten ihre Zukunft gemeinsam gestalten müssen. Der europäische Geist war entfacht und eine neue, europäische Rechtsordnung sollte entstehen.

Und auch wenn das Zivilprozessrecht zu diesem Zeitpunkt noch nicht Gegenstand dieser neuen europäischen Rechtsordnung war, so fand es doch bereits eine Erwähnung: Die Schlussbestimmungen, dort Art. 220 EWGV im letzten Anstrich, enthalten einen Appell[5] oder Auftrag[6] an die bzw. eine Verpflichtung[7] oder Absichtserklärung[8] der Mitgliedstaaten soweit erforderlich untereinander Verhandlungen einzuleiten, um zugunsten, ihrer Staatsangehörigen die Vereinfachung der Förmlichkeiten für die gegenseitige Anerkennung und Vollstreckung richterlicher Entscheidungen und Schiedssprüche sicherzustellen. Gewährte die Norm auch aus sich heraus dem Einzelnen noch keine Rechte, auf die er sich unmittelbar berufen konnte, so definierte sie doch die Vereinfachung der Anerkennung und Vollstreckung von Entscheidungen als gemeinsames Ziel der Europäischen Gemeinschaft und steckte den Rahmen für von den Mitgliedstaaten „soweit erforderlich" untereinander einzuleitende Verhandlungen ab.[9]

Die Thematik fand früh politische Beachtung im Europäischen Parlament[10] und bei der Kommission der Europäischen Wirtschaftsgemeinschaft[11], die daraufhin noch 1959 gegenüber den sechs Gründungsmitgliedstaaten Belgien, Deutschland, Frankreich, Italien, Luxemburg und die Niederlande darlegte, dass Rechtsschutz und Rechtssicherheit im Gemeinsamen Markt wesentlich von einer befriedigenden Regelung der Anerkennung und Vollstreckung gerichtlicher Entscheidungen abhänge, wobei ein echter Binnenmarkt erst dann verwirklicht sein werde, wenn ein ausreichender Rechtsschutz gewährleistet sei.[12] Auch die Mitgliedstaaten erkannten, dass der rechtpolitische Alternativweg, der Abschluss bilateraler Anerkennungs-

---

[3] Vertrag zur Gründung der Europäischen Wirtschaftsgemeinschaft, unterzeichnet am 25.3.1957 (BGBl. 1957 II 766), in Kraft getreten am 1.1.1958 (BGBl. 1958 II 1).

[4] Vertrag zur Gründung der Europäischen Atomgemeinschaft, unterzeichnet am 25.3.1957 (BGBl. 1957 II 1014), in Kraft getreten am 1.1.1958 (BGBl. 1958 II 1).

[5] So Bülow RabelsZ 29 (1965) 473 (474).

[6] So Grabitz/Hilf, Das Recht der Europäischen Union/Schweitzer, 40. ErgLfg. 2009, EGV Art. 293 Rn. 1.

[7] So EuGH 6.10.1976 – 12/76, ECLI:EU:C:1976:133 Rn. 9 (Industrie Tessili Italiana Como/Dunlop AG); von der Groeben/von Boeckh, Kommentar zum EWG-Vertrag II/Thiesing, 1960, Art. 220 Rn. 1; Streinz, EUV/EGV/Leible, 2003, EGV Art. 293 Rn. 2.

[8] Geiger, EG-Vertrag, 1993, EGV Art. 220 Rn. 1.

[9] EuGH 11.7.1985 – 37/84, ECLI:EU:C:1984:134 Rn. 11 (Ministère Public/Mutsch); EuGH 12.5.1998 – C-336/96, ECLI:EU:C:1998:221 Rn. 16 = EuZW 1999, 46 (47) (Eheleute Robert Gilly/Directeur des services fiscaux du Bas-Rhin).

[10] S. die Anfrage von Joseph Illerhaus, MdEP, vom 23.9.1959 an die Kommission der Europäischen Wirtschaftsgemeinschaft (ABl. 1959 P 56, 1123).

[11] Vgl. die Antwort der Kommission der Europäischen Wirtschaftsgemeinschaft vom 17.10.1959 (ABl. EG 1959 P 56, 1124).

[12] Kommission der Europäischen Wirtschaftsgemeinschaft, Note an die Regierungen der Mitgliedstaaten vom 22.10.1959 (IV/4586/59), zitiert nach Jenard-Bericht [zum EuGVÜ] (ABl. 1979 C 59, 1 (3)).

und Vollstreckungsverträge, aufgrund erheblicher Unterschiede zu einer weiteren Zersplitterung der Rechtslage führen und sich potentiell störend auf das Wirtschaftsleben auswirken würde.[13] Eine einheitliche Regelung hingegen würde eine gleichartige Behandlung vergleichbarer Fälle ermöglichen, dem Geist und den Zielen der Gründungsverträge – vor allem dem Prinzip der Nichtdiskriminierung und der Gleichheit der Chancen im Wettbewerb – entsprechen und gleichzeitig einen wichtigen Beitrag zur Rechtsangleichung in der EG leisten.[14] Diese Erkenntnis wird man als die Geburtsstunde des Europäischen Zivilprozessrechts verstehen müssen.[15]

Die Gründungsmitglieder unternahmen daraufhin den ersten revolutionären Schritt und schufen bis 1968 mit dem EuGVÜ[16] – international und über Grenzen hinweg verständlicher nach dem Ort seiner Unterzeichnung bezeichnet als „Brüsseler Übereinkommen" – ein kohärentes Rechtssystem für die gesamte Gemeinschaft. Bereits nach der Erstellung des Entwurfs wurde von den Autoren selbstbewusst vermutet, dass dieser wegen seines Inhalts, „der dem Abkommen ein fortschrittliches Gepräge gibt", über die Grenzen der EWG hinaus Aufmerksamkeit erregen werde.[17] Sachlich war sein Anwendungsbereich noch lückenhaft, zahlreiche spezielle Materien wurden in Art. 1 EuGVÜ aus verschiedenen Gründen ausgeklammert. Entscheidend war jedoch, dass die Mitglieder des Sachverständigenausschusses, die den Text des EuGVÜ ausarbeiteten, über die in Art. 220 EWGV allein benannte Anerkennung und Vollstreckung hinausgingen (auch wenn dies aus Gründen der Anerkennung und Vollstreckung erfolgte) und so die Tür zu einem umfassenden Europäischen Zivilprozessrecht aufstießen. Geschaffen werden sollte ein gemeinschaftsweit einheitliches Exequaturverfahren mit einer abschließenden Liste einheitlicher Anerkennungsversagungsgründe. Man erkannte, dass die Urteilsanerkennung deutlich erleichtert würde, wenn eine Überprüfung der Anerkennungszuständigkeit weitgehend aus dem Exequaturverfahren eliminiert werden könnte und eine Zuständigkeitsentscheidung des Ursprungsstaates im Vollstreckungsstaat nicht mehr zur Diskussion stehen würde. Dies war jedoch allein dann akzeptabel, wenn die Zuständigkeitsentscheidung im Ursprungsstaat nach gemeinschaftsweit anerkannten Regeln erfolgte, so dass sich das EuGVÜ auch der umfassenden Regelung der Internationalen Zuständigkeit widmete.[18] Nach der Ratifikation durch alle Mitgliedstaaten (Art 62 EuGVÜ) konnte es als erster Baustein des Europäischen Zivilprozessrechts 1973 in Kraft treten.

---

[13] Hardung, Die europäische Titelfreizügigkeit, 2020, S. 40.

[14] Arnold AWD 1965, 321.

[15] So wurde die Entstehung eines Europäischen Zivilprozessrechts bereits während der ersten Entwurfsphase des EuGVÜ diskutiert von Nagel, Auf dem Wege zu einem europäischen Prozessrecht, 1963.

[16] Übereinkommen über die gerichtliche Zuständigkeit und die Vollstreckung gerichtlicher Entscheidungen in Zivil- und Handelssachen, unterzeichnet am 27.9.1968, in Kraft getreten am 1.2.1973 (ABl. 1972 L 299, 32).

[17] Bülow RabelsZ 29 (1965) 473, der Vorsitzender des von den Mitgliedstaaten benannten Sachverständigenausschusses war, welcher die Entwurfsausarbeitung übernommen hatte.

[18] Huber FS Kaissis, 2012, 413; Bülow RabelsZ 29 (1965) 473 (478ff.); Jenard-Bericht [zum EuGVÜ] (ABl. 1979 C 59, 1 (7)).

2. Territoriales Mitwachsen mit den Europäischen Gemeinschaften

Da es sich bei dem EuZPR des EuGVÜ nicht um originäres Europarecht handelte, konnte es seinen territorialen Anwendungsbereich nicht automatisch mit dem Beitritt weiterer Staaten zu den Europäischen Gemeinschaften ausdehnen. Vielmehr war ein aufwändiges, eigenständiges Beitrittsverfahren erforderlich. In der Folge einer Erweiterung der Europäischen Gemeinschaft wurde stets ein gesondertes Beitrittsübereinkommen ausgearbeitet und der Ratifikationsprozess in allen Mitgliedstaaten durchlaufen. Diese Beitrittsübereinkommen wurden zugleich für Reformen und Anpassungen des EuGVÜ genutzt, so dass regelmäßig auch inhaltliche Änderungen erfolgten.

Nach dem EG-Beitritt des Vereinigten Königreichs, Irlands und Dänemarks 1973 wurde das erste Beitrittsübereinkommen[19] 1978 geschlossen, nach dem EG-Beitritt Griechenlands 1981 kam das zweite Beitrittsübereinkommen[20] 1982 hinzu, nach dem EG-Beitritt Spaniens und Portugals 1986 folgte das dritte Beitrittsübereinkommen[21] 1989 (jenes von Donostia – San Sebastián) und nach dem Beitritt Schwedens, Finnlands und Österreich 1995 schloss man schließlich das vierte Beitrittsübereinkommen[22] 1996.

Für ein Inkrafttreten wollte man bei der immer größer werdenden Anzahl von Mitgliedstaaten jedoch nicht auf den Letzten warten; man entschloss sich für ein gestuftes Inkrafttreten jeweils zwischen den Staaten, die die Ratifikation vorgenommen haben, sobald nur stets ein Neu-Mitgliedstaat unter diesen war (Art. 39 1. BeitrittsÜbk 1978, Art. 15 2.BeitrittsÜbk 1982, Art. 32 3. BeitrittsÜbk 1989, Art. 16 4. BeitrittsÜbk 1996).

Eine weitere kleine territorial Erweiterung erfolgte ohne einen aufwändigen internationalen Beitrittsprozess. Nach Art. 10 Abs. 1 Einigungsvertrag[23] gelten im Gebiet der ehemaligen DDR mit dem Wirksamwerden des Beitritts die Verträge über die Europäischen Gemeinschaften sowie die internationalen Vereinbarungen, Verträge und Beschlüsse, die in Verbindung mit diesen Verträgen in Kraft getreten

---

[19] Übereinkommen über den Beitritt des Königreichs Dänemark, Irlands und des Vereinigten Königreichs Großbritannien und Nordirland zum Übereinkommen über die gerichtliche Zuständigkeit und die Vollstreckung gerichtlicher Entscheidungen in Zivil- und Handelssachen sowie zum Protokoll betreffend die Auslegung dieses Übereinkommens durch den Gerichtshof, unterzeichnet am 9.10.1978 (ABl. 1978 L 304, 1).

[20] Übereinkommen über den Beitritt der Republik Griechenland zum Übereinkommen über die gerichtliche Zuständigkeit und die Vollstreckung gerichtlicher Entscheidungen in Zivil- und Handelssachen sowie zum Protokoll betreffend die Auslegung dieses Übereinkommens durch den Gerichtshof [...], unterzeichnet am 25.10.1982 (ABl. 1982 L 388, 1).

[21] Übereinkommen über den Beitritt des Königreichs Spanien und der Portugiesischen Republik zum Übereinkommen über die gerichtliche Zuständigkeit und die Vollstreckung gerichtlicher Entscheidungen in Zivil- und Handelssachen sowie zum Protokoll betreffend die Auslegung dieses Übereinkommens durch den Gerichtshof [...], unterzeichnet am 26.5.1989 (ABl. 1989 L 285, 1).

[22] Übereinkommen über den Beitritt der Republik Österreich, der Republik Finnland und des Königreichs Schweden zum Übereinkommen über die gerichtliche Zuständigkeit und die Vollstreckung gerichtlicher Entscheidungen in Zivil- und Handelssachen sowie zum Protokoll betreffend die Auslegung dieses Übereinkommens durch den Gerichtshof [...], unterzeichnet am 29.11.1996 (ABl. 1997 C 15, 1).

[23] Vertrag zwischen der Bundesrepublik Deutschland und der Deutschen Demokratischen Republik über die Herstellung der Einheit Deutschlands – Einigungsvertrag –, unterzeichnet am 31.8.1990 (BGBl. 1990 II 889), in Kraft getreten am 29.9.1990 (BGBl. 1990 II 1360).

sind. Als in Verbindung mit den EG-Verträgen stehend wurden auch die auf Grundlage von Art. 220 EWGV geschlossenen Vereinbarungen, mithin das EuGVÜ und die zugehörigen Rechtsakte, betrachtet.[24]

3. *Territoriale Expansion jenseits der Europäischen Gemeinschaften*

Spannend und exotisch waren stets die Gebiete der Mitgliedstaaten außerhalb ihres europäischen Kerngebietes. Art. 60 EuGVÜ nahm bis zu seiner Streichung durch Art. 21 3. BeitrittsÜbk 1989 zwar eine deutliche Beschränkung des territorialen Anwendungsbereichs auf das europäische Hoheitsgebiet der Vertragsstaaten vor.

Jedoch schloss er zusätzlich für Frankreich alle überseeischen Departements und Gebiete ein, mithin neben Guadeloupe (seinerzeit einschließlich Saint Martin sowie Saint-Barthélemy[25]), Guyana, Martinique, Réunion, auch die Komoren (einschließlich Mayotte), Neukaledonien, Französisch-Polynesien, St. Pierre und Miquelon sowie Wallis und Fortuna. Die Komoren schieden mit ihrer Unabhängigkeit 1975 bereits wieder aus dem Anwendungsbereich aus. Für Mayotte,[26] dass bei Frankreich verblieb und einen eigenen besonderen Status erhielt, bestätigte die Anpassung von Art. 60 EuGVÜ durch Art. 27 1. BeitrittsÜbk 1978 ausdrücklich den fortbestehenden Einschluss.

Eingeschlossen werden sollte für Dänemark auch Grönland. Jedoch erfolgte – nachdem Grönland zum 1.1.1985 aus den Europäischen Gemeinschaften ausgeschieden war[27] – die Ratifizierung durch Dänemark sodann entgegen dem Wortlaut von Art. 60 EuGVÜ (idF von Art 27 1. BeitrittsÜbk 1978) mit der Maßgabe, dass sich das Übereinkommen nicht auf Grönland erstreckt.[28]

Im Übrigen war vorgesehen, dass Vertragsstaaten den Anwendungsbereich auf verschiedene Gebiete erstrecken konnten. Hiervon machten die Niederlande Gebrauch. Ein erstes Mal erfolgte eine Erstreckung des Anwendungsbereichs durch Erklärung vom 30.1.1973 auf Suriname.[29] Mit der Unabhängigkeit Surinams am 25.11.1975 schied dieses Gebiet jedoch schon wieder aus dem Anwendungsbereich des EuGVÜ aus.[30] Ein zweites Mal erfolgte eine Erstreckung durch Erklärung vom 2.6.1986 auf Aruba.[31]

Den Europäischen Gemeinschaften stand in Europa eine zweite Staatengruppe gegenüber. Auch die Entwicklung der Europäischen Freihandelsassoziation (EFTA) gehört zur Geschichte der wirtschaftlichen Integration Westeuropas in der Nachkriegs-

---

[24] Trunk, Die Erweiterung des EuGVÜ-Systems am Vorabend des Europäischen Binnenmarktes, 1991, S. 10; Denkschrift zum Einigungsvertrag, BT-Drs. 11/7760, 355 (361).

[25] Seit 1.1.2012 ein eigenständiges überseeisches Gebiet, Art. 1 Beschluss 2010/718/EU (ABl. 2010 L 325, 4).

[26] Erst seit dem 1.1.2014 änderte sich der Status erneut hin zu einem Departement, welches Teil der EU ist, Art. 1 Beschluss 2012/419/EU (ABl. 2012 L 204, 131).

[27] Vertrag zur Änderung der Verträge zur Gründung der Europäischen Gemeinschaften bezüglich Grönlands, unterzeichnet am 13.3.1984, in Kraft getreten am 1.1.1985 (ABl. 1985 L 29, 1).

[28] Vgl. BGBl. 1986 II 1020.

[29] BGBl. 1975 II 243.

[30] S. dazu Schlosser-Bericht [zum 2.BeitrittsÜbk 1978] (ABl. 1979 C 59, 71 Rn. 254).

[31] BGBl. 1986 II 919; die Erstreckung wurde bei der Hinterlegung der Ratifikationsurkunde für das 4. BeitrittsÜbk 1996 bestätigt (BGBl. 2001 II 1058).

zeit. Die Staaten der EFTA teilten mit denen der Europäischen Gemeinschaften stets das Ziel, einen dynamischen und homogenen europäischen Wirtschaftsraum zu schaffen. Diesem Ziel war auch das EuGVÜ verpflichtet, und übereinstimmend in EWG und EFTA war man der Ansicht, dass es eine Reihe von Grundsätzen enthalte, auf die eine Vertiefung der gerichtlichen und der wirtschaftlichen Zusammenarbeit zwischen den betreffenden Staaten gestützt werden könne.[32] Der Erfolg des EuGVÜ wurde damit jenseits der Grenzen der Europäischen Gemeinschaften anerkannt und, da ein unmittelbarer Beitritt von Drittstaaten aufgrund der aus Art. 220 EWGV hergeleiteten Gemeinschaftsbezogenheit des Instruments ausgeschlossen wurde,[33] in den 1980er Jahren ein Parallelübereinkommen ausgearbeitet. 1988 wurden die Arbeiten am LugÜbk 1988[34] auf einer diplomatischen Konferenz in Lugano abgeschlossen.

Das Vereinigte Königreich hat dem Schweizerischen Bundesrat als Verwahrer am 31.7.1998 die am 1.10.1998 wirksam gewordene Erstreckung des LugÜbk 1988 auf Gibraltar notifiziert; seinen Einspruch hiergegen notifizierte Spanien am 1.10.1998.[35] Jedoch nahm Spanien diesen Einspruch am 21.9.2000 zurück.[36] Eine Erweiterung des LugÜbk 1988 wurde um die Jahrtausendwende vielfach diskutiert,[37] letztlich erfolgte allein der Beitritt Polens zum 1.2.2000.[38]

4. *(Noch) gescheiterte sachliche Expansion*

Mit dem EuGVÜ waren die sachlichen Grenzen von Art. 220 EWGV jedoch lange nicht erreicht, schließlich nahm Art. 1 EuGVÜ zahlreiche Bereiche des Zivilrechts selbst aus seinem Anwendungsbereich aus. Und so wurde bereits früh der Gedanke geäußert, es könne der Kern eines wachsenden EuZPR sein.[39] Bereits parallel wurden die Arbeiten für ein Europäisches Konkursübereinkommen aufgenommen und 1970 konnte ein erster Entwurf vorgelegt werden.[40] Hatte jedoch die Komplexität der Probleme und die Sorge die Arbeiten am EuGVÜ zu verzögern bereits zu einer Aufspaltung der Arbeiten an beiden Übereinkommen geführt,[41] so verschärfte sich die Situation in den Folgejahren. Ein zweiter Entwurf konnte erst 1980 fertiggestellt werden,[42] nachdem die erste EG-Erweiterungsrunde

---

[32] Jenard/Möller-Bericht [zum LugÜbk 1988] (ABl. 1990 C 189, 57 (63)).

[33] Jenard/Möller-Bericht [zum LugÜbk 1988] (ABl. 1990 C 189, 57 (65)).

[34] Übereinkommen über die gerichtliche Zuständigkeit und die Vollstreckung gerichtlicher Entscheidungen in Zivil- und Handelssachen, zur Unterzeichnung aufgelegt am 16.9.1988 (ABl. 1988 L 319, 9, ber. ABl. 1989 L 20, 38 (ABl. 2001 L 148, 86)).

[35] Bekanntmachung vom 24.9.1999 (BGBl. 1999 II 1014).

[36] Bekanntmachung vom 13.9.2001 (BGBl. 2001 II 1060).

[37] S. nur Stankewitsch NJW 1991, 2194 (2195); Kengyel FS Schütze, 1999, 347.

[38] Bekanntmachung vom 31.8.2000 (BGBl. 2000 II 1246).

[39] Habscheid ZfRV 1973, 262 mutmaßte „man werde den 1.2.1973 später einmal als Beginn eines Europäischen Zivilprozeßrechts feiern“; Spellenberg EuR 1980, 329 (347).

[40] Vorentwurf eines Übereinkommens über den Konkurs, Vergleiche und ähnliche Verfahren vom 16.2.1970, EG Dok. 3327/XIV/1/70, abgedruckt in Kegel/Thieme, Vorschläge und Gutachten zum Entwurf eines EG-Konkursübereinkommens, 1988, S. 3.

[41] Noël/Lemontey-Bericht [zum EG-KonkursÜbk-E 1970], EG Dok. 16775/XIV/70.

[42] Entwurf eines Übereinkommens über den Konkurs, Vergleiche und ähnliche Verfahren vom 23.6.1980, EG Dok. III/D/72/80, abgedruckt in Kegel/Thieme, Vorschläge und Gutachten zum Entwurf eines EG-Konkursübereinkommens, 1988, S. 45.

1973 die Wiederaufnahme der Arbeiten in einem erweiterten Ausschuss und eine vollständige Neuverhandlung mit sich brachte.[43] Weitere Verhandlungen und Entwürfe folgten, 1985 die Beratungen jedoch mangels hinreichenden Einvernehmens ausgesetzt.[44] Auf jener Tagung des Europäischen Rates im Mai 1989 in Donostia – San Sebastián reifte erneut der Gedanke, dass die Probleme im Zusammenhang mit der Zahlungsunfähigkeit von Unternehmen einer gemeinschaftsweiten Lösung bedürfen. So wurde dem Wunsch Ausdruck verliehen, die Verhandlungen über ein einschlägiges Übereinkommen zwischen den Mitgliedstaaten wieder in Gang zu bringen.[45] Ein neues EG-InsÜbk wurde von 1991–1995 ausgearbeitet und zur Zeichnung aufgelegt.[46] Allein auch dieser Entwurf wurde nicht von allen Mitgliedstaaten gezeichnet, so dass das Übereinkommen erneut scheiterte.[47]

Mit dem Vertrag von Maastricht[48] sollte 1993 die europäische Integration vertieft werden. Die Europäische Union entstand als übergeordneter Verbund für die bestehenden Europäischen Gemeinschaften, die gemeinsame Außen- und Sicherheitspolitik sowie die Zusammenarbeit in den Bereichen Justiz und Inneres. In der letzten sogenannten 3. Säule fand sich nun auch die justizielle Zusammenarbeit in Zivilsachen wieder (Art. K.1 Nr. 6 EUV 1993); neben Art. 220 EGV gab es damit eine zweite europarechtliche Grundlage, um diese zu organisieren. Sie war sachlich nicht auf die Anerkennung und Vollstreckung und mit dieser im Zusammenhang stehenden Maßnahmen beschränkt. Auch gab es Unterschiede zwischen beiden Grundlagen im Detail – so bestand im Verfahren nach Art. K EUV 1993 ein Initiativrecht der Europäischen Kommission (Art. K.3 Abs. 2 EUV 1993) und das Europäische Parlament war zu unterrichten, anzuhören und seine Auffassung gebührend zu berücksichtigen (Art. K.6 EUV 1993)[49] – jedoch wurden kompetenzrechtlich noch keine Veränderungen vorgenommen. Die Mitgliedstaaten waren zur intergouvernementalen Zusammenarbeit ermächtigt, eine europäische Rechtsetzungskompetenz zum Erlass von Sekundärrecht bestand jedoch nicht. Die in diesem Politikfeld gefassten Beschlüsse mussten weiterhin als eigenständige völkerrechtliche Abkommen umgesetzt und von daher in jedem Einzelfall in jedem Mitgliedstaat ein Ratifikationsverfahren durchlaufen werden.

Das Momentum der vertieften Integration wurde dennoch genutzt. Arbeiten zur sachlichen Ausdehnung des Europäischen Zivilprozessrechts wurden aufgenom-

[43] Stellungnahme der Kommission vom 10.12.1981 [zum vorgenannten Entwurf] (ABl 1981 L 391, 23); Lemontey-Bericht [zum EG-KonkursÜbk-E 1980], EG Dok. III/D/222/80, abgedruckt in Kegel/Thieme, Vorschläge und Gutachten zum Entwurf eines EG-Konkursübereinkommens, 1988, S. 93 (96f.).

[44] Virgos/Schmit-Bericht [zum EG-InsÜbk-E 1995], Rat der EU Doc. 6500/1/96 REV 1, Rn. 3.

[45] Virgos/Schmit-Bericht [zum EG-InsÜbk-E 1995], Rat der EU Doc. 6500/1/96 REV 1, Rn. 1.

[46] Übereinkommen über Insolvenzverfahren, zur Zeichnung aufgelegt am 23.11.1995, abgedruckt in ZEuP 1996, 325.

[47] Generalanwalt Szpunar 26.5.2016 – C-195/15, ECLI:EU:C:2016:369 = BeckRS 2016, 81108 Rn. 20.

[48] Vertrag über die Europäische Union, unterzeichnet am 7.2.1992 (BGBl. 1992 II 1251), in Kraft getreten am 1.11.1993 (BGBl. 1993 II 1947).

[49] Detaillierter s. Müller-Graff, Europäische Zusammenarbeit in den Bereichen Justiz und Inneres/Dittrich, 1996, S. 105f.

men. In den Folgejahren wurden zwei weitere Übereinkommen vollständig ausgearbeitet. Die grenzüberschreitende Zustellung sollte mit dem EG-ZustÜbk[50] erleichtert werden. Den vom EuGVÜ ausgeklammerten Ehesachen widmete sich das Brüssel II-Übk.[51] Zudem ergriff die Europäische Kommission die Initiative und unterbreitete einen vollständig ausgearbeiteten Reformvorschlag für das EuGVÜ.[52] Jedoch konnte keines dieser Übereinkommen den Ratifikationsprozess vollständig durchlaufen, so dass letztlich keines in Kraft trat.

5. *Materielle Entwicklung*

Für die Entwicklung eines wahrlich Europäischen Zivilprozessrechts war es nicht ausreichend die anwendbaren Rechtsnormen zu vereinheitlichen. Da gleiche Rechtstexte bei Anwendung durch Gerichte verschiedener Länder nicht automatisch zu gleichem Recht führen,[53] war vielmehr entscheidend, dass diese auch in gleicher Weise in den Mitgliedstaaten verstanden und angewandt wurden.

Quelle der Interpretation können dabei die zu den einzelnen Übereinkommen veröffentlichten Sachverständigenberichte sein.[54] Bei ihnen handelt es sich um eine konzentrierte Expertendarstellung, welche auch die Gedanken aus dem jeweiligen Gremium zusammenfasst, in dem das Übereinkommen entstand. Vergleicht man diese mit der Vielzahl von Dokumenten, welche zu heutigen Rechtsetzungsverfahren verfügbar sind, mag die Quantität klein sein, jedoch ist die Qualität bis heute beachtlich.[55]

---

[50] Übereinkommen aufgrund von Artikel K.3 des Vertrags über die Europäische Union über die Zustellung gerichtlicher und außergerichtlicher Schriftstücke in Zivil- oder Handelssachen in den Mitgliedstaaten der Europäischen Union, unterzeichnet am 26.5.1997 (ABl. 1997 C 261, 2).

[51] Übereinkommen aufgrund von Artikel K.3 des Vertrags über die Europäische Union über die Zuständigkeit und die Anerkennung und Vollstreckung von Entscheidungen in Ehesachen, unterzeichnet am 28.5.1998 (ABl. EG 1998 C 221, 2).

[52] Vorschlag für einen Rechtsakt des Rates über die Ausarbeitung des Übereinkommens über die gerichtliche Zuständigkeit, die Anerkennung und die Vollstreckung gerichtlicher Entscheidungen in Zivil- und Handelssachen in den Mitgliedstaaten der Europäischen Union vom 22.12.1997 (ABl. 1998 C 33, 20).

[53] So Spellenberg EuR 1980, 329 (338); Müller-Graff, Der Raum der Freiheit, der Sicherheit und des Rechts/Leible, 2005, S. 55 (59).

[54] Zu allgemeinen Zivil- und Handelssachen: Jenard-Bericht [zum EuGVÜ 1968] (ABl. 1979 C 59, 1); Jenard-Bericht [zum AuslProt 1971] (ABl. 1979 C 59, 66); Schlosser-Bericht [zum 1. BeitrittsÜbk 1978] (ABl. 1979 C 59, 71); Evrigenis/Kerameus-Bericht [zum 2. BeitrittsÜbk 1982] (ABl. 1986 C 298, 1); Almeida Cruz/Desantes Real/Jenard-Bericht [zum 3. BeitrittsÜbk 1989] (ABl. 1990 C 189, 35); Jenard/Möller-Bericht [zum LugÜbk 1988] (ABl. 1990 C 189, 57); Pocar-Bericht [zum LugÜbk 2007] (ABl. 2009 C 319, 1); zu Zustellungssachen: Bericht [zum EG-ZustÜbk] (ABl. 1997 C 261, 38); zu Ehesachen: Borrás-Bericht [zum Brüssel II-Übk] (ABl. 1998 C 221, 27); zu Insolvenzsachen: Noël/Lemontey-Bericht [zum EG-KonkursÜbk-E 1970], EG Dok. 16775/XIV/70; Lemontey-Bericht [zum EG-KonkursÜbk-E 1980], EG Dok. III/D/222/80; Virgos/Schmit-Bericht [zum EG-InsÜbk-E 1995], Rat der EU Doc. 6500/1/96 REV 1.

[55] Den Wegfall dieser Berichte als wesentlichen Nachteil des Übergangs von Übereinkommen zu Verordnungen kritisiert deutlich Schlosser, EU-Zivilprozessrecht, 2. Aufl. 2003, Einl. Rn. 27; implizit ähnlich auch Pocar-Bericht [zum LugÜbk 2007] (ABl. 2009 C 319, 1 Rn. 11).

Noch entscheidender ist hingegen die Sicherung einer einheitlichen Rechtsprechung, bestenfalls durch ein gemeinsames Gericht. Das EuGVÜ fußte zwar auf dem Auftrag aus Art. 220 EWGV und beschränkte daher seinen territorialen Bereich grundsätzlich auf die Mitgliedstaaten der EWG.[56] Jedoch handelte es sich letztlich lediglich um ein multilaterales völkerrechtliches Übereinkommen, welches selbst kein Teil des mit und aufgrund der drei Verträge zur Gründung der Europäischen Gemeinschaften geschaffenen Europarechts war. Damit unterlag es insbesondere nicht automatisch der Zuständigkeit des EuGH und seiner Auslegungskompetenz. Diese, heute im Bereich des Europäischen Zivilprozessrechts eine Selbstverständlichkeit, wurde in einer bei Unterzeichnung des Übereinkommens abgegebenen Gemeinsamen Erklärung zunächst nur angedacht. In der Folge bedurfte es der Ausarbeitung, Zeichnung und Ratifizierung einer eigenständigen Regelung, des Auslegungsprotokolls 1971,[57] mittels dessen dem EuGH die Vorabentscheidungskompetenz zugewiesen wurde. Die Arbeiten wurden zwar zügig noch vor dem Inkrafttreten des EuGVÜ abgeschlossen, der Ratifikationsprozess in den sechs Einzelstaaten nahm jedoch erneut eine gewisse Zeit in Anspruch, so dass das Auslegungsprotokoll im Vergleich zum EuGVÜ selbst erst mit einer Verzögerung von ca. 2,5 Jahren in Kraft treten konnte. In der damaligen Zeit für erforderlich erachteten die Mitgliedstaaten, in einer dem Auslegungsprotokoll beigefügten Gemeinsamen Erklärung festzuhalten, dass sie im Benehmen mit dem EuGH einen Austausch von Informationen jedenfalls über die Entscheidungen der jeweiligen obersten nationalen Gerichte in Anwendung des EuGVÜ einrichten.

Das Auslegungsprotokoll wurde in der Folge als integraler Bestandteil des EuGVÜ betrachtet; mit jeder Beitrittsrunde erfolgte stets auch ein Beitritt zum Auslegungsprotokoll und wurde zugleich das Beitrittsübereinkommen selbst dem Auslegungsprotokoll unterworfen (Art. 30 1. BeitrittsÜbk 1978, Art. 10 2. BeitrittsÜbk 1982, Art. 24 3. BeitrittsÜbk 1989, Art. 11 4. BeitrittsÜbk 1996).

Die gleiche Methodik wurde bei den vorgesehenen sachlichen Erweiterungen des Europäischen Zivilprozessrechts vorgesehen. Jedes der fertig ausgearbeiteten Übereinkommen wurde mit einem ähnlichen, eigenen Auslegungsprotokoll versehen,[58] welches ein Vorabentscheidungsverfahren beim EuGH ermöglichen sollte. In Geltung gelangten diese mangels ausreichender Ratifikation keines der weiteren Übereinkommen jedoch nicht.

Die Zuweisung dieser Auslegungskompetenz an ein gemeinsames Gericht war sodann entscheidend für die Ausbildung eines eigenständigen Rechtsgebietes. So bestand die Möglichkeit eine einheitliche Auslegung zu sichern. Fast noch ent-

---

[56] Abgeleitet wird die territoriale Beschränkung auch aus Art. 61 EuGVÜ, vgl. Arnold AWD 1965, 321 Fn. 4.

[57] Protokoll betreffend die Auslegung des Übereinkommens vom 27. September 1968 über die gerichtliche Zuständigkeit und die Vollstreckung gerichtlicher Entscheidungen in Zivil- und Handelssachen durch den Gerichtshof, unterzeichnet am 3.6.1971, in Kraft getreten am 1.9.1975 (ABl. 1975 L 204, 28).

[58] S für das EG-ZustÜbk ABl. 1997 C 261, 18, für das Brüssel II-Übk (ABl. 1998 C 221, 20), in den Entwürfen über das Europäische Konkurs- oder Insolvenzverfahren erfolgte stets eine unmittelbare Aufnahme in die Normen des Übereinkommens Art. 70 EG-KonkursÜbk-E 1980, Art. 43 ff. EG-InsÜbk 1995.

scheidender war jedoch die Entwicklung einer eigenständigen Interpretation ohne Verweis und Rückgriff auf die einzelnen nationalen Rechtsordnungen. In den ersten Jahren mit 6 Mitgliedstaaten waren angesichts geringerer Fallzahlen und zu berücksichtigender Rechtsordnungen unter Umständen detaillierte rechtsvergleichende Analysen im Einzelfall noch vorstellbar. Die Ausbreitung hatte jedoch mit der ersten Erweiterungsrunde bereits begonnen.

Der EuGH nutzte die ihm gegebene Möglichkeit und entwickelte bereits in seiner ersten Entscheidung zum EuGVÜ für Begriffe des Übereinkommens die „autonome Auslegung" als gleichwertige Methode, auch wenn er aus Sorge, mit der Auslegung des Prozessrechts dem anwendbaren Sachrecht vorzugreifen, vor der konkreten Anwendung noch zurückschreckte.[59] Zur Anwendung gelangte sie jedoch wenige Tage später, ohne dass sie als solche bezeichnet würde.[60] Bereits frühzeitig wurde dem Rückgriff auf die lex fori lediglich eine Auffangfunktion zugesprochen.[61] Hielt der EuGH selbst das Dogma der Gleichwertigkeit der Auslegungsmethoden zunächst lange aufrecht,[62] so musste er später doch auch ein Übergewicht der autonomen Auslegung anerkennen.[63] Spätestens in den 1990er Jahren ist daher deutlich eine Trendwende von der Gleichgewichtung der Auslegungsmethoden hin zu einem Grundsatz oder Vorrang der autonomen Auslegung erkennbar.[64]

Diese favorisierte auch der *Jubilar,* der bereits in seiner Dissertationsschrift entgegen dem EuGH für den „Ort, an dem die Verpflichtung erfüllt worden ist oder zu erfüllen wäre" eine autonome Auslegung des Art. 5 Nr. 1 EuGVÜ bevorzugte.[65] Heute ist die autonome Auslegung ein Kernbestandteil des Europäischen Zivilprozessrechts, welches auf diese Weise ein eigenständiges, von den nationalen Rechtsordnungen unabhängiges Rechtsgebiet bilden konnte. Und da die (meist autonomen) Auslegungsentscheidungen rasch zunahmen, führte der *Jubilar* bereits zeitig eine Leitsatzkartei,[66] die die umfassender werdende EuGH-Rechtsprechung erschloss.

---

[59] EuGH 6.10.1976 – 12/76, ECLI:EU:C:1976:133 Rn. 9ff. = NJW 1977, 491 (Industrie Tessili Italiana Como/Dunlop AG).

[60] EuGH 14.10.1976 – 29/76, ECLI:EU:C:1976:137 Rn. 5 = NJW 1977, 489 (LTU Lufttransportunternehmen GmbH & Co. KG/Eurocontrol).

[61] Generalanwalt Capotorti 31.5.1978 – 150/77, ECLI:EU:C:1978:116 Rn. 2 = Slg. 1978, 1447 (1449); so auch die Meinung in der Literatur Kropholler, Europäisches Zivilprozessrecht, 1982, Einl. Rn. 38; Schack, Internationales Zivilverfahrensrecht, 1991, Rn. 93; Kropholler FS 75 Jahre Max-Planck-Institut für Privatrecht, 2001, 583 (589f.).

[62] EuGH 8.12.1987 – 144/86, ECLI:EU:C:1987:528 Rn. 7 = Slg. 1987, 4871 (Gubisch Maschinenfabrik KG/Giulio Palumbo); EuGH 10.3.1992 – C-214/89, ECLI:EU:C:1992:115 Rn. 12 (Powell Duffryn plc/Wolfgang Petereit).

[63] EuGH 19.1.1993 – C-89/91, ECLI:EU:C:1993:15 Rn. 13 = NJW 1993, 1251 (Shearson Lehman Hutton Inc./TVB Treuhandgesellschaft für Vermögensverwaltung und Beteiligungen mbH); EuGH 13.7.1993 – C-125/92, ECLI:EU:C:1993:306 Rn. 10f. (Mulox IBC Ltd/Hendrick Geels); dies hält auch Generalanwalt Léger 17.5.1995 – C-341/93, ECLI:EU:C:1995:139 Rn. 20ff. fest.

[64] So Scholz, Das Problem der autonomen Auslegung des EuGVÜ, 1998, S. 14

[65] Rauscher, Verpflichtung und Erfüllungsort in Art. 5 Nr. 1 EuGVÜ (1984), S. 224; s dazu auch Rauscher, Internationales Privatrecht, 5. Aufl. 2017, Rn. 1809f.

[66] Inzwischen wurde diese auch veröffentlicht: Rauscher/Pelikan, EuGH-Leitsatzsammlung EuZPR/EuIPR, 2. Aufl. 2021.

Und mit dem territorialen wie materiellen Wachstum schon bald griffig nur noch EuZPR genannten Rechtsgebiet trug auch der *Jubilar* selbst die Idee und das Wissen um ein Europäisches Zivilprozessrecht zu den Studenten in Europa. Gastvorlesungen in Oslo, Turku und bald regelmäßig in Budapest, wofür er später von der Eötvös-Loránd-Universität mit der Verleihung des *doctor et professor honoris causa* geehrt wurde, befruchteten den internationalen Austausch und bilden letztlich einen weiteren Baustein für eine einheitliche Anwendung der Normen. Die erheblich gestiegene Bedeutung des EuGH für das EuZPR bringt der Ausspruch des *Jubilars* – getätigt im Rahmen des Erasmus Netzwerkes in seiner Lehrveranstaltung im Februar 1998 an der Turun yliopisto – zum Ausdruck: „The ECJ, The Godfather Himself, – oh, no Itself, The Godfather is a „him" but the ECJ is a „it" – …"

6. *Verbleibende Bedeutung*

Legislativ bestand am Ende das auf Art. 293 EGV, ex-Art. 220 E(W)GV fußende Europäische Zivilprozessrecht allein aus dem EuGVÜ, dem zugehörigen AuslProt idF seiner Beitrittsübereinkommen und dem Parallelübereinkommen LugÜbk 1988. Im Wesentlichen sind diese nach der Vergemeinschaftung (dazu sogleich → II.1.) durch die Brüssel I-VO (→ II.2.) und deren Nachfolgeverordnungen und das LugÜbk 2007 (→ III.2.) ersetzt worden.

Ganz verschwunden ist dieser erste Teil des Europäischen Zivilprozessrechts jedoch heute noch nicht. Es verbleibt ein territorialer Restanwendungsbereich in den erstreckten Gebieten jenseits der heutigen Europäischen Union. Das Europarecht und damit die aktuellen Rechtsinstrumente finden in den französischen Gebieten Saint-Barthelémy,[67] St. Pierre und Miquelon, Wallis und Fortuna, Französisch-Polynesien, Neukaledonien, Französische Süd- und Antarktisgebieten sowie im niederländischen Aruba keine Anwendung. Insoweit konnte die Brüssel I-VO (Art. 68 Abs. 1 Brüssel I-VO) das EuGVÜ und das AuslProt auch nicht ablösen. Beide gelten daher in den hier genannten Gebieten bis heute weiter. Daher wird das EuGVÜ auch heute noch bei nationalen Anpassungen aktuell gehalten.[68] Zur bereits vorgesehenen Ablösung durch das LugÜbk 2007 → III.2.

Das LugÜbk 1988 ist hingegen vollständig durch das LugÜbk 2007 ersetzt worden. In den vorgenannten außereuropäischen Gebieten fand es wohl nie Anwendung.[69] Jedenfalls aber sind diese Gebiete keine eigenständigen Vertragsstaaten des LugÜbk 1988 geworden, Vertragsstaat waren insoweit stets allein Frankreich und die Niederlande. Gegenüber diesen Vertragsstaaten gilt der klare Ersetzungsbefehl in Art. 69 Abs. 6 LugÜbk 2007. Dass das ersetzende LugÜbk 2007 in bestimmten Gebieten dieser Vertragsstaates nicht in Geltung gelangt genügt nicht, um die Ersetzung einschränkend zu verstehen. Wäre dies gewollt gewesen, hätte sie – wie bei

[67] Seit 1.1.2012 ein eigenständiges überseeisches Gebiet, Art. 1 Beschluss 2010/718/EU (ABl. 2010 L 325, 4).

[68] S. dazu zuletzt die Mitteilung Schwedens (ABl. 2016 C 453, 4) sowie die Mitteilung Portugals ABl. 2016 C 453, 4.

[69] Jenard/Möller-Bericht [zum LugÜbk 1988] (ABl. 1990 C 189, 57 (85 Rn. 94)) geht von einer Anwendbarkeit aus; Dasser/Oberhammer, Lugano-Übereinkommen/Domej, 3. Aufl. 2021, Art. 63 Rn. 29 verneint diese mangels Niederschlags im Vertragstext.

Art. 68 Abs. 1 Brüssel I-VO – ausdrücklich formuliert sein müssen.[70] Das LugÜbk 1988 ist damit in vollem Umfang ersetzt worden und damit erloschen. Damit scheidet auch ein Wiederaufleben hinsichtlich des Vereinigten Königreichs nach dem BREXIT aus.[71]

II. Vergemeinschaftung der Rechtsquellen

1. Unionsrechtliche Grundlagen

Nachdem im völkervertraglichem Regime nach dem sehr erfolgreichen EuGVÜ jedenfalls der Umsetzungserfolg häufig im Ratifikationsprozess stecken blieb, war eine signifikante Ausdehnung allein mit einer Änderung des kompetenzrechtlichen Regimes denkbar. Dieser Umbruch kam mit dem Vertrag von Amsterdam 1999.[72] Er nahm das Ziel zur Etablierung eines „Raums der Freiheit, der Sicherheit und des Rechts" in das Europäische Primärrecht auf (Art. 61 EGV 1999) und ordnete diesem auch die justitielle Zusammenarbeit in Zivilsachen zu (Art. 61 lit. c EGV 1999). Damit wurde die Kompetenz zum Erlass der Regelungen des Europäischen Zivilprozessrechts auf den europäischen Verordnungsgeber übertragen. Das EuZPR konnte zu einem Bestandteil des Europäischen Sekundärrechts werden.

Jedoch kam das neue Kompetenzgefüge nicht ohne Schwächen. Dänemark beteiligt sich aufgrund des dem Vertrag von Amsterdam beigefügten Protokolls über die Position Dänemarks nicht an Maßnahmen, welche auf der neu geschaffenen Kompetenz fußen. Der „Raum der Freiheit, der Sicherheit und des Rechts" erstreckt sich daher nicht auf dieses EU-Mitglied, Dänemark steht insoweit einem Drittstaat gleich. Das Protokoll wurde zwar durch den Vertrag von Lissabon,[73] dahingehend angepasst, dass Dänemark zu einem opt-in Modell übergehen kann (Art. 8 Protokoll über die Position Dänemarks idF des Vertrags von Lissabon), jedoch hat es davon bis heute keinen Gebrauch gemacht.

Mit dem ebenfalls dem Vertrag von Amsterdam beigefügten Protokoll über die Position des Vereinigten Königreichs und Irland wurde für diese beiden Länder hinsichtlich der neuen Kompetenz ebenfalls ein Sonderregime geschaffen. Jedoch wird hier nach Vorschlag einer auf der neuen Gemeinschaftskompetenz fußenden Maßnahme die Möglichkeit des singulären opt-in gewährt. Für jede Einzelmaßnahme ist daher ein individueller Entscheidungsprozess möglich.

---

[70] Dasser/Oberhammer, Lugano-Übereinkommen/Domej, 3. Aufl. 2021, Art. 63 Rn. 29.

[71] Dasser/Oberhammer, Lugano-Übereinkommen/Domej, 3. Aufl. 2021, Art. 63 Rn. 27.

[72] Vertrag von Amsterdam zur Änderung des Vertrags über die Europäische Union, der Verträge zur Gründung der Europäischen Gemeinschaften sowie einiger damit zusammenhängender Rechtsakte, unterzeichnet am 2.10.1997 (BGBl. 1998 II 386), in Kraft getreten am 1.5.1999 (BGBl. 1999 II 296).

[73] Vertrag von Lissabon zur Änderung des Vertrags über die Europäische Union und des Vertrags zur Gründung der Europäischen Gemeinschaft, unterzeichnet am 13.12.2007 (BGBl. 2008 II 1038), in Kraft getreten am 1.12.2009 (BGBl. 2009 II 1223).

Damit war mit diesem „Säulenwechsel von Amsterdam"[74] zwar eine „Kompetenzrevolution"[75] verbunden. Mit der konkreten Ausgestaltung der Kompetenzgrundlage stand aber auch fest, dass insbesondere der aufgrund der genannten Protokolle eingeschränkte territoriale Anwendungsbereich des EuZPR innerhalb der EU stets im Blick des Rechtsanwenders wird sein müssen. Dies wurde heftig als Kodifikation des Prinzips „Europa à la carte" gebrandmarkt.[76] Zudem wurde zunächst die Auslegungskompetenz des EuGH beschränkt. Diesem mussten und konnten nur noch letztinstanzliche Gerichte vorlegen, die optionale Vorlagemöglichkeit der Instanzgerichte entfiel (Art. 68 Abs. 1 EGV 1999). Dies war nicht nur im Vergleich zum allgemeinen Europarecht eine Beschränkung, sondern auch im Vergleich zum AuslProt 1971, konnten doch bisher bei Auslegungsfragen zum EuGVÜ auch Rechtsmittelgerichte vorlegen. Die Beschränkung wurde erst mit dem Vertrag von Lissabon 2009 aufgehoben. So wurde die mögliche Vergemeinschaftung des EuZPR anfänglich in der Literatur heftig kritisiert. Es wurde von einem „höchst gefährlichem Sprengsatz" und „rabiater Rechtsvereinheitlichungspolitik" gesprochen.[77] Dennoch wurde bald auch angenommen, dass die weltweite Fachwissenschaft die Kompetenzverlagerung schon sehr bald als „fait accompli" hinnehmen werde.[78]

2. *Verordnungen der „Erste Generation" – sachliche Expansion*

In einem ersten Schritt wurde die Kompetenz genutzt, um den materiellen Gehalt des EuZPR zu steigern. Hierzu konnte auf die zahlreichen Arbeiten innerhalb der intergouvernementalen Zusammenarbeit zurückgegriffen werden. Im Wesentlichen wurden die fertig ausgearbeiteten Übereinkommen genutzt und nunmehr als Verordnungen in das Rechtsetzungsverfahren eingebracht.

Der Ausbau des Europäischen Zivilprozessrechts begann wenige Tage nach dem Inkrafttreten des neuen Kompetenzregimes und wurde mit höchster Geschwindigkeit vorangetrieben. Die Europäische Kommission startete mit Ihren Vorschlägen zur EG-ZustVO 2000[79] und zur Brüssel II-VO[80], Deutschland und Finnland folgten mit Ihrer Initiative zur EG-InsVO[81], für alle drei Verordnungen wurde ein Jahr

---

[74] Geimer, Internationales Zivilprozessrecht, 9. Aufl. 2024, Rn. 245.

[75] So Mansel, Vergemeinschaftung des Europäischen Kollisionsrechts/Mansel, 2001, S. 1 (3); Wagner NJW 2003, 2344

[76] Sauer, Internationale Zuständigkeit für die Auflösung und Lockerung des Ehebandes nach deutschem, französischem und europäischem Recht, 2003, S. 194.

[77] Schack ZEuP 1999, 805 (805, 808); s. zur Kritik auch Jayme/Kohler IPRax 1999, 401; Jayme IPRax 2000, 165; Kohler rev. crit. dip 1999, 1; Beaumont ICLQ 1999, 223 (225ff.).

[78] Basedow FS Lorenz, 2001, 463.

[79] Europäische Kommission, Vorschlag vom 4.5.1999, KOM(1999) 219; VO (EG) Nr. 1348/2000 vom 29.5.2000 über die Zustellung gerichtlicher und außergerichtlicher Schriftstücke in Zivil- oder Handelssachen in den Mitgliedstaaten (ABl. 2000 L 160, 37).

[80] Europäische Kommission, Vorschlag vom 4.5.1999, KOM(1999) 220; VO (EG) Nr. 1347/2000 vom 29.5.2000 über die Zuständigkeit und die Anerkennung und Vollstreckung von Entscheidungen in Ehesachen und in Verfahren betreffend die elterliche Verantwortung für die gemeinsamen Kinder der Ehegatten (ABl. 2000 L 160, 19).

[81] Bundesrepublik Deutschland und Republik Finnland, Initiative dem Rat vorgelegt am 26.5.1999 (ABl. 1999 C 221, 8); VO (EG) Nr. 1346/2000 vom 29.5.2000 über Insolvenzverfahren (ABl. 2000 L 160, 1).

später am selben Tag das Rechtsetzungsverfahren abgeschlossen. Die weitgehende (→ I.6.) Ablösung des EuGVÜ durch die Reform mittels der Brüssel I-VO[82] folgte kurz danach und zur Rechtshilfe wurde die EG-BewVO[83] ergänzt.

Binnen kürzester Zeit hatte sich die zu beachtende und zu bearbeitende Materie vervielfacht. In dieser spannenden Zeit des Neuen, des grundlegenden Um- und Aufbruchs, der großen Erweiterung, die auch zahlreiche neue Rechtsfragen aufwarf, und bald des Experimentierens entstand beim *Jubilar* die Idee eines Großkommentars zum Europäischen Zivilprozessrecht, der tiefgründig alle (Neu)Bestandteile des Rechtsgebiets erfasst. Dem Praktiker wie dem Wissenschaftler und vielleicht auch dem Gesetzgeber sollte Halt und fundierte Orientierung, Diskurs und Austausch in diesem sich rapide entwickelnden Rechtsgebiet gegeben werden. Und der *Jubilar* inspirierte den wissenschaftlichen Nachwuchs, sich für dieses Rechtsgebiet zu begeistern und zu engagieren. Die Arbeit an nahezu einer jeden Dissertation beginnt mit der Suche nach einem geeigneten Thema. In jener Zeit fielen dabei an seinem Leipziger Institut in zahlreichen Fällen die Worte: „Etwas im EuZPR, irgendwie mit den neuen Verordnungen." Es war Das übergreifende Thema, mit dem es sich zu beschäftigen lohnte. Schlussendlich widmeten sich eine Vielzahl seiner Doktoranden diesem Gebiet.[84] Und auch der Verfasser selbst fertigte sodann eine grundlegende Arbeit zu den Ehesachen unter dem Brüssel II-Regime.

3. *Verordnungen der „Zweiten Generation" – Abschaffung des Exequaturs*

Es blieb jedoch nicht bei dieser ersten Runde der Vergemeinschaftung. Nach der Reform des europäischen Primärrechts erhielt das Europäische Zivilprozessrecht auch politische Aufmerksamkeit. Der Europäische Rat am 15./16.10.1999 in Tampere hielt in seinen Schlussfolgerungen fest, dass der Grundsatz der gegenseitigen Anerkennung ein Eckstein der justitiellen Zusammenarbeit innerhalb der Union werden sollte. Er forderte im Anerkennungs- und die Vollstreckungsverfahren zum weiteren Abbau von Zwischenmaßnahmen im ersuchten Staat auf und forderte die Abschaffung des Exequaturs ausdrücklich für Titel aufgrund geringfügiger verbraucher- oder handelsrechtlicher Ansprüche und für bestimmten familienrechtliche Urteile (zB über Unterhaltsansprüche und Besuchsrechte). Damit einhergehend

[82] Europäische Kommission, Vorschlag vom 14.7.1999, KOM(1999) 348; VO (EG) Nr. 44/2001 vom 22.12.2000 über die gerichtliche Zuständigkeit und die Anerkennung und Vollstreckung von Entscheidungen in Zivil- und Handelssachen (ABl. 2001 L 12, 1).

[83] Bundesrepublik Deutschland, Initiative vom Rat zirkuliert am 6.10.2000 (ABl. 2000 C 314, 1); VO (EG) Nr. 1206/2001 vom 28.5.2001 über die Zusammenarbeit zwischen den Gerichten der Mitgliedstaaten auf dem Gebiet der Beweisaufnahme in Zivil- oder Handelssachen (ABl. 2001 L 174, 1).

[84] So sei erinnert an Ina Sauer, Internationale Zuständigkeit für die Auflösung und Lockerung des Ehebandes nach deutschem, französischem und europäischem Recht, 2003, Anna Junghardt, Die Vereinheitlichung des Erb- und Testamentsrechts im Rahmen einer europäischen Verordnung – Rom IV-VO, 2009, und Franziska Rößler-Hecht, Der Eigentumsvorbehalt in der Insolvenz im europäischen Rechtsvergleich, 2009, aber auch an das unvollendete Projekt des Mitherausgebers Guido Kosmehl, Der Gerichtsstand der unerlaubten Handlung im Internet. Alternativ endete die Themenwahl für das anstehende Projekt im Nachbarrechtsgebiet, für welches der *Jubilar* den Begriff „EuIPR" prägte, so bei Alexander Fehre, Vorschlag für ein limitiertes Optionsrecht als europäische Kollisionsregel bei Persönlichkeitsverletzungen – Eine Analyse der Rom-II-Vorschläge, 2007.

könnten Mindeststandards für spezifische Aspekte des Zivilprozessrechts aufgestellt werden.[85] Hierzu wurde zur Erstellung eines Maßnahmenprogramms aufgefordert, welches sodann von vom Rat der EU vorgelegt[86] und in der Folge gemeinsam mit den weiteren europäischen Institutionen abgearbeitet wurde.

Hinzu kamen weitere Veränderungen im Kompetenzgefüge. Mit dem Vertrag von Nizza[87] 2003 fiel in weiten Teilen das im Rat bis dahin bestehende Einstimmigkeitserfordernis (Art 67 Abs. 5 EGV 2003). Künftig konnten Rechtsakte im Mitentscheidungsverfahren vom Rat der EU und dem Europäischen Parlament als Co-Rechtsetzer mit Mehrheit beschlossen werden. Dies beschleunigte die Aktivitäten des europäischen Verordnungsgebers weiter. Eine Ausnahme bildet das Familienrecht, hier bedarf es weiterhin einer Einstimmigkeit im Rat, das Europäische Parlament hat im Gegenzug allein ein Anhörungsrecht (Art. 67 Abs. 1 EGV 2003, Art 81 Abs. 3 AEUV).

Im Familienrecht kam es sogleich zur ersten Reform einer doch gerade erst in Kraft getretenen Verordnung: Die Brüssel II-VO wurde durch die um die elterliche Verantwortung für alle Kinder erweiterte Brüssel IIa-VO[88] ersetzt und dabei die Möglichkeit der Vollstreckbarkeit ohne Exequatur für Umgangs- und Rückgabeentscheidungen mit eingeführt. Im sachlichen Anwendungsbereich der Brüssel I-VO, aber beschränkt auf unbestrittene Forderungen, entstand die EG-VollstrTitelVO[89] mittels derer Titel nach Bestätigung im Ursprungsstaat EU-weit der unmittelbaren Vollstreckung ohne Exequatur zugänglich sind. Eingeführt wurde ein europäisches Mahnverfahren mit der EG-MahnVO[90] und ein europäisches Erkenntnisverfahren bei als geringwertig definierten Forderungen mit der EG-BagatellVO.[91] Auch diese führen zu im Wesentlichen frei zirkulierbaren Titeln. Kurz darauf wurde zudem die EG-ZustVO 2000 durch die EG-ZustVO 2007[92] ersetzt.

---

[85] Ziff. 33ff. Schlussfolgerungen des Vorsitzes, Europäischer Rat in Tampere, 15./16.10.1999, https://www.europarl.europa.eu/summits/tam_de.htm (abgerufen 16.6.2024).

[86] Rat der EU, Maßnahmenprogramm zur Umsetzung des Grundsatzes der gegenseitigen Anerkennung gerichtlicher Entscheidungen in Zivil- und Handelssachen (ABl. 2001 C 12, 1).

[87] Vertrag von Nizza zur Änderung des Vertrags über die Europäische Union, der Verträge zur Gründung der Europäischen Gemeinschaften sowie einiger damit zusammenhängender Rechtsakte, unterzeichnet am 26.2.2001 (BGBl. 2001 II 1666), in Kraft getreten am 1.2.2003 (BGBl. 2003 II 1477).

[88] Europäische Kommission, Vorschlag vom 3.5.2002, KOM(2002) 222; VO (EG) Nr. 2201/2003 vom 27.11.2003 über die Zuständigkeit und die Anerkennung und Vollstreckung von Entscheidungen in Ehesachen und in Verfahren betreffend die elterliche Verantwortung und zur Aufhebung der Verordnung (EG) Nr. 1347/2000 (ABl. 2003 L 338, 1).

[89] Europäische Kommission, Vorschlag vom 18.4.2002, KOM(2002) 159; VO (EG) Nr. 805/2004 vom 21.4.2004 zur Einführung eines europäischen Vollstreckungstitels für unbestrittene Forderungen (ABl. 2004 L 143, 15).

[90] Europäische Kommission, Vorschlag vom 25.5.2004, KOM(2004) 173/3; VO (EG) Nr. 1896/2006 vom 12.12.2006 zur Einführung eines europäischen Mahnverfahrens (ABl. 2006 L 399, 1).

[91] Europäische Kommission, Vorschlag vom 15.3.2005, KOM(2005) 87; VO (EG) Nr. 861/2007 vom 11.7.2007 zur Einführung eines europäischen Verfahrens für geringfügige Forderungen (ABl. 2007 L 199, 1).

[92] Europäische Kommission, Vorschlag vom 1.12.2006, KOM(2006) 751; VO (EG) Nr. 1393/2007 vom 13.11.2007 über die Zustellung gerichtlicher und außergerichtlicher Schriftstücke in Zivil- oder Handelssachen in den Mitgliedstaaten (Zustellung von Schriftstücken) und zur Aufhebung der Verordnung (EG) Nr. 1348/2000 des Rates (ABl. 2008 L 324, 79).

Die politische Aufmerksamkeit blieb über das erste Jahrzehnt des neuen Jahrtausends hoch. Themen des Europäischen Zivilprozessrechts wurden auch 2004 in das nachfolgende mehrjährige „Haager Programm" des Europäischen Rates aufgenommen. Es formulierte 2004 als Ziel die Verbesserung der gemeinsamen Fähigkeit der Union und ihrer Mitgliedstaaten zur Weiterentwicklung der gegenseitigen Anerkennung von Gerichtsentscheidungen und Urkunden sowohl in Zivil- als auch in Strafsachen sowie zur Beseitigung rechtlicher und gerichtlicher Hindernisse bei Rechtsstreitigkeiten in Zivil- und Familiensachen mit grenzüberschreitenden Bezügen.[93]

Die Aktivitäten wurden mit der EG-UntVO[94] fortgesetzt, in welcher erstmals – wenn auch noch ohne eigene materielle Regeln – das Internationale Privatrecht mit adressiert wurde. Die EG-UntVO griff zugleich in den Anwendungsbereich der Brüssel I-VO ein und der Anwendungsbereich der EG-VollstrTitelVO kann bis heute nicht mehr aus dieser selbst heraus bestimmt werden; dies muss mittels Art. 68 Abs. 2 EG-UntVO und (jedenfalls bis zum BREXIT) in Abhängigkeit der Bindung der Mitgliedstaaten an das HUntStProt 2007 bestimmt werden.

Mit dem „Stockholmer Programm" 2009 wurde dann auf höchster politischer Ebene Erreichtes anerkannt, aber auch festgestellt, „dass die Effizienz der Instrumente der Union in diesem Bereich noch weiter verbessert werden muss", Defizite in Form von Überschneidungen und mangelnder Kohärenz wurden erstmals anerkannt.[95]

Im ersten Schritt kam es jedoch zur Reform der Brüssel I-VO durch die Brüssel Ia-VO[96] und der damit verbundenen Abschaffung des Exequatur-Verfahrens. Dennoch gewisse Anerkennungsversagungsgründe, insbesondere der *ordre public*-Einwand blieben – anders als bei Art. 21 EG-VollstrTitelVO – erhalten (Art. 45 Brüssel Ia-VO). Der Verordnungsgeber schuf aber auch neue eigenständige Instrumente und erweiterte das Europäische Zivilprozessrecht im Familienrecht um die EU-SchutzMVO[97] und im allgemeinen Zivil- und Handelsrecht um die EU-KPfVO,[98]

---

[93] Europäischer Rat, Haager Programm zur Stärkung von Freiheit, Sicherheit und Recht in der Europäischen Union (ABl. 2005 C 53, 1).

[94] Europäische Kommission, Vorschlag vom 15.12.2005, KOM(2005) 649; VO (EG) Nr. 4/2009 vom 18.12.2008 über die Zuständigkeit, das anwendbare Recht, die Anerkennung und Vollstreckung von Entscheidungen und die Zusammenarbeit in Unterhaltssachen (ABl. 2009 L 7, 1).

[95] Europäischer Rat, Das Stockholmer Programm – Ein offenes und sicheres Europa im Dienste und zum Schutz der Bürger (ABl. 2010 C 115, 1 (15 [Ziff. 3.3.2], 5 [1.2.3])).

[96] Europäische Kommission, Vorschlag vom 14.12.2010, KOM(2010) 748; VO (EU) Nr. 1215/2012 vom 12.12.2012 über die gerichtliche Zuständigkeit und die Anerkennung und Vollstreckung von Entscheidungen in Zivil- und Handelssachen (Neufassung) (ABl. 2012 L 351, 1).

[97] Europäische Kommission, Vorschlag vom 18.5.2011, KOM(2011) 276; VO (EU) Nr. 606/2013 vom 12.6.2013 über die gegenseitige Anerkennung von Schutzmaßnahmen in Zivilsachen (ABl. 2013 L 181, 4).

[98] Europäische Kommission, Vorschlag vom 25.7.2011, KOM(2011) 445; VO (EU) Nr. 655/2014 vom 15.5.2014 zur Einführung eines Verfahrens für einen Europäischen Beschluss zur vorläufigen Kontenpfändung im Hinblick auf die Erleichterung der grenzüberschreitenden Eintreibung von Forderungen in Zivil- und Handelssachen (ABl. 2014 L 189, 59).

die das EuZPR erstmals in das Gebiet des klassischen Zwangsvollstreckungsrechts hineinentwickelte,[99] sowie die EU-UrkVO[100].

4. *„Misch"-Verordnungen – Einschluss des EuIPR*

Die Regelungen des Kollisionsrechts wurden lange von denen des Prozessrechts getrennt gehalten. Der Beginn der Entwicklung eines Europäischen Kollisionsrechts, eines Europäischen Internationalen Privatrechts oder – wie es der *Jubilar* kurz und prägnant prägte – EuIPR geht zurück auf das Rom I-Übk 1980, welches nach dem Vertrag von Amsterdam ebenfalls von einer Rom I-VO abgelöst und um eine Rom II-VO ergänzt wurde. In Ehesachen kam es sodann zur Rom III-VO, die jedoch bereits nicht für die gesamte EU (mit der Ausnahme Dänemarks) erlassen werden konnte, so dass der Weg der Verstärkten Zusammenarbeit gewählt wurde, welche zunächst mit 14 Staaten startete und heute auf 17 Mitgliedsstaaten angewachsen ist.[101]

Die Idee der Verquickung von EuZPR und EuIPR in einem Rechtsakt, wie erstmals bei der EG-UntVO (wenn auch dort noch allein durch einen Verweis auf das HUntStProt 2007) praktiziert, wurde für die kommenden Aktivitäten des europäischen Verordnungsgebers populär. So regelt die EU-ErbVO[102] Fragen der Zuständigkeit, des anwendbaren Rechts, der Anerkennung und Vollstreckung. Anders als die Verordnungen der zweiten Generation enthält die EU-ErbVO aber wieder ein Exequaturverfahren (Art. 43 EU-ErbVO).

Die Fortsetzung dieser Methodik findet sich bei der EU-EheGüterVO[103] und der EU-LP-GüterVO.[104] Für beide kommt eine weitere Einschränkung hinzu: Als familienrechtliches Instrument wäre zum Erlass eine Einstimmigkeit im Rat erforderlich gewesen (Art. 81 Abs. 3 AEUV), welche nicht erzielt werden konnte. Daher wurden beide Instrumente im Wege der Verstärkten Zusammenarbeit in Kraft ge-

---

[99] S. dazu Lüttringhaus ZZP 129 (2016), 187 (188f.); Rechberger FS Coester-Waltjen, 2015, 651.

[100] Europäische Kommission, Vorschlag vom 24.4.2013, COM(2013) 228; VO (EU) 2016/1191 vom 6.7.2016 zur Förderung der Freizügigkeit von Bürgern durch die Vereinfachung der Anforderungen an die Vorlage bestimmter öffentlicher Urkunden innerhalb der Europäischen Union und zur Änderung der Verordnung (EU) 2016/1191 (ABl. 2016 L 200, 1).

[101] Münchener Kommentar zum BGB/Rentsch, 9. Aufl. 2024, Rom III-VO Vor. Art. 1 Rn. 5f.

[102] Europäische Kommission, Vorschlag vom 14.10.2009, KOM(2009) 154; VO (EU) Nr. 650/2012 vom 4.7.2012 über die Zuständigkeit, das anzuwendende Recht, die Anerkennung und Vollstreckung von Entscheidungen und die Annahme und Vollstreckung öffentlicher Urkunden in Erbsachen sowie zur Einführung eines Europäischen Nachlasszeugnisses (ABl. 2012 L 201, 107).

[103] Europäische Kommission, Vorschlag vom 16.3.2011, KOM(2011) 126; Vorschlag Verstärkte Zusammenarbeit vom 2.3.2016, COM(2016) 106; VO (EU) 2016/1103 vom 24.6.2016 zur Durchführung einer Verstärkten Zusammenarbeit im Bereich der Zuständigkeit, des anzuwendenden Rechts und der Anerkennung und Vollstreckung von Entscheidungen in Fragen des ehelichen Güterstands (ABl. 2016 L 183, 1).

[104] Europäische Kommission, Vorschlag vom 16.3.2011, KOM(2011) 127; Vorschlag Verstärkte Zusammenarbeit vom 2.3.2016, COM(2016) 107; VO (EU) 2016/1104 vom 24.6.2016 zur Durchführung der Verstärkten Zusammenarbeit im Bereich der Zuständigkeit, des anzuwendenden Rechts und der Anerkennung und Vollstreckung von Entscheidungen in Fragen güterrechtlicher Wirkungen eingetragener Partnerschaften (ABl. 2016 L 183, 30).

setzt, an welcher sich bis heute lediglich 18 Mitgliedstaaten beteiligen. Der genaue territoriale Anwendungsbereich und insbesondere gegebenenfalls neu hinzugekommene Mitgliedstaaten müssen insbesondere bei einer begehrten Vollstreckung innerhalb der EU aufwändig ermittelt werden, so dass die Vorhersehbarkeit und Rechtsklarheit für den Rechtsanwender leidet.

Der Weg der „Misch"-Verordnung soll auch in Zukunft fortgesetzt werden. Aktuell befinden sich zwei Projekte im Verordnungsgebungsverfahren, zum einen der Entwurf für eine familienrechtliche, die Einstimmigkeit im Rat der EU erfordernde EU-ElternVO[105] und der Entwurf für eine EU-ErwSVO,[106] wobei der Erwachsenenschutz nicht als familienrechtliche Maßnahme eingeordnet wird, so dass das Mitentscheidungsverfahren mit Mehrheitsentscheidung zur Anwendung gelangt.[107]

5. *Reformverordnungen*

Der Verordnungsgeber beschäftigte sich in diesen Jahren auch mit der Reform bestehender Rechtsinstrumente. Jedoch wurde dabei stets eine Verordnung durch eine neue ersetzt, jeweils verbunden mit einer Neunummerierung und einer Entsprechungstabelle im Anhang. So wurde die EG-InsVO durch die EU-InsVO 2015,[108] die EG-BewVO durch die EU-BewVO 2020,[109] die EG-ZustVO 2007 durch die EU-ZustVO 2020[110] und die Brüssel IIa-VO durch die Brüssel IIb-VO[111] ersetzt. In anderen Rechtsakten enthaltene Verweise werden dabei nicht angepasst. Der Rechtsanwender muss bei Auffinden eines solchen Verweises erkennen, dass die verwiesene Norm durch eine Neufassung ersetzt wurde und sodann anhand der der Neufassung beigefügten Entsprechungstabelle die tatsächliche Zielnorm ermitteln. Bei einem Verweis auf die EG-ZustVO 2000 (zB im Zust EU-DK Abk) oder die Brüssel II-VO ist dieser Vorgang nun bereits zweimal durchzuführen, da

---

105 Europäische Kommission, Vorschlag für eine Verordnung über die Zuständigkeit, das anzuwendende Recht, die Anerkennung von Entscheidungen und die Annahme öffentlicher Urkunden in Elternschaftssachen sowie zur Einführung eines europäischen Elternschaftszertifikats vom 7.12.2022, COM(2022) 695.

106 Europäische Kommission, Vorschlag für eine Verordnung über die Zuständigkeit, das anwendbare Recht, die Anerkennung und Vollstreckung von Maßnahmen und die Zusammenarbeit in Fragen betreffend den Schutz Erwachsener vom 31.5.2023, COM(2023) 280.

107 Europäische Kommission, COM(2023) 280, S. 4.

108 Europäische Kommission, Vorschlag vom 12.12.2012, COM(2012) 744; VO (EU) 2015/848 vom 20.5.2015 über Insolvenzverfahren (Neufassung) (ABl. 2015 L 141, 19).

109 Europäische Kommission, Vorschlag vom 31.5.2018, COM(2018) 378; VO (EU) 2020/1783 vom 25.11.2020 über die Zusammenarbeit zwischen den Gerichten der Mitgliedstaaten auf dem Gebiet der Beweisaufnahme in Zivil- oder Handelssachen (Beweisaufnahme) (Neufassung) (ABl. 2020 L 405, 1).

110 Europäische Kommission, Vorschlag vom 31.5.2018, COM(2018) 379; VO (EU) 2020/1784 vom 25.11.2020 über die Zustellung gerichtlicher und außergerichtlicher Schriftstücke in Zivil- oder Handelssachen in den Mitgliedstaaten (Zustellung von Schriftstücken) (Neufassung) (ABl. 2020 L 405, 40).

111 Europäische Kommission, Vorschlag vom 30.6.2016, COM(2016) 411; VO (EU) 2019/1111 vom 25.6.2019 über die Zuständigkeit, die Anerkennung und Vollstreckung von Entscheidungen in Ehesachen und in Verfahren betreffend die elterliche Verantwortung und über internationale Kindesentführungen (Neufassung) (ABl. 2019 L 178, 1).

sich die Entsprechungstabelle stets nur auf die unmittelbar aufgehobene Verordnung bezieht. Die betroffenen Rechtsnormen sind so nicht mehr aus sich selbst heraus verständlich.[112] Für den Rechtsanwender bleibt die Rechtsklarheit endgültig auf der Strecke. Eine Konsolidierung oder Abstimmung der Verordnungen aufeinander ist jedoch nicht erkennbar.

Zudem wurde die EU-JustDigiVO[113] verabschiedet, sie gelangt in ihren wesentlichen Teilen am 1.5.2025 (Art. 26 Abs. 2 EU-JustDigiVO) in Geltung und hält ganz verschiedene Regelungskategorien bereit: Zum einen sind einige unmittelbar für den Rechtsanwender geltende Regelungen enthalten, so dass die Verordnung selbst in den Kanon von der Praxis regelmäßig zu beachtenden Rechts aufgenommen ist. Zum Anderen wendet sie sich an die Mitgliedstaaten, mit Reformaufträgen für das Justizwesen. Und zum Dritten ist sie Änderungsverordnung im klassischen Sinn und nimmt Anpassungen in anderen Rechtsakten des Europäischen Zivilprozessrechts vor, so in der EG-VollstrTitelVO, der EG-MahnVO, der EG-BagatellVO, der EU-SchutzMVO, der EU-KPfVO, der EU-InsVO 2015 und der EU-ZustVO 2020.

III. Völkerverträge der EU

1. Begrenzte Lösung der Dänemark-Problematik

Die aufgrund der Nichtteilnahme Dänemarks an der Vergemeinschaftung des EuZPR entstandene Situation wurde zumindest punktuell hinsichtlich des Ersatzes des EuGVÜ durch die Brüssel I-VO und die mit dieser in engem Zusammenhang stehende EG-ZustellVO auf völkerrechtlicher Ebene gelöst. Die EU schloss mit Dänemark zwei völkerrechtliche Abkommen, das Brüssel I EU-DK Abk[114] sowie das Zust EU-DK Abk[115], welche die Texte dieser beiden Verordnungen in Gestalt eines völkerrechtlichen Abkommens zwischen der EU und Dänemark zur Anwendung brachte. Auch wenn die Rechtsnatur verschieden ist, ist der territoriale Anwendungsbereich dieser Instrumente damit praktisch seit 1.7.2007 wieder auf die gesamte EU erstreckt.

Die Abkommen wurden so gestaltet, dass Reformen bezüglich der beiden Verordnungen durch Erklärung Dänemarks hier ebenfalls übernommen werden. Die notwendigen Erklärungen hat Dänemark bisher stets abgegeben, so dass auch die

---

[112] Münchener Kommentar zur ZPO/Rauscher, 6. Aufl. 2022, EG-ZustellVO Art. 25 Rn. 1; Rauscher, EuZPR/EuIPR/Fehrenbach, 5. Aufl. 2022, EU-InsVO Art. 91 Rn. 3.

[113] Europäische Kommission, Vorschlag vom 1.12.2021, COM(2021) 759; VO 2023/2844 vom 13.12.2023 über die Digitalisierung der justiziellen Zusammenarbeit und des Zugangs zur Justiz in grenzüberschreitenden Zivil-, Handels- und Strafsachen und zur Änderung bestimmter Rechtsakte im Bereich der justiziellen Zusammenarbeit (ABl. L 2023/2844 vom 27.12.2023).

[114] Abkommen zwischen der Europäischen Gemeinschaft und dem Königreich Dänemark vom 19.10.2005 über die gerichtliche Zuständigkeit und die Anerkennung und Vollstreckung von Entscheidungen in Zivil- und Handelssachen, Ratifikation aufgrund Art. 1 Beschluss 2006/325/EG (ABl. 2006 L 120, 22).

[115] Abkommen zwischen der Europäischen Gemeinschaft und dem Königreich Dänemark vom 19.10.2005 über die Zustellung gerichtlicher und außergerichtlicher Schriftstücke in Zivil- oder Handelssachen, Ratifikation aufgrund Art. 1 Beschluss 2006/326/EG (ABl. 2006 L 120, 23).

Brüssel Ia-VO[116] und in Teilen die EG-UntVO[117] (nämlich soweit diese die Brüssel I-VO ersetzt) sowie die EG-ZustVO 2007[118] und heute die EU-ZustVO 2020[119] hier in Kraft sind.

2. *Umgang mit dem Lugano-Übereinkommen*

Nach der Vergemeinschaftung des EuZPR wurde im Zusammenhang mit der beabsichtigten Reform des LugÜbk 1988 die Frage, ob die Außenkompetenz für den Abschluss von völkerrechtlichen Verträgen der Europäische Union oder den Mitgliedstaaten zukommt, diskutiert und gutachterlich durch den EuGH zugunsten der EU beantwortet.[120] Das reformierte LugÜbk 2007[121] konnte daraufhin von der EU sowie von der Schweiz, Island, Norwegen und Dänemark gezeichnet und der Ratifikationsprozess durchgeführt werden. Im Verhältnis der einzelnen Mitglieder zueinander trat es sodann 2010/2011 in Kraft und ersetzte das LugÜbk 1988 vollständig (→ I.6.). Da die EU selbst die Außenkompetenz besitzt und das Übereinkommen damit innerhalb der EU ein Rechtsakt der EU ist, sind innerhalb der EU auf das Übereinkommen auch die allgemeinen Vorschriften zum Vorabentscheidungsverfahren anwendbar. Der EuGH hat daher zumindest bei Vorlage durch ein Gericht aus einem EU-Mitgliedstaat auch bezüglich des LugÜbk 2007 die Auslegungskompetenz.[122]

Das reformierte LugÜbk 2007 sollte sodann auch im Verhältnis der EU-Mitgliedstaaten und deren außereuropäischen Gebieten, in denen das EuGVÜ noch Anwendung findet, übernehmen (Art 69 Abs. 7 LugÜbk 2007). Zu beachten ist, dass damit für diese Gebiete die Auslegungskompetenz des EuGH, welche heute aufgrund des AuslProt zum EuGVÜ besteht, verloren geht. Jedoch sind diese Gebiete gerade nicht Teil der EU. Die relevanten Mitgliedstaaten haben daher der EU auch nicht die Gesetzgebungskompetenz und damit die Abschlusskompetenz für völkerrechtliche Verträge übertragen. Das LugÜbk 2007 gilt mithin für diese Gebiete nicht automatisch. Um dennoch einen vergleichsweise leichten Übergang zu schaffen, wurde aber ein erleichterter Beitrittsweg für diese Gebiete in Art. 69 Abs. 7 LugÜbk 2007 aufgenommen. Die Norm schafft die Möglichkeit, dass der betroffene Mitgliedstaat einseitig im Namen des betreffenden Gebietes den Beitritt erklären und so das EuGVÜ ablösen kann.[123] Dies ist aber bis heute nicht erfolgt. Zwar wurde zumindest in Frankreich der Übergang von der L'Assemblée Französisch-Polynesiens und dem Congrès Neukaledoniens befürwortet[124] und sodann

---

[116] Mitteilung Dänemarks vom 20.12.2012 (ABl. 2013 L 79, 4).

[117] Mitteilung Dänemarks vom 14.1.2009 (ABl. 2009 L 149, 80).

[118] Mitteilung Dänemarks vom 20.11.2007 (ABl. 2008 L 331, 21).

[119] Mitteilung Dänemarks vom 22.12.2020 (ABl. 2021 L 19, 1).

[120] EuGH 7.2.2006 – Gutachten 1/03, ECLI:EU:C:2006:81 = BeckEuRS 2006, 421995.

[121] Übereinkommen über die gerichtliche Zuständigkeit und die Anerkennung und Vollstreckung von Entscheidungen in Zivil- und Handelssachen, unterzeichnet am 30.10.2007 (ABl. 2009 L 147, 5, ber. ABl. 2009 L 147, 44, ABl. 2011 L 115, 31, ABl. 2014 L 18, 70).

[122] S. zB EuGH 20.12.2017 – C-467/16, ECLI:EU:C:2017:993 = BeckRS 2017, 135796 (Brigitte Schlömp/Landratsamt Schwäbisch Hall); EuGH 30.9.2021 – C-296/20, ECLI:EU:C:2021:784 = EuZW 2022, 177 (Commerzbank AG/E O).

[123] Dasser/Oberhammer, Lugano-Übereinkommen/Domej, 3. Aufl. 2021, Art. 69 Rn. 6.

[124] S. Laufoaulu, Bericht vom 23.5.2018, Sénat: 97 (2016–2017) 498, S. 27.

das nationale Gesetzgebungsverfahren durchlaufen.[125] Eine anschließende Hinterlegung und Notifizierung beim zuständigen Verwahrer, dem Schweizerischen Bundesrat, ist jedoch nicht feststellbar.

Nach dem BREXIT hat sich das Vereinigte Königreich um einen eigenständigen Beitritt zum LugÜbk 2007 bemüht.[126] Nachdem die Schweiz, Island und Norwegen bereits ihr grundsätzliches Einverständnis erklärten,[127] wies die Europäische Kommission das Ersuchen für die EU zurück.[128] Ein Beitritt ist damit vorerst gescheitert.

3. Haager Übereinkommen

Nach Erstattung des Gutachtens durch den EuGH im Zusammenhang mit dem Abschluss des LugÜbk 2007[129] war inzident auch geklärt, dass die EG bzw. später die EU auch im Bereich der Haager Übereinkommen auf dem Gebiet des Europäischen Zivilprozessrechts die alleinige Außenkompetenz besitzt. In der Folge rückten die Rechtsvereinheitlichungsbestrebungen der Haager Konferenz mehr und mehr in den Fokus, bot diese doch die Möglichkeit im EuZPR ein einheitliches Außen-IZPR im Verhältnis zu Drittstaaten, insbesondere bezüglich wichtiger Handelspartner der EU-Mitgliedstaaten, auszubilden. Dieses kann sich insbesondere in der Integrationstiefe vom EU-internen EuZPR erheblich unterscheiden. Um hier selbständig auch eine aktive Rolle bei der Rechtsentwicklung einnehmen zu können und nachdem die Satzung der Haager Konferenz zum 1.1.2007 angepasst wurde, trat die Europäische Gemeinschaft der Haager Konferenz für Internationales Privatrecht am 3.4.2007 bei.[130]

Bereits bei Beitritt waren alle EG-Staaten auch Vertragsstaaten des HApostilleÜbk 1961[131] und des HKindEntfÜbk 1980.[132] Nach Ermächtigung der noch feh-

---

[125] S. Laufoaulu, Bericht vom 23.5.2018, Sénat: 97 (2016–2017) 498; Assemblée nationale: 18.9.2019, texte adopté n° 333.

[126] Notifikation des Verwahrers an die Vertragsstaaten vom 14.4.2020.

[127] Notifikation des Verwahrers an die Vertragsstaaten vom 25.2.2021, vom 18.3.2021, vom 28.4.2021.

[128] Europäische Kommission, Mitteilung vom 4.5.2021, COM(2021) 222, S. 4; Europäische Kommission, Verbalnote an den Verwahrer vom 21.6.2021, https://www.dfae.admin.ch/content/dam/eda/fr/documents/aussenpolitik/voelkerrecht/autres-conventions/Lugano2/20210701-LUG-ann-EU.pdf (abgerufen 15.6.2024); das Tätigwerden der Kommission ohne Abwarten der Stellungnahmen der legislativen Institutionen deutlich kritisierend Kohler ZEuP 2021, 781 (790f.).

[129] EuGH 7.2.2006 – Gutachten 1/03, ECLI:EU:C:2006:81 = BeckEuRS 2006, 421995.

[130] Art. 1 Beschluss 2006/719/EG (ABl. 2006 L 297, 1); Mitteilung der Haager Konferenz vom 3.4.2007, https://www.hcch.net/de/news-archive/details/?varevent=129 (abgerufen 15.6.2024).

[131] Haager Übereinkommen vom 5.10.1961 zur Befreiung ausländischer öffentlicher Urkunden von der Legalisation (BGBl. 1965 II 875).

[132] Haager Übereinkommen vom 25.10.1980 über die zivilrechtlichen Aspekte internationaler Kindesentführung (BGBl. 1990 II 206); die Annahme des Beitritts neuer Drittstaaten erfordert nunmehr jedoch stets die (Einzel-)Ermächtigung der EU-Mitgliedstaaten, vgl. zB für Russland Beschluss (EU) 2015/2355 (ABl. 2015 L 331/14), für Armenien Beschluss (EU) 2015/2358 (ABl. 2015 L 331/23), für Kasachstan Beschluss (EU) 2016/2311 (ABl. 2016 L 345/53), für Südkorea Beschluss (EU) 2016/2313 (ABl. 2016 L 345/59) oder für Tunesien Beschluss (EU) 2022/2450 (ABl. 2022 L 320/39).

lenden EU-Mitgliedstaaten gehören heute ebenfalls alle dem HZÜ[133] und mit Ausnahme von Belgien, Irland und Österreich dem HBÜ[134] an. Auch das KSÜ[135] ist heute für alle EU-Mitgliedstaaten in Kraft. Das ErwSÜ[136] hingegen hatten bisher lediglich 13 EU-Mitgliedstaaten ratifiziert. Da eine Ratifizierung durch alle Mitgliedstaaten aber ein langjähriges Ziel der EU ist, sollen die verbleibenden Mitgliedstaaten nunmehr zur Ratifikation ermächtigt werden.[137]

Neuere Übereinkommen sehen nunmehr unmittelbar den Beitritt der EU als „Organisation der regionalen Wirtschaftsintegration" vor. So hat die EU selbst das HProrogÜbk 2005[138], HUntVerfÜbk 2007[139] und das HAVÜ 2019[140] ratifiziert.

4. *Weitere völkervertragliche Abkommen*

Soweit bei EU-Mitgliedstaaten im Übrigen in Ehesachen, Sachen der Elterlichen Verantwortung und Unterhaltssachen das Bedürfnis entsteht, mit Drittstaaten bilaterale IZPR-Regelungen zu treffen, so hat die EU dafür ein Verfahren für die Aushandlung und den Abschluss von völkerrechtlichen Abkommen in einer VO[141] erlassen, durch welches insbesondere die Europäische Kommission an den Verhandlungen beteiligt wird und vor Abschluss bei dieser ein Prüfungs- und Genehmigungsverfahren zu durchlaufen ist.

---

[133] Haager Übereinkommen vom 15.11.1965 über die Zustellung gerichtlicher und außergerichtlicher Schriftstücke im Ausland in Zivil- oder Handelssachen (BGBl. 1977 II S. 1452); nach Ermächtigung Österreichs und Maltas durch Art. 1 Beschluss (EU) 2016/414 (ABl. 2016 L 75, 1).

[134] Haager Übereinkommen vom 18.3.1970 über die Beweisaufnahme im Ausland in Zivil- oder Handelssachen (BGBl. 1977 II 1452).

[135] Haager Übereinkommen vom 19.10.1996 über die Zuständigkeit, das anzuwendende Recht, die Anerkennung, Vollstreckung und Zusammenarbeit auf dem Gebiet der elterlichen Verantwortung und der Maßnahmen zum Schutz von Kindern, Unterzeichnung aufgrund Art. 1 Entscheidung 2003/93/EG (ABl. 2003 L 48, 1), Ratifikation (soweit noch erforderlich) aufgrund Art. 1 Entscheidung 2008/431/EG (ABl. 2008 L 151, 36).

[136] Haager Übereinkommen vom 13.1.2000 über den internationalen Schutz von Erwachsenen (BGBl. 2007 II 323).

[137] Europäische Kommission, Entwurf ein Beschlusses vom 31.5.2023, COM(2023) 281.

[138] Haager Übereinkommen vom 30.6.2005 über Gerichtsstandsvereinbarungen, Unterzeichnung aufgrund Art. 1 Beschluss 2009/397/EG (ABl. 2009 L 133, 1), Ratifikation aufgrund Art. 1 Beschluss 2014/887/EU (ABl. 2014 L 353, 5).

[139] Haager Übereinkommens vom 23.11.2007 über die internationale Geltendmachung der Unterhaltsansprüche von Kindern und anderen Familienangehörigen, Unterzeichnung aufgrund Art. 1 Beschluss 2011/220/EU (ABl. 2011 L 93, 9), Ratifikation aufgrund Art. 1 Beschluss 2011/432/EU (ABl. 2011 L 192, 39), geändert durch Art. 1 Beschluss 2014/218/EU (ABl. 2014 L 113, 1).

[140] Haager Übereinkommens vom 2.7.2019 über die Anerkennung und Vollstreckung ausländischer Entscheidungen in Zivil- und Handelssachen, Ratifikation aufgrund Art. 1 Beschluss (EU) 2022/1206 (ABl. 2022 L 187, 1).

[141] VO (EG) 664/2009 vom 7.7.2009 zur Einführung eines Verfahrens für die Aushandlung und den Abschluss von Abkommen zwischen Mitgliedstaaten und Drittstaaten, die die Zuständigkeit und die Anerkennung und Vollstreckung von Urteilen und Entscheidungen in Ehesachen, in Fragen der elterlichen Verantwortung und in Unterhaltssachen sowie das anwendbare Recht in Unterhaltssachen betreffen.

IV. Kodifikationsgedanken

Das Europäische Zivilprozessrecht als Rechtsgebiet des Europarechts ist erwachsen geworden. Wenn es auch keine umfassende Verfahrensordnung darstellt und so weiter nationalen Traditionen Raum lässt, so bietet es doch für den europäischen grenzüberschreitenden Rechtsverkehr umfassende Regelungen zu zahlreichen wesentlichen Fragen des Zivilverfahrens. Sachlich hat es das Zivilrecht im weiteren Sinn voll erfasst, vom allgemeinen Zivil- und Handelsrecht über das Insolvenzrecht bis zum Familien- und Erbrecht. Für all diese Gebiete werden für die entscheidenden Verfahrensfragen in grenzüberschreitenden Sachverhalten wie Zuständigkeit, Zustellung, anderweitige Rechtshängigkeit, Beweiserhebung, Anerkennung und Vollstreckbarkeit einheitliche europäische Lösungen bereitgestellt.

Aber zugleich ist es organisch entstanden und gewachsen, stets von politischen Einzelinitiativen getrieben. Eine ganzheitliche Betrachtung ist im Brüsseler Verordnungsbetrieb nie erfolgt. Strukturell gelten die einzelnen Verordnungen doch stets allein für das von ihnen selbst eng umschriebene Teilgebiet. Der Rechtsbestand des Europäischen Zivilprozessrechts ist unübersichtlich geworden. Eine Vielzahl von Einzelverordnungen ist in Kraft, so einige sind bereits wieder abgelöst worden. Popularnamen haben sich im Regelfall etabliert, die Nummer oder den Langtitel kennen nur sehr wenige spezialisierte Wissenschaftler, aber wohl kaum ein Praktiker. Bei Verweisen von Verordnung zu Verordnung wird jedoch idR die Verordnungsnummer angegeben, so dass zunächst Recherche erforderlich ist. Offizielle Kurznamen gibt es selten. Allein das Aufzählen aller heute geltenden Rechtsinstitute des Europäischen Zivilprozessrechts nach Lektüre dieses Beitrages dürfte in der Regel Nicht-Spezialisten schwerfallen.

Materiell kommt hinzu, dass die Bestimmung des Anwendungsbereichs der jeweiligen Verordnung in jedem einzelnem Fall in seinen einzelnen Facetten – territorial, sachlich, zeitlich und personell – von großer Bedeutung ist. Die Beantwortung einer vergleichbaren Rechtsfrage unterscheidet sich im Detail durchaus, je nachdem welche Verordnung konkret zur Anwendung gelangt. Die Rechtsbehelfe des Schuldners im Vollstreckungsverfahren gegen einen Titel zB sind abhängig davon, welcher Verordnung der Titel im Ursprungsstaat entspringt.[142] Es steht zu befürchten, dass die aktuell erfolgende Gesetzgebungspraxis diese Inkohärenz und fehlende Rechtsklarheit weiter verstärkt.[143]

Aber die politische Zielsetzung verschiebt sich langsam. Das sogenannte „Stockholm-Nachfolgeprogramm" 2014 benannte für das Europäische Zivilprozessrecht keine neuen Betätigungsfelder mehr. Jedoch rückt die Verbesserung der Einheitlichkeit und Klarheit der EU-Rechtsvorschriften in den Fokus. Dabei sei das „reibungslose Funktionieren eines echten Europäischen Rechtsraums unter Achtung der verschiedenen Rechtsordnungen und -traditionen der Mitgliedstaaten unverzichtbar für die EU"[144]

---

[142] S. dazu Haubold FS Schütze, 2014, 163.

[143] Hardung, Die europäische Titelfreizügigkeit (2020) S. 50.

[144] Europäischer Rat, Auszug aus den Schlussfolgerungen der Tagung vom 26./27. Juni 2014 betreffend den Raum der Freiheit, der Sicherheit und des Rechts und einige damit zusammenhängende Querschnittsthemen (ABl. 2014 C 240, 13 (15, Ziff. 11)).

Auch im Europäischen Parlament wurde erkannt, dass statt eines einheitlichen Europäischen Zivilprozessrechts ein „regulatorisches Puzzle" besteht aus a) zahlreichen legislativen Maßnahmen der justiziellen Zusammenarbeit in Zivilsachen, b) einer recht umfangreichen Rechtsprechung des EuGH sowie c) einigen sektorspezifischen, detaillierten Vorschriften des EU-Sekundarrechts zu verschiedenen Fragen verfahrensrechtlicher Art auf Grundlage der wettbewerbsrechtlichen Kompetenz (Art. 114 AEUV), die noch zusätzlich hinzutreten.[145] Angemahnt wird eine klare Vision der Funktionsweise eines gemeinsamen Zivilprozessrechts in der europäischen Rechtsordnung und kritisiert die immer wieder neue Reglementierung verfahrensrechtlicher Kernfragen für jeden einzelnen Bereich, da dies zu umständlichen, große Unterschiede aufweisenden und widersprüchlichen Systemen führen könne.[146] Das Europäische Parlament forderte daraufhin die Europäische Kommission auf, einen Vorschlag für einen Rechtsakt zu gemeinsamen Mindeststandards des Zivilprozessrechts vorzulegen.[147]

Statt einer neuen, weiteren Richtlinie ist es jedoch an der Zeit die Materie größer zu Denken. Zur tatsächlichen Herstellung von Rechtssicherheit und Rechtsklarheit ist es erforderlich ein verordnungsübergreifendes Systemverständnis herauszubilden, welches die Vorhersehbarkeit für den Rechtsanwender als zentrales Begriffselement beinhaltet,[148] aber auch die weiteren Leitprinzipien des Europäischen Zivilprozessrechts wie die Parteiautonomie, den Schutz der schwächeren Partei und das Verbot der Gesetzesumgehung im Blick behält.[149] So kann Gewissheit über den Verfahrensablauf, die Auswirkungen von Parallelverfahren oder die richtige Wahl der Rechtsbehelfe gegen die Anerkennung und Vollstreckung und damit Rechtsklarheit geschaffen werden. Dieser wirkt eine Vielzahl von Rechtsnormen und schnelles Tempo des Gesetzgebers bei deren Entwicklung und Erlass entgegen.[150] Übersteigt der Rechtsstoff aber ein gewisses Maß, kann der Rechtsanwender und Normadressat ihn nicht mehr in Gänze im Blick behalten und der Sinn für Zusammenhänge geht verloren.[151]

Nach den vergangenen 25 Jahren des Aufbaus, des Experimentierens und des territorialen und sachlichen Expandierens braucht das Europäische Zivilprozessrecht Ordnung. Die nun folgende Aufgabe muss darin bestehen, den Bestand des Europäischen Zivilprozessrechts zu analysieren, in der Vielzahl der europäische Rechtsinstrumente Überschneidungen und mangelnde Kohärenz zu identifizieren

---

[145] Radev, Rechtsausschuss, Europäisches Parlament, Bericht vom 6.6.2017, A8-0210/2017, S. 35.

[146] Radev, Rechtsausschuss, Europäisches Parlament, Bericht vom 6.6.2017, A8-0210/2017, S. 36.

[147] Europäisches Parlament, Entschließung vom 4.7.2017 (ABl. 2018 C 334, 39 Ziff. 24).

[148] Dies wird auch von der Rechtsprechung regelmäßig als zentrales Ziel bestätigt: EuGH 23.4.2009 – C-533/07, ECLI:EU:C:2009:257 = NJW 2009, 1865 Rn. 22 (Falco Privatstiftung u. Rabitsch/Weller-Lindhorst); EuGH 3.5.2007 – C-386/05, ECLI:EU:C:2007:262 = EuZW 2007, 370 (Color Drack GmbH/Lesese International Vertriebs GmbH); EuGH 13.7.2006 – C-103/05, ECLI:EU:C:2006:471 = EuZW 2006, 667 Rn. 25 (Reisch Montage AG/Kiesel Baumaschinen Handels GmbH).

[149] Lüttringhaus RabelsZ 77 (2013) 31 (38).

[150] Hardung, Die europäische Titelfreizügigkeit, 2020, S. 57; Herschel JZ 1967, 727 (729).

[151] Herschel JZ 1967, 727 (729).

und daraus ein abgestimmtes Werk von konsolidierten Mindeststandards und Regelungen, systematisiert und konsolidiert, zu entwickeln.

Der Europäische Gesetzgeber sollte nun an eine Kodifizierung denken. Hierin liegt die Chance verloren gegangene Rechtssicherheit und Rechtsklarheit wieder herzustellen, denn die Kodifikation erleichtert die Rechtsanwendung, wendet auf gleiche Sachverhalte gleiche Normen an und stellt Ausnahmen ausdrücklich daneben. Erste Ansätze sich mit einer solchen zu beschäftigen, waren in der Vergangenheit bereits zu erkennen. So hat sich das Europäische Parlament bereits 2010 gegenüber dem Rat der EU und der Europäischen Kommission grundsätzlich positiv in dieser Richtung geäußert.[152] Die Europäische Kommission nahm 2014 in ihre Justizagenda 2014 auf, dass „eine Kodifizierung existierender Gesetze und Praxis die Kenntnis, das Verständnis und die Anwendung von Rechtsvorschriften, das gegenseitige Vertrauen sowie die Kohärenz und Rechtssicherheit erhöhen und zu einer Vereinfachung und dem Abbau bürokratischer Hindernisse beitragen kann".[153] In der Wissenschaft wird das Thema bereits intensiver diskutiert.[154]

Ein solches Ansinnen stellt jedoch ein sehr umfangreiches Projekt dar, welches die nächste Generation von EuZPR-Experten beschäftigen kann. Die Rechtsfragen der grenzüberschreitenden Zustellung, Zuständigkeit, Rechtshängigkeit, Verfahrensdurchführung (einschließlich der Beweisaufnahme) Urteilsanerkennung und Zwangsvollstreckung sind in allgemeinen Zivil- und Handelssachen und zum Teil sicher abweichend in Familien- und Erbsachen zu bearbeiten. Ein Großprojekt, sicher zu groß für Einzelne und schwierig mit der erforderlichen politischen Rückendeckung auszustatten. Das konkrete Ergebnis der Rechtsanwendung wird sich wohl nur marginal verändern. Auch wenn die kohärentere Rechtsetzung es zum politischen Ziel geschafft hat, so ist ein solches Projekt kaum für den kurzfristigen politischen Erfolg innerhalb einer Wahl- oder Amtsperiode geeignet.

In einer gemeinsamen Kraftanstrengung von Wissenschaft, Europäischer Verwaltung und Politik ist wohl im ersten Schritt durch Netzwerk- und Lobbyarbeit das Fundament für ein politisches Mandat für die Bildung und (finanzielle) Ausstattung einer Expertengruppe zu legen. Hierin liegt zugleich ein Rückbesinnen auf die Sachverständigenausschüsse des Anfangs des EuZPR. Seine Geschichte begann in einem solchen Ausschuss nationaler Experten, der neue Wege beschritt, aber sich auch einigen musste. Hierfür ließ er sich nicht ewig Zeit, dachte aber auch nicht in politisch zeitlichen und thematisch kurzfristigen Dimensionen. Auch in jüngerer Zeit ist der Einsatz von Expertenkommissionen jedenfalls zur Überprüfung und Ausarbeitung von Reformvorschlägen nicht unbekannt. So geht zB die Reform der Brüssel I-VO durch die Brüssel Ia-VO auf den sogenannten „Heidelberg-Re-

[152] Europäisches Parlament, Entschließung vom 7.10.2010, P7_TA(2010)0304, Ziff. 1.

[153] Europäisches Kommission, Die EU-Justizagenda für 2020 – Stärkung von Vertrauen, Mobilität und Wachstum in der Union vom 11.3.2014, COM(2014) 144, S. 9 (Ziff. 4.2).

[154] Wohlwollend Adolphsen FS Kaissis, 2012, 1 (13); kritisch von Hein/Rühl, Kohärenz im internationalen Privat- und Verfahrensrecht der Europäischen Union/Basedow, 2016, 3 (9).

port“[155] zurück, welcher aufgrund eines Forschungsauftrages der Kommission entstand.

Dabei sollte Kodifizierung hier gar nicht im hergebrachten Sinne einer allumfänglichen Regelung verstanden werden. Soweit auch heute noch Lücken bei den Regelungsgegenständen des EuZPR bestehen, müssen diese durch eine Kodifizierung nicht zwingend geschlossen werden. Die Möglichkeit des Rückgriffs auf eine stets im Hintergrund anwendbare nationale Rechtsordnung lässt auch weiterhin solche Löcher zu. Dies ist wichtig, da auch künftig bei der Schaffung von Regelungen der Kompromiss zwischen den Mitgliedstaaten erforderlich ist und nicht die schlichte Parlamentsmehrheit allein oder in einer Koalition.

Materiell lieferte der *Jubilar* selbst einen möglichen Ausgangspunkt, publiziert etwas versteckt, so dass er nicht die große Aufmerksamkeit erhielt.[156] Kodifizierung sollte hier nicht im Sinne von Vollständigkeit und Abgeschlossenheit verstanden werden, sondern als offenes systematisch durchdachtes, modulares System, in das der Rechtsetzungsbestand vollständig eingestellt wird und in dem später weitere Bausteine hinzugefügt werden können. Der Ruf nach einem „Allgemeinen Teil“ wurde bereits lauter,[157] er kann in einem solchen System hilfreiche Grundlage sein.

Ist dabei der ganz große Wurf erforderlich, sollte das EuIPR auch zugleich in ein solches Kodifikationsprojekt integriert werden? Für diese große Lösung gibt es durchaus Befürworter.[158] Und ohne Frage lassen sich die Kodifikationsideen auch auf das EuIPR übertragen. Dennoch sollte ein solches Projekt auch mit Pragmatismus angegangen werden. Ein Abschichten und die Konzentration können häufig eher zielführend sein, als der Versuch das perfekte Ganze zu erreichen. EuZPR und EuIPR – so häufig im selben Lebenssachverhalt beide Materien benötigt werden – haben bei zwar bestehenden Begriffsüberschneidungen doch wenig gemeinsamen Regelungsgehalt. Bei einer Aufteilung dürften sich die Doppelregelungen bis auf wenige Ausnahmen auf Begriffsdefinitionen beschränken. Hier können Verweisungen ein taugliches Mittel sein. Und im potentiellen Experten- und Bearbeiterkreis mögen sich Spezialisten für das eine und das andere Gebiet finden lassen. Auch für den Rechtsanwender bleiben zwei Kodifikationen erfassbar. Und für den Übergang kann der jeweilige EuIPR-Teil in bestehenden Verordnungen recht unproblematisch allein fortbestehen oder aufgehoben werden wie deren EuZPR-Teil. Ein gleichzeitiger Beginn oder Abschluss der Arbeiten wäre nicht notwendig. Daher spricht doch einiges für den pragmatischen Ansatz, das EuZPR in einem Ausschuss ausgewiesener Prozessrechtler und das EuIPR in einem durch entsprechende Kollisionsrechtler besetzten bearbeiten zu lassen.

---

155 Hess/Pfeiffer/Schlosser, Report on the Application of Regulation Brussels I in the Member States, Study JLS/C4/2005/03, Final Version September 2007, veröffentlicht auch als: Hess/Pfeiffer/Schlosser, The Brussels I-Regulation No 44/2001, 2008.

156 Rauscher FS Machacek & Matscher, 2008, 665 (673).

157 Hardung, Die europäische Titelfreizügigkeit, 2020, S. 70.

158 von Hein/Rühl, Kohärenz im internationalen Privat- und Verfahrensrecht der Europäischen Union/Dutta, 2016, 27 (42f.); Hein/Rühl, Kohärenz im internationalen Privat- und Verfahrensrecht der Europäischen Union/Kadner Graziano, 2016, 44 (59).

Die benannten Kodifikationen würden einen wesentlichen Beitrag zur Verwirklichung eines Raumes der Freiheit, der Sicherheit und des Rechts innerhalb der Europäischen Union leisten. Daher lohnt es sich, sich auf das zurückzubesinnen, was bereits in der Zeit der Entstehung des ersten Bausteins dieses so groß und umfassend gewordenen Europäischen Zivilprozessrecht niedergeschrieben wurde. Folgender Auszug gibt Aufgabe, Erkenntnis und Vision für die Zukunft:

„Jedes System fasst den in der Arbeit an den Einzelproblemen erreichten Erkenntnisstand zusammen: die erkannten Rechtsprinzipien in ihrer gegenseitigen Beziehung ebenso wie die erkannten Sachstrukturen, die uns im Fall, im Gegenstand der Regelung entgegentreten. Es erleichtert damit nicht nur Übersicht und praktische Arbeit; es wird auch Ursprung neuer Erkenntnisse über bestehende Zusammenhänge, die erst das System deutlich macht, und damit Grundlage weiterer Entwicklung des Rechts. Eine Wissenschaft, die nur am Einzelproblem arbeitete, würde nicht in der Lage sein, zur Entdeckung größerer Zusammenhänge von Problemen zu weiteren Prinzipien fortzuschreiten […]. Darum bleibt die Arbeit am System eine dauernde Aufgabe.“[159]

[159] Coing, Grundzüge der Rechtsphilosophie, 2. Aufl. 1969, S. 347.

HONG PHAN-HUY

Einfluss des europäischen Rechts und des deutschen Rechts in Vietnam

2005 schrieb ich einen Artikel im Liber Amicorum für Thomas Rauscher zu seinem 50. Geburtstag[1] und 2006 dann einen weiteren Artikel in der Festgabe für Wolfgang Seiffert.[2] Es war für mich an der Zeit, nach 20 Jahren der Reform in Vietnam eine Zwischenbilanz zum aktuellen Stand des Wirtschaftsrechts (im Allgemeinen) und des Investitionsrechts (im Besonderen) zu ziehen. Anlässlich des 70. Geburtstages von *Thomas Rauscher* habe ich diesmal die Gelegenheit, eine Bestandsaufnahme zum aktuellen Stand dieser Reform in den nächsten, weiteren 20 Jahren vorzunehmen. Vietnam hat sich in den letzten 20 Jahren weiterhin tief in die Weltwirtschaft integriert und gleichzeitig den Aufbau und die Weiterentwicklung der marktwirtschaftlichen Mechanismen im Land erlebt. Obwohl die Einschätzungen von Nadja Marschhausen[3] vor 20 Jahren über „eine unvollendete Transformation in Vietnam" hinsichtlich des politischen Systems Vietnams immer noch gültig zu sein scheint, haben die im Rahmen dieses internationalen Integrationsprozesses aufgebauten beziehungsweise weiterentwickelten marktwirtschaftlichen Institutionen tiefgreifende Auswirkungen auf alle Aspekte des wirtschaftlichen, sozialen, kulturellen und rechtlichen Lebens in Vietnam. Im Rahmen dieses Artikels möchte ich einen interessanten Aspekt dieses Prozesses darstellen, nämlich den positiven Einfluss des europäischen Rechts und des deutschen Rechts auf das vietnamesische Recht, insbesondere auf das Zivilrecht, zu dem Generationen von in Europa ausgebildeten vietnamesischen Juristen maßgeblich beigetragen haben.

I. Kontext des Einflusses des europäischen und deutschen Rechts auf das vietnamesische Recht

1. Die Politik der internationalen Integration

In den oben genannten Artikeln erwähnte ich die Normalisierung der diplomatischen Beziehungen zwischen Vietnam und den Vereinigten Staaten im Jahr 1994 und die Unterzeichnung des Handelsabkommens zwischen Vietnam und den Vereinigten Staaten im Jahr 2000 als Ereignisse, die die Tür für Vietnam nach fast

---

[1] Phan-Huy LA Rauscher, 2005, 131.
[2] Phan-Huy FS Seiffert, 2006, 263.
[3] Marschhausen FS Seiffert, 2006, 445.

20 Jahren der Weltisolation durch das US-Handelsembargo öffneten. Damals waren Grundsätze wie „Meistbegünstigung" oder „Inländerbehandlung" in Handels- und Investitionsbeziehungen konzeptionell noch neu, ganz zu schweigen davon, wie schwierig es war, sie in das nationale Recht umzusetzen. In diesem Zusammenhang mussten zurückkehrende im Ausland ausgebildete Juristen Artikels schreiben, um sie grundlegend und ausführlich zu erläutern, um auch den Gesetzgeber bei der Umsetzung internationaler Verpflichtungen zu unterstützen.[4]

Das Ende des US-Handelsembargos sowie die Normalisierung der diplomatischen Beziehung mit den USA sind auch die Voraussetzung dafür, dass Vietnam seine internationale Wirtschaftsintegrationspolitik umsetzen kann, so dass es Ende 1994 den Verhandlungsprozess für den Beitritt zur Welthandelsorganisation (WTO) beantragte und nach den sich anschließenden Beitrittsverhandlungen Anfang 2007 offiziell Mitglied dieser Organisation wurde. Während eines Jahrzehnts der Verhandlungen über den Beitritt zur WTO hatte Vietnam die Gelegenheit, seinen Verhandlungspartnern politische Reformen und Reformgesetze vorzulegen sowie Voraussetzungen für die Umsetzung künftiger Beitrittsverpflichtungen zu schaffen. In diesem Zusammenhang steht Vietnam weiterhin vor einer Reihe von Herausforderungen bei der Gewährleistung von Transparenz, Offenheit und insbesondere Vorhersehbarkeit der Bildung der Politik und Gesetzgebung.

Die internationale Wirtschaftsintegration zusammen mit der Liberalisierung der eigenen Wirtschaft hat dazu beigetragen, dass Vietnam im Zeitraum 1986–2020 kontinuierlich hohe Wirtschaftswachstumsrate erzielen konnte.[5] Auch der Handel mit dem Ausland floriert, insbesondere in den Beziehungen zu den Vereinigten Staaten, zur EU und zum ASEAN. Die Handelsbeziehungen zwischen Vietnam und der EU entwickelt sich sehr schnell.[6] Die EU ist einer der wichtigsten Handelspartner Vietnams, wobei der gegenseitige Handelsumsatz jährlich um durchschnittlich 15–20% steigt. Sie ist 2016 der viertgrößte Handelspartner und der zweitgrößte Exportmarkt Vietnams.[7] Die EU behauptet derzeit (2023) immer noch ihre Position als viertgrößter Handelspartner Vietnams (nach China, den Vereinigten Staaten und Südkorea); sie ist für Vietnam der drittgrößte Exportmarkt (nach den USA und China) und der fünftgrößte Importmarkt (nach China, Korea, Japan und Taiwan).[8] Deutschland, die größte Volkswirtschaft der EU, ist auch Vietnams größter Handelspartner unter den 27 Mitgliedsländern. Herausragende Merkmale in der Import-Export-Struktur zwischen Vietnam und der EU sind eine erhebliche Kom-

[4] Als Beispiel: Phan-Huy, An Analysis of the principles and standands of treatment in international trade and investment relations on the basis of the U.S.-Vietnam Trade Agreement, Legislative studies magazine N° 6/2002, S. 49.

[5] Die vietnamesische Wirtschaftswachstumsrate betrug 6,51% im Zeitraum 1986–2000, 7,26% im Zeitraum 2001–2010 und 5,9% im Zeitraum 2011–2020 (Vietnam News Agency, https://en.infographics.vn/35-years-of-renewal-process/19877.vna (abgerufen 1.7.2024).

[6] Von 2000 bis 2017 stieg der Handelsumsatz zwischen Vietnam und der EU um mehr als das Zwölffache, von 4,1 Milliarden US-Dollar im Jahr 2000 auf über 50 Milliarden US-Dollar im Jahr 2017; dabei stiegen die Exporte Vietnams in die EU um mehr als das Dreizehnfache (von 2,8 Milliarden US-Dollar auf über 38 Milliarden US-Dollar) und die Importe aus der EU nach Vietnam um das Neunfache (von 1,3 Milliarden US-Dollar auf 12 Milliarden US-Dollar).

[7] Vietnam Export- und Importbericht 2017, S. 92.

[8] Vietnam Export- und Importbericht 2023, S. 95.

plementarität und ein geringer direkter Wettbewerb.[9] Bis August 2023 ist Vietnam 16 Freihandelsabkommen beigetreten.[10] Darunter ist AFTA ein neues Handelsabkommen mit dem höchsten Maß an freiem Warenhandel, das für Vietnam einen großen Markt mit den günstigsten geografischen Bedingungen eröffnet. Unter ihnen gelten CPTPP wie EVFTA[11] als Freihandelsabkommen der neueren Generation mit einem breiten Umfang an Verpflichtungen und einem hohen Maß an Engagement, die einen starken Einfluss auf Vietnam in den Bereichen Handel, Investitionen, Privatsektor sowie in Bereichen wie Umweltschutz, Arbeit, geistiges Eigentum und rechtlich-institutionelle Fragen haben werden.

Vietnam unterzeichnete außerdem mehr als 60 Abkommen über die Förderung und den Schutz von Investitionen, darunter die Abkommen mit 21 einzelnen EU-Mitgliedstaaten, die durch das EU-Vietnam-Investitionsschutzabkommen (EVIPA) ersetzt werden.[12] Das EVIPA gilt auch als Investitionsschutzabkommen neuerer Generation und umfasst vier Kapitel, 92 Artikel und 13 Anhänge, insbesondere detaillierte Bestimmungen zur direkten und indirekten Enteignung von Eigentumsrechten und Schadensersatz sowie Vorschriften über Streitbeilegungsmechanismen zwischen Parteien sowie zwischen Investoren und Investitionsempfängerländern. Dank konsequenter und kontinuierlich verbesserter Politik zur Investitionsförderung und zum Investitionsschutz[13] sind die Zahl der Projekte und der Wert des ausländischen Investitionskapitals, die Vietnam in den vergangenen 35 Jahren seit der Reform anziehen konnte, stetig gestiegen.[14]

In den höchsten politischen Beschlüssen wird bekräftigt, dass Vietnam die Strategie der „Vervollkommnung der Institutionen für eine synchrone Entwicklung, vor allem der Institutionen für die Entwicklung einer sozialistisch orientierten Marktwirtschaft", fortsetzt; die Entwicklungsorientierung des Landes für den Zeitraum

---

[9] WTO-Zentrum, Zusammenfassung des Vietnam-EU-Freihandelsabkommens (EVFTA), https://wtocenter.vn/file/18176/ttwto-tom-luoc-evfta-final–eng.pdf (abgerufen 1.7.2024), S. 2.

[10] Darunter AFTA 1993 (ASEAN), ACFTA 2003 (ASEAN – China), AKFTA 2007 (ASEAN – Korea), AJCEP 2008 (ASEAN – Japan), VJEPA 2009 (Vietnam – Japan), AIFTA 2010 (ASEAN – Indien), AANZFTA 2010 (Vietnam – Australien – Neuseeland), VCFTA 2014 (Vietnam – Chile), VKFTA 2015 (Vietnam – Korea), VN EAEU FTA 2016 (Vietnam – Eurasische Wirtschaftsunion), CPTPP 2018 (Vietnam und 11 weitere Staaten), AHKFTA (Asean – Hongkong), EVFTA 2020 (Vietnam – EU), UKVFTA 2021 (Vietnam – Vereinigtes Königreich), RCEP 2022 (Asean – China – Japan – Korea – Australien – Neuseeland), VIFTA 2023 (Vietnam – Israel); zudem wird verhandelt über 3 weitere Freihandelsabkommen. darunter Vietnam – EFTA (Schweiz, Lichtenstein, Norwegen, Insel) und Vietnam -Vereinigte Arabische Emirate.

[11] Freihandelsabkommen zwischen der Europäischen Union und der Sozialistischen Republik Vietnam, ABl. 2020 L 186, 3.

[12] Dieses Abkommen wurde vom ursprünglichen EVFTA getrennt. Derzeit befindet sich EVIPA noch im Ratifizierungsprozess durch EU-Mitglieder. Vollständiger Text des Abkommens: https://policy.trade.ec.europa.eu/eu-trade-relationships-country-and-region/countries-and-regions/vietnam/eu-vietnam-agreement/texts-agreements_en (abgerufen 1.7.2024).

[13] Vietnam hat in den Jahren 1987 und 1996 jeweils ein Gesetz für ausländische Direktinvestitionen und in den Jahren 2005, 2014 und 2020 jeweils ein allgemeines Investitionsgesetz erlassen.

[14] Von 1988 bis 2021 hat Vietnam 38.349 ausländische Direktinvestitionsprojekte mit 523.918 Mio. US Dollar registriertem Gesamtinvestitionskapital angezogen, von denen 251.192 Mio. US Dollar umgesetzt wurden: Vietnam Statistik Amt, https://www.gso.gov.vn/en/px-web/?pxid=E0411&theme=Investment (abgerufen 1.7.2024).

2021–2030 sei „die umfassende und gleichzeitige Vervollkommnung der Institutionen für die Entwicklung einer sozialistisch orientierten Marktwirtschaft, die Schaffung eines günstigen Umfelds für die Mobilisierung, effiziente Zuteilung und Nutzung von Ressourcen sowie die Förderung von Investitionen, Produktion und Handel".[15]

Diese Entwicklungsstrategien und -orientierungen sind die politische Grundlage dafür, dass Vietnam eine weitestgehende internationale Wirtschaftsintegration fortsetzen und gleichzeitig das Wirtschafts- und Zivilrechtssystem entsprechend den Bedürfnissen des Landes weiterentwickeln wird.

2. Unterstützung durch die Europäische Union und ihre Mitgliedsländer im Prozess der internationalen Integration

Schon sehr früh begleitete die EU Vietnam bei der Reformierung der wirtschaftlichen Institutionen des Landes. Die EU hat Vietnam bei seiner institutionellen Reform durch vier handelsbezogene technische Hilfsprojekte begleitet, darunter das multilaterale Projekt zur Unterstützung der Handelspolitik MUTRAP I (2001–2003), MUTRAP II (2004–2007) und MUTRAP III (2008–2012) und das EU-Projekt zur Unterstützung der Handels- und Investitionspolitik (EU-MUTRAP 2013–2017). Das Projekt MUTRAP I hat dazu beigetragen, ein quantitatives, vergleichendes Wirtschaftsmodell für Vietnam zur Handelsliberalisierung und Investitionsattraktivität (FACTOM-Modell) zu entwickeln und so dazu beigetragen, ein quantitatives Bewertungsinstrument für politische Entscheidungsträger bereitzustellen. Darüber hinaus hat das Projekt auch die Weitergabe von Integrationsinformationen an relevante Behörden und Unternehmen durch Seminare und Dokumentationszentren zum Ziel. Nach MUTRAP I unterstützte das Projekt MUTRAP II Vietnam dabei, den Verhandlungsprozess für den Beitritt zur WTO zu beschleunigen und günstige Bedingungen für den Integrationsprozess Vietnams in der Weltwirtschaftsorganisation zu schaffen. Nachdem Vietnam 2007 offiziell der WTO beigetreten war, unterstützte das Projekt MUTRAP III dann die Stärkung der Kapazitäten des Ministeriums für Industrie und Handel (MOIT) in den Bereichen der handels- und wettbewerbspolitischen Gestaltung (insbesondere die Umsetzung der WTO-Beitrittsverpflichtungen) sowie bei den Verhandlungen und der Umsetzung regionaler Wirtschaftsintegrations- und Freihandelsabkommen in Verbindung mit den WTO-Verhandlungen.

Das Projekt EU-MUTRAP wurde vor dem Hintergrund realisiert, dass Vietnam und die EU bereits das umfassende Partnerschafts- und Kooperationsabkommen (PCA) unterzeichneten und gerade die EVFTA-Verhandlungen aufgenommen hatten.

Das Projekt setzte sich allgemein zum Ziel, Vietnam bei der weiteren Integration in den Welthandel sowie der regionalen Zusammenarbeit zu unterstützen, die Handels- und Investitionsbeziehungen zwischen Vietnam und der EU zu stärken, die Vorteile der wirtschaftlichen Entwicklung, einschließlich eines integrativen Wirt-

[15] Kommunistische Partei Vietnams, Dokumente des 13. Nationalkongresses, Band II, 2021, S. 328f.

schaftswachstums und einer effektiven Armutsbekämpfung zu maximieren. Das spezifische Ziel des Projekts besteht darin, das vietnamesische Ministerium für Industrie und Handel bei der Erleichterung des internationalen Handels und der Investitionen durch die Stärkung der politischen Planung, politischen Konsultation, bei der Verhandlung und Umsetzung der damit verbundenen Verpflichtungen, insbesondere in den Beziehungen zur Europäischen Union, zu unterstützen.

Neben EU-Förderprojekten gibt es auch Projekte vieler EU-Mitgliedsstaaten zur Unterstützung der internationalen wirtschaftlichen Integration Vietnams. Deutschland gehört dabei zu den Ländern mit herausragenden und vielfältigen Förderaktivitäten. Anlässlich des 35. Jahrestages der Aufnahme diplomatischer Beziehungen zwischen Deutschland und Vietnam (1975–2010) resümierte die „Communist Review": „Deutschland ist eines der führenden Länder, die öffentliche Entwicklungshilfe (ODA) für Vietnam leisten". Die von Deutschland für Vietnam bereitgestellten Mittel belaufen sich auf über 1,5 Milliarden US-Dollar und liegen damit an zweiter Stelle in der EU (nach Frankreich). Die ODA-Mittel wurden und werden effektiv in Vietnam in den als vorrangig angesehenen Bereichen wie Hunger- und Armutsbekämpfung, Gesundheitsversorgung, Bildung, Infrastruktur, institutioneller Kapazitätsaufbau, Bildung sowie Umweltschutz eingesetzt. Deutschland wird sich in den kommenden Jahren weiterhin für die Bereitstellung von ODA für Vietnam engagieren und konzentriert sich dabei auf neue Bereiche der Zusammenarbeit wie die Reaktion auf den Klimawandel, wissenschaftliche Forschung und Ausbildung hochwertiger Arbeitskräfte. „Beide Länder pflegen enge, vertrauensvolle Beziehung und gegenseitiges Verständnis, haben ähnliche Ansichten zu internationalen Themen wie Globalisierung, Terrorismusbekämpfung, der Reform der Vereinten Nationen und kooperieren und koordinieren sich regelmäßig eng in multilateralen und internationalen Fragen. Deutschland unterstützte den Beitritt Vietnams zur WTO sowie den Ausbau und die Stärkung der umfassenden Beziehungen zu Europa und der EU. Die beiden Länder einigten sich darauf, die Beziehungen zwischen Vietnam und Deutschland zu einer strategischen Partnerschaft auszubauen".[16] Anlässlich des offiziellen Besuchs von Bundeskanzler Olaf Scholz in Vietnam im November 2022 veröffentlichte die Online-Zeitung der Kommunistischen Partei Vietnams einen Artikel mit dem Titel „Die strategische Partnerschaft zwischen Vietnam und der Bundesrepublik Deutschland entwickelt sich weiterhin positiv",[17] aus dem hervorgeht: Deutschland ist seit vielen Jahren einer der wichtigsten Partner Vietnams in Europa. Das gegenseitige Vertrauen und Verständnis zwischen den beiden Ländern wird durch die Aufrechterhaltung hochrangiger Delegationsaustausche und Kooperationsmechanismen zunehmend gestärkt. Was den Handel betrifft, ist Deutschland derzeit Vietnams größter Partner in Europa (auf ihn entfallen fast 20% der vietnamesischen Exporte in die EU) und ist auch ein wichtiges Transittor für vietnamesische Waren in andere Länder in Europa. Viet-

[16] Communist Review, Bundesrepublik Deutschland in Zusammenarbeit mit Vietnam, 15.9.2010, https://tapchicongsan.org.vn/web/guest/tin-tieu-diem-10-06/-/2018/1223/cong-hoa-lien-bang-duc-trong-quan-he-hop-tac-voi-viet-nam.aspx (abgerufen 1.7.2024).

[17] https://dangcongsan.vn/thoi-su/quan-he-doi-tac-chien-luoc-viet-nam-chlb-duc-tiep-tuc-phat-trien-tich-cuc-624345.html (abgerufen 1.7.2024).

nam ist zum führenden Handelspartner Deutschlands in Südostasien und zum sechstgrößten Partner Deutschlands in Asien geworden. Deutschland spielt eine aktive Rolle im Verhandlungs- und Ratifizierungsprozess des Vietnam-EU-Freihandelsabkommens und des EU-Vietnam-Investitionsschutzabkommens in der EU. Seit 2013 haben beide Seiten vereinbart, die ODA-Zusammenarbeit in drei neuen vorrangigen Bereichen zu stärken: Energie, Berufsbildung im Zusammenhang mit einer nachhaltigen Wirtschaftsentwicklung und Umweltpolitik und nachhaltige Nutzung natürlicher Ressourcen. Ab 2020 wird Vietnam in der deutschen Entwicklungszusammenarbeitsstrategie bis 2030 (BMZ 2030) als „Globaler Partner" eingestuft. Die beiden Länder haben die Zusammenarbeit in Schlüsselbereichen auf „Ausbildung und nachhaltiges Wachstum für hochwertige Arbeitsplätze", „Verantwortung für unseren Planeten – Klima und Energie" und „Schutz unserer Lebensgrundlagen – Umwelt und natürliche Ressourcen" ausgeweitet. Hervorzuheben ist das Projekt „Unterstützung Vietnams bei der Umsetzung des Pariser Abkommens" (VN-SIPA), das die Überprüfung und Aktualisierung der an das UN-Rahmenübereinkommen zum Klimawandel übermittelten Dokumente zum national festgelegten Beitrag (NDC) unterstützt, sowie Vietnam bei der Überprüfung und Aktualisierung der Bestimmungen zur Reaktion auf den Klimawandel im Umweltschutzgesetz 2020 hilft, welche einen wichtigen Rechtsrahmen für die Umsetzung des staatlichen Managements des Klimawandels bildet. Deutschland ist einer der wichtigsten Partner Vietnams im Bereich Berufsbildung und unterstützt das Ministerium für Arbeit, Veteranen und Soziales bei der Entwicklung einer nationalen Berufsbildungsstrategie, der Ausarbeitung des Berufsbildungsgesetzes sowie beim Aufbau von einigen Berufsschulen nach dem erfolgreichen deutschen Modell der parallelen Berufsausbildung. Im Finanzsektor unterstützt die Bundesregierung im Rahmen des Programms „Vietnam Macroeconomic Reform" für den Zeitraum 2006–2014 die State Securities Commission bei der Überarbeitung zahlreicher Bestimmungen des Wertpapiergesetzes. Sie leistet Beratungen bei der Modernisierung von Aktienhandelsbörsen. Seit 2015 unterstützt die Bundesregierung Vietnam weiterhin bei der institutionellen Reform und der Stärkung der Leistungsfähigkeit des Finanz- und Bankensystems, unterstützt den digitalen Transformationsprozess des vietnamesischen Bankensektors, die Entwicklung eines Green-Bond-Marktes und grüner Finanz- und Bankdienstleistungsprodukte, leistet einen Beitrag zur Umsetzung der Green Growth Strategy in Vietnam. Die Kooperationsaktivitäten zwischen den beiden Ländern im Bereich Justiz und Recht begannen 1996. Im Jahr 2008 unterzeichneten die beiden Regierungen eine Gemeinsame Erklärung zur Zusammenarbeit in diesem Bereich. Auf der Grundlage der Gemeinsamen Erklärung vereinbarten das vietnamesische Justizministerium und das Bundesministerium der Justiz die Umsetzung eines Programms zum Rechtsstaatsdialog für die Zeiträume 2009–2011, 2012–2014, 2015–2018 und 2019–2022, und zuletzt am 7.10.2022 ein dreijähriges Programm zum Rechtsstaatsdialog für den Zeitraum 2022–2025. Im Rahmen dieser Programme haben beide Seiten zahlreiche Seminare, Diskussionen sowie Forschungsaufenthalte organisiert, um für Vietnam Erfahrungen zur Überarbeitung und Durchsetzung von Gesetzen in den Bereichen des Zivil-, Straf-, Verwaltungsrechts und der Justiz zu sammeln.

All dies ist nicht nur ein anschaulicher Beweis der Unterstützung der EU sowie der EU-Mitgliedsländer, insbesondere Deutschlands, für die Reform und internationale wirtschaftliche Integration Vietnams. Damit einhergehend sind die Verbreitung europäischer Rechtsstaatlichkeit in Vietnam und ein positiver Einfluss auf seine institutionellen Reformen verbunden. Was Deutschland betrifft, so wirkt sich diese kooperative Unterstützung nicht nur indirekt auf Dutzende von Gesetzen aus, die in jüngster Zeit erlassen wurden, sondern auch direkt auf den Inhalt einiger Gesetze wie das Umweltschutzgesetz von 2020, das Berufsbildungsgesetz, das Wertpapiergesetz von 2019, das Gesetz über Kreditinstitute 2023 oder das Verbraucherschutzgesetz.

3. Das Vorbild des europäischen Rechts und des deutschen Rechts für Vietnam

Die Forschung zum europäischen Rechts wird in Vietnam nicht nur mit dem pragmatischen Ziel durchgeführt, die Spielregeln eines wichtigen Handelspartners zu verstehen, um diesen Markt effektiv zu durchdringen. Darüber hinaus ist das EU-Modell zu einem Vorbild für die ASEAN-Integration geworden. Es scheint, dass ASEAN nie zu einer Union wie die EU wird, insbesondere aufgrund unterschiedlicher Wertesysteme. Das von ASEAN angestrebte Ziel der Schaffung eines gemeinsamen Marktes mit voller wirtschaftlicher Freiheit (einschließlich der Freiheit des Waren- und Dienstleistungsverkehrs, des freien Personenverkehrs sowie des freien Kapitalverkehrs) macht die EU aber zu einer wertvollen Erfahrungsquelle für ASEAN im Prozess der Rechtsharmonisierung seiner Mitgiedsländer. Andererseits ist das EU-Recht auch in verschiedenen Sprachen leicht zugänglich. Daher ist das europäische Recht seit vielen Jahren zu einem beliebten Objekt der rechtsvergleichenden Forschung in Vietnam geworden. Zahlreiche Forschungsprojekte sowie rechtswissenschaftliche Doktorarbeiten befassen sich mit dem europäischen Recht und den Gesetzen einiger EU-Mitgliedsländer als Gegenstand vergleichender Forschung. Eine Reihe von Forschungsinstituten für rechtsvergleichende Wissenschaft sind gegründet worden.[18] Das gängige Argument für die Wahl des EU-Rechts als Vergleichsobjekt ist, dass das EU-Recht darauf abzielt, die Gesetze der Mitgliedstaaten zu harmonisieren, so dass es einen hohen Konsens in den Ansichten der europäischen Gesetzgeber aufweist und damit von hohem Referenzwert für ASEAN- oder vietnamesisches Recht ist.[19] Auch das EU-Recht und die Rechtsprechung des Gerichtshofs der Europäischen Union (EuGH) steht zunehmend im Fokus des Vergleichs.[20]

Das vietnamesische Recht galt früher als Teil des sozialistischen Rechtssystems. Auch dieses Recht ist ein geschriebenes Rechtssystem und weist viele Ähnlichkeiten mit dem kontinentaleuropäischen Rechtssystem auf. Auch das vietnamesische Recht soll vom französischen Recht beeinflusst sein, da Vietnam eine koloniale

---

[18] So etwa das Institute für Rechtsvergleichung der Hanoi Rechtsuniversität, die Ho-Chi-Minh-Stadt Universität für Wirtschaft und Recht und die Ho-Chi-Minh-Stadt Rechtsuniversität (im Aufbau).

[19] Phan-Huy, Journal of State and Law, 1(225)/2007, S. 43.

[20] Wie zB bei Phan-Huy und Nguyen Thanh, Business freedom under the law of the European Union and Vietnam, 2012.

Vergangenheit hatte. Beim nähreren Ansehen lässt sich jedoch erkennen, dass das französische Zivilrecht seit dem vietnamesischen Zivilgesetzbuch (ZGB) von 1995,[21] über das ZGB von 2005 bis zum aktuellen ZGB von 2015, nach und nach seinen Einfluss auf das moderne vietnamesische Zivilrecht verloren hat. Denn das erste Zivilgesetzbuch der Reformzeit war tatsächlich stark vom Zivilgesetzbuch der DDR, einem Gesetz, das selbst viele Wurzeln im BGB hatte, beeinflusst. Eine interessante Tatsache ist, dass die Experten der Japan International Cooperation Agency (JICA) von 1996 bis heute kontinuierlich technische Kooperationsprojekte für Vietnam bezüglich der Rechtstheorien und Rechtsfiguren des deutschen Zivilrechts durchführt. Dies lässt sich damit begründen, dass Japan die Rechtstheorien und Rechtsfiguren des deutschen Zivilrechts in sein Zivilrecht übernommen hat.[22] Hervorzuheben ist insbesondere das JICA-Projekt zur Reform des Rechts- und Justizwesens in Vietnam für den Zeitraum von 2007–2015, welches Vietnam unter anderem beim Aufbau eines neuen Zivilgesetzbuchs (ZGB 2015) begleitet hat. Mit diesem Projekt wurde erstmals im Rahmen eines Gesetzesvorhaben eine mögliche Einführung der Institutionen des Sachenrechts in das Zivilgesetzbuch und damit eine Umstrukturierung des Zivilgesetzbuches in Sachenrecht und Schuldrecht thematisiert. Im Anschluss an dieses Projekt begleitet JICA weiterhin die Umsetzung dieses Kodex mit einem neuen Projekt mit dem Titel „Das Projekt für eine harmonisierte, praktische Gesetzgebung und einheitliche Rechtsanwendung mit dem Zieljahr 2020".[23]

II. Der Einfluss des europäischen Rechts und des deutschen Rechts auf das Zivilrecht Vietnams

1. Einfluss auf gesetzgeberischen Wertvorstellungen

Wie oben erwähnt, erfordert die objektive Notwendigkeit institutioneller Reformen zum Ziel des Aufbaus einer Marktwirtschaft und der internationalen Integration, dass der vietnamesische Gesetzgeber eine Harmonisierung der Gesetze und die Einhaltung internationaler Standards anstrebt und dabei internationale Praktiken insbesondere in den Bereichen Wirtschafts- und Zivilrecht beachten muss. Dies spiegelt sich darin wider, dass im Rahmen der Gesetzesvorhaben der letzten zwei Jahrzehnte jeweils eine Recherche zu ausländischen Rechtserfahrungen durchgeführt wurde. In diesem Zusammenhang sind europäisches Recht sowie das Recht der EU-Mitgliedsländer immer die erste Wahl, sowohl aufgrund vieler

[21] Siehe eine allgemeine Einführung in dieses Zivilgesetzbuch: Rauscher/Phan-Huy ZVglRWiss 97 (1998), 340.

[22] Zur Rezeption von Rechtstheorien und Rechtsfiguren des deutschen Zivilrechts im japanischen Zivilrecht: Sanders, Einführung in das japanische Recht, Humbolt Forum Recht 6/2005, 51 (Rn. 12–26); Wendehorst, Rezeption deutschen Zivilrechts – Was bleibt im 21. Jahrhundert?, in Jehle/Lipp/Yamanaka, Rezeption und Reform im japanischen und deutschen Recht, 2008, S. 19.

[23] https:www.jica.go.jp/Resource/project/english/vietnam/032/index.html (abgerufen 28.06. 2024).

Ähnlichkeiten, da das vietnamesische Rechtssystem auch ein geschriebenes Rechtssystem ist, als auch aufgrund der freundschaftlichen Begleitung der EU und der EU-Mitgliedsländer bei Vietnams institutioneller Reform und internationaler Integration.

Im Rahmen dieses Artikels möchte ich den Einfluss Europas und Deutschlands auf das Konzept der Rechtsquellen in Vietnam erwähnen. In Vietnam wird kein Pluralismus akzeptiert, so dass es auch keine Gewaltenteilung gibt. Es gibt lediglich eine „Aufgabenteilung" zwischen Parlament, Regierung und Gericht. Nach diesem Verständnis müsste die Rechtsprechung sich darauf beschränken, das geschriebene Recht anzuwenden. Eine Rechtsfortbildung durch Rechtsprechung im deutschen Sinne ist nicht möglich. Sogar die Befugnis zur Auslegung von Gesetzen wird von der Verfassung[24] dem Ständigen Ausschuss der Nationalversammlung übertragen.[25]

Um das Gesetz anzuwenden, müsste das Gericht jedoch Gesetze auch auslegen können. Man geht davon aus, dass diese Auslegung Teil der Anwendung des strikt integrierten Rechts ist, so dass sie nur innerhalb eines sehr engen Rahmens vorgenommen werden kann. Sollten Gerichte bei ihren Tätigkeiten Schwierigkeiten mit dem Verständnis der Gesetzesbestimmung haben, könnten sie sich an das Oberste Gericht wenden. Der Richterrat des Obersten Gerichts könnte dazu Beschlüsse zur Erläuterung (in der Regel einiger) Gesetzesbestimmungen erlassen, um eine einheitliche Rechtsanwendung zu gewährleisten. Im vietnamesischen Rechtssystem haben solche Beschlüsse des Richterrates des Obersten Gerichts normativen Charakter[26] und sind somit für Richter bindend. Aufgrund begrenzter Ressourcen kann das Oberste Gericht jedoch nicht einmal einen kleinen Teil der Anfragen der unteren Gerichte beantworten. Der Bedarf an einem Präzedenzrecht wird immer dringlicher. Präzedenzrecht als Rechtsquelle ist in der vietnamesischen Rechtsgeschichte nicht neu, sondern existierte während der französischen Kolonialzeit von 1858 bis 1945.[27]

In jüngerer Zeit wurde das Präzedenzrecht zum ersten Mal in einer Resolution der Kommunistischen Partei[28] erwähnt: „Das Oberste Gericht hat die Aufgabe, die

[24] Art. 74 der Verfassung von 2013 legt fest, dass allein der Ständige Ausschuss der Nationalversammlung die Befugnis hat, die Verfassung, Gesetz und Dekretgesetz auszulegen. Es sollte auch hinzugefügt werden, dass viele Wissenschaftler im Rahmen der Diskussion der Verfassungsnovellierung von 2013 ein Modell des Verfassungsgerichts nach dem Vorbild des Bundesverfassungsgerichts vorgeschlagen haben. Dieser Versuch ist jedoch aus ideologischen Gründen letzlich gescheitert.

[25] Tatsächlich hat der Ständige Ausschuss der Nationalversammlung bereits einige Beschlüsse erlassen, in denen eine Reihe von Gesetzesbestimmungen offiziell ausgelegt werden, beispielsweise die Auslegung des in Art. 241 des Handelsgesetzes von 1997 verwendeten Begriffs „Handelsaktivität", oder die Erläuterung der Straftatsbestände der Straftaten des illegalen Eindringens in Computernetze, Telekommunikationsnetze oder elektronische Geräte einer anderen Person gemäß Art. 289 Strafgesetzbuch 2015.

[26] Art. 4 Abs. 7 Gesetz zum Erlass von Rechtsvorschriften 2015.

[27] Zu dieser Zeit waren einige Präzedenzfallsammlungen erschien, typischerweise die Präzedenzfallsammlungen Tonkin von 1937 und die Präzedenzfallsammlungen Annam von 1941. Es gab bereits manche juristische Fachzeitschrift, die Gerichtsurteile veröffentlichte und kommentierte.

[28] Resolution Nr. 49-NQ/TW vom 2.6.2005 zur Justizreform.

Rechtsprechung auszuwerten, die Rechtsanwendung anzuleiten sowie Präzedenzfälle zu entwickeln." Dies ist die politische Grundlage für die Wiederbelebung von Präzedenzrecht in Vietnam. Die Ergebnisse dieses Justizreformprozesses spiegeln sich in den Bestimmungen des Gesetzes über die Organisation der Volksgerichte von 2014 wieder, in dem der Gesetzgeber dem Obersten Gericht die Aufgabe und die Befugnis überträgt, die Rechtsprechung weiterzuentwickeln, wonach der Richterrat des Obersten Gerichts die Aufgabe hat, „aus Kassationsentscheidungen des Obersten Gerichts sowie Urteilen und Entscheidungen der unteren Gerichte, die Rechtskraft erlangt haben, Präzedenzfälle zu entwickeln, damit die Gerichte sie studieren und anwenden können" (Art. 22 Abs. 2 des Gesetzes über die Organisation der Volksgerichte 2014). Der Oberste Richter des Obersten Gerichts hat daher die Aufgabe, Präzedenzfälle als solche zusammenzufassen und zu veröffentlichen" (Art. 127 Abs. 5 Gesetzes über die Organisation der Volksgerichte 2014). Auf der Grundlage dieser Befugnis hat der Richterrat des Obersten Gerichts bereits zwei Beschlüsse zur Umsetzung erlassen.[29] Gemäß diesen Beschlüssen sind „Präzedenzfälle die Argumente und Urteile in den rechtswirksamen Urteilen und Entscheidungen eines Gerichts zu einem bestimmten Fall, der vom Richterrat des Obersten Gerichts ausgewählt wurden und vom Obersten Richter des Obersten Gerichts als Präzedenzfälle bekanntgegeben, welche Gerichte studieren und in Gerichtsverfahren zur Anwendung bringen können". Anders als im Westen entsteht das Präzedenzrecht in Vietnam somit in einem formellen Prozess und scheint normative Bindungskraft für das Gerichtssystem zu haben.[30]

Das Oberste Gericht hat nun eine elektronische Plattform zur Veröffentlichung von Präzedenzfällen eingerichtet.[31] Als nächstes erkennt das ZGB 2015 zum ersten Mal Präzedenzfälle als eine Quelle des Zivilrechts an (Art. 6 Abs. 2 ZGB 2015); das Zivilverfahrensgesetz von 2015 sieht Präzedenzfälle auch als eine Quelle des Rechts, welche zur Lösung von Zivilsachen angewendet wird (Art. 4 Abs. 2, Art. 45 Abs. 3 Zivilverfahrensgesetz 2015). Das Oberste Gericht hat außerdem eine weitere elektronische Informationsseite zur Bekanntgabe der Urteile von Gerichten auf allen Ebenen eingerichtet.[32] Der Zugriff auf die Rechtsprechung des Gerichts ist dank der rasanten Entwicklung der Informationstechnologie einfacher geworden. Auf dem Markt angebotene Anwendungssoftware mit künstlicher Intelligenz (KI) trägt bereits dazu bei, die Arbeit von Richtern, Staatsanwälten und Rechtsanwälten zu erleichtern und damit einer einheitliche Rechtsanwendung förderlich zu sein.

---

[29] Beschluss Nr. 03/2015/NQ-HDTP vom 28.10.2015 und Beschluss Nr. 03/2015/NQ-HDTP vom 23.5.2019 zur Auswahl, Veröffentlichung und Anwendung von Präzedenzfällen.

[30] Art. 45 Abs. 3 Zivilverfahrensgesetz bestimmt: „Präzedenzfälle werden vom Gericht bei der Lösung von Zivilsachen studiert und angewendet werden, wenn sie vom Richterrat des Obersten Gerichts ausgewählt und vom Obersten Richter des Obersten Gerichts bekannt gegeben werden".

[31] https://anle.toaan.gov.vn (abgerufen 1.7.2024); bis Juni 2024 wurden insgesamt 72 Präzedenzfälle veröffentlicht, darunter 17 Präzedenzfälle im Strafrecht, 4 Präzedenzfälle im Verwaltungsrecht, 35 Präzedenzfälle im Zivilrecht, 5 Präzedenzfälle im Familienrecht, 9 Präzedenzfälle im Handelsrecht und 2 im Arbeitsrecht.

[32] https://congbobanan.toaan.gov.vn (abgerufen 1.7.2024); bis Juni 2024 wurden bereits fast 1,5 Mio. Gerichtsurteile und -entscheidungen veröffentlicht.

Die EU sowie eine Reihe von EU-Mitgliedstaaten haben Vietnams Justizreformbemühungen aktiv unterstützt, einschließlich des Aufbaus eines Präzedenzrechts, und dadurch einen gewichtigen Einfluss auf diesen Prozess ausgeübt. Besonders hervorzuheben ist das von der Europäischen Union geförderte Programm zur Stärkung von Recht und Justiz in Vietnam (EU JULE). Dieses Programm setzt sich zum Ziel, „die Rechtsstaatlichkeit in Vietnam durch ein glaubwürdigeres, vertrauenswürdigeres und zugänglicheres Justizsystem zu stärken“, und wurde von UNDP, UNICEF, UNODC und OXFAM in Zusammenarbeit mit dem vietnamesischen Justizministerium im Zeitraum 2018–2024 umgesetzt.[33]

2. *Der Einfluss auf das Zivilrecht*

In der neueren Zeit wurden in Vietnam drei Zivilgesetzbücher erlassen, die Zivilgesetzbücher von 1995, 2005 und 2015, wobei die Änderung und Ergänzungen jedes Mal sehr bedeutsam waren. Natürlich spiegelt die Verkündung von drei Zivilgesetzbüchern in Abständen von nur zehn Jahren begrenzte Visionen und Gesetzgebungstechniken wider. Dies spiegelt aber auch eine sehr bemerkenswerte Realität wider, nämlich eine rasche Entwicklung der wirtschaftlichen und sozialen Bedingungen in Vietnam in jüngster Zeit. Die Politik des Aufbaus einer Marktwirtschaft und der internationalen Integration erfordert auch, dass sich das Recht schnell an diese veränderten Bedingungen anpassen soll. Daher wurden bei einer Reihe wichtiger Institutionen des vietnamesischen Zivilrechts bedeutende qualitative Reformen durchgeführt.

Zunächst soll eine kurze allgemeine Einführung in die Struktur des vietnamesischen Zivilgesetzbuchs gemacht werden. Die ersten beiden Zivilgesetzbücher der neueren Zeit (ZGB 1995, 2005)[34] haben die gleiche Struktur und bestehen jeweils aus 7 Teilen: (i) Allgemeine Vorschriften, (ii) Eigentum und andere Vermögensrechte, (iii) Zivilrechtliche Pflichten und Verträge, (iv) Erbrecht, (v) Übertragung von Grundstücksnutzungsrechten, (vi) Geistiges Eigentum und Technologietransfer und (vii) Zivilrechtsverhältnisse mit Auslandsberührung. Dieser Gesetzesaufbau weist noch immer Spuren der Tradition sozialistischer Zivilgesetzbücher auf, in denen es kein Familienrecht gibt. Neuerdings wird das ZGB von 2015 umstrukturiert und besteht aus sechs Teilen: (i) Allgemeine Vorschriften, (ii) Eigentum und andere Vermögensrechte, (iii) Zivilrechtliche Pflichten und Verträge, (iv) Erbrecht, (v) Anwendung des Rechts auf Zivilrechtsverhältnisse mit Auslandsberührung und (vi) Übergangs- und Durchführungsbestimmungen. Einige Ziviljuristen in Vietnam halten diesen Gesetzaufbau für eine Anlehnung an das Pandektensystem.[35] Es wurden die Bestimmungen zur Übertragung von Grundstücksnutzungsrechten und des geistigen Eigentums und der Technologieübertragung aus diesem Gesetzbuch herausgenommen, und bereits teilweise in das Bodengesetz und das Gesetz über geisti-

[33] Siehe: Delegation der Europäischen Union in Vietnam, EU Justice and Legal Empowerment Programme in Vietnam (EU JULE), https://www.eeas.europa.eu/projects-eujule_en?s=184 (abgerufen 1.7.2024).

[34] Zum vietnamesischen ZGB 1995, siehe: Rauscher/Phan-Huy ZVglRWiss 97 (1998), 340.

[35] Dinh Trung, Wissenschaftlicher Kommentar zum Zivilgesetzbuch 2015, 2021, S. 26.

ges Eigentum verlagert. Während der Phase der Ausarbeitung dieses neuesten ZGB gab es zahlreiche Vorschläge zur Umstrukturierung des Gesetzbuches, nach denen Teil (ii) in „Sachenrecht“ und Teil (iii) in „Recht der Schuldverhältnisse“ umbenannt und dementsprechend umgestaltet werden sollten. Letztlich scheiterte dieser Vorschlag jedoch, weil er „in Theorie und Praxis als noch nicht reif“ galt.

a) Rechtsinstitut „juristische Person“

Die Regelung der juristischen Personen in den ZGB von 1995 und 2005 wurden durch das Rechtsverständnis des ehemals sozialistischen Gesetzgebers, welcher sich an jeweiligen Zivilgesetzbüchern der Ostblock-Länder orientierte, beeinflusst. Ein typisches Merkmal dieses Rechtsinstituts ist, dass juristische Personen nicht über eine umfassende Rechtsfähigkeit, sondern nur über eine Rechtsfähigkeit, die ihrem Gründungszweck entspricht, verfügen.[36] Im ZGB von 2005 heißt es: „Die zivilrechtliche Rechtsfähigkeit einer juristischen Person ist die Fähigkeit der juristischen Person, Träger von zivilrechtlichen Rechten und Pflichten zu sein, die mit ihrem Gründungszweck im Einklang stehen.“ Dieses Merkmal hat möglicherweise keine Wurzeln in der Ultra-vires-Lehre des angloamerikanischen Rechtssystems, sondern ist lediglich ein zufälliges Zusammentreffen.[37] Nach Maßgabe dieser beiden Zivilgesetzbücher können Transaktionen einer juristischen Person als ungültig angesehen werden, wenn sie als außerhalb des Gründungszwecks der betroffenen juristischen Person stehend oder mit diesem unvereinbar angesehen werden. Bei juristischen Personen der gewerblichen Wirtschaft (Gesellschaften, Genossenschaften) wird der „Gründungszweck“ sogar durch den Inhalt der „angemeldeten und registrierten Geschäftsbereiche“ eingeschränkt. Allerdings wurde im Zuge der wirtschaftlichen Liberalisierung das bereits im Unternehmensgesetz von 1999 anerkannte Recht von Unternehmen, Geschäfte in nicht gesetzlich verbotenen Branchen zu tätigen, im weiteren Sinne als „unabhängig von der Gewerbebescheinigung“ verstanden. Mit dem Unternehmensgesetz von 2014 wurde dann darüber Klarheit verschafft, dass auf der Gewerbebescheinigung die Inhalte „registrierter Geschäftsbereiche“ nicht mehr erscheinen. Solche Vorstellungen von unternehmerischer Freiheit erweiterten den Kompetenzbereich der Unternehmen und führten letztlich zu einem veränderten Rechtsverständnis über der Umfang der Rechtsfähigkeit juristischer Personen im Allgemeinen. Nun legt das ZGB von 2015 klar fest: „Die zivilrechtliche Rechtsfähigkeit einer juristischen Person ist die Fähigkeit, Träger von zivilrechtlichen Rechten und Pflichten zu sein, es sei denn Gesetze sehen etwas anderes vor“ (Art. 86 Abs. 1 ZGB 2015). Die Anerkennung der umfassenden Rechtsfähigkeit juristischer Personen durch das ZGB von 2015 trägt auch dazu bei, Risiken für ausländische juristische Personen zu beseitigen, da gemäß den Bestimmungen des vietnamesischen internationalen Privatrechts die Rechtsfähigkeit ausländischer juristischer Personen stets nach vietnamesischem

[36] Art. 96 S. 1 ZGB 1995, Art. 86 S. 1 ZGB 2005.

[37] Vgl. dazu: Phan-Huy, Das Recht der ausländisch-vietnamesischen Joint-Ventures und die Rechtsverfolgung in Vietnam, 2021, S. 99f.

Recht beurteilt wird, soweit sie in Vietnam Rechtsgeschäfte begründen und realisieren.[38]

Neben den dringenden Bedürfnissen des gesellschaftlichen Lebens trägt die Rechtswissenschaft zum neuesten vietnamesischen Zivilgesetzbuch auch wesentlich zur Innovation juristischer Institutionen bei. Durch eine Reihe veröffentlichter rechtsvergleichender Studien haben vietnamesische Juristen auch etwas über die Rechtspersönlichkeitstheorien von Friedrich Carl von Savigny und Otto von Gierke erfahren.[39]

b) Der Nießbrauch

Im vietnamesischen Zivilrecht wurde das Nießbrauchrecht erstmals im ZGB von 2015 eingeführt. Im Zuge der Ausarbeitung dieses Gesetzbuches wurden zahlreiche rechtsvergleichende Studien veröffentlicht, insbesondere zum französischen und deutschen Nießbrauchrecht, welche Diskussionen über die Einführung dieses Rechtsinstituts in das neue Zivilgesetzbuch vorantrieben.

Im Ergebnis ist ein Nießbrauchrecht in das ZGB 2015 eingeführt worden, und zwar ins Kapitel „Andere Vermögensrechte". In diesem Kapitel sind zunächst „Rechte an angrenzenden Grundstücken", dann der Nießbrauch und schließlich „Rechte an Grundstücksoberfläche" geregelt.

Obwohl der Nießbrauch nun in das ZGB eingeführt worden ist, erscheint er in der vietnamesischen Gesellschaft immer noch fremd. Er stellt selbst für den Gesetzgeber etwas sehr Neues dar. Die Einführung des Nießbrauchrechts in das ZGB geschah wahrscheinlich vielmehr auf Grund des Drucks der akademischen Kreise. Daher ist in diesem Gesetzbuch das Nießbrauchrecht nur in „Grundzügen" geregelt, welche ihrem Wesen nach sowohl dem französischen als auch dem deutschen Nießbrauch vergleichbar sind. Es fehlen in diesem Zivilgesetzbuch jedoch gänzlich Regelung zur Bestellung, Eintragung und zur Beendigung des Nießbrauchs, welche letztlich nötig sind, um einen Nießbrauch zu begründen und zu realisieren. Das neu erlassene Bodengesetz von 2024 enthält auch keine Regelungen dazu. Damit das eingeführte Nießbrauchrecht in der Praxis umgesetzt werden kann, sollten in dem neuen ZGB von 2015 selbst oder in anderen Gesetzen wie zum Beispiel im Bodengesetz Ergänzungen vorgenommen werden.

c) Vertrags- und Haftungsrecht

Das vietnamesische Vertragsrecht war zunächst in zwei parallele Teile gespalten und zwar in das Recht der „Zivilverträge" und das Recht der „Wirtschaftsverträge".[40] Die Vereinheitlichung des Vertragsrechts wurde erst durch den Erlass des

[38] Vgl. Art. 831 Abs. 2 ZGB 1995; Art. 765 Abs. 2 ZGB 2005; Art. 676 Abs. 3 ZGB 2015.

[39] Phan-Huy, Discussion on legal Capacity of Business Legal Entities, Journal of State und Law, Nr. 5/2005, S. 54; Dinh Trung, Wissenschaftlicher Kommentar zum Zivilgesetzbuch 2015, 2021, S. 151–202.

[40] Zur früheren Systematik des vietnamesischen Vertragsrechts vgl. Phan-Huy, Das Recht der ausländisch-vietnamesischen Joint-Ventures und die Rechtsverfolgung in Vietnam, 2021, S. 213–216.

ZGB von 2005 und das gleichzeitig erlassene Handelsgesetz von 2005 geschaffen. Das ZGB von 2005 definierte „zivile Beziehungen" in einem erweiterten Sinne. Demnach schließen sie „zivile Beziehungen" im bisher engeren Sinne sowie die gleichberechtigten Beziehungen in Ehe und Familie, Wirtschaft, Handel und Arbeit ein (Art. 1 Abs. 1 ZGB 2005). Damit wird das Vertragsrecht in diesem Gesetzbuch zum allgemeinen Vertragsrecht mit der Rolle einer *lex generalis* und das Vertragsrecht im Handelsgesetz von 2005 zum Sondervertragsrecht *(lex specialis)*. Das Vertragsrecht des Handelsgesetzes von 2005 seinerseits stellt deutlich eine Übernahme der Konzepte des Wiener Übereinkommens über den internationalen Warenkauf (CISG) dar, obwohl dieses Übereinkommen nur das internationale Kaufrecht regelt. Das UN-Kaufrecht wird in vielerlei Hinsicht als ein Kompromiss zwischen dem anglo-amerikanischen Recht und dem kontinentaleuropäischen Recht angesehen. Vietnam hat das Konzept des UN-Kaufrechts der Rechtsbehelfe bei Vertragsbrüchen in die für alle Handelsgeschäfte geltenden Rechtsbehelfsvorschriften übernommen. Dadurch scheint das Vertragsrecht im Handelsgesetz liberaler zu sein und es kann den Grundsatz der Vertragsfreiheit besser als das frühere Vertragsrecht des ZGB von 2005 gewährleisten.

Interessanterweise ist festzustellen, dass der Gesetzgeber des neueren Zivilgesetzbuchs von 2015 zur Novellierung des allgemeinen Vertragsrechts das Vertragsrecht des Handelsgesetzes als Vorbild herangezogen hat. Damit hat das ZGB von 2015 auch eine Tradition des vietnamesischen Zivilrechts, nämlich in der Schuldfrage des Haftungsrechts, aufgegeben. Nun enthält das ZGB von 2015 die grundsätzliche Bestimmung, wonach die Partei bei Verletzung ihrer Pflichten im Allgemeinen bzw. bei Verletzung vertraglicher Pflichten im Besonderen Schadensersatz leisten muss, unabhängig davon, ob diese Partei ein Verschulden trifft oder nicht (Art. 360 ZGB 2015). Natürlich ist der Bruch mit der Tradition des Haftungsrechts im vietnamesischen Zivilrecht nicht einfach, tatsächlich hat es zu diesem Thema viele heftige Debatten gegeben. Letztlich siegt jedoch die Übernahme der Lösung des Vertragsrechts des Handelsgesetzes, die sich in der Praxis auch im Hinblick der internationalen Integration bewährt hat.[41] Das heutige vietnamesische Vertragsrecht ist daher durch die Übernahme der Konzepte des UN-Kaufrechts sowohl vom angloamerikanischen Vertragsrecht als auch vom kontinentaleuropäischen Vertragsrecht in vielerlei Hinsicht beeinflusst.

[41] Zur Erläuterung der Schuldfrage im Haftungsrecht des vietnamesischen Handelsgesetzes vgl. Phan-Huy, The Fault Principle in the Commercial Law of Vietnam, Journal of State and Law, 11 (270)/2010, S. 19–33.

TAMÁS SZABADOS

Forum Shopping und die EU-Insolvenzverordnung – Das *Galapagos*-Urteil des Europäischen Gerichtshofs

I. Einleitung

Während sich der EU-Gesetzgeber meistens von einer eindeutigen Stellungnahme zur Praxis des *forum shopping* im Internationalen Privat- und Verfahrensrecht enthält, äußerte der Gerichtshof der Europäischen Union (EuGH) schon seine Meinung zum *forum shopping* in einer Reihe von Rechtssachen. Im Allgemeinen betrachtet der EuGH die Möglichkeit der Auswahl der Zuständigkeit vornherein nicht als ein negatives, moralisch zu beurteilendes Phänomen.

Es gibt jedoch ein Gebiet, wo die EU-Gesetzgebung das *forum shopping* ausdrücklich missbilligt: das internationale Insolvenzrecht. Im Mittelpunkt dieses Beitrags steht ein neueres Urteil des EuGH, das *Galapagos*-Urteil,[1] in dem der EuGH wieder auf das *forum shopping* im Zusammenhang mit der EU-InsVO eingehen sollte. Es wird gehofft, dass diese Themenauswahl auch das Interesse des *Jubilars,* des Herausgebers eines der wichtigsten Kommentare zum europäischen Zivilprozess- und Kollisionsrecht, der sich natürlich auch auf das internationale Insolvenzrecht erstreckt,[2] wecken wird.

II. Forum shopping im internationalen Privatrecht der EU

Im Bereich des internationalen Privat- und Verfahrensrechts befassen sich nur wenige EU-Rechtsakte ausdrücklich mit der Frage des *forum shopping.* Die Verordnung über das Gemeinschaftsgeschmacksmuster – wie ihr ErwGr. 30 erklärt – sieht Regel über die internationale Zuständigkeit vor, um das *forum shopping* zu verhindern.[3] Die meisten EU-Rechtsakte, die auf die Zuständigkeit eingehen, schweigen zum Problem des *forum shopping.* Die Annäherung des EU-Rechts, und besonders die Rechtsprechung des EuGH, bleibt neutral, was die Auswahl der Zuständigkeit betrifft, und gibt überwiegend der automatischen Anwendung der europäischen Zuständigkeitsregeln gegenüber einer moralischen Missbilligung des *forum shopping* Vorrang. Das ist in den vom EuGH im Zusammenhang mit der alternativen Zuständigkeit und der Rechtshängigkeit getroffenen Urteilen deutlich erkennbar. Die

[1] EuGH 24.3.2022 – C-723/20, ECLI:EU:C:2022:209 (Galapagos BidCo./DE ua).
[2] Rauscher, EuZPR/EuIPR II-1, 5. Aufl. 2022.
[3] Siehe Verordnung (EG) Nr. 6/2002 des Rates vom 12. Dezember 2001 über das Gemeinschaftsgeschmacksmuster (ABl. 2002 L 3, 1) ErwGr. 30.

EU-Rechtsvorschriften und die Rechtsprechung des EuGH beschränken das *forum shopping* nur in ziemlich engem Kreis.

1. *Alternative Zuständigkeit*

Die EU-Zuständigkeitsverordnungen selbst bestimmen alternative Zuständigkeitsgründe und erkennen damit die Möglichkeit des *forum shopping* an. Es reicht hier aus, auf die besonderen Zuständigkeiten der Brüssel Ia-VO hinzuweisen.[4] Die Brüssel IIb-VO beinhaltet in ähnlicher Weise alternative Zuständigkeitsgründe für die Ehescheidung, die Trennung ohne Auflösung des Ehebandes und die Ungültigerklärung einer Ehe.[5]

Diese Zuständigkeitsgründe, die eine Wahl für den Kläger einräumen, wurden durch den EuGH in zahlreichen Fällen so ausgelegt, dass die Wahlmöglichkeit der Kläger erweitert wurde. Dies kann zB mit Urteilen aus dem Gebiet der deliktischen Haftung illustriert werden. Der Ort, an dem das schädigende Ereignis eingetreten ist, dh der Anknüpfungspunkt für unerlaubte Handlungen im Art. 7 Nr. 2 Brüssel Ia-VO, wurde in mit der Verursachung von Umweltschäden[6] und grenzüberschreitenden Ehrverletzungen[7] verbundenen Angelegenheiten dahin ausgelegt, dass er sowohl den Ort, an dem der Schaden eingetreten ist, als auch den Ort des dem Schaden zugrunde liegenden ursächlichen Geschehens bedeuten kann. Dementsprechend kann der Kläger selbst entscheiden, wo er das Verfahren einleitet.

Nach Art. 3 Brüssel IIb-VO begründet die allgemeine Zuständigkeit für die Ehescheidung, die Trennung ohne Auflösung des Ehebandes und die Ungültigerklärung einer Ehe entweder der gewöhnliche Aufenthalt einer oder beider Parteien oder die Staatsangehörigkeit beider Ehegatten. Der letztere Zuständigkeitsgrund wurde im Fall von doppelter Staatsangehörigkeit in der Rechtsache *Hadadi* so ausgelegt, dass der Kläger die Gerichte seiner beliebigen Staatsangehörigkeit anrufen kann. Als Antwort auf den Verweis auf das *forum shopping* durch die polnische Regierung setzte der EuGH fest, dass keine Rangordnung zwischen den durch Art. 3 Brüssel IIb-VO bestimmten Gerichtsständen bestehe.[8] Er fügte hinzu, dass die Brüssel IIb-VO keine einheitlichen Kollisionsregeln vorsehe, deshalb könne sie die Ehegatten motivieren, ein Gerichtsverfahren da einzuleiten, wo das anzuwendende materielle Scheidungsrecht für sie vorteilhaft ist.[9] Daraus folgt aber nicht, dass die Anrufung eines nach der Verordnung zuständigen Gerichts als missbräuchlich angesehen werden könnte. Es kann hinzugefügt werden, dass im Fall des Unionsrechts die Möglichkeit der Auswahl der internationalen Zuständigkeit und damit des *forum shopping* nicht das Ergebnis des unkoordinierten Bestehens der Zuständigkeitsregeln von verschiedenen Staaten, sondern ein Folgesatz der bewussten Entscheidung des

---

[4] Art. 7 Brüssel Ia-VO.

[5] Art. 3 Brüssel IIb-VO.

[6] EuGH 30.11.1976 – 21/76, Slg. 1976 1735 Rn. 19 (Bier BV/Mines de potasse d'Alsace SA).

[7] EuGH 7.3.1995 – C-68/93, Slg. 1995 I-415 Rn. 20 (Shevill/Presse Alliance SA); EuGH 25.10.2011 – C-509/09 und C-161/10, Slg. 2011 I-10269 Rn. 41 (eDate/X).

[8] EuGH 16.7.2009 – C-168/08, Slg. 2009 I-6871 Rn. 48 (Hadadi/Mesko).

[9] EuGH 16.7.2009 – C-168/08, Slg. 2009 I-6871 Rn. 57 (Hadadi/Mesko).

EU-Gesetzgebers ist.[10] Die gesetzgeberische Freistellung von alternativen Zuständigkeiten ermöglicht eine Wahl zwischen diesen Zuständigkeiten und gilt nicht als ein missbräuchliches *forum shopping.*

Die Alternativität der Zuständigkeit wird nur selten begrenzt. In der Rechtssache *Allianz Elementar* wurde der im Art. 11 Brüssel Ia-VO befindliche alternative Zuständigkeitsgrund so ausgelegt, dass der Kläger mit seinem Anspruch nicht vor irgendwelchem Gericht des Mitgliedstaates vorgehen kann, wo er seinen Wohnsitz hat, sondern nur vor jenem, in dessen Bezirk sich sein Wohnsitz befindet. Art. 11 Brüssel Ia-VO bestimmt also nicht nur die internationale Zuständigkeit, sondern auch die örtliche Zuständigkeit.[11] Der EuGH rechtfertigte diesen Schluss damit, dass weder die Brüssel Ia-VO im Allgemeinen noch ihrer Art. 11 Brüssel Ia-VO das Ziel verfolgen, eine Praxis des *forum shopping* zu ermöglichen.[12]

2. *Rechtshängigkeit*

In den nationalen Rechten wurden herkömmlich verschiedene Korrektiven ausgestaltet, um *forum shopping*-Situationen zu belegen. Solche Mechanismen umfassten *fraude à la compétence* im französischen und belgischen Recht, *forum non conveniens* und *anti-suit injunction* in angelsächsischen Ländern.[13] Die *Gasser,*[14] *Owusu*[15] und *Turner*[16]-Entscheidungen des EuGH schlossen jedoch die Verwendung solcher aus den nationalen Rechten stammenden korrektiven Mechanismen aus. Kein mitgliedstaatliches Gericht kann nämlich von den verbindlichen Bestimmungen der Brüssel Ia-VO abweichen.

Die Bestimmung über die Anhängigkeit der Brüssel Ia-VO sagt eindeutig aus, dass, wenn Klagen wegen desselben Anspruchs zwischen denselben Parteien bei Gerichten verschiedener Mitgliedstaaten anhängig gemacht werden, das später angerufene Gericht das Verfahren von Amts wegen auszusetzen hat, bis die Zuständigkeit des zuerst angerufenen Gerichts feststeht.[17]

Der EuGH legt die Vorschriften über die Rechtshängigkeit strikt aus und hat keine Ausnahmen von ihnen zugelassen, auch nicht für Verfahrensstrategien, die missbräuchlich erscheinen mögen.[18] Ein später angerufenes Gericht muss die Entscheidung des zuerst angerufenen Gerichts über die Zuständigkeit abwarten, auch wenn die Anrufung des zuerst angerufenen Gerichts nur eine Verzögerung der Ent-

---

[10] Raimon La Semaine Juridique éd. G. n° 38, 20 septembre 2000, 1695 (1700).

[11] EuGH 30.6.2022 – C-652/20, ECLI:EU:C:2022:514, NJW-RR 2022, 1140–1144 Rn. 42 (HW/Allianz Elementar).

[12] EuGH 30.6.2022 – C-652/20, ECLI:EU:C:2022:514, NJW-RR 2022, 1140–1144 Rn. 52 (Allianz Elementar).

[13] Siehe Vareilles-Sommières The Mandatory Nature of Article 2 of the Brussels Convention and Derogation from the Rule It Lays Down in: Vareilles-Sommières, Forum Shopping in the European Judicial Area, 2007, i, ix.

[14] EuGH 9.12.2003 – C-116/02, Slg. 2003 I-14693 (Gasser/MISAT).

[15] EuGH 1.3.2005 – C-281/02, Slg. 2005 I-1383 (Owusu/Jackson).

[16] EuGH 27.4.2004 – C-159/02, Slg. 2004 I-3565 (Turner/Grovit).

[17] Art. 29 Abs. 1 Brüssel Ia-VO.

[18] Siehe EuGH 9.12.2003 – C-116/02, Slg. 2003 I-14693 (Gasser/MISAT); EuGH 27.4.2004 – C-159/02, Slg. 2004 I-3565 (Turner/Grovit).

scheidung des Rechtsstreits in der Sache bezweckt, da die Parteien in ihrem Vertrag die Zuständigkeit des später angerufenen Gerichts vereinbart hatten.[19] Das Gericht eines Mitgliedstaates kann weiterhin keine Entscheidung *(anti-suit injunction)* treffen, mit der es einer Partei des bei ihm anhängigen Verfahrens untersagt, ein Verfahren vor einem Gericht eines anderen Mitgliedstaates einzuleiten oder sich als Partei an einem solchen Verfahren zu beteiligen, wenn diese Partei bösgläubig ein Verfahren vor dem Gericht des anderen Mitgliedstaates einleiten oder fortsetzen will, um ein bereits anhängiges Verfahren zu vereiteln.[20] Dies ergibt sich aus dem zwingenden Charakter der Vorschriften der gegenwärtigen Brüssel Ia-VO und daraus, dass ein mitgliedstaatliches Gericht die Zuständigkeit eines Gerichts eines anderen Mitgliedstaates nicht überprüfen kann. Die Beurteilung des missbräuchlichen Charakters des Verhaltens bedeutet auch eine Bewertung, ob die Klageerhebung vor den Gerichten eines anderen Mitgliedstaates zugelassen werden kann. Auch hier gelten die Vorschriften über die Rechtshängigkeit.

Die Anhängigkeitsregel ist außerdem auch auf negative Feststellungsklagen anzuwenden.[21] Das schweizerische Bundesgericht äußerte jedoch im Zusammenhang mit dem Lugano-Übereinkommen von 1988, dass das nationale Verfahrensrecht bei der Anwendung seiner Bestimmung über die Rechtshängigkeit das Vorliegen eines besonderen Feststellungsinteresses verlangen darf, um die Gefahr des Missbrauchs negativer Feststellungsklagen zu verhindern.[22]

In der Literatur wurde die Auffassung vertreten, dass eine Ausnahme von der Anwendung der Zuständigkeitsvorschriften im Allgemeinen oder von der Anwendung der Vorschriften über die Rechtshängigkeit im Falle von Rechtsmissbrauch gemacht werden sollte.[23] Was Letzteres betrifft, wurde bei der Neufassung der Brüssel Ia-VO zwar vorgeschlagen, dass das zuerst angerufene Gericht bei negativen Feststellungsklagen nicht automatisch den Vorrang haben sollte, dieser Vorschlag wurde jedoch nicht angenommen.[24] Es sei darauf hingewiesen, dass eine ähnliche Rechtshängigkeitsregel nicht unbedingt außerhalb des Anwendungsbereichs der Brüssel Ia-VO, im autonomen internationalen Privat- und Verfahrensrecht gilt und sich die Mitgliedstaaten dagegen ein missbräuchliches Verhalten nach ihrem eigenen Gefallen schützen dürfen. Auf die Anwendung eines allgemeinen Verbotes des Rechtsmissbrauchs gehen wir in dem nächsten Abschnitt noch ein.

3. Einschränkung des forum shopping im EU internationalen Privatrecht

In einigen wenigen spezifischen Fällen geben die Brüssel Ia-VO und die Entscheidungen des EuGH Hinweise zur Verhinderung des *forum shopping.* Art. 8 Abs. 2 der Brüssel Ia-VO stellt fest, dass eine Person, die ihren Wohnsitz im Hoheitsgebiet eines Mitgliedstaates hat, auch verklagt werden kann wenn es sich um

[19] EuGH 9.12.2003 – C-116/02, Slg. 2003 I-14693 Rn. 53 (Gasser/MISAT).

[20] EuGH 27.4.2004 – C-159/02, Slg. 2004 I-3565 Rn. 26–31 (Turner/Grovit).

[21] EuGH 8.12.1987 – 144/86, Slg. 1987 4861 (Gubisch Maschinenfabrik/Palumbo); EuGH 6.12.1994 – C-406/92, Slg. 1994 I-5439 Rn. 46–48 (Tatry).

[22] BGE 136 III 523.

[23] Nuyts Global Jurist 2003/1, 31–33.

[24] Gaudemet-Tallon Mélanges en l'honneur du Professeur Bernard Audit, 2014, 384 (393).

eine Klage auf Gewährleistung oder um eine Interventionsklage handelt, vor dem Gericht des Hauptprozesses, es sei denn, dass die Klage nur erhoben worden ist, um diese Person dem für sie zuständigen Gericht zu entziehen. Es kann aus der Rechtsprechung des EuGH auch aufgerufen werden, dass er in der Rechtssache *Kalfelis* im Zusammenhang mit Klagen gegen mehrere Personen (Art. 6 Abs. 1 Brüsseler Übereinkommen; Art. 8. Abs. 1 Brüssel Ia-VO) feststellte, dass es ausgeschlossen werden sollte, „eine Klage gegen mehrere Beklagte allein zu dem Zweck zu erheben, einen dieser Beklagten der Zuständigkeit der Gerichte seines Wohnsitzstaats zu entziehen."[25] Diese Feststellung beabsichtigt, die Verhinderung einer Klageerhebung gegen eine nicht betroffene Person vor dem Gericht des Wohnsitzes des Letzteren nur mit dem Zweck, eine andere Person auch in diesem Staat zu klagen, vorzusehen.[26]

In der Rechtssache *M.S.G.* nahm der EuGH gegen eine fiktive Bestimmung des Erfüllungsortes aufgrund des gegenwärtigen Art. 7 Abs. 1 Brüssel Ia-VO Stellung.[27] Soweit die Festlegung des Erfüllungsortes ausschließlich die Bestimmung des Gerichtsstands zum Ziel hat, ist es zu untersuchen, ob eine solche Bestimmung des Erfüllungsortes den Voraussetzungen einer Vereinbarung über die Zuständigkeit (zurzeit Art. 25 Brüssel Ia-VO) entspricht.

Aus dieser Rechtsprechung folgern einige Autoren, dass das EU-Recht im Allgemeinen die betrügerische Veränderung der und Berufung auf die Zuständigkeit verbietet, und in solchen Fällen die mitgliedstaatlichen Gerichte die Ausübung der Zuständigkeit verweigern müssen.[28] Dies setzt die künstliche Veränderung des Sachverhalts (materielle Voraussetzung) und die Absicht (subjektive Voraussetzung), den Beklagten von dem zuständigen Gericht zu entziehen, voraus.[29]

Eine andere, in der Literatur erwähnte mögliche Schranke des *forum shopping* ist das Verbot des Rechtsmissbrauchs. Nach der Rechtsprechung des EuGH ist das Verbot des Rechtsmissbrauchs ein Grundsatz des EU-Rechts.[30] Es ist untersagt, sich betrügerisch oder missbräuchlich auf die Normen des EU-Rechts zu berufen. Das EU-Recht schützt nicht die missbräuchlichen Praktiken bzw. Vorgänge, die nicht im Rahmen des normalen Geschäftsverkehrs durchgeführt werden, sondern zum Ziel haben, missbräuchlich irgendwelchen aus dem EU-Recht stammenden Vorteil zu ziehen. Die Feststellung des Bestehens des Rechtsmissbrauchs setzt das Bestehen eines objektiven und eines subjektiven Elements voraus. Es geht um Rechtsmissbrauch, wenn „eine Gesamtwürdigung der objektiven Umstände ergibt, dass trotz formaler Einhaltung der gemeinschaftsrechtlichen Bedingungen das Ziel der Regelung nicht erreicht wurde" (objektives Element) und die Absicht besteht, sich einen durch das Unionsrecht bestimmten Vorteil dadurch zu sichern, dass die

[25] EuGH 27.9.1988 – 189/87, Slg. 1988 5565 Rn. 9 (Kalfelis/Bankhaus Schröder, Münchmeyer, Hengst & Co); EuGH 27.10.1998 – C-51/97, Slg. 1998 I-6511 Rn. 47 (Réunion européenne SA/Spliethoff's Bevrachtingskantoor BV und Kapitän des Schiffes „Alblasgracht V002").

[26] Nuyts Global Jurist 2003/1,12.

[27] EuGH 20.2.1997 – C-106/95, Slg. 1997 I-911 Rn. 31–35 (Mainschiffahrts-Genossenschaft (MSG)/Les Gravières Rhénanes SARL).

[28] Nuyts Global Jurist 2003/1,14.

[29] Nuyts Global Jurist 2003/1,14.

[30] EuGH 5.7.2007 – C-321/05, Slg. 2007 I-5795 Rn. 38 (Kofoed/Skatteministeriet).

entsprechenden Voraussetzungen willkürlich geschaffen werden (subjektives Element).[31] Nach der Annäherung des EuGH kann es sich nicht um Rechtsmissbrauch handeln, soweit die fraglichen Handlungen eine andere Erklärung als nur die Erlangung eines Vorteils haben können.[32]

Die Wahlmöglichkeit betreffend verschiedene Gerichte zielt die Sicherung des Zugangs zu Gerichten von dem Kläger ab.[33] Nach einer im Schrifttum vertretenen Auffassung kann das Verbot des Rechtsmissbrauchs aber zur Verweigerung der Ausübung der Zuständigkeit führen, wenn das Ziel der Klageerhebung ist, der anderen Partei einen unverhältnismäßigen Nachteil (mit bedeutenden Kosten oder mit der Verzögerung des Verfahrens im Fall einer negativen Feststellungsklage) zu verursachen.[34] Andere Autoren halten die Unzulässigkeit der Klage für eine angemessene Sanktion.[35] Wie früher schon dargestellt wurde, erklärte der EuGH aber bis jetzt in keiner einzigen Angelegenheit, dass ein mitgliedstaatliches Gericht im Fall des Rechtsmissbrauchs die Ausübung der Zuständigkeit verweigern oder die Klage als unzulässig abweisen sollte. Daraus folgt, dass der Eingriffsradius und die Eingriffsintensität des EU-Rechts gegenüber (missbräuchlichem) *forum shopping* eher beschränkt ist. Die Anwendung des Verbots des Rechtsmissbrauchs wurde bestritten, da es in der Rechtsanwendung Unsicherheit darüber schaffen würde, ob es sich um die Ausübung eines Rechts handelt, das sich aus den Zuständigkeitsvorschriften ergibt *(forum shopping bonus)* oder um ein missbräuchliches Verhalten *(forum shopping malus)*.[36]

Wie wir später sehen werden, bleibt die Einstellung der EU-InsVO, obwohl sie sich ausdrücklich mit dem *forum shopping* befasst, eher neutral und die moralische Beurteilung, ob ein Verhalten als missbräuchlich betrachtet wird oder nicht, ist nur in wenigen Situationen maßgebend.

III. EU-InsVO und das forum shopping

Wie wir oben gesehen haben, macht das internationale Privatrecht der EU nur vereinzelte Äußerungen zum *forum shopping.* Das positive Recht definiert den Begriff des *forum shopping* nicht. Ein Bereich, wo das internationale Privatrecht der EU allerdings auf das Risiko des *forum shopping* ausdrücklich aufmerksam macht, ist das internationale Insolvenzrecht. Unter den Zuständigkeitsverordnungen der EU ist die EU-InsVO die Einzige, die auch eine Definition für *forum shopping* enthält.

Die Definition des *forum shopping* befindet sich trotzdem nicht in dem normativen Teil der Verordnung, sondern unter den Erwägungsgründen. Der ErwGr. 5 be-

---

[31] EuGH 14.12.2000 – C-110/99, Slg. 2000 I-11569 Rn. 52–53 (Emsland-Stärke/Hauptzollamt Hamburg-Jonas).

[32] EuGH 28.7.2016 – C-423/15, ECLI:EU:C:2016:604 Rn. 40 (Kratzer/R+V Allgemeine Versicherung).

[33] Nuyts Global Jurist 2003/1, 25.

[34] Nuyts Global Jurist 2003/1, 26.

[35] Raimon La Semaine Juridique éd. G. n° 38, 20 septembre 2000, 1695 (1699–1701).

[36] Niboyet Journal du droit international 2006, 937 (945–946).

schreibt *forum shopping* als eine Situation, in der die Beteiligten „Vermögensgegenstände oder Gerichtsverfahren von einem Mitgliedstaat in einen anderen [...] verlagern, um auf diese Weise eine günstigere Rechtsstellung zum Nachteil der Gesamtheit der Gläubiger zu erlangen“.[37] Der ErwGr. 29 fügt hinzu, dass Sicherungen geschaffen werden müssen, „um betrügerisches oder missbräuchliches *forum shopping* zu verhindern.“[38] Dies ist eine spezielle, auf das Insolvenzrecht geschnittene Begriffsbestimmung, indem sie auf die Auswirkungen auf die Gläubiger verweist. Die Erwägungsgründe stellen klar, dass die Verlagerung von Vermögensgegenständen oder Gerichtsverfahren, dh *forum shopping* an sich nicht immer rechtswidrig ist. Was die EU-InsVO missbilligt, ist das betrügerische oder missbräuchliche *forum shopping.*

Es ist kein Zufall, dass sich die EU-Gesetzgebung mit dem *forum shopping* in diesem Bereich ausdrücklich beschäftigt. Die Verschiedenheit der nationalen Insolvenzrechte, einschließlich der verschiedenen Regelungen der Rechte von Gläubigern und Arbeitnehmern, kann eine insolvente Gesellschaft dazu verleiten, ein für sie günstigeres Insolvenzregime zu wählen.

Eine Voraussetzung des *forum shopping* ist die Möglichkeit der Auswahl der Zuständigkeit. Das wichtigste Anknüpfungsprinzip der EU-InsVO ist der Mittelpunkt der hauptsächlichen Interessen des Schuldners, der COMI. Der COMI bestimmt nicht nur die internationale Zuständigkeit, sondern auch das anwendbare Recht. Mit der Verlegung des COMI kann ein Schuldner deshalb sowohl den Gerichtsstand als auch das anwendbare Recht beeinflussen. Auf diese Weise kann die Verlegung des COMI ein Mittel des *forum shopping* darstellen. Es muss aber bemerkt werden, dass nicht alle Verlegungen des COMI, nicht einmal kurz vor dem Eintreten der Zahlungsunfähigkeit, ein zu verbietendes missbräuchliches *forum shopping* darstellt. Im Lichte der oben erwähnten Erwägungsgründe sollte *forum shopping* nur dann verhindert werden, wenn es auf die Beeinträchtigung der Rechte von Gläubigern abzielt.

Da die in dem folgenden Abschnitt vorgeführte *Galapagos*-Entscheidung von der Verlagerung des COMI einer Gesellschaft handelt, wird das *forum shopping* hier ausschließlich im Zusammenhang mit insolventen Gesellschaften erörtert. Um den COMI zu verändern, kann eine Gesellschaft seinen Satzungssitz oder Verwaltungssitz oder beide in einen anderen Staat verlegen.[39] Diese Fälle der Sitzverlegung fallen ohne Zweifel in den Geltungsbereich der Niederlassungsfreiheit. Die Rechtsprechung des EuGH zur Niederlassungsfreiheit und neuerdings die Mobilitätsrichtlinie[40] erleichtern die grenzüberschreitende Mobilität von Gesellschaften in der EU und damit die Möglichkeit der Veränderung des COMI und gleichzeitig des *forum shopping,* während einer der Zwecke der EU-InsVO gerade die Verhinderung des *forum shopping* ist.[41] Es ist allerdings nicht zu übersehen, dass die Nieder-

---

[37] ErwGr. 5 EU-InsVO.

[38] ErwGr. 29 EU-InsVO.

[39] Siehe Ringe Hamburg Law Review 2017, 38 (41).

[40] Richtlinie (EU) 2019/2121 des Europäischen Parlaments und des Rates vom 27. November 2019 zur Änderung der Richtlinie (EU) 2017/1132 in Bezug auf grenzüberschreitende Umwandlungen, Verschmelzungen und Spaltungen, ABl. 2019 L 321, 1 (MobilitätsRL).

[41] Siehe Myszke-Novakowska Polish Yearbook of International Law 2017, 203 (220).

lassungsfreiheit nach der ständigen Rechtsprechung des EuGH ua zum Zweck des Schutzes der Interessen der Gläubiger mit der Wahrung des Grundsatzes der Verhältnismäßigkeit eingeschränkt werden kann.

Die EU-InsVO stellt eine Vermutung auf, nach der der COMI bei Gesellschaften bis zum Beweis des Gegenteils mit dem satzungsmäßigen Sitz der Gesellschaft übereinstimmt. Die Vermutung kann nach der Rechtsprechung widerlegt werden, wenn objektive und für Dritte feststellbare Elemente belegen, dass sich der COMI der Gesellschaft anderswo befindet.[42] Wie ErwGr. 30 der EU-InsVO darauf hinweist: „Bei einer Gesellschaft sollte diese Vermutung widerlegt werden können, wenn sich die Hauptverwaltung der Gesellschaft in einem anderen Mitgliedstaat befindet als in dem Mitgliedstaat, in dem sich der Sitz der Gesellschaft befindet, und wenn eine Gesamtbetrachtung aller relevanten Faktoren die von Dritten überprüfbare Feststellung zulässt, dass sich der tatsächliche Mittelpunkt der Verwaltung und der Kontrolle der Gesellschaft sowie der Verwaltung ihrer Interessen in diesem anderen Mitgliedstaat befindet." Diese Auslegung nähert den COMI auf den ersten Blick einer Anknüpfung zum Verwaltungssitz. Der Verwaltungssitz als der Ort, an dem die Entscheidungen des Vorstands getroffen werden, ist jedoch oft nur schwierig feststellbar für Dritte, während andere Anknüpfungen (Geschäftstätigkeit, Büros) schon leichter erkennbar sind.[43] Was entscheidend ist, ist der Gesichtswinkel von Dritten, vor allem der der Gläubiger. Im Fall eines Versuchs, den COMI zu verlegen, mögen die Gläubiger so empfinden, dass sich der COMI noch im Ursprungsland befindet. Damit entnimmt die Wahrnehmung von Dritten die Wirkung der versuchten Veränderung.[44] Da es nicht immer leicht ist, die tatsächlichen Umstände, die den COMI der Gesellschaft begründen, zu verändern, wirkt die Bestimmung des COMI im Einklang mit der EU-InsVO gegen missbräuchliches *forum shopping*.[45] Für einen Schuldner ist es zusätzlich manchmal schwierig vorsehbar, ob das angerufene mitgliedstaatliche Gericht mit Rücksicht auf die tatsächlichen Umstände aus dem Gesichtspunkt von Dritten die Widerlegung der Vermutung feststellt oder den COMI nach satzungsmäßigem Sitz bestimmt. Diese Ungewissheit erschwert die Planung und Durchführung einer *forum shopping*-Strategie.[46]

Die Verlegung des Satzungssitzes löst die Verlegung des COMI im Hinblick auf die Vermutung für die Übereinkunft des COMI und des Satzungssitzes nach Art. 3 Abs. 1 Alt. 2 EU-InsVO ein. Eine Gesellschaft kann jedoch ihren Verwaltungssitz in einen anderen Mitgliedstaat verlegen, ohne dass sie ihren Satzungssitz verlegen würde. Eine solche Struktur nutzt die Möglichkeit der Widerlegung der Annahme, dass der COMI mit dem Satzungssitz als Hauptregel übereinstimmt. Eine gleichzeitige Verlegung des Satzungs- und des Verwaltungssitzes verursacht kein Problem, da sie eindeutig die Veränderung des COMI meldet.

---

[42] EuGH 2.5.2006 – C-341/04, Slg. 2006 I-3813 Rn. 33–34 (Eurofood).

[43] Siehe Armour, Abuse of European Insolvency Law? A Discussion in: de la Feria/Vogenauer, Prohibition of Abuse of Law (2011), 157, 159.

[44] Szydło European Business Organization Law Review 2010, 253 (260).

[45] Ringe European Business Organization Law Review 2008, 579 (595); Szydło European Business Organization Law Review 2010, 253 (258).

[46] Szydło European Business Organization Law Review 2010, 253 (258 und 261).

In solchen Fällen ist es eine Vorfrage, ob der COMI tatsächlich verlegt wurde. Dies erfordert die Feststellung des Ortes des COMI. Die Schuldner können versuchen, die faktische Situation künstlich so zu verändern, dass der Anschein die Veränderung des COMI sei.[47] Wie der BGH bereits festlegte, müssen die manipulativen Tatbestandselemente, einschließlich der künstlichen Veränderung des Verwaltungssitzes des Schuldners (durch die Bestellung eines Geschäftsführers mit einer ausländischen Anschrift) außer Acht gelassen werden.[48] Der BFH legte fest, dass die Anerkennung eines im Vereinigten Königreich eröffneten Insolvenzverfahren in Deutschland nur deswegen zum Schutz der öffentlichen Ordnung nicht verweigert werden kann, dass der Schuldner da eine Restschuldbefreiung (discharge from bankruptcy) schneller erreichen konnte.[49] Zu gleicher Zeit, wenn der Schuldner seinen Wohnsitz und damit seinen COMI nur scheinbar und rechtsmissbräuchlich nach Großbritannien verlegte, um die vorteilhafteren britischen insolvenzrechtlichen Vorschriften und so eine schnellere Restschuldbefreiung auszunutzen, konnte dies schon als ein Grund betrachtet werden, der Anerkennung des britischen Insolvenzverfahrens wegen Unvereinbarkeit mit der öffentlichen Ordnung entgegenzustehen.

Eine Verlegung des COMI ist nicht zwangsläufig missbräuchlich. Es kann vorkommen, dass die Gläubiger der Veränderung des COMI zustimmen, oder sie kann dem Interesse der Gläubiger dienen, wenn sie die Restrukturierung der Gesellschaft so erleichtert, dass die Beibehaltung des Gesellschaftsvermögens zur Befriedigung der Gläubiger beitragen kann. Im Allgemeinen kann es angenommen werden, dass die Verlegung des COMI missbräuchliches *forum shopping* ergibt, wenn das für die Gläubiger verfügbare Vermögen damit vermindert wird und zur Übertragung des Vermögens an die Eigentümer führt oder gewisse Gläubiger gegenüber anderen Gläubigern bevorzugt.[50] Nach einer anderen Auffassung ist nicht die Verminderung des für die Gläubiger verfügbaren Vermögens entscheidend, sondern der unilaterale oder konsensuale Character der Verlegung des COMI. Wenn die Gläubiger der Veränderung zustimmen, gibt es keinen Missbrauch; wenn die Verlegung des COMI das Ergebnis einer unilateralen Entscheidung des Schuldners ist, besteht der Verdacht des Rechtsmissbrauchs.[51]

Im Zusammenhang mit der Anwendung der EU-InsVO sind drei mögliche Fälle des *forum shopping* denkbar. Die Verlegung des COMI kann nämlich (1) vor der Stellung eines Antrags auf die Eröffnung des Hauptinsolvenzverfahrens; (2) zwischen der Antragsstellung und der Eröffnung des Hauptinsolvenzverfahrens; und (3) nach der Eröffnung des Hauptinsolvenzverfahrens stattfinden. Das neuere *Galapagos*-Urteil des EuGH geht von diesen auf die zweite Modalität des *forum shopping* ein.

---

[47] McCormack Cambridge Law Journal 2009, 169 (191).

[48] BGH 13.12.2007 – IX ZB 238/06, BeckRS 2008, 720.

[49] BFH 27.1.2016 – VII B 119/15, BeckRS 2016, 95276.

[50] Eidenmüller, Abuse of Law in the Context of European Insolvency Law in de la Feria/Vogenauer, Prohibition of Abuse of Law, 2011, 137 (147).

[51] Armour, Abuse of European Insolvency Law? A Discussion in de la Feria/Vogenauer, Prohibition of Abuse of Law, 2011, 163.

IV. Das Galapagos-Urteil

Im Zusammenhang mit der Anwendung der EU-InsVO hat sich in einigen Fällen die Frage gestellt, wie die Verlegung des COMI des Schuldners in einen anderen Staat, möglicherweise mit günstigeren rechtlichen Regelungen für ihn, nach dem Einreichen des Antrags auf die Eröffnung des Hauptinsolvenzverfahrens, aber vor seiner Eröffnung zu bewerten ist. Das Problem kann darauf zurückgeführt werden, dass die EU-InsVO den genauen Zeitpunkt für die Feststellung des COMI nicht ausdrücklich bestimmt.

In der neueren Rechtssache *Galapagos* verlegte die Gesellschaft Galapagos, die ihren satzungsmäßigen Sitz in Luxemburg hatte, ihre Hauptverwaltung im Juni 2019 in das Vereinigte Königreich. Zwei Monate später beantragten die Direktoren der Gesellschaft die Eröffnung eines Insolvenzverfahrens vor dem englischen High Court of Justice. Einen Tag später wurden diese Direktoren jedoch abberufen und durch einen neuen Direktor ersetzt, der für Galapagos ein Büro in Düsseldorf errichtete. Am gleichen Tag reichte Galapagos einen neuen Antrag auf Eröffnung eines Insolvenzverfahrens beim Amtsgericht Düsseldorf ein. Dieser Antrag wurde später durch das Gericht mit Rücksicht auf das Fehlen der Zuständigkeit abgewiesen. Zwei andere Gläubiger beantragten am 6. September 2019 die Eröffnung eines Insolvenzverfahrens und das AG Düsseldorf stellte seine Zuständigkeit fest, da sich der COMI von Galapagos – nach seinem Standpunkt – zum Zeitpunkt dieser Antragstellung in Düsseldorf befand. Diese wurde von einer Tochtergesellschaft und Gläubigerin von Galapagos bestritten, die behauptete, dass die Hauptverwaltung der Gesellschaft in dem Vereinigten Königreich gewesen sei. Zum Zeitpunkt des Einreichens des Vorabentscheidungsersuchens entschied der High Court of Justice noch nicht über die Eröffnung des Hauptinsolvenzverfahrens.

Die Vorlagefrage betraf die bereits in der Rechtssache *Staubitz-Schreiber*[52] erörterte Frage, ob das Gericht, zu dem der Antrag auf Eröffnung eines Hauptinsolvenzverfahrens eingereicht wurde, seine ausschließliche Zuständigkeit beibehält, selbst wenn der COMI nach der Vorlage des Antrags, aber vor der Entscheidung über diesen Antrag in einen anderen Mitgliedstaat verlegt wurde. Bei der Beantwortung der Vorlagefrage bestätigte der EuGH, dass die Grundsätze, die im Zusammenhang mit der Anwendung der alten Fassung der EU-InsVO ausgearbeitet wurden, weiterhin einschlägig gelten.[53]

In diesem Geist wies der EuGH auf das bereits oben erwähnte Ziel der EU-InsVO hin, auf die Verhinderung des betrügerischen oder missbräuchlichen *forum shopping.* Wenig überraschend stellte der EuGH aufgrund seiner *Staubitz-Schreiber*-Entscheidung fest, dass das Gericht des Mitgliedstaates, in dem der Antrag auf die Eröffnung des Hauptinsolvenzverfahrens gestellt wurde, weiter ausschließlich zuständig bleibt *(perpetuatio fori),* auch wenn der Schuldner seinen COMI nach Antragstellung, aber vor der Entscheidung über diesen Antrag in einen anderen Mit-

---

[52] EuGH 17.1.2006 – C-1/04, ECLI:EU:C:2006:39 = BeckRS 2006, 70077.

[53] Verordnung (EG) Nr. 1346/2000 des Rates vom 29. Mai 2000 über Insolvenzverfahren (ABl. 2000 L 160, 1).

gliedstaat verlegt.[54] Ein Gericht eines anderen Mitgliedstaates, wenn bei ihm später ein ähnlicher Antrag eingereicht wird, kann sich nicht für die Eröffnung des Hauptinsolvenzverfahrens für zuständig erklären, solange das erste Gericht nicht entschieden und seine Zuständigkeit nicht verneint hat. Andernfalls könnte der Schuldner durch die Verlegung seines COMI sowohl den Gerichtsstand als auch das anwendbare Recht einseitig bestimmen.[55] Wie der EuGH es schon in seinem *Staubitz-Schreiber*-Urteil ausführte, würde die Anerkennung der Veränderung der Zuständigkeit in einem solchen Fall die Gläubiger zwingen, dem Schuldner stets zu folgen, und dort Verfahren zu eröffnen, wo sich der Letztere gerade für kürzere oder längere Zeit niederlässt. Dies würde zur Verlängerung der Verfahren führen. Hieraus ist auch ersichtlich, dass das EU-Recht die Auswahl des Forums nicht toleriert, wenn es, wie im Fall der EU-InsVO, einen ausschließlichen Gerichtsstand für eine gewisse Gruppe von Angelegenheiten bestimmt. Der Abschluss der Wirkung einer Verlegung des COMI nach dem Einreichen des Antrags auf die Eröffnung des Hauptinsolvenzverfahrens, aber vor der Eröffnung des Verfahrens hängt aber gar nicht von der Beurteilung der Handlungsweise als missbräuchlich ab. Die Veränderung der Zuständigkeit wird nach diesem Zeitpunkt im Sinne der *Staubitz-Schreiber*- und *Galapagos*-Rechtsprechung automatisch ausgeschlossen.[56]

Beachtlich sind die Äußerungen des EuGH zur Anwendung der EU-InsVO nach dem Brexit. Gemäß dem Austrittsabkommen sollte die EU-InsVO bis zum Ablauf der Übergangszeit, dh bis zum 31. Dezember 2020 im Vereinigten Königreich angewandt werden, soweit das Hauptinsolvenzverfahren bis zu diesem Zeitpunkt eingeleitet wurde.[57] Nach dem Ablauf der Übergangszeit gilt jedoch das Vereinigte Königreich nicht mehr als Mitgliedstaat. Infolgedessen, falls der High Court bis diesen Zeitpunkt keine Entscheidung über den Antrag auf Eröffnung des Hauptinsolvenzverfahrens entschieden hatte, soll ein Gericht des Mitgliedstaates, wo sich der COMI von Galapagos nach seiner Verlagerung befindet, die Entscheidung des englischen Gerichts nicht abwarten und sich von der Feststellung seine internationale Zuständigkeit nicht enthalten. Dieser Befund kann auf alle Drittstaaten, in denen die EU-InsVO nicht zur Anwendung kommt, verallgemeinert werden.

Nach der Beantwortung der Vorabentscheidungsfragen vom EuGH entschied die Angelegenheit schließlich der BGH.[58] Der BGH stellte fest, dass die EU-InsVO auf den Rechtsstreit anwendbar ist, da sie nur erfordert, dass der COMI des Schuldners in einem Mitgliedstaat sei. Es ist jedoch unerheblich, dass die tatsächlichen Umstände den Sachverhalt an einen Drittstaat knüpfen. Der BGH führte aus, dass Galapagos als eine Holdinggesellschaft, die keine wirkliche selbständige Wirt-

---

[54] EuGH 24.3.2022 – C-723/20, ECLI:EU:C:2022:209 Rn. 36 (Galapagos BidCo./DE ua).

[55] EuGH 24.3.2022 – C-723/20, ECLI:EU:C:2022:209 Rn. 32 (Galapagos BidCo./DE ua).

[56] Eidenmüller, Abuse of Law in the Context of European Insolvency Law in: de la Feria/Vogenauer, Prohibition of Abuse of Law, 2011, 152.

[57] Art. 67 Abs. 3 Abkommen über den Austritt des Vereinigten Königreichs Großbritannien und Nordirland aus der Europäischen Union und der Europäischen Atomgemeinschaft (ABl. 2020, L 29, 7).

[58] BGH 8.12.2022 – IX ZB 72/19, NJW-Spezial 2023, 150.

schaftstätigkeit ausübte, ihren COMI spätestens ab September 2019 in Deutschland hatte. Als eine neue Tatsache wurde festgestellt, dass der englische High Court das Insolvenzverfahren mit einem *windig-up order* am 30. Juni 2022 eröffnete. Der BGH erinnerte daran, dass ein mitgliedstaatliches Gericht, das mit einem Antrag auf Eröffnung eines Hauptinsolvenzverfahrens befasst ist, gemäß der EU-InsVO weiter zuständig bleibt, selbst wenn der COMI des Schuldners nach dem Einreichen des Antrags, aber vor der Eröffnung des Insolvenzverfahrens in einen anderen Mitgliedstaat verlegt wird. Bis der Entscheidung des ersten angerufenen Gerichts sind die Gerichte anderer Mitgliedstaaten für die Eröffnung des Insolvenzverfahrens nicht zuständig.

Die aus dieser Auslegung folgende Sperrwirkung mit dem Austritt des Vereinigten Königreichs aus der EU nach dem Ende des am 31.12.2020 ablaufenden Übergangszeitraums entfiel. Gemäß den Übergangsregeln war die EU-InsVO auf bis zum Ablauf der Übergangsfrist eröffnete Hauptinsolvenzverfahren anwendbar. Bis zu diesem Zeitpunkt entschied aber der englische High Court nicht über die Eröffnung eines Hauptinsolvenzverfahrens. Ab dem Ablauf des Übergangszeitraums schloss der zuvor bei dem englischen Gericht gestellte Insolvenzantrag die Zuständigkeit deutscher Gerichte nicht mehr aus.

Es folgte auch nicht anderes aus den autonomen deutschen Zuständigkeitsregeln, insbesondere § 343 InsO. Die letztere Bestimmung sieht die Anerkennung der Eröffnung eines ausländischen Insolvenzverfahrens vor, beantwortet aber nicht die Frage, wie ein deutsches Gericht vorgehen soll, wenn das ausländische Gericht über die Eröffnung des Insolvenzverfahrens noch nicht entschied, sondern es lediglich um die Wirkungen eines in einem Drittstaat gestellten Insolvenzantrags geht. Soweit die Zuständigkeit eines deutschen Gerichts nach Art. 3 EU-InsVO begründet werden kann und dieses Gericht über die Eröffnung des Insolvenzverfahrens entscheidet, geht die Zuständigkeit des deutschen Gerichts der eines drittstaatlichen Gerichts auch dann vor, wenn der Antrag auf Eröffnung des Insolvenzverfahrens bei dem drittstaatlichen Gericht früher gestellt worden ist. Der Grundsatz des gegenseitigen Vertrauens, der in der Beziehung zwischen den Mitgliedstaaten anzuwenden ist, gilt bezüglich Drittstaaten nicht. Aufgrund dieser Erwägungen gelangte der BGH zu dem Schluss, dass der in England eingereichte Antrag auf Eröffnung des Insolvenzverfahrens unter den Umständen des Falles die internationale Zuständigkeit deutscher Gerichte nicht ausschloss.

Diese Entscheidung erleuchtet gut den Unterschied zwischen den Situationen, wo der erste Antrag auf die Eröffnung des Insolvenzverfahrens bei einem mitgliedstaatlichen bzw. drittstaatlichen Gericht gestellt wird. In dem ersten Fall bleibt das zuerst angerufene Gericht bis zur Entscheidung über die Eröffnung des Verfahrens allein zuständig. Die Verlegung des COMI in einen anderen Mitgliedstaat wird nicht berücksichtigt. Die gleiche Annäherung gilt aber nicht für Anträge, die zuerst bei einem drittstaatlichen Gericht eingereicht wurden.[59] In solchen Fällen sind die mitgliedstaatlichen Gerichte durch das EU-Recht nicht verpflichtet, die Entscheidung der drittstaatlichen Gerichte über die Eröffnung des Insolvenzverfahrens ab-

[59] Baumert LMK 2023, 804828.

zuwarten. Die Entscheidung des BGH wirft zur gleichen Zeit die Gefahr von Parallelverfahren in einem Drittstaat und in einem Mitgliedstaat auf.[60]

Es lohnt sich hier noch eine andere einschlägige Entscheidung des BGH zu erwähnen. In dieser Angelegenheit wurde der Antrag auf die Eröffnung des Insolvenzverfahrens bei einem örtlich unzuständigen deutschen Gericht (AG Cottbus) gestellt, das die Sache an das zuständige Amtsgericht (AG Charlottenburg) verwies.[61] Dies war erforderlich, da es um eine Schuldnerin, eine Gesellschaft ging, die ihren satzungsmäßigen Sitz im Bezirk des AG Cottbus hatte, aber ihre Wirtschaftstätigkeit in Berlin ausübte. Ohne Zweifel war der COMI der Schuldnerin im Zeitpunkt der Antragstellung in Deutschland. Zwischen dem Zeitpunkt der Antragstellung und der Verweisung an das örtlich zuständige Gericht verlegte die Schuldnerin jedoch ihren COMI durch die Veräußerung der Gesellschaftsanteile an eine in Polen ansässige Person und die gleichzeitige Bestellung einer ebenfalls in Polen ansässigen Geschäftsführerin nach Polen. Der BGH stellte fest, dass die Verweisung an das örtlich zuständige Gericht die Bestimmung der internationalen Zuständigkeit nicht verändert. Die EU-InsVO bestimmt nur die internationale Zuständigkeit und sie kommt nicht auf die örtliche Zuständigkeit an. Es ist die Aufgabe der Mitgliedstaaten, zu bestimmen, welches Gericht in dem betroffenen Mitgliedstaat sachlich und örtlich zuständig ist. Die Verweisung bedeutet keinen neuen Antrag auf die Eröffnung des Insolvenzverfahrens. Das örtlich zuständige Gericht setzt das Verfahren fort, das durch das unzuständige Gericht begann. Um das *forum shopping* zu vermeiden, kann ein Schuldner die internationale Zuständigkeit durch die Verlegung seines COMI in einen anderen Mitgliedstaat nicht verändern, selbst wenn ein Gläubiger den Antrag auf die Eröffnung des Insolvenzverfahrens bei einem international zuständigen, aber nach dem mitgliedstaatlichem Recht örtlich unzuständigen Gericht gestellt hatte. Die Verlegung des COMI nach der Antragstellung kann nicht berücksichtigt werden. Die Gläubiger können nicht gezwungen werden, dem Schuldner stets zu folgen und dort ein neues Verfahren einzuleiten, wo der Schuldner sich auch nur vorübergehend niederlässt. Damit verwendete der BGH die gleiche Annäherung, der der EuGH in den Rechtssachen *Staubitz-Schreiber* und *Galapagos* bezüglich der *perpetuatio fori* folgte und stärkte sie für Fälle weiter, wo der Antrag auf die Eröffnung des Insolvenzverfahrens bei einem örtlich unzuständigen Gericht gestellt wird.[62]

V. Weitere Fälle des forum shopping im Zusammenhang mit der Anwendung der EU-InsVO

Wie oben dargestellt, ist eine andere mögliche *forum shopping*-Situation der Fall, wo die Gesellschaft ihren COMI kurz vor dem Einreichen des Antrags auf die Eröffnung des Insolvenzverfahrens verlegt. Die EU-InsVO stellt klar, dass die Vermutung der Bestimmung des COMI aufgrund des Satzungssitzes nur dann gilt,

[60] Baumert LMK 2023, 804828.

[61] BGH 7.7.2022 – IX ZB 14/21, NJW-RR 2022, 1275. Siehe Fritz/Canpolat NZI 2022, 912; Lieberknecht IPRax 2024, 140.

[62] Fritz/Canpolat NZI 2022, 914.

wenn der Sitz nicht innerhalb eines Zeitraums von drei Monaten vor der Antragsstellung in einen anderen Mitgliedstaat verlegt wurde.[63] Diese Vorschrift schließt die Verlegung des COMI nicht aus, sie betrifft nur die Anwendung der Vermutung. Die Regel gilt nur für die Verlegung des Satzungssitzes, aber schließt ein *forum shopping* durch die Verlegung des Verwaltungssitzes, ohne eine gleichzeitige Verlegung des Satzungssitzes, nicht aus.[64] Wenn die Vermutung nicht gilt und der Schuldner sich darauf beruft, dass er seinen COMI innerhalb drei Monate vor der Stellung des Antrags auf die Eröffnung des Hauptinsolvenzverfahrens verlegt hatte, ist es zu beweisen, dass die Verlegung des COMI auch aus dem Blickwinkel der Gläubiger erfolgte.

Diese Lösung der EU-InsVO wurde kritisiert, da sie auch solchen Sitzverlegungen entgegenwirkt, in die auch die Gläubiger einwilligen.[65] Die Nichtanwendung der Vermutung kann weiterhin für die neuen Gläubiger nachteilig sein, die Rechte gegenüber dem Schuldner nach der Verlegung des Satzungsitzes erwarben.[66] Die Einschränkung der Anwendung der Vermutung ist deshalb nicht im Einklang mit der in der EU-InsVO beinhalteten Definition, nach der das *forum shopping* nur solche Verhaltensweisen umfasst, die „zum Nachteil der Gesamtheit der Gläubiger" sind. Die durch die Kommission bestellte Studie weist darauf hin, dass die EU-InsVO objektive und nachprüfbare Kriterien bestimmen sollte, um feststellen zu können, ob die Veränderung des COMI innerhalb des dreimonatigen Zeitraums als missbräuchlich betrachtet werden soll.[67]

Im Fall einer früheren Sitzverlegung müssen die Gläubiger mit Rücksicht auf die Umstände des Falls beweisen, dass die Gesellschaft ihren COMI in dem ersten Mitgliedstaat behielt.[68] Je ferner wir in Zeit von der dreimonatigen Zeitgrenze sind, desto unwahrscheinlicher ist das Bestehen des Missbrauchs. Wie früher erklärt wurde, liegt ein Rechtsmissbrauch vor, wenn die Verlegung des COMI die Eigentümer der Schuldnerin gegenüber den Gläubigern bzw. gewisse Gläubiger gegenüber anderen Gläubigern bevorzugt.[69]

In der Angelegenheit *Galapagos* ging der EuGH davon aus, dass der COMI der Gesellschaft zum Zeitpunkt des Antrags auf Eröffnung des Insolvenzverfahrens im Vereinigten Königreich war und untersuchte nicht die Verlegung der Hauptverwaltung (und wahrscheinlich des COMI der Gesellschaft) von Luxemburg kurz vor dem Einreichen des Antrags.[70]

---

[63] Art. 3 Abs. 1 Alt. 2 EU-InsVO.

[64] Ringe Hamburg Law Review 2017, 48–50.

[65] Ringe Hamburg Law Review 2017, 48.

[66] Ringe Hamburg Law Review 2017, 49.

[67] Study on the issue of abusive forum shopping in insolvency proceedings, Final report, https://commission.europa.eu/document/download/0664f511-6e09-4751-b7be-421fde651091_en?filename=Final%20Report%20-%20Abusive%20Forum%20Shopping_Febr%202022.pdf (abgerufen 14.5.2024), S. 41.

[68] Myszke-Novakowska Polish Yearbook of International Law 2017, 203 (216).

[69] Eidenmüller, Abuse of Law in the Context of European Insolvency Law in: de la Feria/Vogenauer, Prohibition of Abuse of Law, 2011, 149.

[70] EuGH 24.3.2022 – C-723/20, ECLI:EU:C:2022:209 Rn. 25 (Galapagos BidCo./DE ua).

Als ein dritter Fall des *forum shopping* ist es auch vorstellbar, dass ein Schuldner nach der Eröffnung des Hauptinsolvenzverfahrens versuchen würde, das Verfahren in einen anderen Mitgliedstaat zu verlegen. Es ist zu bemerken, dass eine wirksame Eröffnung eines Insolvenzverfahrens durch ein zuständiges mitgliedstaatliches Gericht in allen übrigen Mitgliedstaaten anzuerkennen ist. Dies schließt praktisch das *forum shopping* durch die Veränderung des COMI nach der Eröffnung des Hauptinsolvenzverfahrens aus.

Im Fall der Sitzverlegung durch eine grenzüberschreitende Umwandlung, die zumindest die Verlegung des Satzungssitzes voraussetzt, können die Regeln der neulich angenommenen MobilitätsRL verwendet werden. Die Richtlinie selbst bestimmt gewisse Vorschriften zum Schutz der Gläubiger und fordert die Mitgliedstaaten auf, ein angemessenes Schutzsystem auszugestalten, um den Schutz der Gläubiger zu gewährleisten. Aus der Sicht des *forum shopping* muss es hervorgehoben werden, dass Art. 86j Abs. 4 MobilitätsRL vorsieht, dass die Mitgliedstaaten sicherstellen sollen, dass die Gläubiger, deren Forderungen vor der Offenlegung des Plans für die grenzüberschreitende Umwandlung entstanden sind, innerhalb zwei Jahre nach dem Wirksamwerden der Umwandlung auch in dem Wegzugsmitgliedstaat ein Verfahren gegen die Gesellschaft einleiten können. Damit schafft die Richtlinie selbst einen alternativen Zuständigkeitsgrund und zugleich eine Möglichkeit für *forum shopping* seitens der Gläubiger. Die Richtlinie ist jedoch auf Gesellschaften nicht anzuwenden, die sich in Liquidation befinden und bei denen die Verteilung ihres Vermögens bereits begonnen hatte.[71] Die Mitgliedstaaten können weiterhin so entscheiden, dass die Mobilitätsregeln auf Gesellschaften nicht angewendet werden, die an Insolvenzverfahren oder präventiven Restrukturierungsrahmen beteiligt sind.[72]

Manche Autoren haben verschiedene Vorschläge unterbreitet, um *forum shopping* im Bereich des Insolvenzrechts zu verhindern. Ein Vorschlag ist der Ersatz des COMI durch den Satzungssitz als Anknüpfungspunkt.[73] Der Satzungssitz kann (von den Gläubigern) eindeutig feststellt werden, und damit könnten die Zuständigkeit und das anwendbare Recht auch einfach bestimmt werden.

Zusammenfassend lässt sich festhalten, dass, obwohl die EU-InsVO den Begriff des *forum shopping* definiert und eines der Ziele der Verordnung, die Verhinderung betrügerischer oder missbräuchlicher Verhaltensweisen ist, eine mögliche moralische Beurteilung des *forum shopping* nur eine geringe Rolle spielt. Wie im *Galapagos*-Urteil bestätigt wurde, ist die Verlagerung des COMI zwischen dem Zeitpunkt der Stellung eines Antrags auf die Eröffnung des Insolvenzverfahrens und dem Zeitpunkt der Eröffnung des Verfahrens einfach außer Acht zu lassen. Nach der Eröffnung des Hauptinsolvenzverfahrens ist die Verlegung des COMI aus der Sicht der

[71] Art. 86a Abs. 3 lit. a MobilitätsRL.

[72] Art. 86a Abs. 4 lit. a MobilitätsRL. Die Anwendung der RL kann durch die Mitgliedstaaten auch auf andere „Liquidationsverfahren als denjenigen, die in [Art. 86a] Absatz 3 Buchstabe a genannt sind, ausgeschlossen werden.“

[73] Eidenmüller, Abuse of Law in the Context of European Insolvency Law in: de la Feria/Vogenauer, Prohibition of Abuse of Law, 2011, 154–156; Armour Abuse of European Insolvency Law? A Discussion in de la Feria/Vogenauer, Prohibition of Abuse of Law, 2011, 167; Szydło European Business Organization Law Review 2010, 253 (270).

Zuständigkeit und des anwendbaren Rechts nicht mehr maßgebend. Wo eine moralische Einschätzung noch entscheidend bleiben kann, ist die Veränderung des COMI vor der Antragstellung. Hier sollen die Gerichte – auch neben der Anwendung der dreimonatigen Regel – beurteilen, ob die Verlegung einen missbräuchlichen Charakter hat. Es kann jedoch schwierig sein, zu beweisen, dass das Hauptziel der Verlagerung des COMI eine Vorteilverschaffung durch die übermäßige Benachteiligung der Gläubiger war und dass es keine andere Erklärung für die Handlung gibt. Hier wird erfordert, festzustellen, worauf die Absicht des Schuldners in erster Linie richtete.

VI. Fazit

Die EU-InsVO versucht ein zulasten der Gläubiger beabsichtigtes *forum shopping* zu verhindern. Zu diesem Zweck – allein unter den EU-Rechtsakten auf dem Gebiet des internationalen Privatrechts – definiert sie den Begriff des *forum shopping*. Obwohl die EU-InsVO auf missbräuchliches und betrügerisches Verhalten als *forum shopping* hinweist, bleibt ihre Annäherung eher neutral. In der *Galapagos*-Angelegenheit brachte der EuGH seine frühere Rechtsprechung zum *forum shopping* weiter. Er unterhielt den aus dem *Staubitz-Schreiber*-Urteil anerkennten Grundsatz auch im Kontext der erneuerten EU-InsVO, dass der relevante Zeitpunkt für die Bestimmung der internationalen Zuständigkeit die Stellung des Antrags auf die Eröffnung des Insolvenzverfahrens ist und eine Verlagerung des COMI nach der Antragstellung, aber vor der Eröffnung des Verfahrens einfach außer Acht zu lassen ist. Ohne die Notwendigkeit einer moralischen Beurteilung der Verlegung des COMI bestätigt das *Galapagos*-Urteil die Absicht des EuGH, die Regeln der EU-InsVO über die ausschließliche Zuständigkeit durch die *perpetuatio fori* zu schützen. Ein gleicher Vorrang der Zuständigkeit von drittstaatlichen Gerichten, die mit einem Insolvenzantrag angerufen werden, wird aber nicht gegeben. Eine Entscheidung über die Eröffnung des Hauptinsolvenzverfahrens ist in den anderen Mitgliedstaaten anzuerkennen, deshalb kann die Verlegung des COMI die Zuständigkeit und das anwendbare Recht nach diesem Zeitpunkt nicht mehr beeinflussen. Die Betrachtung einer Verhaltensweise als missbräuchlich kann nur in einem relativ engeren Kreis notwendig sein, wenn der COMI noch vor der Antragstellung verlegt wird, um eine für den Schuldner günstigere rechtliche Position zu schaffen. In diesen Fällen ist es immer eine Vorfrage, ob der COMI tatsächlich verlegt wurde oder es nur um eine künstliche Struktur geht.

Es scheint jedoch, dass sich die Gefahr des *forum shopping* in grenzüberschreitenden Insolvenzfällen nicht nur den EuGH, sondern auch den EU-Gesetzgeber beschäftigt. Die Kommission bestellte die bereits oben erwähnte Studie über missbräuchliches *forum shopping* in Insolvenzverfahren, die Anfang 2022 veröffentlicht wurde.[74] In diesem Zusammenhang muss man ebenso hervorheben, dass die Kom-

[74] Study on the issue of abusive forum shopping in insolvency proceedings, Final report, https://commission.europa.eu/document/download/0664f511-6e09-4751-b7be-421fde6510

mission im Jahr 2023 einen Vorschlag für eine Richtlinie zur Harmonisierung bestimmter Aspekte des materiellen Insolvenzrechts vorlegte.[75] Die Annahme der Richtlinie, selbst wenn sie keine umfassende Regelung des Insolvenzrechts vorsieht, kann gewissermaßen auch zur Verhinderung der Fälle des *forum shopping* beitragen.

91_en?filename=Final%20Report%20-%20Abusive%20Forum%20Shopping_Febr%202022.pdf (abgerufen 14.5.2024).

[75] Europäische Kommission, Vorschlag für eine Richtlinie des Europäischen Parlaments und des Rates zur Harmonisierung bestimmter Aspekte des Insolvenzrechts, Brüssel, 7.12.2022, COM (2022) 702 final.

KINGA TIMÁR

Die neue ungarische Kollisionsregelung für Schiedsvereinbarungen: große Erwartungen – k(l)eine Ergebnisse?

I. Einführung

Ich habe Professor Rauscher vor mehr als 15 Jahren während meines an der Universität Leipzig verbrachten Erasmus-Studienjahres kennen gelernt. Seine Vorlesungen zum Internationalen Privatrecht und Internationalen Zivilverfahrensrecht haben auf mich einen sehr großen Eindruck gemacht: Ich habe in seinen Vorlesungen zuerst wahrgenommen, welche Tiefe und Komplexität diese beiden miteinander eng verwandten Rechtsgebiete aufweisen können. Diese Wahrnehmung hat dann eine entscheidende Rolle dabei gespielt, dass ich meine wissenschaftlichen Recherchen, vor allem meine Dissertation, und teilweise meine anwaltliche Praxis in Ungarn gerade diesen Rechtsgebieten gewidmet habe.

Der 1.1.2018 war für die ungarische Regelung zu den auf die Schiedsvereinbarung anwendbaren Rechten ein Wendepunkt. Dies war der Tag, an dem die neuen ungarischen Gesetze über die Schiedsgerichtsbarkeit bzw. über das internationale Privatrecht – Gesetz Nr. LX von 2017 (ungSchG 2017) und Gesetz Nr. XXVIII von 2017 (ungIPRG 2017) – in Kraft getreten sind und das frühere Regelungsregime verdrängt haben. Im Folgenden werde ich die seit dem 1.1.2018 geltenden neuen Bestimmungen vor allem im Hinblick darauf prüfen und bewerten, wie erfolgreich der ungarische Gesetzgeber die Mängel der früheren Regelung – Gesetz Nr. LXXI von 1994 über die Schiedsgerichtsbarkeit (ungSchG 1994) und Gesetzesverordnung Nr. 13 von 1979 über das internationale Privatrecht (ungIPRGV 1979) – beseitigt hat und welche neuen Fragen sich aus der neuen Rechtslage ergeben.

Das auf die Schiedsvereinbarung anwendbare *Recht* (im Singular) ist das Recht, dem die Schiedsvereinbarung als Vertrag unterliegt. Dieses Recht ist auf alle vertraglichen – materiell-rechtlichen – Elemente der Schiedsvereinbarung anzuwenden, für die es keine separate kollisionsrechtliche Regelung gibt. Die auf die Schiedsvereinbarung anwendbaren *Rechte* (im Plural) umfassen dagegen alle Rechte, die für die verschiedenen Rechtsfragen in Bezug auf die Schiedsvereinbarung maßgeblich sind. Die vier wichtigsten – und in der Praxis am häufigsten aufkommenden – Aspekte der Durchsetzbarkeit (mit der herkömmlichen englischen Terminologie: *enforceability*) der Schiedsvereinbarung sind die Folgenden:

- materielle Gültigkeit,
- Formgültigkeit,

- subjektive Schiedsfähigkeit, dh die Fähigkeit der Parteien, eine Schiedsvereinbarung abzuschließen, und
- objektive Schiedsfähigkeit, die bestimmt, welcher Rechtsstreit (Streitgegenstand) vor ein Schiedsgericht gebracht werden kann.

Diese Rechtsfragen müssen aus einem kollisionsrechtlichen Gesichtspunkt meistens unabhängig voneinander beurteilt werden. Dies kann dazu führen, dass auf die verschiedenen Rechtsfragen unterschiedliche Rechte angewendet werden. Deswegen scheint die Verwendung der Mehrzahl in solchen Fällen, in denen es nicht ausdrücklich um das auf die Schiedsvereinbarung als Vertrag anwendbare Recht (dh das Vertragsstatut der Schiedsvereinbarung) geht, gerechtfertigt zu sein. Ich werde die Neuerungen und die kritischen Punkte der seit dem 1.1.2018 geltenden, neuen Regelung im Zusammenhang mit dieser vier Durchsetzbarkeitsvoraussetzungen untersuchen.

II. Die seit dem 1. 1. 2018 geltenden Kollisionsregeln

1. Die Kollisionsregeln des ungSchG 2017

Das ungSchG 2017 hat die Kollisionsnormen des ungSchG 1994 praktisch unverändert übernommen. Im Vergleich zum ungSchG 1994 brachten die kollisionsrechtlichen Bestimmungen des ungSchG 2017 eine einzige signifikante Änderung mit sich: Die Regelung zur Bestimmung des Rechts, das auf die Hauptsache des Schiedsverfahrens mangels einer Rechtswahl anzuwenden ist (§ 41 ungSchG 2017), wurde mit Art. 28 Abs. 2 UNCITRAL-Modellgesetz über die internationale Handelsschiedsgerichtsbarkeit 1985 (in der Fassung von 2006) in Einklang gebracht.[1] Dies bedeutet, dass Schiedsgerichte seit dem 1.1.2018 das auf die Hauptsache – und eventuell auf die Schiedsvereinbarung[2] – anwendbare materielle Recht mangels einer Rechtswahl der Parteien nicht direkt festlegen, sondern durch die Bestimmung der anwendbaren Kollisionsnorm(en).

Abgesehen von dieser Abweichung enthält das ungSchG 2017 genau dieselben Kollisionsnormen wie das ungSchG 1994. Zur *subjektiven Schiedsfähigkeit* der Parteien enthält das ungSchG 2017, ähnlich wie das ungSchG 1994, keine ausdrückliche kollisionsrechtliche Regelung.[3] In Bezug auf die anderen Aspekte der Durchsetzbarkeit der Schiedsvereinbarung – die in diesem Beitrag geprüft werden – sieht das ungSchG 2017 die folgenden Kollisionsnormen vor:

---

[1] Varga, A polgári perrendtartás és kapcsolódó jogszabályok kommentárja III/III/Király, 2018, Rn. 7474, 7479.

[2] Welche Bedeutung der Kollisionsnorm zur Bestimmung des auf die Hauptsache anwendbaren Rechts bei der Ermittlung des für die Schiedsvereinbarung maßgeblichen Rechts im Schiedsverfahren zukommen kann, wird in diesem Beitrag unten (→ III. 1.) angesprochen.

[3] § 47 Abs. 2 lit. a sublit. aa ungSchG 2017 regelt das Fehlen der Rechts- oder Handlungsfähigkeit einer der Vertragsparteien der Schiedsvereinbarung – in Übereinstimmung mit § 55 Abs. 1 lit. a ungSchG 1994 – als einen Grund für die Aufhebung des Schiedsspruchs, ohne Angabe des auf die Rechts- bzw. Handlungsfähigkeit anwendbaren Rechts.

– Das für die *Gültigkeit* der Schiedsvereinbarung anwendbare Recht wird in der Aufhebungsphase, dh im Verfahren zur Aufhebung des Schiedsspruchs, durch die Kollisionsnorm in § 47 Abs. 2 lit. a sublit. aa ungSchG 2017 ermittelt. Diese Regelung entspricht § 55 Abs. 1 lit. b ungSchG 1994 und bestimmt, dass die Gültigkeit der Schiedsvereinbarung nach dem von den Parteien gewählten Recht oder – mangels einer Rechtswahl – nach ungarischem Recht zu beurteilen ist.
– § 47 Abs. 2 lit. b sublit. ba ungSchG 2017 und § 54 lit. a ungSchG 2017 übernehmen wortwörtlich § 55 Abs. 2 lit. a ungSchG 1994 und § 59 Abs. 1 lit. a ungSchG 1994. Diese Vorschriften bestimmen die auf die *objektive Schiedsfähigkeit* in der Aufhebungs- bzw. Vollstreckungsphase anzuwendenden Regeln, unter Verweis auf das ungarische Recht (dh auf die *lex fori*).

2. *Die Kollisionsregeln des ungIPRG 2017*

Im Gegensatz zum ungSchG 2017 brachte das ungIPRG 2017 erhebliche Änderungen für die Bestimmung der auf die Schiedsvereinbarung anwendbaren Rechte mit sich. Unter der Überschrift „Vertragsschuldverhältnisse" widmet das ungIPRG 2017 einen eigenen Paragraphen den Rechten, die auf die Schiedsvereinbarung und deren Formgültigkeit anzuwenden sind: Die Vorschriften in § 52 Abs. 1–3 ungIPRG 2017 bestimmen das auf die Schiedsvereinbarung als Vertrag anwendbare Recht, und § 52 Abs. 4 ungIPRG 2017 bestimmt die auf die Formgültigkeit der Schiedsvereinbarung alternativ anzuwendenden Rechte im Rahmen einer *favor validitatis* Regelung. Die Ministerialbegründung zu § 52 ungIPRG 2017, die im Gesetzgebungsverfahren dem Gesetzesvorschlag beigefügt wurde, fasst die Gründe für die Einführung dieser neuen Regeln wie folgt zusammen:[4]

„Das Recht der Europäischen Union schließt derzeit den Bereich des Kollisionsrechts für Schiedsvereinbarungen aus seinem sachlichen Anwendungsbereich ausdrücklich aus. Die in diesem Bereich abgeschlossenen und weit verbreiteten internationalen Übereinkommen (insbesondere das New Yorker Übereinkommen und das Genfer Übereinkommen)[5] *regeln die einzelnen Fragen der Bestimmung des auf die Schiedsvereinbarung anwendbaren Rechts nicht allgemein, sondern behandeln nur Teilfragen (wie zB die Rechtswahl). Das geltende ungarische Recht enthält zwar Kollisionsnormen in § 49 des Gesetzes Nr. LXXI von 1994 über die Schiedsgerichtsbarkeit, aber in unseren derzeit geltenden Rechtsvorschriften findet man keine kollisionsrechtliche Regelung zur Bestimmung des auf die Schiedsvereinbarung anwendbaren Rechts. Aus diesem Grund wurde in das Gesetz eine eigenständige kollisionsrechtliche Regelung für Schiedsvereinbarungen aufgenommen."*

---

[4] S. auch Schmidt, Magyar Jog 2020/1, 54 (62).
[5] Übereinkommen über die Anerkennung und Vollstreckung ausländischer Schiedssprüche, abgeschlossen in New York am 10.6.1958 (in Ungarn verkündet durch Gesetzesverordnung Nr. 25 von 1962) bzw. Europäisches Übereinkommen über die internationale Handelsschiedsgerichtsbarkeit, abgeschlossen in Genf am 21.4.1961 (in Ungarn verkündet durch Gesetzesverordnung Nr. 8 von 1964).

§ 52 ungIPRG 2017 verwendet eine mehrstufige Kombination der weit verbreiteten Anknüpfungen zur Bestimmung des auf die Schiedsvereinbarung anwendbaren Rechts, dh des *Vertragsstatuts* der Schiedsvereinbarung.

Auf der ersten Ebene, die in § 52 Abs. 1 ungIPRG 2017 verankert ist, legt die neue Regelung den Schwerpunkt auf die Autonomie der Parteien: Die Parteien können das auf die Schiedsvereinbarung anwendbare Recht wählen.[6] Darin spiegelt sich eindeutig die vertragliche Natur der Schiedsvereinbarung wider, die auch durch die Unterbringung des § 52 ungIPRG 2017 unter der Überschrift „Vertragsschuldverhältnisse" bestätigt wird. Die Anerkennung der Freiheit der Parteien, in Bezug auf die Schiedsvereinbarung eine separate Rechtswahl zu treffen, bedeutet gleichzeitig eine Bestätigung des Grundsatzes der Unabhängigkeit der Schiedsvereinbarung. Eine separate Rechtswahl kann nämlich dazu führen, dass auf die Schiedsvereinbarung ggf. ein anderes Recht anzuwenden ist als das für das zugrunde liegende materiell-rechtliche Rechtsverhältnis (meistens einen Hauptvertrag) maßgebliche Recht.[7] Die Regelung auf dieser ersten Ebene steht im Einklang mit den einschlägigen internationalen Trends.

Auf der zweiten Ebene – dh gemäß der in § 52 Abs. 2 ungIPRG 2017 enthaltenen Kollisionsregel – liegt der Fokus weiterhin auf der vertraglichen Natur der Schiedsvereinbarung, aber anstelle des Grundsatzes der Unabhängigkeit tritt der akzessorische Charakter der Schiedsvereinbarung in Vordergrund:[8] mangels einer Rechtswahl der Parteien für die Schiedsvereinbarung muss jenes Recht angewendet werden, das für das zugrunde liegende Rechtsverhältnis maßgeblich ist. Im Falle einer Rechtswahl durch die Parteien für das zugrunde liegende Rechtsverhältnis ist dieses Recht auch für die Schiedsvereinbarung maßgeblich. In der Ministerialbegründung zu § 52 ungIPRG 2017 wird diese Lösung wie folgt erklärt: *„Bei der Festlegung der Anknüpfungen für die Bestimmung des mangels einer Rechtswahl anzuwendenden Rechts geht das Gesetz davon aus, dass die Schiedsvereinbarung an sich immer ein bestehendes oder zukünftiges, zugrunde liegendes Rechtsverhältnis (typischerweise ein vertragliches Rechtsverhältnis) voraussetzt, und dass der Abschluss der Schiedsvereinbarung (die Annahme der Schiedsklausel) in den meisten Fällen im Rahmen der Regelung des zugrunde liegenden Rechtsverhältnisses (typischerweise im Hauptvertrag) erfolgt."*

Die Anwendung des auf das zugrunde liegende Rechtsverhältnis anwendbaren Rechts auf die Schiedsvereinbarung führt typischerweise zu einer indirekten Anwendung der Kollisionsregeln der Rom I- oder Rom II-Verordnungen auf die Schiedsvereinbarung, obwohl Schiedsvereinbarungen vom Anwendungsbereich

---

[6] S. auch Vékás/Nemessányi/Osztovits, A nemzetközi magánjogról szóló törvény kommentárja/Szabados, 2020, S. 317 (§§ 50–56); Erdős, Ünnepi tanulmányok Király Miklós 60. születésnapja alkalmából, 2021, 187.

[7] S. die Ministerialbegründung zu § 52 ungIPRG 2017; s. auch Vékás/Nemessányi/Osztovits, A nemzetközi magánjogról szóló törvény kommentárja/Szabados, 2020, S. 317 (§§ 50–56); Erdős, Ünnepi tanulmányok Király Miklós 60. születésnapja alkalmából, 2021, 187.

[8] S. Bán/Nemessányi, A választottbírósági szerződésre alkalmazandó jog meghatározása, in: Berke/Nemessányi, Az új nemzetközi magánjogi törvény alapjai – kodifikációs előtanulmányok, 2016, S. 233; Vékás/Nemessányi/Osztovits, A nemzetközi magánjogról szóló törvény kommentárja/Szabados, 2020, S. 318 (§§ 50–56); Erdős, Ünnepi tanulmányok Király Miklós 60. születésnapja alkalmából, 2021, 188–189.

der Rom I-VO ausdrücklich ausgeschlossen sind.[9] In dem Fall, dass das zugrunde liegende Rechtsverhältnis ein Kaufvertrag über eine bewegliche Sache ist, kann die Anwendung des auf das zugrunde liegende Rechtsverhältnis anwendbaren Rechts weitere interessante Konsequenzen haben, nämlich die Anwendung des UN-Kaufrechts[10] auf bestimmte Aspekte, zB auf den Abschluss der Schiedsvereinbarung.[11]

Auf der dritten Ebene – die in § 52 Abs. 3 ungIPRG 2017 geregelt ist –, dh wenn die Parteien den Schiedsort bestimmt haben und das Recht dieses Ortes eine engere Verbindung mit der Schiedsvereinbarung aufweist als das auf das zugrunde liegende Rechtsverhältnis anzuwendende Recht, wird der Schwerpunkt erneut auf den Grundsatz der Unabhängigkeit und zugleich auf die verfahrensrechtliche Natur der Schiedsvereinbarung gelegt: Das Recht des Schiedsortes *(lex loci arbitri)* muss auf die Schiedsvereinbarung angewendet werden. Nach der Ministerialbegründung zu § 52 ungIPRG 2017 *„[besteht] [d]er Vorteil der Anwendung dieser Anknüpfung darin, dass sie die Schiedsvereinbarung, das Schiedsverfahren und den Schiedsspruch einem einheitlichen Statut unterwirft, und kann in dem Fall, dass die Parteien den Schiedsort selbst gewählt haben, besonders geeignet sein"*.

Vergleicht man die zweite und die dritte Ebene, wird sofort deutlich, dass der Gesetzgeber dem Recht, das für das zugrunde liegende Rechtsverhältnis maßgeblich ist, gegenüber dem Recht des Schiedsortes Vorrang einräumen wollte. Während die Anwendung des ersteren automatisch ist, wenn die Parteien das auf die Schiedsvereinbarung anwendbare Recht nicht festgelegt haben, müssen für die Anwendung des letzteren zwei weitere Bedingungen erfüllt sein:

- die Parteien haben den Schiedsort bestimmt, und
- die Schiedsvereinbarung steht mit dem Recht des Schiedsortes in einer engeren Verbindung als mit dem auf das zugrunde liegende Rechtsverhältnis anzuwendenden Recht.[12]

In Bezug auf die *Formgültigkeit* der Schiedsvereinbarung hat der Gesetzgeber eine spezielle *favor validitatis* Regel eingeführt. Gemäß § 52 Abs. 4 ungIPRG 2017 kann eine Schiedsvereinbarung nicht aus formalen Gründen als ungültig betrachtet werden, wenn sie den Formerfordernissen irgendeines der nach § 52 ungIPRG 2017 bestimmten Rechte oder denen des Rechts des Staates des angerufenen Gerichts entspricht. Das „Recht des Staates des angerufenen Gerichts" bezieht sich auf das Recht des Gerichtsforums *(lex fori)*, vor dem die Formgültigkeit der Schiedsverein-

---

[9] S. Art. 1 Abs. 2. lit. e Rom I-VO; s. auch Erdős, Ünnepi tanulmányok Király Miklós 60. születésnapja alkalmából, 2021, 189.

[10] Übereinkommen der Vereinten Nationen über Verträge über den internationalen Warenkauf, abgeschlossen in Wien am 11.4.1980 (in Ungarn verkündet durch Gesetzesverordnung Nr. 20 von 1987).

[11] S. Erdős, Ünnepi tanulmányok Király Miklós 60. születésnapja alkalmából, 2021, 189–190. Die Anwendbarkeit des UN-Kaufrechts auf Schiedsvereinbarungen ist eine umstrittene Frage, s. Born, International Commercial Arbitration, 2014, S. 505–506. Der deutsche Bundesgerichtshof hat die Anwendbarkeit des UN-Kaufrechts auf den Abschluss von Schiedsvereinbarungen bejaht, s. BGH 26.11.2020 – I ZR 245/19, NJW-RR 2021, 376.

[12] Für die Auslegung des Begriffs „engere Verbindung" in diesem Kontext s. Erdős, Ünnepi tanulmányok Király Miklós 60. születésnapja alkalmából, 2021, 190–191.

barung angefochten wird. Das vom Gesetzgeber gewählte *favor validatis* Konzept ist ein progressiver Ansatz, der die Formgültigkeit der Schiedsvereinbarung in der größtmöglichen Breite gewährleistet.[13]

Zusätzlich zu den speziellen Regeln zur Bestimmung der auf die Schiedsvereinbarung bzw. deren Formgültigkeit anwendbaren Rechte müssen ggf. auch die allgemeinen Bestimmungen des ungIPRG 2017 sowie die Kollisionsnormen des ungIPRG 2017 für Verträge angewendet werden. Die Untersuchung, inwieweit und wie genau diese Regeln auf die Schiedsvereinbarung anwendbar sind, geht über den Rahmen dieses Beitrags hinaus, daher werde ich im Folgenden nur eine Auflistung dieser weiteren Regeln des ungIPRG 2017 bereitstellen:

- § 1 stellt klar, dass die Kollisionsnormen des ungIPRG 2017 nur dann anwendbar sind, wenn das Rechtsverhältnis einen ausländischen Bezug aufweist, und dass „Recht" im Sinne des ungIPRG 2017 ausschließlich staatliches Recht bedeutet.
- § 2 gewährt dem Recht der Europäischen Union und internationalen Verträgen Vorrang vor den Bestimmungen des ungIPRG 2017.
- § 3 enthält Begriffsbestimmungen.
- § 4 enthält Regeln über die Qualifikation zur Ermittlung des anwendbaren Rechts.
- § 5 bezieht sich auf die *renvoi* Doktrin.
- § 10 ermächtigt Gerichte in Fällen, in denen der Tatbestand mit einem anderen Recht als dasjenige, das nach den Bestimmungen des ungIPRG 2017 anzuwenden wäre, wesentlich enger verbunden ist, dieses andere Recht anzuwenden (allgemeine Ausweichklausel).
- § 11 regelt die Ermittlung des anwendbaren Rechts, wenn das ungIPRG 2017 für ein bestimmtes Rechtsverhältnis keine ausdrückliche kollisionsrechtliche Regelung vorsieht (allgemeine Hilfsregel).
- § 12 regelt die *ordre public* Ausnahme.
- § 13 behandelt die Anwendung der international zwingenden Bestimmungen des ungarischen Rechts und anderer Rechtssysteme.
- § 14 regelt die Auswirkungen der Änderung des anwendbaren Rechts, wenn sich die Umstände, die das anwendbare Recht bestimmen, ändern.
- §§ 15 und 22 bestimmen das auf die Rechts- und Handlungsfähigkeit natürlicher und juristischer Personen anwendbare Recht (Personalstatut).
- § 50 Abs. 2–3 regeln die Frist für die Rechtswahl der Parteien (eine in der Phase der vorbereitenden Verhandlung vom Gericht festgelegte Frist) sowie die Änderung der früheren Rechtswahl der Parteien.
- § 50 Abs. 4 regelt die Auswirkungen der Wahl eines ausländischen Rechts durch die Parteien in dem Fall, dass der Vertrag nur mit dem Recht eines einzigen Staates verbunden ist (materiell-rechtliche Rechtswahl[14]).
- § 50 Abs. 5 betrifft das Zustandekommen und die Gültigkeit der Rechtswahl.

---

[13] S. Schmidt, Magyar Jog 2020/1, 54 (63).

[14] Die Rechtswahl der Parteien kann die zwingenden Rechtsvorschriften des Staates, mit dem der Vertrag ausschließlich verbunden ist, nicht verletzen bzw. verdrängen.

- § 53 bestimmt das auf das Zustandekommen und die Gültigkeit des Vertrags anwendbare Recht in Fällen, in denen das Zustandekommen oder die Gültigkeit des Vertrags angefochten wird.
- § 54 Abs. 1–2 bestimmen die auf die Formgültigkeit von Verträgen anwendbaren Rechte in Fällen, in denen sich die Parteien oder ihre Vertreter zum Zeitpunkt des Vertragsabschlusses im demselben Staat oder in verschiedenen Staaten aufhalten und dieser Staat bzw. diese Staaten von denen, auf deren Rechte in anderen Bestimmungen des ungIPRG 2017, wie zB § 52 Abs. 4, Bezug genommen wird, abweicht bzw. abweichen.[15]
- § 54 Abs. 3 betrifft die Formgültigkeit einseitiger Willenserklärungen im Zusammenhang mit Verträgen, zB der Vollmacht zur Unterzeichnung einer Schiedsvereinbarung.

III. Die Fragen, die sich aus der seit dem 1. 1. 2018 geltenden Regelung ergeben

Gemäß der oben zitierten Ministerialbegründung des ungIPRG 2017 beabsichtigte der Gesetzgeber, mit der Einführung der neuen kollisionsrechtlichen Regelung für Schiedsvereinbarungen die bestehenden Mängel zu beheben. Wie im Folgenden dargelegt wird, ist es dem Gesetzgeber jedoch nicht vollständig gelungen, die Mängel und Unsicherheiten des früheren Regelungsregimes zu beseitigen, und die neue Regelung wirft über die „geerbten" Probleme hinaus auch weitere Fragen auf.

1. Unvollständige Kollisionsregeln

Die kollisionsrechtlichen Fragen im Zusammenhang mit Schiedsvereinbarungen können in verschiedenen Phasen des schiedsrichterlichen Streitbeilegungsmechanismus aufkommen:

- während des Schiedsverfahrens,
- vor einem staatlichen Gericht in einem gerichtlichen Verfahren – typischerweise Zivilprozess –, das bzw. der bezüglich des Streitgegenstandes trotz der Schiedsvereinbarung eingeleitet wurde,
- bei der Überprüfung der Zuständigkeitsentscheidung des Schiedsgerichts durch ein staatliches Gericht,
- in dem zur Aufhebung des Schiedsspruchs eingeleiteten Verfahren,
- in der Phase der Anerkennung und Vollstreckung des Schiedsspruchs oder
- in einem separaten gerichtlichen Verfahren in Bezug auf das Zustandekommen oder die Gültigkeit der Schiedsvereinbarung.

Die alte Regelung, dh das ungSchG 1994 und die ungIPRGV 1979, ließen Schiedsgerichte und staatliche Gerichte in vielen Situationen – in mehreren Phasen der schiedsrichterlichen Streitbeilegung – ohne klare Antwort bezüglich der Frage, welches Recht auf die Schiedsvereinbarung und die damit verbundenen Rechtsfra-

[15] Für eine Erörterung dieser Vorschriften → III. 5.

gen (Zustandekommen/Bestand, Gültigkeit, Auslegung, subjektive Schiedsfähigkeit, objektive Schiedsfähigkeit, materiell-rechtliche und verfahrensrechtliche Rechtswirkungen usw.) anzuwenden ist. Der Hauptgrund dafür war, dass die kollisionsrechtlichen Bestimmungen des ungSchG 1994 Kollisionsnormen ausschließlich für die Aufhebung und Vollstreckung von Schiedssprüchen enthielten, und dass der Geltungsbereich der alten kollisionsrechtlichen Bestimmungen der ungIPRGV 1979 sich nur auf staatliche Gerichte beschränkte.[16] Mit der Einführung der Kollisionsnormen in § 52 ungIPRG 2017, die spezifisch auf Schiedsvereinbarungen anwendbar sind, hat der Gesetzgeber die bestehenden Regelungslücken in der kollisionsrechtlichen Regelung von Schiedsvereinbarungen nur teilweise gefüllt.

Ähnlich wie in der alten ungIPRGV 1979, ist auch im ungIPRG 2017 nicht ausdrücklich festgestellt, dass die gesetzliche Regelung nur auf die Ermittlung des anwendbaren Rechts durch staatliche Gerichte anzuwenden wäre. Der Wortlaut und die Ministerialbegründung des ungIPRG 2017 sind jedoch insofern noch klarer als die der ungIPRGV 1979.[17] In § 3 lit. a ungIPRG 2017 findet man eine Begriffsbestimmung für das „Gericht". Gemäß dieser Definition umfasst der Begriff „Gericht" im Sinne des ungIPRG 2017 auch andere Behörden, die für Zivilsachen zuständig sind, mangels einer abweichenden Bestimmung des Gesetzes. Nach der Ministerialbegründung zu § 3 ungIPRG 2017 *„erstreckt sich der Gericht-Begriff des Gesetzes nicht auf Schiedsgerichte"*. Schiedsgerichte sind also vom Begriff „Gericht" nach dem ungIPRG 2017 eindeutig ausgeschlossen. Diese Herangehensweise lässt sich auch verfassungsrechtlich rechtfertigen: Nach der konsequenten Rechtsprechung des Verfassungsgerichts Ungarns verzichten die Parteien mit einer Schiedsvereinbarung auf ihr Recht auf Zugang zu einem Gericht, dh auf ihr Recht, sich an ein staatliches Gericht zu wenden. Dementsprechend sind Schiedsgerichte keine Gerichte und auch keine staatlichen Organe.[18]

Die Verwendung des Ausdrucks *„Recht des Gerichtsstaates"* in § 52 Abs. 4 ungIPRG 2017, dh die Bezugnahme auf die *lex fori* als ein auf die Formgültigkeit der Schiedsvereinbarung alternativ anzuwendendes Recht, deutet ebenfalls darauf hin, dass die kollisionsrechtlichen Bestimmungen des ungIPRG 2017 über die auf die Schiedsvereinbarung anwendbaren Rechte ausschließlich an staatliche Gerichte gerichtet sind. Erstens verwendet § 52 Abs. 4 ungIPRG 2017 den Begriff „Gericht". Wie bereits klargemacht, sind Schiedsgerichte vom Begriff „Gericht" im Sinne des ungIPRG 2017 gemäß der Begriffsbestimmung in § 3 lit. a ungIPRG 2017 ausgeschlossen. Zweitens hat das Schiedsgericht keinen eigenen Staat, da es

---

[16] S. Oberster Gerichtshof Ungarns [Datum nicht angegeben] – Pfv. XI. 22.270/2006, BH2007.4.130; Oberhammer, Schiedsgerichtsbarkeit in Zentraleuropa – Arbitration in Central Europe/Varga, 2005, S. 678–683 (Ungarn).

[17] S. § 5 Abs. 1 und 2, § 6 Abs. 2, § 29 Abs. 2 ungIPRGV 1979 sowie die Ministerialbegründung zu §§ 1–9 ungIPRGV 1979.

[18] S. zB die folgenden Entscheidungen: ungVerfG 12.5.2003 – 95/B/2001, Alkotmánybíróság Határozatai (ABK) 2003/5 (V. 31.); 20.10.2009 – 339/B/2003, ABK 2009/10 (X. 31.); 22.11.2011 – 1245/B/2011, ABK 2011/11 (XI. 30.); 23.09.2014 – 3244/2014. (X. 3.), ABK 2014/24 (X. 3.); 23.06.2015 – 3116/2015 (VII. 2.), ABK 2015/15 (VII. 2.); 14.12.2015 – 3263/2015 (XII. 22.), ABK 2015/26 (XII. 22.); 23.5.2016 – 3108/2016. (VI. 3.), ABK 2016/13 (VI. 3.); Oberster Gerichtshof Ungarns 30.6.2008 – Gfv. 30.505/2007, BH2009.10.299.

kein staatliches Organ ist und daher keinem Staat angehört. Daher unterstützt auch die Verwendung des Ausdrucks *„Recht des Gerichtsstaates"* die Annahme, dass § 52 Abs. 4 ungIPRG 2017 ausschließlich an staatliche Gerichte adressiert ist. Wenn dies der Fall ist, gibt es keinen Grund dafür, zu vermuten, dass die Regelungen der weiteren Absätze des § 52 ungIPRG 2017 auch für Schiedsgerichte gelten.

Die Schlussfolgerung, dass die Kollisionsnormen des ungIPRG 2017, einschließlich der Regeln zur Bestimmung des anwendbaren Rechts für Schiedsvereinbarungen, ausschließlich an staatliche Gerichte gerichtet sind,[19] steht im Einklang mit den aktuellen Trends der internationalen Schiedsgerichtsbarkeit. Gemäß diesen Trends ist die traditionelle Auffassung, dass Schiedsgerichte die allgemeinen Kollisionsnormen, also die gleichen Regeln wie lokale Gerichte, anwenden müssen oder zumindest sollten, veraltet und steht im Widerspruch zu den grundlegenden Prinzipien der Schiedsgerichtsbarkeit.[20]

Aus diesen Überlegungen ergibt sich, dass das ungIPRG 2017 die bestehenden Lücken in der kollisionsrechtlichen Regelung von Schiedsvereinbarungen nur teilweise gefüllt hat. Die speziellen Kollisionsnormen zur Bestimmung der auf die Schiedsvereinbarung anwendbaren Rechte wurden nämlich ausschließlich für diejenigen Phasen der schiedsrichterlichen Streitbeilegung eingeführt, die von staatlichen Gerichten durchgeführt werden.[21] Für Schiedsgerichte gibt es jedoch weiterhin keine spezifischen Kollisionsnormen, die sich ausdrücklich auf Schiedsvereinbarungen bezögen.[22]

In Bezug auf die *Gültigkeit* der Schiedsvereinbarung bedeutet dies im Wesentlichen, dass Schiedsgerichte unter der seit dem 1.1.2018 geltenden Regelung grundsätzlich die gleichen Möglichkeiten haben wie unter der früheren Regelung:

- analoge Anwendung der speziellen Kollisionsnorm des § 41 ungSchG 2017 für die Hauptsache des Schiedsverfahrens;
- analoge Anwendung der in § 47 Abs. 2 lit. a sublit. aa ungSchG 2017 für das Aufhebungsverfahren vorgesehenen speziellen Kollisionsnorm;
- analoge Anwendung der speziellen und allgemeinen Kollisionsnormen des ungIPRG 2017, insbesondere § 52 ungIPRG 2017;
- analoge Anwendung der speziellen Kollisionsnorm des Art. V Abs. 1 lit. a New Yorker Übereinkommen.

Es gibt auch die Auffassung, dass mangels spezieller Kollisionsnormen für Schiedsvereinbarungen im ungSchG 2017 die einzig richtige Lösung darin besteht, dass das Schiedsgericht das auf die Schiedsvereinbarung anwendbare Recht gemäß § 41 ungSchG 2017, dh gemäß der Kollisionsnorm für die Hauptsache bestimmt.[23] Meiner Meinung nach ist es äußerst zweifelhaft, ob der Gesetzgeber beabsichtigt

[19] S. auch Varga, A polgári perrendtartás és kapcsolódó jogszabályok kommentárja III/III/Király, 2018, Rn. 7475–7476; Schmidt, Magyar Jog 2020/1, 54 (61).

[20] S. Born, International Commercial Arbitration, 2014, S. 2637–2643.

[21] S. auch Varga, A polgári perrendtartás és kapcsolódó jogszabályok kommentárja III/III/Király, 2018, Rn. 7484.

[22] S. Erdős, Ünnepi tanulmányok Király Miklós 60. születésnapja alkalmából, 2021, 191–193.

[23] S. Varga, A polgári perrendtartás és kapcsolódó jogszabályok kommentárja III/III/Király, 2018, Rn. 7484.

hat, § 41 ungSchG 2017 auch zur Bestimmung des anwendbaren Rechts für Schiedsvereinbarungen zu nutzen. Gemäß dem Wortlaut der Norm ist dies auf die *Substanz* des Rechtsstreits zwischen den Parteien, dh auf die Hauptsache des Schiedsverfahrens anzuwenden.[24] Obwohl die Gültigkeit der Schiedsvereinbarung typischerweise materielle Rechtsfragen aufwirft – insbesondere, wenn die materielle Gültigkeit der Schiedsvereinbarung angefochten wird –, handelt es sich um eine Vorfrage, die die Zuständigkeit des Schiedsgerichts betrifft und nicht zur Hauptsache gehört. Die direkte Anwendung der für die Hauptsache vorgesehenen Kollisionsnorm auf die Schiedsvereinbarung würde zudem die Unabhängigkeit der Schiedsvereinbarung untergraben. Daher ist es sinnvoller, bei der Bestimmung des auf die Schiedsvereinbarung anwendbaren Rechts von einer analogen Anwendung des § 41 ungSchG 2017 zu reden und dies bloß als eine Möglichkeit für das Schiedsgericht zu betrachten.

Ähnlich verhält es sich mit der Bestimmung der auf die subjektive Schiedsfähigkeit der Parteien bzw. auf die objektive Schiedsfähigkeit des Rechtsstreits anwendbaren Rechte. Mangels spezieller Kollisionsnormen zur *subjektiven Schiedsfähigkeit* der Parteien müssen staatliche Gerichte die allgemeinen Regeln des ungIPRG 2017 für die Rechts- und Handlungsfähigkeit natürlicher und juristischer Personen anwenden.[25] Der Geltungsbereich dieser kollisionsrechtlichen Bestimmungen erstreckt sich jedoch nicht auf Schiedsgerichte, die diese Regeln höchstens analog anwenden können. Im Falle der *objektiven Schiedsfähigkeit* fehlt es sogar an einer kollisionsrechtlichen Regelung für staatliche Gerichte: Es gibt nur Kollisionsnormen für das Aufhebungsverfahren und die Vollstreckungsphase. Diese Regelungen richten sich natürlich nur an staatliche Gerichte, sodass für Schiedsgerichte überhaupt keine kollisionsrechtlichen Bestimmungen zur objektiven Schiedsfähigkeit existieren.

2. *Mangelnde Harmonie zwischen den nationalen Kollisionsregeln bzw. mit den internationalen Trends*

Wenn man § 52 ungIPRG 2017 mit § 47 Abs. 2 lit. a sublit. aa ungSchG 2017 vergleicht, wird sofort deutlich, dass zwischen den beiden Bestimmungen ein Widerspruch besteht. Gemäß § 47 Abs. 2 lit. a sublit. aa ungSchG 2017 muss das Gericht im Aufhebungsverfahren, falls keine Rechtswahl der Parteien vorliegt, die Gültigkeit der Schiedsvereinbarung nach ungarischem Recht beurteilen. Im Gegensatz dazu sieht § 52 ungIPRG 2017 vor, dass für eine Schiedsvereinbarung, für

[24] Für einen ähnlichen Standpunkt in Bezug auf § 49 ungSchG 1994, dessen Wortlaut in dieser Hinsicht dem des § 41 ungSchG 2017 entspricht, s. Bán/Nemessányi, A választottbírósági szerződésre alkalmazandó jog meghatározása, in Berke/Nemessányi, Az új nemzetközi magánjogi törvény alapjai – kodifikációs előtanulmányok, 2016, S. 227–228.

[25] In Bezug auf das anwendbare Recht für die Rechts- und Handlungsfähigkeit der Parteien s. Vékás/Nemessányi/Osztovits, A nemzetközi magánjogról szóló törvény kommentárja/Szabados, 2020, S. 310 (§§ 50–56). Szabados weist darauf hin, dass die Frage der Rechts- und Handlungsfähigkeit der Parteien im Zusammenhang mit Verträgen im Allgemeinen als Vorfrage aufkomme und die kollisionsrechtliche Regelung für Verträge in dieser Hinsicht keine speziellen Kollisionsnormen enthalte. Daher müssten die Gerichte die allgemeinen Kollisionsnormen des ungIPRG 2017 anwenden, die auf das Personalstatut verwiesen.

die die Parteien das anwendbare Recht nicht separat vereinbart haben, je nach den Umständen des Falles, entweder das Recht des zugrunde liegenden Rechtsverhältnisses oder das Recht des Schiedsortes gelten soll, wobei die Schiedsvereinbarung nicht nur dann als formal gültig angesehen werden soll, wenn sie den Formerfordernissen des ungarischen Rechts entspricht, sondern auch dann, wenn sie die Formerfordernisse irgendeines der nach § 52 ungIPRG 2017 bestimmten Rechte erfüllt.

Der oben beschriebene Widerspruch stellt nur dann ein Problem dar, wenn der Schiedsort in Ungarn liegt und nur in der Phase der Aufhebung. Der Anwendungsbereich des § 47 Abs. 2 lit. a sublit. aa ungSchG 2017 ist nämlich begrenzt: Diese Bestimmung legt die auf die Schiedsvereinbarung anzuwendende kollisionsrechtliche Regelung ausschließlich für das Aufhebungsverfahren fest (die Ungültigkeit der Schiedsvereinbarung ist ein Grund für die Aufhebung des Schiedsspruchs), und es kann, wie die meisten Bestimmungen des ungSchG 2017, nur dann angewendet werden, wenn der Schiedsort in Ungarn liegt.[26] In dieser Situation sollte nach den allgemeinen Grundsätzen der Gesetzesauslegung § 47 Abs. 2 lit. a sublit. aa ungSchG 2017 als *lex specialis* den Vorrang vor § 52 ungIPRG 2017 haben: Während § 52 ungIPRG 2017 in allen Gerichtsverfahren anzuwenden ist, in denen die Gültigkeit der Schiedsvereinbarung als eine zu prüfende Frage aufkommt, und zwar unabhängig vom Gegenstand des Verfahrens, ist § 47 Abs. 2 lit. a sublit. aa ungSchG 2017 nur dann anwendbar, wenn die Ungültigkeit der Schiedsvereinbarung in einem Aufhebungsverfahren geltend gemacht wird. Das bedeutet, dass ein ungarisches Gericht, das mit einer Klage auf Aufhebung eines in Ungarn ergangenen Schiedsspruchs befasst ist,

- wenn keine Rechtswahl der Parteien vorliegt, immer ungarisches Recht auf die Gültigkeit der Schiedsvereinbarung anwenden sollte, und
- das auf das zugrunde liegende Rechtsverhältnis anwendbare Recht nicht anwenden könnte, das nach dem ungIPRG 2017 die primäre objektive Anknüpfung ist, nicht einmal in dem Fall, dass der Schiedsort (Ungarn) nicht von den Parteien, sondern vom Schiedsgericht bestimmt wurde, und auch dann nicht, wenn dieses Recht enger mit der Schiedsvereinbarung in Verbindung steht als das ungarische Recht.

Das Ergebnis dieser Auslegung steht nicht im Einklang mit dem Zweck der neuen Regelung. Wie es aus dem oben zitierten Absatz der Ministerialbegründung des ungIPRG 2017 eindeutig hervorgeht, wurde die neue Regelung mit Rücksicht darauf eingeführt, dass *„[man] in unseren derzeit geltenden Rechtsvorschriften [...] keine kollisionsrechtliche Regelung zur Bestimmung des auf die Schiedsvereinbarung anwendbaren Rechts [findet]“*. Obwohl dieser Ausgangspunkt nicht vollständig korrekt ist, da § 55 Abs. 1 lit. b ungSchG 1994 eine Kollisionsnorm zur Bestimmung des auf die Schiedsvereinbarung anwendbaren Rechts sehr wohl enthielt, zeigt das obige Zitat, dass das Ziel der neuen Regelung darin bestand, Kollisionsregeln zu schaffen, die

[26] In Bezug auf den räumlichen Anwendungsbereich des ungSchG 2017 s. § 1 Abs. 1, 2 ungSchG 2017.

global in jedem Fall anwendbar sind, in dem ein staatliches Gericht das auf die Schiedsvereinbarung anwendbare Recht bestimmen muss. Dies wird auch durch andere Aussagen der Ministerialbegründung bestätigt, die darauf hinweisen, dass die früheren Kollisionsregeln *„nur Teilfragen berühr[t]en"*, und diese Situation nicht befriedigend gewesen sei. Die Seltsamkeit der Situation wird noch deutlicher, wenn man bedenkt, dass das Aufhebungsverfahren wahrscheinlich die häufigste Situation ist, in der die Gültigkeit einer Schiedsvereinbarung vor einem staatlichen Gericht angefochten wird, und daher ein staatliches Gericht das auf die Schiedsvereinbarung anwendbare Recht bestimmen muss.

Der Widerspruch zwischen § 47 Abs. 2 lit. a sublit. aa ungSchG 2017 und § 52 ungIPRG 2017 könnte möglicherweise dadurch erklärt werden, dass der Gesetzgeber versehentlich versäumt hat, die beiden Regelungen in Einklang zu bringen, und dies darauf zurückzuführen ist, dass die beiden Gesetze in parallelen, gleichzeitigen Gesetzgebungsverfahren verabschiedet wurden.[27] Allerdings ist § 52 ungIPRG 2017 auch mit Art. V Abs. 1 lit. a New Yorker Übereinkommen und Art. VI Abs. 2 sowie Art. IX Abs. 1 lit. a Genfer Übereinkommen nicht vereinbar. Dies legt nahe, dass hinter diesen Widersprüchen Absicht steckt. Das wird auch durch einen Beitrag von *Bán* und *Nemessányi* bestätigt, in der sie einen Vorschlag zur Regelung des auf die Schiedsvereinbarung anwendbaren Rechts unterbreitet haben. Diesen Vorschlag hat der Gesetzgeber akzeptiert und in § 52 ungIPRG 2017 eingearbeitet. In Bezug auf die Anwendung des *lex loci arbitri* mangels einer Rechtswahl der Parteien und anstelle des auf das zugrunde liegende Rechtsverhältnis anwendbaren Rechts verweisen *Bán* und *Nemessányi* ausdrücklich auf das New Yorker Übereinkommen, um zu unterstreichen, dass, wenn zwischen den Parteien keine Vereinbarung vorliege, mit der die Schiedsvereinbarung einem bestimmten Recht unterworfen werde, der Schiedsort eine oft eingesetzte Anknüpfung sei.[28] Daraus folgt, dass die tatsächlichen „Verfasser" des § 52 ungIPRG 2017 sich sehr wohl der Unterschiede zwischen den beiden Lösungen bewusst waren.

Wie auch *Schmidt* zu Recht darauf hinweist bezüglich der Abweichung zwischen § 52 ungIPRG 2017 und Art. V Abs. 1 lit. a New Yorker Übereinkommen, ist diese Abweichung in der kollisionsrechtlichen Regelung für Schiedsvereinbarungen kein bloßer „Schönheitsfehler" – keine Inkonsistenz ohne praktische Konsequenzen –, sondern vielmehr ein echtes Problem, das schwerwiegende Folgen haben kann. Die Anwendung unterschiedlicher Kollisionsnormen auf die Gültigkeit der Schiedsvereinbarung in verschiedenen Phasen der schiedsrichterlichen Streitbeilegung, in denen die Gültigkeit der Schiedsvereinbarung vor einem staatlichen Gericht angegriffen wird, kann zur Anwendung unterschiedlicher Rechte und in Bezug auf die Gültigkeit zu unterschiedlichen Schlussfolgerungen führen.[29] Infolgedessen kann es vorkommen, dass das ungarische Gericht, vor dem eine der Par-

---

[27] Das ungIPRG 2017 wurde am 11.4.2017 verkündet, während das ungSchG 2017 weniger als zwei Monate später, am 8.6.2017.

[28] S. Bán/Nemessányi, A választottbírósági szerződésre alkalmazandó jog meghatározása, in: Berke/Nemessányi, Az új nemzetközi magánjogi törvény alapjai – kodifikációs előtanulmányok, 2016, S. 234.

[29] S. Schmidt, Magyar Jog 2020/1, 54 (62).

teien trotz der Schiedsvereinbarung bezüglich des Streitgegenstandes eine Klage erhoben hat, mangels einer Rechtswahl der Parteien gemäß § 52 Abs. 2 ungIPRG 2017 das auf das zugrunde liegende Rechtsverhältnis anwendbare Recht anwendet – möglicherweise ein ausländisches Recht, nach dem die Schiedsvereinbarung gültig ist –, und die Parteien an das Schiedsgericht verweist.[30] Wenn der Schiedsort in Ungarn liegt, kann die unterlegene Partei die Aufhebung des Schiedsspruchs vor einem ungarischen Gericht beantragen. Dieses Gericht wird die Gültigkeit der Schiedsvereinbarung nach ungarischem Recht beurteilen. Wenn die Schiedsvereinbarung nach ungarischem Recht ungültig ist, wird das Gericht den Schiedsspruch aufheben, auch wenn zuvor ein anderes ungarisches Gericht – oder *horribile dictu* sogar dasselbe ungarische Gericht – die Schiedsvereinbarung für gültig erklärt hat und den Rechtsstreit an das Schiedsgericht verwiesen hat.

Ein weiteres Beispiel, das auch *Schmidt* vorführt:[31] Wenn der Schiedsort nicht in Ungarn liegt, kann es vorkommen, dass eine Partei trotz der Schiedsvereinbarung vor einem ungarischen Gericht bezüglich des Streitgegenstandes Klage erhebt. Mangels einer Rechtswahl kann das ungarische Gericht, das § 52 Abs. 2 ungIPRG 2017 anwendet, zu dem Schluss kommen, dass die Schiedsvereinbarung nach dem auf das zugrunde liegende Rechtsverhältnis anwendbaren Recht ungültig ist, und dass das Gericht daher die Streitigkeit zwischen den Parteien in der Sache entscheiden kann. Wenn parallel zu dem vor dem ungarischen Gericht anhängigen Verfahren auch ein Schiedsverfahren am ausländischen Schiedsort eingeleitet wird und das Schiedsgericht einen Schiedsspruch fällt, da die Schiedsrichter zu dem Schluss kommen, dass nach einem anderen Recht – dem *lex loci arbitri* – die Schiedsvereinbarung gültig ist, und dann die obsiegende Partei in Ungarn Vollstreckung beantragt, wird das Vollstreckungsgericht die Gültigkeit der Schiedsvereinbarung gemäß dem New Yorker Übereinkommen ebenfalls aufgrund der *lex loci arbitri* prüfen. Es wird zu demselben Schluss kommen wie das Schiedsgericht, im Widerspruch zu der früheren Feststellung eines anderen – oder möglicherweise desselben – ungarischen Gerichts, dass die Schiedsvereinbarung ungültig ist und dass das Gerichtsverfahren in der Sache durchgeführt werden kann.

Die Bestrebung des Gesetzgebers danach, auf die Gültigkeit und andere materiellrechtliche Aspekte der Schiedsvereinbarung mangels einer Rechtswahl jenes Recht anzuwenden, das die engste Verbindung zur Schiedsvereinbarung aufweist, ist auf jeden Fall lobenswert. Trotzdem, angesichts der oben dargestellten Komplikationen, die sich aus den Unterschieden zwischen § 52 ungIPRG 2017 und § 47 Abs. 2 lit. a sublit. aa ungSchG 2017 bzw. Art. V Abs. 1 lit. a New Yorker Übereinkommen ergeben können, wäre es wahrscheinlich sinnvoller gewesen, eine Regelung zu verabschieden, die vollständig mit den bestehenden Kollisionsregeln übereinstimmt.

Die Anwendung des auf das zugrunde liegende Rechtsverhältnis anwendbaren Rechts auf die Schiedsvereinbarung widerspricht an sich nicht den internationalen

---

[30] Dh das Gerichtsverfahren wird gemäß § 9 Abs. 1 ungSchG 2017 wegen Unzuständigkeit auf Antrag eingestellt.

[31] S. Schmidt, Magyar Jog 2020/1, 54 (62).

Trends. Die Anwendung des Rechts, das von den Parteien für den Hauptvertrag gewählt wurde, auf die Schiedsvereinbarung – also die Auslegung der Rechtswahl für den Hauptvertrag als eine konkludente Rechtswahl für die Schiedsvereinbarung – ist international weit verbreitet.[32] Allerdings geht § 52 ungIPRG 2017 darüber hinaus, und mangels einer spezifisch für die Schiedsvereinbarung getroffenen Rechtswahl, dh auf der zweiten Ebene der Regelung, sieht er die Anwendung des auf das zugrunde liegende Rechtsverhältnis anwendbaren Rechts auch dann vor, wenn die Parteien hinsichtlich des zugrunde liegenden Rechtsverhältnisses keine Rechtswahl getroffen haben. Es ist auch nicht die beste Lösung, dass die *lex loci arbitri* anstelle des auf das zugrunde liegende Rechtsverhältnis anwendbaren Rechts nur dann angewendet werden kann, wenn die Parteien den Schiedsort bestimmt haben oder wenn das Gericht die allgemeine Ausweichklausel anwendet – was ein außergewöhnliches Instrument ist. Ebenso bedauerlich ist die Tatsache, dass § 52 ungIPRG 2017 nicht eindeutig macht, ob die Wahl der Parteien für den Schiedsort ausdrücklich sein muss oder eventuell auch konkludent erfolgen kann.[33] Diese Umstände erhöhen erheblich das Risiko, dass staatliche Gerichte, die in verschiedenen Phasen der schiedsrichterlichen Streitbeilegung tätig sind, auf dieselbe Schiedsvereinbarung unterschiedliche Rechte anwenden und hinsichtlich der Gültigkeit der Schiedsvereinbarung ggf. zu unterschiedlichen Schlussfolgerungen gelangen. Dies kann insbesondere in den folgenden Fällen auftreten:

- Die Parteien haben weder für die Schiedsvereinbarung noch für den Hauptvertrag das anwendbare Recht gewählt und nicht einmal den Schiedsort bestimmt.
- Die Parteien haben weder für die Schiedsvereinbarung noch für den Hauptvertrag das anwendbare Recht gewählt. Obwohl sie den Schiedsort bestimmt haben, kommt ein ungarisches Gericht, das das ungIPRG 2017 anwendet, zu dem Schluss, dass das Recht des Schiedsortes mit der Schiedsvereinbarung nicht enger verbunden ist als das Recht, das mangels einer Rechtswahl für den Hauptvertrag anwendbar ist.

Das ungarische Gericht, das das ungIPRG 2017 anwendet, wird in beiden Fällen jenes Recht auf die Schiedsvereinbarung anwenden, das auf das zugrunde liegende Rechtsverhältnis mangels einer Rechtswahl anzuwenden ist. Im Gegensatz dazu wird ein Gericht, das Art. V Abs. 1 lit. a New Yorker Übereinkommen oder Art. VI Abs. 2 bzw. Art. IX Abs. 1 lit. a Genfer Übereinkommen anwendet – das entweder ein anderes oder *ad absurdum* dasselbe ungarische Gericht sein kann –, auf die Schiedsvereinbarung in beiden Fällen das Recht des Schiedsortes anwenden.

[32] S. zB [2020] UKSC 38, 9.10.2020 (Enka Insaat Ve Sanayi AS [Respondent] v OOO Insurance Company Chubb [Appellant]); [2019] SGCA 84 (BNA [Appellant] v BNB and BNC [Respondents]).

[33] Für weitere kritische Anmerkungen zu § 52 Abs. 2 und 3 ungIPRG 2017 s. Schmidt, Magyar Jog 2020/1, 54 (62).

3. Die Rechtswirkung der Rechtswahl der Parteien für die Hauptsache bzw. der Wahl des Schiedsortes durch die Parteien

Die Frage, ob mangels einer spezifischen Rechtswahl für die Schiedsvereinbarung die Rechtswahl der Parteien für das zugrunde liegende Rechtsverhältnis bzw. die Wahl des Schiedsortes als eine konkludente Wahl des betroffenen Rechts für die Schiedsvereinbarung betrachtet werden kann, ist durch die Einführung des § 52 ungIPRG 2017 überholt worden. Der Grund dafür liegt darin, dass der Gesetzgeber für beide Fälle ausdrückliche Kollisionsregeln geschaffen hat.[34] Auf diese Weise hat der Gesetzgeber klargestellt, dass für die Bestimmung des auf die Schiedsvereinbarung anwendbaren Rechts sowohl die Rechtswahl der Parteien hinsichtlich des Hauptvertrags als auch die Wahl des Schiedsortes relevant sind.

Wie es aus den oben Dargelegten klar hervorgeht, hat es für die Anwendung der mehrstufigen Regelung des § 52 ungIPRG 2017 eine herausragende Bedeutung, ob die Parteien für die Schiedsvereinbarung eine spezifische Rechtswahl getroffen haben. Wenn die Schiedsvereinbarung selbst eine ausdrückliche und spezifische Rechtswahl enthält (zB „*für diese Schiedsklausel gilt ungarisches Recht*"), ist klar, dass die erste Ebene der Kollisionsregelung anzuwenden ist: Das von den Parteien ausdrücklich und spezifisch gewählte Recht wird für die Schiedsvereinbarung maßgeblich sein. Es ist jedoch sehr selten, dass die Parteien eine solche Rechtswahl im Zusammenhang mit der Schiedsvereinbarung treffen.[35] Aus der zweiten und dritten Ebene der Kollisionsregelung folgt, dass, je nach den Umständen, die Rechtswahl der Parteien hinsichtlich des zugrunde liegenden Rechtsverhältnisses bzw. die Wahl des Schiedsortes durch die Parteien als eine konkludente Rechtswahl für die Schiedsvereinbarung betrachtet werden kann.

Die gemeinsame Auslegung der drei Ebenen der Kollisionsregelung wirft die folgende Frage auf: Wenn die Parteien für die Schiedsvereinbarung keine ausdrückliche und spezifische Rechtswahl getroffen haben, wird dann die zweite oder dritte Ebene der Regelung (dh das Recht des zugrunde liegenden Rechtsverhältnisses bzw. das Recht des Schiedsortes) automatisch angewendet, oder ist es auch möglich, dass die Parteien eine solche konkludente Rechtswahl für die Schiedsvereinbarung treffen, die der zweiten und dritten Ebene der Regelung vorausgeht? Mit anderen Worten: Kann die Rechtswahl der Parteien gemäß § 52 Abs. 1 ungIPRG 2017 nur ausdrücklich sein, oder ist eine konkludente Rechtswahl für die Schiedsvereinbarung, anders als die Wahl eines Rechts für das zugrunde liegende Rechtsverhältnis bzw. die Wahl des Schiedsortes, auch möglich und zulässig?

---

[34] S. Vékás/Nemessányi/Osztovits, A nemzetközi magánjogról szóló törvény kommentárja/Szabados, 2020, S. 318 (§§ 50–56). Szabados weist darauf hin, dass das auf das zugrunde liegende Rechtsverhältnis anwendbare Recht genau das Recht sei, das – bei Anerkennung einer stillschweigenden Rechtswahl – höchstwahrscheinlich ohnehin auf die Schiedsvereinbarung anzuwenden wäre. Dies ist der Fall, wenn die Parteien das Recht für den Hauptvertrag gewählt haben. Mangels einer Rechtswahl für den Hauptvertrag kann jedoch nicht von einer stillschweigenden Rechtswahl für die Schiedsvereinbarung gesprochen werden. S. auch Erdős, Ünnepi tanulmányok Király Miklós 60. születésnapja alkalmából, 2021, 187–188.

[35] S. Vékás/Nemessányi/Osztovits, A nemzetközi magánjogról szóló törvény kommentárja/Szabados, 2020, S. 318 (§§ 50–56).

Gemäß § 9 Abs. 1 lit. a ungIPRG 2017 muss die Rechtswahl der Parteien ausdrücklich sein, sofern das Gesetz nichts anderes bestimmt. Dies bedeutet, dass das ungIPRG 2017 grundsätzlich keine stillschweigende Rechtswahl anerkennt. § 50 Abs. 1 ungIPRG 2017 enthält allerdings eine Ausnahme: Der Vertrag unterliegt dem von den Parteien gewählten Recht, vorausgesetzt, dass die Rechtswahl der Parteien aus den Bestimmungen des Vertrags oder den sonstigen Umständen des Falles ausdrücklich oder zumindest eindeutig hervorgeht. Daher ist gemäß den allgemeinen Kollisionsregeln für Verträge auch eine stillschweigende Rechtswahl zulässig.[36] § 52 Abs. 1 ungIPRG 2017, der eine spezielle Regelung für die Schiedsvereinbarung ist, schweigt darüber, ob die Rechtswahl für die Schiedsvereinbarung ausdrücklich sein muss oder auch stillschweigend erfolgen kann. Da die Schiedsvereinbarung selbst ein Vertrag ist und § 52 Abs. 1 ungIPRG 2017 unter der Überschrift „Vertragsschuldverhältnisse" zu finden ist, ist diese Schweigsamkeit richtig so zu verstehen, dass die Rechtswahl der Parteien gemäß § 52 Abs. 1 ungIPRG 2017 nicht nur ausdrücklich, sondern auch stillschweigend sein kann.[37] Daher sollte – wenn die Parteien für die Schiedsvereinbarung keine ausdrückliche und spezifische Rechtswahl getroffen haben, aber die Umstände des Falles eindeutig darauf hinweisen, dass die Parteien bezüglich der Schiedsvereinbarung die Anwendung eines solchen Rechts gewünscht haben, das sowohl von dem für das zugrunde liegende Rechtsverhältnis gewählten oder darauf sonst anwendbaren Recht als auch von dem Recht des Schiedsortes abweicht – auf die Schiedsvereinbarung nach § 52 Abs. 1 ungIPRG 2017 dieses Recht angewendet werden. Ein Beispiel hierfür könnte der Fall sein, in dem der Kläger, der den Rechtsstreit trotz der Schiedsvereinbarung vor ein staatliches Gericht gebracht hat, die Gültigkeit der Schiedsvereinbarung aufgrund eines bestimmten Rechts angreift (zB der Kläger behauptet, dass die Schiedsvereinbarung nach deutschem Recht nichtig sei), und der Beklagte den Vortrag des Klägers zur Ungültigkeit der Schiedsvereinbarung unter Berufung auf dasselbe Recht (zB deutsches Recht) erwidert.[38]

---

[36] S. Vékás/Nemessányi/Osztovits, A nemzetközi magánjogról szóló törvény kommentárja/Vékás, 2020, S. 94 (§ 9); Vékás/Nemessányi/Osztovits, A nemzetközi magánjogról szóló törvény kommentárja/Szabados, 2020, S. 312 (§§ 50–56).

[37] Vgl. Vékás/Nemessányi/Osztovits, A nemzetközi magánjogról szóló törvény kommentárja/Szabados, 2020, S. 317–318 (§§ 50–56); Erdős, Ünnepi tanulmányok Király Miklós 60. születésnapja alkalmából, 2021, 187. Nach Szabados und Erdős gebe das ungIPRG 2017 keine eindeutige Antwort darauf, ob § 52 Abs. 1 nur eine ausdrückliche Rechtswahl für die Schiedsvereinbarung ermögliche oder auch eine stillschweigende.

[38] Nach der Rechtsprechung im Zusammenhang mit der ungIPRGV 1979 konnte die bloße Tatsache der Erhebung einer Klage vor einem ungarischen Gericht nicht als eine stillschweigende Wahl des ungarischen Rechts betrachtet werden (s. Oberster Gerichtshof Ungarns, [Datum nicht angegeben] – Gfv. IX. 30.214/2006, EBH2006.2.1520; 31.10.2019 – Pfv. 20.067/2019, BH2020.3.72). Bestimmte zusätzliche Umstände, wie zB die ausdrückliche Bezugnahme des Klägers auf das ungarische Recht in seiner Klageschrift und die ausdrückliche Bezugnahme des Beklagten auf das ungarische Recht in seiner Klageerwiderung, oder die Tatsache, dass der Beklagte versäumt hat, fristgerecht (ohne unentschuldbare Verzögerung) Einwände gegen die Anwendung des ungarischen Rechts zu erheben, konnten jedoch dazu führen, dass das ungarische Recht anstelle des ansonsten anwendbaren ausländischen Rechts angewendet wurde. S. Oberster Gerichtshof Ungarns, 31.10.2019 – Pfv. 20.067/2019, BH2020.3.72; Bóka, A Kúria és az ítélőtáblák joggyakorlata a nemzetközi magánjogról szóló 1979. évi 13. törvényerejű rendelettel (Nmjt.)

Aufgrund der oben dargelegten Überlegungen ist mangels einer ausdrücklichen und spezifischen Rechtswahl der Parteien für die Schiedsvereinbarung die Rechtswahl der Parteien für das zugrunde liegende Rechtsverhältnis bzw. die Wahl des Schiedsortes als eine konkludente Rechtswahl für die Schiedsvereinbarung zu betrachten, aber nur dann, wenn aus den Umständen des Falles keine andere konkludente Rechtswahl hervorgeht.

4. Der sachliche Anwendungsbereich der Kollisionsregeln für die Gültigkeit der Schiedsvereinbarung

Im Gegensatz zur ungIPRGV 1979 und der Rom I-Verordnung[39] enthält das ungIPRG 2017 keine Bestimmung, die den Umfang des anwendbaren Rechts für den Vertrag festlegen würde.[40] Aus dem Wortlaut der §§ 50–54 ungIPRG 2017 und des § 47 Abs. 2 lit. a sublit. aa ungSchG 2017 folgt, dass das auf die Schiedsvereinbarung anwendbare Recht zumindest für die folgenden Rechtsfragen gelten soll:

- das Zustandekommen (der Bestand) der Schiedsvereinbarung;[41]
- die materielle Gültigkeit der Schiedsvereinbarung;[42]
- die Formgültigkeit der Schiedsvereinbarung (nicht ausschließlich, sondern alternativ mit anderen Rechten);[43]
- das Zustandekommen (der Bestand) sowie die (materielle und formelle) Gültigkeit der Rechtswahl für die Schiedsvereinbarung.[44]

Jedoch können im Zusammenhang mit der Schiedsvereinbarung zahlreiche weitere Rechtsfragen aufkommen, die materiell-rechtlicher Natur sind und für die daher die Anwendung des Vertragsstatuts der Schiedsvereinbarung gerechtfertigt wäre: die Auslegung, die Übertragbarkeit und die materiell-rechtlichen Auswirkungen der Schiedsvereinbarung. Ob diese Rechtsfragen ebenfalls aufgrund des auf die Schiedsvereinbarung anwendbaren Rechts zu beurteilen sind, ist jedoch nicht eindeutig. In dieser Hinsicht bedeutet die neue Regelung einen Rückschritt gegenüber der alten Regelung, dh im Vergleich zu § 29 Abs. 1 ungIPRGV 1979. Nach dieser alten Regelung erstreckte sich das Vertragsstatut auf alle Elemente des Schuldverhältnisses, einschließlich insbesondere des Zustandekommens (Bestands), der materiellen und formellen Gültigkeit, der schuldrechtlichen Wirkungen und der Übertragbarkeit des Vertrags.[45]

---

kapcsolatban. 2. rész – az alkalmazandó joggal kapcsolatos kérdések. Kúriai Döntések (Bírósági Határozatok), 2015/8, 882 (884 und 886).

[39] S. § 29 Abs. 1 ungIPRGV 1979 und Art. 12 Rom I-VO.

[40] S. Vékás/Nemessányi/Osztovits, A nemzetközi magánjogról szóló törvény kommentárja/Szabados, 2020, S. 315 (§§ 50–56).

[41] S. § 53 ungIPRG 2017.

[42] S. § 53 ungIPRG 2017 und § 47 Abs. 2 lit. a sublit. aa ungSchG 2017.

[43] S. § 50 Abs. 3, § 52 Abs 4, § 53 und § 54 ungIPRG 2017.

[44] S. § 50 Abs. 5 ungIPRG 2017.

[45] Nach Szabados kann Art. 12 Rom I-VO als Ausgangspunkt für die Bestimmung des Umfangs des auf den Vertrag anwendbaren Rechts dienen, s. Vékás/Nemessányi/Osztovits, A nemzetközi magánjogról szóló törvény kommentárja/Szabados, 2020, S. 315 (§§ 50–56).

Gemäß § 55 Abs. 1 lit. b ungSchG 1994 war es nicht vollständig klar, ob der Ausdruck „nicht gültig“ auch die formelle Ungültigkeit umfasste, und ob § 5 ungSchG 1994, dh die Bestimmung über die Formerfordernisse für Schiedsvereinbarungen, bzw. § 55 Abs. 1 lit. b ungSchG 1994 als *lex specialis* für die Anwendung der allgemeinen *favor validitatis* Regelung[46] in § 29 ungIPRGV 1979 auf die Formgültigkeit der Schiedsvereinbarung einen Raum ließen. Leider hat die Einführung der auf die Schiedsvereinbarung anwendbaren, speziellen Kollisionsnormen in § 52 ungIPRG 2017 diese Unsicherheiten im Zusammenhang mit der Formungültigkeit der Schiedsvereinbarung nicht beseitigt. Der Grund dafür ist, dass der Gesetzgeber der Wortlaut des auf die Ungültigkeit der Schiedsvereinbarung basierenden Aufhebungsgrundes im ungSchG 2017 nicht mit der neuen Regelung des ungIPRG 2017 in Einklang gebracht hat.[47] Daher ist weiterhin unklar, ob der Ausdruck „nicht gültig“ in § 47 Abs. 2 lit. a sublit. aa ungSchG 2017 auch die Formungültigkeit mit einschließt. Meiner Meinung nach ist es nicht gerechtfertigt anzunehmen, dass die Kollisionsnorm in § 47 Abs. 2 lit. a sublit. aa ungSchG 2017 die Formungültigkeit der Schiedsvereinbarung nicht abdeckt.[48] In diesem Zusammenhang bleibt die Rechtsprechung der ungarischen Gerichte, die die Formerfordernisse des ungSchG 1994 für die Schiedsvereinbarung eindeutig als eine Gültigkeitsvoraussetzung betrachtet haben, weiterhin maßgeblich.[49]

Wenn man davon ausgeht, dass § 47 Abs. 2 lit. a sublit. aa ungSchG 2017 auch auf die Formungültigkeit der Schiedsvereinbarung hinweist, ist jedoch nicht klar, ob die spezielle *favor validitatis* Regelung in § 52 Abs. 4 ungIPRG 2017 auch in der Aufhebungsphase anwendbar ist. § 47 Abs. 2 lit. a sublit. aa ungSchG 2017 sieht nämlich für die Gültigkeit der Schiedsvereinbarung kategorisch die Anwendung des von den Parteien gewählten Rechts oder, mangels einer Rechtswahl, die Anwendung des ungarischen Rechts vor.

5. *Die neue favor validatis Regel*

Unabhängig davon, ob die *favor validitatis* Regel auch in der Aufhebungsphase angewendet werden kann, wirft die Auslegung dieser Regel weitere Fragezeichen auf. Gemäß § 52 Abs. 4 ungIPRG 2017 kann die Schiedsvereinbarung nicht aus formalen Gründen als ungültig betrachtet werden, wenn sie den Formerfordernissen irgendeines der gemäß § 52 ungIPRG 2017 bestimmten Rechte oder denen des Rechts des Staates des angerufenen Gerichts *(lex fori)* entspricht. Der Ausdruck *„irgendeines der gemäß diesem § bestimmten Rechte“* kann auf zwei verschiedene Weisen interpretiert werden:

– der Ausdruck umfasst alle Rechte, die gemäß § 52 Abs. 1–3 ungIPRG 2017 anwendbar sein können, dh das von den Parteien gewählte Recht (sofern vorhan-

---

[46] § 29 Abs. 2 ungIPRGV 1979.

[47] Für die Diskrepanz zwischen den beiden Regelungen → III.2.

[48] S. auch Varga, A polgári perrendtartás és kapcsolódó jogszabályok kommentárja III/III/Juhász, 2018, Rn. 7500. Juhász verwendet den Ausdruck „nicht gültig“ im weitesten Sinne, einschließlich der formellen Ungültigkeit.

[49] S. Oberster Gerichtshof Ungarns 24.9.2007 – Gfv. 30.176/2007, EBH2007.2.1705; Komitatsgericht Fejér [Datum nicht angegeben] – Gf. 40.049/2002, BDT2004.2.941.

den), das Recht, das auf das zugrunde liegende Rechtsverhältnis anwendbar ist, *und* das Recht des Schiedsortes; oder
- der Ausdruck umfasst nur das Recht, das gemäß § 52 Abs. 1–3 ungIPRG 2017 tatsächlich anwendbar ist, dh das von den Parteien gewählte Recht, das Recht, das auf das zugrunde liegende Rechtsverhältnis anwendbar ist, *oder* das Recht des Schiedsortes.

Während die erste – weitere – Auslegung dazu führen kann, dass neben dem Recht des Staates des angerufenen Gerichts *(lex fori)* drei weitere Rechte alternativ angewendet werden, kann die zweite – engere – Auslegung die Anwendung eines einzigen weiteren Rechts zur Folge haben. Mit Rücksicht darauf ist die erste Auslegung günstiger: Je mehr Rechte man auf die Formgültigkeit der Schiedsvereinbarung alternativ anwendet, desto wahrscheinlicher ist es, dass sie zumindest nach einem dieser Rechte formgültig ist. Die Verwendung des Ausdrucks *„gemäß diesem § bestimmt"* unterstützt jedoch eher die zweite, engere Auslegung. Der Grund dafür ist, dass von den in § 52 Abs. 1–3 ungIPRG 2017 erwähnten Rechten in einem konkreten Fall immer nur ein einziges Recht tatsächlich als das auf die Schiedsvereinbarung anwendbare Recht bestimmt wird. Mit anderen Worten: Gemäß § 52 Abs. 1–3 ungIPRG 2017 bedeutet das auf die Schiedsvereinbarung anwendbare Recht immer ein einziges Recht. Die Verwendung des Ausdrucks *„irgendeines der [...] Rechte"* unterstützt jedoch die erste, weitere Auslegung, da mit diesem Ausdruck eindeutig auf mehrere Rechte Bezug genommen wird, was nur dann sinnvoll ist, wenn der Verweis sich nicht auf das tatsächlich anwendbare (einzige) Recht beschränkt, sondern alle gemäß § 52 Abs. 1–3 ungIPRG 2017 in Betracht kommenden Rechte mit einschließt. Die gleiche Schlussfolgerung kann auch aus der Tatsache gezogen werden, dass § 52 Abs. 4 ungIPRG 2017 auf § 52 ungIPRG 2017 verweist. Wenn die zweite Auslegung korrekt wäre, wäre kein Verweis auf § 52 ungIPRG 2017 erforderlich, da die Verwendung des Ausdrucks *„das auf die Schiedsvereinbarung anwendbare Recht"* angemessener wäre. Allerdings ist auch der Verweis in § 52 Abs. 4 ungIPRG 2017 auf den ganzen § 52 ungIPRG 2017 ungenau und falsch, da er auch § 52 Abs. 4 abdeckt, was eine „sich selbst verschlingenden Schlange" ist. § 52 Abs. 4 ungIPRG 2017 sollte richtigerweise auf *„eines der gemäß Abs. 1–3 anwendbaren Rechte"* hinweisen.

Die Ministerialbegründung zu § 52 ungIPRG 2017 bietet wenig Hilfe beim oben genannten Dilemma. Gemäß der Ministerialbegründung *„sind die Regeln der Formgültigkeit – im Gegensatz zur materiellen Ungültigkeit – typischerweise darauf abgezielt, nachträgliche Beweisschwierigkeiten zu vermeiden. Daher wurde eine Aushilfsregel zur Beseitigung der Formungültigkeit der Schiedsvereinbarung erlassen, vorausgesetzt, dass es zumindest ein anwendbares Rechtssystem gibt, dessen Formerfordernissen die Schiedsvereinbarung entspricht."* Diese Erklärung lässt Spielraum für beide Interpretationen.

Wie die Ministerialbegründung des ungIPRG 2017 ausdrücklich darauf hinweist, stützte sich der Gesetzgeber bei der Kodifizierung auch auf die neuesten internationalen Erfahrungen, insbesondere auf die tschechischen, polnischen, belgischen und schweizerischen Gesetze zum internationalen Privatrecht.[50] Das belgische IPRG 2004 enthält keine Bestimmungen zu dem auf die Schiedsvereinbarung anwendbaren Recht. Daher können für die Auslegung des § 52 Abs. 4 ungIPRG 2017 nur die schweizerischen, polnischen und tschechischen Rechtsvorschriften relevant sein. Leider lässt sich der Ministerialbegründung nicht entnehmen, welches Gesetz als Grundlage für § 52 Abs. 4 ungIPRG 2017 diente. Dies ist besonders deshalb problematisch, da alle drei Regelungen unterschiedliche Ansätze befolgen.

Gemäß Art. 178 Abs. 1 schwIPRG *„[hat] die Schiedsvereinbarung [...] schriftlich oder in einer anderen Form zu erfolgen, die den Nachweis durch Text ermöglicht"*. Gemäß Art. 178 Abs. 2 schwIPRG *„[ist] die Schiedsvereinbarung im Übrigen gültig, wenn sie dem von den Parteien gewählten, dem auf die Streitsache, insbesondere dem auf den Hauptvertrag anwendbaren oder dem schweizerischen Recht entspricht"*. Die in Art. 178 Abs. 2 schwIPRG aufgeführten Rechte sind genau die gleichen, die in § 52 Abs. 1–4 ungIPRG 2017 erwähnt werden. Die Tatsache, dass Art. 178 Abs. 2 schwIPRG anstelle des Rechts des Schiedsortes oder der *lex fori* (dh des Rechts des angerufenen Gerichts) auf das schweizerische Recht verweist, macht keinen wirklichen Unterschied, da das 12. Kapitel schwIPRG, in dem Art. 178 enthalten ist, nur dann anwendbar ist, wenn der Schiedsort in der Schweiz liegt,[51] und das schwIPRG in der Regel nur von den schweizerischen Gerichten angewendet wird.[52] Daher ist der Verweis auf das schweizerische Recht in Art. 178 Abs. 2 schwIPRG praktisch gleichbedeutend mit dem Verweis in § 52 Abs. 3 ungIPRG 2017 auf das Recht des Schiedsortes und dem Verweis in § 52 Abs. 4 ungIPRG 2017 auf die *lex fori*.

Es gibt jedoch zwei wesentliche Unterschiede zwischen der ungarischen und der schweizerischen Regelung. Einerseits erstreckt sich der Anwendungsbereich der Regelung des schwIPRG zur internationalen Schiedsgerichtsbarkeit, einschließlich der Kollisionsregeln, nicht nur auf staatliche Gerichte, wie es bei der Regelung des ungIPRG 2017 der Fall ist, sondern auch auf Schiedsgerichte. Andererseits – und dies ist noch wichtiger – beschränkt sich der Anwendungsbereich des § 52 Abs. 4 ungIPRG 2017 ausdrücklich auf die Formgültigkeit. Dies bedeutet, dass die ungarische *favor validitatis* Regel auf die materielle Gültigkeit der Schiedsvereinbarung nicht angewendet werden kann. Im Gegensatz dazu, obwohl der Wortlaut des Art. 178 Abs. 2 schwIPRG auch eine breitere Auslegung ermöglicht – nämlich die Anwendbarkeit der Kollisionsnorm auf beide Aspekte der Gültigkeit, also sowohl auf die materielle als auch auf die formelle Gültigkeit[53] –, wird Art. 178 Abs. 2

[50] S. den Allgemeinen Teil der Ministerialbegründung des ungIPRG 2017. Die zitierten ausländischen Rechtsvorschriften sind wie folgt: das (tschechische) Gesetz über das internationale Privatrecht, verkündet unter Nr. 91/2012 Coll. am 25. 1. 2012 (tschIPRG 2012), das (polnische) Gesetz vom 4. 2. 2011 über das internationale Privatrecht, verkündet im Polnischen Amtsblatt 2011/80, S. 432; in Kraft getreten am 16. 5. 2011 (plIPRG 2011), das (belgische) Gesetz vom 16. 7. 2004 über das internationale Privatrecht (belgIPRG 2004) und das (schweizerische) Bundesgesetz über das internationale Privatrecht (schwIPRG).

[51] S. Art. 176 Abs. 1 schwIPRG.

[52] Ausländische Gerichte wenden das schwIPRG nur an, wenn die Kollisionsnormen der *lex fori* auf das gesamte schweizerische Recht, einschließlich seiner Kollisionsnormen, verweisen (kollisionsrechtliche Verweisung oder Gesamtverweisung).

[53] Der Ausdruck „im Übrigen" in Art. 178 Abs. 2 schwIPRG kann auch so interpretiert werden, dass, wenn die Schiedsvereinbarung den Formerfordernissen gemäß Art. 178 Abs. 1

schwIPRG konsequent als eine Kollisionsregel ausschließlich für das Zustandekommen (Bestand) und die materielle Gültigkeit der Schiedsvereinbarung interpretiert.[54] Dieser Unterschied in Bezug auf den Anwendungsbereich der beiden Regelungen schließt jedoch nicht aus, dass § 52 Abs. 4 ungIPRG 2017 nach dem Vorbild des Art. 178 Abs. 2 schwIPRG formuliert wurde. Wenn dies der Fall wäre, sollte § 52 Abs. 4 ungIPRG 2017 nach der ersten – weiteren – Auffassung korrekt interpretiert werden.

Im Gegensatz dazu befolgt das plIPRG 2011 ein unterschiedliches Konzept, das dem zweiten – engeren – Verständnis des § 52 Abs. 4 ungIPRG 2017 ähnlich ist. Gemäß Art. 40 plIPRG 2011 *„gilt für die Form der Schiedsvereinbarung das Recht des Staates, in dem der Schiedsort liegt[,] [e]s genügt jedoch, wenn es den Formerfordernissen des auf die Schiedsvereinbarung anwendbaren Rechts entspricht“*.[55] Das auf die Schiedsvereinbarung anwendbare Recht wird nach Art. 39 plIPRG 2011 bestimmt. Gemäß Art. 39 Abs. 1 ist das von den Parteien gewählte Recht vorrangig anwendbar. Mangels einer Rechtswahl der Parteien sieht Art. 39 Abs. 2 plIPRG 2011 vor, dass das auf die Schiedsvereinbarung anwendbare Recht entweder das Recht des Schiedsortes oder – falls die Parteien den Schiedsort nicht bestimmt haben – jenes Recht ist, das auf das durch den Rechtsstreit betroffene Rechtsverhältnis anzuwenden ist. In letzterem Fall kann die Schiedsvereinbarung nicht als ungültig betrachtet werden, wenn sie dem Recht des Staates entspricht, *„in dem das Schiedsverfahren durchgeführt wird oder in dem das Schiedsgericht seinen Schiedsspruch erlassen hat“*, abhängig vom aktuellen Stand des Verfahrens (dh davon, ob ein Schiedsspruch in der Angelegenheit bereits ergangen ist).[56] Daraus ergibt sich, dass gemäß dem plIPRG 2011 die höchste Anzahl der auf die Formgültigkeit der Schiedsvereinbarung alternativ anwendbaren Rechte zwei beträgt, und neben dem Recht des Schiedsortes, das auf die Formgültigkeit der Schiedsvereinbarung alternativ immer anzuwenden ist, ist das andere Recht in jedem Fall das tatsächlich anwendbare – günstigere – Recht anstelle der theoretisch – potenziell – anwendbaren Rechte.[57] Daher sollte § 52

schwIPRG nicht entspricht, sie dennoch als formgültig zu betrachten ist, wenn sie die Formerfordernisse irgendeiner der in Art. 178 Abs. 2 schwIPRG neben dem schweizerischen Recht erwähnten Rechtsordnungen erfüllt.

[54] Zur Rechtsprechung des schweizerischen Bundesgerichts s. schwBG 3.5.2010 – 4A_456/2009, SpuRt 2010, 198; s. auch Conrad FS Kren Kostkiewicz, 2018, 321 und Girsberger/Droese (Zentrum für Konflikt und Verfahren CCR, Universität Luzern), Vernehmlassungseingabe zur Änderung des Bundesgesetzes über das Internationale Privatrecht (Internationale Schiedsgerichtsbarkeit), 31.5.2017, zugänglich unter https://www.ius.uzh.ch/dam/jcr:3de94330-ddb1-4ba6-b64a-5eda9772f072/Gesammelte%20Stellungnahmen%20zur%20Revision%20des%20Schiedsverfahrensrechts.pdf (abgerufen 14.1.2024), Rn. 29–32.

[55] Die offizielle englische Übersetzung des plIPRG 2011 ist zugänglich unter https://sociedip.files.wordpress.com/2013/12/polonia-act-of-4-february-2011-private-international-law.pdf (abgerufen 14.1.2024).

[56] S. Szwedowski, New PIL provisions governing arbitration agreements come into force, 28.7.2011, https://www.lexology.com/library/detail.aspx?g=886495df-f447-4fb7-893d-40fb7c814ebc (abgerufen 14.1.2024).

[57] S. Szwedowski, New PIL provisions governing arbitration agreements come into force, 28.7.2011, https://www.lexology.com/library/detail.aspx?g=886495df-f447-4fb7-893d-40fb7c814ebc (abgerufen 14.1.2024).

Abs. 4 ungIPRG 2017, falls die Regelung durch das plIPRG 2011 inspiriert wurde, nach der zweiten – engeren – Auffassung korrekt interpretiert werden.

Was die tschechische Regelung angeht, folgt sie einem dritten Konzept. Gemäß dem ersten Satz des § 117 Abs. 1 tschIPRG 2012 muss auf die Zulässigkeit der Schiedsvereinbarung tschechisches Recht angewendet werden.[58] Was „Zulässigkeit“[59] bedeutet, ist auf den ersten Blick nicht klar. Wie es in einem tschechischen Beitrag zum internationalen Privatrecht zu lesen ist, *„wenn die lex arbitri (das Recht des Staates, in dem das Schiedsverfahren durchgeführt wird) tschechisches Recht ist, wird die Zulässigkeit der Schiedsvereinbarung nach den Bestimmungen des § 2 des [tschechischen Schiedsgesetzes*[60]*], die sich auf die objektive Schiedsfähigkeit beziehen, beurteilt [...]“.*[61] Daraus folgt, dass nach tschechischem Recht die Zulässigkeit der Schiedsvereinbarung mit der objektiven Schiedsfähigkeit des Rechtsstreits identisch ist. Daher ist diese Bestimmung für die Ermittlung des auf die Formgültigkeit der Schiedsvereinbarung anwendbaren Rechts nicht relevant.

Gemäß dem zweiten Satz des § 117 Abs. 1 tschIPRG 2012 *„sind die übrigen Bestandteile der Schiedsvereinbarung nach dem Recht des Staates zu beurteilen, in dem der Schiedsspruch erlassen wird“.* Genauso wie der Ausdruck „Zulässigkeit“, ist der Ausdruck „übrige Bestandteile“ (oder je nach Übersetzung „übrige Bedingungen“, „übrige Anforderungen“)[62] recht unklar. Einige Autoren sind der Ansicht, dass der Ausdruck „übrige Bestandteile“ die Aspekte der materiellen Gültigkeit der Schiedsvereinbarung umfasst,[63] aber es gibt auch Autoren, die den Ausdruck viel weiter auslegen – so weit, dass er sich beispielsweise auch auf die von staatlichen Gerichten gewährte Rechtshilfe bei der Ernennung von Schiedsrichtern oder bei der Beweiserhebung erstrecken könnte.[64] Es hat keine praktische Bedeutung, ob die Formgültigkeit im Ausdruck „übrige Bestandteile“ mit umfasst ist, da es für die Formgültigkeit der Schiedsvereinbarung in § 117 Abs. 2 tschIPRG 2012 sowieso

---

[58] S. Pauknerová/Pfeiffer, Private International Law in the Czech Republic, 2. Aufl. 2019, Part III Chapter 7 Rn. 474. Die englische Übersetzung des tschIPRG 2012 ist zugänglich unter http://obcanskyzakonik.justice.cz/images/pdf/Act-Governing-Private-International-Law.pdf (abgerufen 14.1.2024).

[59] Auf Tschechisch: *přípustnost.*

[60] Das (tschechische) Gesetz über das Schiedsverfahren und die Vollstreckung von Schiedssprüchen, verkündet unter Nr. 216/1994 Coll (tschSchG 1994).

[61] Pauknerová/Pfeiffer, Private International Law in the Czech Republic, 2. Aufl. 2019, Part III Chapter 7 Rn. 474; Belohlávek, Arbitration Law of Czech Republic: Practice and Procedure, 2013, S. 1734–1735. Belohláveks Aussagen über das auf die objektive Schiedsfähigkeit anwendbare Recht beziehen sich noch auf die alte Rechtslage, dh auf § 36 des tschSchG 1994. Bis zum 31.12.2013 enthielt diese Bestimmung die Regeln zur Ermittlung der auf die Schiedsvereinbarung anwendbaren Rechte mit einem Wortlaut ähnlich wie § 117 tschIPRG 2012.

[62] Auf Tschechisch: *náležitosti.* Für die unterschiedlichen Übersetzungen s. Pauknerová/Pfeiffer, Private International Law in the Czech Republic, 2. Aufl. 2019, Part III Chapter 7 Rn. 474 (auf Englisch: ‚*other constituents*‘); die veröffentlichte Übersetzung des tschechischen Justizministeriums, http://obcanskyzakonik.justice.cz/images/pdf/Act-Governing-Private-International-Law.pdf (abgerufen 14.1.2024) (auf Englisch: ‚*other requisites*‘); Belohlávek, Arbitration Law of Czech Republic: Practice and Procedure, 2013, S. 1735–1736 (auf Englisch: ‚*other requirements*‘).

[63] Briza, New Czech Act on Private International Law, veröffentlicht von Cuniberti am 17.4.2014 auf Conflict of Laws.net, http://conflictoflaws.net/2014/new-czech-act-on-private-international-law-2/ (abgerufen 14.1.2024).

[64] S. Belohlávek, Arbitration Law of Czech Republic: Practice and Procedure, 2013, S. 1736.

eine separate Kollisionsregel gibt. Gemäß dieser Bestimmung *„muss auf die Form der Schiedsvereinbarung das Recht, das auf die übrigen Bestandteile der Schiedsvereinbarung anwendbar ist, angewendet werden; [es ist jedoch ausreichend, wenn sie dem Recht des Ortes oder der Orte entspricht, an dem bzw. denen die Willenserklärung abgegeben wird]"*.

Aus § 117 Abs. 2 tschIPRG 2012 folgt eindeutig, dass § 52 Abs. 4 ungIPRG 2017 nicht vom tschIPRG 2012 inspiriert wurde, sondern – je nachdem, welche Auslegung korrekt ist – entweder vom schwIPRG oder vom plIPRG 2011. Wenn man die schweizerische und die polnische Regelung genauer betrachtet, wird man feststellen, dass sie an einem wichtigen Punkt übereinstimmen: das Recht des Schiedsortes ist nach beiden Regelungen eines der alternativ anwendbaren Rechte. Es ist kein Zufall: Der Schiedsort hat eine entscheidende Bedeutung für die gesamte Schiedsgerichtsbarkeit, und dies ist der Ort (das Rechtssystem), in dem (unter dem) die Schiedsvereinbarung seine primäre – positive – Zuständigkeitswirkung (Begründung der Zuständigkeit des Schiedsgerichts) entfalten muss. Da das ständige Element der *favor validitatis* Regel des ungIPRG 2017 nicht das Recht des Schiedsortes *(lex loci arbitri)*, sondern das Recht des Staates des angerufenen Gerichts *(lex fori)* ist, kommt das Recht des Schiedsortes nur dann als eines der auf die Formgültigkeit der Schiedsvereinbarung alternativ anwendbaren Rechte in Betracht, wenn § 52 Abs. 4 ungIPRG 2017 nach dem ersten – weiteren – Verständnis interpretiert wird oder wenn auf die Schiedsvereinbarung nach der Wahl der Parteien oder gemäß § 52 Abs. 3 ungIPRG 2017 tatsächlich die *lex loci arbitri* anzuwenden ist.

Aus all dem und aus dem Wortlaut des § 52 Abs. 4 ungIPRG 2017 geht insgesamt hervor, dass die Absicht des Gesetzgebers darin bestand, eine Regelung zu schaffen, nach der die auf die Formgültigkeit der Schiedsvereinbarung alternativ anwendbaren Rechte das Recht des Staates des angerufenen Gerichts und daneben jedes Recht umfassen, das gemäß § 52 Abs. 1–3 ungIPRG 2017 anwendbar sein kann: das von den Parteien gewählte Recht (sofern vorhanden), das auf das zugrunde liegende Rechtsverhältnis anwendbare Recht *und* – am wichtigsten – das Recht des Schiedsortes.[65] Ob das Recht des Schiedsortes auf die Formgültigkeit der Schiedsvereinbarung in jedem Fall alternativ anzuwenden ist oder nur dann, wenn die Parteien den Schiedsort bestimmt haben, ist nicht vollständig klar, aber aus den obigen Überlegungen ergibt sich, dass der Verweis auf das Recht des Schiedsortes weit ausgelegt werden sollte.

Hinsichtlich der neuen *favor validitatis* Regel ist schließlich hervorzuheben, dass § 52 Abs. 4 ungIPRG 2017 keine erschöpfende Regelung enthält, sondern eine spezielle Regelung ist, die durch die allgemeinen *favor validitatis* Regeln für die Formgültigkeit von Verträgen ergänzt wird. Diese Regeln befinden sich in § 54 Abs. 1, 2 ungIPRG 2017 und übernehmen die Bestimmungen des Art. 11 Rom I-VO.[66] Gemäß § 54 Abs. 1, 2 ungIPRG 2017 kann ein Vertrag aus formellen Gründen nicht als

---

[65] S. auch Nagy, Nemzetközi magánjog, 3. Aufl. 2017, S. 150, 329. Nach der Aufzählung aller Rechtsordnungen, die gemäß § 52 Abs. 1–3 ungIPRG 2017 auf die Schiedsvereinbarung anwendbar sein können, bezieht sich Nagy auf *„irgendeines der zuvor aufgeführten Rechte oder das Recht des angerufenen Gerichts"*.

[66] S. die Ministerialbegründung zu § 54 ungIPRG 2017; s. auch Nagy, Nemzetközi magánjog, 3. Aufl., 2017, S. 150, 331 und Vékás/Nemessányi/Osztovits, A nemzetközi magánjogról szóló törvény kommentárja/Szabados, 2020, S. 319 (§§ 50–56).

ungültig angesehen werden, wenn er den Formerfordernissen des *„nach diesem Gesetz [ungIPRG 2017] anwendbaren Rechts"* entspricht oder,

- falls sich die Vertragsparteien oder ihre Vertreter zum Zeitpunkt des Vertragsabschlusses im selben Staat aufhalten, den Formerfordernissen des Rechts dieses Staates, oder,
- falls sich die Vertragsparteien oder ihre Vertreter zum Zeitpunkt des Vertragsabschlusses in verschiedenen Staaten aufhalten, den Formerfordernissen des Rechts irgendeines dieser Staaten oder des Rechts jener Staaten, in denen eine der Parteien ihren gewöhnlichen Aufenthalt hat.

In Bezug auf die Formgültigkeit der Schiedsvereinbarung bedeutet *„das nach diesem Gesetz anwendbare Recht"* die gemäß § 52 Abs. 4 ungIPRG 2017 alternativ anwendbaren Rechte. Aufgrund der allgemeinen *favor validitatis* Regel müssen neben den in § 52 Abs. 1–4 ungIPRG 2017 festgelegten Rechten auch ein weiteres oder sogar mehrere weitere Rechte alternativ angewendet werden, je nachdem, ob sich die Parteien oder ihre Vertreter zum Zeitpunkt des Abschlusses der Schiedsvereinbarung im selben Staat oder in verschiedenen Staaten aufhalten und in letzterem Fall abhängig davon, wo sich der gewöhnliche Aufenthalt der Parteien befindet. Wie es in § 55 Abs. 3 ungIPRG 2017 festgehalten wird, ist dabei ausschließlich der gewöhnliche Aufenthalt der Parteien zum Zeitpunkt des Abschlusses der Schiedsvereinbarung relevant. Änderungen des gewöhnlichen Aufenthalts der Parteien nach diesem Zeitpunkt bleiben unberücksichtigt. Der Begriff des gewöhnlichen Aufenthalts wird in § 3 Abs. 3 lit. b ungIPRG 2017 für natürliche Personen (allgemein) definiert,[67] und in § 55 Abs. 1 ungIPRG 2017 für juristische Personen, andere Organisationen mit Rechtspersönlichkeit und natürliche Personen, die durch den Rechtsstreit in ihrer Geschäftstätigkeit betroffen sind.[68]

§ 55 Abs. 2 ungIPRG 2017 definiert den gewöhnlichen Aufenthalt für den Fall, dass der Vertrag im Rahmen des Betriebs einer Filiale, Handelsvertretung oder einer sonstigen Niederlassung geschlossen wurde oder wenn gemäß dem Vertrag die Erfüllung durch eine solche Filiale, Handelsvertretung oder sonstige Niederlassung erfolgen muss. In diesem Fall ist der Staat der Filiale, Handelsvertretung oder sonstigen Niederlassung als gewöhnlicher Aufenthaltsort zu betrachten. Laut der Ministerialbegründung umfasst § 55 Abs. 2 ungIPRG 2017 drei Fälle:

- die Filiale, Handelsvertretung oder sonstige Niederlassung schließt den Vertrag im eigenen Namen und zu eigenen Gunsten;[69]

---

[67] Der gewöhnliche Aufenthaltsort einer natürlichen Person ist im Allgemeinen der Ort, an dem nach allen Umständen des betroffenen Rechtsverhältnisses nachweislich der tatsächliche Lebensmittelpunkt der Person liegt. Bei dessen Bestimmung müssen auch solche Tatsachen beachtet werden, denen die Absicht der betroffenen Person entnommen werden kann.

[68] Der gewöhnliche Aufenthaltsort einer juristischen Person oder eines nicht rechtsfähigen Rechtssubjekts ist der Ort, an dem die zentrale Verwaltung stattfindet. Der gewöhnliche Aufenthaltsort einer natürlichen Person, die im Rahmen ihrer geschäftlichen Tätigkeit handelt, ist der Hauptort ihrer geschäftlichen Tätigkeit.

[69] Der erste Fall ist nur dann möglich, wenn die Niederlassung, Handelsvertretung oder sonstige Niederlassung nach ihrem eigenen Personalstatut über eine von der Muttergesellschaft getrennte Rechtspersönlichkeit verfügt.

- die Muttergesellschaft schließt den Vertrag, aber die Erfüllung muss durch die Filiale, Handelsvertretung oder sonstige Niederlassung erfolgen;
- die Filiale, Handelsvertretung oder sonstige Niederlassung schließt den Vertrag im Namen und zu Gunsten der Muttergesellschaft.

Die in den ersten und dritten Punkten genannten Fälle können auch im Falle einer Schiedsvereinbarung vorkommen, nicht nur im Falle des Hauptvertrags. Wenn die Filiale, Handelsvertretung oder sonstige Niederlassung den Hauptvertrag im eigenen Namen und zu eigenen Gunsten oder im Namen und zu Gunsten der Muttergesellschaft abschließt, gilt das gleiche auch für die Schiedsvereinbarung. Im ersten Fall wird die Filiale, Handelsvertretung oder sonstige Niederlassung als Vertragspartei der Schiedsvereinbarung betrachtet. Dagegen wird die Schiedsvereinbarung – genauso wie der Hauptvertrag – im zweiten Fall die Muttergesellschaft als Vertragspartei binden. Der im zweiten Punkt genannte Fall ist jedoch im Zusammenhang mit Schiedsvereinbarungen nicht relevant. In diesem Fall ist der Begriff „Vertrag" nach § 55 Abs. 2 ungIPRG 2017 als „Hauptvertrag" zu verstehen, selbst wenn die Formgültigkeit der Schiedsvereinbarung angefochten wird. Wenn der Hauptvertrag durch die Muttergesellschaft abgeschlossen wurde, aber die Erfüllung durch die Filiale, Handelsvertretung oder sonstige Niederlassung erfolgen muss, muss der Staat der Filiale, Handelsvertretung oder sonstigen Niederlassung als gewöhnlicher Aufenthalt der betroffenen Partei, dh der Muttergesellschaft angesehen werden, und zwar auch im Zusammenhang mit der Schiedsvereinbarung.

Wie oben klargestellt, wurde die spezielle *favor validitatis* Regelung in § 52 Abs. 4 ungIPRG 2017 offensichtlich nicht von der tschechischen Regelung inspiriert. Jedoch folgt die allgemeine *favor validitatis* Regelung in Bezug auf die Formgültigkeit von Verträgen teilweise dem gleichen Prinzip wie § 117 Abs. 2 tschIPRG in Bezug auf die Formgültigkeit von Schiedsvereinbarungen: Ein Vertrag kann nicht aus formellen Gründen als ungültig betrachtet werden, wenn er den Formerfordernissen des Rechts des Ortes bzw. der Orte entspricht, an dem bzw. an denen die Parteien ihren Willen zum Vertragsabschluss ausgedrückt haben.

IV. Fazit

Mit der Einführung der neuen Kollisionsregelung für Schiedsvereinbarungen hat der ungarische Gesetzgeber im Vergleich zur früheren Regelung einen großen Fortschritt gemacht. Eine klare positive Änderung besteht darin, dass im ungarischen internationalen Privatrecht – neben den zuvor existierenden, zerstreuten und in der neuen Regelung weiterhin vorhandenen speziellen Kollisionsregeln – eine solche Kollisionsregelung eingeführt wurde, die nach der Absicht des Gesetzgebers durch die ungarischen Gerichte in allen Phasen der schiedsrichterlichen Streitbeilegung global angewendet werden soll und speziell auf Schiedsvereinbarungen zugeschnitten ist. Damit hat der Gesetzgeber die Lücken in der früheren Regelung erheblich gefüllt. Für Schiedsrichter gibt es jedoch weiterhin keine expliziten Kollisionsnormen zur Ermittlung der auf die Schiedsvereinbarung anwendbaren Rechte. Dies bedeutet, dass die Einführung der neuen Regelung für Schiedsgerichte in Bezug auf die Bestimmung der auf die Schiedsvereinbarung anwendbaren Rechte keine wesentlichen Änderungen mit sich gebracht hat – lediglich hat sich die Anzahl der analog anwendbaren Regeln erweitert.

Die neue Regelung hat jedoch auch neue Probleme – Fragen – aufgeworfen. Eine der bedeutendsten davon ist, dass der Gesetzgeber neben der Kollisionsregelung in § 52 ungIPRG 2017 auch die früheren, zerstreuten speziellen Kollisionsregeln beibehalten hat, einschließlich insbesondere der Kollisionsnorm in § 47 Abs. 2 lit. a sublit. aa ungSchG 2017, die im Aufhebungsverfahren auf die Gültigkeit der Schiedsvereinbarung anwendbar ist. Die Parallelität der beiden Regelungen wäre unproblematisch, wenn die Regeln miteinander vereinbar wären. Leider ist dies jedoch nicht der Fall: § 52 ungIPRG 2017 und § 47 ungSchG 2017 verwenden weitgehend unterschiedliche Anknüpfungen. Dies kann dazu führen, dass ein ungarisches Gericht, das mit einer Klage auf die Aufhebung des Schiedsspruchs angerufen wurde, die Gültigkeit der Schiedsvereinbarung nach einem anderen Recht prüft als das ungarische Gericht, das in einer anderen Phase der schiedsrichterlichen Streitbeilegung tätig ist, zB das Gericht, vor dem eine der Parteien hinsichtlich des Streitgegenstandes trotz der Schiedsvereinbarung Klage erhebt. Die Anwendung unterschiedlicher Rechte kann zu unterschiedlichen Schlussfolgerungen zu derselben Rechtsfrage – der Gültigkeit der Schiedsvereinbarung – führen.

Das Risiko, dass staatliche Gerichte in Ungarn bezüglich der Gültigkeit der Schiedsvereinbarung unterschiedliche Rechte anwenden und daher zu unterschiedlichen Schlussfolgerungen kommen, wird durch die Tatsache, dass § 52 ungIPRG 2017 mit der Kollisionsregelung des New Yorker Übereinkommens und des Genfer Übereinkommens nicht in Einklang steht, weiter erhöht. Der Hauptgrund dafür ist, dass § 52 ungIPRG 2017 mangels einer Rechtswahl der Parteien für die Schiedsvereinbarung die Anwendung des auf das zugrunde liegende Rechtsverhältnis ohne Rechtswahl anzuwendenden Rechts vorsieht, und aus der Struktur der Regelung folgt, dass diesem Recht gegenüber dem Recht des Schiedsortes Vorrang eingeräumt wird.

Die oben genannten Probleme – ebenso wie die mit der Anwendung der *favor validitatis* Regelung verbundenen Unsicherheiten und die anderen in diesem Beitrag vorgestellten Unsicherheiten – müssen von der gerichtlichen und schiedsrichterlichen Praxis bewältigt werden. Der erste Schritt dabei wird die Wahrnehmung der Notwendigkeit einer kollisionsrechtlichen Prüfung sein: die Wahrnehmung – sowohl von Richtern und Schiedsrichtern als auch von den Parteien –, dass in einem in Ungarn durchzuführenden Gerichtsverfahren oder Schiedsverfahren auf die verschiedenen Aspekte der Durchsetzbarkeit einer Schiedsvereinbarung nicht notwendigerweise ungarisches Recht anzuwenden ist. Diese Wahrnehmung sollte dadurch, dass das ungIPRG 2017 ausdrückliche Kollisionsregeln für Schiedsvereinbarungen enthält, gefördert werden. Angesichts der Tatsache, dass zu § 52 ungIPRG 2017 mehr als 5 Jahren nach seinem Inkrafttreten immer noch keine Rechtsprechung zu finden ist, besteht allerdings Zweifel daran, ob § 52 ungIPRG 2017 diese „didaktische“ Funktion tatsächlich erfüllt hat.

BERNHARD ULRICI

Zustellung über den Europäischen elektronischen Zugangspunkt

I. Einleitung

Dem *Jubilar* verdankt der *Gratulant,* das Europäische Zivilverfahrensrecht zu seinen Forschungsgebieten zu zählen. Dafür blieb rückblickend zwar noch ohne nachhaltige Auswirkungen der Besuch der einschlägigen Vorlesung des Jubilars[1] – die Dogmatik des nationalen Rechts band zu Studienzeiten die Aufmerksamkeit des Gratulanten. Rund eine Dekade später sorgte dann aber ein Zufall dafür, dass der Jubilar als Herausgeber des *Münchener Kommentars zur Zivilprozessordnung* dem Gratulanten die Erläuterung von Teilen des FamFG[2] anvertraute. Dies wiederum zog nach sich, dass der Jubilar etwas später auch noch das Wagnis einging, dem in internationalrechtlichen Fragestellungen unbeleckten Gratulanten die Erläuterung der EG-MahnVO zu übertragen. Aus diesem Anstoß entwickelte sich in der Folge eine ausweitende Befassung des Gratulanten mit dem Europäischen Zivilverfahrensrecht. Dementsprechend hat der Gratulant zuletzt mit Freude auch der Bitte des Jubilars entsprochen und in dem von diesem herausgegebenen Großkommentar zum *Europäischen Zivilprozess- und Kollisionsrecht*[3] die reformierte EU-ZustVO erläutert. Hieran knüpft die vorliegende, dem als großen Kenner des Europäischen Zustellungsrechts ausgewiesenen Jubilar gewidmete Untersuchung an. Sie ist gleichsam ein zeitnaher Nachtrag zur entstandenen Kommentierung des Gratulanten: Durch die Verordnung über die Digitalisierung der justiziellen Zusammenarbeit und des Zugangs zur Justiz in grenzüberschreitenden Zivil-, Handels- und Strafsachen und zur Änderung bestimmter Rechtsakte im Bereich der justiziellen Zusammenarbeit vom 13.12.2023 (EU-JuDigiVO)[4] wird der Katalog der von der EU-ZustVO vorgesehenen Zustellungsarten um die Elektronische Zustellung über den Europäischen elektronischen Zugangspunkt erweitert. Diese neue Zustellungsart wird nach einem einordnenden Überblick über die EU-JuDigiVO (→ II.) und die durch sie bewirkten Änderungen der EU-ZustVO (→ III.) näher vorgestellt (→ IV.).

---

[1] Vorlesung Internationales Zivilverfahrensrecht (Universität Leipzig, Sommersemester 1998).

[2] Sachlich einschlägig hat der Gratulant besucht die Vorlesung des Jubilars zur Freiwilligen Gerichtsbarkeit (Universität Leipzig, Sommersemester 1998).

[3] Rauscher, Europäisches Zivilprozess- und Kollisionsrecht – EuZPR/EuIPR, 5. Aufl. 2020ff. (ursprünglich unter dem Titel Europäisches Zivilprozeßrecht erschienen in 1. Aufl. 2003).

[4] VO (EU) 2023/2844 (ABl. 2023 L 2844); zu den Verordnungszielen vgl. ErwGr. 4 EU-JuDigiVO und auch COM(2021) 759 final, 2f.

II. Digitalisierung der justiziellen Zusammenarbeit und des Zugangs zur Justiz

1. Überblick

Gegenstand der EU-JuDigiVO ist die Digitalisierung von Verfahren mit grenzüberschreitenden[5] Bezügen. Sie schafft einen einheitlichen Rahmen für die Nutzung elektronischer Kommunikation zwischen den zuständigen Behörden in Verfahren der justiziellen Zusammenarbeit in Zivil-, Handels- und Strafsachen sowie für die Nutzung der elektronischen Kommunikation zwischen natürlichen oder juristischen Personen und den zuständigen Behörden in Gerichtsverfahren in Zivil- und Handelssachen. Außerdem wird der Einsatz von Videokonferenz- und anderen Fernkommunikationstechnologien für andere Zwecke als eine Beweisaufnahme nach der EU-BewVO geregelt. Behandlung findet in ihr mithin gleichermaßen die elektronische Kommunikation als Substitut zur physischen schriftlichen[6] Kommunikation (unter Abwesenden) wie auch die elektronische Kommunikation als Substitut zur physischen Präsenz (Anwesenheit). Daneben enthält die EU-JuDigiVO als Ergänzung zur Digitalisierung der schriftlichen Kommunikation Vorschriften zu elektronischen Echtheitszeichen und zu den Rechtswirkungen elektronischer Schriftstücke. Zur Erleichterung des Zugangs zur Justiz befasst sie sich überdies mit der verwandten Frage der elektronischen Zahlung von in den in ihrem Anhang I genannten Verfahren in Zivil- und Handelssachen[7] zu zahlenden Gebühren.

2. Kommunikation zwischen Behörden

In ihrem auf Kapitel I (Allgemeine Bestimmungen: Gegenstand und Anwendungsbereich sowie Begriffsbestimmungen) folgenden Kapitel II (= Art. 3) regelt die EU-JuDigiVO die Kommunikation (unter Abwesenden) zwischen Behörden (verschiedener Mitgliedstaaten bzw. solchen und Stellen der EU) für die in den beiden Anhängen zur Verordnung[8] genannten europäischen Rechtsakte.[9] Als Vorbild dienen dabei die von der EU-JuDigiVO nicht berührten[10] Regelungen der reformierten Verordnungen zur justiziellen Rechtshilfe (Art. 5 EU-ZustVO und Art. 7 EU-BewVO).[11] Der dortige Ansatz wird auf die in den Anhängen der EU-JuDigiVO genannten europäischen Rechtsakte und die nach diesen zwischen Behörden erforderliche Kommunikation ausgedehnt:[12] Im Grundsatz hat (unter Abwesenden) die

[5] Vgl. amtl. Titel der VO, ErwGr. 1, 13 S. 1, 15, 41 S. 1 2. Fall EU-JuDigiVO, Art. 3 Abs. 1 EU-JuDigiVO: „Behörden verschiedener Mitgliedstaaten", Art. 5 Abs. 1 EU-JuDigiVO: „in einem anderen Mitgliedstaat aufhält".

[6] Vgl. auch ErwGr. 16 EU-JuDigiVO.

[7] Vgl. auch Art. 2 Nr. 5 EU-JuDigiVO.

[8] Vgl. auch ErwGr. 13 S. 2 EU-JuDigiVO.

[9] Nach Art. 3 Abs. 6, 7 EU-JuDigiVO können die geschaffenen Kommunikationswege auch für die ohne Überschreitung einer Kompetenzgrenze („intern") erfolgende Kommunikation genutzt werden.

[10] Vgl. ErwGr. 17 S. 1, 2 EU-JuDigiVO.

[11] COM(2021) 759 final, 3f.

[12] Vgl. COM(2021) 759 final, 3f., 12.

Kommunikation zwischen Behörden (verschiedener Mitgliedstaaten) elektronisch über ein dezentrales IT-System zu erfolgen.[13] Ausnahmsweise können in den Fällen der Unmöglichkeit[14] und der Unangemessenheit[15] andere Kommunikationswege genutzt werden (Art. 3 Abs. 2, 3 EU-JuDigiVO). Bei der Übermittlung lediglich von Formblättern nach den in den Anhängen zur EU-JuDigiVO genannten europäischen Rechtsakten (zB Art. 23 Abs. 3 EU-KPfVO) scheidet eine Ausnahme wegen Unangemessenheit allerdings aus (Art. 3 Abs. 4 EU-JuDigiVO).[16]

3. Kommunikation mit Behörden

Gegenstand von Kapitel III (= Art. 4) EU-JuDigiVO ist die Kommunikation (unter Abwesenden) zwischen natürlichen oder juristischen Personen (zB Antragsteller) einerseits und den zuständigen Behörden (insbes. Gerichte) andererseits:

Dazu soll auf dem Europäischen Justizportal ein Europäischer elektronischer Zugangspunkt eingerichtet werden.[17] Bei diesem handelt es sich um eine durch die Kommission bereitzustellende[18] webbasierte Anwendung,[19] welche natürlichen und juristischen Personen bzw. ihren Vertretern nach einer Identifizierung[20] ermöglicht, Anträge zu stellen (zB nach Art. 7 EG-MahnVO), Ersuchen einzureichen, verfahrensrelevante Informationen zu übermitteln (zB Einspruch nach Art. 16 EG-MahnVO) und zu empfangen (zB Aufforderung nach Art. 9 EG-MahnVO), mit den zuständigen Behörden zu kommunizieren (zB Art. 5 Abs. 3 EG-BagatellVO) oder gerichtliche oder außergerichtliche Schriftstücke zugestellt zu bekommen (Art. 4 Abs. 4 UAbs. 1 S. 2, 3 EU-JuDigiVO). Außerdem soll über das Recht auf Prozesskostenhilfe informiert werden.[21]

Genutzt werden kann der Europäische elektronische Zugangspunkt für die Kommunikation in den gesamten (Erkenntnis-)Verfahren nach EG-BagatellVO, EG-MahnVO und EU-KPfVO, im (Vollstreckbarerklärungs-)Verfahren nach der EG-VollstrTitelVO, in den Verfahren zur Anerkennung, Vollstreckbarerklärung bzw. Versagung sowie im Zusammenhang mit der Ausstellung, Berichtigung bzw. dem Widerruf von Auszügen, Zeugnissen bzw. Bescheinigungen jeweils nach Brüssel Ia-VO, Brüssel IIb-VO, EU-ErbVO, EU-EheGüterVO, EU-LP-GüterVO, EU-SchutzMVO und EG-UntVO, für die Forderungsanmeldung durch einen ausländischen Gläubiger gemäß Art. 53 EU-InsVO sowie für die Kommunikation mit den Zentralen Behörden nach der Brüssel IIb-VO und der EG-UntVO bzw. mit den zuständigen Behörden nach Kapitel IV der Prozesskostenhilfe-RL. Der betreffende Kommunikationsvorgang muss nicht (unmittelbar) durch den jeweiligen

---

[13] Vgl. ErwGr. 25 S. 1, Art. 3 Abs. 1 EU-JuDigiVO.
[14] Vgl. dazu ErwGr. 24 EU-JuDigiVO.
[15] Vgl. dazu ErwGr. 25 EU-JuDigiVO.
[16] Vgl. ErwGr. 25 UAbs. 2 S. 3 EU-JuDigiVO.
[17] Vgl. Art. 4 Abs. 1 EU-JuDigiVO.
[18] Vgl. Art. 4 Abs. 3 S. 1 EU-JuDigiVO: entwickeln, verwalten, zugänglich machen, warten und sichern.
[19] Vgl. ErwGr. 10 S. 2, 27 S. 2, Art. 2 Nr. 4 EU-JuDigiVO: Portal.
[20] Vgl. ErwGr. 19 S. 1 aE, Art. 4 Abs. 7, Art. 7 Abs. 3 EU-JuDigiVO.
[21] Vgl. auch ErwGr. 28 EU-JuDigiVO.

Unionsrechtsakt vorgegeben sein. Erfasst ist ebenso ein Kommunikationsvorgang, welcher durch nationale Durchführungsvorschriften vorgegeben ist oder auch nur rein tatsächlich zum Zweck der Förderung eines erfassten Verfahrens erfolgt.

In diesem Umfang wird der Kommunikationsweg über den Europäischen elektronischen Zugangspunkt mit bindender Wirkung für die zuständigen Behörden eröffnet, sie haben ihn tatsächlich einzurichten und ihnen gehen auf diesem Weg übermittelte Erklärungen zu (Art. 4 Abs. 5 EU-JuDigiVO). Natürliche oder juristische Personen sowie ihre Vertreter sind dagegen nicht verpflichtet, diesen Kommunikationsweg zu eröffnen oder zu nutzen (vgl. auch ErwGr. 29 EU-JuDigiVO).[22] Willigen sie allerdings in die Nutzung des Europäischen elektronischen Zugangspunkts zuvor ausdrücklich ein, sollen die zuständigen Behörden mit ihnen über diesen Weg kommunizieren und können natürlichen und juristischen Personen bzw. ihren Vertretern Schriftstücke über diesen Weg zugestellt werden (Art. 4 Abs. 6 EU-JuDigiVO).

4. *Sonstiges*

Kapitel IV EU-JuDigiVO befasst sich mit der Verhandlung oder Anhörung mittels Videokonferenz- oder anderen Fernkommunikationstechnologien (Herstellung virtueller Präsenz) in Zivil- und Handelssachen (Art. 5 EU-JuDigiVO), soweit nicht Rechtsakte des europäischen Zivilverfahrensrechts (zB Art. 20 EU-BewVO) dies gesondert regeln,[23] sowie in Strafsachen (Art. 6 EU-JuDigiVO).

Kapitel V widmet sich als Ergänzung[24] zu Kapitel II, III den ihre physischen Pendants bei der elektronischen Kommunikation vertretenden elektronischen Signaturen und Siegeln (Art. 7 EU-JuDigiVO) sowie in Anlehnung an Art. 6 EU-ZustVO,[25] Art. 8 EU-BewVO[26] den Rechtswirkungen elektronischer Dokumente (Art. 8 EU-JuDigiVO). Außerdem wird behandelt die elektronische Zahlung von Gebühren (Art. 9 EU-JuDigiVO).

Kapitel VI ermächtigt die Kommission zum Erlass von Durchführungsvorschriften (Art. 10 EU-JuDigiVO) im Prüfverfahren nach der Komitologie-VO (Art. 15 EU-JuDigiVO), befasst sich mit der Schulung der Angehörigen der Rechtsberufe und der zuständigen Behörden (Art. 11 EU-JuDigiVO), klärt die Verantwortung und die Kostentragung für die Schaffung einer Referenzimplementierungssoftware, die Errichtung des dezentralen IT-Systems und die Einrichtung eines Europäischen elektronischen Zugangspunkts (Art. 12, 13 EU-JuDigiVO), widmet sich dem Datenschutz (Art. 14 EU-JuDigiVO), verpflichtet die Kommission zur Evaluation (Art. 16 EU-JuDigiVO) und legt den Mitgliedstaaten eine Verpflichtung auf zur Bereitstellung von den Zugang zur Justiz unterstützenden Informationen (Art. 17 EU-JuDigiVO).

---

[22] COM(2021) 759 final, 8, 12; Europäischer Wirtschafts- und Sozialausschuss (ABl. 2022 C 323/77 zu Ziff. 2.1.5, zu Ziff. 2.6.2).

[23] Vgl. ErwGr. 41 S. 1 EU-JuDigiVO.

[24] Vgl. auch ErwGr. 49 S. 1, Art. 7 Abs. 2, 3 EU-JuDigiVO.

[25] Vgl. dazu Rauscher, EuZPR/EuIPR/Ulrici, 5. Aufl. 2024, EU-ZustVO 2020 Art. 6 Rn. 7 ff.

[26] Vgl. dazu Rauscher, EuZPR/EuIPR/von Hein, 5. Aufl. 2022, EU-BewVO Art. 8 Rn. 1 ff.

Kapitel VII und VIII sehen eine Reihe von (Folge-)Änderungen in den von der Anwendung der Verordnung betroffenen Rechtsakten der justiziellen Zusammenarbeit in Zivil- und Handelssachen bzw. Strafsachen vor.[27] Dies umfasst auch den die nachstehend näher zu behandelnden Änderungen der EU-ZustVO bringenden Art. 24 EU-JuDigiVO.

Kapitel IX regelt schließlich das Inkrafttreten und den zeitlichen Anwendungsbereich.

III. Änderungen der Zustellungsverordnung

Änderungen der EU-ZustVO waren im Kommissionsentwurf für die EU-JuDigiVO[28] ebenso wie im dazu erstatteten Bericht des Europäischen Parlaments[29] noch nicht vorgesehen.[30] Sie gehen vielmehr zurück auf die zwischen Kommission, Rat und Parlament geführten Triloggespräche,[31] in welche sie durch den Rat eingebracht wurden.[32] In ihrem Zentrum steht die Ergänzung der EU-ZustVO um einen Art. 19a EU-ZustVO nF, welcher als neue Zustellungsart die Elektronische Zustellung über den Europäischen elektronischen Zugangspunkt (→ IV.) vorsieht.

Begleitend zur Einführung der neuen Zustellungsart wird Art. 12 Abs. 7 EU-ZustVO geändert. Bereits nach dem unveränderten Art. 12 Abs. 6 EU-ZustVO gilt Art. 12 Abs. 1–5 EU-ZustVO auch für die in Kapitel II, Abschnitt 2 EU-ZustVO eingestellte neue Zustellungsart. Als Ergänzung dazu werden durch Änderung von Art. 12 Abs. 7 EU-ZustVO und Nennung von Art. 19a EU-ZustVO nF neben Art. 18, 19, 20 EU-ZustVO die Verantwortlichkeit für die Belehrung des Zustellungsadressaten über sein Annahmeverweigerungsrecht sowie der Adressat der Annahmeverweigerungserklärung geklärt. Geändert wird überdies Art. 13 Abs. 3 EU-ZustVO. Die dort in Ansehung der Kollisionsnorm[33] zur Bestimmung des Zustelldatums angeordnete Gleichstellung der in Kapitel II, Abschnitt 2 EU-ZustVO geregelten anderen Übermittlungs- und Zustellwege mit der Zustellung auf dem einfachen Rechtshilfeweg wird beschränkt und Art. 19a EU-ZustVO nF aus ihr ausgenommen. Dass die Kollisionsnorm zur Bestimmung des Zustelldatums auf die neue Zustellungsart keine Anwendung finden soll, ist vor dem Hintergrund zu sehen, dass Art. 19a Abs. 2 EU-ZustVO nF eine verordnungsautonome Anordnung für die Bestimmung des Zustelldatums enthält.

---

[27] COM(2021) 759 final, 18; ErwGr. 51 EU-JuDigiVO.

[28] COM(2021) 759 final, 36ff.

[29] Vgl. insbes. Radev/Kaljurand, Rechtsausschuss & Ausschuss für bürgerliche Freiheiten, Justiz und Inneres, Europäisches Parlament, A9–0062/2023, 36f. (zu Art. 4).

[30] Es war explizit angestrebt, dass EU-BewVO und EU-ZustVO von der EU-JuDigiVO nicht betroffen werden, vgl. auch ErwGr. 9 Komm-E (COM(2021) 759 final, 21) vs. ErwGr. 17 EU-JuDigiVO.

[31] Vgl. Europäisches Parlament, Provisional agreement resulting from interinstitutional negotiations, PE752.630v01–00, 70f.; Rat der Europäischen Union, Dokument 15899/23, 12 (Änderung in ErwGr. 17), 86f. (Art. 24 eingefügt); Rat der Europäischen Union, Dokument 11779/2/23 REV 2, 8 (Änderung in ErwGr. 9), 70f. (Art. 22c eingefügt).

[32] Vgl. Rat der Europäischen Union, Dokument 8090/23, 22, 281ff. (4-column table).

[33] Münchener Kommentar zur ZPO/Rauscher, 6. Aufl. 2022, EG-ZustellVO Art. 9 Rn. 1.

Abgerundet werden die Änderungen durch die Ergänzung um Art. 37 Abs. 3 EU-ZustVO nF, welche eine Sonderregelung für den zeitlichen Anwendungsbereich der neuen Zustellungsart bringt. Dieser weicht sowohl von dem der übrigen Regelungen der EU-ZustVO als auch um ein Jahr von dem des Art. 4 EU-JuDigiVO ab. Möglich werden Zustellungen über den Europäischen elektronischen Zugangspunkt erst ab dem ersten Tag des Monats sein, der auf den Zeitraum von drei Jahren nach dem Inkrafttreten der auf Grundlage von Art. 10 Abs. 3 EU-JuDigiVO zu den einzelnen in Anhang I der EU-JuDigiVO genannten europäischen Rechtsakte (zB Brüssel Ia-VO, EG-MahnVO, EG-VollstrTitelVO) erlassenen Durchführungsrechtsakte folgt. Da maßgeblich das Inkrafttreten des für den jeweiligen europäischen Rechtsakt, für welchen der Europäische elektronische Zugangspunkt genutzt werden kann, erlassenen Durchführungsrechtsakts ist, wird eine Zustellung über den Europäischen elektronischen Zugangspunkt voraussichtlich nicht in allen erfassten Verfahren ab dem gleichen Zeitpunkt möglich sein. Überschreitet die Kommission die ihr zum Erlass dieser Durchführungsrechtsakte eingeräumten Zeiträume[34] nicht und wird das Inkrafttreten der Durchführungsrechtsakte in diesen auch nicht übermäßig aufgeschoben, werden Zustellungen nach Art. 19a EU-ZustVO nF spätestens ab dem Jahr 2029, 2030, 2031 bzw. 2032 möglich sein. Der so gefasste zeitliche Anwendungsbereich ist allerdings zusätzlich beschränkt durch den zeitlichen Anwendungsbereich von Art. 4 EU-JuDigiVO, weil die Zustellung über den Europäischen elektronischen Zugangspunkt nur erfolgen kann, soweit dieser Zugangspunkt rechtlich (und tatsächlich) auch zur Verfügung steht. Daher kommt eine nach Maßgabe von Art. 37 Abs. 3 EU-ZustVO nF mögliche Zustellung nur in Verfahren in Betracht, welche nicht früher als ein Jahr vor dem in Art. 37 Abs. 3 EU-ZustVO nF genannten Zeitpunkt eingeleitet wurden (Art. 26 Abs. 4 EU-JuDigiVO). In den Blick zu nehmen ist dabei jeweils die Einleitung desjenigen Verfahrens, für welches Art. 4 EU-JuDigiVO die Nutzung des Europäischen elektronischen Zugangspunkts eröffnet (→ II. 3.), dh zB in Bezug auf Art. 43 Abs. 1 S. 1 Brüssel Ia-VO die Einleitung des Bescheinigungsverfahrens nach Art. 53 Brüssel Ia-VO und nicht des vorausgehenden (nationalen) Erkenntnisverfahrens.

IV. Neue Zustellungsart

1. Allgemeines

a) Systematische Einordnung

Die neue Zustellungsart wurde als Art. 19a EU-ZustVO nF eingegliedert in Abschnitt 2 (Art. 16–20 EU-ZustVO) des Kapitels II über gerichtliche Schriftstücke, welcher die Übermittlung bzw. Zustellung eines gerichtlichen Schriftstücks zum Zweck der grenzüberschreitenden Zustellung auf anderen Wegen als der einfachen Rechtshilfe (Kapitel II, Abschnitt 1) behandelt. Wie Art. 17, 18 und 19 EU-

[34] Zwei, drei, vier bzw. fünf Jahre ab Inkrafttreten der EU-JuDigiVO am 16.1.2024.

ZustVO gehört die Neuregelung zu den Vorschriften über direkte,[35] dh nicht unter Einbindung einer Empfangsstelle und auch nicht durch Stellen des Empfangsmitgliedstaats ausgeführte Zustellungen. Gedacht ist sie insbes. als Ergänzung zu Art. 19 EU-ZustVO, der wiederum eine digitale Entsprechung zur in Art. 18 EU-ZustVO geregelten Postdirektzustellung enthält. Anders als die Vorschriften über die Rechtshilfe, zu denen auch Art. 16 EU-ZustVO gehört, regelt Art. 19a EU-ZustVO nF als Form der direkten Zustellung nicht nur die Übermittlung eines zuzustellenden Schriftstücks in einen anderen Mitgliedstaat, um dort eine Zustellung zu ermöglichen. Vielmehr ist vorgesehen eine grenzüberschreitende Bewirkung der Zustellung unmittelbar durch Stellen des Ursprungsmitgliedstaats (Unterschied auch zu Art. 20 EU-ZustVO), weil der als Teil des Europäischen Justizportals eingerichtete Europäische elektronische Zugangspunkt Teil einer anationalen[36] öffentlichen Infrastruktur ist.

Wie durch Art. 19 EU-ZustVO wird auch durch Art. 19a EU-ZustVO nF die Souveränität der Mitgliedstaaten als Empfangsmitgliedstaat im Verhältnis zu anderen Mitgliedstaaten dahin eingeschränkt,[37] dass aus einem Mitgliedstaat (Ursprungsmitgliedstaat) heraus Zustellungen an Personen mit einer bekannten Zustelladresse in einem anderen Mitgliedstaat bewirkt werden können. Dieser Rücknahme des Souveränitätsanspruchs im Verhältnis zwischen den Mitgliedstaaten liegt zu Grunde, dass Zustellungen auf elektronischem Weg im Kern der Information dienen und als solche nicht mit der Ausübung von Zwang ieS verbunden sind. Dies gilt insbes., wenn der Zustellungsempfänger, wie von Art. 19a Abs. 1 EU-ZustVO nF vorausgesetzt (→ IV. 2. d)), der Zustellung vorab zugestimmt hat und die Zustellung erst bewirkt ist, wenn im Nachgang zudem der Empfang des zuzustellenden Schriftstücks bestätigt wurde. Hinzu kommt, dass sich das für die Nutzung des Europäischen elektronischen Zugangspunkts erforderliche Nutzerkonto, über welches Schriftstücke empfangen werden, nicht sinnhaft einem Hoheitsgebiet zuordnen lässt und sich im Falle seiner Nutzung die Ausübung von Staatsgewalt auf einem fremden Staatsgebiet nicht manifestiert. Zustellungen über den Europäischen elektronischen Zugangspunkt tangieren den Souveränitätsanspruch des Empfangsmitgliedstaats mithin nur sehr eingeschränkt, was unter Berücksichtigung des wechselseitigen Vertrauens der Mitgliedstaaten nicht rechtfertigt, dass ein Mitgliedstaat umfassend auf seiner Souveränität beharrt, welche er tatsächlich gar nicht zu verteidigen vermag.

Vergleichbar wie Art. 18 EU-ZustVO[38] für die Postdirekzustellung enthält auch Art. 19a EU-ZustVO nF (für seinen auf bestimmte Verfahren beschränkten Anwendungsbereich) eine verordnungsautonome Zulassung und regelt für die neue Zustellungsart verordnungsautonom auch ihre Ausführung sowie das Zustelldatum.

---

[35] Vgl. auch ErwGr. 17 S. 3 EU-JuDigiVO: „direkt an eine Person".

[36] Vgl. auch ErwGr. 27 S. 1 EU-JuDigiVO („auf Unionsebene"), Art. 14 Abs. 2 EU-JuDigiVO.

[37] Der Rechtshilfeweg folgt dagegen einem abweichenden Ansatz, vgl. dazu Rauscher, EuZPR/EuIPR/Ulrici, 5. Aufl. 2024, EU-ZustVO 2020 Einl. Rn. 58.

[38] Vgl. dazu Münchener Kommentar zur ZPO/Rauscher, 6. Aufl. 2022, EG-ZustellVO Art. 14 Rn. 13.

Hierdurch unterscheidet sich Art. 19a EU-ZustVO nF insbes. auch von Art. 19 EU-ZustVO,[39] welcher die elektronische Zustellung nicht generell, sondern nur nach Maßgabe des Rechts des Ursprungsmitgliedstaats zulässt und sich auf die Vorgabe von einzuhaltenden Mindestbedingungen beschränkt, welche durch den Empfangsmitgliedstaat ggf. angehoben werden können. Nach Art. 19a EU-ZustVO nF ist die elektronische Zustellung über den Europäischen elektronischen Zugangspunkt ohne Rücksicht auf das Recht des Ursprungsmitgliedstaats eröffnet und kann ein Empfangsmitgliedstaat keine zusätzlichen Beschränkungen vorsehen.

b) Anwendungsbereich

Der Anwendungsbereich von Art. 19a EU-ZustVO nF ist verordnungsautonom und anders als der Anwendungsbereich des verwandten Art. 19 EU-ZustVO ohne Verweis auf das Recht der Mitgliedstaaten bestimmt. Vorgesehen ist, dass eine Zustellung über den Europäischen elektronischen Zugangspunkt eröffnet ist, soweit keine abschließenden Sondervorschriften (zB Art. 8 Abs. 2 EU-SchutzMVO, Art. 28 EU-KPfVO) bestehen und sich der Anwendungsbereich der EU-ZustVO mit dem Anwendungsbereich des Europäischen elektronischen Zugangspunkts überschneidet. Es müssen beide Anwendungsbereiche kumulativ eröffnet sein. Dies ergibt sich daraus, dass die Zustellung über den Europäischen elektronischen Zugangspunkt eine Zustellung nach der EU-ZustVO ist und zugleich unter Nutzung des Europäischen elektronischen Zugangspunkts erfolgt, weshalb dessen Nutzung rechtlich (und tatsächlich) möglich sein muss, was seine Bestätigung in der in Art. 37 Abs. 3 EU-ZustVO nF erfolgten Anknüpfung an die einzelnen die Nutzung des Europäischen elektronischen Zugangspunkts betreffenden Durchführungsrechtsakte findet.

Die Eröffnung des Anwendungsbereichs der EU-ZustVO bestimmt sich nach Art. 1 EU-ZustVO[40] und setzt insbes. eine grenzüberschreitende Zustellung zwischen Mitgliedstaaten voraus.[41] Die Nutzungsmöglichkeit des Europäischen elektronischen Zugangspunkts bestimmt sich nach Art. 4 EU-JuDigiVO. Sie ist insbes. auf die in Art. 4 Abs. 2 EU-JuDigiVO genannten „Verfahren, die in den Anwendungsbereich des Unionsrechts im Bereich Zivil- und Handelssachen fallen“,[42] beschränkt. Anders als die sonstigen Zustellungsarten nach der EU-ZustVO steht die Zustellung über den Europäischen elektronischen Zugangspunkt nicht für nationale Verfahren zu Verfügung, auch wenn sich in diesen das Bedürfnis für eine grenzüberschreitende Zustellung ergibt (eine Öffnungsklausel vergleichbar zu Art. 3 Abs. 6 EU-JuDigiVO enthält Art. 4 EU-JuDigiVO nicht). Vielmehr ist sie nur eröffnet in unionsrechtlich gestalteten Verfahren (unabhängig von der Natur

[39] Vgl. dazu Geimer/Schütze, Internationaler Rechtsverkehr/Okonska, 66. EL 1/2023, VO (EU) 2020/1784 Art. 19 Rn. 3f.

[40] Ausführlich dazu Rauscher, EuZPR/EuIPR/Ulrici, 5. Aufl. 2024, EU-ZustVO 2020 Art. 1 Rn. 19ff., 29ff., 33ff., 59ff., 65ff.

[41] Da Irland seine Teilnahme zur EU-JuDigiVO erklärt hat, vgl. Rat der Europäischen Union, Dokument 16726/23, zählt Irland in diesem Kontext zu den Mitgliedstaaten. Dänemark zählt dagegen nicht zu den Mitgliedstaaten, vgl. ErwGr. 59 EU-JuDigiVO.

[42] Vgl. auch ErwGr. 11 EU-JuDigiVO.

der angenommenen Zustellungslast, auch → II. 3.). Zugleich steht sie in diesen aber auch nicht generell, sondern nur zur Verfügung, soweit in diesen eine grenzüberschreitende Zustellung erfolgt, weil nur dann zugleich der Anwendungsbereich der EU-ZustVO eröffnet ist. Der Anwendungsbereich von Art. 19a EU-ZustVO nF bleibt danach iErg. insbes. auch erheblich hinter dem möglichen Anwendungsbereich von Art. 19 EU-ZustVO zurück.

Unbeschadet ErwGr. 27 S. 1, Art. 4 Abs. 4 UAbs. 1 S. 3 EU-JuDigiVO können in Anwendung von Art. 19a EU-ZustVO nF iErg. nur gerichtliche Schriftstücke zugestellt werden. Dies folgt zwar nicht aus einer entsprechenden selbstständigen Beschränkung von Art. 19a EU-ZustVO nF, weil aus der Bezugnahme des Wortlauts allein auf gerichtliche Schriftstücke wegen der Gleichstellung außergerichtlicher und gerichtlicher Schriftstücke durch Art. 21 EU-ZustVO keine Beschränkung des Anwendungsbereichs folgt.[43] Allerdings ergibt sich dies aus der zu beachtenden Beschränkung der Nutzungsmöglichkeit des Europäischen elektronischen Zugangspunkts durch Art. 4 Abs. 2 EU-JuDigiVO auf die dort genannten Verfahren und den Umstand, dass in den genannten (Rechtsschutz-)Verfahren nur gerichtliche Schriftstücke[44] zuzustellen sind, weshalb Art. 19a Abs. 1 EU-ZustVO nF auch die vorherige Zustimmung gerade in Bezug auf ein bestimmtes (Rechtsschutz-)Verfahren erfordert.

2. Möglichkeit zur Zustellung über den Europäischen elektronischen Zugangspunkt

a) Überblick

Aufgrund ihrer verordnungsautonomen Zulassung (→ IV. 1. a)) kann die Zustellung über den Europäischen elektronischen Zugangspunkt ohne Rücksicht auf das Recht des Ursprungs- und des Empfangsmitgliedstaats erfolgen, wenn die verordnungsautonom vorgesehenen Voraussetzungen (→ IV. 2. b) bis d)) erfüllt sind. Keine gesonderte Aussage trifft die Vorschrift zum Verhältnis der Zustellung über den Europäischen elektronischen Zugangspunkt zu anderen Zustellungsarten, insbes. auch nicht zur Zustellung auf dem einfachen Rechtshilfeweg. Die Auslegung der EU-ZustVO ergibt insoweit, dass die Zustellung über den Europäischen elektronischen Zugangspunkt nicht subsidiär zu den übrigen Zustellungsarten der EU-ZustVO ist.[45] Ebenso wenig folgt aus Art. 4 Abs. 6 S. 1 EU-JuDigiVO umgekehrt ein Vorrang der Zustellung über den Europäischen elektronischen Zugangspunkt, wofür zunächst der Wortlaut („können" darüber zustellen) spricht. Weiter spricht dafür das Telos, Zustellungen zu beschleunigen, weil anderenfalls eine Zustellung

---

[43] Vgl. Rauscher, EuZPR/EuIPR/Ulrici, 5. Aufl. 2024, EU-ZustVO 2020 Art. 21 Rn. 17 gegen zB Halfmeier LMK 2009, 288747.

[44] Zum Begriff Rauscher, EuZPR/EuIPR/Ulrici, 5. Aufl. 2024, EU-ZustVO 2020 Art. 21 Rn. 9.

[45] Vgl. die verallgemeinerungsfähigen Aussagen bei EuGH 2.3.2017 – C-354/15, ECLI:EU:C:2017:157 = EuZW 2017, 344 Rn. 71 (Andrew Marcus Henderson/Novo Banco SA); EuGH 11.11.2015 – C-223/14, ECLI:EU:C:2015:744 = EuZW 2015, 947 Rn. 57 (Tecom Mican SL, José Adrias Domíngueez); EuGH 19.12.2012 – C-325/11, ECLI:EU:C:2012:824 = NJW 2013, 443 Rn. 31 (Krystyna Alder, Ewald Alder/Sabina Orlowska, Czeslaw Orlowski); EuGH 9.2.2006 – C-473/04, ECLI:EU:C:2006:96 = NJW 2006, 975 Rn. 19ff. (Plumex/Young Ports NV).

über diesen Weg zunächst stets selbst dann erfolgen müsste, wenn der veranlassenden Stelle bekannt ist, dass der Zustellungsempfänger Bestätigungen nach Art. 19a Abs. 2 EU-ZustVO nF nur unzuverlässig bzw. stark verzögert abgibt, oder dies zB unter Berücksichtigung der Natur eines Verfahrens erwartbar ist (zB Zustellungen nach Art. 43 Abs. 1 S. 1 Brüssel Ia-VO an Schuldner eines Annäherungsverbots).

b) Veranlassende Stelle

Entgegen der hA zur Postzustellung unter Art. 14 EG-ZustVO 2007[46] wird die Zustellung über den Europäischen elektronischen Zugangspunkt im Einklang mit Art. 18, 19 EU-ZustVO[47] nicht lediglich für die Zustellung durch Übermittlungsstellen, sondern ebenso für die Zustellung durch sonstige nach dem Recht des Ursprungsmitgliedstaats zustellungsberechtigte Personen eröffnet. Dafür spricht die Verwandtschaft von Art. 19a EU-ZustVO nF mit Art. 19 EU-ZustVO. Allerdings ist erforderlich, dass die eine Zustellung über den Europäischen elektronischen Zugangspunkt veranlassende Stelle eine zuständige Behörde iSv Art. 2 Nr. 1 EU-JuDigiVO ist. Neben der auf die Kommunikation im Subordinationsverhältnis ausgerichteten Formulierung von Art. 1 Abs. 1 UAbs. 1 2. Fall EU-JuDigiVO und der passiven Formulierung in Art. 4 Abs. 4 S. 3 EU-JuDigiVO aE spricht dafür auch Art. 4 Abs. 6 S. 1 EU-JuDigiVO, welcher die Nutzung des Europäischen elektronischen Zugangspunkts zur Zustellung nur für behördlich veranlasste Zustellungen zulässt.[48] Natürlichen und juristischen Personen als (zB nach § 1111 Abs. 1 S. 4 ZPO) zustellungsberechtigte Stellen ist die neue Zustellungsart nicht eröffnet. Abweichendes ergibt sich auch nicht aus Art. 20 EU-ZustVO, weil dieser nicht die Nutzungsmöglichkeit des Europäischen elektronischen Zugangspunkts ausweitet und außerdem die Zustellung über den Europäischen elektronischen Zugangspunkt nicht durch Stellen des Empfangsmitgliedstaats erfolgt und daher nicht in den Anwendungsbereich von Art. 20 EU-ZustVO fällt. Durch Art. 19a EU-ZustVO nF wird auch nicht eröffnet die Möglichkeit, dass Empfangsstellen zur Rechtshilfegewährung das zuzustellende Schriftstück über den Europäischen elektronischen Zugangspunkt zustellen. Denn die Ausführung von Zustellungen durch Empfangsstellen wird von der Vorschrift nicht erfasst, weil diese eine „direkte" Zustellung anspricht und damit darauf verweist, dass die Zustellung ohne Einschaltung

---

[46] Vgl. dazu zB Generalanwalt Bobek 26.11.2020 – C-307/19, ECLI:EU:C:2020:971 = BeckRS 2020, 32975 Rn. 102f. (Obala i lučice d.o.o./NLB Leasing d.o.o.); OLG Dresden 6.11.2018 – 4 W 940/18, NJW-RR 2019, 319 Rn. 5; OLG Frankfurt/Main 3.11.2021 – 6 W 95/21, NJW-RR 2022, 211 Rn. 11; Münchener Kommentar zur ZPO/Rauscher, 6. Aufl. 2022, EG-ZustellVO Art. 2 Rn. 3, EG-ZustellVO Art. 14 Rn. 4.

[47] Vgl. Rauscher, EuZPR/EuIPR/Ulrici, 5. Aufl. 2024, EU-ZustVO 2020 Art. 18 Rn. 10, EU-ZustVO 2020 Art. 19 Rn. 12; vgl. auch OLG Düsseldorf 24.6.2024 – 20 W 28/24, WRP 2024, 988 Rn. 11; zu Art. 18 EU-ZustVO aA zB Thomas/Putzo, ZPO/Nordmeier, 45. Aufl. 2024, EuZustVO Art. 18 Rn. 1; aA auch Musielak/Voit, ZPO/Stadler/Krüger, 20. Aufl. 2023, EuZustVO Art. 18 Rn. 1 unter verfehltem Verweis auf die nicht die Zuständigkeit für die (Postdirekt-)Zustellung, sondern nur die Zuständigkeit als „Übermittlungsstelle" bestimmende Regelung in § 1069 Abs. 1 Nr. 1 ZPO.

[48] Vgl. auch *e contrario* ErwGr. 13 S. 4 EU-JuDigiVO: Gleichstellung mit Behörden nur für Insolvenzverwalter.

einer Empfangsstelle erfolgt. Zudem ist die Ausführung der Zustellung durch eine Empfangsstelle im Empfangsmitgliedstaat ein innerstaatlicher Vorgang, den die EU-ZustVO im Grundsatz nicht regelt.

c) Empfänger mit bekannter Zustelladresse in einem anderen Mitgliedstaat

Die Zustellung über den Europäischen elektronischen Zugangspunkt setzt voraus, dass der Zustellungsempfänger eine bekannte Zustelladresse in einem anderen Mitgliedstaat hat. In diesem Erfordernis kommt wie in Art. 19 EU-ZustVO[49] parallel zur Wohnsitzanknüpfung in Art. 17 EU-ZustVO und zur Aufenthaltsanknüpfung in Art. 18 EU-ZustVO zum Ausdruck, dass die Direktzustellung über den Europäischen elektronischen Zugangspunkt eröffnet ist ohne Rücksicht auf die Staatsangehörigkeit des Zustellungsadressaten und -empfängers, welcher für die Zugehörigkeit zum Raum des Rechts keine entscheidende Bedeutung zukommt. Die Anknüpfung an die bekannte Zustelladresse anstatt an die Staatsangehörigkeit zielt danach auf eine Ausweitung des Anwendungsbereichs. Zugleich beschränkt jedes zusätzliche Erfordernis aber den Anwendungsbereich. Da der Verordnungsgeber die sich aus einer Anknüpfung an den Wohnsitz ergebenden Beschränkungen für die Direktzustellung über den Europäischen elektronischen Zugangspunkt anders als für die Zustellung durch diplomatische oder konsularische Vertreter als nicht sachgerecht angesehen hat, knüpft die Vorschrift anders als Art. 17 EU-ZustVO nicht an den Wohnsitz an. Zugleich wurde anders als in Art. 18 EU-ZustVO auch nicht an den Aufenthalt angeknüpft, weil die Ausführung einer Zustellung aufgrund der Ubiquität des Europäischen elektronischen Zugangspunkts anders als die Postdirektzustellung (dort im Grundsatz Erfordernis der Abgabe einer Empfangsbestätigung nebst Übergabe an den Postbediensteten) nicht ihrer Natur nach Unsicherheiten darüber mindert, ob der Zustellungsempfänger im maßgeblichen Zeitpunkt gerade einen Aufenthalt in einem anderen Mitgliedstaat hatte.

Für den Zustellungsempfänger muss eine Zustelladresse in einem anderen, dh vom anhand der veranlassenden Stelle bestimmten Ursprungsmitgliedstaat verschiedenen Mitgliedstaat gegeben sein. Maßgeblich ist der Zeitpunkt der Zustellung. Ohne Belang ist, in welchem anderen Mitgliedstaat der Zustellungsempfänger eine bekannte Zustelladresse hat. Es bedarf wie bei Art. 19 EU-ZustVO keiner irgendwie gearteten Beziehung der bekannten Zustelladresse zu dem für die elektronische Zustellung genutzten Nutzerkonto, weil sich elektronische Kommunikation gerade dadurch auszeichnet, dass dem Ort der Speicherung und des Abrufs sowie der „Nationalität" des genutzten Providers/Nutzerkontos (hier letztlich eine „europäische")[50] keine Bedeutung beigemessen wird. Unschädlich ist, dass der Zustellungsempfänger eine bekannte Zustelladresse in mehreren vom Ursprungsmitgliedstaat verschiedenen Mitgliedstaaten hat. Unschädlich ist aber auch, dass der Zustellungsempfänger im Ursprungsmitgliedstaat selbst eine bekannte Zustelladresse hat, weil das Fehlen einer bekannten Zustelladresse im Ursprungsmitgliedstaat auch im Rah-

---

[49] Vgl. dazu Rauscher, EuZPR/EuIPR/Ulrici, 5. Aufl. 2024, EU-ZustVO 2020 Art. 19 Rn. 14.

[50] Vgl. ErwGr. 27, Art. 13 Abs. 6, Art. 14 Abs. 2 EU-JuDigiVO.

men von Art. 1 Abs. 1 EU-ZustVO nur ein halbseitiges Erfordernis für die Eröffnung des Anwendungsbereichs ist.[51]

Der Begriff der bekannten Zustelladresse ist verordnungsautonom in Anlehnung an das entsprechende Erfordernis in Art. 19 EU-ZustVO[52] auszulegen. Er bezeichnet wie im Rahmen von Art. 1 Abs. 1 EU-ZustVO eine Adresse, dh einen durch nähere Angaben individualisierten Ort, an dem der Zustellungsempfänger physisch angetroffen und, wird er dort nicht angetroffen, ein Schriftstück ggf. gleichwohl physisch in seinen Machtbereich gelangen kann. Dagegen bezeichnet er nicht die Angaben zur Individualisierung eines elektronischen Postfachs. Denn elektronische Postfächer eignen sich ihrem Wesen nach nicht zur sinnhaften Verortung eines Zustellungsempfängers in einem Mitgliedstaat, weil elektronische Postfächer auch nach einem grenzüberschreitenden Umzug wohl ganz überwiegend unverändert weitergenutzt werden (der Europäische elektronische Zugangspunkt wird gerade auch dies ermöglichen), während sich eine Postanschrift im Falle eines Umzugs ändert. Abweichendes gilt mit Rücksicht auf die Ausrichtung des Begriffs der Zustelladresse auf die Möglichkeit einer physischen Übergabe auch nicht für Postfächer, welche auf Grundlage spezifischer nationaler Rechtsvorschriften (vgl. §§ 10ff. ERVV: Besonderes elektronisches Bürger- und Organisationenpostfach) eingerichtet und genutzt werden.

d) *Ausdrückliche vorherige Zustimmung*

Bereits nach Art. 4 Abs. 6 S. 1 EU-JuDigiVO kann der Europäische elektronische Zugangspunkt für die Zustellung von Schriftstücken an natürliche und juristische Personen nur nach deren vorheriger ausdrücklicher Zustimmung genutzt werden. Nach Art. 4 Abs. 6 S. 2 EU-JuDigiVO gilt eine entsprechende Zustimmung jeweils nur und muss dementsprechend jeweils erteilt sein für ein konkretes (Rechtsschutz-)Verfahren, in dessen Rahmen der Europäische elektronische Zugangspunkt „als Briefkasten" genutzt werden soll. Sie muss sich ausweislich Art. 4 Abs. 6 S. 2 EU-JuDigiVO gerade auch auf Zustellungen und nicht nur allgemein auf eine verfahrensbezogene Kommunikation beziehen. Die Zustimmung muss vor Einleitung eines Zustellungsverfahrens vorliegen und ausdrücklich, dh unter Verwendung von Zweifeln keinen Raum lassenden Erklärungszeichen erfolgt sein; eine nachgehende Genehmigung genügt nicht. Inhaltlich muss die Erklärung den Willen verlautbaren, über den Europäischen elektronischen Zugangspunkt bewirkte Zustellungen gegen sich bzw. den vom Zustellungsempfänger repräsentierten Zustellungsadressaten gelten zu lassen. Sie ist nicht formbedürftig und kann auch elektronisch erteilt werden (vgl. auch Art. 4 Abs. 6 S. 3 EU-JuDigiVO). Rechtlich ist nicht erforderlich, dass sie ihrerseits über den Europäischen elektronischen Zugangspunkt erklärt wird. Aus dem Regelungszusammenhang ergibt sich, dass Adressat der Zustimmungserklärung die zuständige Behörde ist, welche das jeweilige Verfahren führt. Die Erklärung der Zustimmung bereits in zwischen den Parteien vereinbarten Streitbeilegungsklauseln scheidet danach aus.

---

[51] Rauscher, EuZPR/EuIPR/Ulrici, 5. Aufl. 2024, EU-ZustVO 2020 Art. 1 Rn. 50.
[52] Dazu Rauscher, EuZPR/EuIPR/Ulrici, 5. Aufl. 2024, EU-ZustVO 2020 Art. 19 Rn. 15.

Art. 19a EU-ZustVO nF greift das bereits nach Art. 4 Abs. 6 EU-JuDigiVO für die Nutzbarkeit des Europäischen elektronischen Zugangspunkts bestehende Einwilligungserfordernis auf, wiederholt es und erhebt es zu einer Zustellungsvoraussetzung, ohne ihm weitere Anforderungen beizufügen. Keine ausdrückliche Aussage trifft Art. 19a EU-ZustVO nF dazu, ob die Zustimmung für ein konkretes (Rechtsschutz-)Verfahren auch eingeschränkt erteilt werden kann bzw. welche Bedeutung einer beschränkten Zustimmung zukommt, und zur Widerruflichkeit einer erteilten Zustimmung. Gleichwohl sind diese Fragen anhand des Unionsrechts und nicht des Rechts des Ursprungs- oder Empfangsmitgliedstaats zu beantworten. Mit Rücksicht auf ihre Funktion ist wie zu Art. 19 EU-ZustVO[53] davon auszugehen, dass eine Zustimmung eingeschränkt erteilt und eine erteilte Zustimmung durch Erklärung mit Wirkung für die Zukunft auch ganz oder teilweise widerrufen werden kann. Für die Zulassung eines Widerrufs spricht, dass die EU-JuDigiVO betont, dass die Digitalisierung des Zugangs zu Gericht keine Hürden errichten darf,[54] und für die einwilligende natürliche oder juristische Person gerade auch erst bei einer erfolgten Zustellung Hindernisse offenbar werden können, mit denen sie im weiteren Verfahren nicht erneut konfrontiert werden will. Dass entsprechende Hindernisse nachgewiesen werden, ist für einen Widerruf nicht erforderlich, weil der Verordnungsgeber dem Prinzip gefolgt ist, dass keine natürliche (oder juristische) Person sich für die Ablehnung einer elektronischen Kommunikation rechtfertigen muss (um nicht das Fehlen digitaler Kompetenz offenbaren zu müssen).[55]

3. *Nutzung der Zustellung über den elektronischen Zugangspunkt*

a) *Ausführung der Zustellung*

aa) *Auswahlermessen*

Die Zustellung über den Europäischen elektronischen Zugangspunkt kann bei Vorliegen der hierfür erforderlichen Voraussetzungen erfolgen. Die berechtigte Stelle kann dann nach pflichtgemäßem Ermessen die Zustellung über den Europäischen elektronischen Zugangspunkt ebenso wählen, wie sie eine grenzüberschreitende Zustellung auf dem Weg der einfachen Rechtshilfe oder zB eine Postdirektzustellung wählen kann (auch → IV. 2. a)). Aufgrund des Anwendungsvorrangs der EU-ZustVO kann die Nutzung dieser Zustellungsart nicht durch den Ursprungsmitgliedstaat ausgeschlossen oder beschränkt werden. Ebenso wenig kann ein durch die bekannte Zustelladresse bestimmter Empfangsmitgliedstaat diese Zustellungsart ausschließen oder beschränken. Er kann an eine solche insbes. auch nicht wie nach Art. 19 Abs. 2 EU-ZustVO[56] weitere Anforderungen stellen (bereits die Gestaltung des Europäischen elektronischen Zugangspunkts berücksichtigt abschließend die in Art. 19 Abs. 2 EU-ZustVO angesprochenen Interessen).

---

[53] Dazu Rauscher, EuZPR/EuIPR/Ulrici, 5. Aufl. 2024, EU-ZustVO 2020 Art. 19 Rn. 25.
[54] Vgl. auch ErwGr. 10 S. 1, 12 S. 1, 29 S. 3, 4 EU-JuDigiVO; Europäischer Wirtschafts- und Sozialausschuss, ABl. 2022 C 323/77 zu Ziff. 1.1., zu Ziff. 1.6, zu Ziff. 2.8. lit. c.
[55] Vgl. auch ErwGr. 1 EU-JuDigiVO: „Vermeidung sozialer Ausgrenzung".
[56] Dazu Rauscher, EuZPR/EuIPR/Ulrici, 5. Aufl. 2024, EU-ZustVO 2020 Art. 19 Rn. 30ff.

bb) Maßgeblichkeit der Durchführungsrechtsakte und der technischen Umsetzung

Die tatsächliche Ausführung der Zustellung über den Europäischen elektronischen Zugangspunkt richtet sich in erster Linie rechtlich nach den auf Grundlage von insbes. Art. 10 Abs. 1 lit. g EU-JuDigiVO zu erlassenden Durchführungsrechtsakten sowie tatsächlich nach der Gestaltung der eingesetzten Back-End-Software (insbes. Referenzimplementierungssoftware) und des Europäischen elektronischen Zugangspunkts. Sie wird dadurch erfolgen, dass die veranlassende Stelle ein zuzustellendes Schriftstück als elektronisches Dokument unter Verwendung der Back-End-Software über das dezentrale IT-System dem Zustellungsempfänger in dessen Nutzerkonto ein- und dadurch zum Abruf über den Europäischen elektronischen Zugangspunkt zur Verfügung stellt. Nach den Durchführungsrechtsakten und der technischen Gestaltung des Europäischen elektronischen Zugangspunkts wird sich auch richten, inwieweit der Zustellungsempfänger zusätzlich darüber, dass für ihn ein zuzustellendes Schriftstück zum Abruf bereitgestellt wurde, gesondert benachrichtigt wird (zB per E-Mail).

cc) Empfangsbestätigung

Bewirkt ist die Zustellung noch nicht mit dem Bereitstellen des zuzustellenden Schriftstücks und auch nicht mit Zugang einer ggf. erfolgenden Benachrichtigung hierüber, sondern erst dadurch, dass der Zustellungsempfänger den Eingang des Schriftstücks einschließlich des Empfangsdatums gegenüber der die Zustellung veranlassenden Stelle bestätigt (Art. 19a Abs. 2 S. 1 EU-ZustVO nF).[57] Die Abgabe der entsprechenden Empfangsbestätigung ist Teil des Zustellungstatbestands. Für diesen unerheblich ist dagegen, ob das zuzustellende Schriftstück tatsächlich abgerufen oder gar gelesen wurde. Art. 19a Abs. 2 EU-ZustVO nF gibt nicht vor, dass die Bestätigung des Empfangs in einer bestimmten Form oder auf einem bestimmten Weg erklärt werden muss. Nahe liegt zwar, dass dem Verordnungsgeber die Abgabe über den Europäischen elektronischen Zugangspunkt vorschwebte und der Europäische elektronische Zugangspunkt auch so gestaltet werden wird, dass (automatisch) eine Empfangsbestätigung eingeholt wird. Es spricht aber nichts dagegen, eine auf anderem Weg gegenüber der die Zustellung veranlassenden Stelle abgegebene Erklärung, weist sie den geforderten Inhalt auf und lässt sie die Feststellung des Erklärenden zu, als hinreichend anzusehen. Von Art. 19a EU-ZustVO nF wird nicht angeordnet, dass der die Zustellung veranlassenden Stelle die Empfangsbestätigung übermittelt bzw. zugänglich gemacht wird. Allerdings hat dies der Verordnungsgeber vorausgesetzt und ist ersichtlich davon ausgegangen, dass eine über den Europäischen elektronischen Zugangspunkt abgegebene Empfangsbestätigung der veranlassenden Stelle übermittelt wird und dieser als Nachweis der Zustellung und ihres Zeitpunkts (vgl. zB ErwGr. 32 S. 1, Art. 43 Abs. 1 S. 1 Brüssel Ia-VO) dient, ohne dafür das einzige Nachweismittel zu sein.

Unbeschadet des Umstands, dass die Erfüllung des Zustellungstatbestands von einer aktiven Mitwirkung des Zustellungsempfängers abhängig ist, begründet Art. 19a EU-ZustVO nF (wie auch Art. 4 Abs. 6 EU-JuDigiVO) keine Mitwir-

---

[57] Vgl. Thomas/Putzo, ZPO/Nordmeier, 45. Aufl. 2024, EuZustVO Art. 19a Rn. 2.

kungsverpflichtung oder -obliegenheit des Zustellungsempfängers (anders zB § 31a Abs. 6 BRAO für das beA). Zwar spricht der Verordnungswortlaut tendenziell für eine entsprechende Obliegenheit. Denn hätte in Art. 19a Abs. 2 S. 1 EU-ZustVO nF lediglich zum Ausdruck gebracht werden sollen, dass die Empfangsbestätigung Teil des Zustellungstatbestands ist, hätte die Norm ähnlich wie Art. 18 EU-ZustVO oder Art. 19 Abs. 1 EU-ZustVO formuliert werden können. Andererseits zwingt der Wortlaut von Art. 19a Abs. 2 S. 1 EU-ZustVO nF aber auch nicht zur Annahme einer Mitwirkungsobliegenheit. Für eine solche könnte aber weiter sprechen, dass die Zustellung über den Europäischen elektronischen Zugangspunkt die vorherige ausdrückliche und mit Bezug zu einem konkreten (Rechtsschutz-)Verfahren abgegebene Zustimmung verlangt und eine solche Erklärung bei demjenigen, in dessen Interesse eine Zustellung erfolgt,[58] die Erwartung weckt, dass der Zustellungsempfänger in dem konkreten (Rechtsschutz-)Verfahren der gegebenen Zustimmung entsprechend an der Verwirklichung des Zustellungstatbestands mitwirkt. Indes ist eine solche Erwartung nur in dem Umfang schutzwürdig, in dem der Einwilligung von Rechts wegen eine zur Mitwirkung selbstbindende Bedeutung zukommt. Gegen die Annahme einer Mitwirkungsobliegenheit spricht in systematischer Hinsicht, dass weder Art. 18 EU-ZustVO[59] noch Art. 19 EU-ZustVO eine solche vorsehen. Dem ist größeres Gewicht aber nicht beizumessen, weil Art. 19a EU-ZustVO nF sich von diesen beiden Normen wesentlich unterscheidet, von Art. 18 EU-ZustVO durch das Erfordernis einer vorherigen und auf ein konkretes (Rechtsschutz-)Verfahren bezogenen Einwilligung und von Art. 19 EU-ZustVO durch die verordnungsautonome Ausgestaltung des Zustellungstatbestands. Gegen eine Mitwirkungsobliegenheit sprechen schließlich deutlich und iErg. durchgreifend teleologische Gesichtspunkte. Zunächst steht die Wahl der Zustellung über den Europäischen elektronischen Zugangspunkt im pflichtgemäßen Ermessen der veranlassenden Stelle. Diese kann bei Bedarf eine Zustellung auch auf einem anderen Weg oder unter paralleler Nutzung verschiedener Zustellungsarten bewirken. Für die Herbeiführung des Zustellungserfolgs ist die Annahme einer Mitwirkungsobliegenheit mithin nicht unabdingbar. Hinzu kommt, dass Art. 19a Abs. 2 S. 2 EU-ZustVO nF das Zustelldatum nur für den Fall der erfolgten Mitwirkung, nicht aber unabhängig hiervon auch für den Fall einer treuwidrigen Vereitelung regelt (anders zB § 173 Abs. 4 S. 4, 5 ZPO), weshalb sich im Falle einer Vereitelung weder deren Vorliegen noch ein Zustelldatum mit vergleichbarer Sicherheit[60] bestimmen ließe. Schließlich spricht gegen eine Mitwirkungsobliegenheit der oben für die Widerruflichkeit der Einwilligung angeführte Umstand, dass niemand sich für Defizite im Umgang mit der elektronischen Kommunikation soll rechtfertigen müssen (→ IV. 2. d)), weil sich solche Defizite unbeschadet einer erteilten Zustimmung gerade erst im Zusammenhang mit dem Abruf eines bereit-

---

[58] Vgl. dazu Rauscher, EuZPR/EuIPR/Ulrici, 5. Aufl. 2024, EU-ZustVO 2020 Art. 2 Rn. 19ff.

[59] Vgl. Rauscher, EuZPR/EuIPR/Ulrici, 5. Aufl. 2024, EU-ZustVO 2020 Art. 18 Rn. 30.

[60] Vgl. zu diesem Gesichtspunkt im Zusammenhang mit der Postdirektzustellung EuGH 2.3.2017 – C-354/15, ECLI:EU:C:2017:157 = EuZW 2017, 344 Rn. 81 (Andrew Marcus Henderson/Novo Banco SA).

gestellten Schriftstücks zeigen können. Aufgrund des Fehlens einer Mitwirkungsobliegenheit kann bei ausbleibender oder verzögerter Mitwirkung der Mangel im Zustellungstatbestand nicht unter dem Gesichtspunkt einer treuwidrigen Zustellungsvereitelung kompensiert werden.[61] Abweichendes kommt in Betracht, soweit sich eine entsprechende Obliegenheit aus dem für das Verfahren, in welchem die Zustellung erfolgt, geltenden Recht ergibt.

b) Zustelldatum

Das Datum der Zustellung über den elektronischen Zugangspunkt regelt Art. 19a Abs. 2 S. 2 EU-ZustVO nF verordnungsautonom, dh unabhängig vom Recht des Ursprungs- und des Empfangsmitgliedstaats dahin, dass das in der Empfangsbestätigung angegebene Datum gilt. Diese Angabe gilt ohne Rücksicht darauf, wann das zuzustellende Schriftstück tatsächlich abgerufen oder gelesen wurde. Durch die eine Zustellung veranlassende Stelle und durch denjenigen, in dessen Interesse eine Zustellung erfolgt, kann eine frühere Zustellung nicht nachgewiesen werden; unberührt bleibt, eine Reaktion auf das zuzustellende Schriftstück und das in ihr ausgewiesene Antwortdatum als Empfangsbestätigung und Angabe des Empfangsdatums zu behandeln. Umgekehrt kann durch den Zustellungsadressaten nicht der Nachweis geführt werden, dass in der Empfangsbestätigung ein zu frühes Empfangsdatum angegeben wurde; Abweichendes gilt unter Berücksichtigung des Übermaßverbots, wenn das angegebene Datum vor dem feststehenden Zeitpunkt der Absendung liegt.

Art. 13 Abs. 3 EU-ZustVO nF nimmt vor dem Hintergrund der verordnungsautonomen Regelung des Zustelldatums (Art. 19a Abs. 2 S. 2 EU-ZustVO nF) seinem Wortlaut nach die Zustellung über den Europäischen elektronischen Zugangspunkt aus dem Geltungsbereich des sog. doppelten Datums aus. Dies erweist sich (wie bereits die Beibehaltung des anerkanntermaßen missverständlichen[62] ErwGr. 15 S. 3, 4 EG-ZustVO 2007 als ErwGr. 27 S. 3, 4 EU-ZustVO)[63] als schwerer Missgriff des Verordnungsgebers und beruht auf einem gravierenden Fehlverständnis von Art. 13 EU-ZustVO.[64] Richtig ist zwar, dass es aufgrund der autonomen Regelung des Zustelldatums in Art. 19a Abs. 2 S. 2 EU-ZustVO nF nicht der Anwendung der Kollisionsnorm des Art. 13 Abs. 1 EU-ZustVO bedarf. Dagegen ist die autonome Regelung des Zustelldatums durch Art. 19a Abs. 2 S. 2 EU-ZustVO nF nicht geeignet, Art. 13 Abs. 2 EU-ZustVO zu ersetzen, weil sie sich gar nicht der dort behandelten Problematik widmet. Gerade der Umstand, dass es der Zustellungsempfänger im Rahmen von Art. 19a Abs. 2 EU-ZustVO nF in der Hand hat, das Zustelldatum durch die Angabe in der Empfangsbestätigung mitzubestimmen,

---

[61] Mit Blick auf die Unbestimmtheit des für den ersten Erhalt des zuzustellenden Schriftstücks maßgeblichen Zeitpunkts scheidet auch eine Analogie zu Art. 12 Abs. 5 S. 3 EU-ZustVO (Nichtbestätigung als Annahmeverweigerung) aus.

[62] Vgl. COM(2013) 858 final, 13.

[63] Vgl. dazu Rauscher, EuZPR/EuIPR/Ulrici, 5. Aufl. 2024, EU-ZustVO 2020 Art. 13 Rn. 9.

[64] Unkrit. dagegen Thomas/Putzo, ZPO/Nordmeier, 45. Aufl. 2024, EuZustVO Art. 19a Rn. 2.

fordert in besonderer Weise[65] heraus, dem Schutz desjenigen, in dessen Interesse eine Zustellung erfolgt, Aufmerksamkeit zu widmen. Ersichtlich wird dies zB in dem Fall, dass zur Hemmung der Verjährung (§ 204 Abs. 1 Nr. 1 BGB) eine Widerklage[66] nach Art. 5 Abs. 6 EG-BagatellVO erhoben wird und sich das die Zustellung veranlassende Gericht für eine Zustellung über den Europäischen elektronischen Zugangspunkt entscheidet: durch Angabe eines späteren Zustelldatums könnte der Widerbeklagte die Hemmung der Verjährung vereiteln. Der Verordnungsgeber hat dies aufgrund eines Missverständnisses der Funktion von Art. 13 Abs. 2 EU-ZustVO übersehen. Die sich ergebende planwidrige Regelunglücke ist durch Reduktion von Art. 13 Abs. 3 Hs. 2 EU-ZustVO nF dahin zuschließen, dass Art. 13 Abs. 2 EU-ZustVO als Ergänzung zu Art. 19a Abs. 2 EU-ZustVO nF Anwendung findet.[67] Nur dadurch lässt sich eine sachlich nicht zu rechtfertigende Ungleichbehandlung gegenüber der Nutzung einer anderen Zustellungsart vermeiden. Über den Verweis des Art. 13 Abs. 2 EU-ZustVO finden, weil die im Ursprungsmitgliedstaat geltende EU-ZustVO keine Aussage trifft und das nationale Recht des Ursprungsmitgliedstaats die Zustellung über den Europäischen elektronischen Zugangspunkt nicht regelt, die sachnähesten Vorschriften (insbesondere solche, die für sonstige elektronische Zustellungen gelten) Anwendung.

c) Annahmeverweigerungsrecht

aa) Zuständigkeit für Erteilung der Belehrung und Empfang der Verweigerung

Nach Art. 12 Abs. 6 EU-ZustVO besteht auch bei direkter Zustellung über den Europäischen elektronischen Zugangspunkt keine unbedingte Übersetzungsobliegenheit, sondern ein Annahmeverweigerungsrecht des Zustellungsadressaten. Über dieses ist er zu belehren, wobei die Belehrung nach Art. 12 Abs. 7 EU-ZustVO nF zu erfolgen hat durch die die Zustellung veranlassende Stelle (Behörde). Diese hat dem zuzustellenden Schriftstück die Belehrung beizufügen und sie wie dieses über den Europäischen elektronischen Zugangspunkt zum Abruf bereitzuzustellen. Der Berechtigte hat seine Annahmeverweigerung (unter Abwesenden) zu erklären gegenüber der die Zustellung veranlassenden Stelle, nicht dagegen gegenüber der zu Einrichtung und Betrieb des Europäischen elektronischen Zugangspunkts verpflichteten Kommission oder gegenüber der beauftragten eu-LISA.

---

[65] Ohnehin sollten durch ein Gericht veranlasste Verzögerungen nach Möglichkeit nicht denjenigen treffen, in dessen Interesse eine Zustellung erfolgt.

[66] Bei der primären Verfahrenseinleitung zur Verjährungshemmung (zB Einleitung eines Europäischen Mahnverfahrens) stellt sich das Problem dagegen aufgrund des Erfordernisses einer vorherigen Zustimmung des Empfängers zur Zustellung für ein spezielles Verfahren regelmäßig nicht (vor Zustellung des verfahrenseinleitenden Schriftstücks hat der Schuldner regelmäßig keine Kenntnis vom konkreten Verfahren und keinen Anlass für dieses in eine Zustellung über den Europäischen elektronischen Zugangspunkt einzuwilligen – vom Verordnungsgeber zu Art. 13 Abs. 2 EG-MahnVO nF nicht berücksichtigt).

[67] Vgl. zu Art. 18 EU-ZustVO in diese Richtung bereits Rauscher, EuZPR/EuIPR/Ulrici, 5. Aufl. 2024, EU-ZustVO 2020 Art. 18 Rn. 35.

bb) Heilung und Fristwahrung

Der Verweis in Art. 12 Abs. 6 EU-ZustVO erfasst nicht nur das Annahmeverweigerungsrecht, sondern ebenso die Möglichkeit, eine zurückgewiesene Zustellung nach Art. 12 Abs. 5 EU-ZustVO zu heilen. Dies wird in Art. 19a Abs. 2 S. 3 EU-ZustVO nF zunächst bestätigt und zugleich wird dazu angeordnet, dass die Regelung zum Zustelldatum (Art. 19a Abs. 2 S. 2 EU-ZustVO nF) auch für die Zustellung „verweigerter“[68] Schriftstücke gilt, welche gemäß Art. 12 Abs. 5 EU-ZustVO geheilt wird.

Die Formulierung von Art. 19a Abs. 2 S. 3 EU-ZustVO nF wirft allerdings mehr Fragen auf als sie beantwortet. Sie lässt zunächst nicht erkennen, inwieweit die Regelung Anwendung finden soll, wenn nur entweder die originäre oder[69] die heilende Zustellung über den Europäischen elektronischen Zugangspunkt erfolgt ist. Für den Fall, dass beide Zustellungen über den Europäischen elektronischen Zugangspunkt erfolgt sind, ist ihr nicht zu entnehmen, ob sich das Zustelldatum ausnahmslos nach der Angabe in der Bestätigung zur originären oder nach der Angabe in der Bestätigung zur heilenden Zustellung richten soll. Beide möglichen Verständnisse können zu sachwidrigen Ergebnissen führen: Wäre stets die Angabe zur originären Zustellung entscheidend, könnte eine rückwirkende Heilung möglicherweise noch nach Jahren bewirkt werden und bis dahin eine Schwebelage von unerträglicher Dauer entstehen. Wäre stets die Angabe zur heilenden Zustellung entscheidend, trüge die an der Zustellung interessierte Person entgegen dem Telos[70] von Art. 12 Abs. 5 EU-ZustVO die Folgen einer sich aus einer Annahmeverweigerung ergebenden Verzögerung.

Zu sachgerechten, im Einklang mit dem Telos sowohl von Art. 12 Abs. 5 EU-ZustVO als auch von Art. 13 Abs. 2 EU-ZustVO (dazu → IV. 3. b)) stehenden und eine Ungleichbehandlung gegenüber anderen Zustellungsarten vermeidenden Ergebnissen führt ein Verständnis, nach welchem Art. 19a Abs. 2 S. 3 EU-ZustVO nF lediglich klarstellt, dass sich nicht nur der Zeitpunkt einer originären Zustellung über den Europäischen elektronischen Zugangspunkt, sondern auch der Zeitpunkt einer heilenden Zustellung über den Europäischen elektronischen Zugangspunkt (unabhängig von der Art der für die originären Zustellung gewählten Form) nach dem in der jeweiligen Empfangsbestätigung angegebenen Datum richtet, die Anwendung von Art. 12 Abs. 5 EU-ZustVO aber vollständig unberührt bleibt: Das Datum einer geheilten Zustellung richtet sich dann, ist die heilende Zustellung über den Europäischen elektronischen Zugangspunkt erfolgt, im Ausgangspunkt nach der Angabe in der Bestätigung des Empfangs der heilenden Zustellung

---

[68] Gemeint „zurückgewiesener“ (verweigert werden nicht die Schriftstücke, sondern ihre Annahme); zur Qualität der deutschen Sprachfassung der EU-ZustVO vgl. bereits Rauscher, EuZPR/EuIPR/Ulrici, 5. Aufl. 2024, EU-ZustVO 2020 Einl. Rn. 34. Zum Umgang mit der Rechtssprache im EuZPR/EuIPR ausführlich Rauscher IPRax 2012, 40.

[69] Dazu, dass die Heilung nicht auf demselben Zustellungsweg erfolgen muss, vgl. Geimer/Schütze, Internationaler Rechtsverkehr/Okonska, 66. EL 1/2023, VO (EU) 2020/1784 Art. 12 Rn. 104; Rauscher, EuZPR/EuIPR/Ulrici, 5. Aufl. 2024, EU-ZustVO 2020 Art. 12 Rn. 98.

[70] Vgl. dazu EuGH 8.11.2005 – C 443/03, ECLI:EU:C:2005:665 = NJW 2006, 491 Rn. 42 (Götz Leffler/Berlin Chemie AG); Rauscher, EuZPR/EuIPR/Ulrici, 5. Aufl. 2024, EU-ZustVO 2020 Art. 12 Rn. 18.

(Art. 12 Abs. 5 S. 2 EU-ZustVO). Muss eine Zustellung innerhalb einer bestimmten Frist erfolgen, richtet sich das Datum einer geheilten Zustellung, ist die originäre Zustellung über den Europäischen elektronischen Zugangspunkt erfolgt, dagegen nach der Angabe in der Bestätigung des originären Empfangs, wenn die dafür nach dem die Zustellungslast begründenden Recht bestehenden Voraussetzungen erfüllt sind (Art. 12 Abs. 5 S. 3 EU-ZustVO).[71]

V. Schluss

Die EU-JuDigiVO verfolgt bei der Digitalisierung der justiziellen Zusammenarbeit in Zivil- und Handelssachen einen die einzelne Rechtsakte, welche Verfahren unionsrechtlich ausgestalten, übergreifenden Ansatz. Hierdurch wird nicht nur bestätigt, dass die verschiedenen Rechtsakte nicht beziehungslos nebeneinanderstehen, sondern Teil eines Gesamtsystems des Europäischen Zivilverfahrensrechts sind, dessen Lückenhaftigkeit allein dem Prinzip der begrenzten Einzelermächtigung geschuldet ist, sondern auch die Kohärenz der verschiedenen Rechtsakte gefördert.

In ihrem Kapitel VII sieht die EU-JuDigiVO die Änderung von verschiedenen Verordnungen des Europäischen Zivilverfahrensrechts vor. Für die EU-ZustVO ist vorgesehen insbes. die Ergänzung um eine neue Zustellungsart, die nach derzeitigem Stand wegen der vorgesehenen Einführungsphase praktische Bedeutung allerdings erst in einigen Jahren erlangen wird. Um zu vermeiden, dass die EU bei der Digitalisierung im Vergleich mit anderen Wirtschaftsräumen zurückfällt, wären eine etwas ambitioniertere Ausgestaltung des Zeitplans sowie (zumindest für Zustellungen) ein Verzicht auf die zusätzliche Beschränkung durch Art. 26 Abs. 4 EU-JuDigiVO wünschenswert gewesen. Andererseits gibt der großzügig aufgeschobene Beginn des zeitlichen Anwendungsbereichs Gelegenheit, die vorstehend aufgedeckten Schwächen der zur EU-ZustVO vorgesehenen Änderungen abzustellen.

[71] Zur Auslegung von Art. 12 Abs. 5 S. 3 EU-ZustVO vgl. Rauscher, EuZPR/EuIPR/Ulrici, 5. Aufl. 2024, EU-ZustVO 2020 Art. 12 Rn. 101 ff.

ISTVÁN VARGA

Vor und nach ZF Automotive v. Luxshare: Bedeutungszuwachs für § 1050 ZPO & Co.?

Thomas Rauscher ist in vielerlei Hinsicht ein Transatlantiker. Die Stimmung in den Räumlichkeiten seines Leipziger Instituts war über die Jahrzehnte unserer Zusammenarbeit geprägt durch die Präsenz der wuchtigen amerikanischen Entscheidungssammlungen U.S. Supreme Court Reports, Federal Reporter und Federal Supplement, in seiner Eigenschaft als Sportfliegerpilot machte er nie einen Hehl aus seiner Präferenz für den amerikanischen Luftraum, er war der Taktgeber des Leipzig-Miami Rechtsvergleichenden Seminars. Der didaktische Reichtum seiner internationalprivat- und prozessrechtlichen Vorlesungen nährte sich nicht zuletzt aus der rechtsvergleichenden Durchdringung des Rechtssystems, insbesondere aus dem tiefen Verständnis der Denkweisen- und Regelungsunterschiede zwischen civil law- und common law-Tradition. Aus dem von ihm betreuten Studenten- und Mitarbeiterkreis sind denn auch zahlreiche hervorragende junge Juristen hervorgegangen, deren einige wir – im Umfeld meiner von ihm initiierten Leipziger Gastvorlesungen – in ihren rechtsvergleichenden LLM- oder Promotionsstudien gemeinsam betreut haben. Wertvolles von ihm mitgenommen haben auch zahlreiche Studenten und Nachwuchswissenschaftler in Budapest, wo er nach jahrzehntelanger Lehrtätigkeit auf dem Gebiet des europäischen Zivilprozessrechts zum doctor et professor honoris causa der ELTE Juristischen Fakultät berufen wurde. Besonders gerne erinnere ich mich an einen Satz, den er vor Jahren an einen seiner Assistenten richtete, als jener ihn um Rat bei der Berufsorientierung gebeten hat: Seinen beruflichen Werdegang auf dem Gebiet des weit verstandenen Kollisionsrechts zu planen ist notwendigerweise zugleich eine Entscheidung zugunsten einer Lebensführung, deren Leitmotiv die Offenheit für die Welt, physische und geistige, kulturelle und rechtsvergleichende Reiselust voraussetzt. Damals sicher nicht nur als Antwort an den Wegsuchenden, sondern auch als Bekenntnis des Internationalprivatrechtlers, des Wissenschaftlers formuliert.

Mit dem Schlusspunkt seines Leipziger universitären Wirkens fällt symbolträchtig gerade jene Entscheidung des US Supreme Court aus dem Jahre 2022[1] zusammen, die der Offenheit des US-amerikanischen Zivilverfahrensrechts gegenüber Beweisnöten in internationalen Schiedsverfahren, insbesondere der schiedsfreundlichen Entwicklung der Beweisrechtshilfe seitens US-amerikanischer Bundesgerichte zugunsten ausländischer Schiedsgerichte und Schiedsparteien ein vorläufiges Ende gesetzt hat. Der vorliegende Beitrag möchte den *Jubilar* mit einer Nachzeichnung

[1] ZF Automotive US, Inc. v. Luxshare, Ltd., 142 S.Ct. 2078 (2022).

der zu dieser höchstrichterlichen Entscheidung führenden Rechtsentwicklung, einer kritischen Würdigung der Entscheidung, sowie schließlich einem Ausblick auf die Konsequenzen derselben für die deutsche Praxis ehren.

I. Der deutsch-amerikanische Rechtshilfeverkehr und dessen Bedeutung für internationale Handelsschiedsverfahren

1. Zivilprozessuale Beweisrechtshilfe und Schiedsverfahrensrecht

Die Zugehörigkeit des Zivilprozessrechts zum öffentlichen Recht einerseits und die private Natur der Schiedsgerichtsbarkeit andererseits führen auf den Gebieten zu tiefgreifenden Abweichungen in der Verfahrensweise staatlicher und privater Gerichte, auf denen eine Zwangsanwendung erforderlich werden kann. Die Regeln des Zivilprozessrechts als öffentliches Recht richten sich an den ins Staatsgefüge integrierten und daher mit der selbstverständlichen Befugnis hoheitlicher Zwangsanwendung ausgestatteten Richter, während die Schiedsverfahrensrechtsregeln – auch wenn sie kodifikationstechnisch womöglich in den gleichen Rechtsquellen niedergelegt sind – an Private adressiert sind, denen es an den gleichen Befugnissen mangelt. Stellvertretend für die in diesem Beitrag zur Sprache kommenden beiden repräsentativen Rechtsordnungen, für die deutsche und die US-amerikanische also, mögen diesen Umstand der notwendigen Modifikationen des Verfahrensrechts in privater Umgebung zwei fast gleichzeitig entstandene Worte von Mittermaier und Justice Story veranschaulichen:

„[...] daß das Prozessrecht ein Theil des öffentlichen Rechts sey, ergiebt sich leicht, wenn man erwägt, daß der Prozess mit der Gerichtsorganisation zusammenhängt und die Bestellung der Gerichte durch viele Interessen des öffentlichen Rechts geleitet wird. Daraus erklärt sich, warum zwar die Bürger einer Privatperson als Schiedsrichter sich unterwerfen können, ohne daß deswegen der Schiedsrichter eine wahre jurisdictio erhält, daher kann ein Schiedsrichter keinen Zeugen vorladen, daher den freiwillig erscheinenden Zeugen nicht beeidigen, und das schiedsrichterliche Urtheil nicht selbst vollziehen [...]“[2]

"Now we all know, that arbitrators [...] cannot compel the production of documents, and papers and books of account, or insist upon a discovery of facts from the parties under oath."[3]

Sind den Schiedsgerichten keine hoheitlichen Befugnisse verliehen, so entsteht Handlungsbedarf auf Seiten des das Schiedsverfahren mit der staatlichen Gerichtsbarkeit funktional gleichstellenden[4] Normgebers vor allem auf zwei solchen Gebieten, die die Wahrscheinlichkeit des Notwendigwerdens der Zwangsanwendung in sich bergen: Das eine solche Gebiet ist die Zwangsvollstreckung aus Schiedssprüchen, das jedoch nicht Gegenstand des vorliegenden Beitrags ist, so dass wir uns

[2] Mittermaier AcP 13 (1830), 294.
[3] Tobey v. County of Bristol et al., 23 Fed. Cas. 1313, 1320 (1845).
[4] § 1055 ZPO, collateral estoppel, dazu vgl mit aktualisierter Rspr.: The Preclusive Effect of Arbitration Awards in the US, Westlaw Practical Law Practice Note 1-583-9465.

hier mit der Bemerkung begnügen können, dass diesem Problem weitgehend durch die in den nationalen Rechtsquellen zugesicherte Anerkennung und Vollstreckung durch die Staatsgerichte Rechnung getragen worden ist. Ferner sind internationale Schiedsverfahren und dort erlassene ausländische Schiedssprüche durchweg von völkerrechtlichen Verträgen – vornehmlich vom UNÜ[5] – abgedeckt und der nationalen Zwangsvollstreckung zugänglich gemacht worden.

Dem zweiten problematischen Gebiet soll nunmehr unsere Aufmerksamkeit gelten. Hierbei handelt es sich um das gesamte Gebiet der Informationsbeschaffung durch das Schiedsgericht: um die Beweisermittlung. Die hier interessierende Grundfrage kann auch in Gestalt einer Kollision zwischen schiedsverfahrensrechtlichen Grundsätzen gestellt werden: Wie kann das Schiedsgericht seiner Pflicht nachkommen, den Sachverhalt zu ermitteln[6] und einen begründeten Schiedsspruch zu erlassen, wenn es letztlich keine Zwangsgewalt hat, Beweismittel zu beschaffen bzw. zu sichern? Oder aus der Sicht der Partei: Wie kann ihrem Anspruch auf rechtliches Gehör und auf vollständiges Vorbringen ihrer Angriffs- und Verteidigungsmittel (fair trial, full and fair hearing) Genüge getan werden, wenn die Einführung von ihr günstigen Beweismitteln in das Verfahren an der fehlenden Erzwingungsmöglichkeit scheitern kann?[7] Selbst die Verfasser des UNCITRAL Model Law haben dies noch als Defizit empfunden[8], was in den ersten Entwürfen dergestalt zutage tritt, dass sie international einheitliche Standards schaffen wollten. Im letzten Entwurf ist es dann am Ende beim geltenden Art. 27 UNCITRAL Model Law geblieben, in dem die Ausgestaltung der Rechtshilfe vollständig den einzelstaatlichen Rechten überlassen wird.[9]

Die Schiedsvereinbarung, die den Rechtsstreit den hoheitlich legitimierten Staatsgerichten entzieht, darf keineswegs mit einem Verzicht auf eine durch vollständig – oder doch die begründete Überzeugungsbildung ermöglichend – erforschten Sachverhalt untermauerte Sachentscheidung gleichgesetzt werden. Ist ein Beweismittel für die Sachentscheidung erforderlich und kann das Schiedsgericht dieses Beweismittel nicht über die freiwillige Mitwirkung von Parteien oder Dritten erlangen, so bleiben ihm zwei Wege zur Wahl. Entweder es erlässt eine Entscheidung ohne Auswertung der betreffenden Beweismittel, weil es etwa die die Sachaufklärung sabotierende Haltung der einen Partei hiermit sanktionieren zu können und zu dürfen glaubt. Eine solche Herangehensweise würde jedoch dem

---

[5] New Yorker Übereinkommen über die Anerkennung und Vollstreckung ausländischer Schiedssprüche vom 10.6.1958, im Folgenden UNÜ abgekürzt.

[6] Diese Pflicht wird gerade hinsichtlich der Nichtverfügbarkeit der discovery von amerikanischen Gerichten wiederholt problematisiert. Vgl. zB Chevron Transport Corp. v. Astro Vencedor Compania Naviera S. A., 300 F.Supp. 179 (S.D.N.Y. 1969).

[7] Vgl. Furlong 20 Willamette Law Review (1984), 535, der seine Überlegungen auf diese Kollision aufbaut.

[8] "Because of the lack of power of an arbitral tribunal to compel ... the arbitral proceedings may be blocked." UNCITRAL Documents A/CN. 9/WG II/WP.41 article 27.

[9] "The arbitral tribunal or a party with the approval of the arbitral tribunal may request from a competent court of this State assistance in taking evidence. The court may execute the request within its competence and according to its rules on taking evidence." Vgl. zu den einzelnen nationalen Umsetzungen →II. und III. 2. Zum Problem und zur Entwurfsgeschichte des Art. 27, in: Šarčević, Essays on International Commercial Arbitration/van Houtte, 1989, 113 (124ff.).

Geist und der Natur des ganzen Schiedsverfahrensrechts (typischerweise eine einzige Instanz und die sich daran knüpfende intensivierte Entscheidungsverantwortung, aus der ua ein eingeschränkter Untersuchungsgrundsatz entwickeln lässt[10]) zuwiderlaufen, wie dies auch im gesetzten Recht schön sichtbar wird etwa am Ausschluss der Geständnisfiktion und eines sich daran im staatlichen Zivilprozess womöglich anschließenden Versäumnisurteils.[11] Oder – und diese ist die zu empfehlende Variante – das Schiedsgericht versucht es, mit allen Mitteln an das betreffende Beweismittel heranzukommen und es ersucht letztlich die staatlichen Gerichte um Rechtshilfe bei der Beweisaufnahme, die dann ihrerseits während der Rechtshilfeleistung ihr eigenes Verfahrensrecht und damit sehr wohl ihre üblichen Zwangsmaßnahmen einsetzen können.

Zwar wird die Rechtshilfe in der Regel nur als letzte Zuflucht des Schiedsgerichts zum Zuge kommen, weil sie naheliegenderweise eine Verzögerung des Verfahrens zur Folge haben kann und das Schiedsgericht auch sonst, wie alle anderen Verfahrensprobleme, auch dieses im Einvernehmen mit den Parteien zu lösen versuchen wird. Doch zeigt die internationale und insbesondere die hier zu behandelnde US-amerikanische Praxis, dass Schiedsgerichte bei Bedarf nicht selten zu diesem Mittel greifen. Hinzu kommt, dass sich gegenüber am Verfahren nicht beteiligten Dritten die Notwendigkeit der staatlich-gerichtlichen Rechtshilfe häufiger ergibt. In solchen Verfahrenssituationen, aber auch schon früher, etwa beim Abschluss der Schiedsvereinbarung und der damit zusammenfallenden Wahl des Schiedsortes ist die Kenntnis der Einstellung der in Frage kommenden Rechtsordnungen als leges fori der Rechtshilfe zugunsten von Schiedsgerichten leistenden staatlichen Gerichte von herausragender Bedeutung. Unterschiede können hier auf die Effektivität der Beweismittelbeschaffung und damit auf die Integrität und die Legitimation des individuellen Schiedsverfahrens weitreichenden Einfluss ausüben.[12] Die Kenntnis dieser gerade zwischen Deutschland und den USA stark divergierenden Haltung[13] erleichtert sowohl für die Parteien als auch für die Schiedsrichter die realistische Einschätzung des Ablaufs des Beweisverfahrens. Wissen die Parteien und auch dritte Beweispersonen, sobald sie angesprochen werden, dass die Gerichte des jeweils ersuchten Staates großzügig Rechtshilfe leisten und dabei auch

[10] Dazu Varga, Beweiserhebung in transatlantischen Schiedsverfahren – Eine Suche nach Kompromissen zwischen deutscher und US-amerikanischer Beweisrechtstradition, 2006, S. 86ff.

[11] §§ 1048, 138 I, 331 ZPO.

[12] Für vergleichende Überblicke vgl. zB Meshel 39 ArbInt 2023, 19; Ke Mu 15 Contemp Asia Arb J (2022), 283. Wie verschieden die einzelnen nationalen Einstellungen sein können, zeigt etwa Griffin JIntArb 17(2) (2000), 19 (23ff.).

[13] Für einen ersten Überblick über ausgewählte Rechtssysteme vgl: im deutsch-amerikanischen Kontext zuerst dargestellt in der Arbeit von Saathoff, Möglichkeiten und Verfahren gerichtlicher Hilfe bei der Beweisaufnahme zugunsten fremdnationaler Handelsschiedsgerichtsverfahren mit internationaler Beteiligung, 1987. Allgemein und einführend mit internationalem Überblick: J.-Cl. Proc.civ. Fasc. 1068 (87 pp., par Gaillard, Intervention des juridictions étatiques). Sehr allgemein gehalten: Carpi ZZPInt 2 (1997), 397 (404f.) (knappe Informationen zu England: § 43, 44 Arbitration Act, Spanien: Art. 27 Ley 36/1988 de Arbitraje, Schweiz: Art. 184 IPRG). Zu ausgewählten Staaten (vor allem Frankreich und die Schweiz) vgl. Schlosser, in Böckstiegel, Schiedsgerichtsbarkeit im Umfeld, S. 58ff. Für die aktuelle Rechtslage in Spanien vgl. Mota ZZPInt 4 (1999), 67 (82f.).

vor der Anwendung von Zwang nicht zurückschrecken, wird sich die Beweiserhebung mit größerer Wahrscheinlichkeit einvernehmlich und ohne Sabotage gestalten. Internationale schiedsrichterliche Erfahrung zeigt, dass in der Regel ein Hinweis des Schiedsgerichts auf die Möglichkeit der Anrufung der staatlichen Gerichte genügen wird, um die Partei bzw. Dritte zur ordnungsmäßigen Mitwirkung am Beweisverfahren anzuhalten. Aus der Sicht der Schiedsrichter ist die Kenntnis der jeweiligen Haltung einer Rechtsordnung auch deswegen wichtig, weil es im Falle der Beweisvereitelung davon abhängig früher oder später zu innerprozessualen Sanktionen greifen wird: Weiß das Schiedsgericht, dass die Gerichte des zu ersuchten Staates großzügig Rechtshilfe gewähren, wird es wahrscheinlich nicht eher eine unbegründete Sachentscheidung etwa als Folge von – den Gedanken der §§ 427, 444 ZPO entsprechenden – *negative inferences* zum Zuge kommen lassen, bis es die betreffenden Beweismittel im Wege der Rechtshilfe einzuholen versucht hat. Ist die Rechtshilfe in der gegebenen Situation dagegen aussichtslos, wird es diese nicht unnötig bemühen und früher zu den schiedsspezifischen innerprozessualen Sanktionen[14] greifen.

Schließlich gibt es noch eine wichtige Überlegung, die die Unterschiede hinsichtlich der Einstellung zur Rechtshilfe relevant werden und sogar als Elemente des internationalen Wettbewerbs um beliebte Schiedsorte erscheinen lässt. Wie empfindlich die Art und Weise der Rechtshilferegelung die Beliebtheit eines Schiedsortes beeinflussen kann, zeigt beispielsweise ein Blick auf die englische Gesetzgebungsgeschichte: Die ab 1950 geltende Regelung des früheren Arbitration Act sicherte in § 12(4)-(6)[15] dem High Court die Befugnis zu, eine discovery of documents in Schiedsverfahren bzw. zugunsten von Schiedsparteien auch ohne Rechtshilfeersuchen seitens des Schiedsgerichts und sogar gegen den Willen des Schiedsgerichts anzuordnen. Nicht von ungefähr wurde diese Vorschrift im Zuge der Schiedsrechtsreform im Jahre 1996 ersatzlos gestrichen. Ausschlaggebend war dabei offenbar die Befürchtung, diese Möglichkeit könnte Parteien von der Wahl Londons als Schiedsort abschrecken.[16] Wie gleich zu zeigen sein wird, spielte die Unterscheidung zwischen schiedsgericht- und parteiinitiierten discovery-Ersuchen auch in der hier zu besprechenden neuen Leitentscheidung des US Supreme Court eine wichtige Rolle.

Wie gezeigt worden ist, entstammt das Bedürfnis nach staatlicher Beweisrechtshilfe letzten Endes der privaten Natur der Schiedsgerichtsbarkeit und damit ihrer Unfähigkeit, hoheitlichen Zwang auszuüben. Diese ihre Eigenschaft kann jedoch – vor allem im internationalen Kontext – nicht nur als Defizit angesehen werden. Aus der privaten Legitimation folgt nämlich auch, dass die Beweisaufnahme durch das

[14] Negative inferences als Sanktion etwa nach den Art 9.6 und 9.7 IBA Rules „[...] the Arbitral Tribunal may infer that such evidence would be adverse to the interests of that Party."

[15] "The High Court shall have ... the same power of making orders in respect of ... discovery of documents ... as it has for the purpose of and in relation to an action or matter in the High Court." Dazu vgl. Böckstiegel, Schiedsgerichtsbarkeit im Umfeld von Politik, Wirtschaft und Gerichtsbarkeit/Schlosser,, 1992, S. 60, und Lew, Contemporary Problems in International Arbitration/Hunter, 1987, S. 195 (197).

[16] Vgl. für Einzelheiten Weigand RIW 1992, 361 und Triebel/Zons IDR 2002, 26 (31).

Schiedsgericht „im Ausland“, anders als die des staatlichen Gerichts, keinen hoheitlichen Beschränkungen unterworfen ist. Das bedeutet, dass der ganze internationalbeweisrechtliche Problemkomplex, wie es sich im internationalen Zivilverfahrensrecht darstellt, in schiedsrichterlichen Verfahren größtenteils entfällt. Zwar wird die Schiedsgerichtsbarkeit traditionell in der Rechtsprechung sowohl des BGH[17] als auch US-amerikanischer Gerichte[18] als echte Rechtsprechung oder zumindest deren funktionales Äquivalent angesehen. Dafür spricht als starkes Argument nicht zuletzt die Gleichsetzung der Wirkungen des Schiedsspruchs mit den Urteilswirkungen in § 1055 ZPO und in der herrschenden US-amerikanischen Lehre von der Anwendbarkeit der Doktrinen der issue preclusion, claim preclusion, res iudicata und collateral estoppel auf arbitral awards.[19] Die Schiedsrichter üben aber keine Hoheitsfunktionen aus, sie „setzen keine Hoheitsakte.“[20] Deshalb sind der Beweisaufnahme durch die Schiedsrichter auch vom Völkerrecht her keine territorialen Schranken gesetzt.[21] Die Befürchtungen, die in ausländischen Rechtshilfeersuchen staatlicher Gerichte Souverenitätseingriffe gesehen und damit hauptsächlich den transatlantischen Justizkonflikt genährt haben[22], werden daher im schiedsverfahrensrechtlichen Kontext größtenteils gegenstandslos. Internationale Schiedsgerichte haben damit die Chance, den transatlantischen Justizkonflikt auf dem Gebiet der extraterritorialen Beweisaufnahme abzumildern bzw. sich und Parteien mit den Nachteilen zu verschonen, die sich in der staatlichen Rechtshilfepraxis zeigen. Zu Souvereinitätsbedenken und damit zu mit dem Justizkonflikt vergleichbaren Reibungen kann es allenfalls dann kommen, wenn ein ausländisches Schiedsgericht über die Einschaltung der Gerichte seines Forumstaates Rechtshilfe erreichen will. Aus der Perspektive Deutschlands als ersuchtem Staat dürfte gerade dieser Aspekt mittlerweile weniger gravierend sein, wurde doch der deutsche Vorbehalt gegenüber discovery-Ersuchen US-amerikanischen Stils durch die unlängst – wiederum symbolträchtig praktisch gleichzeitig mit ZF Automotive v. Luxshare – erfolgte Änderung des § 14 HZÜ-HBÜ-AG[23] abgemildert. Aus US-amerikanischer Sicht wiederum war dies nie wirklich ein Problem, kennt doch das US-Recht mit seinen weite Informationspflichten statuierenden discovery-Regeln eines der liberalsten

---

[17] Vgl. aus der ganzen Fülle einschlägiger höchstrichterlicher Entscheidungen nur: BGH 19.12.1968 – VII ZR 83/66, BGHZ 51, 255 (258); BGH 5.11.1970 – VII ZR 31/69, BGHZ 54, 392 (395); BGH 3.7.1975 – III ZR 78/73, BGHZ 65, 59 (61); BGH 5.5.1986 – III ZR 233/84, BGHZ 98, 32 (36).

[18] Vgl. zB Moore v. Conliffe, 7 Cal.4th 634, 636 (Cal. 1994).

[19] Vgl. zB Freecharm Ltd. v. Atlas Wealth Holdings Corp., 499 F.App'x 941, 943 (11th Cir. 2012); Restatement (Third) U.S. Law of Int'l Comm. Arb. § 4.35.).

[20] BGH 3.7.1975 – III ZR 78/73, BGHZ 65, 59 (61).

[21] Vgl. zB Berger IPRax 2001, 522 (523).

[22] Vgl. dazu ausführlich Bertele, Souveränität und Verfahrensrecht – Eine Untersuchung der aus dem Völkerrecht ableitbaren Grenzen staatlicher extraterritorialer Jurisdiktion im Verfahrensrecht, 1998.

[23] Gesetz zur Ausführung des Haager Übereinkommens vom 15. November 1965 über die Zustellung gerichtlicher und außergerichtlicher Schriftstücke im Ausland in Zivil- oder Handelssachen und des Haager Übereinkommens vom 18. März 1970 über die Beweisaufnahme im Ausland in Zivil- oder Handelssachen, geändert mWv 1.7.2022 durch Art. 3 Nr. 3, Art. 23 Abs. 1 Gesetz v. 24.6.2022 (BGBl. 2022 I 959).

und aufklärungsfreundlichsten Systeme der Welt, das dazu noch über eine Öffnungsklausel des Bundesrechts das eigene weitherzige Beweisrechtsregime ausländischen Foren zur Verfügung stellt. Gerade diese Öffnungsklausel ist jedoch Gegenstand der hier zu besprechenden Entscheidung des Supreme Court geworden, womit zugleich das Vertrauen in die erwähnte Schiedsfreundlichkeit des US-amerikanischen Rechts aufs Neue ins Wanken geraten ist. Daher soll unsere Aufmerksamkeit zunächst der Vorschrift selbst gelten.

2. Die Öffnungsklausel des US-amerikanischen Rechts: Extraterritoriale Beweisrechtshilfe

In dem mit der Gerichtsverfassung und dem Verfahrensrecht befassten 28. Titel („Judiciary and Judicial Procedure") des United States Code eröffnet 28 USC § 1782(a) ausländischen Foren den Zugang zu den Beweisermittlungsmethoden des pre-trial discovery US-amerikanischen Rechts:

"Assistance to foreign and international tribunals and to litigants before such tribunals:

(a) The district court of the district in which a person resides or is found may order him to give his testimony or statement or to produce a document or other thing for use in a proceeding in a foreign or international tribunal, including criminal investigations conducted before formal accusation. The order may be made pursuant to a letter rogatory issued, or request made, by a foreign or international tribunal or upon the application of any interested person and may direct that the testimony or statement be given, or the document or other thing be produced, before a person appointed by the court. By virtue of his appointment, the person appointed has power to administer any necessary oath and take the testimony or statement. The order may prescribe the practice and procedure, which may be in whole or part the practice and procedure of the foreign country or the international tribunal, for taking the testimony or statement or producing the document or other thing. To the extent that the order does not prescribe otherwise, the testimony or statement shall be taken, and the document or other thing produced, in accordance with the Federal Rules of Civil Procedure.

A person may not be compelled to give his testimony or statement or to produce a document or other thing in violation of any legally applicable privilege."

Mit dieser Vorschrift hatten die Vereinigten Staaten sowohl in der Ursprungsfassung Mitte des 19. Jahrhunderts, dann in der modernen Fassung von 1958 als auch in der aus unserer Sicht hochrelevanten erweiterten Fassung von 1964 die Absicht gehabt, auf dem Gebiet der internationalen Rechtshilfe früh Weichen zu stellen und in der Staatengemeinschaft eine Art Vorreiter- und zugleich Vorbildrolle einzunehmen. Diese gesetzgeberische Willensrichtung ist reichlich dokumentiert sowohl in der Gesetzgebungsgeschichte als auch in der entsprechenden Auslegung durch die mit der Vorschrift befassten Bundesgerichte: Der am Entwurf maßgeblich beteiligte Philip Amram[24] bezeichnete sie überschwänglich als die liberalste, fort-

[24] In mehrfacher Eigenschaft: United States delegate to the Hague Conference in 1956, 1960, 1964, and 1968. Chairman of the Advisory Committee to the United States Commission on International Rules and Judicial Procedure.

schrittlichste, effizienteste und effektivste Rechtshilfevorschrift auf der ganzen Welt.[25] Die Vorschrift setzt keinerlei Reziprozität oder sonstige Bedingungen für die auf amerikanischem Boden für ausländische Gerichte zu leistende Rechtshilfe voraus[26] und stößt damit die Tür zu den amerikanischen Gerichten als Rechtshilfeorganen für ausländische Gerichte weit auf. Der Kongress hatte damit das erklärte Ziel, durch dieses vorbildliche Beispiel andere Staaten zu ähnlich liberalen Rechtshilferegelungen zu bewegen.[27] Diesem Gedanken entsprechend wird die Vorschrift auch durch die Bundesgerichte ausgelegt[28], was in einer sehr hohen Anzahl von positiv beschiedenen Rechtshilfeersuchen mündet. Dass die genannte Hoffnung, die Vorschrift würde regulatorisch weltweit Pate stehen, unerfüllt bleiben sollte, liegt vor allem an den Unterschieden in der Substantiierungs- und Spezifizierungspflicht der common law- und civil law Verfahrensrechtstraditionen, die hauptsächlich zur Erklärung des discovery-Vorbehalts laut Art. 23 HBÜ seitens europäischer Staaten geführt haben. Dies ändert aber nichts daran, dass die Vorschrift als eine Verkörperung des *doctrine of comity*[29] gilt. Die Liberalität der Einstellung der amerikanischen Rechtsprechung geht so weit, dass sie eine amerikanische discovery auch solchen Ersuchen zugutekommen lässt, deren Gegenstand im ersuchenden Staat selbst kein zulässiges Beweismittel zutage fördern würde.[30] Die Bereitschaft amerikanischer Bundesgerichte, aufgrund § 1782 ausländischen Gerichten Rechtshilfe zu leisten war und ist damit im transatlantischen Rechtsverkehr weit liberaler[31] und unbe-

[25] "... the most liberal, the most advanced, and the most efficient, and the most effective system of judicial assistance in the world." Nachweis übernommen von Weis ZVglRWiss 90 (1991), 411 (412).

[26] Application of Malev Hungarian Airlines, 964 F.2d 97, 100 (Conn. 1992): "We find nothing in the text of 28 U.S.C. § 1782 which would support a quasi-exhaustion requirement ... It would undermine the policy of improving procedures for assistance to foreign and international tribunals ... Additionally, it would undermine the policy of prompting foreign courts to act similarly based on our own generous example."

[27] Vgl. Report No. 1580, 88th Congress, 2d Session (1964), U.S.C.C.A.N. 3782 (3783): "It is hoped that the initiative taken by the United States in improving its procedures will invite foreign countries similarly to adjust their procedures." Vgl. auch die sehr detaillierte Gesetzgebungsgeschichte und Rechtsprechungsübersicht bei Stahr 30 Va.J.Int'l L. (1990), 597 und im deutschen Schrifttum Eschenfelder, Beweiserhebung im Ausland und ihre Verwertung im inländischen Zivilprozess, 2002, S. 245ff.

[28] "The twin aims of the statute are to provide 'efficient means of assistance to participants in international litigation in our federal courts' and to encourage 'foreign countries by example to provide similar means of assistance to our courts'", in re Ishihara Chem. Co., 251 F.3d 120, 124 (2d Cir. 2001).

[29] Entwickelt in Hilton v. Guyot, 159 U.S. 113. Vgl. auch § 102 Restatement Second on Conflict of Laws (1971), und Schütze, Deutsch-amerikanische Urteilsanerkennung, 1992, 9f.

[30] Application of Gianoli Aldunate, 3 F.3d 54, 62 (2d Cir. 1993): "We hold that section 1782 does not contain a requirement that the material requested in the district court be discoverable under the laws of the foreign jurisdiction." Das gleiche Ergebnis fordert übrigens Schlosser für deutsche Schiedsverfahren. Es bestehe nach ihm „... generell kein Grund, Informationen für unverwertbar zu halten, die im Ausland legal erlangt worden sind, selbst wenn sie im Inland unter vergleichbaren Umständen legal nicht hätten erlangt werden können. Für staatliche Gerichte gilt richtigerweise nichts anderes." Schlosser, Das neue deutsche Recht der Schiedsgerichtsbarkeit, 2. Aufl. 1989 S. 202.

[31] Für den äußerst weiten Anwendungsbereich der Vorschrift vgl nur die berühmtesten Leitentscheidungen: In re Request for Judicial Assistance from Seoul District Criminal Court, 555 F.2d

kümmerter, als die Rechtslage und die Praxis in Deutschland und überhaupt in den Rechtsordnungen diesseits des Atlantiks, die amerikanischen Ersuchen lange Zeit zunächst mit der HBÜ-Vorrangigkeit und dem daselbst erklärten Vorbehalt gegenüber discovery-Ersuchen begegneten.[32]

Nun stellt sich die Frage, ob nicht nur ausländische staatliche Gerichtsverfahren, sondern auch ausländische Schiedsverfahren, dh solche, deren Schiedsort außerhalb der USA liegt, in die Gunst dieser Offenherzigkeit des 28 USC § 1782(a) und der sich daran anschließenden Rechtsprechung kommen können. Fallen ausländische, ua also auch deutsche Schiedsverfahren[33] in den Anwendungsbereich des § 1782, so erfährt die Möglichkeit der Sachverhaltsaufklärung in diesen Schiedsverfahren eine weitreichende Bereicherung, sobald Beweismittel aus bzw. in den USA zu beschaffen sind. Eine solche Konstellation ist angesichts des Handelsvolumens und des weit verästelten wirtschaftlichen Austausches zwischen europäischen Staaten, insbesondere Deutschland, und den USA keine Seltenheit in der einschlägigen Schiedspraxis. In der Sprache des deutschen Zivilprozessrechts wäre die Anwendbarkeit des 28 USC § 1782 auf ausländische private Schiedsverfahren nichts anderes bedeuten, als die Vorschrift als vollständige, spiegelbildliche Entsprechung des § 1050 iVm § 1025 Abs. 2 ZPO erkennen zu dürfen: Was das deutsche Recht im Wege der Durchbrechung des Territorialitätsprinzips erreicht, würde das US-amerikanische Recht durch einfache Einbeziehung ausländischer privater Foren in den Wortlaut der primären Regelung erreichen. Und in der Tat sprechen gute Gründe dafür, § 1782 als Öffnungsklausel nicht nur zugunsten fremder staatlicher Gerichtsverfahren, sondern auch zugunsten „fremder", dh mit außer-amerikanischem Schiedsort ablaufender Schiedsverfahren anzusehen. Hierfür sprechen gewichtige Stimmen aus Literatur und Rechtsprechung, die sich vornehmlich an die Gesetzgebungsgeschichte anlehnen:

Es finden sich bereits in der geltenden Fassung der Vorschrift mehrere Anhaltspunkte, die prima facie ihre Anwendbarkeit auf ausländische Schiedsverfahren na helegen. Sicher ist eines der wichtigsten Indizien die 1964 erfolgte Änderung des Wortlauts von ursprünglich *court* zu *tribunal.* Zur Begründung der schiedsfreundlichen Auslegung wird daher nicht von ungefähr zumeist auf die Äußerungen von *Hans Smit* verwiesen. Diese bilden bis heute das Quellgebiet praktisch aller Stimmen, die eine Wirkungserstreckung der Vorschrift auf private Schiedsverfahren mit Schiedsort außerhalb der USA befürworten. Der als Mitglied des beratenden Ausschusses (Advisory Committee to the United States Commission on International Judicial Assistance) maßgeblich an der Neukodifikation des § 1782 mitwirkende *Smit* berichtete vom zentralen gesetzgeberischen Willen, Schiedsverfahren zu för-

720 (C.A. Cal. 1977; In re Court of the Commissioner of Patents for the Republic of South Africa, 88 F.R.D. 75 (D.C.Pa. 1980); John Deere Ltd. v. Sperry Corp., 754 F.2d 132 (C.A.Pa. 1985); Lo Ka Chun v. Lo To, 858 F.2d 1564 (C.A. 11th Circuit 1988). Die Entwicklung der liberalen Rechtsprechung erreicht ihren Gipfel dann in Malev, 964 F.2d 97, 100 (Conn. 1992), der seitdem praktisch für bedingungslose Rechtshilfeleistung sorgt.

[32] Vgl. zum Ganzen detailliert Varga, Beweiserhebung in transatlantischen Schiedsverfahren – Eine Suche nach Kompromissen zwischen deutscher und US-amerikanischer Beweisrechtstradition, 2006, S 234 ff.

[33] Vgl. §§ 1025, 1043 ZPO.

dern. Insbesondere spreche die 1964 in Kraft getretene Änderung des Wortlauts, wonach nicht mehr nur Verfahren vor internationalen Gerichten, die durch internationale Verträge mit amerikanischer Beteiligung errichtet wurden, sondern ganz allgemein „ausländische und internationale" Spruchkörper erfasst sein sollen, eindeutig für eine denkbar liberale Auslegung, und somit für die Anwendbarkeit der Vorschrift auf private Schiedsverfahren.[34] *Smit*s Äußerungen stießen auf großen Widerhall und es wurde seither immer wieder auf ihn zurückgegriffen zur Begründung der weiten, schiedsfreundlichen Auslegung. Seine Argumentation wurde in der wissenschaftlichen Diskussion Schritt für Schritt um weitere Punkte bereichert, wie etwa um den Gedanken, 28 USC § 1782 solle für ausländische Schiedsverfahren sogar noch liberaler angewandt werden als für Ersuchen seitens staatlicher Gerichte, da Schiedsgerichte nicht als Souverenitätsträger in Erscheinung träten und deshalb auch durch die ihnen geleistete Rechtshilfe ein geringerer Eingriff in amerikanische innere Angelegenheiten entstünde.[35]Auch das maßgebliche deutsche Schrifttum ging schon immer recht einheitlich wie selbstverständlich von der Anwendbarkeit von 28 USC § 1782 auf ausländische – und damit auf deutsche – Schiedsverfahren aus. Als erster vertrat *Junker* in seiner grundlegenden Arbeit, nachdem er die grundsätzlich liberale Haltung der USA gegenüber Beweisrechtshilfe dargestellt hatte, die Position, 28 USC § 1782 erfasse ohne Weiteres auch Ersuchen von ausländischen Schiedsgerichten.[36] Ebenso ging bereits *Saathoff* von der gleichen Annahme aus.[37] Seitdem ist die Beurteilung der Frage in der Wissenschaft – soweit ersichtlich und zumindest in der gesamten Zeitspanne zwischen 1964 und 2022, also dem Jahr der Entscheidung in ZF Automotive vs Luxshare – unverändert.[38]

Diese zu einer Wirkungserstreckung neigende Mehrheitsmeinung setzte sich zunächst auch in einem gewichtigen Teil der US-amerikanischen Rechtsprechung auf District- sowie Circuit Court-Ebene durch, wobei sich nach anfänglicher schiedsfreundlicher Haltung vieler Distriktgerichte es bald zu einer Spaltung der Rechtsprechung auf der Ebene der Bundesberufungsgerichte kam. Diese um die Jahrtau-

---

[34] Smit 62 Colum.L.Rev. (1962), 1264: "The term 'tribunal' embraces all bodies exercising adjudicatory powers, and includes investigating magistrates, administrative and arbitral tribunals, and quasi-judicial agencies, as well as conventional civil, commercial, criminal, and administrative courts [...] The increasing number and importance of international tribunals make this liberal provision of assistance in aid of litigation in international tribunals of great significance. New Section 1782 ensures that an important international court [...] and litigants before such a court can be given any reasonable assistance they may require. [...] The new legislation also authorizes assistance in aid of international arbitral tribunals." Vgl. auch Smit 8 Am.Rev.Int'l Arb. (1997),153.

[35] Newman/Castilla JIntArb 9(2) (1992), 61 (69); Schwartz/Johnson JIntArb 15(3) (1998), 53; Lurie/Howard JIntArb 17(3) (2000), 55; Hammond, JIntArb 17(4) (2000), 131. Ebenso bereits aus der Zeit nach ZF Automotive v. Luxshare: van Ginkel 33 ARIA (2022), 187.

[36] Junker, Discovery im deutsch-amerikanischen Rechtsverkehr, 1987, S. 276, Fn. 134.

[37] Saathoff, Möglichkeiten und Verfahren gerichtlicher Hilfe bei der Beweisaufnahme zugunsten fremdnationaler Handelsschiedsgerichtsverfahren mit internationaler Beteiligung, 1987, S. 122.

[38] Vgl. detailliert Varga, Beweiserhebung in transatlantischen Schiedsverfahren – Eine Suche nach Kompromissen zwischen deutscher und US-amerikanischer Beweisrechtstradition, 2006, S. 234ff. und insbesondere noch Schlosser 12 Mich.J.Int'l L. (1990), 150 (170), Fn 84.; Gottwald, Generalbericht, S. 71 unter Bezugnahme auf Carbonneaus Länderbericht. Ferner – freilich mit etwas indirekter Formulierung – Baum FS Böckstiegel, 2001, 21 (23) und McDonald/Wetzler RIW 2000, 212 (214), Fn. 10.

sendwende einsetzende relativierende Haltung einiger Berufungsgerichte führte dann zu jenem etwa zwei Jahrzehnte währenden „Circuit Split", der den Weg zur hier zu besprechenden Supreme Court Entscheidung ebnete und dem wir uns deswegen im Folgenden zuwenden.

3. Die Situation vor dem Supreme Court Shutdown: Der Circuit Split

Die ersten beiden meilensteinartigen Entscheidungen, die zunächst die von der Wissenschaft geforderte positive Einstellung gegenüber ausländischen Schiedsverfahren verwirklichten, ergingen Mitte der 1990er Jahre. In *Technostroyexport* hatte die russische Partei eines in Stockholm stattfindenden Schiedsverfahrens unter Bezugnahme auf 28 USC § 1782 Dokumentenvorlagen und Zeugenvernehmungen in New York beantragt. Das Gericht wies zwar den konkreten discovery-Antrag ab, erklärte dann aber in einem obiter dictum mit folgendem Wortlaut ausländische Schiedsgerichte für „tribunals" im Sinne des 28 USC § 1782:

> *"The court is of the view that an arbitrator or arbitration panel is a 'tribunal' under § 1782. The court further believes that, if Technostroy had obtained a ruling from a foreign arbitrator that discovery should take place, the court would be empowered under § 1782 to enforce that ruling in the United States. However, Technostroy has made no effort to obtain any ruling from the arbitrators. It has come directly to the Federal District Court. The court concludes that, under these circumstances, it would be improper to order the discovery requested."*[39]

Das Gericht differenziert also zwischen discovery-Ersuchen, die vom Schiedsgericht stammen und Anträgen, die die Parteien selbst, ohne Zutun des Schiedsgerichts initiieren. Aus der weiteren Begründung der Entscheidung geht hervor, dass Letzteren deswegen der Erfolg versagt blieb, weil die Kontrolle über das Beweisverfahren letztlich beim Schiedsgericht verbleiben sollte. Wenn die Antragsbefugnis auch den Parteien allein eröffnet würde, wäre diese Kontrolle dem Schiedsgericht entzogen.[40] Zwar ist die Entscheidung wegen der expliziten eigenständigen Antragsbefugnis „jeder interessierten Person" („any interested person") in 28 USC § 1782 rätselhaft, es soll hier für unsere Zwecke genügen, dass damit die Serie der eine Wirkungserstreckung bejahenden Entscheidungen einsetzte. In der zwei Jahre später ergangenen Entscheidung *Bushnak* hielt dann ein anderes Distriktgericht die Parteien selbst für antragsberechtigt und gab dem Antrag einer Partei eines in London stattfindenden Schiedsverfahrens statt.[41] Nach *Technostroyexport* und *Bushnak* folgte eine beträchtliche Anzahl weiterer erstinstanzlicher positiver Entscheidungen[42], die durch die Berufungsgerichte auch bestätigt wurden. Zu den

---

[39] Application of Technostroyexport, 853 F.Supp. 695, 697 (S.D.N.Y. 1994).

[40] Application of Technostroyexport, 853 F.Supp. 695, 698 (S.D.N.Y. 1994).

[41] In re Bushnak, E.D. North Carolina, 19 August 1996. Implizit auch In re Trygg-Hansa Insurance Co., 896 F.Supp. 624 (E.D. Louisiana 1995).

[42] In re Applicaion of Roz Trading Ltd., 469 F.Supp.2d 1221 (N.D.Ga. 2006) bejahend für VIAC aufgrund grammatikalischer Auslegung; In re Application of Hallmark Capital Corporation, 534 F.Supp.2d 951 (D.Minn. 2007) Urkundenvorlage bejaht für israelisches privates Schiedsverfahren; In re Application of Babcock Borsig AG, 583 F.Supp.2d 233, 241 (D.Mass. 2008) grundsätzlich bejahend, im Individualfall scheiterte jedoch der discovery request am Fehlen wei-

bedeutendsten bejahenden Circuit (Appellate) Court-Entscheidungen zählt etwa im 6th Circuit *Abdul Latif Jameel v. FedEx Corporation*[43], die auch noch in der ZF Automotive v. Luxshare-Prozesshistorie eine Rolle spielte. Dort bejahte das Berufungsgericht auf der Grundlage einfacher sprachlicher Auslegung die Gewährung des discovery-Antrags einer saudi-arabischen Partei (ALJ) gegen eine US-amerikanische Partei (FedEx) in einem Schiedsverfahren in Dubai und erteilte der von der Gegenseite ins Feld geführten Argumentation der Differenzierung zwischen „state-sponsored" und „private" auf Normebene eine ausdrückliche Absage, da im Wortlaut der Vorschrift nichts für eine solche Differenzierung und eine damit einhergehende Einschränkung der Wirkung auf staatliche Streitentscheidungsorgane spreche. Etwaige Einschränkungen im Individualfall seien ausschließlich dem richterlichen Ermessen vorbehalten, wie dies die *Intel*-Rechtsprechung des Supreme Court ja auch suggeriert, dies ändert aber nichts daran, dass ausländische private Schiedsgerichte klar vom Wortlaut des 28 USC § 1782 erfasst seien:

"Upon careful consideration of the statutory text, the meaning of that text based on common definitions and usage of the language at issue, as well as the statutory context and history of § 1782(a), we hold that this provision permits discovery for use in the private commercial arbitration at issue. [...] Here, the text, context, and structure of § 1782(a) provide no reason to doubt that the word 'tribunal' includes private commercial arbitral panels established pursuant to contract and having the authority to issue decisions that bind the parties. Therefore, we need look no further to hold that the DIFC-LCIA Arbitration panel is a 'foreign or international tribunal [...]'"[44]

Mit ähnlicher Argumentation ordnete auch der 4th Circuit discovery zugunsten eines englischen Schiedsverfahrens in *Servotronics v. Boeing* an, jedoch bereits unter Einschluss weiterer Argumente, insbesondere einer ausdrücklichen Bejahung der Nähe bzw. der funktionalen Äquivalenz von privaten Schiedsverfahren mit staatlich-gerichtlichen Verfahren:

"[...] arbitration in the United States is a congressionally endorsed and regulated process that is judicially supervised. And it was developed as a favored alternative to the judicial process for the resolution of disputes. Thus, contrary to Boeing's general assertion that arbitration is not a product of 'government-conferred authority,' under U. S. law, it clearly is."[45]

---

terer Voraussetzungen; Jeweils mit ähnlichen Argumenten und unter Rückgriff auf die Smit-Auslegung ferner: Comisión Ejecutiva Hidroeléctrica del Rio Lempa v. Nejapa Power Co., LLC, 2008 WL 4809035 (D.Del. 2008); Ukrnafta v. Carpatsky Petroleum Corp., No 09-MC-265, 2009 WL 2877156 (D Conn 2009); Ex rel application of Winning (HK) Shipping Co. Ltd., 2010 WL 1796579 (S.D.Fla. 2010); In re Application of Reis Veiga, 746 F Supp. 2d 8 (DDC 2010); In re application of Mesa Power Group, 2013 WL 1890222 (D. New Jersey 2013); In re Application of Owl Shipping, LLC, No. 14-CV-5655, 2014 WL 5320192 (DNJ 2014).

[43] In re Application to Obtain Discovery for Use in Foreign Proceedings, (Abdul Latif Jameel v. FedEx Corporation) 939 F.3d 710 (6th Cir. 2019). Vgl. auch in die gleiche Richtung weisend bereits In re Consorcio Ecutroriano de Telecomunicaciones S. A. v. Forwarding (USA), Inc., 685 F.3d 987, 995 (11th Cir. 2012).

[44] In re Application to Obtain Discovery for Use in Foreign Proceedings, (Abdul Latif Jameel v. FedEx Corporation) 939 F.3d 710, 714, 723 (6th Cir. 2019).

[45] Servotronics, Inc. v. Boeing Co., 954 F.3d 209, 214 (4th Cir. 2020).

Parallel zu dieser schiedsfreundlichen Entwicklung an zahlreichen Bundesdistriktgerichten und an den Bundesberufungsgerichten im 4th und 6th Circuit nahm indessen ebenfalls bereits seit Ende der 1990-er Jahre eine entgegengesetzte Tendenz in der Rechtsprechung Gestalt an, die sich mit vergleichbar konstanten Argumenten bis zum letzten Augenblick, dh bis zur wegweisenden Entscheidung des Supreme Court in 2022 gehalten hat. Diese sich mit der Entscheidung *Medway* ankündigende, und seitdem von den Gerichten vielfach bestätigte ablehnende Einstellung gegenüber ausländischen Schiedsverfahren etablierte sich dann ebenfalls auf der Ebene der Berufungsinstanzen in mehreren Circuits, die dementsprechend also eine der Rechtsprechung der 4th und 6th Circuits zuwiderlaufende Auslegung des 28 USC § 1782 zur Geltung brachten. In *Medway* lehnte ein New Yorker Bundesrichter mit etwas ungewöhnlichen, teils auch redundanten Argumenten die Rechtshilfeleistung ab. Hier begehrte eine der Parteien eines in England laufenden Schiedsverfahrens Urkundenvorlagen von General Electric Company („GE“) in New York, die im Schiedsverfahren nicht Partei war. In der Begründung der Zurückweisung des discovery-Antrags führte das Gericht zunächst Folgendes aus:

“At oral arguments, I asked petitioner's counsel a series of hypotheticals concerning what weight he would give to rulings of tribunals, such as a feudal patriarch or a Bet Din (Jewish religious court). A feudal patriarch and a Bet Din may be referred to colloquially as tribunals but are not tribunals in a formal sense. If they were tribunals under Section 1782, the potential discovery problems would be fascinating. A private arbitration generally has not been referred to as a tribunal. … I find that an arbitration is not a tribunal for the purposes of Section 1782. Congress intended this statute to assist official, governmental bodies exercising an adjudicatory function. The legislative history of Section 1782 does not suggest an intent to encompass unofficial, private arbitrations – which Congress and the courts have consistently treated as creatures of a contract which a court should enforce just like any other obligation imposed by private agreement.”[46]

In eindeutiger Abkehr von dem im damals noch frischen Fall *Technostroyexport* vertretenen Standpunkt sollen also nach dieser Entscheidung Schiedsgerichte nicht unter 28 USC § 1782 fallen, da sie lediglich auf einem Schuldverhältnis basierten und daher keine offiziellen staatlichen Streiterledigungsorgane seien. 28 USC § 1782 würde nur solche ausländischen Gerichte erfassen und begünstigen, die unter die letztgenannte Kategorie fielen. Dass Richter *Duffy* dieses Ergebnis gerade über einen Vergleich der Schiedsgerichtsbarkeit mit der feudalen bzw. der traditionellen jüdischen religiösen Gerichtsbarkeit (Beth Din) erreicht, widerspiegelt jedenfalls auch einen gewissen – im internationalen Vergleich doch ungewöhnlichen – grundsätzlichen Unwillen gegenüber internationalen Schiedsverfahren. Im weiteren Gang der Entscheidungsbegründung führt er allerdings zwei neue, eher schon sachliche Kriterien ein. Zunächst verweist er darauf – wie dies in inländischen Fällen auch wiederholt Ablehnungsgrund gewesen ist – dass der Antragsgegner gar nicht Partei im Schiedsverfahren sei und daher für ihn auch keine aus der

[46] Application of Medway Power Ltd., 985 F.Supp. 402, 403 (S.D.N.Y. 1997).

Schiedsvereinbarung resultierenden Pflichten oder Lasten entstehen könnten. Dazu formuliert er:

"… GE is not a party to the Medway arbitration, has not consented to arbitrate any dispute with Medway, and has never agreed to abide by any decision of the English attorney selected as an arbitrator in the Medway matter."[47]

Das weitreichendste, da auch in der ablehnenden Haltung weiterer Gerichte seitdem stets wiederkehrende Argument schöpft das Gericht aber aus einem Vergleich der Reichweite der für inländische Schiedsverfahren geltenden § 7 Federal Arbitration Act (FAA) mit dem für ausländische Verfahren einschlägigen 28 USC § 1782. Während nämlich § 7 FAA die Rechtshilfehandlungen bei der Beweisaufnahme auf einen einzigen Distrikt beschränkt, nämlich auf den Sprengel des Bundesdistriktgerichts, in dem der Sitz des Schiedsgerichts liegt, enthält § 1782 naturgemäß (ausländischer Schiedsort!) keine solche Einschränkung und macht die Rechtshilfe auf dem ganzen Gebiet der Vereinigten Staaten möglich. Ein Unterschied hinsichtlich *venue,* der ja aus der Belegenheit des Schiedsortes außerhalb der USA naturgemäß folgt, der uns aber im Folgenden noch tiefer beschäftigen wird. Eine Geltungserstreckung des 28 USC § 1782 würde also für das *Medway*-Gericht gleichsam bedeuten, dass ausländische Schiedsverfahren unverhältnismäßig besser als inländische gestellt wären. Dieses Ergebnis wird – wie folgender Auszug aus dem Urteilstext zeigt – als untragbar empfunden:

"Section 7 of the Act (FAA) empowers a district court to compel non-parties to produce documents or testimony for an arbitration hearing – but the power granted is limited to witnesses situated in the district in which the arbitration is being held. Medway's construction of the statute would result in assistance to foreign arbitrations throughout the territory of the United States under Section 1782, but assistance for domestic arbitrations only within the district where the arbitration is being held pursuant to the federal statute that specifically addresses judicial assistance to arbitrations."[48]

Die weiteren, discovery-Anträge negativ bescheidenden Entscheidungen der Distriktgerichte in den folgenden Jahren wiederholten größtenteils diese drei, im Urteil *Medway* angeführten Hauptargumente.[49] Das gleiche gilt für die Berufungsinstanzen. Für das Berufungsgericht im für den transatlantischen Rechts(hilfe)verkehr wegen der überdurchschnittlichen Präsenz international tätiger Wirtschaftsunternehmen und Geldinstitute hochrelevanten 2nd Circuit im Fall *NBC v. Bear Stearns* fällt ein ICC-Schiedsverfahren nicht unter 28 USC § 1782, weil das Schiedsgericht der Internationalen Handelskammer nicht als „tribunal" im Sinne der Vorschrift anzusehen sei. Zudem bereichert das *NBC*-Gericht das Argument aus dem

[47] Application of Medway Power Ltd., 985 F.Supp. 402, 404 (S.D.N.Y. 1997).

[48] Application of Medway Power Ltd., 985 F.Supp. 402, 404, 405 (S.D.N.Y. 1997).

[49] La Comision Ejecutiva Hidroelecctrica Del Rio Lempa v. El Paso Corporation, 617 F. Supp.2d 481, 487 (S.D.Tex. 2008); In re Arbitration between Norfolk Southern Corporation, et al. v. ACE Bermuda Ltd., 626 F.Supp.2d 882 (N.D.Ill. 2009); In re Application of Operadora SB Mexico, 2009 WL 2433138 (M.D.Fla. 2009); In re Finserve Grp. Ltd., 2011 WL 5024264 (D. S.C. 2011); In re EWE Gasspeicher GmbH, 2020 WL 1272612 (D.Del. 2020).

Vergleich zwischen § 7 FAA und 28 USC § 1782 um einen weiteren wichtigen Gesichtspunkt. Während es für das Gericht in *Medway* auf den territorialen Aspekt (in personam jurisdiction und venue) des Vergleichs ankam, betont Richter *Cabranes* in *NBC* auch die Unterschiede bezüglich der Antragsberechtigung. Während nämlich § 7 FAA eindeutig nur Schiedsrichtern die Antragbefugnis verleiht, erstreckt 28 USC § 1782 die gleiche Befugnis dagegen auf jede interessierte Person, damit vor allem auf die Schiedsparteien selbst. Wäre 28 USC § 1782 auf ausländische Schiedsverfahren anwendbar, so würde das die Ungleichbehandlung ausländischer und inländischer Schiedsverfahren weiter verschärfen, könnten doch die Parteien in Selbstregie, ohne schiedsrichterliche Kontrolle eine pre-hearing discovery durchführen, was Parteien inländischer Schiedsverfahren wiederum nicht gestattet sei. Für das Berufungsgericht des 2nd Circuit ist das inakzeptabel:

"... § 7 explicitly confers authority only upon arbitrators; by necessary implication, the parties to an arbitration may not employ this provision to subpoena documents or witnesses. ... The limitations in § 7 of the FAA, described above, are consistent with these traditional discovery limits, which would be overridden by the application of § 1782 to proceedings before private arbitral panels. Opening the door to the type of discovery sought by NBC in this case likely would undermine one of the significant advantages of arbitration, and thus arguably conflict with the strong federal policy favoring arbitration as an alternative means of dispute resolution."[50]

Auch das Bundesberufungsgericht für den 5th Circuit beruft sich im Fall *Kazakhstan v. Biedermann International* auf die gleichen Argumente und lässt damit die zugunsten eines Stockholmer Schiedsverfahrens unternommenen Beweisermittlungsversuche erfolglos bleiben. Auch hier dominiert die Sichtweise, nach der die Rechtshilfeleistung nach 28 USC § 1782 nur staatlichen Gerichten, nicht aber Schiedsgerichten, und noch weniger Schiedsparteien zustünde:

"Empowering arbitrators or, worse, the parties, in private international disputes to seek ancillary discovery through the federal courts does not benefit the arbitration process. ... The provision was enlarged to further comity among nations, not to complicate and undermine the salutary device of private international arbitration."[51]

Die in diesem Sinne schiedsfeindliche Entwicklung der Rechtsprechung des 2nd und 5th Circuit erfuhr zuletzt im Jahre 2020 zweifache Bestätigung in den Bundesberufungsinstanzen. Zuerst bestätigte im Juli 2020 der 2nd Circuit seine inzwischen zwei Jahrzehnte alt gewordene NBC-Rechtsprechung in *Hanwei GUO v. Deutsche Bank Securities Inc. et al.*[52] und qualifizierte das CIETAC als eindeutig privates

---

[50] National Broadcasting Co. Inc., v. Bear Stearns & Co. Inc., 165 F.3d 184, 187, 191 (C.A. 2nd Circuit 1999). Lesenswert dazu die Einblicke in die womöglich auch persönliche Abneigungen gegen Hans Smit einschließende Motivation des Berufungsrichters bei van Ginkel 33 ARIA (2022), 187 (209) („Was There a Personal Dimension?").

[51] Republic of Kazakhstan v. Biedermann International, 168 F.3d 880, 883 (C.A. 5th Circuit 1999).

[52] Hanwei GUO v. Deutsche Bank Securities Inc., J.P. Morgan Securities LLC, Merrill Lynch, Pierce, Fenner & Smith Incorporated, Morgan Stanley & Co. LLC, China Publishing Corporation, Ocean Interactive (Beijing) Technology Co., Ltd., Tencent Music (Beijing) Co., Ltd., Ocean Interactive (Beijing) Culture Co., Ltd., Tencent Music Entertainment Group, Aka China Music

Schiedsgericht trotz aller staatlicher Verflechtung und Unterstützung durch die chinesische Regierung. Der NBC-Test bleibt bestimmend, es kommt unverändert auf das Unterscheidungsmerkmal staatliche ("state-sponsored") oder private Eigenschaft an, wobei das Gericht nunmehr neue, funktional anmutende Elemente in den Test einfließen lässt. Danach soll für eine staatliche Einstufung – und damit für den Zugang zur discovery-Rechtshilfe – sogar die staatliche Gründung der Schiedsinstitution nicht unbedingt ausreichen, vielmehr soll von Fall zu Fall eine Prüfung der Funktionsweise und der tatsächlichen Verselbständigung vom Staat ausschlaggebend sein:

"A closer inquiry is required where, as here, the arbitral body was originally created through state action, yet subsequently evolved such that it arguably no longer qualifies as a 'governmental or intergovernmental arbitral tribunal[,]... conventional court[, or]... other state-sponsored adjudicatory bod[y].' We now clarify that the 'foreign or international tribunal' inquiry does not turn on the governmental or nongovernmental origins of the administrative entity in question. No single factor clearly distinguishes a private international commercial arbitration from a state-sponsored one. Rather, echoing the functional approach adopted by the Intel court in determining whether the Directorate General-Competition qualified as a tribunal, See 542 U.S. at 257–58, 124 S.Ct. 2466, we consider a range of factors, including the degree of state affiliation and functional independence possessed by the entity, as well as the degree to which the parties' contract controls the panel's jurisdiction. In short, the inquiry is whether the body in question possesses the functional attributes most commonly associated with private arbitration. Here, considering these factors, it is clear that CIETAC arbitrations are private international commercial arbitrations falling outside the ambit of § 1782.

Beginning with state affiliation, our focus is on the extent to which the arbitral body is internally directed and governed by a foreign state or intergovernmental body. CIETAC was, all parties agree, originally founded by the Chinese government. CIETAC now, however, functions essentially independently of the Chinese government in the 'administration of its arbitration cases.' [...] According to the parties' declarations, CIETAC maintains confidentiality from all non-participants during and after arbitration, limiting opportunities for ex parte intervention by state officials. CIETAC offers parties a pool of arbitrators who are not selected by any entity other than CIETAC and who do not purport to act on behalf of, or have any mandatory affiliation with, the Chinese government. Indeed, the arbitrators appear to come from many different backgrounds and nations. These facts suggest that CIETAC possesses a high degree of independence and autonomy, and, conversely, a low degree of state affiliation"[53]

Hier drängt sich bereits bei einer sachlichen Beschreibung des Circuit Split die Frage auf, ob denn eine stärkere Verflechtung mit der kommunistischen Partei Chinas, also mit dem chinesischen Staat die zum entscheidenden Moment erhobene state-sponsored-Eigenschaft begründet und zu einer umgekehrten, rechtshilfefreundlichen Entscheidung des 2nd Circuit geführt hätte. Auf die Frage wird bei der Kritik von *ZF Automotive v. Luxshare* zurückzukommen sein.

Corporation, 965 F.3d 96 (2nd Cir. 2020), im Weiteren: In Re Guo, 965 F.3d 96, 107 (2nd Cir. 2020).

[53] In Re Guo, 965 F.3d 96, 107 (2nd Cir. 2020).

Der vorläufige Schlussakt des Circuit Split kam dann Ende September 2020, also nur etwa ein Jahr vor der Annahme von ZF Automotive v. Luxshare zur Entscheidung (grant of certiorari) durch den Supreme Court. Diesen Schlussakt lieferte eine weitere, mit der Rechtsfrage bis dahin nie befasste[54] Bundesberufungsinstanz, der Court of Appeals for the Seventh Circuit in *Servotronics v. Rolls-Royce.*[55] Dort schloss sich der 7th Circuit der ablehnenden Haltung der beiden anderen, die mittlerweile zwei Dekaden alten NBC- und Kazakhstan-Entscheidungen (und sinngemäß auch Guo) zeichnenden Circuits vollumfänglich an. Dabei bereicherte der 7th Circuit über den gewohnten Verweis auf das Ergebnis der grammatischen und historischen Auslegung des 28 USC § 1782 hinaus den NBC-Test um weitere rechtsquellentheoretische und normhierarchische Argumente, die eine Wirkungserstreckung auf ein privates Schiedsgericht, wie das im Fall betreffende englische CIArb Schiedsgericht, verböten:

"Section 1782 works in tandem with and supplements § 1781 [...] Once we situate the word „tribunal" in its proper statutory context, the more expansive reading of the term – the one that includes private arbitrations – becomes far less plausible. [...] Service-of-process assistance and letters rogatory – governed by §§ 1696 and 1781 – are matters of comity between governments, which suggests that the phrase 'foreign or international tribunal' as used in this statutory scheme means state-sponsored tribunals and does not include private arbitration panels. [...] the statute provides that the court's discovery order 'may prescribe the practice and procedure, which may be in whole or part the practice and procedure of the foreign country or the international tribunal.' [...] The highlighted phrase parallels the earlier phrase 'foreign or international tribunal.' Harmonizing this statutory language and reading it as a coherent whole suggests that a more limited reading of § 1782(a) is probably the correct one: a 'foreign tribunal' in this context means a governmental, administrative, or quasi-governmental tribunal operating pursuant to the foreign country's 'practice and procedure.' Private foreign arbitrations, in other words, are not included."[56]

Und auch die in den Vorgängerentscheidungen hervorgehobene Problematik der Ungleichbehandlung von in- und ausländischen Schiedssprüchen, also die Besserstellung von ausländischen Schiedsparteien wegen ihrer discovery-Antragsbefugnis in 28 USC § 1782 gegenüber der Beschränkung der gleichen Befugnis auf das Schiedsgericht in § 7 FAA in inländischen Schiedsverfahren wird in einem normhierarchischen Kontext aufbereitet und die Beweisrechtshilfe für die Zwecke des englischen Handelsschiedsverfahrens verweigert:

"[...] what the text and context of § 1782(a) strongly suggest is confirmed by the principle of avoiding a collision with another statute: a 'foreign or international tribunal' within the meaning of § 1782(a) is a state-sponsored, public, or quasi-governmental tribunal."[57]

---

[54] "This is a question of first impression for our circuit, but several other circuits have addressed it and a split has recently emerged." Servotronics, Inc. v. Rolls-Royce PLC, 975 F.3d 689 (7th Circuit 2020).

[55] Servotronics, Inc. v. Rolls-Royce PLC, 975 F.3d 689 (7th Circuit 2020).

[56] Servotronics, Inc. v. Rolls-Royce PLC, 975 F.3d 689, 694–695 (7th Circuit 2020).

[57] Servotronics, Inc. v. Rolls-Royce PLC, 975 F.3d 689, 696 (7th Circuit 2020).

Bekanntlich gab es schließlich während der Jahrzehnte des Circuit Split eine einzige Entscheidung des Supreme Court, in der sich das Höchstgericht zur Frage des subjektiven/institutionellen Anwendungsbereichs von 28 USC § 1782(a) äußerte. In dem im Jahre 2004 entschiedenen Fall *Intel v. AMD*[58] lag jedoch der höchsten Instanz gerade die Frage nicht vor, ob die Vorschrift auf private Schiedsgerichte Anwendung findet. Die Rechtsprechungsspaltung unter den Berufungsinstanzen hat demgemäß auch *Intel* nicht beseitigt. Die Entscheidung soll hier am Schluss der Darstellung des Circuit Split nichtsdestotrotz kurz in ihrem wesentlichen Inhalt referiert werden, weil sie einerseits in vielerlei Hinsicht in der gespaltenen Rechtsprechung der Berufungsgerichte richtungsweisenden Widerhall fand, andererseits nach der hier vertretenen Meinung auch in Zukunft die nach der fragwürdig geratenen Auflösung des Circuit Split durch *ZF Automotive v. Luxshare* nunmehr einsetzende Weiterentwicklung der Rechtsprechung maßgebend beeinflussen wird. Die von Justice *Ginsburg* vorgelegte Opinion hatte ausschließlich über die Qualifikation des wettbewerbsbehördlichen Verfahrens des DG Competition der EU-Kommission zu entscheiden. Das Verfahren und damit die Kommission im Zusammenhang mit einem solchen Verfahren wurden als eindeutig hoheitlich legitimiert eingestuft und damit der im Vorfeld des Verfahrens gestellte discovery-Antrag von AMD gegen Intel rechtshilfefreundlich, also als unter 28 USC § 1782(a) fallend beschieden. Zur Qualifizierung der EU-Kommission – der ja im gegebenen Verfahren jegliche Gerichts- bzw. Streitentscheidungsfunktion abgeht – als „foreign or international tribunal" gelangt der Supreme Court mittels einer beherzigenswert funktionalen Betrachtungsweise eines antizipierten Verfahrensgangs, in dem die Kommission als revisible erste Instanz und zugleich als einzige Tatsacheninstanz eingebettet dargestellt wird:

"We next consider whether the assistance in obtaining documents here sought by an 'interested person' meets the specification 'for use in a foreign or international tribunal.' Beyond question the reviewing authorities, both the Court of First Instance and the European Court of Justice, qualify as tribunals. But those courts are not proof-taking instances. Their review is limited to the record before the Commission. [...] Hence, AMD could 'use' evidence in the reviewing courts only by submitting it to the Commission in the current, investigative stage."[59]

Die breite und funktionale Bestimmung des tribunal-Charakters wird dabei vielsagenderweise unter Befolgung des oben bereits geschilderten Berichts von *Hans Smit,* dem am Entwurf des erweiterten Wortlauts maßgebend beteiligten Professor, über die Entstehungsgeschichte der Neufassung von 28 USC § 1782 erreicht. *Smit*s Gedankengang wird sogar nicht als sonst übliche Fußnote eingefügt, sondern im Entscheidungstext selbst geführt, wo – für *Intel* zwar entscheidungsunerheblich – auch Schiedsgerichte ausdrücklich als erfasst genannt sind:

"Congress understood that change to 'provid[e] the possibility of U.S. judicial assistance in connection with [administrative and quasi-judicial proceedings abroad].' S.Rep. No. 1580, at

[58] Intel Corp. v. Advanced Micro Devices, Inc., 542 U.S. 241.
[59] Intel Corp. v. Advanced Micro Devices, Inc., 542 U.S. 241, 257.

7-8, U.S.Code Cong. & Admin.News 1964, pp. 3782, 3788; see Smit, International Litigation 1026-1027, and nn. 71, 73 ([t]he term 'tribunal'... includes investigating magistrates, administrative and arbitral tribunals, and quasi-judicial agencies, as well as conventional civil, commercial, criminal, and administrative courts."[60]

Im Wesentlichen kam es für den Supreme Court auf die durch den Kongress entsprechend dem Vorschlag der Smit-Kommission in 1964 vollzogene Liberalisierung und Öffnung des Wortlauts gegenüber nicht als (staatliche) Gerichte funktionierenden Foren an. Zur positiven Bescheidung des ex parte discovery-Antrags führte sichtlich die Qualifizierung der EU-Kommission als zumindest eines der Elemente in der Smit-Aufzählung. Es mag dahinstehen, ob die EU-Kommission dabei eher in die Kategorie „investigating magistrate" oder „quasi-judicial agency" (oder in beide[61]) fällt. Der Kontext des Entscheidungstextes spricht jedenfalls für diese Kategorien, während eine Schiedsgerichtseigenschaft der EU-Kommission selbstredend ausscheidet, weswegen der Circuit Split in Intel zwangsläufig unentschieden bleiben musste. *Intel* hat jedoch eine Reihe anderer, bis dahin ebenfalls stark umstrittener Fragen abschließend beantwortet, die für unsere Zwecke auch relevant sind. So bejaht die Entscheidung die Antragsbefugnis von interessierten Personen im Rahmen von 28 USC § 1782 (hier von AMD als erst potenzieller Antragsteller bei der EU-Kommission vor Eröffnung des wettbewerbsbehördlichen Verfahrens) bereits vor der Eröffnung des zu unterstützenden Verfahrens. Das Verfahren vor dem ausländischen bzw. internationalen Forum braucht danach nicht anhängig zu sein, vielmehr reicht für den Erfolg des Rechtshilfebegehrens die Glaubhaftmachung einer absehbaren Verfahrenseinleitung aus:

"In short, we reject the view, expressed in In re Ishihara Chemical Co., that § 1782 comes into play only when adjudicative proceedings are 'pending' or 'imminent.' [...] Instead, we hold that § 1782(a) requires only that a dispositive ruling by the Commission, reviewable by the European courts, be within reasonable contemplation."[62]

Ebenfalls im erweiternden und rechtshilfefreundlichen Sinne verwarf der Supreme Court eine von manchen Untergerichten befürwortete „foreign-discoverability rule", wonach das im Rechtshilfeweg angewandte US-amerikanische Bundeszivilprozessrecht nur in dem Rahmen zum Zug kommen dürfe, in dem eine Beweisermittlung auch im ersuchenden Staat vorgesehen ist. In der liberalen Auffassung des Supreme Court soll der weitherzige discovery-Mechanismus der FRCP dem Ersuchenden (dem Forum oder der interessierten Person) auch dann zugutekommen, wenn dessen Heimatrecht keine vergleichbaren Aufklärungsmöglichkeiten eröffnet:

[60] Intel Corp. v. Advanced Micro Devices, Inc., 542 U.S. 241, 258.

[61] Dafür spricht jedenfalls die Formulierung am Ende der Entscheidung: "[...] entities with similarly blended adjudicative and prosecutorial functions" Intel Corp. v. Advanced Micro Devices, Inc., 542 U.S. 241, 266, 124 S. Ct. 2466, 2484, 159 L. Ed. 2d 355 (2004).

[62] Intel Corp. v. Advanced Micro Devices, Inc., 542 U.S. 241, 259, 124 S. Ct. 2466, 2480, 159 L. Ed. 2d 355 (2004).

"While comity and parity concerns may be important as touchstones for a district court's exercise of discretion in particular cases, they do not permit our insertion of a generally applicable foreign-discoverability rule into the text of § 1782(a). We question whether foreign governments would in fact be offended by a domestic prescription permitting, but not requiring, judicial assistance. A foreign nation may limit discovery within its domain for reasons peculiar to its own legal practices, culture, or traditions – reasons that do not necessarily signal objection to aid from United States federal courts. [...] When the foreign tribunal would readily accept relevant information discovered in the United States, application of a foreign-discoverability rule would be senseless. The rule in that situation would serve only to thwart § 1782(a)'s objective to assist foreign tribunals in obtaining relevant information that the tribunals may find useful but, for reasons having no bearing on international comity, they cannot obtain under their own laws."[63]

Auch umgekehrt darf die Rechtshilfeleistung nicht daran scheitern, dass ein entsprechender discovery-Antrag im US-amerikanischen Recht so, wie vom fremden Forum bzw. von der dortigen Partei erbeten, nicht vorgesehen oder abzulehnen wäre. Auch in dieser Hinsicht überwiegt die auf *comity* basierende, vom Öffnungsgedanken getragene Denkweise des Obersten Gerichts:

"We also reject Intel's suggestion that a § 1782(a) applicant must show that United States law would allow discovery in domestic litigation analogous to the foreign proceeding. Brief for Petitioner 19-20 ('[I]f AMD were pursuing this matter in the United States, U. S. law would preclude it from obtaining discovery of Intel's documents.'). Section 1782 is a provision for assistance to tribunals abroad. It does not direct United States courts to engage in comparative analysis to determine whether analogous proceedings exist here."[64]

Mit alledem bekennt sich der Supreme Court zu einer ausgeprägt weitherzigen, sowohl in institutioneller als auch in zeitlicher und gegenständlicher Hinsicht liberalen Auslegung des 28 USC § 1782 und damit letzten Endes zu einem möglichst weiten Verständnis des *comity*-Gedankens, der hilfsbereiten Achtung und der Förderung des jeweils fremden Verfahrensrechtssystems. Nachdem alle genannten Aspekte in einem für die internationale Rechtshilfe günstigen Sinne beantwortet worden sind, gleicht das Gericht im abschließenden Teil der Entscheidung diese seine grundsätzlich positive und offene Herangehensweise dadurch aus, dass es den unteren Gerichten Anhaltspunkte für ihre Ermessensausübung an die Hand gibt. Die Notwendigkeit dieser seitdem in Literatur und Rechtsprechung als „Intel-Kriterien" bezeichneten Ermessensgesichtspunkte ergibt sich aus der einfachen Tatsache, dass nach dem Wortlaut des 28 USC § 1782 (etwa im Gegensatz zu § 1050 ZPO!) eine Rechtshilfeleistung nicht zwingend, sondern lediglich als eine Möglichkeit („may") vorgesehen ist. Dementsprechend darf und sollte, selbst wenn alle – ua die oben angeführten – Anwendungsvoraussetzungen von 28 USC § 1782 gegeben sind, eine Rechtshilfeleistung versagt werden, wenn dies im Lichte der Intel-Krite-

[63] Intel Corp. v. Advanced Micro Devices, Inc., 542 U.S. 241, 261–62, 124 S. Ct. 2466, 2481–82, 159 L. Ed. 2d 355 (2004).

[64] Intel Corp. v. Advanced Micro Devices, Inc., 542 U.S. 241, 263, 124 S. Ct. 2466, 2482, 159 L. Ed. 2d 355 (2004).

rien geboten erscheint: Erstens ist die Intensität des Informationsbedarfs, und damit die Ermessensausübung zugunsten einer Rechtshilfeleistung prima facie stärker gegenüber Dritten als gegenüber im mit Aufklärungspflichten- bzw. Lasten ausgestatteten Verfahrensrechtsverhältnis eingebundenen Parteien. Zweitens fällt die Art des fremden Verfahrens und insbesondere die Empfänglichkeit desselben gegenüber US-amerikanischer Rechtshilfe ins Gewicht. Drittens darf das Rechtshilfeersuchen nicht einer Zweckentfremdung und insbesondere nicht einer Umgehung ursprungsstaatlicher Beweisverbote dienen. Viertens kann und sollte eine Versagung auch dann erfolgen, wenn das Ersuchen im gegebenen Fall ausufernd, übergriffig oder unverhältnismäßig belastend ist:

"[...] nonparticipants in the foreign proceeding may be outside the foreign tribunal's jurisdictional reach; hence, their evidence, available in the United States, may be unobtainable absent § 1782(a) aid. [...] the character of the proceedings underway abroad, and the receptivity of the foreign government or the court or agency abroad to U. S. federal-court judicial assistance. [...] a district court could consider whether the § 1782(a) request conceals an attempt to circumvent foreign proof-gathering restrictions or other policies of a foreign country or the United States. [...] Also, unduly intrusive or burdensome requests may be rejected or trimmed."[65]

Festzuhalten bleibt nach alledem, dass *Intel* die überwiegende Mehrheit der umstrittenen Fragen der internationalen Beweisrechtshilfe mittels 28 USC § 1782 großzügig, geleitet durch den comity-Gedanken und nicht zuletzt beachtenswert mit ständig wiederkehrendem Verweis auf *Hans Smit* in einem umfassend rechtshilfefreundlichen Sinne beantwortet hat. Lediglich die uns hier näher interessierende Frage der Anwendbarkeit der Vorschrift auf *private* Schiedsgerichte blieb auch in, und noch fast zwei Jahrzehnte nach der Entscheidung offen und damit der geschilderten, Rechtsunsicherheit verursachenden Rechtsprechungsspaltung preisgegeben. Und eine sorgfältige Auswertung der bundesberufungsgerichtlichen Rechtsprechung bis zum Jahr der *ZF Automotive v. Luxshare*-Entscheidung des Supreme Court 2022 zeigt, dass im Zeitpunkt der Annahme der Rechtssache zur Entscheidung durch den Supreme Court die Verfechter der Sache der internationalen privaten Schiedsgerichtsbarkeit eher die schlechteren Karten zu haben schienen: Die – zwar knappe – Mehrheit der Bundesberufungsgerichte stand ausländischen privaten Schiedsgerichten ablehnend gegenüber. Wie oben gezeigt, haben gerade die für den transatlantischen Wirtschafts- und Rechtsverkehr wichtigen Circuits im unmittelbaren Vorfeld der Entscheidung des Supreme Court ihre alte ablehnende Rechtsprechung mit weiter angereicherter Argumentation bestätigt. Zwar überwog im Schrifttum eindeutig die Kritik an dieser restriktiven Rechtsprechung, die unter anderem auch Forderungen nach einer redaktionellen, die Rechtshilfe zugunsten ausländischer Schiedsgerichte ausdrücklich erlaubenden Änderung des 28 USC § 1782 laut werden ließ.[66] Die kritischen Stimmen stammten verständlicherweise

[65] Intel Corp. v. Advanced Micro Devices, Inc., 542 U.S. 241, 265, 124 S. Ct. 2466, 2483, 159 L. Ed. 2d 355 (2004).

[66] Vgl. umfassend dazu Varga, Beweiserhebung in transatlantischen Schiedsverfahren – Eine Suche nach Kompromissen zwischen deutscher und US-amerikanischer Beweisrechtstradition, 2006, S 261 ff. sowie zB Schwartz/Johnson JIntArb 15(3) (1998), 53 und Hammond, JIntArb 17

aus der Feder von inmitten der Schiedspraxis agierenden Wissenschaftlern und Praktikern, die ihr Hauptaugenmerk auf die Gefahr der defizitären Sachverhaltsermittlung und damit eines potenziellen Legitimationsverlusts der internationalen Handelsschiedsgerichtsbarkeit gerichtet hatten. Sie wollten – wie auch der damals am Anfang seiner Zusammenarbeit mit dem Jubilar stehende, dh noch junge, und manchmal eher vom vermeintlich in die richtige Richtung gehenden Wunschdenken als von nüchterner Betrachtung geleitete Autor dieser Zeilen[67] – im Smit-Wort „arbitral tribunals" wie selbstverständlich „private arbitral tribunals" inbegriffen sehen – auch aus der Ferne betrachtet keine Vermessenheit, zumal auch vom engsten Mitarbeiter des entwerfenden Professors nachträglich glaubwürdig bestätigt.[68] Doch die Mehrheit der Circuit Courts maß weder der Entwurfsgeschichte der erweiterten Fassung von 1964 noch einem weit verstandenen, dh auch privaten Schiedsgerichten unverändert wie staatlichen Gerichten zugutekommenden comity-Gedanken entscheidende Bedeutung bei der Auslegung zu, sondern schlug den Weg einer am Wortlaut haftenden, oft überwiegend an Textualismus orientierten Interpretation ein, die dann in der Regel mit der weiteren inhaltlichen Legitimation der angeblich fehlenden funktionalen Äquivalenz zwischen staatlicher und privater Ziviljustiz versehen wurde. So überwog denn die Sichtweise in der Rechtsprechung, dass mit „foreign or international tribunal" immer nur etwas staatlich Getragenes („state-sponsored") gemeint sein könne. Die eine funktionale Äquivalenz, oder zumindest mit inhaltlich schiedsfreundlicher Argumentation die Rechtshilfe zugunsten privater Schiedsgerichte bejahenden Bundesgerichte gerieten in Minderheit, waren aber immerhin mit zwei bejahenden Circuits gegenüber den drei verneinenden vertreten. Damit hing das Schicksal von discovery-Anträgen seitens Schiedsparteien und sonstigen interessierten Dritten, sowie von discovery-Rechtshilfeersuchen seitens privater Schiedsgerichte mit einem ausländischen (außeramerikanischen) Schiedsort grundsätzlich von der Belegenheit des Beweisgegenstands bzw. der Beweisperson ab. Dieses sowohl in regulatorischer als auch in

(4) (2000), 131 sowie Garfinkel/Miller 19 Mealey's Int'l Arb.Rep. (2004), 25; Shore, DAJV-Newsletter 2004, 117f. In der deutschen Literatur wohl von der Hoffnung auf eine schiedsfreundliche Lösung getragen auch (und NBC v. Bear Stearns als Ausreißer („A complication …") betrachtend) Lew/Mistelis/Kröll, Comparative International Commercial Arbitration, 2003, Rn. 22-106); Demeyere SchiedsVZ 2003, 247 (250). Vgl. auch mwN Rieckers RIW 2005, 19. Anders die damalige Mindermeinung, nicht von ungefähr von den verfahrensbevollmächtigten Anwälten, die im ersten negativen Fall (Medway) General Electric, also den die discovery abwehrenden Antragsgegner vertreten haben: Rivkin/Legum 14 ArbInt (1998), 213.

[67] Vgl. Varga, Beweiserhebung in transatlantischen Schiedsverfahren – Eine Suche nach Kompromissen zwischen deutscher und US-amerikanischer Beweisrechtstradition, 2006, S. 261ff.

[68] S van Ginkel 33 ARIA 187, 218 mit Verweis auf den Wortgebrauch und den Umgang von Hans Smit mit der juristischen Sprache: "Professor Smit literally loved Strunk & White's The Elements of Style, a booklet that focused on specific questions of usage of the English language and the cultivation of good writing. Smit especially loved the principles to 'omit needless words' and to 'use the active voice'. […] Following the rule of omitting needless words, and already deeply interested in international arbitration (the New York Convention had just been concluded in 1958), in Professor Smit's mind it was likely perfectly logical to conclude that 'arbitral' tribunals did not need to be specified, as the term 'foreign and international tribunals' naturally included them. Applying 'the Elements of Style,' the word 'arbitral' may thus have been deleted – or may never have made it into the Text – as being redundant."

judizieller Hinsicht unzulängliche, da beträchtliches Rechtsunsicherheitspotenzial bergende Umfeld harrte einer klärenden höchstrichterlichen Entscheidung, zu der im Jahre 2022 ein discovery-Antrag für die Zwecke eines potenziellen DIS-Schiedsverfahrens den Anlass lieferte.

II. Eine kritische Würdigung der Entscheidung des Supreme Court ZF Automotive v. Luxshare

Die Quelle der Rechtsstreitigkeit war die von der Käuferin (Luxshare Inc., Hongkong) behauptete grobe Unverhältnismäßigkeit des Kaufpreises bei einem auf Assets bezogenen Unternehmenskaufvertrag von ZFs amerikanischer Tochtergesellschaft (ZF Automotive Inc., Verkäuferin). Für Rechtsstreitigkeiten aus der Transaktion enthielt der Vertrag der Parteien eine DIS-Schiedsklausel mit Schiedsort München. Um ihre auf den sich nachträglich als überhöht entpuppenden Kaufpreis bezogenen Behauptungen substantiieren zu können, beantragte Luxshare aufgrund 28 USC § 1782 – vor Schiedsklageerhebung, was sie laut *Intel* durfte – sowohl Dokumentenvorlage (production of documents) am Sitz von ZF Inc. in Michigan, als auch die protokollierte Anhörung (deposition) von zwei leitenden Angestellten von ZF ebenfalls in Michigan. Das District Court for the Eastern District of Michigan gab sämtlichen discovery-Ersuchen statt, woraufhin Luxshare die entsprechenden, laut Bundeszivilprozessrecht (Federal Rules of Civil Procedure, FRCP) in Parteibetrieb zuzustellenden Vorlageanordnungen und Ladungen (subpoenas) an ZF zustellte. Sowohl die erste Instanz als auch die Berufungsinstanz (CA 6th Circuit) entschieden ganz im Sinne der schiedsfreundlichen Rechtsprechungslinie zugunsten des discovery-Antragstellers und wiesen den auf Unanwendbarkeit von 28 USC § 1782 auf private Schiedsgerichte gegründeten Einspruch (motion to stay and motion to quash) von ZF zurück. Dies verwundert im Lichte der obigen Beschreibung des Circuit Split nicht: Michigan ist Teil des 6th Circuit mit der zur Zeit der erstinstanzlichen Anhängigkeit von ZF Automotive v. Luxshare praktisch noch druckfrischen schiedsfreundlichen Präzedenz *Abdul Latif Jameel v. FedEx Corporation.*[69] Beide Instanzen gingen daher unter Aufrechterhaltung der Argumentation in *Abdul Latif* ohne Weiteres einheitlich davon aus, dass ein DIS-Schiedsgericht, dessen Verfahren mit Schiedsort Deutschland sich nach dem 10. Buch der ZPO und der DIS-Schiedsordnung richtet, ein *foreign or international tribunal* im Sinne des 28 USC § 1782 sei und daher sich eine potenzielle Schiedspartei, die für die Zwecke eines in Deutschland bevorstehenden Schiedsverfahrens Beweismittel in den USA sammeln will, auf die Vorschrift erfolgreich berufen kann. Zudem standen sichtlich auch die Intel-Kriterien der rechtshilfeweisen gerichtlichen Erzwingung der beantragten Dokumentenvorlage und der Zeugenanhörung nicht

[69] In re Application to Obtain Discovery for Use in Foreign Proceedings, (Abdul Latif Jameel v. FedEx Corporation) 939 F.3d 710 (6th Cir. 2019). Vgl. auch in die gleiche Richtung weisend bereits In re Consorcio Ecutroriano de Telecomunicaciones S. A. v. Forwarding (USA), Inc., 685 F.3d 987, 995 (11th Cir. 2012).

entgegen. Dies (Präklusion ihrer Argumentation durch *Abdul Latif* als circuit precedent) war auch ZF als discovery-Antragsgegnerin während des ganzen Verfahrens bewusst. Sie vertraute indessen darauf, dass der Supreme Court die Sache zur Entscheidung annehmen und die höchstgerichtlich praktisch einzig noch offengebliebene Anwendungsfrage des 28 USC § 1782 klären würde.

So kam es dann auch am 10.10.2021, als die petition for certiorari von ZF zur Verhandlung und Entscheidung angenommen wurde. Sichtlich maß der Supreme Court dem Fall herausragende Bedeutung zu, denn er hat dies sogar im Rahmen eines *certiorari before judgment* getan, des funktional der deutschen Sprungrevision, dem englischen *leapfrog appeal* etc. entsprechenden und entsprechend selten zugelassenen Rechtsmittels.[70] Die Zulassung stand hier indessen selbst in dieser Ausnahmegestaltung angesichts einer besonderen Vorgeschichte des Falles am Supreme Court so gut wie von vornherein fest: Gerade ein Jahr zuvor, am 7.10.2020 ging nämlich beim Supreme Court der certiorari request zur selben Rechtsfrage im oben besprochenen Fall *Servotronics v. Rolls Royce* vom 7th Circuit ein, den der Supreme Court auch zuließ und in dem bis zum *October Term* 2021, für den die mündliche Verhandlung avisiert war, ein erschöpfender Schriftsatzwechsel samt einer Reihe hochkarätiger *amicus curiae briefs* stattfand. Dieser mit großem Aufwand als Entscheidungsgrundlage zustande gekommene Prozessstoff schien plötzlich obsolet geworden zu sein, nachdem Servotronics und Rolls-Royce im September die Einstellung des von ihnen einvernehmlich erledigten Falles (*joint stipulation to dismiss* laut Supreme Court Rule 46.1) beantragt hatten. Mit dem Einstellungsbeschluss verflüchtigte sich die Chance, die Rechtsfrage im bereits in allen Details aufbereiteten *Servotronics v. Rolls-Royce*-Fall einer endgültigen Klärung zuzuführen.[71] Doch wie durch eine Fügung des Schicksals ging bereits zwei Tage nach der ersten Servotronics-Erledigungserklärung der neue, im vor dem 6th Circuit anhängigen ZF Automotive v. Luxshare Fall dieselbe Rechtsfrage problematisierende certiorari request ein, der naturgemäß zugelassen wurde und bei dem wenig überraschend ein durchgängiger Gleichlauf des Inhalts der Schriftsätze mit dem des Servotronics-Falles zu beobachten ist.[72] Unterschiede im Zusammenhang der internationalen Handelsschiedsgerichtsbarkeit beschränken sich praktisch auf Aktualisierungen der – auch ausländischen – Rechtsprechungsnachweise in den Schriftsätzen.[73] Einen leichten

---

[70] U.S. Supreme Court Rule 11: „A petition for a writ of certiorari to review a case pending in a United States court of appeals, before judgment is entered in that court, will be granted only upon a showing that the case is of such imperative public importance as to justify deviation from normal appellate practice and to require immediate determination in this Court." iVm 28 USC § 2101(e): „An application to the Supreme Court for a writ of certiorari to review a case before judgment has been rendered in the court of appeals may be made at any time before judgment."

[71] Zum gesamten Prozessstoff und zur Schritt für Schritt kommentierten Verfahrenshistorie siehe https://www.scotusblog.com/case-files/cases/servotronics-inc-v-rolls-royce-plc/ (abgerufen 7.9.2024).

[72] Siehe auch hier den gesamten Prozessstoff unter https://www.scotusblog.com/case-files/cases/zf-automotive-us-inc-v-luxshare-ltd/ (abgerufen 7.9.2024).

[73] Den anderen Unterschied macht eine Abzweigung der Argumentation in Richtung Investitionsschiedsgerichtsbarkeit aus, denn hier wurde ein aus einem BIT-Schiedsverfahren resultierender Rechtsstreit (Alix Partners LLP v. The Fund for Protection of Investors' Rights in Foreign States) im Verbund verhandelt.

anfänglichen, eher gefühlsmäßigen Unterschied bedeutete das Umsatteln von *Servotronics v. Rolls-Royce* auf *ZF Automotive v. Luxshare* allerdings insoweit schon, dass den Ausgangspunkt des eingestellten ersteren Servotronics-Verfahrens noch eine aus dem schiedsfeindlichen 7th Circuit stammende und zugegebenermaßen alle Negativargumente in ziemlich ansprechender Weise aufführende zweitinstanzliche Entscheidung gebildet hatte, wohingegen der nunmehr zu beurteilende ZF-certiorari request aus einem solchen Verfahren stammte, das vom schiedsfreundlichen Gedankengut geleiteten 6th Circuit positiv beschieden wurde.

Die Vorzeichen muteten dabei für die eine erweiternde Auslegung und damit eine schiedsfreundliche Lösung befürwortenden Vertreter der Schiedszunft auf den ersten Blick trotzdem eher negativ an. Auch hier ist man geneigt, Schicksalhaftes zu erkennen: Bereits mehr als ein Jahr vor dem Zeitpunkt der certiorari-Annahme war Justice *Ruth Bader Ginsburg,* die Berichterstatterin von *Intel* verstorben. Die von vielen Steakholdern gehegte Hoffnung, sie würde, sobald sich die Gelegenheit dazu böte, ihre in *Intel* offenbarte liberale, vom Öffnungsgedanken geleitete und durchgehend an den Smit-Zitaten aufbereitete Rechtsprechung um dieses letzte Element vervollständigen und private Schiedsgerichte ebenso kreativ wie damals die EU-Kommission in den persönlichen-institutionellen Anwendungsbereich des 28 USC § 1782 einbeziehen, schied mit ihrer Person dahin. Acht Tage nach ihrem Tod, am 26. September 2020 wurde an ihre Stelle Bundesberufungsrichterin *Amy Coney Barrett* vom 7th Circuit Court of Appeals berufen, dem Bundesberufungsgericht also, das erst vier Tage zuvor, am 22. September *Servotronics v. Rolls-Royce* mit schiedsrechtshilfefeindlichem Inhalt entschieden hatte. Sie wurde anschließend Berichterstatterin in *ZF Automotive v. Luxshare.* Es blieb somit abzuwarten, ob und wie die negative Rechtsprechung ihrer bisherigen Wirkungsstätte in ihrem höchstrichterlichen Judizieren widerklingen würde. Ferner und insbesondere war aber ebenfalls abzuwarten, welche Gestalt ihr ausgeprägter, am geistigen Vermächtnis ihres Mentors *Antonin Scalia* orientierter Textualismus[74], gewissermaßen der Kontrapunkt zu Ginsburgs Berufsethos, in *ZF Automotive v. Luxshare* annehmen würde.

Und in der Tat kann die Entscheidung überwiegend als eine Verkörperung der textualistischen, am allgemeinen, ja alltäglichen Sprachgebrauch orientierten Gesetzesauslegung (textualist statutory interpretation) bezeichnet werden. Die Entscheidungsbegründung fängt denn auch standesgemäß mit der Auflistung der zum Zeitpunkt der Verkündung des modifizierten Wortlauts von 28 USC § 1782, also Mitte und Ende der 1960er Jahre geläufigen Wörterbucheinträgen zu *tribunal* an. Aufgrund dieser wird zunächst noch aufgezeigt, dass der Begriff an sich sowohl staatliche als auch private Streitentscheidungsorgane erfasst. Würde also die Untersuchung bei der streng textuellen Auslegung des Wortes *tribunal* Halt machen, wäre die Anwendbarkeit der Vorschrift auf ausländische private Schiedsgerichte wohl unproblematisch:

---

[74] Vgl. zB Barrett 84 U. Chi. L. Rev. 2193; Barrett 92 Notre Dame L. Rev. 1921; Barrett 70 Case W. Res. L. Rev. 855.

"[...] the broad meaning of 'tribunal' does not itself exclude private adjudicatory bodies. If we had nothing but this single word to go on, there would be a good case for including private arbitral panels."[75]

Sodann geht die Entscheidungsbegründung auf den „Zusammenhang" ein, in dem das Wort *tribunal* steht. Dabei soll jedoch für den Supreme Court als „Zusammenhang" keineswegs ein primär inhaltlich begriffenes, vielmehr lediglich ein rein sprachlich erfasstes Gefüge der Adjektiv-Substantiv-Verbindung *foreign tribunal* bzw. *international tribunal* sein. Wiederum wird zwar in einem Zwischenschritt – unter Heranziehung weiterer Wörterbücher – bestätigt, dass *foreign* grundsätzlich sowohl „zu einem fremden Staat gehörend" als auch „in einem fremden Staat belegen" bedeuten kann, doch sei die erste Bedeutungsvariante zu bevorzugen, und zwar wegen der – nicht weiter erläuterten[76] – Prämisse, das Substantiv *tribunal* trage das Merkmal der staatlichen Autorität an sich, weswegen ein dieses spezifizierendes Adjektiv (hier: *foreign*) auch am besten als mit dem gleichen Merkmal ausgestattet zu lesen sei.[77] „Ausländisch" ist also nach dieser Lesart immer gleich „fremde staatliche Autorität verkörpernd", wenn nur das spezifizierte Substantiv eine – aus welchen Gründen auch immer bejahte – Souveränitätskonnotation aufweist, wie dies laut Supreme Court bei *tribunal* der Fall ist:

"This is where context comes in. 'Tribunal' does not stand alone – it belongs to the phrase 'foreign or international tribunal.' And attached to these modifiers, 'tribunal' is best understood as an adjudicative body that exercises governmental authority. [...] [T]wo words together may assume a more particular meaning than those words in isolation. Take 'foreign tribunal' first. Congress could have used 'foreign' in one of two ways here. It could mean something like '[b]elonging to another nation or country,' which would support reading 'foreign tribunal' as a governmental body. Black's Law Dictionary, at 775. Or it could more generally mean 'from' another country, which would sweep in private adjudicative bodies too. See, e.g., Random House Dictionary of the English Language 555 (1966) ('derived from another country or nation; not native'). The first meaning is the better fit. The word 'foreign' takes on its more governmental meaning when modifying a word with potential governmental or sovereign connotations. That is why 'foreign' suggests something different in the phrase 'foreign leader' than it does in 'foreign films.' The phrase 'foreign leader' brings to mind 'an official of a foreign state, not a team captain of a European football club.' [...] So too with 'foreign tribunal.' 'Tribunal' is a word with potential governmental or sovereign connotations, so 'foreign tribunal' more naturally refers to a tribunal belonging to a foreign nation than to a tribunal that is simply

[75] ZF Automotive US, Inc. v. Luxshare, Ltd., 596 U.S. 619, 628 (2022).

[76] Vgl. dazu die ausführliche linguistische Kritik bei Collins 122 Mich. L. Rev. 127 (137).

[77] Johann Gottlieb Fichte, Die Bestimmung des Menschen, S. 17: „... zuvörderst sind jene Beschaffenheiten gar nichts an und für sich, sie sind nur etwas an einem andern; Beschaffenheiten eines Beschaffenen, Formen eines Geformten; und ein solches die Beschaffenheit Annehmende und Tragende, – ein Substrat derselben, nach dem Ausdrucke der Schule, – wird für die Denkbarkeit derselben immer vorausgesetzt. Ferner, daß ein solches Substrat eine bestimmte Beschaffenheit habe, drückt einen Zustand der Ruhe, und des Stillestehens seiner Verwandlungen, ein Anhalten seines Werdens aus." Diesen letzteren Aspekt lässt die Opinion außer Acht, indem sie „tribunal" am Staatlichen festnagelt.

located in a foreign nation. And for a tribunal to belong to a foreign nation, the tribunal must possess sovereign authority conferred by that nation."[78]

Wenn man sich die doch etwas simplizistisch geratenen Beispiele (foreign leader, foreign film, foreign football club) vergegenwärtigt (die übrigens ohne Ausnahme den Schriftsätzen des Antragstellers und des als amicus curiae auftretenden Justice Department entnommen sind), ist man geneigt sich zu fragen, nach welchen Kategorien denn im Einzelfall die Souveränitätskonnotation (nicht) zu bejahen und damit Rechtssicherheit zu erreichen ist: *Foreign wine* wäre ja beim ersten Besehen sicher rein privat, das spezifizierte Substantiv scheint ja (nach welchen Kriterien?!) keine Souveränitätskonnotation aufzuweisen. Sollte aber das Regime im Ursprungsland des edlen Tropfens etwa aufgrund seiner Begeisterung für den jungen, dem väterlichen Freund Richard Wagner zuliebe tätig werdenden klassischen Philologen aus Röcken die Hinwendung vom Apollinischen zum Dionysischen[79] soweit vollzogen haben, dass der Dionysoskult mit staatlich produziertem, kredenztem und den Glaubensgenossen staatlich zugeteiltem Wein praktiziert wird, dann wird es wohl für den betreffenden Wein auch nicht mehr auf das vornehmlich geografisch bestimmbare und ohne Rücksicht auf staatliche Grenzen reichlich sonnenbeschienene und Wissen und Pflege von Generationen verkörpernde Weingebiet, sondern auf das souveräne Staatsgebiet ankommen. Ja, ebenso wie im oben beschriebenen Fall *In re Guo:* Nur etwas mehr Einbindung noch in den kommunistischen chinesischen Staatsapparat und plötzlich qualifiziert sich CIETAC für direkte amerikanische Rechthilfe? Die Logik des Supreme Court eröffnet, gelinde gesagt, gewagten Denkperspektiven den Weg. Wie bereits bei *In re Guo* drängt sich hier mit besonderer Intensität auch die Grundsatzfrage auf, ob denn die Distinktion staatlich-privat wirklich als Anwendungsbegründungmerkmal des 28 USC § 1782 taugt und wirklich als solches in die Vorschrift hineinzulesen ist. Ohne die Stütze von willkürlich gewählten Wörterbucheinträgen ist im Wortlaut nichts dergleichen zu finden. Gerade ein strenger Textualist müsste sich die Frage stellen, ob nach der 1964er Reform, mit der just das Wort *court* aus der Vorschrift gestrichen wurde, eine solche Interpretation des Normgehalts haltbar ist, wenn man ja konsequent ausschließlich mit Grammatik und nicht mit Gesetzgebungsgeschichte und schon gar nicht mit systematischen Bezügen als „Zusammenhang" arbeitet.

Noch intensiver drängt sich dieselbe Frage, und damit im breiteren Kontext auch jene nach der methodischen Ehrlichkeit des wörterbuchbasierten Textualismus auf, wenn man beginnt, mit Substantivbildungen in einem wirklich relevanten Kontext zu arbeiten: Wieso kommt die Opinion des Supreme Court eigentlich nicht auf die Idee, statt der fachspezifisch jedes Zusammenhangs barer Substantivbildungen (foreign film, foreign leader) einmal die sich bei einem schiedsverfahrensrechtlichen Fall wohl auch ohne überheizte Vorstellungskraft anbietende und für eine echte

[78] ZF Automotive US, Inc. v. Luxshare, Ltd., 596 U.S. 619, 629 (2022).

[79] Friedrich Nietzsche, Die Geburt der Tragödie aus dem Geiste der Musik. Vgl. lesenswert zu dem hier genannten Aspekt, also zu Nachweisen zur Ermunterung Nietzsches durch Wagner zur Niederschrift des Tragödienbuches ua zwecks (alt)philologischer Untermauerung seines Gesamtkunstwerks: Safranski, Nietzsche, 2019, S. 33ff., 49f.

Sinnermittlung naheliegende und vielversprechende Substantivbildung *foreign arbitral award* als Vergleichsbasis zu nehmen? Diese firmiert ja gleich im Titel der *New York Convention on the Recognition and Enforcement of Foreign Arbitral Awards* vom Jahre 1958 (damit gleiche Generation wie die zitierten allgemeinsprachlichen Wörterbücher, jedoch wohl mit etwas mehr Sachnähe und Aussagekraft). Dort werden Schiedssprüche privater Schiedsgerichte gerade dadurch mit praktisch weltweiter – und damit einer über die der staatlichen Gerichtsurteile hinausgehender – Freizügigkeit ausgestattet, dass die souveränen Staaten sie an einer der wichtigsten Manifestationen ihrer staatlichen Souveränität, nämlich an der Verleihung der Ausübung ihrer Vollstreckungsgewalt teilhaben lassen. Letzten Endes ist das New York Übereinkommen – zusammen mit den einzelnen funktionalen gleichstellenden Normen der *leges fori arbitrationis* wie etwa § 1055 ZPO) – die Verkörperung und zugleich der Garant der funktionalen Gleichstellung von Schiedssprüchen und Gerichtsurteilen. Sind aber gerade die ausschließlich der staatlichen Souveränität entfließenden Wirkungen, insbesondere also die Vollstreckbarkeit von Schiedssprüchen denen der staatlichen Gerichtsurteile gleichgestellt, so ist schwer einzusehen, warum der zum Schiedsspruch führende Weg, also das Schiedsverfahren plötzlich ohne Weiteres als funktional ungleich dastehen und der eine begründete Sachentscheidung garantierenden Beweisrechtshilfe entbehren soll. Die Entscheidungsbegründung des Supreme Court macht diesbezüglich zumindest etwas überraschend Halt bei der zitierten Aussage, dass aufgrund allgemeinen Sprachgebrauchs *foreign* auf fremde staatliche Souveränität hindeutet. Das Potenzial der – gerne auch textualistischen – Auslegung auf der sich anbietenden Basis *foreign arbitral award* und damit zugleich einer dem schiedsrechtlichen Zusammenhang gerecht werdenden inhaltlichen Interpretation bleibt unerkannt, oder – wohlwollend – zumindest ungenutzt. Dies führt dazu, dass ein vielschichtiges Problem künstlich auf ein gewollt Einfaches reduziert wird, wodurch die internationale private Schiedsgerichtsbarkeit in einem verzerrten Spiegelbild wiedergegeben – wenn nicht gar desselben nach Art des Erasmus Spikher verlustig[80] – wird und gerade einem ihrer wichtigsten Wesensmerkmale, der längst anerkannten funktionalen Äquivalenz nicht Rechnung getragen wird.[81]

---

[80] Ernst Theodor Wilhelm (Amadeus) Hoffmann, Die Geschichte vom verlorenen Spiegelbilde – zu lesen Hand in Hand mit Peter Schlemihls wundersamer Geschichte von Adelbert von Chamisso.

[81] Zur Selbstverständlichkeit, dass private Schiedsgerichte als foreign tribunals anzusehen sind vgl nur den amicus curiae brief of George Bermann in Servotronics (und dann gleichlautend und mitgezeichnet durch Robert H. Smit, D. Brian King, Ruth Teitelbaum und Lucas Bento in ZF Automotive v. Luxshare): "It is telling that Congress did not limit assistance under Section 1782 to 'foreign or international courts' or 'foreign or international judicial bodies,' as it easily could have. 'Tribunal' is indisputably the term used to identify the bodies that conduct international arbitral proceedings. Indeed, when the term 'foreign or international tribunal' is mentioned, international commercial arbitral tribunals come immediately to mind. Thus, both before and after 1964, this Court has repeatedly used the term 'tribunal' to identify such bodies. In keeping with accepted canons of statutory construction, a statute is to be interpreted in accordance with the plain meaning of its terms, and the inquiry into meaning should stop there. Bostock v. Clayton Cty., Ga., 140 S. Ct. 1731, 1738 (2020). Courts interpreting Section 1782 must remain faithful to

Die dergestalt stark dem Textualismus verpflichtete Entscheidungsbegründung rief bereits eine Reihe hochkritischer Stimmen in der Literatur hervor.[82] Bemerkenswerterweise bleibt die Mehrheit dieser Stimmen bei einer Verärgerung über die textualistische Methode, insbesondere über die in letzter Zeit in deren Dienst gestellte, stark umstrittene Nutzung linguistischer Datenbanken (*linguistic corpora* als auf Statistik, also auf Nutzungshäufigkeit basierte Ermittlungsmethode des Sinnes von Wörtern bzw. Wortzusammensetzungen[83]) stehen. Im Mittelpunkt der Kritik steht dabei die Beliebigkeit der Wahl des als Ermittlungsgrundlage herangezogenen linguistischen Corpus. Dies deckt sich im Wesentlichen mit der hier oben geäußerten Kritik, zumindest in linguistischer Hinsicht. Indessen würde man der Supreme Court Opinion Unrecht tun, wollte man behaupten, dass sie sich ausschließlich auf das Linguistische beschränkt und so das negative Ergebnis erreicht. Es gibt nämlich einen – wenn auch kurzen und wenig ausgearbeiteten – Teil der Entscheidungsbegründung, der sich um Erweiterung des Horizonts um regulatorisch-inhaltliche Zusammenhänge bemüht. Dem gilt im Folgenden unsere Aufmerksamkeit, denn hier ist die Stelle, wo die inhaltliche Kritik der Entscheidung in voller Schärfe zutage treten kann, dh die bloße Textualismuskritik hinter sich lassend Grundsätzliches zur Thematik beitragen kann und muss.

Der betreffende, ansatzweise auch inhaltliche Zusammenhänge berücksichtigende Teil der Begründung hätte mitnichten zwingend zum negativen Ergebnis der Entscheidung führen müssen. Es ist gewissermaßen der gedankliche Höhepunkt der Entscheidungsbegründung, da hier von der alles andere als zwingenden, ausschließlich am aus Wörterbüchern gewonnenen Wortsinn haftenden Interpretation Abschied genommen und die Brücke zum *comity*-Gedanken geschlagen wird. *Comity* wird jedoch wieder denkbar eng als von der auf Reziprozität gerichteten Erwartungshaltung von Staaten getragene Rücksichtnahme auf das Fremde verstanden. Unter Fremdem wird dabei betont etwas originär Fremdstaatliches, dh unmittelbar der fremden staatlichen Souveränität Entspringendes verstanden. *Comity* wird engherzig – und entgegen führenden Autoritäten[84] – auf unmittelbar Zwischenstaatliches beschränkt und im vermeintlich auch dort nur bezüglich staatlicher Foren existierenden Gegenseitigkeitskontext gesehen. Da erscheint es in der inneren – zirkulären[85] – Logik der Entscheidungsbegründung nur konsequent, dass für aus privatautonomen Parteivereinbarungen entstandene Streitentscheidungsorgane

that precept.", https://www.supremecourt.gov/DocketPDF/20/20-794/179133/20210513153854699_20-794tsacProfessorGeorgeA.Bermann.pdf (abgerufen 11.9.2024).

[82] Vgl. zB Tobia 71 Duke L.J. Online 146 (2021–2022). Dagegen allerdings mit eindeutig positiver Wertung: Philips/Egbert 108 Va. L. Rev. Online 207 (2022) und Szalai 25 Cardozo J. Conflict Resol. (Fall 2023), 13 (51).

[83] Vgl. zur Rolle der modernen *linguistic corpora* bei der Gesetzesauslegung Jensen/Lee 54 Geo. Wash. Int'l L. (2022), 1.

[84] Statt aller s Briggs Recueil des cours 354 (2012), insb 164. (zusammenfassend 182): "Properly understood, the doctrine of comity is separate, distinct from, and unaffected by any reciprocity, or lack of reciprocity, in respect of a foreign State, and accepts that there may be parallel, co-existent reasons for a court to act which are neither mandated by comity nor precluded by it. […] the doctrine of comity does not prevent a court giving effect to private agreements, contracts, or other voluntary relationships assumed by parties inter se […]".

[85] Ebenso Collins 122 Mich. L. Rev. 127, 137.

kein Platz bleibt. Dies wird deutlich an den – an mehreren Stellen der Begründung verstreuten – diesbezüglichen Aussagen des Supreme Court:

"[...] This reading of 'foreign tribunal' is reinforced by the statutory defaults for discovery procedure. In addition to authorizing district courts to order testimony or the production of evidence, § 1782 permits them to 'prescribe the practice and procedure, which may be in whole or part the practice and procedure of the foreign country' [...] The reference to the procedure of 'the foreign country [...] parallels the authorization for district courts to grant discovery for use in a 'foreign or international tribunal' mentioned just before in § 1782. The statute thus presumes that a 'foreign tribunal' follows 'the practice and procedure of the foreign country.' It is unremarkable for the statute to presume that a foreign court, quasi-judicial body, or any other governmental adjudicatory body follows the practice and procedures prescribed by the government that conferred authority on it. But that would be an odd assumption to make about a private adjudicatory body, which is typically the creature of an agreement between private parties who prescribe their own rules. [...] That the default discovery procedures for a 'foreign tribunal' are governmental suggests that the body is governmental too."[86]

Sodann weiter angereichert mit Gesetzgebungsgeschichte und *comity* in jenen Zusammenhang eingebettet:

"[...] From the start, the statute has been about respecting foreign nations and the governmental and intergovernmental bodies they create. From 1855 until 1964, § 1782 and its antecedents covered assistance only to foreign 'courts.' [...] Congress [...] charged the Commission with improving the process of judicial assistance, specifying that the 'assistance and cooperation' was 'between the United States and foreign countries' and that 'the rendering of assistance to foreign courts and quasi-judicial agencies' should be improved. In 1964, Congress adopted the Commission's proposed legislation, which became the modern version of § 1782. Interpreting § 1782 to reach only bodies exercising governmental authority is consistent with Congress' charge to the Commission. Seen in light of the statutory history, the amendment did not signal an expansion from public to private bodies, but rather an expansion of the types of public bodies covered. [...] After all, the animating purpose of § 1782 is comity: Permitting federal courts to assist foreign and international governmental bodies promotes respect for foreign governments and encourages reciprocal assistance. It is difficult to see how enlisting district courts to help private bodies would serve that end. Such a broad reading of § 1782 would open district court doors to any interested person seeking assistance for proceedings before any private adjudicative body – a category broad enough to include everything from a commercial arbitration panel to a university's student disciplinary tribunal. Why would Congress lend the resources of district courts to aid purely private bodies adjudicating purely private disputes abroad?"[87]

An dieser inhaltlich konzipierten Stelle muss sich die Entscheidung wiederum mehrschichtige inhaltliche Kritik gefallen lassen. Zum einen ist es alles andere als so selbstverständlich, wie die Opinion dies hinstellt, dass die Ersetzung des immerhin ein Jahrhundert währenden Wortes *court* durch *tribunal* im Zuge der Reform im

---

[86] ZF Automotive US, Inc. v. Luxshare, Ltd., 596 U.S. 619 (630) (2022).
[87] ZF Automotive US, Inc. v. Luxshare, Ltd., 596 U.S. 619 (631 f.) (2022).

Jahre 1964 keine Erweiterung auch in Richtung nicht-staatlicher Foren bezweckt hätte. Immerhin plädiert eine Reihe hochkarätiger Stimmen aus der nächsten Nähe des damaligen Reformprozesses im Einklang mit dem – zugegebenermaßen selbst nicht zwingenden[88] – Smit-Zitat für eine Erstreckungsabsicht auf private Schiedsverfahren. Zwar spricht der entwerfende Professor „nur" von *arbitral tribunals or single arbitrators,* nicht etwa von *private* or *commercial arbitral tribunals or single arbitrators.* Jedoch hätte gerade ein textualistischer Ansatz unter Zugrundelegung linguistischer Corpora statistisch sehr schnell zum Ergebnis kommen müssen, dass *arbitral tribunal* und *single arbitrator* meistens im Zusammenhang mit *commercial* oder *private dispute resolution* gebraucht wird. Zum anderen erscheint die comity-Auffassung des obersten US-amerikanischen Gerichts hier als eindeutig zu eng. Als *state-sponsored* soll ausschließlich das Primär-(Fremd)Staatliche gelten, und ausschließlich dieses soll von der *comity*-Doktrin erfasst sein. Wie bereits oben angeklungen ist, steht dies in Widerspruch zu maßgebenden Stimmen in der Wissenschaft[89], und bricht in nicht unbedeutendem Maß inhaltlich nicht zuletzt selbst auch mit den Ursprüngen der *comity*-Rechtsprechung des Supreme Court.[90] Auf keines der beiden Aspekte wird in der Entscheidungsbegründung eingegangen, weder führende Literatur noch das weitherzige *comity*-Konzept von *Hilton v. Guyot* wird in irgendeiner Weise relativiert oder gar widerlegt. Stattdessen wird unter Wiederholung des Vorbringens der antragstellenden Partei ohne Weiteres vom Primär-Staatlichem als einzigem Normadressaten ausgegangen. Für ein Sekundär-Staatliches bleibt in diesem inhaltlichen Prüfungsrahmen also nach derselben Logik kein Raum, die schon im formellen, rein linguistischen Prüfungsrahmen zur Außerachtlassung des einzig echten und relevanten Zusammenhangs und damit der einzig legitimen Vergleichsbasis *(foreign arbitral award)* geführt hat. Gewiß, niemand könnte den Sinn der Vorschrift zutreffender und eindringlicher in einer einzigen Wendung auf den Punkt bringen, als die Opinion dies tut: *„After all, the animating purpose of § 1782 is comity."* Ja, das stimmt! Aber wieso darf und soll *comity* nicht auch das Sekundär-Staatliche erfassen?[91] Gerade hier wäre ein weites, von rein etatistischen Vorstellungen befreites *comity*-Verständnis angesagt, das im gegebenen Zusammenhang, dh im Dienste des freien internationalen Wirtschaftsverkehrs und dessen bevorzugten Streitlösungsmechanismus wirklich interessen- und zielgerecht, anstatt zweckentfremdet, angewandt werden sollte. Private Schiedsverfahren sind ja in den modernen, UNCITRAL-harmonisierten Rechtsordnungen durch und durch staatlich eingebettet und vom Souverän an entscheidenden Stellen (Konstitution, Rechtshilfe, Vollstreckung) mitgetragen. Auch dort ist ja nichts anderes als *comity* am Werke, wo der ersuchte Staat dem Sekundär-Staatlichen des ersuchenden Staates bzw. des Staa-

---

[88] Smit spricht von arbitral tribunals, und nicht spezifiziert von private arbitral tribunals.

[89] Briggs Recueil des cours 354 (2012), 164 (zusammenfassend 182).

[90] Hilton v. Guyot, 159 U.S. 113, dort war ja Ausgangspunkt auch ein fremdes Schiedsverfahren und dessen Sanktionierung.

[91] Wie bereits in diese Richtung im oben zitierten Fall Servotronics, Inc. v. Boeing Co., 954 F.3d 209, 214 (4th Cir. 2020): "[...]arbitration in the United States is a congressionally endorsed and regulated process that is judicially supervised. And it was developed as a favored alternative to the judicial process for the resolution of disputes. Thus, contrary to Boeing's general assertion that arbitration is not a product of 'government-conferred authority,' under U.S. law, it clearly is."

tes, aus dem als Schiedsort der Antrag stammt, seine Rücksichtnahme dadurch erweist, dass er den fremden, also am Schiedsort geltenden staatlichen regulatorischen Rahmen des Schiedsverfahrensrechts anerkennt[92] und deswegen Rechtshilfe leistet. Die wirksame Konstituierung und das Verfahren des im Individualfall verfahrenden fremden Schiedsgerichts *(foreign arbitral tribunal)* unterliegen in aller Regel ebenso dem gesetzten Recht des fremden Souveräns, wie die Möglichkeit und Grenzen der Derogierung desselben gesetzten Rechts. Ebenso ist es der fremde Souverän, der durch die jeweiligen funktionalen Äquivalenznormen (in Deutschland § 1055 ZPO) das inhaltliche Ergebnis des Schiedsverfahrens dem des staatlichen Zivilprozesses gleichstellt. Schließlich ist es auch der jeweilige fremde Souverän, der – nicht zuletzt als Folge jener funktionalen Äquivalenz – die Erzwingung des Inhalts des (Leistungs)Schiedsspruchs durch gleiche Anwendung staatlichen Zwangs wie bei staatlichen Gerichtsurteilen ermöglicht. Und wenn diese Wirkungserstreckung gerade durch das im New York Übereinkommen manifestierten Einvernehmen der souveränen Staaten, darunter der sich gern in der Vorreiterrolle sehenden USA immerhin praktisch weltweite Geltung erlangt, dann ist es nicht ersichtlich, warum ausgerechnet die Beweisrechtshilfe zugunsten eines ausländischen (dort vielfach staatlich eingebetteten) Schiedsverfahrens von der *comity*-Doktrin nicht erfasst sein soll. In diesem Zusammenhang sollte man sich nochmal vergegenwärtigen, dass sich der Supreme Court im Ursprungsfall seiner *comity*-Rechtsprechung im Jahre 1895, in *Hilton v. Guyot* gerade deswegen eine großzügige Definition der Doktrin aufstellen konnte, weil er sich an der Andersartigkeit, dh an der der US-amerikanischen Vorstellung von einer staatlich organisierten Ziviljustiz nicht entsprechenden Ausgestaltung des anzuerkennenden französischen Verfahrens nicht störte. Jene Andersartigkeit rührte ja dort von der schiedsverfahrensähnlichen Ausgestaltung des französischen, wesentliche private Züge aufweisenden handelsgerichtlichen Verfahrens her. Die restlose Anerkennung jenes französischen Verfahrens folgte für das Hilton-Court ohne Weiteres gerade aus der übergeordneten, großzügig definierten und demgemäß auch das insoweit Sekundär-Staatliche erfassenden *doctrine of comity.*[93] Das Hauptaugenmerk lag dabei auf der – in *ZF Automotive v. Luxshare* vermissten und hier eingeforderten – Überlegung, dass es sich um ein solches ausländisches, schiedsähnliches Verfahren handelte, das vom fremden Souverän zugelassen, ausgestaltet, mitgetragen, anerkannt und im Ergebnis auch zwangsweise durchgesetzt wurde. Nichts anderes gilt für moderne private Schiedsverfahren, die gerade wegen ihrer vielschichtigen Einbindung in das staatliche Recht und damit in

[92] Ebenso Niedermaier SchiedsVZ 2022, 345 (350). Insb für die Kritik der Bezugnahme des Supreme Court auf die angeblich nur staatliche Gerichte erfassenden practice and procedure of the foreign country or the international tribunal mit richtigem Verweis auf die jeweilige lex fori arbitrationis: „Die Anwendbarkeit jedes von den Parteien unmittelbar oder durch Bezugnahme vereinbarten Regelwerks sowie die Ausübung des schiedsgerichtlichen Ermessens stehen unter dem Vorbehalt der Vereinbarkeit mit den zwingenden Regelungen des anwendbaren nationalen Schiedsrechts."

[93] Vgl. detailliert dazu und zur Kritik einer abweichenden Entwicklung Teitz, in: Clermont (ed), Procedural Stories, Hilton v. Guyot, S. 470f. sowie Briggs Recueil des cours 354 (2011) 65 (182): "[...] the doctrine of comity does not prevent a court giving effect to private agreements, contracts, or other voluntary relationships assumed by parties inter se [...]"

die staatlichen Kontrollmechanismen am Schiedsort ohne Weiteres auf die Anwendung der *comity*-Doktrin Anspruch erheben, sobald sich Grenzüberschreitungen – sei es vor dem Schiedsverfahren (Gedanke des § 1032 iVm § 1025 Abs. 2 ZPO), sei es während des Schiedsverfahrens (Gedanke des § 1050 iVm § 1025 Abs. 2 ZPO) oder in der Anerkennungs- und Vollstreckungsphase nach dem Schiedsverfahren (NYÜ) – ergeben.

Unter Weiterführung dieses letzten Gedankens soll hier abschließend der Aspekt der Durchbrechung des Territorialitätsprinzips unsere kritischen Bemerkungen abrunden. Eine diesbezügliche rechtsvergleichende Umschau verleiht nämlich der hier geäußerten inhaltlichen Kritik weitere Legitimation: Das oben erwähnte Einvernehmen der Staatengemeinschaft, das sich im New York Übereinkommen 1958 hinsichtlich des Endergebnisses des Schiedsverfahrens manifestiert, indem es den privaten Schiedsspruch ganz im Sinne der funktionalen Äquivalenz zwischen staatlicher und privater Ziviljustiz zum weltweit frei zirkulierenden Vollstreckungstitel qualifiziert, findet seinen Pendant hinsichtlich der weit verstandenen Rechtshilfe zugunsten Schiedsverfahren im UNCITRAL Model Law und den diesem folgenden nationalen Gesetzgebungen. Dieser Pendant, nämlich die ausnahmsweise Durchbrechung des Territorialitätprinzips, basiert zweifellos ebenfalls auf *comity*-Überlegungen: Das Wesen der privaten Schiedsgerichtsbarkeit ist entsprechend dem sie auf den Plan rufenden Vertragswillen der Parteien die Derogation nicht nur der staatlichen Gerichtszuständigkeit am Schiedsort oder nur der jeweiligen sonst international zuständigen staatlichen Gerichte, sondern jeglicher staatlicher Ziviljustiz überhaupt, im globalen Sinne. Nimmt man dieses Wesen ernst, so muss man gleichzeitig zur Einsicht gelangen, dass eine schiedsortbasierte Differenzierung zwischen inländischen und ausländischen Schiedsverfahren an jenen Regelungsmeilensteinen des Schiedsverfahrensrechts illegitim ist, von denen die von den Vertragsparteien gewollte und vom jeweiligen Gesetzgeber abgesegnete Funktionsfähigkeit und Effektivität des Schiedsverfahrens abhängen. Diese Einsicht führte gerade in den für die internationale Handelsschiedsgerichtsbarkeit maß- und tonangebenden Rechtsordnungen zur Durchbrechung des Territorialitätsprinzips an den genannten Meilensteinen der weit verstandenen, weil jene Funktionsfähigkeit und Effektivität zusichernden Rechtshilfe: Am Beispiel der deutschen Regelung gehören hierher das zugunsten des Schiedsverfahrens ergehende Prozessurteil gemäß § 1032 ZPO, der zugunsten von Schiedsverfahren ergehende einstweilige Rechtsschutz gemäß § 1033 ZPO, sowie eben die zugunsten von Schiedsverfahren vollzogene Beweisaufnahme durch die staatlichen Gerichte gemäß § 1050 ZPO. Der genannten Einsicht folgend hebt § 1025 Abs. 2 ZPO bei allen drei Prozesshandlungen der staatlichen Gerichte richtigerweise das in § 1025 Abs. 1 ZPO aufgestellte Territorialitätsprinzip auf. Die uns hier näher interessierende Beweisrechtshilfe gemäß § 1050 ZPO wird – geleitet durch den comity-basierten Öffnungsgedanken – von deutschen staatlichen Gerichten also global, schiedsortunabhängig, dem Wesen der privaten Schiedsgerichtsbarkeit entsprechend ohne Differenzierung sowohl zugunsten in- als auch ausländischer Schiedsverfahren geleistet.[94] Die gleiche Regelungstechnik – des

[94] Vgl. mwN Meshel 39 ArbInt 2023, 19, sowie ebenso im vorausgehenden Brief of Professors Tamar Meshel, Crina Baltag, Fabien Gélinas, and Janet Walker as Amici Curiae in Support of

dort traditionell gesondert behandelten internationalen Schiedsrechts – findet sich im französischen Verfahrensrecht, wo Art. 1469 iVm Art. 1506 Code de procédure civile die französische staatliche Beweisrechtshilfe global eröffnet. Nicht anders das auch das internationale Schiedsverfahrensrecht regelnde schweizerische Bundesgesetz über das Internationale Privatrecht (IPRG), dessen ursprünglicher Art. 184 über die Beweisrechtshilfe im Jahre 2020 um den neu eingefügten Art. 185a II IPRG bereichert wurde, indem die schiedsfreundliche Vorschrift ausdrücklich auf ausländische Schiedsgerichte und Schiedsparteien erstreckt wurde.[95] Der Wortlaut der Vorschrift erinnert nicht von ungefähr an unseren Prüfungsgegenstand im US-Recht: „Ein Schiedsgericht mit Sitz im Ausland oder eine Partei eines ausländischen Schiedsverfahrens mit Zustimmung des Schiedsgerichts kann das staatliche Gericht am Ort, an dem die Beweisaufnahme erfolgen soll, um Mitwirkung ersuchen. Art. 184 Absätze 2 und 3 gilt sinngemäß." Auch das österreichische Schiedsverfahrensrecht enthält die gleiche Regelungstechnik in § 602 iVm § 577 Abs 2 östZPO. Ebenso verfährt das englische Schiedsverfahrensrecht und das sich daran anschließende Fallrecht: Section 2(3)(b) des Arbitration Act 1996 eröffnet die Anwendbarkeit der die Beweisrechtshilfe regelnden Section 44(2) für Schiedsverfahren mit Schiedsort außerhalb des Vereinigten Königreichs.[96] Gleiche Regelungen finden sich ferner in einer Reihe weiterer Rechtsordnungen.[97] Angesichts der hier kurz vorgestellten Regelungstechniken lässt sich mit Sicherheit feststellen, dass eine das Territorialitätsprinzip durchbrechende und damit die Beweisrechtshilfe zugunsten ausländischer Schiedsverfahren garantierende Regelung gerade in den führenden Schiedsverfahrensrechtssystemen den Regelfall bildet. Diese Regelungstechnik scheint sogar angesichts der unlängst in dieser Richtung erfolgten Gesetzesänderungen bzw. -ergänzungen einen internationalen Regelungstrend zu bilden. Ebenso sicher darf man davon ausgehen, dass die genannten führenden und traditionell über beträchtliche Regelungsausstrahlung verfügenden Rechtsordnungen sich bei dieser Rechtssetzung hauptsächlich von *comity*-Überlegungen leiten ließen. Und eine einfache, unbefangene Lektüre des 28 USC § 1782 lässt diese US-amerikanische Vorschrift ohne Weiteres als vollkommene Entsprechung der aufgelisteten nationalen Regelungen erscheinen. *ZF Automotive v. Luxshare* führt hingegen dazu, dass sie in Zukunft nicht als solche wird funktionieren können, was auf den ersten Blick schon einen Bruch nicht nur mit der eigenen *comity*-Tradition sondern auch mit dem hier aufgezeigten internationalen Trend bedeutet.[98] Man wird sich aber wohl nicht dazu hin-

---

Respondent Luxshare, Ltd., https://www.supremecourt.gov/DocketPDF/21/21-401/215240/20220301124035547_Luxshare%20Meshel%20Amicus%20-%20eFile.pdf, abrufbar auch über SCOTUSblog https://www.scotusblog.com/case-files/cases/zf-automotive-us-inc-v-luxshare-ltd/ (abgerufen 7.9.2024).

[95] MwN zur schweizerischen Rechtslage, insb zur Rolle der Kantonalgerichtet bei der Rechtshilfe Schroeder/Junge SchiedsVZ 2022, 210 (212).

[96] Mit erweiternder, auch interessierte Dritte erfassender Auslegung durch den UK Court of Appeal: A. v. C. [2020] EWCA (Civ) 409, [2020] 1 WLR 3504. Dazu und zur englischen Rechtsprechung detailliert Cockerill J.B.L. 2021, 3, 246–258.

[97] Etwa Neuseeland, Schweden, Österreich usw, vgl mwN Meshel, 39 Arbitration International 2023, 19.

[98] Manche Autoren bezeichnen die USA daher sogar als outlier vgl zB Greenop/Sanjur 5 ITA in Review (2023), 1 (13) und González-Bueno, 40 under 40 International Arbitration/Bento (2024), 181 (unter Verwertung des von ihnen mitgezeichneten Brief Amici Curiae of George A.

reißen lassen müssen, jenseits des Atlantiks auch einen Trendwechsel allgemein hinsichtlich der schiedsfreundlichen Haltung, gar eine Rückkehr der früher beklagten *judicial hostility* zu vermuten,[99] selbst wenn der unwürdige Vergleich des privaten Schiedsverfahrens mit dem Disziplinarverfahren eines Studentenwerks Eingang in den oben zitierten Entscheidungstext gefunden hat.

Vollständigkeitshalber möge hier noch ein Verweis auf den abschließenden Teil der Begründung stehen. Dort zieht sich die Opinion auf das oben bereits beschriebene, von der restriktiven Circuit-Rechtsprechung befolgte Argument der Unzulässigkeit der Ungleichbehandlung inländischer und ausländischer Handelsschiedsverfahren zurück, ohne der Argumentationslinie gerade mit Blick auf Intel etwas hinzuzusetzen: Würden ausländische private Schiedsverfahren in den Genuss der discovery-Möglichkeiten des 28 USC § 1782 kommen, würde das deren Besserstellung gegenüber § 7 FAA unterfallenden inländischen Schiedsverfahren zur Folge haben, insbesondere in zeitlicher (vor Verfahrenseröffnung bereits möglich) sowie in persönlicher Hinsicht (Antragsbefugnis nicht nur bei Schiedsgerichten sondern auch Parteien und Dritten). Wie gezeigt, war dies über die Jahre des Circuit Split ein wiederkehrendes Argument der abgeneigten Circuits, sei es im Kontext der angeblichen Statutenkollision, sei es unter Berücksichtigung eines nicht weiter erklärten Gleichbehandlungsstrebens. Es erstaunt jedenfalls auch hier, dass die Opinion dieselben Argumente ins Feld führt, ohne auf die in Intel erarbeiteten Kriterien, geschweige denn auf die ganze entgegengesetzte Denkweise von Intel einzugehen.[100] Die Intel-Kriterien sind ja ua gerade dazu erdacht und zum Leitentscheidungsinhalt gemacht worden, damit die US-Gerichte unausgeglichene, ausufernde discovery-Ersuchen aus dem Ausland einfach abschneiden können. Ein Sich-Begnügen mit einem Verweis auf die unveränderte Anwendbarkeit des dritten bzw. vierten Intel-Kriteriums (Versagung bei US-policy-Verstoß und bei ausufern-

---

Bermann, Robert H. Smit, D. Brian King, Ruth Teitelbaum, and Lucas Bento in Support of Respondents Luxshare, Ltd., https://www.supremecourt.gov/DocketPDF/21/21-401/215546/20220302173954546_21-401%2021-518%20bsac%20George%20A%20Bermann%20Robert%20H%20Smit%20D%20Brian%20King%20Ruth%20Teitelbaum%20And%20Lucas%20Bento.pdf, abrufbar auch über, SCOTUSblog https://www.scotusblog.com/case-files/cases/zf-automotive-us-inc-v-luxshare-ltd/ (abgerufen 7.9.2024)).

[99] Wobei manche Stimmen bereits davon ausgehen, so zB Reiss Arbitration: The International Journal of Arbitration, Mediation and Dispute Management 89 (2023), 98 (112) "The decision is a blow to the prestige of international arbitration. One cannot help but cringe when one reads how the US Supreme Court likened international arbitration to a 'university's student disciplinary tribunal'. Almost as disheartening was the US government's assertion, at oral argument, that arbitral panels are 'not administering justice', but rather are only 'trying to divine the intent of two parties to an agreement'. Indeed, it is quite concerning that the Court demonstrated such hostility towards international arbitration."

[100] Grundsätzlich gutheißend, aber ebenso krit wegen der Ausklammerung der Intel-Kriterien Gibbons 27 Suffolk J. Trial & App. Advoc. (2021), 241 (267): "[...] the Intel decision already gave the district courts an analytical framework to accept or reject § 1782 requests for use in private international arbitration. By finding that the statute's language and purpose simply do not encompass private arbitration, the ZF Automative decision relieves them of the need to conduct this assessment in the first place." Auch in der deutschen Literatur galten die Intel-Kriterien als allgemein anerkannte und ausreichende Sicherheiten für eine balancierte Anwendung des § 1782. Vgl. (noch kurz vor ZF Automotive v. Luxshare) Faulhaber/Beimel SchiedsVZ 2022, 1 (7): "The District Courts remain the gatekeepers [...]"

den oder missbräuchlichen Ersuchen) hätte hier eine ausgewogenere Lösung geboten und zur Möglichkeit der im richterlichen Ermessen liegenden Berücksichtigung der (Beweis)Nöte und der berechtigten Interessen im jeweiligen Individualfall verholfen. Und was die Denkrichtung angeht, die an mehreren Stellen in Intel eindeutig wird und die in ZF Automotive v. Luxshare einfach übergangen wird: Im Mittelpunkt der diesbezüglichen Ausführungen von Justice Ginsburg steht eigentlich ein einziger Gedanke: Die Auslegung der die grenzüberschreitende Beweisrechtshilfe regelnden, und damit ganz andere Interessenlagen berücksichtigenden Vorschrift darf nicht davon abhängen, wie inländische Sachverhalte geregelt werden:

"The Court also rejects Intel's suggestion that a § 1782(a) applicant must show that United States law would allow discovery in domestic litigation analogous to the foreign proceeding. Section 1782 is a provision for assistance to tribunals abroad. It does not direct United States courts to engage in comparative analysis to determine whether analogous proceedings exist here. Comparisons of that order can be fraught with danger."[101]

Hier ist wiederum zu erkennen, dass das Leitmotiv der *Intel*-Opinion auch in dieser Hinsicht nichts anderes war als *comity:* Der Umstand, dass eine Möglichkeit für Inlandsfälle nicht vorgesehen ist, darf nicht als Argument für die Versagung der gleichen Möglichkeit in grenzüberschreitenden Fällen verwendet werden. Gerade aus comity-Überlegungen kann es durchaus folgen (wie auch das oben beschriebene Mandat der Rules Commission nahelegt), dass der Gesetzgeber für grenzüberschreitende Fälle ein Mehr zur Verfügung stellen will.[102]

Zusammenfassend lässt sich behaupten, dass ZF Automotive v. Luxshare für den handelsschiedsverfahrensrechtlichen Zusammenhang am Ende nicht mehr geliefert hat, als eine stark vereinfachte Wiederholung der oben dargestellten Servotronics v. Rolls-Royce-Entscheidung des 7th Circuit. Dabei überspringt die neue Leitentscheidung des Supreme Court bedauerlicherweise die in *Servotronics v. Rolls-Royce* noch ausgearbeiteten und die Problematik im ganzen Rechtshilfekontext einbettenden dogmatischen Argumente, und bleibt bei einer sehr vereinfachenden, an einem willkürlich ausgewählten und damit verengten Corpus orientierten grammatischen Auslegung, sowie bei einem unzulänglichen comity-Konzept stehen. Inwieweit eine solche Entwicklung durch das von Justice *Barrett* hochgehaltene geis-

[101] Intel Corp. v. Advanced Micro Devices, Inc., 542 U.S. 241, 244, 124 S. Ct. 2466, 2471, 159 L. Ed. 2d 355 (2004).

[102] Nicht von ungefähr auch hier entsprechend die Sichtweise von Smit 14 ARIA (2003), 295 (311): "The fact that Section 1782, which deals only with assistance on the international level, does not deal with the domestic arena cannot be seriously considered as an argument for limiting its intended purpose in the international arena. On the contrary, if anything, it should move the legislature dealing with domestic adjudication to emulate the reform achieved on the international level. Surely, if the drafters of Section 1782 had been given the mandate also to address the domestic situation, they would readily have advocated that the same assistance it provided for international and foreign tribunals be, a fortiori, extended to domestic tribunals. In fact, the aim of the drafters of Section 1782 was that domestic legislatures adopt the liberalized rules they provided for the international situation. The argument here discussed stands the very purpose of 1782 on its head. It seeks to limit Section 1782 because the domestic lawmaker has fallen short in introducing the same desirable rules into its domestic system."

tige Vermächtnis von Justice *Scalia* vorgezeichnet war, muss und kann offenbleiben. Zum Verständnis der Argumentation der Opinion – die anfangs alles andere als ein Selbstläufer schien, wie dies die letztendliche Einstimmigkeit suggeriert[103] – mag jedoch die von Justice *Scalia* durchaus noch mitgestaltete Vorgeschichte der Rechtsprechung sehr wohl beitragen: Er, der bedeutende Verfechter des Textualismus und damit Gegner allen vermeintlich unnötigen Ausschweifens der Gesetzesauslegung in Richtung Gesetzgebungs-, Entstehungsgeschichte bzw. Wille des Gesetzgebers, war zwar mit der Intel Opinion von Justice *Ginsburg* im Endergebnis, aber auch ausschließlich darin, also mit dem Entscheidungstenor einverstanden. Dieser indessen hätte in seiner Sicht ausschließlich über die grammatische Auslegung des Normtextes erreicht werden müssen und dürfen. Von den funktionalen Gedankengängen mit Verweisen auf die Smit-Kommissionsdokumente und von der kreativen Zerlegung des Verfahrens der Wettbewerbsbehörde als Tatsacheninstanz mit Beweisaufnahmefunktion, die in *Intel* schließlich zur Qualifizierung des DG COMP der EU-Kommission als foreign tribunal geführt hatten, wollte er – wie seine *concurring opinion* bezeugt – schon gar nicht hören:

"As today's opinion shows, the Court's disposition is required by the text of the statute. [...] That being so, it is not only (as I think) improper but also quite unnecessary to seek repeated support in the words of a Senate Committee Report – which, as far as we know, not even the full committee, much less the full Senate, much much less the House, and much much much less the President who signed the bill, agreed with. Since, moreover, I have not read the entire so-called legislative history, and have no need or desire to do so, so far as I know the statements of the Senate Report may be contradicted elsewhere. Accordingly, because the statute – the only sure expression of the will of Congress – says what the Court says it says, I join in the judgment."[104]

Die in unserer Kritik aufgezeigten Stellen, an denen die *ZF Automotive v. Luxshare*-Opinion unnötig und unerklärlich an der Oberfläche Halt macht, und auch noch im Vergleich zur direkten Vorgängerentscheidung *Servotronics v. Rolls-Royce* sichtlich um Weglassen von inhaltlichen Zusammenhängen und um Vereinfachung bemüht ist, lassen zumindest die Annahme zu, dass die Entscheidungsbegründung nicht zuletzt im Gedenken an *Antonin Scalia* und in Entsprechung seinem genannten geistigen Vermächtnis entstanden ist. Ob er selbst auch in ähnlich fragwürdiger Weise die Worte *state-sponsored* und *governmental* trotz ihrer textuellen Abwesenheit in den Normtext hineingelesen hätte, bleibt ebenso in Geheimnis ge-

[103] In der mündlichen Verhandlung waren etwa Chief Justice Roberts, der einflussreiche und sich auch seinerzeit in Intel mit einer dissenting opinion profilierende Justice Breyer sowie Justices Kagan, Kavanaugh und Sotomayor alles andere als überzeugt. Für den äußeren Betrachter schien die Sache aufgrund der Verhandlung eher noch in die schiedsfreundliche Richtung zu gehen. Vgl. den Mitschnitt und Verhandlungsbericht von Minyao Wang, In dispute over discovery requests in international arbitration, justices weigh text, comity, academic literature, and their own role, SCOTUSblog (Apr. 29, 2022, 10:51 AM), https://www.scotusblog.com/2022/04/in-dispute-over-discovery-requests-in-international-arbitration-justices-weigh-text-comity-academic-literature-and-their-own-role/ (abgerufen 7.9.2024).

[104] Justice Scalia concurring in Intel Corp. v. Advanced Micro Devices, Inc., 542 U.S. 241, 267.

hüllt, wie die Antwort auf die Frage, ob eine Mitwirkung seiner langjährigen Weggefährtin und Diskussionspartnerin *Ruth Bader Ginsburg* als Berichterstatterin *ZF Automotive v. Luxshare* einem anderen Entscheidungsinhalt zugeführt hätte.

Das in Gestalt einer Leitentscheidung den grenzüberschreitenden Rechtsverkehr nunmehr mitbestimmende Endergebnis ist ernüchternd: Der Entscheidungstext nennt zwar die comity-Doktrin als Leitmotiv, lässt ihr aber im Endeffekt den ihr gebührenden Spielraum nicht. Dies führt im Ergebnis zu dem oben genannten Bruch und zugleich zum Ausscheren der US-amerikanischen Praxis aus dem internationalen Regelungstrend. Diese Situation verlangt nach kreativen Lösungen der Schiedspraxis, soll das Sachverhaltsermittlungspotenzial des US-amerikanischen Zivilverfahrensrechts für die internationale Handelsschiedsgerichtsbarkeit nicht für immer verloren gehen. In diesem Sinne sollen im folgenden letzten Schritt die nach hier vertretener Ansicht möglichen Lösungswege, die die entstandene Lücke zu füllen vermögen, im Ansatz aufgezeigt werden.

III. Ansätze für mögliche Lösungswege

Sieht man einmal von dem im Schrifttum bereits geforderten[105], und sogar in der mündlichen Verhandlung in einer Frage von Justice *Breyer* anklingenden[106] legislativen Lösungsweg, also der Gesetzesänderung mit klarstellendem, die private Schiedsgerichtsbarkeit ausdrücklich erfassendem Wortlaut ab, so bleiben zwei Lösungswege, mittels derer dem entstandenen Beweisrechtshilfedefizit begegnet werden kann: Zum einen kann man versuchen, § 7 FAA durch eine kreative und erweiternde Interpretation in den Dienst ausländischer privater Schiedsverfahren zu stellen. Zwar erscheint dieser, vom Recht der USA, also vom Recht des ersuchten Staates her operierende Lösungsweg auf den ersten Blick als ein Umgehen von *ZF Automotive v. Luxshare,* stand doch dort für den Supreme Court ua gerade diese Vorschrift des Bundesschiedsverfahrensrechts einer schiedsfreundlichen, dh ein ausländisches privates Schiedsverfahren erfassenden Auslegung des 28 USC § 1782 im Wege. Doch lässt sich, wie sogleich aufzuzeigen sein wird, diese Lösung mit beachtenswerten dogmatischen Argumenten vertreten. Zum anderen bietet sich ein Rückgriff auf die jeweiligen „eigenen", dh am Schiedsort in der *lex fori arbitrationis* enthaltenen Beweisrechtshilfevorschriften (in Deutschland § 1050 ZPO) an, wodurch in einem zweiten logischen Schritt der Weg zur traditionellen Rechtshilfe zwischen den staatlichen Gerichten des Schiedsortes (ersuchender Staat, zB Deutschland bei deutschem Schiedsort) und denen des Beweisaufnahmeortes (ersuchter Staat, USA) eröffnet wird. Dieser zweite, vom Recht des ersuchenden

[105] Vgl. zB van Ginkel 33 ARIA (2023), 187; Collins 122 Mich. L. Rev. 127.

[106] "As Justice Stephen Breyer pointed out, users and targets of Section 1782 are sophisticated companiescapable of lobbying Congress, which may be the most suitable forum for resolution of the dispute." Minyao Wang, In dispute over discovery requests in international arbitration, justices weigh text, comity, academic literature, and their own role, SCOTUSblog https://www.scotusblog.com/2022/04/in-dispute-over-discovery-requests-in-international-arbitration-justices-weigh-text-comity-academic-literature-and-their-own-role/ (abgerufen 7.9.2024).

Staates her einzuschlagende Lösungsweg ist sicherlich der langwierigere und der Schiedspraxis bislang eher fremde, doch scheint er derzeit, wie sogleich unten gezeigt wird, in der Ära nach *ZF Automotive v. Luxshare* im transatlantischen Schiedsrechtsverkehr bei wirklicher und nur mittels in den USA belegener Beweismittel zu stillender Beweisbedürftigkeit der gangbare Weg zu sein.

1. *Lösungsweg vom Recht des ersuchten Staates her: Wiedererfindung des internationalen Rechtshilfewegs über § 7 Federal Arbitration Act*

Der relevante Teil des für US-amerikanische inländische Schiedsverfahren geltenden § 7 FAA, der das oben beschriebene Ungleichbehandlungsargument während des Circuit Split und auch in *ZF Automotive v. Luxshare* lieferte, lautet wie folgt:

"The arbitrators [...] or a majority of them, may summon in writing any person to attend before them or any of them as a witness and in a proper case to bring with him or them any book, record, document, or paper which may be deemed material as evidence in the case. [...] Said summons shall issue in the name of the arbitrator or arbitrators, or a majority of them, and shall be signed by the arbitrators, or a majority of them, and shall be directed to the said person and shall be served in the same manner as subpoenas to appear and testify before the court; if any person or persons so summoned to testify shall refuse or neglect to obey said summons, upon petition the United States district court for the district in which such arbitrators, or a majority of them, are sitting may compel the attendance of such person or persons before said arbitrator or arbitrators, or punish said person or persons for contempt in the same manner provided by law for securing the attendance of witnesses or their punishment for neglect or refusal to attend in the courts of the United States."

Da nach dem Normtatbestand das Schiedsgericht seinen Sitz in dem Sprengel eines US-Bundesdistriktgerichts haben muss, um sich dann an dasselbe Distriktgericht mit einem Rechtshilfeersuchen wenden zu können, ist die in § 7 FAA[107] vorgesehene Beweisrechtshilfemöglichkeit *prima facie* und nach gängiger Auslegung nur auf aus amerikanischer Sicht inländische Schiedsverfahren anwendbar. Es gab zwar vereinzelt Fälle, in denen US-Bundesdistriktgerichte – in Ausnahmesituationen und zumeist implizit – eine Geltungserstreckung von § 7 FAA auf ausländische Schiedsverfahren für möglich hielten,[108] doch hat sich eine solche Praxis auf Berufungsgerichtsebene nie etablieren können, bis es in California zu einer neuen, wiederum etwas schicksalhaft mit *ZF Automotive v. Luxshare* praktisch gleichzeitigen

---

[107] Title 9 U.S.C. Federal Arbitration Act. Dazu detailliert Varga, Beweiserhebung in transatlantischen Schiedsverfahren – Eine Suche nach Kompromissen zwischen deutscher und US-amerikanischer Beweisrechtstradition, 2006, S. 262ff. Für eine Einführung und legislative history vgl. Sturges/Murphy 17 Law & Contemp. Probs. 580, Fn 1.

[108] So wohl in Bergen Shipping Corp. v. Japan Marine Services Ltd., 386 F.Supp. 430, 435 (S.D. N.Y 1974), wo das Gericht wegen der Dringlichkeit discovery-Rechtshilfe zugunsten eines in Tokyo stattzufindenden Schiedsverfahrens anordnete, ohne die für ausländische Verfahren einschlägige Vorschrift des 28 USC § 1782 zu bemühen (freilich auch ohne ausdrückliche Nennung von § 7 FAA): "This was clearly a case of extraordinary circumstances. The allegations to the effect that the crew was about to leave the United States and be reassigned to vessels in international commerce were sufficient to meet the test of necessity."

Entwicklung gekommen ist: Dort hat das 9th Circuit Bundesberufungsgericht am 1. August 2022, also nur anderthalb Monate nach Verkündung von *ZF Automotive v. Luxshare* eine erweiternde Auslegung von § 7 FAA zugunsten internationaler bzw. ausländischer privater Schiedsgerichte vorgenommen. In der Rechtssache *Jones Day v. Orrick, Herrington & Sutcliffe* wird dies gerade mittels jener funktionalen Denkweise begründet, deren Abwesenheit den Kernpunkt unserer obigen Kritik an *ZF Automotive v. Luxshare* bildete. Die private Schiedsgerichtsbarkeit wird hier richtigerweise unabhängig vom Schiedsort als mit der staatlichen Gerichtsbarkeit funktional äquivalent wahrgenommen und im Kontext der durch das New York Übereinkommen bezeugten (oben von uns „sekundär" genannten) staatlichen Souveränitätsverleihung gesehen. Die funktionale Äquivalenz wird dabei nicht nur für die beiden primären Regelungsgegenstände des New Yorker Übereinkommens (Schiedsvereinbarung und Schiedsspruch als Anerkennungsgegenstände) angenommen, sondern sinngemäß für das gesamte Verfahren samt dessen wichtigstem Teil, der rechtshilfeweise bewerkstelligten Beweisaufnahme:

"Not only are these proceedings 'related to' an arbitration agreement falling under the Convention, petitions to enforce a summons issued by the arbitrator are necessary ancillary proceedings that ensure the proper functioning of the underlying arbitration. As Judge Watford has explained, '[c]onsidering the structure of the FAA as a whole, it seems evident ... that Congress envisioned a § 7 petition [to enforce an arbitral summons to a third party] not as a freestanding lawsuit, but as an adjunct to the 'underlying substantive controversy' between the parties in arbitration.' [T]he enforcement of a subpoena brings before the court one aspect of enforcing the parties' agreement to arbitrate – not the right to arbitrate itself, but the enjoyment of a key procedural attribute of the arbitration the parties bargained for." [...]

The New York Convention has been adopted by nearly 200 nations worldwide because of the expanding role arbitration plays in resolving international commercial disputes. The purpose of the Convention is twofold: (1) to ensure that countries recognize and enforce arbitration agreements, and (2) to ensure that countries recognize and enforce foreign arbitral awards. [...] By signing on to the Convention and adopting Chapter Two of the FAA, "the United States sought 'to encourage the recognition and enforcement of commercial arbitration agreements in international contracts and to unify the standards by which agreements to arbitrate are observed and arbitral awards are enforced in the signatory countries.' [...]. Recognizing and enforcing arbitration agreements includes facilitating the arbitration process and providing arbitrators – in both domestic and international arbitrations – with access to the ancillary actions and proceedings necessary to arrive at an arbitration award. This includes arbitral subpoenas and their enforcement."[109]

Diese innovative, eminent funktionale und auf eine tatsächliche Durchsetzung des NYÜ abzielende Denkweise, die seit ZF Automotive v. Luxshare zunehmend auch in der angelsächsischen Literatur propagiert wird[110], wird gerade dem geweihten deutschen Ohr nicht als eine Neuigkeit erscheinen. Arno *Saathoff* plädierte bereits 1987 in seiner in Deutschland erstmals die Problematik detailliert aufgreifen-

[109] Day v. Orrick, Herrington & Sutcliffe, LLP, 42 F.4th 1131, 1139 (9th Cir. 2022).
[110] So zB Meshel 39 ArbInt 2023, 19; Bailey 58 Ga. L. Rev. 845 (Winter 2024).

den Werk für die Anwendbarkeit von § 7 FAA im internationalen Kontext.[111] Nach seiner Argumentation ergebe § 7 FAA in Verbindung mit § 208 FAA die Möglichkeit der Beweisrechtshilfe auch für ausländische Schiedsgerichte, weil das dem FAA später hinzugefügte Chapter 2 – praktisch ein Ausführungsgesetz zum UNÜ[112] – und der darin enthaltene § 208 FAA[113] die Geltungserstreckung des Chapter 1 und des darin enthaltenen § 7 und des dazugehörigen case law auf dem UNÜ unterfallende ausländische Schiedsverfahren anordneten. UNÜ-Schiedsverfahren würden somit vom ganzen FAA erfasst, was praktisch einer Inlandsbehandlung gleichkomme und damit die Anwendung von § 7 FAA ermögliche. *Saathoff* erreichte dieses Ergebnis zum einen aus einer gesetzessystematischen Auslegung des Verhältnisses beider Vorschriften zueinander, zum anderen aber mit der im besten Zweigert-Kötz'schen Sinne funktional-vergleichenden Argumentation, zwar hätte es seinerzeit kein case law zu § 7 FAA in Bezug auf ausländische Schiedsverfahren gegeben, wohl aber zu § 8 FAA (pre-arbitral-attachments), wonach US-Gerichte Arreste zugunsten im Ausland, sogar ohne amerikanische Beteiligung laufender Schiedsverfahren angeordnet hätten.[114] Nicht von ungefähr gründet also auch dieser Gedankengang – wie die hier zitierte neue Entscheidung des 9th Circuit in *Day v. Orrick* – auf der Erkenntnis der funktionalen Äquivalenz prozessualer Rechtsinstitute, hier der Funktionsgleichheit und damit dem „Gleichbehandlungsanspruch" von Arrest und Beweismittelsicherung.[115] Die Erwartung *Saathoffs*, seine Interpretation würde sich im Lichte künftiger bundesberufungsgerichtlicher Rechtsprechung als zutreffend herausstellen, scheint nach langer Durststrecke mit dem Aufkommen der neuen 9th Circuit-Rechtsprechung in *Day v. Orrick* der Erfüllung einen Schritt näher gekommen zu sein. Ergänzend zum Lösungsweg über § 7 FAA lässt sich schließlich vollständigkeitshalber anmerken, dass ein privates Schiedsgericht auch davor nicht verschlossen ist, seinen Sitz zu einem beliebigen Zeitpunkt – uU auch nur vorübergehend – in einen US-Bundesstaat zu verlegen, und zwar sinnvollerweise in denjenigen, in dem die heranzuziehenden Beweismittel aufzufinden sind. Ab diesem Zeitpunkt wird das betreffende Schiedsverfahren als inländisch qualifiziert und es kommt automatisch in den Genuss der nach § 7 FAA („… the district, where the arbitrators are sitting …") gewährleisteten US-bundesdistriktgerichtlichen staatlichen Rechtshilfe.

---

[111] Saathoff, Möglichkeiten und Verfahren gerichtlicher Hilfe bei der Beweisaufnahme zugunsten fremdnationaler Handelsschiedsgerichtsverfahren mit internationaler Beteiligung, 1987.

[112] 9 U.S.C.A. § 201: "The Convention on the Recognition and Enforcement of Foreign Arbitral Awards of June 10, 1958, shall be enforced in United States courts in accordance with this chapter."

[113] 9 U.S.C.A. § 208: "Chapter 1 (also auch § 7 FAA – eigene Einfügung) applies to actions and proceedings brought under this chapter to the extent that chapter is not in conflict with this chapter or the Convention as ratified by the United States."

[114] Andros Compania Maritima S. A. v. Andre & Cie, 430 F.Supp. 88 (S.D.N.Y. 1977); Compania de Navigation v. National Unity Marine Salvage Co., 457 F.Supp. 1013 (S.D.N.Y. 1978).

[115] Vgl. dazu Stürner IPRax 1984, 299 (300); Stein/Jonas, Kommentar zur ZPO/Schlosser, 23. Aufl. 2014, ZPO § 1050 Rn. 1–2 und Saathoff, Möglichkeiten und Verfahren gerichtlicher Hilfe bei der Beweisaufnahme zugunsten fremdnationaler Handelsschiedsgerichtsverfahren mit internationaler Beteiligung, 1987, S. 24.

Ob sich die international schiedsfreundliche *Day v. Orrick*-Rechtsprechung des US Court of Appeals for the Ninth Circuit als bundesweite Praxis verfestigen kann und damit zur wohltuenden Relativierung des negativen Ergebnisses von *ZF Automotive v. Luxshare* längerfristig beitragen kann, steht derzeit offen. Auf eine Wirkungserstreckung des § 7 FAA in anderen Circuits kann sich der Praktiker – also der prozessstrategisch planende Verfahrensvertreter der Schiedspartei, wie der die Sachverhaltsermittlung vorausschauend planende Schiedsrichter – jedenfalls derzeit nicht mit Sicherheit einstellen. Daher ist – entsprechend dem oben Vorausgeschickten – abschließend die zweite und zugleich letzte Relativierungsmöglichkeit im Folgenden noch zu betrachten.

2. *Lösungsweg vom Recht potenzieller ersuchender Staaten her: Bedeutungszuwachs für die hergebrachten Rechtshilferegeln der jeweiligen lex fori arbitrationis*

ZF Automotive v. Luxshare versperrt den in 28 USC § 1782 vorgesehenen Beweisrechtshilfeweg zu US-amerikanischen Bundesgerichten und damit zur Verwertung der weitreichenden Sachverhaltsermittlungsmöglichkeiten im Rahmen des *pre-trial discovery* für ausländische private Schiedsgerichte mit dem Argument, dass diesen das Merkmal der Trägerschaft staatlicher Souveränität abgeht. Im Umkehrschluss folgt sowohl aus der Leitentscheidung als auch aus dem Geist der ganzen, durch *ZF Automotive v. Luxshare* nunmehr nachträglich legitimierten voraufgehenden negativen Rechtsprechungslinie aus der Zeit des Circuit Split, dass Rechtshilfeersuchen seitens Souveränitätsträger auch dann erfüllt werden können und sollen (mit den *Intel*-Kriterien ständig im Hinterkopf), wenn der Zweck der Ersuchen die Hilfeleistung für private Schiedsverfahren ist. Für die im Formalismus und Textualismus verstrickte *ZF Automotive v. Luxshare*-Opinion kommt es ja wie gezeigt nicht auf eine funktional-inhaltliche Betrachtungsweise an, sondern auf den nackten Wortlaut: Das Rechtshilfeersuchen muss, um positiv beschieden zu werden, aus einem staatlichen *(state-sponsored)* Verfahren bzw. von einem staatlich getragenen, mit staatlicher Autorität ausgestatteten Organ *(tribunal imbued with governmental authority)* stammen. Nun ist das „Gerichtliche Unterstützung bei der Beweisaufnahme und sonstige richterliche Handlungen" genannte Zivilverfahren nach § 1050 ZPO:

> *„Das Schiedsgericht oder eine Partei mit Zustimmung des Schiedsgerichts kann bei Gericht Unterstützung bei der Beweisaufnahme oder die Vornahme sonstiger richterlicher Handlungen, zu denen das Schiedsgericht nicht befugt ist, beantragen. Das Gericht erledigt den Antrag, sofern es ihn nicht für unzulässig hält, nach seinen für die Beweisaufnahme oder die sonstige richterliche Handlung geltenden Verfahrensvorschriften. Die Schiedsrichter sind berechtigt, an einer gerichtlichen Beweisaufnahme teilzunehmen und Fragen zu stellen."*

unstreitig ein vor deutschen staatlichen Gerichten ablaufendes Verfahren, dessen Wesensmerkmal es ist, die souveräne judikative Staatsgewalt zum Zuge kommen zu lassen, sobald dies für die Zwecke der erfolgreichen Abwicklung eines – der gleichen Souveränität ermangelnden – privaten Schiedsverfahrens erforderlich und entsprechend beantragt wird. Nun sind ausländische – also auch deutsche – private Schiedsgerichte gerade wegen ihrer fehlenden Souveränitätsträgerschaft „nicht dazu befugt", Beweisrechtshilfe in den USA bei den dortigen Bundesgerichten gemäß § 1782 zu beantragen. Das nach § 1062 Abs 4 ZPO zuständige deutsche Amtsgericht jedoch, das in Ausübung seiner in § 1050 ZPO verliehenen Zuständigkeit gerade seinerseits Rechtshilfe zugunsten eines privaten Schiedsverfahrens mit deutschem Schiedsort leistet, wird ohne Weiteres antragsbefugt sein müssen im Rahmen von 28 USC § 1782. Das Beweisrechtshilfe leistende deutsche Amtsgericht verfährt ja – das Argument ist zwar unnötig, passt aber zur Logik von ZF Automotive v. Luxshare, die ja auf *practice and procedure of the foreign country* pocht – „nach seinen für die Beweisaufnahme oder die sonstige richterliche Handlung geltenden" (wenig überraschend wegen der Zugehörigkeit des Zivilprozessrechts zum öffentlichen Recht: *staatlichen*) Verfahrensvorschriften der ZPO. Entsprechendes gilt für sämtliche – oben zT referierten – Rechtsordnungen (UK, Frankreich, Schweiz, Österreich[116] usw.), die eine § 1050 ZPO vergleichbare innerstaatliche Rechtshilferegel kennen. Diese innerstaatlichen Rechtshilferegeln funktionieren also als Transmissionsriemen und Brücken zur Anrufung und Anwendung des seinerseits auf (angeblich nur primär staatlich-) Grenzüberschreitendes zugeschnittenen 28 USC § 1782, womit über die Zwischenschaltung der „eigenen" (die judikative Gewalt des Schiedsortes tragenden) staatlichen Gerichte die privaten Schiedsgerichte sich weiterhin freien Zugang zur US-amerikanischen Beweisermittlung sichern können.

IV. Schluss und Ausblick

Die Entscheidung des Supreme Court in *ZF Automotive v. Luxshare* wird dem in vielfältiger staatlicher und völkervertraglicher Normgebung definierten und anerkannten Anspruch der privaten Schiedsgerichtsbarkeit auf funktionale Äquivalenz mit der staatlichen Gerichtsbarkeit nicht gerecht, und kann daher einer auf derselben Grundlage beruhenden Kritik nicht standhalten. Das auch in sich nicht schlüssige Festhalten am vermeintlichen inhärenten Sinn des Wortlauts von 28 USC § 1782, wonach er nur Souveränitätsträger als antragsbefugte Ersuchende erfassen würde, führt zu einer unverhältnismäßigen Beeinträchtigung des dogmatisch wie praktisch höherstehenden Wertes der Sicherung der effektiven und wahrheitsstrebenden Sachverhaltsermittlung. Gerade die funktionale Äquivalenz des Ergebnisses des Schiedsverfahrens (Rechtskraftwirkung, globale Vollstreckbarkeit des Schiedsspruchs) verlangt danach, den zum Ergebnis führende Weg, also das Schiedsverfahren selbst auch funktional gleichwertig zu behandeln und sämtliche Möglichkeiten der Beweisermittlung für den Bedarfsfall bereit zu halten. Comity beschränkt sich nicht auf Primär-Zwischenstaatliches. Das Wesen der privaten Schiedsgerichtsbar-

[116] Erhellend dazu die ausdrückliche diesbezügliche Ermächtigung in § 602 S 2 östZPO: „Die Rechtshilfe kann auch darin bestehen, dass das Gericht ein ausländisches Gericht oder eine Behörde um die Vornahme solcher Handlungen ersucht."

keit ist entsprechend dem sie auf den Plan rufenden Vertragswillen der Parteien die globale Derogation jeglicher staatlicher Ziviljustiz. Die Erkenntnis dieses Wesens verbietet eine schiedsortbasierte Differenzierung zwischen inländischen und ausländischen Schiedsverfahren gerade an jenen Regelungsmeilensteinen des Schiedsverfahrensrechts, von denen die von den Vertragsparteien gewollte und vom jeweiligen Gesetzgeber abgesegnete Funktionsfähigkeit und Effektivität des Schiedsverfahrens abhängen. Zur Funktionsfähigkeit und Effektivität gehören sicher auch Zeitersparnis und Kostengünstigkeit[117], doch vermögen diese den übergeordneten Wert der gründlichen und wirklichen, letzten Endes den Inhalt des global vollstreckbaren Schiedsspruchs legitimierenden Sachverhaltsermittlung nicht zu verdrängen. Nach hier vertretener Ansicht können indessen die oben aufgezeigten Umwege über das US-amerikanische Schiedsrecht sowie über die einzelnen, § 1050 ZPO funktionsgleichen Rechtshilferegelungen der Schiedsrechte weltweit Abhilfe leisten.

Zu den eher entmutigenden Langzeitwirkungen der Entscheidung könnte die Bestätigung oder zumindest die Stärkung einer grundsätzlich skeptischen Haltung gegenüber der privaten Schiedsgerichtsbarkeit zählen. Der Supreme Court liegt in diesem Zusammenhang gewissermaßen im Trend der Rechtsprechung des Europäischen Gerichtshofs. Nicht zu verkennen ist hier die Parallelität zwischen der die internationale Beweisrechtshilfe abschneidenden amerikanischen höchstgerichtlichen Entscheidung und der mittlerweile jahrzehntelang währenden schiedsfeindlichen, die funktionale Äquivalenz negierenden Haltung des EuGH[118]: Dieser versagt privaten Schiedsgerichten die Vorlagebefugnis gemäß Art 267 AEUV seit Menschengedenken mit dem Argument, sie seien keine mitglied*staatlichen* Gerichte. Da Schiedsgerichte sehr wohl über EU-rechtlich relevante Fragen entscheiden müssen (etwa Eingriffsnormen des europäischen Wettbewerbsrechts), um ihre Legitimität zu wahren und nicht etwa EU-rechtlich begründeten Aufhebungsklagen ausgesetzt zu sein[119], wird hier aus nunmehr rechtsvergleichendem Anlass die Diskussion wieder eröffnet werden müssen, ob nicht auch hier § 1050 ZPO und die funktionsgleichen Rechtshilferegelungen der Schiedsrechte der Mitgliedstaaten die Lösung zur Wiederherstellung der funktionalen Äquivalenz liefern.[120]

Schließlich tangiert die Entscheidung auch vitale Interessen der in diesem Beitrag aus Zeit- und Raumgründen bewusst ausgeklammerten Investitionsschiedsgerichtsbarkeit. Der mit ZF in Verbund entschiedene AlixPartners-Fall zeigt die gleiche Parallelität mit der Skepsis gegenüber der Investitionsschiedsgerichtsbarkeit

[117] Die Entscheidung des Supreme Court daraus legitimierend Wilske/Krapfl IWRZ 2023, 210 (212) unter Verweis auf Wilske JUVE 2022, 69 („Billing Opportunity für US-Kollegen", was im Einzelfall sicher gestimmt haben mag), obwohl dieser Effektivitäts- bzw Kostenersparnisaspekt in der Entscheidungsbegründung nicht zu Worte kommt.

[118] Vgl. die Rspr. seit EuGH 23.3.1982 – C-102/81, ECLI:EU:C:1982:107 (Nordsee Deutsche Hochseefischerei GmbH/Reederei Mond Hochseefischerei für M Nordstern AG & Co. KG). Die negative Haltung zuletzt manifestiert in EuGH 20.6.2022 – C-700/20, ECLI:EU:C:2022:488 (London Steam-Ship Owners' Mutual Insurance Association Ltd v Kingdom of Spain).

[119] Vgl. EuGH 1.6.1999 – C-126/97, ECLI:EU:C:1999:269 (Eco Swiss China Time Ltd/Benetton International NV).

[120] Vgl. dazu Münchener Kommentar zur ZPO/Münch, 6. Aufl. 2022, ZPO § 1050 Rn 11 („Staatsgericht als Vorlagebote").

seitens des EuGH wie bereits oben gezeigt. Die Entscheidung spricht einem unter den UNCITRAL Rules verfahrenden BIT-Investitionsschiedsgericht die Antragsbefugnis nach 28 USC § 1782 mit dem gleichen Argument ab, wie schon privaten Schiedsgerichten: Es sei kein *state-sponsored* Entscheidungsorgan trotz der völkervertragsrechtlich begründeten Verfahrenslegitimation. Wie also private Schiedsgerichte nicht als *foreign* qualifiziert werden dürfen, so dürfen Investitionsschiedsgerichte nicht als *international* im Sinne von 28 USC § 1782 gelten. Hierdurch wird wohl selbst der International Centre for Settlement of Investment Disputes „gefährdet" werden, denn in der Logik des Supreme Court werden wohl auch ICSID-tribunals trotz der ICSID-Konvention nicht als international tribunal gelten, wie dies die wenige Tage vor der Niederschrift dieser Arbeit ergangene *WeBuild*-Entscheidung des 2nd Circuit[121] zeigt, die sich selbstredend auf ZF Automotive v. Luxshare beruft. Hier bleibt uU auch noch eine höchstrichterliche Klärung abzuwarten, sollte der Fall auch die certiorari-Phase erreichen.

Es steht derzeit viel auf dem Spiel für die internationale Handelsschiedsgerichtsbarkeit. Diese Entwicklung ist nicht beschränkt auf die ungünstige Behandlung des hier geschilderten punktuellen Problems der Beweisrechtshilfe zu betrachten, sondern vielmehr im weiteren Zusammenhang des darin zutage tretenden Wandels der Denkweise über die Schiedsgerichtsbarkeit. Die durch die Rechtsprechung der Höchstgerichte beiderseits des Atlantiks herbeigeführte Situation verlangt nach einer offenen, von Vorurteilen befreiten, fundierten rechtsvergleichenden Diskussion. Nichts war und ist mehr im Sinne des *Jubilars.*

[121] WEBUILD S.P.A., Applicant-Appellant, Sacyr S. A., Applicant, v. WSP USA INC., Respondent-Appellee, Republic of Panama, Intervenor-Appellee, July 19, 2024, 2024 WL 3463380 US Court of Appeals, Second Circuit.

MATTHIAS WELLER/ACHIM CZUBAIKO

Die Urteilsdefinition im Haager Anerkennungs- und Vollstreckungsübereinkommen (HAVÜ 2019) – Zur Einrahmung eines Schlüsselbegriffs im Spannungsfeld zwischen international einheitlicher Auslegung und nationaler Entscheidungstypologie

I. Einleitung: Eine Haager Sprachverwirrung?

Es ist keine Überraschung, dass die genaue Definition des „Urteils" zentral für das Verständnis des jüngsten Rechtsinstruments der Haager Konferenz für Internationales Privatrecht (HCCH) werden würde.[1] Immerhin verkörpert das Anerkennungs- und Vollstreckungsübereinkommen (HAVÜ 2019) vom 2.7.2019[2] das Resultat des seit dem Jahre 1992 verfolgten *judgments project.*[3] Bemerkenswert ist jedoch, dass die hinter diesem – auch hier – in aller Selbstverständlichkeit postulierten Schlüsselbegriff verborgenen Interpretations- und Abgrenzungsfragen bereits im Normtext der einzelnen Sprachfassungen aufscheinen. So verzichtet etwa die zwischen Deutschland, Österreich und der Schweiz abgestimmte Ausfertigung nahezu vollständig auf den Urteilsbegriff und stützt sich stattdessen auf die abstraktere Bezeichnung „Entscheidung".[4]

Hierdurch hebt sie sich deutlich von der nuancierteren Formulierung[5] aller UN-Sprachen ab, unter denen allerdings nur die französische *(jugement)* und englische

---

[1] Treffend Brand/Coffee/Herrup, The 2019 Hague Judgments Convention, 2023, para. 5.05: "the stuff of the Convention is judgments, and it is natural that any discussion […] begins with its concept of a judgment."

[2] Convention on the recognition and enforcement of foreign judgments in civil or commercial matters (HCCH 2019 Judgments Convention) of 2 July 2019, UNTS I-58036 und Tractatenblad 2024, 42 (Verdragsnr. 013672).

[3] Hierzu sogleich → III.; einen Überblick bietet etwa Weller/Ribeiro-Bidaoui/Brinkmann/Dethloff, The HCCH 2019 Judgments Convention/Zhao, 2023, pp. 315, 317 et seq.

[4] Das „Urteil" findet – der nationalen Terminologie entsprechend – nur als Unterfall des Oberbegriffs „Entscheidung" Erwähnung, vgl. Art. 3 lit. b HAVÜ 2019 in der zwischen Deutschland, Österreich und der Schweiz abgestimmten Übersetzung von 2021 (abrufbar unter hcch.net), die inzwischen – neben der Übersetzung in alle übrigen Amtssprachen der EU – Eingang in den Beschluss (EU) 2022/1206 des Rates v. 12. Juli 2022 über den Beitritt der Europäischen Union zum Übereinkommen über die Anerkennung und Vollstreckung ausländischer Entscheidungen in Zivil- und Handelssachen (ABl. 2022 L 187, 4; EU HAVÜ 2019-Beitrittsbeschluss) gefunden hat.

[5] Arabisch: „الحكم" – *al-ḥukm* und nicht „القرار" – *al-qarār*; Chinesisch: „判决" – *pàn jué* an Stelle von „裁判" – *cái pàn*; Englisch: *„judgment"* statt *„decision"*; Französisch: *„jugement"* bevorzugt vor *„décision"*; Russisch: „решения суда" – *reschenja suda* im Unterschied zu beispielsweise „судебное постановление" – *sudebnoe postanovlenie*; Spanisch: *„sentencia"* als Konkretisierung von *„decisión"* (vgl. aber EU HAVÜ 2019-Beitrittsbeschluss (Beschluss (EU) 2022/1206, ABl. 2022 L187, 1): *„resolución"*).

Variante *(judgment)* verbindlich sind.[6] Allein schon aus diesem Grund wäre es sicherlich zu weit gegriffen, gleich von einer Sprachverwirrung zu sprechen. Dennoch verdeutlicht diese geringfügige Divergenz auf der semantischen Oberfläche, mit welchen Herausforderungen die uniforme Anwendung des HAVÜ 2019 selbst in Kernfragen konfrontiert ist. Schließlich entscheidet eine zutreffende Begriffsbestimmung im Vorfeld der Subsumtion darüber, welche Judikate im Einzelnen der Konvention unterfallen und in der Folge zwischen den Vertragsstaaten frei zirkulieren können.

Ziel dieses Beitrages ist es, in dieser Frage methodisch abgesicherte Leitlinien für die international-einheitliche Auslegung zu entwickeln, die in der – seit dem Inkrafttreten des HAVÜ 2019 verstärkt zu erwartenden[7] – Rechtspraxis als Orientierung dienen können. Hierfür wird – in Anlehnung an den klassischen Auslegungskanon – zunächst die Legaldefinition sowie deren systematische Einbettung innerhalb des Rechtsinstruments (→ II.) beleuchtet, bevor die Historie des Begriffs anhand der Genealogie des HCCH *judgments project* (→ III.) nachverfolgt wird. Schließlich sollen die so herausgearbeiteten Urteilsmerkmale in den Kontext der nationalen Zivilprozessrechtsordnungen gesetzt werden (→ IV.), um auf dieser Grundlage eine Einschätzung abzugeben, inwieweit der gewählte definitorische Ansatz geeignet erscheint, tatsächlich die „weltweite Zirkulation ausländischer Entscheidungen“[8] zu gewährleisten (→ V.).

Diese Überlegungen mögen das Interesse des Jubilars finden, den die hiesigen Autoren als Herausgeber des Maßstäbe setzenden Großkommentars zum „Europäischen Zivilprozess- und Kollisionsrecht“ schätzen. Es zeugt dabei von der wissenschaftlichen Weitsicht des Jubilars, die Haager Instrumente zur justiziellen Zusammenarbeit frühzeitig und umfassend in das Gesamtbild der europäischen justiziellen Zusammenarbeit aufgenommen zu haben.[9]

---

[6] Vgl. HAVÜ 2019-Schlussformel; Übersetzungen finden sich unter hcch.net bzw. im EU HAVÜ 2019-Beitrittsbeschluss (Beschluss (EU) 2022/1206, ABl. 2022 L 187, 1).

Der chinesische Text beruht auf einer bereits anlässlich der Verabschiedung des Rechtsinstruments auf der 22. Diplomatischen Konferenz angefertigten Übersetzung von He Qisheng (何其生), der in den hier diskutierten Punkten jedoch mit dem seitens der Volksrepublik China übermittelten Text zur wortlautgleichen Vorschrift der Vorgängerkonvention übereinstimmt (auch hierzu → III.).

[7] Neben den bestehenden Vertragsstaaten der Europäischen Union (mit Ausnahme Dänemarks), der Ukraine und Uruguay, vgl. die Nachweise in den Statustabellen der HCCH (hcch.net) sowie der Vertragssammlung der Vereinten Nationen (treaties.un.org), beruht diese Annahme vornehmlich auf der erst kürzlich vorgenommenen Ratifikation des Übereinkommens durch das Vereinigte Königreich, wodurch ein Großteil der vor dem Brexit im Rahmen der Brüssel-Verordnungen abgewickelten Justizkooperation im Rahmen der HCCH-Instrumente widerbelebt werden dürfte. Zunächst erstrecken sich die Wirkungen des Übereinkommens zwar kraft Erklärung gem. Art. 25 Abs. 1 HAVÜ 2019 nur auf die Gebietseinheiten England und Wales und nicht auf Schottland und Nordirland. Nach dem Plan der Regierung soll dies jedoch bis zum Inkrafttreten des Übereinkommens nachgeholt werden, vgl. HL Int. Agreements Committee, 11th Report of 8 May 2024 “Scrutiny of international agreements: 2019 Hague Convention on the Recognition and Enforcement of Foreign Judgments in Civil or Commercial Matters” (HL Paper 113), paras. 11 and 12.

[8] Vgl. Präambel UAbs. 3 HAVÜ 2019.

[9] Zu einer gewissen „Blindheit“ der EU selbst in diesem Punkt Weller, Judicial cooperation of the EU in civil matters in its relations to non-EU States – a blind spot?, in Uzelac/van Rhee, Public and Private Justice (PPJ) 2017: The Transformation of Civil Justice, 2018, S. 63ff.

II. Legaldefinition und Binnensystematik

Insgesamt drei Gruppen von HAVÜ 2019-Bestimmungen liefern Anhaltspunkte dafür, welche Entscheidungsformen dem Übereinkommen unterfallen. Natürlicher Ausgangspunkt dieser Betrachtung ist zunächst die Legaldefinition des „Urteils" in Art. 3 Abs. 1 lit. b HAVÜ 2019:[10]

„[1]"judgment" means *any decision on the merits given by a court,* whatever that decision may be called, including a decree or order, and a determination of costs or expenses of the proceedings by the court (including an officer of the court), provided that the determination relates to a decision on the merits which may be recognised or enforced under this Convention. [2]*An interim measure of protection is not a judgment.*"

Neben der selbstredenden Beschränkung auf den sachlichen und territorialen Anwendungsbereich des Übereinkommens,[11] insbesondere auf Entscheidungen in Zivil- und Handelssachen, lassen sich dieser Definition drei wesentliche Eigenschaften eines Urteiles iSd HAVÜ 2019 entnehmen: Positiv sind (1) Sachentscheidungen eines (2) Gerichtes erfasst, solange es sich bei diesen nicht, gleichsam negativ, um eine (3) einstweilige Sicherungsmaßnahme handelt.

Wie genau die so gefundenen Mittelbegriffe dieser horizontalen Begriffskette auszulegen sind, lässt sich dem Rechtstext nicht ausdrücklich entnehmen. Leichte Konkretisierungen ergeben sich jedoch im systematischen Zusammenhang mit Vorschriften aus anderen Kapiteln. So wird mit Blick auf die Bereichsausnahme in Art. 2 Abs. 3 HAVÜ 2019 deutlich, dass private Schiedsgerichte jedenfalls keine „Gerichte" iSd Definition darstellen, sondern der relevante Spruchkörper vielmehr Teil der (vertrags-)staatlichen Rechtspflege sein muss.[12] Dies folgt *expressis verbis* auch aus Art. 4 Abs. 1 HAVÜ 2019 („court of a Contracting State"). „Zur Sache trägt" nach Art. 5 Abs. 1 lit. f HAVÜ 2019 nicht vor, wer nur die Zuständigkeit rügt. „[I]n der Sache selbst" darf eine Entscheidung jedoch gem. Art. 4 Abs. 2 HAVÜ 2019 nicht nachgeprüft werden, ohne dass sich hieraus eine Präzisierung des Begriffes ableiten ließe.[13] Jedenfalls sind Versäumnisurteile ausweislich der Verfahrensvorschrift in Art. 12 Abs. 1 lit. b HAVÜ 2019 explizit erfasst. Im Übrigen bleibt festzuhalten, dass sich noch für keines der Tatbestandsmerkmale ein international hinreichend abgesichertes Be-

---

[10] Hervorhebungen nicht im Original.

[11] Die Anerkennung und Vollstreckung von Entscheidungen, die außerhalb des Anwendungsbereiches liegen, bleibt gem. Art. 15 HAVÜ 2019 nach nationalem Recht weitgehend möglich *(favor recognitionis)*. Aufgrund des umfangreichen Ausnahmekataloges in Art. 2 HAVÜ 2019 (insb. Abs. 1 lit. m) – geistiges Eigentum) entscheidet der Anwendungsbereich maßgeblich darüber, welche Judikate effektiv unter dem Übereinkommen zirkulieren können. Da er dennoch nicht im engeren Sinne zur Definition des Urteils beiträgt und dessen Konzeption über das HAVÜ 2019 hinaus auch für weitere HCCH-Übereinkommen und potentiell auch das HCCH *jurisdiction project* Relevanz zeitigt (hierzu → III.), sollen seine Implikationen hier nur kursorisch behandelt werden.

[12] Brand/Coffee/Herrup, The 2019 Hague Judgments Convention, 2023, para. 5.18.

[13] Siehe aber Jacobs, Das Haager Anerkennungs- und Vollstreckungsübereinkommen, 2021, S. 140.

griffsverständnis herausgebildet hat, welches als Grundlage der Begriffsbestimmung dienen könnte.[14]

Gewissheit über den methodischen Weg zur Ausfüllung dieser Leerstelle verschafft allerdings eine zweite Gruppe von Vorschriften, insb. Art. 4 Abs. 3 HAVÜ 2019, welcher vordergründig nur ergänzende Anforderungen an die Zirkulationsfähigkeit des Urteils festlegt:[15]

„A judgment shall be recognised only if it has *effect in the State of origin,* and shall be enforced only if it is *enforceable in the State of origin.*"

Rechtstechnisch sucht der Konventionsgeber an dieser Stelle die unbestimmten Rechtsbegriffe „Wirksamkeit" bzw. „Vollstreckbarkeit" durch eine vertikale Verweisung[16] auf das nationale Zivilprozessrecht im Ursprungsstaat zu bestimmen. Im Umkehrschluss bedeutet dies jedoch, dass es sich bei den übrigen Anerkennungs- und Vollstreckungsvoraussetzungen, einschließlich der Tatbestandsmerkmale des Urteils, um konventionsautonome Kriterien handelt, für die der Grundsatz einheitlicher Auslegung aus Art. 20 HAVÜ 2019 uneingeschränkt Geltung beansprucht.[17]

Lassen sich die Tatbestandsmerkmale des Urteilsbegriffs somit nicht durch Rückgriff auf ein national oder international gefestigtes Begriffsverständnis konkretisieren, ist eine konventions-spezifische Sichtweise zu entwickeln, die sich insbesondere an Zielsetzung und Historie des HAVÜ 2019 orientiert und dessen internationalem Charakter hinreichend Rechnung trägt.[18] Gemessen am weltweiten Regelungsanspruch des Haager Übereinkommens wäre diese optimalerweise durch Vergleich aller wesentlichen Rechtskulturen zu gewinnen, der im Einzelnen auf die konkrete Pflichtenstruktur des HAVÜ 2019 hin abzustimmen ist.[19]

Schließlich erstreckt eine dritte Normgruppe gewisse Rechtsfolgen – insb. die völkerrechtliche Verpflichtung zur Vollstreckung – auf andere Rechtsakte, die unter Mitwirkung eines Gerichtes zustande gekommen sind, und diese somit als *aliud* zur Gerichtsentscheidung ausweisen.[20] Dies gilt zum einen für den Prozessvergleich

---

[14] Brand/Coffee/Herrup, The 2019 Hague Judgments Convention, 2023, para. 5.07; selbst auf regionaler Ebene fällt die Begriffsbestimmung schwer, vgl. etwa Art. 3 Brüssel Ia-VO oder Art. 2 (1) Commonwealth Model Law on the Recognition and Enforcement of Foreign Judgments, CLMM 2017 of 16–19 October 2017 (Nassau).

[15] Hervorhebungen nicht im Original.

[16] Diese Bezeichnung für die bewusste Rücknahme des Anwendungsvorrangs in Ermangelung autonomer internationaler bzw. unionaler Systembegriffe ist entlehnt bei *Roth,* zB Roth IPRax 2006, 338.

[17] Vgl. Brand/Coffee/Herrup, The 2019 Hague Judgments Convention, 2023, para. 8.40 und Garcimartín/Saumier, Explanatory Report on the HCCH 2019 Judgments Convention, 2020, para. 90.

[18] Hierzu umfassend Jacobs, Das Haager Anerkennungs- und Vollstreckungsübereinkommen, 2021, S. 52ff.

[19] Vgl. zu diesem Ansatz im EU-IPR Münchner Kommentar zum BGB/v. Hein, 9. Aufl. 2024, Einl. IPR, Rn. 134f.; deutlich skeptischer jedoch Jacobs, Das Haager Anerkennungs- und Vollstreckungsübereinkommen, 2021, S. 78f.: „Einem solchen Ansatz stünden in einem potenziell weltweiten Übereinkommen auch kaum überwindbare praktische Schwierigkeiten entgegen".

[20] Garcimartín/Saumier, Explanatory Report on the HCCH 2019 Judgments Convention, 2020, para. 322; Rauscher, EuZPR/EuIPR/Weller, 5. Aufl. 2022, HAVÜ 2019 Einf. Rn. 101.

(Art. 11 HAVÜ 2019) und zum anderen – in engen Grenzen – für Kostenentscheidungen im Exequaturverfahren (Art. 14 Abs. 2 HAVÜ 2019):[21]

Article 11 Judicial settlements (transactions judiciaires)

Judicial settlements (transactions judiciaires) which *a court of a Contracting State has approved,* or which have been *concluded in the course of proceedings before a court* of a Contracting State, and which are *enforceable in the same manner as a judgment* in the State of origin, *shall be enforced under this Convention* in the same manner as a judgment.

Article 14 Costs of proceedings

(2) An order for payment of costs or expenses of proceedings, made in a Contracting State against any person exempt from requirements as to security, bond, or deposit by virtue of paragraph 1 or of the law of the State where proceedings have been instituted, shall, on the application of the person entitled to the benefit of the order, be rendered enforceable in any other Contracting State.

Für die Grundzüge der Urteilsdefinition dienen diese Vorschriften als Abgrenzungsposten.

Demgemäß betont Art. 11 HAVÜ 2019, dass nicht jede Streitbeilegung der Parteien durch die bloße Beteiligung eines Gerichtes zum „Urteil“ mutiert. Vielmehr muss der Einfluss des Gerichtes eine solche Qualität erreichen, dass das Einigungsergebnis (auch) ihm als eigene Entscheidung zugerechnet werden kann.[22] Auffallend hierbei ist, dass der englische Wortlaut explizit auf die französische Konzeption verweist, nicht aber *vice versa*. An dieser Stelle scheint der Vertragstext Abgrenzungsschwierigkeiten zu anderen konsensualen Entscheidungsphänotypen (zB „jugement d'accord“ oder „consent decree“) im Grenzbereich des Urteilsbegriffes vorbeugen zu wollen, die besonders dem anglo-amerikanischen Rechtskreis vertrauter sind als der schlichte Prozessvergleich.[23]

Des Weiteren entwirft Art. 14 Abs. 1, 2 HAVÜ 2019 ein Konstrukt interdependenter Gleichstellung: Profitiert der Antragssteller im Exequaturverfahren von der Inländergleichbehandlung bezüglich der Prozesskostensicherheit *(cautio iudicatum solvi)*,[24] so wird eine zugunsten des Antragsgegners ausfallende Kostenentscheidung hinsichtlich ihrer Vollstreckbarkeit dem Urteil eines Vertragsstaates gleichgestellt. Aus der Notwendigkeit dieser positiven Normierung ergeben sich für die Urteilsdefinition *e contrario* zwei Erkenntnisse. Zum einen stellt der Kostenentscheid im Anerkennungs- oder Vollstreckungsverfahren des ersuchten Staates keinen hinreichenden Bezug zur Sachentscheidung im Ursprungsstaat iSd Art. 3 Abs. 1 lit. b HAVÜ 2019 mehr her („related to a decision on the merits“). Dieser Umstand deutet darauf hin, dass Sachurteil und Nebenentscheidung zwar nicht vom selben

[21] Hervorhebungen nicht im Original.

[22] So auch Weller/Ribeiro-Bidaoui/Brinkmann/Dethloff, The HCCH 2019 Judgments Convention/Hau, 2023, pp. 21, 29.

[23] Brand/Coffee/Herrup, The 2019 Hague Judgments Convention, 2023, para. 7.85.

[24] Diese Konstruktion ist Art. 14 und 15 der hier nicht weiter besprochenen Convention on International Access to Justice (HCCH 1980 Access to Justice Convention) of 25 October 1980, 1510 UNTS I-26112 sowie Tractatenblad 1989, 114 (Verdragsnr. 000691) nachempfunden.

Spruchkörper („including an officer of the court"), wohl aber von einer als einheitliches Organisationsgefüge wahrgenommenen Instanz erlassen werden müssen. Zum anderen ist augenfällig, dass die Anerkennungsentscheidung oder Vollstreckbarerklärung nicht selbst Bezugspunkt der Kostenentscheidung sein kann, dh kein „Urteil" iSd HAVÜ 2019 darstellt. Bereits aus der Normenstruktur ergibt sich somit das Verbot des Doppelexequaturs *(l'exequatur sur l'exequatur ne vaut pas).*[25] Angesichts jüngerer Tendenzen zu seiner Aufweichung scheint die Bedeutung dieses Grundsatzes jedoch keineswegs mehr selbstverständlich.[26]

Somit können dem Normbestand des Übereinkommens drei Kernelemente des Urteilsbegriffs entnommen werden, die allerdings nur schwach konturiert sind. Zugleich ergibt sich aus der Binnensystematik jedoch der methodische Rahmen, in dem sich die Konkretisierung dieser Begriffsbestandteile vollzieht. Darüber hinaus etabliert der Normtext zwei Entscheidungs-formen, von denen das Urteil abzugrenzen ist. Auf dieser Grundlage sollen im Anschluss an eine Erläuterung der Begriffsentwicklung im Rahmen des HCCH *judgments project* die einzelnen Tatbestandsmerkmale der Urteilsdefinition im Kontext konkreter zivilprozessualer Erscheinungsformen näher bestimmt werden.

III. Genealogie des HCCH judgments project (1992–2019)

In den Stadien des sog. *jugdments project* der HCCH, dem Arbeitsprozess, der letztendlich in der Verabschiedung des HAVÜ 2019 münden sollte, spiegelt sich auf vielfältige Weise die Historie der HCCH selbst von ihrer Verwurzelung in Europa hin zu ihrer strategischen Neuausrichtung als Organisation mit globalem Zuschnitt und universellem Charakter wider.

Mit der Annahme des Anerkennungs- und Vollstreckungsübereinkommen vom 1.2.1971 (HAVÜ 1971) hatte die HCCH schon einmal – damals noch durch Mehrheitsbeschluss[27] – den Versuch unternommen, die nationalen Zivilprozessrechte im Rahmen einer *convention simple* zu vereinheitlichen.[28] Obwohl das Rechtsinstrument 1979 sogar in Kraft getreten ist, gelangte es letztlich in keinem einzigen Fall zur Anwendung und gilt allgemein als gescheitert.[29] Als Hauptgrund hierfür wird überwiegend die Konstruktion des Mechanismus der *bilatéralisation* identifiziert, der für die Wirksamkeit den Abschluss eines Zusatzabkommens zwi-

---

[25] Dieses Ergebnis wird überwiegend nicht aus der Systematik hergeleitet, sondern aus dem Zweck des Übereinkommens abgeleitet, vgl. etwa Brand/Coffee/Herrup, The 2019 Hague Judgments Convention, 2023, para. 5.15.

[26] Vgl. EuGH 7.4.2022 – C-568/20, ECLI:EU:C:2022:264 Rn. 47 (J. v. H Limited); kritisch hierzu Hess IPRax 2022, 349 (350f.), der anregt, diese Rechtsprechung in der anstehenden Revision des Rechtsinstrumentes zu korrigieren, vgl. Art. 79 Brüssel Ia-VO.

[27] Vgl. etwa HCCH, Procès-verbal No. 1 – séance du 13 avril 1966, dans: Actes et documents de la Session extraordinaire (13–26 avril 1966), 1969, p. 235.

[28] Convention on the recognition and enforcement of foreign judgments in civil and commercial matters (HCCH 1971 Judgments Convention) of 1 February 1971, 1144 UNTS I-17957 sowie Tractatenblad 1972, 144 (Verdragsnr. 002721).

[29] Schack RabelsZ 57 (1993), 224 (226) ordnet es in eine Reihe „kümmerlicher Gewächse ein, die entweder überhaupt nicht zum Leben aufgeblüht sind oder nur ein Schattendasein fristen".

schen den jeweiligen Vertragsstaaten vorsah,[30] wodurch das HAVÜ 1971 effektiv zu einer Rahmen- oder Modellkonvention ohne eigenen Mehrwert verkam.[31]

Auf Anregung der Vereinigten Staaten (USA)[32] im Jahr 1992 setzte die Haager Konferenz daher die Arbeit an einem neuen multilateralem Übereinkommen betreffend die Internationale Zuständigkeit sowie die Anerkennung und Vollstreckung ausländischer Entscheidungen wieder auf die Agenda. Hierfür orientierte sich das Projekt zunächst an dem auf *Arthur von Mehren*[33] zurückgehenden Modell einer *convention mixte,* die Kataloge von allgemein anerkannten ("green list") und verbotenen exorbitanten Gerichtsständen ("red list") enthalten sollte.[34] Zeitgleich bewirkte der Fortschritt des Integrationsprozesses in Europa einen stetigen Kompetenzzugewinn der Europäischen Gemeinschaften auch in Fragen der justiziellen Zusammenarbeit in Zivilsachen, wodurch sich auf organisatorischer Ebene der HCCH eine bequeme Stimmenmehrheit der EG-Mitgliedstaaten und perspektivischer Beitrittskandidaten ergab.[35] Hieraus erklärt sich, warum der im Jahr 1999 erarbeitete Entwurfstext (inkl. Erläuterndem Bericht)[36] deutlich stärker als erwartet an den europäischen Rechtsakten orientiert war und deshalb von Staaten des *common law*-Rechtskreises skeptisch betrachtet wurde.[37] Aufgrund ernsthafter Bedenken der USA[38] musste die 19. Diplomatische Konferenz schließlich verschoben und die Erörterung des Entwurfes auf ein Konsensverfahren umgestellt werden.[39]

---

[30] Dieses Konzept in Art. 21 HAVÜ 1971 ging auf den auf den belgischen Ministerialdirektor Jenard, RBDI 1966, 386 zurück. Zur zeitgenössischen Kritik etwa Jacobs, Das Haager Anerkennungs- und Vollstreckungsübereinkommen, 2021, S. 17ff.; Schack RabelsZ 57 (1993), 224 (249); Weller/Ribeiro-Bidaoui/Brinkmann/Dethloff, The HCCH 2019 Judgments Convention/Zhao, 2023, pp. 315, 317.

[31] Vedie, Arthur T. von Mehren und das internationale Zivilverfahrensrecht im transatlantischen Dialog, 2017, S. 320.

[32] Formaler Ausgangspunkt war ein Brief des Legal Advisor des US Department of State an den damaligen Generalsekretär der HCCH Georges A. L. Droz vom 5. Mai 1992 mit der Bitte, eine solche Konvention auf die Tagesordnung zu setzen (verfügbar unter: https://2009-2017.state.gov/documents/organization/65973.pdf, abgerufen 13.5.2024); vgl. HCCH, Some Reflections of the Permanent Bureau on a general Convention on Enforcement of Judgments, Prel. Doc. No. 17 of May 1992.

[33] Grundlage hierfür war seine unveröffentlichte „Recognition Convention Study", vgl. aber den hieraus hervorgegangenen Beitrag v. Mehren, Law & Contemporary Problems 57 (1994), 271 (286).

[34] HCCH, Conclusions of the Working Group Meeting on the Enforcement of Judgments, Prel. Doc. No. 19 of November 1992, para. 6.

[35] Struycken WPNR 6421 (2000), 735; Brand/Coffee/Herrup, The 2019 Hague Judgments Convention, 2023, para. 3.09.

[36] HCCH, Preliminary Draft Convention on Jurisdiction and Foreign Judgments in Civil and Commercial Matters adopted by the Special Commission on 30 October 1999, Prel. Doc. No. 11 of August 2000, p. 1; Nygh/Pocar, Report of the Special Commission, Prel. Doc. No. 11 of August 2000, p. 19.

[37] Brand/Coffee/Herrup, The 2019 Hague Judgments Convention, 2023, para. 3.07 et seq.

[38] Auslöser war erneut ein Brief des Assistant Legal Advisers des US Department of State an den Generalsekretär der HCCH Hans van Loon vom 22.2.2000, der die Streitpunkte und das Bedürfnis nach mehr Beratungszeit eindringlich auflistete (verfügbar unter: http://www.cptech.org/ecom/hague/kovar2loon22022000.pdf, abgerufen 13.5.2024).

[39] HCCH, Conclusions of the Special Commission of May 2000 on General Affairs and Policy of the Conference, Prel. Doc. No. 10 of June 2000, p. 11.

Durch diese Maßnahmen traten die Gemeinsamkeiten und Divergenzen in den Positionierungen der Delegierten – festgehalten in dem sog. Interim Text 2001[40] – zwar klar hervor, der sich anbahnende Dissens ließ sich jedoch letztlich nicht mehr vermeiden.[41]

Nach dem vorläufigen Scheitern des HCCH-Prestigeprojektes brach zunächst eine Phase der Konsolidierung an. Auf organisatorischer Ebene versuchte die HCCH dem Bedeutungsverlust in Europa zum einen proaktiv durch eine strategische Neuausrichtung hin zu einer Organisation mit universellem Charakter zu kompensieren[42] und zum anderen integrativ durch Einbindung der Europäischen Gemeinschaften als Mitglied sowie die Umstellung ihres Entscheidungsverfahrens auf ein Konsensprinzip zu begegnen.[43] Auf der Arbeitsebene konzentrierte sich das weitere Vorgehen in einer Reihe informeller Arbeitstreffen auf die zuvor als konsensfähig identifizierte Prorogation als Grundlage gerichtlicher Zuständigkeit, welche im Folgenden relativ geräuschlos in das Haager Gerichtsstandsübereinkommen (HProrogÜbk 2005) vom 30.6.2005, eine *convention double,* übersetzt werden konnte.[44]

Bestärkt von diesem Erfolg entschied sich die HCCH im Jahr 2010 das ursprüngliche Projekt wieder aufzunehmen. Nunmehr sollten die einzelnen Aspekte des *judgments project* durch eine Reihe von Komplementärinstrumenten zum HProrogÜbk 2005 verwirklicht werden.[45] Geopolitisch fiel die Ausarbeitung der ersten Entwürfe der anvisierten *convention simple* in einen Zeitraum, der wie selten zuvor vom Rückzug der USA aus internationalen Kooperationsverbünden geprägt war.[46] Dennoch wiesen die Verhandlungen dieses jüngsten Rechtsinstruments durch die intensive Beteiligung von Schwergewichten wie der Volksrepublik China, der Europäischen Union sowie dem Königreich Saudi Arabien eindeutig globalen

---

[40] HCCH, Summary of the Outcome of the Discussion in Commission II of the First Part of the Diplomatic Conference (6–20 June 2001): Interim Text.

[41] Jüngst hat Jueptner, A Hague Convention on the Jurisdiction and Judgments – Why did the Judgments Project (1992–2001) Fail?, 2024, eine umfassende Analyse vorgelegt, in der die Gründe des Scheiterns weniger in Sachfragen, sondern in dem fehlerhaften Management des Ständigen Büros in der „pre-negotiating phase" gesehen werden.

[42] Vgl. HCCH, The Pursuit of Universality as a Strategic Objective of the Hague Conference on Private International Law and Ways to Achieve it, Prel. Doc. No. 1 of March 2016; Wagner RabelsZ 73 (2009), 215 (222) spricht von einer „Marketing-Offensive". Dass die Sorgen der HCCH vor der eigenen Nivellierung in Europa keineswegs unbegründet waren, zeigt der Fall der ehemals in Statusangelegenheiten äußerst bedeutsamen *Commission Internationale de l'Etat Civil* (CIEC), vgl. CIEC, Protocole relatif à la Commission internationale de l'état civil conclu à Berne le 25 septembre 1950, 932 UNTS I-13270.

[43] Vgl. jetzt Art. 8 (2) Statute of the Hague Conference on Private International Law of 31 October 1951 as amended on 30 June 2005, 2993 UNTS A-2997 sowie die EU-Beitrittserklärung v. 3.4.2007, 2432 UNTS A-2432; Hierzu umfassend Schulz ICLQ 56 (2007), 939 et seq.

[44] Convention on Choice of Court Agreements (HCCH 2005 Choice of Court Convention) of 30 June 2005, 3110 UNTS I-53843 und Tractatenblad 2009, 31 (Verdragsnr. 011343).

[45] HCCH, Continuation of the Judgments Project, Prel. Doc. No. 14 of February 2010, para. 1; Lehmann, JPIL 19 (2023), 25 (26) spricht von „Inkrementalismus"; allg. hierzu Block-Lieb/Halliday Brook. J. Int'l L. 32 (2007), 851.

[46] Zur Wahrnehmung einer "withdrawal doctrine" der Trump-Administration als handlungsleitend Bellinger III, Case W. Res. J. Int. L. 7 (2019), 7 (21) et seq.

Charakter auf.[47] Erstmals wurde auch der parallel zur Ausarbeitung entstandene Erläuternde Bericht[48] explizit von den Mitgliedstaaten genehmigt, wodurch die dort vertretenen Auffassungen mit besonderer Überzeugungskraft ausgestattet sind.[49] Schließlich markierte das Inkrafttreten des HAVÜ 2019 zwischen der EU und der Ukraine am 1.9.2023 den erfolgreichen Abschluss des *judgments project*.[50]

Trotz dieser wechselvollen Geschichte zeichnen sich die verwendeten Urteilsdefinitionen durch eine erstaunliche begriffliche Konsistenz aus. So enthält bereits Art. 2 HAVÜ 1971 – trotz verschiedener Wortwahl – eine Vielzahl von inhaltlichen Überschneidungen mit der oben vorgestellten modernen Variante in Art. 3 Abs. 1 lit. b HAVÜ 2019.[51] Lediglich das Erfordernis einer Sachentscheidung findet sich nicht ausdrücklich in der alten Legaldefinition wieder, ergibt sich jedoch – ebenso wie die Erfassung von Kostenentscheiden – aus Art. 15ff. HAVÜ 1971.[52] Im Unterschied zum jüngsten Rechtsinstrument waren *administrative tribunals* damals jedoch ausdrücklich vom Gerichtsbegriff ausgenommen.[53] Zu bedenken bleibt jedoch, dass diese Bestandteile gem. Art. 23 HAVÜ 1971 weitreichend zur Disposition der Parteien *inter se* stehen.[54]

Hingegen nahm Art. 23 Interim Text 2001 die Kostenentscheidung eines Gerichtsbediensteten in die Legaldefinition selbst auf, sah dafür aber – potentiell noch auf eine *convention double* ausgerichtet – ausweislich Art. 23A Interim Text 2021 in zwei Alternativen A-B die Möglichkeit zur Anerkennung und Vollstreckung einstweiliger Sicherungsmaßnahmen vor.[55] Schließlich ist der Text der Legaldefinition in Art. 4 Abs. 1 HProrogÜbk 2005 praktisch identisch zum HAVÜ 2019 abge-

---

[47] Vgl. jeweils die Beiträge von Sun/Wu Chinese JIL 19 (2020), 481 et seq.; Weller/Ribeiro-Bidaoui/Brinkmann/Dethloff, The HCCH 2019 Judgments Convention/Stein/Vysoka, 2023, pp. 145 et seq.; HCCH, "Minutes of the First Commission No. 3 of 19 June 2019", in: Proceedings of the Twenty-Second Session (18 June to 2 July 2019), Tome I: Book 4, 2023, paras. 157 et seq.

[48] Vgl. Brand/Coffee/Herrup, The 2019 Hague Judgments Convention, 2023, para. 8.40 und Garcimartín/Saumier, Explanatory Report on the HCCH 2019 Judgments Convention, 2020, para. 90.

[49] HCCH, Conclusions & Decisions of the CGAP (3.-6.3.2020), para. 36.

[50] Vgl. Art. 28 Abs. 1 HAVÜ 2019 unter Einschluss der Statustabelle des HAVÜ 2019 unter hcch.net.

[51] Art. 2 HAVÜ 1971: „This Convention shall apply to all decisions given by the courts of a Contracting State, irrespective of the name given by that State to the proceedings which gave rise to the decision or of the name given to the decision itself such as judgment, order or writ of execution. However, it shall apply neither to decisions which order provisional or protective measures nor to decisions rendered by administrative tribunals."

[52] Vgl. Fragistas, Rapport explicatif, dans: Actes et documents de la Session extraordinaire (13–26 avril 1966), 1969, 360, 366.

[53] Fragistas, Rapport explicatif, dans: Actes et documents de la Session extraordinaire (13–26 avril 1966), 1969, 366: „Il est donc évident que les décisions des tribunaux administratifs ne tombent pas dans le domaine de la convention, même si, à titre exceptionnel, ils statuent sur une matière de droit civil ou commercial".

[54] Zu diesen Gegenständen zählen der Begriff der Zivil- und Handelssache sowie des Gerichts (Abs. 1) und die Anwendbarkeit auf einstweilige Maßnahmen (Abs. 4), Entscheidungen in Strafverfahren (Abs. 5), Urteile, die nicht auf Geldzahlung lauten (Abs. 15) oder Versäumnisurteile (Abs. 8), vgl. Fragistas, Rapport explicatif, dans: Actes et documents de la Session extraordinaire (13–26 avril 1966), 1969, 364.

[55] Art. 23 lit. b Entwurfstext 1999 sah die einstweiligen Sicherungsmaßnahmen noch vom Begriff des Urteils erfasst an, vgl. hierzu Nygh/Pocar, Report of the Special Commission, Prel. Doc. No. 11 of August 2000, pp. 99 et seq.

fasst.[56] Allerdings verfügt die Schwesterkonvention über keine separate Kostenregelung, die Art. 14 HAVÜ 2019 vergleichbar wäre.

Vor diesem Hintergrund kann im Rahmen des HCCH *judgments project* von einer gefestigten Begriffstradition gesprochen werden, die in den Grenzen des Wortlautes zur Interpretation des HAVÜ 2019 herangezogen werden kann. Hiervon ist insbesondere auszugehen, soweit sich diese Inbezugnahme auf den mutmaßlichen Willen der Verhandlungspartner stützen kann, weil sie sich aus dem von diesen genehmigten Erläuternden Bericht ergibt.[57]

IV. Tatbestandsmerkmale im Kontext des nationalen Zivilprozessrechts

Um dem Zweck der Etablierung eines Rechtsregimes weltweiter Urteilsfreizügigkeit auch nur perspektivisch gerecht zu werden, müssen die Regelungen des HAVÜ 2019 einen angemessenen Ausgleich zwischen Rechtssicherheit und Flexibilität finden. Für die Urteilsdefinition bedeutet dies, dass die einzelnen Tatbestandsmerkmale zum einen so klar umrissen sein müssen, dass ihre einheitliche Anwendung möglich ist, und zum anderen inklusiv genug gefasst sein müssen, dass sie potentiell für Erscheinungsformen des Urteils in den verschiedenen Rechtstraditionen der Welt anschlussfähig sind.

1. Sachentscheidung (any decision on the merits; toute décision sur le fond)

Im Grundsatz besteht Einigkeit, dass ein Gericht in der Sache entscheidet, wenn es sich in einem irgendwie gearteten streitigen Verfahren mit dem zur Disposition gestellten Anspruch ausei-nandersetzt.[58] *Brand/Coffee/Herrup* möchten diesen Ansatz dahingehend konkretisiert wissen, dass die Entscheidung "(1) a resolution of the fundamental dispute, or substantive aspects of that fundamental dispute, presented to a court" enthalten muss, die "(2) based upon a pleading that presents averments of fact, whether or not the court makes independent findings of fact".[59]

Ausgeschlossen sind damit mangels Auseinandersetzung mit dem Streitgegenstand zunächst rein prozessuale Entscheidungen *(procedural rulings)* mit expliziter Rückausnahme zugunsten der Kostenentscheidung.[60] Dies hat zur Folge, dass die nach Abweisung wegen Unzuständigkeit zugesprochenen Kosten selbst dann nicht

---

[56] Wortlautdifferenzen bestehen nur in der Verwendung von "it" statt "that decision"; allgemein zu Art. 4 Abs. 1 HProrogÜbk 2005: Hartley/Dogauchi, Explanatory Report on the Convention of 30 June 2005 on Choice of Court Agreements (abgedruckt in: HCCH, Proceedings of the Twentieth Session (2005) III, 2010, p. 783), paras. 116 et seq.

[57] Zu Recht betonen allerdings Brand/Coffee/Herrup, The 2019 Hague Judgments Convention, 2023, para. 4.34: "The Report cannot trump the face of the text, or considerations of logic, or of practical consequences (including effects of an interpretation on the prospects of widespread implementation)."

[58] Garcimartín/Saumier, Explanatory Report on the HCCH 2019 Judgments Convention, 2020, para. 95.

[59] Brand/Coffee/Herrup, The 2019 Hague Judgments Convention, 2023, para. 5.08.

[60] Garcimartín/Saumier, Explanatory Report on the HCCH 2019 Judgments Convention, 2020, para. 95.

vollstreckt werden können, wenn die hypothetische Entscheidung in der Hauptsache dem Übereinkommen unterfiele.[61] Im Einzelfall ist zu differenzieren, ob die Herausgabe von Dokumenten – etwa als Teil einer britischen *disclosure* oder U.S.-amerikanischen *pretrial discovery* – zu Beweiszwecken erfolgt oder das Klagebegehren in der Hauptsache (ggf. als Stufenklage) ausmacht.[62] Ist das Gericht hingegen berufen, den Vergleich der Parteien einer Sammelklage *(class action settlement)* zu genehmigen, steht weniger die Eigenschaft als Sachentscheidung, sondern vielmehr die Zurechnung des Ergebnisses der Streitbeilegung zum involvierten Gericht in Frage.[63]

Generell kommt es auf das gewählte Verfahren oder die Art des Urteils nicht an („any decision"; „toute décision"). Erfasst werden somit auch Verfahren des kollektiven Rechtsschutzes wie Sammelklagen *(class action),* repräsentative Gruppenklagen oder Musterverfahren,[64] nicht aber selbstständige Beweisverfahren.[65] Ebenso wenig ist für die Urteilseigenschaft – evtl. aber für die Anerkennung – von Belang, ob die Entscheidung eine umfassende Begründung enthält.[66]

Leicht umstritten ist mittlerweile, inwieweit sich Leistungsurteile, die auf Basis des Ergebnisses einer ausländischen Entscheidung ergehen, mit dem Streitgegenstand auseinandersetzen.[67] Hintergrund ist die im *common law* verbreitete *doctrine of obligation,* auf deren Grundlage ein ausländischer Titel im Inland einen materiellen Anspruch begründet, der in einem verkürzten Verfahren *(summary procedure)* im Inland durchgesetzt werden kann.[68] Ausgangspunkt ist hierbei das – bereits aus der Binnensystematik abgeleitete – Verbot des Doppelexequaturs.[69] Rechtstechnisch führt das Institut zwar ein lediglich nationales Leistungsurteil herbei, funktional betrachtet wird jedoch wie bei dem Exequatur die Wirkung des ausländischen Titels auf das Inland erstreckt. Mit anderen Worten setzt sich das Gericht unmittelbar nur mit dem vor das ersuchte Gericht gebrachte Urteil (im Lichte der ggf. einschlägigen Versagungsgründe), nicht mehr aber mit dem Tatsachenvortrag der Parteien aus-

---

[61] Hierauf verweist Jacobs, Das Haager Anerkennungs- und Vollstreckungsübereinkommen, 2021, S. 140f.

[62] Erneut Jacobs, Das Haager Anerkennungs- und Vollstreckungsübereinkommen, 2021, S. 139.

[63] Hierzu sogleich → IV. 2.

[64] Garcimartín/Saumier, Explanatory Report on the HCCH 2019 Judgments Convention, 2020, para. 95; Bei Anwendung des HAVÜ im Übrigen ergeben sich jedoch die strukturell gleichen Probleme wie unter der Brüssel Ia-VO, vgl. hierzu Rentsch RabelsZ 85 (2021), 544 (551ff.).

[65] Vgl. Weller/Ribeiro-Bidaoui/Brinkmann/Dethloff, The HCCH 2019 Judgments Convention/Hau, 2023, p. 25.

[66] Erneut Weller/Ribeiro-Bidaoui/Brinkmann/Dethloff, The HCCH 2019 Judgments Convention/Hau, 2023, p. 24 in Abgrenzung zu 23.2 ALI/UNIDROIT Principles of Transnational Civil Procedure.

[67] In diesem Sinne jedenfalls Weller/Ribeiro-Bidaoui/Brinkmann/Dethloff, The HCCH 2019 Judgments Convention/Hau, 2023, p. 25.

[68] Das traditionelle Verfahren nach dem *common law* ist jedoch von dem ebenfalls verfügbaren Anerkennungs- und Vollstreckungsverfahren auf gesetzlicher Grundlage *(statutes)* durch Registrierung zu unterscheiden, vgl. mit Bezug auf das Vereinigte Königreich Cheshire/North/Fawcett, Private International Law, 15th ed. 2017, p. 525.

[69] Vgl. → II.

einander.[70] Entscheidend gegen die Einordnung solcher Judikate als Sachentscheidung streitet jedoch die Pflichtenstruktur des HAVÜ 2019.[71] Neben der implizit verbürgten Reziprozität enthält das Übereinkommen feingliedrige Mechanismen zur Steuerung gegenseitigen Vertrauens zwischen den Vertragsstaaten (insb. in Art. 29 HAVÜ 2019).[72] Diese drohten effektiv unterlaufen zu werden, wenn ein Vertragsstaat durch entsprechende Ausgestaltung seines Zivilprozessrechts die eigentlich ihm gegenüber eingegangene völkerrechtliche Verpflichtung bzw. das ihm gegenüber erbrachte Vertrauen unter der Hand auf die Judikate aus Drittstaaten erweitern könnte. Im Extremfall könnten dadurch sogar Vorbehaltserklärungen nach Art. 29 Abs. 2 HAVÜ 2019 unterlaufen werden.

Weitaus schwieriger gerät die Einordnung derjenigen Verfahren, welche die Vertragsstaaten zur vereinfachten Durchsetzung unbestrittener Forderungen eingeführt haben. Ergeht etwa ein Gerichtsbescheid zwecks Zahlung auf Betreiben allein einer Partei *(ex parte order)*, so handelt es sich nicht um ein streitiges Verfahren.[73] Gibt die rechtliche Ausgestaltung dem Antragsgegner jedoch ausreichend Gelegenheit zum Widerspruch, kann das Verfahren dennoch nahtlos oder mittelbar in einen Rechtsstreit übergehen.[74] In dieser Konstellation liegt die Parallele zum Versäumnisurteil auf der Hand. Entsprechend ist etwa der Vollstreckungsbescheid eines deutschen Mahnverfahrens nach §§ 699, 700 Abs. 1 ZPO „Urteil" im Sinne der Konvention.[75]

Zuletzt ist es nicht von Relevanz, ob es sich bei der fraglichen Entscheidung um ein Leistungs-, Gestaltungs- oder (ggf. auch Muster-) Feststellungsurteil handelt.[76] Prinzipiell kann der Urteilstenor nicht nur auf Geldleistung (insb. *damages*), sondern auf jedwedes Handeln oder Unterlassen *(specific performance)* lauten[77] und sowohl Strafschadensersatz *(punitive damages)*[78] als auch Zinsen zusprechen. Diese Urteilselemente können jedoch auf Ebene der Versagungsgründe Bedeutung erlangen.[79] Be-

---

[70] Wohl ebenfalls in diesem Sinne Jacobs, Das Haager Anerkennungs- und Vollstreckungsübereinkommen, 2021, S. 141.

[71] Brand/Coffee/Herrup, The 2019 Hague Judgments Convention, 2023, para. 5.15.

[72] Hierzu Weller FS Kronke, 2020, 621, (629) et seq.

[73] Garcimartín/Saumier, Explanatory Report on the HCCH 2019 Judgments Convention, 2020, para. 95; skeptisch hingegen Weller/Ribeiro-Bidaoui/Brinkmann/Dethloff, The HCCH 2019 Judgments Convention/Hau, 2023, p. 26.

[74] Garcimartín/Saumier, Explanatory Report on the HCCH 2019 Judgments Convention, 2020, para. 95, fn. 90.

[75] Weller/Ribeiro-Bidaoui/Brinkmann/Dethloff, The HCCH 2019 Judgments Convention/Hau, 2023, p. 26; Rauscher, EuZPR/EuIPR/Weller, 5. Aufl. 2022, HAVÜ 2019 Einf. Rn. 23.

[76] Jacobs, Das Haager Anerkennungs- und Vollstreckungsübereinkommen, 2021, S. 137f.

[77] Vgl. Zhao 30 SRIEL (2020), 345 (354); Eine Art. 28 der Convention on Contracts for the International Sale of Goods (CISG) of 11 April 1980, 1489 UNTS I-25567 entsprechende Vorschrift enthält das HAVÜ 2019 nicht. Inzwischen hat die Beschränkung auf Geldzahlung im anglo-amerikanischen Rechtskreis jedoch ohnehin an Bedeutung verloren, vgl. Pro Swing v. Elta Golf [2006] 2 S.C.R. 612, para. 66: „The common law should be extended to permit the enforcement of foreign non-money judgments in appropriate circumstances.".

[78] Vgl. Art. 10 HAVÜ 2019 *e contrario.*

[79] Für *punitive damages* ergibt sich dies bereits aus Art. 10 HAVÜ 2019; In islamisch geprägten Jurisdiktionen kann das Zinsverbot „ربا – *riba*", welches auf dem Koran „ٱلْقُرْءَانُ" Sure 2:275 „Die Kuh" „ٱلْبَقَرَة" beruht, im Rahmen der *ordre public*-Kontrolle relevant werden, vgl. Weller/Ribeiro-Bidaoui/Brinkmann/Dethloff, The HCCH 2019 Judgments Convention/Elbalti, 2023, pp. 181, 189.

wusst offen blieb indes, ob auch Zahlungsanordnungen zur Durchsetzung angeordneter Handlungspflichten *(penalty orders)* „in der Sache" ergehen.[80] Anordnungen dieser Art haben in den Rechtsordnungen vielfältige Ausgestaltungen erfahren. So werden sie teilweise im Urteil selbst, teilweise erst im Vollstreckungsverfahren erlassen und können sowohl dem Staat (Ordnungsgeld) als auch der gegnerischen Partei zufließen *(astreinte)*.[81] Aufgrund dieser Unterschiede ließ sich bis zur Diplomatischen Konferenz zum HAVÜ 2019 in diesem Punkt keine Einigung mehr erzielen. Entsprechend enthält der Normtext auch keine Hinweise, wie mit dieser Form der Nebenentscheidung zu verfahren ist. Weil derartige *penalty orders* jedoch der Hauptleistungspflicht dienlich sein sollen, spricht einiges dafür, sie mit *Jacobs* als Akte der Vollstreckung einzuordnen, die sich gem. Art. 13 Abs. 1 S. 1 HAVÜ 2019 allein nach dem Recht des ersuchten Staates richten.[82] Ihre Einbeziehung in Anlehnung an den EuGH nur zuzulassen, soweit sie bereits vom Erstgericht nominell bestimmt angeordnet worden sind, würde hingegen zu einer im Konventionstext nicht angelegten vertikalen Verweisung auf die *lex fori* führen.[83]

2. *Gericht (court; tribunal)*

Um im Sinne des HAVÜ 2019 als vollwertiges Urteil anerkannt zu werden, muss die Entscheidung in der Sache einem „Gericht" zugerechnet werden können. Seit dem Entwurfstext 1999 scheint das gemeinsame Verständnis des Begriffskerns auf Spruchkörper festgelegt, die rechtsprechende Gewalt des Staates ausüben.[84] Ein im Zuge der Verhandlungen verworfener Vorschlag[85] zur Definition seitens der Delegationen aus Ecuador und Uruguay fasste unter den Begriff des „Gerichts" "(i) a tribunal belonging to the Judiciary of a Contracting State at any level, and (ii) any other permanent tribunal that, according to the law of a Contracting State, exercises jurisdictional functions on a particular subject matter, according to pre established procedural rules, being independent and autonomous."

Einigkeit besteht dahingehend, dass der Gerichtszweig, dem ein Spruchkörper angehört, keine Bedeutung zukommt, solange er über eine Zivil- und Handelssache entscheidet.[86] Somit können sowohl Annexentscheidungen im strafrecht-

[80] Garcimartín/Saumier, Explanatory Report on the HCCH 2019 Judgments Convention, 2020, para. 97.

[81] Einen Überblick bietet HCCH, Treatment of penalty orders that are imposed on the non-compliance with non-monetary judgments under the 2018 draft convention, Prel. Doc. No. 3 of February 2019.

[82] Jacobs, Das Haager Anerkennungs- und Vollstreckungsübereinkommen, 2021, S. 145.

[83] Vgl. EuGH, 18.10.2011 – C-406/09, NJW 2011, 3568 (Realchemie Nederland BV v. Bayer); ebenfalls kritisch Garcimartín NILR (2020), 19, 24; ihm folgend Rauscher, EuZPR/EuIPR/Weller, 5. Aufl. 2022, HAVÜ 2019 Einf. Rn. 23.

[84] Nygh/Pocar, Report of the Special Commission, Prel. Doc. No. 11 of August 2000, p. 32; so nun auch Garcimartín/Saumier, Explanatory Report on the HCCH 2019 Judgments Convention, 2020, para. 102.

[85] HCCH, Proposal of the delegations of Ecuador and Uruguay, Work. Doc. No. 166 of February 2017.

[86] Garcimartín/Saumier, Explanatory Report on the HCCH 2019 Judgments Convention, 2020, para. 29.

lichen Adhäsionsverfahren[87] als auch – anders als noch unter dem HAVÜ 1971 – Verwaltungsgerichte, die tatsächlich[88] über privatrechtliche Ansprüche entschieden haben, die Definition erfüllen.[89] Hiervon wird man wohl auch für staatliche Schlichtungsstellen ausgehen dürfen, die – wie bei geringem Streitwert in der Schweiz[90] – obligatorisch angerufen werden müssen und verbindliche Entscheidungen treffen können.[91] Darüber hinaus ist umstritten, welche Eigenschaften der Gerichtsbegriff des HAVÜ 2019 verlangt.

Naheliegend wäre ein Kriterium persönlicher und sachlicher Unabhängigkeit des erkennenden Spruchkörpers.[92] Dass die Entscheidung nicht in der Sache durch sachfremde Gründe und Weisungen von außerhalb beeinflusst sein darf, ergibt sich aus dem Erfordernis prozeduraler Fairness wie es in Art. 7 Abs. 1 lit. b, c HAVÜ 2019 zum Ausdruck kommen. Fraglich ist jedoch, ob diese Erwägungen in der abstrakt generellen Definition des Gerichts zutreffend verortet sind.[93] In diesem Fall könnten jene Jurisdiktionen, die letztlich nur über eine organisatorische Gewaltenteilung verfügen, die jedoch keine rechtliche oder politische Unabhängigkeit von der (Zentral-)Regierung genießen, keine Sachentscheidungen exportieren, sondern stünden nur in der Verpflichtung, die Urteile anderer Vertragsstaaten anzuerkennen.[94] So könnten etwa Urteile aus der Hong Kong SAR oder den Vereinigten Arabischen Emiraten (VAE) frei zirkulieren, während Judikate aus dem Königreich Saudi-Arabien oder der Volksrepublik China nicht im Ausland vollstreckbar wären.[95] Gemessen an der Bedeutung gerade dieser Jurisdiktionen ergäbe sich hieraus

---

[87] Vgl. §§ 403ff. StPO.

[88] Auf die Einhaltung der nationalen Zuständigkeiten kommt es nicht an, vgl. Jacobs, Das Haager Anerkennungs- und Vollstreckungsübereinkommen, 2021, S. 139.

[89] Jacobs, Das Haager Anerkennungs- und Vollstreckungsübereinkommen, 2021, S. 138.

[90] Die Kompetenzen der Schlichtungsbehörde ergeben sich aus Art. 197, 212 Abs. 1 Schweizer ZPO.

[91] So auch Weller/Ribeiro-Bidaoui/Brinkmann/Dethloff, The HCCH 2019 Judgments Convention/Hau, 2023, p. 23 in vorsichtiger Anlehnung an EuGH 20.12.2017 – C-467/16, BeckRS 2017, 135796(Schlömp v. Landratsamt Schwäbisch Hall). Für die Rechtshängigkeit iSd Art. 7 Abs. 2 HAVÜ 2019 mag es auf die Befähigung zur verbindlichen Entscheidung hingegen nicht ankommen.

[92] So mit unterschiedlichen Nuancen Brand/Coffee/Herrup, The 2019 Hague Judgments Convention, 2023, para. 5.18 („independence from other public authorities in reaching decisions"); Weller/Ribeiro-Bidaoui/Brinkmann/Dethloff, The HCCH 2019 Judgments Convention/Hau, 2023, p. 23 wirft die Frage nach der Orientierung an internationalen Standards (zB Art. 6 EMRK) auf, lehnt sie im Ergebnis jedoch ab.

[93] Diesen Ansatz wählte zuletzt im Rahmen von sec. 4 (b) (1) UFCMJRA (2005) der New York Supreme Court in Shanghai Yongrun Inv. Mgt. Co., Ltd. v Kashi GalaxyVenture Capital Co., Ltd, 2021 NY Slip Op 31459(U), als er in Bezug auf China einen *systematic lack of due process* feststellte. Allerdings wurde die Entscheidung inzwischen von der Appellate Division mit Verweis auf die Einflussnahme im Einzelfall wieder aufgehoben, 2022 NY Slip Op 01523.

[94] Die völkerrechtliche Verpflichtung aus Art. 4 HAVÜ 2019 gilt für alle Vertragsstaaten nur dann, wenn auch ein Urteil iSdArt. 3 Abs. 1 lit. b HAVÜ 2019 vorliegt.

[95] Saudi-Arabien ist als absolute Monarchie konzipiert, in der die Letztentscheidung beim König liegt, vgl. Art. 5 Basic Law of Saudi Arabia (النظام الأساسي للحكم). Hingegen genießen die Gerichte der Vereinigten Arabischen Emirate (VAE) ausweislich des Art. 94 der VAE-Verfassung (دستور دولة الامارات العربية المتحدة) vollständige Unabhängigkeit. Ähnlich konstituiert Art. 2 Hong Kong Basic Law die Judikative als unabhängige Gewalt, während die Gerichte der Volksrepublik China unter der generellen politischen Führung der Kommunistischen Partei stehen, vgl. Weller/

eine empfindliche normative Einschränkung der Zielsetzung weltweiter Urteilsfreizügigkeit. Zudem erscheint es doch unwahrscheinlich, dass diese Mitgliedstaaten ihrer aktiven Teilnahme an den Verhandlungen zum HAVÜ 2019 ein Verständnis zugrunde gelegt haben sollen, welches ihre Gerichte vom Anwendungsbereich ausschließen würde.[96] Aus diesem Grund scheint es vorzugswürdig, mit *Tang* zwischen der Makrokontrolle der Justiz durch Leitlinien oder Strategiepapiere *(policy papers)* und der Mikrokontrolle im Einzelfall zu unterscheiden.[97] Somit stünde es der Einordnung als Gericht zwar nicht im Wege, wenn das Justizsystem generell der politischen Führung untersteht, verdichtetet sich diese aber zur Einflussnahme im Einzelfall, wäre das aus diesem Verfahren resultierende Urteil als Verstoß gegen den *ordre public* nach Art. 7 Abs. 1 lit. c HAVÜ 2019 nicht notwendig zu vollstrecken.[98]

Verwandt ist die Fragestellung ob auch Behörden erfasst werden, wenn sie quasigerichtliche Funktionen wahrnehmen. Relevanz könnte dies etwa für Verfahren vor den als Kollektivorgane der Verwaltung ausgestalte Vergabekammern entfalten.[99] Während *Hartley/Dogauchi* eine entsprechende Auslegung im HProrogÜbk 2005 für möglich erachten,[100] schließen *Garcimartín/Saumier* dies für das HAVÜ 2019 aus.[101] Vermittelnd sollten zumindest jene Tribunale der Verwaltung erfasst werden, für deren Entscheidungen der Rechtsweg zu einem Organ der Judikative eröffnet ist, da es nicht nur von der willkürlichen Entscheidung der unterlegenen Partei abhängig sein sollte, ob der Urteilsgläubiger einen Titel erlangt oder nicht.[102] In diesem Fall unterschiede sich die Rolle der Behörde nämlich kaum von der einer obligatorischen Schlichtungsstelle.

Des Weiteren wird zum Teil verlangt, dass ein Urteil in der Hauptsache durch eine Richterin erlassen werden müsste.[103] Gefolgert wird dies aus einem Umkehrschluss zur ausdrücklichen Erwähnung des Gerichtsbediensteten („officer of the court") in Art. 3 Abs. 1 lit. b HAVÜ 2019 für Kostenfestsetzungsbeschlüsse und die Ausstellung von Dokumenten iRd Art. 12 HAVÜ 2019. Indes scheint der Erläuternde Bericht diesen Erwähnungen nur exemplarischen Charakter beizumessen, wenn er etwa auch den Erlass eines Versäumnisurteils durch einen Rechtspfleger

---

Ribeiro-Bidaoui/Brinkmann/Dethloff, The HCCH 2019 Judgments Convention/Tang, 2023, 297 (311).

96 Zur Teilnahme gerade dieser Staaten an den Verhandlungen zum HAVÜ 2019 schon → III.

97 Weller/Ribeiro-Bidaoui/Brinkmann/Dethloff, The HCCH 2019 Judgments Convention/Tang, 2023, 311.

98 In diesem Sinne auch Weller/Ribeiro-Bidaoui/Brinkmann/Dethloff, The HCCH 2019 Judgments Convention/Hau, 2023, p. 24; Weller/Ribeiro-Bidaoui/Brinkmann/Dethloff, The HCCH 2019 Judgments Convention/Tang, 2023, 311.

99 Vgl. § 155ff. GWB; die Unabhängigkeit ergibt sich aus § 157 Abs. 1 GWB; zur Relevanz für zivilrechtliche Ansprüche vgl. etwa VK Bund 27.5.2019 – VK 2–24/19.

100 HCCH, Proceedings of the Twentieth Session (2005) Tome III/*Hartley/Dogauchi,* 2010, para. 116 fn. 146 in Bezug auf Patentbehörden.

101 Garcimartín/Saumier, Explanatory Report on the HCCH 2019 Judgments Convention, 2020, para. 102.

102 Brand/Coffee/Herrup, The 2019 Hague Judgments Convention, 2023, para. 5.20.

103 Weller/Ribeiro-Bidaoui/Brinkmann/Dethloff, The HCCH 2019 Judgments Convention/Hau, 2023, p. 22; aA Jacobs, Das Haager Anerkennungs- und Vollstreckungsübereinkommen, 2021, S. 138.

für möglich hält.[104] Dies erscheint angemessen. Zumal davon auszugehen ist, dass gerichtliche Verfahren in zunehmendem Maße automatisiert ablaufen werden, wie es – ohne überhaupt auf die Entwicklung von *smart courts*[105] rekurrieren zu müssen – für Mahnverfahren bereits jetzt der Fall ist.[106] Da den Zielsetzungen des HAVÜ 2019 langfristig eine gewisse Technologieoffenheit förderlich ist, sollte man nicht auf die Qualifikation einer natürlichen Person beharren, soweit dies nicht das Recht der Parteien auf einen fairen Prozess über Gebühr einschränkt.

Zuletzt ist die Abgrenzung des Prozessvergleiches iSd Art. 11 HAVÜ 2019 zu konsensualen Urteilsformen (*"jugement d'accord"; "consent decree"*) zu erörtern.[107] Nationale Besonderheiten wie die Fähigkeit zur Rechtskraft können die Qualifikation des Begriffes nicht leiten.[108] Autonom kommt es für die Zurechnung der Streitbeilegung maßgeblich darauf an, wem die Entscheidungshoheit darüber zukommt, ob ein Urteil ergeht.[109] Übt das Gericht konkrete inhaltliche Kontrollbefugnisse aus, ist ihm die Entscheidung (auch) zuzurechnen,[110] kommt ihm hingegen eher die Funktion eines Notars zu, handelt es sich um einen Prozessvergleich.[111] Für diese komplexe Würdigung mag die äußere Form als Indiz dienen, sie kann aber nicht primär für das Vorliegen einer Entscheidung herangezogen werden.[112]

3. Keine einstweilige Sicherungsmaßnahme (interim measure of protection; mesures provisoires et conservatoires)

Als letztes darf es sich bei der Sachentscheidung des Gerichtes nicht um eine einstweilige Sicherungsmaßnahme handeln, dh Entscheidungen zur Wahrung des *status quo* während des Verfahrens oder zur Sicherung eines Vermögensgegenstands für eine eventuelle spätere Vollstreckung.[113] Dieses Begriffsverständnis lässt sich bis auf den Entwurfstext 1999 sowie den Interim Text 2001 zurückverfol-

[104] Garcimartín/Saumier, Explanatory Report on the HCCH 2019 Judgments Convention, 2020, para. 95 fn. 88.

[105] Vgl. Tang RabelsZ 87 (2023), 118.

[106] Vgl. § 703c ZPO.

[107] Garcimartín/Saumier, Explanatory Report on the HCCH 2019 Judgments Convention, 2020, para. 296; hierzu → II.

[108] Jacobs, Das Haager Anerkennungs- und Vollstreckungsübereinkommen, 2021, S. 157

[109] Erneut Jacobs, Das Haager Anerkennungs- und Vollstreckungsübereinkommen, 2021, S. 158.

[110] So etwa für die Genehmigung *(approval)* eines *class action settlement* im U.S.-amerikanischen Recht, vgl. hierzu im Rahmen des § 328 ZPO Hess JZ 55 (2000), 373 (377). Rechtsgrundlage ist R. 23 (e) (2): "Approval of the Proposal. If the proposal would bind class members, the court may approve it only after a hearing and only on finding that it is fair, reasonable, and adequate [...]".

[111] Dies ist auch für den Beschlussvergleich nach § 278 Abs. 6 S. 2 ZPO anzunehmen, vgl. Weller/Ribeiro-Bidaoui/Brinkmann/Dethloff, The HCCH 2019 Judgments Convention/Hau, 2023, p. 29.

[112] So aber Jacobs, Das Haager Anerkennungs- und Vollstreckungsübereinkommen, 2021, S. 158: „Für *diese* Frage [Anmerkung: ob eine Entscheidung vorliegt] und damit auch die Abgrenzung zum Prozessvergleich die Bezeichnung oder die äußere Form irrelevant wären, sagt die Vorschrift nicht."

[113] Garcimartín/Saumier, Explanatory Report on the HCCH 2019 Judgments Convention, 2020, para. 99.

gen.[114] Dort waren sie indes noch selbst potentieller Gegenstand der Anerkennung- und Vollstreckung und nicht auf die Funktion als negatives Tatbestandsmerkmal beschränkt.

Kategorisch vom Anwendungsbereich des HAVÜ 2019 ausgeschlossen sind damit Formen des vorläufigen Rechtsschutzes *in rem* (zB der Arrest oder ein US *writ of attachment*) oder *in personam* (bspw. die britische *Mareva injunction* oder Sicherungsverfügung), unabhängig davon, ob sie überhaupt eine extraterritoriale Wirkung bezwecken.[115] Hingegen sind Maßnahmen zur Beweissicherung wie die britische *Anton Piller order* bereits keine Sachentscheidungen.[116] Die deutsche Leistungsverfügung führt zwar über den Sicherungszweck hinaus bereits die (teilweise) Befriedigung des Klägers herbei.[117] Anders als in den zitierten Entwürfen dient die Kategorie im HAVÜ 2019 jedoch vornehmlich dazu, den Urteilsbegriff und die mir ihm korrespondierende völkerrechtliche Verpflichtung von zeitlich nur begrenzt angelegten Maßnahmen zu entlasten.[118] Diese Ratio streitet für den Ausschluss der Leistungsverfügung.

Interessant ist die Einordnung von Prozessführungsverboten *(anti-suit injunction)*. Schließlich müssen diese keinesfalls zeitlich begrenzt sein, sondern können ebenso gut als permanente Anordnungen ergehen.[119] Gegen die Einbeziehung in den Urteilsbegriff wird jedoch wahlweise ihre eigene (vermeintliche) Rechtsnatur als Verfahrensinstrument[120] oder aber die Natur des HAVÜ 2019 als *convention simple,* die sich bewusst den Fragen der direkten Zuständigkeit enthalte, angeführt.[121] Angesichts dieser Argumente erscheint es dennoch erwägenswert, ob nicht die Verfügungen gegen Prozessführungsverbote *(anti-anti-suit injunction),* soweit diese auf einem materiellen Anspruch wegen Verletzung einer absoluten Rechtsposition beruhen, anerkannt werden können.[122] Zumeist wird diese Überlegung jedoch daran scheitern, dass auch diese Ansprüche durch eine Verfügung im einstweiligen Rechtsschutz durchgesetzt werden.

---

[114] Nygh/Pocar, Report of the Special Commission, Prel. Doc. No. 11 of August 2000, p. 70; Art. 13 (3) Alternative A Interim Text 2001.

[115] Einen Überblick bietet HCCH, Note on Provisional and Protective Measures in Private International Law and Comparative Law, Prel. Doc. No. 10 of October 1998.

[116] Vgl. McLachlan ICLQ 36 (1987), 669 (678) et seq.

[117] Im Rahmen des HAVÜ 2019 kann das von der Rechtsprechung analog § 940 ZPO entwickelte Rechtsinstitut etwa für Ansprüche aus Delikt (Art. 2 Abs. 1 lit. j HAVÜ 2019) auf Lohnforderungen, Schmerzensgeldrenten oder Krankentagegeld relevant werden, vgl. Saenger, ZPO/Kemper, 10. Aufl. 2023, ZPO § 940 Rn. 11.

[118] Brand/Coffee/Herrup, The 2019 Hague Judgments Convention, 2023, para. 5.12.

[119] Cheshire/North/Fawcett, Private International Law, 15th ed. 2017, 421 et seq.

[120] Nygh/Pocar, Report of the Special Commission, Prel. Doc. No. 11 of August 2000, p. 72.

[121] Jacobs, Das Haager Anerkennungs- und Vollstreckungsübereinkommen, 2021, S. 152f.

[122] Vgl. OLG München 12.12.2019 – 6 U 5042/19, GRUR 2020, 379 (Ls.): „Die Beantragung einer Anti-Suit Injunction vor einem amerikanischen Gericht mit dem Ziel, die Durchsetzung von Unterlassungsansprüchen wegen Patentverletzung im Inland zu verhindern, stellt eine Beeinträchtigung der eigentumsähnlichen Rechtsposition des Patentinhabers dar."

V. Ausblick: Ein belastbares Begriffsfundament!

In ihrer Gesamtheit erweist sich die Urteilsdefinition des HAVÜ als belastbares Fundament eines hypothetisch weltweit operierenden Rechtsregimes der wechselseitigen Anerkennung und Vollstreckung von Entscheidungen in Zivil- und Handelssachen. Dies ist in erster Linie der Überschaubarkeit ihrer Tatbestandsmerkmale zu verdanken, die hinreichend klar gefasst sind, um dem autonomen Begriffsverständnis inhaltliche Konturen zu verleihen, und sich zugleich – wie soeben gezeigt – als flexibel genug erweisen, um eine Vielzahl der in den Jurisdiktionen dieser Welt entwickelten Herangehensweisen an die justizielle Streitbeilegung zu integrieren, ohne dass ihre grundsätzliche Stoßrichtung hierdurch unkenntlich würde.

Nicht verschwiegen werden sollen jedoch auch die vielen Ungewissheiten, mit denen das Verständnis des Begriffs nach wie vor belastet ist. Erster Prüfstein der autonomen Auslegung könnten – je nach politischer Großwetterlage – die qualitativen Kriterien eines „Gericht" werden. Auch müssen Wortlaut und Systematik nicht selten genug mit allgemeinen Wertungen aus der „Natur der Konvention" oder unausgesprochenen Annahmen auf Seiten der Delegierten der verhandelnden Staaten unterfüttert werden.

Hoffnungsvoll stimmt in diesen Punkten die erstaunliche Konsistenz, die der Urteilsbegriff des HAVÜ 2019 über die Zeiten hinweg mit den zuvor im Rahmen der HCCH angestellten Überlegungen aufweist. Hierdurch steht dem Rechtsanwender bereits seit Verabschiedung des HAVÜ 2019 ein solcher Reichtum an Materialien in Englisch und Französisch (inkl. der Erläuternden Berichte und der Verhandlungsdokumentation der HCCH) zur Verfügung, dass einem Heimwärtsstreben in Fragen der Urteilsdefinition in hohem Maße vorgebeugt sein sollte. Retrospektiv erweist sich die lange Entwicklungsdauer des *judgments project* somit sogar als methodischer Segen.

Mit anderen Worten: Sollte der einst so euphorisch errichtete Turm des *judgments projects* letztlich doch durch die rechtspolitischen Realitäten nicht wirklich zum Leuchtturm werden, wird hierfür sicher nicht seine Konzeption des Schlüsselbegriffs „Urteil" verantwortlich sein.

Schriftenverzeichnis[1]

I. Herausgeber

Münchener Kommentar zur Zivilprozessordnung
gemeinsam mit Wolfgang Krüger
7. Auflage 2025f., 3 Bände (Band 2, 3 in Vorbereitung)
6. Auflage 2020–2022, 3 Bände
5. Auflage 2016/2017, 3 Bände
4. Auflage 2013, 3 Bände
3. Auflage 2007/2008, 3 Bände (gemeinsam mit Peter Wax und Joachim Wenzel)

Münchener Kommentar zum FamFG
4. Auflage 2025, 2 Bände (Band 2 in Vorbereitung)
3. Auflage 2018/2019, 2 Bände
2. Auflage 2013, 1 Band
1. Auflage 2010, 1 Band (als: Band 4 Münchener Kommentar zur Zivilprozessordnung, 3. Aufl.)

Europäisches Zivilprozess- und Kollisionsrecht – EuZPR/EuIPR, Kommentar
5. Auflage 2020ff., 8 Bände (Band IV-1 bis V-2 in Vorbereitung)
4. Auflage 2014–2016, 5 Bände
3. Auflage 2010/2011, 4 Bände
2. Auflage 2006, 2 Bände (als: Europäisches Zivilprozeßrecht)
1. Auflage 2003, 1 Band (als: Europäisches Zivilprozeßrecht)

Schriften des Instituts für Ausländisches und Europäisches Privat- und Verfahrensrecht der Universität Leipzig
Band 1–20 2000–2021

Schriften zum europäischen Kollisions- und Verfahrensrecht
Band 1 2009

Festschrift für Werner Lorenz zum 80. Geburtstag
gemeinsam mit Heinz-Peter Mansel
2001

II. Monografien

Reformfragen des gesetzlichen Erb- und Pflichtteilsrechts (Band 1, 2/1, 2/2)
Habilitationsschrift
1993

Sharī'a, Islamisches Familienrecht der sunna und shī'a
1987

Verpflichtung und Erfüllungsort in Art. 5 Nr. 1 EuGVÜ
Dissertationsschrift
1984

---

[1] Der Jubilar, unprätentiös stets an der Lösung konkreter Rechtsfragen und wenig an der Darstellung und Vermarktung des eigenen wissenschaftlichen Beitrages hierzu interessiert, veröffentlicht seit längerem kein aktualisiertes Schriftenverzeichnis. Die Herausgeber haben nach eigenen Kenntnissen und intensiver Recherche in zahlreichen Quellen versucht, hier dennoch das umfassende und vielschichtige wissenschaftliche Œuvre des Jubilars zusammenzustellen. Einen Anspruch auf Vollständigkeit können sie zu ihrem Bedauern dennoch nicht erheben. Für Ergänzungshinweise sind sie daher dankbar.

III. Lehrbücher

Internationales Privatrecht. Mit internationalem Verfahrensrecht
6. Auflage 2026 (in Vorbereitung)
5. Auflage 2017
4. Auflage 2012
3. Auflage 2009
2. Auflage 2002
1. Auflage 1999 (in zwei Bänden: Internationales Privatrecht, Internationales und Europäisches Zivilverfahrensrecht)

Klausurenkurs im Internationalen Privat- und Verfahrensrecht
5. Auflage 2026 (in Vorbereitung)
4. Auflage 2019
3. Auflage 2013 (als: Klausurenkurs im Internationalen Privatrecht)
2. Auflage 2009 (als: Klausurenkurs im Internationalen Privatrecht)
1. Auflage 2003 (als: Internationales Privatrecht, Fälle und Lösungen)

Familienrecht
Großes Lehr- und Handbuch
2. Auflage 2008
1. Auflage 2001

IV. Kommentierungen

1. Münchener Kommentar

1067–1078 ZPO, EG-ZustellVO, EG-BewVO, Völkervertragliches Zustellungsrecht
in Krüger/Rauscher, Münchener Kommentar zur Zivilprozessordnung
7. Auflage 2026 (in Vorbereitung)
6. Auflage 2022
5. Auflage 2017
4. Auflage 2013
3. Auflage 2008 (Hrsg. Rauscher/Wax/Wenzel)

§§ 183, 184 ZPO
in Krüger/Rauscher, Münchener Kommentar zur Zivilprozessordnung
7. Auflage 2025

Art. 1–61, Art. 74–84 EU–ErbVO, §§ 1–32, §§ 45–47 IntErbRVG
in Rauscher, Münchener Kommentar zum FamFG
4. Auflage 2025 (in Vorbereitung)
3. Auflage 2019

§§ 97–110, §§ 269–270 FamFG
in Rauscher, Münchener Kommentar zum FamFG
4. Auflage 2025
3. Auflage 2018
2. Auflage 2013
1. Auflage 2010 (als Rauscher, Münchener Kommentar zur Zivilprozessordnung, Band 4)

EGGVG
gemeinsam mit Steffen Pabst
in Rauscher/Wax/Wenzel, Münchener Kommentar zur Zivilprozessordnung
3. Auflage 2008

2. Rauscher EuZPR/EuIPR

Einl., Art. 1–6, Art. 52, Art. 65 Abs. 1, Art. 99 Brüssel IIb-VO
in Rauscher, Europäisches Zivilprozess- und Kollisionsrecht – EuZPR/EuIPR
5. Auflage 2025 (in Vorbereitung)

Brüssel IIa-VO
in Rauscher, Europäisches Zivilprozess- und Kollisionsrecht – EuZPR/EuIPR
4. Auflage 2015
3. Auflage 2010
2. Auflage 2006 (als: Rauscher, Europäisches Zivilprozeßrecht)
1. Auflage 2003 (Brüssel II-VO als: Rauscher, Europäisches Zivilprozeßrecht)

EU-KPfVO
gemeinsam mit Denise Wiedemann
in Rauscher, Europäisches Zivilprozess- und Kollisionsrecht – EuZPR/EuIPR
4. Auflage 2014

EG-VollstrTitelVO
gemeinsam mit Steffen Pabst
in Rauscher, Europäisches Zivilprozeßrecht
2. Auflage 2006

3. Julius von Staudingers Kommentar zum Bürgerlichen Gesetzbuch

§§ 1564–1568 BGB
Scheidungsrecht
in Julius von Staudingers Kommentar zum Bürgerlichen Gesetzbuch
Neubearbeitung 2018
Neubearbeitung 2010
Neubearbeitung 2004
13. Bearbeitung 1999
12. Auflage 1996

Art. 223–225, Art. 229 § 10, Art. 230–235 ohne Art. 232 §§ 2–3, Art. 237 EGBGB
Übergangsrecht
in Julius von Staudingers Kommentar zum Bürgerlichen Gesetzbuch
Neubearbeitung 2016
Neubearbeitung 2003 (Art. 223–225, Art. 230–235 ohne Art. 232 §§ 2–3, Art. 237 EGBGB)
13. Bearbeitung 1996 (Art. 230–235 ohne Art. 232 §§ 2–3 EGBGB)
12. Auflage 1993 (Art. 230–235 ohne Art. 232 §§ 2–3 EGBGB), Zweitveröffentlichung als: Die Einführung des BGB und EGBGB in den neuen Bundesländern

§§ 1684–1686a, §§ 1712–1717 BGB
Umgangs- und Beistandschaftsrecht
in Julius von Staudingers Kommentar zum Bürgerlichen Gesetzbuch
Neubearbeitung 2014
Neubearbeitung 2006 (§§ 1684–1686, §§ 1712–1717 BGB)
13. Bearbeitung 2000 (§§ 1684–1686, §§ 1712–1717 BGB, Art. 223 EGBGB)

§§ 1589–1600d BGB
Abstammungsrecht
in Julius von Staudingers Kommentar zum Bürgerlichen Gesetzbuch
Neubearbeitung 2011
Neubearbeitung 2004 (§§ 1589–1600e BGB)
Neubearbeitung 2000 (§§ 1589–1600e BGB, Art 224 EGBGB)
13. Bearbeitung 1997 (§§ 1589–1600o BGB)

V. Gesamtdarstellungen

Einleitung zum Zivilprozessrecht
in Krüger/Rauscher, Münchener Kommentar zur Zivilprozessordnung
7. Auflage 2025
6. Auflage 2020
5. Auflage 2016
4. Auflage 2013
3. Auflage 2008 (Hrsg. Rauscher/Wax/Wenzel)

Durch die COVID-19-Situation verursachte Fragestellungen im Zivilprozessrecht
in Krüger/Rauscher, Münchener Kommentar zur Zivilprozessordnung, Beilage zu Band 1
6. Auflage 2020

Einführung zum EU-ErbVO-Entwurf
in Rauscher, Europäisches Zivilprozess- und Kollisionsrecht – EuZPR/EuIPR
3. Auflage 2010

Länderbericht Algerien
in Geimer/Schütze, Internationaler Rechtsverkehr
37. Ergänzungslieferung 2009
19. Ergänzungslieferung 1998 (Hrsg. Bülow/Böckstiegel/Geimer/Schütze)

Länderbericht Marokko
in Geimer/Schütze, Internationaler Rechtsverkehr
37. Ergänzungslieferung 2009
19. Ergänzungslieferung 1998 (Hrsg. Bülow/Böckstiegel/Geimer/Schütze)

Länderbericht Tunesien
in Geimer/Schütze, Internationaler Rechtsverkehr
37. Ergänzungslieferung 2009
19. Ergänzungslieferung 1998 (Hrsg. Bülow/Böckstiegel/Geimer/Schütze)

Einführung zum EG-MahnVO-Entwurf
in Rauscher, Europäisches Zivilprozeßrecht
2. Auflage 2006

Einführung zum EG-BagatellVO-Entwurf
in Rauscher, Europäisches Zivilprozeßrecht
2. Auflage 2006

Einführung zum EG-UntVO-Entwurf
in Rauscher, Europäisches Zivilprozeßrecht
2. Auflage 2006

Der Europäische Vollstreckungstitel für unbestrittene Forderungen
2004

Einführung zum EG-VollstrTitelVO-Entwurf
in Rauscher, Europäisches Zivilprozeßrecht
2003

Chapter 7: Germany
in Peter Kaye, European Case Law on the Judgments Convention
1998

VI. Beiträge zu Festschriften, Zeitschriften und Sammelwerken

2022

Ausländische Verkehrsunfälle im deutschen Zivilprozess
FS Ekkehard Becker-Eberhard, 2022, 477

2021

Aufhebung von Auslandsehen mit einem minderjährigen Ehegatten, Anmerkung zu BGH 22.7.2020 – XII ZB 131/20
JR 2021, 573

Die Entwicklung des Internationalen Privatrechts 2020 bis 2021
NJW 2021, 3566

Gutachten Nr 39 – Gesellschaftsrecht, Gesellschaft mit beschränkter Haftung – Portugal (Leipzig)
IPG 2018–2020, 2021, 633

Gutachten Nr 31 – Erbrecht, Testament – Griechenland (Leipzig)
IPG 2018–2020, 2021, 453

2020

COVID-19-Pandemie und Zivilprozess
COVuR 2020, 2

Die Entwicklung des Internationalen Privatrechts 2019 bis 2020
NJW 2020, 3632

2019

Vollkaskoversicherung als Rechtsgeschäft iSd § 1357 I BGB, Anmerkung zu BGH 28.02.2019 – XII ZR 94/17
JR 2019, 391

Mutterschaft des Kindes bei Transsexualität, Anmerkung zu BGH 6.9.2017 XII ZB 660/14 sowie BGH 29.11.2017 – XII ZB459/16
JR 2019, 147

Anwendbares Recht bei statusneutraler Klärung der biologischen Abstammung, Anmerkung zu BGH 10.7.2019 – XII ZB 33/18
LMK 2019, 421944

Die Entwicklung des Internationalen Privatrechts 2018 bis 2019
NJW 2019, 3486

Gutachten Nr 32 – Erbrecht, Gesetzliches Erbrecht – Rumänien (Leipzig)
IPG 2015–2017, 2019, 590

Gutachten Nr 25 – Sachenrecht, Bewegliche Sachen – Belgien (Leipzig)
IPG 2015–2017, 2019, 457

Gutachten Nr 13 – Schuldrecht, Gesetzliche Schuldverhältnisse, Unerlaubte Handlung – Italien (Leipzig)
IPG 2015–2017, 2019, 214

Gutachten Nr 1 – Allgemeine Lehren des Zivilrechts, Personenstand – Bulgarien (Leipzig)
IPG 2015–2017, 2019, 1

2018

Rechtskolonialismus oder Zweckverfehlung? Auswirkungen des Kinderehebekämpfungsgesetzes im IPR
FS Jolanta Kren Kostkiewicz, 2018, 245

Die Entwicklung des Internationalen Privatrechts 2017 bis 2018
NJW 2018, 3421

Anmerkung zu BGH 20.6.2018 – XII ZB 369/17
NJW 2018, 2643

2017

§ 1371 Abs. 1 BGB zwischen EU-ErbVO und EU-EheGüterVO
FS Reinhold Geimer, 2017, 529

Die Entwicklung des Internationalen Privatrechts 2016 bis 2017
NJW 2017, 3486

Anmerkung zu BGH 19.7.2017 – XII ZB 72/16
NJW 2017, 2914

2016

Unterhaltszuständigkeit zwischen Sorgerechts- und Ehesachenverbund
IPRax 2016, 215

Anerkennung zweier Väter kraft kalifornischer Leihmuttervereinbarung
JR 2016, 97

Umgang mit dem leiblichen Vater bei Ablehnung durch die rechtlichen Eltern, Anmerkung zu BGH 5.10.2016 – XII ZB 280/15
LMK 2016, 384750

Wahl eines Fantasie-Adelsnamens nach Art. 48 EGBGB, Art. 21 AEUV, Anmerkung zu EuGH 2.6.2016 – C-438/14
LMK 2016, 381541

Die Entwicklung des Internationalen Privatrechts 2015 bis 2016
NJW 2016, 3493

Anmerkung zu BGH 20.4.2016 – XII ZB 15/15
NJW 2016, 2327

Keine Hemmung der Anfechtungsfrist für biologischen Vater, Anmerkung zu OLG Karlsruhe 21.3.2016 – 2 WF 31/16
NZFam 2016, 574

Kindesentführung und Minderjährigenschutzabkommen, Anmerkung zu OLG Bremen 22.12.2015 – 4 UF 183/15
NZFam 2016, 143

Die Eintragungsfähigkeit ausländischer Ehegatten und juristischer Personen im Grundbuch
gemeinsam mit Sven Loose
RPfleger 2016, 617

2015

Nur ein Not-Sitz des Rechtsverhältnisses – Zum gewöhnlichen Aufenthalt im Personalstatut
FS Dagmar Coester-Waltjen, 2015, 637

Von einem getriebenen Gesetzgeber und mehreren Arten von Vätern
GS Manfred Seebode, 2015, 301

Unbilligkeit bei Versorgungsausgleich mit Auslandsbezug
IPRax 2015, 139

Anmerkung zu BVerfG 24.2.2015 – 1 BvR 472/14
JZ 2015, 624

Die Entwicklung des Internationalen Privatrechts 2014 bis 2015
NJW 2015, 3551

Verstoß des iranischen Ehegattenerbrechts gegen den deutschen ordre public, Anmerkung zu OLG Hamburg 4.12.2014 – 2 W 58/14
NZFam 2015, 736

Einseitiges Scheitern der Ehe, Anmerkung zu OLG Brandenburg 12.2.2015 – 9 UF 260/14
NZFam 2015, 379

Internationale Zuständigkeit für Umgangsvollstreckung, Anmerkung zu OLG Bremen 24.11.2014 – 5 WF 67/14
NZFam 2015, 95

2014

Schutzinstrumente bei vorsorgender Rechtswahl nach der Rom III-Verordnung
FS Rolf A. Schütze, 2014, 463

Erbstatuswahl im deutsch-italienischen Rechtsverkehr
IPRax 2014, 51

Exhumierung zur Vaterschaftsfeststellung, Anmerkung zu BGH 29.10.2014 – XII ZB 20/14
LMK 2014, 364604

Verbleib eines Kindes in einer Pflegefamilie statt Sorgerechtsentzug, Anmerkung zu BGH 22.1.2014 – XII ZB 68/11
LMK 2014, 357068

Die Entwicklung des Internationalen Privatrechts 2013–2014
NJW 2014, 3619

Ehegattenzuwendungen
NZFam 2014, 298

2013

Zuweisung der Ehewohnung zum Wohl eines Heranwachsenden, Anmerkung zu OLG Hamm 25.9.2013 – II-2 UF 58/13
FamFR 2013, 549

Widerruf einer Zustimmung zur Verbringung des Kindes nach Art. 13 I lit. a HKÜ, Anmerkung zu OLG Hamm 4.6.2013 – 11 UF 95/13
FamFR 2013, 380

Keine rein verfahrensrechtliche Anerkennung einer in Thailand registrierten Privatscheidung, Anmerkung zu KG 19.3.2013 – 1 VA 12/12
FamFR 2013, 238

Ausschluss der Mutter von Vertretung im Vaterschaftsanfechtungsverfahren, Anmerkung zu OLG Oldenburg 27.11.2012 – 13 UF 128/12
FamFR 2013, 47

Gerichtsstandsvereinbarungen in Unterhaltssachen mit Auslandsberührung
FamFR 2013, 25

Anpassung des IPR an die Rom III-VO
FPR 2013, 257

Zur gesetzlichen Vertretung des Kindes durch den anfechtenden Vater im Statusprozess, Anmerkung zu BGH 21.3.2012 – XII ZB 510/10
JR 2013, 213

Schwerpunktbereich: Kapitalgesellschaften in der Bearbeitung auslandsrechtlicher Fälle
gemeinsam mit Sven Loose
JuS 2013, 683

Anmerkung zu BGH 20.7.2012 – V ZR 135/11
JZ 2013, 308

Die Entwicklung des Internationalen Privatrecht 2012–2013
gemeinsam mit Steffen Pabst
NJW 2013, 3692

2012

Zugewinnausgleich und Versorgungsausgleich: Zweckidentität bei mangelnder Systemabstimmung, Anmerkung zu BGH 18.1.2012 – XII ZB 213/11
DNotZ 2012, 708

Rückforderung von Ehegattenzuwendung bei Täuschung über Abstammung, Anmerkung zu BGH 27.6.2012 – XII ZR 47/09
FamFR 2012, 401

Versöhnung durch Rücknahme des Scheidungsantrags, Anmerkung zu OLG Bremen 2.5.2012 – 4 WF 40/12
FamFR 2012, 332

Zuständigkeitskonzentration bei Unterhaltsverfahren nach der EG-UntVO, Anmerkung zu OLG Frankfurt a.M. 11.1.2012 – 1 UFH 43/11
FamFR 2012, 216

Tatsächlicher Lebensmittelpunkt als gewöhnlicher Aufenthalt des Kindes, Anmerkung zu OLG Hamm 15.12.2011 – 11 UF 240/11
FamFR 2012, 141

Gesamtschuldnerausgleich nach Tod eines Ehegatten, Anmerkung zu OLG Koblenz 14.11.2011 – 12 U 712/10
FamFR 2012, 19

Von prosaischen Synonymen und anderen Schäden
IPRax 2012, 40

Verschweigen anderweitiger Vaterschaft als unterhaltsrechtlich relevantes Fehlverhalten, Anmerkung zu BGH 15.2.2012 – XII ZR 137/09
LMK 2012, 333521

Auskunftsanspruch des Scheinvaters, Anmerkung zu BGH 9.11.2011 – XII ZR 136/09
LMK 2012, 328635

Die Entwicklung des Internationalen Privatrecht 2011–2012
gemeinsam mit Steffen Pabst
NJW 2012, 3490

2011

Voraussetzungen der Ehegattenschutzklausel, Anmerkung zu OLG Brandenburg 7.9.2011 – 13 UF 7/09
FamFR 2011, 524

Enge Rechtsmissbrauchsgrenzen beim Abstammungsklärungsanspruch, Anmerkung zu OLG München 14.6.2011 – 33 UF 772/11
FamFR 2011, 359

Versagung der HKÜ–Rückführungsanordnung wegen Ablehnung durch das Kind, Anmerkung zu AG Hamm 8.11.2010 – 3 F 512/10
FamFR 2011, 94

Zustimmung zur Kündigung der Ehe-Mietwohnung bei Getrenntleben, Anmerkung zu OLG Köln 4.10.2010 – 4 UF 154/10
FamFR 2011, 21

Entwicklungen im europäischen und völkervertraglichen Kollisionsrecht 2009–2010
gemeinsam mit Steffen Pabst
GPR 2011, 43

Vollstreckung von Zivilentscheidungen aus Europa und Drittstaaten in Deutschland – Ein Versuch der Systematisierung
International Journal of Procedural Law 2011, 265

Ehegüterrechtlicher Vertrag und Verbraucherausnahme? – Zum Anwendungsbereich der EuVTVO
IPRax 2011, 484

Prozesskostenhilfe bei Scheidung einer „Scheinehe", Anmerkung zu BGH 30.3.2011 – XII ZB 212/09
LMK 2011, 318616

Unrichtige Belehrung über die Zustellung eines Versäumnisurteils, Anmerkung zu BGH 15.12.2010 – XII ZR 27/09
LMK 2011, 315429

Anmerkung zu BGH 14.9.2011 – XII ZR 168/09 (Heilung eines Zustellungsmangels bei Auslandszustellung nach Haager Zustellungsübereinkommen)
NJW 2011, 3584

Die Rechtsprechung zum Internationalen Privatrecht 2010–2011
gemeinsam mit Steffen Pabst
NJW 2011, 3547

Haager Kinderschutzübereinkommen und Auswanderungsmotive in der Sorgerechtsregelung
NJW 2011, 2332

2010

Keine Wohnungszuweisung bei „Hinausdrängen" ohne ernsthafte Gewalt, Anmerkung zu OLG Köln 27.8.2010 – 4 WF 160/10
FamFR 2010, 524

Inzidentfeststellung der Vaterschaft im Scheinvaterregress, Anmerkung zu BVerfG 27.5.2010 – 1 BvR 2643/07
FamFR 2010, 406

Hilfsanknüpfung an deutsches Unterhaltsstatut, Anmerkung zu OLG Nürnberg 16.4.2010 – 7 WF 492/10
FamFR 2010, 288

Ehebedingter Nachteil wegen Verlustes des erstehelichen Unterhaltsanspruchs, Anmerkung zu OLG Düsseldorf 17.3.2010 – 8 UF 173/09
FamFR 2010, 226

Islamischer talaq und deutscher ordre public, Anmerkung zu OLG Hamm 27.1.2010 – 2 WF 259/09
FamFR 2010, 192

Die Beteiligung des Kindes am Umgangsvergleich
FamFR 2010, 28

Anmerkung zu BGH 2.9.2009 – XII ZB 50/06
JR 2010, 437

Anmerkung zu BVerfG 21.7.2010 – 1 BvR 420/09
JZ 2010, 1010

Belehrung vor zweitem Versäumnisurteil und Europäisches Vollstreckungsurteil, Anmerkung zu BGH 22.9.2010 – VIII ZR 182/09
LMK 2010, 311410

Auswanderung mit dem Kind gegen den Willen des Umgangsberechtigten, Anmerkung zu BGH 28.4.2010 – XII ZB 81/09
LMK 2010, 305039

Die Rechtsprechung zum Internationalen Privatrecht 2009–2010
gemeinsam mit Steffen Pabst
NJW 2010, 3487

Erfüllungsortgerichtsstand (Art. 5 Nr. 1 Brüssel I-VO): Abschied von Tessili und de Bloos
NJW 2010, 2251

Gutachten Nr 26 – Familienrecht, Ehe, Scheidungsfolgen – Griechenland (Leipzig)
IPG 2007/2008, 2010, 331

2009

Scheidungs–IPR von der Brüsseler Baustelle
FS Konstantinos D. Kerameus, 2009, 1113

Entwicklungen im europäischen und völkervertraglichen Kollisionsrecht 2008–2009
gemeinsam mit Steffen Pabst
GPR 2009, 294

Güterrechtliche Auseinandersetzung von Ehegatten, die vor Beitritt der DDR geschieden wurden, Anmerkung zu BGH 6.8.2008 – XII ZR 155/06
JR 2009, 195

Trifft den Unterhaltsschuldner eine Obliegenheit zur Einleitung der Verbraucherinsolvenz?, Anmerkung zu BGH 12.12.2007 – XII ZR 23/06
JR 2009, 65

Ordre public–Verstoß eines ausländischen Unterhaltsurteils wegen Verletzung des rechtlichen Gehörs bei der Vaterschaftsfeststellung, Anmerkung zu BGH 26.8.2009 – XII ZB 169/07
LMK 2009, 293153

Schutzmaßnahme als Zivilsache nach der Brüssel IIa-VO, Anmerkung zu EuGH 2.4.2009 – C–523/07
LMK 2009, 282910

Die Rechtsprechung zum Internationalen Privatrecht 2008–2009
gemeinsam mit Steffen Pabst
NJW 2009, 3614

Technische Reform der Zugewinngemeinschaft – zu kurz gegriffen
in Bayer/Koch, Aktuelle Fragen des Familienrechts, 2009, S. 9

2008

Der Wandel von Zustellungsstandards zu Zustellungsvorschriften im Europäischen Zivilprozessrecht
FS Jan Kropholler, 2008, 851

Ein „Code of EC-Conflict Law"?
FS Rudolf Machacek und Franz Matscher, 2008, 665

Islamisches Erbrecht und ordre pubic, Anmerkung zu KG 26.2.2008 – 1 W 59/07
FamRZ 2008, 1566

Entwicklungen im europäischen und völkervertraglichen Kollisionsrecht 2007–2008
gemeinsam mit Steffen Pabst
GPR 2008, 302

Anmerkung zu BVerfG 1.4.2008 – 1 BvR 1620/04
JZ 2008, 949

Entgeltforderungen für so genannte Telefonsexdienstleistungen, Anmerkung zu BGH 8.11.2007 – III ZR 102/07
LMK 2008, 254388

Die Rechtsprechung zum Internationalen Privatrecht 2007–2008
gemeinsam mit Steffen Pabst
NJW 2008, 3477

Gutachten Nr 43 – Internationales Privatrecht, Anknüpfung der Ehescheidung – Vietnam (Leipzig)
IPG 2005/06, 2008, 575

Gutachten Nr 28 – Familienrecht, Eherecht, Scheidung – Zypern (Leipzig)
IPG 2005/06, 2008, 380

2007

Internationales Familien- und Familienverfahrensrecht – Ein Ehescheidungsfall
Ad Legendum 2007, 16

Entwicklungen im europäischen und völkervertraglichen Kollisionsrecht 2005–2007
gemeinsam mit Steffen Pabst
GPR 2007, 244

Anmerkung zu BGH 11.10.2006 – XII ZR 79/04
JZ 2007, 741

Kein Versorgungsausgleich bei Tod des Berechtigten, Anmerkung zu BGH 15.8.2007 – XII ZB 64/06
LMK 2007, 244592

Die Rechtsprechung zum Internationalen Privatrecht 2005–2007
gemeinsam mit Steffen Pabst
NJW 2007, 3541

Anmerkung zu BGH 12.6.2007 – XI ZR 290/06 (Keine Anwendbarkeit von Art. 15 Abs. 2 EuGVVO, wenn die Zweigniederlassung bereits vor Einreichung der Klage aufgelöst worden ist)
WuB 2007, 883 (WuB VII B Art 15 EuGVVO, 2.07)

Anmerkung zu BGH 21.12.2006 – IX ZB 150/05 (Arrest; rechtliches Gehör; Anerkennung von Entscheidungen der Gerichte anderer Mitgliedstaaten im Verfahren des einstweiligen Rechtsschutzes)
WuB 2007, 385 (WuB VII B Art 34 EuGVVO, 1.07)

BGB–Schenkungsrecht bei Grundbucheintragung eines geschenkten DDR-Grundstücks nach Wiedervereinigung, Anmerkung zu BGH 15.5.2007 – X ZR 109/05
ZEV 2007, 439

Thú tuc tó tung yêu câu thanh toán cúa Liên minh châu Âu và môt sô liên hê vói luât tô tung dân su Viêt Nam
(European Order for Payment Procedure and Some Notes to Vietnamese Law on Civil Procedure)
gemeinsam mit Hông Phan-Huy und Steffen Pabst
Tap Chí Khoa Hoc Pháp Ly Truòng Dai Hoc Luât Thánh phô Hô Chí Minh 10 (2007) 25 (Legal Sciences Journal Ho Chi Minh City University of Law 10 (2007) 25)

2006

Bis dass der Tod Euch scheide?
IPRax 2006, 140

Zustellung eines nicht in der Amtssprache des Empfangsmitgliedstaats abgefassten Schriftstücks, Anmerkung zu EuGH 8.11.2005 – C–433/03
JZ 2006, 251

Anmerkung zu BGH 20.03.2006 – IX ZR 15/05 (Erfüllungsortgerichtsstand nach Art. 5 Nr. 1 lit. b EuGVVO bei Dienstleistungserbringung in mehreren Staaten)
WuB 2006, 681 (WuB VII B Art 5 EuGVVO, 4.06)

Anmerkung zu OLG Koblenz 29.9.2005 – 5 U 131/05 (Internationale Zuständigkeit deutscher Gerichte bei grenzüberschreitendem Termingeschäft)
WuB 2006, 447 (WuB VII B Art 15 EuGVVO, 1.06)

Anmerkung zu BGH 24.10.2005 – II ZR 329/03 (Internationale Zuständigkeit deutscher Gerichte für eine Unterlassungsklage)
WuB 2006, 443 (WuB VII B Art 5 EuGVVO, 3.06)

Das Ende des forum non conveniens unter dem EuGVÜ und der Brüssel I-VO?
gemeinsam mit Alexander Fehre
ZEuP 2006, 459

Gutachten Nr 47 – Insolvenz– und Vergleichsrecht – Schweiz (Leipzig)
IPG 2003/04, 2006, 645

Recent Developments in German Succession Law, report to the XVIIth Congress of the International Academy of Comparative Law, Utrecht 2006
congress–website (nicht mehr verfügbar), Zweitabdruck in EJCL 14 (2010) 10

2005

Zuständigkeitsfragen zwischen CISG und Brüssel I
FS Andreas Heldrich, 2005, 933

Parental Responsibility Cases under the new Council Regulation „Brussels IIA“
EuLF 2005, I–37

Surrogatsthese contra ökonomische Logik
FF 2005, 135

Versorgungsausgleich bei unklarem ausländischen Rentenanrecht.
IPRax 2005, 431

Iranischrechtliche Scheidung auf Antrag der Ehefrau vor deutschen Gerichten.
IPRax 2005, 313

Anmerkung zu OLG Köln 14.5.2004 – 16 W 11/04 (Gerichtsstand für eine Klage des Insolvenzverwalters gegen die Gründungsgesellschafter einer AG wegen Unterkapitalisierung)
WuB 2005, 479 (WuB VII B Art 5 EuGVVO, 2.05)

2004

Heimatlos in Europa? – Gedanken gegen eine Aufgabe des Staatsangehörigkeitsprinzips im IPR
FS Erik Jayme, 2004, 719

Ehevereinbarungen: Die Rückkehr der Rechtssicherheit – zu BGH v. 11.2.2004 – XII ZR 265/02
DNotZ 2004, 524

Reformbedarf im Erbrecht?
FF Sonderheft 2 (2004) 141

Der europäische Vollstreckungstitel für unbestrittene Forderungen
GPR 2003/2004, 286

Unzulässigkeit einer anti-suit-injunction unter Brüssel I
IPRax 2004, 405

Keine Sabotage der CMR-Zuständigkeiten im Konflikt von EG-Zuständigkeiten und CMR
LMK 2004, 75

Europäischer Vollstreckungstitel für unbestrittene Forderungen
RIW 2004, Heft 11, S. I (Die erste Seite)

Anmerkung zu 15.1.2004 – EuGH C–433/01
ZZPInt 9 (2004) 160

Gutachten Nr 13 – Familienrecht, Ehe, Heirat – Pakistan (Leipzig)
IPG 2002, 2004, 189

Gutachten Nr 39 – Gesellschaftsrecht, Gesellschaft mit beschränkter Haftung – Hongkong (Leipzig)
IPG 2000/01, 2004, 593

Gutachten Nr 36 – Erbrecht, Testament – Spanien (Leipzig)
IPG 2000/01, 2004, 562

2003

Wie ordnungsgemäß muß die Zustellung für Brüssel I und Brüssel II sein?
FS Kostas E. Beys, 2003, 1295

§ 28 öst. IPRG und deutsches Fiskalerbrecht
IPRax 2003, 269

Grundfragen des Zugewinnausgleichs
Jura 2003, 465

Anmerkung zu BGH 27.5.2003 – IX ZR 203/02 (Revisibilität der Internationalen Zuständigkeit; Zuständigkeit für Insolvenzanfechtung)
WuB 2003, 913 (WuB VII A § 545 ZPO, 1.03)

2002

Leidet der Schutz der Ehescheidungsfreiheit unter der VO Brüssel II?
FS Reinhold Geimer, 2002, 883

Grenzen der Vertragsfreiheit im Unterhaltsrecht – Konsequenzen aus der Rechtsprechung des BVerfG
DNotZ 2002, 751; Zweitabdruck in NotRV, Vertragsobjekt Ehe und Lebenspartnerschaft, 2002, S. 88

Vaterschaft auf Grund Anerkennung
FPR 2002, 359

Vaterschaft auf Grund Ehe mit der Mutter

FPR 2002, 352

Die Haushaltsführung beim „Neuen" als Surrogat?
FuR 2002, 337

Geisteskrankheit als Scheidungsgrund
JR 2002, 457

Anmerkung zu BGH 7.11.2001 – VIII ZR 263/00 (Prozeßaufrechnung; Widerklage; internationale Zuständigkeit; Erfüllungsort)
WuB 2002, 379 (WuB VII B Art 6 EuGVÜ, 2.02)

Die von beiden Seiten zu vertretende Unmöglichkeit im neuen Schuldrecht
ZGS 2002, 333

Sozialhilferegreß unter Brüssel I?, Anmerkung zu EuGH 14.11.2002 – C–271/00
ZZPInt 7 (2002) 324

2001

Konten deutscher Erblasser bei Banken in New York
FS Werner Lorenz, 2001, 525

Grenzüberschreitende Gewinnmitteilung: Anknüpfung und Internationale Zuständigkeit
gemeinsam mit Clemens Schülke
EuLF 2001, 334

Auswirkungen der Hausfrauenunterhaltsentscheidung des BGH auf Alttitel
FuR 2001, 438

Veränderungen in der Bemessung des Ehegattenunterhalts, Anmerkung zu BGH 13.6.2001 – XII ZR 343/99
FuR 2001, 385

Ein Bärendienst für die Freiheit der Eheschließung – Gedanken zum Urteil des BVerfG 1 BvR 12/92 vom 6.2.2001
FuR 2001, 155

Anmerkung zu BGH 10.5.2000 – IV ZR 171/99
JR 2001, 234

Anmerkung zu BGH 5.7.2001 – IX ZR 327/99 (Rückgabeanspruch aus Miete und Beseitigungsanspruch in der Insolvenz)
LM § 566 BGB Nr 26

Anmerkung zu BVerfG 13.3.2001 – 1 BvR 1974/98 (Verfassungsmäßigkeit der Verlängerung des sachenrechtlichen Moratoriums)
WuB 2001, 857 (WuB IV B Art 233 § 2a EGBGB, 2.01)

2000

Talaq und deutscher ordre public
IPRax 2000, 391

Anmerkung zu BGH V ZR 324/98 (Nutzungsentgelt während Bodensonderungsverfahren)
WuB 2000, 693 (WuB IV B Art 233 § 2a EGBGB, 1.00)

Anmerkung zu BGH 18.1.2000 – XI ZR 46/99 (Aufbauhypothek; Nachweisanforderungen an Valutierung eines DDR-Kreditvertrags; Haftung der Kommunalen Wohnungsverwaltung für DDR–Altschulden)
WuB 2000, 539 (WuB I F 3 – 6.00)

Anmerkung zu EuGH 27.1.2000 – C–8/98
ZZPInt 5 (2000) 240

Deutsch-italienisches Kindschaftsrecht nach der Reform
Jahrbuch für Italienisches Recht 13 (2000) 77

1999

Arbeitnehmerschutz – Ein Ziel des Brüsseler Übereinkommens
FS Rolf A. Schütze, 1999, 695

Anmerkung zu BGH 14.10.1998 – XII ZRT 66/97 (Entscheidung des BGH zur Morgengabe)
DEuFamR 1 (1999) 194

Intertemporale Anwendung des Art. 21 EuGVÜ
IPRax 1999, 80

Anmerkung zu BGH 17.12.1998 – V ZR 200/97 (Bodenreform)
JR 1999, 465

Telefonkommentar: Zwangsvollstreckung aus Auskunftsurteil über mögliche Erzeuger
NJW-Cassetten 1999

Anmerkung zu OLG Dresden 27.5.1998 – 13 U 2656/97 (Überleitung von Konto- und Sparkontoverträgen der DDR)
WuB 1999, 1149 (WuB IV B Art 232 § 7 EGBGB, 1.99)

Anmerkung zu BGH 6.10.1998 – XI ZR 36/98 (Aufbauhypothek; Haftung eines restituierten Grundstücks für Zinsen aus staatlicher Verwaltung; Funktionsnachfolge der Sparkassen der ehemaligen DDR)
WuB 1999, 227 (WuB I F 3 – 2.99)

Gutachten Nr 3 – Schuldrecht, Vertrag – Österreich (Leipzig)
IPG 1997, 1999, 21

1998

Das Umgangsrecht im Kindschaftsrechtsreformgesetz
FamRZ 1998, 329; Zweitabdruck in Schwab, Das neue Familienrecht, 1998, S. 233

Neue verbraucherfreundliche „Spielregeln" im spanischen Markt
RIW 1998, 26

Anmerkung zu BGH 18.3.1998 – XII ZR 251/96 (Zwangsvollstreckung in Gesamtgut eines ausländischen Güterstandes; hier: Niederlande; Übergangsrecht IPR 1986)
WuB 1998, 847 (WuB VI E § 740 ZPO, 1.98)

Anmerkung zu OLG Brandenburg 28.8.1997 – 5 U 69/97 (Belastung eines volkseigenen Grundstücks durch den Rechtsträger mit [Höchstbetrags-Hypothek)
WuB 1998, 459 (WuB IV B Art 233 § 3 EGBGB, 1.98)

An Englishman still remains at liberty at his death – Mutual wills, implied trust and family provisions im englischen Recht (HCJ 23.12.1995)
ZEuP 1998, 140

Die erbrechtliche Stellung nicht in einer Ehe geborener Kinder nach dem Erbrechtsgleichstellungsgesetz und dem Kindschaftsrechtsreformgesetz
ZEV 1998, 41

Das vietnamesische Zivilgesetzbuch vom 28.10.1995
gemeinsam mit Hông Phan-Huy
ZVglRWiss 97 (1998) 340

1997

Vergißt die Reform des Kindschaftsrechts § 1931 IV BGB?
FamRZ 1997, 1121

Neue Fragen zu Art. 27 Nr. 2 EuGVÜ?
IPRax 1997, 314

Sonderregelungen zum Verzugszins im spanischen Recht
RIW 1997, 879

Anmerkung zu BVerfG 8.4.1997 – 1 BvR 48/94 (Fortbestand von Altschulden einer LPG; Verfassungsmäßigkeit von Art. 232 § 1 EGBGB, Art. 25 Abs. 3 Satz 3 Einigungsvertrag; § 16 Abs. 3 DMBilG)
WuB 1997, 615 (WuB I E 1 – 6.97)

Anmerkung zu BGH 29.11.1996 – LwZR 8/95 (Verwendungsersatzanspruch einer LPG gegen den Eigentümer wegen werterhöhender baulicher Veränderungen)
WuB 1997, 459 (WuB IV B Art 232 § 3 EGBGB, 1.97)

Anmerkung zu BGH 20.11.1996 – IV ZR 6/96 (Formunwirksamkeit einer Erbausschlagung in Bezug auf DDR-Grundstücke bei Zugang)
ZEV 1997, 26

1996

Grundrechtsverletzungen bei der Zwangsvollstreckung, Deutsches Recht
DIKE International 1996, 213

Gran Canaria – Isle of Man – Was kommt danach?
EuZW 1996, 650

Eidesstattliche Versicherung durch den Generalbevollmächtigten einer ausländischen Gesellschaft?
IPRax 1996, 179

Anmerkung zu BGH 4.10.95 – IV ZB 5/95 (Qualifikation von Restitutionsansprüchen)
JR 1996, 283

Anmerkung zu BGH 20.3.1996 – IV ZR 366/94 (Verjährungshemmung wegen Hemmung der Rechtsverfolgung)
JZ 1996, 973

Anmerkung zu BGH 24.5.1996 – V ZR 148/94 (Moratorium bei Inanspruchnahme zu öffentlichen Zwecken; Verletzung von öffentlichrechtlichen und zivilrechtlichen Vorschriften der DDR)
WuB 1996, 1207 (WuB IV B Art 233 § 2a EGBGB, 1.96)

Anmerkung zu BGH 15.12.1995 – V ZR 110/94 (Verkauf volkseigener Gebäude; Unwirksamkeit der Eigentumsübertragung am Gebäude wegen unwirksamer Vertretung des VEB; kein Besitzrecht am Gebäude aufgrund eines Nutzungsrechts am Grundstück)
WuB 1996, 627 (WuB IV B Art 233 § 2d EGBGB, 1.96)

Grenzüberschreitende Ehrverletzung durch Presseartikel
ZZPInt 1 (1996) 151

1995

Karteikarten und leere Aktendeckel – zur Kündigung inoffizieller STASI-Mitarbeiter
FS Wolfgang Gitter, 1995, 757

Prozessualer Verbraucherschutz im EuGVÜ?
IPRax 1995, 289

Anmerkung zu BGH 3.5.1994 – VI ZR 278/93 (Verjährungshemmung wegen Unmöglichkeit der Rechtsverfolgung)
JR 1995, 373

Anmerkung zu BGH 16.12.1994 – V ZR 177/93 (Keine Herausgabe von Nutzungsentgelten durch den Verfügungsberechtigten, § 3 VermG)
JZ 1995, 792

Entwicklungen im italienischen Erbrecht
gemeinsam mit Katrin Scheuer
Jahrbuch für italienisches Recht 8 (1995) 59

1994

Rechtshängigkeitseinwand bei belgischem Parallelverfahren
IPRax 1994, 188

Pflichtteilsausgleich für restituierten DDR-Grundbesitz
JR 1994, 485

Iranische Sorgerechtsbestimmungen – Deutscher ordre public
JR 1994, 184

Anmerkung zu LG Mönchengladbach 14.7.1994 – 10 O 87/93 (Keine Vollstreckung aus einem ausländischen Urteil auf Rückzahlung von Darlehen zu Spielzwecken)
WuB 1994, 1001 (WuB VII A § 762 BGB, 1.94)

Anmerkung zu OLG Düsseldorf 14.1.1994 – 17 U 129/93 (Vertragsstatut und Aufklärungspflichten bei ausländischen Börsentermingeschäften;
WuB 1994, 591 (WuB I G 5 – 4.94)

Anmerkung zu BGH 26.10.1993 – XI ZR 222/92 (Fortbestand von Altschulden aus Staatsbankkrediten einer LPG)
WuB 1994, 247 (WuB I E 1 – 4.94)

1993

Keine EuGVÜ-Anerkennung ohne ordnungsgemäße Zustellung
IPRax 1993, 376

Teleologische Grenzen des Art. 21 EuGVÜ?
gemeinsam mit Uta Gutknecht
IPRax 1993, 21

Keine Heilung bei Verstoß gegen Haager Zustellungsabkommen durch tatsächliche Zustellung (Anmerkung zu BGHZ 120, 305)
JR 1993, 413

Verfassungskonforme Auslegung von § 39 FGB (DDR)
JR 1993, 95

1992

Prorogation und Vertragsgerichtsstand gegen Rechtsscheinhaftende (Anmerkung zu OLG Saarbrücken 2.10.1991 – 5 U 21/91)
IPRax 1992, 143

Zustellung durch Brief und Art. 27 EuGVÜ
IPRax 1992, 71

Jugoslawisches IZPR vor deutschen Gerichten? – Zur Beachtlichkeit ausländischer Rechtshängigkeit
IPRax 1992, 14

Neuordnung des gesetzlichen Erbrechts
ZRP 1992, 272

1991

Internationales Bereicherungsrecht bei Unklagbarkeit gemäß Art. VIII Abs. 2 (b) IWF-Abkommen (Bretton Woods)
FS Werner Lorenz, 1991, 471

Die Überleitung des Ehegüterrechts im Einigungsvertrag (Art. 234 § 4 EGBGB)
DNotZ 1991, 209

Intertemporale Bestimmungen zum internationalen Ehegüterrecht im Einigungsvertrag
DtZ 1991, 20

Strikter Beklagtenschutz durch Art. 27 Nr. 2 EuGVÜ
IPRax 1991, 155

Gemeinsames Sorgerecht nach Scheidung – Was bewirkt das Kinder- und Jugendhilfegesetz?
NJW 1991, 1087

Gespaltenes Kindschaftsrecht im vereinten Deutschland
StAZ 1991, 1

Gerichtsstandsbeeinflussende AGB im Geltungsbereich des EuGVÜ
ZZP 104 (1991) 271

1990

Der Arbeitnehmergerichtsstand im EuGVÜ
IPRax 1990, 152

Neues irisches Nichtehelichenrecht, Status of Children Act 1987
IPRax 1990, 65

Gutachten Nr 63 – Devisenrecht – Österreich (München)
gemeinsam mit Werner Lorenz
IPG 1987/88, 1990, 627

Gutachten Nr 38 – Kindschaft, Elterliche Sorge – Marokko (München)
gemeinsam mit Werner Lorenz
IPG 1987/88, 1990, 347

Gutachten Nr 2 – Allgemeine Lehren des Zivilrechts, Namensrecht – Österreich/Schweiz (München)
gemeinsam mit Werner Lorenz
IPG 1987/88, 1990, 7

1989

Regelwidriger Versorgungsausgleich (Art. 17 III 2 EGBGB) und Abgeschlossenheit (Art 220 I EGBGB)
IPRax 1989, 224

1988

Amtspflegschaft für ausländische Kinder
Der Amtsvormund 1988, 758

Qualifikations- und Übergangsfragen im Kollisionsrecht der Scheidungsfolgen, Anmerkung zu OLG Zweibrücken 11.11.1987 – 2 UF 17/87
IPRax 1988, 343

Sachnormverweisungen aus dem Sinn der Verweisung
NJW 1988, 2151

Immobiliarzwangsvollstreckung bei fremdem Güterstand
Rpfleger 1988, 89

1987

Die Ausschaltung fremden interlokalen Rechtes durch Art. 4 III Satz 1 EGBGB
IPRax 1987, 206

Neues Scheidungsstatut in schwebenden Scheidungsverfahren
IPRax 1987, 137; Zweitabdruck in IPRax-Sonderheft 1989

Deliktshaftung des Herstellers für Beschädigung der Kaufsache – BGH NJW 1985, 2420
JuS 1987, 14

Art. 220 III EGBGB verfassungswidrig?
NJW 1987, 531

Anmerkung zu BGH, GSZ 1/86 (Schadensersatz für Nutzungsausfall)
NJW 1987, 53

Neues internationales Kindschaftsrecht – Schwerpunkte der Reform
StAZ 1987, 121

1986

Dingliche Mitberechtigung in der Zugewinngemeinschaft
AcP 186 (1986) 529

Ausländische Rechtshängigkeit und Rechtsschutz – Anmerkung zu BGH 28.11.1985 – III ZR 3/85
IPRax 1986, 274

§ 606b Nr. 1 ZPO, Folgen einer unterbliebenen Nichtigerklärung
JZ 1986, 319

Abschied vom Schadenersatz für Nutzungsausfall?
NJW 1986, 2011

Auflassungsvormerkung für verheiratete Ausländer
Rpfleger 1986, 119

Die Statusfeststellung im deutschen Kollisionsrecht
StAZ 1986, 89

1985

Ehelichkeitsanfechtung und ordre public
Der Amtsvormund 1985, 620

Fristen der accettazione dell'eredità
DNotZ 1985, 204

Rechtshängigkeit nach dem EuGVÜ
IPRax 1985, 317

Doppelstaater und MSA
IPRax 1985, 214

Sicherungsübereignung im deutsch-österreichischen Rechtsverkehr
Juristische Blätter (Österreich) 1985, 321

Haftung der Eltern für Ihre Kinder – BGH, NJW 1984, 1958
JuS 1985, 757

Nichts Neues zu Art. 17 EGBGB?
JZ 1985, 518

Die Ferienhausentscheidung des EuGH – Unbilligkeit oder Konsequenz europäischer Rechtspflege
NJW 1985, 892; Telefonkommentar: NJW-Cassetten Rechtsprechung April 1985

Die Vererblichkeit des Schmerzensgeldanspruches in der Rechtsprechung des BGH
NJW 1985, 596

Zuständigkeitsvereinbarung und rügelose Einlassung nach dem EuGVÜ
RIW 1985, 887

Sicherungsübereignung im deutsch-österreichischen Rechtsverkehr
RIW 1985, 265

Auflassungsvormerkung für verheiratete Ausländer
Rpfleger 1985, 52

Italienisches Kindschaftsrecht im deutschen Geburtenbuch
StAZ 1985, 194

Pakistanisch-islamische Eheschließungen
StAZ 1985, 101

1984

Anmerkung zu BGH 15.2.1984 – IVb ZB 701/81
StAZ 1984, 306

VII. Buchbesprechungen

Peter G. Mayr, Handbuch des europäischen Zivilverfahrensrechts, 2017
ZZP 131 (2018), 402

Burkhard Piltz, Internationales Kaufrecht. Das UN-Kaufrecht in praxisorientierter Darstellung, 2. Aufl. 2008
NJW 2009, 133

Andreas Kurt Pattar, Islamisch inspiriertes Erbrecht und deutscher Ordre pubic, 2007
FamRZ 2008, 1402

Heinrich Honsel/Nedim Peter Vogt/Anton K. Schnyder/Stephen V. Berti, Internationales Privatrecht, 2. Aufl. 2007
FPR 2008, 237

Karsten Schmidt, Münchener Kommentar zum Handelsgesetzbuch Bd. 6, 2. Aufl. 2007
NJW 2008, 908

Franco Ferrari/Eva-Maria Kieninger/Peter Mankowski/Karsten Otte/Ingo Saenger/Ansgar Staudinger, Internationales Vertragsrecht. EGBGB, CISG, CMR, FactÜ. Kommentar, 2007
NJW 2008, 278

Petra Fischer-Langosch, Die Entstehungsgeschichte des Familiengesetzbuches der DDR von 1965, 2007
De processibus matrimonialibus 14 (2007) 462

Matthias Kannengießer, Die Aufrechnung im Internationalen Privat- und Verfahrensrecht, 1998
JR 2001, 350

Martin Frank, Das verfahrenseinleitende Schriftstück in Art. 27 Nr. 2 EuGVÜ, 1998
RabelsZ 64 (2000) 441

Peter Windel, Über die Modi der Nachfolge in das Vermögen einer natürlichen Person beim Todesfall, 1998
AcP 198 (1998) 249

Jahrbuch für Italienisches Recht, Band 7, Familienrecht, Staatsangehörigkeitsrecht, Übernahmeangebote, Strafprozessrecht, 1994
RabelsZ 61 (1997) 610

Hanno Merkt, Abwehr der Zustellung von punitive damages Klagen, 1995
WM 1996, 1379

Karlheinz Muscheler, Die Haftungsanordnung der Testamentsvollstreckung, 1994
AcP 195 (1995) 295

Hartwin Bungert, Das Recht ausländischer Kapitalgesellschaften auf Gleichbehandlung im deutschen und US-amerikanischen Recht, 1994
WM 1995, 1386

Peter Rennpferdt, Die internationale Harmonisierung des Erfüllungsrechts für Geldschulden, 1993
WM 1995, 87

Carsten Thomas Ebenroth, Erbrecht, 1992
ZEuP 1995, 714

Frank Peters, Der Entzug des Eigentums an beweglichen Sachen durch gutgläubigen Erwerb, 1991
JR 1993, 217

Daniel Levin, Konflikte zwischen einer weltlichen und einer religiösen Rechtsordnung, 1991
StAZ 1991, 327

Dieter Henrich/Paul Heinrichsmeier, Fälle und Lösungen nach höchstrichterlichen Entscheidungen, Bd. 5 Familienrecht, 3. Auflage 1990
Jura 1991, 167

Jahrbuch für Italienisches Recht, Band 2, Eherecht, Schadensregulierung, Wiener Kaufrecht, Sprachrisiko, 1989
NJW 1990, 3064

Jahrbuch für Italienisches Recht, Band 1, Konkursrecht, Persönlichkeitsschutz, Kapitalverkehr, 1988
RIW 1988, 928

Heinz-Peter Mansel, Personalstatut, Staatsangehörigkeit und Effektivität, 1988
Rpfleger 1988, 429

Ulrich Magnus, Schaden und Ersatz, 1987
NJW 1988, 2591